Flash™ 5 Bible

Flash™ 5 Bible

Robert Reinhardt and Jon Warren Lentz

Hungry Minds™

Hungry Minds, Inc.

New York, NY ✦ Cleveland, OH ✦ Indianapolis, IN

Chicago, IL ✦ Foster City, CA ✦ San Francisco, CA

Flash™ 5 Bible

Published by
Hungry Minds, Inc.
909 Third Avenue
New York, NY 10022
www.hungryminds.com

ISBN: 0-7645-3515-3

Printed in the United States of America

10 9 8 7 6 5 4 3 2 1

1B/QX/QS/QR/FC

Distributed in the United States by Hungry Minds, Inc.

Distributed by CDG Books Canada Inc. for Canada; by Transworld Publishers Limited in the United Kingdom; by IDG Norge Books for Norway; by IDG Sweden Books for Sweden; by IDG Books Australia Publishing Corporation Pty. Ltd. for Australia and New Zealand; by TransQuest Publishers Pte Ltd. for Singapore, Malaysia, Thailand, Indonesia, and Hong Kong; by Gotop Information Inc. for Taiwan; by ICG Muse, Inc. for Japan; by Intersoft for South Africa; by Eyrolles for France; by International Thomson Publishing for Germany, Austria, and Switzerland; by Distribuidora Cuspide for Argentina; by LR International for Brazil; by Galileo Libros for Chile; by Ediciones ZETA S.C.R. Ltda. for Peru; by WS Computer Publishing Corporation, Inc., for the Philippines; by Contemporanea de Ediciones for Venezuela; by Express Computer Distributors for the Caribbean and West Indies; by Micronesia Media Distributor, Inc. for Micronesia; by Chips Computadoras S.A. de C.V. for Mexico; by Editorial Norma de Panama S.A. for Panama; by American Bookshops for Finland.

For general information on Hungry Minds' products and services please contact our Customer Care department within the U.S. at 800-762-2974, outside the U.S. at 317-572-3993 or fax 317-572-4002.

For sales inquiries and reseller information, including discounts, premium and bulk quantity sales, and foreign-language translations, please contact our Customer Care department at 800-434-3422, fax 317-572-4002 or write to Hungry Minds, Inc., Attn: Customer Care Department, 10475 Crosspoint Boulevard, Indianapolis, IN 46256.

For information on licensing foreign or domestic rights, please contact our Sub-Rights Customer Care department at 650-653-7098.

For information on using Hungry Minds' products and services in the classroom or for ordering examination copies, please contact our Educational Sales department at 800-434-2086 or fax 317-572-4005.

For press review copies, author interviews, or other publicity information, please contact our Public Relations department at 650-653-7000 or fax 650-653-7500.

For authorization to photocopy items for corporate, personal, or educational use, please contact Copyright Clearance Center, 222 Rosewood Drive, Danvers, MA 01923, or fax 978-750-4470.

Library of Congress Cataloging-in-Publication Data

Reinhardt, Robert, 1973–
  Flash 5 Bible / Robert Reinhardt and Jon Warren Lentz.
     p. cm.
  Includes Index.
  ISBN 0-7645-3515-3 (alk. paper)
  1. Computer simulation. 2. Flash (computer file)
  3. Interactive multimedia. I. Lentz, Jon Warren.
  II. Title.
  TR897.7 .R46   2001
  006.6'96--dc21   00-143896

About the Authors

Robert Reinhardt — Robert's curiosity and autodidactic energy have carried him from psychology (University of Toronto) to photography (Ryerson University) to new media authoring, teaching, and writing. After discovering the Internet while studying in the Image Arts department at Ryerson in Toronto, Robert began the journey of discovery that eventually enabled him to fuse his interest in technology and communication with his background in the visual arts.

Robert has developed and taught workshops addressing all aspects of content creation and has become increasingly involved with the development of systems for interactive interfaces and data management. Although his head often leads him into the land of scripting and programming, he remains dedicated to the world of images. The main reward of digital literacy has been the ability to move freely between mediums and tools to share ideas through art and design. Before leaving Toronto, Robert worked as a collage and video artist to create set and screen art for the Warner Bros. feature film, *Gossip*.

During their first year in Los Angeles, Robert and his partner, Snow Dowd, formed a multimedia consulting and design company called the Makers (www.theMakers.com). They created a broadband Web site for *Gossip* with Warner Bros. Online, as well as graphics for a tie-in video with the band Tonic. Recently, the Makers has also created screen graphics for *The Pledge,* a film directed by Sean Penn, and worked with Outlaw Productions on previsualization graphics for the forthcoming Warner Bros. film *Training Day* (to star Denzel Washington and Ethan Hawke). In addition to work for entertainment companies, the Makers has done work for independent artists and nonprofit organizations.

While establishing the Makers, Robert also worked as senior art director and program developer with Rampt.com to create a unique Flash interface and search engine, launched in November 1999. After being recognized as a Macromedia Site of the Day and nominated in the FlashForward film festival in New York, Rampt received the Bandies 2000 award for Best Interface Application, as well as an award of excellence from the New Media Invision Awards 2000.

In addition to design and content creation through the Makers, Robert continues an involvement with teaching, consulting, and writing. He currently develops and teaches Flash workshops with Lynda.com and the Moviola Digital Education Center in California, as well as doing onsite training and seminars for clients in the United States and Canada. Robert was a speaker at the San Francisco and New York FlashForward 2000 conferences, as well as the October 2000 DV Web Expo in Long Beach, California.

Jon Warren Lentz — In addition to the *Flash 5 Bible,* Jon Warren Lentz is involved in a number of Flash-related projects, most notably, Flash-Guru.com. Jon founded Flash-Guru.com because he observed the need for sustained, learner-centered training on a variety of intermediate to advanced Flash topics. The courses at Flash-Guru.com are designed to help you to implement advanced Flash techniques in your workflow and include in-depth information and new developments as they happen.

Jon's favorite movie, Fellini's *Satyricon,* was released the year that he graduated from high school. A decade later, Jon graduated from the Classical Studies program at UCSC, where he first received notice as a poet and translator. He then metamorphosed into a sculptor and began working with sand-carved glass — a process that he helped to define as a fine art medium. Following a disabling accident, he reinvented himself as an artist working with cameras and computers. Jon's images have been featured in the Graphis Poster Annual, Mac Art & Design Magazine (Sweden), IdN — The International Designer's Network Magazine (Hong Kong), and Shutterbug Magazine. His stock photography is represented by two agencies, AGE and SuperBild. Jon's abstract fine art and a selection of his glass sculpture may be viewed online at www.uncom.com.

Jon is an occasional professor at Palomar College. Although he has taught and lectured on digital art, design, and technology at many venues, he prefers to stay home, work on his own projects, and go to the beach. He resides with his family near San Diego, California.

Technical Editors

High school did not represent **Jeffrey Bardzell's** glory years, and it concluded inauspiciously with the release of *Dances With Wolves*, "memorable," he writes, "because it was so popular and I absolutely hated it." A decade later and a Ph.D. Candidate in Comparative Literature (Indiana University), Jeffrey sought a way to pull together his then-conflicting desires to teach, to express himself creatively with vectors, and to sustain himself with electronic publishing. An interesting job listing prompted him to check Flash out. The job didn't materialize, but Jeffrey became taken with Flash's potential for online learning. For him, tools such as Flash and the Internet pose as fundamental a revolution in human communication and teaching as another period he knows something about: the advent of literacy in twelfth century Europe. He has created online learning environments for Indiana University and Ignatius University, while working as a Flash and Fireworks author for Flash-Guru.com and eHandsOn. He is also coauthoring *Fireworks 4 Expert Edge* with Lisa Lopuck. In addition to his computer-related publications, he has published on education finance reform, early reading intervention, and epic poetry. Not only did Jeffrey work as a technical editor for the *Flash 5 Bible*, but he also drafted the Quick Start section and formatted the initial Generator chapters.

From his first introduction to the ever-changing world of computing in his sophomore year of high school, **Shane Elliott** has found a familiarity in expressing his designs and code ideas using a computer. While his years at North Carolina State University revealed a certain duality between his fascination with computer programming and his growing interest in acting and writing, he found a way to express himself both creatively and logically through animation and design on computers. He was introduced to Flash around the time Flash 4 was released, and learning the program wasn't ever a problem. As Shane puts it, "I had the author of the Flash Bible (Robert Reinhardt) sitting next to me at work every day. How can you not learn Flash in that situation?" Coming from an extensive background in the internet realm, including starting his own company, Webshock, he quickly found a great value in Flash as a creative tool and internet utility. "Robert suggested I begin teaching, and at first I was scared to death, but the idea of sharing my knowledge with others was so fascinating, I couldn't pass it up." And so he began teaching Flash part-time while continually pursuing his acting and writing endeavors, which are still very much a part of his life. "I found that creating designs in animation and movies on the internet isn't such a far cry, on a creative level, from acting or any other type of creative expression. Currently Shane is finishing up his first screenplay as well as working to continue his experimentation with Flash technology involving other applications and languages such as Java, XML, and the list goes on.

Credits

Acquisitions Editor
Michael Roney

Project Editor
Julie M. Smith

Technical Editors
Jeffrey Bardzell
Shane Elliot
Ellen Finkelstein

Copy Editors
Richard H. Adin
Laura Stone

Proof Editors
Cindy Lai
Patsy Owens

Project Coordinators
Louigene A. Santos
Danette Nurse

Permissions Editor
Carmen Krickorian

Media Development Specialist
Angela Denny

Media Development Coordinator
Marisa Pearman

Graphics and Production Specialists
Robert Bihlmayer
Rolly Delrosario
Jude Levinson
Michael Lewis
Victor Pérez-Varela
Ramses Ramirez

Quality Control Technician
Dina F Quan

Book Designer
Drew R. Moore

Illustrators
Gabriele McCann
Ronald Terry
John Greenough
Karl Brandt
Brian Drumm

Proofreading and Indexing
York Production Services

Cover Image
Lawrance Huck

To Snow, Stella, and Al. I won't forget the year 2000.

RJR

I dedicate my efforts on this book to the memory of my mother-in-law, Phyllis Rogers.

I would also like to thank my family — near and far — for their unconditional love, support, and encouragement, especially my wife, Roanne; my son, Rob; and my mother and father. In addition, I am also thankful for my newfound friends, Jeffrey Bardzell and Nik Schramm, for their wisdom, expertise, and encouragement.

JWL

Foreword

The Web has certainly changed the way that people work, live, and communicate. One cannot help but draw parallels between the digital revolution and other innovations that changed and shaped generations of people — the telephone, radio, and television. Though each of these technologies were rather crude when they started, they eventually became much more dynamic, powerful and attractive to use. The telephone changed from a two-piece handset box to a tiny wireless communication device that acts as mobile office. Television has evolved into high-definition systems that are akin to a movie theater experience in a living room. The Web started out and for many people is still a slow-loading, static, uncompelling experience. Macromedia Flash has revolutionized the way in which designers, animators, and developers alike can express their creativity, enabling over two hundred million viewers worldwide to catch a glimpse into what the Web can be.

With each evolution of Macromedia Flash, we have seen a larger audience of users take advantage of the many innovative features it has to offer. First there were illustrators and animators creating amazing vector work, and then there were Web designers creating interactive navigation systems, motion graphics, and full Web pages. Developers started creating cutting-edge Web applications and database front-ends. Others create rich-media advertisements, viral marketing content, screensavers, and product simulations. Still others are using Macromedia Flash to create original cartoon series for television and short films. It is no wonder the Macromedia Flash community has grown to include over half a million users, with dozens of dedicated resource Web sites and thousands of attendees at regional conferences, all sharing a common thread — the Macromedia Flash authoring tool. Our users have never ceased to amaze and encourage me with the innovative works they are developing with each release of Flash, continuing to push the envelope of what can be done. The incredible user base and the content they create is the inspiration that drives our team at Macromedia to improve and iterate the Flash platform.

It has been my privilege to know and work with the coauthors of this book — Jon Warren Lentz and Robert Reinhardt — two of the most respected experts in the Flash community. To bring greater breadth and depth to this book, they assembled a team of over forty guest tutorialists; a group that includes some of the finest artists, developers, and authors working with Flash. The *Flash 5 Bible* is an essential all-purpose reference guide for Macromedia Flash, providing insights and tips for mastering the creation of all types of Flash content. It is one book any serious Web designer, developer, or animator should own.

Jeremy Clark
Flash Product Manager
Macromedia

Preface

In 1997, Macromedia acquired a small Web graphics program, FutureSplash, from a company named FutureWave. FutureSplash was a quirky little program with the astounding ability to generate compact, vector-based graphics and animations for delivery over the Web. With Macromedia's embrace, Flash blossomed. Now Flash has obtained ubiquity. The Flash Player plug-in ships with most major browsers and operating systems. Now Flash graphics appear all over the Web, and the number of Flash users continues to increase at an astounding pace.

Flash 5 has greatly expanded the interactive and programmatic features of Flash movies. Flash movies can now communicate directly with server-side scripts and programs, using standard URL-encoded variables or XML-formatted structures. Sounds can be imported and exported as MP3 audio, for high-quality music on the Web at the smallest file sizes. The Flash interface now looks and feels like other Macromedia products, with tool options contained in user-configurable panels. Third-party developers are creating applications that output to the Flash movie format, .SWF files. Flash is poised to be the central application for generating hot, low-bandwidth, interactive content for delivery over the Web.

Is there any other Flash book for you?

The *Flash 5 Bible* is the most comprehensive and exhaustive reference on Flash. It helps you get started on your first day with the program and will still be a valuable resource when you've attained mastery of the program. When you are looking for clues on how to integrate Flash with other programs so that you can deliver unique and compelling content in the Flash format, you'll know where to turn.

+ **Exhaustive coverage of Flash.** We spent a great deal of time covering every aspect of Flash functionality. The first part of the book is entirely dedicated to the Flash interface, and Parts II and III explain how to integrate animations and sound into your Flash movies.

+ **Flash is not just one tool.** You can think of Flash as a multitasking application: It's an illustration program, an image and sound editor, an animation machine, and a scripting engine, all rolled into one. In this book, we dissect Flash into each of these components and explain how each works with the other parts.

+ **This is a real-world book.** We've gone to great lengths to make sure that our lessons, examples, and explanations are based in reality (not that the Web isn't real!). We have continued the use of expert tutorials to bring you tips and techniques from some of the top names in the Flash industry, so that you can benefit their years of expertise.

✦ **The CD-ROM.** The CD-ROM that accompanies this book includes many of the source .FLA files and original artwork for the examples and lessons in the book. It also includes trial versions of Flash 5 and other Macromedia products, as well as many of the applications discussed in this edition.

✦ **The book's Web site.** In order to create a forum for the delivery of updates, notes, and sample files, we have also established a Web site:

www.flash5bible.com

Jon Warren Lentz has his own Flash Bible Web site: www.theflash5bible.com

At the Web site, you'll find a detailed evaluation form for the Flash 5 Bible. We invite you to contribute your comments and suggestions for this edition, so that we can continue to improve our material.

How to get the most out of this book

Here are two things to know so you can get the most out of this book.

First, regarding menu and keyboard commands, here's the convention for indicating that you're going to need to select a command from a menu: The menu and command are separated by an arrow symbol. For example, if we tell you to open the Info Panel from the Flash Menu Bar, the instructions will say to choose Window ⇨ Panels ⇨ Info.

Second, jump in anywhere. Although this book was written to take a beginner by the hand, starting from page one, you can also use it as a reference. Use the index and the table of contents to find what you're looking for, and just go there. If you already know Flash and want to get some details on sound, for example, just go to the sound sections.

Icons: What do they mean?

Although the icons are pretty standard and self-explanatory (they have their names written on them!), here's a brief explanation of what they are and what they mean.

 Tips offer you extra information that further explains a given topic or technique, often suggesting alternatives or workarounds to a listed procedure.

 Notes provide supplementary information to the text, shedding light on background processes or miscellaneous options that aren't crucial to the basic understanding of the material.

 When you see the Caution icon, make sure you're following along closely to the tips and techniques being discussed. Some external applications may not work exactly the same with Flash on different operating systems.

 If you want to find related information to a given topic in another chapter, look for the cross-reference icons.

The New Feature icons point out any differences between Flash 5 and previous versions of Flash.

 This icon indicates that the CD-ROM contains a related file in the given folder.

How this book is organized

Based on feedback from our readers, we have greatly expanded the content in this edition of the Flash Bible, so much in fact that the book has doubled in page count. This book has been written in a format that gives you access to need-to-know information very easily in every section (or Part) of the book. If you are completely new to Flash, then you'll want to read Parts I through V. After you have developed a familiarity with the Flash interface, then you can proceed to Parts VI, VII, and VIII. However, if you've already used Flash 4, then you may want to review the changes to the Flash 5 interface in Part I, and then jump right into Parts V through VIII to learn more about ActionScript, working with Generator, creating artwork and content in other applications, and integrating Flash with HTML. Part VII is especially useful if you have a favorite application such as Dreamweaver or Director in which you want to use Flash movies.

Part I — Mastering the Flash Environment

The first part of this book explores the Flash file format and the interface of Flash 5, explaining the context in which Flash movies interact on the Web (Chapter 1), and working with the new panels and tools (Chapters 2-7). Specifically, you can read about the new Pen Tool in Chapter 4, and you learn how to use the new Mixer Panel in Chapter 6.

Part II — Creating Flash Graphics

After you've learned how to work your way through the Flash interface, you can read about the timeline structures (Chapter 8) and the Flash Library (Chapter 9), where you learn about the symbol types in Flash 5. You can learn how to draw with Flash (Chapter 10), animate with Motion and Shape Tweens (Chapter 11), and incorporate external media files such as JPEGs and GIFs into your Flash artwork (Chapter 12). You see how to structure content on the Main Timeline and create a simple scrolling text interface (Chapter 13).

Part III — Sound Planning

Because Parts I and II focus mainly on the visual presentation of a Flash movie, you need to start thinking about the effect of sound within a Flash movie. In Chapter 14, you learn the basics of digital sound and see which file formats can be imported into Flash. Chapter 15 shows you how to control the playback of sounds within a Flash movie, and you learn how to create interactive buttons with rollover sounds. Chapter 16 explains how to adjust and optimize audio compression in an exported Flash movie.

Part IV — Adding Basic Interactivity to Flash Movies

Not everyone wants to use Flash to create animating buttons for HTML documents on the Web. In Part IV, you learn how to start using Flash actions to create interactive and responsive presentations. You learn the difference between Normal and Expert Modes of the Actions Panel (Chapter 17). Flash 5 has greatly increased the capacity of a Flash movie to communicate with its own internal elements, such as nested Movie Clips (Chapter 18). Properties and methods of the Movie Clip Object are introduced (Chapter 19), and you master the art of preloading and sharing Flash .SWF files (Chapter 20).

Part V — Programming Flash Movies with ActionScript

Flash 5 brings with it a whole new interactive language and syntax called ActionScript. While Flash 4 implemented new interactive functions and controls, Flash 5 enables interactive designers to write code much more easily and fluidly. You learn about solving interactive problems (Chapter 21), making functions and arrays (Chapter 22), detecting Movie Clip collisions and using Smart Clips (Chapter 23), creating Flash forms and loading XML (Chapter 24), and using HTML text fields and properties (Chapter 25). Part V ends with an entire chapter dedicated to advanced Flash movie examples (Chapter 26).

Part VI — Using Flash with Generator and Other Server Technologies

As the Web and Flash mature together, developers increasingly need more dynamic content and data-driven systems for faster updates and maintenance of Web sites, especially for large sites with hundreds (if not thousands) of pages and assets. Macromedia Generator can create and load dynamic graphics and data into Flash movie templates. Chapters 27–29 show you how to get up and running with Generator 2 and other server-side technologies.

Part VII — Using Flash with Other Programs

Every multimedia designer uses Flash with some other graphics, sound, and authoring application to create a unique workflow that solves the problems of daily interactive project development. Part V shows you how to create content in popular applications such as Macromedia Fireworks, Freehand, and Director, as well as Adobe Photoshop and Discreet 3D Studio Max — just to name a few. We're sure that you'll find our coverage of RealPlayer, QuickTime 4, and QuickTime Flash movies particularly interesting.

Part VIII — Distributing Flash Movies

Finally, you need to learn how to export (or publish) your Flash presentations to the .SWF file format for use on a Web page, or within another presentation such as a floppy disk or CD-ROM project. Chapter 25 details every option in the Publish Settings of Flash 5, as well providing tips for optimizing your Flash movies in order to achieve smaller file sizes for faster download performance. If you prefer to hand-code your HTML, then read Chapter 26, which describes how to use the <EMBED> and <OBJECT> tags, how to load Flash movies into framesets, and how to create plug-in detection systems for your Flash movies. If you want to find out how to create a Flash standalone projector, or use the Flash standalone player, then check out Chapter 27.

Appendixes

You'll find directions for using the *Flash 5 Bible* CD-ROM and a listing of our contributors' contact information in the appendixes.

Getting in touch with us

Unlike many authors, we aren't going to make any promises about answering every e-mail that comes to us. We already have more mail than we can *possibly* begin to answer. However, if you have a really, really good tip or idea that you want to share with us, we'd like to hear from you. You can also send us comments about the book to:

    robert@theMakers.com
    jon@theFlashBible.com

Also check Appendix B for more information on contacting this book's various contributors and technical editors.

You can help make Flash better!

The latest version of Flash is more powerful, has more robust capabilities, and is easier to use than any previous version of Flash. It's also the best program that's capable of creating highly-compact, vector-based content for transmission over the Web (although FreeHand can also export to the .SWF file format). We're convinced that Flash 5 is a *great* program. (That's why we wrote this book!) But we also know that Macromedia is probably already planning the next version. So, if you have an idea or feature request for the next version, let the folks at Macromedia know. Send an e-mail to:

    wish-flash@macromedia.com

The simple fact is this: If more users request a specific feature or improvement, it's more likely that Macromedia will implement it.

Acknowledgments

Robert Reinhardt: This book would not have been possible without the help and talent of many people. I am grateful for the added breadth and depth the tutorials bring to this second edition. First and foremost, I would like to thank the Flash development community. In my six years of multimedia research and production, I haven't seen another community that has been so open, friendly, and willing to share advanced tips and techniques. It was a wonderful experience to meet many of you at the FlashForward 2000 conferences in San Francisco and New York.

Along the lines of communal experiences, I would like to thank my award-winning Flash team from Rampt.com. All of them have contributed to this book in one way or another. With Scott Brown, Daniel Cluff, Sandro Corsaro, and Shane Elliott, I learned more about real Flash production in one short year than any books, tech notes, or tutorials could ever describe.

I would like to thank everyone at Hungry Minds (formerly IDG Books Worldwide) who saw this book through a tough production schedule. As anyone in a creative team can attest, a great manager can make or break a project — or, in this case, a book. Julie Smith, our development editor, was always there (on ICQ and at the phone, weekdays and weekends) to answer questions and steer us in the right direction. A great deal of gratitude must also go to Mike Roney, our acquisitions editor. Even when I was pushing deadlines, Mike trusted that I would do whatever it took to see this book, doubled in size from its previous edition, to print.

I find it hard to believe that some authors can go without a literary agent. If it weren't for David Fugate, our agent at Waterside Productions, this book wouldn't have been written — at least, not before the next release of Flash. David, I couldn't have gotten through this without your invaluable guidance and encouragement.

Of course, a book about Flash would not be very useful if it wasn't technically accurate. Many thanks to the developers, engineers, and support staff at Macromedia, especially Gary Grossman and Jeremy Clark, who answered my questions during the development of Flash 5. Also, I am indebted to Jeffrey Bardzell and Shane Elliott for their watchful eyes and keen observations of the material.

Finally, even though this book was considered a "revision" of the first edition, the extensive new features of Flash 5 made the writing process no less grueling. There were many weeks that I missed dog walks to the top of Runyon Canyon and weekend outings to see a movie or swim in the ocean. I couldn't have finished this project without the love, support, and understanding of my partner, Snow Dowd.

Jon Warren Lentz: Over a year ago, when Robert and I were in the early phases of development for the original Flash 4 Bible, I came up with the idea of solicitung Expert Tutorials from eminent Flash artists in order to augment and deepen our coverage of the program. At that time, I had no idea how popular and effective that concept would be – but, judging by the emails from readers and comments to me in person, the idea was clearly a huge success. Accordingly, this book is graced with nearly 50 tutorials which are the contributions of nearly 40 guest tutorialists. In soliciting these contributions, I've had the pleasure of collaborating with and editing the wisdom of some of the finest minds in the Flash world. (The contact information for these contributors is listed in Appendix C.) These contributions have added immeasurable breadth and depth to our book. On behalf of my readers, my co-author, and myself, I want to thank all of you tutorialists for your generosity and genius: you gals and guys ROCK!

I also owe an incredible debt to all of my friends and associates; both on the Flash beta, and also the denizens of the many Flash lists and communities — your unthreatened willingness to share your knowledge and ideas, confident that you have an endless supply better ideas, is what makes our Flash community so vibrant and personally rewarding.

I would like to thank my co-author, Robert Reinhardt for his unflagging support and solidarity throughout all phases of this intensely demanding project. I would also like to thank our agent, David Fugate of the Waterside Agency, for his insight and counsel. I am also grateful to my students and readers: Your questions and ideas have helped me to revise and improve this book on each and every page.

For all the people at Macromedia — especially Jeremy Clark, Flash product manager — I heap high praise and infinite thank yous.

Finally, I would like to thank all of the people at IDG/Hungry Minds, Inc., for the extraordinary efforts which they brought to this project. Thanks to Walt Bruce, our publisher, for allocating so much special attention to this book. Thanks to Andy Cummings for his careful management. Thanks to Michael Roney, our Acquisitions Editor, for keeping us on track and for resolving so many natty details that threatened to impinge on our progress. Thanks to Julie Smith, our Developmental Editor, for your clear and consistent handling of our submissions. Thanks to all of the other amazing people at IDG/Hungry Minds, Inc., for carrying this project from manuscript to the book that you now hold in your hands.

Bravo.

Contents at a Glance

Contents

Part II: Creating Flash Graphics   201

Part III: Sound Planning   389

Chapter 14: Understanding Sound for Flash 391

Chapter 15: Importing and Editing Sounds in Flash 403

Chapter 16: Optimizing Flash Sound for Export 417

Flash in a Flash

The tutorial in this chapter provides a working overview of Flash 5. It guides you through a simple Flash project, from start to finish. Along the way, you'll gain experience with common tools, learn the location and use of many of the new Flash 5 panels, and gain more than passing familiarity with key Flash concepts.

To get the most out of this tutorial, you are strongly encouraged to first work through the tutorials that ship with Flash 5 — including those located in the Help menu as well as the kite tutorial found in *Using Flash 5*. Let's get started!

The Tutorial

In this tutorial, you create a bouncing ball and a button to control the ball. It sounds simple, but completing this tutorial will give you experience with all the major features of Flash.

Starting Flash projects

To begin, let's open a new movie in Flash and prepare it for our project.

1. Open Flash if it isn't already open, or open a new file (File ➪ New).

2. Open the Move Properties dialog. From the main menu, go to Modify ➪ Movie. You can also use Ctrl+M/Command+M to open this dialog, and you'll work more efficiently if you form a habit of learning as many keyboard shortcuts as possible.

3. Set the Frame Rate to 12, if it is not already (this is the default). The frame rate determines the speed at which the animation will run. Although in theory a higher frame rate generally smoothes animation, higher frame rates can also bog down Flash files, which are built to be lean.

♦ ♦ ♦ ♦

In This Quick Start

Planning projects

Setting up .FLAs

Introducing timelines, layers, keyframes, and frames

Creating Graphic, Button, and Movie Clip symbols

Using basic ActionScript

Using Motion Tweens

Editing strokes and fills

Adding sounds

Using frame labels and comments

Sizing and positioning with the Info Panel

Editing gradients

♦ ♦ ♦ ♦

4. Set the movie dimensions to 670(w)×490(h). This size should fit well in the browser windows of those using the common 800×600 resolution. For those running at a smaller resolution, such as 640×480, these dimensions could be a problem. However, as you progress through this book, you learn ways of embedding Flash movies so that they scale to fit. In this tutorial, we chose the larger size to give you plenty of room in which to work.

5. Click OK.

Now you are staring at an empty Stage and timeline.

The Stage should present no particular difficulties — it looks like what you'd find in a drawing or page-layout program, or, for that matter, even in a word processor. But for many of you, the timeline might be something new. A clear understanding of the timeline is critical to productive work in Flash, so let's take a moment to look it over.

The timeline is best understood if you imagine that this tool is used to order graphic information across two dimensions: time and depth.

✦ Arranged horizontally, from left to right, is the sequence of frames as they appear in time. Thus, if your movie is set to 12 frames per second, then the frame 24 occurs at the 2-second mark of your animation.

✦ Arranged vertically, from bottom to top, are layers. The timeline layers enable you to separate different content items on discrete layers. They also enable you to separate content from actions, comments, labels, and sounds, which are another kind of content. Items placed on layers above will block out any items beneath them, without otherwise affecting each other. In the editing environment, you can set layer visibility (the Eye icon), editablility (the Lock icon), and the color of its outlines (the Square icon) — note, however, that these settings do not affect the final movie — all layer content, regardless of visibility or outline settings, is included in the final movie.

The red rectangle with a line extending down through all layers is the Playhead. The *Playhead* indicates which frames are currently displayed on the Stage. Drag it to activate and display another area of the timeline. You can also drag it for a preview of your animation; this is called scrubbing the timeline.

As you'll see soon, a powerful feature of the timeline is that a quick glance at the frames of the timeline provides a lot of information about what is on those frames. Sounds are represented by their waveforms, tweens are colored, actions are designated with an **a**, and labels are marked with a red flag.

Before we actually start populating these frames with items, let's take a moment to plan ahead. Flash is one of those programs that makes you stick to your early decisions, for better or worse, so a moment spent planning can save hours down the line.

There are really two ways in which you can plan your file. The first is to use a consistent way of structuring your Flash files. One way to do that is to use a standard set of layers in *every* new .FLA. These layers will be the same in every movie you make. The second way to plan your file is to think through what items will populate your movie and make room for them ahead of time by adding layers for them in advance. These layers, of course, will vary by movie.

Tip Always give every layer a meaningful name—Flash movies can get complex fast, and one of the best ways to ensure that you're putting everything where it belongs is to give all of your layers a meaningful name.

Let's cover the standard layers first. You can always add more later, but we suggest you always begin with the following set of layers:

✦ **Labels:** In this layer, you'll place frame labels. You can use frame labels to identify certain timeline segments both for your own ease of reading the timeline and to enable Flash to address specific frames. This is done with actions, which we cover in more detail later in this tutorial.

✦ **Comments:** Frame comments are notes visible in the timeline that you make to yourself and your collaborators. Flash ignores them.

✦ **Actions:** Although you can attach actions to any frame in Flash, it is not advisable. Keep all of your actions in one layer because this will make your file much easier to author and maintain.

✦ **Content layers:** Under the preceding three layers you place all of the layers that have content.

Inserting and naming layers is easy.

1. Double-click the name of the original (and only) layer in your timeline (Layer1) to select it.

2. Type **contents**. Flash is case-sensitive, and although that does not make much difference for layers, it does make a difference for other assets. It is probably easier to keep everything lowercase.

3. On the lower left-hand side of the timeline, and beneath your new contents layer, are two folded page icons, one white (with a plus sign) and one blue (with a wavy line). These add new layers: The white adds regular layers, and the blue adds guide layers.

4. Click the white Insert Layer icon to add a new layer.

5. Following Steps 1 and 2, rename the layer **actions**.

6. Now add two more layers, calling the first **comments** and the second **labels**. If you can't see all the layers in your timeline, you can either scroll up and down or drag the gray line across the bottom of the timeline downward to give it more room.

7. Locking layers prevents you from adding items — be it artwork, symbols, or sounds — but it does not prevent you from adding labels, comments, or actions. Thus, one way to make sure that you do not accidentally put a Button in the actions layer is to lock it. Now lock the labels, comments, and actions layers.

Now that you have your standard layers set up, it's time to identify the items that you intend to use in your project. Of course, these may well change during authoring, and you can make changes if necessary. But for now, you can still add new layers for the different kinds of content that you'll be creating.

Here is the plan for the final output of this tutorial. You'll create a simple interface in which users can click a button and make a ball fall and bounce several times before resting. They can click again, and the ball will go away. Onscreen directions will explain this information to them.

You know from this plan that your content will include two Buttons, a bouncing ball, and some text. Thus, a reasonable next step is to add new layers to accommodate these items.

1. Double-click the contents layer name and change it to buttons.

2. Insert two new layers above the buttons layer and call them text and ball. The ball layer should be between the actions and text layers, and the buttons layer should be on the bottom, as shown in the Figure QS-1.

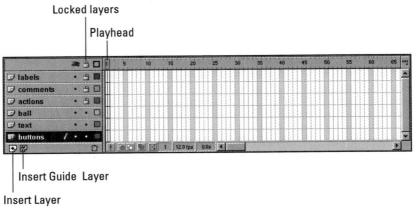

Figure QS-1: The timeline layers that we'll be using in this tutorial.

The width of a circle

In this section of the tutorial, you draw a circle, fill it with a gradient so that it looks like a ball, and then animate the ball.

Drawing, strokes, and fills

Now you have an empty Stage and all these empty layers just begging to be filled. Let's get to work. Our first major task is to create the ball animation.

1. Click the first frame of the ball layer.

2. Click to activate the Oval Tool in the Toolbox on the left. Alternatively, you can press O to activate it.

3. Draw a circle anywhere on the screen. To constrain the oval to a perfect circle, hold down the Shift key as you drag. (This also works for drawing perfect squares with the Rectangle Tool, for constraining lines to 45-degree angles, and other operations.

If you have not changed Flash's default settings, your circle is probably red with a black border going around it. (If it is not — don't worry, because we'll change it in a moment anyway.) The red color that fills the circle is called the fill, and the black border around the circle is called the stroke. Every closed vector item (squares, parallelograms, irregular polygons, and so on) is made up of these two components (though you can set both stroke and fill to none).

Let's modify this circle and make it look more like a ball.

1. Click the edge of the circle (in other words, the stroke). Notice that you can select both the fill and the stroke separately simply by clicking them. Also, you can double-click either to select both. For now, just select the stroke.

2. Using the Launcher Bar (at the bottom-right corner of the screen), click the Show Info icon to open the Info Panel, if it isn't already open.

3. Click the Stroke tab to open the Stroke Panel.

4. In the first drop-down list (Stroke Style), Solid should already be chosen for you by default. Before continuing, why don't you check out some of the alternatives? Then, when you're done, select Solid.

5. Below the Stroke Style drop-down are two other controls. The first, Stroke Height, which has a two-headed arrow beside it, is used to set the thickness of the stroke. Set it to 2.

6. The third control is Stroke Color, which previews the current stroke color. It should display the default to black, which is what we want. This control is also a button. So, if another color is displayed, click the Stroke Color button to invoke the swatches pop-up and choose black.

7. Next, click the fill of the ball to select it (and deselect the stroke), and then click the Fill tab (beside the Stroke tab) to open the Fill Panel.

8. From the Fill Style drop-down, choose Radial Gradient.

9. Unless your installation of Flash has been reconfigured, the default black and white spectrum appears in the dialog. The extreme left of the gradient is black, and the extreme right of the gradient is white. This gradient should change the fill of the ball immediately. Between the two extremes of this gradient, black fades into white. However, to make our circle appear spherical, we want a red ball that fades to black around the edges.

10. Click the black Color Pointer located at the extreme left of the gradient. At right, a Pointer Color control appears.

11. Click the Pointer Color control to open a color palette and choose the bright red swatch midway down the left side of the palette. Your circle's fill becomes red fading to white.

12. Next, click the white Color Pointer, and change it to black. Now your circle looks more like a ball!

13. But there's one problem: The highlight of the ball is exactly in the center, which isn't very realistic. The most likely light source is from above the ball and off to one side, so the lighting of the ball should reflect that. In the Toolbox, choose the Paint Bucket Tool, which is used to modify fills.

14. Notice the Fill Color control in the Color Tray beneath the Toolbox; the gradient is shown. This indicates that it's the active fill, so any shapes that you fill with the Paint Bucket Tool will have this fill.

15. This may take some experimentation, but click within the ball about three-quarters up from the bottom and a little off to the side until you have a more realistic-looking ball (see Figure QS-2).

Sizing and positioning the ball

Now that the ball looks the way you want it to, let's resize it and position it. Although you can resize by using the Scale Tool in the Options Tray (when the Arrow Tool is active) at the bottom of the Toolbox, and you can position simply dragging items, it is more precise to use the Info Panel.

1. From the Launcher Bar, open the Info Panel (it is in the same set as the Stroke and Fill Panels, so it might already be open).

2. The first two controls (W and H) are entry fields that enable you to set the physical dimensions. In both fields, enter 75.

3. The next pair of controls (X and Y) enable you to modify the selected item's positioning, relative to the top-left corner of the Stage. Just like in high school geometry, X modifies the item's horizontal positioning and Y modifies its vertical positioning. However, before we modify these settings, let's talk about the Alignment Grid. The Alignment Grid is located just to the left of the numeric entry fields that are used for adjusting the X and Y location of any selected item. This Alignment Grid consists of nine small squares. Together,

these squares represent an invisible bounding box that encloses the selected item. Every shape created in Flash, even circles, resides in a square or rectangular bounding box that includes the extremities of the shape. Now, this alignment grid enables you to position the selected item relative to either its upper-left corner or its center. Click either square to define which point to use for positioning. Because this is a circle, which by definition doesn't have any corners (although it is still surrounded by an invisible bounding box), it makes more sense to position it relative to its center. Click the center square of the alignment grid, which should turn the middle square black, and the upper-left square to white.

4. Enter 450 for the X position and 75 for the Y position. When you're done, the ball should appear at a new size, near the upper-right corner of the Stage. This will be the origin point of the ball before it falls in the animation.

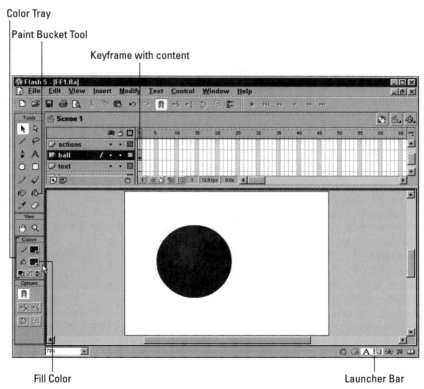

Figure QS-2: You can use off-center radial gradients to make a circle look like a sphere.

Your first animation

Now that you have created and positioned the ball, you're ready to set it in motion. As you may be aware, Flash offers several different methods of animation, including Frame-by-Frame and both Motion and Shape Tweens. For now, we'll work with Motion Tweening, which is perhaps the easiest of the three.

In the next couple of steps, we cover the full mechanics of a Motion Tween. For now, what you need to know is that a Motion Tween enables you to make an item move from one location to another over time. Now, for Flash to Motion Tween an item over time, it has to understand that the item in the first frame of the animation and the item in the last frame (and all the other items between) are all the same item. In our case, we need Flash to know that the ball in the air at the beginning is the same ball as the one hitting the ground at the end of the first Tween.

Simple graphics versus symbols and instances

To enable Flash to recognize that the item that occurs at the beginning and end of a Motion Tween is the same, you need to change the ball from a standard piece of art-work to a symbol, so that you can reuse the artwork throughout the movie. In other words, by converting the artwork into a symbol, you make it possible for Flash to recognize two pieces of art that are located in different frames on the timeline as two instances of the same item. Once Flash sees that the ball in the air at the beginning of the Motion Tween is the same ball as the one striking the ground at the end of the Motion Tween, it's capable of tweening, or drawing, the intervening positions for you; that is, the series of ball pictures that change incrementally as it falls to the ground. Tweening saves you a lot of time and work.

Converting artwork to symbols also saves you bandwidth. Because Flash refers to the singular symbol to generate multiple instances, your user will only have to download the ball once, even if you use it hundred of times on your site. Similar to the programming distinction between an item class and an item based on that class, when you create an instance of a symbol, behind the scenes you're literally reusing the same code. Flash keeps track of this by creating a link between your many instances and the one symbol they are based upon — and every time you deploy an instance, Flash simply inserts a copy of the symbol. Another bonus is that if you decide that you need to edit the symbol, it will automatically update all of the instances, saving you some painstaking work.

While it may be conceptually difficult to understand what symbols are and the possibilities they enable, actually making your graphic into a symbol is quite easy. So, let's get started working with symbols now and develop more of the conceptual background as we go:

1. Select the sphere (make sure you select both the fill and the stroke by double-clicking the fill).

2. Then choose Insert ➪ Convert to Symbol. In the Symbol Properties dialog, name it **ball**, then click the Graphic radio button, and then click OK or press Enter to continue.

Notice that your ball is no longer selected with gray hatching; instead, there is a blue bounding box around it. This change in the appearance of the selection indicates a change in the architectural status of the item. The ball on screen is no longer a piece of artwork. The ball is now an instance of the ball symbol that you just created and which resides in your Library. Choose Window ➪ Library, or Ctrl+L in Windows, or Command+L on a Mac, to open the Library panel.

Frames, keyframes, and frame sequences

In a tweened animation, an instance of a symbol is either moved or manipulated across a span of frames, with incremental changes displayed in the intervening frames. So, now that you understand the reason for symbols and instances and understand the logic of tweening, you're probably wondering how to designate beginning and ending frames. In other words, how does Flash know when to start and when to stop a tween?

The answer is that there are different kinds of frames in the timeline, and you use these different frames to establish and define changes of content across a given layer of the timeline.

✦ **Keyframes:** A keyframe is a frame in which something changes in a layer of the timeline. The first frame of every layer is, by default, a keyframe. Keyframes can be empty or they can have any number of items in them. You can use empty keyframes as a way to stop the display of existing content on a given layer.

✦ **Frames:** Also known as static frames, regular frames depend on keyframes. By definition, no new content can be added in a regular frame. Thus, if a ball appears in a keyframe, and is followed by ten static frames, the ball would remain motionless throughout that span of ten frames (unless the first keyframe initiates a tween).

✦ **Frame Sequences:** The new Flash 5 timeline makes heavy use of this concept: A frame sequence is a keyframe and all of the static frames that follow it, up to, but not including, the next keyframe in a layer. Frame sequences are selectable as an entity, which means that they can be easily copied and moved in the timeline.

To answer the question of how Flash knows when to begin and end a tween, the answer is simple: keyframes. The item in one keyframe is tweened across the intervening static frames until it reaches the next keyframe, which contains the item in the final position of the tween. In this scenario, the intervening static frames become tweened frames.

Creating a Motion Tween

Motion Tweens are animations between two keyframes. These animations can involve a change in color, shape, size, space, or any combination of the preceding. As regards an animation through space, the placement of the item in the first keyframe determines the starting point of the item, and its placement in the second keyframe determines the item's ending point.

Now, let's create a simple Motion Tween with the ball, wherein the ball will appear to fall down to the bottom of the Stage. Before you can do that, you'll need to insert a second keyframe in the timeline, which will designate where the ball will land.

1. Click frame 20 in the timeline of the stage. Then, to insert a keyframe, choose Insert ⇨ Keyframe from the main menu, or press F6.

2. Notice that the ball is still at the top of the screen, just where it was in frame 1. Actually, this is a new instance of the same ball symbol. That's because Flash automatically creates a new instance of any placed instance that occurs on the preceding keyframe, every time you create a new keyframe.

3. With frame 20 selected, drag the ball down so it is near the bottom of the Stage. Remember that before you click and drag, you should hold down the Shift key and then drag to force the ball to go straight down — you don't want a wobble, or for it to fall at a diagonal!

4. Now that the ball is correctly positioned in both keyframes, insert a Motion Tween to let Flash do the animating. Click the first keyframe of the ball layer.

5. Next, from the main menu, choose Insert ⇨ Create Motion Tween, or open the Frame Panel (Windows ⇨ Panels ⇨ Frame, or Ctrl/Command+F). In the Tweening drop-down menu, choose Motion.

6. You now have a Motion Tween (see Figure QS-3). Note that the span in the timeline extending from one keyframe to the other is now blue and has an arrow pointing from the first keyframe to the second.

7. You can preview your Tween by dragging the Playhead back and forth across frames 1 through 20. This kind of preview is called scrubbing the timeline.

Motion Tween

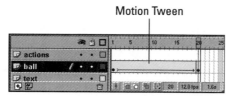

Figure QS-3: Motion Tweens appear in the timeline as a blue-shaded region with an arrow pointing from the first keyframe to the second.

If you had a steady hand while you were scrubbing the timeline, you probably noticed something. When a real-life ball is dropped, it accelerates. That is, it is moving faster when it hits the ground than it was when it left your hands. However, your ball moves uniformly to the ground and stops. Is this just a case of a computer not being able to animate as well as a human can?

Although there is no substitute for hand-drawn animation, Flash does have a few tricks. One trick is *Easing,* which enables you to control acceleration and deceleration in Motion Tweens.

Easing is an option that appears in the Frame Panel on the frame in which a Motion Tween is initiated.

1. Click the first frame of the ball layer of the timeline.

2. Using the Launcher Bar, open the Instance Panel and then click the Frame tab to open the Frame Panel.

3. In the Tweening drop-down menu, you should see Motion already selected.

4. Beneath that is a control labeled Easing, as shown in Figure QS-4. The drop-down arrow pulls up a slider, which you can drag down into negative numbers, or up into positive numbers. Positive Easing, called Easing Out, causes the tweened item to start quickly and to slow toward the end — just the opposite of what we want. Drag the slider all the way down to the bottom, so that the number is –75.

If you scrub the timeline again, with a steady hand, you'll see the effect of the Easing.

Frame Panel is in the Instance Panel group

Easing slider

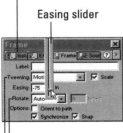

Rotation options (partially obscured)

The Tweening drop-down menu (partially obscured)

Figure QS-4: The Easing slider on the Frame Panel

Of course, most balls, when dropped, bounce back up — and fall back down, and bounce back up. Let's add a few bounces, so that the ball goes up and down a few times before resting on the ground.

If you think about it for a moment, you'll realize that the bounces are going to require more tweens — twice as many tweens as there are bounces. Also, you'll have to reverse the effect of Easing for each tween, because when the ball is falling, it accelerates, and while it is rebounding, it decelerates.

In addition, you know that every time you add a keyframe, Flash simply copies the contents of the last keyframe, which means that half of your work is already done for you. The ball will bounce or land from the same spot on the ground each time, meaning that the location of the ball in frame 20 will also be the location of the ball in every other keyframe until (and including) the final keyframe, in which the ball stops.

Let's make the ball bounce three times and come to a rest on the fourth.

1. Press F6 to insert keyframes in frames 40, 55, 70, 80, 90, and 98. Notice that we are shortening the span of time each bounce requires — because with each bounce, the ball won't travel as high as the previous bounce, the ball will need less time to rise and fall.

2. Click frame 1 and note where the ball is. Then click frame 40 and drag the ball about three-fourths of the way up — don't forget to constrain with the Shift key! (If you're mathematically inclined, you can use the Y position in the Info Panel to figure out *exactly* where the three-quarter mark is.)

3. Click frame 20 and from the Frame Panel, insert a Motion Tween, and set the Easing to 100, to make the ball Ease Out.

4. Scrub the timeline to preview the effect.

5. Click frame 55. How convenient! The ball is already back on the ground.

6. Click frame 40 and insert a Motion Tween, setting the Easing at –75.

7. Click frame 70 and drag the ball to about half the height it was in frame 1.

8. Return to frame 55 and insert a Motion Tween, setting the Easing to 100.

9. Again, the ball in frame 80 is already where it needs to be. Click frame 70 and insert a Motion Tween, setting the Easing to –75.

10. In frame 90, drag the ball up so that it is one-quarter the height it was in frame 1.

11. Returning to frame 80, insert a Motion Tween and set the Easing to 100.

12. Finally, click frame 90, insert a Motion Tween, and set the easing to –75.

13. Scrub the timeline from beginning to end to watch the animation!

The animation of the ball is now completed, but we're not quite through with it.

Movie Clip Symbols

Working with a Movie Clip is in many ways like working with the main movie. Each Movie Clip has its own Stage, timeline, and layers. All of the drawing tools work in the same ways that they work on the main Stage. You can even place other symbols (for example, Button instances and other Movie Clips) inside Movie Clips. In short, Movie Clips are like full-blown Flash movies that can be placed in a single frame of the main movie. It's this nesting that gives Flash Movie Clips their power.

A primary (and initially most obvious) structural benefit of Movie Clips is that Movie Clip timelines play independently of the Main Timeline. This independence facilitates great flexibility in the overall development of your movie. It enables your movie to stop and keep moving at the same time. Later in this lesson, you'll end up with only two frames of content on your Main Timeline. In one of the two keyframes, there will be the Movie Clip of the bouncing ball animation you've just created, and the ball will bounce even though the Playhead of the Main Timeline has stopped!

Convert the timeline-based animation to a Movie Clip

Enough theory — it's time to find out how simple it is to convert a Main Timeline animation into a Movie Clip.

1. Click any of the static frames in the ball layer (any blue-shaded nonkeyframe) to select the entire animation from beginning to end.

2. Now, copy the frames: Proceeding from the Main Menu, choose Edit ⇨ Copy Frames; or, from the keyboard, Ctrl+Alt+C/Option+Command+C; or right-click/Ctrl+click and choose Copy Frames.

3. Next, create a new Movie Clip symbol. Choose Insert ⇨ New Symbol (Ctrl+F8/Command+F8).

4. In the Symbol Properties dialog, name your symbol **bb** for bouncing ball. Leave the behavior at its default, which is Movie Clip.

5. You should now be viewing a blank Stage with an empty timeline. You have entered Symbol Editing Mode, which simply means that you're authoring in a symbol, and not in the main movie. One indication of this change in authoring environments is the appearance of a new tab at the upper-left of the timeline. This tab displays the Movie Clip icon, together with the title of this Movie Clip, bb. Thus, both the timeline and Stage that you now see belong to the symbol only. Click the first frame of the timeline (be sure that it is selected, which is indicated by its being displayed with black), and choose Edit ⇨ Paste Frames, Ctrl+Alt+V/Option+Command+V, or right-click/Ctrl+click and choose Paste Frames.

6. Notice that the first (and only) layer of the Movie Clip's timeline is called Layer1, which is not the most descriptive name in the world. Double-click the name and rename it **ball**.

Your animation is now in a Movie Clip. But there's one hitch; this Movie Clip is just sitting in your Library, and the original animation is still on the Main Timeline. Let's replace the Main Timeline animation with an instance of the Movie Clip animation.

1. Return to the main movie by clicking the Scene 1 button just above the left-hand side of the timeline, shown in Figure QS-5. Alternatively, you can choose Edit ➪ Movie from the main menu (Ctrl+E/Command+E).

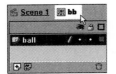

Figure QS-5: These tabs above the timeline help you determine which Stage you are editing—that of the main movie or that of a symbol

2. Click any static frame in the tweened animation to select the entire animation sequence. (Note: This selection method works only if the Flash 5 Selection Style and Frame Drawing have been left as the default in Edit ➪ Preferences ➪ General.)

3. Choose Insert ➪ Remove Frames to remove both the contents of each of the frames and the empty frames (including keyframes) themselves. When you're done, the entire layer should be entirely empty, lacking even a keyframe in frame 1.

4. Now, insert a keyframe in frame 1 by pressing F6.

5. Then, open your Library (Ctrl+L/Command+L), if it isn't already open.

6. Finally, with frame 1 of the ball layer still active, click and drag the bb Movie Clip out of the Library and drop it on the main Stage.

All 98 frames of the bb Movie Clip are now placed entirely within frame 1 of the ball layer of the Main Timeline. If the movie were to stop in frame 1, the complete ball animation would still play, because all 98 of its frames are encapsulated in the bb Movie Clip placed on frame 1.

Position the Movie Clip

The only problem now is that the ball is wherever you dropped it, and not where we placed it so precisely using the Info Panel in an earlier step. Let's reposition the ball with the Info Panel again.

You can't simply use the same numbers that you used earlier, though. Ensuring that the bb Movie Clip is selected, you'll notice a small crosshair symbol below and to the left of the ball. This crosshair represents the center of the Movie Clip. This might seem strange because the ball animation at no time even passes through this crosshair. What is going on?

Here is what happened: When you converted the ball animation to a Movie Clip, Flash remembered the positioning of the ball relative to the center of the Stage. In short, this crosshair now marks where the center of the Stage was before the conversion. It follows, then, that to reposition the ball again, you would need to position this crosshair exactly at the center of the Stage.

With the bb Movie Clip still selected, open the Info Panel and look at the Alignment Grid. Make sure that the center box is still selected. Next, enter the center coordinates of the movie: Set X to **335** and Y to **245** (half of 670 and 490, which are the dimensions of the movie, as set at the beginning of this tutorial). The crosshair is now at the exact center of the movie, and the ball is in its original position.

The bb Movie Clip is complete and in place. So now, with our star item ready, it is time to flesh out the rest of the movie. But first, have you saved your project yet?

Frame labels and comments

We begin by defining different segments of our timeline using labels and comments. Although this is not a complex movie, it is a good place to start developing good work habits. As you develop long movies with many things going on at once, interpreting the timeline becomes more difficult. Labels and comments are two ways to make logical divisions and help you (and Flash — as we'll see shortly) keep track of what is going on.

In the case of the movie we are developing — a simple interface in which users can click a button and make a ball fall and bounce several times before resting, and click again to make the ball go away — you'll need to divide your timeline into two major segments: One segment will have a button and some text indicating that pressing the button will activate the ball animation, and the other segment will be where the ball animation is accessed and played.

You can use frame labels and comments much like you might use bookmarks: to identify sections or events (for example, the beginning of a given tween, or transition between an intro animation and a stopped frame in which the user has to click a button to continue).

Labels or comments?

Why have two different kinds of timeline bookmarks? To serve two different purposes, of course!

✦ **Labels:** Labels actually communicate with Flash. You can use frame labels as targets of Go To actions (simple ActionScripts that move the Playhead to a specified location). Consequently, labels are exported in .SWF movies — they are necessary for the functioning of ActionScript. For this reason, you should keep labels short.

✦ **Comments:** Comments, much like comments in programming, are simply notes that you can make to yourself or others developing the movie with you. They are not exported in .SWF movies, so they neither add file size nor have any functional impact. They simply help you keep track of what is going on in complex timelines.

Inserting labels and comments

Let's insert a couple frame labels:

1. Click frame 1 of the labels layer.

2. Using the Launcher Bar, click the Instance Button and click the Frame tab to invoke the Frames Panel.

3. Enter **intro** in the Label text field.

4. In the timeline, if there is room to display it, a red flag will appear with the text you entered next to it. In your file, there probably is not room yet.

5. Click frame 10 of the labels layer and insert a keyframe. Now you can see that intro label!

6. Add a label to frame 10 as well, calling it **ball.** Again, you probably cannot see the label, because there aren't enough frames. You can click frame 20 and press F5 to insert some extra frames.

All of the items in this movie will be placed within keyframes in two places: The first set of keyframes will be in various layers of frame 1, while the others will be in frame 10. For this reason, you could put the entire movie in the first two frames. The only reason that we don't is to provide room to view our labels and comments. The extra frames (frames 2 to 9, which are empty in all layers) do not affect file size or movie performance. If we wanted to (we don't), we could put the second set of keyframes on frame 100 or even on frame 15,999 — but 16,000 is the limit.

Although we aren't going to insert any comments just yet, the process is nearly the same as for adding labels, with one modification:

1. Follow the previous directions for entering a label.

2. Insert two slashes // before the text in the Label text field.

In the timeline, if there is room to display it, a green //, rather than a red flag, will appear with the text that you entered next to it.

Working with text

Some interfaces are so well designed that users just know where to click. In our simple movie, however, we'll provide simple directions.

1. Click the first frame of the text layer to activate that layer.
2. Choose the Text Tool from the Toolbox.
3. Click just inside the left edge of the Stage at about the same height as the ball.
4. Type the following (we'll format the text in a moment): **The button below controls a cool animation.**
5. Select the entire text that you just typed.
6. Using the Launcher Bar, open the Character Panel.
7. Use the Font Name drop-down menu to choose a sans-serif font such as Arial or Helvetica.
8. Using the Font Size control, type in the field or drag the slider bar so that the font size is 44.
9. Your text block probably runs right across the bb Movie Clip and off the Stage! See Figure QS-6.

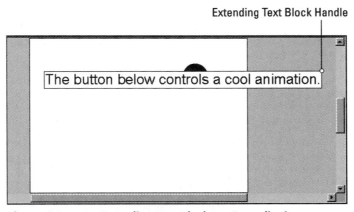

Figure QS-6: An Extending Text Block . . . Extending!

10. To resize the text block, and change its behavior to a Fixed Text Block, simply drag the circle in the top-right corner of the text block to the left. As you drag, the text block adds lines as necessary to wrap the text. When you let go, this round corner-handle becomes a square corner-handle.

Note

The (circle) Extending Text Block Handle indicates that the text block is expandable, and as you add text, the text block simply widens. The (square) Fixed Text Block Handle indicates that the text block has a fixed width, and that — as you add text — the block creates additional lines for new text below. By default, when you first create a text block, it has an Extending Text Block Handle. After you manually set the width of a text block, it automatically converts to a Fixed Text Block Handle.

These directions will appear in both frames of the movie; that is, even after the user has clicked the button and started the animation, the text will still be visible. Because the text won't change, you don't need a second keyframe in that layer.

The Button symbol

Buttons are one of the three symbol types. Buttons are used primarily for interactivity, often triggering some sort of event. As you will soon see, Flash makes it easy to create slick, responsive Buttons. The interactivity is where it gets more complicated. Still, you can easily create interactive movies with Buttons and simple ActionScripts — in fact, we do that next.

Buttons in Flash 5

The next step is to add the buttons, and from there, to add the ActionScripts that will make the Buttons interactive. Let's begin by going over some Button basics.

Like Movie Clips, Buttons are symbols and have their own timelines. Also like Movie Clips, Button timelines run independently of the Main Timeline. But that's pretty much where the similarity ends.

Unlike Movie Clip timelines, Button timelines never run at 12 (or whatever) frames per second. You cannot tween items across the frames of the Button timeline. (You can, however, have animation — including tweens — within a Button.)

The major difference between Buttons and Movie Clips — and the most important fact you can know about Buttons — is that Button timelines always have exactly four frames. These frames aren't played over time elapsed; rather, they are displayed in response to user interaction with the Button. Table QS-1 explains each of the four frames of a Flash Button.

Table QS-1 Button Frames and Functionality	
Frame Name	**Functionality**
Up	This is the natural state of the Button; the way the Button appears when the page is first loaded.
Over	Commonly called the *rollover*, this frame appears on screen when the user's cursor rolls over (without clicking) the Button.
Down	The Down state appears during the moment that the user clicks the Button (lasting only until the user releases it). As you learn later, this state is the most common state during which an action (or behavior) is triggered.

Frame Name	Functionality
Hit	This refers to the hot (or clickable) area of the Button. The user never sees what is in this frame, but neglecting it can have some unpleasant consequences.

Creating a Button

The first step in making a Button is drawing the shape itself.

1. Begin by clicking to select the first frame of the buttons layer.

2. Choose the Rectangle Tool from the Toolbox.

3. The Round Rectangle Radius button appears in the Options Tray at the bottom of the Toolbox. Click this button to open the Rectangle Settings dialog.

4. Enter **11** as the Corner Radius setting. This rounds the corners of any rectangles you draw, and it is a good way to make rectangular items look more buttonlike.

5. In the Color Tray, set the stroke to none and the fill to bright red.

   • To set the color of the stroke or fill, click the adjacent Stroke or Fill Color button, which will invoke either the Stroke or Fill swatches. Notice that when you drag your cursor over either of the swatches, or elsewhere within the interface, the cursor turns into an Eyedropper. Furthermore, as you move over the colors in the palette or anywhere on screen, you'll notice a six-digit number in the hex field above the colors — it updates to display the values for the color immediately beneath the dropper, as you move. This number is the color's hexadecimal value, which is simply the unique color description that identifies each color. To the right of the hex field is a white button with a red slash through it. Click this button to set the stroke to none.

   • For the red fill color, choose #FF0000 (this red can be found in the leftmost column of colors, about halfway down; or, you can simply type the number in the hex field).

6. Draw a rectangle in the bottom half of the Stage. Don't worry too much about positioning just yet; eyeballing it is sufficient for now.

7. Select both the stroke and fill of the rectangle.

8. Using the Launcher Bar, open the Info Panel.

9. Set the rectangle's width to 137 pixels and height to 55 pixels.

10. With the rectangle still selected, convert it to a Button symbol, as follows:

    • Choose Insert ⇨ Convert to Symbol.

    • In the Symbol Properties dialog, name your Button **button** and choose Button as its behavior. Whenever you have the option to name something (for example, layers, symbols, and instances), use simple, meaningful names — you will thank yourself in the end.

    • Click OK.

11. The hatching that previously indicated that a drawing was selected has now turned into a blue bounding box, indicating that it is now a symbol instance.

12. In the Library, double-click the button symbol icon to view it in Symbol Editing Mode.

13. You'll see that the timeline has changed; there are now four frames, labeled Up, Over, Down, and Hit. Notice also that layers work the same way and that there is a keyframe in the Up frame only. Keyframes work the same way in Buttons as they do in other timelines: A keyframe signifies a change in the content of a layer. Remember, too, that all subsequent layers up to the next keyframe have the same content as this keyframe.

Modifying the Button

The next step is to turn this simple red rectangle graphic into a Button that responds to the user. For this exercise, we'll have the Button brighten when users roll over it and appear to be depressed when users click it.

Of course, the graphic is already bright red! So, rather than brighten the Button further, let's darken the Button in the Up frame. Before you start modifying the graphic in the four frames, though, you need to place it in the remaining three frames. To do this, you *could* simply insert a keyframe in each of the frames, because you know that Flash will copy the contents of the first keyframe into the next, unless you insert a blank keyframe.

But copying the keyframes is not the most efficient way. If you distribute the artwork across all four keyframes, then Flash will have to include *four* different pieces of artwork, even though they are really all the same (albeit with minor modifications, which are covered in the next step).

You already know that you should use symbols whenever possible to keep file sizes small. So, go ahead and convert this red rectangle in the Up frame into a Graphic symbol. Then you can place instances of this symbol within each Button keyframe and save Flash (and yourself, if you should later decide to make any edits to the graphic) some work.

1. You should still be in Symbol Editing Mode for the Button, and if it's not already selected, select the rectangle artwork (hatching should cover the Button to indicate that it is selected).

2. Proceeding from the main menu, choose Insert ⇨ Convert to Symbol. This time, call it **button shape** and set its behavior to Graphic.

3. After it is converted, the selection style changes again, from hatching to a blue bounding box.

4. Now, enter a keyframe (press F6) in each of the three remaining frames. New instances of the button shape Graphic symbol will be inserted for you in each frame.

Now you have identical instances of the same graphic symbol in each of the four frames of your Button symbol. This is our first nested symbol — you are becoming a bona fide Flash architect.

Next, let's complete the visual design of the Button so that it brightens on rollover and then, when clicked, appears depressed.

The Up frame, or Up state

The instance of our rounded rectangle that appears in this frame will be how the Button looks when the page first loads, before the user approaches or clicks it. It's going to be darker than it will be on rollover, having a subdued appearance that will beg users to click it.

Here is the catch: You cannot directly edit an instance of a symbol, so you cannot change the fill to a darker color. In addition, changing the fill of the symbol itself changes all instances, making it impossible to distinguish between the instances in the three frames of the Button animation. What you need, then, is some special way to distinguish among the symbol instances on the Button frames.

Flash provides just such a tool: Instance Effects. Instance Effects alter the appearance of an instance without actually requiring Flash to redraw the graphic from scratch; it simply modifies an existing symbol. These effects include Brightness, Tint, Alpha (transparency), and a combination of these, which is called Advanced. Each effect modifies the color of the instance. Although they may not be the most robust graphics tools in the world, in concert with the other capabilities of Flash, they pack a lot of punch.

In this step, we're going to use the Tint Effect, which will mix another color with the instance that will darken the rounded rectangle graphic (without forcing Flash to download and draw it from scratch).

1. With the Up frame selected, click to select the button shape instance on the Stage.

2. Using the Launcher Bar, click the Show Instance Button. Then click the Effect tab to display the Effect Panel.

3. In the drop-down menu, choose Tint. The Tint Effect will tint your instance with the color you select.

4. Click the Tint Color button to choose black (hex: #000000). Your instance is now completely black. We said dark, but we don't want it *that* dark!

5. There are four sliders on the right side of the dialog. The lower three (R, G, B) enable you to custom mix a color, while the first controls the percentage of tint applied to the original color of the instance. A Tint setting of 100 percent, the default, tints the instance completely with the tint color you selected: in this case, black. At the other end of the spectrum, 0 percent (not surprisingly) won't tint the instance at all. Drag the slider up and down just to get an interactive sense for how the black tint affects the button instance. (You might even try another tint color, such as a bright yellow, just to get an even better sense for how the Tint Instance Effect works.) When you're done experimenting, set the tint color back to black and use the slider to set the tint amount to 34 percent, as shown in Figure QS-7. Now, the Up state of your Button is a deep burgundy color.

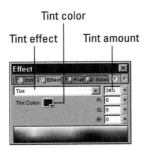

Figure QS-7: The Effect Tab with the Tint Effect selected.

The Over frame, or Over state

This frame is to be the brightest of the frames, and the rectangle is already quite bright. Other than remembering that this frame is the one shown on rollover, you need do nothing else for this frame.

The Down frame, or Down state

The rectangle in this frame is going to be the same color as it was on rollover, so there is no need for you to add any instance effects. What you need, instead, is to move it to give it the appearance that it's been pushed down when clicked.

1. Click the rectangle in the Down frame to select it.

2. Working with the arrow keys on your keyboard, press the down arrow three times, and the right arrow four times. You can use your arrow keys to nudge items in small increments. Nudging this instance of the button downward and to the right will create the effect that, when the Down state is displayed, the button has been pushed.

The Hit frame, or Hit state

The Hit state is a bit trickier; because your users will never see it, it might be tempting to ignore the Hit state altogether. The Hit state determines the hot area of the Button.

The appropriate use of Hit states can eliminate a few common pitfalls. These happen when your Button frames meet one of the following situations:

✦ Buttons with different shapes or shapes in different locations on each of the four frames.

✦ Buttons made of shapes with no fills.

✦ Buttons made of text only without a surrounding shape.

In each of these cases, clicking the Buttons can create some embarrassing problems that could have been easily avoided with good Hit frames.

Usually, the problem with these buttons is that there is no consistent, clear, clickable area throughout all states of the Button. As regards text Buttons, the problem is that the spaces between the letter shapes are not active. For example, the user must click precisely upon the shape of the O, — as clicking in the center of the letter is not defined as hot. The solution is to make a shape in the Hit frame that extends to include the aggregate outline of all preceding button states, and that is a little bit larger.

Because the Button you're making does not meet either of the previous criteria in the Up or Over states, it won't hurt just to leave it as is.

Using the Align Panel to position the Button

Exit Symbol Editing Mode (Edit ➪ Edit Movie [Ctrl+E/Command+E]). Your Button should be on the Stage of the Main Timeline. If not, drag an instance of the Button onto the Stage. Now, let's position the button.

1. Drag the button so that it is near the bottom of the Stage, with a little white space beneath.

2. Next, we use the Align Panel (shown in Figure QS-8) to center the button left-to-right on the Stage. Open the Align Panel (Window ➪ Panels ➪ Align or Ctrl+K/Command+K).

3. Click the To Stage button on the right side of the panel. You can use this panel to align items relative to each other or relative to the Stage. We want the Button centered left-to-right on the Stage, so we'll align relative to the Stage.

4. Click the Align Vertical Center button.

Align Horizontal Center

Align Vertical Center

To Stage

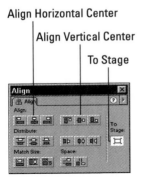

Figure QS-8: The Align Panel

Pushing your Buttons

Graphically, your Button is complete. Of course, you'll need to attach some ActionScript in order to make it do anything. Some sort of button label would also help. But you should first test your Button, just to make sure everything looks the way it should.

You can test buttons in the authoring environment by selecting Control ➪ Enable Simple Buttons (Ctrl+Alt+B/Option+Command+B).

Roll your cursor over the Button and then click it. Cool! (We recommend unchecking Enable Simple Buttons as soon as you're done testing; otherwise, you cannot select the Button to move, modify, or attach actions to it.)

Adding a Button label

As a plain rectangle, the Button is a little nondescript, so let's add a simple button label so users know that it's a Button.

1. Open the Button again in Symbol Editing Mode. (Double-click the button icon in the Library.)

2. Right now, your Button only has one layer, called by default Layer1. Double-click the name in the Layer Bar and rename it **rectangle.**

3. Next, insert a new layer (click the white page icon beneath the first layer). A new layer should appear above the rectangle layer.

4. Rename this layer **label.**

5. If it's not already selected, click the Up frame of the label layer.

6. Choose the Text Tool to activate it and then open the Character Panel.

7. Choose a sans-serif font, such as Arial or Helvetica, if it isn't already selected. Set the font size to 27. Set the font color to white. Click the B button to make it Bold.

8. With the Up frame of the label layer still selected, and with the Text Tool still selected, click over the rectangle and type **Click Me!**

9. Now, switch to the Arrow Tool in the Toolbox.

10. Using the Arrow Tool, click the text block (that you just created) and then Shift+click the rectangle (that is, the button), so that both are selected.

11. Using the Align Panel (Ctrl+K/Command+K), click To Stage and then click both the Align Vertical Center and Align Horizontal Center buttons (if you're not sure which buttons these are, hold your cursor over the buttons for a pop-up message indicating each button's name). This will align both the button and its text label perfectly to the center of the Stage (and to each other).

12. Next, insert keyframes in the Over and Down frames of the label layer. You do not need to enter a keyframe in the Hit layer, because no one will ever see it, and you know that the button area is already sufficiently covered.

13. Click the Down keyframe of the label layer. Oops! The text doesn't line up with the rectangle.

14. With the text selected, use your arrow keys to nudge the text down three times and to the right four times.

15. Return to Movie Editing Mode (Ctrl+E/Command+E) and test the Button again.

At this point, your Stage and timeline should look like Figure QS-9.

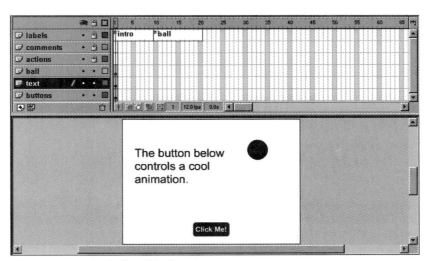

Figure QS-9: The ball and its button

The sound and the fury

Now that your button *looks* good, let's add some sounds to it, which will enhance your user's experience.

Although Flash has many options for using sound, many designers simply neglect to add sound to their Flash movies. Yet, adding simple sounds to Buttons can be a very effective way to provide users with feedback and to improve their experience. Adding a quick sound to your Buttons is easy to do and, if done with a little intelligent restraint, won't affect your file size too much.

Sound basics in Flash 5

To import a sound into a Flash movie, simply use the Import dialog (File ⇨ Import [Ctrl+R/Command+R]) and navigate to the file. Flash 5 can import any of these sound file types: .WAV, .AIFF, and .MP3. Upon import, sounds are placed in the Library.

Sounds, like any other Library item, have to be placed into a frame of a timeline (including the Main Timeline, any Movie Clip timeline, or any Button timeline). Also, like any other symbol, you can deploy as many instances of the original sound symbol as you like without affecting file size.

Because sounds, like animations, occur over time, audio synchronization is important. In other words, you need your sounds to start and stop in sync with what's going on in the rest of the movie. Flash offers several ways to handle synchronization as well as other sound options in the Sounds Panel.

> ✦ **Event:** Event sounds begin on the keyframe to which they are added and play independently of the timeline.
>
> ✦ **Stream:** Stream sounds are locked to the timeline. In a browser, Flash will force the frames and sounds to play in sync, even if it needs to drop frames of animation to keep up.
>
> ✦ **Start/Stop:** These options simply start a sound (again, if it is still playing) or stop it where it is.

Import and deploy two sounds

On the CD-ROM in the 00_QS folder are two sounds: buzz.wav and pop.wav. You'll need both of these sounds for the following steps.

1. Import both the buzz.wav and pop.wav sound clips from the 00_Flash in a Flash folder on the CD-ROM. Choose File ⇨ Import (Ctrl+R/Command+R) and navigate to the each sound file. Select it and click Open.

2. The imported sound goes to your Library. Notice that sounds in the Library have a speaker icon next to them.

Add sounds to the Button

When you import a sound, it goes directly to your Library. It will not appear in your movie — even if you have a keyframe selected — until you drag it from your Library to any keyframe on a Button, the Main Timeline, or a Movie Clip. Now, let's associate the sounds with the proper frames of the Button.

1. Enter Symbol Editing Mode to edit the Button.

2. Add a new layer to the Button timeline and call it **sounds.**

3. Insert a keyframe in both the Over frame and the Down frame of the sounds layer.

4. Click the Over frame of the sounds layer to select it.

5. With the Library open, drag buzz.wav onto the Stage and let go. Note that nothing appears to be different on the Stage, but the squiggly blue line representing the sound waveform in the previously empty Over frame of the sounds layer on the Button timeline indicates that you've successfully placed the sound.

6. Following the preceding steps, add the pop.wav sound to the Down frame of the sounds layer.

If you like, you can return to the main Stage (Edit ➪ Edit Movie), enable Buttons (Control ➪ Enable Simple Buttons), and test your Button. Irresistible!

Figuring items over time

With your frame labels set up, your timeline now logically divided into two sections, and your text, Movie Clip, and Button items in place, you need to put these items in their appropriate section(s).

Again, in our plan, the user will only see the text block and Button when the movie first displays. The ball animation will only become visible after the Button has been pressed, which will advance the Playhead to the ball label section. To begin, then, the bb Movie Clip should not be visible in the first frame.

Of course, it's currently visible in the first frame, so you'll need to move the keyframe to frame 10, so that it's under the ball label.

1. Click the first frame of the ball layer.

2. Drag the keyframe itself to frame 10. The first frame no longer has a black circle in it, indicating that it's empty. Now, frame 10 does have a black circle in it, and all of the intervening frames have been filled with empty frames.

3. Optionally, you can click frame 20 and press F5 to insert extra frames. While the Playhead will only alternate between frame 1 and frame 10, you've added extra frames to make the ball frame label visible. Adding these frames does little more than make your timeline look tidier. They add no function and add nothing additional to the file size of the exported .SWF.

The text block that you entered previously should be visible at all times. It should not change when the Playhead is advanced to frame 10 (the ball label section). When you dragged the bb Movie Clip to frame 10, you probably noticed that the Stage was otherwise blank. Where did the text block go?

Well, look at the text layer in the timeline — it only has one frame. If you want the text block to be visible in frame 10, then you should make sure that the frame sequence extends at least that far, although extending it to frame 20 would be more consistent with the rest of the movie.

1. Click frame 20 of the text layer.

2. Press F5 to insert frames up to and including frame 20.

3. Drag the Playhead back to frame 10. You can now see the text block.

The last concern is the Button. Certainly, we want the button to be visible at all times, just like the text. However, if we have only one Button instance — the one in the first keyframe — the Button can only point to frame 10, and never back to frame 1. Thus, we need to add a second instance (in a new keyframe) in frame 10, so that the two Button instances can point to different frames.

1. Click frame 10 of the buttons layer.

2. Press F6 to insert a keyframe.

3. Again, optionally, you can click frame 20 and press F5 just to make your timeline appear tidier.

All of your items are fully created, positioned on the Stage, and located in their proper places on the timeline. All that's missing are the ActionScripts to drive your buttons and to make the movie work.

An ActionScript primer

ActionScript in Flash 5 is a robust object-oriented scripting language in its own right. Rebuilt from the ground up for Flash 5, ActionScript closely resembles JavaScript.

ActionScript is what makes things happen in Flash. Unless told otherwise, Flash movies play through the timeline sequentially and at a steady rate (the frame rate). In a word, ActionScript is *how* you tell Flash otherwise. If you want the movie to stop at some point — so your readers can, for example, read some text, fill out a form, or make a navigational decision — you use ActionScript. If you want the movie to loop temporarily while the rest of the movie loads in the background (this kind of loop is called a preloader), you need ActionScript. If you want your users to be able to drag and drop a product into a shopping cart at your Flash e-commerce site, you use ActionScript to accomplish this high level of interactivity.

ActionScript enables you to make your Flash movies truly interactive, so that users can go where they want, see what they want, and get what they want — on demand.

Events and event handlers

You may be wondering how ActionScript works. Every action comprises two distinct items: event handlers and events.

- ✦ Event handlers are instructions that tell Flash to do something on a given event: on (release) and on (rollover) are event handlers. When the user clicks an item that has an on (release) event handler, something happens.

- ✦ Events are the triggered behaviors or actions. An example of an event is the Go To And Stop action, which tells Flash to skip to a different frame (advance the Playhead to a specified frame) and stop.

Consider the following short script:

```
on (release) {
   stopAllSounds ();
}
```

The first line is an event handler; the action is triggered when the user releases the mouse button after clicking the item. The curly bracket at the end of the first line opens the list of actions that occurs on this event. In this case, there is only one action, namely, Stop All Sounds. The second curly bracket (the only character in the third line) indicates that there are no more actions associated with the mouse release event for this item. You might see a script like this one on a mute button in a movie that plays a looping soundtrack.

You might be surprised to learn how much you can do with just a handful of short, easy scripts similar to this one. In short, ActionScript simply joins a predefined event to a programmed response. This enables you to make your Flash movie fully interactive.

Frame actions versus object actions

You can put ActionScripts in two different kinds of locations, and, not surprisingly, the nature of the events that trigger them are also somewhat different.

+ **Frame actions:** These actions are associated with frames. The event that triggers these actions is simply that the Playhead has come to the frame. *Example*: Assume that you have a 20-frame movie with a simple Motion Tween spanning all 20 frames. When converted to a .SWF, the movie will play to frame 20 and then automatically loop back to frame 1. To stop the animation after one play-through, you'd need to add a Stop action at frame 20. That way once the Playhead reaches frame 20, the event is triggered, and Flash stops the play.

+ **Object actions:** These actions are attached to objects (such as Buttons and Movie Clips) and require some kind of user interaction, such as clicking, rolling over, or dragging, before the event is triggered.

You'll add both frame and object actions to your movie shortly.

Add object actions to instances, not symbols

One final note, before we actually start adding some ActionScripts: For object actions to work, they must be placed on a Stage. You cannot, for example, add an action to a Button symbol in Symbol Editing Mode. Why?

Object actions are all user triggered — through mouse clicks, rollovers, key entry, and so on — but symbols, by definition, reside in the Library. Flash does not generally export unused Library assets to .SWF files — only placed instances. Therefore, if your user has no access to a Library object in the .SWF movie, then your user cannot trigger an event embedded in such an object.

The bottom line: Attach actions only to *frames* and to Button or movie *instances*, never to symbols.

The Actions Panel

The Actions Panel (see Figure QS-10) is divided into three major sections, and you use each to write an ActionScript.

The Toolbox List (top half, left side) is used to add or subtract lines of code.

+ **To add an action:** Either click the Add a Statement (+) button, which will bring up a menu of code categories (Basic Actions, Actions, Operators, Functions, and so on) and select the desired action from the list, or use the categorized actions list from the window to find an action, and then double-click it to insert it.

+ **To remove a line of code:** Select the line of code in the right window and click the Delete a Statement (–) button.

Toolbox list

Actions list

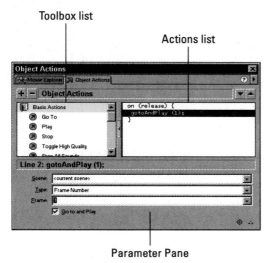

Parameter Pane

Figure QS-10: The Actions Panel

The Actions List (top half, right side) contains the script itself in a script pane; the script is color coded to make reading easier. You can click individual lines of code and delete them or modify them (see next paragraph).

In the Parameters Pane (bottom half), you can fill out an action-specific form to modify the line of script selected in the script pane above.

Adding actions

As you may know by now, in the broadest terms, there are two types of actions in Flash 5: frame actions and object actions. Frame actions are added directly to frames, and they are usually triggered when the Playhead reaches the frame that contains the action. Object actions are attached to Objects, including Buttons and Movie Clips, and they can be triggered a number of ways.

Adding frame actions

By default, a Flash movie plays through all frames, in order, and at the specified frame rate. When it reaches the end of the Main Timeline, it goes to the next Scene, if there is one. When it has reached the end of the last timeline, it loops back to the beginning and replays the movie. For this reason, there are a couple of basic and common commands that you'll need to force the Playhead to stop.

In the interface we are developing, we need to give users time to click the button. If we do not stop the Playhead, they'll have less than a second to click the button; otherwise, the ball animation Movie Clip will appear anyway. Therefore, we need to stop the movie on the first frame.

The Playhead of a Movie Clip timeline functions the same way. Thus, once the ball animation plays, rather than coming to a rest, the ball will suddenly be jerked to the top and start falling all over again. You need to stop the animation in the last frame of that Movie Clip.

Let's make an action to stop the Main Timeline first.

1. Click frame 1 of the actions layer.

2. Open the Actions Panel from the Launcher Bar.

3. Double-click to open the Basic Actions list.

4. Double-click Stop. A small a will appear in the frame to which you just added the action.

5. If you like, you can add extra frames so that this layer has 20 frames as well.

To help yourself remember what action is in the first frame, you can add a comment above the action, indicating what it is.

1. Click the first frame of the Comments layer.

2. Open the Frame Panel.

3. In the Label text field, enter //stop. The two slashes tell Flash that this is a comment and not a label. If there is room, two green slashes and your comment will appear in the timeline. However, there probably is insufficient room for it to appear.

4. Click frame 20 and press F5 to insert frames — now the comment is visible!

Next, let's add a Stop action to the end of the Movie Clip, to prevent it from looping.

1. Double-click the bb Movie Clip icon in the Library to open it in Symbol Editing Mode.

2. Insert a new layer above all the others, and rename it **actions.**

3. In this new actions layer, click the frame over the last frame of animation (frame 98) and insert a keyframe (F6).

4. Use the Actions Panel to add a Stop action.

5. Return to the main movie.

Your final timeline should appear as shown in Figure QS-11. (By the way, have you saved your project recently?)

Non-empty frame sequence
Empty frame sequence
Frame action
Comment
Frame label

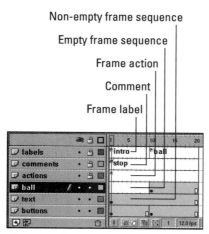

Figure QS-11: The final timeline

Adding object actions

Earlier we claimed that all actions have both Events and Event Handlers, yet the frame actions described previously had only events. This is because the event handler is implied when the frame loads.

With object actions, however, the event handler is not implied; instead, it must be made explicit. This makes the scripts a little longer. Let's add a `GoTo` action to the first Button instance, so that when the button is clicked, the Playhead is advanced to the ball frame label.

1. Click the Button instance in the first frame of the buttons layer, so that it's selected.

2. Using the Launcher Bar, open the Actions Panel. The Object Actions Panel opens. It looks and works just like the Frame Actions Panel.

Caution

Make sure that the title of the panel says Object Actions and not Frame Actions — Flash sometimes opens the wrong one. The way to ensure that it selects the right panel is to make sure an instance is selected rather than an individual frame.

3. Double-click `GoTo` from the Basic Actions list.

4. In the right pane, a script appears. Its first line should say `on (release) {`, the second line should say `gotoAndPlay (1);`, and there should be a close curly bracket in the third line. In the bottom half of the dialog are several options that you need to modify.

5. In the Parameters Pane, leave the Scene drop-down menu alone, because your movie has only this scene.

6. In the Type drop-down menu, change from the default Frame Number to Frame Label.

7. In the third drop-down, choose ball. You might be wondering why you even bothered with labels, because you can use frame numbers. Why not just enter frame number 10 in the GoTo script? There are two reasons: first, frame number 10 is not terribly descriptive, and when you start making sophisticated movies, labels will help you keep track of what content is where. Second, if you decide to edit your movie later and add five frames between the intro and ball labels, then any scripts that depend on those numbers would no longer work. However, if you add 5 frames between the labels, the labels will move, too, and your GoTo actions will still point to the right place.

8. Finally, uncheck the Go to and Play option at the very bottom. Unchecking it changes the script (see the right pane above) to a GoTo And Stop action, which ensures that your movie stops at the ball label, rather than playing, which — when it ran out of frames in less than one second — would send the Playhead looping back to the beginning.

9. When you're finished, close the Object Actions Panel; it will save your changes.

10. Following the same steps, add a GoTo And Stop action to the Button instance in frame 10. Be sure that it points to frame label intro.

Save your work.

Testing movies

You've already seen that you can scrub the timeline, that is, preview the movie by dragging the Playhead. If you were to scrub this timeline, however, you wouldn't get much of a preview. The animation in a Movie Clip would never be seen, the sounds and animation in the Buttons wouldn't be visible, and, of course, interactivity cannot be previewed this way. At this point, you should probably test your movie for real. You can test your movie by choosing Control ⇨ Test Movie from the Main Menu, or by pressing Ctrl+Enter/Command+Enter to have Flash export the movie as a .SWF file so that you can experience your movie as your users will.

Tips for Effective Flash Development

To conclude this introductory Flash in a Flash, let's go over some Flash authoring tips. Most of the tips fall into one of two categories: (a) taking a *process approach* to Flash authoring will both expedite authoring and lead to more mature final products, and (b) take advantage of the *Flash's inherent nature* as a vector-authoring program.

A process approach to Flash authoring

Here are some ideas for taking a process approach when creating a Flash movie:

✦ Plan your files before you start authoring! This will not only save you development time (and increase your profitability), it will also free your mind to add creativity and sophistication to your final product.

✦ Storyboarding is a great way to get started. Just remember that you can sketch in Flash, any vector drawing program (particularly FreeHand), and/or scan drawings and place bitmaps.

✦ Remember that all human documents are supposed to be communicative, which means that one party is communicating a message to a defined audience.

✦ Use frame labels, rather than frame numbers, as a way to enable significant flexibility without requiring major revision. Use comments to help you keep track of what is going on. They are not exported with .SWF files, so be as verbose as you need.

✦ When you first create a new file, before doing anything else, create a layer scheme similar to the one in Table QS-2.

Table QS-2		
Recommended Layer Scheme for All New .FLAs		
Layer Name	**Purpose**	**Comments**
guides	Place your fpo (for placement only) items in this layer	Make it a Guide Layer
labels	Place all of your frame labels on this layer	Lock this layer — it will not prevent you from adding labels, but it will prevent you from adding items that belong in content layers
comments	Add comments in this layer; one tip is to add comments above frame actions that say what the actions do	Lock this layer
actions	Add all your frame actions to this layer	Lock this layer
content	Add content to designated content layers	Don't forget to give these layers meaningful names!

Know Flash 5's capabilities and limitations

Knowing Flash 5's capabilities and limitations will make available all its possibilities while avoiding problems:

✦ Take full advantage of the power of symbols. Never draw the same shape twice.

✦ Vector file sizes (such as the text and lines that Flash draws) are unaffected by changes in scale. So be bold and make it big, if that's what you want.

✦ Because the contents of the Library are generally not exported with the movie, you can put as much in the Library as you need.

✦ Make full use of layers to gain maximum control over your items (and to keep them organized and easily editable!). Flash flattens them when it exports, so layers are yet another feature that add great depth to development without adding bytes to your final product.

✦ New for Flash 5, ActionScript is now a full-blown object-oriented language, much like JavaScript. This improvement has many implications. In addition to the enhanced power that you have at your fingertips, it also means that you need to structure your movies in architecturally savvy ways to take advantage of the power of ActionScript.

✦ Flash is an unusually architectural program: You need to think and plan vertically (layers), horizontally (timeline frames), and structurally (symbols). Mastery of all three axes is mastery of Flash architecture.

✦　　✦　　✦

Mastering the Flash Environment

While the Quick Start introduced you to many of the new features in Flash 5, you'll probably want to start examining individual components of the authoring environment. The first chapter of Part I acquaints you with the overall structure of a Flash movie and the features of the .SWF format. Chapter 2 provides an overview of the Flash toolbars, menus, and preferences, so that you'll know where to go when you need to access a certain tool, command, or setting. Chapter 3 covers every option of the navigation tools (Magnifier and Hand Tools, as well as zoom control and magnification commands). If you used previous versions of Flash, then you'll want to read Chapter 4 for information about the selection tools and the new Pen Tool, for precise control over vector drawings. In Chapter 5 you learn how to use the new Stroke and Fill Panels (among other options) for the artwork creation tools in Flash. Because Web color limitations still remain a primary concern for many designers and Web surfers, we introduce you to Flash color (and gradients) with the Mixer and Swatches Panels in Chapter 6. We end Part I with a discussion of the Text Tool and the new types of text in Flash 5.

Understanding the Flash Framework

In this chapter, we introduce Flash. We discuss the nature of the Flash application and why it is so unique and powerful. We discuss both its similarity and dissimilarity to other programs with which you may be familiar. Then, to wrap up, we talk about the capabilities of Flash. Let's get started.

Introducing the Flash 5 Framework

Flash is a hybrid application that is like no other application. On the immediate surface, it may seem (to some) to be a simple hybrid between a Web-oriented bitmap handler, and a vector-drawing program, such as Macromedia Freehand or Adobe Illustrator. But while Flash is indeed such a hybrid, it's also capable of much, much more. It's also an interactive multimedia-authoring program. Also, it's a sophisticated animation program suitable for creating a range of animations — from simple Web ornaments to broadcast-quality cartoons. As if that weren't enough, it's also the host of a scripting language — Flash now supports a robust, fully featured ActionScript language, grounded in the JavaScript standard. This language enables Flash 5 to couple with XML (Extensible Markup Language), HTML (Hypertext Markup Language), and other content in many ways. So it's also a scripting language that's capable of communication with other parts of the Web. Furthermore, in alliance with Macromedia Generator, Flash 5 is also capable of serving as the front end and graphics engine for the premiere, robust solution for the delivery of dynamic Web content (graphics, charts, sounds, personalized

Flash movies) from databases and other back-end resources. A final note to our list of Flash capabilities: Just as this manuscript was going to press, we learned that Macromedia has collaborated with the makers of ColdFusion to create a toolkit that will enable dynamic data-driven Flash interfaces that are based on CFML (ColdFusion Markup Language) or JSP (JavaServer Pages).

So, what's this hybrid we call *Flash* capable of? That's a question that remains to be answered by developers such as you. In fact, we're hoping that you will master this application and show us a thing or two. That's why we've written this book: to point out the facets of the tool, hoping that you will take the tool in your hands and amaze us — and the world!

So, if Flash is a hybrid application, and if this application is capable of just about anything, a good place to start working with this powerhouse is to inquire: What are the components of this hybrid? And if they were separated out, how might their capabilities be described? Those are the questions that we answer in this chapter.

Bitmap handler

In truth, Flash has limited capabilities as an image-editing program. It is more accurate to describe this part of the Flash application as a bitmap handler. Bitmap images are composed of dots on a grid of individual pixels. The location (and color) of each dot must be stored in memory, which makes this a memory-intensive application and leads to large file sizes. However, for photographic-quality images, bitmap formats are indispensable. One more drawback to bitmap images is that they cannot be scaled without adversely affecting the quality (clarity and sharpness). The adverse effects of scaling an image up are more pronounced than when scaling down. Because of these two drawbacks — file sizes and scaling limitations — bitmaps images are not ideal for Web use.

Vector program

Much of the Flash application is a vector-based drawing program, with capabilities similar to either Macromedia Freehand or Adobe Illustrator. A vector-based drawing program doesn't rely upon individual pixels to compose an image. Instead, it draws shapes by defining points that are described by coordinates. Lines that connect these points are called *paths,* and vectors at each point describe the curvature of the path. Because this scheme is mathematical, there are two distinct advantages: Vector content is significantly more compact, and it's thoroughly scalable without image degradation. These advantages are especially significant for Web use.

Vector animator

The vector animation component of the Flash application is unlike any other program that preceded it. Although Flash is capable of handling bitmaps, its native file format is vector-based. So, unlike all other animation and media programs, Flash relies on the slim and trim vector format for transmission of your final work. Instead of storing megabytes of pixel information for each frame, Flash stores compact vector descriptions of each frame. Whereas a bitmap-based animation program (such as Apple's QuickTime) struggles to display each bitmap in rapid succession, Flash quickly renders the vector descriptions as needed and with far less strain on either the bandwidth or the recipient's machine. This is a huge advantage when transmitting Flash animations and Flash content over the Web.

Authoring program

You might say that the body of Flash is a multimedia-authoring program, or multimedia-authoring environment. It authors movies that can contain multiple kinds of media, such as sound, still graphics, and moving graphics. Yet it is also an interactive multimedia program because it has the capability to assign action commands to the movies that it authors.

Animation sequencer

Most multimedia-authoring programs have a component for sequencing content as animation, and Flash is no exception. But in Flash, the animation sequencer is the core of the application. The organization of sequences, also known as movies, is as follows:

✦ The Movie may have any number of *scenes*, which may be arranged (or rearranged) into a sequence to create a playing order. Scenes play through from first to last (unless Flash's interactive commands, known as "actions," dictate otherwise).

✦ Each scene may contain an unlimited number of *layers*, which are viewed from front-to-back in the scene. The stacking order of these layers is arranged in the timeline: The topmost layer in the timeline appears at the front of the scene, while the bottom layer is at the back.

✦ Furthermore, each layer may also have a stacking order of the objects within it. Always at the *bottom* level are ungrouped vector lines and shapes. Above, in the *overlay* level, are bitmaps, text, groups, grouped items, and symbol instances. *Groups* are one or more items that have been selected and "grouped." *Symbol instances* may be one or more references to an item that resides in the Library. Any of these items may be moved in front or behind others on that layer without moving them to another layer.

Cross-Reference   Groups and grouping are covered in Chapter 8, "Exploring the Timeline," while symbols and symbol instances are covered in Chapter 9, "Checking Out the Library: Symbols and Instances."

✦ The units that are responsible for the illusion of time in an animation are *frames*. Each layer may be composed of a sequence of one or more frames that are controlled by the timeline.

✦ Finally, there are two basic kinds of frames: *static frames* and *keyframes*. Each layer must begin with a keyframe, which may be empty. Static frames simply repeat the content of the prior frame. Keyframes are where content or emptiness is either placed or changed. (Emptiness, or an empty keyframe, functions as a *stop frame*.) Animation is achieved either by changing the contents on a frame-by-frame basis — which is called *frame-by-frame animation* — or by establishing two keyframes and instructing Flash to interpolate the change between them — which is called *tweening*.

Cross-Reference   With the upgrade to Flash 5, the timeline has seen considerable changes to both its terminology and functionality, as well to the options for controlling various timeline behaviors. For detailed coverage of all this and more, please refer to Chapter 8, "Exploring the Timeline."

Programming interface and database front end

With Flash 4, Macromedia expanded the capabilities of Flash to include limited — but powerful — programming capabilities that were capable of controlling the nature and quality of Flash interactivity. Furthermore, these capabilities — augmented with Generator 2 — gave Flash the ability to work as the database front end for sophisticated interactive applications such as online shopping, forms, and other activities not normally associated with an animation program. In fact, there were many ingenious creations that melded code with vector content in ways that no one could have imagined! But that was Flash 4.

Flash 5 has changed all of that in ways that we cannot begin to describe — simply because there is little, if any, limitation to what Flash 5 is now capable of. All one need add is a dash of genius, and genius is in good supply among Flash aficionados. What are we talking about? Well, with Flash 5:

✦ ActionScript matured from a limited quasi-scripting vocabulary to a robust scripting language that's backward compatible with Flash 4, yet based in JavaScript. To be accurate, Macromedia developed Flash 5 ActionScript from the ECMA-262 specification. (The ECMA is the European Computers Manufacturers Association — www.ecma.ch.) This ECMA-262 specification was derived from JavaScript to establish an international standard for the JavaScript language. (Thus, *technically*, Flash ActionScript is not 100 percent compliant with JavaScript.)

✦ Support for XML was added. You can now send and receive XML data from Flash movies. You can also open live sockets for a constant XML data feed.

✦ Math operations have been greatly expanded with the Math Object, including common sine, cosine, and tangent methods.

✦ The color and sound properties of Flash symbols can be controlled with scripting.

✦ Using Symbol Linkage, Sounds and Movie Clips are now directly accessible from the Library without appearing on the authoring timeline.

Viewing Flash movies

Generally, Flash movies are played back in one of three ways. The most common implementation is for Flash movies to be played back within Web browsers — either as part of an HTML page, or as a 100-percent Flash Web page that contains no visible content other than the Flash Movie. Flash movies can also be played through a separate application called the *Flash Player*. In addition to the Flash Player, Flash movies can also be created as Stand Alone Projectors that facilitate playback without the need for either the player or the browser.

There are several other ways in which Flash movies, or their parts, can be played back or displayed. Since Flash 4, the Publish feature has offered provisions for the export of movies, or sections of movies, to either the QuickTime digital video format, the QuickTime Flash layer vector format, or to the Animated GIF format. Parts of movies can also be exported as a series of individual bitmaps or as vector files. Single frames can also be exported to these formats. Recently, methods were developed that enable Flash content to be used as screensavers.

Cross-Reference
Using Flash content for separate deployment — including screensavers — is covered in Chapter 42, "Using Players, Projectors, and Screensaver Utilities." QuickTime is covered in Chapter 34, "Working with QuickTime."

Finding Applications for Flash 5 Movies

A Flash movie can be many things, depending on the function and design of a project. Because Flash has only just hit its adolescence, things are definitely getting interesting. Already Flash has unforeseen relationships with all forms of communication, around the world. And Flash's popularity continues to grow, unabated. But that's all based on Flash 4!

If you were to compare the functionality of a Flash 4 movie to that of a Flash 5 movie, you'd agree that, yet again, Flash movies have come a long way — but in an even shorter time than when we last said that. There's already an impressive legacy of Flash movies and we don't usually refer to youths as having a legacy. Here's a short list of the (known) possibilities for Flash 5:

✦ A splash page animation for a Web site

✦ An interactive map

✦ An interactive form on a Web page

✦ An interactive database that sends and retrieves information with server-side scripts; this has been a function since Flash 4

✦ A live, multiuser game or chat with XML sockets that allows real-time communication between Internet users

✦ An online jukebox that can play MP3 audio that is delivered dynamically via Macromedia's Generator 2 application

✦ Stand-alone Web applications — check out the calculator sample in the Flash Samples menu

✦ Entire Web sites, presented without *any* HTML-based graphics or textual content — which means absolute control over scaling and placement of items, including fonts

✦ Interactive art presentations that involve 3D transformations and multiuser experiences (check out www.yugop.com)

✦ Web installation art that offers access to high-quality bitmapped artwork and rich audio experiences

✦ Interactive QuickTime Flash movie trailers that allow user feedback while watching

✦ Stand-alone Presentations or Slide Shows on either CD-ROM or floppy disk

✦ With the help of third-party tools, screensavers for both Windows and Macintosh made from Flash movies

✦ Web cartoons — in the last 18 months, there has been an explosion of Flash cartooning

✦ Broadcast-quality cartoons — of which Turnertoons' *Weber*, *The Murkeys* and Richard Bazley's *Journal of Edwin Carp* are groundbreaking examples

✦ As a platform for QuickTime editing and enhancements — there's a world of possibilities in the synergy of QuickTime and Flash 5 (We've developed workflows about which even Macromedia said, "It can't be done.")

✦ Flash movies can be integrated into a larger Shockwave Director movie that can play QuickTime movies, MIDI audio, and other media formats that Flash doesn't support

As you can probably tell from this list, if you can imagine a use for Flash, it can probably be accomplished.

Planning interactive Flash projects

Before you attempt to construct interactive projects in Flash, you should be familiar with the structure of the authoring environment. Even if you already know Flash 4, this is advisable. That's because with the release of Flash 5, Macromedia has again added many new features to the interface, and either moved or improved other features and functionalities. So, to get a firm footing with the new interface, we strongly suggest that you work your way through this book — from the beginning.

Moreover, you need to proactively plan your interactive projects before you attempt to author them in Flash. An ounce of preplanning goes a long way during the production process. Don't fool yourself — the better your plan looks on paper, the better it will perform when it comes to the final execution.

Cross-Reference

Interactive planning is discussed in several areas of the Flash 5 Bible, including in Eric Jordan's Expert Tutorial, "Interface Design," which is located in Chapter 13. You'll also find this topic discussed in Chapters 26 and 38.

In this edition of the Flash Bible, we've opted to include a number of ways to approach interactive planning. In general, you can teach yourself how to organize interactive elements by creating simple flowcharts, such as Figure 1-1, that describe the Flash-authoring environment.

Figure 1-1 shows how Flash movies are made up of individual scenes that, in turn, contain keyframes to describe changes on the Stage. What you can't see in the figure is the efficiency created (or time saved) by being able to share Flash Libraries between Flash projects (.FLA files) and by linking other Flash movies to a parent Flash movie using the Load Movie action, as well as other scripting methods that are discussed in Part V. Before you start to try to do that level of interactivity, though, you need to know the difference between Flash movies and .SWF movies.

Looking at Flash movie file types

Flash movie (.FLA) files are geared to work in an efficient authoring environment. Within this environment, content can be organized into scenes, and the ordering of scenes can be rearranged throughout the production cycle. Layers provide easy separation of graphics within each scene, and, as guide or mask layers, they can also aid drawing or even provide special effects. The timeline shows keyframes, motion and shape tweens, labels, and comments. All imported bitmaps and sounds are stored in the Flash Library (which can be shared with other Flash movie files). The quality of these Library files (or symbols) is identical to that of the originals.

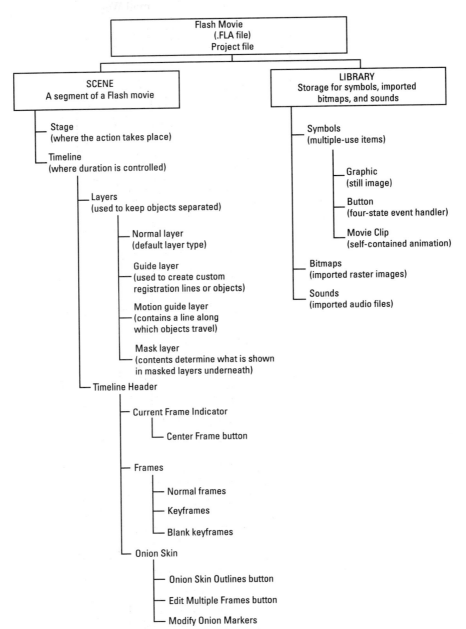

Figure 1-1: Elements of the Flash Environment

However, when a Flash movie (.FLA) is exported to a Small Web Format file (.SWF), much of this information is discarded in order to create small .SWF files (or as small as possible) for network delivery (for example, the Internet or intranets). In fact, just about everything that's stored in the original FLA file will be transformed in some way. The elements in the Library are loaded and stored on the first frame of their use — while unused Library elements are simply discarded. (They are *not* exported to the .SWF file.) Thus, for maximum efficiency, elements that are reused are saved into the .SWF file only once because they are referenced from one location in the SWF file. Layers and scenes are "flattened" in the order that is established in the .FLA file. In other words, the .SWF file contains the all the elements from the original .FLA in one layer, controlled by a single timeline. Technically, .SWF files are not compressed like ZIP or SIT/HQX files — only individual bitmaps and sounds are compressed according to the settings specified for each element in the Library and/or during the export process.

Refer to Figure 1-2 for a graphic explanation of the characteristics of the Shockwave Flash movie (.SWF) Format.

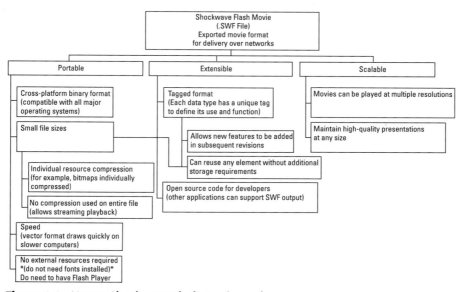

Figure 1-2: How a Shockwave Flash movie works

Note Flash movie (.FLA) files are referred to as *Flash editor documents* by some documentation included with the software. Also, the term "Shockwave Flash" no longer exists in the Macromedia Flash documentation — Flash movies for the Web are simply called .SWF files. Originally, SWF stood for Shockwave Flash but later, according to one source, Macromedia revisited the acronym and tweened it to mean, Small Web File. (Because "Shockwave" originally referred to Shockwave Director movies, perhaps Macromedia is trying to avoid confusion between the two?) Still, to the general public, it appears that Flash movies are still considered to be Shockwave movies; our position is to simply refer to Flash movies, when distributed for download, as .SWFs (and avoid the unimportant controversy).

Summary

✦ Flash is a hybrid program that has combined many of the most powerful features of various other types of programs, and then mixed them with some unique capabilities.

✦ Flash is recognized as one of the most robust and capable programs available for the creation of content for the Web.

✦ Flash is not limited to the Web. In fact, Flash is the software of choice in numerous other niches.

✦ With Flash 5, ActionScripting has risen to a new level of robust capability, modeled on JavaScript.

Now that we've given you a taste of the capabilities and distinctions of the Flash Authoring Environment, and shown you how some of the larger pieces fit together; it's time for you to look at some of the particulars.

✦   ✦   ✦

Exploring the Interface: Panels, Settings, and More

CHAPTER 2

◆ ◆ ◆ ◆

In This Chapter

Learning Flash
Toolbox Basics

Getting to know the
fundamental Flash
interface

Demystifying
preferences and
keyboard shortcuts

Working with menus
and panels

◆ ◆ ◆ ◆

This chapter tours all Flash menus and panels. In some cases, the basic function of a panel or menu item is discussed, while the deeper explanation is deferred to another chapter or area of the book that's dedicated to that particular function — or group of functions. In most cases, however, we've tried to deliver a full explanation right here in this chapter. We hope you use it as both a learning device and as a reference tool.

Learning Flash Tool Basics

Terminology: A book about a software program must be clear and consistent in the terms and names that are used to describe the various thingamajigs and doohickeys that make the program work. As with the last edition of the Flash Bible, we considered carefully before we settled upon the terminology that has — we hope — been applied consistently throughout this book. So, here's our logic: Wherever possible, we use terms derived from the Flash interface and Macromedia's documentation. When we've discovered inconsistencies, we've tried to choose terminology that's most consistent with other Macromedia products.

The Toolbox

The default location for the Flash Drawing Toolbox is in the upper-left corner of the Flash Program window. However, if you haven't just installed Flash, or if someone else has changed the defaults in Flash, you may not be able to find the Drawing Toolbox.

The Toolbox consists of four main sections. The top section contains all 14 Flash Tools, from left to right and top to bottom: Arrow, Subselect, Line, Lasso, Pen, Text, Oval, Rectangle, Pencil, Brush, Ink Bottle, Paint Bucket, Dropper, and Eraser. The second section contains the Flash View Tools: the Hand and Magnifier. Beneath the View Tools is the Color Tray, and beneath that is the Options Tray.

Using Tool options

Depending on the tool selected, the Options Tray may display some of the options, or properties, that control the functionality of each particular tool — while other controls may appear in the new Flash 5 panels. Of the options that are located in the Options Tray, some appear as a pop up or drop-down menus with multiple options, while others are simple buttons that toggle a property on or off. Thus, if an option turns a property on or off, then it's a button. (For example, if the Lasso is selected, the Magic Wand option can be turned on or off by clicking its button in the Options Tray.) But if an option has more than two options, then it's a menu.

New Feature   With the release of Flash 5, Macromedia has introduced an extensive panels system for the comprehensive control of many operations. These panels are introduced and discussed in general within this chapter. Their functionality will be discussed in relationship with specific tools, both in the subsequent chapters of Part I and throughout the *Flash 5 Bible.*

Most of the options that appear within the Options Tray of the Toolbox can also be accessed from menus on the Menu Bar, or with keyboard combinations. However, all of the controls for the Line, Pen, Text, Oval, Rectangle, Pencil, and Ink Bottle Tools are now located in the new panels system. The new Subselect Tool has no options or controls. All of the controls and options for each tool are described in detail in subsequent chapters of Part I.

Making the Drawing Toolbox visible

If the Drawing Toolbox is not visible on the PC Flash screen, it can be opened from the Flash Menu Bar by choosing Window ➪ Tools. Conversely, when the Toolbox is visible, unchecking the Tool menu item hides it. On the Mac, the Drawing Toolbox is always a floating panel that can be dragged anywhere in the screen.

Docking the Flash Drawing Toolbox on the PC

On the PC only, the Drawing Toolbox can be deployed as either a floating panel or as a panel that's docked to either edge of the Flash program window. *Docking* means that a floating panel is dragged to the edge of the program window, where it then melds to the border of the window. It remains docked there until it is either moved to another docked position, floated off to resume usage as a panel, or is closed. You can drag the panel anywhere around the screen, or you can drag it to the edge of the Flash program window, which docks it there.

Tip   On the PC, to drag the Drawing Toolbox to the edge of the program window, yet prevent it from docking, press the Control key while dragging.

Quick work with keyboard shortcuts

All of the tools that are accessed from the Drawing Toolbox have keyboard equivalents, or shortcuts, that are single keystrokes (see Figure 2-1). For example, to access the Arrow Tool—which is the tool with the black arrow icon, located in the upper-left corner of the Drawing Toolbox—you can simply press the V key when the Stage or timeline is in focus. *Thus, the V key is the keyboard shortcut for the Arrow Tool on both the Mac and the PC.* This is easier than moving the mouse up to the Drawing Toolbox to click the Arrow Tool, and it saves mouse miles, besides. Henceforth, throughout this book, when we mention a new tool, the keyboard shortcut for that tool follows in parentheses, as follows: Arrow (V).

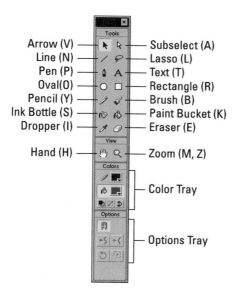

Figure 2-1: The PC Drawing Toolbox is shown here with the keyboard shortcuts for each tool. With the release of Flash 5, the Toolbox is now identical on both the Mac and the PC.

Using tooltips

On both PC and Mac platforms, each tool has a cursor icon that resembles the tool's icon in the Toolbox. For example, when you select the Brush by clicking the Brush button on the Toolbox, the cursor (or mouse pointer) turns into an icon similar to the Brush icon in the Toolbox. In most other programs, these cursor icons are referred to as *tooltips*: When you are working with a particular tool, the cursor icon for that tool appears on screen. In Flash, this kind of tooltip cannot be turned off. That's because Flash uses the term tooltip to refer to a text label that appears onscreen, adjacent to the cursor, when the cursor is paused over a tool button in the Toolbox. These text labels—Flash Tooltips—tell you the name of the tool and its keyboard shortcut. You can personalize Flash so that these Flash Tooltips are either visible or hidden.

✦ To change the Tooltips setting on the PC, choose Edit ⇨ Preferences to open the Preferences dialog; then, on the General Tab, in the Selection Options area, either check or uncheck Show Tooltips.

✦ To change the Tooltips setting on the Mac, choose Edit ⇨ Preferences to open the Preferences dialog; then, on the General Tab, in the Selection area, either check or uncheck Show Tooltips.

Tooltips display information only about the tools that are part of the actual Flash program itself, and not about buttons that are part of a scene in a Flash movie. (If you are familiar with Macromedia Director, then you know that Sprites—which can be similar to buttons in Flash—can show or hide information about their properties. Flash does not offer this type of "tip.")

Color and Flash tools

The Color Tray and other colorful matters are discussed in depth in Chapter 6, "Applying Color."

Getting to Know the Fundamental Flash Interface

Before discussing the Flash menu items, panels, and miscellaneous dialogs, we take a look at the interface and its default array of toolbars and panels. We look at the way the program looks when first opened after installation, and some of the basic possibilities for arranging these and other fundamental panels and toolbars.

Cross-platform consistency

There's much to celebrate in this new version of Flash, and one improvement that really shows is the consistency between the Mac and PC versions of Flash 5. Although there are a few inconsistencies, many of them are attributable to the nature of the divergent operating systems, and none of them are even remotely as bothersome as with prior versions.

Figure 2-2 shows how Flash looks on the Mac. Note the Launcher Bar at the bottom right, which can be used to invoke the default groupings of Flash panels. These are, from left to right: Instance, Mixer, Character, Info, Explorer, Frame Actions, and the Library.

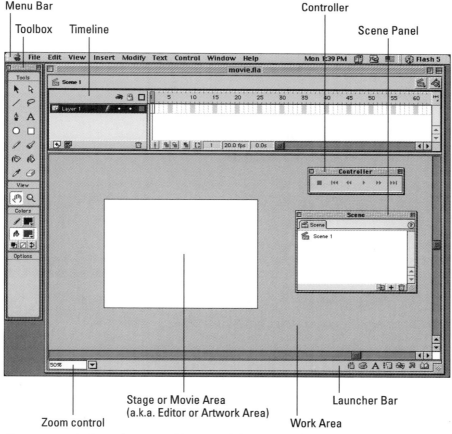

Figure 2-2: Flash on the Mac with most of the panels closed

Figure 2-3 shows Flash on the PC with the panels closed. There are three optional features that are absent from the Mac version. These include the Main Toolbar, the dockable Controller, and the Status Bar. However, note the consistency especially as regards the Toolbox (Tools), timeline, Launcher Bar, and the overall feel of the interface.

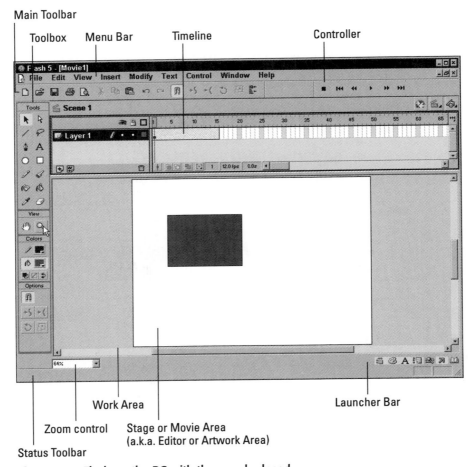

Figure 2-3: Flash on the PC with the panels closed

Note One of the minor ways in which the PC version differs from the Mac version is that the Toolbox and the Controller can be docked (or undocked) to the program window. As in Figure 2-3, the Toolbox and Controller were dragged to the edge of the program window, where they're docked seamlessly to the interface. Note that the Toolbox docks only to the sides, while the Controller can also dock to the top and bottom, as well as mesh with other toolbars. To move either the Toolbox or Controller, yet prevent docking, press the Control key while dragging.

With Flash 5, Macromedia significantly altered the look and feel of Flash by replacing the inspectors and palettes of Flash 4 with a comprehensive system of panels. As was mentioned previously with regard to the Toolbox, some tool options have also migrated to the panels system. The implementation of panels is consistent across both the Mac and the PC. Throughout the book, we discuss each panel in context with the tools and operations where it is used. As shown in the following figures, there are many ways to arrange these panels for a customized workflow. For examples of panels viewed simultaneously, see Figure 2-4 for the Mac version and 2-5 for the PC version.

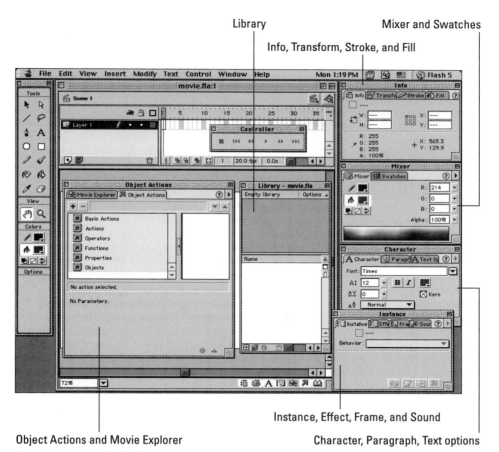

Figure 2-4: Here's Flash on the Mac with the panels viewed simultaneously.

Info, Transform, Stroke, and Fill

Mixer and Swatches

Instance, Effect, Frame, and Sound

Align and Scene

Library

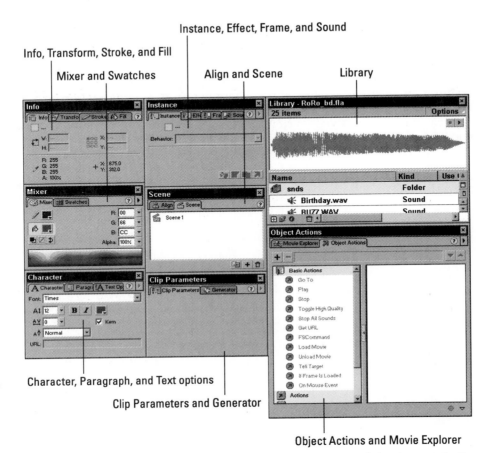

Character, Paragraph, and Text options

Clip Parameters and Generator

Object Actions and Movie Explorer

Figure 2-5: Here's Flash on the PC with all of the panels viewed simultaneously. Four additional panels that are not included in the default groupings are also displayed.

On both the Mac and the PC, you can drag the panel tabs off the panels or onto another panel. Figure 2-6 shows an alternative mega-panel grouping in which all of the Flash panels have been joined using this method. This grouping is most suited for a dual-monitor system, and has the advantage of displaying all of the information within a single panel without scrolling.

Contextual menus

Flash contextual menus pop-up in response to a right-click (Control+click for the Mac) on a selected item in the timeline, Library window, or on the Stage. Contextual menus duplicate most functions and commands that are accessible either through the drop-down menus of the Menu Bar, or through the many panels and dialogs, which are discussed in this chapter.

Movie Explorer   Library

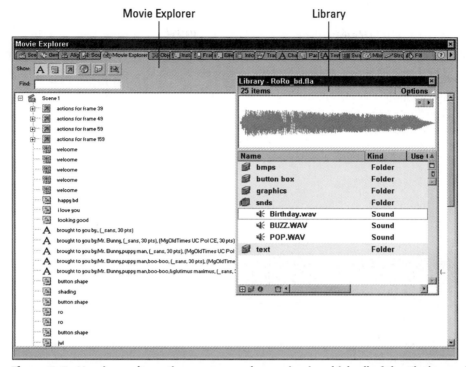

Figure 2-6: Here's an alternative mega-panel grouping in which all of the Flash panels have been dragged together.

Cross-Reference Although the Flash timeline is a central axis of the Flash interface, we defer discussion of the timeline for two reasons. First, the timeline has changed considerably since Flash 4 and, as such, deserves more attention. Second, the Flash drawing tools and most of the menus and panels can be introduced more clearly (at first) without the complication of the timeline. If you must check out the timeline, see Chapter 8, "Exploring the Timeline."

Using the Menu Bar

Now that we've introduced most of the *major* elements of the Flash interface, we begin at the far left of the Menu Bar and work through the major points of all the drop-down menus, submenus, and panels. It's a gruesome, tedious job, but someone has to dive in and make sense of all these interrelated and (sometimes) seemingly duplicate or parallel operations.

Note   Prior to Flash 4, there was only one area of the application that required users to pay attention to focus—when selecting colors for either the stroke or fill—when it was easy to confuse the two. Now, with the increased power and robust scripting environment of Flash 5, focus has become an important aspect of the program. What is focus? *Focus* is a term used to describe which part of the application has priority, or focus, at a given time. For example, all panels, such as the Actions Panel, do not automatically "have focus"—this means that you have to click within the panel to commence working there. Similarly, to return to the movie editor (or screen), you must click there to return focus to that aspect of the application. So, if a panel or dialog box doesn't seem to respond, just remember to FOCUS on what you are doing.

The File Menu

The Flash File Menu (Figure 2-7) is like the front door of the program. Most of what comes into or out of Flash passes in some fashion through the File Menu.

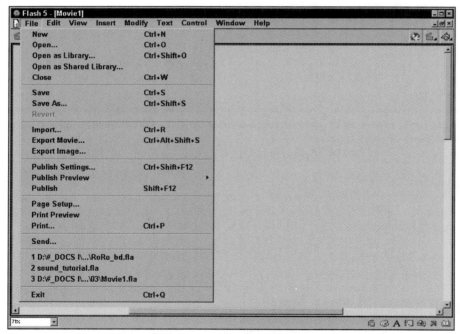

Figure 2-7: File Menu on the PC

✦ **New:** By default, Flash opens a new Flash document whenever the program is launched (unless Flash is launched from an extant movie). But once the program is open, File ➪ New generates all new documents.

✦ **Open:** File ➪ Open launches the Open dialog, which is used to browse and locate a Flash-compatible file. Compatible formats are:

- Flash Movie — .FLA

Caution

As of this writing, a number of lingering issues impact reverse compatibility between Flash 5 and legacy Flash movies that were authored in earlier versions of Flash. Although we anticipate that there will be a fix for this, it would be *impossible* for us to stress the following too strongly: ALWAYS (*always!*) make a copy of any legacy Flash movie *before* opening it in Flash 5. Otherwise, if there is a problem with the file in Flash 5 and you have saved it as a Flash 5 .FLA, and you don't have a copy in the legacy flavor . . ., you will be stuck (and there will be no alternative but to start over, from zero).

- Futuresplash Movie — .SPA
- SmartSketch Drawing — .SSK
- Flash Player Movie — .SWF

✦ **Open as Library:** Use File ➪ Open as Library to launch the Open as Library Dialog and browse for the Flash Movie whose Library you want to open. This makes the components of that Movie available for use within another movie. For more about working with the Flash Library, refer to Chapter 9, "Checking Out the Library: Symbols and Instances."

✦ **Open as Shared Library:** Use File ➪ Open as Shared Library to launch the Open as Shared Library dialog and browse for the Flash Movie that you want to open as a Shared Library, which is a powerful new functionality of Flash 5. For more about working with the Flash Library, refer to Chapter 9, "Checking Out the Library: Symbols and Instances."

✦ **Close:** Close any open movie with File ➪ Close.

✦ **Save:** Save an open movie with File ➪ Save.

✦ **Save As:** To save an open movie to another location or with another name, use File ➪ Save As.

Tip

To make saving a quickly accomplished task, File ➪ Save appends any changes to the end of the .FLA file. So, if you delete a handful of bitmaps from your project and then save, your file size may actually increase. By doing a File ➪ Save As, Flash restructures and writes a new file from scratch, resulting in a cleaner, smaller file. Consequently, File ➪ Save As takes a little longer to complete.

✦ **Revert:** Made a big goof that Edit ➪ Undo can't undo? Use File ➪ Revert to revert to the previously saved version of the current movie. Of course, this won't spare you much grief unless you *save often and incrementally*.

✦ **Import:** Many compatible formats can be opened directly into Flash. Use File ➪ Import to launch the Import dialog for these formats:

- Adobe Illustrator — .EPS, .AI
- AIFF Sound — .AIF

- AutoCAD DXF — .DXF
- Bitmap — .BMP, .DIB (Mac with QuickTime 4 installed)
- Enhanced Metafile — .EMF
- Flash Player — .SWF, .SPL
- FreeHand — .FH7, .FH8, .FH9, .FT7, .FT8, .FT9
- GIF Image — .GIF
- JPEG Image — .JPG
- Macintosh PICT Image — .PCT (Windows with QuickTime 4 installed)
- MacPaint Image — .PNTG (only with QuickTime 4 installed)
- MP3 Sound — .MP3
- Photoshop 2.5, 3 Image — .PSD (only with QuickTime 4 installed)
- PNG Image — .PNG
- QuickTime Image — .QTIF (only with QuickTime 4 installed)
- QuickTime Movie — .MOV
- Silicon Graphics Image — .SGI (only with QuickTime 4 installed)
- Sun AU — .AU
- TGA Image — .TGA (only with QuickTime 4 installed)
- Tiff Image — .TIFF (only with QuickTime 4 installed)
- WAV Sound — .WAV
- Windows Metafile — .WMF

✦ **Export Movie:** Flash can also directly export to several compatible formats. Use File ⇨ Export to write your movie to any of these formats:

- Adobe Illustrator Sequence — .AI
- Animated GIF — .GIF
- Bitmap Sequence — .BMP
- DXF Sequence — .DXF
- EMF Sequence — .EMF
- EPS 3.0 Sequence — .EPS
- Flash Player — .SWF
- Futuresplash Player — .SPL
- Generator Template — .SWT

- GIF Sequence — .GIF
- JPEG Sequence — .JPG
- PNG Sequence — .PNG
- QuickTime — .MOV
- WAV Audio — .WAV
- Windows AVI — .AVI
- WMF Sequence — .WMF

✦ **Export Image**

- Adobe Illustrator — .AI
- AutoCAD DXF — .DXF
- Bitmap — .BMP
- Enhanced Metafile — .EMF
- EPS 3.0 — .EPS
- Flash Player — .SWF
- FutureSplash Player — .SPL
- Generator Template — .SWT
- GIF Image — .GIF
- JPEG Image — .JPG
- PNG Image — .PNG
- Windows Metafile — .WMF

Publishing

One of the most celebrated features of Flash 4 was the Publish feature, which replaced Aftershock. This is a powerful, robust aspect of Flash that required no changes in this upgrade to Flash 5. So if you're familiar with Flash 4, you'll be thoroughly at home with the Publish workflow, which is covered in depth in Chapter 41, "Integrating Flash Content with HTML." The areas of the File Menu which pertain to the Publish feature are:

✦ Publish Settings
✦ Publish Preview
✦ Publish

Printing

Although Flash is considered a Web and animation program, it fully supports printed output. The functionality and specific dialogs vary slightly from the Mac to the PC — while other variations are subject to which printers and printer drivers are installed on your machine. The Flash Page Setup dialog is the most standard aspect of the program and the choices for paper size, margins, center positioning, and orientation are pretty intuitive. However, the Layout area of the PC Page Setup Dialog deserves a little more attention. The options here are:

✦ **Frames:** Use this drop-down menu to choose to print either **All Frames** of the animation or the ecological default, which is to print the **First Frame Only.**

✦ **Layout:** There are three basic options:

• **Actual Size:** This prints the Frame at full size, subject to the accompanying Scale setting: At what scale do you want to print your frames? Enter a percentage.

• **Fit on One Page:** This automatically reduces or enlarges the Frame so that it fills the maximum printable area, without distortion.

• **Storyboard:** This enables you to print several thumbnails per page in the following arrangements: Boxes, Grid, or Blank. There are accompanying settings for Frames Across, Frame Margin, and Label Frames. This is a great tool for circulating comps and promotional materials.

Tip   When printing Storyboard Layouts, use File ⇨ Print Preview to ensure optimal results.

✦ **Print Margins (Mac Only):** Refer to the prior discussion (immediately preceding) of Frames, Layout, and Actual Size for an explanation of these equivalent options on the Mac. Note the **Disable PostScript** check box.

Note   When printing single large areas of color surrounded by complex borders, problems may occur on PostScript Printers. If you encounter such problems, try using the Disable PostScript check box in the Mac Print Margins dialog (Edit ⇨ Print Margins) or in the PC Preferences dialog (Edit ⇨ Preferences ⇨ General ⇨ Printing Options). Otherwise, divide the complex area into several simpler areas and use the Modify commands (Modify ⇨ Smooth / Straighten / Optimize) to reduce the complexity of these areas (which may, however, drastically alter your artwork — so save first!).

✦ **Print Preview:** Use Print Preview to see an onscreen preview of how the printed output looks, based upon the options you've chosen in the Page Setup and Print Margins (Mac Only) dialogs.

✦ **Print:** Just print it!

✦ **Send** (PC only): This is a new command that invokes the default e-mail client so that that you can readily send the Flash file as an attachment.

✦ **Exit/Quit:** Finally, at the very bottom of the File Menu is the command to close Flash. On the PC, it's File ⇨ Exit; the Mac equivalent is File ⇨ Quit.

The Edit Menu

The Edit Menu (Figure 2-8) isn't nearly as complex as the File Menu. Still, it's an important menu because many of these commands are central to so many Flash operations.

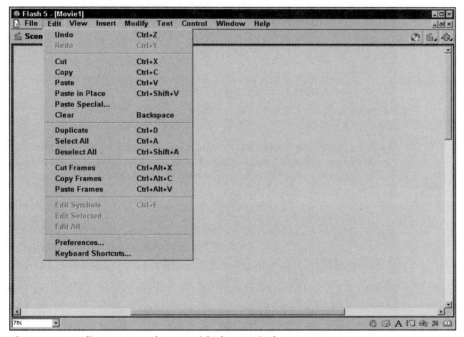

Figure 2-8: Edit Menu on the PC with the Equivalent Mac Menu Inset

✦ **Undo:** When you make a mistake, before you do anything else — Do the Undo.

Note Flash generates an Undo stack for several different parts of the interface: Each timeline (Main Timeline and Movie Clip timelines) has its own undo stack, as does the ActionScript Panel. Furthermore, Undo does not transcend Focus: You cannot Undo work on the Stage from the ActionScript Panel — you must first return focus to the Stage to exercise Undo.

✦ **Redo:** The anti-Undo, this undoes what you just undid.

✦ **Cut:** This removes any selected item(s) and places it on the clipboard.

✦ **Copy:** This copies any selected item(s) and places it on the clipboard, without removing it.

✦ **Paste:** Disabled if nothing has been copied or cut, this pastes items from the clipboard into the currently active frame on the currently active layer. You can also paste into panel controls.

✦ **Paste in Place:** This is like Paste, except that it pastes the object precisely in the same place (with regards to X and Y coordinates) from which it was copied.

✦ **Paste Special (PC only):** This is like Paste on steroids, with version control. It pastes or embeds contents from the Clipboard in a specified format; it can also paste and simultaneously generate a link to information in another movie. The Paste Special Dialog has these fields:

   • **Source:** This displays the local path to the source of the item that is on the clipboard.

   • **Paste:** This pastes the data on the clipboard.

   • **Paste Link:** This pastes data on the clipboard, maintaining a link to the original document, but is generally not available.

   • **As:** This field may have several choices, depending both on the nature of the item (including the application that created it) that is on the clipboard, and also on which radio button is activated.

Tip   In the *As* section: (1) Flash Drawing pastes a portion of a Flash drawing. (2) Object pastes an object together with the information needed to edit it. (You convert the object to an editable Flash element with Modify ➪ Break Apart.) (3) Picture (Metafile) pastes in a form that Flash can edit. (4) Text (ASCII) pastes unformatted text. (5) Text (Native) pastes text with formatting intact.

   • **Result:** This indicates the result of the selected combination of the Paste / Paste Link and As options.

   • **Display as Icon:** This check box is enabled when any combination of the options permits the selected item to be pasted as an Icon.

   • **Change Icon:** This button is evoked when Display as Icon is enabled. Click this button to open the Change Icon dialog (complete with browse capability), which facilitates selection of an alternate icon.

   • **OK:** Once these settings have been determined, click OK.

✦ **Clear:** This removes a selected item(s) from the Stage *without* copying it to the Clipboard.

✦ **Duplicate:** This command duplicates a selected item or items, without burdening the Clipboard. The duplicated item appears adjacent to the original.

✦ **Select All:** Does what it says.

✦ **Deselect All:** Does what it says.

✦ **Cut Frames:** Cut a selected Frame or Frames with this command.

✦ **Copy Frames:** Copy a selected Frame or Frames with this command.

✦ **Paste Frames:** Pastes the Frame(s).

✦ **Edit Symbols:** Select an instance of a symbol and choose this command to edit in symbol-editing mode. For more about symbols and editing symbols, refer to Chapter 9, "Checking Out the Library: Symbols and Instances."

✦ **Edit Selected:** This is only enabled if a group or symbol is selected on the Stage. It opens a group or symbol for editing in a separate *tab* while dimming the rest of the Flash Stage — similar to Edit in Place with symbols.

✦ **Edit All:** When editing a group, Edit All is used to go back to editing the normal Flash scene.

✦ **Preferences:** The Preferences item of the Edit Menu invokes a tabbed dialog. A full explanation of this dialog follows.

Preferences

The Preferences dialog is one of the places where you get to tell Flash how you want it to behave. After you've established your preferences, this is how the program will be configured for every movie that you make. Nearly all options are identical on both platforms — with the exception of the clipboard settings, which are a reflection of the different ways that the two platforms handle their clipboards.

As shown in Figure 2-9, options for the General tab of the Preferences dialog are:

✦ **Undo Levels:** This sets the number of undos that Flash holds in memory to cover your mistakes. The maximum combined number of undos is 200. The default is 100. Undo levels devour system memory, so if you work smart and save incrementally, you can set your undos between 10 and 25. The only limitation here is the RAM on your machine.

✦ **Printing Options (PC only):** As discussed previously in this chapter, in context with the Printing commands of the File Menu, when printing single large areas of color surrounded by complex borders, problems may occur on PostScript Printers. If you encounter such problems, try checking this option to Disable PostScript. The equivalent option is available on the Mac by choosing File ⇨ Print Margins.

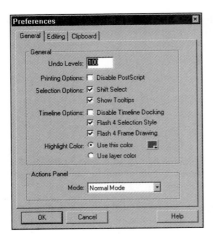

Figure 2-9: The General tab of the Preferences dialog for the PC

✦ **Selection Options:**

- **Shift Select:** Shift Select controls how Flash accumulates multiple selections. When Shift Select is **ON**, Flash behaves normally: Hold down the Shift key to select and acquire additional elements. When **OFF**, simply click, click, click to continue adding elements to the selection. (Veteran users of Flash may recall that this is also how Flash implemented Select when it was Futuresplash and Flash 2.)

- **Show Tooltips:** Tooltips are little labels that appear adjacent to the cursor when the cursor is held over a tool, prior to clicking the tool. These labels tell the name of the tool and related keyboard shortcut. Deselect this option to turn this feature off.

✦ **Timeline Options:**

- **Disable Timeline Docking:** This option prevents the timeline from attaching to the application window once it's been deployed as a floating panel.

- **Flash 4 Selection Style:** Flash 5 introduced a new methodology for selecting frames in the timeline. This option toggles that functionality back to Flash 4 Selection Style. For in-depth coverage of the timeline, refer to Chapter 8, "Exploring the Timeline."

- **Flash 4 Frame Drawing:** Flash 5 also introduced a new methodology for drawing frames in the timeline. This option toggles that functionality back to the Flash 4 style. For in-depth coverage of the timeline, refer to Chapter 8, "Exploring the Timeline."

✦ **Highlight Color:** This preference controls the highlight color for selected objects: groups, symbols, or text — but not shapes.

- **Use this color:** Check this option to choose a highlight color for selections from the Swatches pop-up.

- **Use layer color:** Check this option to use the layer color as the highlight color for selections. This option enables you to distinguish selected items according to their associated layer color. For a more detailed explanation of the advantages of this option, refer to Chapter 8, "Exploring the Timeline."

✦ **Actions Panel:** This drop-down menu has two options that configure the Frame Actions Panel each time you launch Flash. The options are Normal or Expert Mode. For a detailed explanation of the Actions Panel, refer to Chapter 17, "Understanding Actions and Event Handlers."

As shown in Figure 2-10, options for the Editing tab of the Preferences dialog are:

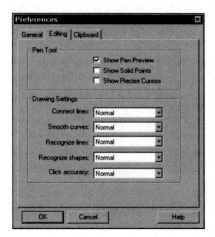

Figure 2-10: The Editing tab of the Preferences dialog for the PC

✦ **Pen Tool:** With the release of Flash 5, Macromedia added a robust Pen Tool to the Flash Toolbox. Three preferences to control the performance of the Pen Tool are located here. Because fine, accurate use of the Pen Tool often involves the use of selection tools in order to move and adjust control points, we've chosen to introduce the Pen Tool at the end of the chapter on selections, immediately prior to the chapter on drawing tools. For a detailed discussion of the Pen Tool in context, refer to Chapter 4, "Working with Selections and the Pen Tool."

- **Show Pen Preview:** With this option checked, Flash will display a preview of the next line segment, in response to moving the pointer, prior to clicking to make the next end point and create the line segment.

- **Show Solid Points:** Check this option to display selected anchor points as solid points, and unselected points as hollow points. The default, which is unchecked, displays anchor points in the opposite manner: The default is for selected points to be hollow and for unselected points to be solid.

- **Show Precise Cursors:** This option toggles the Pen tool cursor between the default Pen Tool icon and a precision crosshair cursor. We advise that you check this option to use the precision cursor.

✦ **Drawing Settings:** Previous versions of Flash had a drawing control that was referred to as the Assistant. It controlled the performance of one of Flash's most celebrated features, the "automated helpers" that aid drawing, which include Line Processing and Shape Recognition. With Flash 5, these controls have been relocated — intact — here as the Drawing Settings. For more about the principles of Line Processing and Shape Recognition, please refer to Chapter 5, "Working with the Drawing and Painting Tools." In all cases, the Assistant controls the degree of "automatic help" for each of six categories of assistance. For all assistants, the options range from off, to lax, to moderately aggressive, to aggressive. Only one assistant has an option that's equivalent to always on. Regardless of the particular assistant, here's a universal translation for these somewhat quirky settings:

Off = OFF

Must be close / Rough / Strict = Lax

Normal = Moderately Aggressive

Can be distant / Smooth / Tolerant = Aggressive

Always snap = Always ON

- **Connect lines:** Controls snapping between an extant line and a line that's being drawn. If the line that's being drawn is within the threshold, it snaps to the nearest point of the other line. This setting also controls vertical and horizontal line recognition, which is the aspect of Line Processing that makes nearly vertical or horizontal lines absolutely vertical or horizontal.

- **Smooth curves:** When drawing with the Pencil Tool, with the mode set to either Straighten or Smooth, this setting controls how much smoothing will be applied to curved lines.

- **Recognize lines:** This setting determines how nearly straight a line segment needs to be in order for Flash to make it perfectly straight.

- **Recognize shapes:** In Flash, roughly drawn circles, ovals, squares, rectangles, and arcs of either 90 or 180 degrees can be recognized as geometric shapes and automatically redrawn with absolute precision. This is called *Shape Recognition*, and this setting controls the degree of what is "permissible."

- **Click accuracy:** This setting controls how close the cursor must be to an item before Flash recognizes the item. A tolerant setting means that you either inadvertently select an item, which is a bother, or that you can be close and easily select an item, which may be cool. We think Normal is the best setting for this.

As shown in Figure 2-11, options for the Clipboard tab of the Preferences dialog are:

Figure 2-11: The Clipboard tab of the Preferences dialog for the PC

✦ **Bitmaps (PC) / PICT Settings (Mac):**

- **Color Depth (PC):** Choose **None** if you are only pasting back into Flash. This only copies the Flash vector format, which is faster and conserves system memory. Otherwise, if you want to copy bitmaps to the clipboard (in addition to the default Windows Metafile), choose a bitmap format — which is only useful when pasting to and from bitmap applications, such as Photoshop. In which case, choose the appropriate bit depth for your use.

- **Type (Mac):** As with the PC, choose **Objects** if you are only pasting back into Flash. This only copies the Flash vector format, which is faster and conserves system memory. Otherwise, choose a bitmap format if you want to copy bitmaps (in the PICT format) to the clipboard — which is only useful when pasting into bitmap applications, such as Photoshop. As with the equivalent setting for the PC, chose the appropriate bit depth for your use.

- **Resolution:** Choose the resolution at which you want to capture bitmaps.

- **Size Limit (PC):** Use this entry box to limit the amount of RAM (memory) that will be gobbled up by bitmaps on the clipboard.

- **Smooth (PC):** Smooth is antialiasing, which means that the edges of shapes and lines are dithered to look smooth on screen. Check Smooth to turn antialiasing on.

- **Include PostScript (Mac):** Although mostly unused now, the original Pict format had the capability to include postscript items.

- **Gradients on Clipboard (PC):** The Quality drop-down controls the quality of the gradient fills that are created when copying to the Windows Clipboard. Copying higher quality gradients can be slow and consumes system RAM. If you're only pasting back into Flash, choose **None,** because full gradient quality is preserved regardless.

- **Gradients (Mac):** As with the PC, the Quality drop-down controls the quality of gradient fills that are created when copying to the Mac Clipboard. Copying higher quality gradients can be slow and consumes system RAM. Choose **None** if you're only pasting back into Flash, as full gradient quality is preserved regardless.

✦ **FreeHand Text:** This command confirms the marriage between Flash and FreeHand. For more information about using FreeHand with Flash, refer to Chapter 31, "Working with Vector Graphics."

- **Maintain Text as Blocks:** When pasting text from a FreeHand file, if this option is checked, the pasted text remains editable.

✦ **Keyboard Shortcuts:** This final item of the Edit Menu invokes the Keyboard Shortcuts dialog, which is a powerful new feature of Flash 5. As shown in Figure 2-12, the Keyboard Shortcuts dialog enables you to customize your Flash keyboard shortcuts to maintain consistency with other applications or to develop a personalized workflow. Not only can you choose keyboard shortcuts developed from other applications, you can also save your modifications and custom settings. A full explanation of this dialog follows.

Keyboard shortcuts

There is one major reason to applaud the inclusion of this feature in Flash 5: It enables the disabled. Imagine how wonderful this facility might be for someone who has lost the use of one of his or her hands. For other disabilities, this feature could make the difference between the ability to work effectively in Flash or not. We have a friend who is a quadriplegic; having the use of neither his hands nor his feet, this intrepid fellow accomplishes amazing feats in Flash — with a mouth stick! These keyboard commands enable him, and others with disabilities, to use the program with a little more ease.

Another reason to celebrate this feature is that it facilitates the development of a custom workflow — for example, drawing tablet with one hand, keyboard with the other. The disadvantage of this feature is that, in a busy studio where artists are swapping seats like musical chairs, irresponsible keyboard changes can lead to team grief. In a studio, Keyboard Shortcuts must be implemented with regard for others working in the same environment. But this is a small detraction from the greater value of this feature. We hope that Macromedia will build upon their example and continue to lead the way, and will offer greater accessibility for the disabled with subsequent releases.

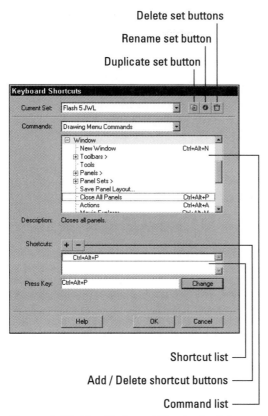

Delete set buttons

Rename set button

Duplicate set button

Shortcut list

Add / Delete shortcut buttons

Command list

Figure 2-12: The Keyboard Shortcuts dialog

To create a new keyboard shortcut, you must first duplicate an existing set, from which you can then add or subtract existing shortcuts to form your custom shortcut set. Here's the process:

1. Select a shortcut set from the Current Set pop-up menu. This is now the active set.

2. Duplicate the active set by clicking the Duplicate Set button. The Duplicate dialog appears. Enter a new name for this set in the Duplicate Name field and click OK.

   A similar procedure is employed to rename a shortcut set. Simply click the Rename Set button and enter the new name in the ensuing dialog. (But you cannot rename the built-in sets that ship with the program.)

3. Select a commands list from the Command pop-up menu (Drawing Menu Commands, Drawing Tools, or Test Movie Menu Commands) either to add a command or to modify it.

4. Next, in the Command list, choose either a grouping or a command from one of the previously chosen commands lists. Note that some lists have sublists. Click the Plus sign (or small arrow on the Mac) to expand a particular category. Figure 2-13 shows commands for the Window Menu.

5. Now choose a command that you want to add (or subtract) — a description of the selected command appears in the Description area.

6. To delete the existing shortcut, click the (–) Shortcut button.

7. To add a shortcut for this command, click the (+) Shortcut button, and then enter the shortcut key combination in the Press Key entry box. Click Change, and then OK to close the dialog.

8. Or, to change an existing command, select the command and click the Change button.

9. To delete a shortcut set, click the Delete set button, then select the set to be deleted from the ensuing Delete Set dialog and click the Delete button. (Because you cannot delete the built-in sets that ship with the program, they do not appear in the Delete Set dialog.)

Tip   Keyboard Shortcut sets are stored within the installed Flash 5 program folder, within the Keyboard Shortcuts folder. You can navigate to this location on your hard drive and copy, backup, restore, delete, or otherwise manipulate any of these files from this folder. Keyboard Shortcuts are transferable between machines, although we had no success transferring them across platforms.

The View Menu

As shown in Figure 2-13, the View Menu is dedicated to controlling how movies — and some tools — are viewed in Flash. There are also a few controls that toggle functionality.

✦ **Goto:** The Goto command leads to a Pop-up menu of scenes in the current movie, including four handy shortcuts to the First, Previous, Next and Last scenes.

Cross-Reference   The next three commands — Zoom In, Zoom Out, and Magnification — are covered in greater detail in Chapter 3, "Using Tools for Navigation and Viewing."

✦ **Zoom In:** This increases the view by 50 percent.

✦ **Zoom Out:** This decreases the view by 50 percent.

✦ **Magnification:** This command leads to eight preset magnification levels. See Chapter 3, "Using Tools for Navigation and Viewing," for more detail.

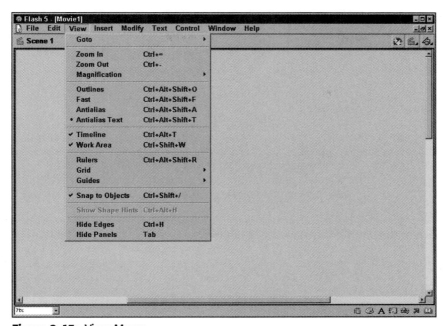

Figure 2-13: View Menu

The next four commands: Outlines, Fast, Antialias, and Antialias Text have *no* effect on the way in which Flash exports your movie. Quality decisions are made in the Publish Settings, which are covered in Chapter 40, "Publishing Flash Movies." These settings only affect screen quality and screen speed — meaning, "How much longer until this picture appears?"

✦ **Outlines:** Use this command to display all shapes as outlines, and to show all lines as thin lines. This command is useful for reshaping graphic elements, and for getting the general timing and sense of a movie. It also speeds up the display of complex scenes. It is a global equivalent of the outlines toggle of individual frames.

✦ **Fast:** This command also speeds up display. It turns off both antialiasing and dithering. Although the default is Off, the recommended setting is On. Unfortunately, this setting is *not* saved as a preference — it must be set for every movie.

✦ **Antialias:** Not to be confused with the wife of your outlaw cowboy uncle, antialiasing dithers the edges of shapes and lines so that they look smoother on screen. It also slows the display. It works best with fast, 24-bit video cards. This is really a toggle in opposition with the *Fast* command: turn this On and *Fast* goes Off. The setting we recommend for Antialias is Off.

✦ **Antialias Text:** As with Antialias, this is also a toggle in opposition to the *Fast* command. It smoothes the edges of text *only* and works best with large font sizes — it can be dreadfully slow when there's a lot of text.

✦ **Timeline:** Use this toggle to show or hide the timeline.

✦ **Work Area:** This command makes the light-gray area that surrounds the Stage (or Movie Area) visible. This can be useful when your movie has items that are either partially or completely off stage — as, for example, when you have something move into or out of a scene. To work with these items (to place or manipulate them) off stage, use View ➪ Work Area. To see the maximum Stage/Work Area, use View ➪ Work Area, and then use View ➪ Show All.

A good example of the utility of the Work Area feature can be seen in both the Weber movie, and the Journal of Edwin Carp; examples of both are on the CD-ROM in the ch37 folder. Cartoonists such as Turner and Bazley rely upon this capability of Flash for creating effects (such as long pans) in which very large background artwork hangs off the Stage (or view area) until called upon or tweened through.

Caution

You cannot deselect items that are selected and offstage when View ➪ Work Area is toggled off. This can lead to inadvertent deletions, so be careful!

✦ **Rulers:** This command toggles the Rulers (which display at the top and left edges of the Work Area) on or off — use Modify ➪ Movie to change units of measurement.

✦ **Grid:** Click this command to access three commands that control the parameters and use of both Snapping and the Flash Grid.

  • **Show Grid:** This command toggles the Drawing Grid on or off.

  • **Snap to Grid:** This command toggles the Snap to Grid function on or off. Snap to Grid works regardless of whether the Grid has been made visible with View ➪ Grid ➪ Show Grid — if the Grid has not been made visible, it just snaps to the *invisible* Grid.

  • **Edit Grid:** Use this command to invoke the Grid dialog, where you can change Grid Color, Spacing, and the settings for Snap accuracy. Snap accuracy controls how close an item, symbol, or — while drawing — the end of a line must be to a Grid intersection before the item, symbol, or line endpoint snaps to the Grid. Both Show Grid and Snap to Grid check boxes are also included in this dialog. Edited Grid settings can be saved as the default by clicking the Save Default button, which enables you to have these setting as presets for all subsequent Flash movies.

Note

The default Grid size of 18 pixels is inherited from the origins of Flash in the SmartSketch program — it's because 18 pixels equals 0.25 inch! But you aren't stuck with that. Grid units can be changed by entering the appropriate abbreviation (for example: 25 pt., .5", .5 in, 2 cm, and so on) in the Grid Spacing entry boxes. Although the specified units *will* be applied to the grid, they will be translated into the current unit of measurement for the Ruler. Thus, if the Ruler is set to pixels, and the Grid units are changed to .5 in, then, on reopening the Grid dialog, the Grid units will be displayed as 36 pix (because pixels are allocated at 72 pix = 1"). Changing Ruler Units via Modify ➪ Movie also changes Grid Units.

✦ **Guides:** When Rulers are turned on, Guides, a new feature for Flash 5, can be dragged onto the Stage from either ruler. These four commands control the parameters of these Guides.

- **Show Guides:** This is a simple toggle to either show or hide the Guides.

- **Lock Guides:** This is a toggle that either locks or unlocks all current Guides.

- **Snap to Guides:** This is a toggle that extends Snap behavior to Guides. It works independently of the other Snap toggles — so, if Snap to Grid is turned off in the Edit Grid dialog, and Snap to Objects is also turned off, Snap to Guides is still active, unless, of course, it, too, is toggled off.

- **Edit Guides:** This command invokes the Guides dialog box, where Guide Color and Guide-specific Snap accuracy can be adjusted. Also included are check boxes for the other three Guide commands: Show Guides, Snap to Guides, and Lock Guides. This enables you to establish Guide settings and then click the Save Default button to have these setting as presets for all subsequent Flash movies.

✦ **Snap to Objects:** Due to the recent trend among high-end Flash developers to structure their Flash authoring as *Object-Oriented Flash,* it's advisable — for the sake of future clarity — to think of this command as a Snap to Items command. Snap to Items means that, when moving or manipulating an item, the item snaps into alignment with items already placed on the stage.

✦ **Show Shape Hints:** This toggles Shape Hints to make them visible or invisible. It does not disable shape hinting. Shape Hints are used when tweening shapes. For more about Shape Tweens (or Shape Morphing) refer to Chapter 11, "Animating in Flash."

✦ **Hide Edges:** Use this command to hide selection highlights, so that you can edit items without the added confusion of their selection highlights.

Tip

If you want to Hide Edges permanently, in every movie you make, a similar, more permanent effect can be obtained by first creating a Color Swatch with a Zero Alpha, and then setting the Highlight Color to that color in the General tab of the Edit ➪ Preferences dialog. For more about Color Swatches, refer to Chapter 6, "Applying Color."

✦ **Hide Panels:** This command hides all visible panels. However, it is not a toggle because repeating the command does not return the panels to visibility. To return the panels to visibility, you must invoke them from either the Launcher Bar or the Window Menu. However, pressing Tab hides and returns your currently visible set of panels.

The Insert Menu

As shown in Figure 2-14, the Insert Menu is used to insert Symbols, Layers, Guides, Frames, and Scenes into the current Movie.

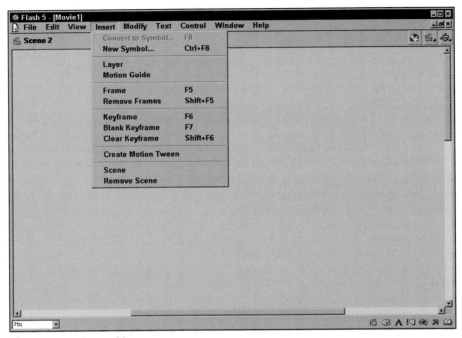

Figure 2-14: Insert Menu

✦ **Convert to Symbol:** Use this command to convert a selected item (or items) on stage into a new Symbol and evoke the Symbol Properties Dialog. Refer to Chapter 9, "Checking Out the Library: Symbols and Instances," for a full explanation of symbols.

✦ **New Symbol:** Use this command to create a new symbol in Symbol-editing Mode. To use this command, first make sure that nothing is selected by using Edit ➪ Deselect All. Refer to Chapter 9, "Checking Out the Library: Symbols and Instances," for a full discussion of symbols.

✦ **Layer:** This command creates a new layer directly above the currently active layer. The new layer becomes the active layer.

✦ **Motion Guide:** Use this command to add a Motion Guide layer (also referred to as a Motion Path). The Motion Guide layer appears above the selected layer. For more information about using Motion Guides to tween along a path, refer to Chapter 8, "Exploring the Timeline."

✦ **Frame:** Use this command to insert a new frame at any selected point on the timeline. If a frame is selected, then that selected frame (together with all frames to the right on that layer) are shifted to the right to accommodate the new frame — other layers are left alone. But if no layers (or frames) are selected, then all layers get a new frame at the current position of the Playhead (indicating the active frame) and preexisting frames on all layers shift right.

✦ **Remove Frame:** This command deletes the selected Frame.

✦ **Keyframe:** Use this command to convert a selected Frame into a Keyframe.

✦ **Blank Keyframe:** This command inserts a new Keyframe at a selected point on the timeline. If a frame is selected, then that selected frame (together with all frames to the right on that layer) shift to the right to accommodate the new frame — other layers are left alone. If no layers (or frames) are selected, then all layers get a new frame at the current frame marker's position and pre-existing frames on all layers shift right.

✦ **Clear Keyframe:** This command changes a Keyframe back into a simple Frame, whereupon the contents of the former Keyframe are replaced with copies of the Keyframe immediately previous in the timeline.

✦ **Create Motion Tween:** This command is one step in the process of creating a tweened animation. Refer to Chapter 8, "Exploring the Timeline," for the full scoop on tweened animation.

✦ **Scene:** This command inserts a new, empty Scene immediately following the currently active Scene. By default, new Scenes are numbered — use the Scene panel to rename and to organize Scenes.

✦ **Remove Scene:** This command deletes the currently active Scene.

The Modify Menu

As shown in Figure 2-15, the Modify menu is thick with commands that invoke pop-ups, submenus, and panels. Not shown are the pop-ups for the first five items on the menu: Instance, Frame, Layer, Scene, and Movie. Although all of these are introduced here, substantial discussion of these items has been deferred until they can be handled in context with the Flash workflow.

✦ **Instance:** The Modify ⇨ Instance command evokes the Instance Panel, which is used to control independent behaviors of Symbol Instances. In its default configuration, the Instance Panel is accompanied by the Effect Panel. Together, they have fields for Instance Behavior, Options, Name, and Color Effect. These topics are introduced in greater depth in Chapter 9, "Checking Out the Library: Symbols and Instances."

✦ **Frame:** The Modify ⇨ Frame command, opens the Frame Panel. In its default configuration, the Sound Panel accompanies the Frame Panel. Together, they have fields for the control of frame labels, tweening, and sound. These topics are introduced in greater depth in Chapter 11, "Animating in Flash," and in Part III, "Sound Planning."

✦ **Layer:** The Modify ⇨ Layer invokes the Layer Properties dialog, which is used to control and edit the properties of the active layer of the timeline. The timeline is discussed fully in Chapter 8, "Exploring the Timeline."

✦ **Scene:** Modify ⇨ Scene opens the Scene Properties panel, which has only one function: to rename the current scene.

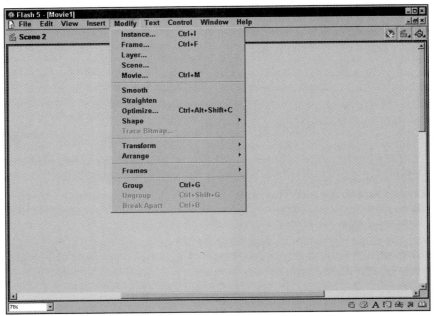

Figure 2-15: The Modify Menu

✦ **Movie:** Modify ➪ Movie leads to the Movie Properties dialog, which is used to change Frame Rate, Movie Dimensions, Background Color, and Ruler Units.

• **Frame Rate:** Changes the Frame Rate.

• **Dimensions:** Establishes the Dimensions of the Movie.

• **Match:** The Match Printer button matches the Movie Dimensions to the currently selected printer's maximum printable dimensions. The Match Contents button adjusts the Movie Dimensions to include all active items, from the upper left-hand corner to the lower right-hand corner of the entire movie (including animation, and the space it may cover during such movements). The expanse includes a narrow zone of white (stage) around it.

• **Background Color:** Click the chip to choose a color from the Swatches pop-up.

Tip   The Background Color can be changed at any time during an animation by adding a new layer at the bottom of the layer stack, and then creating a Keyframe at the point where you want the color to change. Next, draw a rectangle the size of the stage (or larger) position it to cover the stage, and fill with the new color. Subsequent changes of background color can be accomplished with the insertion of another Keyframe and changing the color of the rectangle at that point. For more information, see Chapter 9, "Checking Out the Library: Symbols and Instances."

- **Ruler Units:** Use this drop-down menu to specify units for the movie. Remember, Ruler Units also changes Grid Units — and impacts Snap to Grid behavior.

- **OK:** Applies changes to the current movie only.

- **Save Default:** Click this button to add these settings to the preferences. They become the default for all subsequent movies created with File ⇨ New.

The next group of commands replaces the prior grouping of commands that were located within the Curves submenu. These commands aren't only for manipulating curves — they're useful for manipulating other things, too. See Chapter 10, "Drawing in Flash," for detailed explanations in context. These commands are as follows:

✦ **Smooth:** Reduces curves and bumps.

✦ **Straighten:** Straightens out lines and curves.

✦ **Optimize:** Lessens the number of curves in a shape. Use this command to reduce the size of Flash files.

✦ **Shape:** Lets you convert lines to fills, expand and shrink fills, and soften the edges of fills.

✦ **Trace Bitmap:** Use this command to convert an imported bitmap into a vector graphic with editable, discrete areas of color. Please refer to Chapter 12, "Using Bitmaps and Other Media with Flash," for a full treatment of the use of various media — including bitmaps — within the Flash vector environment.

✦ **Transform:** Use Modify ⇨ Transform to access the Transform submenu, home to the following commands: *Scale, Rotate, Scale and Rotate, Rotate 90 °* CW, *Rotate 90 ° CCW, Flip Vertical, Flip Horizontal, Remove Transform,* and *Edit Center.* These are explained in context in Chapter 10, "Drawing in Flash." As for the remaining commands, *Add Shape Hint* and *Remove All Hints* are explained in Chapter 11, "Animating in Flash."

✦ **Arrange:** Use Modify ⇨ Arrange to open the Arrange submenu, which is used to move selected items, symbols, and groups either forward or backward in the stack of items that are layered in the currently active Layer. The options — which are intuitive — are:

  - **Bring to Front:** This moves the selected item to the absolute front of the active layer's stack.

  - **Bring Forward:** This moves the selected item one step forward in the stack.

  - **Send Backward:** This moves the selected item one step backward in the stack.

- **Send to Back:** This moves the selected item all the way back to the hinterlands of the stack.

- **Lock:** Use this to lock the selected item in its current position in the stack.

- **Unlock:** Use this to release the selected item from its locked status in the stack.

✦ **Frames:** Modify ➪ Frames yields the Frames submenu, with four commands:

- **Reverse:** To reverse an animation sequence, first check that there's a keyframe at the beginning and end of the sequence. Next, select the entire sequence — keyframe to keyframe — and choose Modify ➪ Frames ➪ Reverse.

- **Synchronize Symbols:** Sometimes an animation sequence is encapsulated as a symbol and used as a graphic instance in a movie. If the number of frames occupied by this graphic instance doesn't jive with the number of frames in the original sequence, erratic looping occurs. Although this command is supposed to adjust timing and ensure synchronous looping, it rarely works. The optimal solution is to synchronize the animations manually.

- **Convert to Keyframes:** Use this command to convert a range of selected frames into keyframes. This command is an obvious candidate for a custom keyboard shortcut.

- **Convert to Blank Keyframes:** Use this command to downgrade a range of selected keyframes to blank keyframes. This command is another obvious candidate for a custom keyboard shortcut.

✦ **Group:** Use this command to Group two or more selected items. Details and advantages of grouping are discussed in Chapter 6, "Applying Color," and Chapter 7, "Working with Text."

✦ **Ungroup:** This command ungroups items that have been grouped — it's also discussed in Chapter 6, "Applying Color," and Chapter 7, "Working with Text."

✦ **Break Apart:** This command is used to separate groups, blocks of type, instances, bitmaps, and OLE items. It can be used to reduce the file size of imported graphics. However, it may not be reversible, and it also has some unintuitive effects, so refer to the discussion of this command in Chapter 7, "Working with Text," before using! Furthermore, because this command turns blocks of type into graphics, applying it to type increases file size — sometimes significantly.

The Text Menu

This menu (see Figure 2-16) contains duplicate commands for text controls that are available in one of the three Text Panels.

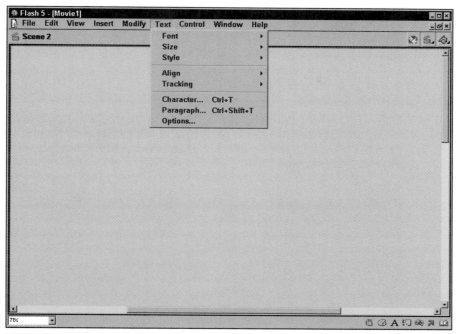

Figure 2-16: The Text Menu

These commands are:

> ✦ **Font:** Although this command duplicates the Font drop-down menu located at the top of the Character Panel, it's much easier to work with — if you know your fonts. That's because Text ⇨ Font invokes a scrolling pop-up menu that extends from top to bottom of your screen. The only disadvantage of this menu is that it lacks the additional display that the Text Panel offers, which shows the font name in the character set of the highlighted font.

> ✦ **Size:** This command offers 13 preset sizes ranging from 8 points to 120 points. Although it's quick and easy, it lacks the infinite precision of the Size control located on the Text Panel, which presents both a numeric entry field and a slider bar for the selection of point size.

> ✦ **Style:** This command gives you the easiest access for changing the style of selected text. The options are Plain, Bold, Italic, Subscript, and Superscript.

> ✦ **Align:** This command duplicates the function of the upper pane of the Paragraph Panel. Here the options are Align Left, Align Center, Align Right, and Justify.

> ✦ **Tracking:** This command offers abbreviated control of text tracking. It isn't nearly as robust or as precise as the lower pane of the Paragraph Panel. That's because the options are limited to Increase, Decrease, and Reset.

✦ **Character:** This command invokes the Character Panel.

✦ **Paragraph:** This command invokes the Paragraph Panel.

✦ **Options:** This command invokes the Text Options Panel.

The Control Menu

Despite the Control Menu's alluring title (see Figure 2-17), this is not the menu for Type A personalities. Rather, like the VCR controller, which Type A's always seem to finagle onto their armrest, the Control Menu displays buttons that control the movie playback features within Flash.

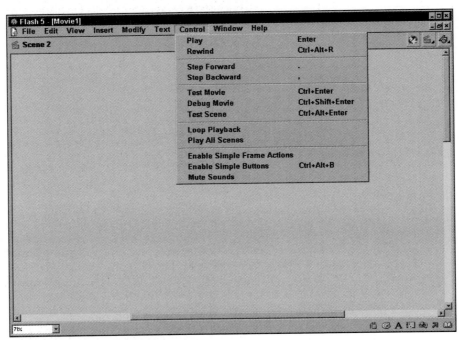

Figure 2-17: The Control Menu

✦ **Play:** This command plays the movie in the authoring environment.

✦ **Rewind:** This command returns the movie back to frame 1.

✦ **Step Forward:** Use this command to step the movie forward one frame.

✦ **Step Backward:** Use this command to step the movie one frame backward.

✦ **Test Movie:** Some interactive functions will not work when the movie is played within the Flash playback environment. This command uses the settings established in the Publish Settings dialog to export the current movie and instantly play it within a new Flash Player window. The exported movie is *not* a temporary file; it is saved to the same folder as the parent .FLA file. The Keyboard Shortcut for this command is Ctrl+Enter/Command+Return.

Tip

If you're doing a lot of coding and are accustomed to using the default keyboard shortcut to do Test Movie, you must first return focus from the Actions Panel to the Editor. But that's a pain! The easy fix is to use the Keyboard Shortcuts dialog to assign a custom key for Control ⇨ Test Movie.

✦ **Debug Movie:** This is a new feature of Flash 5 that enables developers to debug a Flash movie for problems in their code. It launches the Debugger Panel. Use of the Debugger is discussed in detail in Chapter 21, "Planning Code Structures."

✦ **Test Scene:** This command is similar to the Test Movie command; the only exception is that it tests the current scene only, whereas Test Movie runs the whole shebang.

✦ **Loop Playback:** This command is a toggle that enables looping with all subsequent implementations of the *Play, Test Movie,* and *Test Scene* commands.

✦ **Play All Scenes:** The default within the Flash Movie Controller is to play the current scene only. So, like *Loop Playback,* this is another toggle — it overrides the default single-scene playback and enables all scenes to be played with subsequent implementations of the *Play, Test Movie,* and *Test Scene* commands.

✦ **Enable Frame Actions:** This is a toggle that controls whether Frame Actions are enabled. Use *Enable Frame Actions* only during tests and playback within Flash; otherwise, it may be difficult to edit a movie.

✦ **Enable Simple Buttons:** Like *Enable Frame Actions,* this toggle controls whether buttons are enabled. It would be impossible to edit, move, or manipulate buttons if they were continually enabled. So, enable buttons only during tests and playback within Flash. This is limited to simple buttons because complex buttons cannot be effectively tested within the Flash Editor environment.

✦ **Mute Sounds:** This command toggles sound on or off, within the Flash Editor environment.

The Window Menu

The Window Menu, shown in Figure 2-18, is the launch pad for a number of key panels and dialogs. It has several commands that are used to arrange the display of multiple movies.

✦ **New Window:** This command opens the currently active movie in a new window.

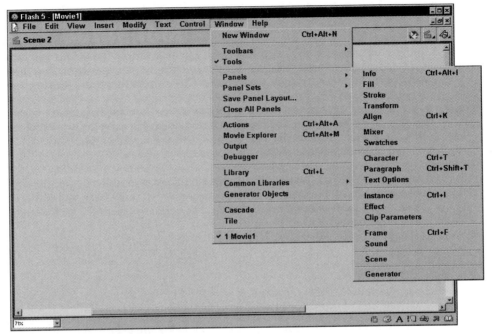

Figure 2-18: The Window Menu

✦ **Toolbars (PC Only):** This command opens the Toolbars subpanel, which contains the following commands.

- **Main:** The Main Toolbar is the just the Standard Toolbar from Flash 4, with a different name. As shown earlier in Figure 2-3, this toolbar is similar to the production toolbars of many programs. It duplicates commonly used tools for easier access, and is generally for those who are unfamiliar with the program. Because it devours precious screen space, we urge that it be disabled.

- **Status:** The Status Toolbar, shown in Figure 2-3, gives text readouts that may explain the use of tools, buttons, and many interface elements. Generally, the text is too limited to be much help. Leave this option disabled; it, too, devours precious screen space and retards learning.

✦ **Controller (PC placement):** This command toggles the display of the Controller Toolbar. With buttons similar to a VCR, the Controller is used to test animations within the Flash Movie Editor. (It can be used instead of the commands on the Control Menu to play a movie within Flash.) From right to left, the buttons are: *Stop, Rewind, Step Back One Frame, Play, Step Forward One Frame,* and *Fast Forward.*

✦ **Tools:** On both the Mac and the PC, this command toggles display of the Toolbox, which was shown earlier in Figure 2-1.

✦ **Controller (Mac placement):** On the Mac, this command, which toggles display of the Controller Toolbar, is in the front lineup of the Window Menu commands.

Note Experienced users usually disable these additional toolbars: Main Toolbar and Status Toolbar.

✦ **Panels:** This command opens the Panels submenu, which leads to groupings of most of the primary panels of Flash 5, which are:

• **Info:** The top pane of this panel has a readout for the width and height of a selected item, as well as the x and y coordinates. These readouts are also, numeric entry fields, permitting a numeric transformation of both the dimensions and position of the selected item. There's also an alignment grid that's used to toggle the x,y coordinates between the item's center and the top-left corner of the item. The bottom pane delivers the information about the (pixel precise) current mouse location: R, G, B, and Alpha values as well as x,y coordinates. The Info Panel is discussed in context in Chapter 10, "Drawing in Flash."

• **Fill:** This panel is used to select or create fills — Solid, Gradient, or Bitmap — that are applied with the Paint Bucket (K) Tool. Fills are discussed in context in Chapter 5, "Working with the Drawing and Painting Tools," and in Chapter 6, "Applying Color."

• **Stroke:** Strokes are lines created by the Pen (P) or Pencil Tool (Y), as well as the outlines of filled shapes. Three controls handle the qualities that define a stroke: Stroke Style, Thickness, and Color. Like fills, strokes are first discussed in context in Chapter 5, "Working with the Drawing and Painting Tools," and Chapter 6, "Applying Color."

• **Transform:** This panel is a complement to the numeric transformation capabilities of the Info Panel. The Transform Panel facilitates changing the dimensions of a selected item according to percentage, with a check box to constrain transformations to the original aspect ratio of the item. Controls for Skew and Rotate are also located here. The Transform Panel is discussed, in concert with the Info Panel, in Chapter 10, "Drawing in Flash."

Tip With the default panel layout, you can use the Info Panel button on the Launcher Bar to invoke the default Info/Transform/Stroke/Fill cluster.

• **Align:** The Align Panel is used to align multiple selected items according to various criteria. This panel has intuitive, visual buttons that can be used to align, resize, and evenly distribute two or more selected items. These options can be used separately or in combinations. This panel is discussed in context in Chapter 10, "Drawing in Flash."

- **Mixer:** The Mixer Panel is used to mix colors and save them as color swatches. Colors may be assigned to either the Stroke or Fill Color Chips of the Color Tray. Additionally, the readout for the color space can be chosen from RGB (Red, Green, Blue), HSB (Hue, Saturation, Brightness), or hex (hexadecimal) color specification types. The Mixer Panel is discussed in concert with the Swatches Panel in Chapter 6, "Applying Color."

- **Swatches:** The Swatches Panel is used to load, organize, save, and remove both individual Color Swatches and Color Sets. See Chapter 6, "Applying Color."

Tip With the default panel layout, use the Mixer Panel button on the Launcher Bar to invoke the default Mixer/Swatches cluster.

- **Character:** The Character Panel offers control over the following aspects of text in Flash. Controls include font; point size; bold and italic; color; tracking; kerning; character position; and URL entry. The Character Panel is discussed — in concert with the Paragraph and Text Option Panels — in Chapter 7, "Working with Text."

- **Paragraph:** The Paragraph Panel controls the alignment and placement of text in Flash. The controls include Align (Left, Center, Right, or Full Justification), Left Margin, Right Margin, Indentation, and Line Spacing. The Paragraph Panel is discussed in context in Chapter 7, "Working with Text."

- **Text Options:** The Text Options Panel is used to select the type of text that you will be using in Flash. The choices are Static, Dynamic, or Input Text. There are other choices as well, subject to the type of text you will be using. These details are introduced in Chapter 7, "Working with Text."

Tip With the default panel layout, use the Character Panel button on the Launcher Bar to invoke the default Character/Paragraph/Text Options cluster.

- **Instance:** The Instance Panel is used to control various fundamental properties of Symbol Instances. These properties vary according to whether the instance Behavior is as a Movie Clip, Button, or Graphic. The Instance Panel is first discussed in context in Chapter 9, "Checking Out the Library: Symbols and Instances."

- **Effect:** The Effect Panel controls color effects for symbol instances. The choices are Brightness, Tint, Alpha, and Advanced, which is a combination of the preceding three choices. These controls are first introduced in Chapter 9, "Checking Out the Library: Symbols and Instances."

- **Clip Parameters:** The Clip Parameter Panel is where Smart Clips are made. Smart Clips are a new feature of Flash 5, whereby Clip Parameters can be defined for each movie clip in the Library. By defining attributes (and default values for each attribute), a developer can create templates for interactivity, for ease of use by designers, and other purposes yet to be discovered by the indefatigable legions of Flash genius. The Clip Parameter Panel is discussed in context in Chapter 40, "Publishing Flash Movies."

- **Frame:** The Frame Panel has two functions: It is used to add labels and comments to individual frames, and to hold the controls that manage the finer aspects of Motion and Shape Tweening. The labeling aspect of the Frame Panel is discussed in Chapter 8, "Exploring the Timeline," while the Tweening controls are discussed in Chapter 11, "Animating in Flash."

- **Sound:** Controls for Flash sound are located in the Sound Panel, the Library, and the Publish Settings. The Sound Panel controls are used to set the Effect, Sync, and Loop for each sound, while the Edit button launches the Edit Envelope. Sound is covered in depth in the three chapters of Part III, "Sound Planning."

Tip With the default panel layout, use the Instance Panel button on the Launcher Bar to invoke the default Instance/Effect/Frame/Sound cluster. (For better workflow, we suggest that you consider adding Clip Parameters to this cluster. The procedure for accomplishing this feat is discussed later.)

- **Scene:** The Scene Panel duplicates the function of the Edit Scene button, which is located at the right side of the Timeline Header. When working with Flash Movies that have two or more scenes, the Scene Panel facilitates switching from one scene to another, as well as duplicating, adding, and deleting them.

- **Generator:** If you have Generator installed, the Generator Panel displays common (as well as any custom) Generator Objects that have been installed. Generator and the Generator Panel are discussed in Chapter 27, "What Is Generator?," and Chapter 28, "Revving Up Generator."

✦ **Panel Sets:** This command invokes the Panel Sets submenu, which displays the command for the Default Layout, as well as any custom panel layout that may have been saved.

✦ **Save Panel Layout:** Select this command to launch the Save Panel Layout dialog, which has a Name field and rudimentary buttons. Enter a name with which to save the current arrangement of panels. If you enter a name that's been saved previously, Flash queries whether you want to overwrite it.

✦ **Close All Panels:** This command closes all open panels. However, repeating this command does not reopen those same panels — so it is *not* a toggle.

Tip There is a toggle that closes and then reopens all open panels. On both platforms, the shortcut key for this toggle is the Tab key.

✦ **Actions:** The Actions panel is used for assigning and authoring ActionScript. Although excluded from the Panels submenu, both the Actions Panel and the Movie Explorer Panel, which follows, can be arranged together with the other panels and saved into a panel set. The Actions Panel — and ActionScript — is covered in exhaustive depth in Part V, Programming Flash Movies with ActionScript.

✦ **Movie Explorer:** The Movie Explorer is a powerful new feature of Flash 5. It's like the helpmate of the Library because it provides an asset overview (in a file menu environment, analogous to the Mac Finder or the Windows Explorer) of the current Flash Movie, and offers many shortcuts for editing, updating, and troubleshooting many of the same items that would be much more difficult to sleuth out from the Library. A good example of the utility of the Movie Explorer is changing text and font choice. Doing operations like this from the Movie Explorer can be a *serious* time-saver. The Movie Explorer is introduced in Chapter 9, "Checking Out the Library: Symbols and Instances."

Working with Panels

Depending upon your point of view, the proliferation of panels in Flash 5 can be either an enhancement to or the bane of your workflow. Even if you have dual 21" monitors, or a cinema display, here are some tips that can make your work with panels a lot more productive:

✦ Double-click the title bar of any panel to collapse it upward into just a title bar with the panel tab(s) showing. Unfortunately, collapsed status is not retained when closing the program, nor when saving a panel set.

✦ Use the Launcher Bar. As shown at the beginning of this chapter, in Figures 2-2 and 2-3, the Launcher Bar is located at the lower-right corner of the Flash Editor. It's a default that cannot be excluded from your working environment. It is very handy for launching specific panels as needed, and then closing them.

✦ Alt/Option+Click the close box of any panel to close all panels simultaneously.

✦ Just because you open a panel doesn't mean that it has focus. You have to click in the field where you want to start typing, even if there is only one field.

✦ After you've typed text in a panel field (whether in the Actions Normal mode or other panel), either hit Tab or Enter to make the change take. This is especially useful when entering Frame Labels or Comments, or when entering a number of Instance Names for Movie Clip instances. However, you still must have the field selected or else hitting Tab just toggles all the panels on and off.

   • If a panel isn't open, choosing it from the Panels submenu, tapping the keyboard shortcut, or clicking its Launcher button opens it.

   • If a panel is open and is at the back in the stacking order of other panels, then choosing it from the Panels submenu, tapping the keyboard shortcut, or clicking its Launcher button brings it to the front.

   • If a panel is open and is at the top of the stacking order of other panels, then choosing it from the Panels submenu, tapping the keyboard shortcut, or clicking its Launcher button closes that panel.

   • You can rearrange panels into new panel groups by dragging the panel of choice by its tab. Because panels cannot be regrouped within an existing set, you must plan the order for a panel group before you assemble the group.

   • Alt/Option+double-click any item brings up all relevant panels.

Tip

Both the Actions Panel and the Movie Explorer have buttons on the Launcher Bar to access them without hesitation.

✦ **Output:** Unlike so many of the commands available from the Windows menu, this one isn't a panel — it really is a window, and cannot be ganged together with the panels. After export to .SWF, this opens the Output Window, which shows precise file-size reports on every scene, symbol, text, and so on. It's very helpful for analyzing download problems and testing the effectiveness of preloaders.

✦ **Debugger:** Another new addition to Flash 5, the Debugger Panel is used for troubleshooting Flash ActionScript code, and/or to monitor the properties of Flash movies and symbols. The debugger can be enabled within Flash using Control ⇨ Debug Movie, or it can be evoked from a Web page in a browser. By using the latter method, the Flash application gets focus and the Debugger Panel becomes active (meaning that you don't get a Debugger window/Panel in the browser). This is intended for advanced authoring and can get complex, quickly. For a full explanation of the Debugger, refer to Chapter 21, "Planning Code Structures."

✦ **Library:** The Library is also a true window and not a panel. As was shown earlier in Figures 2-4 and 2-5, the Library is the repository of all recurring elements, known as Symbols, that are placed as Instances within a Flash movie. Imported sounds and bitmaps are automatically placed in the Library. Upon creation, both buttons and Movie Clips (which are symbols) are stored in the Library. It's a smart practice to make a Symbol for nearly *every* item within a Flash movie. The Library is covered in depth in Chapter 9, "Checking Out the Library: Symbols and Instances." Although it differs from the Common Libraries discussed next, they are related. The Windows ⇨ Library is specific to the current movie, whereas Common Libraries are available whenever Flash is open.

✦ **Common Libraries:** The Libraries Menu is the one menu over which the user has real control. That's because — in addition to the Library items that are placed there in the process of a default installation of Flash — you have the option of placing your own items there, too. The default Libraries contain a selection of buttons and symbols to get you started. These are located in the Libraries folder of the Flash application folder. (And when you're tired of them, you can remove them!) To add your own buttons, symbols, or libraries for specific projects, first save them in a Flash file with a descriptive name, then place that Flash file in the Libraries folder within the Flash Program folder on your hard drive. Because these default Common Libraries have such obvious names, we won't waste valuable pages to describe them. They are **Buttons, Graphics, Learning Interactions, Movie Clips, Smart Clips,** and **Sounds.**

✦ **Generator Objects:** This is another true window, and not a panel. This command is disabled, unless you have Generator installed. Generator is a separate program, with a database engine that melds to the Flash's pictorial and animation engine. Refer to Chapter 27, "What Is Generator?," for an introduction to Generator.

    ✦ **Cascade:** This command cascades all open windows so that they overlap in a cascade descending from the top left to the bottom right, like fanned out playing cards.

    ✦ **Tile:** This command tiles all open movie windows so that they are arranged, side-by-side like an eclectic tile job. (Panels and application windows are not tiled.)

The Help Menu

There are so many varied forms of Flash help that it's astounding. In this chapter, we look at a few of the sources for help. The Flash Help Menu, shown in Figure 2-19, directs users to two kinds of help, offline and online. Unless you've opted for a custom install or have removed the help files from your Flash installation, there are a number of offline Help resources directly accessible from the Help Menu. First, beginners may benefit from the lessons and samples. In addition, there are four Flash Help Topics, a sophisticated help system that's viewed offline in your Web browser. Finally, a vast array of online resources are available on the Web—some of which are also linked directly from the Help Menu.

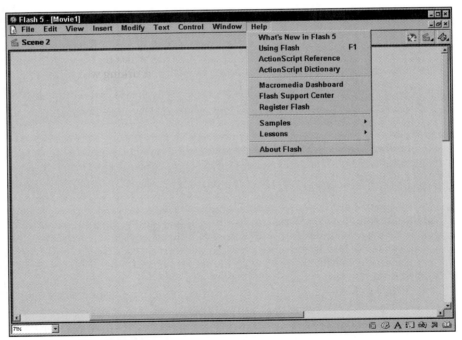

Figure 2-19: The Help Menu

Offline learning resources

Aside from the normal Help files, Flash offers a beginner's course with eight lessons, sample movies, and ActionScript resources.

Lessons and samples

If you accepted the default installation, these are available to you from the Help Menu. (Note, however, that you may not have the Lessons or Samples installed if you chose to do a custom install. In this case, you'll probably want to reinstall Flash in order to have access to these terrific resources.) These excellent, free Lessons and Samples are near the bottom of the Help Menu and are highly recommended for all new Flash users.

Help resources

From the Menu Bar, any of the following four resource topics launch your Web browser and open an offline Web page. Like the Lessons and Samples, these are installed as a default with the program. (If you don't have Flash Help Topics installed, you have to reinstall Flash if you want to access this resource.) The four main topics offer help and instruction in the following areas:

✦ **What's New in Flash 5:** This is an overview of new features and tools. The topics are linked to the relevant areas of the offline manual Using Flash.

✦ **Using Flash:** This is the offline manual, presented as a series of self-paced seminars on the principal tools and methods of working with Flash.

✦ **ActionScript Reference:** This is a reference to the new, robust, Flash 5 Action-Script language.

✦ **ActionScript Dictionary:** This is a dictionary of the new Flash 5 ActionScript language.

Online learning resources

The Flash Help Menu also leads to three resources that are viewed online through a Web browser; these are the new Macromedia Dashboard and the Flash Developers Center.

✦ **Macromedia Dashboard:** This resource is like a mini-browser, built in Flash. The menu has the following Flash-related items: News, Community, Support, Resources, Training, Feedback, and Flash Player. The Dashboard is designed to include a current featured site and a featured community. It also provides an Auto-Update feature, to help you stay current on all features. Technically, the Dashboard is another panel, so it can be grouped with any panel set.

If you have your monitor set to a high resolution (or if you happen to be getting on in years) you may find the text at Dashboard a bit difficult to read. If so, remember that this is scalable vector content: Simply grab any corner of the panel with your mouse and drag out the Dashboard to a more legible size.

✦ **Flash Support Center:** This is Macromedia's original online resource, the Flash Support Center, sometimes also referred to as the Developer's Resource Center. This is Macromedia's primary vehicle for the distribution of up-to-date information about Flash and Flash related topics, so check here regularly for the latest developments. This is a searchable area with current (and archived) articles on many Flash topics. There are also links to downloads, documentation, forums, and many other gems.

✦ **Register Flash:** Although this isn't exactly a resource for help, Macromedia isn't going to give you direct help unless you register your copy of Flash — enough said?

Summary

✦ Flash 5 is the most consistent, cross-platform version yet.

✦ Flash 5 had many enhancements to the interface, preferences, and sundry settings that help to make the program clearer and more powerful.

✦ Some of the most obvious changes are the addition of panels and the inclusion of the new Movie Explorer, while keyboard shortcuts enable users to personalize Flash to facilitate their workflow.

✦ There's not much to be done in Flash that doesn't rely on these menus, panels, settings, and preferences to get it accomplished. So, use this chapter as a reference.

✦ Now that you've toured the Flash menus, panels, settings, and preferences, you're ready to step on out into Flashland and start *creating*.

✦   ✦   ✦

Using Tools for Navigation and Viewing

Before you embark on a project in Flash, you need to know how to get to the action — in a scene, a symbol, or any other element in the movie. You need to know how to change the size of your viewing area (not everyone has 21" monitors). You also need to know how to move efficiently and quickly to areas of the scene that might be off-screen. That's because (surprise!) scrollbars aren't necessarily the easiest way to shift among the contents of the screen. Flash offers familiar navigation and viewing tools for changing the viewable area of a scene and for moving to different areas of a scene.

The Magnifier Tool

The Flash Magnifier Tool (Z) is similar to the zoom tool of many other programs. It has two options, Zoom In and Zoom Out. The Z key is the keyboard shortcut for the Magnifier Tool on both the Mac and the PC. Although this may seem counter-intuitive, the Magnifier Tool is nearly synonymous with the Zoom Tool — furthermore, this keyboard shortcut brings Flash into alignment with usage established in other major software. Keyboard shortcuts for tools located in the Drawing Toolbar are single keystrokes. For example, simply press the Z key to activate the Magnifier Tool. Throughout this book, we indicate keyboard shortcuts with the following notation: Magnifier Tool (Z).

Note Due to the redesign of Flash 5, keyboard shortcuts are now subordinate to what is called *focus,* the active part of the Flash interface. When the Main Timeline and Stage have focus, then the keyboard shortcuts work as they did previously: Simply tap the appropriate key and the related tool is invoked. However, if you are working in any of the various new panels, because that panel has focus, the keyboard shortcuts will not respond—in this case, Flash is not broken. Simply click anywhere on the Stage to switch focus and reenable the function of the keyboard shortcuts.

Zoom In/Zoom Out

Zoom In brings you closer to the drawing so that you're viewing it at a higher level of magnification, whereas *Zoom Out* pulls you away from the drawing by showing it at a lower level of magnification. Each level of *Zoom In* brings you in twice as close, and each level of *Zoom Out* pulls you away in increments of one-half. In addition, here's a less obvious use of the Zoom Tool: If you double-click the Magnifier Tool (see Figure 3-1), it forces the movie to display at 100 percent.

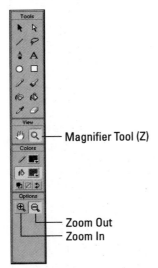

— Magnifier Tool (Z)

— Zoom Out
— Zoom In

Figure 3-1: The Magnifier Tool's options are Zoom In and Zoom Out.

To toggle the Magnifier Tool between the Zoom In and the Zoom Out options on the PC, press Alt+click. On the Mac, press Option+click.

New Feature Flash 5 has added these keyboard zoom commands that bring Flash further into alignment with other Macromedia programs. To Zoom In, press Ctrl/Command with the plus (+) key. To Zoom Out, press Ctrl/Command with the minus (–) key.

Another way of working with the Zoom Tool, which is useful when you want to zoom in on a specific area of your work, is to activate the Magnifier Tool either by clicking it in the Drawing Toolbar or by pressing the (Z) key and then dragging out a rectangle with the Magnifier Tool in the Flash work space. Flash opens the rectangular area at the highest level of magnification that includes the entire area of the rectangle.

The Hand Tool

When you're zoomed in close on the screen, you have two methods for moving around the stage. You can use the scroll bars, or you can use the Hand Tool, which looks like a little gloved hand. Although the scroll bars might be more familiar, especially if you are unfamiliar with drawing and graphics applications, you'll probably find that you can navigate the Flash workspace contents more accurately and intuitively by using the Hand Tool (H). Use this tool by clicking and dragging (while holding down the mouse) in the direction that you want to move the screen. It's important to note that the Hand Tool does not move items in a scene to a new location — the Arrow Tool does that. Rather, the Hand Tool shifts the viewable portion of a scene to reveal another section that may be positioned awkwardly or somewhere off-screen. In addition to this functionality, there's a less obvious use of the Hand Tool — it will fit the Stage in the frame.

Tip The Hand Tool can also be activated temporarily by pressing the space bar; this is a toggle that causes the Hand Tool mouse pointer (the little gloved hand) to appear, regardless of what tool is currently selected in the Tool Palette.

Zoom Control and View Commands

In addition to the use of the Magnifier Tool, similar operations of magnification can also be accomplished with either the Zoom Control (PC only) or with the View Command. The only real difference between these tools and the Magnifier Tool is where they are located within the program and the manner in which they are used to control the level of magnification.

Note With the release of Flash 5, the Zoom Control has changed considerably. Although it has been retained as an integral part of the PC version of Flash, it's been moved to the bottom left of the Stage, where it resides as part of the Launcher Bar. It has been removed entirely from the Mac version.

The Zoom Control

On the PC, the Zoom Control is a numeric entry box and pop-up menu, located at the bottom-left corner of the Stage, as part of the Launcher Bar (see Figure 3-2). The Zoom Control can be used as either a pop-up menu or a numerical entry box. Click the pop-up to display a series of preset Zoom levels, or enter a number in the numerical entry box and press Enter to view the Flash workspace at any other zoom percentage that you desire.

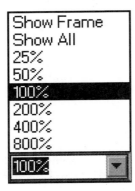

Figure 3-2: The Zoom Control and Zoom Control pop-up menu on the PC

The following preset Zoom levels can be selected from the Zoom Control drop-down menu: Show Frame, Show All, 25%, 50%, 100%, 200%, 400% and 800%. Also, a specific zoom level, such as 122%, can be obtained by typing the exact value in the entry box. Selecting Show Frame or Show All often results in a zoom level other than the evenly incremented zoom percentages available in the Zoom Control drop-down menu. That's because these selections are determined by two factors: The pixel size of a given movie and the pixel area available to the scene on a given computer monitor.

The Magnification commands

In addition to the Magnifier Tool, the new keyboard shortcuts, and the Zoom Control (PC only), the Magnification commands, shown in Figure 3-3, are also available to adjust your screen view. On both the Mac and PC, the Magnification commands are accessed from the Menu Bar, View ⇨ Magnification.

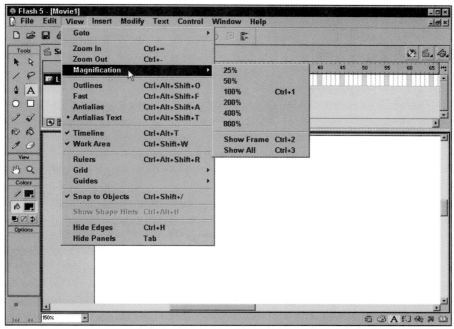

Figure 3-3: The Magnification commands include three presets with keyboard shortcuts. Also, note that the Work Area command is accessed from the View Menu.

The Magnification menu contains the following preset commands: 25%, 50%, 100%, 200%, 400%, 800%, Show Frame, and Show All. (For those of you on the PC, three of these Magnification commands are equivalent to settings available through the Zoom Control drop-down menu.) Three view commands also have corresponding keyboard shortcuts:

✦ **100% (Ctrl/Command+1):** Depending on your monitor resolution and video card, this setting shows your work at actual size. For example, if your movie size is 500 pixels × 400 pixels and your screen size is 800 × 600, then your movie will occupy roughly 40 percent of your total screen area in Flash.

✦ **Show Frame (Ctrl/Cmnd+2):** This setting adjusts the zoom to show everything within the frame boundary, as defined by the movie properties.

✦ **Show All (Ctrl/Cmnd+3):** This setting adjusts the zoom to fit the contents of the current frame. If the frame is empty, the entire scene is displayed.

How Zoom Affects Tool Size

Zoom has a counterintuitive effect on brush sizes and other tools. For example, identical brush sizes draw at different sizes, depending on the Zoom level that you have set! Similarly, the Paint Bucket's interpretation of *gap* (meaning, is that a big gap or a small gap?) is entirely dependent on the zoom setting. It's best to think of brush size and gap size as a fixed *screen image* size. (Caution: This is *unlike* Photoshop and many other programs with fixed *image pixel* size.) Whatever size the brush appears to be on the screen or Work Area *is the effective size of that brush*. Its size is not measured in fixed pixels.

Other tools and functions that are affected by the Zoom setting are those that modify shapes, such as the Smooth option and the functions available by choosing Modify ➪ Curves.

For optimum accuracy when manually placing or aligning items on Stage, use a consistent Zoom setting. For example, if you are arranging several items around a particular point, unless you use the same Zoom setting when you place each item, the accuracy of your positioning may be compromised, which may result in an unwanted jitter in your animation. (Gap is discussed at length in Chapter 4, "Working with Selections and the Pen Tool.")

Another related command, also accessible from the View Menu, View ➪ Work Area, is the Work Area command. (On prior versions of Flash, this command was included with the Magnification commands.) This command adjusts the view to include the work area displayed in gray outside the Stage. It's useful when you're working with items that are completely or partially out of the scene (or out of view). This command enables you to work with items positioned off-screen.

Tip To see the broadest possible Work Area and Stage, choose View ➪ Work Area, and then select either 50% or 100%, depending on your screen size and movie size.

Figure 3-4 compares two brush strokes made with the same exact brush at two different levels of Zoom. Using the third largest brush, the stroke on the left was painted at a Zoom level of 100%, while the stroke on the right was painted at a Zoom of 200%.

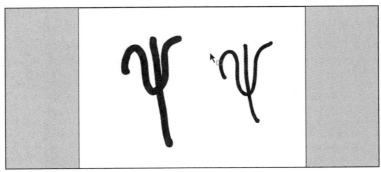

Figure 3-4: How Zoom affects effective Tool Size

Summary

✦ Two basic tools that are common to many other programs, the Magnifier Tool and the Hand Tool, facilitate moving around in Flash.

✦ The Magnifier Tool enables you to either zoom in or zoom out of the Flash Stage. Similar functionality is also offered by the Magnification and Work Area commands, which are accessed from the View menu.

✦ The Hand (or Grabber) Tool enables you to scoot areas of the Flash Stage in or out of the viewable area of zoom.

✦ The level of zoom has a direct, counterintuitive effect upon both the apparent Tool size and also the accuracy of positioning and aligning of items on stage.

✦　　✦　　✦

Working with Selections and the Pen Tool

Flash has a pair of tools — the Lasso Tool and the Arrow Tool — that can be used to select lines, shapes, groups, symbols, buttons, and other items. The Lasso Tool is primarily used to make free-form selections and to select odd-shaped sections of a drawing. The Arrow Tool is used primarily to select discrete lines, shapes, groups, symbols, buttons, and other items. In combination with the Magnet option and the Shape Recognition options, the Arrow Tool has many unique capabilities not found in any other program. In addition to these tools, the new Subselect Tool, which also looks like an arrow, can be used (in a limited way) to select these items. However, the Subselect Tool is primarily a companion for the Pen Tool, which is introduced at the end of this chapter. We've chosen to address the Pen Tool among the selection tools because the Pen Tool draws lines by laying down editable points. Additionally, both the Pen Tool and the Subselect Tool are used to manipulate those points, and, thereby, edit lines. Nevertheless, both the Pen Tool and the Subselect Tool are equally useful for selecting and editing all lines and shape, so they're selection tools, too.

The Lasso Tool

The Lasso Tool (L) is used to group-select odd or irregular-shaped areas of your drawing. After areas are selected, they can be moved, scaled, rotated, or reshaped as a single unit. The Lasso Tool can also be used to split shapes, or select portions of a line or a shape. As shown in Figure 4-1, it has three options in the Options Tray: the Polygon Lasso, the Magic Wand, and the Magic Wand properties.

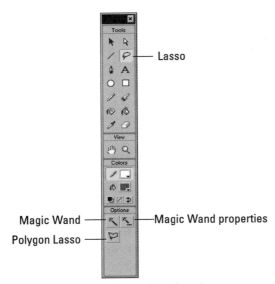

Figure 4-1: The Lasso Tool and options

The Lasso Tool works best if you drag a loop around the area you wish to select. (Hence the tool name Lasso!) But if you slip or if you don't end the loop near where you started, Flash closes the loop with a straight line between your starting point and the end point. Because you can use the Lasso Tool to define an area of *any* shape — limited only by your ability to draw and use the multiple selection capabilities of Flash — the Lasso Tool gives you more control over selections than the Arrow Tool.

Tip   To add to a previously selected area, hold down the Shift key before initiating additional selections.

Using the Polygon option with the Lasso Tool

The Polygon Lasso affords greater precision when making straight-edge selections, or — in mixed mode — selections that combine freeform areas with straight edges. To describe a simple polygon selection, click the Polygon option to toggle the Lasso Tool *on* and commence Polygon selection mode. In Polygon Mode, selection points are created by a mouse click, causing a straight selection line to extend between mouse clicks. To complete the selection, double click.

Mixed mode usage, which includes Polygon functionality, is available when the Lasso Tool is in Freeform Mode. To work in Freeform Mode, the Polygon option must be in the *off* position. While drawing with the Freeform Lasso, press the Alt (Option) key to temporarily invoke Polygon Mode. (Polygon Mode continues only as long as the Alt (Option) key is pressed.) Now, straight polygonal lines can be described between selection points that are created by a mouse click. That is, *as long as the Alt (Option) key is pressed, a straight selection line extends between mouse clicks.* To return to Freeform Mode, simply sneeze — or release the Alt (Option) key. Release the mouse to close the selection.

Note

Sometimes aberrant selections — selections that seem inside out, or that have a weird, unwanted straight line bisecting the intended selection — result from Lasso selections. That's usually because the point of origination of a Lasso selection is the point to which the Lasso will snap when the selection is closed. It usually takes a little practice to learn how to *plan* the point of origin so that the desired selection will be obtained when the selection is closed.

Using the Magic Wand option with the Lasso Tool

The Magic Wand option of the Lasso Tool is used to select ranges of a similar color in a bitmap that has been broken apart. After you select areas of the bitmap, you can change their fill color or delete them. Breaking apart a bitmap means that the bitmap image is subsequently seen by Flash as a collection of individual areas of color. (This is not the same as *tracing* a bitmap, which reduces the vast number of colors in a continuous-tone bitmap to areas of solid color.) After an image is broken apart, you can select individual areas of the image with any of the selection tools, including the Magic Wand option of the Lasso Tool. You can restore a broken bitmap by selecting the entire image (this causes it to look like a negative relief), and then choosing Modify ➪ Group from the Menu Bar. The equivalent shortcut is Ctrl (Command)+G.

Cross-Reference

Techniques and settings for using the Magic Wand when working with Bitmaps, as well as Tracing Bitmaps, are covered in Chapter 12, "Using Bitmaps and Other Media with Flash."

Using Magic Wand properties

The Magic Wand properties option has two modifiable settings: Threshold and Smoothing. To set them, click the Magic Wand properties button while the Lasso Tool is active.

The Threshold setting of the Magic Wand option

The Threshold setting defines the breadth of adjacent color values that the Magic Wand option includes in a selection. Values for the Threshold setting range from 0 to 200: The higher the setting, the broader the selection of adjacent colors. Conversely, a smaller number results in the Magic Wand making a narrower selection of adjacent colors.

Note   A value of zero results in a selection of contiguous pixels that are all the same color as the target pixel. With a value of 20, clicking on a red target pixel with a value of 55 selects all contiguous pixels in a range of values extending from red 35 to red 75. (For those of you who are familiar with Photoshop, it is important to note that the Flash Threshold is unlike Photoshop in which a Threshold setting of 20 selects all contiguous pixels in a range of values extending from red 45 to red 65.)

The Smoothing setting of the Magic Wand option

The Smoothing setting of the Magic Wand option determines to what degree the edge of the selection should be smoothed. This is similar to antialiasing. (Antialiasing dithers the edges of shapes and lines so that they look smoother on screen.) The options are Smooth, Pixels, Rough, and Normal.

The Arrow Tool

The Arrow Tool is used to select and move an item — or multiple items — on the Stage. The Arrow Tool is also used to reshape lines and shapes, as those users familiar with prior versions of Flash may remember. The Arrow Tool's new neighbor, which is also an arrow, but a white one, is the Subselect Tool. Its debut in Flash was occasioned by the addition of the Pen Tool. Thus, it is most useful for moving and editing anchor points and tangents on Bézier curves, as well as *single* items.

New Feature   Now, with the addition of a new Pen Tool, Flash 5 enables you to draw and manipulate lines and shapes using Bézier curves (or Bézier handles), much like other vector-based programs. Often, this manipulation is accomplished with the Subselect Tool. Because the Subselect Tool is technically a selection tool, and because it is used in concert with the Pen Tool, which can also be used to select and edit points on lines created by any of the other drawing tools, we present a full discussion of both tools at the end of this chapter.

Use the Arrow Tool to reshape a line or shape by pulling on any unselected line (or shape), or on its end points, curves, or corners. The Arrow Tool is also used to select and move Flash elements, including lines, shapes, groups, symbols, buttons, and other items. Five options appear in the Option Tray when the Arrow Tool (A) is selected (see Figure 4-2): Magnet (or Snap), Smooth, Straighten, Rotate, and Scale.

Tip   When you are busy with another tool, you can temporarily toggle to the Arrow Tool by pressing and holding down the Ctrl (Command) key.

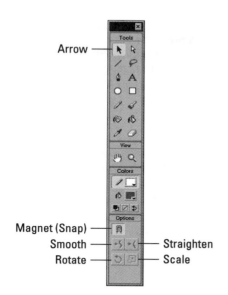

Figure 4-2: The Arrow Tool and its five options

Arrow

Magnet (Snap)
Smooth ——— Straighten
Rotate ——— Scale

Using the Arrow Tool to select items

The Arrow Tool is the primary selection tool in Flash. When you click a line or shape, a checkered pattern appears, covering it, to indicate that the line or shape has been selected. If the item is either a Symbol or a Group, a thin, colored border (called the Highlight) indicates selection status. This Highlight Color may be set in the Preferences dialog by choosing Edit ➪ Preferences ➪ General.

Figure 4-3 shows a shape, a group, and a symbol as they look both when unselected (the top items) and selected (the bottom items). The hatched pattern covers and surrounds the square indicating that it is a selected graphic, while the thin borders that surround the group and the symbol indicates that they have been selected.

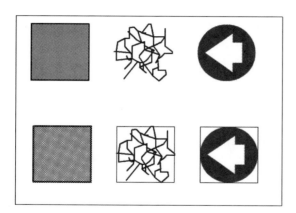

Figure 4-3: Using the Arrow Tool to select items

In addition to clicking on a line to select it, you can also select one or more items by dragging a rectangular marquee over them using the Arrow Tool. This operation is called *drag-select*. Additional items can be added to a current selection by pressing the Shift key and clicking the items. When you drag-select to select, previously selected items are deselected and excluded from the selection. To include previously selected items, press the Shift key as you drag-select.

Note Prior to Flash 4, the implementation of Shift Select was unlike other graphics applications: Additional lines were added to a selection simply by clicking them. Since Flash 4, the Shift key must be pressed in order to add to the current selection. To change this default setting for Shift Select, go to Edit ➪ Preferences, and click the General tab. Then, in the Selection Options section, uncheck Shift Select.

Deselect one or more items by using any of these methods:

✦ Pressing the Escape key

✦ Choosing Edit ➪ Deselect All

✦ Using the keyboard shortcut Ctrl+Shift+A (Command+Shift+A)

✦ Clicking anywhere outside all the selected items

Using the Magnet option of the Arrow Tool

The Magnet (or Snap to Objects) option button is a toggle that causes items being drawn or moved on screen to snap to existing items on the Stage. Click the option button to toggle snapping on or off, or choose View ➪ Grid ➪ Snap to Objects.

As shown in Figure 4-4, the rectangular shape is being moved to the right with the Arrow Tool and is snapping to the invisible grid. When snap is turned on, Flash snaps the item to existing items. You can tell that an item is snapping by the presence of an o icon beside the Arrow mouse pointer. For some shapes, the icon or snap function will not work unless, when clicking to grab the shape before moving, the shape is clicked either at the center, corner, or side.

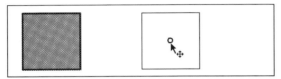

Figure 4-4: Using the Magnet (Snap to Objects) option of the Arrow Tool

Even if the Magnet option is turned on, you can temporarily override the Snap function by holding down the Shift key as you drag or move an item.

The functionality and degree of precision of the Magnet (or Snap) button are controlled by settings that can be customized in the Grid field of the Grid dialog, which can be accessed by choosing View ➪ Grid ➪ Edit Grid. The settings are measured in pixels, relative to the movie size (*not* the screen size).

Understanding shape recognition

Shape recognition is the general term for a set of options that can be set to assist accurate drawing and manipulation of basic shapes. These options are the Smooth and Straighten options, which are used in conjunction with the Arrow Tool to clean up drawings by clicking their respective buttons to invoke their smoothing or straightening action. This is fully explained in the sections that follow.

When used in conjunction with the Pencil Tool, more powerful shape recognition can be invoked — the only real difference is that, with respect to the Pencil Tool, shape recognition processes the lines automatically. For example, a crude lumpy oval will be automatically recognized and processed into a true oval. Using shape recognition with the Pencil Tool is explained in greater detail in the first section of Chapter 5, "Working with the Drawing and Painting Tools."

For the Arrow and the Pencil Tools, both the degree to which shape recognition processes your drawings and also the strength with which the Smooth and Straighten options interact with your drawings may be adjusted with the Drawing Settings pane of the Editing tab of the Preferences dialog: Edit ➪ Preferences ➪ Editing.

Here's how shape recognition works with the Arrow Tool: Sketch something spontaneously (but not too wildly!). Then use shape recognition to transform your sketch into precision geometric forms. Start by sketching a rough circle, square, or rectangle. Then click the Arrow Tool and select the item you've just sketched. Then click either the Straighten or Smooth button to begin shape recognition. For hard-edged items such as a polygon, click the Straighten option button repeatedly until your rough sketch is a recognizable and precise geometric form. For smooth-edged items that approximate an oval, click the Smooth option button repeatedly until your rough sketch becomes an exact circle.

 In addition to the treatment here in this chapter, shape recognition is detailed elsewhere in the book. The settings that control shape recognition are first explained in Chapter 2, "Exploring the Interface: Panels, Settings, and More." Shape recognition is also discussed further, in context with drawing processes, in Chapter 10, "Drawing in Flash."

Using the Smooth option with the Arrow Tool

The Smooth option is a button that simplifies selected curves, as shown in Figure 4-5. Smoothing reduces the number of bumps and variations (or points of transition) along the span of a complex curve so that the curve spans the same distance with fewer points. Repeated use of the Smooth button on a line results in a curve with only two points, one at either end. To use this option, a line must first be selected with the Arrow Tool, and then the Smooth button can be used to reduce the points in the selected line (or line segment). Action similar to the Smooth button can also be accessed by choosing Modify ⇨ Smooth.

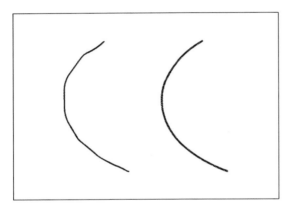

Figure 4-5: Using the Smooth option with the Arrow Tool: The curve on the left was drawn with the Pencil Tool (in Ink Mode). Then the curve was selected by clicking it with the Arrow Tool and smoothed by hitting the Smooth option button twice. That result is shown on the right.

Using the Straighten option with the Arrow Tool

The Straighten option is a button that is used to make selected line segments less curved. The Straighten button operates on the same principle as the Smooth button, except that it's used for straightening (instead of smoothing) a selected line segment. Repeated use of the Straighten button turns a curvy line into a series of angled lines. Action similar to the Straighten button can also be accessed by choosing Modify ⇨ Straighten.

In Figure 4-6, the Pencil Tool (in Ink Mode) was used to draw the rough, freehand T on the left. After selecting this rough T by clicking with the Arrow, the Straighten option button was clicked once to create the refined T shown on the right.

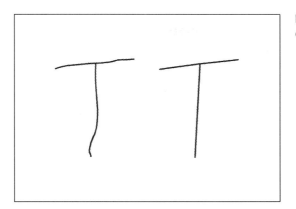

Figure 4-6: Using the Straighten option with the Arrow Tool

The degree of the Smoothing or Straightening adjustments that can be made with the Smooth or Straighten button is regulated by the number of times that the button is clicked. Although it may appear that the degree of automatic Smoothing or Straightening can be adjusted by choosing Edit ➪ Preferences ➪ Editing and then selecting one of the four choices (Off, Rough, Normal, or Smooth), these options *only* affect smoothing or straightening done *during* the drawing process (with shape recognition turned on), *not* adjustments made with the Smooth or Straighten buttons.

Using the Rotate option with the Arrow Tool

The Rotate option enables you to rotate, skew, or slant a selected line, group, symbol, or item. With the graphic element selected, click the Rotate option to put it into Rotation Mode. Eight circular handles appear. Drag a corner handle to rotate the item. Drag either a middle or side handle to skew or slant. You can also rotate items by choosing Modify ➪ Transform ➪ Rotate.

In Figure 4-7, the Rectangle Tool was used to draw the square shown at the upper left. After it was selected by clicking with the Arrow Tool, the Rotate button was clicked, resulting in the superimposed checker pattern and bounding box with eight *circular,* draggable handles, as shown at the upper right. Then, the square was rotated counterclockwise by click-dragging one of the four circular handles located at the corners of the square, as shown at the bottom left. Click-dragging any of the four internal handles (the handles not on the corners) results in a skewing of the shape, as shown at the bottom right.

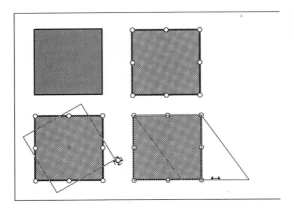

Figure 4-7: Using the Rotate option with the Arrow Tool

Tip

When reshaping, scaling, or rotating a solid item with fills, Flash handles the filled area as if a line of zero thickness enclosed it. As you readjust such an item to a new shape, the fill either expands or contracts accordingly.

Using the Scale option with the Arrow Tool

The Scale option button enables you to scale or stretch a selected line, shape, group, symbol, button, or other item. With the graphic element selected, click the Scale button. Eight square handles appear around the selected graphic element. Click and drag a corner handle to scale the item. Click and drag either a middle or side handle to stretch the item. You can also scale by choosing Modify ⇨ Transform ⇨ Scale.

As shown in Figure 4-8, after drawing the square on the upper left with the Rectangle Tool, the square is first selected with the Arrow Tool and then the Scale button is clicked, resulting in the superimposed checker pattern and bounding box with eight square, draggable handles, as shown at the upper right. Clicking and dragging on any corner handle, as shown at the lower left, symmetrically resizes the square. Asymmetrical scaling is accomplished by clicking and dragging on any of the side handles, as shown at the lower right.

Using the Scale and Rotate dialog

Choosing Modify ⇨ Transform ⇨ Scale and Rotate elicits a dialog that combines the properties of both the Rotate and Scale option buttons in one dialog, enabling you to input numeric values for the amount of scale and transformation. (It's very much like the Photoshop Numeric Transform Tool.) The keyboard shortcut for this hybrid is Ctrl+Alt+S (Command+Option+S). This functionality is further duplicated in the Transform Panel (Window ⇨ Panels ⇨ Transform). Although using either numeric transform dialog may seem unintuitive and hard to use unless you already know what you want to accomplish, they are *extremely* valuable for repetitive production tasks.

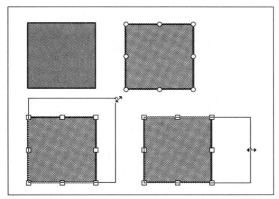

Figure 4-8: Using the Scale option with the Arrow Tool

Using arrow states to reshape and reposition drawings

In addition to the actions accomplished by selecting a line (or line section) and clicking an option, three arrow states — Move Selected Element, Reshape Curve or Line, and Reshape Endpoint or Corner — enable you to reshape and move parts of your drawings. It works like this: As you move the Arrow Tool over the Flash Stage, the Arrow Tool changes the state of its cursor to indicate what tasks it can perform in context with various items (the line or fill) closest to the Arrow Tool's current position.

Tip

> When reshaping brush strokes and similar items with the Arrow Tool, make sure that you don't select the entire brush stroke before trying to reshape the outline. If you do, you'll only be able to move the entire brush stroke – you won't be able to reshape it.

Figure 4-9 shows a series of images that demonstrate the various Arrow states in context with several kinds of shapes. These shapes are a filled shape, a brush stroke, and a brush stroke with an outline applied. In the upper left, the *Move Selected Element* Arrow state appears when the Arrow is passed over either one of these shapes. In the upper right, the *Reshape Curve or Line* Arrow state appears when the Arrow is hovered over any line or over the perimeter of a brush stroke. At the lower left, the *Reshape Endpoint or Corner* Arrow state appears when the Arrow is hovered over a corner. At the lower right, an Arrow state cursor is being used to reshape each item.

Figure 4-10 shows the completion of the reshape operations indicated in Figure 4-9.

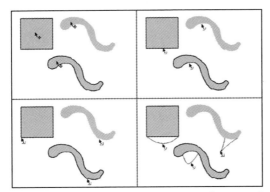

Figure 4-9: Using Arrow states to reshape and reposition items

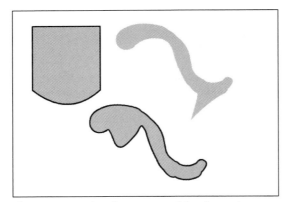

Figure 4-10: The changes resulting from the reshaping shown in Figure 4-9.

To make your reshaping go even easier, try these techniques:

✦ Press the Ctrl+Alt (Command+Option) keys, click a line or segment of a line, and drag to create a new corner point.

✦ Selected lines cannot be reshaped. Click anywhere (outside all selected items) to deselect, and then reshape the line by clicking it with one of the different states of the Arrow Tool.

✦ Smooth complex lines to make reshaping easier.

✦ Increase magnification to make your reshaping easier and more accurate.

✦ Prior to reshaping, select any group of elements (as a multiple selection, using Shift+select) that you want to change in unison.

Moving grouped and ungrouped elements with the Arrow Tool

Text and Groups are selected as single elements and move as a single unit. After you create text in a given frame (text functions are discussed in Chapter 7, "Working with Text"), Flash treats the text as one block, or group, meaning that all the individual letters move together when the box is selected. Similarly, a group of graphic elements — such as lines, outlines, fills, or shapes — can be grouped and moved or manipulated as a single element. However, when you move an item that is not grouped, only the selected part is moved. This can be tricky when you have ungrouped fills and outlines, because selecting one without the other could result in detaching the fill from the outline or vice versa. To move separate elements (such as a rectangular line and its colored fill area) in the same direction simultaneously, group them first. To group separate elements, first select them all, and then group them with Modify ⇨ Group. If necessary, they can be ungrouped later. Grouping is further discussed in Chapter 10, "Drawing in Flash."

Duplicating items with the Arrow Tool

The Arrow Tool can also be used for duplicating items. Simply press the Alt (Option) key while dragging a selected item (or line segment) with the Arrow Tool. The original item remains in place, and a new item is deposited at the end of your drag stroke.

Introducing the Pen Tool

Finally, Flash has a Pen Tool. Some developers groused over the addition of this new feature, saying that the original drawing set was fine and that this was only being added to attract new users who might be more familiar with FreeHand or other drawing programs. Frankly, these people sounded like members of a child's club, comfortable in their tree fort, as they haul up the rope ladder. The inclusion of the Pen Tool and its close associate, the Subselect Arrow, shown in Figure 4-11, has made the Flash drawing tools far more robust and gives artists more options for creating, editing, and optimizing their art.

For example, previously, when trying to the reduce file size of a movie, an artist might resort to one of the Optimize commands, hoping to reduce the number of points in a drawing. But this had the disadvantage of being both unpredictable and uncontrollable. Now, with the Pen Tool, an artist can select individual points and delete them one by one, resulting in aesthetic precision and reduced file size!

Figure 4-11: Neither the Pen Tool nor the Subselect Tool has options in the Options Tray.

Subselect

Pen

Using the Pen Tool

The Pen Tool (P) is used to draw precision paths that define straight lines and smooth curves. These paths define adjustable line segments, which may be straight or curved — the angle and length of straight segments is completely adjustable, as is the slope and length of curved segments. To draw a series of straight-line segments with the Pen Tool, simply move the cursor and click successively: Each subsequent click defines the end point of the line. To draw curved line segments with the Pen Tool, simply click *and drag:* The length and direction of the drag determines the depth and shape of the current segment. Both straight- and curved-line segments can be modified and edited by adjusting their points. In addition, any lines or shapes that have been created by other Flash drawing tools can also be displayed as paths (points on lines) and edited with either the Pen Tool or the Subselect Tool.

The Preferences for the Pen Tool are located in the Pen Tool section of the Preferences dialog. (Choose Edit ➪ Preferences ➪ Editing.) There are three settings: Pen Preview, Point display, and Cursor style. These settings are covered in detail in Chapter 2, "Exploring the Interface: Panels, Settings, and More." As regards your preference for Cursor style, although you can choose between a precise crosshair cursor and a tool icon cursor, you can also use a keyboard shortcut to toggle between the two: Caps Lock toggles Pen Tool cursors between the precise crosshair and the Pen icon.

As Figure 4-12 shows, the Pen Tool cursor displays a number of tiny icons to the lower right of the Pen Tool. These are the Pen states. Four of these Pen states are shown in this composite image, which is a detail of a path describing a white line over a light-gray background, shown at a zoom of 1600.

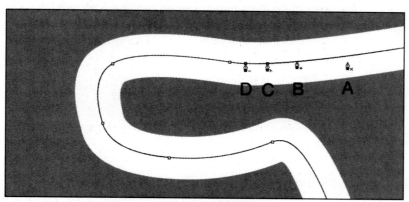

Figure 4-12: In addition to the choice between the cursor icon and crosshair, the Pen Tool displays seven Pen states that indicate the Pen's function under various circumstances.

✦ The Pen displays a small (x) when it's simply over the stage (A).

✦ When the Pen is over a path, it displays a (+) to indicate that clicking there will add a point to the path (B).

✦ When the Pen hovers over an existing point, it displays a (^) to indicate that clicking that point will turn it into a corner point (C).

✦ When the Pen hovers over a corner point, it displays a (–) sign to indicate that clicking this corner point will delete it (D).

Tip   Working with the Pen Tool in a movie whose background color is set to black can seem to be nearly impossible—if your Layer Outline Color is set to black! Change the Layer Outline Color to contrast with your background and Pen away! This same principle applies if your background is red (or any other color) and the Layer Outline Color is set to that same color.

As shown in Figure 4-13, there are three more Pen states and a number of details to be defined about the Pen Tool.

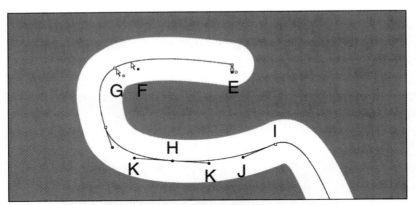

Figure 4-13: More Pen states are shown in this composite image, together with other functions of the Pen Tool.

✦ When the Pen is hovered over an end point, it displays an (o) to indicate that this is an end point (E). Click this point to connect a continuation of this path or, when making a closed shape, to close the path.

✦ With the Ctrl (Command) key pressed, when the Pen hovers over a path or line, it displays as a hollow arrow with a filled black box (F). In this manner, the Pen Tool is mimicking the Subselect Tool.

✦ With the Ctrl/Command key pressed, when the Pen hovers over a point, it displays the same hollow arrow, but with a hollow box (G). In this manner, too, the Pen Tool is mimicking the Subselect Tool.

✦ When adjusting a path with either the Pen Tool or the Subselect Tool, the default for selected points is a filled circle (H), while unselected points display as a hollow squares (I). Note that the unselected points display a single tangent handle (J), bound toward the selected point, which displays two tangent handles (K).

Now that we've toured the various Pen Tool icons and Pen states, and have defined the fine details, points, and tangent handles, it's time to start drawing with the Pen Tool. To draw and adjust a straight-line segment with the Pen Tool, follow these steps:

1. Click to initiate the beginning of your line.

2. Then, click to create subsequent points and define individual line segments.

3. Each subsequent click creates a *corner* point on the line that determines the length of individual line segments.

4. To adjust straight segments, press the Ctrl (Command) key and click a point to select it. Continue pressing the Ctrl (Command) key as you drag and move the point to change the angle or length of the segment.

5. Or, with the Ctrl (Command) key pressed, click and drag on the tangent handles of the point to adjust the line. Remember that corner points occur on a straight segment or at the juncture of a straight segment and a curved segment.

Tip

When drawing with the Pen Tool, press the Shift key to force constrain drawing to either 45-degree or 90-degree angle.

To draw and adjust a curved line segment with the Pen Tool, follow these steps:

1. In one continuous motion, click to create the first anchor point.

2. Then, drag the Pen Tool in the direction you want the curve to go.

3. Repeat this process to create subsequent *curve* points for curved segments.

4. Or simply click elsewhere to change to make the subsequent segment a straight line with a *corner* point.

5. As with adjusting straight segments, press the Ctrl (Command) key and click a point to select it, continue pressing the Ctrl (Command) key as you drag and move the point to change the angle or length of the segment.

6. Or, with the Ctrl (Command) key pressed, click and drag on the tangent handles of the point to adjust the depth and shape of the curve.

Although both corner points and curve points may be adjusted, they behave differently:

✦ Because a corner point defines a corner, adjusting the tangent handle of a corner point only modifies the curve that occurs on the same side as the tangent handle that is being adjusted.

✦ Because a curve point defines a curve, moving the tangent handle of a curve point modifies the curves on both sides of the point.

✦ You can also use the arrow keys, located on your keyboard, to nudge corner and curve points into position. Press the Shift key to augment the arrow keys and to make them nudge 10 pixels with each click.

Note

You can also reshape any lines or shapes created with the Pen, Pencil, Brush, Line, Oval, or Rectangle Tools by dragging with the Arrow Tool, or by optimizing their curves with Modify ⇨ Optimize.

Using the Subselect (Arrow) Tool

The Subselect Tool (A) has two purposes:

1. **To either move or edit individual anchor points and tangents.** (You can use the Subselect Tool to display points on both lines and shape outlines and modify them by adjusting their points.)

2. **To move individual objects.** When moving the Subselect Tool over a line or point, the hollow arrow cursor displays one of two states: When over a line it displays a small, filled square next to it; when over a point, it displays a small, hollow square. When either cursor appears, the item can be clicked and moved about the stage.

Note   If you use the Subselect Tool to drag a selection rectangle around two items, you'll find that although both may be selected, you can only move one of them.

Figure 4-14 shows the use of the Subselect Tool to move a path (A), to move a single point (B), to select a tangent handle (C), and to modify a curve by adjusting its tangent handle (D). Note that both the before and after are shown before releasing the handle.

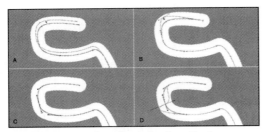

Figure 4-14: Using the Subselect Tool

The Subselect Tool is most useful for modifying and adjusting paths. To display anchor points on a line or shape outline created with the Pencil, Brush, Line, Oval, or Rectangle Tools, simply click the line or shape outline with the Subselect Tool. This reveals the points that define the line or shape. Click any point to cause its tangent handles to appear. If you have a shape that is all fill, without any stroke, you'll need to position the Subselect Tool precisely at the edge of the shape in order to select or move it with the Subselect Tool.

To convert a corner point into a curve point, follow these steps:

1. Click to select the point with the Subselect Tool.

2. While pressing the Alt (Option) key, click and drag the point.

3. A curve point with tangent handles appears, replacing the original corner point.

Note By holding down the Ctrl (Command) key, the Pen Tool can also be used to mimic the function of the Subselect Tool — except when converting a corner point.

An important use of the Pen Tool/Subselect Tool combo is editing lines for optimal file size. The simpler your shapes, the smaller your file size and the faster your movie downloads. Most often, this involves deleting extraneous points. There are a couple of ways to delete points:

✦ Choose the Subselect Tool from the Toolbox, and then click to select the line with the Subselect Tool, which causes the individual points to appear as hollow circles along the line. Select the point that you wish to delete. Click the delete key.

✦ Choose the Pen Tool from the Toolbox, which causes all paths on the current layer to be selected. Bring the Pen Tool over the point that you want to delete. The cursor updates and displays a small inverted v (^) to the lower right, which is the Corner Point cursor. Click the point with the Corner Point cursor, and continue to hover over the point. After clicking with the Corner Point cursor, the cursor updates and displays a small minus sign (–) to the lower right, which is the Delete Point cursor. Click the point with the Delete Point cursor to delete it.

✦ When deleting more than one point from a closed shape, such as an oval or polygon, use the Subselect Tool to drag and select any number of points. Press Delete to eliminate the selected points. The path heals itself, closing the shape with a smooth arc or line.

Tip If you used the Subselect Tool to select a path and then Shift+select several points on it, those points will show handles, turning from solid squares to hollow circles, which indicates that they are now moveable. However, if you attempt to move all of the points simultaneously with the Subselect Tool, only one point will move. However, all the points *can* be moved in unison by tapping the arrow keys.

Stroke and color

You may have noticed that we've been discussing the Pen Tool and the Subselect Tool in a relative vacuum — that is, there's been no mention yet of either stroke or color. Well that's easy enough to do, because both *those* controls are sequestered off in the Stroke Panel. But that's not why we've refrained from discussing the more colorful aspects of the Pen Tool. Rather, in this chapter, we focused on the aspects of the Pen Tool that are most closely related to selecting. We begin the next chapter, "Working with the Drawing and Painting Tools," with a rudimentary discussion of color as it applies to all Drawing Tools. This is a discussion of the settings for the Stroke and Fill Panels, which involve Stroke Height and Stroke Color — the color settings for the Pen Tool. See you there.

Shifting Points? Too Many Points?

We've heard reports of perceived problems with the new Pen Tool. Some users noted that Pen paths seemed to "add points" when adding keyframes, or between sessions. Naturally, this seemed very odd, so we did some research through a contact at Macromedia—and here's what we found out.

The Macromedia Flash Player is driven by quadratic curves, which differ from Bézier curves in two ways: They are faster drawing and they result in a more compact file. This is partially because they employ a single tangent handle for each node, rather than the two tangent handles per node in a Bézier format.

The Flash Editor is also driven by quadratics, and even when drawing with the Pen Tool, the internal curve descriptions are still in quadratics—so, you can always push and pull on those Pen Tool curves, and do many other things in the customary *Flash* manner. Therefore, each time you choose the Pen Tool, Flash converts selected lines to an onscreen Bézier representation in order to support Bézier-style curve editing. When the editing is done, Flash converts the curve back to quadratics for storage and display—the Bézier nodes aren't stored.

At the next Pen Tool editing session, the Bézier representation is created, on the fly from the stored quadratic definition. This can lead to some confusion, because it may appear as though the number of points has increased. However, there's no worry about too many points, or changed points, because—in the strict Flash sense—those points don't really exist in the file. What is important is the overall shape complexity that is stored in the saved quadratic representation. When you optimize a line by reducing points with the Pen Tool, this reduces complexity and that is retained when the file is saved. Summary: You will see your shapes accurately retained, but because the Bézier nodes are calculated on demand and only appear while editing, the points may display differently between sessions.

Summary

✦ Flash provides a range of tools that are used to select and modify items on the Stage.

✦ The Lasso Tool is useful for making free-form selections, while the Magic Wand option is a powerful tool for selecting a range of colors — particularly when working with imported bitmaps that you break apart.

✦ The Arrow Tool has multiple uses. With its shape-recognition features, it can be used to smooth or straighten selected drawings — which simplifies their forms to create smaller file sizes.

✦ The Arrow Tool is also used to rotate, scale, and skew selected items.

✦ The Arrow states enable you to simply click lines, fills, and corners to reshape items with rapid ease.

✦ The new Flash Pen Tool and its companion, the Subselect Tool, enhance the Toolbox with their precision path-drawing and point-editing capabilities.

✦ ✦ ✦

Working with the Drawing and Painting Tools

Flash 5 significantly revamped the former Toolbar and renamed it the *Toolbox*. Flash 5 also added two new tools: the *Pen Tool* and the *Subselect (Arrow) Tool.* Both of these new tools were described in detail in Chapter 4, "Working with Selections and the Pen Tool." In this chapter, we look at the rest of the drawing tools — the Pencil, Line, Oval, Rectangle, Brush, Dropper, Ink Bottle, Paint Bucket, and Eraser Tools.

Perhaps the most significant renovation of the Toolbox is in the area formerly referred to as the Modifier Tray. This is now called the *Options Tray.* Although that, in itself, is not a big deal, *this* is: For most tools, many of the former modifiers (or options) have been relocated to individual panels. General routines for accessing and managing panels were discussed in the Window menu section of Chapter 2, "Exploring the Interface: Panels, Settings, and More."

Choosing Colors

Whenever any Flash Drawing or Painting Tool is used, the stroke and fill colors are determined by the current settings of the color controls located in the Flash Toolbox. These controls are present regardless of which tool is being used. Although these controls operate like color chips that indicate the current color, they're really buttons: Click either Color button to open the current Swatches pop-up, shown in Figure 5-1, and select a new stroke or fill color.

In addition to the basic reorganization of the Toolbox, the color controls include three new buttons, arrayed across the bottom of the Color Tray. These are, from left to right, buttons for Default Stroke and Fill, None, and Swap. The Default button sets the stroke to black and the fill to white. The None button (only active with the Pen, Oval, and Rectangle Tools) sets the active control to apply no color. The Swap button swaps the current colors between the Stroke and Fill controls.

Figure 5-1: This is the current Swatches pop-up for the Pencil Tool.

Clicking either the Stroke or Fill Color buttons invokes the current Swatches pop-up. This pop-up displays the same Swatch that is currently loaded in the Swatches Panel. It includes a hexadecimal color entry box, another iteration of the None button, and a button that launches the Color Picker. For all drawing tools, elementary color selection is accomplished by clicking either the Stroke or Fill Color buttons and then choosing a color from the Swatches pop-up. More advanced color usage is detailed in the next chapter.

We've devoted Chapter 6, "Applying Color," to an explanation of Flash Color. It includes not only the details of working with Flash Color, but also a little primer on color theory, computer color, and Web color.

The Stroke and Fill Panels

Users of prior versions of Flash, when beginning to use the Drawing and Painting Tools, might well inquire about the disappearance of the controls for Line Thickness and Line Style, as well as the Fill Color control. But that's because these controls now reside in the Stroke and the Fill Panels, where they are now referred to as the Stroke Height, Stroke Style, and Fill Style controls. These panels, and the controls they contain, are consistently available regardless of which tool is being used. Panels are accessed from the Window menu, by choosing Window ⇨ Panels and then choosing the individual panel from the submenu.

Stroke Color

To select a color for a stroke that you are about to draw, click the Stroke Color button of the Stroke Panel (see Figure 5-2) to invoke the Swatches pop-up and then select a color. To change the color of a stroke that's already drawn, first select the item with the Arrow Tool, click the Stroke Color button of the Stroke Panel, and then select a new color from the Swatches pop-up.

Note   Selecting stroke color and changing stroke color can be accomplished with either the Stroke Color button in the Toolbox or in the Stroke Panel. This same procedure can also be applied to paths drawn with the Pen Tool.

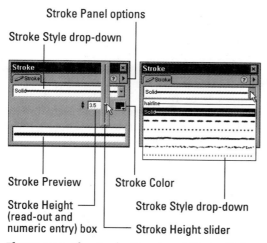

Figure 5-2: The Stroke Panel and Stroke Style drop-down

Stroke Height

In Flash 5, for all tools that draw or display a line or outline, the thickness of the line—or *stroke*—is controlled by either dragging the Stroke Height slider or by entering a value in the Stroke Height numeric entry box. When dragging the slider, the numeric entry box updates and displays a height readout analogous to the current position of the slider. This also functions as a precise numeric entry field. Simply enter a value to create a stroke with a specific height, or thickness. Permissible values range from 0 to 10, with fractions expressed in decimals.

Note   Depending upon the level of zoom, some lines may not be visible on screen— even though they will print correctly on a high-resolution printer.

Stroke Style

The Stroke Style drop-down offers seven stroke, or line, styles: Hairline, Solid, Dashed, Dotted, Ragged, Stippled, and Hatched.

Using the custom stroke styles

Click the Stroke Panel options (the triangular button at the upper right of the Stroke Panel) and then choose Custom (the only option) to access the Line Style dialog. The Line Style dialog, which remains unchanged from Flash 4, is used to generate custom line styles by selecting from a range of properties for each preset line. Basic properties include Stroke Weight and Sharp Corners. Depending on the preset line style, additional properties are available for each style.

Note   Points are the default unit of measurement for determining lengths in the Line Style dialog.

To closely examine a custom line before you begin drawing with it, click the Zoom 4× check box beneath the preview area of the Line Style dialog. Note the Sharp Corners check box, which toggles this Line Style feature on and off. The Sharp Corners feature ensures that the end of a line component (such as a dash), rather than a space, extends to each corner, so that the corners appears sharp.

Tip   Although there is no way to save custom line styles within Flash, you can create a separate .FLA file and save your favorite lines there. This will ease your workflow if you want to make more extensive use of Custom Line Styles. You can apply these styles quite easily to other lines by using the Dropper Tool in conjunction with the Ink Bottle Tool. For more information, see the sections on both the Dropper and the Ink Bottle Tools in this chapter.

Hairline line style

If you need a line that always appears one pixel wide, and does not scale subject to zoom, choose Hairline from the Stroke Style drop-down.

Solid Line Style

The Solid Line Style draws a solid, unbroken line. The customization variables for the Solid Line Style are limited to Thickness and Sharp Corners. These two variables are always available in the Line Style dialog, regardless of which Line Style is being customized.

> **Note**   The Solid Line Style is the optimal Line Style for Web viewing because it requires fewer points to describe it and, consequently, is less file intensive. The smaller file sizes theoretically translate into faster download times when the artwork is transmitted over the Web. However, the difference in file size may be so nominal that the difference in download time that it saves is negligible.

Dashed Line Style

The Dashed Line Style draws a solid line with regularly spaced gaps. Customization variables that appear in the Line Style dialog for the Dashed Line Style are Line Thickness, Sharp Corners, Dash Length, and Gap Length. Both Dash Length and Gap Length are precisely adjustable by changing the numeric entries in their respective fields.

Dotted Line Style

The Dotted Line Style draws a dotted line with evenly spaced gaps. At first glance, the Dotted Line Style appears to have only one variable — Dot Spacing. Change the numeric entry in this field to control the quality of the custom dashed line. But don't overlook the Thickness drop down, which offers a range of settings for Dot Thickness.

Ragged Line Style

The Ragged Line Style draws a ragged line with various gaps between the dots. The quality of both the raggedness and the gaps are adjustable. The Ragged Line Style has three parameters unique to ragged lines: Pattern, Wave Height, and Wave Length. Each has a drop-down menu with multiple variables that, in combination, afford myriad possibilities.

Stippled Line Style

The Stippled Line Style draws a stippled line that goes a long way toward mimicking an artist's hand-stippling technique. The qualities of stippling are adjustable with three variables unique to the nature of stippled lines: Dot Size, Dot Variation, and Density. Each variable has a drop-down with multiple settings that can be combined to generate a staggering array of line effects.

Hatched Line Style

The Hatched Line Style draws a hatched line of amazing complexity that can be used to accurately mimic an artist's hand-drawn hatched-line technique. As shown in Figure 5-3, the numerous hatching qualities are highly adjustable, making this perhaps the most complex of all the Flash drawing tools. The Line Style dialog has six parameters unique to hatched lines: Thickness (hatch-specific), Space, Jiggle, Rotate, Curve, and Length.

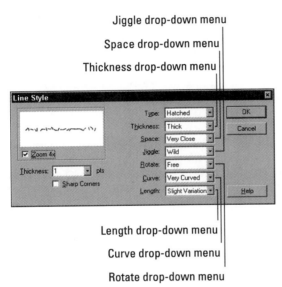

Figure 5-3: The Hatched Line Style wins the prize for the most variables. With these six drop-down lists, a plethora of unique line effects can be hatched.

Note The Hatched Line Style thickness settings are in addition to the usual Thickness settings that are available as a default with the Line Style dialog. Combined, they offer a much higher level of adjustment. The default thickness (measured in points) defines the thickness of the overall hatched line, while this additional thickness setting defines the thickness of the individual scrawls that comprise the aggregate hatched line.

Applying and changing fills with the Fill Panel

The Oval, Rectangle, Brush, and Paint Bucket Tools all rely on the Fill Panel (shown in Figure 5-4) to set or customize the type and color of fill applied to a new shape that is about to be drawn, or to change the color of a selected shape (or shapes).

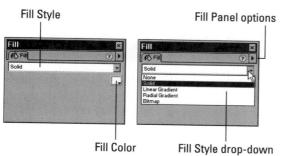

Figure 5-4: The Fill Panel and the Fill Style drop-down, which offers five kinds of fills: None, Solid, Linear Gradient, Radial Gradient, and Bitmap.

The Fill Style can be changed as follows: Choose a Fill Style from the drop-down of the Fill Panel. Then click the Fill Color button on the Toolbox to invoke the Swatches pop-up. If you've chosen a Solid Fill Style, then select a color for your fill. If you've chosen either gradient, clicking the Fill Color button causes a row of gradient color chips to appear at the bottom of the Swatches pop-up. Choose a gradient for your fill. For a more exhaustive discussion of color, including working with swatches, and creating and selecting gradients, please refer to Chapter 6, "Applying Color."

Adjusting Stroke and Color

Changes in stroke and color apply to lines or curves drawn with the Pen, Line, Pencil, Oval, and Rectangle Tools. For ovals and rectangles, the changes apply only to the outline, not to the fill.

Changing Stroke Height

To change the Stroke Height, or Thickness, of a line, follow these steps:

1. Use the Arrow Tool to select the line.

2. If it's not already open, access the Stroke Panel from the Window menu by choosing Window ➪ Panels ➪ Stroke.

3. Choose a new Stroke Height either by using the Stroke Height slider or by entering a new Stroke Height in the numeric entry field and pressing Enter.

Changing Stroke Color

To change the Stroke Color of a line, follow these steps:

1. Select the line with the Arrow Tool.

2. Then, locate either one of these Stroke Color controls:

- The Stroke Color in the Color Tray area of the Toolbox
- The Stroke Color on the Stroke Panel (Window ⇨ Panels ⇨ Stroke)

3. Finally, choose a new color from the Swatches pop-up.

The Pencil Tool

The Pencil Tool is used to draw lines and shapes in any given frame of a scene and—at first glance—operates much like a real pencil. (A frame is the basic unit of a Flash creation. Frames and scenes are described in the Chapter 8, "Exploring the Timeline.") But a deeper examination reveals that—unlike a real pencil—the Flash Pencil Tool can be set to straighten lines and smooth curves as you draw. It can also be set to recognize or correct basic geometric shapes. Or, you can use the Pencil Tool options to create specific shapes. In addition, you can modify lines and shapes manually.

When the Pencil Tool is active, one option appears in the Options Tray. This is the Pencil Mode pop-up menu, shown in Figure 5-5, which sets the Pencil Tool's current drawing mode. Users of prior versions of Flash might inquire about the disappearance of the controls for Stroke Weight and Line Style—these now reside in the Stroke Panel, where they are referred to as the Line Style and Stroke Height controls.

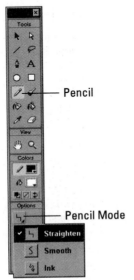
— Pencil

— Pencil Mode

Figure 5-5: The Pencil Tool and the Pencil Mode option are shown here with pop-up, which reveals the Straighten, Smooth, and Ink processing options.

Using the Pencil Mode pop-up options

The Pencil Mode pop-up menu has options that control how Flash processes the lines that you draw. That's right, unlike any other program we know of, Flash can *p-r-o-c-e-s-s* the lines that you draw, as you draw them! We call this *line processing* — it's a kind of shape recognition specific to the Pencil Tool that may make drawing easier for artists who are draftsmanship-challenged. It also has the benefit of generating drawings that are simpler and less complex (meaning that they are described by fewer points). As a result, the drawings transmit across the Web at greater speed because they require less data, which means a smaller file size, to describe them. The Pencil Tool has three processing options. Two are Straighten and Smooth; the third, for those who prefer the characteristics of hand drawing, is Ink Mode. Working in Ink Mode lets you turn off all line processing.

Understanding line processing

So, what is meant by processing the lines? Processing differs from shape recognition in that it is automatic and occurs while the line is *in the process of being drawn*. This differs from shape recognition with the Arrow Tool because that occurs after the line is drawn — in fact, it can be done at any time after the line is drawn. (For more information on shape recognition, refer to the section on the Arrow Tool, in Chapter 4, "Working with Selections and the Pen Tool.") The Straighten, Smooth, and Ink processing options of the Pencil Tool control the degree to which automatic processing occurs. Each of these options is detailed in subsequent sections of this discussion of the Pencil Tool. These options are also affected by the settings in the Drawing Settings Panel of the Editing tab of the Preferences dialog (choose Edit ➪ Preferences and click the Editing tab).

Cross-Reference In addition to the treatment here, the settings that control line processing and shape recognition are explained in Chapter 2, "Exploring the Interface: Panels, Settings, and More."

Straighten option

Drawing with the Straighten option processes your drawings while taking into account line and shape recognition. This means that separate lines are automatically connected, lines that approximately straight are straightened, and wobbly curves are smoothed. In short, approximate shapes are recognized and automatically adjusted.

Smooth option

Drawing with the Smooth option reduces the zeal with which Flash automatically processes your drawings. With Smooth option, line straightening and shape recognition are disabled. You can draw curved lines, and they will be smoothed slightly. Additionally, a line that ends near another line will be joined to it.

Ink option

Drawing with the Ink option turns off all Flash processing. You're left with the lines as you've drawn them. Your lines are *not* smoothed, straightened, or joined.

Caution   For Web deployment, lines drawn with the Ink option can become unnecessarily complex. If this happens to you, these lines can be selected with the Arrow Tool and then slightly optimized by choosing either Modify ➪ Smooth or Modify ➪ Optimize from the menu.

You can also choose to smooth, straighten, or join lines and shapes that have been drawn with the Ink option simply by using the Arrow Tool to select what you've drawn and then using either the Arrow Tool's Smooth or Straighten options. Or, for maximum control, manually edit extraneous points with either the Pen or the Subselect Tool.

The Line Tool

Drawing with the Line Tool creates a perfectly straight line that extends straight from the starting point to the end point, simply choose the tool and start drawing. As shown in Figure 5-6, the Line Tool has no options on the Options Tray. Line Thickness is chosen from the Stroke Height control of the Stroke Panel, while the basic Line Style may be chosen from the Stroke Style drop-down. As shown in Figures 5-2 and 5-3, Custom Line Styles may be created with the Line Style dialog, which is accessed from the Stroke Panel options.

Figure 5-6: The Line Tool has no options.

Tip Depress the Shift key while drawing to constrain the Line Tool to angles of 45 degrees or 90 degrees.

The Oval Tool

Drawing with the Oval Tool creates a perfectly smooth oval. Ovals are drawn by dragging diagonally from one "corner" of the oval to the other. Press the Shift key at any time while the shape is being drawn to constrain the shape to a perfect circle. As shown in Figure 5-7, the Oval Tool has no options.

Figure 5-7: The Oval Tool has no options.

To either choose or change the Stroke Height or Style, use the Stroke Panel. To choose or change the fill of an oval, use the Fill Panel.

The Rectangle Tool

Drawing with the Rectangle Tool creates a perfect rectangle, which means that all four of the corners are at 90-degree angles. Rectangles are drawn by dragging from one corner of the rectangle to the other. Pressing the Shift key at any time while the shape is being drawn creates a perfect square. As shown in Figure 5-8, the Rectangle Tool has one option — Rounded Rectangle Radius.

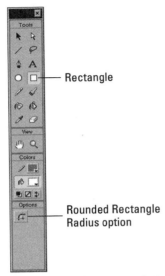

Rectangle

Rounded Rectangle
Radius option

Figure 5-8: The Rectangle Tool
has one option in the Options Tray:
Rounded Rectangle Radius.

As with the Oval Tool, to choose or change the Stroke Height or Style of a
Rectangle, use the Stroke Panel. To choose or change the fill, use the Fill Panel.

The Rounded Rectangle Radius Tool is useful for making rounded rectangles —
a.k.a. interactive button shapes. Click this option to elicit the Rectangle Settings
dialog (shown in Figure 5-9), which accepts numeric values between 0 and 999.
Subsequent rectangles will be drawn with this value applied to the corner radius,
until the value entered in this dialog is either changed or returned to zero. Note
that this button is *not* a toggle; to turn off rounded rectangle drawing, click the
option and enter a value of zero.

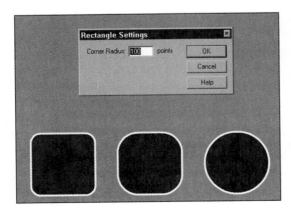

Figure 5-9: The Rectangle
Settings dialog with three
shapes drawn with the following
Corner Radius settings: (from
right to left) 25, 50, and 100.

Using the (Paint) Brush Tool

The Brush Tool is used to paint with brushlike strokes and to fill enclosed areas. Unlike the Pencil Tool, which creates a single, solid line, the Brush Tool creates filled shapes with outlines of zero thickness. (This is easily demonstrated by painting a stroke with the Brush, then choosing a new color for the Ink Bottle, and then clicking that brushed line with the Ink Bottle. The Brush line of zero thickness will acquire the line thickness and color from the Ink Bottle — if there were no line, the Ink Bottle would be unable to alter the stroke in this manner.) The fills can be solid colors, gradients, or fills derived from bitmaps. Additionally, the Brush Tool options permit you to paint in unusual ways: You can choose to paint in front of or behind an element, or you can apply paint only within a specific filled area, or within a selection. The Brush Mode option drop-down reveals five painting modes that are amazingly useful for a wide range of effects when applying brush strokes: Paint Normal, Paint Fills, Paint Behind, Paint Selection, and Paint Inside, as shown in Figure 5-10.

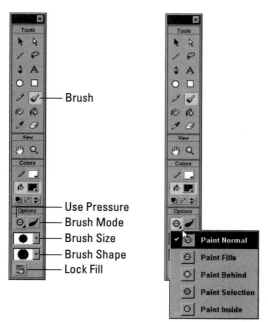

Figure 5-10: The Brush Tool and options (left); the Brush Mode drop-down (right)

Depending on whether you have a pressure-sensitive tablet connected to your computer, four or five options appear in the Options Tray when the Brush Tool is active. The Use Pressure option — which only appears if you have a pressure-sensitive tablet attached to your computer — and the Brush Mode are both unique to the Brush Tool. The Lock Fill option is common to both the Brush Tool and the Paint

Bucket (which is discussed subsequently in this chapter). Although similar to Stroke Weight and Line Style, the Brush Size and Brush Shape drop-downs are also fairly unique to the Brush Tool. In the following sections, we run through all of the Brush options — just to make certain that we're clear on all points, even if there is some review.

> **Note** Painting with the background color (such as white) is not the same as erasing. Painting with the background color may appear to accomplish something similar to erasing. However, you are, in fact, creating a filled item that can be selected, moved, deleted, or reshaped. Only erasing erases!

To choose or change the Brush Color, either click the Fill Color button on the Toolbox, or use the Fill Panel. Because the Brush Tool creates filled shapes with outlines of zero thickness, the Stroke Color button is defunct when the Brush Tool is active.

Using the Brush Mode option

The Brush Mode option is a drop-down menu with five modes for applying brush strokes: Paint Normal, Paint Fills, Paint Behind, Paint Selection, and Paint Inside. Used in conjunction with selections, the Brush Modes option yields a broad range of sophisticated paint masking capabilities. True masking is fully described and defined in Chapter 10, "Drawing in Flash."

The following images depict various ways in which the Brush Modes interact with drawn and painted elements. The base image is a solid gray rounded rectangle drawn with a black, hatched outline. Three white lines of various widths are drawn on top of the gray fill of the rectangle.

Paint Normal Mode

Paint Normal Mode, shown in Figure 5-11, applies brush strokes over the top of any lines or fills.

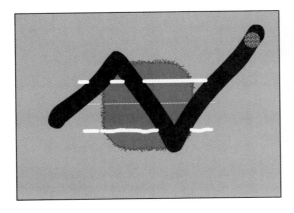

Figure 5-11: In Paint Normal Mode, a black scrawl covers all elements: background, outline, fill, and drawn lines.

Paint Fills Mode

Paint Fills Mode, shown in Figure 5-12, applies brush strokes to replace any fills, but leaves lines untouched.

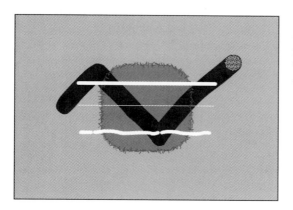

Figure 5-12: In Paint Fills Mode, a black scrawl covers both the gray fill and the background — which, surprisingly, is considered a fill in this case.

Paint Behind Mode

Paint Behind Mode applies brush strokes only to blank areas and leaves all fills, lines or other items untouched. As shown in Figure 5-13, the only parts of the stroke that cover are those over the background. Effectively, the scrawl has gone behind the entire shape. If the stroke had originated within the gray fill, it would have covered the fill and gone behind the drawn white lines.

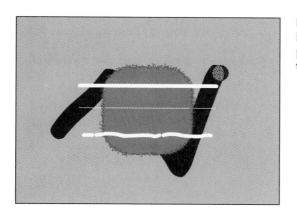

Figure 5-13: Scrawling again in Paint Behind Mode, the only parts of the stroke that cover are those over the background.

Paint Selection Mode

Paint Selection Mode applies brush strokes only to selected fills. In Figure 5-14, a selection was made by shift-clicking both the gray fill and the upper white line.

The same black scrawl has been drawn with the selection described in the previous figure still active, using Paint Selection Mode.

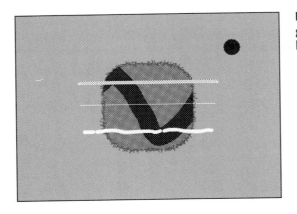

Figure 5-14: Only the selected gray fill has been covered by the brush stroke.

Paint Inside Mode

Paint Inside Mode, shown in Figure 5-15, applies brush strokes only to the singular fill area where the brush stroke was first initiated. As the name implies, Paint Inside never paints over lines. If you initiate painting from an empty area, the brush strokes won't affect any existing fills or lines, which approximates the same effect as the Paint Behind setting.

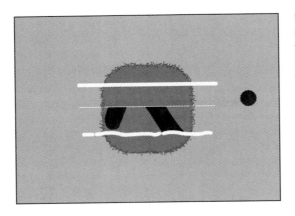

Figure 5-15: Another scrawled stroke with Paint Inside Mode — the only difference between this stroke and the others is that it was initiated over the gray fill.

Using the Brush Size option

The Brush Size option, shown in Figure 5-16, is a simple pop-up menu with a range of ten preset brush sizes. Although the sizes are shown as circles, the diameter size applies to all brush shapes. In the case of an oblong brush, the diameter size refers to the broadest span of the brush. You can combine brush sizes and shapes for a great variety of custom brush tips.

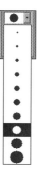

Figure 5-16: The Brush Size drop-down reveals ten well-distributed brush sizes, ranging from pin line to humongous.

In Flash, the apparent brush size is always related to the Zoom setting. Therefore, identical brush diameters applied at different Zoom settings result in different-sized brush marks.

Using the Brush Shape option

The Brush Shape option, shown in Figure 5-17, is a simple pop-up menu with nine possible brush shapes that are based on the circle, ellipse, square, rectangle, and line shapes. The oval, rectangle, and line shapes are available in several angles. Although no custom brush shapes are available, you can combine these stock brush shapes with the range of brush sizes to generate a variety of nearly custom brush tips. When using shapes other than circles, note that the diameter sizes indicated in the Brush Size drop-down apply to the broadest area of any brush shape.

Figure 5-17: The Brush Shape drop-down is loaded with nine preset brush shapes.

Using the Brush Lock Fill option

The Lock Fill option is a toggle that controls how Flash handles areas filled with a gradient or bitmap fill. Once this button is pressed, all subsequent areas (or shapes) that are painted with the same gradient or bitmap fill appear to be part of a single, continuous filled shape. This option locks the angle, size, and point of origin of the current gradient so that it remains consistent throughout the scene. This capability is useful, for example, if you are creating a gradated sunset sky with gradated clouds, and the clouds must appear to be part of one continuous gradient, while the sky needs to appear to be another.

Cross-
Reference

Working with gradient colors is discussed in Chapter 6, "Applying Color."

To demonstrate the distinction between painting with or without the Brush Lock Fill option, as shown in Figure 5-18, on the left, we created five shapes and filled them with a gradient, using the Paint Inside setting — with Lock Fill off. The gradient is noticeably not aligned from one shape to the next. On the right, those same shapes were repainted with that same gradient, still using the Paint Inside setting — but with Lock Fill on. Note how the gradient is now aligned from one shape to the next.

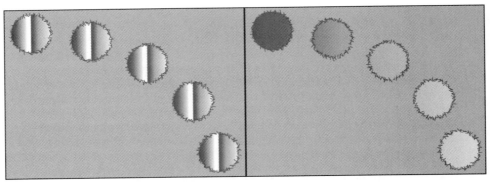

Figure 5-18: The Lock Fill option

Note

When the Dropper Tool is used to pick up a fill or gradient from a scene, the Lock Fill button is automatically engaged.

Using the Brush Pressure option

The Brush Pressure option appears only if you have a pressure-sensitive tablet. This option button is a simple toggle that is used to enable or disable the finer capabilities of a pressure-sensitive tablet. With pressure-sensitivity enabled, the size of the brush stroke increases with increased drawing pressure.

The difference between the Brush Tool and the Pencil Tool

A pencil stroke has no fill, whereas a brush stroke is technically a filled outline of zero thickness. Regardless of the width of a pencil stroke, when viewed as an outline, it will *always* appear as a single vector. Conversely, when viewed as outlines, brush strokes of varied thickness will be exhibited as outlines whose breadth varies according to the thickness of the stroke. Yet the outlines themselves will always be outlines (or vectors) of zero thickness.

Figure 5-19 displays a pencil line and a brush line, each drawn with a Stroke Height of 10, (A) in what is regarded as regular mode (View ⇨ Antialias), and again (B) as outlines (View ⇨ Outlines). The same lines are displayed both above and below. This demonstrates the technical detail that brush strokes are filled vector outlines of zero thickness, while a pencil stroke is a stroked vector of zero thickness.

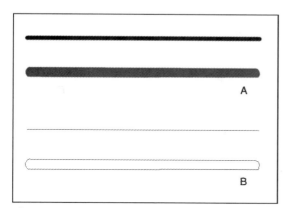

Figure 5-19: Comparing the Brush and Pencil Tools

As shown in Figure 5-20, these differences have demonstrable consequences when pencil strokes and brush strokes are edited with the selection tools: A brush stroke can be pulled out of shape, whereas a pencil stroke can only be bent. The results of each operation are shown at the right.

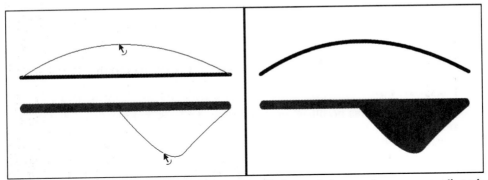

Figure 5-20: A brush stroke (bottom) can be pulled out of shape, whereas a pencil stroke (top) can only be bent.

The Dropper Tool

The Dropper Tool (shown in Figure 5-21), which is found at the bottom of the Toolbox tools, is used to acquire (or copy) the color and style information from existing pencil lines, brush strokes, and fills. The Dropper Tool has no options, but then it doesn't need options. That's because the Flash Dropper Tool performs a function entirely unlike any dropper tool in any other program that we know of.

— Dropper

Figure 5-21: The Dropper Tool is an amazingly useful "one-trick pony." It has no options.

When the Dropper Tool isn't hovering over a line, fill, or brush stroke, its cursor is similar to the Dropper icon in the Drawing Toolbox. However, the Dropper Tool's cursor changes as follows to indicate when it is over a line or a fill:

✦ When the cursor is over a line, a tiny pencil appears to the lower right of the standard Dropper Tool cursor.

✦ When the cursor is over a fill, a tiny brush appears to the lower right of the standard Dropper Tool cursor.

When the Dropper Tool is over a line, fill, or brush stroke, and the Shift key is pressed, the cursor changes to an inverted U shape. In this mode (that is, when you Shift+Click), use of the Dropper Tool changes the attributes for all editing tools in Flash (for instance, the Pencil, Brush, Ink Bottle, and Text Tools) to match the attributes of the area clicked. That's right! . . . Shift-clicking with the Dropper Tool acquires the attributes of the clicked item and simultaneously changes the color and style settings for the Ink Bottle Tool, as well as the Pencil Tool and the Text Tool.

✦ When the clicked item is a line, the Dropper Tool is automatically swapped for the Ink Bottle Tool, which facilitates the application of the acquired attributes to another line. Similarly, when the clicked item is a fill, the Dropper Tool is automatically swapped for the Paint Bucket Tool. This facilitates the application of acquired fill attributes to another fill.

✦ When the Dropper Tool is used to acquire a fill that is a bitmap, the Dropper Tool is automatically swapped for the Paint Bucket Tool and a thumbnail of the bitmap image appears in place of the Fill Color option in the Color Tray of the Toolbox.

This composite image shown in Figure 5-22 shows all Dropper Tool cursors as they appear when the Dropper is brought to hover over various types of lines and fills. The figure shows the Dropper Tool:

✦ Alone (A)

✦ Over a gradient fill created with the Rectangle Tool (B)

✦ Over a white line created with the Rectangle Tool (C)

✦ Over a line painted with the brush (D)

✦ Over a line drawn with the Pencil Tool (F)

✦ After pressing Shift and clicking to acquire the attributes of the clicked item and simultaneously change the color and style settings for the Ink Bottle Tool, as well as the Pencil Tool and the Text Tool (E)

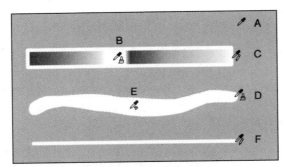

Figure 5-22: The Dropper Tool cursors

Note   The Dropper Tool can be extremely helpful when changing the attributes of multiple lines. However, the Ink Bottle cannot apply acquired attributes to lines that are grouped. To work around this limitation, you must first ungroup the lines, then apply the attributes to the lines (either individually or as a multiple selection), and then regroup the lines.

The attributes of a group can be acquired using the Dropper Tool if the contents are being edited. For more information on editing groups, please refer to Chapter 8, "Exploring the Timeline."

New Feature   When used to acquire colors, the Toolbox Dropper Tool is limited to acquiring colors from the Flash interface, which includes not only items created in Flash (that is, on or next to the Stage), but also icons, buttons, and menus of the Flash application. However, the Droppers that are accessed from the Color Palettes of the Mixer, Stroke, Fill, and Character Panels can acquire colors from anywhere on the entire computer interface, such as the system background, items on the desktop, or items that are open in other applications. For more information about this new feat, refer to Chapter 6, "Applying Color."

The Ink Bottle Tool

The Ink Bottle Tool, shown in Figure 5-23, is used to change the color, style, and thickness of existing outlines. It is most often used in conjunction with the Dropper Tool. When the Ink Bottle Tool is in use, attention to three options may be required: The current Stroke Color option on the Toolbox or the Stroke Panel, and both the Line Height and Stroke Style options of the Stroke Panel.

Note   The Ink Bottle Tool reveals the underlying consistency in the way that Flash "sees" lines. Lines, outlines, and those *lines of zero thickness* that describe strokes of the Brush are all treated as lines by the Ink Bottle Tool.

Figure 5-23: The Ink Bottle Tool has no options on the Toolbox.

Ink Bottle

Caution   When you click a selected line with the Ink Bottle Tool, all other *selected* lines (if any) are changed simultaneously.

The Ink Bottle is especially useful for applying custom line styles to multiple lines. You can build a collection of custom line styles either off-screen, or in a special custom line palette that is saved as a single-frame Flash movie. You can then acquire these line styles whenever necessary.

Caution   Depending on the level of zoom, some lines may not appear on the screen— although they will print correctly on a high-resolution printer. Stroke Weight may also be adjusted in the Stroke Style dialog that is accessible by choosing Custom from the Stroke Style option drop-down list (the arrow at the top right of the panel).

The Paint Bucket Tool

The Paint Bucket Tool is used to fill enclosed areas with color, gradients, or bitmap fills. Although the Paint Bucket Tool is a more robust tool than the Ink Bottle, and can be used independently of the Dropper Tool, it's often used in conjunction with the Dropper Tool. That's because, as was discussed earlier in the section on the Dropper Tool, when the Dropper Tool is clicked on a fill, it first acquires the fill attributes of that fill and then automatically swaps to the Paint Bucket Tool. Because this *acquire and swap* function of the Dropper Tool readily facilitates the application of acquired fill attributes to another fill, the Bucket Tool is frequently used in tandem with the Dropper. When the Paint Bucket Tool is active, as shown in Figure 5-24, four options are available from the Toolbox: Lock Fill, Transform Fill, Gap Size, and Fill Color. The Gap Size drop-down, which is shown at the right, offers four settings to control how Flash handles gaps when filling with the Bucket Tool.

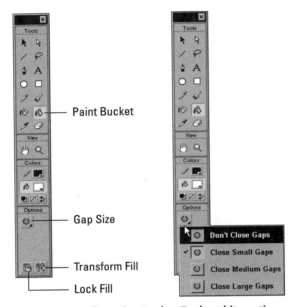

Figure 5-24: The Paint Bucket Tool and its options

When the Dropper Tool is used to acquire a fill that is a broken-apart bitmap, the Dropper Tool is automatically swapped for the Paint Bucket Tool and a thumbnail of the bitmap image appears in place of the Fill Color Option chip. This procedure also automatically engages the Paint Bucket Lock Fill Option. For more information about working with bitmap fills, refer to Chapter 12, "Using Bitmaps and Other Media with Flash."

Caution   Using the Paint Bucket to paint with white (or the background color) is not the same as erasing. Painting with white (or the background color) may appear to accomplish something similar to erasing. However, you are, in fact, creating a filled item that can be selected, moved, deleted, or reshaped. Only erasing erases!

Like the Ink Bottle, the Paint Bucket can be especially useful for applying custom fill styles to multiple items. You can build a collection of custom fill styles either off-screen or in a special, saved, custom-fills-palette, single-frame Flash movie. You can then acquire these fills whenever necessary.

Caution If you click with the Paint Bucket Tool on one of several selected fills, *all* of the selected fills will be changed with the new fill.

Using the Paint Bucket Gap Size option

As shown in Figure 5-24, the Gap Size option drop-down offers four settings that control how the Paint Bucket Tool treats gaps when filling. These settings are Don't Close Gaps, Close Small Gaps, Close Medium Gaps, and Close Large Gaps. These tolerance settings enable Flash to fill an outline if the end points of the outline aren't completely joined, leaving an open shape. If the gaps are too large, you may have to close them manually.

Note The level of zoom changes the apparent size of gaps. Although the actual size of gaps is unaffected by zoom, the Paint Bucket's interpretation of the gap is dependent upon the current Zoom setting. Thus, the Paint Bucket's behavior in relation to Gap Size is liable to change with the Zoom setting.

Using the Paint Bucket Lock Fill option

The Paint Bucket's Lock Fill option is the same as the Brush Lock Fill option — it controls how Flash handles areas filled with gradient color or bitmaps. When this button is turned on, all areas (or shapes) that are painted with the same gradient will appear to be part of a single, continuous, filled shape. The Lock Fill option locks the angle, size, and point of origin of the current gradient to remain constant throughout the scene. For further information, please refer to the earlier discussion of the Brush Tool.

Tip When the Dropper Tool is used to pick up a fill or gradient from the scene, this Lock Fill button is automatically engaged.

Using the Paint Bucket Transform Fill option (a.k.a. the Reshape Arrow cursor)

The Transform Tool option button is used to adjust the size, angle, and center of a gradient or fill, including bitmap fills. When the Transform Tool option is selected, the Paint Bucket Tool automatically becomes a *Reshape Arrow cursor*. (This Reshape Arrow cursor is different from either of the Arrow Tool's Rotate or Scale options.) This is a lot like scooting, rotating, or skewing a larger piece of material so that a different portion is displayed within a smaller frame. To use the Reshape Arrow to transform a fill, first select the Transform Tool option, and then simply click an existing gradient or fill. A set of three or four adjustment handles appears, depending on the type of fill. With this option, three transformations can be performed on a fill: adjusting the fill's center point, rotating the fill, and scaling the fill.

Adjusting the center point with the Reshape Arrow

To adjust the center point, follow these steps:

1. Deselect the fill if it has been previously selected.

2. Choose the Paint Bucket Tool.

3. Choose the Transform Fill option.

4. Click the fill.

5. Bring the Reshape Arrow Cursor to the small circular handle at the center of the fill until it changes to a four-arrow cursor, pointing left and right, up and down like a compass, indicating that this handle can now be used to move the center point in any direction.

6. Drag the center circular handle in any direction you want to move the center of the fill.

Figure 5-25 shows the Reshape Arrow cursor (A). It transforms into a compass point when it's brought near the round center handle of a gradient or fill (B). Click the center handle and drag to move the center point (C).

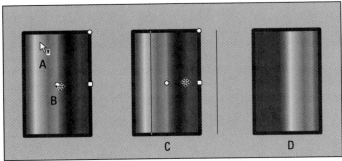

Figure 5-25: Repositioning a gradient fill's center

Rotating a fill with the Reshape Arrow

To rotate a gradient or bitmap fill, find the small circular handle that's at the corner of the fill. (In a radial gradient, choose the middle circular handle.) This circular handle is used for rotating a fill around the center point. Click the handle and four circular arrows appear, indicating that this handle will rotate the fill about the center point.

Figure 5-26 shows how the Reshape Arrow cursor becomes a Rotate cursor when it is brought near the circular handle at the corner of a gradient fill (A). Click the circular handle with the Rotate cursor and rotate the gradient fill (B).

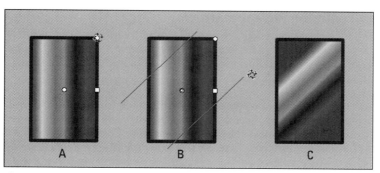

Figure 5-26: Rotating a gradient fill

Reshape Arrow Anomalies

Fills can differ in their characteristics when you use the Reshape Arrow, primarily in the placement of their handles, subject to a number of variables, including whether they are applied horizontally or vertically:

✦ Some fills may not have the full complement of Reshape Arrow cursors available.

✦ For a horizontally applied fill: To rotate the fill, find the small circular handle that is at the *upper right*, at the top of the hatched line. This circular handle is used for rotating a horizontally applied gradient or fill around the center point. Click the handle and four circular arrows appear, indicating that this handle will rotate the fill about the center point.

✦ For a vertically applied fill: To rotate the fill, find the small circular handle that is at the *upper left*, at the end of the hatched line. This circular handle is used for rotating a vertically applied gradient or fill around the center point. Click the handle and four circular arrows appear, indicating that this handle will rotate the fill about the center point.

✦ These general characteristics may differ if a fill (or bitmap fill) has been variously copied, rotated, or pasted in any number of ways. The fundamental rule is this: Round center handle moves the center point; round corner handle rotates; round edge handles skew either vertically or horizontally; square-edge handles scale either vertically or horizontally; and the square-corner handle scales symmetrically.

✦ Skewing and scaling of bitmap fills may have a counterintuitive effect: If the bitmap fill is scaled *smaller,* it will tile to fill the space of the original fill.

✦ Due to their nature, gradient fills don't support skewing; they can only be scaled on the horizontal axis.

Skewing the fill with the Reshape Arrow

To skew a bitmap fill horizontally, find the small round handle at the middle of the right-hand border. This round handle is used to skew the gradient or fill. Click the handle and arrows appear, parallel to the edge of the fill, indicating the directions in which this handle will skew the fill.

Figure 5-27 shows how the Reshape Arrow cursor changes to the Skew Arrow cursor when it is brought near a small round horizontal skew handle (first image). Click and drag the round horizontal skew handle with the Skew Arrow cursor to skew the bitmap fill (second image). Release the skew handle to view the result (third image). Note that the skew procedure is still active, meaning that the skew may be further modified—this behavior is common to all functions of the Reshape Arrow. To skew a bitmap fill vertically, locate the vertical skew handle. Vertical skew is functionally equivalent to skewing horizontally.

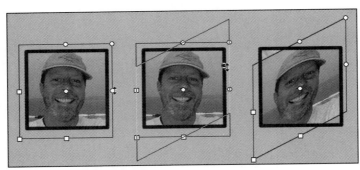

Figure 5-27: Skewing a bitmap fill

Figure 5-28 hones in on radial gradients. A radial gradient has slight variations from a linear gradient, mostly as regards the placement of the handles. So here's a quick tour: The Reshape Arrow cursor (A); Center Point cursor (B); Skew cursor (C) and Skew handle (G); Radius cursor (D, F) and Radius handle (H); and, finally, the Rotate cursor (E) and Rotate handle (I).

Symmetrically adjusting the scale with the Reshape Arrow

To resize a bitmap fill symmetrically, find the small square-corner handle, which is usually located at the lower-left corner of the fill. This square-corner handle is used to resize the fill while retaining the aspect ratio. The Symmetrical Resize cursor, shown in Figure 5-29, has diagonal arrows, and appears when the Reshape Arrow cursor is brought into proximity of this square-corner handle, indicating the direction(s) in which the handle will resize the fill. Click and drag the square-corner handle to scale the fill symmetrically.

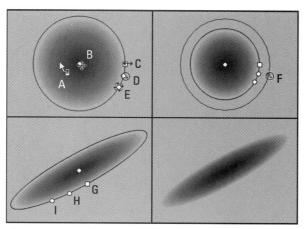

Figure 5-28: Adjusting radial gradients: The final skewed, scaled (with the Radius handle), and rotated gradient is shown in the lower right.

Figure 5-29: The Symmetrical Resize cursor appears when the Reshape Arrow cursor is the square-corner handle.

Asymmetrically adjusting the scale with the Reshape Arrow

To resize a bitmap fill asymmetrically, find a small square handle on either a vertical or a horizontal edge, depending whether you want to affect the width or height of the fill. The Asymmetrical Resize cursor, which has arrows that appear perpendicular to the edge, appears when the Reshape Arrow cursor is brought into proximity of any one of these square-edge handles, indicating the direction in which this handle will resize the fill, as shown in Figure 5-30. Click and drag a handle to reshape the fill.

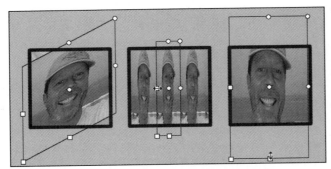

Figure 5-30: The Asymmetrical Resize cursor appears when the Reshape Arrow cursor is brought into proximity of the square-edge handle.

Note   The center of Figure 5-30 is a good example of a situation in which scaling a bitmap fill with the Reshape Arrow cursor may have a counterintuitive effect. When a bitmap fill is scaled in either dimension so that it is *smaller* than the shape that encloses it, this causes it to tile — or repeat — and fill the space of the original fill. As you can see, your author takes a rather narrow view of this feature.

The Eraser Tool

Although the Eraser Tool is neither a Drawing nor a Painting Tool, we feel that it belongs together with the Drawing and Painting Tools rather than orphaned in a category of its own. After all, without the Eraser Tool to complement the Drawing and Painting Tools, the process of Drawing and Painting might get impossibly complex — one mistake and you'd have to start over. The Eraser Tool is used in concert with the Drawing and Painting Tools to obtain final, usable art. As the name implies, the Eraser Tool is primarily used for erasing. When the Eraser Tool is active, three options appear in the Options Tray, as shown in Figure 5-31. The Erase Mode option and the Eraser Shape option are both drop-down menus with multiple options. The third option, the Faucet button, is used to clear enclosed areas of fill.

The only alternative to using the Eraser Tool to remove graphic elements or areas of drawings is to select them and then delete them by pressing either the Delete or the Backspace key.

Caution   As has been mentioned previously, in context with various Drawing and Painting Tools, Drawing or Painting with white (or the current background color) is *not* the equivalent of erasing. Only the Eraser Tool erases! Either use the simple Eraser Tool or harness the power of the Faucet option to take away filled areas and lines. Of all the things that we have repeated about the Flash Tools, if you don't "get" this one, it can really come back to bite you!

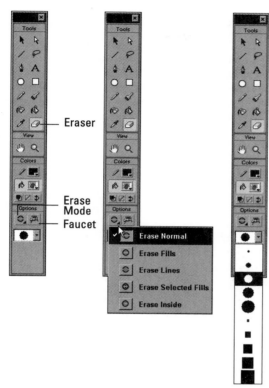

Figure 5-31: The Eraser Tool has three options:
the Erase Mode, Eraser Shape, and the Faucet.
Both the Mode and Shape options have menus.

The Eraser Tool only erases lines and fills that are in the current frame of the scene. It won't erase groups, symbols, or text. When you need to erase a part of a group, you have two options: Select the group and choose Edit ➪ Edit Selected from the Menu Bar, or select the group and choose Modify ➪ Ungroup from the Menu Bar.

Using the Eraser Shape option

The Eraser Shape option defines both the size and shape of the eraser. As shown in Figure 5-31, it's a simple drop-down menu with ten brushes available in two shapes: circular and square. These are arrayed in two banks of five sizes each, ranging from small to large.

Using the Eraser's Faucet option

The Eraser Tool's Faucet option is Flash's version of selective annihilation — kind of like a neutron bomb. The Faucet option deletes an entire line segment or area of fill with a single click. Using the Faucet option is the equivalent of selecting and deleting an entire line or fill in a single step. Select the Eraser Tool, and then choose the Faucet Option button. Click the offending item to say goodbye. Clicking a selected line or fill erases all selected lines or fills.

Using the Erase Mode option

The Erase Mode option both controls and limits what and how the Eraser Tool erases. As shown in Figure 5-31, the Erase Mode pop-up reveals five options: Erase Normal, Erase Fills, Erase Lines, Erase Selected Lines, and Erase Inside. These function in a similar manner to the Brush Mode options:

✦ **Erase Normal:** With this, the Eraser Tool functions like a normal eraser. It erases all lines and fills that it passes over, as long as they are on the active layer.

✦ **Erase Fills:** In Erase Fills Mode, the Eraser Tool becomes a specialty eraser, erasing only fills and leaving lines unaffected.

✦ **Erase Lines:** When in Erase Lines Mode, the Eraser Tool works by erasing lines only and leaving fills unaffected.

✦ **Erase Selected Fills:** In Erase Selected Fills Mode, the Eraser Tool becomes even more specialized. In this mode, it only erases fills that are currently selected, leaving unselected fills and all lines unaffected.

✦ **Erase Inside:** With Erase Inside Mode, the Eraser Tool only erases the area of fill *on which you initiate erasing*. This is much like the Erase Selected Fills Mode, except that the selection is accomplished with the initial erasure. In this mode, the eraser leaves all other fills and all lines unaffected.

Caution To quickly erase everything in a scene, double-click the Eraser Tool in the Drawing Toolbox. (Don't click in the scene! You have to double-click the Eraser Tool button in the Drawing Toolbox. Okay?)

Summary

✦ The Flash 5 drawing tools are more robust and more capable than they were in any previous version of Flash.

✦ The process for choosing colors and for editing Stroke Height and Style has been streamlined. Lines drawn with the Pen Tool can be easily modified with the Color options and with the controls on the Stroke Panel.

✦ The Pencil Tool is used to draw expressively with natural ease. A range of options enable a user to fine-tune the manner in which Flash applies shape recognition to lines and shapes drawn with the Pencil Tool.

✦ The Line and the Oval Tools are useful for creating perfect geometric shapes.

✦ The Brush Tool applies strokes of color to Flash artwork. Brush strokes can be applied with a number of mask settings, called Brush Modes, that control how color is applied.

✦ The Dropper Tool is used to acquire color from Flash art so that it may be applied to other items with either the Paint Bucket or Ink Bottle Tools.

✦ The Ink Bottle Tool is used primarily to apply acquired color to lines, outlines, and lines of zero thickness.

✦ The Paint Bucket is used to fill shapes and closed areas of drawings. It can also edit the colors and properties of such fills.

✦ The Eraser Tool is used to erase anything that's been drawn on the Flash Stage. Like the Brush Tool, it has powerful masking capabilities that make it easier to erase specific items without endangering other portions of your Flash art.

✦   ✦   ✦

Applying Color

Before we get into the specifics of applying color with Flash, we think it's essential to discuss some of the fundamental theory behind working with color that's destined for display on the Web. In the process, we also introduce some cool resources that may be helpful to you, both in concert with Flash and as bona fide Web resources on their own. Then we look at how the Flash Tools access Flash Color; and we show you how to work with the new Flash Color Panels to select, change, mix, and apply both colors and gradients.

Introducing Color Basics

Computer monitors display color by using a method called *RGB color*. A monitor screen is a tightly packed array of pixels arranged in a grid, where each pixel has an address. For example, a pixel that's located 16 rowsdown from the top and 70 columns over from the left might have an address of 70,16. The computer uses such an address to send a specific color to each pixel. Because each pixel is composed of a single red, green, and blue dot, the colors that the monitor displays can be "mixed" at each pixel by varying the individual intensities of the red, green, and blue color dots. Each individual dot can vary in intensity over a range of 256 values: starting with 0 (which is *off*) to a maximum value of 255 (which is *on*). Thus, if red is *half-on* (a value of 127), while green is *off* (a value of 0), and blue is fully *on* (a value of 255), the pixel appears reddish-blue.

This is the description for unlimited, full color, which is sometimes referred to as 24-bit color. However, many computer systems are still incapable of displaying full color. Limited color displays are either 16-bit or 8-bit displays. Although a full discussion of bit-depth is beyond the scope of this book, it is important to note several points.

✦ 24-bit color is required to accurately reproduce photographic images.

✦ Because 8-bit and 16-bit systems are color challenged, they can only display a limited number of colors, and they must dither-down anything that exceeds their gamut, which is their expanse of possible colors. *Dithering* means that, in order to approximate colors that are missing from the palette, two near colors are placed in close proximity to fool the eye into seeing intermediate colors.

✦ Although most color-challenged systems have the capability to adequately handle a few out-of-gamut colors without exceeding their palette, serious problems occur once their palette is exhausted. This means that your Flash site might look okay on a color-challenged system if it's the first site visited when the system is started up. However, the site may look much worse after an hour of browsing the Web.

✦ Some image formats, such as GIF, use a color palette, which limits them to 256 colors. This is called *indexed color*.

✦ Calibration of your monitor is essential for accurate color work. For more information check out www.colorpar.com.

Discussing Web-Safe Color issues

Web-Safe Color is a complex issue but what it boils down to is this: The Mac and PC platforms handle their color palettes differently, thus the browsers don't have the same colors available to them across platforms. This leads to inconsistent, unreliable color — unless one is careful to choose their colors for Web design from the Web-Safe Palette. The Web-Safe Palette is a palette of 216 colors that's consistent on both the Mac and the PC platforms for the Netscape, Explorer, and Mosaic browsers. The Web-Safe Palette contains only 216 of 256 possible indexed colors because 40 colors vary between Macs and PCs. Use the Web-Safe Palette to avoid color shifting and to ensure greater design (color) control.

The Swatches Panel has an option, Web 216, which is accessible from the options triangle at the upper right of the panel. Web 216 restricts the color palette to Web-Safe Colors. However, intermediate colors (meaning any process or effect that generates new colors from two Web-Safe Colors) such as gradients, color tweening, transparent overlays, and alpha transitions, will not be snapped to Web-Safe Colors.

Using hexadecimal values

Any RGB color can be described in hexadecimal (hex) notation. *Hexadecimal notation* is used with HTML code and some scripting languages to specify flat color, which is a continuous area of undifferentiated color. Hex code is used because it describes colors in an efficient manner that HTML and scripting languages can digest. In HTML, hexadecimal is used to specify colored text, lines, background, borders, frame cells, and frame borders.

A hexadecimal color number has six places. It allocates two places for each of the three color channels: R, G, and B. So, in the hexadecimal example 00FFCC, 00 signifies the red channel, FF signifies the green channel, and CC signifies the blue channel. The corresponding values between hexadecimal and customary integer values are as follows:

16 integer values:	0 1 2 3 4 5 6 7 8 9 10 11 12 13 14 15
16 hex values:	0 1 2 3 4 5 6 7 8 9 A B C D E F

Applying ColorSafe and other solutions

There are a couple of valuable tools used to create custom-mixed Web-Safe Colors. They build patterns composed of Web-Safe Colors that fool the eye into seeing a more desirable color. These are essentially blocks of preplanned dithers, built out of the Web-Safe Palette, that augment the usable palette while retaining cross-platform, cross-browser color consistency.

✦ ColorSafe is an Adobe Photoshop plug-in that generates hybrid color swatches with this logic. ColorSafe (Mac and Win) is available directly from BoxTop software at www.boxtopsoft.com. Furthermore, the ColorSafe demo is included in the software folder of the Flash 5 Bible CD-ROM.

✦ ColorMix is an easily used online utility that interactively delivers hybrid color swatches, much like ColorSafe. It is free at www.colormix.com.

Note

Now that we've arrived at the millennium, there's a growing trend among developers to consider the art of designing with Web-Safe Color something like building Web sites for the Ice Age. As Dorian Nisinson remarked, "What can you *do* with that many shades of weird green? Even a lime would be embarrassed." We *are* inclined to agree. It is true, especially in North America and Europe, that even the most inexpensive systems are equipped to display full color. But we also feel compelled to ask: What about the rest of the world? What about the poorer areas of North America — as, for example, most school systems? <soapbox> If we are to survive through this next century, then *inclusion* — no matter how inconvenient for the privileged — needs to become a planetary priority. </soapbox> We urge you to know your audience and design accordingly, but with a dash of generosity.

Expert Tutorial: Using Hybrid Color Swatches in Flash, *by Jon Warren Lentz*

Both ColorSafe and ColorMix can be teamed up with the Flash Dropper Tool to expand the available palette yet retain Web-Safe Color consistency. It takes a little fussing, but once you've built a set of Flash hybrid color swatches they can be reused from the library, and once you get the knack, new swatches are more easily created. (Note: In order to illustrate the principle of hybrid swatches, the images that illustrate this tutorial were created at high zoom levels. In normal practice, the checkered appearance would not be noticeable.)

Whether you use ColorMix online or use the ColorSafe plug-in for Photoshop, the optimal size for your hybrid color swatch is about ten pixels square, as shown in the following figure. Some swatches for this tutorial were saved as TIFFs, others as GIFs. The optimal workflow is to generate all of your swatches first. Then, before proceeding further, open the Photoshop Preferences dialog with File ⇨ Preferences ⇨ General, and make sure that Export Clipboard is enabled. Don't close Photoshop.

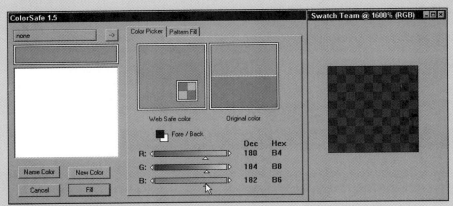

BoxTop Software's ColorSafe Photoshop plug-in creates Web-Safe hybrid color swatches.

Next, open a new Flash document and name it *HybridSwatches.FLA*. Next, turn off Flash's default dithering by unchecking the View ⇨ Fast Toggle, and then save the document. Return to Photoshop and open all of your Hybrid Color Swatches, as seen in the following figure. Working with the topmost swatch, select and then copy the entire swatch as follows: Select ⇨ All and then Edit ⇨ Copy. Now return to Flash and paste the swatch (that you've just copied) into the Hybrid Swatches document with Edit ⇨ Paste. Use the Arrow Tool to position the swatch. Repeat this procedure for each swatch until they've all been pasted into Flash. Save the PhotoShop document as a layered .PSD for possible reuse, and then close Photoshop.

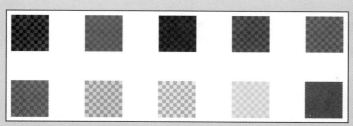

Ten hybrid color swatches were imported into Flash and arranged on the Stage. For convenience, these were moved into the offstage Work Area.

Now for a few examples to show how this works: Add a new layer to your Hybrid Swatches document and use the Rectangle Tool to drag out a rectangle, filled with any color. Return to the Swatches layer and use the Arrow Tool to select a swatch with which to fill the rectangle. When the swatch is selected, break it apart with Modify ⇨ Break Apart. (A bitmap that's broken apart is signified by a fine grid pattern that covers the bitmap.) Then use the Dropper Tool to acquire the bitmap fill of this swatch. When you click the swatch, the Dropper Tool is automatically swapped to the Paint Bucket Tool, as shown here. Click inside the rectangle with the Paint Bucket — the fill has been replaced with the hybrid bitmap fill!

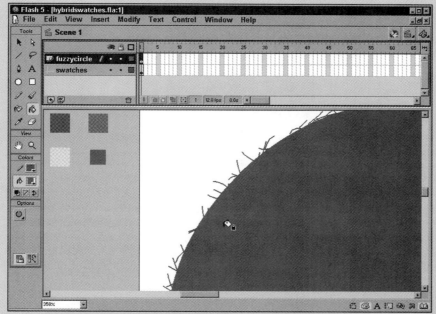

The edge of the shape on stage and to the right is an enclosed area, described by a custom line — it has just been filled with the hybrid swatch.

Continued

Continued

Follow the same procedure to fill other shapes—either on the same layer or on different layers—with Web-Safe hybrid bitmap fills. (Note that a swatch layer can be saved with a project and be excluded from the final animation simply by turning that layer into a Guide layer.) As regards the procedure, the most common problem encountered in acquiring the bitmap fill is either forgetting to break apart the bitmap or failing to do so properly.

The following figure shows a detail of the checkered pattern of our hybrid fill, accompanied by a view of the Library that contains each of our bitmaps.

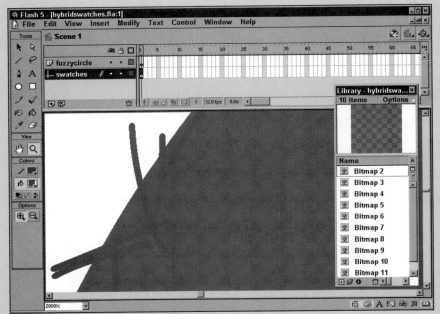

When bitmaps are brought into Flash, they automatically reside in the Library.

Before we leave our document behind, let's see a little more about the way these imported bitmaps behave. In the following figure, the same fill is selected, and the Fill Panel is shown, with the Bitmap menu open, revealing all of the bitmaps that are currently used in the .FLA—including those offstage. We've drawn a rectangle around the bitmap fill that was originally broken apart and applied to the shape, which is also highlighted above the cursor in the Fill Panel.

With the fill selected on Stage, the second bitmap in the Fill Panel was clicked. This caused the bitmap to become highlighted in the Fill Panel. It also caused this newly activated fill to be swapped in as the fill for our selected shape. This replacement fill is clearly different, as the grid pattern is much larger than the grid of the original swatch.

Furthermore, the second fill has also replaced the original bitmap swatch (around which we drew the rectangle), as shown in the following figure. Note, however, that swapping bitmaps from the Fill Panel only works when the bitmaps are present on the Stage.

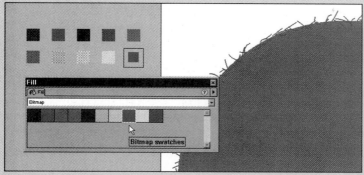

The Fill Panel's Bitmap menu

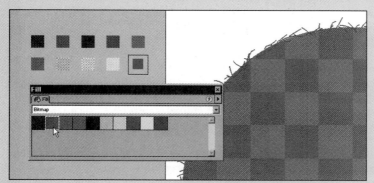

Use the Fill Panel's Bitmap menu to swap one bitmap fill for another.

Finally we need to prepare and save the Hybrid Swatches document so that it can be used as a Library: To do this, add a new layer, leave it blank, and then delete all of the other layers, including the layer into which the swatches were originally pasted, because they aren't on any layer. Or if you've arranged your swatches off stage, you'll need to select and delete them, since they aren't visible on any layer.

How does this work? Well, because imported bitmaps reside in the Library, and because we want this document as a Library, you don't need to keep them on Stage. Save the document and close it. Now you can open a new Flash document and then access the hybrid swatches library with File ➪ Open as Library and use the dialog to locate and open Hybrid Swatches.FLA. As long as you open this file as a Library, all of the bitmap fills saved in HybridSwatches.FLA will be available for use within any new Flash document.

Continued

Continued

With the Library open, to use a hybrid swatch, select the appropriate swatch from the Library and drag the swatch from the Preview window onto the work area, or onto any active layer. If the swatch is not selected, use the Arrow Tool to select it, and then use Modify ⇨ Break Apart to break it apart. Next, use the Dropper Tool to acquire the bitmap fill, which loads the Paint Bucket Tool. As we've shown, the Paint Bucket can now be used to fill any shape with hybrid Web-Safe Color.

On the CD-ROM
If you'd like to see the example swatches and associated Flash file for this tutorial, open the Hybrid Swatches folder located in the ch6 folder of the *Flash 5 Bible* CD-ROM.

Using color effectively

According to some developers, the issue of color on the Web has been seriously confused by the misperception that people can set numbers to give them Web-Safe Colors, and that — if they do that — they will have *good* color. It's given a lot of people the idea that color has some absolute quality.

But when there over 16 million possible colors, why settle for a mere 216? Or, if you do settle for 216 colors, you must understand that the value of color in Web design (or any design or art for that matter) has to do with color perception and design issues, and numbers have little to do with that. Humans perceive color relative to the context of other colors in which the color is set.

Most art schools offer at least one course about color. They often start with color experiments that are conducted with pieces of colored paper. An early assignment is to make three colors look like more than three colors — this is done by placing small scraps of the same color on larger pieces of different colors. Students are always amazed to learn how much a person's perception of a single color is tainted by placing it on those different-colored backgrounds. The lesson is that color is *not* an absolute — it never was before computers and never will be. Just step into a computer classroom and note the range of variation between monitors. Do you think it's any different out on the Web?

Perhaps there is one thing that is more important than color: contrast. Here's a good test: Take a colorful design that you admire and render it to grayscale — does it still work? Contrast is a major factor in good color composition. Good design almost doesn't need color because it leverages contrast instead.

So what's the point? Consider your audience. Choose a color strategy that will enable the preponderance of your viewers to view your designs as you intend them.

For example, if your audience is the public schools, then you must seriously consider limiting your work to the Web-Safe Palette. (If you choose this route, then hybrid swatches may enable you to access colors that are technically unavailable, while remaining within the hardware limitations of you audience.) On the other hand, if you are designing an interface for a stock photography firm whose clients are well-equipped art directors, then please use the full gamut. But in either case, understand that no one will see the exact same colors that you see. The variables of hardware, calibration, ambient light, and environmental decor are insurmountable.

Here's the bottom line: To achieve good Web design you'll need to use color — to achieve *great* Web design your colors should leverage contrast as well.

Working with Flash Color

Flash 5 has three levels for working with Flash Color. The first level is Toolbox Color, which is discussed in this chapter and which was briefly introduced in Chapter 5. At the intermediate level are the Stroke and Fill Panels, which can be used to set any predefined color, or immediately capture a color from anywhere on screen with the Eyedropper Tool, or invoke the system color picker. At the third level are the Mixer and Swatches Panels, where Alpha can be set for individual swatches, colors can be mixed and edited, and color sets can be added to, subtracted from, or loaded into the Swatches Panel. For many operations, proceeding from any of these panels, you can use existing swatches or any onscreen color, or set a color without needing to access any other panels. Other more complex operations, such as creating a gradient, require adjustments across several panels.

Using Toolbox Color

Just as there are several ways to approach the subject of color, there are also a number of ways to access the various — but fundamentally similar — color-handling tools in Flash 5. The quickest, and perhaps most convenient route is to approach color from either of the Color buttons located on the Toolbox: the Stroke Color and the Fill Color buttons located in the Color Tray. As we discussed in Chapter 5, these options serve double duty: Although these controls appear to be Color Chips that indicate the current color, they're also buttons. Click either Color button to open the current Swatches pop-up and select a new stroke or fill color. Whenever any Flash drawing or painting tools are activated, the current stroke and fill colors are represented by the Color controls located in the Flash Toolbox. These controls are present regardless of which tool is being used.

As shown in Figure 6-1, clicking either the Stroke or Fill Color button opens the current Swatches pop-up. This pop-up displays the same Swatch set that is currently loaded in the Swatches Panel. It includes a hexadecimal color entry box — which facilitates keyboard entry, as well as cut-and-paste of hex values — and a button that launches the Color Picker. Depending upon the tool selected, the Fill Color pop-up may also display a No Color button. The Swatches pop-up for Fill Color also includes a row of Gradients at the bottom of the solid colors. For all Drawing Tools, elementary color selection is accomplished by clicking either the Stroke or Fill Color buttons, and then choosing a color from the Swatches pop-up. If the color you want is not there, you may opt to invoke the Color Picker by clicking the Color Picker button. Alternatively, you may also open the Mixer Panel to create a new color and add it to the Swatches.

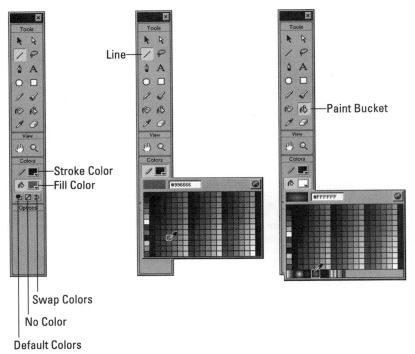

Figure 6-1: The Toolbox Color Tray and the Stroke and Fill Swatches Panels

New Feature

In addition to the basic reorganization of the Toolbox, the Color Controls include three new buttons, arrayed across the bottom of the Color Tray. As shown at the left of Figure 6-1, these are buttons for Default Colors (Stroke and Fill), No Color, and Swap Colors. The Default button sets the stroke to black and the fill to white. The No Color button sets the active control — which may be either the Stroke or the Fill — to apply no color. The Swap button swaps the current colors between the Stroke and Fill controls.

Tools that create a line include the Line Tool, Pencil Tool, Ink Bottle Tool, Pen Tool, and — because they draw outlines around their fills — both the Oval and Rectangle Tools. Each tool relies upon the Stroke Color button, which appears in the Toolbox

Color Tray. Click the Stroke Color button to open the Swatches pop up, which contains all colors in the current color set, including any new colors that have been temporarily added to the set. It is identical for any tool that has a stroke color.

In addition to tools that create lines, there are also fill tools. The fill tools include the Brush, Paint Bucket, Oval, and Rectangle Tools. Each of these tools is accompanied by the Fill Color button, which also resides in the Color Tray of the Toolbox. Clicking the Fill Color button invokes the Swatches pop up. Although the Fill Swatches pop-up is similar to the line pop up, it has one significant difference: It has another row of swatches at the bottom, which are gradient swatches — click one to fill with that gradient. The Fill Swatches pop-up contains all of the colors and gradients in the current color set, including any new colors or gradients that have been temporarily added to the set. It is identical for any tool that has a fill color.

Applying color from the Stroke and Fill Panels

You won't need to keep all of the color panels open to use colors. That's because, for most color operations, the colors are already present in any panel you're using. Flash 5 color works best if you use the Mixer Panel to create new colors, and the Swatches Panel to manipulate the display of colors that are available in the other panels. If you already have a predetermined palette for your project (which is a smart workflow), you may find that you do most of your color work from the Stroke and Fill Panels. The Stroke and Fill Panels each have a single option available from their options triangles: The Stroke option invokes the Line Style dialog, which was discussed in Chapter 5, while the Fill Panel option invokes Add Gradient. In Figure 6-2, the Fill Panel is set for solid colors only. For more information, please see Chapter 5.

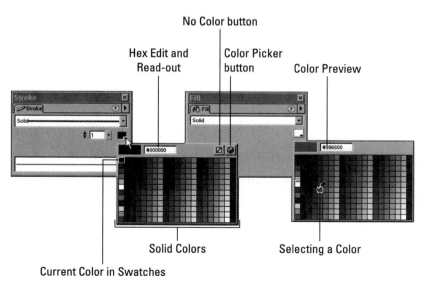

Figure 6-2: The Stroke and Fill Panels

The Fill Panel is also used for working with bitmap fills. This topic is covered in detail in Chapter 12, "Using Bitmaps and Other Media with Flash."

Working with the Swatches Panel

Think of the Swatches Panel (Figure 6-3) as a way to organize your existing swatches and to manipulate the display of colors that are available in the other panels. Use the Swatches Panel to save color sets, import color sets, and reorder or change selected colors.

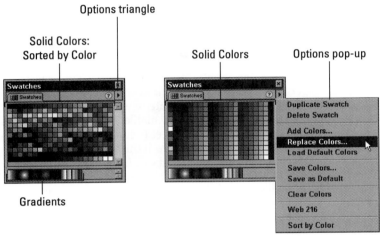

Figure 6-3: On the left, the Swatches Panel is shown after using the Sort by Color option. On the right, it's shown with the default sort, and with the Options pop-up displayed.

The Options pop-up of the Swatches Panel has options that are used to manipulate and administrate individual swatches as well as various color sets:

✦ **Duplicate Swatch:** Use this to duplicate a selected swatch. This can be useful when you want the make a range of related color swatches by duplicating and then editing subsequent swatches from the Mixer Panel.

✦ **Delete Swatch:** Botched a swatch? Select and delete it here.

✦ **Add Colors:** Opens the Import Color Swatch menu, which is a simple dialog used to locate, select, and import color sets. Add Colors retains the current color set and appends the imported color set at the bottom.

✦ **Replace Colors:** Also opens the Import Color Swatch menu. However, Replace Colors drops the current color set when it loads the selected color set. If the current set has not been saved it will be lost.

✦ **Load Default Colors:** Clears the current color set and replaces it with the default Flash color set. Again, if the current set has not been saved it will be lost.

✦ **Save Colors:** Opens the Export Color Swatch Menu, which is used to name and save color sets to a specific location on your hard drive. Color sets may be saved in either the Flash color set — on the PC (.clr), on the Mac (.fclr) — or Color Table (.act) format.

Note

By default, colors are saved *within* your Flash document, rather than as an external file. Using the Add Colors, Replace Colors, and Save Colors menu options, Flash can import and export solid colors from files in the Flash color set (.clr) format. But Flash can also import and export solid colors from files in the Fireworks-savvy Color Table (.act) format, which can be imported by Photoshop, and imported and exported from Fireworks. Flash can also import solid colors from GIF files. If it isn't already obvious, this means greater workflow flexibility, which is a boon to project management because you can save a specific color set for a project and load different color sets as needed. Gradients may only be imported and exported with the Flash color set (.clr) format.

✦ **Save as Default:** Saves the current color set as the default — this action replaces the original default Flash color set.

✦ **Clear Colors:** When Clear Colors is selected, the swatches in the current colors window are removed, leaving only black and white.

✦ **Web 216:** Upon initial installation, this is the default Flash color palette that is displayed in the Swatches Panel. Select this option to replace any current color set with the Web-Safe Palette of 216 colors.

Tip

You can override the default Web 216 Palette by switching the Mixer Panel to either the RGB or HSB (Hue, Saturation, Brightness) color spaces. You can then mix your own fresh colors; add them to the Swatches; and save that palette as the default. Another alternative is to locate the Photoshop Color Tables on your hard drive (or download a specialty color table from the Web) and replace the default set with a broader gamut.

✦ **Sort by Color:** Click this button to rearrange an accumulation of custom colors into a palette that is freshly reordered according to color. It sorts by hues, with the values of each are arranged together from light to dark in declining order. However, once you've sorted a palette in this manner there is no toggle to return to the other view — so save your palette before sorting, and then save the sorted palette, too.

Caution

Be careful about creating huge color sets! On some systems (for example, a 17-inch monitor set at 800×600 resolution),the Toolbox Color pop-ups may extend beyond the visible screen and you'll be forced to use the Swatches Panel to choose colors that are hidden offscreen. This can get really bad if you add colors from a GIF image.

Working with the Mixer Panel

The Color Mixer, which is shown in Figure 6-4, enables you to create new colors, working within any of these three color spaces — RGB, HSB (Hue, Saturation Brightness, or hex — using either the interactive Color Bar or the Color Value slider controls. All colors are handled with four channels, which are RGBA (Red, Green, Blue, Alpha). New colors can be added to the current Swatches, which causes a new swatch to appear in the Fill, Stroke, and Character Panels — just select Add Swatch from the Options pop-up. When working with the Mixer Panel, to add a new color just select Add Swatch from the Options pop-up.

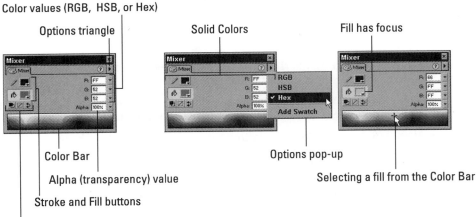

Color values (RGB, HSB, or Hex)

Options triangle

Solid Colors

Fill has focus

Color Bar

Alpha (transparency) value

Stroke and Fill buttons

Default Colors, No Color, and Swap Color buttons

Options pop-up

Selecting a fill from the Color Bar

Figure 6-4: The Color Mixer gives you precise control over the creation of new colors, including Alpha values.

There are two ways to change the Alpha value for a selected color: Either drag the Alpha Slider until the Alpha readout looks right or enter a numeric value in the Alpha readout. Numeric entry is useful when you already know what level of transparency is required, while the slider is useful for interactive fiddling with transparency to get it just right — as indicated in either the Stroke or Fill Color button. In Figure 6-5, a copy of the Flash icon is donating its orange color to our palette. On the right, this orange is shown with the Alpha — or transparency — of the color set to 30 percent. Before proceeding, this swatch was saved from the Options pop-up by clicking Add Swatch.

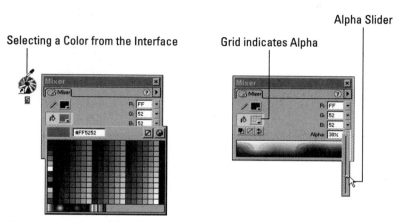

Figure 6-5: When selecting a color from the Swatches pop-up of the Mixer Panel, the Dropper Tool enables you to pluck a color from anywhere in the interface.

New Feature

When working in the Mixer, Stroke, Fill (including Color Pointers), and Character Panels, the Dropper associated with these panels enables you to pluck color information from anywhere in the interface. Simply click the Color button of any of these three panels, which will cause the mouse to display as a Dropper. Then drag the Dropper over any open application — or panel of the Flash interface itself — and click to acquire the color that's at the end of the Dropper. (Although the Toolbox Dropper doesn't facilitate this move, it does have a unique trick of its own: It adds a new swatch to the Swatches pop-up whenever a color is acquired.)

Figure 6-6 shows the Mixer and Swatches Panels on the left. Previous to this shot, we used the Duplicate Swatch command of the Swatches Panel to duplicate the 30-percent-orange swatch. You can see this duplicate swatch highlighted at the bottom of the Swatches Panel on the left. Using the Mixer, we returned the Alpha of this swatch to 100 percent. Then, as shown on the right in Figure 6-6, we used the Save Colors command to add both swatches to the current color set.

Tip

If you're working with a color and want to make it just a little darker, HSB color will come to your rescue! You can do this dynamically, too. Here's how: Click the options arrow of the Mixer Panel and choose HSB. Now make sure your color is selected on Stage and hide the selection with Ctrl/Command+H. Then, from the Color values of the Mixer Panel, reduce the B value, which is brightness, either numerically or by dragging the slider.

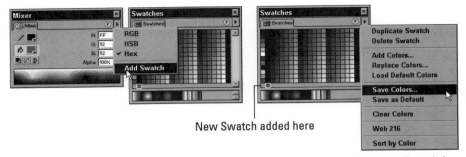

New Swatch added here

Figure 6-6: Use the Mixer and Swatches Panels to add a new color Swatch and then save the new color(s) to the current color set.

As shown in Figure 6-7, the new color — an Orange with an Alpha value of 30 percent — is selected for a ten-point solid line. This same color may also be used as a solid fill. However, to create gradients with new colors, including transparent colors, you need to use the drop-down menu of the Fill Panel, as explained in the next section.

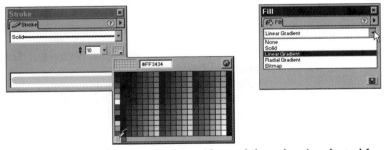

Figure 6-7: A newly created color, with an Alpha value, is selected for a solid line (left). The drop-down menu of the Fill Panel is used to initiate the creation of custom gradient fills (right).

Creating gradient colors

Often you'll find that creating a custom gradient swatch requires that you use several panels. In addition to the Fill Panel, this usually requires the Mixer, and sometimes the Swatches Panel. The drop-down list of the Flash 5 Fill Panel lists two gradient styles: Linear and Radial. When editing or creating a gradient, the current changes can be saved by clicking the Save button at the bottom right of the Panel, which adds another gradient to the Swatches Panel. The gradient shown in Figure 6-8 is being modified from a default black and white linear gradient.

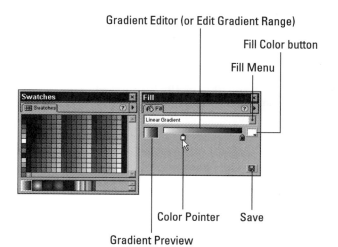

Gradient Editor (or Edit Gradient Range)

Fill Color button

Fill Menu

Color Pointer   Save

Gradient Preview

Figure 6-8: The Pointer Color button displays the color of the active Color Pointer.

Tip   Working with the tiny default Fill Panel to create or edit a complex gradient can be tedious. Want a bigger work area? Simply grab any corner of the panel to resize it — and expand the gradient editor simultaneously.

To change the color of the active pointer, which has focus, click the Pointer Color button and then select a color from the Swatches pop-up. The Fill Color button is updated to reflect the change. Note that the Swatches pop-up contains all of the solid colors in the current color set, including any new colors that may have been temporarily added to the set. As shown in Figure 6-9, the left-hand pointer is being changed to a color that has an Alpha value, which is indicated by the grid pattern in both the Color Preview and, upon release of the pointer, by the Fill Color button.

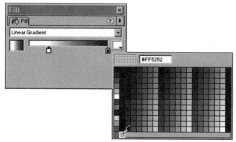

Figure 6-9: Changing the color of the active pointer for a gradient

To customize another point of an existing gradient, click that Color Pointer to give it focus. In the example shown in Figure 6-10, the right-hand Color Pointer was given *focus* — which means that it is active and can be edited. Switching from one Color Pointer to another changes the Fill Color button to display the color of the pointer that has focus. While the Color Pointer has focus, click the Fill Color button and choose a color from the Swatches pop-up, or drag the Dropper out into the interface to acquire a color from any item onscreen, including any color displayed in any open Flash panel.

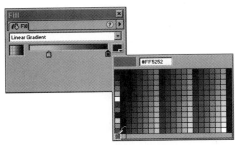

Figure 6-10: Changing the second point of the gradient

Note A new color may also be specified in the Mixer Panel by numeric or hex entry in the RGB entry fields.

In Figure 6-11, the gradient from the previous figure was applied to this simple composition of a circle described by a custom, fuzzy stroke. On the layer behind is a black pattern of black lines, which is visible through the transparent portions of the gradient fill that's been applied to the circle on the top layer. Note the active swatch in the Swatches Panel, and the Gradient Preview of the left-hand Color Pointer in the Mixer Panel, which has focus in the Fill Panel.

Figure 6-12 was changed to a radial gradient and then the left-hand Color Pointer of the previous figure was moved to the right by clicking and dragging it to a new position. The Gradient Preview adjusts immediately to reflect this change. To add a new color to a gradient, you need to add a new pointer to the Gradient Editor, by clicking slightly beneath the bar. To remove a pointer, drag it downwards, away from the bar of the Gradient Editor.

Tip Here's how to obtain an interactive preview while adjusting the quality of an existing gradient fill: First select the fill, and then hide the selection grid with Ctrl/Command+H. Next, open the Swatches, Mixer, and Fill Panels, and select the appropriate gradient in the Swatches Panel. Next, in the Fill Panel, choose a Color Pointer to edit and proceed to edit that color in the Mixer. As each Mixer slider is released, the adjustment will be updated in all relevant Color buttons *and* in the selected fill on the Stage. This same functionality also works with new gradients: Simply make a new single color gradient, apply it as a fill, and then proceed to edit — adding more colors and finessing Alphas to suit.

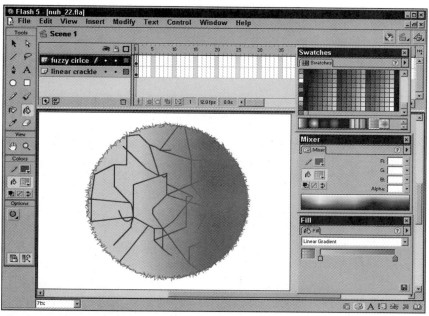

Figure 6-11: Applying a new gradient, with a transparent color, to an object

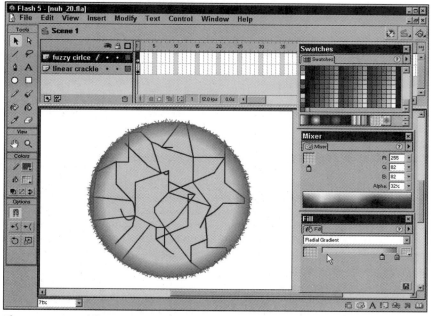

Figure 6-12: Adding a new pointer to the Gradient Editor

As shown in Figure 6-13 more pointers have been added to the gradient. In this figure, the center Color Pointer is active and white is being selected from the Swatches pop-up. Next, the Alpha for this pointer will be reduced to 30 percent by entering this number into the numeric entry field of the Alpha value of the Mixer Panel.

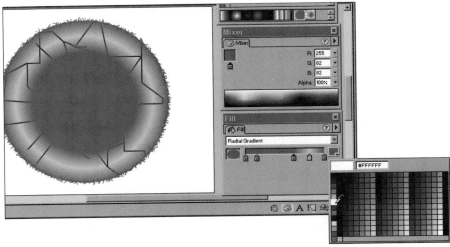

Figure 6-13: Changing the gradient type and adding more complexity to the gradient.

Note   The Alpha (or relative opacity, or transparency) of a Color Pointer may be adjusted either by entering a numeric value or by dragging the Alpha Slider. When using the slider, the Alpha value is displayed as a percentage in the numeric entry box. When adjusting Alpha, a visual cue for the level of transparency is the appearance of a faint grid in the Mixer's active Color button (Stroke Color, Fill Color, or Color Proxy). If visible, other related Color buttons will also update as the Alpha is adjusted, particularly in the Fill Panel's Gradient Preview, the active Color Pointer, and the Gradient Fill Color button.

Figure 6-14 shows our final radial gradient, which is opaque at the center and proceeds through variations of transparency and color as it radiates to the outer edge. The procedure for making a radial gradient is similar to those for creating a linear gradient. The only real difference is that the Gradient Editor bar — when used in conjunction with radial gradients — must be considered as a radius, or slice from the center out to the edge, of the circular gradient. Color Pointers at the left end of the Gradient Editor bar represent the center — or inside — of the radial gradient, while Color Pointers at the right end represent the outside.

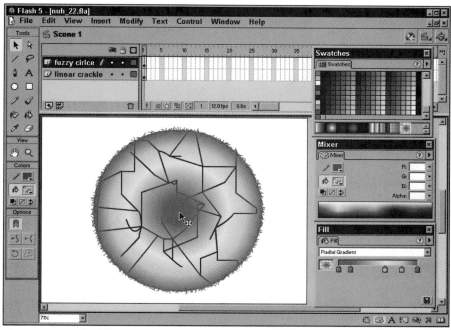

Figure 6-14: The final radial gradient applied to an object in Flash 5.

New Feature

When applying a gradient, it's now easy to interactively orient the direction of the gradient as it is applied: Simply click with the Paint Bucket and drag. A direction line is drawn between the click point and the drag point. If you aren't satisfied with the orientation of the gradient, simply repeat the procedure and reorienting the direction arrow as you drag.

Expert Tutorial: Creating Color Schemes
by Molly E. Holzschlag

Comparing Adobe LiveMotion to Macromedia Flash is like comparing proverbial apples and oranges. Both offer something special and unique. Maybe you like them both, as I do. Each has features that empower designers seeking to add life to their Web sites. In the realm of color, LiveMotion (LM) offers one tool that is especially intriguing. Part of LM's appeal is that it is used for static as well as motion graphics for the Web, so the application has a lot of color support built-in. One very tasty feature that will serve to inspire you in your color goals is a specialty palette known as the *Color Scheme*. In fact, if you were to use LM for nothing else, you might find that the Color Scheme palette is a worthwhile companion to Flash.

Continued

Continued

Color Scheme palette, Triangle view

Think of a color wheel—you know, those standard wheels of color that you've certainly seen before. With that wheel in your mind: Analogous colors are those that are next to each other. Complementary colors are those that are across from each other.

LM works on the concept of analogous and complementary colors to make schemes, which are especially helpful if you're new to working with color, or for those design newcomers and veterans who need inspiration in terms of setting up a palette for a design. Schemes combine colors in interesting ways, and can really help you get creative. The Color Scheme palette shows off its colors via two views, which are known as *Triangle view* and *Honeycomb view*. Use the view that you like best. Sometimes I switch views. Variety, after all, is the one true spice. Along with the views, there are six combinations of color available in the palette:

✦ **Analogous:** This scheme provides a view of the original (referred to as *base*) color plus any analogous colors.

✦ **Split Complementary:** This scheme shows the base color, its complement, and its complement's analogous colors.

✦ **Complementary Analogous:** Using this scheme shows a base color, its analogous color, and the analogous color's complements.

✦ **Triad:** This is a base color and two equidistant colors.

✦ **Tetrad:** This is a base color and three colors chosen at equal intervals along the color wheel.

✦ **Sextet:** This is the base color plus five colors placed at equal distances from one another along the color wheel.

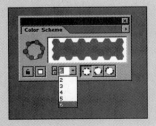

Views and numeric combinations can be employed to create a Color Scheme palette (Honeycomb view).

Getting excited? Great! If you already have LM, open it up because you're about to create your own color scheme. And, if you don't have it, you can download a full-feature, 30-day demo from Adobe. To begin a color scheme, follow me:

1. Select Window ➪ Color Scheme to bring up the Color Scheme palette.

2. Choose a color for your base color. To do this, select the Foreground color box in the Toolbox. Open the Color Palette (Window ➪ Color Palette), and then choose the color you like using the Color Picker.

3. In the Color Scheme palette, choose a number and scheme combo. There are lots of combinations — play around until you find one you really like.

4. As you create your scheme, you'll find that it appears in the Color Scheme portion of the Toolbox. Got a scheme you're happy with? Lock that puppy so that it stays until further commands are given by clicking the Scheme Lock icon on the Color Scheme palette.

5. Got a scheme that you want to use in Flash? Simply open your Color Scheme and make a set of rectangular swatches on the LM stage. Then save it as a .SWF. When you open this .SWF in Flash, you can access those colors with the Dropper and save it out as a Flash color set.

Pretty creative, indeed. But what happens when you don't know much about color and what it represents? Well, here's a little guide I created some time back, and I'm including it here for you to enjoy. Color meanings and perceptions vary, and color meanings are often paradoxical. I've kept this information very basic because getting more detailed would end up taking up a whole, well, book. Instead, use this as a starting point and then put your own savvy to work to come up with fun and interesting colors and color combinations for your designs. For a basic introduction to the psychological responses to various colors, refer to the following table.

Color	Psychological Response
Red	Power, energy, warmth, passions, love, aggression, danger
Blue	Trust, conservative, security, technology, cleanliness, order
Green	Nature, healthy, good luck, jealousy ("green with envy"), renewal
Yellow	Optimism, hope, philosophy, dishonesty, cowardice (a coward can be described as "yellow"), betrayal
Purple	Spirituality, mystery, royalty, transformation, cruelty, arrogance
Orange	Energy, balance, warmth
Brown	Earth, reliability, comfort, endurance
Gray	Intellect, futurism, modesty, sadness, decay
White	Purity, cleanliness, precision, innocence, sterility, death
Black	Power, sexuality, sophistication, death, mystery, fear, unhappiness, elegance

Continued

Continued

For a deeper examination of the complex subject of color, especially within the context of World Wide Web design and the variegated impact of color on different cultures, check out my recent article for Web Techniques, *Color My World*, at `www.webtechniques.com/archives/2000/09/desi/`.

Honored as one of the Top 25 Most Influential Women on the Web, Molly Holzschlag was onto Flash from the start. She first encountered it when, "It was Futuresplash, from a little company in San Diego called FutureWave." She's the author of 15 books, including *Teach Yourself Adobe LiveMotion in 24 Hours* (New York: Macmillan, Sam's Publishing 2000). Some of the sites she's worked on include The Microsoft Network, Desert.Net, RedMeat.Com, and, of course, Molly.Com. Here are her answers to other questions: "Born: Brooklyn. Raised: New Jersey. Do you have a problem with that?" And, after tremendous prodding about her last days as a teenager, she reminisced, "If there was anything worth remembering, I don't remember it. Hey, it was the 70s!"

Tip   You can obtain functionality similar to what is available from the Color Scheme Palette of LiveMotion without the expense of owning LiveMotion. It's found in a Photoshop plug-in called Color Harmony. The plug-in is from Hot Door, Inc.— `www.hotdoor.com`. Although currently available only for the Mac, a Windows version is planned for 2001.

Flash Symbols: Tweened Color Effects and Color Objects

Flash Symbols can be tweened so that they will change color over time. Although this involves color, the selection of colors for the keyframes of the tween is merely a rudimentary application of fill and line color, as described in this chapter. For information regarding the tweening and keyframe aspects of Symbols and Tweened Color effects, including the new Negative Alpha, please refer to Chapter 11, "Animating in Flash."

New Feature   One brilliant aspect of the improvements to ActionScript is that Flash 5 now has a new Color object. This means that color is scriptable. As one developer remarked, "Ahhh, the lengths to which we will no longer have to go in order to simulate this effect!" Although beyond the scope of this chapter, some mention of it does belong here. Technically, it means that you can use the methods of the predefined Color object to change the color and transparency of any movie clip. This is covered in detail in Chapter 19, "Controlling Movie Clips."

Summary

✦ The science of color on the computer is far from accurate. There are many variables involved in the presentation of color over the Web. One variable revolves around the issue of Web-Safe Color. When targeting color-challenged audiences, one solution is to use Hybrid Color Swatches.

✦ Toolbox Color is available to every Flash drawing tool. It gives immediate, intuitive access to the currently loaded swatches and all temporary colors. It also permits direct insertion of hexadecimal values.

✦ At their basic level, the Stroke and Fill Panels are used to access deeper features of the Flash Color system. They both permit sampling of color from anywhere in the interface. Additionally, the Fill Panel is used to create and edit gradients.

✦ The Swatches Panel is used to save out color sets, import color sets, and reorder or change selected colors and gradients.

✦ The Color Mixer is used to create new colors, and adjust the Alpha of new or existing colors. It's also used to choose from three color spaces: RGB, HSB, or hex. New colors can be added to the current Swatches, which causes them to appear in the Fill, Stroke, and Character Panels.

✦ Although Flash doesn't directly support Color Schemes, they can be developed outside Flash, imported (as either a .SWF from LiveMotion, or as an .ACT from Color Harmony) and then sampled and saved into a color set with the Swatches Panel.

✦ Advanced Color capabilities of Flash include color tweening, scriptable color, and negative Alpha. These topics are discussed in depth in subsequent chapters.

✦   ✦   ✦

Working with Text

Type and text are often needed to convey information in a Flash movie. In this chapter, we explain how to create text and avoid font display problems.

Understanding Font Display Problems

TrueType, Type 1 PostScript, and bitmap fonts can be used in Flash. Although Flash exports the system information about the fonts that are used, fonts may still appear incorrectly on other platforms — if the end-user doesn't have the font installed, the font may appear incorrectly (even on the same platform). Often this is a due to the fact that although Flash can display the font within the editor, it does not recognize that particular font's outline and can't export the text. One way to check for this is to momentarily switch your view to View ⇨ Antialias Text. If the text appears jaggy, that's a problem font.

Such problems can be avoided by using the _device fonts (_sans, _serif, and _typewriter fonts), which can be chosen either from the Text ⇨ Font Menu or from the Character Panel. These _device fonts tell the Flash player to use whatever equivalent font is available on the local computer. For example, _sans usually becomes Arial or Helvetica, while _serif becomes Times or Times New Roman, and _typewriter becomes Courier. Because these settings utilize the default fonts on the user's machine, these fonts also make the final movie size smaller, because Flash doesn't have to export their outlines in the .SWF when the movie is exported. Of course, the result of smaller movies is faster downloads.

Characteristics of these _device fonts are that they are always available, always fast, never rotate, and may vary slightly in their metrics from player to player. You can use _device fonts for text fields and areas of text that you don't want *antialiased* (processed for smoother edges).

Tip Another way to avoid system conflicts with fonts is by breaking apart all text, which turns it into shapes instead of fonts. (Breaking apart text is indispensable for creating the text effects explained in Chapter 10, "Drawing in Flash.") However, broken-apart text usually increases the file size considerably, so use it sparingly. Furthermore, text cannot be edited after it's been broken apart—everything must be written correctly before investing the time required to break the text apart and to apply special effects to it.

Because Flash is a vector program, it enables the integration of most fonts within the movie, without fuss. For normal blocks of text, this means that fonts don't have to be rendered into bitmap elements. The .SWF files that Flash publishes (or exports) include all of the necessary information for the font to display properly on every browser.

Problems with fonts on the Mac

Adobe PostScript fonts usually function on the Mac without problems. However, if a font is not properly installed, it may appear to function and display properly within the .FLA, yet falter when the movie is published. Often this is due to the editor using what is called the screen font while you are working in the editor. If, however, the actual font to which the screen font refers cannot be found when the movie is published, that causes problems.

Problems with fonts on the PC

On the PC, it is reported that PostScript fonts that are used with Adobe Type Manager can cause problems when publishing the movie. For this reason, it's often recommended that PC Flash users limit themselves to TrueType fonts. This is especially relevant for block text. But if a text block has been broken apart, this restriction does not apply, because breaking type apart renders it into a vector shapes (or objects) that will ship with the .SWF when the project is published. But the primary disadvantages of breaking text apart are that it may increase the file size considerably, and that once it's broken apart, the text is no longer editable.

Cross-platform issues and codevelopment problems

Sometimes a project from the Mac will open on the PC with the Times font displayed in substitution for all of the text! This isn't anything strange—at least in terms of how Flash is trying to help you—because Flash knows that you don't have the font on your machine.

Resources for Further Study in Typography

Although Flash offers the capability to deliver finely designed typography to 90 percent of the Web-browsing population, too many Flash artists are *typography challenged*. Unfortunately, it shows. If you are unfamiliar with typography, here are two excellent resources:

The Non-Designer's Type Book (Berkeley: Peachpit Press, 1998) by Robin Williams. This is a must-read (and study) for anyone who really wants to take their Flash Web designs to the next level.

The Elements of Typographic Style (Vancover, B.C.: Hartley & Marks, 1997) by Robert Bringhurst. This is a manual of typography and book design that concludes with "appendices of typographic characters and currently available digitized fonts [and] a glossary of terms."

If you select a text block and check you'll most likely see the name of the original font that was used, even though the text is displayed in the Times font. As long as you don't edit the text, Flash will continue to try to use the named font. You may have the same font installed on both the Mac and the PC and notice (now) that there is a slight difference in their names. Usually, there's an extra space or an underscore messing up the font sync.

The Text Tool

The Text Tool is used to create and edit text. Although Flash is neither a drawing program like FreeHand, nor a page-layout program, its text-handling capabilities are well thought-out and implemented. The Text Tool, shown in Figure 7-1, delivers a broad range of control for generating, positioning, tuning, and editing text. Although the basic Text Tool is located in the Flash Toolbox, the controls for working with Text are located in three text panels: the Character, Paragraph, and Text Options Panels.

Tip   Use the Eyedropper Tool to acquire text: Click extant text to acquire all of the formatting and attributes and apply these settings to subsequently entered text.

Cross-Reference   If your handling of text demands a more robust and thorough environment, you can generate your text in Freehand (or Illustrator) and import that more refined text into Flash. For more information on this type workflow, refer to Chapter 31, "Working with Vector Graphics."

Flash handles text as a group. This means that when you create type, you can use the Text Tool to edit the individual letters or words inside the text area at any time. But if you click once anywhere on the text, the entire text block is selected.

Figure 7-1: The Text Tool has
no options in the Toolbox.

Working with Flash text boxes

Flash now generates three flavors of text in three kinds of text boxes: Label Text
(A), Block Text (B), and Editable Text (C), shown in Figure 7-2. The bottom example
shows an Editable Text box as it is being resized (D).

Each of the three kinds of text blocks has its own characteristics:

✦ **Label Text:** With Label Text, Flash creates text blocks that widen as you continue to add text. As shown in the top example of Figure 7-2, Label Text has a
round handle at the upper-right corner. To create a Label Text box, click once
in the movie area with the Text Tool and then commence typing. If you keep
typing without making line breaks in Label Text Mode, the Label Text box continues beyond the right edge of the movie area. When this happens, the text is
not lost. To regain view of this off-movie text, add line breaks, move the Label
Text box, or select View ⇨ Work Area from the Menu Bar, to make the off-
movie area Label Text box entirely visible.

✦ **Block Text:** Flash creates Block Text when you *drag out* the text box as you create it in the movie area. As shown in the second example in Figure 7-2, a Block
Text box has a square handle at the upper-right corner. The Block Text box has
a fixed width, and wraps words automatically. You create a Block Text box by
simply selecting the Text Tool, clicking, and then dragging out a box of the
desired width in the movie area. When you commence typing, the text wraps
automatically and the box extends downwards as you add more lines of text.

✦ **Editable Text:** With Editable Text fields, the content is variable. This means that the page viewer can change the contents of an Editable Text field: for example, when used in a password entry box or a form field. As shown in the third and bottom examples in Figure 7-2, an Editable Text box has a square handle at the lower-right corner that can be dragged in or out to resize it. Create Editable Text by choosing either Dynamic or Static Text from the Text Behavior drop-down of the Text Options Panel, and then click in the movie area to drag out and define the text box. Because the use of Editable Text involves interactivity and is rather complex, detailed discussion of Editable Text is deferred to Chapter 25, "Understanding HTML and Text Field Functions in Flash."

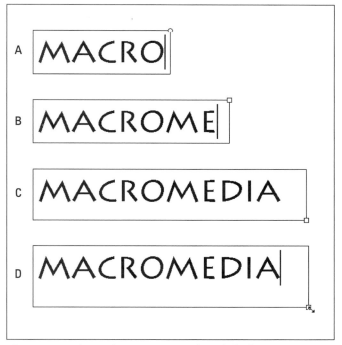

Figure 7-2: Shown here are examples of Flash text in three kinds of text boxes, from top to bottom: Label (or Extending) Text, Block (or Fixed) Text, and Editable (or Dynamic or Input) Text.

A Label Text box can be converted into a Block Text box. Place the cursor over the round text handle at the upper-right corner of the Label Text box. A double-ended arrow appears, indicating that you can modify the Label Text box's width. Drag to reshape the Label Text box. When you release the mouse, the text handle at the upper-right corner will now be square (formerly, it was round), indicating that this is now a Block Text box. To revert back to Label Text, double-click the square text handle.

Tip   Can't tell if it's Label or Block Text? That's because it's not in Edit Mode. To return the text item to Edit Mode, either double-click the item with the Arrow Tool or click it once with the Type Tool.

Using the Character Panel

The Character Panel, shown in Figure 7-3, is readily accessed from the Launcher Bar, or from the Window Menu with Window ➪ Panels ➪ Character. The main feature of this panel is the Font Name drop-down, which is use to select fonts.

Tip   The Character Panel can also be accessed from the keyboard by pressing Ctrl+T/Command+T.

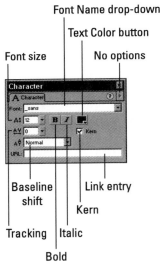

Figure 7-3: The Character Panel is one of three panels used to select and modify manipulated text.

✦ **No options:** There are no options for this panel. The options button here is vestigial.

✦ **Font Name drop-down:** When the Text Tool is active, this displays the name of the current font. Click the button (which is a downward-pointing triangle) to invoke a scrolling menu of available fonts. Choose a font from this scrolling menu to set the font for the next text element that you create. Or, to change the font of existing text, first select the text in the movie area, and then choose a different font from the scrolling menu. When selecting a font from the Character Panel, the currently highlighted font is previewed in its typeface.

Tip

The font of existing text can also be changed from the Menu Bar with Text ⇨ Font. The advantage of this method is that the list is more expansive and easier to scan. The disadvantage of this list is that it doesn't preview the fonts in their typefaces.

✦ **Text Color button:** Click this button to invoke the Current Swatches, which — in addition to current and temporary swatches — also enables you to acquire a color from anywhere within the interface.

✦ **Kern Check box:** If the font includes built-in kerning information, which evens out the spaces between letterforms, check this to activate automatic kerning.

✦ **Bold and Italic:** The Bold option is a simple button that toggles selected text between either Normal or Bold. The Italic option is another simple button. It toggles selected text between Normal and Italic.

Note

Many computer programs (including Flash) that deal with type permit you to fake a Bold and/or Italic version of fonts that you do have; this has led to a lot of confusion. Each typeface has a basic or Normal form. The shape of the Bold version of that typeface is not the same as the Normal form. Nor is the Italic simply a slanted version. The shapes and proportions are different. With a well-designed font, the real bold font will always look better than a Normal letter shape thickened with an outline. A real Bold or Italic version of a typeface will be appropriately named and will be selected as a *separate* font.

✦ **Font size:** This is both a pop-up and a text entry field. When the Text Tool is active, it displays the current font size in a text entry field. You can change the font size by entering a specific font size in this text entry field. If you click the arrow to the immediate right of the text entry field, a pop-up displays a slider of available font sizes.

✦ **Tracking:** In addition to the other controls that Flash affords for the arrangement and adjustment of text, text can be manually tracked. *Tracking* is the process of adjusting the space between two or more text characters. To track characters from the Character Panel, first select the characters that you want to adjust, and then either enter a numeric value in the read out, or drag the interactive slider. The Text menu also has its own Tracking menu suboptions. Menu tracking has the additional advantage that it can be applied either: (a) to selected (highlighted) text characters or (b) to the pair of text characters on either side of the cursor:

• **Decrease Spacing by One Half-Pixel:** To decrease text character spacing by one half-pixel, press Ctrl+Alt+Left Arrow (Command+Option+Left Arrow).

• **Decrease Spacing by Two Pixels:** To decrease text character spacing by two pixels, press Ctrl+Shift+Alt+Left Arrow (Command+Shift+Option+Left Arrow).

• **Increase Spacing by One Half-Pixel:** To increase text character spacing by one half-pixel, press Ctrl+Alt+Right Arrow (Command+Option+Right Arrow).

- **Increase Spacing by Two Pixels:** To increase text character spacing by two pixels, press Ctrl+Alt+Right Arrow (Command+Shift+Option+Right Arrow).

- **Reset Spacing to Normal:** To reset text character spacing to normal, press Ctrl+Alt+Up Arrow (Command+Option+Up Arrow).

✦ **Baseline shift:** There are three options in this drop-down menu. Normal resets text to the baseline, while Superscript and Subscript shift the text either above or below the baseline.

✦ **Link entry:** This is used to link selected text as a hyperlink to another URL. To do this, first select a text block on Stage, and then enter the URL in this Link entry field.

Figure 7-4 shows several uses of the Character Panel, such as previewing and selecting fonts, and adjusting the font size. On the left, this composite image shows selected Block Text as the font is being changed from the _sans device font to Lithos Regular. Note that the font preview displays the selected text, rather than the font name, which is the default display when no text is selected. On the right, the point size is being adjusted by dragging the Font size slider. As the text resizes, the Block Text box, which has a constrained width, forces the text to break and stack vertically, leaving only the M visible on stage.

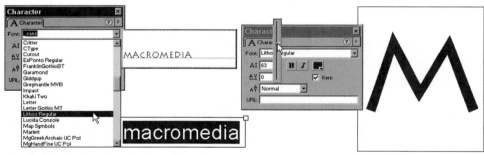

Figure 7-4: Using the Character Panel

Using the Style submenu

Some of the settings of the Character Panel are also available from the Style submenu that appears when you choose Text ➪ Style from the Menu Bar. These include:

✦ Plain — Ctrl(Command)+Shift+P

✦ Bold — Ctrl(Command)+Shift+B

✦ Italic — Ctrl(Command)+Shift+I

✦ Subscript

✦ Superscript

Using the Paragraph Panel

The Paragraph Panel, shown in Figure 7-5, can be directly invoked from the Window Menu with Window ➪ Panels ➪ Paragraph. If you use the default panels layout, you can click the Character Panel button on the Launcher Bar and then select the Para-graph tab to bring it forward in the panel stack. This Panel features alignment controls that can be used to align selected text. When entering new text, if you predetermine the alignment settings before text entry, subsequently entered text will be aligned accordingly.

Tip　　The keyboard shortcut for the Paragraph Panel is Ctrl/Command+Shift+T.

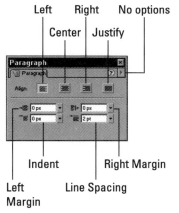

Figure 7-5: The Paragraph Panel is used to set, edit, and adjust the alignment of selected characters and paragraphs.

✦ **No Options:** There are no options for this panel. The options button here is vestigial.

✦ **Alignment Options:** The top area of the panel displays four buttons for the arrangement of text: Left, Center, Right, and Full Justification. When editing, alignment affects the currently selected paragraph(s) only. When entering text, use these options to predetermine the alignment before text entry, and all subsequent text will be aligned accordingly.

✦ **Right Margins:** Use this numeric entry field (or click the arrow button to invoke the interactive slider) to define the space between the text and the right border of the text box. By default, this space is described in pixels.

✦ **Line Spacing:** Use this numeric entry field or associated slider to adjust line spacing. By default, Line Spacing is described in points. Regardless of settings for individual fonts, the largest font on a line will always determine line spacing for that line.

✦ **Indentation:** Use this numeric entry field or associated slider to adjust the indent, also described by default in pixels, of the first line of a paragraph. The indent is relative to the left margin.

✦ **Left Margins:** Use this numeric entry field (or click the arrow button to invoke the interactive slider) to define the space between the text and the left border of the text box. By default, this space is described in pixels.

Figure 7-6 shows how selected text can be realigned, formatted, and edited for size, color, and other attributes. Here, the lower line of text is selected; it's point size reduced; and, as shown, its alignment set to Center.

Figure 7-6: Using the Character and Paragraph Panels to format selected text.

Note   The default units of measurement for both the Margin and Indentation entries of the Paragraph Properties dialog are determined by the Ruler Units for the movie. Ruler Units can be reset in the Movie Properties dialog, which is accessed from the Menu Bar with Modify ➪ Movie or from the keyboard by pressing Ctrl+M (Command+M).

Using the Alignment submenu

Some of the settings of the Paragraph Panel are also available from the Alignment submenu that appears when you choose Text ➪ Align from the Menu Bar:

✦ **Align Left:** Ctrl(Command)+Shift+L

✦ **Align Center:** Ctrl(Command)+Shift+C

✦ **Align Right:** Ctrl(Command)+Shift+R

✦ **Justify:** Ctrl(Command)+Shift+J

Using the Text Options Panel

The Text Options Panel can also be directly invoked from the Window menu with Window ➪ Panels ➪ Text Options. Or, if you use the default Panels layout, you can click the Character Panel button on the Launcher Bar and then select the tab to bring Text Options forward in the panel stack. This is the most varied of the text-related panels. Depending upon your choice of Text Behavior, it displays three option sets: Static, Dynamic, or Input Text.

Tip

There is no keyboard shortcut for the Text Options Panel, but you can make one with the new Flash 5 Keyboard Shortcuts dialog, Edit ➪ Keyboard Shortcuts.

As shown in Figure 7-7, when the Text Behavior is set to Static Text, the Text Options Panel has only two options (left). To choose another behavior, click the Text Behavior drop-down (right).

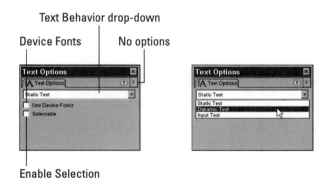

Text Behavior drop-down

Device Fonts   No options

Enable Selection

Figure 7-7: The Text Options Panel

Note

As with the other text-related panels, the options button is disabled on this panel.

Static (noneditable) text behavior

The default behavior for any text block created in (or pasted into) Flash is static. So, for display text and many of the more ordinary implementations of text in Flash, it's unnecessary to use the Text Options Panel. Nevertheless, you may encounter a situation that requires a text field to display information, but also enables users to select and copy the information. Or you might want to fine-tune the display quality of some text. That's when the Static Text Behavior of the Text Options Panel becomes indispensable:

✦ **Selectable:** Check this box to make selected text, or text that's entered subsequently, selectable when displayed on users' machines.

✦ **Use Device Fonts:** This little check box is the secret to a poorly documented, yet extremely powerful enhancement to the way in which Flash 5 handles text. *It is* not *a substitute for selecting one of the three_ device fonts that appear at the top of the Font Menu.* Rather, it's an innovative way in which Flash enables you to use many common fonts without embedding the characters. It also provides a mechanism that improves text display at small point sizes. For more details refer to the following sidebar.

As shown in the composite Figure 7-8, the chosen font is present on the system. The variations are the result of different settings in the Text Options Panel for Static Text. At the top, Use Device Fonts was unchecked. For the following two examples, Use Device Fonts was checked. However, in the middle example, Global Activation of the Type Manager was on, whereas for the bottom example, Global Activation of the Type Manager was off.

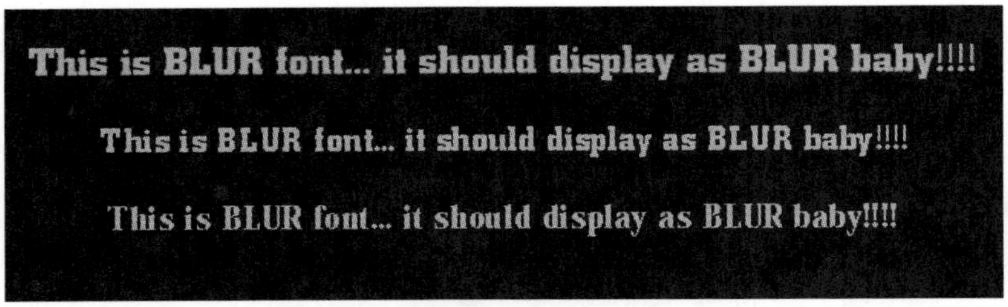

Figure 7-8: Using various Device Font settings

Editable Text fields

All Flash Text is created in text blocks or text boxes. Editable Text is no different except that Editable Text boxes are referred to as text fields, or Input Text boxes — that's probably because they are often used as empty fields in which users can input text, as with a form or a password entry. Think of an Editable Text field as an empty window with a variable — which is a name — attached to it. When text or data is sent to the Flash Movie, it is sent to the variable, which ensures that it will be displayed in the proper window. Flash 5 supports two kinds of editable text fields: Dynamic Text and Input Text. Both of these are introduced in the subsequent sections of this chapter.

Use Device Fonts

When Use Device Fonts is checked, the font is not embedded—only the Font Name, Font family/type (serif/sans serif/monospace), and other information are added to specify the font—which adds no more than 10 or 15 bytes to the .SWF file. This information is used so that the player on the user's system will know if it has the font or not. If the font is not present, it lets the system know whether the substitute font should be serif/sans serif.

Without Use Device Fonts checked, the font metrics for used characters are embedded, which results in a larger file size.

However, even if the user has the font installed, the same test file with Use Device Fonts checked and Use Device Fonts unchecked will not look the same:

✦ A font that is installed but has Use Device Fonts enabled renders better at smaller sizes. That's because there is no antialiasing or smoothing applied to any _device font (including _device fonts), regardless of its existence on your system.

✦ If the font is installed, but does *not* have Use Device Fonts enabled, then the characters from that font are embedded. This means that all text is smoothed (regardless of the fact that the font is available). Smoothed text can be illegible at small point sizes.

Finally, to accurately preview this Use Device Fonts setting on your machine, if you have a font manager (as most Web designers do), then you'll need to make sure you're careful about your font activation settings—make sure Global activation is turned off.

For best results with this specific Use Device Fonts option, we suggest that you limit your font selection to those that most of your audience is likely to have, or which will translate into one of the default _device fonts without disrupting the look of your design. Otherwise, for unusual fonts, we suggest that you either embed the characters (Device Font option unchecked) or, especially for headlines and display text, that you break the text apart.

Cross-Reference

Editable Text field's content is variable. Depending on how it is set up, the content of an Editable Text field can be selected, edited, or changed by the user, as in a password entry field or a form field. Some of the advanced applications of Editable Text fields are discussed in detail in Chapter 25, "Understanding HTML and Text Field Functions in Flash."

Dynamic Text fields

Dynamic Text fields are often fed data from a server. Common uses for this are stocks, sports scores, or weather updates. Creative uses might include a daily memo, frequently updated statements, an introduction, journal, or a randomly selected poem. This content can be supplied from a database, read from a server-side application, or be loaded from another movie or another part of the same movie. Figure 7-9 shows the Text Options Panel when Dynamic Text is chosen from the Text Behavior drop-down list.

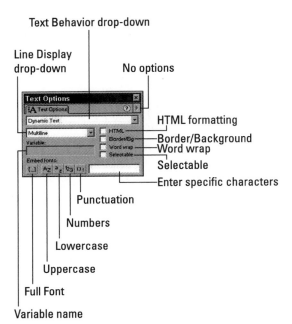

Text Behavior drop-down

Line Display
drop-down

No options

HTML formatting

Border/Background

Word wrap

Selectable

Enter specific characters

Punctuation

Numbers

Lowercase

Uppercase

Full Font

Variable name

Figure 7-9: Dynamic Text fields are used to display dynamically updating text, such as stocks, sports, or weather updates.

✦ **Line Display:** Use this drop-down to choose between a Single Line and a Multiline field.

✦ **HTML:** By enabling this check box, Flash preserves rich text styles when displaying Dynamic Text. This includes font, font style, hyperlink, paragraph, and other formatting consistent with permissible HTML tags. You can also enable HTML in Text Options so that the entry field will accept formatting that has been assigned to it in the Actions Panel. For more information on this, refer to Chapter 25, "Understanding HTML and Text Field Functions in Flash."

✦ **Border/Background:** Use this to draw the text field with a border and a background.

✦ **Word wrap:** With a Multiline text field, Word wrap will break lines at the end of the box.

✦ **Variable:** This is where you name the text field, so that your dynamic data will know where it is supposed to go.

✦ **Embed Fonts:** When embedding a font, Flash 5 gives you have control over how much of the font is actually embedded. Choose one or more character categories for the font — by clicking buttons for Full Font, Uppercase, Lowercase, Numbers, and/or Punctuation. Or, simply enter specific characters in the text field.

Permissible HTML tags

You can use the following HTML tags to control the display of Dynamic and Input Text:

`<A>`	`<P>`	`<FONT FACE>`
`<B>`	`<U>`	`<FONT SIZE>`
`<I>`	` `	`<FONT COLOR>`

Caution The `<B>` and `<I>` tags may cause text to disappear if you've included the font out-lines. Apparently this is because the bold and italic variations of fonts are handled as separate fonts by Flash. (Technically, they *are* separate!)

Input Text fields

When users fill out forms and answer Web surveys, or enter a password, they are using Input text fields. Figure 7-10 shows the Text Options Panel when you choose Input Text from the Text Behavior drop-down list.

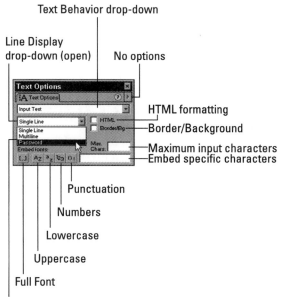

Figure 7-10: The Input Text Behavior has many of the same options as Dynamic Text. In addition to Single Line and Multiline, there is also an option to display the text as a Password.

Here are the options for Input Text fields:

✦ **Line Display:** In addition to Single Line and Multiline, there is also an option to display text as a Password.

✦ **HTML:** By enabling this check box, Flash preserves rich text styles when displaying Dynamic Text. This includes font, font style, hyperlink, paragraph, and other formatting consistent with permissible HTML tags. For specifics, see the explanation of Dynamic Text earlier in this chapter.

✦ **Border/Background:** Use this to draw the text field with a border and a background.

✦ **Maximum Input Characters:** Use this to limit the number of characters that a user can enter in this particular text field. Simply enter the maximum number of characters. This is most common when working with passwords.

✦ **Variable:** This is where you name the text field, so that your dynamic data will know where it is supposed to go.

✦ **Embed Fonts:** When embedding a font, Flash 5 gives you have control over how much of the font is actually embedded. Choose one or more character categories for the font — by clicking buttons for Full Font, Uppercase, Lowercase, Numbers, and/or Punctuation. Or, simply enter specific characters in the text field.

New Feature Flash 5 enables you to use a Font as a Shared Library item, which means that you can link to the font and use it without embedding the font. This is covered in depth in Chapter 20, "Sharing and Loading Assets."

Reshaping and Manipulating Text Characters

In addition to all of the powerful text-handling capabilities previously discussed, Flash also gives you the ability to reshape and distort standard text to suit your taste (or lack thereof). To manipulate text, the text must first be converted to its component lines and fills. Then it can be reshaped, erased, manipulated, and distorted. Converted text characters can be grouped or changed to symbols. These items can also be animated. However, after text characters have been converted to lines and fills, they can no longer be edited as text. Even if you regroup the text characters and/or convert the text into a symbol, you can no longer apply font, kerning, or paragraph options. For more information on reshaping, manipulating, and animating text, see Chapter 10, "Drawing in Flash," and Chapter 11, "Animating in Flash." But just to get you started, here are a few tips and guidelines for manipulating text in Flash:

✦ To convert text characters to component lines and fills: First, the text characters that you want to convert must be selected, or highlighted. Then choose Modify ➪ Break Apart from the Menu Bar. To undo, choose Edit ➪ Undo from the Menu Bar.

✦ Rotation and Break Apart can only be applied to outline fonts such as TrueType fonts.

✦ On Macs, PostScript fonts can only be broken apart if ATM (Adobe Type Manager) is installed.

✦ Bitmap fonts disappear from the screen if you attempt to break them apart.

✦ Test whether a font is a bitmapped font by choosing View ➪ Antialias from the Menu Bar. If the text still appears with ragged edges, it is a bitmapped font and will disappear when broken apart.

Summary

✦ Although minor issues may come up when working with text in Flash, it is relatively simple to work cross-platform and deliver high-quality textual presentations to users on both Macs and PCs with many varied configurations.

✦ The Text Tool is used to create and edit text. Flash's text-handling capabilities are robust and well implemented. There are many improvements to the text handling in Flash 5.

✦ The Text Tool delivers a broad range of control for generating, positioning, fine-tuning, and editing text.

✦ The most powerful controls for working with text are located in the Character, Paragraph, and Text Options Panels.

✦ Flash offers three kinds of text fields for use in interactive projects and for delivering dynamic textual content: Editable Text, Dynamic Text, and Input Text.

✦ Although textual characters and words are complex outlines, they can broken apart in Flash so that they can be reshaped, morphed, manipulated, and animated.

✦   ✦   ✦

Creating Flash Graphics

◆   ◆   ◆   ◆

◆   ◆   ◆   ◆

Now that you know how to navigate the Flash interface, you're ready to learn how to use Flash tools in combination with one another to quickly create artwork. Before you can begin work on art production, though, you'll need to know how to work with time in Flash movies. Chapter 8 discusses the Timeline window and its components: frames, keyframes, Onion Skins, and so on. In Chapter 9 you learn how to start organizing your Flash movie elements with the Library using symbols and symbol instances. Chapter 10 shows you how to create shapes and groups. The different types of animation that can be applied to shapes, groups, and images are discussed in Chapter 11. Chapter 12 introduces you to the process of importing external bitmap files to your Flash movies and optimizing bitmap settings for exported .SWF files. Finally, you begin your exploration of Flash interface design by creating a Flash movie with a button menu and discrete interactive sections.

Exploring the Timeline

The timeline is the backbone of Flash. A clear understanding of the timeline is critical to productive work in Flash. As you'll soon learn, one of the most powerful features of the timeline is that a quick glance at the timeline frames provides a lot of information about what is on those frames.

Viewing the Timeline

The timeline graphically orders Flash content across two dimensions: time and depth.

✦ **Time:** The sequence of frames is arranged horizontally, from left to right, as they appear in time. Thus, if your movie is set to 20 frames per second, frame 40 occurs at the 2-second point of your animation.

Note   Although they say that time and space are without limits, there are limits to nearly everything, including the number of frames (time) on any one Flash timeline. You get 16,000 frames—which will result in a timeline so unwieldy that it will extend into next Christmas. If that's not enough timeline for you, you should be working with scenes and movie clips.

✦ **Depth:** The timeline layers enable you to separate content on discrete layers. These layers are arranged vertically, from bottom to top. They also enable you to separate content from actions, comments, labels, and sounds. Any items placed on layers above will block out any items in layers beneath them, without otherwise affecting each other. In the editing environment, you can set layer visibility (the eye icon), editability (the lock icon), and the display mode—regular or just outlines (the square icon). Note, however, that these settings do not affect the final movie: All layer content, regardless of visibility or outline settings, is included in the final movie.

At this point, it's worth noting that Flash 5 occasioned several changes to the way the timeline works. These changes were designed to make frame spans more easily recognized and manipulated. (A frame span is the group of frames ranging from one keyframe to, but not including, the next.)

Because the frames between two keyframes do not add any new information to the movie, they really depend on the keyframes preceding them. Thus, in a logical sense, it's reasonable to be able to select them as a singular entity (the keyframe and all of the frames that depend on it), rather than individually. This group selection also makes moving frame spans easier — clicking a frame span turns the cursor into a hand and enables dragging.

Tip   Although some accomplished Flash artists say that they find the new Flash 5 timeline confusing, we recommend that you use the new timeline because it really is better. But, if you've tried and find that you are more comfortable with the Flash 4 timeline, you'll be happy to know that you may revert to some of the Flash 4 functionality. To revert to Flash 4 functionality, Choose Edit ⇨ Preferences ⇨ General, check the Flash 4 Selection Style and Flash 4 Frame Drawing check boxes, and then click OK.

Figure 8-1 shows the many features, options, and controls of the timeline.

As shown in Figure 8-1, the principal parts of the timeline are:

✦ **Title Bar:** This identifies the timeline if the timeline is not docked near the top of the screen.

✦ **Active Layer Toggle:** This is more of an icon, really. To make a layer active, either click the layer's name, or select a frame or group of frames. Then the pencil icon appears, indicating that the layer is now active — that's in addition to this more obvious clue: The Layer Bar of the active layer is black, whereas inactive Layer Bars are gray. Only one layer can be active at a time.

✦ **Show/Hide Layer Toggle:** This is a true toggle. Click the dot beneath the eye icon to hide the contents of this layer from view on the stage. When the layer is hidden, a red X appears over the dot. To return the layer to visibility, click the X.

Caution   Hidden layers export, and any content on stage within a hidden layer will become visible upon export. Even if the content is offstage and not visible, it may add considerably to the file size when a Flash movie is published, so you should save your .FLA and then purge these layers before your final export.

✦ **Lock/Unlock Layer Toggle:** This toggle locks or unlocks the layer to either prevent (or enable) further editing. As with Show/Hide, when the layer is locked, a red X appears over the dot.

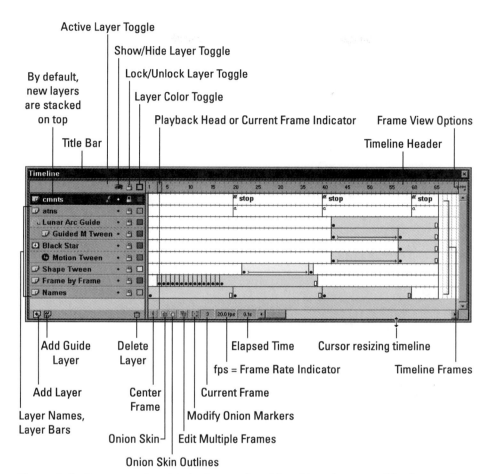

Figure 8-1: Because animation is the art of making things happen with pictures that change over time, the timeline might be considered the backbone of Flash. The timeline uses layers and frames to organize and control a movie's contents.

✦ **Layer Color Toggle:** This toggles the colored layer outlines on or off. When on, the dot changes into a small square outline of the same color as the outlines for the layer. When on, the items in the layer are displayed only as colored outlines, which can be useful for analyzing and finessing animated effects. The Layer Color can be changed with the Outline Color control of the Layer Properties dialog (shown in Figure 8-7), which is accessed by choosing Modify ➪ Layer.

✦ **Playhead or Current Frame Indicator:** The red rectangle with a line extending down through all layers is the Playhead. The Playhead indicates the current Frame. Drag it left or right along the timeline to move from one area of the timeline to another. Push it beyond the visible area to force-scroll the timeline. You can also drag the Playhead at a consistent rate for a preview of your animation; this is called "scrubbing the timeline."

✦ **Timeline Header:** The Timeline Header is the ruler that measures the time of the timeline — each tick is one frame.

✦ **Frame View options button:** This button, at the far right end of the timeline, accesses the Frame View options pop-up, which — as shown in Figures 8-8 and 8-9 — affords many options for the manner in which both the Timeline Header and the Frames are displayed.

✦ **Add Layer:** Simply click this button to add a new layer above the currently active layer. By default, layers are given numeric names. Double-click the Layer name in the Layer Bar to change the name.

✦ **Add Guide Layer:** Guide layers are used to move elements along a path. This button adds a Guide Layer directly above (and linked to) the currently active layer. To learn about using Guide Layers, refer to Chapter 11, "Animating in Flash."

✦ **Delete Layer:** This button deletes the currently active layer, regardless of whether it is locked. Of course, the final layer cannot be deleted.

✦ **Center Frame:** Click this button to shift the timeline so that the current frame is centered in the visible area of the timeline.

✦ **Onion Skin:** The Onion Skin feature enables you to see several frames of animation simultaneously. (Onion skinning is further described in the next section of this chapter.)

✦ **Onion Skin Outlines:** This enables you to see the outlines of several frames of animation simultaneously.

✦ **Edit Multiple Frames:** Normally, onion skinning only permits you to edit the current frame. Click this button to make each frame between the Onion Skin Markers editable.

✦ **Modify Onion Markers:** Click this button to evoke the Modify Onion Markers pop-up, as shown in Figure 8-15. In addition to manual adjustments, the options are used to control the behavior and range of onion skinning.

✦ **Current Frame:** This indicates the number of the current frame. It's most useful when working with small frame sizes, which, as shown in Figure 8-8, can be specified from the Frame View options.

✦ **Frame Rate Indicator:** This indicates the Frame Rate of the movie, measured in fps, or frames per second. Although the program default is 12 fps, usually 20 fps is a good starting point. The Frame Rate is specified in the Movie Properties dialog, which is accessed by choosing Modify ⇨ Movie (Ctrl/Command+M). You can also double-click the Frame Rate Indicator to invoke the Movie Properties dialog.

Note

The fps setting is not a constant or absolute — it means maximum frame rate. The actual frame rate is dependent upon a number of variables, including download speed, processor speed, and machine resources — these are variables over which you have no control. However, another factor, over which you do have control, is the intensity of the animation: Complex movement with multiple moving parts is more processor intensive than simple movement. It is *very* important that Frame Rate be established — with a little testing on various machines — early on in your development process.

✦ **Elapsed Time:** This indicates the total movie time, measured in fps, which would elapse from frame 1 to the current frame — provided that the movie is played back at the specified speed.

Manipulating the Timeline

The position, size, and shape of the timeline can be manipulated to better suit your workflow, much like any other Flash window or panel. On a dual monitor system, the timeline can be exiled to the second monitor, together with all the panels — leaving the stage clear and unencumbered for wild creativity.

✦ Move the timeline by dragging it by the Timeline Title Bar, which is the bar at the top that says timeline. If the timeline is docked, click anywhere in the gray area above the layer stack to undock the timeline and reposition it.

✦ If undocked, resize the timeline by dragging on the lower right corner (PC), or the size box (Mac), which is also in the right corner. If docked, drag the bar at the bottom of the timeline that separates the layers from the application window, either up or down.

✦ To resize the name and icon controls (either to accommodate longer names or to apportion more of the timeline to frames), click and drag the bar that separates the name and icon controls from the frames area.

Layer specifics

Knowing how to work with layers makes the Flash creation process flow much more smoothly.

By default, new layers are stacked on top of the currently active layer. To rearrange layers, click in the blank area (between the layer name and the layer toggle icons), and drag the Layer Bar to the desired position in the layer stack and release.

For enhanced functionality and control, as well as to enable reliable interactivity and ActionScripting, it's a good habit to give your layers meaningful names. Simply double-click the layer's name on the Layer Bar and enter a meaningful name.

Timeline specifics

The new Flash 5 timeline still offers you many clues about what's going on with your animation, as shown in Figures 8-2 and 8-3.

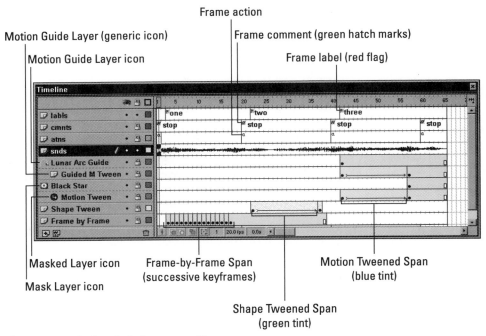

Figure 8-2: Flash 5 Style Layer specifics

✦ **Keyframe:** A keyframe is any frame in which the contents of the frame may differ from the contents of either the previous or subsequent frames. Solid circles designate keyframes with content.

✦ **Keyframe spans:** Keyframe spans — newly designated in Flash 5 — are the sections from one keyframe up to (but not including) the next keyframe, which are separated from each other by vertical lines. Thus, as shown, the span between frames 3 and 6 in the buttons layer is a keyframe span. Note that these spans can now be dragged intact, as a whole to a different location. This functionality is shown in the selected span between frames 8 and 13 in the buttons layer.

 • **Final keyframe:** The final frame of a keyframe span with content is marked with an empty rectangle (that is, frame 6 of the buttons layer), and a vertical line to the right of the rectangle.

Empty keyframes

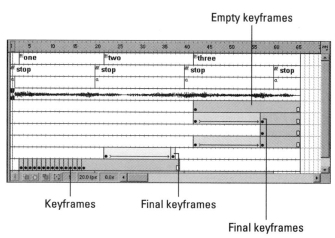

Keyframes   Final keyframes

Final keyframes

Figure 8-3: Here's the same timeline that was shown in Figure 8-2, except that it's cropped to show just the frames area of the timeline, with three varieties of keyframes called out.

- **Intermediate frame(s):** The intermediate frames of a nonempty keyframe span are gray.

- **Empty span(s):** Empty spans are white (for example, the visible portion of the sweep mc layer).

✦ **Frame-by-Frame Animation:** Frame-by-Frame Animation is animation composed entirely of keyframes. In a Frame-by-Frame Animation, the contents of each individual frame differs from both the previous and subsequent frames. For more information on Frame-by-Frame Animation, refer to Chapter 11, "Animating in Flash," and Chapter 37, "Creating Cartoon Animation with Flash."

✦ **Tweened Animation:** Tweened Animation is an animation where the movement or change is interpolated, or tweened, over a range of frames that extend between two keyframes. (For more information refer to Chapter 11, "Animating in Flash.") An arrow stretching across a colored keyframe span designates a Tween, of which there are two varieties:

- **Motion Tweens:** Motion Tweens are indicated by a blue tint.

- **Shape Tweens:** Shape Tweens are indicated by a green tint.

✦ **Motion Guide Layer:** A Motion Guide Layer is used to guide an animated item along a path, which can be drawn with either the Pencil or the Line Tool. For more about Motion Guide Layers, refer to Chapter 11, "Animating in Flash."

✦ **Mask Layer:** A Mask Layer is a layer that is used to selectively obscure the layers beneath it. For more about Mask Layers, refer to Chapter 10, "Drawing in Flash," and Chapter 11, "Animating in Flash."

✦ **Label:** Labels are used to give layers meaningful names, rather than using frame numbers. The advantage of this is that named layers can be moved without breaking ActionScript calls assigned to them. Upon export, Labels are included as part of the .SWF, so it makes sense to keep them short. Use the Frame Panel to add a Label to a selected frame. Press Enter/Return after typing a frame label or comment to ensure that the label takes.

✦ **Comment:** Comments are special Labels, preceded by a double-slash "//" — Comments do not export, so you can be verbose (within the confines of the timeline) without adding to the .SWF. Use the Frame Panel to add a Comment, which is merely a label preceded by "//," to a selected frame.

Tip

Jon begins nearly *every* Flash project with the creation of four labeled layers at the top of the layer stack of the new timeline. The consistency of his working methodology ensures clarity and simplicity when returning to edit old files or when sharing files with other contributors. These abbreviations are as follows (it's not important that you adopt *these* conventions, but it is important that you institute some conventional consistency to structure your work): lbls = labels, cmnts = comments, atns = actions, and snds = sounds.

✦ **Waveform:** This squiggly blue line in the snds layer is the waveform of a placed sound.

✦ **Frame Actions:** The small a's in frames 1, 20, 40, and 60 of the atns layer designate the presence of frame actions.

Caution

If you copy multiple frames extending down through multiple layers and paste them into another timeline, you'll usually lose your layer names.

General preferences

The General Tab of the Flash Preferences dialog, which is accessed from the Main Menu by choosing Edit ⇨ Preferences, has two sections specifically related to the timeline and its behavior in Flash 5. These are Timeline Options and Highlight Color. For more about the other aspects of the Flash Preferences dialog, refer to Chapter 2, "Exploring the Interface: Panels, Settings, Preferences, and More." Otherwise, you'll find that the relevant timeline behaviors are discussed in greater detail here.

Timeline options

The Disable Timeline Docking option prevents the timeline from attaching to the application window after it's been deployed as a floating panel.

On both the Mac and PC, to undock the timeline and deploy it as a floating palette as shown in Figure 8-4, click the gray area to the left of the eyeball icon and then, with the mouse still depressed, drag the palette away from the application window. To prevent the timeline from docking, press the Control key while dragging. To permanently disable timeline docking, use Edit ⇨ Preferences and, under Timeline Options, check the Disable Timeline Docking check box. As shown in Figure 8-4, the timeline can be dragged away from its docked position by clicking the Timeline Header and dragging the timeline away from the edge of the Flash application.

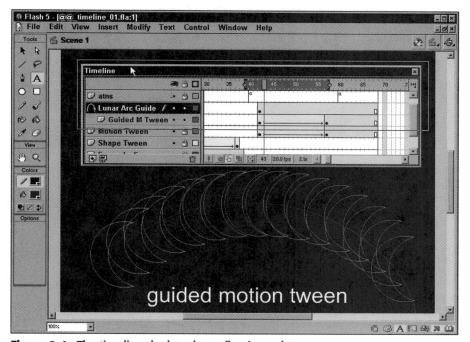

Figure 8-4: The timeline deployed as a floating palette

The next two options in the Preferences dialog let you revert to the Flash 4 timeline style:

- ✦ **Flash 4 Selection Style:** Flash 5 introduced a new methodology for selecting frames in the timeline. This option toggles that functionality back to Flash 4 Selection Style.

- ✦ **Flash 4 Frame Drawing:** Flash 5 also introduced a new methodology for drawing frames in the timeline. This option toggles that functionality back to the Flash 4 style.

Figures 8-5 and 8-6 show the difference between the timelines in Flash 5 and Flash 4.

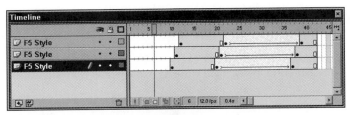

Figure 8-5: Flash 5 frame drawing

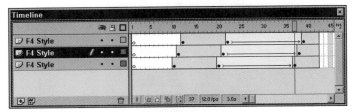

Figure 8-6: Flash 4 frame drawing

Highlight color

The Highlight Color options in the Preferences dialog control which colors are used for selected objects:

✦ **Highlight Color:** This preference controls the highlight color for selected groups, symbols, or text — excluding shapes.

✦ **Use this color:** Check this option to choose a Highlight Color for selections from the Swatches pop-up.

✦ **Use layer color:** Check this option to use the layer color as the Highlight Color for selections. This option enables you to distinguish selected items according to their associated layer color (which you set in the Layer Properties dialog).

Layer Properties

Layer Properties dialog is most readily accessed by Right/Ctrl+clicking any Layer Bar and then choosing Properties from the layer contextual menu. It can also be invoked by choosing Modify ➪ Layer.

The layers contextual menu

As shown in Figure 8-7, the layers contextual menu affords convenient access to a number of layer-specific operations, many of which are duplicated elsewhere.

✦ **Show All:** Shows all layers. If some layers have had their visibility turned off, this makes them all visible.

✦ **Lock Others:** Unlocks the active layer and locks all other layers.

✦ **Hide Others:** Makes the currently active layer visible, if it is not visible, and hides all others.

✦ **Insert Layer:** Inserts a new layer above the currently active layer.

✦ **Delete Layer:** Deletes the active layer.

✦ **Properties:** Invokes the Layer Properties dialog for the currently active layer.

✦ **Guide:** Transforms the current layer into a Guide Layer.

 Note

A Guide Layer differs from a Motion Guide Layer. A Motion Guide Layer is linked to a Guided Layer, which usually has a Motion Tweened animated item that follows a path that is drawn on the Guided Layer. A Guide Layer is independent. A Guide Layer is most often used for placing a bitmap design composition, or other items that should not export with the project. Neither a Guide Layer nor a Motion Guide Layer export with the project.

✦ **Add Motion Guide:** Inserts a new Motion Guide Layer directly above the current layer and automatically links the current layer to the Guided Layer.

✦ **Mask:** Transforms the current layer into a Mask Layer.

✦ **Show Masking:** Use this command on either the Mask or the Masked Layer to activate the masking effect — essentially, this command locks both layers simultaneously, which enables the masking effect.

The Layer Properties dialog

The Layer Properties dialog is used to control and edit the properties of the active layer and to facilitate routine layer operations.

✦ **Name:** Use this option to change the name of the layer.

✦ **Show:** With this option checked, the layer is visible; otherwise, it's hidden.

✦ **Lock:** This option enables you to lock or unlock the layer.

✦ **Type:** These options are used to set the type of layer:

• **Normal:** This is the default, used for drawing and animation.

• **Guide:** Guide Layers have two purposes. They can be used either as Motion Guides or as drawing guides. Guide Layers aren't exported, so they aren't visible and they don't add to the exported file size. Guided Layers are linked to a Guide Layer.

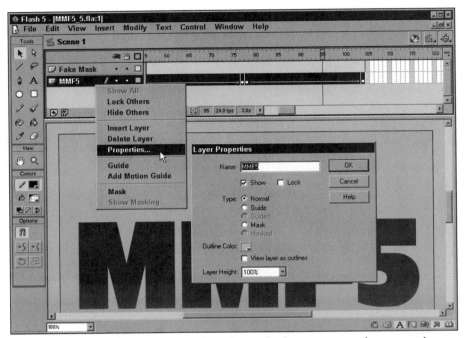

Figure 8-7: This composite screen shot shows the layer contextual menu and ensuing Layer Properties dialog.

Tip   An empty Guide Layer can be used to organize multiple layers of related content for better timeline organization. It can also be used as a repository for custom strokes and fills.

   - **Mask:** A Mask Layer is used in conjunction with a Masked Layer to create special effects. The Masked Layer is hidden except beneath filled areas of the Mask Layer that it's linked to.

✦ **Outline Color:** Use this to choose the color of the layer's outlines.

✦ **View layer as outlines:** When this is checked, all items on the layer appear as outlines, according to the color chosen in the previous option. Viewing as outlines speeds the display while editing because all items are shown as thin outlines. As discussed in the previous section regarding General Preferences, this option can be used in conjunction with the Highlight Color options of the General tab of Edit ➪ Preferences, to either give each layer a unique color, or to employ a global color for all outlines.

✦ **Layer Height:** Use this to increase the height of the *individual* layer. This means that you can have most layers displayed tiny, and yet have others display with more visible content. This is useful if you use the Preview or Preview in Context Timeline options on the Frame View options pop-up. It's also useful when viewing the waveforms of sound files.

Frame View options

As shown in Figure 8-8, the Frame View options pop-up is used to customize the size, color, and style of frames displayed within the timeline. These features can prove very helpful when you are working with cartoon animation, and want to see each frame previewed. Or, if you are working on an extremely long project with a huge timeline, it can be helpful to tweak the size of the individual frames, so that you can see more of the timeline at a single glance.

Figure 8-8: The Frame View options pop-up is used to customize the size, color, and style of frames displayed within the timeline.

When used in conjunction with the Layer Height option of the Layer Properties dialog, you can customize your timeline in myriad ways to better suit your particular project. Your options include:

✦ **Tiny, Small, Normal, Medium, Large:** These options afford a range of sizes for the width of individual frames. When working on extremely long animations, narrower frames facilitate some operations.

✦ **Short:** This option makes the frames shorter in height, permitting more Layer Bars to be visible in the same amount of space. When working with many layers, short layers help squelch the tedium of scrolling through layers of layers.

✦ **Tinted Frames:** This option toggles tinted frames on or off. With Tinted Frames on, the tints are as follows:

• **White:** Empty or unused frames (for any layer). This is the default. The white color of empty or unused frames is unaffected regardless of whether Tinted Frames is on or off.

• **Gray:** There are two kinds of gray frames: (a) The grayed-out gray frames in the default (empty) timeline are a quick visual reference that indicates every fifth frame, like the tick marks on a ruler. These tick frames appear regardless of whether Tinted Frames are enabled. (b) The solid gray color, which appears when Tinted Frames are enabled, indicates that a frame is either filled or otherwise used. Frame usage means that the frame has something in it, which may be either visible or invisible as, for example, an item with an alpha of 0 percent, or a hidden symbol.

• **Blue:** Indicates a Motion Tween span.

• **Green:** Indicates a Shape Tween span.

Note Regardless of whether Tinted Frames is enabled, Flash displays tween arrows (and keyframe dots) to a tween. However, with Tinted Frames disabled, tweened spans are indicted by a faintly checked gray pattern, and the arrows display in color to the indicate the type of tween:

> • **A red arrow:** Indicates a Motion Tween span, when Tinted Frames are off.
>
> • **A green arrow:** Indicates a Shape Tween span, when Tinted Frames are off.

✦ **Preview:** As shown at the top of Figure 8-9, the preview option displays tiny thumbnails that maximize the element in each frame. Thus, the scale of elements is not consistent from frame to frame. (Frame 1 of the animation is shown in Figure 8-9.) In this Frame-by-frame animation, the phases of the moon increase over a span of 15 frames.

✦ **Preview in Context:** As shown at the bottom of Figure 8-9, when previewed in context, the same animation is seen with accurate scale from frame to frame (because elements are not maximized for each frame).

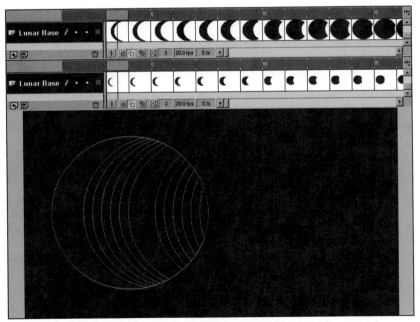

Figure 8-9: In this composite screen shot, the Frames are shown with Preview option (top) and Frames shown with Preview in Context option (middle) for the same animation (bottom).

Scene and Symbol Bar

Nested between the Menu Bar and the top of the timeline is the Scene and Symbol Bar shown in Figure 8-10. This bar is also shown in context in Figure 8-1 and elsewhere in this chapter. The Scene Name button, at the far left, indicates the name of the current scene. When in Symbol Editing Mode, click this button to return to the current scene. To the right is the Edit Scene button, and at the far right is the Edit Symbols button. Click either button to evoke a menu of scenes or symbols that are editable within the current movie.

For more about Symbols, and the Symbol Editing Mode in particular, refer to Chapter 9, "Checking Out the Library: Symbols and Instances."

Figure 8-10: The Scene and Symbol Bar

Scenes are used to organize a Flash project into logical, manageable parts. By default, on export Flash plays back all of the scenes within the movie in the order in which they are listed in the Scene Panel.

Since Flash 4, with the increasingly robust power of ActionScript, there's been a trend among many advanced developers to move away from Scene-based architectures. Although this may require a shift in thinking, it has been shown to result in files that download more efficiently and that are easier to edit due to their modular organization. It's like the difference between one huge ball of all-purpose twine that's the size of a house, and a large drawer filled with manageable spools — sorted neatly according to color and weight. The primary area in which this shift doesn't apply is among more traditional cartoon animators, such as Richard Bazely or Bill Turner, whose work is exampled in Chapter 37, "Creating Cartoon Animation with Flash."

To navigate to other scenes from within the Movie Editor:

✦ Click the Edit Scene button at the far right of the Scene and Symbol Bar, and then click the desired scene.

✦ Navigate to a specific scene from the View Menu with the View ➪ Go To command.

Use the Scene Panel, shown in Figure 8-11, to manage your scenes. The Scene Panel may be accessed with either of these commands: Modify ➪ Scene or Window ➪ Panels ➪ Scene.

Figure 8-11: The Scene Panel

When your movie is published to .SWF, the scenes play in the order in which they are listed in either the Scene Panel or the Scene pop-up.

✦ To delete a scene, either use the Scene Panel's delete button or, from the Insert menu, use the Insert ⇨ Remove Scene command.

✦ To add a scene, either use the Scene Panel's add button or, from the Insert menu, use Insert ⇨ Scene.

✦ Use the duplicate button on the Scene Panel to duplicate a scene.

✦ To rename a scene, simply double-click the scene name and type the new name.

✦ To rearrange scene order, simply click and drag a scene to alter its position with in the Scene Panel. You can use actions to force the movie to access scenes outside the default linear order. For more about actions, refer to Part IV, "Adding Basic Interactivity to Flash Movies."

Caution There are several limitations to the use of scenes in more advanced, ActionScript environments. For example, you can't issue a command from within a Movie Clip to go to and play a frame in another scene.

The Timeline/Stage Relationship

So far in this chapter, we have focused on the features of the timeline and we have shown how the timeline offers detailed control of Flash functionality, especially as regards its ordering of time from left to right. Now we are going to look at the manner in which timeline relates to the depth of a Flash movie, or the arrangement of items from the front to the back of the Stage.

Stacking order

Within a single layer, Flash stacks like items in the order in which they are placed or created, with the most recent item on top, subject to the *kind* of item. The rules that control the stacking order of various kinds of items are simple:

✦ Within a layer, ungrouped, drawn lines and shapes are always at the *bottom* level, with the most recently drawn shape or line at the top of that layer's stack. Furthermore, unless you take precautions, drawn items either compound with, or cut into, the drawing beneath them.

✦ Groups and symbols (including bitmaps) stack above lines and shapes in the *overlay* level. To change the stacking order of several drawings, it's often advisable to group them first, as described in the next section of this chapter.

To change the stacking order within a layer, first select the item that you want to move. Then, do one of the following:

✦ Select Modify ➪ Arrange ➪ Bring to Front or Send to Back to move the item to the top or bottom of the stacking order.

✦ Select Modify ➪ Arrange ➪ Move Ahead or Move Behind to move the item ahead or back one position in the stacking order.

Remember the stacking order rules: You won't be able to bring an ungrouped drawing above a group or symbol — if you need that drawing on top, group it and then move it.

Layers are another factor in the stacking order. To stack an item in a lower layer above an item in a higher layer you simply change the order of the layer among the other layers: First activate the layer, and then drag the Layer Bar to the desired position in the layer stack of the timeline.

Tip

Although having a million layers in your Flash movie might be hard to manage and will, most likely, result in a huge and unwieldy .FLA that requires massive RAM, neither the file size nor the performance of the final .SWF will be adversely impacted because Flash flattens movies upon export to .SWF.

Grouping

Grouping drawings makes them easier to handle. Rather than manipulating a single drawing, group several drawings to work with them as a single item. Grouping also prevents shapes from being altered by other shapes. Furthermore, the stacking of groups is more easily controlled than ungrouped drawings. Here's how to create groups:

1. Use Shift+click to select everything that you want to group — any combination of items: shapes, lines, and symbols — even other groups.

2. Select Modify ➪ Group (Ctrl+G or Command+G). The selected elements are now grouped.

3. To ungroup everything, select the group then use Modify ➪ Ungroup (Ctrl+Shift+G or Command+Shift+G).

Caution

Be careful when ungrouping — your newly ungrouped drawings may alter or eliminate drawings below in the same layer.

Editing groups

To edit a group:

1. Either select the group and then choose Edit ⇨ Edit Selected, or double-click the group.

2. Everything on stage — except for the parts of the group — is dimmed, indicating that only the group is editable.

3. Make the changes in the same way you would edit any items.

4. To stop editing the group, choose Edit ⇨ Edit All (or double-click an empty part of the stage). Items on stage return to normal color.

Editing on the Timeline

After you create your artwork and animations, you may find that you need to edit it. Flash has features that make such edits quick and easy. You can move frames and keyframes, copy and paste frames and keyframes, insert frames and keyframes, delete frames and keyframes, change the sequence of an animation, and edit the contents of a keyframe. You can also use onion skinning to view frames at one time, and you can even edit multiple frames at once.

✦ **Selecting Frames:** The methods for selecting single frames and spans of frames differ slightly. For users of previous versions of Flash, this may take a little getting used to. Overall, however, we find the new methodology is an improvement. Of course, if you aren't happy with the Flash 5 timeline, you can use Edit ⇨ Preferences ⇨ General, to make your timeline behave more like the familiar Flash 4 timeline (as explained earlier in this chapter).

If you're comfortable with Flash 4, you need to know this: Selecting multiple frames and then hitting F6 to generate multiple keyframes no longer works. Instead, select your multiple frames and then use this command, Modify ⇨ Frames ⇨ Convert to Keyframes. If you still want F6 to generate multiple keyframes, then make a custom Keyboard Shortcut with Edit ⇨ Keyboard Shortcuts. (For more on Edit ⇨ Keyboard Shortcuts, refer to Chapter 2, "Exploring the Interface: Panels, Settings, and More.")

• **Frame Spans:** To select a span of frames extending between two keyframes, click anywhere between the keyframes. The cursor will switch to a hand and the entire span will be selected.

• **Single Frames within a Span:** To select a single frame within a span, press the Ctrl/Command key and click a frame. Keyframes at either end of a span can usually be selected with a simple click.

• **Single Frames not within a Span:** To select a single frame that is not implicated with a span, simply click to select it.

✦ **Moving Frames:** Select the frame(s) that need to be moved, and drag them to the new location.

✦ **Extending the Duration of a Span:** To extend the duration of a span, which is the same result as extending a keyframe, select the keyframe and then drag the keyframe to the position where you want the span to end.

✦ **Copying Frames:** Select the frame(s) that you want to copy. Either Choose Edit ➪ Copy Frames from the menu, or press the Alt/Option key and drag to copy the selected frames to another location in the timeline.

Note

You can select a range of frames that you want to copy and drop them anywhere in the timeline — even if there are no frames in the destination area. Any gaps that might result in the timeline will be automatically filled with static frames. In addition, you can Alt/Option+Drag from one layer to another, or even select frames from multiple layers and drag and drop to multiple layers — provided the destination layers exist prior to the operation!

✦ **Pasting Frames:** Select the frame(s) that you want to paste the copied frame(s) into, and select Edit ➪ Paste Frames from the menu.

✦ **Inserting Frames:** Select the point at which you would like to insert a new frame, and select Insert ➪ Frame (F5) from the menu.

✦ **Inserting Keyframes:** Select the point at which you would like to insert a new keyframe, and select Insert ➪ Keyframe (F6) from the menu. Or, you can Right+Click/Ctrl+Click the frame that you want to make a keyframe and then, in the contextual menu, select Insert Keyframe.

✦ **Inserting Blank Keyframes:** Select the point at which you would like to insert a new blank keyframe, and select Insert ➪ Blank Keyframe (F7) from the menu. Or, you can Right+Click/Ctrl+Click the frame that you want to make a keyframe and then, in the contextual menu, select Insert Blank Keyframe.

Note

If you already have content in the current layer and you insert a keyframe, a new keyframe will be created that duplicates the content of the keyframe immediately prior. But if you insert a blank keyframe, the static content of the prior keyframe will cease and the blank keyframe will, as its name implies, be void of content. For a hands-on example, refer to the keyframes folder within the ch8 folder of the CD-ROM.

Figure 8-12 shows a timeline that illustrates some editing points. The top layer shows the original layer, which has content in the first frame, followed by 19 empty frames. This layer was copied into all three lower layers, with the result that the initial content of all four layers was the same. When a keyframe was inserted at Frame 10 of the Keyframe layer, the content of keyframe 1 was copied into the new keyframe, and the gray color of the subsequent frames indicates the continuity of static content. But, when a blank keyframe was inserted at frame 10 of the Blank Keyframe layer, a blank keyframe was inserted and the continuity of content was stopped, as indicated by the white frames extending from frame 10 to frame 20. The dotted line running through the frames of the bottom layer shows what happens when a tween is missing the final keyframe, which often happens when editing on the timeline.

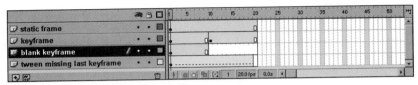

Figure 8-12: Editing on the timeline

✦ **Adding Content from the Library:** To add content from the Library to a selected keyframe, drag an instance of the item from the Library and onto the Stage.

✦ **Deleting Frames (Remove Frames):** Select the frame(s) that you want to delete, and then select Insert ⇨ Remove Frames (Shift+F5), or else Right/ Ctrl+click the frame and select Remove Frames from the contextual menu. This no longer works for deleting keyframes; instead, it will remove an intervening frame and scoot the keyframe backward toward frame 1.

✦ **Clearing a Keyframe:** To obliterate a keyframe and its contents, use Clear Keyframe. Select the keyframe and use Insert ⇨ Clear Keyframe (Shift+F6), or use the contextual menu, Right/Ctrl+click, and choose Clear Keyframe. When deleting a keyframe, the deleted keyframe and all of the frames following, up to the next keyframe, are replaced with the static contents of the previous keyframe.

✦ **Reversing Animation:** Select the animation sequence that you would like to reverse, and select Modify ⇨ Frames ⇨ Reverse from the menu. For this to work, you must have keyframes at both the beginning and the end of the selected sequence.

✦ **Editing the Contents of a Keyframe:** Select the keyframe that you want to edit. Then, on the Stage, edit the contents of the keyframe.

Caution

There are several issues regarding single-frame movies, which are movies whose architecture has shifted all content off of the Main Timeline and, via Movie Clips, has planted that content in a single frame on the Main Timeline: (a) Netscape can have a problem loading these movies properly. (b) Because ActionScripts on frames are evoked before the frame itself is drawn, the player can have problems if it has not finished loading all the necessary components before it starts to run the script. The fix for both issues is to delay contents and scripts by placing them at the second frame of the Main Timeline.

Onion Skinning

Onion skinning enables you to view multiple frames at once. When any of the three Onion Skin buttons is clicked, Onion Skin Markers appear on the timeline, centered over the current frame. These markers indicate the range of frames that will be displayed with onion skinning applied. To reposition either of these markers manually, click and drag it to another location on the timeline. Or, you can use the Modify Onion Markers pop-up to manage the manner in which onion skinning displays. By default, the current frame is displayed in full color, while the remaining frames are dimmed out. As shown in Figure 8-13, they appear as if they were each drawn on a sheet of onion skin paper and then stacked in order. (Note how the frames are dimmed with increasing opacity as they move farther away from the current time marker. This is an important visual clue that works both in filled and outline modes.) Only the selected frame can be edited, but this feature is useful because it enables you to see how your edits will affect the flow of the entire selected animation. It's also useful for Frame-by-Frame Animation, because you can see each part of the animation without having to switch back and forth.

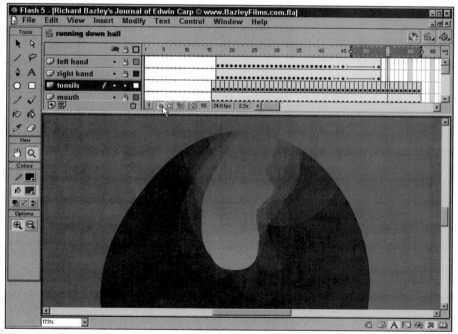

Figure 8-13: With onion skinning turned on, the current frame is shown normally, while the surrounding frames are successively dimmed. The Onion Skin Markers are visible here on the Timeline Header, which surrounds the Playhead.

For examples of the implementation of the onion skinning feature, refer to the "Animating Figures with MetaCreations Poser" section of Chapter 33, "Working with 3D Graphics," and also Chapter 37, "Creating Cartoon Animation with Flash."

Figure 8-14 shows how you can view the Onion Skin as Outlines, which is useful for complex animations. (If you have trouble seeing the outlines, remember that the color of the outlines can be changed with the Layer Properties dialog.)

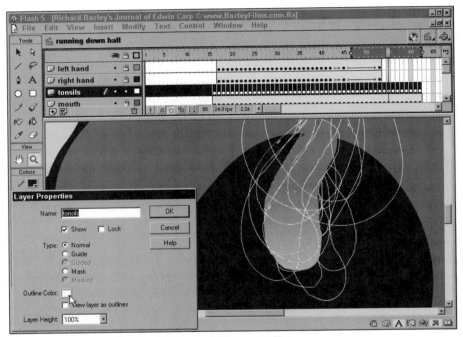

Figure 8-14: You can view the Onion Skin as Outlines.

To set up onion skinning, you first turn onion skinning on, and then adjust the features to suit you, following these steps:

1. Click the Onion Skin button.

2. Move the Start Onion Skin and End Onion Skin markers to contain the frames that you want to view simultaneously.

3. If you'd like to view the Onion Skin as outlines, as shown in Figure 8-14, click the Onion Skin Outlines button.

4. To edit frames between Onion Skin markers, click the Edit Multiple Frames button.

Caution

It has been reported that everything moves, except whatever's on the last frame, if you choose to Edit Multiple Frames, and then set the Start and End Onion Skin Markers to encompass the whole timeline, and then select all and try to nudge everything with the arrow keys. So, we suggest that you first save a copy of your working file. Then, before proceeding after such an adjustment, confirm that this was *not* a problem.

5. Change the display of the Onion Skin Markers by clicking the Modify Onion Markers button. Choose one of the following from the menu:

- **Always Show Markers:** Check this option to always show the Onion Skin Markers, regardless of whether onion skinning is on or not.

- **Anchor Onion:** Usually, the Onion Skin Markers follow the position of the current frame. Check this option to anchor the Onion Skin Markers at their current position on the timeline, thus preventing the Onion Skinning effect to move in relation to the position of the current frame pointer.

- **Onion 2, Onion 5, and Onion all:** These options apply the onion skinning effect as follows: (2) to two frames on either side of the current frame, (5) to five frames on either side of the current frame, or (All) to All frames.

Note

When you enable onion skinning and drag the Onion Markers to display a specific range of frames, the range will migrate in unison with the Playhead. This way, you can always see the same span of frames relative to the current frame, while you are working. If this annoys you, you can click the Anchor Onion Markers to lock the markers at their current position.

In Figure 8-15, the Onion 5 option was clicked. If you compare this figure to the previous figure, you'll note that the range of the Onion Markers has changed accordingly.

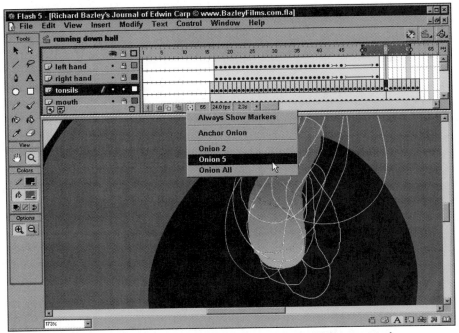

Figure 8-15: In addition to manual adjustments, the Modify Onion Markers pop-up offers several other options for managing Onion Markers.

Summary

✦ The timeline is the backbone of Flash. A clear understanding of both the logic and the many features of the Flash timeline is essential to competency with Flash.

✦ The timeline organizes Flash content with regards to both time and depth.

✦ On the timeline, time is incremented from left to right, while depth is organized in the stacking order of layers, as well as the order of content within each individual layer.

✦ Animations are organized and controlled by using various kinds of frames on the timeline. The characteristics of these frames can be edited, and the frames themselves can be moved, copied, and adjusted on the timeline.

✦ There are three kinds of animation possible in Flash: Frame-by-Frame, Shape Tweened, and Motion Tweened Animation.

✦ The content of the individual frames can be created, edited, manipulated, and otherwise orchestrated on the Stage.

✦ Onion skinning is useful for the manipulation of the content of frames in the context of surrounding frames.

✦   ✦   ✦

Checking Out the Library: Symbols and Instances

Symbols are the key to both the file-size efficiency and the interactive power in Flash. A *symbol* is a reusable element that resides in the current movie's Library, which is accessed with Window ⇨ Library. Each time you place a symbol on the stage or inside of another symbol, you're working with an *instance* of that symbol. Unlike using individual graphic elements, you can use many instances of a given symbol, with little or no addition to the file size.

Using symbols helps reduce the file size of your finished movie because Flash only needs to save the symbol once. Each time that symbol is used in the movie, Flash refers to this original profile. Then, to support the variations of an instance, Flash only needs to save information about the differences — such as size, position, proportions, and color effects. If a separate graphic were used for each change, Flash would have to store a complete profile of all the information about that graphic — not only the size and color, but also what the graphic looks like.

Furthermore, symbols can save you a lot of time and trouble, particularly when it comes to editing your movie. That's because changes made to a symbol are reflected in each instance of that symbol throughout the movie. Let's say that your logo changes halfway through production. Without symbols, it might take hours to find and change each copy of the logo. However, if you've used symbol instances, you need only edit the original symbol — the instances are automatically updated throughout the movie.

With the advent of the increasingly robust Flash ActionScript language, symbols can be considered as objects within an object-oriented authoring environment.

In this chapter, you learn to create and edit symbols. You also learn to use symbols, both within the movie and within other symbols, and to modify each instance of a symbol. Flash stores symbols, as well as imported sounds, bitmaps, and QuickTime movies, in the Library. Understanding how to use the Library is crucial to working with symbols — so to start, let's take a tour of the Library itself.

The Library and Its Features

The Library is the repository of all recurring elements, known as symbols, that are placed as Instances within a Flash movie. Imported sounds and bitmaps are automatically placed in the Library. Upon creation, both Buttons and Movie Clips are also stored in the Library. It's a smart practice to make nearly *every* item within a Flash movie a symbol, and to develop every item within a Flash movie from component symbols.

The Library is also a true window, not a panel. As shown in Figure 9-1, the Library Window (left) — Window ➪ Library — is not the same as the six default asset Libraries (right) that are accessed from the Menu at Window ➪ Common Libraries. However, they are related. When you choose Window ➪ Library, you open a Library specific to the current movie, while Common Libraries are available whenever Flash is open.

Choose Window ➪ Common Libraries to open the submenu of Common Libraries that ship with Flash. The Libraries menu is the one menu over which the user has real control. That's because — in addition to the Library items that are placed there in the process of a default installation of Flash — you can place your own items there, too. The default Libraries contain a selection of buttons and symbols to get you started. These are located in the Libraries folder of the Flash application folder. (And when you're tired of them, you can remove them!) To add your own buttons, symbols, or libraries for specific projects, first save them in a Flash file with a descriptive name, and then place that Flash file in the Libraries folder within the Flash Program folder on your hard drive. Because these default Common Libraries have such obvious names, we won't waste valuable pages to describe them here. They are Buttons, Graphics, Learning Interactions, Movie Clips, Smart Clips, and Sounds.

New Feature

In previous versions of Flash, when working with more than one .FLA movie open at a time, it was easy enough to get confused and start working in the wrong Library. This is no longer possible. Although it's still possible to drag items from the Library of a movie that does not have focus, in Flash 5 that Library is grayed out, indicating that it is not associated with the current movie. Furthermore, double-clicking a symbol within that Library will not transport you to the associated movie.

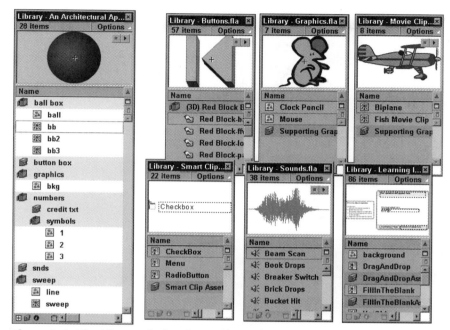

Figure 9-1: The Library window is specific to the current movie, while the other windows, known as the Common Libraries, are available whenever Flash is open.

Working with the Library

Every Flash movie has its own Library, which is used to store and organize symbols, sounds, bitmaps, and other assets such as video files. As shown in Figure 9-2, the item highlighted—or selected—in the *Sort Window* is previewed in the *Preview Window*.

If the item selected in the Library is an animation or sound file, you'll see a controller in the upper-right corner of the Preview window. This Preview Stop/Play controller pops up to facilitate previewing these items. It's almost equivalent to the Play option that's found in the *Options* menu. The Options menu is accessed by clicking the Options triangle, which is located at the upper right of the Library window. As shown in Figure 9-3, the Library options pop-up menu lists a number of features, functions, and controls for organizing and working with items in the Library.

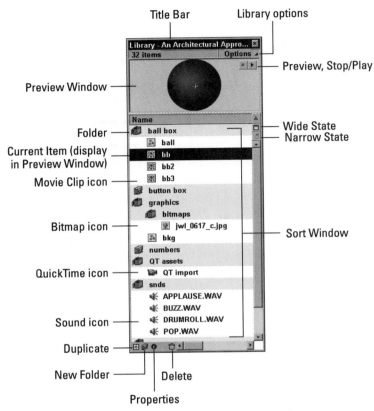

Title Bar   Library options

Preview, Stop/Play

Preview Window

Folder

Current Item (display in Preview Window)

Movie Clip icon

Bitmap icon

QuickTime icon

Sound icon

Duplicate

New Folder   Delete

Properties

Wide State
Narrow State

Sort Window

Figure 9-2: The Library window as viewed in Normal state.

✦ **New Symbol:** Choose this item from the Options menu to create a new symbol. When a new symbol is created, it is stored at the root of the Library Sort window. To create a new symbol in a folder, select the desired folder first—the new symbol will be placed in the selected folder.

✦ **New Folder:** Items in the Library can be organized in folders. The New Folder button simply creates a new folder within the Sort window.

✦ **New Font:** Use this option to invoke the Font Symbol Properties dialog, which is the first step in creating a Font Symbol for use within a Shared Library. For more information about Shared Libraries and Font symbols, refer to the end of this chapter, as well as to Chapter 20, "Sharing and Loading Assets."

✦ **Rename:** Use the Rename option to rename an item.

✦ **Move to New Folder:** Use the Move to New Folder to open the New Folder dialog.

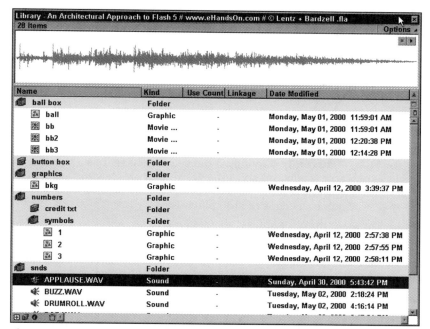

Figure 9-3: Library window and the Options pop-up menu

Note   Library items can also be moved between folders by dragging.

✦ **Duplicate, Delete:** Click Duplicate to duplicate an item and Delete to delete an item.

✦ **Edit:** Click Edit to access the selected symbol in Symbol Editing Mode.

Tip   Double-clicking a symbol on stage takes you to Edit in Place Mode, which is variant of Symbol Editing Mode.

✦ **Edit With:** Provided that you have appropriate external applications installed, most imported assets (such as sounds, bitmaps, and vectors) will have this command available to jump to the external editing environment.

✦ **Properties:** Click to invoke the related Properties dialog for the particular symbol type—Sound Properties, Bitmap Properties, Symbol Properties, or (for QuickTime) Video Properties.

✦ **Linkage:** Use this command to invoke the Linkage Options menu. Linkage means that you can assign an identifier string to a Font symbol or to a sound so that it can be accessed as an object with ActionScript. This is an aspect of Shared Libraries. For more information about Shared Libraries and Linkage, refer to the end of this chapter, as well as to Chapter 20, "Sharing and Loading Assets."

✦ **Define Clip Parameters:** With Flash 5, you can now assign clip parameters to a movie clip to create a Smart Clip. This control invokes the Define Clip Parameters dialog, which is used to assign variables with values to movie clips. Smart Clips are discussed in Chapter 25, "Understanding HTML and Text Field Functions in Flash."

✦ **Select Unused Items:** Select Unused Items to find unused items within the Library.

✦ **Update:** Use this option if you've edited items subsequent to importing them into Flash. Items will be updated without the bother of reimporting.

✦ **Play (or Stop, if currently playing):** If the selected asset has a timeline or is otherwise playable (such as a sound), click this to preview the asset in the Library Preview window. If the asset is currently playing, this option is updated to Stop — in which case, click to stop playing.

✦ **Expand Folder/Collapse Folder:** Use this command to toggle the currently selected folder open or closed.

✦ **Expand All Folders/Collapse All Folders:** Use this command to toggle all folders open or closed.

✦ **Shared Library Properties:** Use this command to invoke the Shared Properties dialog, which is another aspect of Shared Libraries. For more information about Shared Libraries, refer to the end of this chapter, as well as to Chapter 20, "Sharing and Loading Assets."

✦ **Keep Use Counts Updated:** Use this command to tell Flash to continuously keep track of the usage of each symbol. If you are working with multiple, complex graphics and symbols, this feature generally slows things to a crawl.

✦ **Update Use Counts Now:** Use this option to tell Flash to update the usage of each symbol. This command is a one-time check, and is probably less of a drain on system resources than the previous command, which checks continuously.

As shown in Figure 9-4, the Library can also be expanded. Expand the Library by clicking the Wide State button. When displayed in this manner, all of the column headings are visible in the Sort Window. Click any heading to sort the window by Name, Kind, Usage Count, or Date.

Selecting New Symbol, Duplicate, or Properties from the Options Menu launches the Symbol Properties dialog, shown in Figure 9-5. Use this dialog to give the symbol a unique name and assign it a behavior (as a symbol type — graphic, button, or Movie Clip). However, if the Properties Option is chosen for a sound asset, then the Sound Properties dialog appears. For more information on Sound Properties, refer to Part III, "Sound Planning."

Tip   If you're having trouble moving elements from the Library to the Stage on the Mac version of Flash, you may have a corrupt folder on your system. This problem is not due to Flash — it seems to be related to Mac OS 9. For more information, refer to the Macromedia technote at www.macromedia.com/support/flash/ts/documents/cantdrag.htm.

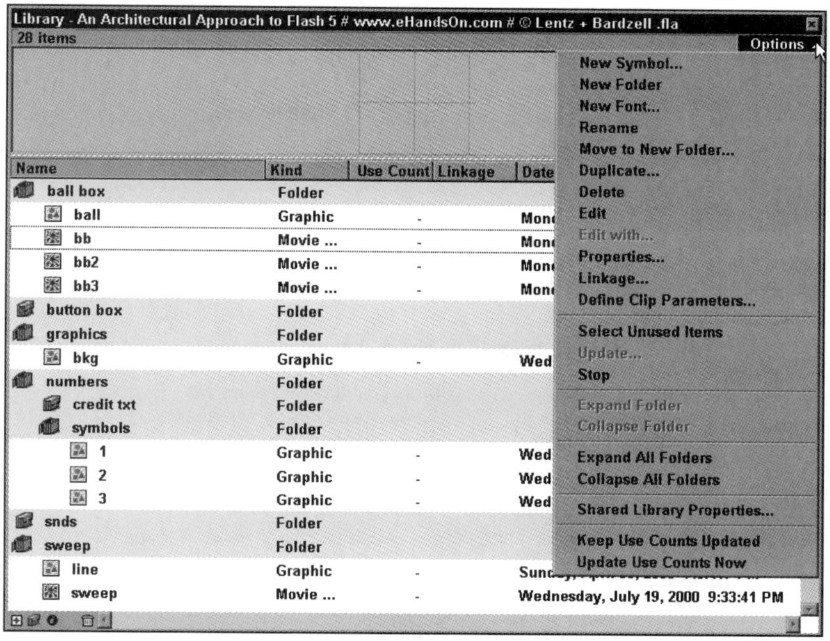

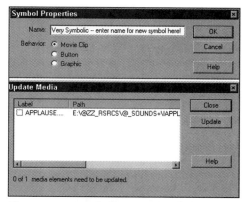

Figure 9-4: The Library deployed in Wide State with the waveform of a sound shown in the Preview window.

Figure 9-5: Symbol Properties dialog (top), and the Update Media dialog (bottom)

Symbol Types

There are three types of symbols. Each type is unique and suited for a particular purpose. Figure 9-6 illustrates the icons associated with each type of symbol.

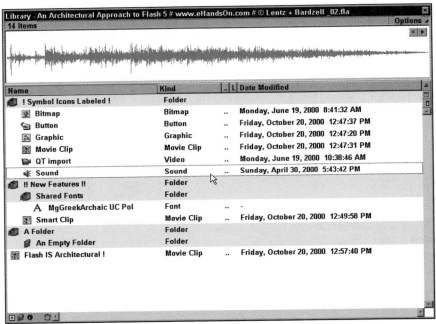

Figure 9-6: Each symbol type has an icon associated with it.

Native symbols

A typical Flash Library may contain these objects that are created within Flash:

✦ **Graphic symbols** are great for static images and simple animations controlled by the main movie's timeline. However, Flash ignores sounds or actions inside a Graphic symbol.

✦ **Movie Clips** are actually like movies within a movie. They're good for animations that run independently of the main movie's timeline. They can contain actions, other symbols, and sounds. Movie Clips can also be placed inside of other symbols and are particularly useful for creating animated buttons.

✦ **Button symbols** are used for creating interactive buttons. Buttons have a specialized timeline with four frames, which are referred to as states. These states are Up, Over, Down, and Hit. Each of these button states can be defined with graphics, symbols, and sounds. After you create a button, you can assign actions to its instances within both the main movie and Movie Clips.

✦ **Shared Fonts** are a new feature of Flash 5. Refer to the end of this chapter as well as to Chapter 20, "Sharing and Loading Assets," for more details.

✦ **Smart Clips** are another new feature of Flash 5. Refer to Chapters 23, "Understanding Movie Clips as Complex Objects," for more details.

Imported symbols

A typical Flash library may also contain these imported objects:

✦ **Bitmaps** are handled as symbols. The topic of importing and using bitmaps in Flash is covered in detail in both Chapter 12, "Using Bitmaps and Other Media with Flash," and Chapter 30, "Working with Raster Graphics."

✦ **Sounds** are also handled as symbols. Importing and using sounds effectively is a complex subject. This critical topic is covered in Part III, "Sound Planning," as well as in Chapter 32, "Working with Audio Applications."

✦ **QuickTime Assets** are handled as symbols, too. Chapter 34, "Working with QuickTime," is devoted to using QuickTime with Flash.

Importing sounds, bitmaps, vectors, and QuickTime

When you import a sound, a bitmap, or a QuickTime (QT) asset (which may be either a QT Movie, or a Sound Only QT Movie), Flash stores these assets in the Library. The advantage of this is that you only need one copy of each asset — regardless how many times, or how many different ways, it might be used throughout your movie. Although each of these assets will be covered in greater depth within their own chapters, we introduce them here, in context with the Library.

Sounds

Flash can import (and export) sounds in a range of sound formats. Upon import, these sound files reside in the Library. To use a sound, drag an instance of the sound out of the Library and onto the stage. Export settings for sound files are managed from within the Library by choosing Properties from either the contextual menu or the Library Options menu. For more information about sounds, refer to Part III, "Sound Planning."

Bitmaps and vectors

Flash can also import (and export) a range of artwork formats, of both vector and bitmap type. Upon import, bitmaps reside in the Library. To use a bitmap asset, drag an instance out of the Library and onto the Stage. Export settings for individual bitmaps are managed in the Bitmap Properties dialog, which is invoked by choosing Properties from either the contextual menu or the Library Options Menu. Bitmaps are discussed in greater detail in Chapter 12, "Using Bitmaps and Other Media with Flash," and again in Chapter 30, "Working with Raster Graphics."

Unlike bitmaps, upon import, vectors arrive on the Flash stage as a group, and may be edited or manipulated just like a normal group drawn in Flash. Vectors are discussed in greater detail in Chapter 12, "Using Bitmaps and Other Media with Flash," and again in Chapter 31, "Working with Vector Graphics."

 Caution Use care in managing the properties of 8-bit images in the Flash Library. The Smoothing option renders custom predithered hybrid Web colors differently from the original colors.

QuickTime

If you have QuickTime 4 or later, you can import QuickTime assets into Flash in the form of either a QT Movie, or a Sound-only QT Movie. QuickTime assets also reside in the Library. Using QuickTime in concert with Flash is covered in Chapter 34, "Working with QuickTime."

Graphic Symbols

Graphic symbols are the simplest kind of Flash symbol. Use them for static images, as well as animations. Note, however, that animations within Graphic symbols are tied to the Main Timeline of the movie—when you stop the movie, the animated Graphic symbol stops, too. Furthermore, actions and sounds don't work within Graphic symbols. You can create an empty symbol first and then add the elements to the symbol or you can convert existing elements into a Graphic symbol.

To create an empty symbol, use the following steps:

1. Use Insert ➪ New Symbol (Ctrl+F8) to initiate a new, empty symbol. This opens the Symbol Properties dialog.

2. Enter a name for your symbol and select a Behavior—Graphic, Button, or Movie Clip. The Behavior setting specifies the default behavior of this symbol as a Graphic, a Button, or a Movie Clip. For this symbol, set the Behavior to Graphic, and then press OK.

3. Click OK. Flash switches to Symbol Editing Mode, in which you can create content for your symbol just as you might normally do in the Movie Editor.

4. When you've finished the symbol and are ready to return to the Stage, use Edit ➪ Edit Movie (Ctrl+E/Command+E) to exit Symbol Editing Mode.

To create a Graphic symbol from existing elements do the following:

1. Select the element or elements that you want to include in the symbol.

2. Use Insert ➪ Convert to Symbol (F8) to access the Symbol Properties dialog.

3. As shown in Figure 9-7, type a name and select a Behavior for the symbol. Then click OK. The Behavior setting specifies the default behavior of this symbol as a Graphic, a Button, or a Movie Clip. For this symbol, set the Behavior to Graphic, and then press OK.

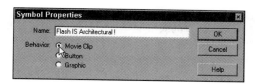

Figure 9-7: Type a name in the Symbol Properties dialog, and then select the Behavior type.

Movie Clips

Movie clips are nested movies inside the main movie. You can add animation, actions, sounds, other symbols, and even other Movie Clips to Movie Clips. Movie Clips have their own timelines, which run independently of the Main Timeline. This can be useful for animations that continue running after the main movie has stopped. Unlike animated Graphic symbols, Movie Clips only need a single keyframe (the initial one) in the timeline of the main movie to play.

Note   A Movie Clip with 40 frames will run to its conclusion, even if it is placed at the first frame of a Main Timeline that has only a single frame.

Creating a Movie Clip using existing animation

You can create a Movie Clip from an empty symbol, as explained in the previous section. However, the simplest way to create a Movie Clip is to use existing animation from the Main Timeline. To do this:

1. Select every frame of every layer of the existing animation that you want to turn into a Movie Clip.

2. Copy the animation by doing one of the following:

   • Right-click or Ctrl+click and select Copy Frames from the pop-up menu.

   • Select Edit ➪ Copy Frames (Option+Command+C or Ctrl+Alt+C) from the Main Menu.

3. Select Insert ➪ New Symbol (Command+F8 or Ctrl+F8) from the Main Menu.

4. Again, as shown previously in Figure 9-7, the Symbol Properties dialog appears. Give the symbol a name and select Movie Clip as the Behavior. Click OK.

5. Now select the first frame of the -timeline in the new symbol that was just created, and paste the frames you copied by doing one of the following:

   • Right-click (Ctrl+click) and select Paste Frames from the pop-up menu.

   • Select Edit ➪ Paste Frames from the Main Menu.

6. Use Edit ➪ Edit Movie (Command+E or Ctrl+E) to return to the main movie.

7. Select the frames from the main movie's timeline (if they aren't still selected from the first step), and delete them with Insert ➪ Delete Frame (Shift+F5).

Expert Tutorial: Graphic Symbols versus Movie Clips, by *Robin and Sandy Debreuil*

A very important yet often confused aspect of Flash 5 are the different methods, and relative advantages of those methods, for storing information — both graphic images and interactivity. This is especially true about Graphic symbols and Movie Clip symbols. In this tutorial, the Debreuils discuss the general nature of the types of information handled by Flash. They then focus on the advantages and disadvantages of both Graphic symbols and Movie Clip symbols.

Flash Information Types

There are six main types of information created by Flash: raw data, groups, buttons, Graphic symbols, Movie Clips, and loaded movies.

Raw Data — These are the raw shapes that are drawn right on the stage. Each separate keyframe of the Main Timeline can contain and display raw data. Note, however, that every time the Flash player encounters a new piece of raw data, even if that same data was displayed in the previous frame, it will be reloaded across the Internet. That's a no-no. For absolute maximum file efficiency, never (ever) leave raw data in the Main Timeline.

Groups — Groups are very useful, but they are not symbols and they don't have any trimming effect on file size. Why? Because, as commonly implemented, groups are usually just groups of raw data. They are only there for your convenience; unfortunately, they give the illusion of being symbols. Just like raw data, placing groups on the stage of the Main Timeline will cause your file size to swell very quickly. That's no-no number two.

Button symbols — Buttons are a straightforward special case — use them for making buttons! (They are also useful for creating other types of interactivity.) Although buttons are symbols, the optimal practice is to use other symbols as the graphic material to build buttons.

Graphic symbols: *static* — These are collections of data that reside in the Library and that are given a name and ID number. When a Graphic symbol is used, essentially the Flash Player says something like, "get the Contents symbol number 47 from the Library and put it right here."

Graphic symbols: *animated* — These are nearly the same as static Graphic symbols, except that these symbols have more than one frame. Accordingly, now the Flash Player must say, "put the contents of the *n*th frame of symbol 47 right there" — and it must say this for each frame. And that tedious statement gets longer for each frame that has raw data in it. This causes the Flash player to think evil thoughts. Another reason to always use symbols, even as that the components that make up your symbols.

Movie Clip symbols: *static* — Error! By definition, all Movie Clips should animate. If a Movie Clip just contains raw graphic, information it should be a Graphic symbol (although a single frame Movie Clip containing other Movie Clips is fine). The reason for this rule is that Movie Clips require slightly more overhead (bytes) to store and to render because they include a new timeline. Again, placing raw graphics on *any* timeline should make you squeamish, even if the file size is not terribly affected.

Movie Clip symbols: *animated*—These are similar to Graphic symbols, but with a few differences. The big difference is that Movie Clips have their own timeline that runs independently of the Main Timeline. This means the Flash player just says, "Oh, hi, Mr. Movie Clip. I see that you're here, so do what you do." Thus, the Movie Clip does its own thing, in its own sweet time. Because of this -timeline independence, you can give the Movie Clip a name and tell it what to do. This is where ActionScript comes into play with things like:

```
bob.gotoAndPlay(4);
judy._rotation=45;
```

(If you run out of aunt and uncle names, you can use cousins and close friends.) One downside of authoring with Movie Clips is that ActionScript only runs while the .SWF is playing, so it isn't possible to scrub or preview the Main Timeline and view a placed Movie Clip while designing.

Loaded movies—These behave much like Movie Clips, except that (a) they are separate .SWF files and (b) each loaded movie is inserted into a new level, so they can't appear be beneath the Main Timeline. Also, loaded movies have an *obvious* restriction: Because they are loaded from a separate file, there needs to be a mechanism to verify that they *are* loaded before giving them instructions. (It's a big Internet and all kinds of things can happen.) There are other differences, between Movie Clips and loaded movies, but those are the main ones.

Graphic versus Movie Clip

That brings us to the difference between Graphic symbols and Movie Clip symbols: Graphic symbols are a quick and tidy way of placing static information into a timeline, while Movie Clips animate independently on their own timeline. Graphics should be used to hold single frames of raw data, or multiple frames when it is important to preview your work while designing it, as with linear animation. Movie Clips must be used when ActionScript is involved, or when an animation must run regardless of what is happening around it. However, the use of one type of symbol rather than the other may not always involve clear-cut choices, because often either will work. Consequently, to use symbols effectively, it's important to know the pluses, minuses, and absolutes of both Graphic symbols and Movie Clips. Here are some tips to keep in mind:

✦ Instance properties of graphics (height, color, rotation, and so on) are frozen at design time, whereas Movie Clips can have their instance properties set on the fly. This makes Movie Clips essential for programmed content such as games.

✦ Scrubbing (previewing while working) is not possible with Movie Clips, although it is possible with Graphic symbols. This makes Graphic symbols essential for animating cartoons. Eyes open, eyes closed—it's that big of a difference.

✦ Movie Clips can't (easily) be exported to video or other linear medium. This is only significant if you plan to convert your .SWF's to another medium.

Continued

Continued

✦ A Graphic symbol's instance properties are controlled (modified) at design time, in the Effect and Instance Panel. One advantage is that this is simple and sure, because you have an instant preview of what's happening. In addition, this information is embedded right in that particular instance of the Graphic symbol — meaning that, if it is either moved or copied, all of this information comes with it.

✦ A Movie Clip's instance properties are set with ActionScript. This gives it great flexibility, although it's a little more abstract to work with. One advantage is that the actions do not need to be directly linked to the Movie Clip, which has the concurrent disadvantage that care must to be taken when moving Movie Clips.

✦ Graphic symbols that are animated (have more than one frame) and are nested (a.k.a. nested animated graphic symbols) may have problems with synchronization. For example: (a) If you have a pair of eyes that blink at the end of a ten-frame Graphic symbol, and you put the graphic symbol containing those eyes within a five-frame Graphic symbol of a head . . . the eyes will never blink. The Graphic symbol will run from frame 1 to frame 5, and then return to frame 1. (b) If you put them in a 15-frame Graphic symbol, they will blink on the 10th frame, and then every 15 frames. That's ten frames, then blink, and then they loop back to frame 1; however, when reaching frame 5 this time, the movie they are in loops back to frame 1 (it's a 15-frame movie), and thus resets the eyes to frame 1.

✦ Movie Clips do not have the problem/feature described in the preceding bullet point.

✦ When using Graphic symbols, looping actions that occur over long timelines result in larger file sizes. While this may seem trivial, understanding this goes a long way toward understanding the Graphic symbol/Movie Clip issue. To understand why the use of Graphic symbols for looping actions is more file intensive, it helps to visualize what the Flash Player is being told to do. The next section goes over this in some detail.

Now that we've given you some background information on Graphic symbols and Movie Clips, let's put our knowledge into practice!

How Flash Sees the World

The miracle that we know as the .SWF format performs two functions: It stores graphical information, and it displays it.

The majority of the file is consumed with information that both defines the symbol and places it. The definition information describes shapes, fills, bitmap fills, and sounds, while the placement information includes instructions for locating these objects, which includes setting their x,y coordinates, scaling, rotating, skewing, coloring, or otherwise manipulating their properties with ActionScript.

Drawing creates shape information. Try drawing a head — this creates lots of curves, and color information as well. If this drawing is confined to a single frame, Flash will play this frame by saying "curve-curve-color-etc."

However, if, at this point, before making it into a symbol, you animate it in a new keyframe, that new keyframe will be required to *duplicate* (or reload) all the curve and color information again. That is, for each frame, Flash will be required to reiterate, completely, "curve-curve-color-etc." (Don't be fooled by groups; although they look like symbols, they are not symbols—all the information inside the group is duplicated in *each* keyframe in which the group appears.)

However, if you make this drawing a Graphic symbol (press F6), and call it head, and then distribute instances of head in those same frames, something different occurs. Things will look the same, but there has been an important change. Now, instead of that first frame containing "curve-curve-color-etc.," it contains these instructions: "head placed at 37,42." And the "curve-curve-color-etc." data is stored in the Library as the head definition. Consequently, all subsequent appearances of head in another keyframe will only require a few bytes of reference and placement data, not all the shape information.

Flash will only rewrite this information when something changes. Adding a keyframe and changing nothing only adds 2 bytes for the keyframe.

However, if, in this new keyframe, you move head to a new position the reference will now be something like "head placed at 45,51" and this will animate the head. Furthermore, because head is a symbol, you can also scale it ("head placed at 45,51, scaled 110 percent"), rotate it ("head placed at 45,51, scaled 110 percent, rotated 45 degrees") and modify its color instance ("head placed at 45,51, scaled 110 percent, rotated 45 degrees, tinted with light blue 20 percent"). Any of these instructions will add information to the placed instance but this is typically very compact, and not something to worry too much about. The savings in file size, compared to animation without Graphic symbols, is tremendous. If a symbol is just moved, very little new data is added, scaling adds a bit more—about 5 bytes, and once it is rotated, skewed, or colored a matrix function kicks in and 10 bytes are added.

What about symbols inside symbols? Let's make a hat for the head—make it a Graphic symbol called hat. We'll put this hat on the head symbol, and then select both symbols and make them into a third Graphic symbol called hatAndHead. Now the timeline contains a reference to the hatAndHead symbol along with its placement information (rotate, scale, and so on), as well as a reference to the hat symbol, its placement information, and lastly a reference to the head symbol, and its placement information. Whew. That might seem like a lot, but it's really only about 35 bytes of new information.

Now things start to get interesting. Just remember, we're still working with a Graphic symbol. If you insert another keyframe into the hatAndHead symbol and move things around, this new information won't be added to the exported .SWF. That's because the Main Timeline is still only one frame, so only the first frame of the hatAndHead symbol is exported. In fact, the Mona Lisa could be added to frame 2 of hatAndHead, and the exported .SWF would never know about it.

Continued

Continued

However, if you now extend the Main Timeline to 100 frames, Flash would repeat the first frame's data into the Main Timeline 50 times (frames 1, 3, 5, 7 . . .) and would also repeat the Mona Lisa frame's data 50 times (frames 2, 4, 6, 8 . . .). With an average of 35 bytes per frame, that would come to $35 \times 100 = 3500$ bytes, or about 3.4KB (1024 bytes per kilobyte). Although that might seem reasonable enough, note that a simple animation of a person running can easily require 20 symbols, which would be something like 34KB over 100 frames. As you can see, this can get significant.

How can Movie Clips accomplish a smaller file size with these looping Graphic symbols? Well, the only thing that really changes is they have a separate timeline. Imagine, the hatAndHead symbol is now a Movie Clip. It has its own two-frame timeline that runs independently of the Main Timeline, so if the Main Timeline is back to being one frame long, the exported .SWF will contain both frames. This means that, even though the .SWF will just sit on frame one of the Main Timeline, hatAndHead will loop through it's own timeline. It will bounce back and forth between its own two frames, because a Movie Clip's timeline is not affected by what is happening around it, it just plays on its own. Unless told otherwise, a Movie Clip will loop, which is the default setting.

But because it's a Movie Clip, another interesting difference occurs. Even if a stop action is placed on frame one of hatAndHead, so that the Mona Lisa frame will never be displayed, it will still be loaded. This is necessary, because a movie can be told to go to any of its frames by other movies, by button clicks, or even by JavaScript in the browser, so it must be loaded and ready to play.

Finally, even though this seems to be a one-frame movie, there are actually three keyframes here: one in the Main Timeline, and two in the hatAndHead timeline. Consequently, at this point it is slightly bigger than had it been a graphic, because Movie Clips must load all their frames, and because making a new timeline involves an extra overhead. However, it is animating, and equivalent Graphic symbol wouldn't be. So, to compare them properly, the timeline for both examples should be extended by 100 (or more) frames. Now we see that the size of the Movie Clip version only increased by about one or two kilobytes, while the Graphic symbol version has increased by $30 +$ KB.

Why is the Movie Clip so much more efficient than the Graphic symbol? It's because the Movie Clip only has 3 frames with information in it, while the Graphic symbol has 100.

In the example mentioned previously of an animated runner, if the running animation loop required 6 frames, there would be about 35 bytes in each of the 6 frames inside the runner Movie Clip, and 1 frame in the Main Timeline placing it, so the file size for that animation would be about $(6 \times 35) + (1 \times 5) = 215$ bytes. This is much better than 3500. But the downside is that there is now no preview while you are designing it, so it's hard to determine whether the running feet will be sliding or not. On the other hand, if the Movie Clip were subjected to a tween (especially a Rotating Tween), much of the benefit would be lost. That's because each frame of the tween would need to contain placement information for the Movie Clip. The important thing is to understand how Graphic symbols and Movie Clips differ in size and functionality, and choose accordingly.

The Debreuil brothers, Robin and Sandy, are from Miami, Manitoba, Canada — and they are still there. Understandably, they reported that their favorite thing to do is: Robin, "Not drive a combine," and Sandy, "Not drive a swather." They also confided that they enjoy an occasional rough game of scrub hockey. They discovered Flash in the olden days of Flash 2, through the fabled RealFlash Animation Festival. In the ensuing years, they have worked on "theromp.com, honkworm.com, FoxSports . . . various animation sites." Responding to our attempt to place them chronologically via the memorable pop music and/or film of the year they graduated from high school, they returned, unsurprisingly, "Eh?" Their other interests include, "travel, travel, travel, children, children, children, Flash, Flash, Flash."

Button Symbols

Button symbols have four states, based on the mouse states, which are:

- ✦ **Up:** The mouse is neither over nor clicking on the button
- ✦ **Over:** The mouse is over the button
- ✦ **Down:** The mouse is clicking on the button
- ✦ **Hit:** This represents the active area of the button

Each button state can present a different image. Buttons can also have actions assigned to them for each of the four mouse states. The images are set inside of the button symbol, while the actions are set in each of the button's instances. Actions cannot be assigned directly to the button symbol itself — only to an instance (or instances) of the symbol. Instances are discussed later in this chapter.

Refer to Chapter 17, "Understanding Actions and Event Handlers," for more about adding actions to button instances.

The timeline for a Button symbol, as illustrated in Figure 9-8, is different from other symbols. It consists of four frames, each one labeled for a mouse state: Up, Over, Down, and Hit. These are the only frames that can be used when creating a button; but you can use as many layers as you like — go ahead, get crazy.

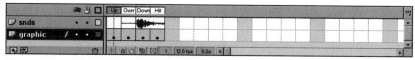

Figure 9-8: The Button symbol timeline always consists of four keyframes labeled Up, Over, Down, and Hit. This button has sounds associated with the Over and the Down states.

The source file for this button discussion is included on the CD-ROM. It's in the button folder of the ch09 folder.

Creating a button

Here are the steps for creating a simple button:

1. Select Insert ⇨ New Symbol to create a new (empty) symbol and launch the Symbol Properties dialog. Name the button and set the Behavior to Button. Click OK.

2. A Button Symbol Editing window opens. It displays each of the four states as a separate frame: Up, Over, Down, and Hit. By default, the initial state automatically has a keyframe. Draw a graphic for this initial state of the button—the Up state. Note that a Graphic symbol or imported graphic (including a bitmap) may also be used or pasted into the keyframe for the Up state.

3. Next, insert a keyframe (Insert ⇨ Keyframe) in the Over state. This is the frame that appears when the mouse passes over the button. If you'd like your button to do something interesting on mouseover, this is where you make it happen. A Graphic symbol, imported graphic, or bitmap (or even a Movie Clip) may also be used or pasted into this keyframe for the Over state—as well as for the next two states.

4. Insert a keyframe in the Down state. This is the frame that appears when the button is clicked. If you don't want the button to change when it's clicked, just insert a frame here instead of a keyframe.

5. Finally, insert a keyframe in the Hit state. This frame defines the effective hit area of the button. If you're only using text for your button, this is particularly important, because without a Hit state the effective hit area is limited to the letter shapes of the text itself—which makes it very hard to hit the button. So, in this frame, draw a shape to define the hit area. Because the user never sees this state, it doesn't matter what it looks like, as long as it defines a usable hit area. It's good practice to add a Hit state to every button you make—this way you won't forget to add one when it's necessary.

For another pass at creating a button, refer to the button section of the QuickStart, "Flash in a Flash."

Adding animation to a button

To add an animated state to a button:

1. Follow the procedure outlined previously to make a new button.

2. Next, follow the procedures outlined earlier in this chapter to create a Movie Clip for the animated state.

3. Now, open the Library with Window ⇨ Library (Ctrl+L or Command+L) and select the button that you've just made, and then open it in Symbol Editing Mode by right-clicking it and then selecting Edit from the contextual menu.

4. For the sake of clarity, add a new layer to the button and name it **MC**, for Movie Clip. Give it four keyframes to match the keyframes of the button states.

5. Select the frame to which you want to add an animated state. This can be the Up, Over, or Down state. (As you already know, the Hit state is *never* seen in the movie, so there's no reason to animate it.)

6. Now, return to the Library with Window ➪ Library (Command+L or Ctrl+L), and select the Movie Clip that you created for the animated state. Then, with the appropriate keyframe active for the desired state, drag the Movie Clip into place, as shown in Figure 9-9.

7. Finally, test your work by selecting Control ➪ Test Movie (Ctrl+Enter or Command+Enter).

Figure 9-9: This figure illustrates a Movie Clip added to the Over state of a Button symbol.

Adding sound to a button

Here's how to add sound to a button:

1. Make a button with all the necessary states, as described previously, and then add an animated state or two if you want.

2. Now, create a second layer to put your sounds in. Although this isn't absolutely necessary, it's recommended because it keeps the button organized.

3. In the new layer, add a keyframe to each state for which you want a sound.

4. Import the sound(s) that you'd like to add to the button state(s).

5. Add the appropriate sound to each state that requires sound. Figure 9-10 shows a button with a sound in both the Over and Down states. Commonly, the Over and Down states have sounds associated with them, but you can add sound to the Up state too.

Figure 9-10: This is the Button to which we previously added the animated state. Now, it also has a sound in the Over and Down states.

Follow these steps for each state that you want associated with a sound:

a. Select the keyframe in the sound layer of the desired Button state.

b. Open the Library and drag the sound onto the Stage.

c. Open the Sound Panel (Window ➪ Panels ➪ Sound), select your sound in the Sound drop-down menu, and set the Synch to Event (it's actually the default).

Cross-Reference

Refer to Part III, "Sound Planning," for more information about importing external sound files.

6. After you've added all your sounds, test the Button (Control ➪ Test Movie) to see how well it works with the sounds.

Organizing Your Library

When your movies start to become complex, you'll find that the Library gets crowded, and it can be hard to find symbols. When this happens, you'll probably appreciate the capability to create and name folders for your symbols. You can organize your Library folders however you like, but here are a few suggestions for greater productivity:

✦ Create a separate folder for each Scene.

✦ Create folders for certain kinds of symbols, such as Buttons, sounds, or bitmap imports.

When you nest complex symbols with each other — a Graphic symbol on the first frame of a Button symbol, with a text symbol on the layer above it — the Library doesn't indicate this hierarchy. But you can — just put all the associated symbols in a folder! You can even nest folders within other folders. Organizing with folders is easy:

✦ To create a folder, click the folder icon at the bottom-left corner of the Library.

✦ To move a file or folder into another folder, simply drag it over the target folder.

✦ To move a folder that's been nested within another folder back to the top level of the Library, drag the folder until it is just above the Library list and over the word Name and release.

Note Putting symbols in different folders does not affect the links between them and their instances (in the same way, for example, that moving a graphic file into a new folder will break an existing link on a Web page). Flash tracks and updates all references to Library items whenever they are renamed moved into separate folders.

The new Flash 5 Movie Explorer gives you a view of the nested interrelationship of symbols, Movie Clips, and other items. Refer to the end of this chapter for more on the Movie Explorer.

Caution There is one Library action for which there is neither undo nor escape: Delete. Any item that is deleted from the Library is gone forever, including all instances throughout the current .FLA editor file.

Adding Symbols to Movies

Now that you've created some symbols, you can use them in movies and modify each instance. Use the Library to put them in a movie. But remember that, in addition to putting symbols on the stage of the main movie, you can also add them to or include them within other symbols as well.

When you add a symbol to the Stage, you are placing an *instance* of the symbol on the Stage rather than the symbol itself. An instance is simply a copy of the original symbol. To put symbols on the stage:

1. Add a Keyframe to the appropriate layer at the point in the timeline where you want the symbol to appear.

2. Use Window ➪ Library (Command+L or Ctrl+L) to open your Library.

Note Don't choose Common Library from the Windows menu. Those libraries come with Flash and—unless you've put them there—won't contain your symbols.

3. Use the Library to find and select the symbol that you want to add to the movie.

4. Drag the symbol onto the Stage by dragging either the graphic of the symbol from the Preview window or the symbol's name as it appears in the Sort window.

Editing Symbols

Because every instance of a symbol is a copy of the original, *any* edit applied to that original is applied to every instance. There are several ways to edit a symbol.

Editing a symbol in Symbol Editing Mode

On the Stage, select an instance of the symbol that you want to edit, and then do one of the following:

1. Choose Edit ➪ Edit Selected from the Edit Menu.

2. Right-click (Ctrl+click) the instance and choose Edit (or Edit in Place) from the contextual pop-up menu.

3. Double-click the instance on stage.

4. Select a symbol from the Library, right-click (Ctrl+click) and choose Properties, and then click the Edit button in the Symbol Properties dialog, as shown in Figure 9-11.

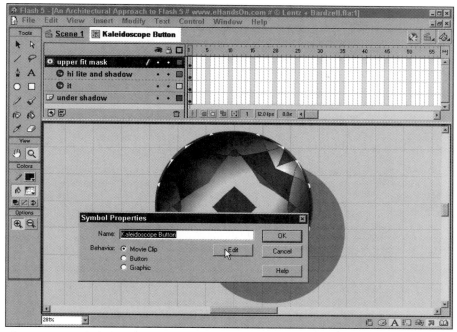

Figure 9-11: Click the Edit button in the Symbol Properties dialog to open Symbol Editing Mode (shown behind).

Editing and Developing

Development in Flash occurs in one of two places: (a) in the Main Timeline and on the Main Stage; or (b) within a symbol, which has its own Stage and a timeline. You can always tell in which mode you are authoring in a couple ways:

The Main Stage (if it is not too large to fill up your screen) is surrounded by a gray area; this is the Work Area, which indicates the edges of the movie, as defined in the Movie Properties. The dimensions of the Main Stage, however, do not limit the symbol Stage. If you make your symbols too large, when you place them on the Main Stage, portions that fall outside of the Main Stage will not appear in the final .SWF. In that event, you can scale the symbol.

Continued

Continued

But how do you know when you are on the Main Stage or when you are in Symbol Editing Mode? Here's one clue: At the upper-left of the timeline is a tab. If you're working on the Main Stage, you will see a single tab with the name of the scene. Unless you name your scenes, this tab should simply say, Scene 1 (or Scene 2). However, in Symbol Editing Mode, a second tab appears to the right of the scene name: This tab displays the name and symbol icon (Movie Clip, Button). If you have nested symbols, more tabs may appear. In this manner, you have convenient access to the hierarchy of your files, no matter how deeply you nest your symbols.

Symbol Editing Mode is much like working on the regular Stage. You can draw with any of the drawing tools; add text, place symbols, import graphics, and sound, and (within limitations) use ActionScript. When you're done working with a symbol, you have an encapsulated element, whether it is a static Graphic, a Movie Clip, or a Button. This element can be placed as many times as needed on your Stage or within other symbols. Each time you place it, the symbol's entire Stage and timeline (if it is a Button or a Movie Clip) will be placed as well, identical to all other instances and the symbol itself.

Editing a symbol in a new window

This method is useful if you want to quickly open a new window to work in. When editing in a new window, the movie remains open and available. You can switch between these windows by choosing from the Window menu. Or, you can divide the workspace between both windows by choosing Window ➪ Arrange All.

1. Select an instance on the Stage of the symbol that you want to edit.

2. Then right-click (Ctrl+click) the instance, and select Edit In New Window from the contextual pop-up menu.

Editing a symbol in place

Edit in Place Mode is very useful. The advantage is that, rather than opening the Symbol Editing Mode, you simply edit your symbol in context with the surrounding movie. Everything else on the stage is visible, but dimmed out. To do this:

1. Select an instance of the symbol that you want to edit.

2. Right-click (Ctrl-click) the instance and select Edit In Place from the contextual pop-up menu.

Editing symbols from the Library

You might not have an instance of your symbol available to select for editing, but you can still edit it. Just edit it from the library.

1. Open your movie's library with Window ➪ Library (Command+L or Ctrl+L) from the Main Menu.

2. Select the symbol that you want to edit and do one of the following:

    • Double-click the symbol.

    • Right-click (Ctrl+click) and select Edit from the contextual pop-up menu.

3. Flash switches to Symbol Editing mode. Edit your symbol any way you want.

Returning to the movie after editing a symbol

After you've edited your symbol, you'll want to go back to the movie to make sure that your changes work properly. Just do one of the following:

✦ Select Edit ➪ Edit Movie (Command+M or Ctrl+M) from the Main Menu.

✦ Select the scene name in the left corner of the timeline as shown in Figure 9-12.

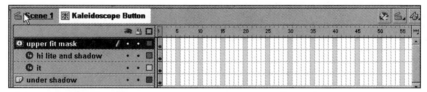

Figure 9-12: Select the scene name to return to editing the movie.

Modifying Instance Properties

Every instance of a symbol has specific properties that can be modified. These properties only apply to the specific instance — not to the original symbol. Properties such as the brightness, tint, alpha (transparency), and behavior can all be modified. An instance can also be scaled, rotated, and skewed. As previously discussed, any changes made to the original symbol will be reflected in each instance — this still holds true even if the instance's properties are modified.

Modifying color effects with symbols

Each instance of a symbol can have a variety of color effects applied to it. The basic effects are changes of brightness, tint, and alpha (transparency). Tint and alpha changes can also be combined for special effects. To apply color effects to a symbol instance:

1. Select the instance that you want to modify.

2. Open the Effect Panel with Window ➪ Panels ➪ Effect.

3. Select one of the options from the drop-down menu. Figure 9-13 shows the Effect Panel drop-down with the Tint option selected.

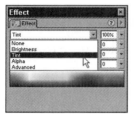

Figure 9-13: The Effects Panel has several options to choose from. Shown here is the Effect drop-down with the Tint option selected.

The options available from the Effect drop-down are as follows:

- **None:** No effect is applied.

- **Brightness:** Adjusts the relative brightness or darkness of the instance. It ranges from 100 percent (black) to 100 percent (white). Use the slider to change the value or just type a numeric value into the entry field.

- **Tint:** Enables you to change the color of an instance. Either select a hue with the color picker, or enter the RGB values directly. Then, select the percentage of saturation (Tint Amount) by using the slider or by entering the percentage in the entry field. This number ranges from 0 percent (no saturation) to 100 percent (completely saturated).

- **Alpha:** Enables you to modify the transparency of an instance. Select a percentage by using the slider or by entering a number directly. The Alpha percentage ranges from 0 percent (completely transparent) to 100 percent (no transparency).

- **Advanced:** Enables you to adjust the tint and alpha settings of an instance. The controls on the left reduce the tint and alpha values by a specified percentage, while the controls on the right either reduce or increase the tint and alpha values by a constant value. The current values are multiplied by the numbers on the left, and then added to the values on the right.

Note The Advanced option includes the potential for negative alpha values. Potential uses for this capability, together with more information about using the Effects Panel, are detailed in Chapter 11, "Animating in Flash."

Changing the behavior of an instance

You don't need to limit yourself to the native behavior of a symbol. There may be times when you want an animated Graphic symbol to have the behavior of a Movie Clip. You don't have to go through the extra effort of creating a new symbol — just change the behavior of the instance as needed:

1. Select the instance that you want to modify.
2. Open the Instance Panel with Window ➪ Panels ➪ Instance, or click the Instance Button on the Launcher.
3. From the Behavior drop-down, select the desired behavior. As shown in Figure 9-14 you can select Graphic, Button, or Movie Clip, which is the default behavior.

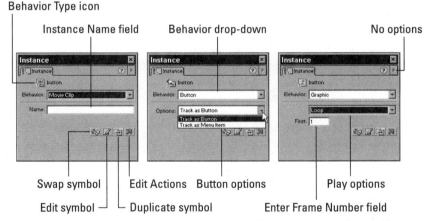

Figure 9-14: As this composite screen shot indicates, you can change the Behavior of an instance from the Instance Panel.

 Cross-Reference Working with Symbol Instances is covered in great depth in Parts IV, "Adding Basic Interactivity to Flash Movies," and V, "Programming Flash Movies with ActionScript."

Switching symbols

There may be times when you need to replace an instance of one symbol with another symbol. You don't have to go through and recreate your entire animation to do this — just use the Switch Symbol feature. This feature only switches the instance of the symbol for an instance of another symbol — all other modifications previously applied to the instance will remain the same. Here's how to switch symbols:

1. Select the instance that you want to switch.

2. Open the Instance Panel with Window ➪ Panels ➪ Instance (or use the Instance Button on the Launcher).

3. Click the Swap Symbol button and, from the ensuing Swap Symbol dialog (shown in Figure 9-15), select the symbol that you want to switch to.

4. Click OK to swap symbols.

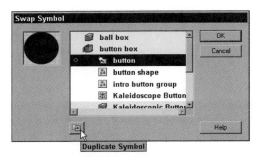

Figure 9-15: Click the Swap Symbol button of the Instance Panel to invoke this Swap Symbol dialog.

The Movie Explorer

The Movie Explorer Panel is a powerful new tool for deciphering movies and finding items within them. It can be opened from the Launcher Bar, or from the Main Menu by choosing Window ➪ Movie Explorer (Ctrl+Alt+M/ Option+Command+M).

New Feature

The Movie Explorer is one of the best new features of Flash 5. It will help you to organize, build, and edit your projects with greater clarity and efficiency. For example, if your client decides to change the font at the last minute, you can use the Movie Explorer to locate and update all occurrences of the original font — without a tedious manual search.

The Movie Explorer is an especially useful tool for getting an overview and for analyzing the structure of a Flash movie. This means that you can now see every element in its relationship to all other elements, and you can see this all in one place.

However, it's also useful for troubleshooting a movie, for finding occurrences of a particular font, and for locating places where you refer to a certain variable name in any script throughout a movie. As an editing tool, you can use it as a shortcut to edit any symbol, for changing the properties of an instance, or even for doing multiple selections and then changing the attributes of the selected items. Furthermore, the Find function is an incredible timesaver.

The new Movie Explorer has so many features that it may be difficult to get used to — however, it's well worth the effort to become familiar with this organizational powerhouse. Figure 9-16 shows the Movie Explorer as well the Movie Explorer Settings dialog, which you can open by clicking the Customize Which Items to Show button in the Movie Explorer.

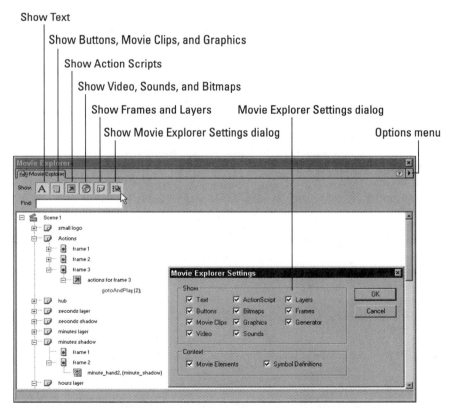

Figure 9-16: The Movie Explorer displays the file structure for Jake Smith's Flash Clock, featured in an Expert Tutorial in Chapter 26.

Filtering Buttons

As shown in Figure 9-16, there are several icon buttons across the top of the Movie Explorer Panel. These are called Filtering Buttons and they have icons representative of their function. Click any button to toggle the display of those elements in your file. Note, however, that the Movie Explorer's display becomes more crowded as you select more buttons — and that it performs more slowly because it has to sift more data. From left to right, the buttons filter the display of the following kinds of content:

✦ Text

✦ Buttons, Movie Clips, and Graphics (placed instances)

✦ ActionScripts

✦ Video, Sounds, and Bitmaps (placed instances)

✦ Frames and Layers

✦ Customize which Items to Show

Note also the Find entry field, which enables you to search for movie items by name.

The Display List

Below the icons is a window with the Display List. Much like Windows Explorer, or the Mac Finder, the Movie Explorer displays items hierarchically, either by individual scene or for all scenes. These listings are expandable, so if you have selected the Text button, a plus sign will appear beside the name of any Scene that includes text. Clicking the plus sign (or right-pointing arrow on the Mac)displays all of the selected items included in that Scene. At the bottom of the Display List, a status bar displays the Path for the currently selected item.

In Figure 9-17, two buttons have been selected: Text, and ActionScripts. As shown, clicking the plus sign beside the ActionScript icon displays the entire ActionScript. Note, too, that the complete text appears, including basic font information.

The contextual menu

Select an item in Movie Explorer and right-click/Ctrl+click to invoke the contextual menu related to that particular item. Irrelevant commands are grayed-out, indicating that functionality is not available in context with the item.

Figure 9-18 shows the contextual menu of the Movie Explorer. Among the most useful commands is the Goto Location option at the top. When you can't find an item (because it's on a masked layer or is invisible), this command can be a lifesaver.

Next, we cover the Movie Explorer Options menu.

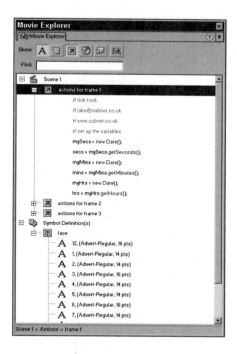

Figure 9-17: The Movie Explorer for one of Jake's Clocks, from Jake Smith's Expert Tutorial, "Using getTimer to Make a Flash Clock," in Chapter 26.

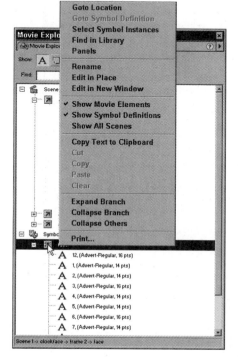

Figure 9-18: The Movie Explorer's contextual menu

The Movie Explorer Options menu

The Options menu is accessed by clicking the Options triangle, which is located in the upper-right corner of the Movie Explorer Panel. These commands are the same as the commands that are found in the Movie Explorer's contextual menus:

✦ **Goto Location:** For a selected item, this transports you to the relevant layer, scene, or frame.

✦ **Goto Symbol Definition:** (For this to work, both Show Movie Elements and Show Symbol Definitions must be toggled on.) This jumps to the symbol definition for the symbol that's selected in the Movie Elements area. *(At the time of this writing, this feature was not functional.)*

✦ **Select Symbol Instances:** Jumps to the scene containing instances of the symbol that is selected in the Symbol Definitions Area. (For this to work, both Show Movie Elements and Show Symbol Definitions must be toggled on.)

✦ **Find in Library:** If the Library Window is not open, this opens the Library and highlights the selected item. Otherwise, it simply highlights the item in the Library.

✦ **Panels:** Click this to open all relevant panels (or panel) for the selected item.

✦ **Rename:** Enables you to easily rename selected items.

✦ **Edit in Place:** Use this to edit the selected symbol in context on the Stage.

✦ **Edit in New Window:** Use this to edit the selected symbol in Symbol Editing Mode.

✦ **Show Movie Elements:** One of two broad categories for how filtered items are viewed in the Display List, Show Movie Elements displays all elements in the movie, organized by scene.

✦ **Show Symbol Definitions:** This is the other category of the Display List, which shows all of the components that are related to each symbol. Both Show Movie Elements and Show Symbol Definitions may be displayed simultaneously.

✦ **Show All Scenes:** This toggles the display of Show Movie Elements between selected scenes, or all scenes.

✦ **Copy Text to Clipboard:** Use this command to copy selected text to the clipboard. Text may then be pasted into a word processor for editing, spell checking and other textual operations not found in Flash.

✦ **Cut:** Use this command to cut selected text.

✦ **Copy:** Use this command to copy selected text.

✦ **Paste:** Use this command to Paste text that has been copied from Flash or another application.

✦ **Clear:** Use this command to clear selected text.

✦ **Expand Branch:** This expands the hierarchical tree at the selected location; it's the menu equivalent of clicking the tiny + sign/right-facing arrow.

✦ **Collapse Branch:** This collapses the hierarchical tree at the selected location; it's the menu equivalent of clicking the tiny – sign/down-facing arrow.

✦ **Collapse Others:** This collapses the hierarchical tree everywhere except at the selected location.

✦ **Print:** The Movie Explorer prints out, with all of the content expanded, displaying all types of content selected.

Make sure to use Movie Explorer! When planning or looking for ways to improve a project, this tool can provide an excellent map to the structure and function of what you've already accomplished. Whenever relevant, print out the Movie Explorer; this document can function as a project file for finished work, providing a reference of all scripting and Movie Clip placement. As such, it can make it much easier to return to a project months later. It can also facilitate collaboration amongst developers, whether they share the same office or are geographically distributed. Finally, for all of the reasons listed previously, the Movie Explorer can also be used as a tool for both learning and teaching.

Shared Library and Shared Fonts

Shared Library is a new feature of Flash 5. The idea behind this is very good. It is intended to enable you to create a Library of assets that can be uploaded to the server and then share those assets with multiple movies. These assets would include any asset that is normally included in a Flash movie, with the inclusion of shared fonts. Furthermore, because an asset file is not added to the movie that references it, this method would enable a developer to trim bandwidth and also obtain a more streamlined authoring procedure.

Unfortunately, *at the time of this writing*, some users have reported that it does not seem to perform consistently in some intensive situations.

Caution Exercise *extreme* care when using any aspect of the Shared Library. If you want to use the Shared Library feature, we suggest that you research the Macromedia site for any technotes on the topic, and that you also search Flash user groups for information, before you commence work.

Cross-Reference For more information about Shared Libraries, refer to Chapter 20, "Sharing and Loading Assets."

Summary

✦ Symbols are the building blocks of Flash. They save you time, reduce your file size, and add flexibility to your movies. With the advent of the increasingly robust Flash ActionScript language, symbols can be considered as objects within an Object Oriented authoring environment.

✦ Flash handles imported sounds, bitmaps, and QuickTime assets as symbols. They reside in the Library and instances of these assets are deployed within a Flash project.

✦ In addition to imported assets, there are three other kinds of symbols that can be created within Flash: Graphic symbols, Movie Clips, and Buttons.

✦ The Library can be organized with folders and symbols and assets can be rearranged without breaking their linkage to instances deployed within the project.

✦ Using symbols within a project is as easy as dragging an asset or symbol from the Library and onto the stage, although it's usually best to have a new layer ready and to have the appropriate keyframe selected.

✦ Symbols can be edited in a number of ways. Any edits to a symbol are reflected by all instances of that symbol throughout the project.

✦ The color and transparency of individual instances of a symbol can be modified, via the Instance Panel. Furthermore, specific instances can be switched for other symbol instances by using the Behavior Panel.

✦ The new Flash 5 Movie Explorer is a powerful new tool for deciphering movies and finding items within them.

✦ Shared Libraries and Shared Font symbols are a promising new feature of Flash 5.

✦   ✦   ✦

Drawing in Flash

Flash has a variety of drawing tools that enable you to create whatever you need for your projects. You should already know how to use these drawing tools from your reading of Chapter 1, "Understanding the Flash Framework." This chapter provides a more in-depth look at using these tools — and several others — when working with your drawings. We manipulate drawings, create special effects, and more.

Simple Shapes and Items

To learn Flash, it's essential to know how to create simple shapes and items with the drawing tools, as described in Part I, "Mastering the Flash Environment." Drawing simple shapes with Flash has always been easy, but with the addition of the Pen Tool in Flash 5, drawing has become even easier. Individually, these basic drawing tools are quite powerful, but when used in combination, they enable you to create an endless variety of complex shapes.

Creating shapes

In Flash, it takes little effort to draw most primitive shapes such as circles or rectangles. But what happened to the Triangle Tool? And how do you create irregular shapes?

Creating complex shapes requires adding or removing parts. If you've already been playing around with shapes, you may have noticed that by joining or overlapping two shapes of the same color on the same layer, a brand new shape is created. (To pull the pieces apart you need to use the Undo [Edit ➪ Undo] command a few times.) This feature is used to create irregular and complex shapes.

Creating shape combinations

Add a rectangle to a circle of the same color (on the same layer) and you'll combine them into a new shape (as shown in

Figure 10-1). This can be accomplished by either drawing the second shape directly over the first, or by selecting the second shape elsewhere on the stage and then dropping it over the first shape. If you find that this doesn't seem to work, be sure that you aren't trying to combine shapes that have been grouped. Remember that even single shapes can be grouped, and thereby protected from shape combination.

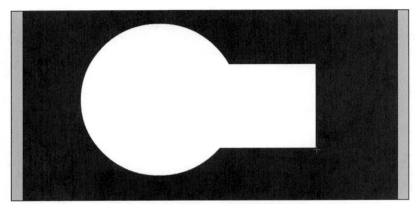

Figure 10-1: Using shape combinations to generate a complex shape from primitive shapes.

Creating shape cutouts

Another effect that can be created by playing around with shapes is a cutout, by combining shapes of different fill colors. For example, add the same circle to a rectangle of a different color, and the circle acts like a cookie cutter, creating another brand-new shape. A similar result is obtained by drawing a shape of a different color directly over the top of an existing shape: the one drawn last (or dropped) acts as the cutter. Drop a collection of selected lines on a rectangle, then deselect, and then reselect and move them away — and you'll create a filigree knockout.

On the CD-ROM The Flash resource files for this example are located in the Moon folder of the ch10 folder on the CD-ROM.

As shown in Figures 10-2 through 10-4, a moon shape is achieved by drawing the cutout shape, then dragging it over the top of the background shape, and then deleting the cutout, as follows:

1. Let's begin with a black background, as if it were the night sky. This is accomplished by using Movie Properties (Modify ➪ Movie Properties).

2. Select the Oval Tool, change the fill color to white for the moon, set the stroke color to transparent, and then hold down the Shift key and draw a perfect circle.

3. Now, copy the original circle as follows: Select the circle with the Arrow Tool, and then hold down the Alt/Option key while dragging a copy of the circle off to the side. This second circle will be the shape cutter.

4. Next, with the new circle still selected, change its fill color by choosing a new color (gray) from the Fill Color control of the Toolbox (as shown in Figure 10-2). If you don't change the fill color for this secondary circle, it will merge and become part of the original circle shape (as in the preceding example) in our next step.

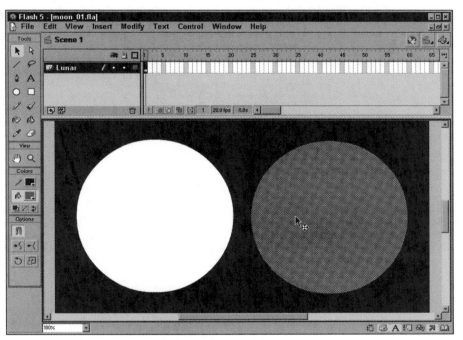

Figure 10-2: The full moon and the shape cutter

5. Use the Arrow Tool to drag the gray circle over the top of the original white circle and position it so that it reveals a sliver of crescent-shaped white (as shown in Figure 10-3). After the gray circle is positioned appropriately, deselect it by clicking off the circle at the edge of the stage.

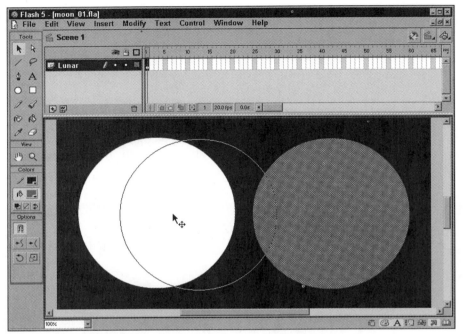

Figure 10-3: Dragging the shape cutter over the full moon

6. Use the Arrow Tool to click the gray shape-cutter circle to select it and drag it away (see Figure 10-4). Then delete the gray circle. What remains? You should now have a sliver of white in the shape of a crescent moon.

You can apply this technique to any number of shapes, limited only by your ingenuity and patience.

Grouping

Here's how to use grouping so that items won't cut out the shapes that occur beneath them.

In the previous example, cutting into the full-moon shape with the gray shape cutter created a sliver of moon. In such cases, there's always a potential for problems if the shape cutter is accidentally deselected. The potential for problems is increased if more than one shape is being used as a cutter. However, if the cutter shape (or shapes) is grouped before it is placed over the shape that's being cut, the problem is eliminated. Furthermore, the group enables you to nudge and align until the cutter is precisely where you want it. And you don't have to decide immediately, either. If you choose the appropriate color for the cutter shape(s), you can wait until later to commit to the cut. When you're ready to make the final cut, simply ungroup the cutter shape(s), and then deselect before selecting and finally deleting them.

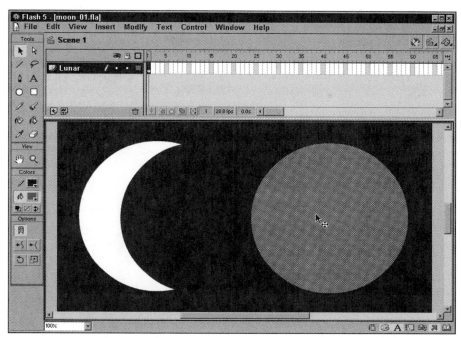

Figure 10-4: With the shape-cutter circle dragged away, the original circle is cut, leaving a crescent moon shape.

Note

Although grouping doesn't usually add significantly to file size, it certainly does not reduce file sizes. Here are a few facts: Although the "grouping" itself requires only a few more bytes, the vectors hidden behind a group do mount up. Because Flash doesn't distinguish between what is in front and behind, it renders everything both within and behind a group. Thus, for the smallest possible files, it makes sense to ungroup most groups before final publication of your project. This will let all of the grouped pieces cookie-cutter themselves down into one unified piece of artwork. Nevertheless, before ungrouping to trim file size, be sure to save an archive of the file with all of the components grouped.

Drawing a triangle

The easiest way to create a triangle is to take the Pencil, draw three lines to outline the shape, and then fill it in. However, you might be interested in drawing a more precise triangle, as follows:

1. Select the Rectangle Tool. Set your Line Color to No Color, and select a fill color. Press the Rounded Rectangle modifier to open the Rectangle Settings dialog, and make sure that the Corner Radius is set to 0 points.

2. Draw a rectangle that's about twice the size of the triangle that you want to create.

3. Choose View ➪ Snap to Objects to turn on object snapping.

4. Use the Line Tool to draw a line from the top-left corner of the rectangle to the bottom-right corner as shown in Figure 10-5.

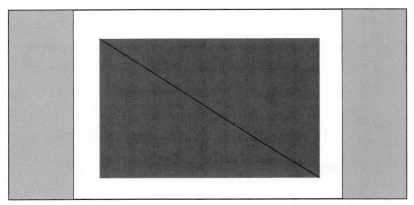

Figure 10-5: Draw a line from the top-left corner of the rectangle to the bottom-right corner.

5. The line has bisected the rectangle into two triangular filled areas. Use the Arrow Tool to select one of the triangular filled areas and drag it away from the rest of the shape. Then select the rest of the shape (the remaining triangle and bisecting line) and delete it. The finished triangle is resting on its side; we discuss how to change that later in this chapter.

Here's how to draw a similar triangle using the Line Tool and the Grid with Snap enabled:

1. From the View Menu, enable both View ➪ Grid ➪ Show Grid and View ➪ Grid ➪ Snap to Grid.

2. Select the Line Tool from the Drawing Toolbox. Choose your line color using the Stroke Color control, and then choose a Stroke Height and Weight from the Stroke Panel.

3. Beginning at one intersection of the Grid, draw a baseline for the triangle, and then draw one of the sides, either by eyeballing the center point above the base line, or by quickly counting grid spaces.

4. Finally, as shown in Figure 10-6, draw the final side of the triangle; the Line Tool will snap to close the shape. When drawing with Snap enabled, a small circle appears adjacent to the cursor whenever snap is active.

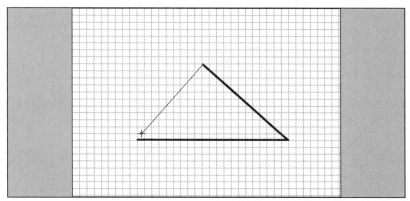

Figure 10-6: This triangle was created with the Line Tool, using Snap to Grid, with the Grid's visibility enabled with View ⇨ Grid ⇨ Show Grid.

Drawing a polygon

A polygon is a flat shape with four or more sides. Polygons are more complicated to make than triangles, but they're not difficult. Figure 10-7 shows a five-sided polygon, drawn directly in Flash.

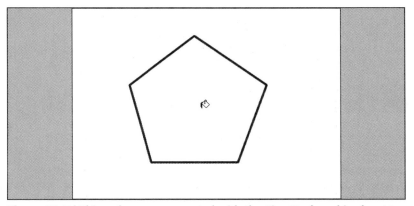

Figure 10-7: This polygon was created with the Line Tool, and is about to be filled with the Paint Bucket.

The simplest way to draw a polygon is to use the Line Tool to draw an outline, and then fill it in with the Paint Bucket Tool. Another method is to draw several rectangles, rotate and adjust them — using the Scale and Rotate Tools — and then place them on top of each other. Yet another method is to draw a rectangle and then chop its corners off by drawing intersecting lines, as demonstrated in the earlier section on Drawing a Triangle. Furthermore, the shape of any polygon can be modified and perfected using:

✦ The Line Processing and Shape Recognition techniques described in Chapter 4, "Working with Selections and the Pen Tool," and Chapter 5, "Working with the Drawing and Painting Tools."

✦ The Pen Tool and Subselect Tool techniques discussed in Chapter 4, "Working with Selections and the Pen Tool," and Chapter 5, "Working with the Drawing and Painting Tools."

✦ The Arrow Tool techniques discussed in Chapter 4, "Working with Selections and the Pen Tool."

On the CD-ROM The Flash resource files for the following tutorial are located in the Larry D. Larsen folder of the ch10 folder on the CD-ROM.

Expert Tutorial: Pill Technique, *by Larry D. Larsen*

Larry has contributed to many sites, including The Poynter Institute, Flash Foundry (content), Machoman Randy Savage, The Alien Containment Facility, E-Hands on Flash tutorial, and Kung Foo Flash.

Making Pill-Shaped Buttons

Pill-shaped buttons are particularly valuable for text buttons. That's because it can be pretty hard to make circular buttons look good with text on them and because rectangular buttons are just plain boring. It's very easy to create oval buttons in Flash, but pill-shaped buttons take a little bit more work. Thus, the procedures used in this tutorial are valuable not only as a solution to the pill problem, but also for their delivery of an advanced way of *thinking* with the Flash drawing tools.

Start by opening a new Flash file with File ⇨ New, which should default to a single, active layer. We want to create a gradient fill that can be applied so that the circle will look three-dimensional. Select the Oval Tool, and then, proceeding from the Window menu, use Window ⇨ Panels ⇨ Fill to access the Fill Panel (shown in the following figure). Choose Radial Gradient from the Fill Style drop-down. The default black-and-white Radial Gradient should appear. If not, click the Swatches tab and choose the default black-and-white Radial Gradient from the bottom of the panel, and then return to customize this Radial Gradient with the Fill Panel.

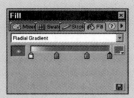

Click twice just beneath the Edit Gradient Range to add two new Color Pointers and position them as shown. (If you have any problems with the color terminology or operations, please refer to Chapter 6, "Applying Color," for a complete explanation before proceeding further.) Next, change the colors of the Color Pointers: From left right, change the first Color Pointer to light yellow, the second and fourth to bright orange, and the third to dark red. Finally, click Add Gradient in the option pop-up (which is the triangle near the upper-right corner of the panel) to add this Radial Gradient to the Swatches Panel. Hold down the Shift key and draw a perfect circle, filled with the new gradient color (see the following figure).

If you've drawn a circle with an outline, click to select and then delete the outline. The circle doesn't look very dimensional, does it? The next step is to reapply the same gradient to this circle in a more convincing way.

Choose the Paint Bucket Tool and confirm that the custom gradient is still the fill color. (If not, return to the Swatches Panel and reselect it.) Now, click somewhere in the upper-left corner of the circle. The light yellow highlight of the gradient should appear in the upper left and there should be a dark red shadow in the lower right. The resulting orange ball (shown in the following figure) will be used as the basis from which the pill shape is created.

Continued

Continued

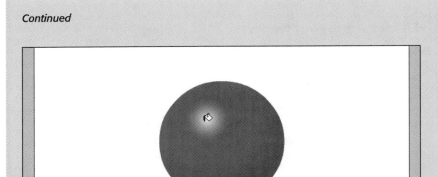

Finally, the dimensional orange ball needs to be centered on the Stage. Select the ball with the Arrow Tool, and then use Edit ⇨ Cut to cut it. Center the stage by double-clicking the Hand Tool. Then, paste the ball back onto the stage using Edit ⇨ Paste. (Don't use the Ctrl+Shift+V (Command+Shift+V) keyboard shortcut because that pastes the ball in its original location!) This process centers the ball.

Create a new layer above Layer 1. (When you create this new layer — Layer 2 — Flash will make it the current layer, which is what we want.) Then select the orange ball and copy it with Edit ⇨ Copy. Next, we need to paste a new copy of the orange ball onto Layer 2, directly over the original. This is easily accomplished with Edit ⇨ Paste in Place, which pastes a copy in the same exact position that it was copied from. Now we're going to use a vertical line to bisect the orange ball on Layer 2. To do this, draw a vertical line off to the side of Layer 2 that's taller than the orange ball, as shown in the following figure.

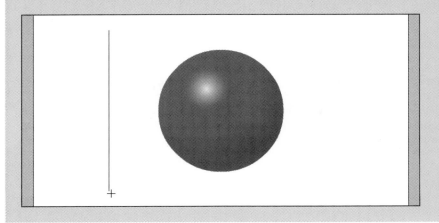

Then, select the line with the Arrow Tool and — as with the ball in the previous step — cut it with File ⇨ Cut. Paste the line back into Layer 2 using Edit ⇨ Paste. This will paste the vertical line in the center of the stage directly over the center of the orange ball, which is also centered on the stage (see the following figure).

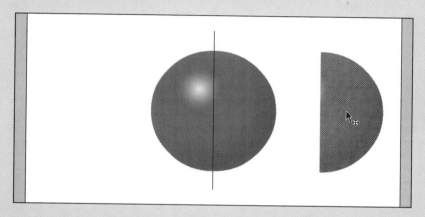

Deselect the vertical line so that it will bisect the ball. Now, select the right side of the orange ball. (Only the right half of the orange ball should be selected.) Hold down the Shift key (to constrain the movement to the horizontal axis) and move this half to the right. Repeat this procedure for the left half of the ball. Then, use the Arrow Tool to select and delete the line (as shown in the following figure).

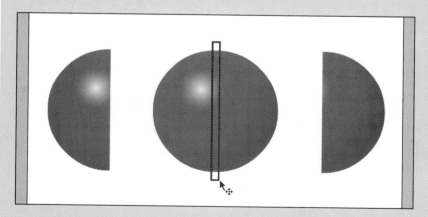

Now, make Layer 1 the current layer. Working off to the side, use the Rectangle Tool — with the fill color set to no fill — to draw a very narrow, empty vertical rectangle, taller than the orange ball. Repeat the procedures used with the line to copy and paste this rectangle over the center of the orange ball on Layer 1. The lines of the vertical rectangle have cut the orange ball into three pieces (as shown in the following figure).

Continued

Continued

Because we only need the center piece, use the Arrow Tool to select both the left and right pieces of the orange ball on Layer 1 and delete them, and then delete the rectangle.

Select the remaining vertical slice of the orange ball on Layer 1 with the Arrow Tool, and then click the Scale option. Now, drag the right-middle handle to the right until it snaps to the left edge of the orange ball half on Layer 2 (as shown in the following figure). Then, repeat the procedure on the left side. Drag the left-middle handle to the left until it snaps to the left edge of the orange ball half on Layer 2.

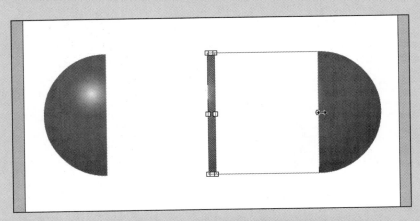

Finally, select all, cut, and then paste into Layer 1. Then delete Layer 2. This will take all of the pieces and put them on the same layer. Group them and you have your pill shape (shown in the following figure).

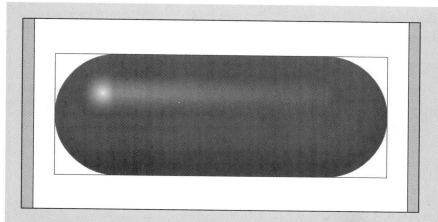

Turn it into a symbol and you won't have to repeat these steps again. (For a discussion of Symbols, refer to Chapter 9, "Checking Out the Library: Symbols and Instances.")

A native of St. Petersburg, Florida, Larry D. Larsen is a true Flash pioneer. This is evident in his claim that "Flash found me." He says that in the year that he graduated from high school, the most memorable media production was the movie *Die Hard*. "I don't know what was on the radio, but I was listening to The Police — "Ghost in the Machine." It was old at the time."

The Drawing Panels

When drawing in Flash, the drawing panels — Info, Transform, and Align — can be your best friends. Use the Info Panel to modify the coordinates and dimensions of an item. Or use the Transform Panel to scale, rotate, and skew an item. Use the Align Panel to align, regularize (match the sizes of), or distribute several items on Stage either relative to each other or to the Stage.

The Info Panel

Use the Info Panel, shown in Figure 10-8, to give precise coordinates and dimensions to your items. Type the numbers in the spaces provided, and your item will be transformed relative to its top-left corner. Or, when working with groups and symbol instances, use the Alignment Grid to apply changes from the center. To open the Info Panel, use Window ➪ Panels ➪ Info.

Symbol type

Alignment Grid

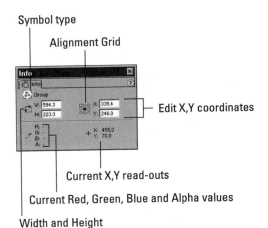

Edit X,Y coordinates

Current X,Y read-outs

Current Red, Green, Blue and Alpha values

Width and Height

Figure 10-8: Use the Info Panel options to change the location and dimensions of an item.

The Info Panel has these controls:

✦ **Width:** Use this numeric entry field to alter the width of a selected item.

✦ **Height:** Use this numeric entry field to alter the height of a selected item.

Units for both Width and Height are measured in the units (pixels, inches, points, and so on) as set in Ruler Units option of the Movie Properties dialog. Note, however, that upon changing the unit of measurement, the item must be deselected and then reselected in order for these readouts to refresh and display in the current units.

✦ **Alignment Grid:** The alignment grid is located just to the left of the numeric entry fields that are used for adjusting the X and Y location of any selected item. This alignment grid consists of nine small squares. Together, these squares represent an invisible bounding box that encloses the selected item. Every shape created in Flash, even circles, resides within an imaginary rectangular bounding box that includes the extremities of the shape. The alignment grid enables you to position the selected item relative to either the upper-left corner or to the center of its bounding box. Click either square to define which point to use for positioning.

The X (horizontal) and Y (vertical) coordinates are measured from the upper-left corner of the Flash Stage, which is the origin with coordinates 0,0.

✦ **X:** Use this numeric entry field to either read the X coordinate of the item or to reposition the item numerically, relative to the center point on the X (or horizontal) axis.

✦ **Y:** Use this numeric entry field to either read the Y coordinate of the item or to reposition the item numerically, relative to the center point on the Y (or vertical) axis.

✦ **RGBA:** This sector of the Info Panel gives the Red, Green, Blue, and Alpha values or graphic items and groups at the point immediately beneath the cursor. Values for symbols, the background, or interface elements do not register.

✦ **+ X: / + Y:** This sector of the Info Panel gives the X and Y coordinates for the point immediately beneath the cursor — including offstage values. A negative X value is to the left of the Stage, while a negative Y is located above the Stage.

To scale or reposition an item, select the item and then open the Info Panel with Window ➪ Panels ➪ Info, as shown in Figure 10-8:

✦ First you must choose to scale or reposition the item relative to either the center, or to the upper-left corner. (The selected square turns black to indicate that it is selected.)

• To work relative to the center, select the center square of the Alignment Grid.

• Or to scale relative to the upper-left corner, click that square of the Alignment Grid.

✦ To scale the item numerically, enter new values in the Width and Height fields, and then click elsewhere or press Enter to effect the change.

✦ To reposition the item numerically, enter new values in the X and Y fields (located in the *upper* half of the panel), and then either press Enter or click elsewhere, outside the panel, to effect the change.

The Transform Panel

This panel gives precise control over scaling, rotation, and skewing of an item. With this panel, instead of using manual techniques — which may be imprecise — numeric values are entered in the appropriate fields and applied directly to the item. However, once transformations are applied to an item, these numbers disappear when it is deselected.

With an item selected, open the Transform Panel with Window ➪ Panels ➪ Transform, as shown in Figure 10-9.

Figure 10-9: Use the Transform Panel to scale, rotate, and skew items.

The Transform Panel has several options that relating to scaling, rotating, and skewing:

✦ **Scale:** Use this to scale the selected item numerically by percentage. Enter a new number in the Scale field and press the Return or Enter key. The shape scales to the specified percentage of its previous scale. To constrain the shape to its current proportions, click the Constrain check box. To restore the shape to its original size, press the Reset button However, once the shape is deselected, it cannot be Reset. The only way to get back your original object's size is to immediately choose Edit ⇨ Undo (probably more than once) or exit your movie without saving your changes (in which case you'll probably lose other work as well).

Tip   When using the Transform Panel with groups and symbol instances, the original settings can be reset even after the item has been deselected.

✦ **Rotate:** Click the radio button and then apply a rotation to the selected item by entering a number in the Rotate field, and then pressing the Return or Enter key.

✦ **Skew:** Items can be skewed (slanted in the horizontal or vertical direction) by clicking the Skew radio button, and then entering values for the horizontal and vertical angles. Click Apply and the item will be skewed to the values entered.

✦ **Copy and Apply Transformation:** Note this Copy button! It's the left button at the bottom-right corner of the panel. Press it and Flash makes a copy of the selected item (including shapes and lines), with all Transform settings applied to it. The copy is pasted in the same location as the original, so select it with the Arrow Tool and scoot it to a new position.

✦ **Reset:** This button, at the bottom-right corner of the panel, removes the transformation you just performed on a selected object. However, once the object is deselected, this button does not work. For simple items, this is really an Undo button, rather than a Reset button. However, you can use the Reset button for instances, groups, or type blocks even after they have been deselected (but not after you save your movie).

The Transform submenu

If you've already mastered Part I, "Mastering the Flash Environment," you know that the Arrow Tool options enable you to interactively scale, rotate, or skew an item relative to its center point. In conjunction with a watchful eye over either the Transform Panel, or the Info Panel, the Arrow Tool options can be used for a measure of numeric control over these processes. But there's another area of Flash (only briefly mentioned in Part I) that can be indispensable. It's the Transform submenu, Modify ⇨ Transform, shown in Figure 10-10.

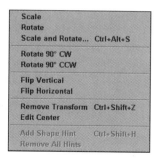

Scale	
Rotate	
Scale and Rotate...	Ctrl+Alt+S
Rotate 90° CW	
Rotate 90° CCW	
Flip Vertical	
Flip Horizontal	
Remove Transform	Ctrl+Shift+Z
Edit Center	
Add Shape Hint	Ctrl+Shift+H
Remove All Hints	

Figure 10-10: The Transform submenu of the Modify menu

The Transform submenu has these items:

✦ **Scale:** Use this command to interactively scale an item, several selected items, or a group.

✦ **Rotate:** Use this command to interactively rotate an item, several selected items, or a group.

✦ **Scale and Rotate:** Use this command to invoke the Scale and Rotate dialog to numerically scale and rotate an item, several selected items, or a group.

✦ **Rotate 90° CW:** Use this command to rotate an item, several selected items, or a group 90° clockwise.

✦ **Rotate 90° CCW:** Use this command to rotate an item, several selected items, or a group 90° counterclockwise.

✦ **Flip Vertical/Flip Horizontal:** Use either Flip command to flip an item, several selected items, or a group on either their vertical or horizontal axis — while leaving the relative position of the item intact, as shown in Figure 10-11.

Figure 10-11: The item on the left is the original. The item in the middle has been flipped vertically, while the item on the right was flipped horizontally.

✦ **Remove Transform:** Use this command to remove previous transformations. Depending on the item transformed, this command remains viable as follows:

- Simple items — until deselected.
- Instances, groups, and type blocks — until the movie is saved.

✦ **Edit Center:** Use this command to relocate the center, or axis, of a group, instance, type block, or bitmap to a position that is off-center. This command does not work on simple graphic shapes.

Tip   While nearly all the commands of the Transform submenu are redundant of commands that might be more easily accessed elsewhere in Flash, Edit Center is a unique and powerful command because it enables you to freely decentralize the axis about which an item (a group, instance, type block, or bitmap) will transform — or animate! For example, by moving the center of a grouped rectangle to its lower-right corner, the rectangle could be animated so that it expands from that corner, and then rotates around that same point.

Figure 10-12 shows the same item as in the previous figure, except that the center, as shown on the left, is being edited, so that the new center will be at the lower right. As shown in the middle, this affects the way that it responds to a rotation as well as how it sits when scaled, as at the right.

Figure 10-12: Changing an item's center for rotation and scaling.

The Align Panel

The Align Panel, shown in Figure 10-13, is one of many features for which you'll be grateful every time you use it. It enables you, with pixel-perfect precision, to align items to each other and the Stage and to distribute items evenly on the Stage. To open the Panel, choose Window ➪ Panels ➪ Align (Ctrl+K/Command+K).

Figure 10-13: Use the Align Panel to both size and line up items without fuss.

The Align Panel has five controls. The icons on the buttons are relatively self-explanatory:

✦ **Align:** There are six buttons in this first control. The first group of three buttons is for horizontal alignment, and the second group of three is for vertical alignment. These buttons align two or more items (or one or more items with the Stage) horizontally (top, middle, bottom) or vertically (left, middle, right).

✦ **Distribute:** This control also has six buttons, three for horizontal distribution and three for vertical distribution. These buttons are most useful when you have three or more items that you want to space evenly (such as a set of buttons). These buttons distribute items equally, again vertically or horizontally. The different options enable you to distribute from edge to edge, or from item centers.

✦ **Match Size:** This control enables you to force two or more items of different sizes to become equal in size; match items horizontally, vertically, or both.

✦ **Space:** This option enables you to space items evenly, again, vertically or horizontally. You might wonder how this differs from Distribute. Both are similar in concept, and if your items are all the same size, they will have the same effect. The difference becomes more apparent when the items are of different sizes:

  • Distribute evenly distributes the items according to a common reference (top, center, or bottom). For example, if one item is larger than the others, it may be separated from the other items by less space, but the distance between its top edge and the next item's top edge will be consistent with all the selected items.

  • Space ensures that the spacing between items is the same; for example, each item might have exactly 36 pixels between it and the next.

✦ **To Stage:** On the right, you will also notice a To Stage button. By clicking this, you include the full Stage in the operation.

To align an item to the exact center of the Stage, do the following:

1. Click to select the item that you wish to center.

2. Click To Stage in the Align Panel.

3. Click the Align horizontal center button.

4. Click the Align vertical center button.

Fill and Stroke Effects

Gradient fills are one kind of important fill effect. They give extra depth and richness to shapes that are drawn in Flash and are commonly used to give a three-dimensional effect to shapes.

Cross-Reference Colors are discussed in great detail in Chapter 6, "Applying Color." Refer to that section to learn more about creating and working with gradient fills.

Spheres

Spheres are very easy to make. To make one, draw a circle on the stage, and then apply a radial gradient fill to it — but don't just stop there! Learn to use the gradient fill to give it some depth by adding highlights and shadows.

As shown in Figure 10-14, starting with a simple sphere (left), a highlight effect is added to the sphere (middle). Then, working with the Radial Gradient drop-down of the Fill Panel, a unique radial fill is generated to apply highlight and shadow effects to the sphere (right).

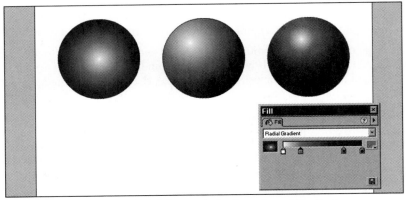

Figure 10-14: Creating highlights and shadows for a 3D effect.

Here's how to make a simple sphere look more realistic.

1. Select the Oval Tool and choose a radial gradient for the fill. (Refer to Chapter 6, "Applying Color," for more about working with fills.)

2. Shift-drag across the stage with the Oval Tool to make a circle, which should look like the sphere shown at the left.

3. To give the sphere a little highlight effect, transform the fill by reapplying it with the Bucket Tool, so that the lightest part is at the top left of the circle, as shown in the middle sphere of the figure.

4. Now play around with the colors in the fill until you get a nice looking sphere, as shown in the figure at the right. Add colors to the radial gradient to tweak the effect of highlight and shadows.

Refer to Chapter 6, "Applying Color," for more information on using fills, as well as modifying gradients. Also, refer to Chapter 5, "Working with the Drawing and Painting Tools," for information about Transform and Lock Fill modifiers, which are useful when modifying fills.

The sphere illustrates a very simple 3D effect created with gradient fills. Although it's not really three-dimensional, it does give the illusion of it. More complex and detailed 3D effects can be created by judiciously combining the power of gradient fills.

Refer to Chapter 33, "Working with 3D Graphics," for a look at creating 3D effects in Flash.

Stroke effects

Stroke effects — which are controlled by the Stroke Panel in concert with the Line, Oval, Rectangle, and Pencil Tools — can be used to give more life to lines. One really neat way of using this effect is to apply a stroke style (stipple, hatch, custom) to a line, and then turn the line into a fill (Modify ➪ Shape ➪ Convert Lines to Fills) and apply various effects to the resulting fill. Then you can apply both Gradients and Bitmap Fills to your lines. Beware that overuse of this technique on complex styles can significantly increase .SWF file size and download **time**. On slower machines, it may also cause the animation to drag.

Strokes are discussed in detail in Chapter 5, "Working with the Drawing and Painting Tools." Refer to the "Using the custom stroke styles" section to learn how to control strokes and how to customize their styles.

Expert Tutorial: Using Modify ⇨ Curves, by Dorian Nisinson

To see the examples for Dorian's tutorial in a real Flash (.FLA) file, open the DNCurves.fla in the ch10 folder on the CD-ROM.

Lines to Fills

Here are three examples where the Modify ⇨ Shape ⇨ Convert Lines to Fills command is indispensable. The following figure shows an example of using Convert Lines to Fills to create square corners.

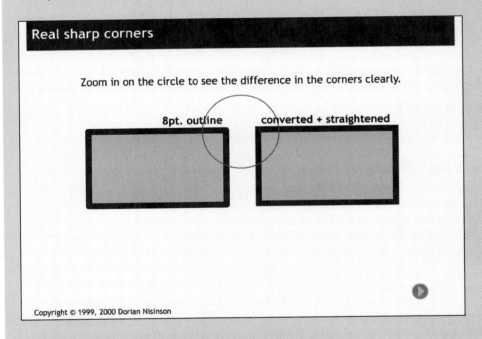

Real sharp corners

Zoom in on the circle to see the difference in the corners clearly.

8pt. outline   converted + straightened

Copyright © 1999, 2000 Dorian Nisinson

Here's how to get real square corners:

1. First, select the Rectangle Tool and draw a square complete with both an outline and a fill.

2. Then, with the Arrow Tool, double-click the outline to select the entire outline.

3. With only the outline selected, use Modify ⇨ Shape ⇨ Convert Lines to Fills.

4. Now, reselect the converted line with the Arrow Tool and click the Straighten option. The corners will be nice and sharp.

If you create a complex shape, put a line around it, and then use this process, the results are less predictable. Some corners may gain an extra facet or two.

Scalable Lines

What about real scalable lines? In the old days of Flash 3, an item created with lines would look fine at 100 percent view, but if an instance was made of that item (which was constructed of lines) and then reduced to 20 percent, the thin lines would not scale properly. Instead, they looked huge and ugly. And because lines (unlike fills) can never be represented by anything smaller than one whole pixel, reducing the line width in the original would not improve the scaled appearance. Well, here's a solution, shown in the following figure:

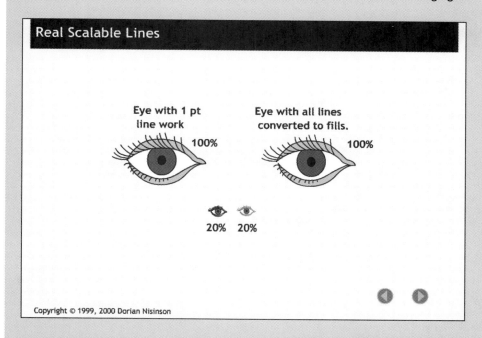

Real Scalable Lines

Eye with 1 pt line work — 100%

Eye with all lines converted to fills. — 100%

20%   20%

Copyright © 1999, 2000 Dorian Nisinson

1. If a symbol will appear at different scales, convert those pesky lines to fills.

2. Then, fill the lines as you choose; they will scale with the artwork!

Converting Styled Lines Retains Style

Now, converting styled lines retains style! That's right, you can convert a dashed or dotted line yet maintain the line style (see the following figure)!

Here's how:

1. Select the Pencil Tool, choose 8 points for the line width, and create a line using the dotted line style. This will draw a line with a row of big dots.

2. Next, use Modify ⇨ Shape ⇨ Convert Lines to Fills. You'll notice that, although you converted the line to fills, the dots are still there.

Continued

Continued

3. Click a single dot; each dot is a separate item that can be filled. But each dot can also be edited much more extensively than if it were a line.

4. So what about lines? As you can see in the example .FLA, even plain lines can be filled with gradients, and even the opacity can be controlled.

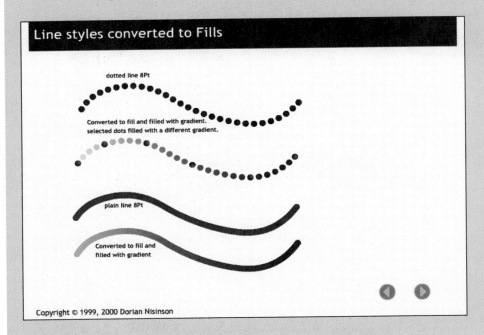

Faux 3D

Now we look at making a slightly 3D rectangle. Here's how to create the effect shown at the left in the following figure:

1. Start with a light gray for the movie background and draw a rectangle with rounded corners set to 10 and no outline.

2. Fill this rectangle with a linear gradient that goes from blue-green to white and back to blue-green.

3. With the Paint Bucket Tool selected, choose the Transform Fill Option. Click the gradient to select it and then rotate it to approximately 45 degrees.

4. Next, expand or contract the gradient so that the full color ends of the gradient are at opposite corners of the filled shape.

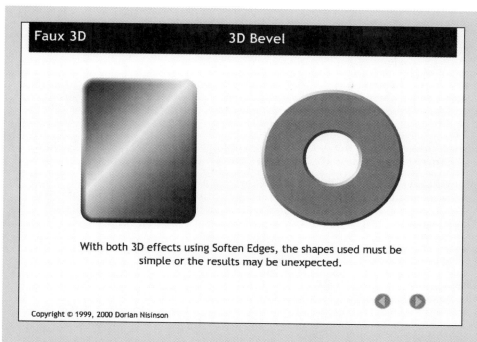

Faux 3D   **3D Bevel**

With both 3D effects using Soften Edges, the shapes used must be simple or the results may be unexpected.

5. Now, we're ready to make our 3D effect. To do this, select the rectangle with the Arrow Tool and use Modify ⇨ Shape ⇨ Soften Fill Edges with the following settings: Distance: 16, Steps: 6 px, Expand. Click OK to apply.

6. Then, with the Arrow Tool, select the outer band of this softened shape and copy it. Create a new layer, drag it beneath the first layer, and use Edit ⇨ Paste in Place to put the outermost band in the same position as the original rectangle (but on the new layer underneath it).

7. Now, return to the top layer and click the eye icon (in the Layers Panel) of the top layer to hide it, so that you can see what you're doing to the lower layer in the next step.

8. Next return to the bottom layer, make it the active layer, and then fill the center of the pasted shape with a white-to-black opaque gradient.

9. Then edit this lower gradient to a 45-degree angle and squeeze it so that 25 percent of the filled area is either pure white or pure black. (This can be adjusted later.)

10. When you make the top layer visible again, you'll notice a 3D effect.

Continued

Continued

Making a 3D bevel

Here's how to create the effect shown at the right of the figure:

1. Start with a circle of 150 pixels in diameter filled with an intermediate color. (To draw a perfect circle, remember to hold down the Shift key to constrain the Oval Tool.)

2. Select the circle (with the Arrow Tool) and use Modify ➪ Shape ➪ Soften Fill Edges with these settings: Distance: 140, Steps: 2, Inset. Click OK to apply.

3. Now, select the center of the circle and delete it, leaving a donut shape with a perfectly centered hole. Because Soften Fill Edges works by creating a series of bands that are the same color as the original shape, yet of gradually decreasing opacity, it's necessary to fill this donut with a new color that's 100 percent opaque.

4. Choose the Paint Bucket Tool and a fill with a middle value color, and then use it to fill the donut hole.

5. Next, select the donut shape and apply Modify ➪ Shape ➪ Soften Fill Edges with these settings: Distance: 20, Steps: 2, Expand. Click OK. This results in a donut shape with a band 10 pixels wide around both the inside and outside edges.

6. Now, in the Linear Gradient drop-down of the Fills Panel, create a linear gradient that goes from white to a darker shade of the original donut color. Use this gradient to fill first the outer and then the inner band of the donut. Take care, as the bands must be filled individually and with the Lock Fill Modifier turned off in order to enable subsequent manipulation of these fills — which will complete the 3D effect.

7. Next, with the Paint Bucket Tool and Transform Fills option, click the outer band and edit the application of the gradient. Assuming a light source from the upper left, rotate the gradient approximately 45 degrees until the outer band is whitest at the upper left edge and darkest color at the lower right.

8. Finally, edit the gradient for the inner band. As a dimensional item, the upper left of the inner band would be in shadow, while lower right would be illuminated — so, rotate this gradient until the inner band to opposes the orientation of the outer band.

9. Now the donut is 3D!

The Settings in the Soften Edges Panel are:

✦ **Distance:** The number of pixels the selected shape will expand or contract

✦ **Number of steps:** The number of bands around the edges of a shape

✦ **Expand or Inset radio buttons:** Tells Flash whether to enlarge or contract the original shape

When working with circular shapes, the width of each band will be equal to the Distance number divided by the number of steps. For example:

✦ If the distance is 10 and the number of steps is 2, then each band will be 5 pixels larger or smaller, depending on whether Expand or Inset is checked. However, the innermost band (the band closest to the original shape) will become the same color as the original shape. (This means that the inner band automatically becomes part of the original shape.)

✦ But with an original circle of 40 pixels in diameter with Expand checked, distance set to 10 and number of steps set to 2, the result will be a circle 45 pixels in diameter with a band of 5 pixels surrounding it — for a total diameter of 50 pixels.

✦ Using those same original numbers but with Inset rather than Expand, the result will be a circle 35 pixels in diameter, with a 5-pixel band — for a total diameter of 40 pixels.

✦ Finally, note that transparency increases successively with each larger band. If Distance is 20 and number of steps is 6, then the inner band will be opaque, while the next smallest band will have 80 percent opacity, the next band will have 60 percent opacity, the next band will have 40 percent opacity. The final band, with the largest diameter, will have an opacity of 20 percent.

When asked how near she lives to New York City, Dorian once replied, "You couldn't get any closer, I was born and raised and live there — right uptown." This was the perfect answer from the woman who perfected the methodology for using the new Flash 5 hitTest method in Chapter 23. In the year that she graduated from high school, "the movie [she] remember[s] most from that time was not new — quite old, in fact: Murders of the Rue Morgue with Bela Lugosi, with gorgeous black and white cinematography." She discovered Flash when it was still Future Splash, just before MM bought it. It was love at first sight. Her favorite thing is, "I don't have one favorite. Draw, design, sing, talk, learn, write, creative problem solving." She's the cofounder of www.FlashCentral.com and designed the graphic intro for www.flashability.org. She has her own motion graphics company, Dorian Nisinson Design.

Static Masks

In the real world, a mask is used to selectively obscure items beneath it. In Flash, a Mask layer is used to selectively obscure items on the specific layers beneath it. To create a mask effect, a Mask layer is used in conjunction with a Masked layer, or multiple Masked layers.

When a mask is enabled, everything on the Masked layer is hidden except what's beneath filled areas of the Mask that it's linked to. Almost any content, (excluding lines) may be used to create a mask. Masks may be animated or static. The only limitation is that motion paths cannot be used to animate a mask, nor can layers within buttons be masked. Animated masks are covered in Chapter 11, "Animating in Flash."

Caution Although groups, text, and symbols can be used as a mask, such items fail to mask when they share a masking layer with a simple shape that's also applied as a mask.

The source files for the next three examples are located in the ch10 folder on the CD-ROM, in the Static Masks subfolder. You can also refer to the sample file, 10_Mask Tests, and examine all of the scenes, for more complex examples of the exceptions to masking.

Masking with a graphic

Here's how to create the simplest form of mask:

1. To begin with, the content that will be visible through the mask should be in place on its own layer, with visibility turned on. This is called the Masked layer.

2. Next, create a new layer above the Masked layer.

3. Then, create the aperture through which the contents of the Masked layer will be viewed. This aperture can be any filled item, text, or placed instance of a symbol. The only constraint is that the aperture must be a filled item. (Of course, lines *can* be used as masks if they are first converted to fills with the Modify ➪ Shapes ➪ Convert Lines to Fills command.) This layer is called the Mask layer.

4. Now, situate your Mask over the contents of the Masked layer so that it covers the area that you will want to be visible through the mask.

5. Finally, right-click/Ctrl+Click the layer bar of the Mask layer to invoke the contextual menu, and then choose Mask from the menu.

6. The Masked layer will become subordinated to the Mask layer and both layers will become locked. The contents of the Masked layer are now visible only through the filled portion(s) of the Mask layer (as shown at the left in Figure 10-15.)

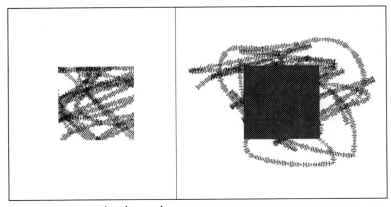

Figure 10-15: A simple mask

7. To reposition the Mask layer, unlock it (as shown at the right in Figure 10-15.)

8. To reactivate masking, lock the Mask layer (and confirm that the Masked layer is locked, too).

Masking with a group

A group can also be used as a mask, as long as it consists of filled shapes and as long as the mask doesn't also include simple ungrouped shapes:

If a mask is composed of multiple items, using a group usually facilitates positioning the mask, as shown in Figure 10-16.

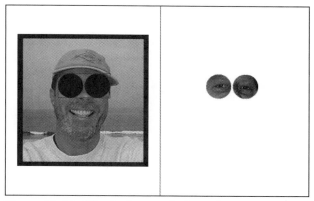

Figure 10-16: Who is that masked man?

Masking with a symbol

Working with symbols is working smart because doing so can help to reduce file size. Because symbols comprised of filled items can be used as masks, there's no reason *not* to use a symbol from your Library to make a mask. Let's return to our moon example from earlier in this chapter and see what we might be able to do with our primitive shapes.

Figure 10-17 shows the original shapes that we used to create a moon shape. The only difference here is that the shape that was used to cut out the bulk of the moon (the gray shape cutter), leaving only a sliver of moon, is now on its own separate layer — and the layers are set up as a Mask layer and a Masked layer.

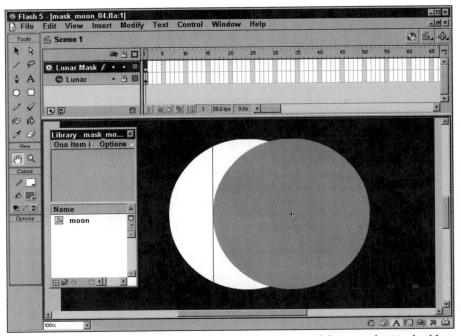

Figure 10-17: Using a circular moon shape for both a Mask layer and a Masked layer

Unfortunately, when we enable masking (by locking both layers), we don't get a sliver of moon. Instead, as seen in Figure 10-18, we get a silly lemon shape! What happened? Well, if you think about it, you'll notice that the upper shape *reveals* the content beneath it. So, as you can see, masking involves a logic that's the opposite of the cookie-cutter interaction that we used to create shapes earlier in this chapter. As you learn in the Chapter 11, "Animating in Flash," a clear understanding of this principle is critical to animating masks.

Masking text

Not only can text be masked, it can also be used to mask. To mask text, simply set up your layers as described in the previous section, with the text to be masked on the Masked layer, and the filled item that you'll use for your aperture on the Mask layer, as shown in Figure 10-19.

On the CD-ROM

The source files for these examples are located in the ch10 folder on the CD-ROM, in the Static Masks subfolder.

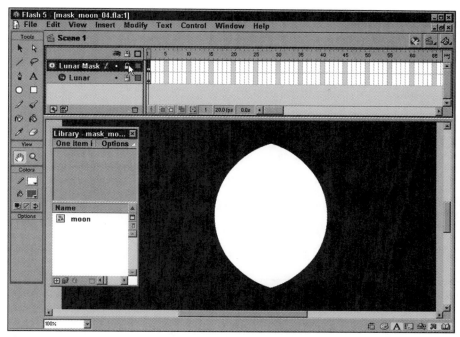

Figure 10-18: The upper circle reveals only the part of the lower circle that it covers.

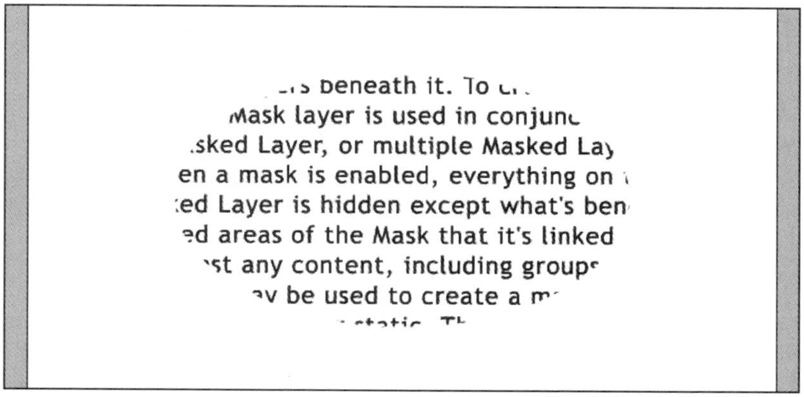

...s beneath it. To cr...
...Mask layer is used in conjunc...
...sked Layer, or multiple Masked Lay...
...en a mask is enabled, everything on ...
...ed Layer is hidden except what's ben...
...ed areas of the Mask that it's linked...
...st any content, including group...
...ay be used to create a m...
...static. Th...

Figure 10-19: Masking text

To use text as a mask, the layers should be set up as described previously. In this situation, the text (which goes on the Mask layer) will look as though it were filled by whatever is place on the Masked layer. For this to be effective, a larger point size and fuller, bold letterforms are advised, as shown in Figure 10-20.

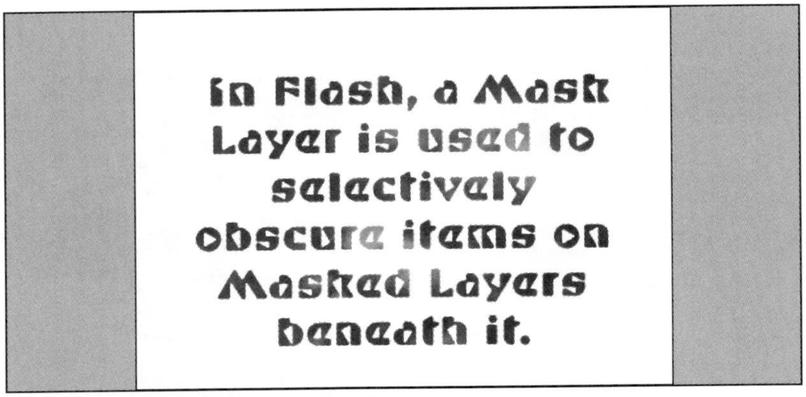

Figure 10-20: Using text as a mask

Creating Type and Text Effects

Whenever you set out to create a Type or Text effect, you'll want to make sure that the text you're working with is the final copy. Do this before you apply any effects, because once you're done, the text will no longer be editable. Thus, if changes need to be made, you'll have to redo both the text and the effect.

Text with an outline

The text used as a mask in the previous example didn't stand out as sharply as it might. The effect could be helped a lot by adding a faint outline to the letters. Here's how to do it:

1. First, turn off the visibility of the sky, which is the Masked layer, and then unlock the Text Mask layer and copy the contents. Then relock the Text Mask layer.

2. Add a new, normal layer beneath the Sky layer. If you inadvertently create a Masked layer, use the contextual menu to access the Properties dialog and assign the layer as a normal layer. Rename the layer Outline. Then paste the copied text in perfect alignment with the Text Mask by using Edit ➪ Paste in Place.

Tip Do you find that you rely heavily on Paste in Place? Do you wish that this was the default, instead of Paste, for the keyboard shortcut Ctrl/Command+V? You could try using the new Flash 5 keyboard shortcuts (Edit ➪ Keyboard Shortcuts) to customize your shortcuts. Or did you know that when you right-click/Ctrl+Click anywhere on the Stage, the contextual menu offers both the Paste and Paste in Place commands?

3. Select the text on the Outline layer and then break it apart using Modify ➪ Break Apart. Then, with the text still selected, choose Modify ➪ Shape ➪ Expand Fill. In the ensuing Expand Fill dialog, enter a value of 3 pixels, and check that the Direction is set to Expand. Click OK.

4. Check to ensure that none of your letters have been obliterated by this process; sometimes, if the expand value is too high, the letterforms become corrupt.

5. Reactivate the masking, as previously described. If you've done it right, your letters should now have a thin outline.

Figure 10-21 shows the effect of adding a thin outline to the text that has been used as a mask.

In Flash, a Mask Layer is used to selectively obscure items on Masked Layers beneath it.

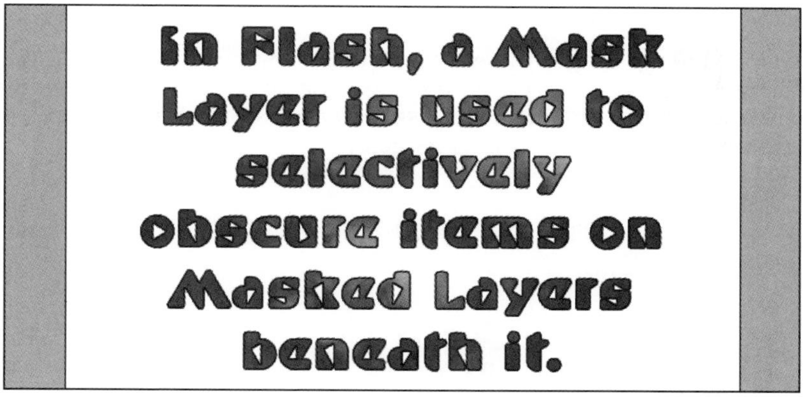

Figure 10-21: Adding a thin outline to text that has been used as a mask helps to sharpen the letters.

The source files for these examples are located in the ch10 folder on the CD-ROM, in the Text Effects subfolder.

Text with drop shadows

Drop shadows are special effects that can be added to text to make the text stand out. There are many ways to achieve such effects. We discuss two of them here.

Type some text. Then, with the text still selected, copy the text with Edit ➪ Copy.

1. Paste the copied text onto the Stage. Then, select it and change its color to something appropriate for a drop shadow — perhaps dark gray, or something slightly transparent.

2. Now, position the shadow on the Stage, and then send it to the back of the stacking order (behind the original text) with Modify ➪ Arrange ➪ Move Behind or Modify ➪ Arrange ➪ Move to Back.

3. Finally, select the original text and position it over the shadow text. Move the text and the shadow around until the shadow effect is optimal. To join the shadow and the text, select both and use Modify ➪ Group.

   But that shadow is too crisp, and it doesn't look convincing. So:

4. For a softer shadow, repeat the preceding steps, and then break apart the shadow text using Modify ➪ Break Apart.

5. You may find that it's easier to manage Text Effects if you move the Text and the Shadow onto separate layers.

6. Soften the shadow's edges by selecting Modify ➪ Shape ➪ Soften Fill Edges. Either leave the settings in the Soften Edges dialog at their defaults, or play around with them to obtain an ideal, soft shadow. Another alternative is to reduce the Alpha value to 75 or 80 percent.

Figure 10-22 shows the result.

Figure 10-22: Drop shadows make text stand out from the page.

Tip   Although a soft drop shadow looks good, it can add a lot to the file size — particularly if the edges are softened with a lot of steps. This may cause long waits during download and slow animations on less-capable processors. So use this effect sparingly!

More text effects

Text effects aren't limited to plain drop shadows. Any of the effects and modifications that have been discussed in this chapter can also be applied to text. You can skew, rotate, and scale text just like any other item. Break text apart and the use the Soften Edges and Expand Shape commands to invent your own effects. Or break text apart to apply fills. Finally, to radically reshape text use the methods discussed in Chapter 5, "Working with the Drawing and Painting Tools," regarding both processing lines and shape recognition.

Tip   Don't sacrifice readability for cool effects. The special effects listed in this section are great for text that really needs to stand out, such as headings and button labels. However, the effects aren't advisable for large blocks of text. Although the final decision is up to you, consider the impact that your decision will have on the readability of your project.

Glowing text

You can also give text a glowing look with a method similar to the Drop Shadow effect. First, break apart the shadow text. Then apply a light-colored fill to it. Now, soften the edges — just increase the distance in the Soften Edges dialog, and make sure that the Direction is set to Expand. Then, move this modified text squarely behind the original text. Or modify this technique to create an embossed look by using a dark fill for the shadow text.

Gradient fills in text

Adding gradient fills to text can also make it stand out. Here's how:

1. Select the text and then break it apart with Modify ➪ Break Apart (Ctrl+B or Command+B). The text appears as selected shapes on the stage. Be careful to keep these shapes selected.

2. Choose the Paint Bucket Tool and select a gradient fill from one of the Gradient drop-downs of the Fill Panel.

3. Apply the gradient fill to the selected shapes of the broken-apart text. The gradient will fill the text as if it were one shape. To add the gradient to each text character individually, deselect the text and apply the fill to each character.

4. A similar effect can be accomplished by choosing a Bitmap Fill, instead of a Gradient Fill, from the Fill Panel.

Summary

✦ Once you've mastered the basics of drawing, there are innumerable manipulations, effects, and combinations of them that can be used to develop your drawings.

✦ Using the basic Flash drawing tools, you can create irregular shapes, modify simple and complex strokes and fills, and apply many effects to those strokes and fills.

✦ Nearly anything that you can draw or create in Flash can be masked or even be used as a mask.

✦ Using these same Flash drawing tools, you can also create custom text and apply multiple effects to it.

✦　✦　✦

Animating in Flash

In this chapter, we discuss the basic methods and tools used to create animations in Flash. Animation is the process of creating the effect of movement or change over time. Animation can be the movement of an item from one place to another, or it can be a change of color over a period of time. The change can also be a morph, or change in shape, from one shape to another. Any change of either position or appearance that occurs over time is animation. In Flash, changing the contents of successive frames (over a period of time) creates animation. This can include any or all of the changes discussed previously, in any combination. There are two basic methods of Flash animation; frame-by-frame and tweened animation:

✦ **Frame-by-frame animation** is achieved by changing the individual contents of each of any number of successive frames.

✦ **Tweened animation** is achieved by defining the contents of the end points of an animation, and then allowing Flash to interpolate the contents of the frames in between. As discussed previously, this is often referred to as tweening. There are two kinds of tweening in Flash — shape tweening and motion tweening.

There's a growing trend among many Flash developers to regard animation as a form of programming. After all, computer animation is the art of orchestrating items according to various properties over time. Perhaps this is a shift in thinking occasioned by the increasingly robust implementations of ActionScript that have accompanied these last two releases of Flash? It is worth mentioning, however, that a tremendous amount of animation is possible by using Movie Clips instead of simple groups and graphics. But before you can go *there,* you need to know how to animate on the Main Timeline with those simple groups and graphics.

Frame-by-Frame Animation

The most basic form of animation is frame-by-frame animation. Because frame-by-frame animation employs unique drawings in each frame, it's ideal for complex animations that require subtle changes — for example, facial expression. However, frame-by-frame animation also has its drawbacks. It can be very tedious and time-consuming to draw unique art for each frame of the animation. Moreover, all those unique drawings contribute to a larger file size. In Flash, a frame with unique art is called a *keyframe*. As shown in Figure 11-1, frame-by-frame animation requires a unique drawing in each frame, which makes every frame a keyframe.

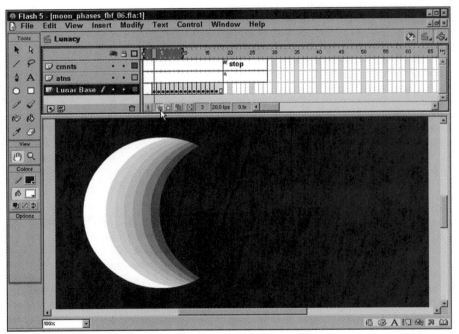

Figure 11-1: You can see the progression across seven frames because onion skinning has been activated. (Note the cursor, having just clicked the Onion Skinning button.)

All of the source files, including the files that were used to generate these shapes for the lunar phases, are included on the CD-ROM — they're in the frame-by-frame folder of the ch11 folder. The timeline shown in Figure 11-1 is from the file named moon_phases_fbf_06.fla. If you examine the files leading to this animation, you'll gain an insight into one process for generating unique drawings. The final .SWF plays like an elapsed time-shot of the moon; 14 days in less than 1 second!

Adding keyframes

To add a keyframe to the timeline, select the frame that you would like to turn into a keyframe. Then, do one of the following:

✦ Right-click or Control+click the keyframe and select Insert Keyframe.

✦ Select Insert ➪ Keyframe from the main menu.

✦ Press F6 on the keyboard.

Creating frame-by-frame animation

Here are the steps for creating a frame-by-frame animation:

1. To create your own frame-by-frame animation, start by selecting the frame in which you'd like your frame-by-frame animation to begin.

2. If it's not already a keyframe, use Insert ➪ Keyframe (F6) to make it one.

3. Then, either draw or import the first image for your sequence into this keyframe. Wherever possible, use symbols and flip, rotate, or otherwise manipulate them to economize on file size.

4. Then click the next frame and make it another keyframe. Change the contents of this second keyframe.

5. Continue to add keyframes and change the contents of each keyframe until you've completed the animation. Finally, test your animation by returning to the first keyframe and then selecting Control ➪ Play from the menu.

Deciphering Flash Source Files

This sidebar is based substantially on content that was developed by Jon Warren Lentz and Jeffrey Bardzell for their interactive Flash curricula at www.Flash-Guru.com. *They've taken a uniquely structural approach to teaching Flash, and the course is titled accordingly:* Flash Five, An Architectural Approach.

There's an old saying, "Give a man a fish, and he'll eat for a day. Teach a man to fish, and he will eat for a lifetime." We think the same concept applies to Flash. There's limited value in delivering linear examples that don't explore the innumerable possibilities for variation at every step—unless you want to duplicate the example precisely, you are headed for unknown territory . . . and you're heading there without a guide.

Beginning with the preceding chapter, we've pointed you toward many source files that are located on the CD-ROM. Many of these source files were designed to lead you from the general example in the book to more particular variations of the same concept. Others are just plain indispensable, because you won't understand the concept until you've seen it in Flash.

Continued

Continued

But examining these Flash source files requires that you decipher them. In a manner of speaking, after you learn how to decipher Flash source files, you are ready to fish with Flash. So, if you aren't familiar with the process of deciphering source files, or if you'd like a few tips, this sidebar is for you.

When you take the time to decipher a Flash file, and persevere until you get the methodology, you'll discover that this process has numerous advantages. Although deciphering source files can be a daunting task for beginners, knowing how to decipher a .FLA is definitely a skill that you want in your Flash repertoire. With this skill, you'll be able to

✦ Understand what your colleagues have done, even if they weren't careful enough to give all symbols and layers meaningful names.

✦ Learn from others, especially by taking advantage of the innumerable online Flash resource sites that offer .FLAs for this purpose.

✦ Engage with Flash architecture by examining a file from a top-down viewpoint, in which you increasingly and systematically discover its functionality.

✦ Explore a file by using the full Flash interface (timeline, Library, Actions Panel, Movie Explorer). This helps you make the kinds of connections among disperse interface elements that will enable you move forward into creative and powerful Flash development

Preliminary Steps

Start with these steps when preparing to decipher a .FLA file:

1. Open the .FLA file.

2. View the .SWF by choosing Control ⇨ Test Movie (Ctrl+Enter/Command+Enter). The best way to understand a .FLA is to know what the final movie looks like!

3. Return to the .FLA and make sure that the timeline and the Library are visible (View ⇨ Timeline and Window ⇨ Library).

Kinds of Information

When deciphering a .FLA, you seek different kinds of information:

✦ There are three structural axes that organize and structure any Flash architecture: the horizontal timeline; the vertical layers; and the deploying and nesting of symbols:

- The timeline organizes content, from left to right, according to time.

- The layers organize content, from front to back, according to space — or depth.

- Symbols, Movie Clips, and nested symbols and Movie Clips organize reusable content through the magic of instances. Generally, this is the most difficult axis to comprehend and decipher.

✦ An understanding each axis is a prerequisite to a thorough understanding of:

- The functionality of a Flash movie — meaning, how users can interact with it.
- How (or how well) the movie was created.

Deciphering Procedures

In most Flash movies, the information that you seek is found in a few predictable locations of the Flash interface, as schematized in the following table:

Kind of Information	Likely Interface Location
What elements are in the file?	Main Timeline and layers (don't forget to look at all the Scenes, if appropriate)
What is the *structural nature* of the elements in the file?	Library and Symbol Editing Mode
How does the movie *function*?	Actions, Labels, and Comments in the timeline; Actions attached to objects (such as Buttons)
All of the above	Movie Explorer (discussed in depth in Chapter 9)

Tweening

Tweening is great for a couple of reasons. Tweened animation is a huge time-saver because it doesn't require that you draw out your animation frame-by-frame. Instead, you establish endpoints and make drawings for each of those end points. Then you let Flash interpolate, or *tween,* the changes between them. Tweening also minimizes file size because you do not have to save the contents for each frame in the animation. Because you only define the contents of the frames at each end point, Flash only has to save those contents, plus the values for the changes between the end points. Two kinds of tweens can be created in Flash — Shape Tweens and Motion Tweens — each with its own unique characteristics.

The Frames Panel

To work with tweens, you need to become familiar with the Frames Panel, shown in Figure 11-2, which is used for choosing the kind of tween and for assigning the properties for each tween. Additionally, the Frames Panel is used for adding labels and comments to keyframes, which is most often associated with ActionScripting operations. For more information on ActionScript, refer to Part V, "Programming Flash Movies with ActionScript."

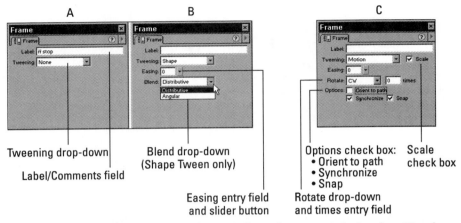

Tweening drop-down

Label/Comments field

Blend drop-down
(Shape Tween only)

Easing entry field
and slider button

Options check box:
• Orient to path
• Synchronize
• Snap

Rotate drop-down
and times entry field

Scale
check box

Figure 11-2: The Frames Panel, in three configurations: as a Label maker (A), when used for assigning properties for a Shape Tween (B), and when assigning properties for a Motion Tween (C).

Shape tweening

Shape tweening is useful for morphing basic shapes between end points. Flash can only shape tween shapes, so don't even try to shape tween a group, symbol, or editable text — it won't work. You can shape tween multiple shapes on a layer, but for the sake of organization it's clearer (and advised!) that each shape be put on its own layer. This makes it much easier to return to the animation later and to make changes, because it can be nearly impossible to figure out what's going on if a number of tweens share the same layer. Shape tweening also enables you to tween colors.

In Figure 11-3, you can see the progression across seven frames because onion skinning has been activated. Although this appears similar to the frame-by-frame example as shown in Figure 11-1, the two animations play quite differently.

The source file for this example is located on the CD-ROM, in the shape tweening folder of the ch11 folder. Take some time to compare this file, and how it plays, to the frame-by-frame previous example.

Here are the steps for creating a Shape Tween:

1. Select the frame in which you'd like to start the animation. If it's not already a keyframe, make it one.

2. Next, before drawing anything, add a second keyframe at the point on the timeline where you want the tween to complete.

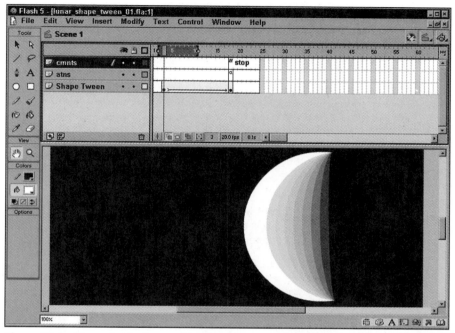

Figure 11-3: Shape tweening enables you to accomplish easy morphing of basic shapes.

3. Now reselect the first keyframe, and then draw your starting image on the stage. Always remember that shape tweening only works with *shapes* — not groups, symbols, or editable text. To shape tween such an element, you first need to break it apart into shapes (Modify ➪ Break Apart).

4. Next, select the second keyframe and draw your ending image on the stage.

5. Open the Frames Panel by choosing Window ➪ Panels ➪ Frames. You can also select a frame between the end points and right-click to invoke the contextual menu. Choose Panels from the menu and then choose Frames from the ensuing submenu.

6. Choose Shape from the Tweening drop-down menu. The panel updates to present several options for modifying the shape tween, as shown in Figure 11-2:

   • Set the Easing slider if necessary. Easing determines the rate of your animation from start to finish. This is useful if you want to create the effect of acceleration or deceleration. If you want your animation to start slowly and progressively speed up, push the slider down. This will cause In to display adjacent to the slider and will also cause a negative number to display in the numeric readout. For an animation that starts out fast, and then progressively slows, push the slider up, causing it to display Out and a positive number in the readout. If you want the rate of your animation to stay constant, leave the slider in the middle. You can also type in a number for the Easing value (–100 to 100).

- Select a Blend Type. Distributive blending creates smoother interpolated shapes, whereas Angular blending creates interpolated shapes with corners and straight lines. If your end points contain shapes with corners and lines, select Angular blending. Otherwise, select Distributive blending, which is the default.

7. Test the animation by selecting Control ➪ Play (Enter) from the menu.

Shape hints

Shape hints give you more control over complex Shape Tweens. As shown in Figure 11-4, they link corresponding points on each shape at both end points of the Shape Tween. The best way to see why shape hints are so useful is to actually work with them.

Caution When copying a span of frames and then pasting that span of frames elsewhere — into a Movie Clip — Flash 5 drops the shape hints (in addition to dropping any layer names). When pasting is confined to the Main Timeline, hints are retained.

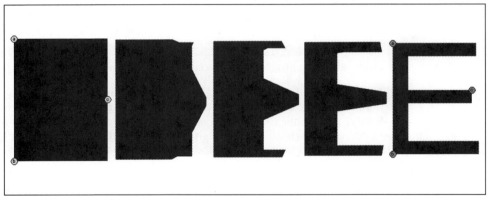

Figure 11-4: Shape hints are small, circled letters at the end points of a Shape Tween.

Using shape hints in a Shape Tween

To use shape hints, follow these steps:

1. Create a more complex Shape Tween using the method described previously — one that would not succeed without a few hints. For example, satisfactorily tweening from the shape of one numeral to another would usually require shape hints.

2. Select the starting frame of your Shape Tween (you can't initiate shape hints from the ending frame). Use Modify ➪ Transform ➪ Add Shape Hint, or press Ctrl/Command+Shift+H to add a shape hint. At first, theshape hint will appear as a red circle with a letter inside of it (the letters start with *a* and go to *z*) as shown in Figure 11-4.

3. Move the shape hint to where it's needed — try to visualize points that must correspond from shape to shape over the course of the tween.

4. Now go to the last frame of your tween. You'll see another small red circle with the same letter as your starting shape hint. Move this shape hint to the corresponding point to which the first shape hint will move during the Shape Tween. After you've placed the second hint, the initiating hint turns yellow and the final hint turns green.

5. Play your movie (Control ⇨ Play) to see how the shape hint affects the tweening.

6. Continue adding shape hints until you're satisfied with the results. Remember to match shape hints at the start and end frames — *a* goes with *a*, *b* with *b*, and so on.

   To get a better idea of just what shape hints do, take a look at the sample in the shape hints folder of the ch11 folder on the CD-ROM. A good experiment is to compare the hinted example to the same example with all hints removed. You just might be amazed!

7. After you've added the first hint, you can simply return to the initiating frame and right-click/Control+click the hint to invoke a contextual menu with options for further shape hinting, including Add Hint, Remove Hint, Remove All Hints, and Show Hints — which is a toggle that's on by default. When you want to see the shape hints again, just use this toggle or View ⇨ Show Shape Hints. To remove all the shape hints, you can also use Modify ⇨ Transform ⇨ Remove All Hints.

Tip

Surprising and interesting results can be obtained by using Shape Tweens in, ahem, unconventional ways. Although the results can be unpredictable, a certain amount of experimentation will yield shapes that might be difficult to obtain through other means. When encapsulated within a Movie Clip, a specific slice of a tween can be captured, by using the Behavior Options of the Instance Panel, or by attaching a `stop` or using a `gotoAndStop` action, and used with few limitations. For more information on Actions, refer to Part IV, "Adding Basic Interactivity to Flash Movies." For example source files, refer to the weird hinted shape tween folder, within the ch11 folder on the CD-ROM.

Motion tweening

Motion tweening is useful for animating groups, symbols, and editable text; however, it cannot animate regular shapes. As the name suggests, motion tweening is used to move an item from one place to another, but it's capable of much more. Motion tweening can be used to animate the scale, skew, or rotation of items; it can also animate the color and transparency of a symbol.

Note

Motion tweening can only be applied to one item per layer — use multiple layers to motion tween multiple items.

A motion tweened item can be started and stopped as much as you want — simply insert a keyframe for each change of pace. Using the easing controls can further finesse this pacing control of Motion Tweens. Furthermore, the kind of tween can be changed; for example, the symbol can be tweened to rotate in the opposite direction. So, if you use a tween to move a symbol from frame 1 to frame 10 and stop the tween on frame 11, you can have the symbol sit still for 10 frames, and then start a new tween (of this same symbol on same layer) from frames 20 to 30. The possibilities are almost endless.

A Motion Tween, such as the one shown in Figure 11-5, is more efficient because it doesn't require unique content for each frame of animation. Yet it is *not* appropriate for all effects — sometimes you'll need to use either frame-by-frame or shape tweening to accomplish what you have in mind.

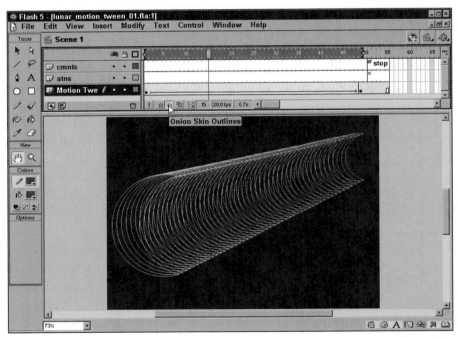

Figure 11-5: The extent of a Motion Tween is revealed here with Onion Skin outlines.

Create a Motion Tween

Here's how to create a Motion Tween:

1. Select the frame in which you'd like to start your animation. If it's not already a keyframe, make it one by selecting Insert ➪ Keyframe (F6).

2. Draw or import the image that you want to tween. Just remember that you can only motion tween groups, symbols (including imported bitmaps — which are, by default, symbols), and editable text (a text block).

   • If you are using an image, group it or turn it into a symbol (refer to Chapter 9, "Checking Out the Library: Symbols and Instances," for a review of creating symbols).

   • If you already have the image as a symbol in your movie's Library, you can just drag it from the Library onto the stage.

   • If you are using editable text, you don't have to do anything — it's already an item.

3. Select the frame where you want the tween to end and make it a keyframe by selecting Insert ➪ Keyframe (F6).

4. Position your images in the two end points. Remember that you can move tweened elements, as well as scale, skew, and rotate them. If your end point images are symbols, you can also use the Effects Panel to apply color effects to them.

5. Right-click/Control+click a frame between your two end points and select Create Motion Tween. Test your animation by choosing Control ➪ Test Movie.

6. Open the Frames Panel by choosing Window ➪ Panels ➪ Frames. You can also select a frame between the end points and right-click to invoke the contextual menu. Choose Panels from the menu and then choose Frames from the ensuing submenu.

7. Choose Motion to make it a Motion Tween. The animation shown in Figure 11-6 involves both diminishing scale and deceleration to mimic the moon as it moves further away.

   Open the easing source file folder located in the ch11 folder on the CD-ROM. Look inside the Frame Properties dialog, under the Tweening tab. Pay special attention to the Easing option.

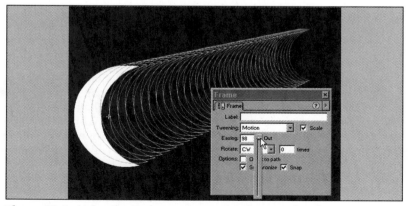

Figure 11-6: Using the Easing option to decelerate animation

- **Rotate:** You can rotate your items using this option. Select a rotation type from the drop-down menu and then type the number of rotations in the entry field. Automatic rotation rotates your item in the direction that requires the least amount of motion, while Clockwise and Counterclockwise rotate your item in the indicated direction. In both cases, the rotation will be completed as many times as you specify in the entry field. If you type 0 in the entry field, or select None from the drop-down menu, no rotation will occur.

- **Orient to path:** When your item follows a path, turning this selection on forces the item to orient its movement to that path. We discuss paths in the next section of this chapter.

- **Synchronize:** This option ensures that your animation loops properly in the Main Movie. It forces the animation to loop properly even if the sequence is not an even multiple of the number of frames occupied by the symbol in the Main Movie's Timeline. This is only important if your animation is contained within a graphic symbol.

- **Snap:** This option snaps your animated item to a Motion Guide. Motion Guides are discussed later in this chapter.

Flash 4 added a feature that automatically adds new keyframes between the end points of a Motion Tween. This is very useful if you decide to add a third point to your animation (you aren't stuck with only two!). Just select the frame that you want to turn into an end point, and move the item that it contains to the desired location — a new keyframe appears like magic.

Tweened Zooms (where an item is initiated at a reduced scale and then tweened to full-scale or larger) and tweened alpha effects can be both CPU and bandwidth intensive — not only do they result in larger files that take longer to download, but they also require more computing horsepower on the user's machine. Our advice: Use such effects judiciously, and always double-check them for performance spikes by using the bandwidth profiler when testing your work. The bandwidth profiler is accessed from the Test Movie player (Control ➪ Test Movie) with View ➪ Bandwidth Profiler. For more discussion about the Bandwidth Profiler, refer to Chapter 20, "Sharing and Loading Assets," and Chapter 40, "Publishing Flash Movies."

Motion Tweened effects

Because symbol instances have properties that can be manipulated separately from their root symbol, it's possible to scale, rotate, and skew an instance. This feature of symbols makes it possible to generate a wide range of animated effects that rely almost entirely upon the file efficiency of Flash symbols. While this is indeed great, it gets even better: There's one more class of instance properties that can be tweaked — these properties are tint, brightness, alpha (or opacity), and advanced combinations of all three.

Using the chromatic options of the Effects Panel in concert with motion tweening gives you great control over the color and opacity of symbol instances in your animations, with good file size economy too. In Figure 11-7, our lunar example has been modified to slowly become the fabled blue moon.

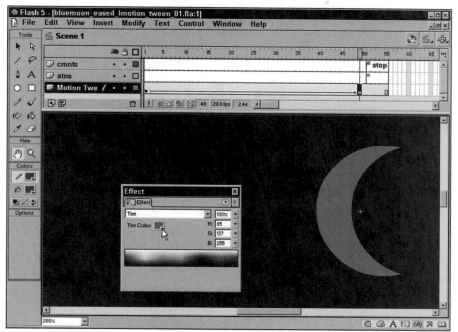

Figure 11-7: Using the chromatic options of the Effects panel along with motion tweening

As shown in Figure 11-8, the Effects Panel enables you to control color and opacity of motion tweened symbol instances. There are five iterations of this panel, each of which is accessed from the Effect drop-down. If you look closely, you'll notice that nearly all of the sliders have the capability to reduce a value by a negative percentage.

On the CD-ROM   The source file for the examples discussed in this section can be found in the effects folder, which is located in the ch11 folder on the CD-ROM.

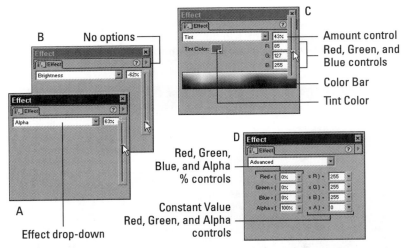

Figure 11-8: The Behavior drop-down of the Effects Panel is shown with four of the five Behaviors and their many options. The fifth behavior, None, has been omitted.

Here's a rundown on the gamut of controls that are available in this colorful workhorse of a panel:

✦ **None:** Use this when you don't want to use this control.

✦ **Brightness:** Use this control to adjust the brightness of the selected instance, on a relative scale that ranges from black to white, which is represented as –100 percent to +100 percent.

✦ **Tint:** Use this control to color (or tint) an instance with a singular color. The tint color that's to be applied can be chosen from the Swatches Panel, which is accessible from the Tint Color button. Alternative methods of choosing the tint color are by entering numeric values in the R, G, B fields, or by adjusting the associated R, G, B sliders. After the tint color is set, the intensity of the tint can be adjusted with the Amount control—which can also be operated as an entry field or as slider.

✦ **Alpha:** Use this control to adjust the alpha, or transparency, of the selected instance on a relative scale that ranges from completely transparent to fully visible, which is represented as 0 percent to 100 percent.

Tip Alpha effects in Motion Tweens will slow most fps settings. The only way to make sure that the fps is honored, no matter what, is to use a stream sync sound that loops over the course of any critical fps playback. For more on the relationship between streaming sounds and fps rate, see Chapter 16, "Optimizing Flash Sound for Export."

✦ **Advanced:** This truly is the advanced control, and it may take some getting used to. It enables you to adjust the R, G, B, and alpha values independently. The controls on the left are used to adjust values on a *relative* scale — meaning that adjustments are relative to the current colors. The colors on the right are used to adjust values subject to *constant* values — meaning that an absolute value, ranging from 0 to 255, can be assigned for R, G, B, or A. When used independently (that is, without tweaking the other bank of controls) these controls are intuitive. When used in conjunction with each other, they become quite powerful, albeit confusing at first blush. We suggest that you take some time, experiment, and take notes — your effort will be repaid in many colorful instances.

New Feature Animating with negative alpha: If you take a close look at the Advanced option of the Effect drop-down of the Effects Panel you'll notice that, in this implementation, alpha can be assigned a *negative* value. Huh? Of course, an instance can't get any less visible than invisible. So what's that good for? A little experimentation yielded this one of many possible answers: Suppose you want to make a motion tweened item go from invisible to visible, but that you want it to commence visibility part way through a 100-frame tween. If you set the alpha to negative 100 in frame 1 and then, in frame 100, set the alpha to a positive 100, then the item will *begin* to be visible at frame 50. A similar logic might be employed to cause a tweened item to rotate only one-half rotation — simply make it invisible for the first half of it's rotation. For more information, refer to the examples on the CD-ROM in the negative alpha folder of the ch11 folder. (This same logic applies to negative brightness, which can be applied from the Brightness option of the Effects Panel.)

Guide Layers

Guide layers make it easy to keep the layout of your movie consistent, or to trace images, drawings, or other materials from which you want to develop an item. When employed as Motion Guides, you can use Guide layers to create the complex motion of a frame-by-frame animation with the ease of a tweened animation. Guide layers are not exported with the rest of the movie — they're just guides. So use them as much as you want.

On the CD-ROM The source file for the examples discussed in this section can be found in the guide layers folder, which is located in the ch11 folder on the CD-ROM.

Using Guide layers for layout

Guide layers are great when you need a little help drawing in Flash. Use them as guides for your layout, as aids for drawing a complex graphic, or for anything else that you might need. To reemphasize, because Guide layers aren't exported with the movie, they do not add to the file size of the final .SWF. As shown in Figure 11-9, Guide layers are marked with unique icons next to the layer name.

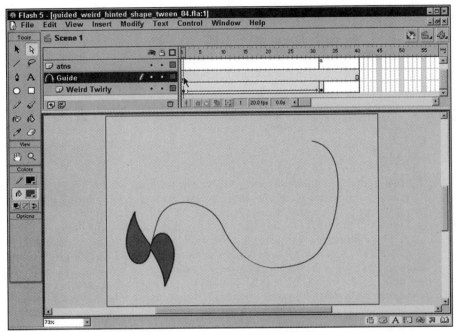

Figure 11-9: Guide layers have unique icons next to the layer name. Shown here is a guided Movie Clip together with its motion path. Note that the motion path is static.

Adding a Guide layer

Here are the steps for adding a Guide layer:

1. Draw or import your guide art into a layer by itself. This can be anything from a hand-drawn sketch of your layout to a full-blown prototype of your design.

2. Open the Layer Properties dialog for this layer by double-clicking the icon to the left of the layer's name.

3. Set the Layer Type to Guide, as shown in Figure 11-10 (using either the Layer Properties or the Contextual Menu, which is accessed with a right-click/Control+click on the Layer name), and then press OK.

4. Use Control ➪ Test Movie to test the movie. Do you see the guide art in the movie? You shouldn't! Remember, because it's a guide layer, it isn't exported with the rest of the movie.

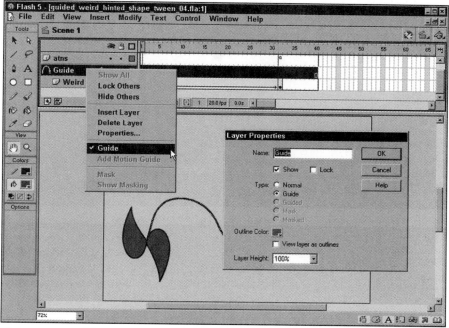

Figure 11-10: This composite screen shot shows how you can choose Guide from the contextual menu, or set the type to Guide in the Layer Properties dialog.

Motion Guides

You already know how to move an item from point A to point B. What if you don't want to move it in a straight line? This is when tweening along a path comes in handy. Motion tweening along a path requires a Motion Guide layer, which defines the path. One or more guided layers that follow the path accompany this Motion Guide layer. The Guide layer does not export with your movie — it's only visible within the editing environment. Figure 11-11 shows an item and its motion path.

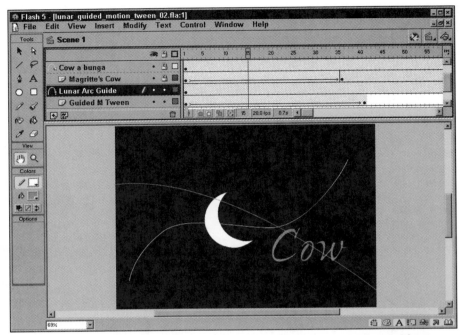

Figure 11-11: Moving items along a path is simple! Just use a Motion Guide. For multiple (as shown) guided items, use multiple Guide layers.

Create a Motion Tween along a path

Follow these steps to create a Motion Tween along a path:

1. Create a Motion Tween as described previously in this chapter.

2. Select the layer containing the tween, and then insert a Guide layer by doing one of the following:

   • Click the Add Guide Layer icon.

   • Right-click or Control+click the layer and select Add Motion Guide from the pop-up menu.

   • Use Insert ⇨ Motion Guide from the main menu.

3. Draw a path in the Guide layer. You can use the Line, Pen, Oval, Rectangle, Pencil, or Brush Tools to do this.

4. Snap the center of the items in the end-point keyframes to the path. If you selected Snap to Guide in the Tweening tab of the Frame Properties dialog, it should snap automatically to the item in the starting keyframe.

5. If you want the item to orient itself to the path it's following, select a frame between your Motion Tween's end points, open the Frame Properties dialog, choose the Tweening tab, and make sure that the Orient to path direction option is selected. This forces the item to move so that its center remains parallel to the path.

Tip

If the item ends up oriented sideways or upside down when you orient it to path, simply rotate it and reattach it to the path.

On the CD-ROM

Be sure to look at the Guide layer source files in the ch11 folder on the CD-ROM. They are commented with useful notes to help you understand this process a little better.

Organizational Guides

An empty Guide layer can be used to organize multiple layers of related content for better timeline organization. It can also be used as a repository for custom strokes and fills. To use a Guide layer for organizational purposes:

1. Create an Organizational Guide layer.

2. Give the Guide Layer a meaningful name.

3. Arrange subordinate layers as Guided layers by:

- Using the Layer Properties dialog; click the Guided radio button to set the layer type to Guided, or

- Clicking and dragging the layer bar until it hovers just underneath the Guide layer, and then releasing.

Masking Animations

When animating with Flash, a mask can be used either to hide or to reveal elements, with the added complication of movement. As with static masks, an animated mask effect is created by integrating a Mask layer with one or more Masked layers. The Mask and the masked content can be moved at varied rates or in different directions — the possibilities are endless. For more background on static masks, see Chapter 10, "Drawing in Flash."

Some obvious possibilities for masked animations include: spotlights, moonbeams, text that is progressively revealed, a view through a periscope (or binoculars), simulated x-ray vision, navigational devices, and many more. Aside from your imagination, the only limitations upon animated masks are that motion paths cannot be used to animate a mask, and that layers within buttons cannot be masked.

Be sure to look at the masking animation source files in the masking animations folder of the ch11 folder on the CD-ROM. There are several advanced examples that will inspire you to learn this process, as well as to test your facility with the deciphering of source files. In order of complexity, the examples are animated mask, masked moon animation, masked line animation, and kaleidoscopic button animation.

Animated mask text

Here's how to create one of the simplest forms of animated mask:

1. To begin with, we need to make the content that will be visible on its own layer beneath the mask and the mask content. For this example, we mask some text so that it appears to be spot lit. The text we use is MMF5. Create this text on frame 1 and make it big and bold! See Figure 11-12.

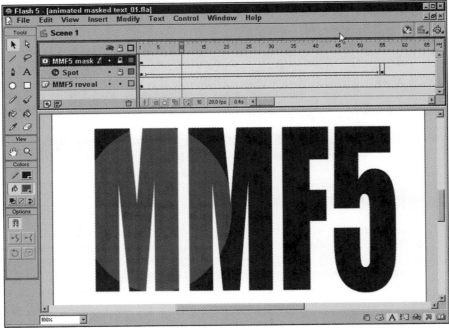

Figure 11-12: This example of animated mask text is among the simplest uses for animated masks.

2. Name this layer **MMF5 reveal**. Then give it about 55 frames, by clicking frame 55 and then hitting the F5 key, to insert a frame.

3. Add another layer above MMF5 reveal, and name it **MMF5 mask**. Make sure that visibility is turned on. Then return to the first layer that you created, MMF5 reveal, and click in the middle of the frame span in order to select all 55 frames.

4. Next, press the Alt/Option key and drag this span of frames up over the MMF5 mask (which is the second layer that you created) to copy the span of frames.

5. Now you're ready to make your masked content, which will be the spotlight. As with static masks, this is called the Masked layer. But first, turn off the visibility for the MMF5 Mask layer.

6. Add a new layer between the two previous layers, and name it **Spot**. Then, with frame 1 selected, use Insert ⇨ New Symbol to create a symbol. For this exercise, any behavior and name is fine.

7. Next, use the Oval Tool to draw a red circle. Click the Scene 1 button to return to the Main Timeline. Open the Library (Window ⇨ Library) and drag an instance of your symbol onto the Stage. This red circle should be as tall as the text, so adjust its size, if necessary. Position it off to the left, so that it is next to the first M, almost touching, as shown in Figure 11-13.

Figure 11-13: Position the red circle to the left, so that it's next to the first M, almost touching the M.

8. Next, select frame 55 of the Spot layer and press F6 to add a keyframe there.

9. Then select the Arrow Tool to reposition the red circle so that it is on the opposite side of the 5, almost touching the 5. If you use the arrow keys to move the item or press Shift to constrain the movement, you will be assured that the circle will animate in a smooth, straight line.

10. Now click anywhere in the middle of the Spot frame span, and then proceed to the Frame Panel and choose Motion from the Tweening drop-down.

11. Now, return to MMF5 Mask layer, and then right-click/Control+click the layer name and choose Mask (as the layer type) from the ensuing contextual menu. The icons of both this layer and the Spot layer beneath it should update to indicate that they are the Mask and Masked layers, respectively. Both layers should automatically lock.

12. Save your work, and then use Control ⇨ Test Movie to preview your work. It should appear as though the Black MMF5 text is being lit by a red spot that moves from left to right.

Now you've probably succeeded with this example, but you might still be wondering how this animated mask text works. Well, here's an explanation.

The first layer that you created, MMF5 reveal, which is at the bottom of the layer stack, is a simple static text layer — it just sits there showing text.

The layer just above MMF5 reveal, which is named Spot, is a simple Motion Tween — the red circle moves from the left of the Stage to the right. Nothing fancy about this, either.

The uppermost layer, MMF5 mask, is the Mask layer, and it's responsible for the effect that you see. As a mask, this layer defines which portions of the Masked layer — which is Spot — will be seen. As Spot moves across the text *beneath* it, the text forms above Spot define where Spot will be seen: only within the shapes of letterforms. So, as Spot moves from left to right, it appears to be illuminating dimensional letterforms, and the "light" falls off the edges where there are no letters.

Masked moon phases

Here's another way in which the phases of the moon might be animated with Flash: by using an animated mask. This is a little more complex because it involves the use of an inverse shape to obtain the desired effect. Consequently, it's a lot less intuitive than the previous example. We strongly urge you to study the sample file on the CD-ROM until you understand why this works.

Figure 11-14 shows the setup for a masked animation of the phases of the moon. The background is black. Shown here are the Masked layer (A), the mask (B), the mask over the Masked layer — but with the layers unlocked and masking consequently disabled (C), and finally, the composite effect with the mask enabled and at frame 30 (D).

Here's the explanation. As shown in Figure 11-14, the Mask layer begins in perfect alignment with the masked shape of the full moon — which is the white circle shown in (A). Because the Mask layer is the inverse of the moon, it covers none of that shape and, consequently, the moon is not revealed. As the mask is moved to the right, a sliver of the mask covers the moon and causes it to be revealed. This continues until the moon is fully masked and, thus, fully revealed. Then the mask is reversed and the moon continues through the other half of its cycle.

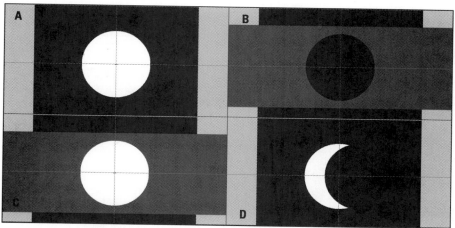

Figure 11-14: The setup for a masked animation of the phases of the moon

Masked line progression

This is a relatively simple effect that's simply repeated to create the effect of a line that appears progressively. Creating such an effect requires either a good bit of clarity before you set to work, or a willingness to tinker and tweak until all of the hiccups are smoothed out. When you decipher this file, and its variations, located in the masking animations folder of the ch11 folder on the CD-ROM, take care to notice how the entire effect was built with multiple instances derived from two symbols.

The animation shown in Figure 11-15 begins with a blank white screen. Starting at the upper-right corner, the first mask moves onscreen from right to left and progressively reveals the hatched line. The effect continues around the screen, until the complete line has been revealed.

This effect is accomplished by creating a stack of four pairs of mask and outline. The first pair is revealed above the others — this mask is Mask 1, together with Outline 1. The only part of Outline 1 that will be revealed is this upper portion.

Next, beginning at frame 25, the left-side portion of Outline 2 is progressively revealed as Mask 2 slides down from the upper offscreen area. Following this, at frame 50, Mask 3 progressively reveals the bottom portion of Outline 3. Finally, the right side of Outline 4 is revealed. Each of these reveals is accomplished with a simple linear Motion Tween.

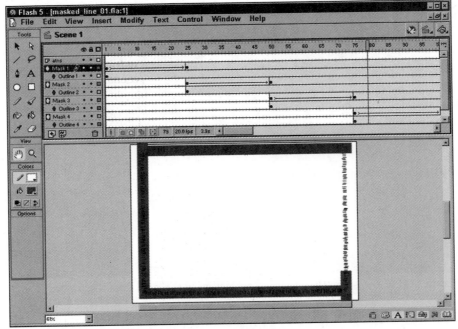

Figure 11-15: Progressively revealing a hatched line

Final notes about animated masks

If you find that these masked animations are a little hard to grasp, don't panic. For most people, the logic of animated masks is slightly inverted. That's because

✦ The mask goes above the item that is revealed by it.

✦ Flash uses an opaque window to reveal items below.

✦ Items that are not covered by the opaque window will not be visible when the mask is enabled by locking the Mask layer together with the Masked layer.

✦ Sometimes mild confusion over the elementary aspects of animation, compounded with the nature of masks, can lead to trouble. If this happens to you, just be patient — separate the animation from the masking. Then, when you've got them both working separately, combine them.

Summary

✦ Animation is an integral part of almost any Flash movie. There are three basic ways to create animated effects, including frame-by-frame animation and two kinds of tweened animation: Shape and Motion Tweens.

✦ More sophisticated animations often involve a combination of all three types of animation. The kind — or combination — that you use will depend on what you're trying to achieve, as demonstrated by the examples in this chapter.

✦ Unless you are working with Shape Tweens, you should always endeavor to work more efficiently by using the Symbols and Instances capability of the Library.

✦ Guide layers can be used in two ways with animations: to organize content and to create Motion Guided Tweens, or motion along a path.

✦ The final ingredient, aside from imagination and creativity, which Flash offers for the creation of animations, is the animated mask.

✦ Combined, these several types of animation, together with guides and masks, can be used to create an endless variety of expressions, effects, and styles. If you have any doubt, just look at the range of Flash animation available for your viewing pleasure on the Web!

✦   ✦   ✦

Using Bitmaps and Other Media with Flash

Although the Flash drawing tools give you a powerful environment in which to create a variety of graphics, you don't have to limit yourself to the capabilities of Flash. That's because Flash also has the capability to import artwork from a wide range of sources. You can import both vector and bitmap graphics, and you can use both types in a variety of ways. In this chapter, we discuss the differences between vector and bitmap graphics. We also learn how to import external artwork so that it can be used in a Flash movie, as well as the Flash features that can be used to handle imported bitmap images.

Understanding Vector versus Bitmap Images

Flash supports two types of image formats: vector and bitmap.

Vector graphic files consist of an equation that describes the placement of points and the qualities of the lines between those points. Using this basic logic, vector graphics tell the computer how to display the lines and shapes, as well as what colors to use, how wide to make the lines, where to put it on the Stage, and at what scale.

Flash is a vector program. Thus, anything that you create with the Flash drawing tools will be described in vector format. Vector graphics have some important benefits: They're small in file size and they scale accurately without distortion. However, they also have a couple of drawbacks: Highly complex vector graphics may result in very large file sizes, and vectors aren't really suitable for creating continuous tones, photographs, or artistic brushwork.

Bitmap (sometimes also referred to as Raster) files are described as an arrangement of individual pixels which are mapped in a grid like a piece of graph paper with tiny squares. Each square represents a single pixel, and each of these pixels has specific color values assigned to it. So, as the name implies, a bitmap image maps out the placement and color of each pixel on the screen.

Note   Do not be confused by the name bitmap. You might already be familiar with the bitmap format used by Windows, which has the file extension .BMP. Although *bitmap* may refer to that particular image format, it's frequently applied to raster images in general, such as .GIF, .JPEG, .PICT, and .TIFF files, as well as many others.

Although bitmap images aren't created in Flash, they can be used within Flash projects. To do this, you need to use an external bitmap application and then import the bitmaps into Flash. Unlike vector graphics, bitmap images aren't very scalable, as shown in Figure 12-1. Simple bitmap images are often larger in file size than simple vector graphics, but very complex bitmap images, for example a photograph, are often smaller (and display better quality) than comparable vector graphics.

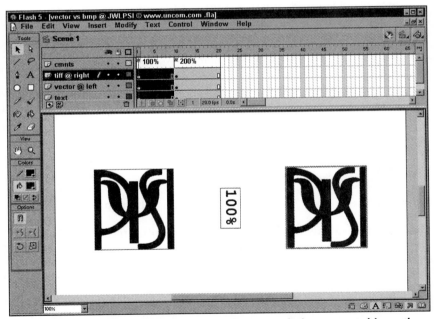

Figure 12-1: Here's JWL's logo — compare the unscaled vector graphic on the left to the unscaled bitmap image on the right. They both look almost equally acceptable, although the vector graphic is sharper.

The rule of thumb is to use scalable, bandwidth-efficient, Flash-compatible vector graphics as much as possible within Flash projects, except for situations in which photographs — or photographic quality, continuous-tone images — are either desired or required.

Figure 12-2 shows the difference between vector and bitmap graphics when scaled.

Figure 12-2: Here's JWL's logo again. Now compare the scaled vector graphic on the left to the scaled bitmap image on the right — the vector is *clearly* superior.

Tip

Most 8-bit raster images are .GIFs, and they are most frequently used for images with large areas of solid color, such as logos and text. Rather than use this image type in Flash, consider re-creating or tracing this artwork with Flash drawing tools. The final .SWF will not only be smaller, it will also look better in Flash.

Importing External Media

Flash can use a variety of external media, including vector graphics and bitmap images. You can import this media directly, or you can copy from another application and paste directly into Flash.

For a complete listing of all importable media supported by Flash 5, refer to section "The File Menu" in Chapter 2, "Exploring the Interface: Panels, Settings, and More." For a full discussion of the importation and handling of sound media, refer to Part III, "Sound Planning." For further discussion of the use of Flash with bitmap applications refer to Chapter 30, "Working with Raster Graphics." For now, take a look at the Table 12-1 for image formats for Flash Import.

Table 12-1
Image Formats for Flash Import

File Type	Extension	Description	Win	Mac	QuickTime
Adobe Illustrator	.ai, .eps	Adobe Illustrator files are imported into Flash as vector graphics (unless they contain bitmap images). Flash supports import of files saved as Adobe Illustrator files.	X	X	
AutoCAD DXF	.dxf	.DXF is the original inter-program format for AutoCAD drafting software. It was subsequently used for the original AutoCAD 3D Studio, now known as Kinetix 3DS MAX. This format is used by most other CAD, 3D, and modeling programs for transferring drawings to other programs.	X	X	
Bitmap	.bmp, .dib	Bitmap is a Windows format for bitmap images. Don't be confused by the format name — not all bitmap images are Windows Bitmaps. Can be used with all PC and some Mac applications. Variable bit depths and compression settings with support of alpha channels. Supports lossless compression. Ideal for high-quality graphics work.	X		Mac with QT4
Enhanced Metafile	.emf	Enhanced Metafile is a proprietary Windows format that supports vectors and bitmaps internally. This format is generally used to import vector graphics.	X		

File Type	Extension	Description	Win	Mac	QuickTime
Flash Player	.swf, .spl	Flash player files are exported Flash movies. The movie is flattened into a single layer and scene, and all animation is converted to frame-by-frame animation.	X	X	
FreeHand	.fh7, .fh8, .fh9	This is the vector-based format of Macromedia's FreeHand 7, 8, or 9.	X	X	
GIF Image	.gif	Graphic Interchange Format (.GIF was developed by Compuserve) is a bitmap image type that uses lossless compression. Limited to a 256-color (or less) palette. Not recommended as a high-quality Flash export format, even for Web use. (See Caution.)	X	X	
JPEG Image	.jpg	Joint Photographic Experts Group (JPEG) images are bitmap images that use lossy compression. Supports 24-bit RGB color. No alpha channel support. Recommended for most high-quality graphics work. Note that this format does throwout color information due to its lossy compression method.	X	X	
MacPaint Image	.pntg	This is a legacy format for the old Mac Paint program.			Mac and Win with QT4

Continued

Table 12-1 (continued)

File Type	Extension	Description	Win	Mac	QuickTime
PICT Image	.pct, .pict	Can be used with many PC and all Mac applications. Variable bit depths and compression settings with support of alpha channels (when saved with no compression at 32 bits). Supports lossless compression. Can contain vector and raster graphics. Ideal for high-quality graphics work.		X	Win with QT 4
PNG Image	.png	The Portable Network Graphic format (.PNG) is another type of bitmap image. Supports variable bit depth (PNG-8 and PNG-24) and compression settings with alpha channels. Lossless compression schemes make it an ideal candidate for any high-quality graphics work. This is the best media type for imported images with alpha settings.	X	X	
Photoshop 2.5, 3, 5, 5.5, 6 Image	.psd	This is the layered format for most versions of Photoshop – from version 2.5 through version 6. Although it is possible to import .PSD files, it's not the best alternative. If you have the .PSD, open it in Photoshop, optimize it for use in Flash, and then export it as either a .JPEG or a .PNG for ideal import into Flash.			Mac and Win with QT4
QuickTime Image	.qtif	This is the image format created by QuickTime.			Mac and Win with QT4

File Type	Extension	Description	Win	Mac	QuickTime
QuickTime Movie	.mov	QuickTime is a video format created by Apple Computers. Flash imports it with a link to the original file.	X	X	Mac and Win with QT4
Silicon Graphics Image	.sgi	This is an image format specific to SGI machines.			Mac and Win with QT4
TGA Image	.tga	The .TGA, or Targa, format is a 32-bit format that includes an 8-bit alpha channel. It was developed to overlay computer graphics and live video.			Mac and Win with QT4
Tiff Image	.tiff	.TIFF is probably the most widely used image format for photography and printing. It's available across Mac and PC platforms.			Mac and Win with QT4
Windows Metafile	.wmf	Windows Metafile is a proprietary Windows format that supports vectors and bitmaps internally. This format is generally used to import vector graphics.	X		

Caution

Although you can use the Publish settings to export to the .GIF format from Flash, this should be considered as a utility for information transfer, as raw .GIFs — and not as a means for creating final .GIF art. For optimal quality and control, Flash-created .GIFs should be brought into Fireworks for fine-tuning and optimization. An even better workflow is to avoid the Flash .GIF entirely by exporting as a .PNG sequence and bringing that into Fireworks for fine-tuning and output to .GIF. For more information, refer to Chapter 30, "Working with Raster Graphics."

Importing Vector Graphics

Vector graphics from other applications can be easily imported into Flash. These graphics are imported as groups, as illustrated in Figure 12-3 and can be used just like a normal group drawn in Flash.

Most vector graphics are imported as grouped items. FreeHand vectors may be imported as a flattened group or as discrete, aligned, layers. The lovely, craftsman-inspired logo shown in Figure 12-3 is from Nik Scramm's www.industriality.com, which is featured in his expert tutorial, "Scripting for Interfaces," in Chapter 26.

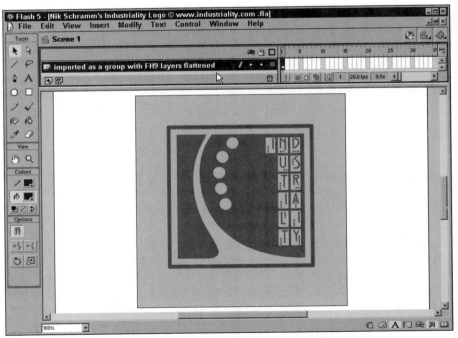

Figure 12-3: Most vector graphics are imported as grouped items.

Cross-Reference Refer to Chapter 8, "Exploring the Timeline," for more information about using grouped items in Flash. Refer to Chapter 31, "Working with Vector Graphics," for more information about working with vector graphics from other applications, such as FreeHand.

Importing a vector file into Flash

To import a vector file into Flash, follow these steps:

1. Make sure that there's an active, unlocked layer. If no layer is available for placement of the imported item, the Import command will be dimmed and you won't be able to import anything.

2. Select File ⇨ Import (Ctrl+R/Command+R).

3. The Import dialog opens, as shown at the left of Figure 12-4. Navigate to the file that you'd like to import, and then select it and click the Open button. If it's a FreeHand file, then — as shown at the right in Figure 12-4 — the FreeHand Import dialog opens.

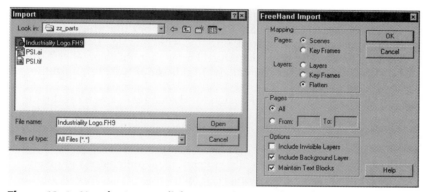

Figure 12-4: Use the Import dialog to navigate to the file that you'd like to import. FreeHand files receive special care upon import.

Preparing Bitmaps for Flash

Flash is a vector-based application, but that shouldn't stop you from using bitmaps when you *need* to use a bitmap. There are many situations in which either the designs or the nature of the client require that photographic images be included in a Flash project. You can import a wide variety of bitmap image types, including .JPEG, .GIF, .BMP, and .PICT using the method described previously in this chapter.

Considering that it's a vector-based program, Flash 5 supports bitmap graphics extraordinarily well. However, because the most common use of Flash movies is for Web presentations, you always need to keep file size in mind — slower Internet connections still dominate the Web. Here's what you can do to offset this problem:

✦ Limit the number of bitmaps used in any one frame of a Flash movie.

✦ Remember that, regardless how many times the bitmap is placed on Stage, the actual bitmap (or its compressed version in the .SWF file) is downloaded during the first occurrence of the bitmap (or its symbol instance).

✦ Try spreading out bitmap usage, or hide a symbol instance of the bitmap in an earlier frame before it is actually needed.

Tip

If you need to include several high-resolution bitmap images in your Flash movie, consider the use of an ActionScript preloader (see Chapter 20, "Sharing and Loading Assets"), or try breaking up the Flash movie into several linked Flash movies. These linked movies could use the Load Movie action to appear in the main (or parent) Flash movie.

Basic tips for preserving bitmap quality

When you choose to use bitmap images, remember that they won't scale as well as vector drawings. Furthermore, bitmaps will become distorted if your movie is resized so that the bitmap is displayed larger than its original size. Here are a few points to consider so that you can avoid this, or at least minimize the effects:

✦ Know your audience and design for the largest screen (at the highest resolution) that your audience may have. (Or, if you deviate from this, know that audience members with optimal equipment will see a low-quality version of your work.)

✦ Measure your hypothetically largest image dimensions in pixels. (One way to determine these dimensions is to take a screen capture of your mockup, and then measure the intended image area in Photoshop. Another way is to use the Info Panel.)

✦ Create or resize your bitmap image to those hypothetical dimensions. If there are any rotations or skews to be applied, do them within your image-editing application — prior to importing into Flash.

✦ Import it into Flash at that size, and then scale it down in Flash to fit into your movie.

The advantage of the previous method, or similar methods, is that the movie can be allowed to scale for larger monitors without causing the bitmap images to degrade. The disadvantage is that it will require sending the same large bitmap to all users. A more sophisticated solution is to use JavaScript to detect browser dimensions and then send the appropriate bitmaps to each user. Other, simpler — albeit partial — solutions might include the following:

✦ Just don't let your movie resize!

✦ Set the bitmap's compression to lossless.

✦ Trace the bitmap to convert it to a vector graphic (covered later in this chapter).

Raster Images: Resolution, Dimensions, and Bit Depth

Resolution refers to the amount of information per a given unit of measurement. Greater resolutions mean better quality (or better resemblance to the original). With respect to raster images, resolution is usually measured in pixels per inch (when viewed on a monitor) or dots per inch (when output on film or paper).

What is Resolution?

The resolution of an original image changes whenever the dimensions of an image are changed, while the pixel dimensions remain fixed. Thus, if an original photograph is scanned at 300 pixels per inch (ppi) with dimensions of 2"×2", subsequently changing the dimensions to 4"×4" will result in a resolution of 150 ppi. Although a 4"×4" image at 300 ppi could be interpolated from the original image, true resolution will be *lost* in such a jump. When an image is enlarged like this, the graphics application simply doubles every pixel, which softens the image considerably. Conversely, reducing the scale of an image has few undesirable side effects — although a smaller version of the original may display reduced (or destroyed) fine details.

Because all raster images consist of pixels, and because resolution simply describes how closely those pixels should be packed, the most accurate way of referencing raster images is by using the absolute pixel width and height of an image. For example, a 4000×5000 pixel image can be printed or displayed at any size with variable resolution. This image could be 4"×5" at 1000 ppi, or it could be 8"×10" at 500 ppi — without any loss of information. Remember that resolution simply describes how much information is shown per unit. When you reduce the pixel width and height of an image, the resolution becomes lower as well. However, once any pixels are thrown out, discarded, or interpolated, they're gone for good.

Bringing Images into Flash

When you want to bring raster images into Flash movies, you should know what portion of the Flash Stage the image occupies. Let's assume that you are working with the default Flash movie size of 550×400 pixels. If you want to use a bitmap as a background image, it won't need to be any larger than 550×440. So, assuming that you are starting with a high-resolution image, you would downscale the image to the largest size at which it will appear in the Flash movie *before* you import it into Flash; for our example, that would be 550×440.

Continued

Continued

Use an image-editing program such as Macromedia Fireworks or Adobe Photoshop to downsize the pixel width and height of your image.

If you mask bitmaps with a Mask layer in the Flash timeline, the entire bitmap is still exported. Consequently, before import you should closely crop all images that will be masked in Flash. For example, if all you need to show is a face, crop the image so that it shows the face with a bare minimum of extraneous detail.

Raster Images: Bit Depth

Bit depth is another factor that influences image quality and file size. Bit depth refers to the amount of information stored for each pixel of an image. The most common bit depths for images are 8-bit and 24-bit, although many others exist. An 8-bit image contains up to 256 colors, while a 24-bit image may contain 16.7 million color values. Depending on their file format, some images can also use an 8-bit alpha channel, which is a multilevel transparency layer. Each addition to an image's bit-depth is reflected in a great file size increase: A 24-bit image contains three times the information per pixel as does an 8-bit image. Mathematically, you can calculate the file size (in bytes) of an image with the following formula (all measurements are in pixels):

```
width×height×(bit depth ÷ 8) = file size
```

Author's Note: You divide bit depth by 8 because there are 8 bits per byte.

The optimal bit depth for us in Flash movies is 24-bit. This is due to the fact that Flashes defaults to 24-bit JPEG compression for all exported bitmaps. You can, however, import 8-bit images in formats such as .GIF, .BMP, and .PICT. In this circumstance, especially for people viewing your Flash artwork with 8-bit video adapters, you'll have a greater degree of viewing predictability with 8-bit images that use Web-safe color palettes.

More about preparing bitmaps

Before sizing and importing bitmaps, you need to consider how you will set the Dimensions for the Flash movie in the HTML tab of the Publish Settings. You also need to know whether the bitmap is to be scaled in a Motion Tween. If the Flash movie scales beyond its original pixel width and height (or if the bitmap is scaled in a tween), then any placed bitmap images will be resized and appear at a lower resolution with a consequent degradation of image quality. Scaling of Flash movies is discussed in the Publishing sections of Chapter 40, "Publishing Flash Movies," and Chapter 41, "Integrating Flash Content with HTML."

If you are unsure of the final size that you need for a bitmap in Flash, then import a low-resolution version of the image into Flash (being careful not to erase or overwrite your high-resolution version in the process!). Then, make a symbol with a graphic behavior and place the low-resolution bitmap into that symbol. Whenever you need to use the bitmap, place its symbol on the Flash Stage. Then, during final production and testing, after you've determine what pixel size is required for the better quality bitmap, create and import a higher resolution image, as follows:

✦ Double-click the icon of the original low-resolution bitmap in the Flash Library to access the bitmap's properties.

✦ In the Bitmap Properties dialog, click the Import button and select the new, higher resolution version of the bitmap.

✦ Upon reimport, all symbols and symbol instances will update automatically.

Although .TIF is now a supported file format for import, it's not a listed file format when you try to use the Import button in the Library properties of a bitmap. To import a .TIF from the Library Properties, you have to switch the file menu to display All Files, instead of All Formats. Consequently, when you select a .TIF and want to import a new .TIF to replace the original image, it only works if All Files is selected.

Be aware that Flash doesn't resize (or resample) an image to its viewed or placed size when the Flash movie (.SWF file) is created. We tested the same source image, resized it into two different pixel dimensions, and placed it in two different Flash movies. In both movies, the image was viewed at 200×300 pixels. The first version of the image had a 400×600 pixel dimension, while the second version had a 200×300 pixel dimension — exactly half the size of the first. In one Flash movie (we'll call it Movie A), the first version was imported and resized (using the Info Panel) to the size of the second. In the other Flash movie (Movie B), the second version was imported and placed as is, occupying the same portion of the Flash Stage as Movie A. Even though both Flash movies contained a bitmap of the same view size on the Flash Stage, the resulting .SWF files, which used the same level of .JPEG compression on export, had drastically different file sizes. Movie A was 44.1KB, whereas Movie B was 14.8KB! Movie A is nearly three times larger than Movie B. However, when a view larger than 100 percent was used within the Flash Player, the difference in resolution was readily apparent in the higher quality of Movie A.

Importing Bitmap Images

There are two ways to bring bitmap images into Flash. You can import bitmap images, as we describe next, or you can copy them from an external application, such as Fireworks, and then paste them directly into Flash. Although the latter process is quick and easy, it doesn't capture any transparency settings, so it may not be the best choice for all of your needs.

When importing bitmaps, Flash 5 supports all of the formats that QuickTime supports — as long as QT4 is installed (refer to Table 12-1). However, the implementation of this reliance upon QuickTime can be confusing. If you attempt to import any previously unsupported format, the following dialog appears: "Flash doesn't recognize the file format of Image.PSD. Would you like to try importing via QuickTime?" If you ignore this dialog and click Yes, the image is imported as a bitmap. According to

Macromedia, you will always get this warning (which you must override in order to complete the import) so that you will be aware that QuickTime is used to complete the import. Other than this rather odd work flow, there are no adverse consequences to importing .PSDs in this manner.

New Feature

With QuickTime support, Flash 5 now enables you to import .TIF images, which is a widely used professional image format in the world of print graphics. .TIFs can also include alpha channels similarly to .PICT and .PNG files. To import a .TIF, you must choose All Files from the Files of type drop-down menu of the Import dialog.

Importing a bitmap file into Flash

To import a bitmap into Flash, follow these steps:

1. Make sure that there's an active, unlocked layer. If no layer is available for placement of the imported item, the Import command is dimmed and you can't import anything.

2. Select File ⇨ Import (Ctrl+R or Command+R).

3. The Import dialog opens. Navigate to the file that you'd like to import, select it, and click the Open button.

As shown in Figure 12-5, the Import dialog also appears when importing bitmaps. Note that any file that requires QuickTime support will invoke the dialog shown at the right — in this case, it's OK to click Yes; the file will import properly.

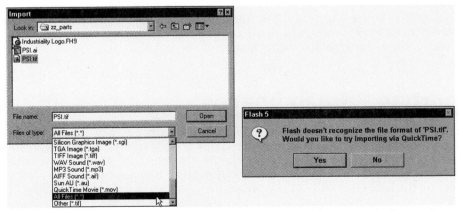

Figure 12-5: The Import dialog, along with the message that you see when trying to import files that require QuickTime support.

If you attempt to open a file that has a number at the end of its name, and there are additional files in the same location with sequential numbers at the ends of their names, Flash prompts you to import the files as a sequence. If that's what you want to do, select Yes when prompted. Flash imports all the files in sequential frames on the timeline. Otherwise, select No, and only the single file that you've selected will be opened.

Copying and pasting a bitmap into Flash

Here's how to use the Clipboard to import a bitmap into Flash:

1. Copy the bitmap from the other application.

2. Return to Flash and make sure that you have an active, unlocked layer that you can paste the bitmap into.

3. Paste the bitmap onto the stage by selecting Edit ⇨ Paste from the menu (Ctrl+E/Command+E). When pasting a selected area from Photoshop, any transparency (alpha channel) is ignored.

Because Flash 5 offers full support for the .PNG image format (including lossless compression and multilevel transparency), .PNG is the ideal format for images that you intend to import into Flash. The .PNG format has two types, PNG-8 and PNG-24. While both provide greater flexibility with compression, only PNG-24 images support 24-bit color and an alpha channel. The .PNG format is discussed in depth in the Photoshop section of Chapter 30, "Working with Raster Graphics."

Caution   When using a .PNG image with a transparent area masked by an alpha channel, many 16-bit systems may display the background appearing behind the masked area with a faintly dithered variation of the actual background color. For more information, refer to the tech notes at www.macromedia.com/go/13524 and www.macromedia.com/go/13901.

Setting Bitmap Properties

The Bitmap Properties dialog, shown in Figure 12-6, has several options that are used to control the quality of your bitmaps.

Follow these steps to use the Bitmap Properties dialog:

1. Open the movie's library with Window ⇨ Library and select the bitmap.

Smoothing (dither) check box

Preview   Name   Image Path, Date, Dimensions

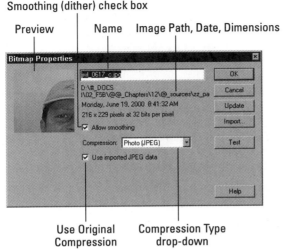

Use Original   Compression Type
Compression   drop-down

Figure 12-6: The Bitmap Properties dialog

2. Double-click the bitmap's icon, or right-click/Ctrl+click the bitmap's name and select Properties to open the Bitmap Properties dialog. You can also select Properties from the Library's Options menu or, with the bitmap highlighted, click the Properties button. Now, set the properties of your bitmap as desired:

- **Preview Window:** This displays the bitmap according to the current settings.

- **Name:** This is the name of the bitmap, as indicated in the Library. To rename the bitmap, highlight the name and enter a new one.

- **Image Path, Date, Dimensions:** Beneath the name Flash lists the local path, dimensions, and date information for the source of the imported image (not available if you pasted the image from the Clipboard).

- **Update:** This feature enables you to reimport a bitmap if it's been altered outside of Flash. Flash tracks the original location of the imported bitmap and will look for the original file in that location when the Update button is clicked.

- **Import:** This opens the Import Bitmap dialog. When using this button, the new bitmap will replace the current bitmap (and all instances, if any), while retaining the original's name.

- **Test:** This button updates the file compression information, which appears at the bottom of the Bitmap Properties dialog. Use this information to compare the compressed file size to the original file size.

- **Compression Type drop-down:** The compression setting enables you to set the bitmap's compression to either Photo (.JPEG) or Lossless (.PNG/.GIF). Photo is good for very complex bitmap images (photographs for example); Lossless is better for bitmap images with areas of flat color. Play around with these settings to see which works best for each particular image.

- **Use imported .JPEG data/Use document default quality:** If the imported image is a .JPEG, the first option will appear — check this check box to avoid double-JPEG compression. If the image is not a .JPEG, the second option will appear — check this check box to retain the original compression of the image.

- **Allow Smoothing (dither):** Check this check box to enable Flash to attempt to dither, or smooth, the image. Results may vary according to the image. Generally, this is ill advised because it blurs an image. If you've imported and placed a perfectly optimized image, at 100 percent scale, this will noticeably degrade the image quality. It's better to optimize images outside of Flash and then insist that Flash doesn't mess with them.

3. Click OK. All copies of this bitmap used in Flash are updated to the new settings.

Using Bitmaps as Fills

Procedures for working with bitmaps as fills have changed significantly since Flash 4. Upon import, a bitmap appears on the Stage in the current frame of the active layer. However, it also lands in the Library, where it truly resides. In fact, you can delete the bitmap from the Stage without clearing it from the Library. However, you might not have noticed that, on import, the bitmap was also deposited in the Bitmap Swatches drop-down of the Fill Panel, shown in Figure 12-7. Bitmaps that appear in this new Bitmap Swatches are automatically broken apart on import and may be modified with any of the Flash drawing and painting tools.

Figure 12-7: This is the Bitmap Swatches drop-down of the Fill Panel.

New Feature

Flash 5 offers improved handling of bitmap fills. Now they live where they are easily accessed, as swatches in the Bitmap Swatches drop-down of the new Fills Panel and are automatically broken apart on import. This means that they don't have to be brought out onto the stage and acquired with the Eyedropper in order to reuse them, as was the case with prior versions of Flash. Nice touch!

Here's how to acquire and apply a bitmap fill (of a bitmap that's already been imported) in Flash 5:

1. Open the Fill Panel and choose Bitmap from the Fill drop-down menu. A display of all imported bitmap swatches appears.

2. Click to select the bitmap swatch that you want from the Bitmap Swatches. (If there is only one, it is automatically selected for you.) The Fill Color button in the Toolbox automatically updates to display the selected bitmap fill.

   • If a fill is currently selected, it is updated with the bitmap you have selected.

   • If no fill is currently selected, choose the Paint Bucket Tool and use it to fill any shape.

3. In either case, as shown in Figure 12-8, the resulting fill contains your bitmap, which can be manipulated with the Paint Bucket Transform Fill modifier, as described in Chapter 5, "Working with the Drawing and Painting Tools."

Figure 12-8: Using a bitmap as a fill can produce some interesting designs.

Caution   If you drag a bitmap from the Library and position it onstage and then attempt to acquire the bitmap fill by first tracing the bitmap and then clicking with the Dropper Tool, you may obtain the following unexpected, undesired results. If the bitmap is still selected, clicking with the Dropper acquires the color immediately beneath the Dropper, and replaces the entire bitmap with a solid fill of the acquired color. If the bitmap is not selected, the Dropper simply acquires the color immediately beneath the Dropper.

Breaking a bitmap apart

Breaking apart a bitmap means that the bitmap image is subsequently seen by Flash as a collection of individual areas of color. After an image is broken apart, it may be modified with any of the Flash drawing and painting tools. You can select individual areas of the broken apart image with any of the selection tools, including the Magic Wand option of the Lasso Tool. (This is not the same as tracing a bitmap, which reduces the vast number of colors in a bitmap to areas of solid color and turns it into vector format.) The command duplicates the new Flash 5 automatic conversion of an imported bitmap as it arrives as a swatch in the Bitmap Swatches of the Fills Panel. You cannot use Modify ⇨ Break Apart to generate a variant fill from the same bitmap.

The Magic Wand Option of the Lasso Tool is used to select ranges of a similar color in either a bitmap fill or a bitmap that's been broken apart. After you select areas of the bitmap, you can change their fill color or delete them, without affecting the Bitmap Swatch in the Fills Panel. For more information about the Lasso Tool, refer to Chapter 5, "Working with the Drawing and Painting Tools." Click the Magic Wand option in the Toolbox to invoke the Magic Wand Settings dialog.

The Threshold setting of the Magic Wand

The Threshold setting defines the breadth of adjacent color values that the Magic Wand will include in a selection. Values for the Threshold setting range from 0 to 200 — the higher the setting, the broader the selection of adjacent colors. Conversely, a smaller number results in the Magic Wand making a narrower selection of adjacent colors. To see the threshold settings see Figure 12-9.

A value of zero results in a selection of contiguous pixels that are all the same color as the target pixel. With a value of 20, clicking a red target pixel with a value of 55 will select all contiguous pixels in a range of values extending from red 35 to red 75. (For those of you who are familiar with Photoshop, it's important to note that the Flash Threshold is unlike Photoshop, in which a Threshold setting of 20 will select all contiguous pixels in a range of values extending from red 45 to red 65.)

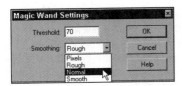

Figure 12-9: The Magic Wand
Settings dialog

The Smoothing setting of the Magic Wand option

The Smoothing setting of the Magic Wand option determines to what degree
the edge of the selection should be smoothed. This is similar to antialiasing.
(Antialiasing dithers the edges of shapes and lines so that they look smoother on
screen.) The options are Smooth, Pixels, Rough, and Normal. Assuming that the
Threshold setting remains constant, the Smooth settings will differ as follows:

✦ **Smooth:** delivers a selection with more rounded edges

✦ **Pixels:** the selection clings to the rectangular edges of each pixel bordering
similar colors

✦ **Rough:** the edges of the selection are even more angular than with Pixels

✦ **Normal:** results in a selection that's somewhere between rough and smooth

Tracing Bitmaps

Trace Bitmap is used to convert a Library image from a bitmap to a native Flash
vector graphic with discrete, editable areas of color. This unlinks the image from
the original in the Library (and also from the Bitmap Swatch in the Fills Panel). It
is possible to create interesting bitmap-based art with this command. However, if
your intention is to preserve the look of the original bitmap with maximum fidelity,
you will have to work with the settings—and you will most likely find that the original bitmap is less file intensive than its traced cousin. Here's how to trace a bitmap:

1. Use the Arrow Tool to select the bitmap that you want to trace—it should be
   either a symbol, in Edit Symbol Mode, or on the Stage.

2. Use Modify ⇨ Trace Bitmap to invoke the Trace Bitmap dialog and set the
   options according to your needs:

   • **Color Threshold:** This option controls the number of colors in your
     traced bitmap. It limits the number of colors by averaging the colors
     based on the criteria chosen in Color Threshold and Minimum Area.
     Color Threshold compares RGB color values of adjacent pixels to the
     value entered. If the difference is lower than the value entered, then adja-
     cent pixels are considered the same color. By making this computation
     for each pixel within the bitmap, Flash averages the colors. A lower
     Color Threshold delivers more colors in the final vector graphic derived
     from the traced bitmap.

- **Minimum Area:** This value is the radius, measured in pixels, that Color Threshold uses to describe adjacent pixels when comparing pixels to determine what color to assign to the center pixel.

- **Curve Fit:** This value determines how smoothly outlines are drawn. Select Very Tight if the curves in the bitmap have many twists and turns. If the curves are smooth, select Very Smooth.

- **Corner Threshold:** The Corner Threshold is similar to the Curve Fit, but it pertains to the corners in the bitmap image.

3. Click OK. Flash traces the bitmap, and the original bitmap disappears. If the bitmap is complex, this may take a while. The traced bitmap does not look exactly like the original bitmap.

Tip

If your objective is for your traced bitmap to closely resemble the original bitmap, then set a low Color Threshold and a low Minimum Area. You'll also want to set the Curve Fit to Pixels and the Corner Threshold to Many Corners. Be aware that using these settings may drastically slow the tracing process for complex bitmaps and result in larger file sizes. If animated, such bitmaps may also retard the frame rate dramatically. Furthermore, if the image is noisy (grainy) it should be smoothed (despeckled) as much as possible prior to tracing to save time, as well as to reduce file size.

As shown in Figure 12-10, the traced bitmap (right) looks quite different from the original bitmap (left). While you can change the settings in the Trace Bitmap dialog to make a traced bitmap look more like the original, it often requires a lot of work from your computer. This comparison was done with the Trace Bitmap settings at a Color Threshold of 25, Minimum Area of 10 pixels, Curve Fit of Very Smooth, and Corner Threshold of Few Corners.

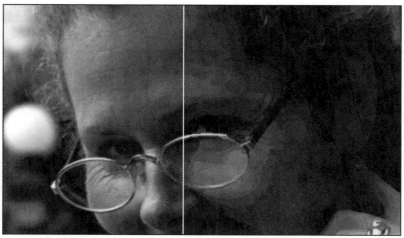

Figure 12-10: The traced bitmap (right) looks quite different from the original bitmap (left).

Cautionary Notes

Flash retains existing .JPEG compression levels on any imported .JPEG image, but, unless specified otherwise in the Library, it reapplies .JPEG compression when the movie is published or exported. Recompressing an image that has already been compressed usually leads to serious image degradation, due to the introduction of further compression artifacts. When importing .JPEGs (and other bitmaps), you'll note that Use document default quality in the Library is checked by default. This is a feature, not an annoyance. That's because (a) Flash has a relatively generic .JPEG compression engine, which is easily surpassed by both Fireworks and Photoshop, and because (b) as mentioned previously, recompressing a .JPEG is routinely disastrous to image quality.

 Tip

If you import .JPEG images, make sure that you either test the results of further .JPEG compression or else choose the Lossless compression setting in Bitmap Properties dialog, which is accessible from the Flash Library.

Apply compression settings to each individual bitmap in the Flash Library to determine the quality that you need before you use the general .JPEG settings in the Export Movie or Publish Settings dialog. You'll find .JPEG export settings for Flash movies (.SWF files) discussed in greater detail in Chapter 40, "Publishing Flash Movies."

Bitmap shift

There is a known problem in Flash that's referred to as *bitmap shift*, which means that colors may shift slightly from one instance to another of the same image. This has been attributed to several reasons. Some developers have reported that turning off compression has, at times, eliminated problems with bitmap shift. Another reported method for eliminating bitmap shift is to make the image a symbol, and then assign it an alpha of 99 percent. Yet the clearest explanation, and related fix, are as follows: Flash renders a bitmap while animating or transforming it, and then rerenders the bitmap as a static image when the motion or transformation ceases. Often, the two don't quite match. From this perspective, the optimal solution is to set the final bitmap's scaling to 99 percent. The advantage of this solution (aside from the fact that it works) is that it's less processor intensive, because any alpha adjustment burdens the processor with computations.

Cross-browser consistency

We've received more than a few queries about image formats and Flash's capability to transcend issues of browser inconsistency, so here's the answer. Many image formats, such as .PNG, are not supported across all browsers. When you import such an image format into Flash and publish or export to the .SWF format, you have accomplished browser independence—because the .SWF is browser independent and because the image has been encapsulated within the .SWF format. (The image is not being sent to the browser in the imported format and then magically empowered to display.) Conversely, if you export any .FLA to .PNG or to any other format that's subject to cross-browser inconsistency, browser independence is lost.

Color Insert: Bitmap Comparisons

The color insert of this *Flash 5 Bible* is dedicated to comparing bitmap quality within Flash, subject to various settings. Using two example photographs, we've generated a series of bitmap examples to help you understand the consequences of some of the procedures that have been discussed in this chapter.

To facilitate your deeper exploration into the subject of bitmap settings and their impact upon image quality, we've included the .SWF's that were built to collect and test our sample shots. They are located in the folder titled, BitMap_Comparison_8-SWF's, which is located in the ch12 folder on the CD-ROM. Because this is all about how images look on screen (and print is merely an approximation of this), we encourage you to use the Flash Player's zoom facility to take a good look at these examples. We've chosen to supply these as eight separate .SWF's because this will enable you to open several pages simultaneously for side-by-side comparison.

Generation of comparison images

Before you can make intelligent use of bitmaps in Flash, it's imperative to know about the options for creating bitmaps for use within Flash. That's because all bitmaps are *not* created equal. A bitmap from one program, created with similar settings, can be twice the file size — with no appreciable increase in quality — of a bitmap created in another program. It makes no sense to study optimization constraints within Flash if you ignore your exposure to fatty imports.

To create a set of controlled images that could be used for comparison, we chose a portrait (with a background that shifts contrast) and a landscape (with a broad expanse of graduated color). Both images were derived from high-quality film shots, scanned at a very high resolution, down-sampled to equivalent dimensions and resolution, 227×287 pixels at 96 ppi, and saved as uncompressed .TIFs. These files were used as the source files from which all other variations were derived (with the sole exception of the double-JPEG example, in which an image that had been previously .JPEG'd was used as the source image for the double-JPEG example).

Note   Because the native resolution of most PC monitors is 96 ppi, we used 96 ppi as the originating resolution in order to circumvent the possibility that Flash would need to scale these images in order to display them on the PC. This means that the image is scaled down to display on the Mac, which has a native resolution of 72 ppi. Unfortunately, this procedure also requires a slight bit of extra care when placing images, because Flash has a tendency to import these images ballooned out. Thus, when working with images at 96 ppi, it's advisable to check the Info Panel to ensure that the image dimensions, as measured in inches, has been retained. If the image dimensions haven't been retained, then the image must be scaled down to the image dimensions that correlate with the resolution of 96 ppi.

Our principal comparisons were done with Adobe Photoshop and Macromedia Fireworks, simply to establish a comparison of the quality and degree of compression available from each program. However, when preparing .JPEGs for comparison, we added a choice alternative, BoxTop Software's ProJPEG, which is a Photoshop-compatible plug-in. Because each program offers different options and different combinations of options, it is absolutely impossible to perform a direct one-for-one comparison. As such, our results are necessarily subjective and may not equate with your findings.

Tip   BoxTop Software's ProJPEG plug-in is available for both the Mac and the PC. It may be obtained online from www.BoxTopSoft.com.

The BoxTop interface

As shown in Figure 12-11, the interface for the BoxTop ProJPEG Photoshop-compatible plug-in is roomy and clear. For the purpose of our comparison we retained all settings as shown — except for the Quality setting, which was set at 94, 60, and 30 for the High, Medium, and Low samples.

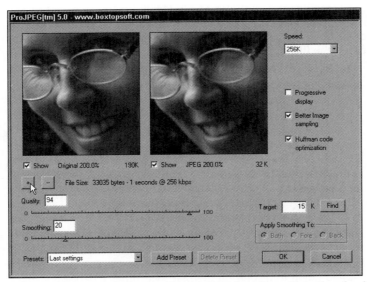

Figure 12-11: Here's the BoxTop ProJPEG interface. Note the check box options at the right for both Better Image Sampling and Huffman code optimization.

The Fireworks interface

As shown in Figure 12-12, Fireworks' Export Preview interface is also roomy and clear. It also provides the option — which we did not use — of comparing the before image with three other previews. Again, for this comparison we retained all settings as shown — except for the Quality setting, which was set at 94, 60, and 30 for the High, Medium, and Low samples. The Fireworks' Export Preview has several options that may have tipped the compression contest in its favor. Note that we used the default, No Smoothing, and that we left the Remove Unused Colors check box activated.

Figure 12-12: The Fireworks Export Preview

The Photoshop interface

The Photoshop Interface that was used for these comparisons is shown in Figure 12-13. In all fairness, it should be noted that Photoshop also sports a roomy interface complete with preview, which is accessed from Photoshop with the File ➪ Save for Web command. (But it should also be noted that, in preliminary testing, the Save for Web interface, in multiple configurations, failed to deliver competitive compressions.) For this comparison we retained all settings as shown — except for the Quality setting, which was set at 11, 9, and 7 for the High, Medium, and Low samples. The deviation in these settings is due to the Quality range of 1 to 12, rather than 1 to 10.

Figure 12-13 shows the familiar Photoshop .JPEG dialog. Note that the Quality range is from 1 to 12, rather than the expected 1 to 10. However, this difference was not the deciding factor in Photoshop's failure to produce competitive compression — we experimented with multiple settings and with the Save for Web dialog. In all cases, Photoshop delivered much heavier .JPEGs than either Fireworks or the BoxTop plug-in ProJPEG.

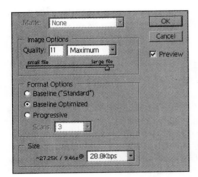

Figure 12-13: The Photoshop .JPEG dialog

Compression Results

To make reasonable sense of the results of our compression tests on the portrait and road images, we assembled the results into Table 12-2.

Table 12-2 Compression Comparison				
Image and Type	**Quality**	**BoxTop**	**Fireworks**	**Photoshop**
Base Tif: Portrait	Uncompressed	–	–	196KB
Base Tif: Road	Uncompressed	–	–	196KB
Jpeg Variations: Portrait	L (=30%)	7KB	6KB	15KB
	M (=60%)	11KB	10KB	19KB
	H (=94%)	33KB	27KB	50KB
Jpeg Variations: Road	L (=30%)	3KB	3KB	10KB
	M (=60%)	5KB	5KB	12KB
	H (=94%)	16KB	13KB	28KB
Png: Portrait	24-bit	–	112KB	128KB
Png: Road	24-bit	–	66KB	76KB

Observations and notes about the results of the settings

When we set out to create this test, we had some preconceptions — based on prior experience — that dissolved in the face of this metrical analysis. In some instances, the results were even counterintuitive, or clearly subject to the specific nature of the bitmap's final use.

As shown in Figure 12-14, in all cases, unless specified otherwise (for smoothing comparisons and to demonstrate double-JPEG corruption), the settings in the Flash Bitmap Properties dialog were maintained to preserve the compression and quality of the imported image. Unless otherwise noted, the .JPEGs and .PNGs were generated with Fireworks from the same Photoshop source .TIF.

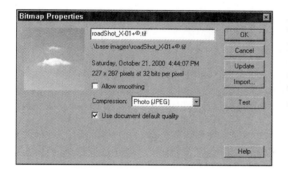

Figure 12-14: Regardless of the kind of image imported, these settings in the Flash Bitmap Properties dialog usually deliver the highest quality image while preserving the imported compression.

Basic image-type comparisons in the color insert

The following is a description of each image in the color section, plate by plate. To see the images discussed, flip to the insert.

Color Plate 1: At the top left, the uncompressed Photoshop .TIF source file is displayed, as rendered by Flash with no compression. In the adjacent panel, this original .TIF is compared to 24-bit .PNGs from both Fireworks and Photoshop; note the slight color shift in the Photoshop .PNG. In subsequent panels, high quality (94 percent) and low quality (30 percent) .JPEGs are compared. Although the quality is nearly the same, on close inspection, at 200 percent zoom (right-click/Ctrl+click), the BoxTop images are slightly less chunky, with less artifacts.

High-quality .JPEG smoothing comparisons

Color Plate 2: Here, high-quality .JPEGs are compared when deployed in the Flash Bitmap Properties dialog either with or without smoothing enabled. At 100 percent, the unsmoothed image is superior. However, if you intend to scale the image smoothing may, as shown, improve the quality. The difference is more noticeable with the portrait.

High-quality Fireworks .JPEG scaling comparisons (no smoothing)

Color Plate 3: Here the high-quality .JPEGs of both images are compared to the same image, when scaled to 200 percent. Note how the horizon detail of the landscape is adversely affected by the zoom, while the portrait is chunky but almost acceptable.

Medium-quality Fireworks .JPEG scaling comparisons (no smoothing)

Color Plate 4: Here the medium-quality .JPEGs of both images are compared to the same image, when scaled to 200 percent. At 100 percent, both images are acceptable. But at 200 percent, it's a different story: Here, you'll note that the portrait is too chunky and unacceptable—many areas have a marked checkerboard pattern. Conversely, the zoomed horizon detail of the landscape isn't much worse than the same view of the high-quality version.

Low-quality Fireworks .JPEG scaling comparisons (no smoothing)

Color Plate 5: Here the low-quality .JPEGs of both images are compared to the same image, when scaled to 200 percent. At 100 percent you'll note that the portrait is barely usable—too many areas of soft transition have been chopped and flattened. At 200 percent, the portrait is so corrupted and badly discolored that it's unusable. It's easier to tolerate distortion in landscapes, thus the 100 percent view of the landscape is still usable, although not advisable for anything more than a background or an incidental shot. However, the zoomed horizon detail of the landscape is far worse than the zooms of both the high- and medium-quality versions—note, especially, the shimmer of artifacts both immediately above the horizon and around the clouds.

Medium-quality double-JPEG corruption comparisons (no smoothing)

Color Plate 6: This image was created by first saving a low-quality .JPEG from Photoshop, then opening it in Fireworks, and then saving it as a low-quality .JPEG from Fireworks. Although the portrait faired worse than the landscape, the results weren't nearly as monstrous as we had expected. The double-.JPEGs *are* chunkier and have more artifacts in transition areas, but they aren't as bad as the print world's admonition that precedes them.

Bit depth and color comparisons

Color Plate 7: These images demonstrate the effect of reduced bit depth—or range of color—through a series of three reductions. The 24-bit .PNG is a full-color image, with a range of millions of possible colors. Subsequent images have been reduced to 256, 128, and 64 colors. Note the increased posterization (or clumping of flattened color) in the transition of the cheek from light-to-dark, as well as the blue sky. Also note the successive banding of the accompanying spectrum.

High-quality JPEG rotation comparisons

Color Plate 8: This is perhaps the trickiest comparison to analyze. We had this problem when building our Web site for the *Flash 4 Bible*. When the animation resolved and the book was displayed at a slight, 14-degree angle, it was distorted—and it was distorted regardless of whether it was rotated in Photoshop and imported with the angle, or if it was imported into Flash on the square and subsequently rotated — the manner of the distortion changed, but not the perception of distortion!

✦ When rotated in Flash, hard edges, such as text, may appear choppy — as if they had been cut out with pinking shears. Yet, when zoomed, this effect is less problematic.

✦ When rotated in Photoshop, prior to import into Flash, hard edges are less choppy, although the file will increase (to accommodate the larger overall shape), the background will become a fixed color, and a certain flutter may occur along the edges of the transition between the background and the image. Yet, other straight lines and text will appear smoother and more acceptable. However, at 200 percent zoom, text looks worse than the same image rotated in Flash.

Before rotating a bitmap in Flash, you should perform a few tests to see how your specific bitmap will be affected by the combination of compression, zoom, smoothing, and rotation (either in or out of Flash). Your choices and your decision will certainly vary, subject to the nature of the bitmap and the manner in which it will be used within Flash.

Summary

✦ Flash can use a variety of external media, including vector graphics, bitmap images, and sounds.

✦ Importing external media, such as vector graphics and bitmaps is very easy.

✦ Preparing bitmaps for use within Flash requires considerable forethought and some preliminary design work in order to determine the optimal dimensions. Otherwise, bitmaps may be subjected to unsightly degradation of quality.

✦ A basic understanding of both bitmap resolution and bitmap depth is a prerequisite for the successful implementation of bitmaps within a Flash project.

✦ Bitmap properties are controlled in the Bitmap Properties dialog, which is accessed from the Flash Library.

✦ Bitmaps can be used as fills within vector shapes and drawings. With Flash 5, the new Bitmap Swatches drop-down of the Fills Panel greatly simplifies the application of bitmap fills.

✦ Bitmaps can also be traced to convert them into vector art, although usually with a loss of detail. If a traced bitmap is forced to approximate photographic quality it may incur a larger file size than the original photograph.

✦ The Bitmap Comparisons in the color insert of this *Flash 5 Bible* are dedicated to comparing bitmap quality within Flash at various settings.

✦   ✦   ✦

Designing Interfaces and Interface Elements

Now that you've learned the basic principles behind
Flash artwork creation, you probably want to start creating a presentation to put on a Web site. For this edition of
the *Flash Bible*, we decided to write a chapter that teaches
you how to make a simple interactive Flash movie that has
basic navigation and text functionality, before we get into
the nitty gritty of ActionScript in Part IV of the book.

The Main Timeline as the Site Layout

Before you can start digging into Flash, you need to know what
you're excavating — what is the basic concept of the experience? Is this an all-Flash Web site? Is this a Flash animation
that introduces some other type of content (HTML, Shockwave
Director movies, and so on)? For the purposes of this chapter,
we create a Flash movie for a basic all-Flash Web site.

Creating a plan

Once you know what goals you want to achieve with your
Flash content, you should map the ideas on paper (or with
your preferred project planning or flowchart software). We
create a basic site for a computer parts company that has four
areas: main menu (and welcome page), products, services, and

contact information. Our organizational chart for this site has four discrete areas, as shown in Figure 13-1.

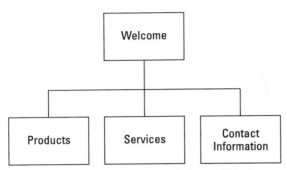

Figure 13-1: Our organizational chart will help us plan our Flash movie architecture.

Flowchart creation and project planning are discussed with greater detail in Chapter 38, "Planning Flash Production with Flowcharting Software."

Determining Flash movie properties

After you've made your organizational chart, you'll want to determine the frame rate, size, and color of the Flash movie. We've skipped much of the "real-life" planning involved with Flash Web sites, which is discussed in Chapter 38, "Planning Flash Production with Flowcharting Software." For this example, we use a frame size of 640×400 (a cinematic aspect ratio), a relatively fast frame rate of 20 fps (for smoother animations), and a white background color. These are set in the Movie Properties dialog, shown in Figure 13-2, which is accessed by Modify ⇨ Movie (Ctrl+M or Command+M).

Figure 13-2: The Flash Movie Properties

Mapping site areas to keyframes

After you have set up your Flash movie properties, you can create a Main Timeline structure for the site. Because we have four areas in our site (main menu, products, services, and contact information), we'll have keyframes on the timeline that indicate those sections.

1. Rename Layer 1 to **labels**, by double-clicking the Layer 1 text in the timeline window.

2. With the Arrow Tool, select frame 10, and press F6. This creates a keyframe on frame 10.

Tip   Always leave some empty frame space in front of your "real" Flash content. We can later use these empty frames to add a preloader, as discussed in Chapter 20, "Sharing and Loading Assets."

3. With the keyframe selected, open the Frame Panel (Ctrl+F or Command+F). In the Label field, type **welcome**. After you have typed the text, press Tab (or Enter) to make the name "stick."

4. Repeat Steps 2 and 3 with frames 20, 30, and 40, with the frame labels **products**, **services**, and **contactInfo**, respectively.

5. Select frame 50 of the labels layer, and press F5. This will enable you to read the very last label, contactInfo. Your Main Timeline should resemble Figure 13-3.

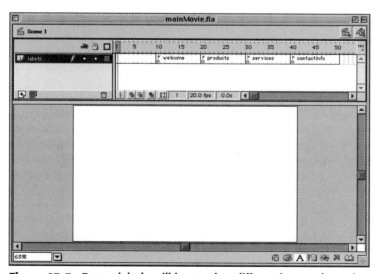

Figure 13-3: Frame labels will be used to differentiate each section of the site.

6. Save your Flash movie as **mainMovie.fla**.

7. Make a new layer, and rename it **actions**. Add a keyframe on frame 10, and open the Frame Actions Panel (Ctrl+Alt+A or Option+Command+A). Make sure the Actions Panel is in Normal Mode by clicking the menu option in the top-right corner and selecting Normal Mode.

8. Click the Basic Actions booklet (located in the left-hand column of the Actions Panel) to expand the actions contained there. Double-click the Stop action. This adds the following code to the Actions list in the right-column of the Actions Panel:

```
stop();
```

9. Close the Actions Panel, and open the Frame Panel. In the Label field, type **//stop**. The // characters assign a frame comment instead of a frame label. Although this step isn't necessary for the functionality of the movie, frame comments can provide quick and easy access to the designer's or programmer's notes. Your Main Timeline should now look like Figure 13-4.

Figure 13-4: Unlike labels, frame comments can not be used in ActionScript. Comments can provide quick visual references for ActionScript code.

10. Save the Flash movie again.

At this point, the Flash movie has a skeleton architecture (a blueprint) for our interactive functionality. Now, let's add some content to each section of the movie.

Main Timeline versus Scene Structure

Arguably, you might be wondering why we are using keyframes to delineate each section, instead of new scenes. There are two reasons to use one scene (in other words, one Main Timeline):

1. We can see the entire layout of our site very easily on one timeline.

2. We can blend interstitials (transitions between each area of the site) over two sections more easily. It's much easier to have one Movie Clip instance span the area between two section keyframes on the Main Timeline.

Ultimately, the decision is yours. Make sure that you determine your Flash architecture well before you start production within the Flash authoring environment. It's not a simple task to rearchitect the layout once production has begun.

Creating content for each area

For the purposes of this example, we add placeholder elements that would be filled in with actual content for live production.

In the ch13 folder of the *Flash 5 Bible* CD-ROM, you'll find a Flash file called content.fla that contains Graphic symbols of computer parts. Copy this .FLA file to your local hard drive.

1. Using the File ⇨ Open as Library command, select your copy of the content.fla file from the *Flash 5 Bible* CD-ROM. This opens the Library of the content .fla file.

2. Move the playhead in the timeline window of your mainMovie.fla movie to the welcome label (frame 10).

3. Create a layer named **companyLogo**. Add a keyframe at frame 10 of the companyLogo layer.

4. Drag an instance of the companyLogo Graphic symbol from the content.fla Library window to the Stage of your mainMovie.fla movie. Place the symbol instance near the top-left corner of the Stage, as shown in Figure 13-5.

5. Create a new layer named **heading**. Add a keyframe on frame 10 of this layer.

6. On frame 10 of the heading layer, use the Text Tool to add the text **Welcome**. For this example, we use the typeface Verdana at 36 points (using the Character Panel). We place the text near the top-center of the movie Stage, as shown in Figure 13-6.

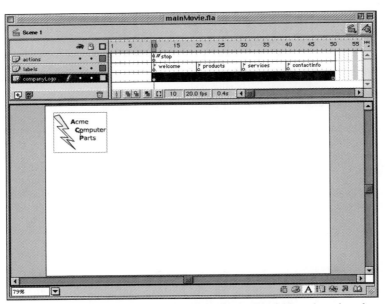

Figure 13-5: The Acme Computer Parts logo should be placed at the top-left corner of the Stage.

Figure 13-6: Use the Text Tool to add a welcome heading to the movie.

7. Add a keyframe at frame 20 of the heading layer. The Welcome text block from the previous keyframe will be copied into this keyframe. Change the text to **Product Catalog**, as shown in Figure 13-7.

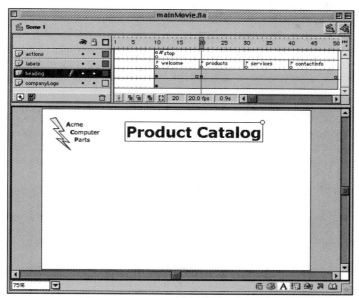

Figure 13-7: Change the text block on frame 20 to indicate the current frame label section.

8. Repeat Step 7 for frames 30 and 40 of the heading layer. Change the text block to indicate the appropriate section of the site (for example, Assembly Services, Contact Information).

   Now lets add a slide show of the computer parts that the company sells. For this, we create a Movie Clip symbol that has each product graphic on a separate keyframe.

9. Create a new symbol using Insert ➪ New Symbol (Ctrl+F8 or Command+F8). Leave the Behavior option at the default Movie Clip setting, and give it a name of **productMovie**.

10. Flash automatically switches to Symbol Editing Mode, on the productMovie timeline. Rename Layer 1 to **products**.

11. Add keyframes to frames 2, 3, 4, 5, and 6 of the products layer. We have six computer parts in the content.fla Library, and each product graphic is put on its own keyframe.

12. Move the playhead to frame 1 of the productMovie timeline, and drag the monitor_1 Graphic symbol from the content.fla Library to the Stage of the productMovie symbol, shown in Figure 13-8.

13. Continue moving the playhead to the next frame, dragging another computer part to the Stage for each frame. When you're finished, press the < and > keys to review your frames. You may want to center each graphic on the Stage using the Align Panel (Ctrl+K or Command+K).

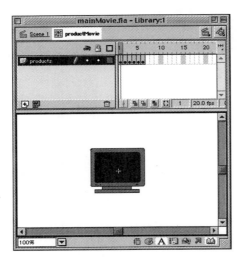

Figure 13-8: You should have six filled keyframes on the products layers of the productMovie timeline.

14. Now we need to insert an actions layer for this Movie Clip symbol. Create a new layer, and rename it **actions**. Select frame 1 of the actions layer, and open the Actions Panel. Add a Stop action:

```
stop();
```

15. Return to the Main Timeline (Scene 1) by clicking the Scene 1 tab in the upper-left corner of the timeline window.

16. Create a new layer, and rename it **productMovie**. Insert a new keyframe on frame 20 of the productMovie layer.

17. Open the mainMovie.fla Library by pressing Ctrl+L or Command+L. Drag the **productMovie** symbol from the Library to the Stage. Place it just left of the center of the Stage, as shown in Figure 13-9.

18. Select frame 30 of the productMovie layer, and press F7. This inserts a blank keyframe. Now, the productMovie instance will only show in the product area of the timeline.

19. Save your .FLA file.

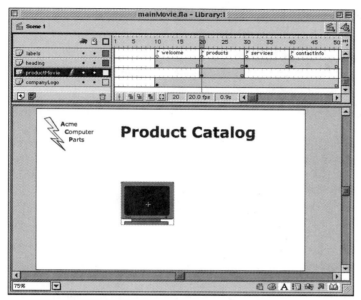

Figure 13-9: The productMovie instance will only be present in the product section of the movie.

Now we have some content in the Flash movie. The following Expert Tutorial provides an excellent overview of the design process for Flash user interfaces. If you want to continue with the demo site, then skip to the next section, "Adding Navigation Elements to the Main Timeline."

Expert Tutorial: Interface Design, *by Eric Jordan*

An important aspect of delivering content on the Web is the method in which it is presented to the audience. In the relatively short period of time since Flash first hit the market, interface design has become an art in and of itself. Now, Flash 5 has empowered designers with the ability to create rich Web-based environments with more interactivity and sophistication than ever before. In the pursuit of attracting attention to information, designers seek to package content within an intuitive *interface*, through which the user can navigate and react with on a new level. Designing a Flash interface is much like designing a product package, as it attempts to represent its contents in the most fashionable way possible. By tapping the new enhancements of the Flash 5 toolsets and property panels, designers now have a much more efficient approach to interface design.

Continued

Continued

Conceptualization and implementation

Whenever I begin the process of creating a Flash interface, I keep in mind one important factor: Once an interface is animated, it is intensely difficult to backtrack if the client should desire a change in the overall design layout. Although the greatest impact of a Flash site normally comes from it's animated elements, it is important to lock down an interface design that pleases the client from the very start. We have developed a process at Design Insites that works very effectively for conceptualizing and finalizing an interface design. This process normally begins with three *roughs*, which are three stylistically different interface concepts envisioned by the designer. These designs vary in look and feel, to give the client an opportunity to settle on a general aesthetic style for the Web site. Then we move onto the next phase, in which we provide three *comprehensive* designs that follow the same aesthetic theme of the chosen rough, yet vary in their execution of the layout structure. After the client has selected the final *comprehensive*, we then proceed to create a working model of the interface that includes the use of animated elements and functionality.

Aesthetic considerations

In my time as a Flash designer, I've developed many different types of interfaces, with a wide range of navigation types, thematic approaches, and bandwidth considerations. Based on the individual requirements of each project I undertake, I attempt to create the most aesthetically pleasing and intuitive interfaces I can, while still maintaining control over the boundaries that have been set forth. Technical requirements aside, the visual appearance of an interface is a creative endeavor that is entirely subjective. It is a matter of one's style. Although my imagination tends to run wild at times, it is a designer's duty to execute a site design that properly delivers it's content based on the branding strategy, corporate mentality, and goals of the client. At Design Insites, our strength lies in our ability to implement interfaces that organize content in a fashionable, yet straightforward manner. To showcase this, we began development of our new site — www.designinsites.com, shown in the following figure — using the enhancements of Flash 5. In doing this, we considered the same design principals that we follow when constructing interfaces for our clients. My implementation of an interface tends to lean toward emulating an operating system, as with www.2advanced.com. The new Design Insites interface uses some of the same concepts, as I have found that draggable panels and drop-down menus provide the user with more interactive navigation and a sense of control over the environment. These elements are by no means a requirement for an interface design; they simply lend themselves to my style of design and layout. The key is to provide the user with straightforward navigation and organized content, and couple it with a visually pleasing environment.

Color is also an indispensable factor for successful interface design. It is an integral part of the visual appeal, and it plays a crucial role in functionality.

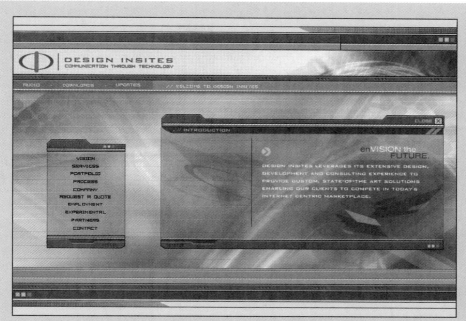

The Design Insites Web site, after the opening animation has completed and the interface has peaked.

The correct colors attract the eye to the most important areas of the interface. They enhance readability and diminish optical exhaustion. Incorrect colors distract the user and decrease the level of comprehension. In all user-interface designs, we concentrate on four issues simultaneously: optical effects, symbolism, aesthetics, and technological components. Paying attention to color theory as it applies to interface design will help you to successfully communicate your message to the audience.

Beginning the design process

Typically, I create my conceptual rough layouts within Flash itself. With the addition of the new Bézier pen tools in Flash 5, sophisticated interfaces can be created easily, without the aid of an illustration program such as Freehand. The new Pen and Sub-Selection Tools enable precise control over strokes, curves, and so on by allowing manipulation of point-to-point drawing. I find that the Flash 5 drawing tools are more than sufficient for creating the overall interface.

Continued

Continued

However, if I choose to implement the use of raster graphics in combination with the vector graphics of Flash, then I have to use a raster-based authoring application such as Photoshop. Then, with feedback from the client, I begin my three rough designs, keeping in mind the various aspects of the decided GUI traits, which include:

✦ Target resolution (640×480, 800×600, and so on)

✦ Color palette support

✦ Navigation (horizontal, vertical, drop-down, draggable, and so on)

✦ Color scheme

✦ Percentage relation of graphics to text

Once these elements have been established, I begin laying out interface concepts using the drawing tools in Flash. However, I continue to pay attention to every factor that may affect the outcome of the final file. The most prominent advantage of using Flash to develop an interactive environment is its combined capability to carry out the construction of graphical layout, content delivery, and functionality, all in one place. This does, however, require careful planning on the part of the designer to ensure that he doesn't back himself into a corner by making a few wrong turns within the complete design process. Without forethought, a Flash site can quickly become an ill-fated nightmare full of unforeseen hurdles such as non-linear navigation and file size limits.

Roughs

Although the three roughs that I create are simply conceptual interfaces, I still maintain constant scrutiny of the file size during the design process. I am well aware that two of the designs are likely to be thrown out, but if I do not pay attention to the optimization of the file from the very start, the chosen rough might have to be redesigned in order to ensure that it makes efficient use of symbols, and other structural elements. While designing the new version of the Design Insites Web site, my main concern was file size. Although this site was a project of our own undertaking, and would not come under the scrutiny of a client, we used the same rough-and-comp approach to ensure that we thoroughly explored the possibilities for our own branding in a similar fashion. As I envisioned the site, the main background of the interface would consist of a large raster graphic that would add a great deal of size to the Flash file. The upper and lower portions of the interface would be built in vector to accommodate navigation and so on. To avoid further bloating the file size, I focused my efforts on using symbols wherever possible. This included reusing simple shapes such as rectangles, lines, and circles within the upper and lower interface bars. Although these areas of the interface appear to consist of 13 gray rectangular shapes, each was derived from a singular symbol. If some rectangles needed to be a different color or size, I didn't draw another. (This is what eventually causes the file size of a Flash movie to inflate.) Instead, I simply used instances of the same symbol, while changing the tint (in the Effect Panel) and size (in the Info or Transform Panel) of the instance. The advantage of this method is that the final movie needs to load only 1 shape during playback, rather than 13 different shapes of various colors and sizes. I used the same technique with lines. Everywhere a line appears, no matter what color or size, it's always an instance of the same symbol. Changes are only made to each particular instance, by using the Effect panel to modify the tint color and by using the Info panel to modify the length. By paying close attention to details such as this, many design headaches can be eliminated from the process. Thus, I end up with three optimized designs that are ready to be refined and built out.

Comprehensives

Once a rough has been chosen, we move onto the comprehensive phase. In this stage, we develop three new designs that have their aesthetic roots based in the stylistic elements of the rough. The only variance is the way in which these elements are structured. Using the symbols that I've already created, I shift the layout around and come up with three distinctly different renditions of the same basic theme. In this phase, we have already locked down the visual feel of the site, and we are developing options to offer the client further choices for the way in which that feel will be executed. A comprehensive can be thought of as the *peak* of the Web site, where animation ceases and the full interface is revealed in all its glory.

The following figure is a view of the source .FLA for the completed Design Insites Web site. Note how many layers appear in the Main Timeline, yet how many more are obscured — as evinced by the scroll bar to the far left of the timeline. In this shot, the playhead is halfway to the peak of the interface animation.

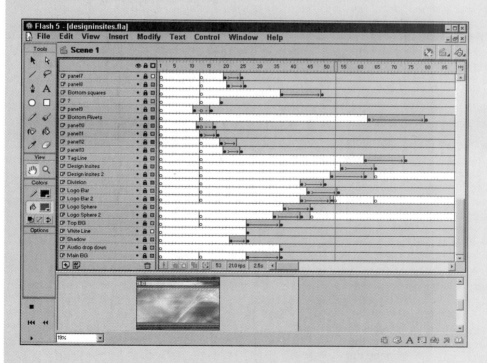

Continued

Continued

I use layers to design the basic levels of the interface elements, so that when it comes time to animate the site, everything is organized on it's own layer and ready for movement and/or functionality. As I add elements to the timeline, each layer is labeled in order to provide clarity for the execution of the animation process. At the end of this phase, I will have a series of layers with one keyframe on each layer. Each keyframe consists of a single symbol that makes up a different part of the interface.

Build out

After our client has chosen one of the three comprehensives, we begin the process of Flashing the interface. In this phase, we add motion and functionality to the site design. Because I've placed each element of the layout on a different layer, it's easy for me to now animate each symbol so that the design will move and manifest into the peak design that I've created. It is almost like deconstructing the interface, so that it may reconstruct itself through animation when played back. I typically insert a set of new keyframes about 100 frames deep in my Flash timeline to be the predetermined peak moment when the site will have achieved its full manifestation. I then proceed to set the properties for the symbol instances at frame 1. This is the very beginning of the animation, where the interface begins to manifest itself. Usually, I set items to have an alpha value of 0, a tint value similar to that of the background, or — if I want the element to slide into place — a position off stage. After I create my Motion Tweens for each animated element of the interface, I set values for easing in the Frame Panel to ensure fluid motion of each symbol. For aggressive and energetic interfaces, I usually have elements ease in and use short Motion Tweens to simulate fast movement. For calmer, more relaxed interfaces, I have elements ease out and use longer Motion Tweens to simulate conservative motion. These techniques are, of course, completely subjective, and each project may follow a different style and/or feel. Of course, some interfaces may not require animation at all, and some interfaces may only use Flash for its implementation of functionality through ActionScripting.

Now that we have a semianimated site, with a key moment in time acting as the peak of the interface, we begin developing content sections either within the main movie (using scenes) or externally for sections that will be loaded into the main movie (using `loadMovie`). The Design Insites interface requires the use of `loadMovie` to introduce additional content into the host Flash movie. Thus, the steps that were pursued during the design and build out process differed from the normal process. The navigation and content windows for the Design Insites Web site were intended to consist of draggable panels, and would be externally loaded into the host movie to avoid bloating it's file size. But rather than design the navigation panel and the content window blindly in a separate movie file, I created them on their own layers within the host movie. This working method enabled me to see how they would appear aesthetically within the main interface. During build out, I simply copied the frames being used by the navigation and content panels and pasted them into their own Flash file, which was then saved out as a separate .SWF file to be externally loaded using button triggers in the main movie. By copying and pasting the frames, I was able to retain all positioning or animation properties they possessed while in the main movie.

After the layout was completed and the file structures established for the externally loaded interface elements (the navigation and content windows), we began ActionScripting to make everything function, such as the navigational elements or the loading of the external .SWF's into the host movie.

Within the upper navigation panels of the main movie, drop-down menus were utilized to control audio, offer downloads, and provide site updates. These are implemented as movie clips that begin with an empty frame on keyframe one of their individual timelines. This allows them to be initially invisible in the interface, and to become visible only when their respective navigation buttons are rolled over. Using drop-down menus is an effective way to organize an interface because they avoid cluttering the main GUI. Considerations such as these are important for providing an intuitive interface that is easily navigable and that doesn't overwhelm the user with too many options at once.

Author's Note: For more information on loading external .SWF files with the `loadMovie` action, see Chapter 20, "Sharing and Loading Assets."

Reflection

Interface design within Flash concerns two factors: (a) how effectively users complete tasks (in other words, comprehend content), and (b) how well-represented the content is aesthetically. Flash 5 has accelerated our ability to create new forms of advanced interactive environments. Without a fundamental understanding of interfaces in general, however, it can be difficult to make these environments become a reality. Our current understanding of interface design, usability, and layout in non-Web–based interfaces can be applied and expanded to maximize the impact and comprehension of information on the Web. To take full advantage of Web efficiency, it is important to explore the use of guidelines, develop new methods of interactivity, and push beyond the existing boundaries of conventional interface design.

"I came across Flash when viewing Gabocorp.com — which was one of the first Flash sites. I set forth to purchase the program and engulf myself in its powerful ability to deliver a new level of interactivity and atmosphere," says Eric Jordan of his indomitable pursuit of Flash. In the year that he graduated from San Clemente High in southern California, Eric says that, "The most memorable movie was Mission Impossible — which, through its use of futuristic interfaces, actually greatly influenced my design style." Eric's personal site, `2advanced.com`, was nominated for best interface at Flash Forward 2000, featured in the launch issue of CreateOnline Magazine: The Web Designers Bible, and has received various design awards throughout the past year. Other sites that he has worked on include `www.centrata.com`, `www.createlabs.com`, and `www.cyberspaceguide.com`. Eric says that his single most favorite thing is to "turn out the lights, boot up the system, and pursue the creation of the ultimate user experience." This tutorial is a reflection upon the general process that led to the interface design for `www.designinsites.com`.

Adding Navigation Elements to the Main Timeline

In the last section, we created a Flash movie timeline for a computer parts Web site. We inserted content placeholder for the welcome, services, and contactInfo sections of the timeline, and we made a Movie Clip with product graphics to place in the product section. However, we had no way of actually getting to any section except the welcome frame. In this section, we create a menu that will control the position of the playhead on the Main Timeline.

Creating text buttons for a menu

In this part of the exercise, you make menu buttons that will enable the user to navigate to the different areas of the Flash movie.

1. On the Main Timeline of your mainMovie.fla movie, add a new layer and rename it **menu**. On this layer, we create text buttons to navigate the site.

2. Insert a keyframe on frame 10 of the menu layer. Select the Text Tool, and, with a 16-point Verdana font face, type the word **Home**. Place this text underneath the company logo graphic, on the left-hand side of the Stage (see Figure 13-10 for placement).

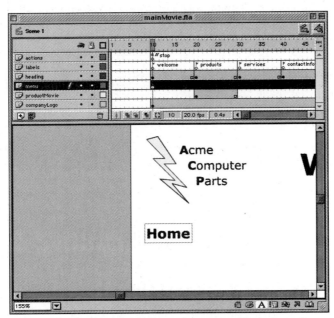

Figure 13-10: The homeButton instance will always take us to the welcome area of the site.

3. With the Arrow Tool, select the Home text block. Press F8 to convert this text into a symbol. In the Symbol Properties dialog, name the symbol **homeButton**. Assign it a Button behavior.

4. Now we need to add a Hit state to the homeButton timeline. By default, Flash will use the last frame of a Button symbol timeline for the Hit state, unless content is added to the Hit state keyframe. Double-click the homeButton instance on the Main Timeline to switch to Symbol Editing Mode.

5. Select the Hit frame of Layer 1 on the homeButton timeline, and press F7 to insert an empty keyframe.

6. Click the Onion Skin Outlines button in the timeline window toolbar. This enables you to view the previous frames of the homeButton timeline, as shown in Figure 13-11.

Figure 13-11: Onion skinning enables you to accurately align the contents of several keyframes.

7. Select the Rectangle Tool, and draw a filled rectangle that covers the same area of the Home text block. You can use any fill color because the user never sees the Hit state. Your button's timeline should resemble the one shown in Figure 13-12.

Figure 13-12: The Hit state defines the "active" area of the Button instance in the movie. If the user's mouse pointer enters this area, then the Over frame of the Button will be displayed.

8. Next we add an Over state to the homeButton, so that the user knows it's an active button. Select the Over frame of Layer 1, and press F6. This copies the contents of the previous keyframe into the new one. Select the Home text block with the Arrow Tool, and change the fill color to blue. You can also turn off Onion Skin Outlines at this point.

9. Return to the Main Timeline of your movie, and save your Flash movie file. Select Control ➪ Test Movie to test the states of the homeButton.

You can also use Control ➪ Enable Simple Buttons to preview the graphical states of a Button instance.

10. Now we put an action on the homeButton instance. Select the homeButton instance, and open the Actions Panel. In Normal Mode, double-click the Go To action in the Basic Actions booklet. Flash automatically adds the `on(release){}` code to store the Go To action, in the right-hand Actions list. In the parameter area of the Actions Panel, uncheck the Go to and Play option. In the Type drop-down menu, select Frame Label. In the Frame drop-down menu (located at the end of the field), select welcome. Your Actions Panel options should match those shown in Figure 13-13.

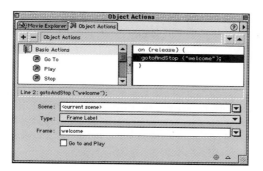

Figure 13-13: With these actions, the homeButton instance will move the Main Timeline playhead to the welcome frame label.

11. If we test our movie at this point, our homeButton won't do anything — our playhead is already on the welcome frame label. Let's add a button for each section on the site. Repeat Steps 2 to 8 for each section name in our movie. You should end up with four buttons: Home, Products, Services, and Contact Us.

12. Repeat Step 10 for each new button instance. For each button instance, change the Frame drop-down menu selection to match the name of the button's area (for example, `gotoAndStop("products");` on the productsButton).

13. Save your Flash movie, and test it (Ctrl+Enter or Command+Enter).

When you test your Flash movie, you should be able to click each button to go to each area of the movie. If a button isn't functioning, double-check the code on the instance. Make sure that each Button instance has a Button behavior in the Instance Panel. In the next section, we add buttons to the productMovie Movie Clip symbol, so that the user can browse the pictures of the computer parts.

Browsing the product catalog

In this section, we go inside the productMovie symbol and add some navigation buttons for our product catalog.

1. From the Main Timeline of our mainMovie.fla, double-click the productMovie instance on frame 20 of the productMovie layer. Flash switches to Symbol Editing Mode.

2. Make a new layer on the productMovie timeline, and rename the layer to **buttons**.

3. Open the Buttons Library (Window ⇨ Common Libraries ⇨ Buttons). In the Buttons Library window, double-click the (circle) Button Set folder. Drag the Circle with arrow Button symbol to the productMovie Stage. Place the Button instance below and to the right of the monitor_1 Graphic symbol.

4. With the Circle with Arrow instance selected, open the Actions Panel. Double-click the Go To action to add this action to the Actions list. In the parameters area of the panel, change the Type menu option to Next Frame. This action moves the productMovie playhead one frame forward with each mouse click on the Button instance.

5. With the Circle with Arrow instance selected, press Ctrl+D (Command+D) to duplicate the instance on the Stage. Move the duplicate instance to the left of the original arrow button. With the Arrow Tool selected, enable the Rotate modifier in the Toolbar. Rotate the duplicated button 180 degrees. Press the Shift key while rotating, to lock in 45-degree steps.

6. Select both arrow buttons, and align them horizontally to each other, as shown in Figure 13-14, by using the Align Panel.

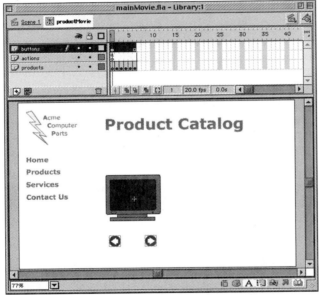

Figure 13-14: Position the arrow Buttons underneath the product graphic.

7. Select the left arrow, and open the Actions Panel. Select the nextFrame(); action in the Actions list. In the parameter area, change the Go To action's Type menu option to Previous Frame.

8. Save your Flash movie, and test it. Click the Products button, and try the new navigation arrows for your product catalog.

You can further enhance your presentation by adding more information in the productMovie Movie Clip symbol. After the following Expert Tutorial, we add a scrolling text window to the catalog that displays text descriptions of the products.

Expert Tutorial: Interface Usability, by *Merien Quintus Kunst*

This tutorial's focus is on the use of Flash as a tool for creating straightforward, serviceable, functioning Web sites. In the past year, Flash design has been under attack by Web usability experts. Although bad interface design is by no means limited to Flash movies, planning and designing interfaces should be a primary concern before building Flash movies.

Looking at Flash

For the last two years I have been running the Quintus Flash Index, which is a rather large collection of links to Flash sites. The reason I started it was simple enough: At the time, there weren't any decent collections of Flash work on the Web. Yet, I wanted to check sites out to see what Flash could do. So I went searching, exploring the world of Flash. As I explored, I decided to bookmark all the Flash sites that I came across. I ended up with a categorized, static list of about 150 links, which I then posted as a Web page, thinking that others might find it useful. Suddenly, I was getting 150 visitors a day to my Web site, which is really not bad for a 1-page site. As part of my internship, my supervisor suggested that I implement the site in ASP, add some ding-dongs, and put it online like that. So I did—and it took off. Today, the QFI has links to over 2,200 Flash sites, and (amazingly) over 12,000 visitor comments.

The comments area was just something I added because I thought it would be a nice feature for people to show their approval or disapproval of a site, which would be very useful for the developers. At first, I posted a lot of comments myself, trying to inspire people to follow my example. I focused mainly on overall impression and user friendliness, not really from an expert point of view, but rather like a regular user. However, the more sites I reviewed, the more I found similar errors and mistakes that would confuse visitors. Over time, many other people at my site also helped the site developers by indicating what elements of the sites were unclear, confusing, or even irritating.

Usability: The user experience

Consequently, I have had the opportunity to learn a lot about Internet usability and interface design. I found that many the site critiques on the Quintus Flash Index could be traced back to basic usability design rules. Not a big surprise, but rather a very clear indication of the value of some of these rules.

Usability may sound mystifying to some people, and some best-selling books may champion the obscurity of this subject, but there's really nothing too complex about it. Usability is the extent to which a system supports its users in completing their tasks efficiently, effectively, and satisfactorily—which may also include the experience of aesthetic pleasure. On the Web, this leads to topics such as navigation, speed, clarity, and readability. The real trick about usability is the horrible task of letting it seep through in your design. Usability extremists call out for Web sites with barely any graphics, using only default browser fonts (and default colors), and certainly no plug-ins.

But the fact is that Flash is one of the best design tools to effectively break most of those extreme rules of usability—and in a very short time. This tutorial attempts to steer both beginning and experienced Flash designers toward a more responsible use of Flash.

Continued

Continued

While this may sound a bit loaded, you should realize that, by now, quite a few sites have banned the use of Flash entirely—simply because they had the unfortunate experience of having Flash implemented on their behalf, but in the *wrong* way. When Flash is used the wrong way, it creates havoc. However, the same can be said of HTML. (The designers should have been blamed, rather than the tool!) So, to help Flash designers avoid making the same errors all over again, I've written out some pointers, highlighting many of the common errors I've encountered when reviewing Flash sites. I hope these hints will be useful to you.

Flash is a tool, not a platform

Flash sites are either sites with Flash elements or 100 percent Flash sites. The latter is a very decent option for small sites such as personal sites or sites that are meant purely for entertainment by animation and sound. But you may want to develop a more elaborate site with features such as a forum, chat room, response forms, user registration, content management, or a search option. While doing this strictly in Flash is certainly a great technical challenge, it's not a very wise decision. The fact is that Flash is just a tool that offers a means for designers to turn their ideas into reality. It is not a platform on which to build a Web site.

The best sites out there combine Flash with other techniques and formats such as DHTML, streaming video, MP3, Java, and the common image formats such as JPEG and GIF, as well as any other medium that will offer the needed content in the most appropriate way to the visitor. The magic rule is to consider every possible medium for each element you want to develop. If you understand the strengths and weaknesses of Flash, you can apply it where it is suitable, or decide when it may not be the best solution.

Button hit area: Number 1 mistake

The single most common error should be mentioned first. When a text button is created, it is essential that the *hit area* frame of the button be filled with a solid shape in roughly the same size as the button text field. The effect of an empty *hit area* frame is a very jerky reaction of the mouse pointer. Often, such buttons require surgical precision to simply use the button. When creating any button, it is best to choose a filled shape that covers the maximum dimensions of your button and put it in the *hit area* frame of the button.

Author's Note: Flash 5 adds a new option for Static Text fields in the Character Panel: URL links. If you need simple text buttons, then you don't need to make a Button symbol—simply specify a URL in the Character Panel. You won't experience hit area problems with this URL-linked Static Text fields. For basic coverage of Button symbols, refer to Chapter 9, "Checking Out the Library: Symbols and Instances."

Font size, font type: Squint, ignore

Designers often choose to use a Flash movie to display textual content in their Web site or presentation. Whenever large pieces of static text are involved, you should question whether Flash is the best medium to present this information to your audience. The downside of embedding large text areas in your Flash movies is mostly an issue of legibility, but there are also concerns about further processing of the information by the viewer.

Often, users aren't prepared to read through pages of small, antialiased text, and usually choose to skip this information — which may be vital information. One technique to solve this problem in Flash 5 is offered in the form of Dynamic Text fields.

Dynamic Text fields are presented as aliased, selectable text that increases the legibility of small fonts while providing a more useful way to present the text. That's because this technique enables users to select an area of text and copy it to the clipboard. This is more user friendly, because it provides better access to the information. Many visitors will want a way to extract specific pieces of information. This technique enables them to store this information wherever they want, exactly like copying text from HTML pages. (For more about Dynamic Text fields, refer to Chapter 7, "Working with Text.")

For large amounts of text, Flash is usually not the best medium, and other media, such as HTML, plain text, Adobe Acrobat, or word processor documents, should be considered. Think twice before you start pasting long passages of text into your Flash movie.

Menu look and feel: Is this a button?

To hang a painting you need a hammer and a nail (and a wall); to water plants you need a hose. How about this one: To find a phone number, you need to start reading each page in the phone book from page one until you reach the page where the wanted name is listed. No? To view your favorite TV show, you zap to the right channel, watch 30 seconds of a creepily familiar introduction video clip, and then the show starts. If you change the channel, but then come back again, you get to watch the introduction all over again. Does that sound right? When you take the elevator, you just press any of the new symbols that are displayed on a huge array of buttons to learn what each does. You keep pressing them, one by one, until you reach the right floor. Oh, and the buttons look like chewing gum stuck to the wall. In fact, some of the buttons aren't even buttons — that *is* gooey chewing gum that you just stuck your finger in! Getting annoyed yet? Well, you're not alone.

Usability is all about offering people something they are looking for. That means offering it quickly, correctly, and with maximum accessibility. On a Web site, accessibility depends on factors such as loading times, user requirements, and navigation. Navigation breaks down into buttons, structure, and guidance. Flash offers wonderful tools to create menus, navigation tricks, and really exotic buttons. Everyone who is working with Flash will think about interfaces such as an interactive phone for a menu, or a tree, a remote control, body parts, cubes, balls, subway maps, giant fruit baskets, planetary models — but remember, no matter how cute or cool or ingenious *your* interface might seem to you, it doesn't work if it doesn't work.

Not many people think, "Gray, square buttons . . ."

Yet, the gray, square buttons are what people know and understand, just like blue, underlined text. Not very exciting, so we need to work out how to merge our galaxy model (or fruit basket) with the user's idea of a menu, and motivate them to navigate through the Web site with it. A solution might be to reconsider your ideas and shape them into a more recognizable menu scheme, making your menu items look a bit more like classic buttons and placing them on the top, side, or bottom of the screen.

Continued

Continued

A less drastic solution might be to have people test your interface. This way, you could see how (or if) they figure out that those thingies are functional buttons, and then make design improvements based on that information.

A menu design can often be improved by adding pointers, like small pop-ups with your buttons, or a help function that delivers a quick explanation. You should expect that Web site visitors aren't very patient, so make sure that a minimal effort is required to *use* your brilliant interface.

Finally, you won't really be testing your navigation with people if you help them, as this will make this a useless test — unless, of course, you also have an ingenious plan to be there to help everyone that visits your site. If you want to design usable Web sites, you must be hard on yourself — because your visitors will certainly be unforgiving of your self-indulgent design lapses.

Some pointers based on problems I often recognize in Flash menus:

✦ Transitions should be short. It doesn't help if the needed segment takes 10 seconds or more to unfold . . . only to show submenu items.

✦ Try to have the current location highlighted in the menu; this visual cue helps people figure out where they are.

✦ Avoid moving or rotating buttons. Even buttons that stop when you move the mouse over them are often very confusing. Slow movement is sometimes acceptable.

✦ Have buttons show their function. Sometimes, buttons don't reveal their function until they're clicked, which is *not* user friendly. If a square shape takes me to the links page, does the triangle shape mean I can send an e-mail? What about the donut? Good practice is to use the right icons, or add text to your buttons.

Skip intro: All the way

If you really want an animated Flash introduction, start it with a SKIP button. In general, don't make intros. They can be interesting for some entertainment sites, or designer agencies, but it's not right to assume that:

✦ The visitor wants to wait for the loading of the intro

✦ The visitor *will* be entertained for 30 seconds

✦ The visitor will *then* wait for the first page to load

✦ The visitor will *stay* long enough to access your information

Intelligent, clear, user-friendly employment of Flash on your Web site is a much better reference than an indulgent intro that takes too long to load. Furthermore, *if* that visitor decides to return to your site, it's not very useful to force them through that intro again.

The only fully justified intro is a light one that entertains the visitor while the main Web site loads. But visitors with fast connections should still be able to skip it—all of it. I could take the next ten pages to tell you the long, long story about how the Flash intro phenomenon started, but that's not very useful, either. However, if I were to tell that story, at least you'd have the mechanism—by turning the page—to move on to the real content. The best advice on this subject is to consider what, if any, added value an intro animation will give to your site.

Finally, here's one option that's not really used often enough. If you really feel driven to create animations that delight and amaze, why not create a separate area of your site for Flash experiments? In such an area, there is no reason to hold back because in that context, your animation *is* the content, rather than an impediment to content.

Browser navigation: Back, Help!

It doesn't seem likely that Flash will ever be well enough integrated into the browsers to eliminate this problem: Using browser navigation buttons is disastrous! When someone's found their way to the information they needed from your Flash site, and then decides to hit the *Back* button to return to the previous segment, they usually end up somewhere unexpected.

A similar annoying result occurs when a visitor attempts to bookmark a particular moment in your Flash movie—the bookmark will only return the visitor back to the start of your Flash movie.

Although a self-made *Back* button can be included in your Flash movie, visitors aren't likely to get used to such features very quickly. Your regular visitors may get the hang of it, but seeing two buttons with the same label (that is, the browser's *Back* button, plus your own *Back* button) may confuse first timers.

To facilitate bookmarking of specific parts of the Flash content drastic measures would be required: Split your movie into several segments, and distribute them over Web pages that can be individually bookmarked. Usually this effort is worth the extra work, because it has additional advantages. Of course, it saves visitors the drag of navigating back to the point of interest every time they visit the site. However, it also helps improve the speed of your Web site. Plus, if you update just one of the movies, you'll be working on a less complex .FLA. And, finally, when the update is completed, caching can still be used to retrieve the other pages. Only the changed page will have to be reloaded from the server.

Site statistics: Split up your movies or go blind

The method indicated previously to facilitate the bookmarking of your Flash pages could also solve the analysis problem of fully Flashed sites. Because a single movie is grabbed from the Web server, it's virtually impossible to tell what people are doing inside your site. What segments attract most visitors, what are the common exit points, and which pages are never viewed? Web site statistics are a valuable developer tool for Web site improvements and visitor analysis. Complex schemes can solve this problem, involving database logging and/or posting to forms from within your Flash movies, which I do not discuss.

Continued

Continued

The easiest, if somewhat crude, way to generate proper statistics is by splitting your movie into segments that reflect the structure of your site. This enables you to use classic tools to view the statistics of your site, because every segment sits in it's own HTML page. Furthermore, this solution, when coupled with <META> tags, can also ensure that your Flash site is properly represented among the search engines.

Use of sound: Music on demand

With every release, Flash delivers better support for sounds and music. The new support for MP3 import in Flash 5, makes it even easier to balance quality sound with streaming and small file sizes. Sounds can be used to add effects to navigation elements, create cool background music loops, or to offer sound samples to visitors. However, because many people without audio available on their systems view the Internet, the best way to incorporate the sounds with your Web creations is to make the sounds passive. Even if your guests have sound on their system, it may not be turned on. If the experience of your movie depends on the sound effects and music that come with it, tell everybody that they need to turn on their speakers. If you use items such as a background loop, it's thoughtful to make the sound optional *before* your visitor starts loading the (often large) music files into your Flash. That way those with sound-challenged systems won't have to wait for it to download even though they have no way to enjoy it.

Always consider whether Flash is the best way to offer your music items. In many cases, other techniques (or technologies) may have better support. For example, if you want to present a streaming audio clip, then you might want to use RealAudio instead of Flash. (See Chapter 32, "Working with Audio Applications," for alternate means of delivering sound in concert with Flash. Methods for deploying sound with both Beatnik and the MP3 Player are discussed in Expert Tutorials.)

Another setting that deserves mention is the volume of your sound clips. Test the audio elements in a movie with normal system volume, to ensure that it's not too low or doesn't cause hearing discomfort.

It's tempting to use sound bytes as a way to improve navigation. For example, a button that tells you all about it's functionality would be nice to add extra clarity to a menu. However, as useful (and impressive) as this technique might be, don't rely on it too much. As mentioned before, much of the Web population relies purely on the visual part of Web sites.

Print option: Will people understand?

Flash offers a great way to embed specific content into your Flash movie that can be sent directly to a user's printer. A common example for this technique is a small Flash banner that sends a full-page advertisement to the printer when the user hits the print button in the movie. It's a nice way to avoid cluttering Web pages with sundry advertisement details, but it's also a way to offer any single- or multipage document (poster size images, spreadsheets, background details) with the click of a small button. (For more information about Flash printing capabilities, refer to Mike Richards' Expert Tutorial, "Creating Printable Paper Airplanes," in Chapter 19, "Controlling Movie Clips.")

Unfortunately, Flash printing is a functionality that's quite new on the Web, and it's a functionality that can't be properly explained in one or two words. So, if you choose to use this feature, make sure to give a clear indication of its function, with button text similar to "Send the details of this product to my printer" or "Print a full-page version of this image."

Progress indicators: What's going on?

This topic is easily dealt with. It comes down to this: Even though loading bars aren't a pleasant sight to look at (a funny or informational preloader is much better), some movies give no indication of what's happening during download. "Are we there yet?" For modem users, this can be especially frustrating, because there is no way of knowing whether the movie has ended, or the connection was lost, or the last bit is being loaded in the background. (A blank or frozen screen is not very entertaining either.) Progress bars are not the most aesthetic solution. If they are designed properly, they'll at least provide clarity about loading time. Many good tutorials can be found online to help you create a reliable progress indicator.

Obviously, the best loading scheme is one that goes unnoticed. But for heftier movies (or really slow connections) a loading scheme and a progress indicator are needed. A great solution is a small game or animation that also indicates progress (percentage). In case you're wondering, yes, Pong has been done, just like Memory, Simon Says, and Tic-Tac-Toe. But you just can't beat the classics!

Forms: Better let them know

Flash offers reasonable support to embed forms. Many elements, such as drop-down lists and the use of the Tab button, don't respond as they do in classic HTML forms. To get around these problematic defaults, some clever ActionScript is needed.

Another problem worth mentioning is that forms in Flash aren't always easily recognized as *forms*. This is attributable to the two issues: The design of the form is rarely that of a classic Web form, and users are not (yet) used to Flash forms. So, some help is required. Try putting a blinking cursor in the first entry field, or, better yet, something like a big arrow that says *Please Use This Form*, to reduce the chance that people will leave the page mystified. (For more information about Flash forms, refer to Chapters 21, "Planning Code Structures," and 24, "Sending Data In and Out of Flash.")

There are few examples on the Web in which Flash forms really use the specific advantages of the Flash medium. Good examples are chat room applications with interactive characters and interactive games that require keyboard input. One clear advantage of Flash is its capability to make form posts without (re)loading a page. This is a feature that can be exploited in clever ways, but consider the visitors' expectations (based on classic HTML forms): Give clear feedback about post results after submission, or they'll wait forever for a form to submit.

Conclusion: The Flash experience

This tutorial has addressed only a few of the many topics that are relevant to Flash developers who care about the user friendliness of their creations.

Continued

Continued

Although some of the topics may be very obvious, this is no guarantee that they aren't easily overlooked. Flash has become so versatile that it's hard to tell people how they should use it, largely because it is used for so many different goals. The focus of this article has been on the use of Flash as a tool for creating rather straightforward Web sites. These are sites that want to inform, entertain, and maybe educate their visitors.

The most important concept to realize about Flash is that it really is just a tool. If you need to create something, first think about what you want to make; then think about how you're going to realize it afterwards. It's bad practice to assume that Flash is such a cool program that it will be a good way to create anything that you might conjure. If the project has elements that would benefit from the features Flash offers, use it the best way possible. Again, that doesn't mean using all the imaginable tween effects that you can think of; it does mean, however, thinking about the user experience you want to create.

That user experience is dependent on overall impression, entertainment value, ease of navigation, loading times, and the sense of control by the visitor. These criteria pose quite a challenge to the best designers and developers. At times, it may be boring or frustrating to address these criteria, but in the long run, it will make your Flash masterpieces more durable and appreciated.

Online reference

This tutorial wouldn't be complete without some interesting links. To ensure that they remain current, I've added an area to the Quintus Flash Index where you'll find additional information about this subject: `www.quintus.org/use`.

A native of Utrecht, Netherlands, Merien Quintus Kunst wins the prize for the most amazing name. He says that his middle name is an old family tradition. In fact, it's Latin for "fifth," while his last name, Kunst, is Dutch for art. So, we might expect him to know a thing or two about art and design. When he came of age, he was rockin' to Nature Boy by Primus, while the rest of Holland succumbed to Let The Beat Control Your Body, by 2 Unlimited. Merien's single most favorite thing to do is snowboarding. He also enjoys, "inline skating, buying CDs, my girlfriend, renting videos, being online, English and American literature, and modern art." Currently employed at BSUR Concepting & Communications Amsterdam, he's also the man behind QFI, the Quintus Flash Index — `www.quintus.org` — and has worked on many other sites, including `www.sarah.nl` and `www.vastned.nl`. How did Quintus find Flash? "Like half the world, through `www.gabocorp.com`. He introduced Flash to the masses."

The topic of Flash usability has received a lot of press lately, particularly because many Flash interfaces are considered experimental or nonintuitive to the average Web user. In December 2000, Macromedia released a new section to their Web site — Macromedia Flash Usability. You can read their usability tips and view examples of interface design at:

`www.macromedia.com/software/flash/productinfo/usability`

Basic Text Scrolling

Continuing from our previous Flash movie example with the computer parts catalog, we demonstrate basic scrolling text using Motion Tween animation and Button actions. We demonstrate this technique for one product in the catalog to get you started.

1. In the mainMovie.fla from the previous section, double-click the productMovie instance on the productMovie layer, located on the Main Timeline. Flash switches to Symbol Editing Mode.

2. Add a new layer, and rename it **scrollingText**. On frame 1 of the scrollingText layer, draw a filled rectangle shape (with any fill color) to the right of the product graphic, as shown in Figure 13-15. The size of the rectangle should match the size of the text area you wish to display in the scrolling text window. The rectangle shape will become a Mask Layer inside another symbol for the text.

3. Select the rectangle shape, and press F8 to convert it into a symbol. Give the new symbol the name **scrollingText**, and keep the default Movie Clip behavior.

4. Double-click the instance on the Stage, and Flash switches to Symbol Editing Mode. The timeline of the scrollingText symbol will be displayed.

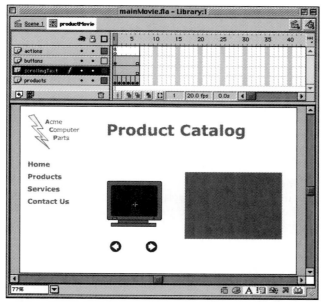

Figure 13-15: This rectangle will be used to mask the text in our scrolling text window.

5. Rename Layer 1 to **textMask**. Add a new layer, rename it **text**, and move this layer below the textMask layer. Switch the viewing mode of the textMask to Outline Mode by clicking the colored square at the right end of the textMask layer options. Also, lock the textMask layer so that you won't accidentally alter its shape or position. The outline of the shape will indicate where our text should be placed.

6. Select the first frame of the text layer, and, using the Text Tool, insert the text that follows into a Static Text block, as shown in Figure 13-16. You can copy and paste this text from the monitor_1_text symbol in the content.fla Library. Keep the right margin of the text block at the right edge of the outlined rectangle in the textMask layer, and don't worry about the text that extends below the Stage edge:

```
This generic flat-screen CRT 22" monitor is optimal for
intense graphics production, ideal for desktop publishing,
video, and 3D art professionals. With a premium dot pitch and
a large viewable area, this monitor can handle all the
demands of accurate color-calibrated output.

Viewable area:

21"

Dot pitch:

.23 mm

Refresh rates:

640 x 480, 67 Hz
800 x 600, 85 Hz
1024 x 768, 85Hz
1152 x 870, 75 Hz
1280 x 1024. 75Hz
1600 x 1200, 75Hz
```

7. Select the Static Text block you created in Step 6, and press F8. This new symbol will be named monitor_1_text, and will have a Graphic symbol behavior.

8. Now we create a Motion Tween over ten frames. We add buttons that will move the playhead one frame with each click. Therefore, nine clicks will get us to the end of the text. Select frame 10 in both the textMask and text layers, and then press F5. Then, select just the frame 10 of the text layer, and press F6. Right-click (or Ctrl+click on the Mac) any frame between frames 1 and 10 of the text layer, and select Create Motion Tween from the contextual menu.

9. On frame 10 of the text layer, select the monitor_1_text instance, and move the instance toward the top edge of the Stage, until the bottom edge of the text aligns with the bottom edge of the mask outline, as shown in Figure 13-17. For greater accuracy, use the up arrow key (with the Shift key pressed) to move the instance.

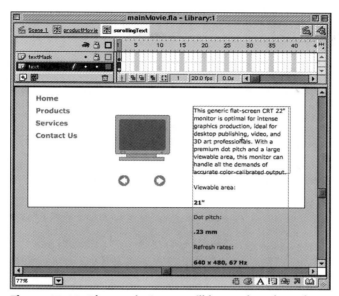

Figure 13-16: The text in Step 6 will be too lengthy to keep within the area of the rectangle outline. Don't worry—we'll be adding scroll buttons that will enable the viewer to see the text outside of the mask.

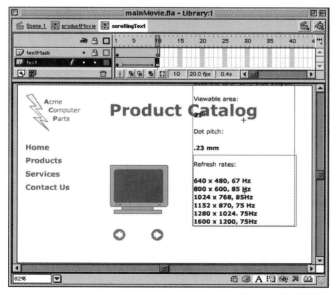

Figure 13-17: By aligning the contents of the end keyframe, you are setting the lower limit of the scrolling window.

10. To complete the masking effect, right-click (or Ctrl+click on the Mac) the label name for the textMask layer. Select Mask from the contextual menu. This automatically nests the text layer with the textMask layer.

11. Now, add two Button instances to this timeline, just like we did in the product Movie symbol. Create a new layer named **buttons**, and place it above the textMask layer. Open the Buttons Library (Window ➪ Common Libraries ➪ Button), and drag an arrow button from the Library on to the scrollingText Stage.

12. If necessary, rotate the arrow instance so that it points upwards.

13. With the arrow instance selected, open the Actions Panel, and add a Go To action, changing the Type to Previous Frame. The Actions list should read:

```
on(release){
    prevFrame();
}
```

14. Select the arrow instance and duplicate it (Ctrl+D or Command+D). Move this instance below the original arrow instance, and rotate the arrow so that it points downward. With the instance selected, open the Actions Panel. Select the prevFrame() action in the Actions list, and, in the parameters area, change the Type menu to Next Frame. The Actions list should now read:

```
on(release){
    nextFrame();
}
```

15. Now we should draw a visual frame from our scrolling text area. Create a new layer, and rename it **frame**. Place this layer underneath the buttons layer, but above the textMask layer. Draw an unfilled rectangle with a 1-point black stroke, just slightly larger than the original rectangle used to create the textMask.

16. Finally, we need to stop this timeline from automatically playing. Add a new layer, and rename it **actions**. Place this layer above the buttons layer. Select frame 1 of the actions layer, and open the Actions Panel. Add a Stop action (stop();) to this keyframe, as shown in Figure 13-18. Optionally, you can add a frame comment of **//stop** in the Label field of the Frame Panel.

17. Go back to the productMovie symbol timeline, and select frame 2 of the scrollingText layer. Press F7 to add a blank keyframe. This restricts the scrollingText layer to the first keyframe, for the monitor_1 graphic.

18. Save your Flash movie, and test it. You should be able to click the Products button, and scroll the description text for the first monitor graphic in the catalog.

To add more descriptions for each product, simply duplicate the scrollingText symbol, change the text (and alignment) in the duplicate symbol, and place it on the corresponding keyframe in the productMovie symbol. Of course, this example is just a functional prototype with placeholder graphics. The next step in real production would be to finesse the artwork, and to add transitional effects between each area of the movie. Perhaps some sound effects would be useful, too. The next chapter introduces Part III of the *Flash 5 Bible*, "Sound Planning."

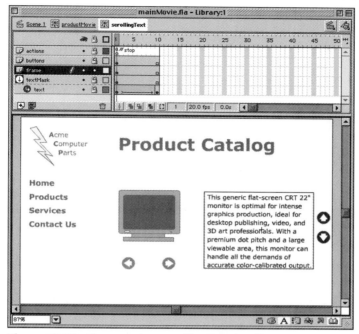

Figure 13-18: The complete scrollingText timeline

Summary

✦ Before you can start to create an interface in Flash, you need to have a plan for your Flash movie timeline. Create an organizational chart outlining the sections of the presentation.

✦ Determine your Flash movie properties (frame size, frame rate, and background color) before you undergo production in Flash.

✦ If you don't have final art for a Flash production, you can still create a functional prototype of the presentation using placeholder graphics. When the final artwork is ready, replace the placeholder graphics with the final artwork.

✦ You can create simple slide shows or product catalogs using sequential keyframes and buttons with nextFrame() and prevFrame() actions.

✦ The Hit area of a text-based Button symbol should always be defined with a solid shape.

✦ Basic nonscripted scrolling can be added to a presentation with simple Motion Tweens and buttons using nextFrame() and prevFrame() actions.

✦   ✦   ✦

Sound Planning

One of the most neglected (or perhaps understated) aspects of multimedia development is sound. Because the majority of people who use Flash (or create multimedia) come from graphic-arts backgrounds, it's no surprise that sound is often applied as the last effect to a visually stunning presentation — there may be little or no consideration for the soundtrack in early stages of development. Moreover, it's the one element that is usually taken from a stock source, rather than being original work by the Flash designer. (Exceptions exist, of course, as many Flash designers have demonstrated time and time again.)

With this in mind, we sought to provide you with a basic overview of digital sound and sound quality in Chapter 14, so that you would know how to judge the quality of different bit depths and sampling rates. Chapters 15 and 16 guide you through the use of audio within a Flash movie and suggest tips for getting the most bang per byte in the final .SWF file.

Understanding Sound for Flash

✦ ✦ ✦ ✦

In This Chapter

Sampling and quality

Distinguishing sample rate from bit resolution

Calculating audio file sizes

Working with audio formats

✦ ✦ ✦ ✦

This chapter introduces the basics of digital audio for Flash. Properly implemented, the integration of sound with your Flash project adds dimension to your creation. That's because sound introduces another mode of sensory perception. Coordinated with visual form and motion, sound deepens the impact and can even enhance the ease of use of your Flash creation. With careful planning and attention to technical detail, sound can be leveraged to great advantage. Rather than add sound as an afterthought, we encourage you to create a seamless multisensory experience for your audience. In this chapter, we explain sample rate and bit resolution, and the difference between the two. We also discuss how audio files sizes are calculated, and the audio formats that are supported by Flash.

Basics of Sampling and Quality

Before you begin integrating sound with your Flash project, it's important to understand the basics of digital audio. To help you with this, we've dedicated this chapter to an introduction to sampling, bit resolution, and file size — and the relevance of these topics to sound in Flash 5.

What is sound?

Sound, or hearing, is one of our five principal sensations; it's the sensation that's produced when vibrations in the air strike the aural receptors located within our ears. When we hear a sound, the volume of the sound is determined by the intensity of the vibrations, or sound waves. The pitch that we hear — meaning how high (treble) or low (bass) — is determined by the frequency of those vibrations (waves). The frequency of sound is measured in hertz (which is abbreviated as Hz).

Theoretically, most humans have the ability to hear frequencies that range from 20 to 20,000 Hz. The frequency of the sound is a measure of the range of the sound—from the highest high to the lowest low. It's important to note here that, when starting to work with sound, the most common error is to confuse the frequency of the sound with the recording sample.

What you should know about sound for Flash

When integrating sound with Flash, a number of factors affect the final quality of the sound and the size of the sound file. The quality of the sound is important because it determines the aesthetic experience of the sound, while the file size is important because it determines how quickly (or not) the sound will arrive at the end user's computer. The primary factors that determine the quality and size of a sound file are sample rate and bit resolution.

Sample rate

The sample rate, measured in hertz (Hz), describes the number of times an audio signal is sampled when it is recorded digitally. In the late 1940s, Harry Nyquist and Claude Shannon developed a theorem that determined that, for optimal sound quality, a sampling rate must be twice the value of the highest frequency of a signal. Thus, the higher the sample rate, the better the audio range. Generally, higher sample rates result in a richer, more complete sound. According to Nyquist and Shannon, in order for the audible range of 20 to 20,000 Hz to be sampled correctly, the audio source needs to be sampled at a frequency no lower than 40,000 Hz, or 40 kHz. This explains why CD audio—which closely resembles the source sound—is sampled at 44.1 kHz.

Note

A sound sample refers to one "analysis" of a recorded sound, whereas a sound file refers to the entire collection of samples recorded, which comprise a digital recording.

The less a sound is sampled, the further the recording will deviate from the original sound. However, this tendency toward loss of the original quality of the sound yields one advantage: When the sample rate of a sound file is decreased, the file size drops proportionately. For example, a 300KB, 44.1 kHz sound file would be 150KB when saved as a 22.05 kHz file. See Table 14-1 for more details on how sample rate affects quality.

Table 14-1
Audio Sample Rates and Quality

Sample Rate	Quality Level	Possible Uses
48 kHz	Studio quality	Sound or music recorded to digital medium such as miniDV, DAT, DVCam, and so on
44.1 kHz	CD quality	High-fidelity sound and music

Sample Rate	Quality Level	Possible Uses
32 kHz	Near-CD quality	Professional/consumer digital camcorders
22.05 kHz	FM radio quality	Short, high-quality music clips
11.025 kHz	Acceptable for music	Longer music clips; high-quality voice; sound effects
5 kHz	Acceptable for speech	"Flat" speech; simple button sounds

Because the native playback rate of all audio cards is 44.1 kHz, sound that is destined for playback on any computer should be a multiple of 44.1. Thus, we recommend sample rates of 44.1 kHz, 22.05 kHz, and 11.025 kHz for *any* use on computers. (Although sample rates that deviate from the rule of 44.1 may sound fine on your development platform, and may sound fine on many other computers, some may have problems. This simple rule will go a long ways toward reducing complaints of popping and distorted sound.) This becomes more important with Flash. When Flash imports sounds that are not multiples of 11.025, the sound file is resampled, which causes the sound to play at a lower or higher pitch than the original recording. This same logic applies to sound export, which is discussed later in this chapter. Finally, although Flash menus list sample rates as 11, 22, and 44, these are abbreviations for the truly precise sample rates of 11.025, 22.05, and 44.1 kHz.

Bit resolution

The second key factor that influences audio quality is bit resolution (or bit depth). Bit resolution describes the number of bits used to record each audio sample. Bit resolution is increased exponentially, meaning that an 8-bit sound sample has a range of 2^8, or 256, levels, while a 16-bit sound sample has a range of 2^{16}, or 65,536, levels. Thus, a 16-bit sound is recorded with far more information than an 8-bit sound of equal length. The result of this additional information in a 16-bit sound is that background hiss is minimized, while the sound itself is clearer. The same sound recorded at 8 bits will be noisy and washed out.

Reducing file size

Another point to remember is that the 16-bit sound file is twice the size of the same file saved at 8-bit quality. This is due to the increase in the amount of information taken to record the higher quality file. So, if your sound is too big, what can you do? Well, a sound that's been recorded at a higher bit resolution can be converted to a lower bit resolution, and a sound with a high sample rate can be converted to a lower sample rate. Although a professional studio might perform such conversions with hardware, either of these conversions can also be done with software. For more information on down sampling and conversion, refer to Chapter 32, "Working with Audio Applications."

Tip

If you're having difficulty understanding the significance of bit depths yet are familiar with the intricacies of scanning photographic images, consider the difference between an 8-bit grayscale image and a 24-bit color image of equivalent dimensions. The file size for the 8-bit grayscale image (such as a black and white photograph) is much smaller than the 24-bit color image (such as a color photograph). The gray scale image doesn't have as much tonal information—only 256 levels of gray—yet the 24-bit color image records a range of 16.7 million colors. Unlike photographs, sound samples don't require anything close to a range of 16.7 million values. Sixteen-bit sound samples deliver a dynamic range of over 64,000 values, which is more than the human ear can detect.

Table 14-2 lists the various bit depths of sound along with their quality level and possible uses.

Table 14-2		
Audio Bit Resolution and Quality		
Bit Depth	**Quality Level**	**Possible Uses**
16-bit	CD quality	High-fidelity sound and music
12-bit	Near-CD quality	Professional/consumer digital camcorder audio
8-bit	FM radio quality	Short, high-quality music clips
4-bit	Acceptable for music	Longer music clips; high-quality voice; sound effects

Refer to Figures 14-1 and 14-2 for a comparison of the differences between sounds at different sample rates and bit depths. Both figures show a wave form derived from the same original sound file, differing only in their sample rates and bit depths. The waveform of the 16-bit 44.1 kHz sound has twice as many "points"—or samples of information—as the 8-bit 11.025 kHz sound. Because the 16-bit 44.1 kHz sound has more samples, the gap between each sample isn't as large as the gaps of the 8-bit 11.025 kHz sound. More samples result in a much smoother, cleaner sound.

Tip

A common mistake that novices make with sound is the assumption that 8-bit audio is acceptable, especially because it ought to result in a much smaller file size than 16-bit sound. This is wrong for at least two reasons. First, 8-bit is unacceptable because it sounds incredibly worse than 16-bit sound. Second, the horrible sound will not pay for itself in diminished file size because most compression codecs won't work on 8-bit sound.

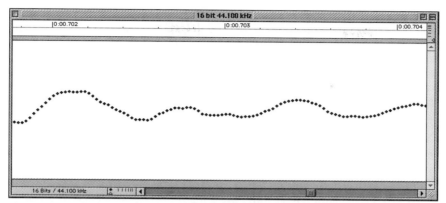

Figure 14-1: This is a waveform of a sound sampled at 44.100 kHz with a 16-bit resolution, as displayed in a high-end sound application.

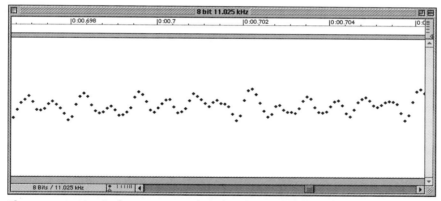

Figure 14-2: Here's the same sound as shown in Figure 14-1, but down sampled to 11.025 kHz with an 8-bit resolution.

Channels

Audio files are either mono (single channel) or stereo (dual channel: left and right). Stereo files are twice the size of mono files because they have twice the information. Most audio-editing applications offer the option to mix the two stereo channels together and either save or export a stereo sound to a one channel mono sound. Most audio applications also have the ability to save the right or left channel of a stereo sound separately as a .WAV or .AIF file.

With the more robust, multitrack-editing applications, such as Deck II, ProTools, or AudioLogic, it's not unusual to work with eight or more audio tracks — limited only by your system configuration. As you might imagine, these applications give the sound artist greater control over the final sound mix. For use in Flash, these multi-track audio project files need to be "bounced" or mixed down to a stereo or mono file in order to be saved as WAV or AIF files. For a more detailed description of this process, refer to Chapter 32, "Working with Audio Applications."

File size

You should be concerned about the file size of your audio clips for a several reasons.

✦ Sound files require a large amount of drive space.

✦ Managing large sound files, and importing them into Flash can be cumbersome and slow.

✦ Download times for large, elaborate sound clips (even when heavily compressed upon export from Flash) can be detrimental to the appreciation of your Flash project, even if you have what might be considered a high speed Internet connection.

Production tips

When working with audio clips, it's important to create the shortest audio clips possible. That means trimming off any excess sound that you don't need, especially any blank lead-in or lead-out *handles* (also called in and out points) at the either the beginning or the end of a clip. This procedure is discussed briefly in Chapter 15, "Importing and Editing Sounds in Flash," with reference to Flash's sound tools, and then again in greater detail in Chapter 32, "Working with Audio Applications," where external audio applications are introduced.

If you plan to have a background music track in your Flash project, it's a good idea to use a small audio clip that can be looped. Looping audio clips are described in both Chapter 15, "Importing and Editing Sounds in Flash," and in Chapter 32, "Working with Audio Applications."

Here is a simple formula to determine the file size, in bytes of a given audio clip:

```
Seconds of audio × sample rate* × # of channels × (bit depth ÷
8**) = file size

*Expressed in hertz, not kilohertz.
**There are eight bits per byte.
```

Thus, a 20-second stereo audio loop at 8 bits, 11 kHz would be calculated like this:

20 sec × 11,025 Hz × 2 channels × (8 bits ÷ 8 bits/byte) = 441,000 bytes = 430 KB

There are two schools of thought regarding the ideal quality of sound files for import into Flash. These schools are pretty much divided into those who have high-end sound-editing tools and those who don't. In an effort to delineate the best path for each group, we've noted the following: (a) If you *don't* have high-end sound tools available, then you may be among those who *always* prefer to start with audio source files of the highest possible quality (16 bit, 44.1 kHz is ideal), and then use the Flash sound settings to obtain optimal compression upon export. See Chapter 16, "Optimizing Flash Sound for Export," for detailed information on the Flash sound export settings for .SWF movies. (b) If you *do* have high-end sound tools available, then you may prefer to compose most of your clients' music from scratch and that you very rarely work with the MP3 format before importing into Flash. You may also disagree with those who advise that one should bring their sound into Flash at the highest quality before optimizing. This workflow difference may be attributable to the plethora of options that are available to those with high-end sound tools. We know of one sound engineer who converts all of his audio to 16-bit 22.1 kHz mono files, "with major bass reduction," *before* importing into Flash. For more information on high-end sound tools, refer to Chapter 32, "Working with Audio Applications." As with so many things, individual mileage may vary.

Sound File Import Formats

Prior versions of Flash could import several different file formats — but the format you chose depended primarily on the platform you were using to develop your content. Flash still supports those formats and, regardless of whether a sound file was imported on a Mac or PC, the resulting .FLA file can still be edited on either platform. The big news with Flash 5 is that it imports MP3.

 Flash 5 now supports direct import of MP3 sound files!

Flash supports more than just MP3 files. Here's the entire list:

✦ **MP3 (MPEG-1 Audio Layer 3):** Among the many advantages of MP3 sound files for Flash 5 users, the most obvious is that they are cross-platform. Flash 5 can import MP3 sound on either the PC or the Mac. This single advantage improves Flash workflow in cross platform environment. Other advantages are the efficiency of MP3 compression and the resultant wealth of sound files that are increasingly available in this format. For more information about MP3's please seen the sidebar at the end of the section.

✦ **.WAV (Windows Wave):** Until the recent support for MP3, .WAV files reigned for nearly a decade as the standard for digital audio on Windows PCs. Flash can import .WAV files created in sound applications and editors such as Rebirth, SoundForge, and Acid. The imported .WAV files can be either stereo or mono, and can support varying bit and frequency rates. Unassisted, Flash 5 for Macintosh cannot import this file format. But with QuickTime 4 installed, .WAV files can be imported into Flash 5 on a Mac. Flash 5 recognizes, properly opens, and can edit .FLA files created on a Windows PC that contain .WAV sounds — with the limitation that any previously imported .WAV sound cannot be updated or edited.

✦ **.AIFF or .AIF (Audio Interchange File format):** Much like .WAV on the PC, prior to the success of the MP3 format, the .AIFF format was the most commonly used digital audio format for the Mac. Flash can import .AIFF sounds created in sound applications and editors such as PEAK, DECK II or Rebirth. Like .WAV, .AIFF supports stereo and mono, variable bit, and frequency rates. Unassisted, Flash 5 for PC cannot import this file format. But with QuickTime 4 installed, .AIFF files can be imported into Flash 5 on the PC. Flash 5 recognizes, properly opens, and can edit .FLA files created on the Mac that contain .AIFF sounds — with the limitation that any previously imported .AIFF sound cannot be updated or edited.

✦ **QuickTime:** Unfortunately QuickTime Audio files (.QTA or .MOV files) cannot be imported directly into Flash. However, QuickTime audio files can be prepared for import into Flash by saving them as either .WAV or .AIFF files. This requires that you have QuickTime Pro 4.0 (or greater) installed. QuickTime Pro is available from Apple at `www.apple.com`.

Note If you're working in a cross-platform environment, unless you're importing MP3 sounds exclusively, it may be important to take a few precautions to ensure that the sound aspect of your .FLA's will be editable on both platforms. Don't rely upon the imported sound that's embedded in the .FLA as your master sound file. Do make sure that the master sound is retained as both a .WAV and as an .AIFF, and that both sound sources are distributed with the .FLA. Of course, this becomes a moot point in environments where QuickTime 4 is installed and maintained on all machines.

MP3s Demystified

MP3 is a noteworthy technology as well as a file format. It excels at the compression of a sound sequence — MP3-compressed files can be reduced to nearly a twelfth of their original size, without destroying sound quality. MP3 was developed under the sponsorship of the Motion Picture Experts Group (MPEG) using the following logic: CD-quality sound is typically sampled at a bit depth of 16 (16-bit) at sample rate 44.1 kHz, which generates approximately 1.4 million bits of data for each second of sound — but that second of sound includes a lot of data for sounds that most humans cannot hear! By devising a compression algorithm that reduces the data linked to imperceptible sounds, the developers of MP3 made it possible to deliver high-quality audio over the Internet without excessive latency (the delay between playing a sound and hearing it back). Another way of describing this is to say that MP3 uses perceptual encoding techniques that reduce the amount of overlapping and redundant information that describe sound. As implemented by Flash 5, MP3 has the added advantage that it streams longer sounds, which means that the sound begins to play before the sound file has been received in its entirety. Shockwave Audio, the default audio compression scheme for Director-based Shockwave movies, is actually MP3 in disguise.

Sound Export Formats Used by Flash

Although the default in Flash 5 is to export all audio as MP3, sound can also be exported in the ADPCM format. You can also decide what export format to use for audio when exporting .FLA project files to .SWF movies (see Chapter 39, "Working with Authoring Applications"). The benefits and drawbacks of each format are noted in the list that follows.

Regardless of the format that you choose for exporting your sounds, you can individually specify a compression scheme for each sound by using the Flash Library. Furthermore, each format has specific options and settings. For more information on the export settings for sound, see Chapter 16, "Optimizing Flash Sound for Export."

✦ **ADPCM (Adaptive Differential Pulse-Code Modulation):** ADPCM is an audio compression scheme that converts sound into binary information. It is primarily used for voice technologies, such as fiber-optic telephone lines, because the audio signal is compressed, enabling it to carry textual information as well. ADPCM works well, because it records only the difference between samples, and adjusts the encoding accordingly, keeping file size low.

Note ADPCM was the default setting for older versions of Flash, such as Flash 2 and 3. It isn't as efficient as MP3 encoding, but is the best choice for situations in which compatibility is required with *all* older Flash Players.

✦ **MP3 (MPEG-1 Audio Layer 3):** Over the last 18 months, MP3 has become the standard for digital audio distributed on the Internet. Although MP3 compression delivers excellent audio quality with small files, it's much more processor-intensive than other compressors. This means that slower computers may gasp when they encounter a high-bit-rate MP3 audio while simultaneously processing complex animations. As always, it's wise to know your audience, and, when in doubt, to test your Flash movie with MP3 audio on slower computers. As a final note, the Flash Player only supports MP3 at versions 4 and above.

✦ **RAW (Raw PCM):** Flash can export sound to .SWF files in a RAW format. If you use this setting Flash won't recompress any audio. However, uncompressed sound makes very large files that would be useless for Internet-based distribution. Even for those people who develop Flash content for QuickTime, it's more effective to use either Premiere or Final Cut to add uncompressed sound to a Flash animation. The only advantage of exporting RAW sounds might be backward compatibility with earliest versions of Flash.

Table 14-3 shows the compatibility of Flash's audio import formats with various platforms.

Table 14-3
Audio Import Formats in Flash 5

Import Formats	Mac Compatibility	PC Compatibility	Flash 4 Compatibility	Comments
.MP3	Yes	Yes	No	Cross-platform, wealth of available sources
.AIF	Yes	No	Yes	Default sound format for Macintosh
.WAV	No	Yes	Yes	Default sound format for PC

Table 14-4 shows the compatibility of Flash's audio export formats with various platforms.

Table 14-4
Audio Export Formats in Flash 5

Export Format	Mac Compatibility	PC Compatibility	Flash 4 Compatibility	Comments
ADPCM	Yes	Yes	Yes	Good encoding scheme; Flash Player 3 and earlier compatibility
MP3	Yes	Yes	Yes	Best encoding scheme; not compatible with versions 1, 2, and 3 of Flash Player
RAW	Yes	Yes	Yes	No compression; lossless; large file sizes

Summary

✦ The sample rate (or sampling rate) of a sound file describes the number of times the source sound is "analyzed" per second. The higher the sample rate, the better the sound quality.

✦ The bit resolution, or bit depth, of a sound file describes the breadth of information recorded at each sample. The higher the bit depth, the better the sound quality.

✦ Because the unaided human ear can perceive frequencies between 20 and 20,000 Hz, the best sampling rate for sound reproduction is 44.1 kHz. This is the sampling rate that's used for high-fidelity audio, such as CDs.

✦ Sound files with high sampling rates and bit depths result in ideal sound quality, but they also have large file sizes. In order to transmit audio over the Internet effectively, without losing your audience, most sounds need to be down sampled or encoded with processor-intensive audio compression schemes. For this, the MP3 format is ideal.

✦ Flash 5 can now import MP3, the most popular audio format.

✦ Flash can import .WAV files in the Windows version of Flash, and .AIFF files in the Macintosh version. However, after the audio files have been imported, the Flash movie (.FLA files) can be exchanged between platforms with the sounds intact in the Flash Library. In such cases, everything is editable except the previously imported, foreign-platform sounds.

✦ Flash .SWF movies have three types of audio compression: ADPCM, MP3, and RAW. Although ADPCM is compatible with earlier versions of the Flash Player, MP3, which is compatible with versions 4 and 5 of the Flash Player, delivers the best sound quality with the least addition to file size.

✦   ✦   ✦

Importing and Editing Sounds in Flash

Sound can be used in Flash to enhance interactive design with multisensory elements such as buttons, to layer the visitor's experience with a background soundtrack, to add narrative, or for more experimental uses. This chapter focuses on the fundamentals of importing and integrating sound files into your Flash project.

Importing Sounds into Flash

In Chapter 14, we explained the basic principles relevant to the use of digital sound within Flash. We also discussed the various sound formats that Flash can import and export. We championed the inclusion of .MP3 among the sound formats that Flash 5 can import. In addition to our discussion of the merits of .MP3 sound, we also explained the uses of platform specific .AIFF (Mac) and .WAV (PC) audio files. But we didn't delve into the process of importing sound into Flash. So, let's get started.

> **Note**
>
> When working with sound, you may encounter some interchangeable terminology. Generally, these terms — sound file, sound clip, or audio file — all refer to the same thing, a single digital file in one of several formats, which contains a digitally encoded sound.

Unlike other imported assets, such as bitmaps or vector art, Flash doesn't automatically insert an imported sound file into the frames of the active layer on the timeline. In fact, you don't have to select a specific layer or frame before you import a sound file. That's because all sounds are sent directly to the Library immediately upon import. At this point, the sound becomes part of the .FLA editor file, which may make the file size balloon significantly if the sound file is large. However, the sound does not become part of the .SWF, nor will it add to the size of the .SWF file unless it is assigned to a keyframe, as an instance. Although this may seem peculiar, it does serve a useful purpose: It helps to ensure that instances of the sound will be employed within your project, rather than duplicates of the same large sound file, which keeps the .SWF file size down. So, to use an imported sound within Flash you must first import the sound, and then assign an instance of that sound to a specific layer and keyframe.

Refer to Chapter 9, "Checking Out the Library: Symbols and Instances," to learn more about how to organize and access sound assets in the Library, as well as how to work with instances.

To import a sound file into the Flash authoring environment:

1. Choose File ➪ Import.

2. From the Files of Type drop-down, choose All Sound Formats.

3. Select the .MP3, .AIFF, or .WAV file that you want to import.

4. Click Open.

   The selected sound file is imported into your Flash editor document (.FLA) and arrives in the Flash Library with its filename intact. If the Library is closed, you can open it by choosing Window ➪ Library, or by using the keyboard shortcut (Ctrl/Command+L). With the Library open, locate the sound, and click it to highlight the name of the sound file where it appears in the Library Sort Window. The waveform appears in the Library Preview Window, as shown in Figure 15-1. Click the Play button above the waveform to audition the sound.

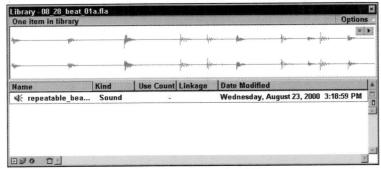

Figure 15-1: This is a stereo sound in the Flash Library.

Refer to Chapter 16, "Optimizing Flash Sound for Export," for an explanation of how unique compression settings can be specified for each sound in the Flash Library.

Sounds may also be loaded from a shared library. Refer to Chapter 9, "Checking Out the Library: Symbols and Instances," to learn how to assign an identifier string to an asset, such as a sound file, in the Flash Library. Refer to Chapter 20, "Sharing and Loading Assets," to learn how to load an asset, such as a sound, from a shared Library.

Assigning a Sound to a Button

The experience of interactivity is enhanced by the addition of subtle effects. The addition of sounds to correspond with the various states of a button is perhaps the most obvious example. Although this effect can be abused, it's hard to overuse an effect that delivers such meaningful user feedback. Here, we show how different sounds can be added to both the Over (mouseover) and the Down (click) states of a button. For more general information about creating the buttons themselves, see Chapter 9, "Checking Out the Library: Symbols and Instances," and Chapter 13, "Designing Interfaces and Interface Elements." Because buttons are stored in the Library, and because only instances of a button are deployed within the Flash movie, sounds that are assigned to a button work for all instances of that button. However, if different sounds are required for different buttons, then a new button symbol must be created. You can create a new button symbol from the same graphic symbols as the previous button (provided it was built out of symbols) or duplicate it in the Library using the Duplicate command on the Library's Option menu.

To add a sound to the Down state of a Flash button:

1. From the Common Library, choose a button to which you want to add sound effects. Open it for editing by either double-clicking it, or by choosing Edit from the Library Options menu. Both methods invoke the Symbol Editing mode.

2. Add a new layer to the button's timeline, label the new layer Sound, and then add keyframes to this layer in the Over and Down columns. Your timeline should look similar to Figure 15-2.

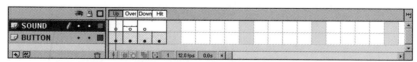

Figure 15-2: The timeline for your button should resemble this timeline.

3. Next, select the frame of the button state where you want to add a sound for interactive feedback (such as a clicking sound for the down state), and then access the Sound Panel by doing one of the following: (a) right-click/Ctrl+click the selected frame, choose Panels from the ensuing contextual pop-up, and then choose Sound; or (b) proceed from the menu with Window ➪ Panels ➪ Sound. An alternative method (with the frame selected) is to simply drag the sound from the Library and onto the stage.

You should now have the new Flash 5 Sound Panel open, as shown in Figure 15-3. For more information about the Flash 5 Panels, refer to Chapter 7, "Working with Text."

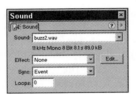

Figure 15-3: The new Flash 5 Sound Panel.

4. Choose the sound clip that you want to use from the Sound drop-down menu. This menu lists all of the sounds that have been imported and that are available in the Library of the current movie.

5. The next step is to use the Sync drop-down menu to choose *how* you want the sound to play. For this lesson, simply use the default, which is the Event option. We defer our exploration of the other options in the Sync pop-up for a later section.

You have now added a sound to your button state. Remember, you're still in Symbol Editing mode, so to test the button, return to the movie editor either by clicking the scene tab at the upper-left of the timeline or by pressing Ctrl+E (Command+E). From the movie editor, choose Control ➪ Enable Simple Buttons, or Control ➪ Test Scene.

To add a sound to the Over state of a Flash button, simply retrace the previous steps, referencing the Over state of the button wherever appropriate. Remember that different sounds can be assigned to the Over, Down, and Hit states of a button.

On the CD-ROM

For a completed example of this button, refer to the Flash movie push_bar_button_ 01.fla located in the ch15 folder of the *Flash 5 Bible* CD-ROM. This movie has a button with sounds attached and was made with the same technique described in this section.

Adding Sound to the Timeline

In addition to the use of sounds to enhance the interactivity of buttons, another popular use of sound in Flash is to provide a background "score." The simplest way to achieve this is to place the sound within its own layer in the timeline, at the precise frame in which you want the sound to begin. To do this, you must first import the sound (as described earlier in this chapter) and also create a new layer for it.

On the CD-ROM If you don't have access to sounds, you can use the sample sound *counting 123*, or *repeatable beat* to practice. These sounds are in the ch15 folder of the *Flash 5 Bible* CD-ROM. They are available in both .WAV and .AIF formats. There's also a silly example, titled jwl_silly_soundtest, that may help you get started in your work with sounds.

Adding sound files to the timeline is similar to assigning sound to a button. To add sounds to a movie's timeline, follow these steps:

1. Add a new layer to the timeline and label the layer with the name of the sound.

2. Create a keyframe on the sound layer at the frame where you want the sound to begin.

3. With that keyframe selected, either (a) right-click/Ctrl+click the selected frame, choose Panels from the ensuing contextual pop-up, and then choose Sound; or (b) proceed from the menu with Window ➪ Panels ➪ Sound.

   You should now have the new Flash 5 Sound Panel open. (See how similar this is to the methodology for adding sound to a button?)

4. If you remembered to import the sound that you want to use, you can now choose that sound clip from the Sound drop-down menu. If you find yourself stuck at this point, review the preceding steps and/or retrace your steps through the methodology for adding sound to a button.

5. From the Event pop-up, choose how the sound should be handled by Flash. The Event pop-up offers several preset effects, plus custom, which invokes the Edit Envelope. For no special effect, choose None. For more about the Event presets and the Edit Envelope, refer to the subsequent section, "Applying Effects from the Effect Pop-up of the Sound Panel."

6. From the Sync pop-up, choose one of four options — Event, Start, Stop, or Stream — to control how you want to the sound to be synchronized. (See the next section for a detailed explanation of Sync options.)

7. Specify how many times you want the sound to loop. To loop indefinitely, enter a high number, such as 999. (For specific information about looping stream sounds, refer to the next section.)

8. Perform any last minute editing or finessing of the sound file (see "Editing Audio in Flash," later in this chapter). Then return to the Main Timeline and save your work.

Your sound is now part of the timeline. Its waveform is visible on the layer to which it was added. Test your sound by pressing Enter on your keyboard, which plays the timeline. Or, for sound with a Sync setting of Stream, manually "scrub" the sound by dragging the Playhead across the timeline. To perform the most accurate test of the sound, use either Control ⇨ Test Scene or Control ⇨ Test Movie to see and hear it as a .SWF file.

Tip

If you sync a sound to the timeline using the Stream feature, you should test your .SWF movie on various platforms and machines with different processor speeds. What looks and sounds good on the latest Power Mac G4 Cube might be less impressive on an underpowered legacy machine.

Organizing sounds on the timeline

There is no technical limit to the number of sound layers; each layer functions like a separate sound channel, and Flash mixes them on playback. (This capability of Flash might be considered an onboard, economy sound mixer.) There is, however, a practical limit, because each sound layer increases the movie's file size, while the mix of multiple sounds may burden the computer it's being run on.

Tip

If you can't recall the *name* of a particular sound in the timeline, remember that with Tooltips enabled from the Preferences dialog (Edit ⇨ Preferences), the file-name of the sound will pop-up whenever the cursor is allowed to settle over the waveform.

Enhanced viewing of sound layers

Because sound is different from other types of Flash content, some users find that increasing the layer height of the sound layers eases working with multiple sounds in the timeline. That's because a taller layer height provides a better visual cue due to the unique waveforms of each sound. To increase the layer height for individual layers:

1. Right-click/Ctrl+click the layer bar, and then choose Properties from the contextual pop-up.

2. At the bottom of the ensuing Layer Properties dialog, change the layer height from the default 100 percent to either 200 or 300 percent.

3. Note that these percentages are relative to the settings chosen in the Frame View Options pop-up. For more information on the intricacies of the timeline, see Chapter 8, "Exploring the Timeline." For an actual example of this, open the file titled, jwl_silly_soundtest.fla, located in the ch15 folder on the CD-ROM in the counting 123 folder.

Tip   Your movie's frame rate, as specified in the Movie Properties dialog, affects the expanse (or number) of frames that a sound occupies on the timeline. For example, at Flash's default setting of 12 frames per seconds (fps), a 30-second sound clip extends across 360 frames of the timeline. At 18 fps, the same 30-second clip expands to 540 frames—but in either case, the time length of the sound is unchanged.

Organizing sound layers with a mask

A helpful trick for organizing sounds is to use a Mask layer. Because Flash doesn't have a utility to group, nest, or collapse multiple sound track layers (or other content, for that matter), a Mask layer (or a Guide layer) can be used to achieve a similar result. Here's how:

1. Create a new empty layer above the sound track layers.

2. From the layer bar, right-click/Ctrl+click to open the Layer Properties dialog. Give it a meaningful name, such as Sound Gang, and change the layer type to Mask. (Leave this Mask layer empty.) Click OK.

3. Drag each of the sound track layers up to the Sound Gang layer. They'll indent beneath the Sound Gang layer, neatly organizing sound content within the timeline.

Cross-Reference   For more information about working with the timeline and Mask layers, refer to Chapter 8, "Exploring the Timeline."

Synchronizing Audio to Animations

In film editor's lingo, to *synchronize*, or *sync*, means to precisely match picture to sound. It's a conjunction of the Greek words *syn*, meaning *with*, and *chronos*, meaning *time*. In Flash, sound is synchronized to the visual content of the timeline. Flash sync affords several options for the manner in which the audio component is related to animation on the timeline. Each of these sync options is appropriate for particular uses, which are discussed in the following section.

Types of sound synchronization in Flash

The Sync options on the Sound Panel control the behavior of sound in Flash, relative to the timeline in which the sound is placed. The Sync option you choose will depend on whether your sound is intended to add dimension to a complex multimedia presentation or to add interactivity in the form of button-triggered sound, or whether it is intended to be the closely timed sound track of an animated cartoon.

✦ **Event:** Event is the default Sync option for all sounds in Flash, so unless you change this default to one of the other options, the sound will automatically behave as an Event sound. Event sounds begin contemporaneously with the keyframe in which they occur, and then play independently of the timeline. If an event sound is longer than the timeline movie, it will continue to play even though the movie has stopped. If an Event sound requires considerable time to load, the movie will pause at that keyframe until the sound has loaded completely. Event sounds are the easiest to implement, and are useful for background soundtracks and other sounds that don't need to be synced. Event is the default Sync setting in Sound Panel.

Note   Event sound can degrade into a disturbing inharmonious round of out-of-tune sound loops. If the movie loops before a sound has completed, the sound may begin again — over the top of the initial sound that has not finished playing. After several loops, this can become intolerable — although in some circles, among the unsound, it may be an esteemed feature. To avoid this effect, use the Start Sync option.

✦ **Start:** The Start Sync option is similar to an Event sound, but with one crucial difference: If it's already playing, a sound that is assigned the Start option will stop and begin over again. A good example of the utility of this option is buttons. Suppose you have three identical buttons that play the same two-second sound on the mouseover. In practice, the sound will begin when any button is moused over. When a second or third button is moused over, the sound will play again with each mouseover.

✦ **Stop:** The Stop Sync option is similar to the Start Sync option, except that the selected sound stops playing when the Sync event occurs. The Stop Sync option can also be used to stop a specific sound.

✦ **Stream:** Stream sounds are similar to a traditional track in a video-editing application. A Stream sound locks to the timeline, and is given priority over visual content. When Stream sound is chosen, the Flash player attempts to pace the animation in sync with the sound. However, when animations either get too complex or are run on slower machines, Flash will skip — or drop — the frames as needed to stay in sync with the Stream sound. A Stream sound will stop once the animation ends (at the end of the timeline) or, more specifically, when the playback head reaches the last frame that includes the waveform of the streamed sound. A Stream sound can be *scrubbed*; by dragging the Playhead along the timeline, the Stream sound will play in direct relationship to the content as it appears, frame by frame. This is especially useful for lip-synch and coordinating the perfect timing of sound effects with visual events. See Chapter 37, "Creating Cartoon Animation with Flash," for more information on lip-synch.

To use sound effectively, it's important to understand how stream sounds work. When the Sync option for a sound is set to Stream, on export or publish, Flash breaks the sound into chunks that are tied to the timeline. Although this is transparent to you, it is nearly the equivalent of breaking a single sound file into many separate files and adding them to the timeline as individual pieces — but that would be a lot of work. Luckily, Flash does this for you.

Tip   When adding sounds to the timeline, no matter how many times you tell a Stream sound to loop, a Stream sound will stop at the end of its timeline. To extend a Stream sound's looping capacity, add as many frames as necessary to a stream sound's layer.

Stopping Sounds

The default behavior of event sounds is for them to play through to the end, regardless of the length of the timeline. However, there's a trick that can be used to stop any sound, including event sounds. Place another instance of the same sound at the keyframe where the sound should stop and assign this instance as a Stop Sync sound. This Stop setting can be on any layer, it will stop all instances of the sound.

Stopping a single instance of a Stream sound

A single instance of a sound can also be stopped, if it's sync option is set to Stream. To do this, simply place an empty keyframe in the sound layer at the point where the sound should stop.

Stopping all sounds

You can stop all sounds that are playing in any timeline (including Movie Clips) at any point by doing the following:

1. If there isn't already an actions layer on your timeline, add a new layer, label it **Actions** (or **atns**), and then select the frame that occurs at the point where you want all sounds to stop. Make this frame into a keyframe.

2. With the keyframe selected, proceed to the Frame Actions panel by either clicking the Show Actions Icon near the far-right end of the Launcher Bar, or by navigating to Window ➪ Actions.

3. From the Basic Actions group in the left side of the Normal Mode (or in Expert Mode, for the Action group) double-click the Stop All Sounds action. The following ActionScript code,

```
stopAllSounds ();
```

   appears in the right side of the Frame Actions panel, as shown in Figure 15-4.

4. Return to the Movie Editor, save your work, and then test it with Control ➪ Test Movie.

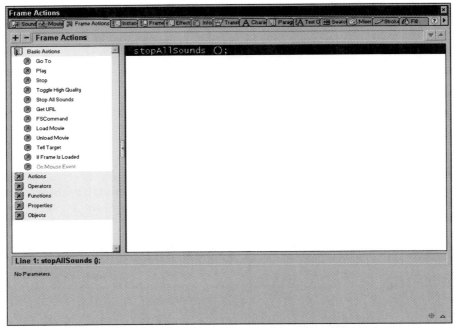

Figure 15-4: Any sound that's currently playing stops when the movie reaches a keyframe with a Stop All Sounds action. Note that all of the panels are ganged here into a mega-panel.

Editing Audio in Flash

Although Flash was never intended to perform as a full-featured sound editor, it does a remarkable job with basic sound editing. If you plan to make extensive use of sound in Flash, we recommend that you consider investing in a more robust sound editor. You'll have fewer limitations and greater control over your work. In Chapter 19, "Controlling Movie Clips," we discuss several popular sound editors that are commonly used in concert with Flash.

Sound editing controls in Flash

Flash has basic sound editing controls in the Editing Envelope control, which is accessed by clicking the Edit button of the Sound panel. (As you may recall from previous sections, you must first select the keyframe containing the sound, and then open the Sound Panel by choosing Window ➪ Panels ➪ Sound.) The Time In control and the Time Out control, or Control Bars, in the Editing Envelope enable you to change the In (start) and Out (end) points of a sound, and the Envelope Handles are used to create custom Fade-in and Fade-out effects.

Note Edits applied to a sound file in the Edit Envelope only affect the specific instance that has been assigned to a keyframe. The original file that resides in the Library is neither changed nor exported.

Setting the In and Out points of a sound

A sound's In point is where the sound starts playing, and a sound's Out point is where the sound finishes. The Time In control and the Time Out control are used for setting or changing a sound's In and Out points. Here's how to do this:

1. Start by selecting the keyframe of the sound you want to edit, and then access the Sound Panel, either from the menu by choosing Window ⇨ Panels ⇨ Sound, or from the contextual menu, with a right-click/Ctrl+click on the keyframe.

2. Open the Edit Envelope dialog, shown in Figure 15-5, by clicking the Edit button of the Sound panel.

3. Drag the Time In control and Time Out control (located in the horizontal strip between the two channels) onto the timeline of the sound's waveform in order to define or restrict which section will play.

4. Use the Envelope Handles to edit the sound volume, by adding handles and dragging them up or down to modulate the volume.

5. Click the Play button to hear the sound as edited before returning to the authoring environment. Then, rework the sound if necessary. When you've finessed the points and are satisfied with the sound, click OK to return to the Sound Panel. Then return to the Movie Editor and save your work.

Applying effects from the Effect pop-up of the Sound Panel

You can apply a handful of preset fades and other effects to a sound by selecting the effect from the Effect pop-up of the Sound Panel. (For many uses, the Flash presets will be more than sufficient, but if you find yourself feeling limited, remember that more subtle effects can be created in an external sound editor.) Flash's preset effects are described in detail here:

✦ **None:** No effect is applied to either of the sound channels.

✦ **Left Channel/Right Channel:** Plays only the right or left channel of a stereo sound.

✦ **Fade Left to Right/Fade Right to Left:** This effect lowers the sound level of one channel while raising the level of the other, creating a Panning effect. This effect occurs over the entire length of the sound.

Edit button (invokes Edit Envelope control)

Envelope handles (left channel)

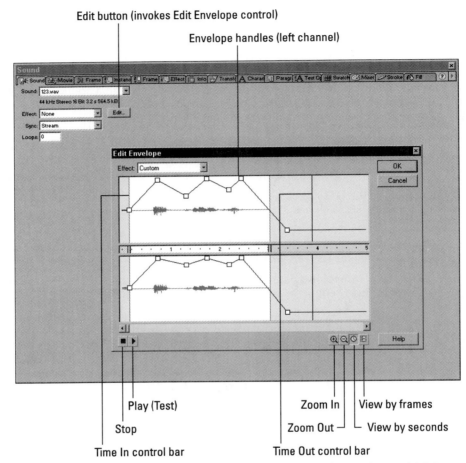

Play (Test)

Stop

Time In control bar

Zoom In

Zoom Out

View by frames

View by seconds

Time Out control bar

Figure 15-5: The sound-editing tools and options of the Edit Envelope, which is accessed from the new Sound panel.

✦ **Fade In/Fade Out:** Fade In gradually raises the level of the beginning of a sound clip. Fade Out gradually lowers the level at the end of a sound. The default length for either effect is approximately 25 percent of the length of the clip. We've noticed that even if the size of the selection is edited with the control bars, the duration of the Fade In/Fade Out will remain the same. (Thus, a 35-second sound clip with an original default Fade In time of 9 seconds, still has a 9-second Fade In time even when the selection's length is reduced to, say, 12 seconds.) This problem can be resolved by creating a Custom Fade.

✦ **Custom:** Any time you manually alter the levels or audio handles on this screen, Flash automatically resets the Effect menu to Custom.

Creating a custom Fade In or Fade Out

For maximum sound-editing control within Flash, use the envelope handles to create a custom fade or to lower the audio levels (or amplitude) of a sound. In addition to creating custom fades, the levels can be lowered creatively to create subtle, low-volume background sounds. Here's how:

1. Select the keyframe of the sound you want to edit.

2. Access the Sound Panel by either (a) right-clicking/Ctrl+clicking the selected frame and choosing Panels ⇨ Sound from the ensuing contextual pop-up, or (b) proceeding from the menu with Window ⇨ Panels ⇨ Sound.

3. Click the Edit button of the Sound Panel to open the Edit Envelope control. Click the envelope lines at any point to create new envelope handles.

4. After handles have been created, you can drag them around to create your desired volume and fading effects. The lines indicate the relative volume level of the sound. When you drag an envelope handle down, the line slopes down, indicating a decrease in the volume level, while dragging an envelope handle up has the opposite effect. The Edit Envelope control is limited to eight envelope handles per channel (eight for left and eight for right).

 Tip

Envelope handles may be removed by dragging them outside the Edit Envelope.

Other controls in the Edit Envelope control

Other useful tools in the Sound tab warrant mention. See Figure 15-5 for their locations.

✦ **Zoom In/Zoom Out:** These tools either enlarge or shrink the view of the waveform, and are particularly helpful when altering the In or Out points or envelope handles.

✦ **Seconds/Frames:** The default for viewing sound files is to represent time in seconds. But viewing time in frames is advantageous for syncing sound with the Stream option. Toggle between viewing modes by clicking either the Seconds or Frames button at the lower right of the Edit Envelope control.

The Loop control

This control appears on the Sound panel, yet a measure of its functionality occurs in conjunction with the Edit Envelope control. The Loop numeric entry field is used to set the number of times that a sound file will loop (or repeat). A small looping selection, such as a break beat or jazz riff can be used for a background soundtrack. A short ambient noise can also be looped for an interesting effect. To test the quality of a looping selection, click the Edit button, which will take you to the Edit Envelope control where you can click the Play button for a preview of your loop. If the loop isn't perfect, or has hiccups, use the Control Bars and envelope handles to trim or taper off a blank or adversely repeating section. In Chapter 32, "Working with Audio Applications," we show you how to create precise loops with Sonic Foundry's Acid Pro and other sound editors and mixers.

Tip   Flash links looped sounds and handles them as one long sound file (although it's really one little sound file played repeatedly). Because this linkage is maintained within the editing environment, the entire expanse of a looped sound can be given a custom effect in the Edit Envelope. For example, a simple repeating 2-measure loop can be diminished over 30 loops. This is a subtle effect that performs well, yet is economical as regards file size.

Summary

✦ When sound is imported to a Flash movie, it's added to the Library. You assign sounds from the Library to a keyframe on a timeline.

✦ Different sounds can be assigned to the Over, Down, and Hit states of a Flash button.

✦ The Sync settings control how a sound will play with relation to the rest of the Flash timeline. Event sounds play in their entirety, regardless of the timeline's playback. Stream sounds are frame-exact, meaning that they are locked to the timeline's playback. Start sync initiates a new instance of a sound, and can be useful when the same sound is used on multiple buttons. Stop sync stops an instance of a sound, if it is playing.

✦ Because sounds are measured and played in seconds (not frames), the frame rate of a Flash movie affects a stream sound's apparent duration in the timeline.

✦ Use the Loop setting in the Sound Panel to repeat a soundtrack in the timeline. Because there's no infinite loop setting, use high numbers for extended playback.

✦ Stream sounds force the Flash Player to keep the timeline in pace with the sound. If the Player can't play every frame (especially with faster frame rates), some frames may be dropped from playback to insure that the sound stays in sync.

✦ Use a Stop All Sounds action to stop all sounds that are currently playing in any current timeline. This is useful during transitions between scenes. For more information about using actions to control sounds, refer to Part V, specifically Chapter 19, "Controlling Movie Clips."

✦ The Effect menu of the Sound panel contains useful presets for sound channel playback. Click the Edit button of the Sound Panel to access the Edit Envelope and create a custom effect.

✦ Basic sound editing can be easily done within the Edit Envelope. Sounds can be trimmed with the Time In and Out Control Bars, or faded in or out with the envelope handles.

✦   ✦   ✦

Optimizing Flash Sound for Export

After you have added sound to buttons and timelines in a Flash movie, you need to know how to modify the audio's export settings for optimal sound quality and file size. In this chapter, we discuss the intricacies of controlling audio output, with particular attention to MP3 bit rates. We also discuss how to use the Publish Settings dialog and compare that with the enhanced control that is available for customizing compression from within the Sound Properties dialog of the Flash Library. Finally, we discuss sound export and the methods available for converting Flash sounds into QuickTime sound tracks.

Sound Optimization Overview

There are several considerations to be cognizant of when preparing Flash sound for export. For Web-based delivery, the primary concern is to find an acceptable middle ground between file size and audio quality. But the concept of acceptability is not absolute; it is always relative to the application. Consider, for example, a Flash Web site for a record company. In this example, sound quality is likely to be more important than file size because the audience for a record company will expect quality sound. In any case, consideration of both your audience and your method of delivery will help you to determine the export settings you choose. Luckily, Flash 5 has new capabilities that can enhance the user's experience both by optimizing sounds more efficiently and by providing improved programming features to make download delays less problematic.

There are two ways of optimizing your sound for export. sThe quickest, simplest way is to use the Publish Settings and apply a one-setting-optimizes-all approach. This works well only if all of your sound files are from the same source. It also will not deliver the highest possible level of optimization.

If you demand that your Flash movie has the smallest possible file size, or if your Flash project includes audio from disparate sources, or uses a combination of audio types — such as button sounds, background music, speech — it's better to fine-tune the audio settings for each sound in the Library. This method gives you much better control over output.

Cross-Reference This chapter discusses the Publish feature of Flash 5, which is explained in greater detail in Chapter 39, "Working with Authoring Applications."

Publish Settings for Audio

Choose File ➪ Publish Settings to access the Publish Settings and to take a global approach to the control of audio output quality. Then choose the Flash tab of the Publish Settings dialog, shown in Figure 16-1. This dialog has three areas where the audio quality of an entire Flash movie can be controlled *globally*.

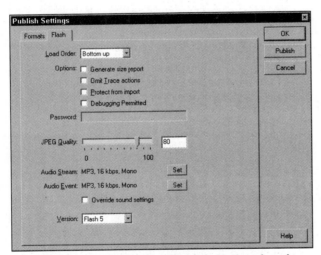

Figure 16-1: The Flash tab of Publish Settings has three options to control audio quality.

The Flash tab of the Publish Settings dialog has three options for controlling audio quality:

✦ **Audio Stream:** Controls the export quality of Stream sounds (see Chapter 15, "Importing and Editing Sounds in Flash," for more information on Stream sounds in Flash.) To customize, click Set. This gives you a number of options, which are described in the section that follows. Flash 5 supports .MP3, which is the optimal streaming format.

✦ **Audio Event:** Controls the export quality of Event sounds. (See Chapter 15, "Importing and Editing Sounds in Flash," for more information on Event sounds in Flash.) To customize, click Set. This gives you a number of options, which are described in the section that follows.

✦ **Override Sound Settings:** If this box is checked, Flash uses the Publish Settings, rather than the individual audio settings that are fine-tuned in the Library. For more information, see the section "Fine Tuning Sound Settings in the Library," later in this chapter.

The Set options

Audio Stream and Audio Event have individual compression settings, which can be specified by their respective Set button options. If you click ether Set button on the Flash Tab, the same Sound Settings dialog appears — it is identical for both Audio Stream and Audio Event, which means that the same options are offered for both types of sound. The Sound Settings dialog, shown in various permutations in Figure 16-2, displays numerous settings related to the control of audio quality and audio file size. The type of compression chosen governs the specific group of settings that appear.

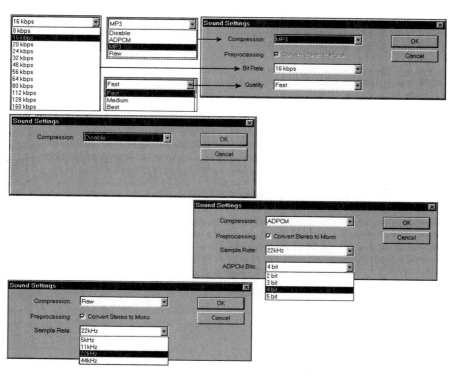

Figure 16-2: The Sound Settings dialogs

Note The impact of individual sound settings may be overridden by another setting. For example, a Bit Rate setting of 160 Kbps will not result in good sound if the Quality is set to Fast. Optimal results require attention to *all* of the settings. This is like a set of interlinked teeter-tooters: A little experimentation will reveal the cumulative or acquired impact of each setting on the others. However, the need to experiment here is hobbled by the lack of a preview mechanism. By contrast, tuning a sound in the Library is much more serviceable, because there's a sound preview button adjacent to the settings controls. For more about this workflow, refer to the following section of this chapter, "Fine-tuning Sound Settings in the Library."

The specific options that are available in the Sound Settings dialogs are always related to the compression, or audio-encoding scheme, selected in the Compression drop-down menu. That's because different compression technologies support different functionalities:

✦ **Disable:** This option turns off all sounds that have been assigned — in the Sound panel — to Sync as either Audio Stream or Audio Event. If this option is selected, no sound of that Sync type will be exported when the .SWF movie is published. There are no further options for this setting.

✦ **ADPCM:** With ADPCM selected in the Compression menu, the following options are available:

- **Convert Stereo to Mono:** Mixes the right and left channel of audio into one (mono) channel. In sound engineer parlance, this is known as "bouncing down."

- **Sample Rate:** Choose from sampling rates of 5, 11, 22, or 44 kHz. (Increasing the sample rate of an audio file to something higher than the native sample rate of the imported file simply increases file size, not quality. For example, if you import 22 kHz sounds into the Flash movie, selecting 44 kHz will not improve the sound quality. For more information on sample rates, see Chapter 14, "Understanding Sound for Flash.")

- **ADPCM Bits:** Set the number of bits that ADPCM uses for encoding. You can choose a rate between 2 and 5. The higher the ADPCM bits, the better the audio quality. Flash's default setting is 4 bits.

✦ **MP3:** If you select MP3 in the Compression menu, you can set the following options:

- **Convert Stereo to Mono:** Mixes the right and left channel of audio into one (mono) channel. This is disabled at rates below 20 Kbps, because the lower bit rates don't support stereo.

- **Bit Rate:** MP3 measures compression in kilobits per second (Kbps). The higher the bit rate, the better the audio quality. Because the MP3 audio compression scheme is very efficient, a high bit rate still results in a relatively small file size. Refer to Table 16-1 for a breakdown of specific bit rates and the resulting sound quality.

- **Quality:** Choose Fast, Medium, or Best quality. Fast optimizes the audio file for faster delivery on the Internet, although there's usually a significant loss in quality. The truth about the Fast setting is this: Unless you're only using the sound as a rudimentary button click, or (in conjunction with the 8 Kbps bit rate) as the voice track for a simulated moonwalk, this setting is useless. Medium is a usable setting that delivers acceptable quality but sacrifices some speed in favor of quality. Best is the highest quality setting, chiefly intended for files distributed through broadband connections, intranets, or on CD-ROMs.

✦ **Raw:** When Raw (a.k.a. Raw PCM audio) is selected in the Compression menu, there are two options:

- **Convert Stereo to Mono:** Mixes the right and left channel of audio into one (mono) channel.

- **Sample Rate:** This option specifies the sampling rate for the Audio Stream or Audio Events sounds. For more information on sample rate, please refer to Chapter 14, "Understanding Sound for Flash."

	Table 16-1 MP3 Bit Rate Quality		
Bit Rate	**Sound Quality**	**Good For**
8 Kbps	Very bad	Best for simulated moonwalk transmissions. Don't use this unless you want horribly unrecognizable sound.
16 Kbps	Barely acceptable	Extended audio files where quality isn't important, or simple button sounds.
20, 24, 32 Kbps	Acceptable	Speech or voice.
48, 56 Kbps	Acceptable	Large music files; complex button sounds.
64 Kbps	Good	Large music files where good audio quality is required.
112–128 Kbps	Excellent	Near-CD quality.
160 Kbps	Best	Near-CD quality.

As a general rule, if you use the Publish Settings to control audio export globally, we recommend choosing MP3 at 64 Kbps. This will result in moderate to good sound quality (suitable for most Flash projects), and the ratio of file size-to-quality will give reasonable performance.

Supporting the MP3 Player

Although this is becoming less of an issue with the release of Flash 5, it may still be important to consider that MP3 is not supported by Flash 3 (or earlier) players. There may be a number of users in your audience that haven't upgraded their Flash Player plug-in to version 4, much less to version 5. Although, as Flash developers, it would be nice to assume that your audience will eventually upgrade, it's more realistic, and therefore advisable, to consider implementing a transitional solution. For example, you could provide both a Flash 3 movie with ADPCM-encoded audio and a Flash 5 movie with MP3-encoded audio. Include information on the splash page about the benefits of the Flash 5 player: reduced download time and increased audio quality. This is an incentive for you users to upgrade. You'll also want to provide a link to Macromedia to download the new plug-in. Another, more "invisible" solution is to add intelligence to your splash page with a "plug-in detection" script that automatically serves users the movie that corresponds to the version of the Flash Player they have installed.

To add plug-in detection to your Flash movies, use one of the HTML templates installed with Flash 5. HTML templates are discussed in the "Using the HTML settings" section of Chapter 40.

Fine-tuning Sound Settings in the Library

The Publish Settings menu is convenient because it permits you to tweak a minimal set of sound adjustments, whereupon Flash exports all of your "noncustomized" Stream sounds or Event sounds at the same rate. However, if you have many sounds and you are seriously concerned about obtaining the ideal balance of both optimal sound quality and minimum file size, you will need to export them at different rates. Consequently, for the fullest level of control over the way in which Flash compresses sound for delivery, we recommend that each sound should be optimized, individually, in the Library. In fact, it would be impossible for us to overemphasize this bit of sound advice: *We recommend that each sound should be optimized, individually, in the Library.*

Settings for audio in the Library

Audio settings in the Library are similar to those discussed previously for the Publish Settings. These settings appear in the Sound Properties dialog, shown in Figure 16-3. To access these settings, either (a) double-click the icon of the sound in the Library, or (b) select the sound as it appears in the Library and (i) click the Properties button, or (ii) choose Properties from the Library Options popup.

There are four groupings of information and controls in the Sound Properties dialog: Status, Export Settings, Estimated Results, and Buttons.

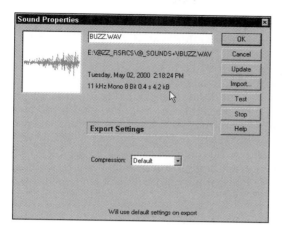

Figure 16-3: The Sound Properties dialog enables you to control the compression settings and to precisely balance all other related settings for each individual sound in the Library.

The top half of the Sound Properties dialog displays status information about the sound file: To the far left is a window with the waveform of the selected audio; to the right of the waveform is an area that displays the name of the file together with its location, date, sample rate, channels, bit depth, duration, and file size.

The lower half of the dialog is titled Export Settings. The first setting is a drop-down menu that is used to select the Compression scheme. The Compression options, and the subsequent compression related options that appear in the other settings, are exactly the same as the sound options of the Publish Settings dialog, discussed earlier in this chapter.

Beneath the Export Settings is where Estimated Results are displayed. Here, the estimated final file size (after compression) of the clip is displayed, together with the compression percentage. This is an extremely important tool that is easily overlooked.

The buttons to the right of the Sound Properties dialog offer the following options:

✦ **Update:** Click this button to have Flash check for an update of the audio file, if the original .MP3, .WAV or .AIFF file has been modified, and update it accordingly. Generally, this only works on the machine the audio file was originally imported to.

✦ **Import:** Enables you to import another audio file into the Flash environment. For more information on importing audio files, see Chapter 15, "Importing and Editing Sounds in Flash."

✦ **Test:** This excellent feature enables you to audition the export quality of the sound based on the options that you've selected from the Compression drop-down list.

✦ **Stop:** Click this button to stop (silence) the sound Test.

✦ **Help:** Launches the Flash Help system within your default Web browser.

There are three benefits to fine-tuning your audio in the Sound Properties dialog of the Library. Foremost of these benefits is the ability to set specific compressions and optimizations for individual each sound. Another benefit is the Test button — this is an excellent way to audition your audio file and to know what it will sound like when it is exported with different compression schemes and bit rates; hearing is believing. Finally, the Estimated Results, which display how each setting will affect the compressed file size, is a powerful tool that helps to obtain the desired balance of quality and file size. In contrast, optimizing sounds with the Publish Settings is more of a blind process — it is not only more global; it's also more of a painful trial-and-error method.

Combining methods for controlling sounds

One of the coolest things about Flash audio is that you can combine the two methods of controlling sounds, using both the Publish Settings and the Library Sound Properties dialog to streamline your work flow while still maintaining a relatively high degree of control over sound quality. (This method works best if you already have some experience with sound behavior in Flash.)

For example, let's assume that you have three different Event sounds in your Flash project. Two of these are simple button sounds. You decide that you won't require optimal sound for buttons, so based on your prior experience of sound behavior in Flash, you go directly to the Publish Settings and set Event sounds to publish as .MP3 at 48 Kbps with Medium Quality. Then, in the Library, by setting the Compression to default, you tell Flash to handle the compression for these sounds with the Publish Settings. But the third sound is a loop of background jazz that you want to be heard at near-CD quality. For this sound, you return to the Sound Properties tab and try a number of combinations — and test each one — until you find a balance between file size and audio quality that pleases your ears. You assign this sound to export as an .MP3, stereo at 112Kbps, with Quality set to Fine.

Expert Tutorial: Sound Clipping on the Flash Player, by William Moschella

William Moschella is a sound engineer with extensive Flash experience. He's provided a number of Expert Tutorials for this edition of the Flash 5 Bible. *Refer to Chapter 32, "Working with Audio Applications," to read his other contributions, as well as to scoop his personal information.*

If you've spent much time with Flash, you've probably noticed an annoying clipping sound that sometimes occurs with event and stream sounds (especially on Windows PCs) in previous versions of Flash. Well, I've volunteered to report that it's still there.

Here's the reason: Flash Player acts as a preamp to its sounds, which means that the sound becomes a few decibels louder *after* the movie is published. It's important to know this, because it means that what you put in isn't what really comes out. This clipping sound is more noticeable with certain types of sounds and instruments than others. Particular offenders include heavy bass, deep vocals, and ultrahigh twangy sounds. This happens because these sound waves tend to peak above and below the threshold of both the Player and sound cards. When overamplified by the Flash Player, this will even happen with sounds that you may have already have optimized. Although the ultimate fix lies with Macromedia, there are a few workarounds. These solutions apply to projectors, CD-ROMs, and Web browsers.

If your clipping is minimal, you may get good results with a custom setting in the Edit Envelope Control to lower volume (stereo channels have two volumes which must be lowered). Move the envelope handles down evenly for both channels; this acts like a volume knob. By testing and making adjustments, you should be able to minimize, if not eliminate the clipping entirely. For more about the Edit Envelope Control, refer to Chapter 15, "Importing and Editing Sounds in Flash."

When the clipping sound is more pronounced, you might need to take additional steps to optimize your sound. Start by using a third-party sound editor, such as Sound Forge, SoundEdit, or Cool Edit to normalize the sound. By removing the high peaks in the sound wave, you help to reduce clipping. For more about using sound applications, refer to Chapter 32, "Working with Audio Applications."

The previous steps usually help, but they aren't the true solution to the problem. Unfortunately, certain sound cards will clip Flash audio at most settings. This is due to a communication issue between the Flash Player and the sound card. So far, there's no way to prevent this before publishing your movie. However, there is a way that this particular clipping can be eliminated after your movie is published. Unfortunately, it means devising a mechanism for moving the user through another step before they finally enter your movie. The answer lies with the mouse. I've determined two actions that clear the communication path between the Flash player to the sound card. Once either of these mouse actions has been performed, the annoying sound clipping will go away.

While an audio track is playing, the viewer must either execute a right mouse-click over the movie, or else act to either minimize or maximize the screen. Although the first of these options is the most user friendly, it will not work if the movie is viewed full-screen. This "fix" will clear up the clipping problem for the current movie as well as for any other movie that is subsequently loaded into the current projector—but it will not work if you open another projector.

The ultimate solution will come from users who choose not to accept this flaw. Send an e-mail to Macromedia at wish-flash@macromedia.com. Perhaps this problem will be resolved in Flash 6.

The Options pop-up menu of the Library has new sound features. When a sound is selected in the Library, the pop-up displays one or two menu items related to editing the selected sound. These menu items will either directly open the sound in a sound-editing application, or lead to the Select External Editor dialog. One such menu item is Edit With; however, the particular menu items that are available will vary depending on both the platform and the software installed on the host computer. For more information on the use of an External Editor with sounds, refer to Chapter 32, "Working with Audio Applications."

Publish Settings for QuickTime Sound

Flash 4 introduced a hot new feature: the capability to export your Flash movies as QuickTime Flash (or Windows AVI) movies. With the release of Flash 5, this is an important and growing area of Flash usage. This section offers brief coverage of the audio options available from within Flash for export to the QuickTime (QT) architecture. Note that these options only pertain to a Flash sound that's converted to a QuickTime sound track. The resulting QuickTime sound track is a new sound track—it is *not* merged with preexisting QT sound tracks. When authoring for export to QuickTime, there is no limit to the number of sounds or sound channels. That's because all sounds are combined into a single sound track upon export to QuickTime (or Windows AVI). When exporting to QuickTime, neither the lack of sounds nor the number of sounds has any effect upon the size of the final file. When exporting a Flash movie (or sound track) to QuickTime, you have two choices:

✦ If you want to export Flash sounds (such as background music) to use compression schemes currently unavailable in Flash 5, then you can opt to convert the Flash sound to a QuickTime-supported audio codec such as QDesign Music.

✦ If you are exporting your Flash movie to QuickTime but want to keep the Flash sound embedded with its original Flash media track, you can disable QuickTime sound compression.

Cross-Reference For more information on QuickTime support in Flash, see Chapter 34, "Working with QuickTime."

To access the QuickTime audio export Settings:

1. Choose File ➪ Publish Settings.

2. In the Formats tab, check the QuickTime option.

3. A QuickTime tab appears. Click the QuickTime tab.

4. Now, at the Streaming Sound setting, check Use QuickTime Compression.

Finally, click the Settings button. The Sound Settings dialog appears, shown in Figure 16-4, with several options to select your audio compression settings. Depending upon the configuration of your machine, different QuickTime audio-encoding options appear. Depending upon the intended use of your QuickTime movie, you may want to choose different options. Table 16-2 explains some of the popular QuickTime encoding methods and their intended uses. Table 16-3 demystifies alternative formats.

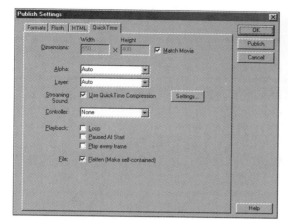 

Figure 16-4: The QuickTime tab of Publish Settings has options to control the conversion of Flash sounds into QuickTime audio tracks with the Streaming Sound setting.

Table 16-2		
QuickTime Sound Compressors		
Popular Codecs	**Best For**	**Description**
Qdesign Music Codec	Internet	Very good compression ratio, great for music. Downloads progressively.
Qdesign version 2	Internet	Excellent compression ratio, great for music, streaming audio.
Qualcomm PureVoice	Internet	Excellent compression ratio. Very good for voice.
IMA	CD-ROM	Good quality, only encodes 16-bit audio. Inadvisable for low frequencies (booming bass) or Web use.

Table 16-3
Alternative Formats

Other Formats	Description
24-bit Integer, 32-bit Integer	Increases bit rate to 24- and 32-bit, respectively.
32-bit Floating Point, 64-bit Floating Point	Increases bit rate to 32-bit and 64-bit, respectively. Note that current computer systems generally are only capable of playing back 16-bit sound.
. ALaw 2:1	European standard compression scheme. Low quality, not recommended.
MACE 3:1, MACE 6:1	Old Macintosh standards. Low quality, high file size. Forget about using these codecs.
uLaw 2:1	Old Internet standard for Japan and North America. Low quality, high file size.

Final Sound Advice and Pointers

Here are a few final notes about sound and some pointers to more complex sound-related topics that are presented later in the book.

VBR (Variable Bit Rate) MP3

Flash 5 has licensed the Fraunhofer MP3 codec, which supports streaming MP3 with a constant bit rate. However, Flash 5 does not support Variable Bit Rate (VBR), or VBR MP3. VBR MP3 is a variant of MP3 that utilizes specialized algorithms to vary the bit rate according to the kind of sound that is being compressed. For example, a soprano solo would be accorded a higher bit rate than a crashing drum sequence, resulting in a superior ratio of quality to file size. There are a number of sound applications, such as the Xing Audio Catalyst 2.1 codec, that export VBR MP3. If you have access to a sound application that exports VBR MP3, you'll be happy to know that you can import your VBR MP3 sound files, which are (theoretically) optimized for file size and quality beyond the compression capabilities of Flash, and that the compression of such files can be maintained by doing the following:

✦ In the Flash tab of the Publish Settings, leave the option to Override Sound Settings unchecked.

✦ In the Sound Properties dialog, which is accessed from the Library, choose Default for the Compression option in Export Settings.

✦ The Sync Option in the Sound Panel may not be set to Stream.

If you choose to use VBR in your Flash projects, please refer to Table 16-4 for a guide to the optimal use of this format.

Table 16-4			
Quick Guide to Common VBR Quality Settings			
VBR	*CBR Bitrate +/– 10%*	*Supported Channels*	*Recommended Use*
Low	96kbits/s	Mono Joint Stereo Stereo	Near-CD quality; good choice for portable MP3 Players (smallest file size). Use when storage space is a consideration; when playback is performed with low-end sound equipment and listening environment, such as portable players or car players.
High Frequency	Not supported at this rate	Not supported at this rate	Not supported at this rate.
Low/Normal	112 Kbits/s	Mono Joint Stereo Stereo	CD-quality; best choice for portable MP3 players where file size is limited.
Normal	128 Kbits/s	Mono Joint Stereo Stereo	CD-quality; best choice for most users. Normal use; similar to encoding moderately difficult to difficult content with a CBR of 128 Kbits/s.
Normal/High	160 Kbits/s	Mono Joint Stereo Stereo	Archival quality; for high-end stereo (larger file size). Compromise between Normal and High settings.
High	192 Kbits/s	Mono Joint Stereo Stereo	Archival quality; for highest-end stereo unlimited file size. Use when storage space is not a consideration; when playback is performed with high-end sound equipment and listening environment; and when heavy equalization adjustments might be used on playback.

Continued

| | Table 16-4 *(continued)* | | |
VBR	CBR Bitrate +/− 10%	Supported Channels	Recommended Use
Very High	224 Kbits/s	Mono Joint Stereo Stereo	Archival quality; for highest-end stereo unlimited file size.
Ultra High	256 Kbits/s	Mono Joint Stereo Stereo	Archival quality; for highest-end stereo unlimited file size.

Extracting a sound from a .FLA editor file

Sometime you may be handed a .FLA file that has sound embedded within it, and told that the original sounds have either been lost or are no longer available. Here's how to extract a sound from such a file:

Note Unfortunately, an equivalent process does not exist for the Macintosh. However, for users with QuickTime Player Pro, a workaround is to export the movie as a QuickTime Video movie and then use QuickTime Player Pro to extract the audio channel.

1. Back up the file. If the original file is named, Mess.fla, then you might resave it as Mess_Sound_Extraction.Fla.

2. Add a new layer in the timeline, at the top of the layer stack. Label this layer **Sound Extraction**. Add nine empty frames to this layer by selecting frame 10 and then using the keyboard shortcut, which is F5. (If it's a long sound, you'll probably want to add more frames.)

3. Delete all other layers.

4. Open the Library and locate the sound that needs to be extracted from the file. In this case, the sound is named Buzz.wav. Note that any other assets within this file are irrelevant to this process. That's because Flash will only utilize Library items that have been actually used within the movie.

5. Double-click Buzz.wav to invoke the Sound Properties dialog. Set the Compression to default, if it's not that way already. This ensures that the Library won't alter the sound upon export. Note the sound specifications just to the right of the waveform display, as you'll be double-checking for these specifications in only a few steps. See Figure 16-5.

6. Click frame 1 of the Sound Extraction layer to select it. This should now be the only keyframe on the only layer in this file.

7. With frame one selected, drag Buzz.wav onto the Stage. Assuming it's a short sound, the waveform will appear in the timeline across the ten frames of the Sound Extraction layer.

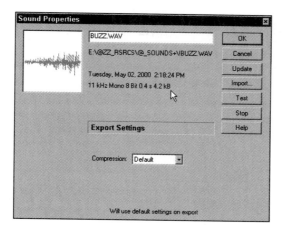

Figure 16-5: The Sound Properties dialog, which is accessed from the Library, includes the original specifications for each sound, located down and to the right of the waveform.

8. Next, on the Flash tab of the Publish Settings dialog, make sure that the Override Sound Settings check box is *not* checked.

9. Now we're ready to extract Buzz.Wav from this .FLA. We've created a .FLA that will ignore all other assets in the Library except this sound, and we've told Flash to honor all of the original specifications of the sound. Choose File ⇨ Export Movie, and specify a file location, name, and file type — in this case, .WAV — and click Save.

10. The Export Windows WAV dialog appears with those sound specifications. If you've done everything correctly, these should match the original specifications that appeared in the Library Sound Properties dialog. If not, go back and recheck your work.

Several sound-related topics must be deferred until after our discussion of Flash 5's enhanced Action Scripting capabilities. Work your way forward to Chapter 19, "Controlling Movie Clips," for a discussion of the following topics:

✦ How to determine whether a sound is currently playing: Despite powerful enhancements to Flash's scripting capabilities, there is no method to determine whether a sound is currently playing. We've found a simple workaround that fits into the Smart Clip, a new Flash 5 feature.

✦ Using the Flash 5 sound control: The Flash 5 Sound Object supports pan and zoom control. Expert tutor Jay Vanian shows how to make sound fade and move from side to side, with incredible realism as a bouncing basketball follows your mouse from side to side and in and out of a virtual basketball court.

✦ Loading sounds from the Library: By using the power of the Flash Library and Movie Clips, sounds can be preloaded from the Library and started and stopped. Robert's soundLib.fla method provides that any asset will be available when it's required to play.

Summary

✦ Audio compression for Flash movies is controlled on the Flash tab of the Publish Settings dialog. The compression settings here are applied to all sounds used in the Flash movie, unless the sound is given custom settings in the Flash Library.

✦ You can use the Override sound settings check box in the Flash tab of the Publish Settings dialog to cancel the custom settings applied to sounds in the Flash Library.

✦ Flash 5 enables you to compress sound files as MP3-encoded audio. MP3 provides near-CD quality at higher bit rates.

✦ Generally, MP3 bit rates below 20 Kbps produce low-quality audio. Use bit rates between 20 and 32 Kbps for acceptable quality audio with the smallest file-size gains.

✦ While MP3 provides the best sound quality with the smallest file sizes, it is not compatible with Flash 3 Players. You may want to create two versions of your Flash movie: one with ADPCM audio encoding, and another with MP3 audio encoding. Both movies could be available to Web visitors to choose from. Alternatively, a JavaScript plug-in detector could automatically deliver the right movie to the visitor's browser.

✦ Use the Flash Library to customize the audio compression schemes of individual sounds.

✦ The Sound Properties dialog enables you to test different compression settings and to hear the results. Useful file size information is also provided in the Export Settings section of this dialog.

✦ Variable Bit Rate (VBR) MP3 sound files can be brought into Flash and exported without degrading the encoding; however, Flash itself cannot encode using VBR.

✦ Orphaned or lost sound files that are embedded within a .FLA file can be extracted without degrading the original sound file.

✦ Flash sounds can be converted to QuickTime sound tracks in QuickTime Flash movies. If you are creating QuickTime Flash movies, then you can access a wide range of Apple and third-party audio compressors.

✦   ✦   ✦

Adding Basic Interactivity to Flash Movies

P A R T

IV

◆ ◆ ◆ ◆

In This Part

Chapter 17
Understanding
Actions and
Event Handlers

Chapter 18
Navigating
Flash Timelines

Chapter 19
Controlling
Movie Clips

Chapter 20
Sharing and
Loading Assets

◆ ◆ ◆ ◆

So far you've been learning how to make *things* — drawing shapes, creating symbols, working with frames, and adding sound. In the next four chapters, you're going to learn how to make things *happen*. If you can't wait to make buttons work, sounds play and stop, Web pages load, or animations really go, you've come to the right place. Start with Chapter 17, which introduces you to the concepts that you should know when adding interactivity to your movies. Chapter 13 also examines the fundamental Flash actions (*Go to*, *Play*, *Stop*, and *Get URL*) and event handlers (button clicks and general mouse/button interaction, keypresses, and keyframes). Once you're ready to get your hands a bit more dirty, move on to Chapter 18, where we see how to target multiple timelines in a Flash movie, using the new Flash 5 Dots notation. As Flash develops a mature programming language and structure, you will need to understand how to work with Objects, on the Stage and in ActionScript. Chapter 19 introduces you to the Movie Clip Object, its properties, and its methods. As you create Flash movies for a Web site, preloading .SWF files will become more of an issue. Chapter 20 provides a breakdown of preloaders (by Flash Player version), and introduces the new Shared Library feature of Flash 5.

Understanding Actions and Event Handlers

Interactivity in a Flash movie can broadly be thought of as the elements that react and respond to a user's activity or input. A user has many ways to give input to a Flash movie, and Flash has even more ways to react. But how does interactivity actually work? It all starts with actions and event handlers.

Actions and Event Handlers

Even the most complex interactivity in Flash is fundamentally composed of two basic parts: (a) the behavior (what happens), and (b) the cause of the behavior (what makes it happen). Here's a simple example: Suppose you have a looping sound-track in a movie and a button that, when clicked, turns the soundtrack off. The *behavior* is the sound turning off, and the *cause* of the behavior is the mouse clicking the button. In Flash, behaviors are referred to as *actions*. The first step in learning how to make interactive movies is becoming familiar with the list of possible actions. However, actions can't act without being told to act *by* something. That something is often the mouse coming in contact with a button, but it can also be a keystroke, or simply a command issued from a keyframe. We refer to any occurrence that can cause an action to happen (such as the button click in the preceding example) as an *event*. The mechanism we use to tell Flash what action to perform when an event occurs is known as an *event handler*.

This cause-and-effect relationship seems obvious, but it is an extremely important concept. For the purposes of creating basic interactivity, the difference between an action and the cause of an action is merely a practical detail. But with

Flash 5's new programmatic actions and the scripting capabilities that they provide, understanding the relationship between actions and the things that cause them can be the key to adding more sophisticated behavior to your movies with traditional programming techniques.

Don't worry, we're taking it one step at a time. First, we set up the new Frame and Object Actions Panel. Then we look at the Basic Actions booklet. Later, we see how to call these actions in various ways with three kinds of event handlers: button manipulation, keyframes, and keystrokes.

What is ActionScript?

Every interactive authoring system uses a language (or code) that enables elements within the system to communicate. Just as there are several languages that people use to speak to one another around the globe, there are hundreds of programming languages in use today. In an effort to make Flash more usable to computer programmers, Flash's scripting language, called ActionScript, has changed much of its formatting to mirror JavaScript, a fundamental component for DHTML and HTML Web pages. Right now, we focus on using the most basic Flash ActionScript.

We look at more advanced ActionScript in Chapters 19 through 26.

Setting up the Actions Panel

Unlike previous versions, Flash 5 has a new way of adding interactive commands to Flash movies — the Actions Panel. Unlike with previous versions of Flash, you do not have to double-click frames and buttons to access actions. Also, you don't have to use menus to select Actions — you can type them by hand in or out of Flash! To open the Actions Panel, go to Windows ➪ Actions (Option+Command+A or Ctrl+Alt+A). If you have a frame selected in the timeline, you will see the Actions Panel with the name Frame Actions (see Figure 17-1). If you have a Button or Movie Clip symbol selected on the stage, you'll see the name Object Actions. Don't be confused — there is only one Actions Panel. Flash simply lets you know the event handler to which you are assigning actions.

Most actions have user-definable parameters that can be set in the gray area below the left and right panes of the Actions Panel. You can show or hide this area by clicking the arrow in the lower-right corner of the panel. You can also hide the left pane of the Actions Panel by clicking the arrow on the divider line between the left and right panes.

In the *Flash 5 Bible*, we do not differentiate between the Frame and Object Actions Panel. We simply use the term *Actions Panel*.

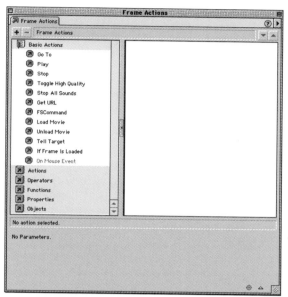

Figure 17-1: The new Actions Panel enables you to instantly add, delete, or change Flash interactive commands.

Normal versus Expert Mode

Flash has two authoring modes for actions: Normal and Expert. By default, Flash uses the Normal Mode (Command+N or Ctrl+N when the Actions Panel is active). In this mode, Flash arranges actions in the left pane into six booklets, each booklet containing sets of ActionScript. You can choose actions from any of the sets by double-clicking a specific action. For this chapter, we work entirely within the first booklet, Basic Actions. In Expert Mode (Command+E or Ctrl+E when the Actions Panel is active), Flash eliminates the Basic Actions booklet (they're all included in the Actions booklet), and enables you to type, copy, cut, and paste code at will into the right pane of the Actions Panel. You can change the mode setting by accessing the Actions Panel options, located at the upper-right corner of the panel (see Figure 17-2).

You can add actions by dragging them from the left pane to the right pane, by selecting them from the plus (+) menu button in the upper-left corner of the Actions Panel, or by double-clicking them from an Action booklet. To delete actions, select the action line(s) in the right pane, and press the Delete key on the keyboard. Or you can select the action line(s) and push the minus (–) button in the upper-left corner.

Shortcut to action menus

Deletes selected actions in right pane

Action window options

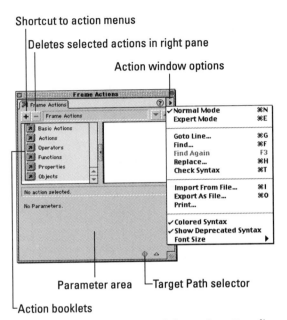

Parameter area — Target Path selector

Action booklets

Figure 17-2: You can control the Actions Panel's look and feel by switching between Normal and Expert Modes.

The Basic Actions are listed as unsorted groups according to the functions they can perform. The first group, comprised of Go To, Play, and Stop, control the playback of the movie. The second group, which includes Toggle High Quality and Stop All Sounds, provides global tools for handling sounds and visual quality. The third group—Get URL, FSCommand, and Load/Unload Movie—let movies load external files and communicate with the browser, a Web server, or the standalone player. The fourth group is effectively made up of Tell Target and If Frame Is Loaded. These two actions afford, respectively, communication between Movie Clips and control over the display of movies as they are downloading.

> **Note**
> We omit On Mouse Event from the Basic Actions list because it's not an Action in and of itself—it's an event handler for buttons.

The remaining Action booklets primarily offer extended ActionScript programming capabilities. We discuss their use in later chapters.

Deprecated and Incompatible Actions: What Are They?

As the ActionScript language of Flash continues to expand and encompass new functionality, older actions will coexist with newer and better actions (or methods, which we discuss later). While the Flash 5 Player will continue to support older Flash 4 and earlier actions, it's better not to use these older actions, which are called deprecated actions. If your Publish Settings for the Flash format are set to Flash 5, certain actions such as `tellTarget` and `ifFrameLoaded` will be highlighted in green (in all but the Basic Actions booklet), as shown in the following figure. Why shouldn't you use these actions? As we see in more advanced scripting, Flash 5 has introduced new ways of targeting Movie Clips and determining if certain frames have loaded.

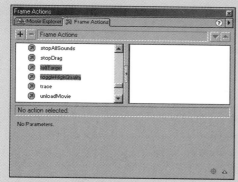

Actions that are highlighted in green should be avoided if possible. However, the Flash 5 Player will support these older actions.

Flash 5 will also let you know if certain actions are not supported with the Player version that is selected in the Flash format's Publish Settings. These actions are highlighted in yellow as shown in the following figure.

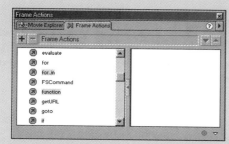

The Flash 4 Player will not support the for...in or function actions (among others), as these actions have been introduced to Flash in Version 5.

Continued

Continued

Finally, Flash will tell you if you have added conflicting actions to one keyframe or object. For example, if you have several Go To actions on one frame or button, Flash will highlight the offending action(s) in red, as shown in the following figure. The red highlighting will only appear in Normal Mode.

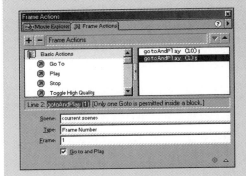

Highlighted actions are in conflict with previously added actions. You must remove or correct the parameters if you want your movie to behave correctly.

Your First Six Actions

So, now that you have a general picture of what actions do, let's look at the first six in detail (the remaining actions are covered in later chapters). At this point, we're only describing the functionality of each action, not how to add an action to your movie. Information on adding an action is covered in the next section, "Making Actions Happen with Event Handlers."

As they appear in the Flash interface, the actions are coincidentally sorted from top to bottom roughly according to their complexity. Let's take it from the top.

Go To

The Go To action changes the current frame of the movie to the target frame specified in the Go To settings. The Go To action has two variations:

✦ **Go to and Stop:** Changes the current frame to the frame specified and then halts playback. Go to and Stop is often used to produce toolbar-style interfaces where the user clicks buttons to view different areas of content in a movie.

✦ **Go to and Play:** Changes the current frame to the frame specified, and then executes a Play Action. Like Go to and Stop, Go to and Play can be used to create toolbar interfaces, but provides the capability to show animated intro sequences as preludes to individual content areas. Go to and Play also gets frequent use in choose-your-own-adventure style animations, in which the user guides an animated character through different paths in a narrative. Note that Go to and Stop is the default type of Go To action. To create a Go to and Play action, you must first add a Go To action, and then check the Go to and Play option in the Parameters area of the Actions Panel.

Each Go To action enables you to jump to certain areas of the Flash movie. The parameters of the Go To actions start with the largest time unit, the Scene, and end with the smallest one, the Frame.

You can specify frames in other scenes as the target of Go To actions with the Scene parameter. In the Scene drop-down menu, you can find a list of all the scenes in your movie, as well as built-in references to <current scene>, <next scene>, and <previous scene>, as shown in Figure 17-3. The Scene drop-down can be used together with the Type and Frame parameters to target a frame in any Scene in a movie.

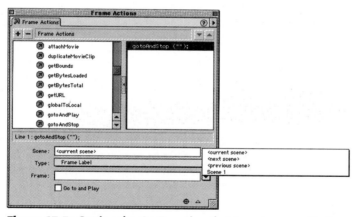

Figure 17-3: Setting the Go To action that targets a specific Scene.

There are five methods of specifying the frame to which the movie should go when it receives a Go To action. You set the method by selecting the appropriate Type and Frame parameters. After you've chosen the method to use to refer to your target frame, enter or select the frame's name or number under that setting's options (see Figure 17-4).

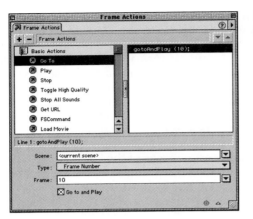

Figure 17-4: Setting the Go To action with a Frame Number type.

The methods for specifying the frame are:

✦ **Number:** Specify the target frame as a number. Frame 1 is the beginning of the movie or scene. Number spans scenes, so if you have a movie with two scenes, each containing 25 frames, and you add a Go to action with Frame Number set to 50, your action advances the movie to the 25th frame of the second scene.

Using frame numbers to specify the targets of Go To actions can lead to serious scalability problems in Flash movies. Adding frames at the beginning or in the middle of a movie's timeline causes the following frames to be renumbered. When those frames are renumbered, all Go to Frame Number actions must be revised to point to the correct new number of their target frames.

In the vast majority of cases, Go To actions that use Label to specify target frames are preferable to Go To actions that use Number to specify target frames. Unlike numbered frame targets, Go To actions with labeled frame targets continue to function properly even if the targeted frame changes position on the timeline.

✦ **Label:** Individual keyframes can be given names via the Label text field in the Frame panel. Once a frame is labeled, a Go To action can target it by name. To specify a label as the target of a Go To action, select Frame Label in the Type drop-down menu. Then either type the name of the frame into the Frame text field, or select it from the automatically generated list of frame labels in the Frame drop-down menu as seen in Figure 17-5.

The automatically generated list of labels that appears in the Label drop-down can include labels from other scenes, but cannot include labels that are inside Movie Clips. To target a label in a Movie Clip, you have to embed the Go To action in a Tell Target action and type the label in manually. However, Flash 5 offers a new way of targeting Movie Clips and their frame labels. For more information, see Chapter 18, "Navigating Flash Timelines."

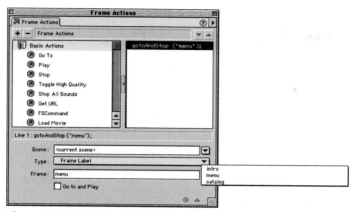

Figure 17-5: Setting the Go To action with a Frame Label.

✦ **Expression:** Specify the target frame as an interpreted ActionScript code segment. Expressions are used to dynamically assign targets of Go To actions. Expressions are covered in Chapter 21, "Planning Code Structures."

✦ **Next Frame:** Specify the target frame as the frame after the current frame. Next Frame can be used in conjunction with Previous Frame to quickly set up a slide-show-style walkthrough of content, where each of a series of contiguous keyframes contains the content of one "slide."

✦ **Previous Frame:** Specify the target frame as the frame before the current frame.

Play

This simple action is one of the true foundations of Flash. Play sets a movie or a Movie Clip in motion. When a Play action is executed, Flash starts the sequential display of each frame's contents along the current timeline. The rate at which the frames are displayed is measured as frames per second, or fps. The fps rate can be set from 0.01 to 120 (meaning that the Play Action can cause the display of as little as 1 frame every 100 seconds to as many as 120 frames in 1 second, subject to the limitations of the computer's processing speed). The default fps is 12. Once Play has started, frames continue to be displayed one after the other, until another action interrupts the flow, or the end of the movie or Movie Clip's timeline is reached. If the end of a movie's timeline is reached, the movie either loops (begins playing again at frame 1, scene 1), or stops on the last frame. (Whether a movie loops or not depends on the Publish settings described in Chapter 40, "Publishing Flash Movies.") If the movie is set to loop, once the end of the Movie Clip's timeline is reached, playback loops back to the beginning of the clip, and the clip continues playing. To prevent looping, add a Stop action to the last frame of your Movie Clip.

Note A single Play action affects only a single timeline, whether that timeline is the main movie timeline or the timeline of a Movie Clip instance on the Main Timeline (Scene 1). For example, a Play action executed inside a Movie Clip does not cause the Main Timeline to begin playing. Likewise, any Go To action on the Main Timeline doesn't migrate to the Movie Clips that reside there. A timeline must be specifically targeted to control it. If there is no specified target, then the action is referring to its own timeline. However, this is not the case for animations within Graphic symbol instances. An animation in a Graphic symbol is controlled by actions on the timeline in which the symbol instance is present—Flash ignores actions on a Graphic symbol's timeline.

Stop

Stop, as you may have guessed, halts the progression of a movie or Movie Clip that is in a Play state. Stop is often used with buttons for user-controlled playback of a movie, or on frames to end an animated sequence.

Tip Movie Clip instances placed on any timeline will begin to play automatically. It's important to remember to add a Stop action on the first frame of a Movie Clip if you don't want it to play right away.

Toggle High Quality

Here's a straightforward action that changes the entire movie's visual rendering quality setting to High if it is currently set at Low, and to Low if it is currently set at High. In High-Quality Mode, the edges of lines and text appear smooth because they are antialiased (or blurred slightly between shifts in color). In Low-Quality Mode, the edges of lines and text appear choppy because they are not antialiased. Low Quality is occasionally set on movies that are played back on slower computers because it causes animation to play back more quickly. See the difference for this toggle setting in Figure 17-6. Toggle High Quality is considered a deprecated action because of the new Flash 5 _quality and _highquality properties. All quality settings are global, which means that every timeline (including Movie Clip timelines) will be affected regardless of where the action is executed.

Tip The Toggle High Quality Action is most frequently used to set the Quality of standalone Flash movies. (On the Web, the quality of a movie can be set with HTML attributes.) If the Quality is not explicitly set to High, it defaults to an automatic mode where the Quality shifts between High and Low depending on how demanding each frame of the movie is on the computer. The effect is rather jarring, so most designers avoid it by simply choosing the often slower, but more attractive High Quality.

Figure 17-6: Low Quality (left) versus High Quality (right)

Stop All Sounds

A simple but powerful action that mutes any sounds playing in the movie at the time the action is executed. Stop All Sounds does not disable sounds permanently — it simply cancels any sounds that happen to be currently playing. It is sometimes used as a quick-and-dirty method of making buttons that shut off background looping soundtracks. Stop All Sounds is not appropriate for controlling whether multiple sounds are played or muted. For information on more accurate control over sounds, please see Chapter 18, "Navigating Flash Timelines," and Chapter 19, "Controlling Movie Clips."

Get URL

Want to link to a Web page from a Flash movie? No problem. That's what Get URL is for. Get URL is simply Flash's method of making a conventional hypertext link. It's nearly exactly the equivalent of an Anchor tag in HTML, except that Flash's Get URL also allows for form submission. Get URL can be used to link to a standard Web page, an ftp site, another Flash movie, an executable, a CGI script, or anything that exists on the Internet or on an accessible local file system. Get URL has three parameters that are familiar to Web builders (the first one, URL, is required for this Action to work):

✦ **URL:** This is the network address of the page, file, script, or resource to which you are linking. Any value is permitted (including ActionScript expressions), but the linked item can only be displayed if the reference to it is correct. URL is directly analogous to the HREF attribute of an HTML Anchor tag. You can use a relative or absolute URL as well. Examples:

```
http://www.yoursite.com/
ftp://ftp.yoursite.com/pub/documents.zip
menu.html
/cgi-bin/processform.cgi
```

Since Flash 4, Get URL can now link to documents on the Web from the standalone Flash player. Execution of a Get URL action in the standalone player causes an external Web browser to launch and load the requested URL (see Figure 17-7).

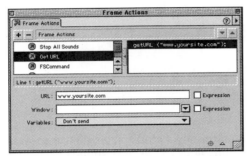

Figure 17-7: Setting the URL of a Get URL action

✦ **Window:** This is the name of the frame or window in which you wish to load the resource specified in the URL setting. Window is directly analogous to the TARGET attribute of an HTML Anchor tag. In addition to enabling the entry of custom frame and window names, Window provides four presets in a drop-down menu:

- **_self:** Loads the URL into the same frame or window as the current movie.

- **_blank:** Creates a new browser window and loads the URL into it.

- **_parent:** Removes the current frameset and loads the URL in its place. Use this option if you have multiple nested framesets, and you want your linked URL to replace only the frameset in which your movie resides.

- **_top:** Loads the URL into the current browser and removes all framesets in the process. Use this option if your movie is in a frame, but you want your linked URL to be loaded normally into the browser, outside the confines of any frames.

Note   Frame windows and/or JavaScript windows can be assigned names. You can target these names by manually typing the name in the Window field. For example, if you had a frame defined as `<FRAME NAME="main". . .>`, you could load specific URLs into "main" from a Flash movie.

✦ **Variables:** This option enables Get URL to function like an HTML form submission. For normal links, the Variables setting should be left at its default value, Don't Send. But in order to submit values to a server-side script, one of the submission methods (Send Using GET or Send Using POST) must be selected. For a complete tutorial on using Get URL to submit data to a server, see the "Creating a Flash Form" section in Chapter 24, "Sending Data In and Out of Flash."

Tip

Get URL functions in the Test Movie environment. Both the Flash stand-alone player and the Test Movie command give you access to external and/or local URLs.

Although this chapter focuses on using Basic Actions, you should start familiarizing yourself with the ActionScript notation that Flash uses for each action (see Table 17-1). As you use Flash for more advanced interactivity, you'll need to have a firm grasp of code notation. Part V, "Programming Flash Movies with ActionScript," teaches you how to start building code from the ground up.

Table 17-1
Basic Actions and ActionScript Notation

Action	ActionScript Notation	Arguments
Go to and Stop	`gotoAndStop(arguments);`	Scene Name (Frame Label, Number, or Expression)
Go to and Play	`gotoAndPlay(arguments);`	Scene Name (Frame Label, Number, or Expression)
Go to Next Frame	`nextFrame();`	None
Go to Previous Frame	`prevFrame();`	None
Go to Next Scene	`nextScene();`	None
Go to Previous Scene	`prevScene();`	None
Play	`play();`	None
Stop	`stop();`	None
Toggle High Quality	`toggleHighQuality();`	None
Stop All Sounds	`stopAllSounds();`	None
Get URL	`getURL(arguments);`	URL, Target frame or window, Variable send method

Making Actions Happen with Event Handlers

The first six Basic Actions — Go To, Play, Stop, Toggle High Quality, Stop All Sounds, and Get URL — provide all the behaviors that you need to make an interesting interactive Flash movie. But those six actions can't make your movies interactive on their own. They need to be told when to happen. To tell Flash when an action should occur, you need event handlers. Event handlers specify the condition(s) under which an action can be made to happen. For instance, you might want to mouse-click a button to initiate a Play action, or you might want a movie to stop when a certain frame in the timeline is reached. Creating interactivity in your movies is simply a matter of deciding what event you want to detect (mouse click, keystroke, and so on), adding the appropriate event handler to detect it, and specifying the action(s) that should be performed when it happens.

Before we describe each event handler in detail, let's see an example of exactly how an event handler merges with an action to form a functioning interactive button.

Combining an action with an event handler to make a functioning button

Imagine that you have a short, endlessly looping movie in which a wire-frame cube rotates. Now imagine that you want to add a button to your movie that, when clicked, stops the cube from rotating by stopping the playback of the looping movie. Here's what you need to do.

On the CD-ROM For this exercise, you can use the rotatingCube.fla file located in the ch17 folder on the *Flash 5 Bible* CD-ROM. The finished file is named rotatingCube_complete.fla.

1. Open your Flash movie (.FLA file), and make a new layer called **button**.

2. Place a button on the button layer. (You could use Flash 5's sample VCR stop button found in Window ➪ Common Libraries ➪ Buttons, in the (circle) VCR Button Set folder.)

3. Bring up the Instance Panel for the button (as shown in Figure 17-8) by selecting the symbol instance on the Stage and choosing Modify ➪ Instance (Command+I or Ctrl+I). If the Instance Panel was already open, then this command will close the panel. Reapply the command to open it again. With the button selected, make sure that the Behavior menu reads Button. If some other Behavior is shown, then change it to Button.

Tip Selecting buttons and editing button properties can be sometimes be tricky if buttons are enabled in the Flash authoring environment. For easier button manipulation, disable buttons by unchecking Enable Simple Buttons under the Control menu.

4. Open the Actions Panel (Option+Command+A or Ctrl+Alt+A), and then open the Basic Actions booklet in the left pane. A list of all the Basic Actions appears.

5. Double-click the On Mouse Event action, or drag it to the right pane. A list of parameters for On Mouse Event appears on the lower portion of the Actions Panel. This list contains all the event handlers for buttons.

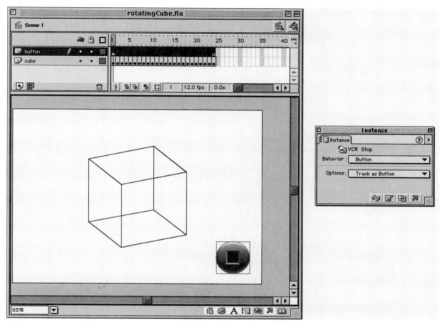

Figure 17-8: The Instance Panel for the VCR Stop button.

6. By default, the Release option of the Event setting (shown in Figure 17-9) is already checked. The Release event handler is one of two kinds of mouse-click handlers (the other is Press; both are described later in this chapter in the section titled "The Flash event handlers"). You should notice that the Actions list in the right pane indicates the event handlers that are selected. You've now told Flash that you want something to happen when the mouse clicks the button. All that's left is to tell it what should happen. In other words, you need to nest another action with the on (release){ and } code.

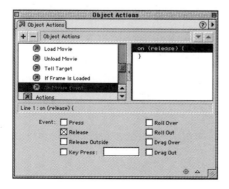

Figure 17-9: Adding a Release event handler

7. Now we try another method for adding an action to the Actions list. Select the top line on (release){ in the Actions list (in the right pane). Then, click the plus (+) button in the top-left corner of the Actions Panel. From the pop-up menu, highlight Basic Actions, and select Stop from the submenu. A Stop action will be placed between the code on (release){ and }. The Actions list box should now read as follows:

```
on (release){
     stop();
}
```

The Stop action, represented by the code stop() shown in Figure 17-10, is contained by the curly braces { and } that mark the beginning and end of the list of actions that are executed when the release event occurs (there could be any number of actions). Each action line must end with the semicolon (;) character.

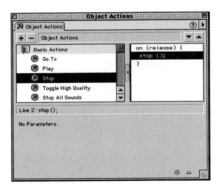

Figure 17-10: This code will stop the Main Timeline playback when the button is clicked.

Tip   In this example we selected the event handler before adding our action. This helped illustrate the individual role that each of those components plays. During real production, however, you may simply drag or add any action to the right pane without first specifying an event handler—Flash automatically adds a Release event handler to actions that are added to buttons.

We now have a button in our Flash movie that stops the movie's playback when it is clicked. You can use the Control ⇨ Test Movie command to see if the button is working correctly. To make any interactivity in your movies, you simply have to apply the basic principles we used to make the stop button: Decide which action (or actions) you want to happen, and then indicate when you want that action to happen with an event handler.

In the first part of this chapter, we explored six actions. Let's look now at the list of Event Handlers you can use to make those actions happen.

The Flash event handlers

Three primary event handlers exist in Flash. Those that detect mouse activity on buttons (button manipulation), those that recognize when a key is pressed on the keyboard (key presses), and those that respond to the progression of the timeline (keyframes).

Note Flash 5 adds some new event handlers such as onClipEvent and data-driven events such as XML.loaded and XMLSocket.onConnect. There is also a new Key Object and methods associated with it (for example, Key.isDown and Key.isToggled). We look at advanced actions in later chapters.

Button manipulation

Event handlers that occur based on the user's interaction with a button rely entirely on the location and movement of the mouse pointer. If the mouse pointer comes in contact with a button's Hit area, it changes from an arrow to a hand symbol. At that time the mouse is described as "over" the button. If the mouse pointer is not over a button, it is said to be *out* or *outside* of the button. General movement of the mouse *without* the mouse button depressed is referred to as *rolling*. General movement of the mouse *with* the mouse button depressed is referred to as *dragging*.

New Feature Event handlers and actions on buttons must be placed only on Button instances on the Stage, not on the four frames in the timeline of the original Button symbol. Flash 5 will not allow you to place actions on any event handlers in the Button symbol timeline.

Here are the mouse-based event handlers for Flash buttons.

Press

A single mouse click can actually be divided into two separate components: the downstroke (the *press*) and the upstroke (the *release*). A Press event occurs when the mouse pointer is over the Hit area of a button *and* the downstroke of a mouse click is detected. Press is best used for control panel-style buttons, especially toggle switches. Press is not recommended for important user moves (such as irreversible decisions or primary navigation) because it does not give users an opportunity to abort their move.

Release

A Release event occurs when the mouse pointer is over the Hit area of a button *and* both the downstroke and the upstroke of a mouse click are detected. Release is the standard button click Event Handler.

Release Outside

A Release Outside event occurs in response to the following series of mouse movements: The mouse pointer moves over a button's Hit area; the mouse button is pressed; the mouse pointer is moved off the button's Hit area; and the mouse button is released. Release Outside can be used to react to an aborted button click.

Roll Over

A Roll Over event occurs when the mouse pointer moves onto the Hit area of a button without the mouse button depressed.

The Roll Over event handler should not be used to make visual changes to a button (such as making it appear "active" with a glow or size increase). Flash has a built-in method of handling strictly visual changes on buttons that is described in Chapter 9, "Checking Out the Library: Symbols and Instances." The Roll Over event handler should only be used to initiate actions.

Roll Out

A Roll Out event occurs when the mouse pointer moves off of the Hit area of a button without the mouse button depressed.

Drag Over

A Drag Over event occurs in response to the following series of mouse movements: The mouse button is pressed while the mouse pointer is over the Hit area of a button; the mouse pointer moves off the Hit area (mouse button still depressed); and the mouse pointer moves back over the Hit area (mouse button still depressed). Drag Over is rather obscure, but could be used for special cases of interactivity such as revealing an Easter egg in a game (for example, when the mouse button is held down and mouse movement occurs over a specific area, then ActionScript can detect the coordinates of the mouse movement and reveal a Movie Clip instance that is otherwise invisible on the Stage).

Drag Out

A Drag Out event occurs in response to the following series of mouse movements: The mouse button is pressed while the mouse pointer is over the Hit area of a button; and the mouse pointer moves off the Hit area (mouse button still depressed).

Key Press (or keystroke)

The Key Press event handler for an On Mouse event action lets you execute an action (or series of actions) when the user presses a key on the keyboard. The implementation method for a Key Press event handler may be confusing: To add a Key Press event handler, you must first place a button onstage at the frame where you want the keyboard to be active. You then attach the keystroke event handler to the button.

If you are only using the button as a container for your keystroke event handler and you do not want the button to appear on Stage, you should make sure that (in Symbol Editing Mode) all the frames of the button are blank.

The Key Press event handler, which was introduced with Flash 4, opens up many possibilities for Flash. Movies can have keyboard-based navigation, buttons can have keyboard shortcuts for convenience and accessibility, and games can have keyboard-controlled objects (such as ships and animated characters). But watch out for some potential "gotchas" to keyboard usage, *specifically with On Mouse event actions*. If you're planning ambitious keyboard-based projects, you may want to check this list of potential issues first:

✦ The Esc key does not work as a key press.

✦ Multiple key combinations are not supported. This rules out diagonals as two-key combinations in the classic four-key game control setup. It also means shortcuts such as Ctrl+S are not available. Uppercase is functional, however.

✦ If presented in a browser, the Flash movie must have "focus" before keystrokes can be recognized. To "focus" the movie, the user must click anywhere in the space it occupies. Keyboard-based movies should include instructions that prompt the user to perform this initial mouse click.

Note When a Flash movie is loaded into a Web browser, Key Presses cannot function until the user has clicked at least once somewhere in the Flash movie.

✦ Because the Enter, less than (<), and greater than (>) keys are used as authoring shortcuts in the Test Movie environment, you may want to avoid using them as control keys in your movies. If you need to use those keys in your movies, make sure that you test the movies in a browser.

✦ Key Press events are case sensitive. For example, an uppercase letter "S" and a lowercase letter "s" can trigger two different actions. No case-insensitive keystroke event handler exists (one that would enable both cases of a letter to trigger the same action). Achieving case-insensitivity would require duplication of event handler and action statements.

Note Flash 5's new Key Object and its methods enable you to do much more with Key Press events than the On Mouse event action does. You can find .FLA files that demonstrate the Key Object in the ch25 folder on the CD-ROM. The Key Object is discussed in the *Macromedia ActionScript Reference Guide* (which ships with the software) on pages 279–288.

Keyframes

The keyframe event handler depends on the playback of the movie itself, not on the user. Any action (except On Mouse event) can be attached to any keyframe on the timeline. An action attached to a keyframe is executed when the playhead enters the keyframe, whether it enters naturally during the linear playback of the movie or as the result of a Go To action. So, for instance, you may place a Stop action on a keyframe to pause the movie at the end of an animation sequence.

In some multimedia applications, keyframe event handlers can differentiate between the playhead *entering* a keyframe and *exiting* a keyframe. Flash has only one kind of keyframe event handler (essentially, on enter). Hence, as an author, you do not need to add keyframe event handlers explicitly — they are a presumed component of any action placed on a keyframe. As mentioned in an earlier note, Flash 5 has a new `onClipEvent` handler, which allows an argument of `enterFrame`. We look at this new handler in Chapter 19, "Controlling Movie Clips."

Tip

Complex movies can have dozens, or even hundreds of actions attached to keyframes. To prevent conflicts between uses of keyframes for animation and uses of keyframes as action containers, it is highly advisable to create an entire layer solely for action keyframes. Name the layer **actions** and keep it on top of all your layers for easy access. Remember not to place any symbol instances, text, or artwork on your actions layer. You can also create a labels layer to hold—you guessed it—frame labels.

Summary

✦ ActionScript is Flash's interactive language. It is a set of actions that enables Flash to communicate with internal elements (timelines, symbols, sounds, and so on) and external Web pages and scripts.

✦ Flash interactivity is based on a relatively simple structure: An event handler waits for something to happen (a playback point being reached or the user providing input), and when that something does happen, it executes one or more actions (which alter the movie's playback, behavior, or properties; loads a file; or executes a script).

✦ There are two authoring modes for adding actions in Flash: Normal and Expert. Normal Mode enables you to add interactivity easily by clicking action names and using menus to set parameters. Expert Mode enables experienced Flash users to type actions directly and to copy text from other applications into Flash.

✦ The Basic Actions booklet contains the fundamental actions for navigating Flash playback through multiple scenes and keyframes, as well as controlling soundtracks and accessing external Web resources such as HTML pages and ftp downloads.

✦ All actions need an event handler to activate them. Event handlers include keyframes on a timeline, button clicks, mouse movements, and key presses. More advanced event handlers are discussed in later chapters.

✦   ✦   ✦

Navigating Flash Timelines

Unlike most multimedia authoring applications, Flash has the capability to use multiple timelines simultaneously. So far, most of the examples in this book have only one timeline and one scene. You've seen how to add basic actions to your movies to make them interactive. Now, we begin exploring the world of multiple movie timelines using the Movie Clip symbol.

Movie Clips: The Key to Self-Contained Playback

A powerful addition to Flash was the Movie Clip symbol, which was introduced in version 3. Movie Clips enabled Flash developers to create complex behaviors by nesting self-contained sequences of animation or interactivity inside each other. These sequences could then be placed as discreet, self-playing modules on the Main Timeline. The key to the power of Movie Clips was their capability to communicate with and control each other via the Tell Target action. In Flash 4, the role of Movie Clips was expanded — they could be used with Action Script. That capability put Movie Clips at the foundation of advanced interactivity in Flash.

How Movie Clips interact within a Flash movie

Previous chapters have dealt with Flash movies as a single sequence of frames arranged along a single timeline. Whether the playback along that timeline was linear (traditional animation) or nonlinear (where the Playhead jumps arbitrarily to any frame), our example movies have normally comprised only the frames of a single timeline. Ostensibly, a single timeline may seem to provide everything you'd need to create any Flash behavior, but as you get more inventive or ambitious, you'll soon find yourself conceiving ideas for animated and interactive segments that are thwarted by the limits of a single timeline.

Suppose you want to create a looping animation of a character's face. You decide that the character's eyes should blink every 2 seconds, and that the character's mouth should yawn every 15 seconds. On a single timeline, you'd have to have a loop of 180 frames for the mouth (assuming a frame rate of 12 frames per second), and repeating keyframes for the closed eye artwork every 24 frames. Although creating your face in that manner would be a bit cumbersome, it wouldn't be impossible — until your character's face had to move around the screen as an integrated whole. Making the mouth and eyes loop while the whole face moved around complex paths for extended periods of time would quickly become impractical, especially if the face were only one part of a larger environment.

Now imagine that you could make your character's face by creating two whole separate movies, one for the eyes and one for the mouth. Could you then place those movies as self-contained animating objects on the timeline of your main movie, just like a graphic or a button? Well, you can — that's what Movie Clips are all about. Movie Clips are independent sequences of frames (timelines) that can be defined outside the context of the main movie timeline and then placed onto it as objects on a single frame. You create Movie Clips the same way you create a Graphic symbol (in the Edit Symbol environment). Unlike a Graphic symbol, a Movie Clip (as the name implies) acts in most cases just like a fully functional .SWF file, meaning, for instance, that frame actions in Movie Clip timelines are functional. After you have created a Movie Clip as a symbol, you drop instances of it into any keyframe of the main movie timeline or any other Movie Clip timeline. The following are some general Movie Clip principles:

✦ During playback, a Movie Clip instance placed on a timeline begins to play as soon as the frame on which it occurs is reached, whether or not the main movie is playing.

✦ A Movie Clip plays back autonomously, meaning that as long as it is present on stage it is not governed by the playing or stopping of the Main Timeline.

✦ Movie Clips can play when the Main Timeline is stopped, or stay halted when the Main Timeline plays.

✦ Like a Graphic or a Button symbol, Movie Clips can be manipulated on the stage — you can size them, skew them, rotate them, place effects such as Alpha blending on them, or tween them, all while the animation within them continues to play.

✦ All timelines play at the frame rate specified by the Modify Movie dialog. However, it is possible to control a timeline's frame rate with ActionScript routines.

In our character face example, the animated eyes and mouth could be looping Movie Clips, and then those movie clips could be grouped and tweened around the Stage on the Main Timeline to make the whole face move. The same principle could be used to move a Movie Clip of a butterfly with flapping wings along a motion path.

One movie, several timelines

Because a Flash movie can have more than one timeline existing in the same space and time, there needs to be away of organizing Movie Clips within the Main Timeline (Scene 1) of your Flash movie. Just like artwork can be placed inside of any symbol, symbol instances can be "nested" within other symbols. If you change the contents of the nested symbol, the parent symbol (the symbol containing the other symbol) will be updated as well. Although this may not seem special, it's of extreme importance to movie clips and Flash interactivity. Because the playback of each Movie Clip timeline is independent from any other timeline, you need to know how to tell Flash which Movie Clip you want to control.

The Flash movie diagram in Figure 18-1 illustrates multiple timelines. This Flash movie has two layers on the Main Timeline, Layer 1 and Layer 2. Layer 1 has a Movie Clip (instance "A") which exists for 19 frames on the Main Timeline. Layer 2 has a Movie Clip (instance "B") which exists for 10 frames on the Main Timeline, but also contains a nested Movie Clip (instance "C").

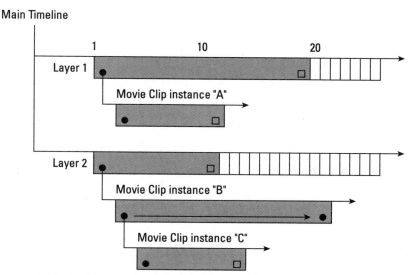

Figure 18-1: This figure shows one method of diagramming Flash timelines.

In Figure 18-1, if the Main Timeline has a Stop action on the first frame, then all three Movie Clips will continue to play unless there are Stop actions on their first frames or they are told to stop by actions targeted to them. If the Main Timeline plays to frame 20, then instance "A" will no longer be on the Stage, regardless of how many frames it may have on its timeline. A more practical diagram of a time-line hierarchy can be found in Figure 18-2.

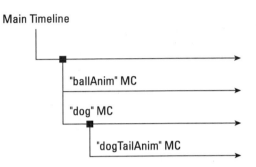

Figure 18-2: Flash movies can be flow-charted in this fashion. This diagram is similar to the new Movie Explorer's method of displaying Flash movie information.

In Figure 18-2, you can see three Movie Clips. Two of them, ballAnim and dog, occupy space on the Main Timeline. The other one, dogTailAnim, is nested within the dog Movie Clip. Each Movie Clip instance on any given timeline needs to have a unique name—you can't have the two Movie Clip instances on the same timeline with the same name. The instance name is specified in the Instance Panel, shown in Figure 18-3.

Figure 18-3: Among other things, the Instance Panel enables you to name each Movie Clip instance that appears on the Stage.

Now that you understand how multiple timelines can exist within a Flash movie, let's see how you can make Movie Clips communicate with one another.

Flash 4 into Flash 5: Targets and Paths Explained

If you already studied Movie Clips in Chapter 9, "Checking Out the Library: Symbols and Instances," you probably know that they provide the solution to our animated face problem. However, you might not have guessed that Movie Clips can also add logic to animation and Flash interfaces. Let's take our animated face example a little further: When people yawn, they generally close their eyes for as long as they are yawning. Our hypothetical character's face may look strange if it is blinking and yawning at the same time. Suppose we wanted to make our character's eyes stay closed during every yawn. We'd have to have some way for the mouth Movie Clip to control the eyes Movie Clip so that we could tell the eyes to go to a "shut" frame when the mouth opens, and then tell them to return to their blink loop again when the mouth closes.

Well, we have a few ways to control the eyes Movie Clip from the mouth Movie Clip. In Flash 3 and 4, the Tell Target action was used to let actions on any timeline (including Movie Clip timelines and the Main Timeline) control what happens on any other timeline. How? Tell Target simply provided a mechanism for extending actions, enabling them to specify (or *target*) the timeline upon which they should be executed. Targets are any Movie Clip instances that are available at any given frame in a Flash movie. In addition to Tell Target, Flash 5 enables you to direct actions to specific timelines by attaching the same actions as methods to the Movie Clip object. If you're new to scripting, please read the "The New and Improved ActionScript" sidebar.

The Tell Target action is a deprecated action; it's still supported in Flash 5, but it's been replaced with more versatile actions and syntax that make its use outdated. For an overview of deprecated actions, see the sidebar in the previous chapter. We show you how to use both Tell Target and Flash 5 methods in this chapter. First, however, you need to understand how targeting works in Flash movies.

The New and Improved ActionScript

Flash 5 has introduced a new method of writing all ActionScripts called *dot syntax*. Earlier versions of Flash used a natural-language scripting environment that was menu-based, in which actions could be read and understood easily and accessed via pop-up menus. While most people prefer easy-to-use scripting environments, the production demands of complex interactive projects are often compromised by such menu-driven scripting environments. Computer programmers prefer to create, edit, and debug scripting with a language that can be accessed and modified easily. Consequently, we see the best of both worlds with Flash 5.

Flash 5 ActionScript adheres closely to the ECMA-262 specification that is based on JavaScript, the universal scripting language used by most browsers for interactive HTML and DHTML documents. Therefore, Flash ActionScript uses a dot syntax. What does that mean? It means that all actions are written within a standard formula that is common with object-oriented programming (OOP) languages:

```
Object.property = value;
```

or

```
Object.method();
```

Continued

Continued

The examples beg four things to be defined: objects, properties, methods, and values. An *object* is any element in a program (in this case, the Flash movie) that has changeable and accessible characteristics. Objects can be user-defined (in other words, you create and name them) or predefined by the programming language. Flash has several predefined Objects, meaning that they're already built into the ActionScript language. We look at both types in more detail in later chapters. An important object (and perhaps the easiest to conceptualize) is the Movie Clip Object. Any Movie Clip instance on the Stage is an object, such as `ballAnim` or `dogTailAnim`. An object has characteristics, or *properties*, that can be updated or changed throughout the movie. An example of a Movie Clip property is scale, which is referred to as `_xscale` and `_yscale`. We look at Movie Clip properties in the next chapter. Properties always have some data accompanying them. This data is called the property's *value*. Using the previous example, at full size, a Movie Clip's `_xscale` is 100 (the scale property uses percent as the unit of measure). For a Movie Clip instance named `ballAnim`, this would be represented in ActionScript syntax as:

```
ballAnim._xscale = 100;
```

Finally, objects can be enacted upon by procedures that do something to or with the object. These procedures are called *methods*. One method for the Movie Clip object is the `gotoAndPlay()` method, which we used as a Basic Action in the previous chapter. In Flash 5, methods can be created for your own objects or predefined for existing Flash objects. Any Basic Action can be attached as a method to any Movie Clip instance, as in:

```
ballAnim.gotoAndPlay("start");
```

The preceding example tells the `ballAnim` Movie Clip to direct its playback head to the frame label `start` on its timeline. This chapter helps you understand how to use the `gotoAndPlay` method for Movie Clips.

Paths: Absolute and relative modes

Earlier in this chapter, you learned how multiple Movie Clip timelines appear on the Flash Stage. It's entirely possible to nest several Movie Clips within another Movie Clip. To understand how Movie Clips communicate with one other by using actions, you need to have a firm grasp on Movie Clip paths. A path is simply that — the route to a destination, an address per se. If you have a Movie Clip instance named dogTailAnim inside a dog Movie Clip instance, how is Flash supposed to know? What if there was one than one dogTailAnim in the entire movie, with others nested in other Movie Clips besides the dog instance? You can specify a Movie Clip's path in an absolute or a relative mode.

An *absolute path* is the full location (or target) information for a given Movie Clip instance from any other location (or target). Just like your postal address has a street name and number and a zip code so that people can find you on a map, all Movie Clips have a point of origin: the Main Timeline (Scene 1). Before Flash 5, the Main Timeline was represented in a Movie Clip path as a starting forward slash (/) character. The absolute path of a Movie Clip instance named dog on the Main Timeline is:

```
/dog
```

Any nested Movie Clips inside of the dog instance would be referenced after that starting path. For example, the absolute path to dogTailAnim, an instance inside the dog Movie Clip instance would be:

```
/dog/dogTailAnim
```

Another / character was put between the two instance names. Think of the / as meaning "from the timeline of," as in dogTailAnim is from the timeline of dog. Use of the / character in Movie Clip paths is known as the *Slashes* notation.

In Flash 5, you can use either the Slashes or *Dots* notation with absolute paths. The Dots notation follows the new ActionScript language conventions. With Dots notation, the Main Timeline becomes:

```
_root
```

Using our previous example, a Movie Clip instance named dog on the Main Timeline (or _root) would have an absolute path of:

```
_root.dog
```

And, following in suit, a Movie Clip instance named dogTailAnim that is nested within the "dog" Movie Clip would have the absolute path of:

```
_root.dog.dogTailAnim
```

Just like Tell Target is considered a deprecated action in Flash 5, the Slashes notation is deprecated syntax. It will still work with the Flash 5 Player, but subsequent versions of the Flash authoring program will be built of the new Dots notation.

A *relative path* is a contextual path to one timeline from another. From a conceptual point of view, think of a relative path as the relationship between the location of your pillow to the rest of your bed. Unless you have an odd sleeping habit, the pillow is located at the head of the bed. You may change the location of the bed within your room or the rooms of a house, but the relationship between the pillow and the bed remains the same.

With Flash, relative Movie Clip paths are useful within movie clips that contain several nested movie clips. That way, you can move the container (or parent) Movie

Clip from one timeline to another, and expect the inner targeting of the nested movie clips to work. As with absolute paths, there are two methods of displaying relative paths: Slashes and Dots notations. To refer to a timeline that is above the current timeline in Slashes notation, use:

```
../
```

The two dots here work just like directory references for files on Web servers; use a pair of .. for each timeline in the hierarchy. You can use relative Slashes notation to refer up and down the hierarchy at the same time. For example, if you have two nested movie clips, such as dogTailAnim and dogPantingAnim, within a larger Movie Clip named dog, you may want to target dogTailAnim from dogPantingAnim. The relative Slashes path for this is:

```
../dogTailAnim
```

This path tells Flash to go up one timeline from dogPantingAnim to the dog timeline, and then look for the instance named dogTailAnim from there.

The relative Dots path for a timeline that is located above the current timeline is:

```
_parent
```

To target one nested Movie Clip from another nested movie clip in the same container Movie Clip instance, you would put the targeted Movie Clip's name after _parent, as in:

```
_parent.dogTailAnim
```

As with absolute paths, we recommend that you become familiar with using the Dots notation for relative paths.

Okay, that's enough theory. We're going to let Colin Moock ease the transition of Flash 4 to Flash 5 targeting by showing how he uses Tell Target and Movie Clips with GWEN!, the star of his online animated series by the same name. (If you want to see more of GWEN! after you've finished the tutorial, you can visit www. moock.org/gwen/.) Note that Colin's material from the previous edition of the Flash Bible has been updated to reflect the Flash 5 look and feel of adding ActionScripts to Movie Clips. We have kept his original procedure intact. In addition to the intrinsic value of his methodology, we're also using this tutorial as an example of one way to migrate Flash 4 content to Flash 5. As you'll see later, though, ActionScript offers new ways to address targets in Flash 5.

On the CD-ROM To do this tutorial, you need the gwen.fla file in the ch18 folder on the *Flash 5 Bible* CD-ROM. If you want to see the finished product, open gwen-finished.fla located in the same folder.

Expert Tutorial: Making GWEN!'s Eyes Shut When She Yawns, *by Colin Moock*

Colin's tutorial uses the Flash 4–compatible action `tellTarget` *to enable communication between multiple timelines. If you wish to retain backward compatibility with Flash 4, then you cannot use Dots notation to enable actions of Movie Clips (for example,* `_root.mcName.gotoAndStop()` *will not work in the Flash 4 Player). While you can use the Dots notation as the path name to a Movie Clip instance, you will need to use* `tellTarget` *if you're "targeting" a Flash 4 audience.*

GWEN! was born as a Flash 2 animation. In Episode One, she didn't blink much, or yawn at all. By the time Episode Two was nearly finished, Flash 3 had hit the streets, and oh, the joy to GWEN! when she discovered Movie Clips and Tell Target. Now, after much convincing, GWEN! has agreed to be dismantled a little so that you can see how her eyes and mouth work. We're going to show you how to put her back together in this tutorial. Don't worry, GWEN!, this won't hurt a bit.

Begin by opening gwen.fla (it's in the ch18 folder on the *Flash 5 Bible* CD-ROM). Open the Library for gwen.fla by choosing Window ➪ Library. In the Library, are five symbols and one folder: gwen's face, gwen's eyes, gwen's eyes shut, gwen's mouth, gwen's mouth open, and the folder face artwork. Drag a copy of the gwen's face graphic symbol, shown in the following figure, from the Library onto the Stage.

Gwen's face graphic symbol

Next we're going to make a Movie Clip with GWEN!'s eyes blinking. Make a new Movie Clip by choosing Insert ➪ New Symbol. In the Symbol Properties dialog, enter the name **eyes** and keep the Movie Clip option of the Behavior setting, as shown in the following figure. Click OK.

Continued

Continued

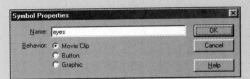

Enter the name of the Symbol and leave the Behavior option set to Movie Clip.

When you create a new Movie Clip symbol, you are automatically taken into Symbol Editing Mode where you work on your Movie Clip. Rename Layer 1 to **Eyes Blinking**. Click Frame 24 of the Eyes Blinking layer, and then select Insert ➪ Frame. While still on Frame 24, select Insert ➪ Blank Keyframe. You can add a blank keyframe to frame 24 by selecting it and pressing the F7 key (see the following figure).

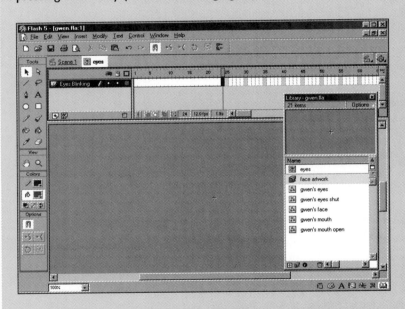

Click Frame 1 and drag the symbol gwen's eyes onto the Stage. Make sure gwen's eyes is still selected, and then open the Align Panel (Ctrl+K/Command+K). Center the symbol on the Stage by clicking To Stage, and then clicking the middle button in the left and right sets of the Align buttons, shown in the following figure.

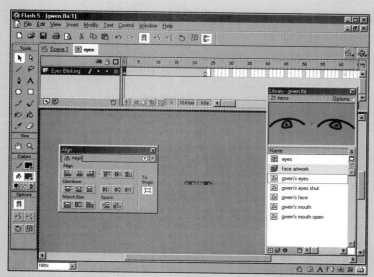

The new Align Panel features a To Stage button, along with the familiar Align Modes.

Click Frame 24 and drag the symbol gwen's eyes shut onto the Stage. Center the symbol on Stage as you did in the previous step.

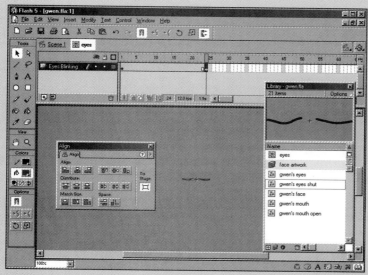

Drag the symbol gwen's eyes shut onto the Stage.

Continued

Continued

Next we need to label our eyes shut frame so that we can move to it whenever GWEN!'s mouth opens. Add a new layer by choosing Insert ➪ Layer. Name the new layer **Labels**. Labels should always be kept on their own layer. Click Frame 24 of the Labels layer, and then select Insert ➪ Blank Keyframe (or press F7). Open the Frame Panel by choosing Modify ➪ Frame (Ctrl+F or Command+F). In the Label text field, type **shut** (as in the following figure). Make sure you press Enter or Return after typing any frame label name to make sure it "sticks" to the current frame.

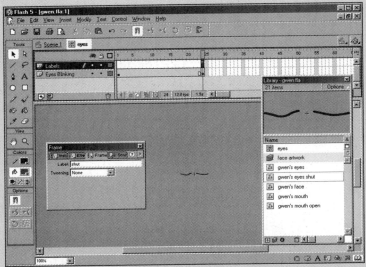

It's better to refer to frame labels (rather than frame numbers) in any Go To actions.

We're done with the eyes, so let's make the mouth. Make a new Movie Clip by choosing Insert ➪ New Symbol. In the Symbol Properties dialog, enter the name **mouth** and select the Movie Clip option of the Behavior setting, as shown in the following figure. Click OK.

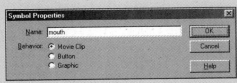

Name the symbol and select the Movie Clip option.

As with the eyes, you are automatically taken into Symbol Editing Mode for your new Movie Clip. Rename Layer 1 to **Mouth Yawning**, as in the following figure. Click Frame 180 of the Mouth Yawning layer, and then select Insert ➪ Frame. Click Frame 160 and select Insert ➪ Blank Keyframe.

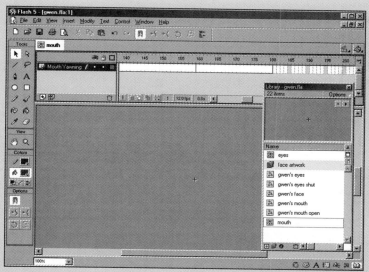

Get in the habit of giving yourself a timeline "workspace" with many frames to prepare your Flash content.

Click Frame 1 and drag the symbol "gwen's mouth" onto the Stage. Make sure "gwen's mouth" is still selected, and then open the Align Panel. Center the symbol on the Stage as you did with previous symbol instances.

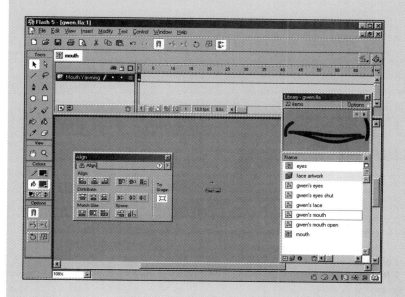

Continued

Continued

Click Frame 160 and drag the symbol. Center the symbol on Stage with the Align Panel, shown in the following figure.

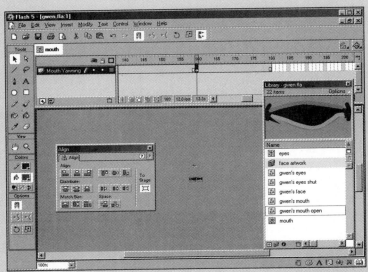

Drag gwen's mouth open onto the Stage and use the Align Panel to center the symbol.

It's time to place our eyes and mouth onto GWEN!'s face. Return to the main stage by choosing Edit ➪ Edit Movie (Ctrl+E or Command+E). Create two new layers, and name them **eyes** and **mouth**. Drag the newly created Movie Clip symbols, eyes and mouth, out of the Library onto GWEN!'s face, as shown in the following figure. Make sure you select their respective layer before dragging each onto the Stage.

At this point, you have a functional animated girl. If you test your movie now, you'll see that GWEN!'s eyes blink, and her mouth opens for her yawn, but we still have to add the interactivity that lets the mouth tell the eyes when to shut and reopen. To do that, we first have to name the instance of the eyes Movie Clip you created and dragged onto the Stage so that the mouth Movie Clip instance can identify it. Then we have to add the Tell Target actions that control the eyes instance. Hang on GWEN!, we're almost there!

Select the eyes Movie Clip on Stage, and then open the Instance Panel by choosing Modify ➪ Instance (Ctrl+I or Command+I). In the Instance Panel, you see a text field next to Name (see the following figure). That text field is where we give our Movie Clip instance a unique identification. Instance names are something like serial numbers—they enable actions in the movie to address a specific copy of a Movie Clip. Type **her-eyes** in the Name text field, and then press Enter or Return.

Drag the eyes and mouth symbols out of the Library and onto GWEN!'s face.

Remember that, like any symbol, a Movie Clip that is placed on Stage is only a reference to the symbol in the Library. That's why you name the symbol instance on the Stage, rather than simply referring to the symbol by name in the Library. You could place multiple copies of GWEN!'s eyes on the Stage and give them all different names so that each could be individually controlled and manipulated without any effect on the others. With eyes, the results can be a little trippy . . . look at Episode Two of GWEN! at www.moock.org/gwen/.

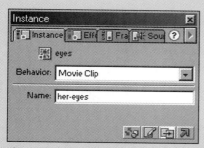

The Name text field in the Instance Panel

Now that the eyes Movie Clip instance is named her-eyes, we can return to the mouth to add the Tell Targets that control the her-eyes instance. Deselect all selections by clicking in a blank area of the Stage. Now, select only the mouth symbol. Choose Edit ➪ Edit Selected to resume work on the mouth Movie Clip. Add a new layer by choosing Insert ➪ Layer. Name the new layer **Actions**. Actions should always be kept on their own layer.

Continued

Continued

Author's Note: You can also deselect all selections by pressing the Esc key.

Click Frame 160 of the Actions layer, and then select Insert ⇨ Blank Keyframe. Open the Frame Actions Panel by double-clicking frame 160 or by right-clicking (Ctrl+clicking on Mac) the frame and selecting Actions from the contextual menu. Click the plus (+) button at the upper left of the Frame Actions Panel, shown in the following figure, select the Basic Actions menu item, and then select Tell Target. In the parameters area of the Actions Panel, find the Target text field and type **/her-eyes**. Now every Action we add between the `tellTarget` `("/herEyes"){` line and the `}` closing line in the Actions list is applied to the Movie Clip instance named her-eyes on the Main Timeline. We're now ready to add the action that controls the playback of the her-eyes instance.

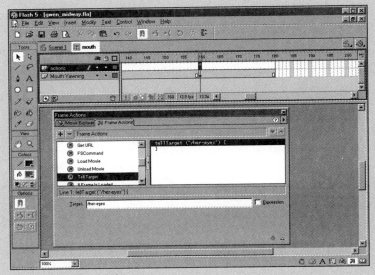

Frame Actions Panel

With the line `tellTarget("/her-eyes"){` highlighted in the actions list, click the plus (+) button, select the Basic Actions menu item, and select Go To. In the parameters area, select the Frame Label option in the Type drop-down menu, and type **shut** in the Frame text field. This makes the her-eyes instance playhead move to the shut frame label and stay there until told otherwise. Make sure that you uncheck the Go to and Play option, as shown in the following figure.

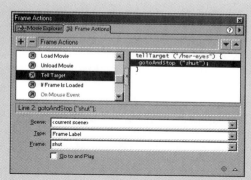

Frame Actions Panel with the parameters area displayed

The Actions list should now read as follows:

```
tellTarget ("/her-eyes"){
    gotoAndStop ("shut");
}
```

Click Frame 180 of the actions layer, and select Insert ➪ Blank Keyframe. Again, open the Frame Actions Panel by double-clicking frame 180. Click the plus (+) button at the upper left of the Frame Actions Panel, select the Basic Actions menu item, and then select Tell Target. In the Target text field type **/her-eyes** (as in the following figure). With the line `tellTarget("/her-eyes"){` highlighted in the Actions list, click the plus (+) button and select Play from the Basic Actions menu. This will make the eyes resume their two-second blink loop.

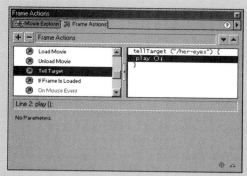

This simple tellTarget action nest will tell the her-eyes instance to play.

Continued

Continued

That's it. Test your movie with File ➪ Publish Preview ➪ Flash, or by using Control ➪ Test Movie (Ctrl+Enter or Command+Enter). You should now see GWEN!'s eyes close when she yawns. If things aren't working perfectly, compare your work closely with the finished version of GWEN!, called gwen-finished.fla, in the ch18 folder of the *Flash 5 Bible* CD-ROM.

A final hint: Tell Targets can be a little finicky—always be sure to check your target names and instance names to be sure that they match, that they are in the correct location, and that they are referred to correctly. You may make a few mistakes at first, but it won't be long before you'll know where to look to find the cause of the most common problems. Oh, and if you want to play with GWEN! some more, visit her at www.moock.org/gwen/. She's kind of snooty, but you never know . . . she might pay more attention to you now that you've seen how she works. Don't forget to pinch her cheeks.

Although we asked Colin Moock the same questions that we asked the other tutorialists, Colin won the prize for the fewest, most evasive answers. He first encountered Flash when, "Futurewave mailed it to me as a trial while I was working at Softquad (makers of Hotmetal Pro)." When we inquired, what was the most memorable movie or song in the year that he graduated from high school, Colin replied, "Can't remember." When we explained that we are doing a media-date thing this time, rather than spell out the ages of all the contributors, he insisted, "Honestly, I didn't really watch movies or listen to hit songs at the time." So, we have little information to give you about Colin Moock; except that he lives in Toronto, is highly regarded among the Flasheratti, and that he has worked on many Flash sites, most notably: www.moock.org/webdesign/portfolio and www.moock.org/webdesign/flash/sandbox.

Using Tell Target and Movie Clips with interfaces

GWEN! is an example of using Tell Target to create enhanced animation. However, the same technique can also be used to produce interfaces. Interface-based Tell Targets are often implemented on buttons. Just as you used Tell Targets with actions on keyframes in Colin's tutorial, so can you also use Tell Targets with actions on buttons. While working at ICE during the spring of 1999, Colin produced much of the interactive component of McClelland and Stewart's *The Canadian Encyclopedia 1999* CD-ROM in Flash. Most of the interactive pieces used Movie Clips and Tell Targets extensively. A simple but good example of using Tell Targets to enhance an interface comes from the Painting Retrospective in the encyclopedia as seen in Figure 18-4.

Figure 18-4 depicts the Painting Retrospective in action. Painting thumbnails are shown on a carousel that the user moves by clicking the right and left arrows. Below the carousel is a status window that displays the painting title, date, and artist when the user rolls their mouse over a painting. The status window is a Movie Clip that has one frame for each of the painting descriptions. The painting thumbnails in the carousel are all buttons. When the user points to a painting, the button's Roll Over event handler initiates a Tell Target action that makes the status window Movie Clip go to the frame that contains the appropriate painting description. Even when the paintings are moved along the carousel, the status window stays put because it's a separate Movie Clip, not a part of the thumbnail buttons.

Targeting Movie Clips in Flash 5

With Flash 5's new ActionScript syntax comes a new way to target and control movie clips. In the last section, you learned about the difference between the Slashes and Dots notations for absolute and relative paths. In Colin's tutorial, you learned how to use the Slashes notation with the Tell Target action to control movie clips. Now, you'll see how to make Movie Clips interact with one another with the Dots notation and Flash 5 ActionScript.

Caution

If you want your Flash movies to retain compatibility with the Flash 4 Player, then you need to use Tell Target actions. The methods described in this section will only work with Flash 5 Player and subsequent releases of it.

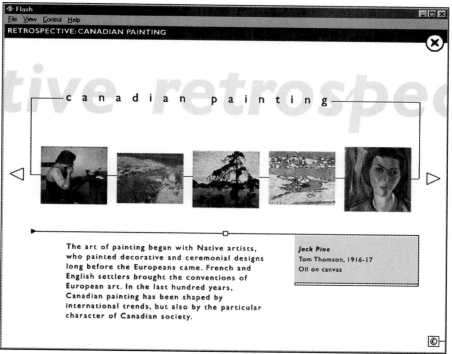

Figure 18-4: The Painting Retrospective from McClelland and Stewart's *The Canadian Encyclopedia 1999*

Using Movie Clips to create Sound Libraries

In Chapters 14 through 16, the ins and outs of sound import and use in Flash movies was discussed. In this chapter, we show you to create sound Movie Clips that are nested within a larger Sound Library Movie Clip. With Sound Library Movie Clips, you can transport sets of sounds easily between timelines and other Flash movies. In this section, you learn the importance of:

✦ Consistent timeline structure

✦ Naming conventions for Movie Clip instances

✦ Nested Movie Clip instances

✦ Streamlining Movie Clip production

These production principles are rather straightforward, and relatively simple to learn.

> You'll find sound files (.WAV and .AIFF) in the ch18 folder of the *Flash 5 Bible* CD-ROM. You can use the pianoKeys_starter.fla file or one of your own Flash movies for this exercise.

Overview of the pianoKeys Movie Clip

Open the pianoKeys_starter.fla file from the *Flash 5 Bible* CD-ROM. A pianoKeys Movie Clip instance is already on the Stage of the Main Timeline. Double-click the pianoKeys instance to enter the Symbol Editing Mode, as shown in Figure 18-5.

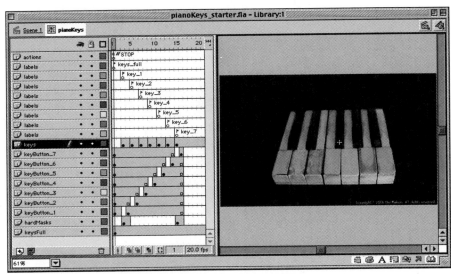

Figure 18-5: The timeline of the pianoKeys Movie Clip

The timeline for pianoKeys has several layers, with Button instances and Label layers. If you test this movie using Control ⇨ Test Movie (Ctrl+Enter or Command+Enter), you'll see that the Button instances over each piano key will tell the playback head of the pianoKeys timeline to go to that key's frame label. For the first key on the left, the button on layer keyButton_1 has the following action list:

```
on (press, keyPress "a") {
    gotoAndStop ("key_1");
}
on (rollOver) {
    gotoAndStop ("keys_full");
}
```

These actions don't use any Tell Target actions — they are simple navigation actions that you learned in the last chapter. When the keyButton_1 Button instance is clicked with the mouse, the playback head moves to the key_1 label on the current timeline, which is the pianoKeys timeline. Unless targeting is used, all actions on a Button instance will target the timeline on which the Button exists.

When the timeline goes to the key_1 frame label, a new .PNG bitmap of a "pressed" piano key (key_01.png on the keys layer) appears on top of the pianoKeys_full.png bitmap that is placed on the bottom keysFull layer. Note that the pianoKeys_full.png bitmap is present throughout the entire pianoKeys timeline. Each Button instance in the pianoKeys Movie Clip sends the playback head to the appropriate piano key frame label.

Now that you have an understanding of what's happening in this Movie Clip, let's create some sound Movie Clips that the pianoKeys instance can target.

Making sound Movie Clips

Before we start making new Movie Clip symbols, we need to establish *a naming convention* for our sounds. A naming convention is simply a way of consistently identifying components in any project, in or out of Flash. As a member of a Web production team, the importance of naming conventions can not be overemphasized — everyone involved with the project should know how to give names to images, sounds, symbol names, instance names, and so on. Even if you work by yourself, a naming convention provides a system of integrating elements from project to project, and enables you to identify elements much more easily when you open old files.

1. For each key on the piano, we'll make a unique sound. Each sound will be on its own timeline where it can be targeted to play. Because there are seven keys on the piano, we need to import seven sounds into Flash. Using File ⇨ Import, locate the ch18 folder on the *Flash 5 Bible* CD-ROM. Import each of the key sounds (.AIFF or .WAV) into your Flash movie.

Cross-Reference

Imported sounds do not show up on the timeline — they go straight into the movie's Library. If you need to know how to import sound files into Flash, refer to Chapter 15, "Importing and Editing Sounds in Flash."

2. Create a new Movie Clip symbol (Insert ➪ New Symbol) and give it the name **sound_1**, as shown in the Figure 18-6. This Movie Clip's timeline will be dedicated to the key_1 sound that you imported in the previous step.

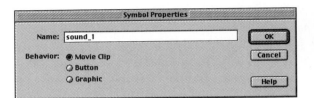

Figure 18-6: The Symbol Properties dialog with the Movie Clip behavior selected

3. Flash will automatically move you into the Symbol Editing Mode for the sound_1 Movie Clip symbol. Rename Layer 1 to **labels** and make a new layer called **sound**. On the labels layer, we need to establish three "states" or positions for the sound: no sound, initiate sound, and mute sound. Why? Remember that all Movie Clips will try to play as soon as they appear on a timeline. So, we need to make sure there's nothing on the first frame (no sound state). For the remaining two states, add two frame labels: one called **start** on frame 3, and another called **mute** on frame 15 (see Figure 18-7). Make sure that you add these labels to unique keyframes — if you try to add a label to a regular frame, the label will be attached to an earlier keyframe. Add an empty frame (F5) on frame 30 for both the labels and sound layers.

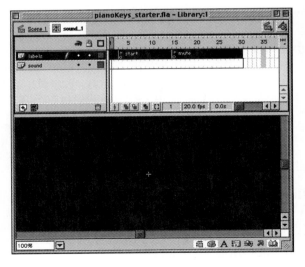

Figure 18-7: Each sound will use the same structure as the sound_1 Movie Clip: an empty first frame and two labels for starting a sound and stopping a sound.

4. Add an empty keyframe (F6) on frame 3 of the sound layer. With that frame selected, open the Sound Panel (Window ⇨ Panels ⇨ Sound), and select the key_1.aif (or key_1.wav) sound from the Sound drop-down menu. Leave the Sync setting at Event so that multiple instances of the key_1 sound can over-lap (play on top of one another). See Figure 18-8 for reference.

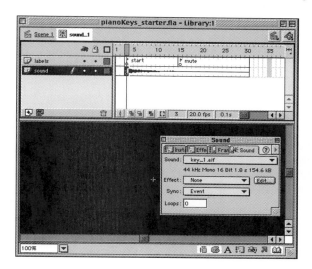

Figure 18-8: When the start label is played on the sound_1 timeline, the key_1 sound will play.

5. Repeat Step 4 for frame 15 on the sound layer. This time, however, change the Sync setting to Stop, as shown in Figure 18-9. When this keyframe is played, all instances of the sound key_1 will stop playing.

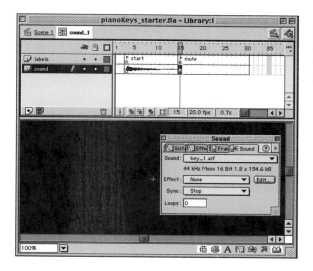

Figure 18-9: Whenever the Stop Sync setting is selected, the sound graphic on the timeline will appear as a short blue line.

6. Now we need to add some Stop actions to the timeline. Because we want each sound Movie Clip to play each time its respective key is pressed, we need to make sure playback from one action doesn't run into the timeline space of other labels. Add a new layer called **actions** and move it above the other two layers. Double-click its first frame to open the Actions Panel. Select the **Stop** action from the Basic Actions booklet, and drag it to the right pane of the Actions Panel, as shown in Figure 18-10.

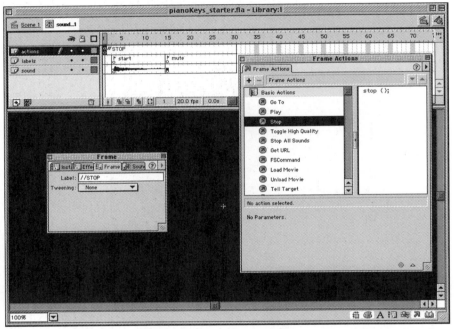

Figure 18-10: This Stop action will prevent the sound's timeline from playing when the Flash movie first loads.

7. With the first frame of the actions layer selected, open the Frame Panel and type **//stop** in the Label text field. Labels that start with // are considered comments and cannot be targeted like ordinary frame labels. The //stop comment gives you a quick indication of what this keyframe does.

Many thanks to Shane Elliott, one of the technical editors of this book, for sharing his //stop frame comment technique.

8. Copy the Stop keyframe on frame 1 by selecting the keyframe and pressing Ctrl+Alt+C (Option+Command+C). You can also right-click (Ctrl+click) the keyframe and select Copy Frames from the contextual menu. Then, select frame 10 of the actions layer and press Ctrl+Alt+V (or Option+Command+V) to paste the Stop keyframe. Repeat for frame 20. The placement of these Stop actions is a bit arbitrary — we only need to stop the playhead from playing into labels that occur later in the timeline. When you're finished with this step, your timeline should resemble the one shown in Figure 18-11.

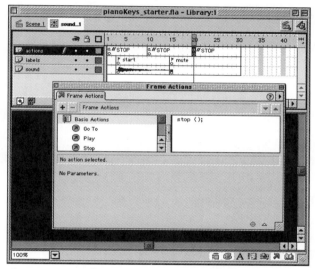

Figure 18-11: These Stop actions will keep each area of the timeline from playing into the others.

9. Next, we add an icon to this Movie Clip so that it can be seen on the Stage. Make a new layer and name it **icon**. On its first frame, draw a white rectangle. Then, use the Text Tool to add the text **Sound** (with a black fill color) on top of the rectangle. Select both items and align them to the center of the Stage using the Align Panel. With both items still selected, choose Insert ➪ Convert to Symbol (F8). In the Symbol Properties dialog, name the symbol **soundIcon**, and select the **Graphic** Behavior, as shown in Figure 18-12. Click OK.

10. Add keyframes for the soundIcon Graphic instance on frames 3, 10, 15, and 20 of the icon layer, as shown in Figure 18-13.

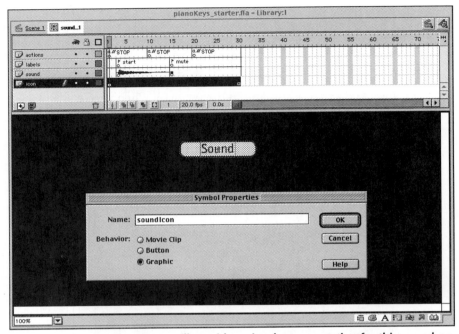

Figure 18-12: The soundIcon will provide a visual representation for this sound on the Stage.

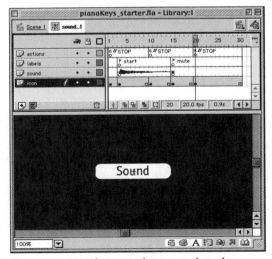

Figure 18-13: The soundIcon needs to have dedicated instances for each state of the sound_1 timeline.

11. Select the instance of soundIcon on frame 3, and open the Effect Panel. Choose the Advanced option from the drop-down menu, and type **255** in the second column text field for the **Green** color channel (see Figure 18-14).

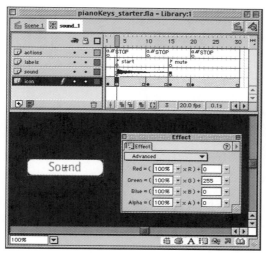

Figure 18-14: When the sound_1 timeline reaches the start label, the soundIcon will turn green.

12. Repeat Step 11 for the instance of soundIcon on frame 15. This time, however, type **255** in the **Red** color channel (see Figure 18-15). This step completes the first sound Movie Clip.

    Now, we need to repeat this process for key sounds 2 through 7 — but don't worry! Because we created a coherent structure for the sound_1 timeline, creating the other Movie Clips will be relatively painless.

13. Open the movie's Library (Ctrl+L or Command+L). Right-click (Ctrl+click) the sound_1 Movie Clip and choose Duplicate from the contextual menu (see Figure 18-16).

14. Name the new Movie Clip copy **sound_2**, and make sure that the Movie Clip behavior is selected. Click OK.

15. Double-click the sound_2 Movie Clip in the Library to edit this symbol's timeline. Remember that we're no longer working on the sound_1 timeline.

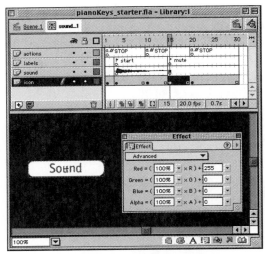

Figure 18-15: When the sound_1 timeline reaches the mute label, the soundIcon will turn red.

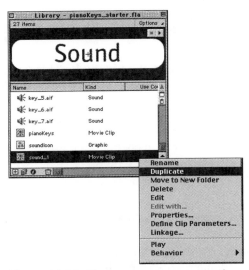

Figure 18-16: You can access many options by right-clicking (Ctrl+clicking) Symbols in the Library.

16. Select frame 3 of the sound layer, and open the Sound Panel (shown in Figure 18-17). Choose key_2.aif (or key_2.wav) from the Sound drop-down menu. Leave all other settings the same.

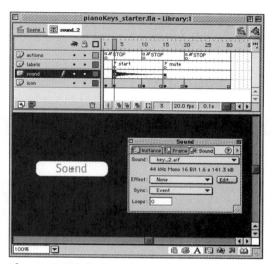

Figure 18-17: In Step 16, you're changing the sound that will be played back on the sound_2 timeline.

17. Repeat Step 16 for frame 15 of the sound layer (see Figure 18-18).

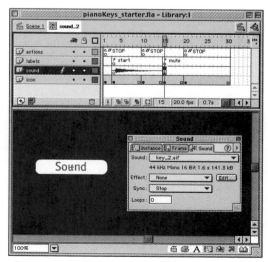

Figure 18-18: In Step 17, you're changing the sound that will be muted to key_2.aif (or key_2.wav).

That's it! You can now easily create the remaining sound Movie Clips (3 through 7) by repeating Steps 13 through 17 and incrementing the Movie Clip's name by one number each time. When you've finished creating all seven sound Movie Clips, you're ready to create a Sound Library Movie Clip.

You can refer to the pianoKeys_starter_sounds.fla file located in the ch18 folder of the *Flash 5 Bible* CD-ROM. This file has the seven sound Movie Clips in the Library, sorted in the keySounds folder.

Nesting sounds into a Sound Library Movie Clip

We have seven sound Movie Clips all ready to go, but we need somewhere to put them on the Stage. It's feasible to place each sound Movie Clip on the Main Timeline's Stage, but your Stage will start to get cluttered if many Symbols populate that space. So, we'll make a Movie Clip container for all those sounds. We refer to a container for sounds as a Sound Library, or soundLib for short.

1. Create a new Symbol by choosing Insert ➪ New Symbol (Ctrl+F8 or Command +F8). Name the symbol **soundLib** and give it a Movie Clip behavior. Click OK. The Stage switches to Symbol Editing Mode for the soundLib Movie Clip timeline.

2. Rename the first layer to **sound_1** and drag an instance of the sound_1 Movie Clip to the Stage. Open the Instance Panel and give the name **sound_1** to the instance, as shown in Figure 18-19.

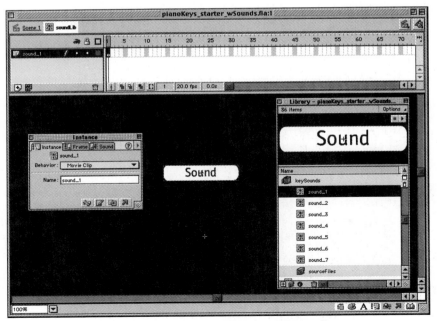

Figure 18-19: The sound_1 instance on the soundLib timeline.

Note

For consistency, it's not a bad idea to give your instance (and the layer it occupies) the same name as its parent symbol in the Library. If the sound is not going to be replicated on the same timeline more than once, then you won't have any targeting issues. It makes it simpler to match up instances with their symbols in the Library as well.

3. Create six more layers in the soundLib Movie Clip, named **sound_2** through **sound_7**. Drag an instance of each remaining sound Movie Clip onto its respective layer. Make sure that you name each instance after its symbol in the Library, just as you did in Step 2. Place each instance on the Stage from top to bottom, with the sound_1 instance at the top (see Figure 18-20 for reference). Use the Align Panel to center the instances horizontally and to space them evenly.

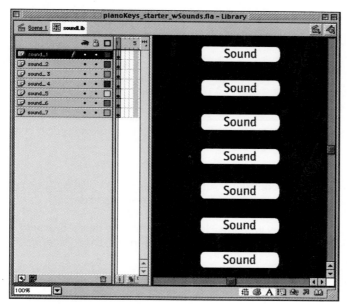

Figure 18-20: The soundLib timeline contains all seven sounds as individual instances.

4. Go to the Scene 1 timeline (the Main Timeline). Create a new layer called **soundLib**. Place an instance of the soundLib Movie Clip on the first frame of the soundLib layer. Give the instance the name **soundLib** in the Instance Panel, as shown in Figure 18-21. You may need to resize the soundLib instance so that it fits on the Stage.

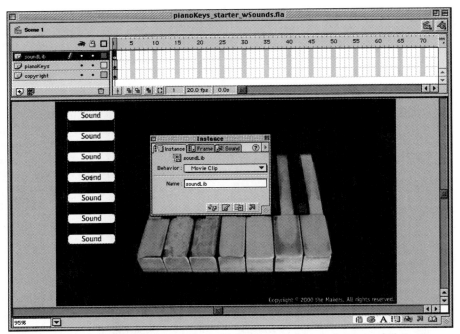

Figure 18-21: The sound Movie Clips will be accessed from the soundLib instance on the Main Timeline.

Our Sound Library is now complete. All that remains is to add actions to our pianoKeys Movie Clip to target the sounds in the correct order.

You can compare your working Flash movie to the finished Sound Library in the pianoKeys_starter_soundLib.fla file, located in the ch18 folder of the *Flash 5 Bible*.

Targeting sounds with ActionScript syntax

Now you have a Movie Clip instance called soundLib along with the instance pianoKeys, both located on the Main Timeline. Instead of using the Tell Target action, we show you how to use the Movie Clip Object in ActionScript. You may want to the review the sidebar "The New and Improved ActionScript" earlier in this chapter before you proceed. The remainder of this exercise shows you how to add Flash 5 actions to the pianoKeys timeline that will target the sounds in the Sound Library.

There will be more than one actions layer in this timeline. The actions layer in Step 1 is a new layer in addition to the existing actions layer (with the //stop comment).

1. Enter the Symbol Editing Mode by double-clicking the pianoKeys instance in Scene 1. On its timeline, add a new layer and name it **actions**. Move this new actions layer underneath the layer that contains the key_1 frame label, as shown in Figure 18-22.

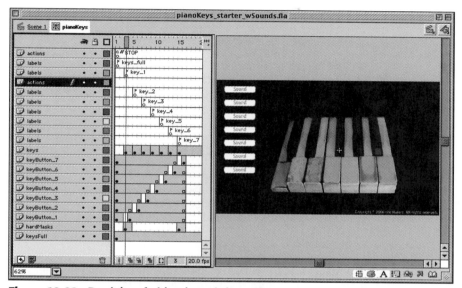

Figure 18-22: Don't be afraid to keep information separated on actions and labels layers. Separating the information will make it much easier for you to access the appropriate sections of your timelines.

2. On frame 3 of the new actions layer, we need to add actions that will play the first sound in our Sound Library. Remember that the button Instances on the pianoKeys timeline already move the playback head to each key's label. Insert a blank keyframe (F7) on frame 3.

3. Double-click the keyframe to open the Actions Panel. In the panel's options menu (located in the right corner), switch to Expert Mode (Ctrl+E or Command+E). Click the Actions list area of the panel (on the right side), and type the following ActionScript:

```
_root.soundLib.sound_1.gotoAndPlay("start");
```

See the Actions Panel in Figure 18-23 for reference. This code looks at the Main Timeline (_root), and then looks for a Movie Clip named soundLib. Then, it tells the timeline of sound_1 instance inside of soundLib to move the playback head from the stopped first frame to the start label keyframe.

Note

For the sound to play more than once, we use the `gotoAndPlay()` action instead of the `gotoAndStop()` action. If a timeline goes to and stops on a keyframe, any other actions that tell the timeline to go to the same keyframe won't work. Why? Because the playback head is already on that frame, it doesn't need to go anywhere. By using `gotoAndPlay()`, the playback head on the sound_1 timeline will go to the frame label and continue playing until it reaches the Stop keyframe just after the frame label.

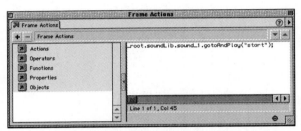

Figure 18-23: This one line of ActionScript is equivalent to the three lines of code using Tell Target (as in, `tellTarget("/soundLib/sound_1"){gotoAndPlay ("start");}`).

4. Click the Stage, and open the Frame Panel. In the Label text field, type **//play sound**. Your stage should resemble Figure 18-24.

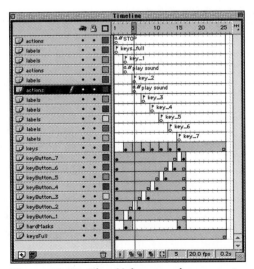

Figure 18-24: The //play sound comment lets you know what the actions on this keyframe do.

At this point, you will want to test your movie to see if the action is finding the target and playing the sound. Save your movie, and use Control ➪ Test Movie to create a .SWF movie. Make sure that the action on the keyframe works, and that you hear a sound. Notice that you'll also see the soundIcon Graphic change to green when you hit the first key.

5. Now, we need to enable all the other sounds in the soundLib instance. Create a new layer and name it **actions**. Place the new layer underneath the label layer that contains the key_2 frame label. Copy the //play sound keyframe from the previous actions layer, using the method described in Step 8 of the "Making Sound Movie Clips" section. Then, paste the copied keyframe to the new actions layer, on frame 5.

6. Double-click the new //play sound keyframe underneath the key_2 frame label layer. In the Actions Panel, we need to change the sound's target to sound_2:

```
_root.soundLib.sound_2.gotoAndPlay("start");
```

See Figure 18-25 for reference.

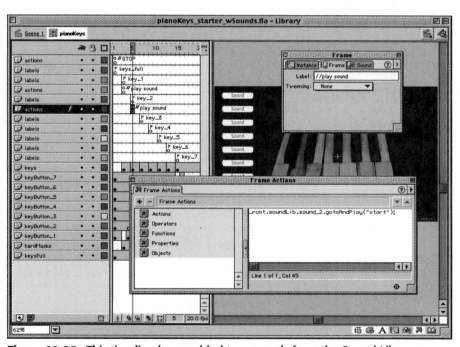

Figure 18-25: This timeline has enabled two sounds from the Sound Library.

7. Repeat Steps 5 and 6, for each key and sound. Each key_ frame label should have its own actions layer with a //play sound keyframe. When you're finished with this task, your pianoKeys timeline should resemble the one shown in Figure 18-26. Test your movie each time you add a new keyframe with Action Script. If a particular key doesn't work, then check two things: the target's name in the ActionScript, and the instance name of the sound in the soundLib Movie Clip. Most errors occur as a result of not naming a Movie Clip instance.

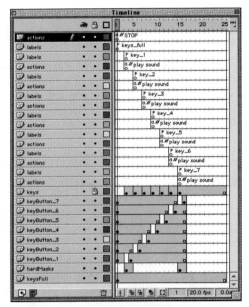

Figure 18-26: The completed pianoKeys timeline

When you've finished adding frame actions for every key, save the movie and test it. After all's been said and done, you should have a functional Flash piano that plays a sound whenever you click a piano key. If you want to change the sounds, you can either update the sound file in the Flash Library or import new ones.

How Movie Clips can add logic to a movie

A not so obvious yet significant aspect to Movie Clips is that they do not need to have any content in them. They can be used solely as empty devices that instigate interactive behavior. A Movie Clip can be just a string of empty frames with only Labels and Actions. Tell Targets from other timelines can move the playhead of empty Movie Clips in order to achieve basic levels of memory and logic in a Flash movie. We refer to these empty Movie Clips as *Logical Movie Clips*. An example of interactivity with a Logical Movie Clip is keeping score in a simple game.

Suppose you have a movie consisting of three true-or-false questions with a true button and a false button for each question. The user answers each question by clicking one or the other button. You also have a Logical Movie Clip with four keyframes. The first frame has a Stop action on it. The last frame has a Tell Target action on it that tells the main movie timeline to go to a keyframe that has a congratulations message. Finally, all the "correct" answer buttons have Tell Target actions that tell the Logical Movie Clip to go to the next frame. Here's what happens when the user plays and gets all the questions right: question one, the user clicks the correct button, and the Logical Movie Clip moves to frame 2; question two, the user clicks the correct button, and the Logical Movie Clip moves to frame 3 and so on. When the user gets to frame 4, the last frame of the Logical Movie Clip, it tells the Main Timeline to go to the congratulations frame, which says, "Congratulations, you got a perfect score!" So, what happens if the user gets a question wrong? Well, when the user gets any of the questions wrong, the Logical Movie Clip does not advance, so by the end of the game, the playhead never reaches frame 4, and the Tell Target action that causes the congratulations message to be displayed is not executed.

Tricks such as the score keeper were common tools for Flash 3 developers. Using Logical Movie Clips, inventive developers produced impressive results — even a primitive version of Pac Man exists as a Flash 3 movie (see www.spookyand thebandit.com/ for the game and to download the free .FLA file). However, now that Flash 4 and 5 movies support variables and scriptable Movie Clip properties, those kinds of Movie Clip uses are less important. Nevertheless, conceptually, it's useful to understand that Movie Clips can serve as more than just devices for embedded animation. They can also serve as containers for meta-information stored in movies.

Summary

✦ Movie Clips are the key to Flash interactivity. Each Movie Clip has its own independent timeline and playback.

✦ Each Movie Clip instance needs a unique name on any given timeline. You cannot reuse the same name on other movie clips on a timeline. You can, however, use the same instance name on different timelines.

✦ There are two types of target paths for Movie Clips: absolute and relative. Absolute paths start from the Main Timeline and end with the targeted instance name. Relative paths start from the timelines that's issuing the action(s) and end with the targeted instance name.

✦ The Slashes and Dots notations are formats for writing either absolute or relative paths. The Slashes notation is considered deprecated, and should be avoided unless you are authoring for Flash 4 or earlier players. The Dots notation is new to Flash 5 and has a more complete syntax for programming in ActionScript.

✦ The Tell Target action can be used to control Movie Clip playback in all Flash Players, while the Movie Clip Object method introduced with the new version of ActionScript works only in Flash 5 or later players.

✦ All movie clips and Flash movie elements should adhere to a naming convention.

✦ The use of a Sound Library Movie Clip enables you to store sounds in one area, and target them from others. Sounds used in a Sound Library can be updated easily, and reused in other Flash movies.

✦   ✦   ✦

Controlling Movie Clips

◆   ◆   ◆   ◆

In This Chapter

Understanding the Movie Clip Object

Using the Color Object

Accessing the Sound Object

Creating Mouse Drag behaviors

Printing Flash movie frames

◆   ◆   ◆   ◆

In the previous chapter, we established the key role that Movie Clips have within the Flash movie structure. By having a timeline that plays separately from other timelines, Movie Clips enable multiple events to occur — independently or as part of an interaction with other Movie Clips. This chapter explores how to manipulate movie clips beyond navigation actions such as `gotoAndPlay` or `stop`.

Movie Clips: The Object Overview

Flash 5's implementation of ActionScript mirrors true object-oriented programming languages. Much like JavaScript, each element in a Flash movie has a data type. A data type is simply a category to which an element belongs. According to the Flash 5 documentation, there are five data types available: Boolean, number, string, object, and Movie Clip. For our purposes, the Movie Clip *is* an object, and we'll refer to it as such throughout the remainder of the book. An object is any element in Flash 5 that has changeable and accessible characteristics *through ActionScript*. Objects can be user-defined (you create and name them) or predefined by the programming language. The Movie Clip Object is a predefined object, meaning that all of its characteristics are already described in the ActionScript language.

Cross-Reference For a brief overview of object-oriented programming concepts, please review the sidebar titled *The New and Improved ActionScript* located in Chapter 18, "Navigating Flash Timelines."

A Movie Clip Object is the same Movie Clip instance we've seen in previous chapters. Any instance of a Movie Clip is a unique object in ActionScript. However, we haven't treated it like an object in our scripting. Before we can proceed with a discussion of Movie Clips as Flash movie assets, you need to understand what predefined characteristics are available in the Movie Clip Object. See Figure 19-1 for more information.

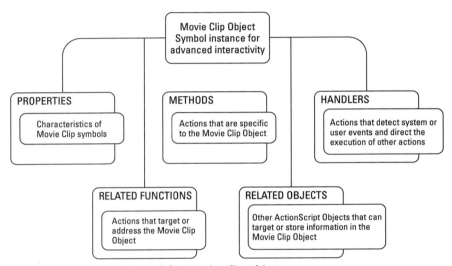

Figure 19-1: An overview of the Movie Clip Object

Movie Clip properties

Each Movie Clip instance has definable properties, or attributes, that control its appearance, size, and position. For example, you can move a Movie Clip instance to a new position on the Stage by changing the value of its X or Y coordinate. This property in ActionScript is denoted as _x or _y, respectively. Some properties have values that are read-only, meaning that these values can't be altered. One read-only property is _url, the value of which indicates the download location of the Movie Clip (or .SWF file) such as http://www.yourserver.com/swf/background.swf. Figure 19-2 is a summary of the properties of the Movie Clip Object. For more information on each property, please refer to Table 19-1.

All properties are preceded by the underscore (_) character. In Table 19-1, each property has an "R" (as in "read") and/or "W" (as in "write") designation. All properties can be read, which means that you can retrieve that property's current value. In Flash 4, these properties were retrieved using the getProperty action. The values of some properties can also be changed, through ActionScript. The table represents these properties with the "W" designation.

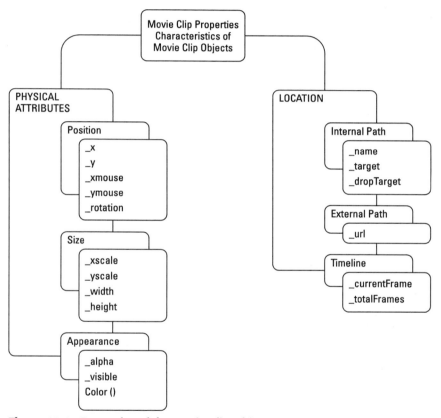

Figure 19-2: Properties of the Movie Clip Object

On the CD-ROM   Use the propInspector Movie Clip in the Library of the property_inspector.fla file on the *Flash 5 Bible* CD-ROM to see the values of Movie Clip or Movie properties.

Table 19-1
Flash Movie and Movie Clip Properties

Category	Property	Timeline	Flash 4	Flash 5	Definition
Position	_x	MC Movie	RW RW	RW RW	The horizontal distance between a Movie Clip's center point and the top-left corner of the stage upon which it resides. Increases as the clip moves to the right. Measured in pixels.
	_y	MC Movie	RW RW	RW RW	The vertical distance between a Movie Clip's center point and the top-left corner of the stage upon which it resides. Increases as the clip moves downward. Measured in pixels.
	_xmouse	MC Movie	N/A N/A	R R	The horizontal distance (in pixels) between the zero point of a Movie Clip (or the Movie) and the current position of the mouse pointer.
	_ymouse	MC Movie	N/A N/A	R R	The vertical distance (in pixels) between the zero point of a Movie Clip (or the Movie) and the current position of the mouse pointer.
	_rotation	MC Movie	RW RW	RW RW	The amount (in degrees) that a Movie Clip is rotated off plumb. Returns values set both by the Transform Panel (or Rotation modifier of the Arrow Tool) and by ActionScript.
Size	_xscale	MC Movie	RW RW	RW RW	The width of a Movie Clip instance (or Movie) as a percentage of the parent symbol's actual size.
	_yscale	MC Movie	RW RW	RW RW	The height of a Movie Clip instance (or Movie) as a percentage of the parent symbol's actual size.
	_width	MC Movie	R R	RW R	The width (in pixels) of a Movie Clip or the main Movie Stage. Determined not by the width of the canvas but by the width of the space occupied by elements on the Stage (meaning it can be less or greater than the canvas width set in Movie Properties).

Category	Property	Timeline	Flash 4	Flash 5	Definition
Size	_height	MC Movie	R R	RW R	The height (in pixels) of a movie clip or the main movie stage. Determined not by the height of the canvas but by the height of the space occupied by elements on the Stage.
Appearance	_alpha	MC Movie	RW RW	RW RW	The amount of transparency of a Movie Clip or Movie. Measured as a percentage: 100 percent is completely opaque, 0 percent is completely transparent.
	_visible	MC Movie	RW RW	RW RW	A Boolean value that indicates whether a Movie Clip instance is shown or hidden. Set to 1 (or true) to show; 0 (or false) to hide. Buttons in "hidden" movies are not active.
	Color()*	MC Movie	N/A N/A	RW RW	Color() is a Flash Object, not a property of the Movie Clip Object. Because Movie Clips can be specified as the target of the Color Object, color values of a Movie Clip can be treated as a user-definable property.
Internal Path	_name	MC Movie	RW R	RW R	Returns or reassigns the Movie Clip instance's name (as listed under the Instance Panel).
	_target	MC Movie	R R	R R	Returns the exact string in Slashes notation that you'd use to refer to the Movie Clip instance. To retrieve the Dots notation, use eval(_target).
Internal Path	_droptarget	MC Movie	R R	R R	Returns the name (in Slashes notation) of the last Movie Clip upon which a draggable Movie Clip was dropped. To retrieve the Dots notation, use eval(_droptarget). For usage, see "Creating Draggable Movie Clips" in this chapter.
External Path	_url	MC Movie	R R	R R	Returns the complete path to the .SWF file in which the Action is executed, including the name of the .SWF itself. Could be used to prevent a movie from being viewed if not on a particular server.

Continued

Table 19-1 *(continued)*

Category	Property	Timeline	Flash 4	Flash 5	Definition
Timeline	_currentframe	MC Movie	R R	R R	Returns the number of the current frame (for example, the frame on which the playhead currently resides) of the Movie or a Movie Clip instance.
	_totalframes	MC Movie	R R	R R	Returns the number of total frames in a Movie or Movie Clip instance's timeline.
	_framesloaded	MC Movie	R R	R R	Returns the number of frames that have downloaded over the network.
Global	_highquality	Movie	W	W	The visual quality setting of the Movie. 0=Low, 1=High, 2=Best. For details, see "Toggle High Quality" in Chapter 17. This is considered deprecated syntax in Flash 5.
	_quality	Movie	N/A	RW	The visual quality of the Movie. The value is a string equal to: "LOW" (no antialiasing, no bitmap smoothing), "MEDIUM" (antialiasing on a 2×2 grid, no bitmap smoothing), "HIGH" (antialiasing on a 4×4 grid, bitmap smoothing on static frames), "BEST" (antialiasing on a 4×4 grid, bitmap smoothing on all frames)
	_focusrect	Movie	W	W	A Boolean value that indicates whether a yellow rectangle is shown around buttons when accessed via the Tab key. Default is to show. When set to 0, the Up state of the button is shown instead of the yellow rectangle.
	_soundbuftime	Movie	W	W	The number of seconds a sound should preload before it begins playing. Default is 5 seconds.

R = Read property (cannot be modified); W = Write property (can be modified)

Movie Clip methods

Although the name might sound intimidating, don't be scared. Methods are simply actions that are attached to objects. As you well know, Movie Clips qualify as objects in Flash. A method looks like a regular action except that it doesn't (and in most cases, can't) operate without a Dots notation reference to a target or an object:

Action: gotoAndPlay("start");

becomes

Method: _root.gotoAndPlay("start");

As actions, interactive commands are executed from the timeline on which they are written. As methods, interactive commands are tied to specific (or dynamic) targets. Figure 19-3 lists the methods and Table 19-2 reviews every method associated with the Movie Clip Object. Some methods can be used with Movie Clip instances and with the entire Flash movie (_root, _level0, and so on), while others can only be used with Movie Clip instances. The "Flash 4" column indicates if the method (when used as an action) is compatible in the Flash 4 Player. Some commands need to be written in Dots notation, as a method (designated as "M" in the table) of a timeline or Movie Clip Object. Other commands can be used as actions (designed as "A" in the table), meaning that the Movie Clip Object name need not precede the command.

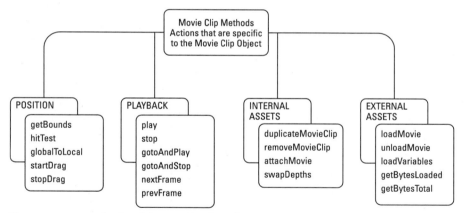

Figure 19-3: Methods of the Movie Clip Object

onClipEvent: The Movie Clip Object handler

Yet another exciting addition to Flash 5 ActionScript is the onClipEvent handler. In previous versions of Flash, our only event handlers were keyframes and Button instances. Now, we can add Actions to the wrapper of a Movie Clip instance — meaning that these actions are not added to keyframes on the Movie Clip's timeline. Nine events can be used with the onClipEvent handler. Refer to Table 19-3 for a summary of these events.

Table 19-2
Flash Movie and Movie Clip Methods

Category	Method	Flash 4	Definition	Usage

Position	getBounds M	No	Returns an object containing the minimum and maximum X and Y coordinates, as properties of that object: xMin, xMax, yMin, and yMax. These values can be used to compare the positions of two or more Movie Clips.	*timeline.getBounds(target space):*
				myBounds = myMovieClip.¬
				  getBounds(_root);
				current_xMin = myBounds.xMin;

	hitTest M	No	Returns a true value if the Movie Clip touches or overlaps a specified coordinate space or target.	*timeline.hitTest(x, y, shapeFlag):*
				timeline.hitTest(target space):
				var isTouching = myMC.¬
				  hitTest(otherMC);
				trace("isTouching is " + ¬
				  isTouching);

	globalToLocal M	No	Translates coordinates from the Main Timeline's stage to a specified Movie Clip's stage. Requires the creation of a new Object with X and Y properties.	*timeline.globalToLocal(object reference):*
				_root.myPoint = new Object();
				_root.myPoint.x = _root.¬
				  _xmouse;
				_root.myPoint.y = _root.¬
				  _ymouse;
				_myMC.globalToLocal(_root.¬
				  myPoint);

	localToGlobal M	No	Translates coordinates from a Movie Clip's stage to the Main Timeline's stage. Same requirements as globalToLocal.	*timeline.localToGlobal(object reference):*
				myMC.myPoint = new Object();
				myMC.myPoint.x = myMC._x;
				myMC.myPoint.y = myMC._y;
				myMC.localToGlobal(myMC.¬
				  myPoint);

Category	Method	Flash 4	Definition	Usage

Position	startDrag
	M, A
		Yes	Enables the user to move a Movie Clip instance on the Stage. The Movie Clip moves (or drags) in tandem with the movements of the mouse. You can specify whether the mouse pointer locks to the center of the Movie Clip instance and if the drag area is constrained to a range of X and Y coordinates (in the parent symbol or timeline space). Constraining the drag area is useful for slider controls.	*timeline.startDrag(lock, min X, min Y,*
				    max X, max Y);
				myMC.startDrag(false, ¬
				    200,0,200,200);

	stopDrag **M, A**	Yes	Stops any startDrag action currently in progress. No target needs to be specified with this action.	*timeline.stopDrag();* myMC.stopDrag();

Playback	play
	M, A
		Yes	Starts playback from the current position of the playhead on a specified timeline.	*timeline.play();*
				// plays the Main Timeline
				_root.play();
				// plays myMC
				_root.myMC.play();

	stop
	M, A
		Yes	Stops playback on a specified timeline.	*timeline.stop();*
				// stops the Main Timeline
				_root.stop();
				// stops myMC
				_root.myMC.stop();

	gotoAndPlay
	M, A
		Yes	Jumps the playhead of a specified timeline to a label, frame number, or expression, and starts playing from there.	*timeline.gotoAndPlay(position);*
				// plays from the "start"
				// label of the myMC timeline
				_root.myMC.gotoAndPlay ¬
				    ("start");

Continued

Table 19-2 (continued)

Category	Method	Flash 4	Definition	Usage
Playback	gotoAndStop M, A	Yes	Jumps the playhead of a specified timeline to a label, frame number, or expression, and stops playback.	*timeline.gotoAndStop(position):* `// stops playback on the // "mute" label of myMC _root.myMC.gotoAndStop¬ ("mute");`
	nextFrame M, A	Yes	Moves the playhead of the specified timeline to the next frame.	*timeline.nextFrame():* `_root.myMC.nextFrame();`
	prevFrame M, A	Yes	Moves the playhead of the specified timeline to the previous frame.	*timeline.prevFrame():* `_root.myMC.prevFrame();`
Internal Assets	duplicate MovieClip M, A	Yes	Makes a copy of a Movie Clip instance on the Stage (or nested in another Movie Clip). The new copy is placed directly above the parent instance, at a specified depth. Higher depth numbers appear above lower depth numbers (for example, a Movie Clip at depth 2 is stacked above a Movie Clip at depth 1).	*timeline.duplicateMovieClip (new name*, depth):* `myMC.duplicateMovieClip¬ ("myMC_2", 20); myMC_2._x = 200;` *You should not specify a new path for the copy. It will be located from the same root as the parent MC instance.
	removeMovieClip M, A	Yes	Deletes a previously duplicated Movie Clip instance. When used as a method, you do not need to specify a target. You can not remove a Movie Clip instance that is manually inserted on any timeline frame from the Library.	*timeline.removeMovieClip():* `myMC_2.removeMovieClip();`
	attachMovie M	No	Places an instance of a Movie Clip symbol from the Library into the specified timeline. Each attached instance requires a unique name and depth. Attached Movie Clip instances can be deleted with removeMovieClip.	*timeline.attachMovie(ID*, new name, depth):* `_root.attachMovie("eye", ¬ "eye_1", 1);` *You need to specify a unique identifier to attached MC symbols in the Library, using the Linkage Properties.

Category	Method	Flash 4	Definition	Usage

Internal Assets	swapDepths
	M
		No	Switches the depth placement of two duplicated or attached Movie Clips. This method is useful for placing one Movie Clip instance in front of (or behind) another instance.	*timeline.swapDepths(depth);*
				timeline.swapDepths(target);
				`// depth`
				`eye_1.swapDepths(10);`
				`// target`
				`eye_1.swapDepths(eye_2);`

External Assets	loadMovie M, A	Yes	Loads an external .SWF file into the main movie. As one of the most powerful features of Flash, this method enables you to break up your Flash movie into several smaller components, and load them as needed. This method can load .SWF files into Movie Clip targets.	*timeline.loadMovie(path, send variables*);* `myMC.loadMovie("menu.swf");` *You can also send Flash variables to the newly loaded .SWF file with an optional "GET" or "POST" parameter. This is discussed in Chapter 24.

	loadMovieNum
	M, A
		Yes	Same functionality as loadMovie. This method can load .SWF files into Levels instead of Movie Clip targets.	*timeline.loadMovieNum(path, send variables*);*
				`_level1.loadMovieNum`
				`("menu.swf");`
				*See note in loadMovie.

	unloadMovie M, A	Yes	Removes an externally loaded .SWF file from the main movie .SWF. This method enables you to dump .SWF assets when they are no longer needed. Use this method for assets loaded into Movie Clip targets.	*timeline.unloadMovie();* `myMC.unloadMovie();`
	unloadMovieNum M, A	Yes	Same functionality as unloadMovie. This method is used to remove externally loaded .SWFs that exist in Levels, not Movie Clips.	*timeline.unloadMovieNum();* `_level1.unloadMovieNum();`

Continued

Table 19-2 (continued)

Category	Method	Flash 4	Definition	Usage

External Assets	loadVariables M, A	Yes	Loads external text-based data into the main movie .SWF. This method enables you to access data (in the form of variable name/value pairs) from server-side scripts or text files, and place it in a Movie Clip target.	*timeline.loadVariables(path, send variables*);*
				`myMC.loadVariables¬`
				`("info.txt");`
				See note in loadMovie.

	loadVariablesNum M, A	Yes	Same as `loadVariables`, except that this method is used to load data into Levels, not Movie Clips.	*timeline.loadVariablesNum(path, send variables*);*
				`_level1.loadVariablesNum¬`
				`("info.txt");`
				See note in loadMovie.

	getBytesLoaded M	No	Returns the number of bytes that have streamed into the Flash Player for a specified Movie Clip (or main movie).	*timeline.getBytesLoaded();*
				`loadBytes = ¬`
				`myMC.getBytesLoaded();`

	getBytesTotal M	No	Returns the total file size (in bytes) for a loading movie or Movie Clip. Combined with `getBytesLoaded()`, you can use this method to calculate the movie's loaded percentage.	*timeline.getBytesTotal();*
				`totalBytes = ¬`
				`myMC.getBytesTotal();`
				`loadBytes = ¬`
				`myMC.getBytesLoaded();`
				`newPercent = (loadBytes/¬`
				`totalBytes)*100;`

Note: Throughout this table the ¬ character indicates continuation of the same line of code.

M = Method, A = Action

Table 19-3
onClipEvent Handler for Movie Clip Objects

Category	Event	Definition	Usage

Playback	load	This event is triggered when (a) a Movie Clip instance first appears on the Stage; (b) a new instance is added with attachMovie or duplicateMovieClip; or (c) an external .SWF is loaded into a Movie Clip target.	`onClipEvent(load){`
			`    trace( _name + " has loaded.");`
			`}`

	unload	This event occurs when (a) a Movie Clip instance exits the Stage (just after the last frame has played on the Main Timeline), or (b) an external .SWF is unloaded from a Movie Clip target. Actions within this handler type will be executed *before* any actions in the keyframe immediately after the Movie Clip's departure keyframe.	`onClipEvent(unload){`
			`    trace( _name + " has unloaded.");`
			`}`

	enterFrame	This event executes when each frame on a Movie Clip instance's timeline is played. The actions within this event handler will be processed *after* any actions that exist on the keyframes of the Movie Clip timeline. Note that enterFrame events will execute repeatedly (at the same rate as the movie's frame rate), regardless of whether any timelines within the movie are actually playing frames.	`onClipEvent(enterFrame){`
			`    trace( _name + " is playing.");`
			`}`

User Input	mouseMove	This event is triggered each time the mouse moves, anywhere on the Stage. Combined with the hitTest method, this event can be used to detect mouse movements over Movie Clip instances. All Movie Clip instances with this event handler receive this event.	`onClipEvent(mouseMove){`
			`    myX = _root._xmouse;`
			`    myY = _root._ymouse;`
			`    if(this.hitTest(myX, myY, ¬`
			`        true) == true){`
			`        trace("Mouse move over MC.");`
			`    }`
			`}`

Continued

Table 19-3 (continued)

Category	Event	Definition	Usage
User Input	mouseDown	This event occurs each time the left mouse button is pressed (or down) anywhere on the Stage. All Movie Clip instances with this event handler receive this event.	```onClipEvent(mouseDown){` ` myX = _root._xmouse;` ` myY = _root._ymouse;` ` if(this.hitTest(myX, myY, true) ==` ` true){` ` trace("Mouse press on MC.");` ` }` `}```
	mouseUp	Each time the left mouse button is released (when the user lets up on the mouse button), this event is triggered. All Movie Clip instances with this handler receive this event.	```onClipEvent(mouseUp){` ` myX = _root._xmouse;` ` myY = _root._ymouse;` ` if(this.hitTest(myX, myY, true)` ` == true){` ` trace("Mouse release on MC.");` ` }` `}```
	keyDown	When the user presses a key, this event occurs. Combined with the Key.getCode method, you can use this event handler to detect unique key presses.	```onClipEvent(keyDown){` ` newKey = Key.getCode();` ` myKey = Key.UP;` ` if(newKey == myKey){` ` trace("UP arrow is pressed.");` ` }` `}```

Category	Event	Definition	Usage
User Input	keyUp	This event happens when the user releases a key (when the finger leaves the key). Same functionality as the keyDown event.	```onClipEvent(keyUp){` ` newKey = Key.getCode();` ` myKey = Key.LEFT;` ` if(newKey == myKey){` ` trace("LEFT arrow released.");` ` }` `}```
External Input	data	This event is triggered when (a) the loadMovie action retrieves an external .SWF and puts it in a Movie Clip target, or (b) the data from a file or script with the loadVariables action (targeted at a Movie Clip instance) is finished loading.	```onClipEvent(data){` ` trace("New data received.");` `}```

Note: Throughout this table the ¬ character indicates continuation of the same line of code.

Other objects that can use the Movie Clip Object

Movie Clips can be used with other ActionScript objects to control appearance and sounds, and to manipulate data.

Color Object

This object requires a Movie Clip as a target. After a new object is created with the Color() action, you can control the color effects of the targeted Movie Clip. We'll look at the Color Object more closely in this chapter.

Sound Object

With this object, you can create virtual sound instances on a Movie Clip timeline, and target them for later use. We'll explore this object later in the chapter as well.

Mouse Object

This object controls the appearance of the mouse pointer within the Flash movie Stage. After the Mouse Object is hidden, you can attach a Movie Clip Object to the X and Y coordinates of the mouse pointer.

XML Object

If you're working with XML (Extensible Markup Language) data from a server-side script or file, then you can store the output within a Movie Clip instance for better data management. The XML Object is discussed in Chapter 24, "Sending Data In and Out of Flash."

Related functions that target the Movie Clip Object

Some ActionScript functions work directly with Movie Clip instances for printing and targeting. Refer to Table 19-4 for a summary of these functions.

Table 19-4
Related Functions with a Movie Clip Target

Function	Definition	Options
print() printNum()	This action prints a frame (or series of frames) in the targeted timeline. The printNum function is used when targeting Levels. Each frame prints to one piece of paper. Use this function to print high-quality artwork. Note that alpha and color effects do not print reliably with this method. We discuss this function later in the chapter.	*print(target, ["bmovie","" bmax", or "bframe"]);* where: *target* is the path to Movie Clip instance. Each frame of the Movie Clip is printed unless you designate printable frames with a #p frame label. and one of the following options: "bMovie" assigns a cropping area for printing, by placing artwork sized to the printable area on a keyframe with the label #b "bmax" uses the frame with the largest-sized artwork to determine the printable area. "bframe" prints each frame at its largest size to fill the paper width.
printAsBitmp() printAsBitmapNum()	Same functionality as the print() function. Use this action to print artwork that employs alpha or color instance settings. We discuss this function later in the chapter.	*print(target, ["bmovie","bmax", or "bframe"]);* See the print() function earlier in this table for descriptions of options.

targetPath()	This function is an advanced substitute for the Flash 4 tellTarget action. Actions within the curly braces are targeted at the Movie Clip instance.	*targetPath(path to Movie Clip instance){ [actions here] }*
		targetPath(_root.myMC){
		    stop();
		}

tellTarget()	This Flash 4 action can direct actions to a specific Movie Clip timeline. To be compatible with Flash 4, you need to use Slash notation for the target path.	*tellTarget(path[[actions here] }*
		tellTarget("/myMC"){
		    stop();
		}

with()	This function enables you to avoid needless replication of object references and paths. By specifying a target for the with function, you can omit the path from nested actions.	*with(path to Object){ [actions here] }*
		with(_root.myMC){
		    stop();
		}

Working with Movie Clip Properties

Now that you have a sense of what a Movie Clip can do (or be told to do), let's get some practical experience with the Movie Clip properties. This section shows you how to access Movie Clip appearance properties that control position, scale, and rotation.

Note   The following exercises use Button Symbols from the prebuilt Common Libraries that ship with Flash 5. To access buttons from the Common Libraries, use Window ➪ Common Libraries ➪ Buttons to open the .FLA library file, and drag an instance of any button into your Flash movie.

Positioning Movie Clips

You can change the location of Movie Clip instances on-the-fly with position properties such as _x and _y. How is this useful? If you want to create multiple Movie Clip instances that move randomly (or predictively) across the Stage, then you can save yourself the trouble of manually tweening them by writing a few lines of Action-Script code on the object instance:

1. Create a new movie file (Ctrl+N or Command+N).

2. Draw a simple shape such as a circle. Select the shape and press F8 to convert it into a symbol. Accept the default Movie Clip behavior in the Symbol Properties dialog, and give the new Movie Clip symbol a unique name such as **circle**.

3. With the Movie Clip instance selected on the Stage, open the Actions Panel (Ctrl+Alt+A or Option+Command+A). Turn on Expert mode (Ctrl+E) and type the following code:

```
onClipEvent(enterFrame){
     this._x += 5;
}
```

4. Save your movie as a new .FLA file, and test the movie (Ctrl+Enter or Command+Enter). The Movie Clip instance moves across the Stage.

How does this code work? In step 3, you specified that the onClipEvent (enterFrame) handler should be assigned to the Movie Clip instance. Because this particular Movie Clip has only one frame (with no stop() action in it), the enterFrame event is triggered continuously. Therefore, any actions nested within the handler will be executed repeatedly.

Our nest contains one action: this._x += 5. On the left side of the action, this refers to the object instance to which this handler and code has been applied. In our case, this refers to our circle Movie Clip instance. Immediately after this is the property for X position, _x. By adding the property _x to the object this, Flash knows that we want to change the value of this property.

On the right side of the action are the operators += and the value 5. By combining the + and = operators, we've created a shortcut to adding the value of 5 to the current X position of the circle Movie Clip instance. Each time the enterFrame event occurs, the circle Object moves 5 pixels to the right.

We dissect operators and expressions in Chapter 21, "Planning Code Structures."

To show how quickly you can replicate this action on multiple Movie Clips, select the instance of the circle Movie Clip on the Stage, and duplicate it (Ctrl+D or Command+D) as many times as you wish. When you test your movie, each instance moves independently across the Stage.

To move the instance diagonally across the Stage, add the action this._y += 5 to the onClipEvent handler nest. This moves the instance down 5 pixels each time the handler is processed.

Scaling Movie Clips

In the last example, you learned how to access the _x and _y properties of the Movie Clip Object. The next example shows you how to use a Button symbol to enlarge or reduce the size of a Movie Clip on the Stage.

1. Create a new movie file (Ctrl+N or Command+N).

2. Draw a shape (or multiple shapes), select the shape(s), and press F8 to convert the artwork into a symbol. Give the Movie Clip symbol a distinct name to identify it in the Library.

3. Select the instance of the Movie Clip on the Stage, and open the Instance Panel. Give the Movie Clip a unique name. In this example, we've named the instance **circle**.

4. From the Button Library, drag an instance of a button onto the Stage.

5. Now we create an ActionScript that will enlarge our circle Movie Clip instance. Select the Button instance on the Stage, and open the Actions Panel. In Expert mode, type the following code:

```
on (release){
    with (circle){
        _xscale += 10;
        _yscale += 10;
    }
}
```

This code uses the `with()` function to target the circle Movie Clip instance with a nested group of actions. In this case, we've increased the values of the `_xscale` and `_yscale` properties by 10 percent. With each release event on the Button symbol, the scale properties of the circle instance will be changed.

6. Save your movie as a new .FLA file, and test the movie (Ctrl+Enter or Command+ Enter). Each time you click the Button instance, your circle Movie Clip instance enlarges by 10 percent.

7. Duplicate the Button instance (Ctrl+D or Command+D). With the new copy of the Button instance selected, change the code in the Actions Panel so that it reads:

```
on (release){
    with (circle){
        _xscale -= 10;
        _yscale -= 10;
    }
}
```

By changing the += operator to -=, each click on this Button instance will reduce (shrink) the circle Movie Clip instance by 10 percent.

8. Resave your Flash file and test the movie again. Make sure that each Button instance behaves appropriately. If one doesn't work (or works in an unexpected manner), go back to the Flash movie file and check the code on both Button instances.

Caution In this simple exercise, we haven't placed any limits on the how much the Movie Clip can be reduced or enlarged. If you click the reduce button enough times, the Movie Clip instance will actually start enlarging again. We look at creating conditions and logic for Movie Clips in Chapter 21, "Planning Code Structures."

Rotating Movie Clips

Let's move along to the rotation property, `_rotation`, which is used to control the angle at which our Movie Clip is shown. In this sample, we'll use the same .FLA file that we created in the previous section.

Note If you had drawn a perfect circle in past exercises for the Movie Clip Object, then you will want to edit your Movie Clip symbol to include some additional artwork that provides an indication of orientation and rotation. If you try to rotate a perfect circle, you won't see any visual difference on the Stage. Because the value of the rotation property is determined from the center point of the Movie Clip, you can also move the contents of the Movie Clip (in Symbol Editing Mode) off-center to see updates in the `_rotation` value.

1. Select the Button instance we used to enlarge the circle Movie Clip instance. Change the button's ActionScript in the Actions Panel to:

```
on (release){
    circle._rotation += 10;
}
```

2. Now, select the Button instance we used to shrink the circle Movie Clip instance. Change the button's ActionScript in the Actions Panel to:

```
on (release){
    circle._rotation -= 10;
}
```

3. Save your movie as a new .FLA file, and test the movie. Each button should rotate the circle Movie Clip instance accordingly.

At this point, you should have a general knowledge of how to access a Movie Clip's properties. Repeat these examples using other properties that can be modified, such as _width and _height. Try combining all the properties into one Button instance or one onClipEvent handler.

Manipulating Color Attributes

The new Color Object in Flash 5 gives you unprecedented control of your Movie Clip Objects. By controlling the color (and transparency) of your artwork with ActionScript's Color Object, you can:

✦ Create on-the-fly color schemes or "skins" for Flash interfaces.

✦ Enable users to select and view color preferences for showcased products on an e-commerce site.

✦ Instantly change the color attributes of a Flash design-in-progress for a client.

Because color is controlled through the Color Object, we'll quickly review the unique methods available to this object. Refer to Table 19-5 for more information. Note that this table is organized by order of practical use.

Table 19-5
Methods for the Color Object

Method	Definition	Options
setRGB	Changes the RGB offset for the specified Color Object (and targeted Movie Clip). This method changes all colors in the targeted instance to one solid RGB color.	*colorReference.setRGB(0xRRGGBB);* where: *colorReference* is the name of the Color Object. We'll discuss the creation of Color Objects in this section. *RR*, *GG* and *BB* are the offset values (in hexadecimal) for the Red, Green, and Blue channels, respectively.
getRGB	Retrieves the values established with the last setRGB execution. If you want to reapply RGB offsets to a new Color Object, use this method.	*colorReference.getRGB();* No options or arguments for this method.
setTransform	Changes the RGB offset and percentage values for the specified Color Object (and targeted Movie Clip). This method produces visual results that resemble both left- and right-hand color controls in the Advanced section of the Effect Panel.	*colorReference.setTransform(colorTransformObject);* where: *colorTransformObject* is the name of a Object that has percentage and offset properties for Red, Green, Blue, and Alpha channels. We'll discuss the intricacies of these properties in the following sections.
getTransform	Retrieves the values established with the last setTransform execution. Use this method to reapply color transforms to new Color Objects.	*colorReference.getTransform();* No options or arguments for this method.

Creating a Color Object

To manipulate the color attributes of a Movie Clip instance, you need to create a new Color Object that references the Movie Clip instance. In the following steps, you learn to use the constructor for the Color Object. Constructors are explained in more detail in Part V, "Programming Flash Movies with ActionScript." For now, we'll work out the steps required to take control of color properties.

For the exercises with the Color Object, use the dog.fla movie in the ch19 folder of the *Flash 5 Bible* CD-ROM. Thank you, Sandro Corsaro of spanktoons.com, for supplying the artwork of the dog!

1. Select the instance of the dog graphic on the Stage. Open the Instance Panel and name this Movie Clip instance **dog**.

2. Open the Button library (Window ➪ Common Libraries ➪ Buttons) and drag an instance of a Button symbol onto the Stage. In this example, we used the Grey button-stop in the (rectangle) Button Set.

3. Select the Button instance on the Stage, and open the Actions Panel. In Expert Mode, type the following actions:

```
on(release){
redSolid = new Color(_root.dog);
redSolid.setRGB(0xFF0000);
}
```

With the on(release) handler, this Button instance's actions create a new Color Object called redSolid, which refers to the _root.dog Movie Clip instance we made in step 1. Once the redSolid Object is initiated, we can access methods of the Color Object, such as setRGB. In this example, we changed the color of the Movie Clip instance to pure red, designated by FF in hexadecimal.

4. Save the movie as a new .FLA file, and test the movie. Click the Button instance on the Stage. The color of the dog Movie Clip should change to bright red. Close the test .SWF, and return to the Flash authoring environment.

5. To see the getRGB method in action, let's create some trace messages for the Output window. Select the Button instance on the Stage, and open the Actions Panel. Add the following line of code to the end of the nest of actions inside the on(release) handler:

```
trace("redSolid's RGB numeric value = " + redSolid.getRGB());
```

6. Save the .FLA file and test the movie. When you click the button, the Output window should open and display the following text:

```
redSolid's RGB numeric value = 16711680
```

7. To change this value back to the hexadecimal value that we entered in the setRGB method, we need to convert the value to base 16. Add the following action to the on(release) action nest:

```
trace("redSolid's RGB hex value = " +
redSolid.getRGB().toString(16));
```

8. Save the .FLA file and test the movie. When you click the button, the Output window should open and display the new value:

```
redSolid's RGB numeric value = 16711680
redSolid's RGB hex value = ff0000
```

9. However, you won't need to convert getRGB's native return value to set another Color Object equal to a previous setRGB value. Duplicate the dog Movie Clip instance on the Stage, and name the new instance **dog2**. Duplicate the Button instance on the Stage. Change the new Button instance actions to:

```
on (release) {
    redSolid2 = new Color(_root.dog2);
    redSolid2.setRGB(redSolid.getRGB());
}
```

10. Save the FLA file and test the movie. When you click the first button, the dog Movie Clip instance turns red. When you click the second button, the dog2 Movie Clip instance turns red.

If you click the second button first, the dog2 Movie Clip instance will turn black. Why? Because the first button's actions were not executed, there was no previous setRGB method execution for the getRGB method to refer to. Moreover, there was no redSolid Object either. Consequently, Flash returns a zero or null value for the getRGB method. In hexadecimal color, zero is equivalent to black.

Now that you've had some experience with the Color Object's setRGB and getRGB methods, let's move on to the more complex colorTransformObject. We'll use the.FLA file from this exercise, so keep the dogs on the Stage!

Creating a Transform Object

The two remaining methods of the Color Object, setTransform and getTransform, require a more thorough understanding of RGB color space. Before the setTransform method can be used with a Color Object, we need to create a generic object using the object constructor. This generic object will become a colorTransformObject once we have assigned color properties to the generic object.

The properties of the colorTransformObject are:

✦ **ra**, the Red channel percentage

✦ **rb**, the Red Channel offset

✦ **ga**, the Green channel percentage

✦ **gb**, the Green channel offset

✦ **ba**, the Blue channel percentage

✦ **bb**, the Blue channel offset

✦ **aa**, the Alpha channel percentage

✦ **ab**, the Alpha channel offset

The *a* properties are percentage-based, ranging in value from –100 to 100. The *b* properties are offset-based, ranging from –255 to 255 (derived from 24-bit RGB color space, in which each 8-bit color channel can have a range of 256 values).

While these properties and values may seem complex, refer to the Advanced options of the Effect Panel for guidance. With the Advanced option chosen in the Effect Panel drop-down menu, the left-hand color controls are percentage-based, while the right-hand controls are offset-based. Admittedly, color is difficult to visualize from numbers. To accurately predict the color changes with setTransform, we'll use the Effect Panel to help us out.

1. Using the same .FLA file from the previous exercise, select the original dog Movie Clip instance on the Stage. Open the Effect Panel (Window ⇨ Panels ⇨ Effect), and select the Advanced option in the drop-down menu. Enter the following value on the left-hand side: **–100% Blue**. On the right-hand side, enter these values: **37 G** and **255 B**. With these values, the dog instance should be a monochrome blue with yellow eyes. Normally, you would want to write these values down so that you had them to use later. Because you have them printed here, erase them by choosing None from the Effect Panel drop-down menu.

2. Duplicate one of the existing Button instances on the Stage. On this new instance, we'll create some code that will initiate a new Color Object, and a new colorTransformObject. The colorTransformObject will be given properties that have the same values as those determined in Step 1. Then, we'll execute the setTransform method for the Color Object, using the colorTransformObject's data for the color change. Select the new Button instance, and add the following code in the Actions Panel:

```
on (release) {
    dogColor = new Color(_root.dog);
    rabidLook = new Object();
    rabidLook.ba = -100;
    rabidLook.bb = 255;
    rabidLook.gb = 37;
    dogColor.setTransform(rabidLook);
}
```

In the preceding code, we created two objects: dogColor and rabidLook. rapidLook is assigned the ba, bb, and gb colorTransformObject properties. Each of these properties is given the values we determined in Step 1. Then, we specified that the rabidLook Object be used as the target for dogColor's setTransform method.

3. Save the Flash movie file, and test the movie. Click the new Button instance that you added in Step 2. The colors of the dog Movie Clip instance should change to match those we saw in Step 1. Close the .SWF file, and return to the Flash authoring environment.

4. Now let's create a button that restores the original look of the dog Movie Clip instance. The code structure resembles that of Step 2, but we use a different way to assign color properties to the colorTransformObject. Duplicate the button created in Step 2, open the Actions Panel, and change the ActionScript code to:

```
on (release) {
    dogColor = new Color(_root.dog);
    restoreLook = new Object();
    restoreLook = {
        ra: '100',
        rb: '0',
        ga: '100',
        gb: '0',
        ba: '100',
        bb: '0',
        aa: '100',
        ab: '0'
    }
    dogColor.setTransform(restoreLook);
}
```

In the restoreLook Object, we defined all the default properties using name/value pairs separated by the colon character (:). Notice that all the properties of the restoreLook Object can be declared and given values within a {} nesting.

5. Save the .FLA file, and test the movie. Click the Button instance you created in Step 2. After the dog Movie Clip instance changes color, click the Button instance you created in Step 4. Voila! The dog Movie Clip instance reverts to its original color. Click the first Button instance that you created in the previous section. This Button instance (which uses the setRGB method) changes the appearance of the dog Movie Clip instance to a solid red color. Now click the Button instance with the restoreLook Object—the dog Movie Clip instance reverts to its original look!

While the setRGB method can alter basic color properties of Movie Clip Objects, the setTransform method is the color-control powerhouse. Any look that you can accomplish with the Effect Panel, you can reproduce with the setTransform method and the colorTransformObject.

Tip Just as the getRGB method can retrieve the values of a past setRGB method, you can transfer past setTransform values using the getTransform method.

Enabling Sound with ActionScript

Flash 5 offers many new object types, and one of the most exciting objects to use is the Sound Object. Like most objects, the Sound Object has predefined methods that you can use to control each new Sound Object. Table 19-6 provides an overview of the Sound Object and its methods.

Reasons for using Sound Objects over traditional Sound Movie Clips or keyframe sounds:

✦ Dynamic event sounds that play in a random or user-defined order.

✦ Precise control over volume and panning.

✦ The ability to dump (or erase) a Sound Object when the sound is no longer needed.

Note All Sound Objects are treated as Event sounds. You can not use Sound Objects for Stream sounds. For more information on Synch modes for sound, please refer to Chapter 15, "Importing and Editing Sounds in Flash."

Unlike the Color Object that uses Movie Clips as targets, the Sound Object uses sounds directly from the movie's Library. You cannot use the Sound Object to control sounds that are specified in the Sound Panel for any given keyframes.

The next section shows you how to create Sound Objects, using the object constructor with the attachSound and start methods.

Table 19-6
Methods for the Sound Object

Method	Definition	Options
attachSound	Creates a new instance of a sound file (.AIF or .WAV) available in the Library. The new instance becomes a part of the Sound Object and can be targeted with Sound Object methods. Unlike attached Movie Clips, attached sounds do not require a depth number.	soundObject.attachSound(libraryID); where: soundObject refers to the sound Object's name libraryID is the name of the sound in the Symbol Linkage properties (available in the Library)
start	Plays the targeted Sound Object. A sound must be attached to the Sound Object before it can play.	soundObject.start(inPoint, loopFactor); where: inPoint is the time (in seconds) in the sound where playback should begin. loopFactor is the number of times the sound should be repeated. Both of these parameters are optional and can be omitted.
stop	Stops playback of the targeted Sound Object. If no target is specified, then all sounds will be stopped. Note that this is not equivalent to pausing a sound. If a stopped sound is played later, it will start at the beginning (or at the inPoint).	soundObject.stop(libraryID); where: libraryID is the name of the sound in the Symbol Linkage properties (available in the Library)
setVolume	Changes the overall volume of the specified Sound Object. This method accepts values between 0 and 100 (in percentage units). You can not enter percentages greater than 100 percent to increase sound output beyond its original recording level.	soundObject.setVolume(volume); where: volume is a number between 0 and 100

Method	Definition	Options
getVolume	Retrieves the values established with the last *setVolume* execution. If you want to reapply RGB offsets to a new Color Object, use this method.	*soundObject.getVolume();* No options or arguments for this method.
setPan	Changes the offset of sound output from both the left and right channels.	*soundObject.setPan(panValue);* where: *panValue* is a value between −100 (full left-speaker output) and 100 (full right-speaker output). Use a value of 0 to balance sound output evenly.
getPan	Retrieves the values created with a previous setPan execution. Use this method to apply Pan settings consistently to multiple Objects, or to store a Pan setting.	*soundObject.getPan();* No options or arguments for this method.
setTransform	Changes the volume for each channel of the specified Sound Object. This method also enables you to play the right channel in the left channel and vice versa.	*soundObject.setTransform(soundTransformObject);* where: *soundTransformObject* is the name of an object that has percentage properties for left and right output for the left channel, and left and right output for the right channels.
getTransform	Retrieves the values established with the last setTransform execution. Use this method to reapply sound transforms to new Sounds Objects, or to store setTransform values.	*soundObject.getTransform();* No options or arguments for this method.

Creating sound libraries with ActionScript

In the previous chapter, you learned how to create a sound library Movie Clip that stored several individual sound Movie Clip instances. You learned how to target these sounds in order to play them (or mute them). From a conceptual point of view, manually creating each sound Movie Clip enabled you to see each sound "object" on the Stage very easily. However, we can produce the sounds for a sound library much more quickly using ActionScript.

In this section, we start with the soundLibrary Movie Clip that you made in the previous chapter. You can also open the pianoKeys_complete.fla file from the ch18 folder of the *Flash 5 Bible* CD-ROM.

1. Using the Open as Library command in the File menu, select the pianoKeys.fla file that you made in the previous chapter. Opening a Flash file as a Library enables you to access symbols and media in that file.

Caution   Do not use the Open as Shared Library command in Step 1. This is a special option that we explore in the next chapter.

2. If you don't have a new untitled Flash document open, then create a new Flash file (Ctrl+N or Command+N). Drag the soundLib Movie Clip from the pianoKeys Library onto the Stage of your new movie. If you open the Library for your new movie, you'll see that all the elements contained within the soundLib Movie Clip have been imported into your new movie. Close the pianoKeys Library window, and save your new Flash movie as **soundLib_ActionScript.fla**.

3. Select the soundLib instance on the Stage, and open the Instance Panel. Give the instance the name **soundLib**. Press the Return or Tab key to make the name "stick."

4. Double-click the soundLib instance on the Stage. In Symbol Editing Mode, create a new blank layer and delete all of the sound layers. (You always need to have at least one layer in a Movie Clip.) On the empty layer, draw an icon representing the soundLib Movie Clip. In this example, we made a white-filled rounded rectangle with soundLib black text. Center the icon elements to the Movie Clip Stage.

5. Go back to the Main Timeline (click the Scene 1 tab in the upper right, or choose Edit ⇨ Movie). Before we can attach sounds to the soundLib instance, each sound in the Library needs to be given a unique ID name in order for ActionScript to see it. Open the Library (Ctrl+L or Command+L), and select key_1.aif (or key_1.wav). Right-click (or Contrl+click on the Mac) the highlighted item, and choose Linkage in the contextual menu. In the Symbol Linkage Properties dialog, check the Export this symbol option and type **sound_1** in the Identifier text field, as shown in Figure 19-4. Click OK.

6. Repeat the naming routine from Step 4 on each sound in the Library. Increase the number that you append to the end of sound_ for each new sound (for example, sound_2 for key_2.aif, sound_3 for key_3.aif, and so on).

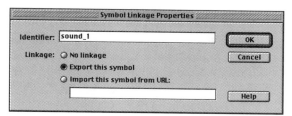

Figure 19-4: The attachSound method can only use sounds that have been set to export with the Flash .SWF file.

7. Now, we need to add the ActionScript code that will create our Sound Object. We will construct a function that, when executed will form a list of sound instances. Create a new layer named actions and double-click its first keyframe. This will open the Actions Panel. With Expert Mode turned on, type the following code:

```
function createLib(num){
    for(i=1;i<=num;i++){
```

These first lines establish the name of our function, createLib. We will want to dynamically change the number of sounds we create with this function. Therefore, we assign an optional parameter (called an argument) num that will be passed to the nested actions within the function.

The second line starts a for loop that cycles its nested actions until the condition i<=num is no longer true. i starts (or initializes) with a value of 1, and the syntax i++ tells i to increase by 1 with each pass of the for loop.

In the next step, we want the for loop to (a) create an array to store a reference to each sound instance; (b) create a new instance of the Sound Object for each sound in the Library; and (c) attach each sound in the Library to its new instance.

Note   We do not discuss the overall structure and purpose of functions, arrays, and logic in this exercise. We do, however, use these mechanisms in this exercise.

8. In the Actions Panel, add the following ActionScript to the code from Step 6:

```
        if(i==1){
            this.snd = new Array();
            trace("new array created.");
        }
        trace("this="+this);
        this.snd[i] = new Sound(this);
        this.snd[i].attachSound("sound_"+i);
    }
}
```

The first line of code in Step 7 checks whether i's current value is 1. During the first pass in the for loop, this will be true. So, the contents of the if nest will be executed.

The second line of code occurs within the if nest. This line creates a new Array named snd and is made a property of this. this refers to the object that targets (or evokes) the createLib function. Because we're only defining our function, we haven't made this function a target for any Movie Clip instance. This line will only be executed once, while the value of i is 1. When i's value increases in subsequent passes of the for loop, this line will be ignored.

The third line executes a trace action, which sends alert messages to the Output window (in the Test Movie environment). The trace action in the third line will tell us that the actions in the if nest have been executed by sending new Array created to the Output window.

The fourth line is also a trace action that tells us what object is evoking (or executing) the createLib function.

The fifth line makes a new element in the snd array. The new element is a new Sound Object that is targeted at the this timeline. Ultimately, our Sound Objects will be tied to the soundLib Movie Clip instance, which you'll see later. Each element in an array has a number indicating its position in the array. Because the value of i increases with each pass of the for loop, each Sound Object will have a unique position within the snd array.

The sixth line uses the attachSound method to take a sound element in the Library and attach it to the Sound Object in the snd array. The target for the attachSound method is specified as "sound_" + i. On each pass of the for loop, this expression will return "sound_1", "sound_2", and so on until our limit prescribed by the num argument is reached.

The complete block of code on the first keyframe of the actions layer should look like this:

```
function createLib(num){
    for(i=1;i<=num;i++){
        if(i==1){
            this.snd = new Array();
            trace("new array created.");
        }

        trace("this="+this);

        this.snd[i] = new Sound(this);

        this.snd[i].attachSound("sound_"+i);
    }
}
```

9. Now that we have a function defined to create all the Sound Objects on a this Object (or timeline), we need to have an object (for this to refer to) that uses the createLib function. In the Actions list for frame 1 of the Actions layer, type the following code after the function createLib:

```
soundLib.createLib = createLib;
soundLib.createLib(7);
```

The first line of code defines a *method* called `createLib` that used the function `createLib` as a value. Because `createLib` is a function, the `createLib` method of soundLib will execute the `createLib` function whenever the method is evoked.

The second line of code evokes the `createLib` method—the use of `()` after the method name indicates that the method is being executed, *not* defined. In addition to executing the `createLib` method, we're also sending the function the number **7** as the `num` argument. Therefore, seven Sound Objects will be created.

10. Save the Flash movie file and test it (Ctrl+Enter or Command+Enter). The Output window should open and display the trace statements:

```
new array created.
this = _level0.soundLib
```

11. Close the Test Movie window and return to the authoring environment. Double-click frame 1 of the actions layer, and add this last bit of code to the Actions list:

```
soundLib.snd[1].start();
soundLib.snd[2].start();
```

The first line of code targets the first declared element, 1, of the `snd` array, and tells it to begin playback with the start method. Remember that element 1 in the array is a Sound Object, which references the sound_1 ID in the Library.

The second line of code targets the second declared element, 2, of the `snd` array, and tells it to start.

12. Save the Flash movie and test it. Both lines of code will execute simultaneously. So, you will hear sound_1 (which is key_1.aif or key_1.wav) and sound_2 (key_2. aif or key_2.wav) play together.

Now you should practice targeting these Sound Objects with Button instances and other keyframes. To access a different sound, simply change the number in the array brackets. In the next chapter, you'll learn to load a Flash movie (a .SWF file) into another Flash movie. You can use the `loadMovie` action to place this sound library file into another movie.

You can view the completed sound library movie, soundLib_AS.fla, located in the ch19 folder of the *Flash 5 Bible* CD-ROM.

The next tutorial introduces the pan methods of the Sound Object, and shows you how to use Sound Objects with interactive projects.

During our testing of Flash 5 and the Sound Object methods, we learned that you should only attach one sound per timeline (or Movie Clip instance). While you can create more than one Sound Object instance on a timeline, you can not use the `setVolume` to control each individual sound—the volume will be set for all Sound Object instances on the targeted timeline.

Expert Tutorial: Sound Control, *by Jay Vanian*

Jay's tutorial introduces the `setPan` *method, and provides a compelling use of Sound Objects with draggable Movie Clips, which are discussed in more detail near the end of this chapter. Note that Jay's tutorial uses some Flash 4 syntax for Slash notation and property usage. As such, the tutorial will help those making the transition from Flash 4 Actions to Flash 5 ActionScript.*

Sound is one of the most powerful tools available to a designer with which to enhance a Flash project, yet it's probably been the most overlooked aspect of Flash. I think this will change with the introduction of Flash 5's new sound controls. But to use these controls (and to begin this tutorial), you first need a compelling reason to adjust either the volume or the left-to-right pan of Flash sound. Randomly setting the audio to go wild in your Flash movie won't endear you to anyone, and isn't likely to encourage repeat visits to your site. So, for this tutorial, I've chosen to use a bouncing basketball to create an interactive design situation that demonstrates this control appropriately.

For the first time, Flash 5 delivers the means to dynamically adjust the sound levels of movies by using the new sound object to control both the volume and to alter the left-to-right pan of a sound.

1. Before we get started, I'd like to offer a little bit of advice: Always determine the dimensions of your movie before you do anything else. Set these dimensions in the Movie Properties dialog. You might eventually learn this the hard way, but once you've had to resize an entire movie, you won't readily repeat the mistake. For this project, set the movie dimensions to 500×300. Also, be sure to save frequently as you work through these steps!

2. With the file size set, the first task is to import the background image, floor.jpg, position it on the default layer, and then rename this layer as **Floor**.

3. Next, import the vector basketball, gfx_basketball.ai, convert it to a graphic symbol and name it **gfx_basketball**. Follow the same procedure for the shadow, gfx_shadow. Now create a movie clip and name it **mov_basketball**; then drag an instance of gfx_basketball into the movie clip, and animate the basketball (along with a shadow) with a Motion Tween so that it bounces up and down. Be sure to use the easing controls for a more realistic bounce. (For more information on animating a bouncing ball, refer to the introductory Quick Start section of the book, "Flash in a Flash.")

   Author's Note: You'll find the source .FLA and related assets for this tutorial in the ch19 folder on the accompanying CD-ROM.

4. The last asset to be imported is the ball-bounce sound; name this **ballbounce**. In the Library, double-click the ballbounce icon to access the Sound Properties Panel, where the properties for this sound can be adjusted and tested until an acceptable balance between quality and file size is achieved. Click OK and return to the Library. Now, right-click the sound and choose Linkage from the pop-up menu. In the ensuing Symbol Linkage Properties dialog, type **ballbounce** in the Identifier box, and under Linkage options choose the radio button for Export this symbol.

5. Still working within the basketball movie clip, add a keyframe on the sixth frame. The bounce sound needs to be in synch with the bounce animation. For our sound, the sixth frame is the appropriate synchronized frame. With that keyframe selected, open the Actions Panel (Ctrl+Alt+A/Commnad+Option+A). There, we'll add actions to link this keyframe to the sound that was identified in the previous step as `ballbounce`.

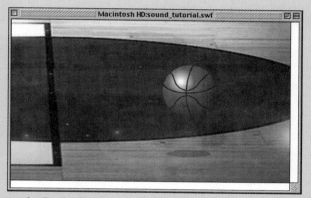

As the basketball bounces and follows the cursor, the sound mimics the change in space: The sound fades or rises as the ball moves backward and forward, and moves from left to right in synch with the position of the ball.

6. For the first action, in Normal Mode, under the Objects ➪ Sound menu of the left pane of the Actions panel, set the value for the variable `s` to `new Sound`.

7. Still, within the same menu (Objects ➪ Sound), double-click `attachSound` and enter **ballbounce** as the idName, and then scroll back to add **s** to the beginning of this action.

8. For the last action in this menu, click `start`, and then delete both `secondsOffset` and `loops` from inside the brackets. Finally, scroll back again and add **s** to the beginning of this action. The actions for the sixth frame of the basketball movie clip should now look like this:

```
s = new Sound();
s.attachSound("ballbounce");
s.start();
```

9. Now return to the Main Timeline and drag an instance of this basketball Movie Clip onto the stage and center it by using the Align Panel (Ctrl+K/Command+K). Name this instance, **basketball**. Save your work!

Continued

Continued

10. To make the basketball respond to mouse movements, we're going to make it into a draggable object. To do this, select the first frame of the top layer (labeled A for actions) and add a `startdrag` action from the Objects ⇨ Movie Clip menu, located within the Actions Panel. The target will be the basketball Movie Clip, /basketball. Both options, `Constrain to rectangle` and `Lock mouse to center` must be checked at the bottom of the panel. Coordinates for the `Constrain to rectangle` options should be Left: 10, Top: 10, Right: 490, Bottom: 200. These settings lock the Movie Clip to the center of any mouse movement, while constraining it to remain within an area of the Stage, as defined by the coordinates. The actions for the first frame of the Main Timeline now look like this:

```
startDrag ("/basketball", true, 10, 10, 490, 200);
```

Author's Note: Because this movie uses Flash 5-specific ActionScript, you may opt to use Dots notation for target names. In Step 10, /basketball would be _root.basketball.

11. On the second frame of the Actions layer, add the following actions:

```
basketball.s.getVolume();
basketball.s.getPan();
```

These actions are used to get (and then store) the volume and pan properties for the sound inside of the movie clip, basketball.

12. Next, set the variable n to equal the _y position of the basketball Movie Clip. This variable is used to scale the basketball with relationship to the mouse as it moves forwards and backwards. But because the basketball shouldn't be allowed to scale down too small, an If (n<=50) statement is used to set the variable n back to 50 if it is recognized as being any value less than 50. The code is as follows:

```
n = getProperty("/basketball", _y);
if (n<=25) {
    n = 25;
}
```

Author's Note: The value for n in Step 12 could also be written as n = _root. basketball._y; (in Flash 5 Dots notation).

13. With n set, the _xscale and _yscale properties of /basketball must now be set to equal n. When setting these properties, it's important to check the Expression box for the value n; otherwise, the movie attempts to set these properties to equal the name n instead of to the value derived from the mouse's _y position (which is what n is set to be). Here's the code:

```
setProperty ("/basketball", _xscale, n);
setProperty ("/basketball", _yscale, n);
```

Author's Note: You can change property values with the following Dots notation:
`_root.basketball._xscale = n;` and `_root.basketball._yscale = n;`.

14. (If you still haven't saved the .FLA, you are courting disaster.) For the volume to be dynamic, the sound must change with the movement of the viewer's mouse. The mechanism for this is much like the scaling of the basketball, shown previously. Because n has already been set to equal the value of the _y position, this can also be used to set the volume. All that's needed is to set the pan. To do this, a variable is assigned to get the _x position of the basketball Movie Clip:

```
s1 = (getProperty ("/basketball", _x));
```

Author's Note: *In Flash 5 ActionScript, the preceding code could be written as* `s1 = _root.basketball._x;`.

15. This variable, which equals the _x position of the viewer's mouse, is used to set the variable that returns the value for the left-to-right pan. Before setting this value, it's important to understand the sliding scale for the pan. The pan is controlled by a scale of values that range from −100 to 100, with 0 being equal balance. This works fine, on a one-to-one relationship for movies that are precisely 200 pixels wide. But for movies where the range of possible value for the _x position exceeds 200, there will be a discrepancy between the possible values of the _x position and the scale of 200 units that is used for controlling the sliding pan. Thus, if a movie is anything other than 200 pixels wide, an adjustment has to be made for the difference. A magic number must be conjured that, when multiplied by 200, will equal the width of the movie. For this particular movie, we divide the width of our movie by 200. Because the width of this movie is 500, the magic number is 2.5.

16. Now, to set s2, which will be the final value of the pan, divide the value of s1 (which is the _x position of the mouse) by the magic number, 2.5. This equation scales the width of the movie to synch with the pan scale of 200. For example, if the _x position of the mouse is 350 (in our 500-pixel-wide movie), we divide by 2.5 to get a value of 140. We always subtract 100, because our scale goes from −100 (full left) to 100 (full right). This delivers a final value of 40 for s2; in other words, 40 percent full right pan. If the _x position is 50 (in a 500-pixel-wide movie), the value for s2 is 80 percent full left pan ((50/2.5 = 20) − 100) = −80. Thus:

```
s2 = ((s1/2.5)-100);
```

If your movie were less than 200 pixels wide, you would substitute multiplication for division. In other words, if your movie was 100 pixels wide and the _x position of the viewer's mouse was at 50, you would multiply 50×2 (which is the number that, when multiplied by the width of your movie, gives you 200), and then subtract 100 — giving you a final value of 0, or equal left-right balance.

Continued

Continued

17. Next, to keep the value of the pan between –100 and 100 without any slop in either direction, an `if` statement is added to ensure that `s2` will not be greater than 100 or less than –100:

```
if (s2<=-100) {
    s2 = -100;
}
if (s2>=100) {
        s2 = 100;
    }
```

18. Finally for the last actions in this keyframe, the volume of `/basketball` is assigned to the value of `n`, and the pan to the value of `s2`. As follows:

```
basketball.s.setVolume(n);
basketball.s.setPan(s2);
```

19. In the third and final keyframe, an action is added to continuously return the movie to the second frame, whereupon the variables are reevaluated and the properties are reset:

```
gotoAndPlay (2);
```

20. The scripting is done. Have you saved your movie yet? If not, save it, and then publish the movie and bounce on!

Jay Vanian's single most favorite thing to do is actually three things, foremost of which is "taking pictures of buildings." He's also prone to "plan world strategies." Jay also enjoys Krav Maga, practice of which includes frequent visits to the emergency room. Perhaps these interests explain why he has no memories of popular culture from the year (1992) that he graduated high school, in his home town of Newport Beach, CA. Jay is billed as a multimedia artist with Pixelpushers, Inc. He was inspired to learn Flash because he "saw two sites that really stood out — Balthaser's and Shiny Entertainment's." He's worked on a number of sites, including: 11th Hour (www.hourtogo.com), THQ/Evil Dead (www.evildeadgame.com), Rhythmcraft (www.rhythmcraft.com), Crave Entertainment (www.cravegames.com), 2thebiz (www.2thebiz.com), Irvine Barclay Theatre (www.thebarclay.org), Ghosts (www.vanian.com/ghosts), and Alien Dog (www.alien-dog.com).

You can also use the `getPan` method to store values of the `setPan` method. In the tutorial example, you could create a hovering object that follows the basketball wherever you drag it. Instead of duplicating the value of the `setPan`, you could use `getPan` to retrieve the current Pan value of the sound of the basketball. The next section provides an overview of the ultimate sound control methods, `setTransform` and `getTransform`.

Creating a soundTransformObject

The two remaining methods of the Sound Object, setTransform and getTransform, work in the same manner as the transform methods of the Color Object. You need to create a generic object using the object constructor before the setTransform method can be used with a Sound Object. This generic object will become a sound TransformObject once we have assigned sound channel properties to the generic Object.

Luckily, the soundTransformObject doesn't have as many properties as the colorTransformObject, and they're much simpler to predict with trial and error testing. The properties of the soundTransformObject are:

✦ **ll**, the percentage of left channel output in the left speaker

✦ **lr**, the percentage of right channel output in the left speaker

✦ **rr**, the percentage of right channel output in the right speaker

✦ **rl**, the percentage of left channel output in the right speaker

The first letter of each property determines which physical speaker is being affected. The second letter determines which channel's output (or its volume) is played in that speaker. Each property can have a value between –100 and 100.

The steps to produce and incorporate a soundTransformObject are nearly the same as the colorTransformObject. The only difference is that you specify paths to Sound Objects rather than Movie Clip Objects for the setTransform and get Transform methods. Refer to the steps described earlier in this chapter for colorTransform Objects.

Tip   Use the soundTransformObject to vary the output of the sounds in the soundLib example you created in this section. Just like the setTransform example for the Color Object, create buttons that create and execute unique transform settings.

Creating Draggable Movie Clips

Flash 4 introduced the drag'n'drop feature, which enables the user to pick up objects with the mouse pointer and move them around the movie stage. Flash 5 has added some new ways to use drag'n'drop with the new onClipEvent Movie Clip handler. Drag'n'drop in Flash is based entirely on Movie Clips. The only objects that can be moved with the mouse are Movie Clip instances. So, if you want a drawing of a triangle to be moveable by the user, you have to first put that triangle into a Movie Clip, and then place a named instance of that clip onto the Stage. Flash's drag'n'drop support is fairly broad, but more-complex drag'n'drop behaviors require some ActionScript knowledge. We'll cover building drag'n'drop Movie Clips in two parts: "Drag'n'Drop Basics" and "Advanced Drag'n'Drop."

Drag'n'drop basics

In mouse-based computer interfaces, the most common form of drag'n'drop goes like this: A user points to an element with the mouse pointer, clicks the element to begin moving it, and then releases the mouse button to stop moving it. In Flash 4, drag'n'drop functionality could only be achieved with the use of a nested Button instance in a Movie Clip symbol. Why? The Button symbol was the only Flash symbol that responded to mouse clicks. Furthermore, because Buttons couldn't be targeted like Movie Clips, a Button instance needed to exist within a Movie Clip in order for it be draggable. Then, a Drag Movie Clip Action (in Flash 4) was added to that Button instance. This method still works in Flash 5 (with the startDrag method or action), and uses the least amount of ActionScript to enable drag behavior. Here's how:

1. Start a new movie. Create a new Movie Clip named **dragObject**.

2. Create a simple button and place it on Frame 1, Layer 1 of the dragObject Movie Clip.

3. Return to the main stage by choosing Edit ➪ Edit Movie (Ctrl+E or Command+E). Place a copy of the dragObject Movie Clip on Stage and, with it still selected, open the Instance Panel (Ctrl+I or Command+I). Type **dragObject** in the Name text field, and then press the Enter or Tab. This names our Movie Clip instance so that it can be referred to by the startDrag action.

4. Return to the Symbol Editing Mode for the dragObject Movie Clip by double-clicking the instance. Select the Button instance on the Stage, and open the Actions Panel. In the upper right-hand corner of the Actions Panel, make sure Normal Mode is selected in the options menu.

5. Click the plus (+) button in the top-left corner of the Actions Panel and select Actions ➪ startDrag. In the parameter area of the Actions Panel, type **_root.dragObject** in the Target text field. The Target option specifies which Movie Clip should begin dragging when the startDrag action is executed. Note that though our startDrag action will be applied to the same Movie Clip that houses our button, a startDrag action can target any Movie Clip from any button, or from any keyframe.

Note You can also specify an empty string (in other words, leave the Target field blank) to refer to the current timeline on which the Button instance exists. Another way of specifying the current timeline (or Movie Clip Object) is to use the term this.

6. Now remember that we want to make our Movie Clip start moving as soon as the user presses the mouse button. So, change the button's Event Handler from on (release) to on (press) by selecting the on (release) line in the Actions list, unchecking the Release option of the Event setting, and then checking Press.

7. At this point, our button, when clicked, causes the dragObject Movie Clip instance to start following the mouse pointer. Now we have to tell the Movie Clip to stop following the pointer when the mouse button is released. With the last curly brace (}) highlighted in the Actions list, click the plus (+) button and select Actions ⇨ stopDrag. The default Event Handler added is on (release), which is what we want, so that's all we have to do. The stopDrag action stops any current dragging Movie Clip from following the mouse pointer.

It is possible to use a button that is not contained in the draggable Movie Clip to stop the dragging Action. If you use a button like that, remember that when your only Event Handler is on (release), your Action will not be executed if the mouse button is released when it is no longer over the button (which is likely to happen when the user is dragging things around). You should also add an on (releaseOutside) event handler to capture all Release events.

8. Test your movie with File ⇨ Publish Preview ⇨ Flash or Control ⇨ Test Movie (Ctrl+Enter or Command+Enter).

Did it work? Great! Now we can tell you about the other basic settings for the startDrag action.

Constrain to rectangle

Check this setting in order to specify the limits of the rectangular region within which a draggable Movie Clip instance can be dragged. After you've checked Constrain to Rectangle, enter the pixel locations of the four corners of the rectangle. The pixel coordinates are set relative to the top-left corner of the Stage upon which the draggable Movie Clip instance resides. For example startDrag ("drag-me", false, 0, 0, 300, 300) would constrain the draggable Movie Clip instance named drag-me to a 300-pixel square region in the top-left corner of the Main Timeline's Stage.

If the draggable Movie Clip instance is located outside of the defined drag region when the Drag Movie Clip action occurs, then the instance is automatically moved into the closest portion of the drag region.

Lock mouse to center

This setting makes the dragged Movie Clip instance center itself under the mouse pointer for the duration of the drag. If the dragged Movie Clip instance is not already under the mouse pointer when the Drag Movie Clip action occurs, the instance will automatically be moved under the pointer, providing that the pointer is not outside the region defined by Constrain to Rectangle. When checked, this setting will add a Boolean value of true just after the specified instance name in the startDrag action.

Detecting the drop position: Using _dropTarget

In "Drag'n'Drop Basics," we showed you how to make Movie Clip instances that the user can move around. But what if we wanted to force the user to move a Movie Clip Object into a certain location before we let them drop it? For instance, consider a child's shape-matching game in which a small circle, square, and triangle should be dragged onto corresponding larger shapes. If the child drops the small circle onto the large square or large triangle, the circle returns to its original location. If, on the other hand, the child drops the small circle onto the large circle, the small circle should stay where it is dropped, and the child should receive a "Correct!" message. That kind of game is quite possible in Flash, but it requires some understanding of Movie Clip properties.

Here's how it works — we'll use the circle as an example. First, create a draggable instance of the little circle Movie Clip just as you did earlier in the "Drag'n'Drop Basics" section (put a button in a Movie Clip, put a named instance of that clip on stage, and then add the startDrag and stopDrag actions to the button). Then, you create a large circle graphic Symbol, put it into a Movie Clip, and place an instance of that Movie Clip onto the Main Timeline's Stage. Name the large circle Movie Clip **circleBig**. Here's where the Movie Clip properties come in: When the user drops any Movie Clip instance, the instance's _droptarget property is updated. The _droptarget property specifies the name of the Movie Clip instance upon which the dragged Movie Clip instance was last dropped. So if the user dropped the little circle Movie Clip instance onto the large circle instance, the _droptarget property for the little circle instance would be set to /circleBig. Knowing that, we can add an if . . . else condition to check whether the little circle was dropped onto the big circle. If it was, we simply let the little circle stay dropped, and we display a "Correct" message by targeting a Movie Clip to update a status-message contained within it. If the little circle wasn't dropped onto the big circle, we return the little circle to its place of origin by setting the X and Y coordinate properties of the little circle instance. Here's what the code on the little circle button would look like (note that the stopDrag action must occur before we check the _droptarget property):

```
on (press){
    startDrag ("_root.circle")
}
on (release){
    stopDrag();
    if (_root.circle._droptarget ) eq "/circleBig"){
        _root.status.gotoAndPlay ("correct");
    } else {
        _root.circle._x = 112;
        _root.circle._y = 316;
    }
}
```

For further study, we've included this basic child's drag'n'drop game as a sample movie called dragndrop.fla on the *Flash 5 Bible* CD-ROM in the ch19 folder.

Making alpha and scale sliders

A compelling use of a draggable Movie Clip is a slider that can alter the properties of another object. By checking the position of a Movie Clip, you can use the position's X or Y coordinate value to alter the value of another Movie Clip. In this section, we create two sliders (one for alpha and another for scale) that will dynamically change the transparency and size of a Movie Clip instance on the Stage. Many thanks to Sandro Corsaro of spanktoons.com for supplying the artwork of Robert's dog Stella and the park sign.

You need to copy the slider_basic_starter.fla file from the ch19 folder of the *Flash 5 Bible* CD-ROM. You'll use premade artwork to understand the functionality of `startDrag`, `stopDrag`, `duplicateMovieClip`, and the `colorTransform` `Object`.

Assembling the parts

In this section, we set up the basic composition of the Stage, using elements from the slider_basic_starter.fla Library. You will add artwork of a dog and a park sign to the movie. The dog artwork will be duplicated using the `duplicateMovieClip` method, and the duplicate instance will be manipulated by the sliders that we create in the next section. The park sign will be used to remove the duplicate instance using the `_dropTarget` property and the `removeMovieClip` method.

1. Open your copy of the slider_basic_starter.fla. Rename Layer 1 to **dog_1**.

2. Access the movie's Library by pressing Ctrl+L (Command+L). Open the dogElements folder, and drag the dog Movie Clip symbol onto the Stage. Place the instance in the upper-left corner of the Stage.

3. With the dog instance selected, open the Instance Panel. In the Name field, type **dog_1**, as shown in Figure 19-5.

4. Using the Text Tool, add the words **Original Dog** under the dog_1 instance. You don't need to make a new layer for this artwork.

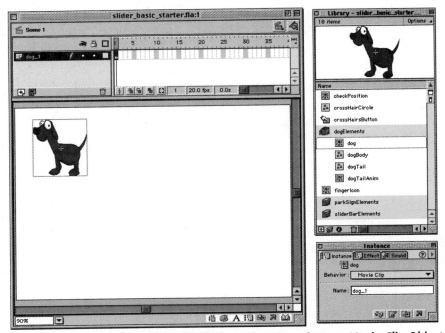

Figure 19-5: The dog_1 instance will be used as our reference Movie Clip Object. The scale and transparency of this dog instance will not be changed.

5. Create a new layer and name it **parkSign**. Move this layer below the dog_1 layer. Drag the parkSign Movie Clip symbol, located in the parkSignElements folder in the Library, to the lower-right corner of the Stage. In the Instance Panel, assign the instance the name **parkSign**. In the Transform Panel, reduce the size of the parkSign instance to **50.0%**, as shown in Figure 19-6.

6. Create a new layer called **actions**, and place it above all the other layers. Double-click the first keyframe of this layer. In the Actions Panel (in Expert Mode), add the following actions:

```
_root.dog_1.duplicateMovieClip ("dog_2", 1);
_root.dog_2._x = 350;
_root.dog_2._y = 175;
```

The first line of code duplicates the instance dog_1, names the new instance dog_2 and places it on the first depth layer of the _root timeline.

The second and third lines of code position the dog_2 instance at the X coordinate of 350 (350 pixels from the left corner of the Main Timeline Stage) and the Y coordinate of 175 (175 pixels down from the left corner).

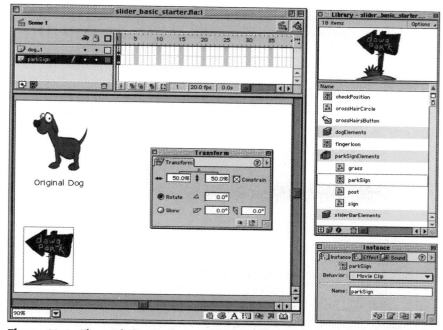

Figure 19-6: The parkSign instance will be used to remove duplicates of the dog_1 Movie Clip instance.

7. Save your movie as a new .FLA file, and test the movie (Ctrl+Enter or Command+Enter). You should see a new instance of the dog_1 Movie Clip appear on the right side of the Stage (see Figure 19-7).

Now that we have some artwork on the Stage, we can manipulate the duplicated Movie Clip with a pair of dynamic sliders.

Building the sliders

In this section, you'll create two sliders: one for scale, and one for transparency. We'll only need to make one slider Movie Clip symbol, and use a new instance for each slider. The basic "problems" of a dynamic slider are to (a) retrieve the position value of an object on the slider (we'll call this the **slider bar**), and (b) set the value of another object equal to (or some factor of) the position value of the slider bar. Finding the position of a slider bar is relatively straightforward. The difficulty lies in creating the value scale for the slider.

Figure 19-7: The duplicateMovieClip method creates a new instance of a Movie Clip Object. Unless you alter the new instance's X and Y position, it will appear directly above the parent instance.

Because we have already determined the properties that will be altered (scale and transparency) we need to establish a range of values that each property can use. Luckily, both scale (as _xscale and _yscale in ActionScript) and transparency (as _alpha) use percentage units. However, scale can be any value that's greater than 0 percent and less than 3200 percent. Alpha has a range of 0 to 100 percent. If we want to use the same parent slider for each property slider, then we need to manipulate the position values of the slider bar differently for each property. Let's start with building the basic slider.

1. Create a new Movie Clip symbol (Ctrl+F8 or Command+F8) and name it **slider**. In Symbol Editing Mode, rename the first layer **sliderRule**. On this layer, drag an instance of the sliderRule Graphic symbol (located in the sliderElements folder of the Library) onto the Movie Clip Stage.

Note

The sliderRule artwork contains a line that is 200 pixels long, bound with a circle on each end. The length of this line determines the position range for the slider bar. Therefore, our absolute range is between 0 and 200.

2. With the sliderRule Graphic selected, open the Info Panel. On the right side of the Info Panel (on the diagram of the square bounding box), make sure that the registration point is set to the top-left corner of the selection's bounding box. Then, enter the values **–28.4** for the X coordinate and **–12.4** for the Y coordinate, as shown in Figure 19-8.

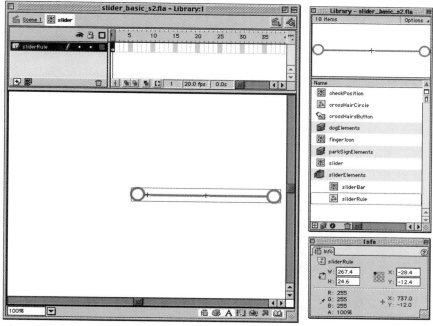

Figure 19-8: The sliderRule's starting point (just to the right of the first left-hand circle) needs to be at the slider Movie Clip's zero X coordinate.

3. Create another layer for the slider Movie Clip and name it **position**. Drag an instance of the sliderBar Movie Clip (located in the sliderElements folder of the Library) to the slider Movie Clip Stage.

4. With the sliderBar instance selected, open the Transform Panel. Type **90** in the Rotate field, and press Enter. In the Info Panel, click the center registration point in the bounding box diagram (on the right side), and enter **100** for the X coordinate and **–0.3** for the Y coordinate.

5. To see the position of the sliderBar instance, we need to assign a unique instance name. Select the sliderBar instance and type **position** in the Name field of the Instance Panel, as shown in Figure 19-9.

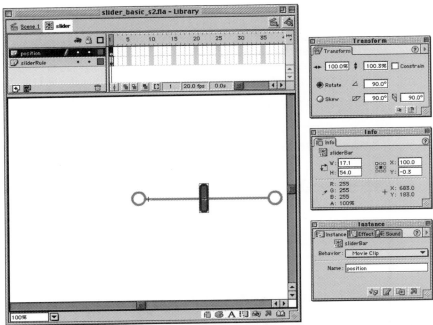

Figure 19-9: The starting X coordinate for the position Movie Clip instance is set to 100. When the Flash movie starts, this value will be applied to the scale and alpha properties of the dog_2 instance on the Main Timeline.

6. Now we need to make the position Movie Clip instance draggable. In earlier sections of this chapter, you saw how to embed an invisible button in the draggable Movie Clip in order to receive `mouseDown` and `mouseUp` events. In this example, we're going to make a button-free draggable Movie Clip instance, using the new `onClipEvent` handler for Movie Clip Objects. Select the position Movie Clip instance and open the Actions Panel. Add the following code to the Actions list:

```
onClipEvent (mouseDown) {
    if(this.hitTest(_root._xmouse,_root._ymouse, true)){
        this.startDrag (true, 10, 0, 200, 0);
        _root.state = "down";
    }
}
```

To make the position instance draggable, we need to detect the `mouseDown` event. Any Movie Clip that has the `onClipEvent(mouseDown)` handler will receive any and all mouse clicks on the Stage. Because this is the case, we need to determine whether the mouse click occurs within the space that the position instance occupies on the Main Timeline Stage.

The first line of code uses the onClipEvent handler to detect the mouseDown event (the act of pressing down on the left mouse button). When a mouse click occurs, the actions nested within the onClipEvent action will be executed.

The second line of code uses an if action to test whether the mouse click occurs on the position instance. The hitTest method can test the overlap of spaces in one of two ways: (a) by comparing a specific X and Y coordinate to an instance's occupied space, or (b) by comparing one Movie Clip instance's occupied space to another Movie Clip instance's space. If the hitTest method is used in the first way, then you can also check whether the X and Y coordinate intersects with the bounding box of the instance (false) or the entire shape of the instance (true). In this example, we use the hitTest method to retrieve the current X and Y coordinates of the mouse pointer (_root._xmouse and _root._ymouse) and compare them to the occupied space of this, which is a reference to the current instance of the position Movie Clip. If the mouse pointer is over the position instance on a mouse click, then the hitTest method will return a true condition, and execute the nested if actions.

Caution

Don't confuse the true argument of the hitTest method with the return value of the hitTest method. In this example, we have omitted the condition to check for hitTest. By doing this, ActionScript knows to infer a true comparison, meaning that the actions below the if action will only occur if hitTest returns a true value.

The third line of code will execute only if the if condition on the second line is true. Here, we enable the dragging behavior of the position instance by using the startDrag method on this. Because it's used as a method and not as an action, we don't need to specify a target instance in the arguments. The arguments prescribed here lock the mouse to the center of the object and constrain the draggable region to a bounding box defined by 10, 0 and 200, 0. This effectively keeps the position instance confined to the line of our sliderRule Graphic.

Note

We've limited the left end of the startDrag to the X coordinate of 10. This keeps the scale properties from going below 10 percent. If you try to assign a value of 0 or less to the scale properties, Flash will start scaling the instance back up to positive values in an unpredictable manner.

The fourth line of code sets a variable called state on the Main Timeline (_root) to the value of down. Because we'll be using two instances of the slider Movie Clip symbol, we need to know whether any instance has received the mouseDown event. We'll see why we need this code in later steps.

7. Now we need to be able to stop dragging the position Object when the left mouse button is released. Again, we'll use the `onClipEvent` handler to define our actions. Open the Actions Panel for the position instance:

```
onClipEvent (mouseUp) {
  if(this.hitTest(_root._xmouse,_root._ymouse, true)){
    this.stopDrag ();
    _root.state = "up";
  }
}
```

This block of code performs in the same manner that our code in Step 6 did. Once a `mouseUp` event (the act of releasing the left mouse button) is detected (line 1), we check whether the event occurred over the space of the position instance (line 2). If it did, then we stop the dragging of the position instance initiated in Step 6 (line 3). Finally, we set the `state` variable on the Main Timeline (`_root`) to `up`.

Next, we'll create two instances of the slider Movie Clip symbol on the Main Timeline Stage: one for scale, and one for alpha.

8. Exit the Symbol Editing Mode, and return to the Scene 1 timeline (the Main Timeline). Create a new layer called **scaleSlider**. Open the Library and drag an instance of the slider Movie Clip to the Stage. Name this instance **scaleSlider** in the Instance Panel.

9. Rotate the scaleSlider instance **180°**, so that the registration point is on the right side of the slider. Move the scaleSlider instance to the lower right of the Stage.

10. Create another layer called **alphaSlider**. Drag another instance of the slider Movie Clip on to the Stage, and name the instance **alphaSlider**. Rotate this instance **–90°**. Place the instance near the right edge of the Stage, as shown in Figure 9-10.

11. Save your Flash movie file and test it. You should be able to drag the position instances on both sliders.

Checking the positions of the sliders

Once we have a slider bar that is draggable, we need to access the new values of the position instance and apply the values to the properties of the dog_2 instance. To do this, we need to have a Movie Clip whose sole job is to check the X coordinate of the position instance. In this section, you'll learn how to make a Movie Clip that uses the `onClipEvent(enterFrame)` handler.

1. Create a new layer on the Main Timeline, and name it **checkPosition**. In the Library, you'll find a Movie Clip symbol with the same name. If you double-click this symbol in the Library, you'll find that there's nothing inside of this symbol except some artwork indicating the symbol's name on a single keyframe.

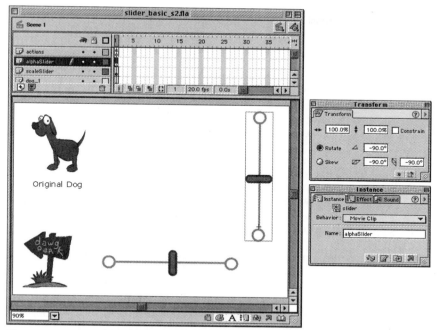

Figure 19-10: At this point, your Flash movie Stage should contain the dog and parkSign artwork, as well as two instances of the slider Movie Clip symbol.

2. Name the new instance **checkPosition** in the Instance Panel. Select the instance, and open the Actions Panel. In the Actions list, type the following code:

```
onClipEvent(enterFrame){
    _root.dog_2._xscale = _root.scaleSlider.position._x;
    _root.dog_2._yscale = _root.scaleSlider.position._x;
    _root.dog_2._alpha = _root.alphaSlider.position._x;
}
```

Because the event `enterFrame` is specified for the `onClipEvent` handler, this block of code will execute continuously in our Flash movie. Why? Any timeline will continuously enter a frame for playback, even if a `stop()` action is applied to all timelines. The speed at which the `enterFrame` event occurs is determined by the frame rate of the Flash movie (as defined by the Modify ➪ Movie dialog). The frame rate of 20 fps was already set in the sample file before you opened it. Therefore, this block will execute 20 times each second.

What happens on each execution of the `enterFrame` event? The second and third lines of code set the X and Y scale properties of the dog_2 instance to the value returned by the current X coordinate of the position instance (relative to the coordinates within the slider Movie Clip symbol).

Notice that the target path for the position instance is the scaleSlider instance in lines 2 and 3. The fourth line sets the alpha property of the dog_2 instance equal to the X coordinate of the position instance within the alphaSlider instance.

3. Save your Flash movie, and test it. When you drag the bar on the bottom scale slider, notice how the *size* of the dog_2 instance increases as you drag it to the left. Remember that we rotated this instance 180°, so it increases from right to left, not left to right. When you drag the bar down on the left alpha slider, you'll see that the *opacity* of the dog_2 instance decreases.

Note

You may be wondering why the X coordinate of the position instance is used for the alphaSlider instance, instead of the Y coordinate. Indeed, you do drag the bar on a vertical axis instead of a horizontal one. However, the position instance exists within the space of the slider Movie Clip symbol, which has a horizontal orientation in the Symbol Editing Mode. The X coordinate is derived from the stage of the Symbol Editing Mode, regardless of the instance's orientation.

Okay, we have the sliders changing the size and opacity of the dog_2 instance. However, nothing happens as we drag the bar on the alphaSlider instance toward its upper limit. Because the X coordinate of the position instance starts at 100, we won't see any visual effect to the alpha property as it increases beyond 100 percent. The lower limit of the alpha slider is 10 percent — it's prevented from going below that value by the coordinate arguments of the startDrag method. Therefore, it would be better to have the alphaScale slider convert the X coordinate of the position instance to a true 0 to 100 range of values.

To do this, we need to develop an equation that will do the work of automatically remapping values to a 0–100 scale. We know that the lowest X coordinate of the position instance is 10, and that the highest X coordinate is 200. If we want the highest position of the bar to provide 100 percent opacity, then we need to divide 200 by a number that will give us 100. Dividing 200 by 2 gives us 100. How does that work for the low end? If the X coordinate returns the lowest value of 10, then our lowest opacity value will be 5.

4. Open the Actions Panel for the checkPosition instance, and modify the fourth line to read:

```
_root.dog_2._alpha = (_root.alphaSlider.position._x)/2;
```

5. Save your movie and test it. Now, as you drag up with the bar for the alphaSlider, the opacity increases. As you drag down, it decreases.

So far, so good. However, it would be useful if the alphaSlider's position instance started with an X coordinate of 200. This would initialize the dog_2 instance with an opacity of 100 percent. We could physically move the position instance within the slider symbol to an X coordinate of 200, but that would increase the scale of the dog_2 instance to 200 percent at the start. To change only the alphaSlider's position instance at the start of the movie, we'll add an onClip Event(load) handler to the position instance in the slider Movie Clip symbol.

load events will be triggered as soon as a Movie Clip Object appears on the Stage. Within the onClipEvent action, we'll check whether the position instance is within the alphaSlider instance. If it is, then we'll move the position instance to an X coordinate of 200; otherwise, nothing will happen to the position instance.

6. In the Library, double-click the slider Movie Clip symbol. In Symbol Editing Mode, select the position instance. Open the Actions Panel and add the following code to the Actions list:

```
onClipEvent (load){
    if(_parent._name == "alphaSlider"){
        this._x = 200;
    }
}
```

This block of code will execute once, when the position instance (a Movie Clip Object) first appears (or loads) on the Stage. Remember that the position instance occurs twice: once inside scaleSlider, and again inside alphaSlider. The second line of code checks which slider instance is executing this code. We use the _parent target to access the properties of the outer Movie Clip containing the position instance. Then, we access its name property (_name) to see if its name is alphaSlider. If it is, then, in line 3, we'll change the X coordinate (_x) of this (which is the position instance) to 200.

7. Save the Flash movie and test it. This time, the alphaSlider's bar (its position instance) will immediately start at the upper limit.

Removing Movie Clips

At this point in the chapter, you have two sliders that dynamically control the scale and alpha of the dog_2 Movie Clip instance on the Stage. What if you wanted to get rid the dog_2 instance? How would you delete it? The only way to remove a duplicated Movie Clip instance is to use the removeMovieClip method or action. In this section, we show you how to use the _dropTarget property and the remove MovieClip method of the Movie Clip Object.

1. Select the dog_1 instance in the upper-left corner of the Stage, and open the Actions Panel. Type the following code into the Actions list:

```
onClipEvent (mouseDown) {
    if(this.hitTest(_root._xmouse,_root._ymouse, true) ¬
&& this._name != "dog_1"){
        this.startDrag (true, 0, 0, 550, 400);
    }
}
onClipEvent (mouseUp) {
    if(this.hitTest(_root._xmouse,_root._ymouse, true)){
        this.stopDrag ();
    }
    if(eval(this._dropTarget) == _root.parkSign){
        this.removeMovieClip();
    }
}
```

Most of this code is already familiar to you. Here we want to make only our duplicate dog instance (dog_2) draggable. We don't want to be able to remove our original dog. Even if we wanted to, we couldn't delete the dog_1 instance, as it is physically placed on the Stage of the Flash movie. Only duplicated Movie Clip instances can be removed with ActionScript.

When a mouseDown event is detected, this code uses the hitTest method to see if the mouse pointer is over the current dog instance (this) and if the current dog instance (this) is *not* named dog_1. If both of these conditions are true, then the startDrag method of the current dog instance (this) will be enabled and constrained to the dimensions of the Flash movie Stage.

When a mouseUp event is detected over the dog instance, then the stopDrag method will be executed. The last if statement checks whether the _drop Target property of the current dog instance is equal to the target path of the parkSign instance. If the dog instance is over the parkSign instance on the Stage when the dragging stops, then the current dog instance is removed.

Note We use the eval() action on the _dropTarget property because _dropTarget returns the path of the target in Slashes notation (for Flash 4 compatibility). If we use eval() on the _dropTarget property, then Flash will return the target path in Dots notation.

2. Save your Flash movie and test it. When you drag the dog_2 instance over the parkSign instance, it disappears.

Duplicating Movie Clips with new colors

What do we do after we've removed the dog_2 instance? How do we get more dog instances to use in the movie? This next section explores using the duplicate MovieClip method on a Button symbol. Not only will we duplicate the dog instance, but we'll also change its color attributes using the colorTransformObject.

Cross-Reference Please see the Color Object coverage earlier in this chapter for details on the colorTransformObject.

1. On the Main Timeline, create a new layer and name it **duplicateButton**. Drag the crossHairsButton symbol from the Library onto the Stage. Place it in the lower-right corner, between the two sliders, as shown in Figure 19-11.

2. With the crossHairsButton instance selected, open the Actions Panel and type the following code:

```
on (release) {
    _root.dog_1.duplicateMovieClip ("dog_2", 1);
    _root.dog_2._x = 350;
    _root.dog_2._y = 175;
    dogColor = new Color(_root.dog_2);
    colorTransform = new Object();
```

```
colorTransform = {
        ra: randomPercent(),
        rb: randomOffset(),
        ga: randomPercent(),
        gb: randomOffset(),
        ba: randomPercent(),
        bb: randomOffset()
}
dogColor.setTransform(colorTransform);
}
```

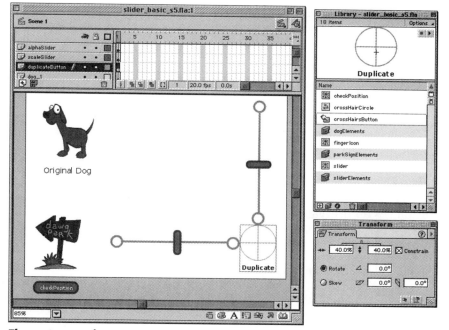

Figure 19-11: The crossHairsButton will contain actions that duplicate the dog_1 instance and apply different color attributes to the new instance.

Because we already covered the colorTransformObject earlier in this chapter, we won't explain its use here. However, we will describe the use of two new user-defined functions, randomPercent() and randomOffset(). These functions will be added to the Main Timeline (_root) in the next step. Instead of assigning fixed values to the color attributes, we supply new random values each time this button is clicked.

3. Return to the Main Timeline and select the first keyframe in the actions layer. Open the Actions Panel, and add the following code to create the `randomPercent()` and the `randomOffset()` functions:

```
function randomPercent(){
    newPercent = Math.round(Math.random()*100 + 1);
    return newPercent;
}
function randomOffset(){
    newOffset = Math.round(Math.random()*255 + 1);
    return newOffset;
}
```

Both of these functions work the same way. When each function is evoked, it will return a new random percent or offset value to the line of code that called the function. Each percent attribute (ra, ga, ba) evokes the `randomPercent()` function, while each offset attribute (rb, gb, bb) accesses the `randomOffset()` function. The only difference between the two functions is the number multiplied to the `Math.random()` method. For percent, we need a value between 1 and 100. For offset, we need a value between 1 and 255.

4. Save your Flash movie and test it. Click the Duplicate button and the dog_2 instance will be replaced with another instance of the same name. The new instance will have random color attributes.

Using the Mouse Object

While the `onClipEvent(mouseDown)` handler can be used instead of nested Button instances for draggable behavior, you may have noticed one small difference: The mouse pointer does not change the finger icon when you rollover a Movie Clip Object with `onClipEvent(mouseDown` or `mouseUp)` event handlers.

In Flash 4, we could emulate new mouse pointers by using the `startDrag` behavior (with lock to center `true`) on Movie Clips containing icon graphics. However, this technique did not hide the original mouse pointer — it would appear directly above the dragged Movie Clip instance. In Flash 5, there is a Mouse Object, which has two simple methods:

✦ `show()`: This method reveals the mouse pointer. By default, the mouse pointer will appear at the start of a movie.

✦ `hide()`: This method turns off the mouse pointer's visibility. To reveal the mouse pointer again, execute the `show()` method.

Once the Mouse Object (the mouse pointer) is hidden, you can lock a Movie Clip Object (containing a new icon graphic) to the position of the mouse pointer. If you have only one Movie Clip Object that works like a Button symbol, then attaching a new Movie Clip instance to the mouse pointer is relatively straightforward. However, in our slider example, we have two different sliders with draggable bars. If we want to enable a custom icon, we need to know which bar is being moused over, and which bar isn't.

1. On the Main Timeline, select the checkPosition Movie Clip instance. Open the Actions Panel, and add the following code to the Actions list:

```
onClipEvent(load){
    overSlider = false;
}

onClipEvent(mouseMove){
 scaleSliderOver = _root.scaleSlider.position.hitTest ¬
   (_root._xmouse,_root._ymouse,true);
 alphaSliderOver = _root.alphaSlider.position.hitTest ¬
   (_root._xmouse,_root._ymouse,true);
 if (scaleSliderOver == true || alphaSliderOver == true){
   if (overSlider != true){
     _root.attachMovie("fingerIcon","fingerIcon",2);
     Mouse.hide();
     overSlider = true;
   }
   _root.fingerIcon._x = _root._xmouse;
   _root.fingerIcon._y = _root._ymouse;
 } else {
   if(_root.state != "down"){
     Mouse.show();
     _root.fingerIcon.removeMovieClip();
     overSlider = false;
   } else {
     _root.fingerIcon._x = _root._xmouse;
     _root.fingerIcon._y = _root._ymouse;
   }
 }
}
```

The first onClipEvent handler detects the load event. Remember that the load event happens when a Movie Clip instance first appears on the Stage. When the Movie Clip instance checkPosition appears on the Stage, the variable overSlider will equal false. This variable remembers if we're currently mousing within one of the position instances.

The second onClipEvent handler detects any mouse movements on the Stage with the mouseMove event. The two variables, scaleSliderOver and alphaSliderOver, will be either true or false, depending on the return of the hitTest method for the mouse pointer and the position instances.

The first if statement checks to see if either hitTest returned a true value. The || operator indicates that only one hitTest needs to return a true value for the nested actions after the if statement to execute.

If the mouse is over either slider, then the next if statement checks whether overSlider is *not* equal to true. When the checkPosition instance first loads, overSlider is equal to false. Therefore, the actions in this second if statement will execute.

If `overSlider` is `false`, then the `attachMovie` method will be executed from the Main Timeline (_root). In this example, we are attaching the fingerIcon Movie Clip from the Library to a new instance of the same name. This new fingerIcon instance is a child of the _root timeline, and is located on its second depth layer — the dog_2 instance occupies the first depth layer. After the fingerIcon is attached to the _root timeline, we need to hide the mouse pointer. The code line `Mouse.hide();` does just that. Then, we set `overSlider` to equal `true` so that these nested actions are not repeated until we leave a position instance and reenter its space.

Note

To use `attachMovie` on Movie Clip symbols in the Library, you need to assign a unique identifier to the symbol. You can assign an identifier to a symbol by right-clicking the symbol in the Library and choosing Linkage. In our example, the identifier fingerIcon was already assigned as the identifier. We discuss Linkage Properties in more detail in Chapter 20, "Sharing and Loading Assets."

Then, we need to change its X and Y coordinates to match the position of the mouse pointer — we can still track its position even if it's hidden. The next two lines of code set the X and Y coordinates of the fingerIcon to the X and Y coordinates of the mouse pointer.

If the mouse pointer is *not* over either of the sliders, then the `else` condition tells Flash what to do on `mouseMove` events: If the mouse isn't currently dragging a slider's bar (`_root.state != "down"`), then show the mouse pointer, remove the fingerIcon Movie Clip instance, and set `overSlider` back to `false`. If the mouse has clicked a position instance *and* is overdragging the area of the position instance (see the following Tip), we still want the fingerIcon to move with the hidden mouse pointer.

Tip

Why do we need to check the state variable if the mouse isn't over the position instance in either slider? If you start to drag the position on a slider, your mouse pointer might move ahead (or beyond) the entire slider as you drag. If the mouse is dragging a position instance, we don't want to see the mouse pointer — only the fingerIcon instance should show.

2. Save the Flash movie, and test it. When you mouse over the bar of each slider, you should see the fingerIcon instance appear instead of the mouse pointer.

That might have seemed like a lot of work to hide a mouse pointer, but in the process, you learned how to attach your own icons to the mouse pointer. If you want more than two Movie Clip instances to use the fingerIcon instance, you would add them to the first `if` statement that checks `hitTest` with the mouse pointer.

Printing with ActionScript

Table 19-4, earlier in this chapter, summarizes the printing functions of ActionScript. Using the `print` and `printAsBitmap` functions, you can enable your Flash movies to output Flash artwork, text and bitmaps. With these actions, you can:

✦ **Create Flash ads that have printable specifications for e-commerce merchandise.** Imagine if the next car ad you saw on your favorite Web site automatically printed dealer locations and maps without having going to the car manufacturer's Web site?

✦ **Make Flash coupons.** You could design printable coupons for e-tailers on the Web that can be printed and redeemed at their brick-and-mortar stores.

✦ **Automate dynamic Web-generated invoices and receipts at e-commerce sites.** With Flash 5, you can format ordered items and add dynamic data to printable sheets.

✦ **Print rich vector illustrations or photorealistic bitmaps from a Web site.** Design Flash portfolio sites that print samples of stock images, or create personalized vector artwork that can be print unique images for each visitor.

✦ **E-mail printable Flash artwork to clients.** The next time you have proof of concepts or finished artwork that needs final approval, you can e-mail your clients the Flash artwork in a standalone projector or .SWF file.

✦ **Design custom contact information pages.** Sick of HTML tables that won't print your nice row-and-column–formatted pages of information consistently from browser to browser? Printable Flash frames will print beautifully each time. You could even add a visitor's contact information to a dynamic database and print it.

Although we can't describe how to do all these tasks in the space of this chapter, we will show you how to get started with the last idea. The following Expert Tutorial by Mike Richards shows you how to add `print` and `printAsBitmap` functions to his cool Flash paper airplane creator.

> **Note**
>
> Because Flash natively uses vector artwork, it translates best when output to a PostScript printer. Nevertheless, both `print` and `printAsBitmap` actions will produce high-quality output to both PostScript and non-PostScript printers.

Expert Tutorial: Creating Printable Paper Airplanes, by *Mike Richards*

Mike's tutorial provides a great example of distributing interesting printable content on the Web. Instead of formatting and printing text and standard layouts, this tutorial shows you how to print Mike's paper planes. He has already prepared a paperplane_starter.fla *file that you can find in the ch19 folder of the* Flash 5 Bible *CD-ROM. We invite you to review this file's contents and timeline structure, and copy the file to your hard drive before you start this tutorial.*

This tutorial focuses on printing using the `print` and `printAsBitmap` actions, which can print frames in any timeline within the Flash movie. These actions become a powerful tool for creating printable content for the Web.

Using the print action to print content in the Main Timeline

When completed, this first section will demonstrate how to print content located on the Main Timeline using the basic `print` action. Additionally, we will control the printable area using the Flash movie's bounding box option in conjunction with the frame labels #b and #p.

1. First we set the printing boundary box for the paper wing folding instructions. Open your copy of paperplane_starter.fla and select frame 54 on the layer print content.

2. With frame 54 of the layer print content selected, drag the Graphic symbol named bounding box from the Library to the Stage. In the Frame Panel, enter **#b** for its label name.

3. Next, we specify the frame to be printed. With frame 55 of the layer print content selected, drag paper wing to the Stage. In the Frame Panel, enter **#p** for it's label. It is important to note that all frames on the Main Timeline will print if #p is not used to designate printable content.

4. Because we will specify a bounding box to define the printable area, it is necessary to horizontally and vertically center the two symbol instances. At the bottom of the timeline window, click the Edit Multiple Frames icon and select the two symbols that we previously placed on the Stage. With both symbols selected, align the horizontal and vertical centers to the Stage using the Align Panel. When finished aligning to center, be certain to click again on the Edit Multiple Frames icon to disable its function.

6. Now we are ready to add the `print` action to the button in our movie. Move the playhead on the timeline to frame 65 and select the printer button in the lower-right corner of the Stage. Choose Window ⇨ Actions to add actions to the Button instance. With the Actions Panel open, click the Actions booklet on the left-hand side of the panel. Double-click print to place the `print` action in the Actions list on the right side, as shown in the following figure. Because there are no alpha effects to preserve in the printed material, choose As vectors in the Print drop-down menu. Because our content resides on the Main Timeline, select Target for the Location option and enter **_root** in the field. Finally, because we specified a bounding box on the Main Timeline, select Movie for the Bounding box option.

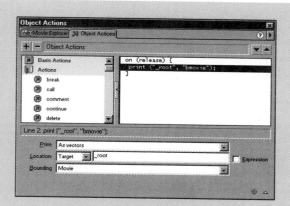

6. Save your Flash movie file and select Control ⇨ Test Movie to view the results. In Test Movie mode, select standard wing and click the printer icon in the lower-right corner to print the one page of wing folding instructions.

Using the printAsBitmap action with content in a Movie Clip instance

This next section demonstrates how to print content residing in a Movie Clip using the `printAsBitmap` action. The print area is controlled by using the Frame bounding box option. The Frame bounding box option scales the print area for each frame of content, thus ensuring that every page is printed at its maximum printable size. Note that Movie Clip instances can use either `print` or `printAsBitmap` actions, depending on the contents of the Movie Clip symbol. For purposes of demonstration, we use the `printAsBitmap` action.

1. With frame 27 of the layer print content selected, drag the Movie Clip symbol named paper shuttle from the Library to the work area located to the right of the Stage. With the instance still selected, enter **shuttle** in the Name field of the Instance Panel. It is not necessary to designate printable frames with #p in the Movie Clip Symbol time-line because we intend to print all frames within this timeline.

2. Now we are ready to assign actions to our print button. Move the playhead on the Main Timeline to frame 27 and select the printer button in the lower-right corner of the Stage. With the Actions Panel open, click the Actions booklet at the left side. Double-click print to place the `print` action in the Actions list on the right side. For the Print option, choose As bitmap because the Movie Clip symbol contains alpha effects on the second frame artwork. For the Location option, choose Target. Our print-able content resides in the shuttle instance on the Main Timeline. Therefore, we enter **_root.shuttle** to correctly target the movie, as shown in the following figure. Finally, we choose Frame for our Bounding box option because we want to scale each page of printable content to it maximum size.

Continued

Continued

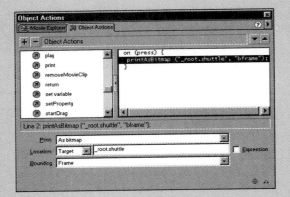

3. Save your Flash movie and select Control ➪ Test Movie to view the results. In Test Movie mode, select the first plane and customize the paper plane with art and text. To print the plane and instructions, press the printer icon in the lower-right corner of the Stage.

Printing a loaded .SWF file

For this last example, we walk through the basics of printing Flash content that is loaded into a target. This method is optimal if the content that you intend on printing is significant in size. The *Flash 5 Bible* discusses loading .SWF files in Chapter 20, "Sharing and Loading Assets."

1. Move the playhead on the Main Timeline to frame 47 and select the printer button in the lower-right corner of the Stage. Choose Window ➪ Actions to view the Actions list for the Button instance. In this example, the `loadMovie` action is used to load a two-frame .SWF file, classic_instructions.swf.

2. Next, with the Actions Panel open, select the word Placeholder, which is located just outside the top-right corner of the Stage. The `onClipEvent(load)` handler, along with `this._visible = 0`, is used to make the content invisible during playback. Even though it is hidden, this Movie Clip instance is still printable. Because content needs to be completely loaded to print, the clip event `data` is used in conjunction with the methods `getBytesTotal` and `getBytesLoaded` to confirm the completion of load before printing. For the Print option, As vectors was chosen because the printable content does not contain alpha effects. For Location, Target was chosen. The printable content will load into this Movie Clip with an instance name of classic_placeholder. Therefore, _root.classic_placeholder was entered to correctly target the movie, as shown in the following figure. Finally, the Bounding box option of Frame was chosen because we want to scale each page to its maximum printable size.

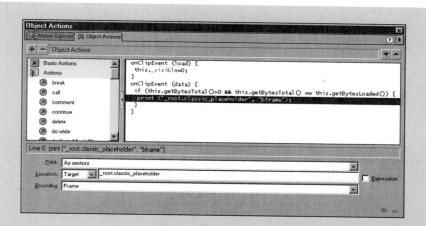

3. Save the Flash movie and select Control ⇨ Test Movie to view the results. In Test Movie mode, select the center plane and customize the paper plane with art and text. Press the printer icon in the lower-right corner of the Stage to print the plane and instructions.

Mike Richards claims that his most favorite thing to do is, "Using Flash." Perhaps that explains why he relocated to San Francisco last year to work for Macromedia. Prior to that move, he worked for American Greetings (american greetings.com) creating animated flash cards and games. It was there that he discovered Flash, "when we were looking for an alternative to Macromedia Director that artists could easily learn and use." From the year that he graduated from High School in Cleveland, Ohio, Mike deems the Chocolate War as the most memorable movie. In addition to his work for Macromedia, Mike's current site development is devoted to www.hipid.com.

Summary

✦ The Movie Clip Object has unique properties, methods, and handlers. Using Dots notation, you can access these characteristics of the Movie Clip Object.

✦ You can change a Movie Clip instance's position, scale, and rotation using ActionScript. Most physical attributes are accessed by specifying the Movie Clip's path followed by the property name, as in _root.myMCinstance._rotation.

✦ The Color Object can store new color values and apply them to Movie Clip instances using the setRGB and setTransform methods.

✦ Sound libraries can be created in less time by using ActionScript and the Sound Object. Sound Objects are created by using Linkage identifiers for sound files in the movie's Library.

✦ Flash 5 enables you to change the volume and pan values of any Sound Object at any point in your Flash movie.

✦ You can add mouse drag behaviors to your Movie Clip symbols in two ways: (a) by using nested Button instances; or (b) by using the new `onClipEvent (mouseDown)` handler combined with the `hitTest` method.

✦ The `_dropTarget` property of Movie Clip instance (instance A) indicates the path of the Movie Clip instance (instance B) upon which a Movie Clip instance (instance A) is dropped.

✦ As the sliders example demonstrated, you can use the values of one Movie Clip instance's properties to change the property values of another Movie Clip instance.

✦ The `onClipEvent(mouseMove)` event handler does not give any visible representation of a `mouseOver` on Movie Clip instances with `onClipEvent (mouseUp` or `mouseDown)` handlers. The Mouse Object can be hidden, and a custom Movie Clip instance can be attached to the coordinates of the mouse pointer.

✦ By using the `print` and `printAsBitmap` functions, you can output high-quality artwork to a PostScript or non-PostScript printer.

✦   ✦   ✦

Sharing and Loading Assets

Because most Flash movies are downloaded and viewed over the Web, Flash 5 has a number of advanced actions that are dedicated solely to controlling the download and display of movies and Library assets. Actions that check movie frame counts and file size properties let developers prevent a movie from playing before a specified portion of it has finished loading. The `loadMovie` and `unloadMovie` actions enable movies to be broken into small pieces or assets that are downloaded only if required by user choice.

Managing Smooth Movie Download and Display

When Flash movies are played back over the Internet, they *stream*, meaning that the plug-in shows as much of the movie as it can during download, even if the whole file has not been transferred to the user's system or browser cache. The benefit of this feature is that users start seeing content without having to wait for the entire movie to finish downloading.

Nevertheless, streaming has potential drawbacks. First, during streamed playback, the movie may unexpectedly halt at arbitrary points on the timeline because a required portion of the movie has not yet downloaded. Second, ActionScript code is ignored when it refers to segments of the movie that have not downloaded. These drawbacks can lead to unpredictable and often undesired playback results.

Thankfully, there's a solution. You can regulate the playback of the movie by using ActionScript code to prevent the movie from playing until a specified portion of it has downloaded. This technique is often referred to as *preloading*. A common preload sequence, or *preloader* involves displaying only a short message, such as "Loading . . . Please Wait," while the movie loads. Once the appropriate amount of the movie has been retrieved, the movie is allowed to play. Flash 5 provides basic and advanced methods of producing a preloader. This section of the chapter shows you how to use three different actions (or methods) to check the download status of a Flash movie:

✦ `If Frame is Loaded` **or** `ifFrameLoaded`: This action has been around since Flash 3, and enables you to check whether a specified frame label in the Flash movie has been downloaded by the plug-in. This is the simplest action to use to check a movie's download progress.

✦ `_framesLoaded` **and** `_totalFrames`: Introduced with Flash 4, these properties can be checked on a Movie Clip timeline or the main movie timeline (Scene 1, Scene 2, and so on). `_framesLoaded` returns the current number of frames that have downloaded into the plug-in, while `_totalFrames` returns the number of frames that exist on the specified target timeline.

✦ `getBytesLoaded()` **and** `getBytesTotal()`: These methods are new to Flash 5 ActionScript. The most accurate way to check the progress of a Flash movie download is to use these methods with other ActionScript code.

The following examples show you how to use each of these actions to monitor the download of a Flash movie over the Web.

Note   Technically, Flash movies are a progressive download file format, similar to original QuickTime 3 video movies. A progressive download is one that can be viewed before the entire file has been received by the browser. Streaming file formats are never saved as actual files in the browser cache. You can't save a streaming file, but you can typically save a shortcut or link to the file's location on the Web.

Building a basic preloader with ifFrameLoaded

In this example, we explain how to create a preloader for a 100-frame movie, where the movie doesn't begin playing until all 100 frames have been downloaded. For this exercise, make sure the Actions Panel is in Normal Mode.

1. Create a new movie with 100 frames. Rename Layer 1 to **actions**.

2. Create a new layer and name it **labels**. On the labels layer, create a blank keyframe on frames 2, 5, and 100. Label those frames **preload_loop**, **begin_movie**, and **minimum_loadpoint**, respectively.

3. Create a new layer and name it **content**. Create blank keyframes at frame 5 and frame 100. On each of those keyframes, place a large symbol such as a complex vector shape or a bitmap (you need some content in order to see the load sequence working in Test Movie Mode). See Figure 20-1 for reference.

Figure 20-1: Add content to the Main Timeline that will be preloaded.

4. On frame 1 of the Content layer, use the Text Tool to type the words **Loading . . . Please Wait**.

5. On the actions layer, create a blank keyframe at frames 3, 4, and 100.

6. Edit the actions of frame 3 by double-clicking it in the timeline. This opens the Actions Panel. Click the plus (+) button in the top-left corner of the panel and select Basic Actions ➪ If Frame is Loaded. Choose the Frame Label option in the Type setting, and select minimum_loadpoint from the Frame drop-down menu.

7. With the line `ifFrameLoaded ("minimum_loadpoint"){` highlighted in the Actions listbox, click the plus (+) button and select Basic Actions ➪ Go To. Choose the Frame Label option of the Type setting, and then select begin_movie from the Frame drop-down menu. Then check the Go to and Play option at the bottom of the parameter area. This `Go To` action, which starts playback of the real movie, will only be executed if the frame labeled minimum_loadpoint has been downloaded.

The `ifFrameLoaded` action is a one-time check. If the frame specified in `ifFrameLoaded` action has already downloaded, then the action(s) contained within the `ifFrameLoaded` statement are executed. If, on the other hand, the frame specified has not yet downloaded, then the action(s) contained are not executed, and the movie simply continues playing. In most cases, however, you won't want the movie to carry on playing until your desired frame has been downloaded, so you have to force the movie to perform the `ifFrameLoaded` check repeatedly until the specified frame is loaded.

8. To loop the `ifFrameLoaded` action, edit the frame actions of frame 4 on the actions layer by double-clicking the frame in the timeline. In the Actions Panel, add a `Go To` action to the Actions list. Choose Frame Label from the Type menu, and select preload_loop from the Frame drop-down menu. Then check the Go to and Play option.

9. Finally, add a `stop()` action on frame 100 of the actions layer. Now you're ready to test your movie and see the preloader work its magic. Choose Control ➪ Test Movie (Command+Enter or Ctrl+Enter). Once in Test Movie Mode, you'll have to configure the environment a bit to watch the simulated download. Enable the Bandwidth Profiler by checking View ➪ Bandwidth Profiler. Click frame 1 in the Profiler timeline. Select View ➪ Frame by Frame Graph. Choose Control ➪ 28.8 (2.3KB/s) (this simulates a 28.8-baud modem). To watch your movie playback as it would over the Web, choose Control ➪ Show Streaming. You'll see the playhead in the timeline looping around your `ifFrameLoaded` action while it waits for the movie to download. The green bar in the timeline indicates how much of the movie has downloaded.

On the CD-ROM

For further study, we've included this basic preloader movie as a sample movie called preloader_1.fla on the Flash 5 Bible CD-ROM in the ch20 folder.

There are some general guidelines to keep in mind when you make a preloader. First, preloaders do not work inside Movie Clips. You cannot preload individual portions of a Movie Clip. If a Movie Clip instance is placed on a frame, the frame is not considered loaded until the entire instance has finished loading. Second, you don't need to preload the entire movie when using preloaders. In our previous example, you could move the `minimum_loadpoint` keyframe to any point in the movie after frame 5. By using the streaming emulator in Test Movie Mode, you can determine approximately how much of your movie should be loaded before you allow it to play. Also, by using more than one preloader you can show the first part of a movie and then reenter a loading state before showing any subsequent parts.

Preloading with _framesLoaded and _totalFrames

In Flash 3, the only tool developers had to create preloaders was the If Frame is Loaded action. Using multiple preloaders, developers attempted to simulate a percentage-loaded feature that told the user how much of the movie had been downloaded. Although they demonstrated the ingenuity of the developers, these percentage-loaded indicators were mostly inaccurate. With the introduction of ActionScript in Flash 4, developers had a way to precisely determine the percentage of *frames* that have been downloaded to the user's system. In this section, we convert the preloading mechanism of the preloader_1.fla movie to the _framesLoaded and _totalFrames method.

1. Open the preloader_1.fla that you created in the last section. If you didn't do that exercise, then open a copy of the same file from the *Flash 5 Bible* CD-ROM.

2. On frame 3 of the actions layer, remove the ifFrameLoaded and Go To actions.

3. On frame 4 of the actions layer, remove any existing actions and add the following ActionScript in the Actions list (in Expert Mode):

```
loadedFrames = _root._framesloaded;
totalFrames = _root._totalframes;
if (loadedFrames < totalFrames){
    percentageOutput = int((loadedFrames / totalFrames)ù
        * 100);
    gotoAndPlay("preload_loop");
else{
    gotoAndPlay("begin_movie");
}
```

4. Create a new layer called **textField**. On this layer, create keyframes on frames 2 and 5. On frame 2 of the textField layer, create a text block with the Text Tool. In the Text Options Panel, change the text type to Dynamic Text, as shown in Figure 20-2. In the Variable field, enter the name **percentageOutput**. Uncheck the Selectable option.

5. Save your Flash movie as **preloader_2.fla** and test the movie.

When the playhead reaches frame 4, Flash executes the script. If, at that time, it finds that the number of frames downloaded is fewer than the number of total frames in the movie, it sends the playhead back to the preload_loop keyframe. Then it updates the percentageOutput variable to show, as a percentage, how many frames have loaded relative to the total number of frames in the movie. If, on the other hand, the number of frames loaded is not less than the total number of frames in the movie (in other words, if all the frames have loaded), then the playhead is moved to the begin_movie keyframe, and the movie proper starts playing.

An interesting variation on this advanced style of preloading is a graphical preload bar. A preload bar would simply be a small Movie Clip that contains a rectangle shape. Once placed on stage, the width of the bar would be set using the _xscale property to adjust the width percentage of the rectangle Movie Clip instance. The following steps show you how to do this.

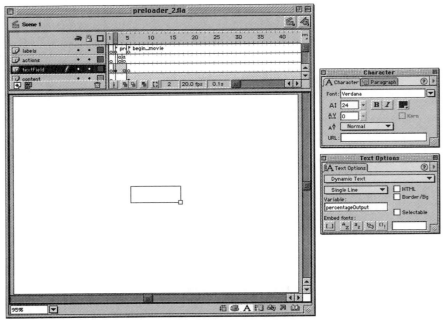

Figure 20-2: Make sure you change the text block into a dynamic text field.

6. Create new layer called **loaderBar**. Create keyframes on frames 2 and 5 of the loaderBar layer. On frame 2, draw a long rectangle, as you want it to be appear when the movie has finished loading. Select the rectangle, and press the F8 key. Call this Movie Clip symbol **loaderBar**.

7. With the loaderBar instance selected on the Stage, open the Instance Panel and name the instance loaderBar. Double-click the instance to enter the Symbol Editing Mode, and position the rectangle shape so that the left edge is at the zero X coordinate, as shown in Figure 20-3.

8. Go back to the Main Timeline, and reposition the loaderBar instance so that it's centered on the Stage.

9. Double-click frame 4 of the actions layer, and change the ActionScript to the match the following code block:

```
loadedFrames = _root._framesloaded;
totalFrames = _root._totalframes;
if (loadedFrames < totalFrames){
    percentageOutput = int((loadedFrames / totalFrames)ù
        * 100);
    _root.loaderBar._xscale = percentageOutput;
    gotoAndPlay("preload_loop");
}
else{
    gotoAndPlay("begin_movie");
}
```

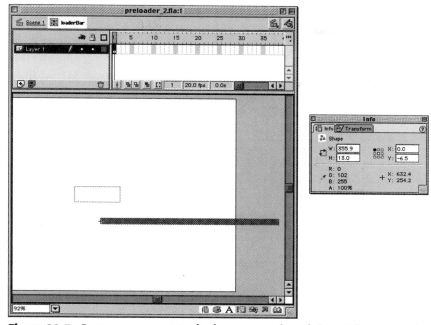

Figure 20-3: Because we want to the bar to grow from left to right, we need to make sure that the registration point is on the left edge of the rectangle.

10. Save your Flash movie, and test it.

On the CD-ROM

You can examine the finished Flash movie, preloader_2.fla, located in the ch20 folder of the Flash 5 Bible CD-ROM.

Both the text-based and graphical preloaders are not accurate measurements of downloaded file size. They measure only the number of frames that have been downloaded. So, if the content of your movie is distributed evenly over the frames of the timeline, the frames-based percentage values will closely match the real file-size transfer percentage.

If, however, your heaviest content occurs only on sporadic frames (as our examples have demonstrated), then the frames-based percentage values may appear imprecise to the user. When such a movie is streamed, the progress bar will jump to discrete sizes regardless of connection speed or duration. Our next example demonstrates a new Flash 5 method for measuring the load progress of a Flash movie.

Using getBytesLoaded() and getBytesTotal() in Flash 5

By far the most accurate way to check the loading progress of a streaming Flash movie is to use the new Flash 5 methods getBytesLoaded() and getBytesTotal(). As their names indicate, you can now access the actual number of bytes that have downloaded to the browser or stand-alone player. With these new methods, we don't need to try to disperse content evenly over frames on the Main Timeline — we can simply place our content where and when we want it.

We continue with the preloader_2.fla that we created in the last exercise. If you want to open a fresh file, use a copy of the preloader_2.fla file from the Flash 5 Bible.

1. Double-click frame 4 on the actions layer. In the Actions Panel, change the Actions list to match the following code block. Pay particular attention to the new variable names we've assigned:

```
loadedBytes = _root.getBytesLoaded();
totalBytes = _root.getBytesTotal();
if (loadedBytes < totalBytes){
    percentageOutput = int((loadedBytes / totalBytes)ù
        * 100);
    _root.loaderBar._xscale = percentageOutput;
    gotoAndPlay("preload_loop");
}
else{
    gotoAndPlay("begin_movie");
}
```

In Step 1, we've changed loadedFrames to loadedBytes, and more importantly, we've made the value of loadedBytes equal the current number of bytes of the main movie file (_root) that have loaded into the Flash Player. Likewise, we've switched totalFrames to totalBytes, and made its value equal to the total number of bytes for the main movie file. Make sure you've also changed the if condition to indicate the new variable names, as well as the math expression for the percentageOutput variable.

2. Save your Flash movie as **preloader_3.fla**, and test it. Make sure the Bandwidth Profiler is in Show Streaming Mode.

After you've tested your movie, you'll see that the loaderBar displays the true loading progress of the Flash movie. Not only can you check the progress of the Main Timeline, but you can also use getBytesLoaded() and getBytesTotal() on loaded .SWF movies. The following Expert Tutorial by Gareth Pursehouse shows you how to check the progress of .SWF files that are loaded into the main movie .SWF. We discuss the actual process of loading external .SWF files later in this chapter.

Expert Tutorial: Preloading Audio .SWF Files, by *Gareth Pursehouse*

Gareth's tutorial demonstrates the new `getBytesTotal()` *and* `getBytesLoaded()` *methods of the Movie Clip Object. He also uses the* `loadMovie` *action, which is discussed in more detail in the next section of this chapter. Gareth's ActionScript code uses a combination of Flash 4 and 5 syntax. You will want to make a copy of the music_preloader.fla and stream.swf files located in the ch20 folder of the Flash 5 Bible CD-ROM.*

Ever need to play and control music in a Flash movie? Unfortunately, it's not as easy as just dropping a song on to the Stage, with a prebuilt interface or control bar that Web visitors can access to control the sound. You need a loading display, a progress display for playback, and playback controls. Otherwise, your Flash movie might end up on worstsites.com, in which case, you're out of a job and your kids never get braces. Luckily you bought this book because we're going to show you how to control your external music .SWF files.

This example focuses on several new Movie Clip Object methods such as `getBytesTotal()` and `getBytesLoaded()`. You learn to create a loop to evaluate properties of an external .SWF file that is loaded into a target, how to display loading and playblack progress on a display bar, and how to create play control buttons for .SWF files that use Stream audio synch modes.

Concept overview

Open a copy of the music_preloader.fla file located in the ch20 folder of the *Flash 5 Bible* CD-ROM. You'll see three top layers on the Main Timeline, named !song, _song and song. The instances !song and _song use the same Movie Clip symbol, `load checker`, found in the Library. We will use this Movie Clip symbol to show the loading status and the playback status. In order to let the ActionScript routine know which status to display, we name the instance with either an _ or a ! as the first character.

A simple check of the first character of the instance's _name value will tell the script inside of `load checker` which routine to run:

```
if (substring(_name, 1, 1) eq "_") {
    // insert actions for playback status display...
} else if (substring(_name, 1, 1) eq "!") {
    // insert actions for loading status display...
}
```

Because the whole idea of programming is to make code as flexible and dynamic as possible, we will have the routine check the _name of the instance to define whether to display the loading progress, or the playback progress.

After the initial _ or ! character, the word *song* is used in the name of both instances. We'll use this suffix to also indicate the Movie Clip instance that is being targeted with a `loadMovie` action (which we'll see later).

Continued

Continued

The Movie Clip instance that will display the playback progress will be called _song, and the instance that will display the loading progress on the display bar !song. These names will also direct our ActionScript code to check the loading or playing status of the Movie Clip instance named song.

The load checker Movie Clip symbol, which has two unique instances on the Stage, will continuously check the progress of the loading .SWF file, targeted at the instance song. Because we don't want the ActionScript code to display status information before the Movie Clip has been loaded, we put a variable in the first frame of the song Movie Clip instance (which is the load placeholder symbol in the Library) to define that the load has not yet begun:

```
loading = false;
```

In our load checker Movie Clip symbol, we start the ActionScript routine on frame 2 with an if statement that checks for that variable:

```
if (_parent[substring(_name, 2, -1)].loading != false) {
```

By referring to a substring (a particular section) of the current instance's name, we can access a completely different instance nested outside of the current instance. This method of addressing Movie Clip instances allows easier alterations to the code and display mechanisms, so that you can reuse the load checker in different sections of your .SWF movie.

This advanced syntax for addressing Movie Clip objects is discussed in Chapter 18, "Navigating Flash Timelines" and Chapter 19, "Controlling Movie Clips."

Building the progress bar

To display the results of the ActionScript code within the load checker symbol, some other Movie Clips are needed. One of the Movie Clips, which we call msize, will be the background for the loading and playback display bars. This Movie Clip must be the exact size of the full display bar, as its width is used within the routine to determine placement and length of the marker Movie Clip. With an instance of the display bar named msize in the load checker symbol, we set a variable called mw that stores the width value (in pixels) of the display bar:

```
mw = msize._width;
```

This line of code occurs on the first frame of the load checker Movie Clip symbol.

The marker Movie Clip will be our second Movie Clip for the display bars. In this example, we use a simple rectangle. Because it will be continually stretched (or moved, depending upon the instance) along the background msize Movie Clip, its size shouldn't interfere with any artwork or design on it.

Initiating the loadMovie action

On the loadButton layer of the Main Timeline, we have a Button instance with the text Load. If you select this instance and open the Actions Panel, you'll see the following code:

```
on (release) {
    loadMovie (loadfile, "song");
    song._visible = 0;
}
```

When a user clicks the button, a loadMovie action will execute. It will load a .SWF file, whose name will be determined by the loadfile variable, into the song Movie Clip instance. The loadfile variable, in our example, is actually the text field located on the loadfile layer of the Main Timeline. You'll see that the text field already contains the text stream.swf. Therefore, the stream.swf file will be loaded into the song Movie Clip instance.

The second action on the Button instance will set the _visible property of the song Movie Clip instance to 0, which makes it hidden on the Stage.

Once the stream.swf file starts to load into the song instance, the !song instance will start to monitor the loading progress.

Loading progress display

Once the loadMovie action has been initiated, the loading variable in the song Movie Clip instance will no longer exist. Therefore, the first if statement on the second frame of the !song and _song instances will no longer prevent the remaining if . . . else statements from executing. The !song instance, which monitors our loading progress, will execute the code within the

```
} else if (substring(_name, 1, 1) eq "!") {
```

nest. The first line of code after the else . . . if statement will set a variable named check to the path of the song instance on the Main Timeline:

```
check = eval("_parent." + substring(_name, 2, -1));
```

Then, we get to use the new getBytesLoaded() and getBytesLoaded() methods now available in Flash 5. The getBytesLoaded() method will evaluate what percentage of the .SWF has loaded:

```
loaded = check.getBytesLoaded();
total = check.getBytesTotal();
percentage = int(loaded/total)*100;
currentKB = int(loaded/1024);
totalKB = int(total/1024);
```

Continued

Continued

After the loaded and total variables are determined, we can find the current percent loaded by dividing the current loaded amount by the total amount, and then multiplying by 100, to return a true percent. By using the int function, we get the whole-number integer of the percent in order to cut off any trailing decimals.

We also use the loaded variable to determine the kilobyte equivalent of getBytesLoaded(), by declaring another variable named currentKB which divides the value of loaded by 1024—there are 1024 bytes to 1 kilobyte. We establish another variable called totalKB, whose value is equal to the total size (in bytes) divided by 1024.

Then, our ActionScript will display the percent that has loaded into the main movie by (a) putting the percentage, totalKB and currentKB variables into our text field named disp within the !song instance, and (b) stretching the width of the marker Movie Clip instance to the same width as the msize Movie Clip instance. As the stream.swf file loads into the song instance, the marker Movie Clip instance will extend itself over the width of the msize instance:

```
disp = percentage + "% of " + totalKB + "kb ù
    loaded.(" + currentKB + " kb)";
marker._x =0;
marker._width = mw*(percentage/100);
```

Playback progress display

When the stream.swf file has fully loaded into the song instance, then the _song instance will start to execute its portion of the ActionScript code in the loader check Movie Clip symbol. Because there is no stop() action on the timeline of the stream.swf file, the contents of stream.swf will begin play automatically.

Because stream.swf has just one sound set to Stream Synch Mode, the timeline has as many frames as required to play the sound on its timeline. That means that there is a playhead whose position we can check. Using _totalframes and _currentframe properties, we can retrieve the playhead's position in the audio clip currently being played:

```
total = check._totalframes;
current = check._currentframe;
percentage = int((current/total)*100);
```

Using the percentage variable, we can display what percent of the audio clip has played, and also change the position of our marker Movie Clip, compared to the msize width, to display a graphic representation of the songs progress:

```
disp = "at " + percentage + "% of " + total + ù
    " frames. (frame " + current + ")";
marker._x = (mw-10) * (percentage/100);
marker._width = 10;
```

Audio control buttons

To achieve the playback control over the audio clip in our `song` instance, a variable is established to know whether the audio is playing or has been stopped.

The first example of this type of variable will be used in the Rewind button. Just like in programs such as Winamp, or hardware such as your car CD player, the Rewind and Fast Forward buttons scan through the music and begin playing as soon as you release the mouse button. To correctly gauge how each control button should work, we need to know whether the song timeline is playing. We'll use a variable named `play` on the Main Timeline (_root). If play is equal to a Boolean value of `false`, then we know playback is paused or stopped. If it's equal to `true`, then we know the timeline is playing. Let's start with the Rewind button.

The Rewind button code looks like this:

```
on (press, keyPress "<Left>") {
    if (_root.play == false) {
        song.gotoAndStop(song._currentframe-5);
    } else {
        song.gotoAndPlay(song._currentframe-5);
    }
}
```

If the song timeline is currently stopped, then a `gotoAndStop` method is used. If the timeline is playing, then a `gotoAndPlay` method is used.

With the Play button, two outcomes are possible: (a) If the Play button is pressed while the audio is playing, then the song will start over at the beginning; or (b) if the audio is in a paused state, then the playback will resume from the current frame. The Play button code contains the following ActionScript:

```
on (press, keyPress "x") {
    if (play == false) {
        song.play();
    } else {
        song.gotoAndPlay(1);
    }
    play = true;
}
```

The Pause button uses the following code:

```
on (press, keyPress "c") {
    play = false;
    song.stop();
}
```

Continued

Continued

The remaining buttons use similar ActionScript to fast forward or stop the audio clip. Select the remaining Button instances to see their code in the Actions Panel.

That wraps up this tutorial on preloading and controlling playback of streamed audio in Flash movies. For further enjoyment, you might want to try adding ActionScript that enables you to drag'n'drop the marker Movie Clip instance to your desired playback position.

Hanging out in San Diego, California, Gareth Pursehouse's single most favorite thing to do is practice Capoeira, which is considered, by some, a type of martial art. Capoeira blends dance, music, rituals, acrobatics, and fighting. This blend originates in Brazil, where it is played like a game. We wouldn't be surprised if Gareth conquered Flash ActionScript with the help of some good mojo from Capoeira. He earned his Flash recognition with one of his first Flash sites, www.infinovation.com.

Loading Flash Movies

Long sequences of animation in Flash naturally require the preloading described in the previous section to guarantee smooth playback. But traditional information-based Web sites done in Flash require a different kind of download management. Suppose you're building a Web site with three sections: products, staff, and company history. Each section is roughly 100KB in size. In a normal Flash movie, you'd place those sections in a sequential order on the main movie timeline. The last section you place on the timeline would, of course, be the last section to download. Might sound fine so far, but here's the problem: What if the section that appears last on the timeline happens to be the first and only section the user wants to see? They'd have to wait for the other two sections to download before they could view the one they want — but they don't even want to see the other two sections, so really they're waiting for nothing. The solution to this problem is the loadMovie action.

loadMovie provides a means of inserting one or more external .SWF files into a Flash movie (whether that movie resides in a browser or on its own in the standalone player). loadMovie can be used to replace the current movie with a different movie or to display multiple movies simultaneously. It can also be used, as in our company Web site example, to enable a parent movie to retrieve and display content kept in independent .SWF files on a need-to-retrieve basis (similar to the way a frame in an HTML frameset can call external pages into different frames).

Basic overview of Flash site architecture

There are two primary ways to produce and distribute straight Flash content on the Web: (a) create several small .SWF files, each one living within a standard HTML page on a Web site; or (b) create one HTML page that hosts one main .SWF file that loads additional content through the Flash Player plug-in. Figure 20-4 illustrates these alternatives.

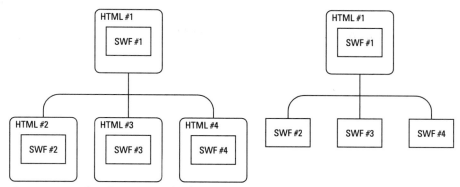

Figure 20-4: The diagram on the left illustrates a Web site that uses multiple HTML pages, each with an individual .SWF file. The diagram on the right shows a Web site that uses one HTML page (or frameset) that has one primary .SWF file, which loads other .SWF files as needed.

If you decide to break up your Flash movies across several HTML pages, your Web visitors will experience:

✦ Short download times for each page

✦ Easier bookmarking of discrete sections of your Web site

✦ Abrupt transitions between each section of the Web site

However, if you use one primary Flash movie in one HTML page (or frameset), your visitors will benefit from:

✦ Short download times for each .SWF file (download times vary with file size)

✦ Seamless integration of new Flash content

✦ Controllable transitions between .SWF asset changes

Which method should you use for your Flash projects? The answer depends on the specifics of each Web project. You may decide to use a combination of both methods, especially for larger sites that use several Web technologies (QuickTime, Flash, RealPlayer, Windows Media, and so on). In either scenario, you can use the `loadMovie` action to manage Flash content more easily.

Where are the multiple movies stored?

You may already be wondering how these newly loaded movies are managed relative to the original movie. Flash uses the metaphor of *levels* to describe where the movies are kept. Levels are something like drawers in a cabinet; they are stacked on top of each other, and can contain things; you can place things in any drawer you like, but once a drawer is full you have to take its contents out before you can put anything else in. Initially, the bottom level, referred to as _level0 ("Level 0"), contains the original movie. All movies subsequently loaded into the Flash Player must be placed explicitly into a target Level. If a movie is loaded into Level 1 or higher, it appears visually on top of the original movie in the Player. If a movie is loaded into Level 0, it replaces the original movie, removing all movies stored on Levels above it in the process. When a loaded movie replaces the original movie, it does not change the frame rate, movie dimensions, or movie background color of the original Flash stage. Those properties are permanently determined by the original movie and cannot be changed.

Tip   You can effectively change the background color of the stage when you load a new movie by creating a rectangle shape of your desired color on the lowest layer of the movie you are loading.

Loading an external .SWF file into a movie

A new movie is imported onto the main movie Stage when a loadMovie action is executed. Here's how to make a button click load an external movie named movie2.swf:

1. Place a Button instance on the Stage of your main movie. Bring up the Actions Panel for the Button by selecting the instance and pressing Ctrl+Alt+A (PC) or Option+Command+A (Mac). Make sure the Actions Panel is in Normal Mode (see Figure 20-5).

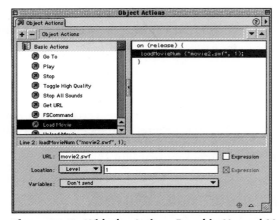

Figure 20-5: With the Actions Panel in Normal Mode, you can clearly see the options and settings of the loadMovie action.

2. Click the plus (+) button in the top-left corner of the Actions Panel, and select Basic Actions ⇨ Load Movie. Type **movie2.swf** (or your external .SWF file name) into the URL text field. The URL text field contains the network path to the movie file that you want to load. That path must be specified relative to the location of the page that contains your main movie, not relative to the location of the movie itself.

3. Select the Level option in the Location menu, and type **1** into the Location text field. This instructs Flash to load movie2.swf into _level1. If there had already been a movie loaded into _level1, it would automatically have been replaced by movie2.swf.

4. Click OK.

Caution Internet Explorer 4.5 (or earlier) for the Macintosh does not resolve paths correctly. For more information, please see Macromedia's tech note at: www.macromedia. com/support/flash/ts/documents/mac_ie_issues.htm

Note When a movie is loaded above any other movie (including the main movie), the Buttons in the movies on lower levels will continue to be active, even though they may not be visible. To prevent this undesired behavior, you need to send movies on lower levels to an idle or blank frame where no buttons are present. Do that by adding a Go To action before your loadMovie action that sends the current movie to the idle frame. This technique is known as "parking" the movie. If you have to park multiple movies, you'll need to know how to communicate between movies on different levels. This will be discussed shortly.

_level0 or _root: What's the Difference?

Until now, we have referred to the Main Timeline as _root in ActionScript. If you don't employ Levels in a Flash movie, then _root will always refer to the Main Timeline of the Flash movie that is loaded into a browser. However, if you start to use Levels to load external .SWF files, _root will be relative to the Level that's executing actions.

For example, if the main movie uses a _root reference in an action, such as:

```
_root.gotoAndStop(10);
```

then the Main Timeline playhead will go to frame 10 and stop.

If a loaded Movie has the same action within its timeline, then it will go to frame 10 on its timeline and stop.

While this works with movies that are loaded into Level locations, it will not work with Movie Clip instance targets. As you'll see in the following sections, a movie that is loaded into a Movie Clip target becomes an instance located within Level 0. Therefore, _root will still refer to the main movie's timeline (the Scene 1 timeline).

How Flash handles loaded movies of differing sizes

A movie loaded onto Level 1 or above that is smaller than the Level 0 movie is positioned in the top-left corner of the Stage. In this situation, elements on the Level 1 movie's Stage are displayed even when they go beyond the bottom and right dimensions of the Level 1 movie. To prevent objects from being displayed off Stage you would have to create a curtain layer above all the other layers in the Level 1 movie that covers up the work area (the space outside the movie's Stage).

Movies loaded onto Level 0 that are smaller than the original Level 0 movie are automatically centered and scaled up to fit the size of the original movie (the manner in which they are scaled depends on the Scale setting in the Publish settings).

Movies loaded onto Level 0 that are larger than the original Level 0 movie are cropped at the right and bottom boundaries defined by the original movie dimensions.

Placing, scaling, and rotating externally loaded .SWF files

Especially when your movies are different sizes, it's not very convenient to have newly loaded movies dropped ingloriously in the top-left corner of the Stage. To give you more flexibility with the placement, rotation, and scale of your loaded movies, Flash provides the capability to load a movie into a Movie Clip instance. So far, this may not make a whole lot of sense. Loading a movie into a Movie Clip instance seems like a strange feature at first, until you find out what it can do — then it seems indispensable. The easiest way to understand what happens when you load a movie into a Movie Clip is to think of the `loadMovie` action as a Convert Loaded Movie-to-Movie Clip action.

When a movie is loaded into a Movie Clip instance, many attributes of the original Movie Clip instance are applied to the newly loaded movie:

✦ The timeline of the loaded movie completely replaces the original instance's timeline. Nothing inside the original Movie Clip (including actions on keyframes) remains.

✦ The loaded movie assumes the following Properties from the original Movie Clip instance:

• Name

• Scale percentage

• Color effects, including alpha

• Rotation degree

• Placement (X and Y position)

• Visibility (with respect to the `_visible` property)

✦ Any `onClipEvent` handlers (and actions within them) that are written for the original Movie Clip instance will still be available (and executing) on the loaded Movie.

We like to refer to Movie Clips that are used to load other movies as Movie Clip holders. Usually, you will load movies into empty Movie Clips that don't have any artwork or actions. However, because you'll need a physical reference to the actual area your loaded movie will occupy on the Stage, it's useful to create temporary guides or artwork that indicate this area. The following steps show you how to create a Movie Clip holder, and how to load an external .SWF file into it.

1. Create a new Movie Clip symbol (Ctrl+F8 or Command+F8) that contains a square or rectangle. This shape can be drawn with the Rectangle Tool. The shape should have the same dimensions as the external .SWF movie's Stage, as defined in the Movie Properties dialog.

2. Place the shape so that its top-left corner is at the 0,0 X,Y coordinate. To do this, select the shape and open the Info Panel. Click the top-left corner of the bounding box diagram, and type 0 in the X and Y fields. Make sure that you press Enter after you type each zero.

3. Go back to the Main Timeline (Scene 1), and place an instance of this Movie Clip on the Stage. In the Instance Panel, give this Movie Clip instance the name **movieHolder**. Position it where you want the external .SWF movie to appear. At this point, you can also tween, scale, or apply color effect to the instance as well.

4. Add a `loadMovie` action to a Button instance or keyframe.

5. Specify the loaded movie's network path and filename in the URL field. Select the Target option in the Location menu. Type **movieHolder** into the Location field. The field specifies the name of the Movie Clip instance into which you want to load your external .SWF file.

> **Note**
>
> The instance must be resident on Stage at the time the `loadMovie` action occurs. Any instance can either be manually placed on the timeline, or created with ActionScript code, such as the `duplicateMovieClip` or `attachMovie` method. If any specification of the `loadMovie` action is incorrect, then the movie will fail to load. Flash will *not* start a request for an external .SWF file if the Movie Clip instance target is invalid.

6. Save the Flash movie file and test it. Your .SWF file's top-left corner will match the top-left corner of the original Movie Clip instance.

7. You may have noticed that there was a quick flash of the original Movie Clip's rectangle artwork before the external .SWF loaded into it. To avoid this, go into the Movie Clip symbol for movieHolder and turn the layer containing the rectangle artwork into a Guide Layer. Guide Layers will not export with the .SWF file.

loadMovie versus loadMovieNum

You may have noticed that a `loadMovie` action will be shown as `loadMovieNum` when a Level location is chosen. Because you can specify variables (that point to dynamic targets) as a Location value, Flash ActionScript needs a way to distinguish a numeric Level location from a Movie Clip instance.

Consequently, if you choose a Level location for a `loadMovie` action (in Normal Mode), then the action will show as:

```
loadMovie("external_1.swf", "movieHolder");
```

which specifies that the file `external_1.swf` be loaded into Level 1.

If you specify the Movie Clip target as `movieHolder` for the `loadMovie` action, then the action will appear as:

```
loadMovie ("external_1.swf", "movieHolder");
```

If you need to add functionality to the loaded movie, then use ActionScript to control the new loaded movie instance. The next section shows you how to communicate with loaded movies.

On the CD-ROM For further study, we've included a `loadMovie` example as a group of files on the *Flash 5 Bible* CD-ROM in the ch20 folder. Open movie1.html in a browser to view the files in action.

Communicating between multiple movies on different levels

After a movie or two are loaded onto different levels, you may want each timeline to control the other, just as Movie Clips can control each other. To communicate between different Levels, you simply need to address actions to the proper Level. The method for addressing a Level that controls a timeline on a different Level is identical to the method for addressing a Movie Clip target that controls the timeline of another Movie Clip instance, except for one small change. You have to indicate the name of the Level you want target rather than the name of the Movie Clip. Level names are constructed like this: First, there's an underscore (_), then there's the word *level,* and then there's the number of the Level that you want your Action to occur on.

This tells the movie loaded onto Level 1 to go to frame 50:

```
_level1.gotoAndStop(50);
```

This tells the main movie timeline to go to frame 50:

```
_level0.gotoAndStop(50);
```

You can also target Movie Clips that reside on the timelines of movies on other levels. Here's an example:

```
_level3.products.play();
```

This sends a `play()` action to the Movie Clip named `products` on the timeline of the movie loaded onto Level 3.

Unloading movies

Even though a movie loaded into an occupied Level (one that already contains a loaded movie) will automatically be removed before the new movie is displayed, the transition can be choppy. To ensure a smooth transition between movies, or to lighten the memory required by the Flash player, you can explicitly unload movies in any Level or Movie Clip target by using the `unloadMovie` action. The only option for `unloadMovie` is the path to the desired location (for example, `_level1`, `_root.instanceName`).

Loading External Files through Proxy Servers

If you are creating Flash movies that will be loaded through proxy servers on the Internet, then you'll need to know how to trick them into loading "fresh" .SWF files every time a user visits your site. What is a proxy server? With the growth of high speed Internet connections such as DSL and cable, many Internet service providers (ISPs) will process all outgoing HTTP requests through a go-between computer that caches previous requests to the same URL. Anytime you type a Web site URL into a browser, you're making an HTTP request. If that computer, called a proxy server, sees a request that was made previously (within a certain time frame), then it will serve its cached content to the end user, instead of downloading the actual content from the remote server.

Similarly, when a Flash movie makes an HTTP request with a `loadMovie` action, then a proxy server may serve the cached .SWF file instead of the one that actually exists on your server. Why is this a problem? If you are updating that .SWF file frequently, or if you want precise Web usage statistics for your Flash movies and content, then you'll want users to download the actual .SWF file on your server each time a request is made.

Continued

Continued

The question remains: How do you trick a proxy server into serving the real .SWF file instead of its cached one? The proxy server knows what's in its cache by the URL for each cached item. So, if you change the name of the loaded Flash movie each time you make a request for it, then the proxy server won't ever see an identical match with its cached content.

To change the name of a loaded Flash movie, simply add a random number to the end of the movie's name in the loadMovie action. This random number won't actually be part of the movie's filename. Rather, it will appear as a query at the end of the filename. Place the following actions on a Button instance that initiates a loadMovie action:

```
on(release){
    randomNum = Math.round(Math.random()*9999999999);
    loadMovie("external_1.swf?" + randomNum, "movieHolder");
}
```

In the preceding example, a variable called randomNum is established and given a random value, a number in the range of 0 to 9999999998. Each time a user presses this button, a different number is appended to the filename of the loaded movie. The proxy server will think that each request is a different, and route the request to your Web server.

Not only does this method prevent a proxy server from server a cached Flash movie file, but it also prevents most browsers from caching the loaded movie in the user's local cache folder.

loadMovie as a method or action for Movie Clip targets

Both loadMovie and unloadMovie can be used as either an ActionScript method or action for Movie Clip targets. What does this mean? You can apply actions in Flash 5 in two ways: as methods of a Movie Clip Object (or some other ActionScript Object), or as a stand-alone action.

As an action, loadMovie and unloadMovie start the ActionScript line of code. When you use actions in this manner, the target of the action is specified as an argument (option) within the action. In the following example, the file external_1.swf is loaded into Level 1:

```
loadMovie ("external_1.swf", "movieHolder");
```

As a method, actions are written as an extension of the object using the action. Therefore, the target is already specified before the action is typed. The same example shown previously could be rewritten as a method of the movieHolder Movie Clip Object:

```
movieHolder.loadMovie("external_1.swf");
```

or

```
_root.movieHolder.loadMovie("external_1.swf");
```

Because we have specifically referenced the movieHolder instance as an object, the loadMovie action (now a method) knows where to direct the loading of external_1.swf.

Expert Tutorial: Keeping Content Fresh and Dynamic Using the Load/Unload Movie Action, *by Derek Franklin*

Derek's tutorial shows you how to randomize the external files that load into a Flash. He provides some examples of interesting uses of the loadMovie *action for creative projects.*

A quick way to lose visitors who are returning to your Web site is for them to realize that every time they visit your site, nothing has changed. The graphics are always the same, the text is always the same, and — after only two visits — they feel that another visit to your site is an utter waste of time. This is known as boredom, and we all know that it's sacrilege to mix the term boredom with Flash site, but it happens.

There are numerous reasons why a Flash developer might not want to update or revise a completed project. One reason is fear of messing up something that already works, especially if it has a complex structure. Or, it could be just the drudgery of having to refamiliarize themselves with a movie's structure, which is often no small task.

To combat the issue of stale Flash content, Macromedia developed Generator. Generator creates dynamic Flash movies on the fly, complete with custom text and graphics. While Generator is a very cool development tool for keeping Flash content fresh, it's not for everyone. Generator involves learning new concepts, and the price of the software may be prohibitive to a lot of Flash. Luckily, there's a functionality already built into Flash that gives you power to deliver dynamic, Generator-like presentations with very little extra effort. It's the loadMovie action, which is part of the Flash 5 ActionScript arsenal. Due its power to enable you to keep content fresh and exciting, I think of this action as the "pseudo-Generator" action. How does it do this?

Continued

Continued

How loadMovie works

The `loadMovie` action enables you to compartmentalize different elements of your movie by enabling you to separate them into separate .SWF's that can be loaded at any time into the main movie. While the `loadMovie` action is commonly used for loading .SWF's that are complete productions in themselves, you can just as easily use it to load:

✦ Navigational controls

✦ The movie's soundtrack

✦ A background image

✦ Any single image

✦ Any text content

✦ An ActionScript functionality

The significance of this is twofold:

First, updating and keeping content fresh becomes much easier. For example, you could create a separate .SWF file for the text content that first displays on your site. You could name this movie text.swf and then place a `loadMovie` action in your main movie that loads text.swf into level 1 (the main movie is always Level 0). Then, whenever you want to edit or update the text content, you wouldn't have to go through the hassle of reopening the main authoring file, finding the text on the timeline, changing the text, making sure you don't mess anything up, testing, and then finally reexporting and uploading the entire movie again. Instead, by using the `loadMovie` action, you could simply open and edit the text.swf, reexport it to the same name (`text.swf`), and then upload the updated .SWF to your server. When the main movie plays again and text.swf gets loaded, it will reflect the updated text. You can just as easily use this trick for updating a graphic or even a soundtrack in your movie. By making your movie modular, updating or changing content becomes less of a hassle.

The second functionality that `loadMovie` offers is to make your movie truly dynamic — each time a visitor returns to your site! Believe me, after learning this trick, you'll never look at Flash construction the same way.

Imagine how unique and fresh a user's experience would be if you could randomly play 1 of 10 different soundtracks each time a visitor stops by; or, if you could pack 24 different bitmaps, 1 for each hour in the day, and have the proper one displayed depending on the hour of the day a user visits. I know what you're thinking, "That sound's great, but with that much content in a single movie, the user would have to wait a week for the whole movie to download." Think again! Using the `loadMovie` action along with some additional, yet very simple, ActionScripting you can accomplish amazing feats of dynamism without adding any more download time to your users' experience than if you'd placed a single soundtrack or bitmap inside a single movie. Let me show you how:

A random soundtrack

The first step in building a movie that contains a randomly generated soundtrack is to create ten different .SWF files (could be more or less for your purposes). Each .SWF will contain a single frame with a looping soundtrack in that single frame. Export these soundtrack .SWF's as soundtrack0.swf, soundtrack1.swf, soundtrack2.swf, and so on. Save them in the same directory in which the main .SWF will be placed. Next, in your main movie, place the following ActionScript wherever you would like the music to begin:

```
randomNum = random(10);
loadMovie ("soundtrack" + randomNum + ".swf", 1);
```

Note that the preceding code is derived from Flash 4. Ideally, you should use the recommended Flash 5 version of the script, which requires a bit more code to generate a random number:

```
randomNum = Math.Round(Math.random () * 10);
loadMovie ("soundtrack" + randomNum + ".swf", 1);
```

When this script is run is a random number is generated between 0 and 9 (not 0 and 10, as you might suspect, because 0 is one of the possible numbers generated) and placed in the variable `randomNum`. Next, using an expression, the `loadMovie` action uses the `randomNum` variable to load one of the soundtrack movies into Level 1. This delivers a randomly generated soundtrack each time someone visits the site, yet download is not increased any more than if you had given them only a single choice.

Placing your soundtrack in it's own Level is an easy way to facilitate sound on/off functionality. That's because turning the music on or off simply involves loading/unloading it from that Level.

A time-based image

The first step in building a Flash movie that will load 1 of 24 images at the appropriate hour, is to create 24 different .SWF files: Each .SWF should contain a single bitmap graphic, placed on frame 1. (There are 24 .SWF's to represent each hour of the day.) The graphic can be any size that your design requires. Export the .SWF's with meaningful file names, such as: hour0.swf, hour1.swf, and so on. Save these into the same directory in which the main .SWF will be placed. Then, in your main movie, place the following ActionScript in the appropriate frame, wherever you would like the picture to appear:

```
myDate = new Date()
currentHour = myDate.getHours();
loadMovie ("hour" + currentHour + ".swf", 1);
```

This script first creates a Date Object that is named `myDate`. Next, using the `getHours` method of the Date Object, Flash determines the current hour on the user's system and places a number representing that hour into the variable `currentHour` (0 = 12 a.m., 23 = 11 p.m.). Then, using an expression, the `loadMovie` action uses the `currentHour` variable to load the appropriate .SWF, which represents the particular hour, into Level 1 of the main movie.

Continued

Continued

If you want the image in the loaded .SWF to appear in particular place in the movie window, add the following code to the end of the previous script:

```
setProperty (_level1, _x, 100);
setProperty (_level1, _y, 100);
```

(This particular code example will cause the top-left corner of the loaded movie to be placed 100 pixels from the top and 100 pixels from the left of the main movie's top-left corner.)

And that's the joy of authoring Flash with pseudo-Generator! Harness the power and flexibility of this command by creating separate .SWF's for different parts of your movie, and you'll find many ways to keep your site fresh and dynamic. Whatever you do, have *loads* of fun with the `loadMovie` action.

The .SWF file format that's used with the `loadMovie` action has become a standard file format in its own right. This means that you have even more tools to help you make your movie modular with separate .SWF files. For example, there are a growing number of tools that enable you to export content directly from them to the .SWF format, including:

✦ **Macromedia Fireworks:** Fireworks 3 allows you to export bitmaps created within its environment as .SWF files. This enables you to easily update individual bitmap graphics in your movie.

✦ **Macromedia FreeHand:** FreeHand 9 not enables you to create vector graphics, as well as simple animations that can be exported to the .SWF format.

✦ **Adobe LiveMotion:** LiveMotion is Adobe's entry into the Web animation market. Although it's interactive capabilities don't compete with Flash, its interface is fabulous and it enables you to quickly create beautiful graphics or animations that can be exported as .SWF files.

✦ **Adobe Illustrator:** Illustrator 9 enables you to create vector graphics as well as simple animations, along the same lines as FreeHand, and then export them to the .SWF format.

✦ **Swift 3D:** Want to add 3D elements to your project? This great software creates 3D objects, complete with animation, that can be exported as .SWF files. You can find it at `www.swift3d.com`.

✦ **SWiSH:** Very cool text effects are what SWiSH is all about. SWiSH provides an amazing assortment of effects that are all configurable and that are easily exported to the .SWF format. You can find it at `www.swishzone.com`.

Derek Franklin is the coauthor of *"Flash 5!" Creative Web Animation,* (Berkeley: Peachpit Press, 2000) one of the most authoritative and usable books on the subject. Born in Illinois and raised in Bloomington, Indiana, he recently moved back to Bloomington. He recalls Kenny Loggin's "Footloose" as the most memorable tune from his last year of high school. Derek claims to have found Flash "by accident really. At first glance (Flash 2), I wasn't all that impressed. But when I saw what people were doing with it, there was no turning back." He says his favorite pastime is "either playing my drums or being the life of the party—they kind of go hand-in-hand."

Accessing Items in Shared Libraries

Flash 5 adds an exciting new feature to asset management in Flash movies: the capability to link external .SWF files (and the symbols, sounds, bitmaps, and font symbols within) to each Flash movie that you use on your Web site. These external .SWF files, called *Shared Libraries*, are different than loaded .SWF files.

A Shared Library .SWF doesn't load into a Level or a Movie Clip instance location. Instead, you set up a the Library of a Flash movie (.FLA file) with assets that you want to use in other Flash movies. This movie is the basis of the Shared Library .SWF file. After you assign an identifier to each asset in the Library, you save the .FLA file, publish a .SWF file, and close the .FLA file. Then, you open another Flash movie .FLA file, and using File ⇨ Open as Shared Library, you open the Shared Library .FLA file. Its Library window will open (in a dimmed gray state), and you can drag and drop assets to your new Flash movie file.

 Note Even though the assets are linked to the external Shared Library .SWF file, the Flash movie will actually store copies of the assets in its .FLA file. However, they will not be exported with the .SWF file that is published.

After you have established a Shared Library file, any changes to the actual contents of the Shared Library .FLA and .SWF files will propagate to any Flash movie that uses the shared assets. In the following sections, you learn how to create a Shared Library file and use it with other Flash movies.

 Caution At the time of this writing, the Shared Library feature of Flash 5 has proven to work very inconsistently. It is recommended that you use only small (low byte size) elements in your Shared Libraries, to ensure that they are downloaded and available for Flash movies that use them. As with any Web production, make sure that you test early and often before you develop an entire project that fails upon final delivery.

Setting up a Shared Library file

To share assets among several Flash files, you need to establish a Shared Library file (or files) that is available to other Flash movie files. To create a Shared Library file:

1. Open a new Flash movie (Ctrl+N or Command+N).

2. To place Flash artwork into the Library, draw the shapes and other elements (text, lines, gradients, and so on). Select the artwork and convert it to a Flash symbol. Choose a symbol type (for example, Graphic, Button, or Movie Clip) that best suits the nature of your artwork.

3. To place bitmaps and sounds into the Library, import the source files as you normally would, using File ⇨ Import (Ctrl+R or Command+R).

4. Delete all artwork that you have placed on the Stage. Every asset that you want to share should be in the Library.

5. To place an entire font (or typeface) into the Library, open the Library (Ctrl+L or Command+L), and choose New Font from the Options menu, located at the top-right corner of the Library window. In the Font Symbol Properties dialog, type a reference name for the font, choose the font face from the Font menu, and select a faux font Style (Bold or Italic) to be applied (optional). (See Figure 20-6.)

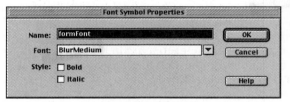

Figure 20-6: Give each embedded font face a descriptive name that indicates its functionality within the Flash movie.

Assigning names to assets

After you have placed each asset into the Library of your starter .FLA file, you'll need to assign a unique identifier to each asset.

1. Select the symbol, bitmap, sound, and font in the Library. Choose Linkage from the Library's Options menu.

2. In the Symbol Linkage Properties dialog, shown in Figure 20-7, choose Export this symbol for the Linkage option. This forces the asset to export with the published .SWF file. Then, type a unique name in the Identifier field. Click OK.

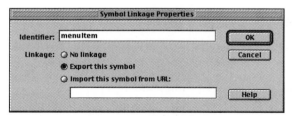

Figure 20-7: Each asset in the Library of the Shared Library .FLA file needs a unique name.

3. Repeat Steps 1 and 2 for each asset in the Library.

Specifying the Shared Library's location

An optional setting for the Shared Library .FLA is the relative or absolute path (as a URL) to the Shared Library .SWF on your Web server. You only need to specify this URL if you plan to store the Shared Library .SWF file within a different directory on the Web server, or on a completely different Web server.

1. In the Options menu in the Library window, choose Shared Library Properties.

2. In the URL field, type the location of the Shared Library .SWF file (or where you intend to publish it on the Web). This location will be preappended to each shared asset's identifier in the movies that use the assets.

 Caution   Make sure that you specify this URL before you start using the Shared Library .FLA file with other .FLA files. The URL location is stored within the each movie that uses the Shared Library .SWF file, and will not update if you decide to change the URL later in the Shared Library .FLA file.

Publishing the Shared Library .SWF file

After the assets of the .FLA file have been assigned identifiers and the URL of the Shared Library has been set (optional), you need to publish a .SWF version of the .FLA file.

1. Save the .FLA movie. Use a descriptive name that notifies other members of your Web production team that this is a Shared Library file, such as `sharedLib.fla`.

2. Publish the Flash movie as a .SWF file. No other publish formats are necessary. In the Publish Settings (File ➪ Publish Settings), select only the Flash format in the Format tab. Click OK. Choose File ➪ Publish to create a .SWF file from your .FLA file.

3. Close the .FLA file.

Linking to assets from other movies

After the Shared Library .SWF file is published, you can use the shared assets in other Flash movies.

1. Create a new Flash movie, or open an existing one.

2. Using the File ➪ Open as Shared Library command, browse to the folder where your Shared Library .FLA was saved. For testing purposes, you should keep this .FLA file in the same folder as the .FLA files that share it. Select the Shared Library .FLA file, and click Open. A separate grayed-out Library window for the Shared Library .FLA file will open in the Flash authoring environment.

3. Drag the asset(s) that you wish to use into the new Flash movie's Library and onto its Stage. Even though Flash will copy the contents of each shared asset, the asset will load from the separate Shared Library .SWF file.

4. To see whether an asset is native to the Flash movie or from a Shared Library .SWF file, right-click (or Control-click on the Mac) the symbol or asset in the Library. Select Linkage from the contextual menu. The Symbol Linkage Properties dialog, shown in Figure 20-8, will indicate whether the symbol (or asset) will be imported from an external Shared Library .SWF file.

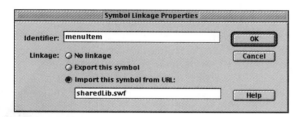

Figure 20-8: If a Shared Library asset is used in another movie, the Symbol Linkage Properties will indicate the name (and path) of the Shared Library .SWF file.

Caution   Do not try to use the Open as Shared Library command when the Shared Library .FLA file is already open. Likewise, you cannot open a Shared Library .FLA file with File ⇨ Open if it's already opened as a Shared Library. Close the grayed-out Library window before you attempt to open the Shared Library .FLA to edit its contents.

When you are done dragging the assets from the Shared Library file, close its Library window. When you publish the new Flash movie(s) that use the Shared Library .SWF file, make sure you put all of the files on your Web server for live testing.

Summary

✦ If you want to make sure that your larger Flash movies don't pause during playback over the Web, then you may want to make a preloader for each Flash movie you make.

✦ Preloaders can use three different ways to test the download progress of the Flash movie .SWF file: ifFrameLoaded, _framesLoaded/_totalFrames, and getBytesLoaded()/getBytesTotal. The most accurate mechanism uses the new Flash 5 getBytesLoaded()/getBytesTotal() methods.

✦ You can breakup large Flash projects into several smaller Flash movie components that are loaded into a primary .SWF file when they're needed.

✦ The loadMovie action enables you to download .SWF files into Level or Movie Clip instance locations.

✦ Flash 5 offers a new way to share movie assets with the Shared Library feature. As this is a new mechanism to load assets, we recommend that you thoroughly test any Shared Libraries on live production servers before you make the content accessible to the public.

✦   ✦   ✦

Programming Flash Movies with ActionScript

◆ ◆ ◆ ◆

◆ ◆ ◆ ◆

At this point in the book, you have learned the basics of Flash artwork, sound, and interactivity. While Part IV covered Basic Actions, fundamental Movie Clip properties and methods, and Flash movie management, Part V has been written for interactive designers who want to learn about Flash ActionScript programming. Chapter 21 introduces problem-solving techniques for interactivity and discusses the use of variables in a Flash movie. If you seek to understand data types, functions, and arrays, then read Chapter 22, where we show you how to create a dynamic menu system. Since many Flash developers create online games, we dedicated Chapter 23 to understanding complex Movie Clip interactions using the hitTest method. In Chapter 24, you learn how to create Flash forms using the loadVariables action and a fully functional CGI script. There, you can also find information on the new XML features of Flash 5 and the use of extensions from the Flash Exchange. You can discover the new world of HTML formatting and the Selection Object for Flash text fields in Chapter 25. For Chapter 26, we have gathered three expert Flash developers to contribute their understanding and workflow of Flash movie production.

Planning Code Structures

For many serious Web developers, Flash 5's enhanced programming capabilities are the single most important new feature of the product. Now, more than ever, elements inside Flash movies can be dynamic, have machine-calculated properties, and respond to user input. Movies can now communicate with server-side applications and scripts by sending and receiving processed and raw data. What does this mean for your movies? It means you now have the tools that you need to produce truly advanced movies (such as Flash asteroids, a multiplayer role-playing adventure game, or a navigational interface with a memory of the user's moves are entirely possible). It also means that Flash can be used to produce many complex Web applications (such as database-driven e-commerce product catalogs) without the need for Macromedia Generator. This chapter introduces you to the new programming structure of ActionScript and explains how to start using code within your Flash movies.

Breaking Down the Interactive Process

Before you can become an ActionScript code warrior, you need to realize that this isn't just a weekend activity — if you want to excel at Flash ActionScripting, you'll need to commit the time and energy necessary for the proper revelations to occur. It's not likely that you'll understand programming simply by reading this chapter (or the whole book). You need to create some trials for yourself, to test your textbook knowledge and allow you to apply problem-solving techniques.

You might be thinking, "Oh no, you mean it's like geometry, where I'm given a problem, and I have to use theorems and postulates to create a proof?" Not exactly, but programming, like geometry, requires strong reasoning and justification skills. You need to be able to understand how values (for example, the height of a Movie Clip instance) are determined, what type of changes you can perform on those values, and how changes to one value might affect another value. Confused? Don't worry, we take this one step at a time.

 Cross-Reference See Chapter 38, "Planning Flash Production with Flowcharting Software," for more detailed information regarding project planning and management.

Define your problems

Regardless of what interactive authoring tool you use (DHTML and JavaScript, Flash, Director, and so on), you can't begin any production work until you have a clear idea of the product. What is it that you are setting out to do? At this point in the process, you should use natural language to describe your problems; that is, define your objective (or problem) in a way that you understand it. For example, let's say that you want to make a quiz. You'll have to run through a list of goals for that interactive product:

+ Is it a true/false test?

+ Or will it be multiple choice?

+ Or fill-in-the-blank?

+ An essay test?

+ How many questions will be in the quiz?

+ Will there be a time limit for each question?

+ Will you notify the person of wrong answers?

+ How many chances does the person get to answer correctly?

There are other questions, of course, that could help define what your product will encompass. Don't try to start Flash production without setting some project parameters for yourself.

Clarify the solution

After you have defined the boundaries for the project, you can start to map the process with which your product will operate. This step involves the procedure of the experience (in other words, how the person will use the product you are creating). With our quiz example, you might clarify the solution as:

1. User starts movie, and types his/her name.

2. After submitting the name, the user will be told that they have 10 minutes to complete a 25-question quiz that's a combination of true/false and multiple-choice questions.

3. Upon acknowledging the instructions (by pressing a key or clicking a button), the timer starts and the user is presented with the first question.

4. The timer is visible to the user.

5. The first question is a true/false question, and the correct answer is false.

6. If the user enters a true response, then a red light graphic will appear and the sound of a buzzer will play. The user will be asked to continue with the next question.

7. If the user enters a false response, then a green light graphic will appear and the sound of applause will play. The user will be asked to continue with the next question.

8. This process repeats until the last question is answered, at which point the score is tallied and presented to the user.

The preceding eight steps are very close to a process flowchart, as discussed in Chapter 38 "Planning Flash Production with Flowcharting Software." In real-life production, you would want to clarify Step 8 for each question in the same amount of detail as Steps 5 to 7 did. As you can see, once you start to map the interactive experience, you'll have a much better starting point for your scripting work. Notice, that we're already using logic, with our if statements in Steps 6 and 7. We're also determining object properties such as _visible in Step 4. While we may not know all the ActionScript involved with starting a timer, we know that we have to learn how time can be measured in a Flash movie.

Translate the solution into the interactive language

After you have created a process for the movie to follow, you can start to convert each step into a format that Flash can use. This step will consume much of your time, as you look up concepts and keywords in the *ActionScript Reference Guide*. It's likely that you won't be able to find a prebuilt Flash movie example to use as a guide, or if you do, that you'll need to customize it to suit the particular needs of your project. For our quiz example, we could start to translate the solution as:

1. Frame 1: Movie stops. User enters name into a text field.

2. **(a)** Frame 1: User clicks a submit Button symbol instance to initiate the quiz. The instructions are located on frame 2. Therefore, the Button action uses a gotoAndStop(2) action to move the playhead to the next frame.

2. **(b)** Frame 2: Static text will be shown, indicating the guidelines for the quiz.

3. Frame 2: User clicks a start quiz Button symbol instance. An action on the Button instance starts a timer and moves the playhead to frame 3.

4. Frame 3: The current time of the timer is displayed in a text field, in the upper-right corner of the Stage.

5. Frame 3: The first question is presented in the center of the Stage. A button with the text True and a button with the text False are located just beneath the question. The correct answer for the question is hidden in a variable name/value. The variable's name is answer, and its value is false. This variable declaration appears as a Frame Action on frame 3. A variable, called score, will also be declared to keep track of the correct answer count. Its starting value will be 0.

6. (a) Frame 3: If the user clicks the True button, then an if/else action will check whether answer's value is equal to true. If it is, then an action will set the _visible of a greenLight Movie Clip instance to true, and initiate and play a new Sound Object for the applause.wav file in our Library. Also, the value of score will increase by 1. If the value of answer is not true, then an action will set the _visible of a redLight Movie Clip instance to true, and initiate and play a new Sound Object for the error.wav file in our Library. The value of score will be left as is.

6. (b) Frame 3: A Button instance will appear, and when clicked, take the user to frame 4.

7. (a) Frame 3: If the user clicks the False button, then an if/else action will check whether answer's value is equal to true. If it is, then an action will set the _visible of a greenLight Movie Clip instance to true, and initiate and play a new Sound Object for the applause.wav file in our Library. Also, the value of score will be increased by 1. If the value of answer is not true, then an action will set the _visible of a redLight Movie Clip instance to true, and initiate and play a new Sound Object for the error.wav file in our Library. The value of score will be left as is.

7. (b) Frame 3: A Button instance will appear, and when clicked, it will take the user to frame 4.

While there is more than one way we could have translated this into ActionScript-like syntax, you'll notice that a few key concepts are presented in the translation: where events occur (frames or buttons), and what elements (for example, Button symbols or Movie Clip instances) are involved.

Most importantly, you'll notice that we used the same procedure for both the True and the False buttons. Even though we could hardwire the answer directly in the Button actions, we would have to change our Button actions for each question. By placing the same logic within each Button instance, we only have to change the value of the answer variable from frame to frame (or from question to question).

Granted, this example was already translated for you, and 90 percent of your scripting woes will be in the translation process — before you even have a testable Flash movie. You need to learn the basic terminology and syntax of the ActionScript language before you can start to write the scripting necessary for Steps 1 to 7. And that's exactly what the rest of this chapter (and the rest of Part V) do.

Expert Tutorial: Object-Oriented Design in Flash: The Fundamental Concepts, *by Philip Fierlinger*

As the scale and sophistication of your Flash projects increase, you will want to streamline your development process. You will need to find ways to optimize your projects, making them more efficient, more flexible, more manageable, and more scalable. One of the best techniques to do this is called object-oriented design.

The basic concept

In object-oriented design, a project gets divided into self-contained modules, simply called objects. In software, each object can be duplicated infinitely, without increasing the file size of your project. Each duplicate of an object can operate independently and be modified independently from the source object. However, making changes to the single source object will automatically apply those changes universally to every duplicate of the object. In object-oriented design, you can easily add or subtract objects to your project or make changes to an object without breaking the overall system. Objects can exchange data directly with each other and they can form complex interconnected relationships.

At its core, Flash is an object-oriented tool. You may not even realize it, but every time you place a Symbol from the Library onto the Stage, you are using an object-oriented design process. Symbols are object based, which means that you can create infinite Instances of the same Symbol without increasing the file size of your movie. In addition, you can modify the properties of each Instance independently.

Think of an object as a worker. Imagine that you can infinitely clone one worker, but you only have to pay for the first one, the rest are free. Then imagine that you can assign each cloned worker to an independent task, so that no two workers have to duplicate the same exact work. That's one stunningly efficient and flexible worker.

All three types of Symbols—Graphic, Button, and Movie Clip—let you independently modify certain properties of their respective Instances while authoring in Flash. These properties include the scale, position, color, and opacity. In the case of Graphic and Button instances, after you export your Flash file as a .SWF movie, those properties are fixed. Those properties cannot be changed despite dynamic conditions such as user input, loaded data, or the state of other properties in your movie.

Dynamic objects

On the other hand, Instances of a Movie Clip can be changed dynamically during runtime. Movie Clips are objects that you can explicitly target. The properties of Movie Clips can be queried and changed at any time. Most important of all, you can also query and set variables within any Movie Clip.

Continued

Continued

Because Movie Clips can be changed dynamically, they can be constructed as general-purpose templates that are customized during runtime. For instance, you can build an object-oriented menu system using Movie Clips in which the buttons have no predefined names. Instead, the button names are created as Movie Clips containing empty text fields that can be dynamically set during runtime, based on specific conditions in the movie. You can also duplicate the entire menu system, at no cost data wise, and apply entirely different values to the button names each time.

Using Movie Clips in this way makes your project very flexible, scalable, and efficient. Because your menu system is object oriented, you can easily reuse and infinitely duplicate the menu system without affecting the project's file size. It also makes your project more manageable. You only need to test and debug a single general-purpose object—the menu system—rather than testing and debugging numerous unique menu items. By the same token, changes made to the foundation object are applied to all of its derivatives, so that fundamental changes to the system are easy to implement.

In most large-scale Flash projects common user interface features such as preloaders, menus, floating windows, and scroll bars are usually built as object-oriented systems. In fact, there's a new feature in Flash 5.0 called Smart Clips. Smart Clips enable you to set variable properties and data values of a Movie Clip through a convenient editor, rather than having to modify the source code of your Movie Clips in ActionScript. This makes project management easier. It provides developers with a simple system to package, reuse, and share Smart Clip objects. Smart Clips can be reused within a single movie, but they can also be shared across multiple projects with numerous team members.

Nesting: Parent-child relationships

Nesting is another powerful technique in object-oriented design. When you place one object inside of another object you are linking the objects in something called a parent-child relationship. The "host" object is called the parent; the nested object is the child. Parent-child relationships are extremely powerful because child objects inherit properties from the parent. However, child objects also maintain their own separate properties, independent of the parent.

To demonstrate the concept of nesting let's use an animated character as an example. Let's say that we nest a character's finger object inside of its hand object, which is nested inside of the arm object, that's nested inside of the body object. All the subsequent child objects will inherit any property that we change in the parent object. Scaling the body scales the arm, hand, and finger accordingly. Moving the body moves the arm, hand, and finger accordingly. However, moving the hand only affects the finger, not the arm or the body, because child objects can act independently of their parents (remember, the arm and the body are *parents* of the hand). That's exactly how our own human anatomy works: Our fingers must go wherever our body takes them, but they can also move independently from our body.

Object-oriented Flash site architecture

These same fundamental principles of object-oriented design also apply to the development of your entire site. By building your Flash site in modular object-oriented components, you can dramatically improve site performance, site management, and site scalability.

Flash sites should be segmented into small, self-contained Flash movies that are treated as independent objects within the overall site structure. These independent movies are loaded and nested into the site by using the `loadMovie` command.

When loading in a new movie you must specify and replace an existing Movie Clip. Often, the Movie Clip that you will want to target and replace will be designed as an empty placeholder, a blank Movie Clip that serves only to load external movies.

Like all other nested objects, your nested movies will be linked through a parent-child relationship. It's very important to remember that the nested movie will inherit the position, scale, color, and opacity of the targeted Movie Clip.

The primary advantage of segmenting your Flash site into independent objects is the ability to load content only if and when it is needed, on demand, rather than forcing users to download your entire site all at once. A word to the wise: For optimum performance, the first movie that users download, the parent movie, should contain only code and graphics that are absolutely necessary for the user to navigate the rest of your site.

In terms of site development, by segmenting your site into independent objects you only need to edit, test, and debug the specific file that needs attention, rather than having to handle one enormously confusing file. It also makes the site infinitely scalable, making it easy to add or remove new content to your site simply by adding or removing individual movies. In a team environment, it's much, much easier to divide development among multiple team members.

Object-oriented scripting

In most software development, object-oriented programming (OOP) is fundamental. Although OOP could be simulated in version 4.0, ActionScript in Flash 5.0 is now a full-fledged OOP language.

The protocol, syntax, and strategy for using object-oriented scripting (OOS) in Flash can get extremely complex. You will find more in-depth coverage of this topic elsewhere in this book. For this section, the general concept is what we want to cover.

Fundamentally, OOS serves the same purpose as all other object-oriented techniques that we've covered so far: OOS makes project development more efficient, more manageable, more scalable, and more flexible.

The basic idea is to avoid writing code that is hardwired, meaning code that is written for only one purpose that can only be used one time, under one set of conditions. Instead, it's better to compartmentalize your code into general-purpose routines that can be accessed and reused multiple times, for multiple purposes, in multiple combinations.

Continued

Continued

In Flash, code objects are known as *functions*. A function describes a specified set of procedures that will be run whenever the function is invoked. The objective is to build functions that have an explicit task, but the data that they process is relative to the current conditions of the movie. By treating all data as relative, your function is flexible — it can operate under many conditions, producing dynamic results that are based on the specific conditions at hand. In addition, you can combine and nest functions to produce very complex and dynamic results.

As an example, let's take the object-oriented menu system that was used as an example earlier. You would probably want to build a number of functions to handle the operation of the menu system. One function would put the menu system Movie Clip on Stage and position it properly. Another function would fill in the button names. An additional function would handle the actions to be performed based on which Button was pressed.

By segmenting various functions into specialized objects, you can reuse each function for other purposes. For instance, the function that puts the menu on stage and positions it could be reused in order to place a character on stage and position it. A well-written function performs a specialized task, but it handles data in a relative manner, so that the Function will be flexible, scalable, manageable, and efficient.

Final thoughts

Over the years, Flash has evolved from a quirky little animation tool into a mighty Internet platform. Its key to success has been the capability to deliver dynamic content in an extremely small file format. While the vector graphics technology behind Flash usually gets all the credit for its zippy performance and slender file size, there is a deeper concept inherent to Flash that is more sublime and ultimately more powerful.

Flash is an intrinsically object-oriented development environment. I hope that you now understand that by using object-oriented design techniques you can dramatically improve your site's performance — making it more efficient and more dynamic. At the same time, you will improve your development process by making your site more manageable, flexible, and scalable.

Born and raised in Penn Wayne, Pennsylvania, Philip Fierlinger's single most favorite thing to do is to spend time with his wife and their baby. Philip works at Turntable (www.turntable.com), a multimedia company in San Francisco, where he has created Flash experiences for De La Soul and the Beastie Boys (for www.shockwave.com); interactive demos of Palm Computing's Palm III; and iTV development for Disney, among other exciting projects. During his final year of high school, Philip remembers seeing *Robocop* and seeing U2 perform at the Meadowlands for their Joshua Tree tour. Philip recognizes the value of "laughing with good friends, eating great food, visiting beautiful places, listening to great music, watching great movies, being inspired by great design, and incorporating all of the above into great work."

The Basic Context for Programming in Flash

With the new Actions Panel in Flash 5, you can program interactivity in two ways: by using a drag'n'drop menu-based set of actions (Normal Mode), or by writing interactive commands directly into the Actions list pane of the Actions Panel (Expert Mode).

Normal Mode

This mode consists primarily of attaching actions to keyframes and buttons, and selecting parameters for those commands from drop-down menus (or Action booklets) and/or entering parameters by hand into option fields. Although this method of programming can feel unnatural to traditional programmers, the resulting ActionScript looks and reads the same as the code produced with Expert Mode.

Expert Mode

In Expert Mode, you can type your code from scratch, as well as insert your code with the help of Action booklets. Syntactically, ActionScript looks and feels very much like JavaScript. Macromedia has gone to great lengths to make ActionScript compatible with ECMA-262 (the standard programming guidelines derived from JavaScript). And like other object-oriented languages, ActionScript is composed of many familiar building blocks: variables, operators, conditionals, loops, expressions, built-in properties, subroutines, and native functions.

Accessing ActionScript commands

All of the ActionScript commands are found easily in the Flash interface in the Action booklets or plus (+) button menu in the Actions Panel. However, the assembly of actions with one another is not something Flash automatically performs. Although it is beyond the scope of this chapter to fully explain fundamental programming principles, we can give a sense of the whole of ActionScript by providing you with an organized reference to each of its parts.

Tip

If you use the plus (+) menu to access ActionScript commands, you'll notice that shortcut keys are defined after the name of the command. You can use these shortcuts in either Normal or Expert Mode. For example, loadMovie has a keyboard shortcut of Esc+lm. If you give the Actions Panel focus and press Esc+lm, then the loadMovie action will appear in the Actions list, complete with placeholders for arguments

Actions list organization in the Actions Panel

In Normal Mode, you can add a line of code below any existing statement by high-lighting the existing statement in the Actions list, and then adding your action. If you accidentally add your code in the wrong place, or if you want to move code around, simply select the lines that you want to move and drag them with the mouse. You can also cut, copy, and paste code within the Actions list or from one list to another using Ctrl+X (Command+X), Ctrl+C (Command+C), and Ctrl+V (Command+V), respectively.

In Expert Mode, the highlighting mechanism for selected actions changes. You are free to select partial or entire lines of code, and modify the code in any way you want. With Flash 5, you can even edit your code in your preferred text editor! If you want to create your own programming macros in other programming applications, then you can write your scripts outside of Flash and copy the final code into the Actions Panel when you're done.

Tip   To make sure that you don't have any syntax errors after reorganizing code in Expert Mode, temporarily switch to Normal Mode. Flash will alert you if there are scripting errors, and won't let you enter Normal Mode until the error(s) has been fixed.

Using the New #include Action

Flash 5 ActionScript now has an action that enables you to insert external text files (with an .AS file extension). Now, you can write ActionScript in any text or script editor and save that text separately from the Flash movie (.FLA file). When you publish a .SWF movie from the .FLA file, Flash 5 will retrieve the .AS file, and insert the actions to the Action list where the #include action was issued. For example, the following code could be written in a contact.as file, which, as the name implies, contains a person's contact information for the Flash movie:

```
contactName = "Joseph Farnsworth";
contactStreet = "675 Locust Street";
contactCity = "Chicago";
contactState = "IL";
contactPhone = "312-555-1342";
contactEmail = "jfarnsworth@mycompany.com";
```

In a Flash movie, you could insert this code into a Main Timeline (or a Movie Clip timeline) keyframe* by using the #include action (you can use the #include action within any Flash event handler including keyframe, Button instance, onClipEvent, and so on):

```
#include "contact.as"
```

Make sure you do *not* insert a semicolon at the end of the #include line. Think of the #include action as a special tag for Flash 5, letting it know that it should replace the #include line of code with all the code within the referred file. The following code will result in a "malformed" error in the Output window, upon testing or publishing the Flash movie:

```
#include "contact.as";
```

Why is the #include action useful? For experienced programmers, the #include command allows freedom to write ActionScript in any text editor. You can define entire code libraries of custom functions. These .AS libraries can then be reused from movie to movie.

Note that the #include action is only executed upon publishing or testing the Flash movie. You can not upload .AS files to your Web server for "live" insertion of Flash ActionScript. Anytime you change the .AS file, you will need to republish your .SWF file.

One Part of the Sum: ActionScript Variables

After you have a clear understanding of Movie Clip instances and how to control their playback and properties, you can move on to the fundamentals of learning a system of composing more complex scripts with Flash actions. If you are familiar with JavaScript or Director Lingo, then your transition to Flash's scripting environment will be smoother.

Cross-Reference
If you are new to scripting, we highly recommend that you review Part IV, "Adding Basic Interactivity to Flash Movies," before you begin this chapter. Also, you may want to review Chapters 1 and 2 of the Flash 5's *ActionScript Reference Guide*.

In any scripting or programming language, you will need some type of "memory" device — something that can remember the values and properties of Objects or significant data. This type of memory device is referred to as a *variable*.

Variables are named storage places for changeable pieces of data (numbers and letters). One of the first obstacles for designers learning a scripting language to overcome is the concept that variable names in and of themselves have no meaning or value to the computer. Remember that the computer can't perform anything unless you tell it to. Even though any given scripting language has a certain set of "built-in" properties and functions, variables can simplify our scripting workload by creating shortcuts or aliases to other elements of the ActionScript language of the script. One prime example of a shortcut variable is the pathname to a deeply nested Movie Clip instance, such as:

```
_root.birdAnim.birdHouse.birdNest.birdEgg
```

truncated to a variable named pathToEgg as:

```
pathToEgg = _root.birdAnim.birdHouse.birdNest.birdEgg;
```

Once pathToEgg is declared and given a value, then we can reuse it without referring to the lengthy path name, as in:

```
with(pathToEgg){
    gotoAndPlay("start");
}
```

The important concept here is that you could just as easily have given `pathToEgg` a different name, such as `myPath`, or `robPath`, or whatever word(s) you'd like to use. As long as the syntax and formatting of the expression is correct, then you have nothing to worry about.

New Feature — Variables in ActionScript are now "typed," meaning that their value is explicitly set to be either a string, number, Boolean, or object. When working with variables, you must therefore know what data type the value is. We discuss data typing in the next chapter.

Variables in Flash are attached to the timeline of the movie or Movie Clip instance on which they are created. If you create a variable x on the Main Timeline, that variable is available for other scripting actions on that timeline. However, from other Movie Clip timelines, the variable is not directly accessible. To access the value of a variable on another timeline (such as a Movie Clip instance), enter the target path to the clip instance in which the variable resides, a dot (.), and then enter the variable name. For instance, this statement sets the variable x to be equal to the value of the variable y in Movie Clip instance named `ball`:

```
x = _root.ball.y;
```

Whereas this statement sets the variable y to be equal to the value of the variable x on the Main Timeline:

```
y = _root.x;
```

Tip — Variables in ActionScript are not case sensitive and cannot start with a number.

String literals

In programmer speak, a string is any combination of alphanumeric characters. By themselves, they have no meaning. It is up to you to assign something meaningful to them. For example, giving a variable the name `firstName` doesn't mean much. We need to assign a value to the variable `firstName` to make it meaningful, and we can do something with it. For example, if `firstName = "Susan"`, then we could make something specific to "Susan" happen.

You can also use much simpler name/value pairs, such as i = 0, to keep track of counts. If you want a specific Movie Clip animation to loop only three times, you can increment the value of i by 1 (for example, i = i + 1, i += 1, and i ++ all do the same thing) each time the animation loops back to the start. Then, you can stop the animation when it reaches the value of 3.

Expressions

Flash uses the term *expression* to refer to two separate kinds of code fragments in ActionScript. An expression is either (a) a phrase of code used to compare values in a Conditional or a Loop (these are known as *conditional expressions*), or (b) a snippet of code that is interpreted at runtime (these are known as *numeric expressions* and *string expressions*). We discuss conditional expressions later in this chapter.

Numeric and string expressions are essentially just segments of ActionScript code that are dynamically converted to their calculated values when a movie runs. For instance, suppose you have a variable, y, set to a value of 3. In the statement $x = y + 1$, the $y + 1$ on the right side of the equal sign is an expression. Hence, when the movie runs, the statement $x = y + 1$ actually becomes $x = 4$, because the value of y (which is 3) is retrieved (or "interpreted") and the calculation $3 + 1$ is performed. Numeric and string expressions are an extremely potent part of ActionScript because they permit nearly any of the options for Actions to be set based on mathematical calculations and external variables rather than requiring fixed information. Consider these two examples:

1. The Type option of a `Go To` action could be set as an expression that returns a random number in a certain range, sending the movie to a random frame

2. The URL option in a `getURL` action could be made up of a variable that indicates a server name and a literal string, which is the file path.

To change all the URLs in your movie from a staging server to a live server you'd just have to change the value of the server variable. Anywhere that you see the word *expression* in any Action options, you can use an interpreted ActionScript expression to specify the value of the option. Just enter the code, and then check the Expression option.

To use a string inside an expression, simply add quotation marks around it. Anything surrounded by quotation marks is taken as a literal string. For example, the conditional: `if (status == ready)` wrongly checks whether the value of the variable `status` is the same as the value of the nonexistent variable `ready`. The correct conditional would check whether the value of status is the same as the string "ready" by quoting it, as in: `if (status == "ready")`.

You can even have expressions that indirectly refer to previously established variables. In Flash 5, you can use the new Dots notation (and array access operators) to indirectly refer to variables, or you can use Flash 4's `eval()` function (to maintain backward compatibility).

Array access operators

If you have a variable called name_1, you can write the expression _root["name_" + "1"] to refer to the value of name_1. How is this useful? If you have more than one variable, but their prefix are the same (for example, name_1, name_2, name_3, and so on), you can write an expression with two variables as a generic statement to refer to any one of the previously established variables: _root["name" + i], where i can be any predefined number.

Eval( )function and Flash 4's Set Variable

If you want to use old-fashioned ActionScript to indirectly refer to variable names and values, then you have two ways to go about it:

1. Use the Set Variable action, specifying the variable name as a Slash-notated expression as:

   ```
   set("/name_" add i, "Robert Reinholdt");
   ```

2. Use the eval() function, specifying the variable as an expression:

   ```
   eval("_root.name_" add i) = "Robert Reinholdt";
   ```

Variables as declarations

In most scripting languages, you usually don't have to declare a variable without its value; that is, you don't need to say variable firstName and then address it again with a value. In Flash, you don't need to preestablish a variable in order to invoke it. If you want to create a variable on the fly from a Movie Clip to the Main Timeline, you can. Most variables that you use in Flash will be declared in a timeline's keyframes.

Variables as text fields

Since Flash 4, text could be specified as *text fields*. A text field can be used as a dynamic text container whose content can be updated via ActionScript and/or the intervention of a server-side script (known in Flash 5 as *Dynamic Text*), or it can accept input from the user (known in Flash 5 as *Input Text*).

You can access its properties by selecting a text field and opening the Text Options Panel. In this panel, you can define the parameters of the text variable, including its name.

An Input Text field is editable when the Flash movie is played; the user can enter text into the text field. This newly typed text becomes the value of the text field variable. On a login screen, you can create an Input Text field with a name login, where the user enters his/her name, such as Joe. In ActionScript, this would be received as login = "Joe". Any text that you type into a text field during the authoring process will be that variable's initial value.

Declaring Variables in Flash

There are several ways to establish, or declare, variables in a Flash movie. You can create them directly with ActionScript (or with Text Fields, as seen in the last section), load them from a text file or CGI (Common Gateway Interface) script, or include them in HTML tags.

Using actions to define variables

The most common way to create a variable is to type the variable's name and value in the Actions list of the Actions Panel, on a specific timeline's keyframe, accessed in the Frame Properties or Instance Properties dialog. Most basic variables will have values that are string literals.

If you are using Normal Mode in the Actions Panel, then a var action has one option: variables. Note that the var action is used for local variables that only exist for the duration of a function execution.

Cross-Reference We discuss local variables in the next chapter.

Loading variables from a predefined source

You can also establish variables by loading them from an external source, such as a text file located on your Web server or even through a database query. By using the loadVariables action, you can load variables in this fashion. There are three primary options for the loadVariables action: URL, Location, and Variables (see Figure 21-1).

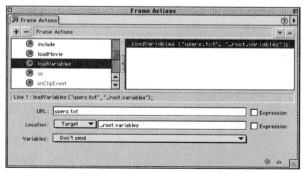

Figure 21-1: The options of the loadVariables action

URL specifies the source of the variables to be loaded. This can be a relative link to the variable source (you don't need to enter the full path of the resource). You can specify whether this URL value is a literal value (`"http://www.theMakers.com/cgi-bin/search.pl"`) or an expression that uses a variable or a combination of variables (`serverURL + scriptPath + scriptApp`). If you want to point to a specific file, type its relative path and name here. If you want to access a database that returns dynamic data, insert the path to the script, such as `"http://www.domain.com/cgi-bin/search.pl"`.

The Location option determines where the variables are to be loaded. You can send the name/value pairs to a level or a timeline target. If you want the variables to be available on the Main Timeline, use `_root` or `_level0`. You can also specify a Movie Clip target using a relative or absolute address. To load to the current Movie Clip (the one initiating the `loadVariables` action), use the target `this`.

The last option is Variables, and this drop-down menu specifies whether you are sending and loading (in other words, receiving) variables. If you want to load variables from a static source, like a text file, you should choose Don't Send. If you are sending a query to a database-driven engine, then you will need to choose either GET or POST. Note that the use of `loadVariables` in GET or POST method means that you are sending variables declared on the active timeline to the specified URL, which, in turn, will send name/value pairs back to the Flash movie.

The formatting of name/value pairs is standard URL-encoded text. If you want to encode name/values in a text file (or a database), you need to use the following format:

```
variable=value&variable=value...
```

Basically, in URL-encoded text, name/value pairs are joined by an ampersand (&). To join multiple terms in a value, use the plus (+) symbol, as in:

```
name1=Joe+Smith&name2=Susan+Deboury
```

Sending variables to URLs

You can also send variables to a URL by using the `getURL` action. Any name/value pairs that are declared on the active timeline will be sent along with the `getURL` action, if a variable send method is defined (GET or POST). Note that `getURL` is only used to send variables out of a Flash movie — it will not retrieve or load any subsequent name/value pairs. If you use a getURL action on a Movie Clip timeline as follows:

```
firstName = "Robert";
getURL("/cgi-bin/form.cgi", "_blank", "GET");
```

then the Flash movie will send the following request to your server:

```
http://www.server.com/cgi-bin/form.cgi?firstName=Robert;
```

The output of the `form.cgi` script would be opened in a new browser window
(`"_blank"`).

Establishing variables with HTML

You can also send variables to Flash movies in the `<EMBED>` and `<OBJECT>` tags that
call the Flash movie. In the SRC attribute of `<EMBED>` or the `PARAM NAME=movie` subtag
of the `<OBJECT>` tag, attach the name/value pairs to the end of the Flash movie
filename, separated by a question mark (?).

```
<OBJECT...>
<PARAM NAME=movie VALUE="flash.swf?name=Rob">
<EMBED SRC="flash.swf?name=Rob">
```

Cross-Reference   We discuss data sending and receiving with greater detail in Chapter 24, "Sending
Data In and Out of Flash."

Creating Expressions in ActionScript

You can write expressions either by manually typing in the primary option fields of
ActionScript commands, or by dragging and dropping Actions from Action Booklets
in the Actions Panel. There are no scripting wizards in Flash; Flash 5 will not automatically script anything for you. However, it will provide you with Booklets of
operators and functions available in Flash 5.

Operators

Operators are used to perform combinations, mathematical equations, and to
compare values.

General and numeric operators

These operators are used for common mathematical operations of adding, subtracting, multiplying, and dividing. You can also use these operators to compare numeric
values, such as > or <.

```
if (results > 1)
name = "Robert";
_root["name_" + i] = newName;
```

String operators

These Flash 4-specific operators are used to declare, join, or compare string literals with other string literals or expressions. If you want to concatenate two variables to create a new variable, use the string operators.

```
set ("fullName", "firstName" & " " & "lastName");
```

Logical operators

These operators join several expressions to create conditions. We discuss these further in the "Checking conditions: If...Else actions" section of this chapter.

```
// Flash 5 syntax below

if (results > 1 && newResults < 10){
   // do something...
}

// Flash 4 syntax below

if (results > number("1") AND newResults < number("10")){
   // do something...
}
```

Table 21-1 describes the ActionScript operators available in both Flash 4 and 5 syntax.

Table 21-1
ActionScript Operators

Flash 5	Flash 4	Definition
+	+	Adds number values and joins (concatenates) strings in Flash 5
-	-	Subtracts number values
*	*	Multiplies number values
/	/	Divides number values
=	=	Equals; used for assignment of variables, properties, methods, and so on in Flash 5; can be used for comparison in Flash 4
==	=	Equals; used for comparison in if/else . . . if conditions
!=	<>	Does not equal

Flash 5	Flash 4	Definition
<	<	Less than
>	>	Greater than
<=	<=	Less than or equal to
>=	>=	Greater than or equal to
( )	( )	Group operations together, as in x = (x+y) * 3;
" "	" "	Indicate that the enclosed value should be interpreted as a string, not as an expression
==	eq	Is equal to; for example, if (name == "derek"){ or if (name eq "derek"){
!=	ne	Is not equal to
<	lt	Alphabetically before; if the strings compared have multiple characters, then the first character determines the alphabetical position
>	gt	Alphabetically after
<=	le	Alphabetically before or the same as
>=	ge	Alphabetically after or the same as
+	add	Join two strings together or add a string to a variable
&&	and	Logical comparison; requires that two or more conditions be met in a single comparison
||	or	Logical comparison; requires that one of two or more conditions be met in a single comparison
!	not	Logical comparison; requires that the opposite of a condition to be met in a single comparison

Checking conditions: If...Else actions

Conditions lie at the heart of logic. In order to create an intelligent machine (or application), we need to create a testing mechanism. This mechanism (called a conditional) needs to operate on rather simple terms as well. Remember the true/false tests that you took in grade school? if/else statements work on a similar principle: If the condition is true, then execute a set of actions. If the condition is false, then disregard the enclosed actions and continue to the next condition or action.

You can simply create isolated if statements that do not employ an else (or then) statement. Solitary if statements are simply ignored if the condition is false. Else statements are used as a default measure in case the tested condition proves false.

Else if statements continue to test conditions if the previous if (or else if) was false. Refer to following examples for more insight.

✦ **Basic** if **statement:** The code between the curly braces is ignored if the condition is false.

```
if (condition is true){
    then execute this code
}
```

✦ **Extended** if/else if/else **statement:** If the first condition is true, then code immediately after the first condition is executed and the remaining else if and else statements are disregarded. However, if the first condition is not true, then the second condition is tested. If it is true, then its code executes and all other statements in the if group are ignored. If all conditions prove false, then the code between the curly braces of the final else is executed.

```
if ( first condition is true){
    then execute this code
} else if (second condition is true){
    then execute this code
} else {
    otherwise, execute this code
}
```

In production, you could have an if/else structure that assigned the value of one variable based on the value of another, such as:

```
if (x == 1){
    name = "Margaret";
} else if (x == 2){
    name = "Michael";
} else {
    name = "none";
}
```

Caution

Do not use a single = sign in a condition, as this will actually set the variable's value. For example, if you wrote if (x = 1){}, then Flash will actually set x = 1, and not check whether x's value is equal to 1.

In Normal Mode, you can add an if statement in ActionScript by choosing the if action from the plus (+) button in the top-left corner of the Actions Panel, or by selecting it from the Actions Booklet. In the Condition text field, enter the expression that identifies what circumstance must exist for the statements in your conditional to be executed. Remember that, in your expression, literal strings must be quoted, and the == operator must be used for string or numeric comparisons. To add an else clause, select the first line of the if statement, and then double-click the else or else if action in the Actions Booklet.

You can join two conditions using Logical compound operators such as and (&&), or (||), or not (!), as in:

```
if (results >1 && newResults < 10){
    gotoAndPlay ("end");
} else if (results > 1 ! newResults < 10) {
    gotoAndPlay ("try_again");
}
```

Loops

A loop is a container for a statement or series of statements that are repeated as long as a specified condition is exists. A basic loop has three parts: the condition, the list of statements to be repeated, and a counter update. There are four types of loops in Flash 5 ActionScript:

✦ while

✦ do . . . while

✦ for

✦ for . . . in

Each of these loop types has a specific use. Depending on the repetitive actions you wish to loop, you need to decide how best to accommodate your code with loop actions.

while(*condition*){ *actions* }

This loop was called the Loop While action in Flash 4. In this loop type, the condition of the loop is evaluated first, and, if it is true, then the actions within the curly braces will be executed. The actions will loop indefinitely (causing a script error) unless there is a way out of the loop — a counter update. A counter update will increment (or decrement) the variable used in the while condition. Here you see a breakdown of a typical while loop. Note that a variable used in the condition is usually set just before the while action is executed.

Initial variable	count = 1;
Condition	while (count <= 10){
Statements to be repeated	_root["clip_" + count]._xscale = 100 / count;
Counter update	count = count + 1;
Termination of loop	}

In this example, a variable named `count` starts with a value of 1. The first time the `while` action executes, counter's value is less than (or equal to) 10. Therefore, the actions within the curly braces are executed. The first action in the loop uses the `count` value to form the name of a Movie Clip instance, clip_1, and alter it's X Scale property by a value of 100/1 (which is equal to 100). Then, the `count` variable is incremented by 1, giving it a new value of 2. The `while` condition is then reevaluated.

The second time the `while` action executed, `count`'s value, 2, is still less than (or equal to) 10. Therefore, the actions within the curly braces are executed again. This time, though, the first action in the loop will address the "clip_2" instance's X Scale property, and make that property's value 50 (100/2 = 50). Then, `count` will be incremented by 1, giving it a new value of 3. Again, the `while` condition is reevaluated.

The `while` condition will continue to execute its nested actions until `count` exceeds a value of 10. Therefore, clip_1 through clip_10 will show a decrease in X Scale.

do { *actions* } while(*condition*);

This type of loop is very similar to the `while` loop discussed previously, with one important exception: The actions in the `do{}` nesting will always be executed at least once. In a `do . . . while` loop, the condition is evaluated after the actions in the loop are executed. If the `while` condition is `true`, then the actions in the `do{}` nesting will be executed again. If the `while` condition is `false`, then the loop will no longer execute.

Initial variable	`count = 1;`
`do` loop	`do{`
Statements to be repeated	`_root["clip_" + count]._xscale = 100 / count;`
Counter update	`count = count + 1;`
Condition	`} while (count <= 1);`

In this example, the actions within the `do{}` nesting will execute automatically without checking any condition. Therefore, the X Scale of "clip_1" will be set to 100, and the `count` value will increase by 1, giving it a new value of 2. After the actions execute once, the condition is checked. Because the value of `count` is not less than (or equal to) 1, the loop does not continue to execute.

for (*initialize; condition; next*) { *actions* }

The `for` loop is a supercondensed `while` loop. Instead of assigning, checking, and reassigning a variable action in three different actions, a `for` loop enables you to define, check, and reassign the value of a counter variable.

Initial variable value, condition, and update	`for(i = 1; i <= 10; i++){`
Statements to be repeated	`    _root["clip_" + i]._xscale = 100 / i;`
Termination of loop	`}`

This `for` loop does exactly the same as the `while` loop example we used earlier. When the loop is started, the variable `i` is given a starting value of 1. A condition for the loop is specified next, `i <= 10`. In this case, we want the loop to repeat the nested actions until the value of `i` exceeds 10. The third parameter of the `for` loop, `i++`, indicates that `i`'s value should be increased by 1 with each pass of the loop. Note that this parameter can use ++ (to increase by 1) or -- (to decrease by 1) operators. You can also use expressions like `i = i*2` for the update.

for(*variableIterant* in *object*){ *actions* }

The final type of loop, `for . . . in`, is the most complex looping mechanism. A `for . . . in` loop does not need a condition statement. Rather, this loop works with a find-and-replace keyword mechanism. Basically, a *variableIterant* is declared, which is simply a placeholder for a property or position index within an object or array, respectively. For every occurrence of the variableIterant, the actions within the `for . . . in {}` nesting will be executed. The `for . . . in` loop can only be used with objects and arrays, and even then, not all properties of this elements can be enumerated.

Placeholder and object	`for(name in _root){`
Statements to be repeated	`    _root[name]._xscale = 50;`
Termination of loop	`}`

In the preceding code example, the word name is used to designate a property of the _root timeline. In this case, we want to change all Movie Clip instances on the Main Timeline to a 50 percent X Scale value. We don't need to specify the actual target paths of each individual instance—the `for . . . in` loop will search for all instances on the Main Timeline, apply the change, and exit the loop.

Although this might look a bit confusing, it can be more helpful than you can imagine. Have you ever had a bunch of nested Movie Clip instances that all need to play at the same time? In Flash 4, you would have had to use several `tellTarget(){}` actions, each one specifying the target path. You could use a while loop to shorten the lengthy code, but, even still, you would need to list the specific parts of the each Movie Clip path, as in:

```
count = 1;
while(count <= 10){
    path = eval("_root.clip_" + count);
```

```
tellTarget(path){
    play();
}
count++;
}
```

The preceding code block would tell clip_1 through clip_10 to start playing. But what if you didn't know (or care to remember) all the paths to several differently named Movie Clip instances? For example, if you had a Movie Clip instance named nestAnim with several nested Movie Clip instances with different names (for example, squareAnim, triangleAnim, and circleAnim), then you would have to specifically name these instances as targets. In Flash 5, the for . . . in loop would let you control any and all nested Movie Clip instances simultaneously:

```
for(name in nestAnim){
    nestAnim[name].play();
}
```

With just three lines of code, all Movie Clip instances in the nestAnim Movie Clip instance will start to play. How? Remember that the variableIterant name is simply a placeholder for a property of the nestAnim Movie Clip object. The for . . . in loop will find every occurrence of an instance inside of nestAnim. And the word name has no significance. We could use a variableIterant myName, and everything would still work fine. Think of the variableIterant as a wildcard in file searches or directory listings in MS-DOS or UNIX:

```
nestAnim[*].play();
```

Although this syntax won't work with ActionScript, it does illustrate the processing of a for . . . in loop. Everything and anything that is playable on the nestAnim timeline will play.

On the CD-ROM Check out the mcPlay.fla and forInLoop.fla files, located in the ch21 folder of the *Flash 5 Bible* CD-ROM.

break

The break action is not a type of loop — it is an action that enables you to quickly exit a loop if a subordinate condition exists. Suppose you wanted to loop an action that hides, at most, clip_1 through clip_10 (out of a possible 20 Movie Clip instances), but you want to have a variable control the overall limit of the loop, as upperLimit does in the following code block. upperLimit's value could change at different parts of the presentation, but at no point do we want to hide more than clip_1 through clip_10. We could use a break action in a nested if action to catch this:

```
count = 1;
while(count <= upperLimit){
    if(count > 10){
        break;
    }
```

```
    _root["clip_" + count]._visible = false;
    count++;
}
```

Break statements, though, should be reserved for catching errors (such as during a debug process) or the need for an immediate exit from the loop.

continue

Like the break action, continue enables you to exit the execution of actions within a loop. However, a continue action won't exit the loop action. It simply restarts the loop (and continues evaluating the current condition). Usually, you will place a continue action with an if nest — otherwise, it will always interrupt the actions within the loop action. For example, if you wanted to omit a particular value from going through the loop actions, you could use the continue action to bypass that value. In the following code block, we will hide clip_1 through clip_10, except for clip_5:

```
count = 1;
while(count <= 10){
  if(count == 5){
    count++;
    continue;
  }
  _root["clip_" + count]._visible = false;
}
```

Adding a loop to your Actions list

To create a loop, add one of the loop-type actions in the Actions Panel, using the plus (+) button in the top-left corner of the panel (or selecting it from the Actions booklet). In the Condition text field, enter an expression that describes the conditions under which the loop should continue repeating. Before the end of the loop, be sure to update whatever the loop relies on in order to continue, usually a counter. If you forget to update a counter, you will be stuck forever in the loop, and Flash will imperiously stop the script from continuing.

Loops in Flash are not appropriate for running background processes that listen for conditions to become true elsewhere in the movie. While a loop is in progress, the screen is not updated and no mouse events are captured, so most Flash actions are effectively not executable from within a loop. Loop Actions are best suited to abstract operations such as string handling (for example, to check each letter of a word to see if it contains an @ symbol) and dynamic variable assignment.

Loops to execute repetitive actions, which affect tangible objects in the movie, should be created as repeating frames in Movie Clips. To create a permanently running process, make a Movie Clip with two keyframes. On the first frame, call the subroutine or add the statements that you want to execute; on the second frame use a gotoAndPlay(1); action to return to the first frame. Alternatively, you can use Flash 5's new onClipEvent(enterFrame) handler to execute repetitive actions.

The onClipEvent handler is first discussed in Chapter 19, "Controlling Movie Clips."

Properties

Properties are characteristics (such as width and height) of movies and Movie Clips that can be retrieved and set. You can use variables to store the current value of a given property, such as:

```
xPos = _root._xmouse;
```

which will store the current X position of the mouse pointer (relative to the stage coordinates of the Main Timeline) in the variable xPos.

See Chapter 19, "Controlling Movie Clips," for detailed tables and explanations of Movie Clip (and movie) properties.

Built-in functions

Flash 5's ActionScript contains a number of native programming commands known as *functions*. Among others, these functions include getTimer, getVersion, parseFloat, parseInt, int, string, substring, escape, and unescape. It's beyond the scope of this chapter (and this book) to discuss the practical use of every new function and ActionScript element in Flash 5. We do, however, discuss many built-in functions throughout this part of the Flash Bible.

Creating and calling subroutines

Whether they're called functions or subroutines, most programming languages provide a mechanism for programmers to create self-contained code modules that can be executed from anywhere in a program. ActionScript supports subroutines by using the new Flash 5 ActionScript function constructor. You can create functions on any timeline, and, just like Movie Clip instances, functions have absolute or relative paths that must be used to invoke them. For example, if you have the following function on a Movie Clip named Functions, located on the Main Timeline:

```
function makeDuplicate(target, limit){
   for(i=1;i<=limit;i++){
      _root[target].duplicateMoviecClip(target+"_"+i, i);
   }
}
```

then to invoke it from another timeline, you would execute it as follows:

```
_root.Functions.makeDuplicate("clip",5);
```

Executing it would create five duplicates of the Movie Clip instance named "clip", naming the duplicates "clip_1", "clip_2", "clip_3", "clip_4", and "clip_5".

Subroutines in Flash 4

To create a subroutine in Flash 4-compatible movies, first attach an action or series of actions to a keyframe. Next, give that keyframe a label. That's it, you've got a subroutine. To call your subroutine from any other keyframe or button, simply add a `Call` action, and then enter the name of the subroutine into the Frame text field using the following syntax: Start with the target path to the timeline on which the subroutine keyframe resides, enter a colon (:), and then enter the subroutine name (for example: `Call ("/bouncingball: getRandom")`). When you call a subroutine, all the actions on the specified keyframe are executed. The subroutine must be present on the movie timeline (either as an keyframe or an embedded Movie Clip instance) for it to work.

Subroutines in Flash do not accept passed parameters, nor do they return any values. To simulate passing and receiving variable values, set the necessary variable values in the action list that calls the subroutine before it is called, and then have the subroutine set other variables that can be retrieved afterward by any other actions.

Cross-Reference We discuss functions in greater detail in the next chapter.

Make a Login Sequence with Variables

In this section, we show you how to use variables to create an interactive form in Flash that accepts or rejects user input. You will create two Input Text fields into which Web visitors will type a username and password. Using ActionScript, we will check the values of the entered data with predefined name/value pairs.

Caution Do not use the following example for secure information over the Web. You could use a login sequence like this in a Flash adventure game, or modify it to work in a Flash quiz. The login information is not secure within the confines of a Flash .SWF movie.

1. Open a new Flash movie. Assign a frame rate of 20 fps, using the default width and height. Use your preferred background color.

2. Create two text fields on one layer called **Text Fields**. Make each text field long enough to accommodate a single first name and/or password. For demonstration purposes, make the text in the text fields large, around 36 points. Make sure that you use a nonwhite fill color for the text.

3. Access the properties for each text field by selecting the text field (with the Arrow Tool) and opening the Text Options Panel, shown in Figure 21-2. In the top drop-down menu, select the Input Text option for both fields. For the top text field, assign the variable name `userEnter`. For the other text field, assign the variable name `passwordEnter`, enable the Password option, and restrict the text length to 8 characters.

Figure 21-2: The passwordEnter variable will be an Input Text field with the Password option enabled and a restricted character length of 8 characters.

4. On a separate layer in the Main Timeline, create text blocks that describe the two text fields, as shown in Figure 21-3. For example, make a text block with the word **Login:** and another one with the word **Password:**. Align these text blocks to the left of the text fields. Note that these text blocks do not need the Input Text behavior; they should be Static Text blocks.

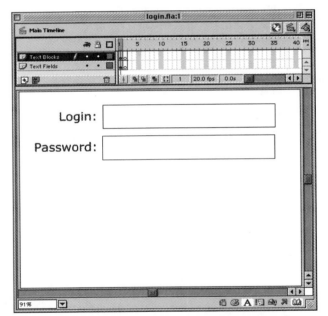

Figure 21-3: Here we have four text areas: two Static Text blocks on the left, and two Input Text fields on the right. The Static Text cannot be altered and/or "read" by ActionScript.

5. Create a new Movie Clip symbol (Ctrl+F8 or Command+F8), called **errorMessage**, that displays an error message, such as INVALID or LOGIN ERROR. Rename Layer 1 of its timeline to **actions**. On that layer, the first frame of the Movie Clip should be blank with a stop() frame action.

6. Create another layer called **labels**. On frame 2 of this layer, make a keyframe and assign it the label start in the Frame Panel.

7. Then, create a new layer called **anim** and move it underneath the actions layer. On this layer, create a tweening animation of your message fading in and out (or scaling up and down, and so on). Start the Motion Tween on frame 2 of the anim layer, underneath the start label of the actions layer. You'll need to make the message a Graphic symbol of its own in order to tween the alpha state. Add enough frames and keyframes to cycle this message animation twice. The very last frame of the animation should have a frame action (on the actions layer) `gotoAndStop(1);`. When you are finished with this step, your Movie Clip timeline should resemble the one shown in Figure 21-4.

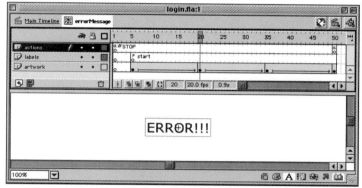

Figure 21-4: The errorMessage Movie Clip symbol contains an empty first frame, and an animation that begins on the start label. This animation will only play if the user enters an incorrect login.

8. In the main movie timeline (Scene 1), create a new layer called **errorMessage**. Drag the Movie Clip symbol from the Library on to the Stage. Position it underneath the user and password text fields. Select the Movie Clip instance on the Stage and access its settings in the Instance Panel. Assign the instance name of errorMessage.

9. Create a new layer on the Main Timeline called **button**, and make a Button symbol on it. You can make one of your own, or use one from Flash's Button library (Window ➪ Common Libraries ➪ Buttons). Place it to the right of or underneath the user and password fields. Select the Button symbol instance, and open the Actions Panel. Add the following ActionScript code in the Actions tab (note that the ¬ character indicates a continuation of the same line of code; do not type or insert this character into your actual code):

```
on (release){
  if (userEnter == "Sandra" && ¬
    passwordEnter == "colorall"){
      gotoAndStop ("success");
  } else {
      _root.errorMessage.gotoAndPlay("start");
  }
}
```

You can change the `userEnter` and `passwordEnter` values to whatever string you desire.

10. On the Main Timeline, create an actions layer, and place it at the top of the layer order. On the first frame, add a `stop()` frame action.

11. Create another layer named **labels**. Assign a frame label of start to frame 1 of the labels layer. Add a keyframe to the frame 2 of the labels layer, and label it **success**. Make sure all other layers on frame 2 have empty keyframes.

12. Make a new layer called **success** and place a text block and/or other graphics suitable for a successful login entry. It should only appear on frame 2, so, if necessary move its initial keyframe to that frame. When you're finished with the step, your Stage and Main Timeline should resemble Figure 21-5.

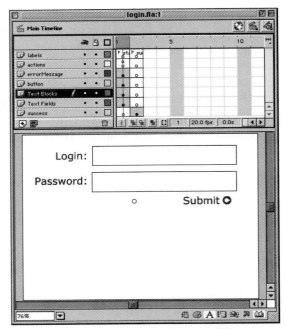

Figure 21-5: Your Main Timeline should have three "states": a login page, an error message, and a success page.

13. Test the movie's functionality with the Test Movie command (Control ➪ Test Movie).

Most login forms like this work with the Return or Enter key active to submit the information. However, this key press also has functionality in the Test Movie environment, so only assign a key press to the Button symbol instance *after* you have tested the initial ActionScript code.

Debugging Your Code

As you start to program your Flash movies with the latest and greatest ActionScript, you'll likely encounter more than one error or experience frustration something you've written isn't working as it should. You can track down errors in your code in three different ways:

✦ **Debugger Panel:** Flash 5 has added a new comprehensive dedicated debugging tool to the authoring environment. The Debugger Panel can be activated in two ways:

- **Debug Movie command:** Accessed with the Control ⇨ Debug Movie command, this method of testing .SWF files enables the Debugger Panel.

- **Remote Debugging:** You can now debug Flash movies from the Flash Player plug-in (or ActiveX Control), as the Flash movie plays in a Web browser window. You'll need to take some steps to enable this feature, though. We discuss the Debugger Panel in more detail shortly.

✦ **Output window:** The Output window will automatically open upon using the Test Movie (or Debug Movie) command when a trace action occurs (see the description later in this list) or when a syntax error is detected in the ActionScript. Syntax errors will appear in the Output window as soon as the export process for the .SWF file is completed. You can also manually update the Output window with useful moving information by using the List Objects and List Variables commands:

- **List Objects.** While in Test Movie (or Debug Movie) mode, use Debug ⇨ List Objects to obtain a list of every element currently present on the movie stage, including Movie Clip instances, buttons, graphics, shapes, and text. List Objects displays the full names and paths of any Movie Clip instance or loaded movies. Useful for checking target names.

- **List Variables.** While in Test Movie (or Debug Movie) mode, use Debug ⇨ List Variables to obtain a list of all variables currently initialized, and to find out their locations and values. This is very useful for checking whether a variable is resident at specific points on the movie timeline and for checking the name of the timeline upon which the variable resides.

- `trace(expression)`. Add a `trace` action to send a string or the value of an interpreted expression to the Output Window during Test Movie (or Debug Movie) mode. The value is sent when the `trace` action occurs. As a debugging tool, `trace` is analogous to `alert()` in JavaScript.

✦ **Custom debugging interfaces:** You can also create your own debugging windows within a Flash movie, using draggable Movie Clips (such as the propInspector.fla from Chapter 19, "Controlling Movie Clips"). Usually, Flash programmers will employ a temporary text field variable to display code output during development. Put temporary text fields on their own layer and make that layer a Guide Layer when exporting the production version of your movie.

Caution   If you think whole sets of actions are being ignored, you may have a simple syntax error in just one line of your code. If any syntax errors are detected in any container (a frame, Button instance, or Movie Clip onClipEvent handler), then the entire list of actions for that container will be effectively disabled. After you correct the syntax error and retest (or republish), the actions in that container will all function again.

Using the Debugger Panel

When you use the Control ➪ Debug Movie command, Flash 5 will create a .SWF file from your .FLA movie file, and open the Debugger Panel. The Debugger Panel (see Figure 21-6) provides useful information about your .SWF file as it plays:

Figure 21-6: When it comes to tracking down scripting problems, the Debugger Panel is a welcome addition to Flash 5.

The elements of the Debugger Panel are as follows:

✦ **Status Bar:** Located at the top of the Debugger Panel, the Status Bar indicates where the .SWF file resides. If you used the Test Movie (or Debug Movie) command within Flash 5, then the Status Bar will read Test Movie. If you are debugging a .SWF file from a Web browser, then the Status Bar will show the full path (or URL) to the .SWF file.

✦ **Display List:** The top pane of the Debugger Panel lists the absolute path (and nesting of) all of the current playing timelines for the Flash movie, including all native Movie Clip instances, all loaded .SWF files (in Levels or Movie Clip targets), and all duplicated or attached Movie Clips (created with ActionScript).

✦ **Properties tab:** This first tab in the lower-left portion of the Debugger Panel lets you view all properties of a selected timeline in the Display List. You can even alter the values of the properties with string, numeric, or Boolean values. You cannot enter expressions (for example, $x + 50$) as a value of any property.

✦ **Variables tab:** This middle tab in the lower portion of the panel enables you to view the variables on a selected timeline in the Display List. As with properties in the Properties tab, you can alter the values of any variable (with the same data type restrictions).

✦ **Watch tab:** This right tab in the lower portion of the panel enables you to monitor specific variables on any timeline. You can add variables to the Watch list in one of two ways:

   1. By right-clicking (or Ctrl+clicking on the Mac) the variable name in the Variables tab and choosing Watch from the contextual menu

   2. By right-clicking (or Ctrl+clicking on the Mac) the empty area of the Watch list and choosing Add from the contextual menu.

You can remove variables from the Watch list by right-clicking (or Ctrl+clicking on the Mac) the watched variable, and choosing Remove from the contextual menu.

Enabling remote debugging

As mentioned previously, you can now debug your Flash 5 .SWF files (served over the Web or from your local disk) as they play live in a Web browser. To enable debugging from a Web browser, you need to do two things:

   1. **Allow debugging in the Publish Settings.** Open the Publish Settings dialog (File ➪ Publish Settings), and select the Flash tab. Check the Debugging Permitted option, and enter a password if you are uploading the .SWF file to a live Web server. You do not need to supply a password, but we highly recommend it for security purposes.

   2. **Install the Flash Player (Debug Version) for your preferred Web browser(s).** You will find the plug-in installer (or ActiveX Control installer) inside the Debug folder of the Players folder, located in the Flash 5 application folder. Make sure you delete any previously installed plug-ins or ActiveX Controls before attempting to install the Debug Player.

After you have enabled debugging and installed the Debug Player, you can point your browser to the .SWF's location on the Web (or on your local disk). Alternatively, you can use the Publish Preview command (File ➪ Publish Preview ➪ HTML) to load the .SWF file (and supporting HTML file) into your preferred Web browser. After the movie has loaded into the browser, right-click (or Ctrl+click on the Mac), the movie's Stage and select Debugger from the contextual menu. Focus will go back to the Flash 5 application, and you will be prompted to enter the debugging password as you supplied it in the Flash format tab of the Publish Settings dialog. If you left the password field blank, then simply click OK. Flash will open the Debugger Panel, providing you instant access to your movie's timeline information, properties, and variables!

Caution You need the Flash 5 application installed on any machine from which you wish to debug your Flash movies. The Debugger Panel can only be displayed within the Flash 5 authoring environment.

Make sure that you disable debugging (or use a password-protected debugger) before you launch your Flash movies on your live Web server. Otherwise, other people can debug your Flash movie.

Summary

✦ Before you begin to add complex interactivity to your Flash movie, you need to break down the steps in the interactive process in a natural language that you can understand.

✦ After you know what you want your presentation to do, you can start to clarify the interactive steps, and translate those steps into Flash-compatible actions.

✦ You can add Flash ActionScript to your Flash movie with the Actions Panel. The Actions Panel operates in two modes: Normal and Expert. If you want to see the options of each action in fields and drop-down menus, then add actions with Normal Mode. If you want the most flexibility with editing your code, then use Expert Mode.

✦ Variables are a programming device that enable you to store property values, strings, paths, or expressions in order to reduce the redundancy of code and to simplify the process of computing information.

✦ Variables can be declared with actions, Input or Dynamic Text fields, or by loading them from an external data source, such as a CGI script, text document, or HTML query.

✦ Expressions are equations that refer to a mathematical operation, a string concatenation, or an existing code object (another variable or object value).

✦ You can use `if/else if/else` actions to add intelligence to your interactive actions. These actions test a condition and execute a certain set of actions if the condition is true.

✦ Loop actions execute a given set of actions repeatedly until a loop condition is no longer true.

✦ You can debug your ActionScript code with the new Debugger Panel, the Output window, or your own debugging interfaces (for example, temporary text fields that display Flash ActionScript data).

✦   ✦   ✦

Creating Subroutines and Manipulating Data

Once you understand how to work with basic data in the form of variables, you can start to explore the programming concepts behind subroutines and arrays. This chapter introduces you to data types, subroutines, arrays, and complex uses of functions.

What Are Data Types?

In Flash 4, any data that you had in Flash movie was not "typed." A data type is a classification or group to which a piece of data belongs. Some data types cannot be converted into other data types, but some can. To illustrate data typing, take this working example in a Flash 4 movie:

```
Set Variable: "path1" = "/ballAnim/ballPath"
Set Variable: "path2" = "/ballAnim"
Begin Tell Target (path1)
    Stop
End Tell Target
Begin Tell Target (path2)
    Stop
End Tell Target
```

In this code example, we have two Flash 4 variables, `path1` and `path2`. The values of these variables are string paths to two different Movie Clip instances, ballAnim and ballPath. In Flash 4, we could use `path1` and `path2` as the target paths in a Tell Target action. In Flash 5, this code would still work:

```
path1 = "_root.ballAnim.ballPath";
path2 = "_root.ballAnim";
tellTarget(path1){
    stop();
}
tellTarget(path2){
    stop();
}
```

Because the `tellTarget` action is Flash 4-compatible, it can accept string data (for example, `"_root.ballAnim.ballPath"`) for a target path in Flash 5. However, if we try to use Flash 5's new Movie Clip Object methods to control the targets, then `path1` and `path2` will not work:

```
path1 = "_root.ballAnim.ballPath";
path2 = "_root.ballAnim";
path1.stop();
path2.stop();
```

Why? Because `path1` and `path2` have string values, Flash 5 does not "see" `path1` and `path2` as a reference to a real object in ActionScript. If we change the code to:

```
path1 = _root.ballAnim.ballPath;
path2 = _root.ballAnim;
path1.stop();
path2.stop();
```

then Flash 5 will see `path1` and `path2` as references to the `ballPath` and `ballAnim` Movie Clip Objects. At this point, you might be wondering how you can use the old-fashioned `eval()` statement to refer to dynamic Movie Clip paths. In Flash 4, you could do this:

```
Set Variable: "i" = 1;
Set Variable: "path1" = "/ballAnim/ball_" + i;
Begin Tell Target (path1)
    Stop
End Tell Target
```

In Flash 5, if you want a variable to point to a Movie Clip object, then the value of the variable must be an object type. To do the same thing in Flash 5 with Movie Clip methods, you would change the preceding code to:

```
i = 1;
path1 = eval("_root.ballAnim.ball_" + i);
path1.stop();
```

By using `eval()`, Flash 5 will evaluate the string concatenation of `"_root.ballAnim.ball_"` + `i`, which will produce the final string of `"_root.ballAnim.ball_1"`. At this point, Flash doesn't "know" that the string refers to a Movie Clip Object. When this is evaluated, Flash will change the string data into object data, referring to the Movie Clip instance `_root.ballAnim.ball_1`.

But even the `eval()` function is a little dated for Flash 5. In the last chapter, we discussed the use of array access operators — the `[ ]` — to bypass the `eval()` function. As with variables, the array access operators can be used to refer to Movie Clip expressions:

```
i = 1;
_root.ballAnim["ball_" + i].stop();
```

This code will join the `"ball_"` string to the value of `i`, and look for `ball_1` Movie Clip object on the `ballAnim` timeline.

So far, we have seen two data types at work: strings and objects. If a variable's value is in quotes, as in `"_root.ballAnim"`, then Flash 5 sees this value as a string. If the variable's value is evaluated or referenced directly, as in `_root.ballAnim`, then Flash 5 sees this value as an object. Flash 5 has a built-in action, `typeof`, which tells you the data type of a value or an expression. We discuss this action later in this section. Before we look at `typeof`, let's examine the five data types in Flash 5 ActionScript.

string

We've seen string data types throughout the *Flash 5 Bible* already. Anytime you have a value in quotes, it is typed as a string. If you have an expression that refers to string data types, then its data type will be a string as well. All of the following examples have a string data type:

```
firstName = "Frank";
lastName = "Houston";
fullName = firstName + lastName;
pathSuffix = "1";
```

Tip   All Input and Dynamic Text fields have a data type of string. If you need to perform numeric operations with text field values, then make sure you convert the string data to number data. We discuss the number data type in the next heading.

If a variable has a string data type, then any of the String methods can be used with that data. For example, if you want to convert the case of all characters in the value of `firstName` to uppercase (turn "Frank" into "FRANK"), then you could do the following operation:

```
firstName = "Frank";
firstName = firstName.toUpperCase();
```

Here, the String method `toUpperCase()` converts any lowercase characters in a string value to uppercase characters. Likewise, you can extract specific information from a string. For example, if you wanted to find where a space occurs within a string, and return the value of the string from the point in the value to the end of the value, you could use the following code:

```
myVersion = "Netscape 4.71";
startChar = myVersion.indexOf(" ") + 1;
myVersion = myVersion.slice(startChar, -1);
trace("myVersion = " + myVersion);
```

In the preceding code, the `indexOf()` method searches for the first occurrence of a space (" ") within the string value for `myVersion`. `indexOf(" ")` for `myVersion` will return the position (as a number, counting from left to right) of the space character. For this example, `indexOf(" ")` will return a 9. Then, we add 1 to this value to the character position after the space. In our example, the tenth position of `myVersion`'s value is a "4." Then, by using the `slice()` method, we can extract the rest of the string from the `startChar` value of 10. The –1 option tells Flash to continue all the way to the end of the string's value, from the starting point of `startChar`. Note that in this example, the final value of `myVersion` is a string value of "4.71."

Cross-Reference

For more information on methods that can be performed upon String objects and string values, see pages 376–383 of the Macromedia *ActionScript Reference Guide*.

number

A `number` data type is any value (or expression value) that refers to a discrete numeric value in Flash. A value must be typed as a number in order for it to work properly in mathematical operations. Note in the following code that the ¬ indicates a continuation of the same line of code. Do not insert this character into your actual code.

```
myAge = "27";
futureYears = "5";
myAge = myAge + futureYears;
trace("I will be " + myAge + " years old in " ¬
    + futureYears + " years.");
```

If this code was added to a Flash movie and tested, the following trace information would appear in the Output window:

```
I will be 275 years old in 5 years.
```

Obviously, this isn't the answer we were looking for. Because `myAge` and `future Years` were specified as string values (with quotes), Flash simply concatenated (joined) the two string values as "27" + "5", which is "275". To see these values as numbers, we need to change the code to the following (note that the ¬ indicates a continuation of the same line of code; do not insert this character into your actual code):

```
myAge = 27;
futureYears = 5;
myAge = myAge + futureYears;
trace("I will be " + myAge + " years old in " ¬
    + futureYears + " years.");
```

Now, the values of myAge and futureYears appear as real numbers to Flash, and the mathematical operation will add the values of myAge and futureYears correctly. The trace output will now read:

```
I will be 32 years old in 5 years.
```

You can convert string data values to number data values by using the Number() function. In our string example from the last section, we could convert the myVersion string value to a number value by adding this line of code:

```
myVersion = Number(myVersion);
```

So, we can now perform mathematical operations on the "4.71" value of myVersion, which is now simply 4.71.

boolean

There will be times when you will designate a variable's value as either true or false. Variables that use true or false are said to have a Boolean value. Boolean values are useful for either/or situations, or when you need a toggle switch — just like a light switch, which is on or off. In the code below, a variable named isLoading is initialized with a true value, but later switched to a false value when loading is complete:

```
onClipEvent(load){
    _root.isLoading = true;
    trace("isLoading's type = " + typeof(_root.isLoading));
}
onClipEvent(enterFrame){
    if(this._framesLoaded >= this._totalFrames){
        _root.isLoading = false;
    }
}
```

This code could be placed on a Movie Clip instance (as Object actions). When the Movie Clip instance appears on the Stage, the load event will occur, and the Output window will display:

```
isLoading's type = boolean
```

movieclip

As the data type name implies, Movie Clip instances on the Stage have a data type of movieclip. You can check the data types of declared variables and objects with the typeof operator. Flash distinguishes Movie Clip Objects from other code-based objects so that you can more easily detect Movie Clip Objects in your code. The following variable value will be typed as movieclip:

```
path = _root.ballAnim;
```

As long as a physical Movie Clip instance named ballAnim exists on the Main Timeline, then path's data type will be movieclip. If ballAnim did not exist, then path's data type would be undefined.

object

This data type refers to any code-based objects that you create with ActionScript. For example, in previous chapters, we used the Color and Sound Objects to enhance interactive presentations. The following code would be typed as object:

```
myColor = new Color(_root.ballAnim);
mySound = new Sound();
myObject = new Object();
```

If you used this code in your Flash movie, you would see object types in the Output window when Debug ⇨ List Variables is used in the Test Movie environment:

```
Level #0:
  Variable _level0.$version = "MAC 5,0,30,0"
  Variable _level0.myColor = [object #1] {}
  Variable _level0.mySound = [object #2] {}
  Variable _level0.myObject = [object #3] {}
Movie Clip:  Target="_level0.ballAnim"
```

function

In Flash 5, you can define your own subroutines of ActionScript code. We discuss subroutines and constructor functions later in this chapter. The function data type will be assigned to any ActionScript code that begins with the function command, such as:

```
function myGoto(label){
gotoAndStop(label);
}
```

undefined

If you check for the data type of a nonexistent code element, then Flash 5 ActionScript will return a data type of undefined.

Checking data types with typeof

Now that you know the various data types in Flash 5 ActionScript, you'll want to know how to check the data type of a given piece of information. Using the typeof operator, you can determine the data type of an ActionScript element. The typeof operator accepts only one option: the name of the ActionScript element that you wish to test. For example, you can trace a variable (or object) type in the Output window:

```
firstName = "Robert";
trace("firstName has a data type of " + typeof(firstName));
```

When this movie is tested, the Output window will display:

```
firstName has a data type of string
```

You can use typeof in for . . . in loops, so that actions will be executed with specific data types. The following ActionScript code will take any string variables on the Main Timeline and move them to an object (or Movie Clip instance) named globalVar:

```
for(varName in _root){
    if(typeof(_root[varName])=="string" && ù
    _root[varName] != _root["$version"]){
        _root.globalVar[varName] = _root[varName];
        delete _root[varName];
    }
}
```

The preceding code block will move all variables except the native $version variable to the Movie Clip instance (or object) named globalVar.

 On the CD-ROM You can see the returned values of the typeof operator in the typeof_simple.fla, typeof_advanced.fla, and moveVariables.fla files, located in the ch22 folder of the *Flash 5 Bible* CD-ROM.

Overview of Functions as Subroutines

A primary building block of any scripting or programming language is a subroutine. A subroutine is any set of code that you wish to reserve for a specific task. A subroutine is useful for code that you wish to reuse in multiple event handlers (for example, Button instances and keyframes). In Flash ActionScript, subroutines are called functions, and are created with the function action.

What functions do

A function (or subroutine) sets aside a block of code that can be executed with just one line of code. Functions can execute several actions, and pass options (called arguments) to those actions. All functions must have a unique name, so that we know what to reference in later lines of code. In a way, functions are equivalent to your own custom additions to the Flash ActionScript language. In Flash 4, we used the `call` action to execute code blocks located on other keyframes in the Flash movie. In Flash 5, we can define a function on a specific timeline, and refer to its path and name to execute it.

When to create a function

For people new to scripting, perhaps the most confusing aspect of functions is knowing when to create them in a Flash movie. Use the following guidelines to help you determine when a function should be created:

✦ If you find yourself reusing the same lines of code on several Button instances, Movie Clip Objects, or keyframes, then you should consider moving the actions to a function. In general, you should not pile up ActionScript on any single Button instance or keyframe.

✦ If you need to perform the same operation throughout a Flash movie, such as hiding specific Movie Clip instances on the Stage, then you should consider defining a function to take care of the work for you.

✦ When you need to perform complex mathematical operations to determine a value, then you should move the operations to a function.

How to define a function

When you add a function to a keyframe on the Main Timeline or a Movie Clip timeline, you are defining the function. All functions have a target path, just like other Objects in Flash. All functions need a name followed by opening and closing parentheses, but arguments (options to pass to the function) inside the parentheses are optional.

Tip Functions are usually defined at the very beginning of a Flash movie (or within a Movie Clip instance that loads within the first frames of Flash movie). You should only place functions on timeline keyframes — you can, however, execute functions from any event handler in Flash.

As a simple example, let's say you wanted to create a function that has one `goto AndStop()` action. This function will have a shorter name than `gotoAndStop()`, and will be faster to type and use in our ActionScript code. We'll place this on the first keyframe of our Main Timeline.

```
function gts(){
_root.gotoAndStop("start");
}
```

This function, when evoked, will send the Main Timeline playhead to the start label We could further expand the functionality of gts() by adding an argument, which we'll call frameLabel:

```
function gts(frameLabel){
    _root.gotoAndStop(frameLabel);
}
```

In this version of the gts() function, instead of hard-coding a frame label such as start into the actual gotoAndStop() action, we specify an argument with the name frameLabel. Just like variable names, the names of your function and its arguments are entirely up to you—the name frameLabel has no significance. Flash simply knows that if we pass an argument to the gts() function, that it should place that argument where the frameLabel term occurs in our actions. An argument acts as a placeholder for information that will be supplied to the function on a per-use basis; that is, we can specify a different value for frameLabel each time we evoke the gts() function.

Caution   Beware of naming your functions (and arguments) after already existing ActionScript terms. If in doubt, you should probably choose a word that does not resemble any JavaScript syntax (with later upgrades to ActionScript in mind). You'll see many examples in tutorials or books in which programmers always prefix names with my, as in myColor or myLabel, to avoid any potential naming conflicts.

How to execute a function

After you have defined a function on a timeline's keyframe, you can create actions that refer to the function's actions. The standard method for executing a function is:

```
[path to function].functionName(arguments);
```

At the end of the previous section, we defined a function named gts() on the Main Timeline. If we added a Button instance to our movie, we could then execute the function from the Button instance with the following code:

```
on(release){
_root.gts("start");
}
```

When this Button instance is clicked, then the function gts() on the _root timeline (the Main Timeline) is executed, and passed the argument "start". In our function gts(), we defined frameLabel as an argument that occurs in the gotoAndStop() action. Therefore, the Main Timeline will go to and stop on the "start" frame label.

Later in this chapter, we use functions to create a dynamic reusable menu system in a Flash movie.

Caution A function cannot be executed unless it was previously defined and recognized by the Flash Player. The keyframe containing the function declaration needs to be "played" before the function is available for use. For example, if you define a function on frame 10 of a Movie Clip instance that has stopped on frame 1 (and never played to frame 10), then Flash will not have registered the function in memory.

Expert Tutorial: Using ActionScript with a Games Focus, *by Mark Burrs*

Since the introduction of Flash, one of its most exciting effects has been the wealth of dynamic capabilities that it has brought to the Web. Flash 4 expanded our horizons by enabling users to actively participate in the Web experience. With this expansion of capability, it's no wonder that there has been an explosion of Flash games on Web sites and distributed in our e-mails as Projector files. Now that Flash 5 has increased our available tools exponentially, I think we've only seen the tip of the iceberg.

This tutorial helps you make a little ice. It takes you systematically through a nontechnical analysis of architecting a game using a case study, followed by a technical look at how Flash 5 helps solve some of the challenges this case study presents.

The source .FLA and other assets relevant to this tutorial can be found in the ch22 folder of the CD-ROM.

Keys to success
Before opening Flash, a few tasks must be completed. Use a procedure such as the following to help give your development time better focus and structure. A whiteboard is very helpful at this stage, especially if it's a team project.

  ✦ Write out a complete functional specification for what you want to create.

  ✦ Identify major components.

  ✦ List properties of those components.

  ✦ List methods (actions) that each component needs to be able to do.

Case study: An air hockey game
The following steps take you through the creation process for an air hockey game such as the one in the following figure.

Basic Image Type Comparisons

Uncompressed Photoshop TIFF

Fireworks PNG 24   Photoshop PNG

JPEG @ High (94%):
BoxTop   Fireworks   Photoshop

JPEG @ Low (30%):
BoxTop   Fireworks   Photoshop

Color Plate 1
(For more information on Plates 1-8, see the "Basic image-type comparisons" section in Chapter 12)

High Quality JPEG: Smoothing Comparisons

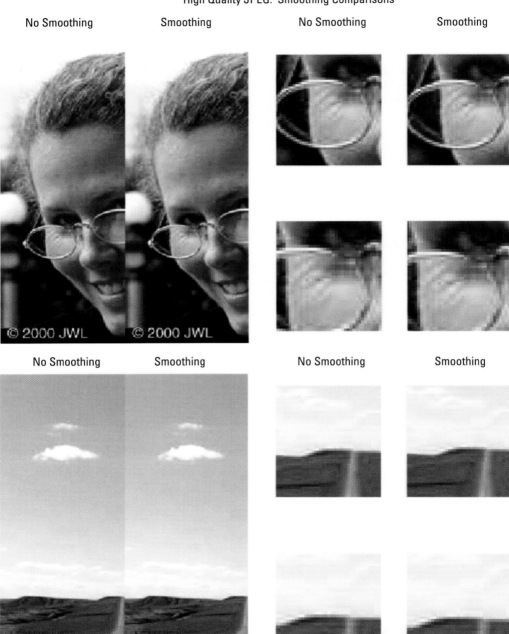

Color Plate 2

High Quality Fireworks JPEG Scaling Comparisons (no smoothing)

100%   200%

100%   200%

Color Plate 3

Medium Quality Fireworks JPEG Scaling Comparisons (no smoothing)

100%

200%

100%

200%

Color Plate 4

Low Quality Fireworks JPEG Scaling Comparisons (no smoothing)

100%   200%

100%   200%

Color Plate 5

Medium Quality Double JPEG Corruption Comparisons (no smoothing)

Double JPEG @ 200%

Double JPEG @ 200%

Double JPEG @ 200%

Double JPEG @ 200%

Color Plate 6

Bit Depth and Color Comparisons

24-bit PNG

256-color 8-bit PNG

128-color, 8-bit PNG

64-color, 8-bit PNG

Color Plate 7

High Quality JPEG Rotation Comparisons

Rotated in Photoshop

100%   200%

100%   Rotated in Flash   200%

Color Plate 8

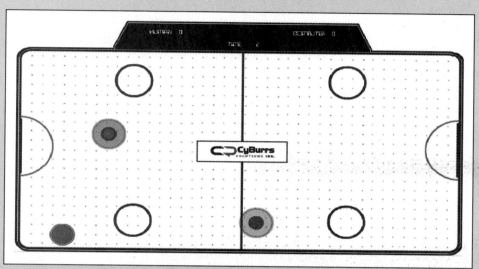

Here's the graphic layout of the air hockey game.

Step 1: Write out a complete functional specification for what you want to create. You should include wish-list items as well. You may not know now if or how to do them, but that can be evaluated more fully later. If you don't list it, it won't happen. The idea here is to start formulating what you want to do so that your brain can start planning a path to get there. Here are some examples:

✦ Human versus computer play mode

✦ Persistent (on the screen all the time) scoreboard with score and time remaining

✦ Demo mode

✦ At start — player-selectable sides (right or left)

✦ At start — player-selectable difficulty settings

✦ At start (or maybe even during a game) — player-selectable ice conditions (fast, slow, or maybe a slider for anything in between)

✦ At start — player-selectable win conditions: first to x, or high score after x minutes

✦ At start — player-selectable paddle color

✦ Ricochet sound

✦ The player and computer should be able to score by knocking the puck into the goal (It may seem silly to have to say it, but so far, while I'm writing this, my prototype does just about everything but this).

Continued

Continued

Step 2: Now that you have a functional specification, it's time to identify the major components that will be necessary to realize that functionality. To do this, simply start a descriptive listing of all the major components that come to mind after creating the functional specifications. Remember that this is a brainstorming session, so don't hold back:

✦ Graphically pleasing rink

✦ Player paddle

✦ Computer paddle

✦ Player goal

✦ Computer goal

✦ Puck

✦ Scoreboard

✦ Opening screen

✦ Ricochet sounds

✦ Game settings screen

Step 3: Now it's time to get more specific by listing the properties of those components. (Understand that this procession of steps does not need to be completed in a single meeting, or in a single day. In fact, your preplanning will probably be enhanced if you take some time between steps, or revisit the completed process after you've given your subconscious some time to gnaw on the details. You may be surprised at how your creativity can be sparked in the interim!):

✦ Graphically pleasing rink

  • Height

  • Width

  • Friction — how much constant drag will affect the puck

✦ Paddle — player or computer

  • `xLocation`

  • `yLocation`

  • `xSpeed`

  • `ySpeed`

  • `maxSpeed` — this is a cap on the `xSpeed` and `ySpeed`

  • `color`

  • `size`

  • `type` — human or computer

✦ Goal — player and computer

- x
- y
- owner — player or computer
- width (visually height, mentally width)

✦ Puck

- xLocation
- yLocation
- xSpeed
- ySpeed
- color
- size
- maxSpeed — this is a cap on the xSpeed and ySpeed

✦ Scoreboard

- playerScore
- computerScore
- timeRemaining

✦ Opening screen

- status — visible, invisible

✦ Ricochet sounds

- Panning — should correspond with horizontal position of the ricochet

✦ Game settings screen

- playMode — "Human versus Computer" or "Demo"
- playerSide — "right" or "left"
- playerColor — "red", "blue", ...
- difficultyLevel — options: 0–10
- friction — options: 0–10
- gameType — "timed" or "first to score x"

Continued

Continued

You may have noticed that, in this step, I got rather technical. How
technical. If you are not the team's ActionScript guru, but are, inst
still describe the action in clear, natural language that commu
other team members.

Step 4: At this step, we list the methods (or actions) that each component needs to be
capable of doing. Again, this list can be written in natural language. The primary purpose of
all these preliminary steps is to clarify what will be built in Flash and how its many parts will
interrelate:

- ✦ Graphically pleasing rink — none
- ✦ Paddles — player and computer
  - Calculate xSpeed and ySpeed — these represent how fast the player is moving
    the paddle and what direction
  - Calculate whether a collision has occurred with the puck
  - Stay within the rinks boundaries
  - The player paddle must be draggable
  - The Computer paddle must have some level of artificial intelligence
- ✦ Goals — player and computer — none
- ✦ Puck
  - Animate within the boundaries of the rink with proper rebounds
  - Rebound off the paddle when a collision is indicated by the paddle
  - Calculate the locations of the goal and indicate to the score board if a score
    occurred
- ✦ Scoreboard
  - Display Player and Computer scores
  - A countdown timer
- ✦ Opening screen — initialize the game
- ✦ Ricochet sound
  - Play
- ✦ Game settings screen — none, it is an information-gathering screen
- ✦ Challenges

Now that we have created an outline of the programming challenges we will face with our Flash movie, we need to start thinking about how we will solve these challenges. We work with the puck animation challenge next.

Puck animation

Challenge: Animate the puck within the boundaries of the rink and make it react when hit by paddles.

To control the puck animation I will make an ActionClip and call it Puck Director. This is a Movie Clip that has no graphical elements; it is a container for ActionScript code only. This Puck Director Movie Clip will be attached to the Puck, so all references made to the actual Puck Movie Clip will be referenced using the `_parent` object. By using the keyword `_parent`, I automatically refer to the Movie Clip that contains my current Movie Clip. To do any kind of animation in Flash, I follow the same basic guidelines:

Get current value:

```
curX = _parent._x
```

Modify current value by applying velocity and friction:

```
newX = curX + xSpeed - friction
```

Check flags — This means to check for various boundaries that exist. In this case, we need to make sure that the puck stays within the confines of the rink. This is usually a series of `if` statements to check whether the new value has reached or exceeded a boundary. If the boundary has been reached or exceeded then the new value is usually set to that boundary.

```
if(newX+(_root.puck1._width*0.5) >= _root.dir_scene:bottom){
  newX = _root.dir_scene.bottom - (_root.puck1._width * .5);
}
```

Set properties:

```
parent._x = newX;
```

It is possible to do all of these actions in one frame, but that can easily become unwieldy. To avoid that, I usually use one frame that has a list of Call actions. A Call statement will execute the ActionScript found in the specified frame. This could also be accomplished by executing a function, but I prefer this method because it keeps everything in one, easy-to-manage location. I use functions in another situation. As shown in the following figure, the loop frame contains these call statements:

```
call ("getCurrent");
call ("modify");
call ("setFlags");
call ("setProperties");
```

Continued

Continued

By using a call command, you are able to break out the basic animation functions and keep them in one easy-to-manage location.

I've often observed the process of other developers. I've observed that other developers work to a point of frustration, whereupon they either start over or try a new approach. (That's one of the reasons why I do so much preplanning!) Using this model, if the confusion is in calculating a new X location based on some trigonometry or physics equation, you can focus on just the `modify` frame. If you want to refine the puck's boundaries, you would go to the `setFlags` frame.

Translating paddle activity

Challenge: Translate the movement of the paddle into values that convey direction and power to the puck upon collision.

If the paddle is moving fast when it hits the puck, then the puck should move fast. Conversely, if the paddle hits the puck lightly, then the puck should move a small amount. The challenge is to calculate how fast and in what direction the paddle was moving when it collided with the puck. To do this, we need a snapshot of its movement over time:

```
counter=counter+1;
if(counter==2){
    oldPad1X = curPad1X;
    oldPad1Y = curPad1Y;
    counter=0
}
curPad1X = pad1._x;
curPad1Y = pad1._y;
```

This code is located in an ActionClip that I call the Puck Director. It keeps track of the paddles and detects for collisions with the puck. The difference between `oldPad1X` and `curPad1X` is equal to the distance along the X axis that the paddle has moved in two frames. This is similar to miles per hour but the units are more arbitrary, pixels per two frames. (If you want a long sampling just increase this number of frames.) If a collision is detected, then these values are translated to `xPaddleSpeed` and `yPaddleSpeed` and then transferred to the Puck Director ActionClip located inside the puck so that it reacts appropriately.

Computer player artificial intelligence

Challenge: Create a "mind" for the computer opponent that will give the user a fun and variable experience.

An interesting challenge in creating a game that has a computer opponent is the creation of the artificial intelligence (AI) code. Several levels of complication can be put into creating AI. For some excellent reading on this subject, as well as several other game programming concepts, I highly recommend *Tricks of the Windows Game Programming Gurus* by André LaMothe, SAMS Publishing. For this example, I've used a very simple play profile for the AI. It consists of three variables:

✦ `skill`: How good it is at perceiving puck position.

✦ `aggr`: How aggressive it is at pursuing the puck.

✦ `maxSpeed`: This is a cap on how fast it can deliver the puck.

Additional options might include thresholds for changing play profiles. For instance, if the computer gets down five points it goes from low aggressiveness to high aggressiveness, or, if it is losing and only ten seconds are left on the clock, it gets very aggressive, but skill goes down. The number of options is only limited by your imagination (and project budget).

An ActionClip accomplishes this AI with the same setup as the Puck Animation: In the first frame there are three different play profiles and one is selected at random.

```
playType=random(3)
//Fast sharp player
if(playType == 0){
    skill = 1;
    aggr = 1;
    maxSpeed = 60;
}
//Medium player
if(playType == 1){
    skill = 20;
    aggr = 7;
    maxSpeed =30;
}
//Poor player - I hope he can get the puck across the ice
if(playType == 2){
    skill = 20;
    aggr = 20;
    maxSpeed =20;
}
```

In this example, a low number means a good aptitude. Of course, I could have used randomization for each attribute, but I wanted some distinct identifiable play styles so I could tell if it was working.

The `modify` frame includes checking for the *perceived* location of the puck using skill as a variable. Then, based on that location, a new paddle location would be calculated using appropriate *aggression*.

Continued

Continued

The `setFlags` frame contains boundary checking to make sure the paddle stays in the rink.

Creating a demo mode

Challenge: Create a demo mode in which the game runs with two computer opponents.

After the Artificial Intelligence ActionClip has been created, it's very simple to create this demo mode for the game. Here is some code from the `initGame` function:

```
_root.attachMovie( "paddle", "paddle1", 201 );
c = new Color( _root.paddle1 );
c.setRGB(parseInt("666699", 16) );
_root.paddle1.side="right";
_root.paddle1.control="computer";
_root.attachMovie( "paddle", "paddle2", 1 );
_root.paddle2.side="left";
if (playMode == "demo"){
    _root.paddle2.control="computer";
} else {
    _root.paddle2.control="human";
}
```

Notice that, in the `if` statement, `_root.paddle2.control` is set to `human` or `computer`. This works because in the Paddle Movie Clip, this code is found in the first frame:

```
if (control eq "computer") {
    this.attachMovie( "ai", "ai", 210 );
}
```

The `ai` Movie Clip that is being attached is the Artificial Intelligence Movie Clip. That would mean that each paddle would have its own AI Movie Clip controlling it. Sounds like a demo mode. (Note, too, that this code also demonstrates how to change the color of a Movie Clip.)

Detecting paddle/puck collision

Challenge: Detect whether the paddle and puck have collided.

There are many ways to detect collision. Flash 5 has introduced a new Movie Clip method called `hitTest`.

Author's Note: For a more detailed implementation of the new Flash 5 `hitTest` Movie Clip method, refer to Dorian Nisinson's Expert Tutuorial, *Using `hitTest` for a Range of Movie Clips*, in Chapter 23, "Understanding Movie Clips as Complex Objects."

The syntax for `hitTest` is:

```
myMovieClip.hitTest(target);
```

Unfortunately, because my objects (pucks!) are round, the `hitTest` method is not very effective. That's because it checks whether the rectangular regions occupied by the Movie Clips have overlapped. This is shown in the following figure.

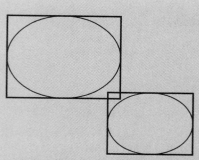

Collision detection using the hitTest method would report this as a collision because the boundaries overlap. Collision detection using Pythagorean Theorem would not register this as a collision because the circles do not overlap.

I used the Pythagorean Theorem to calculate the distances the centers of each object were from each other and then compare that calculation's result to the total of their radii. The Pythagorean Theorem states that $a^2 + b^2 = c^2$. (See the following figure.) We want c, which is the distance between the centers of the two objects.

```
a = the difference between paddle._y and puck._y
b = the difference between paddle._x and puck._x
c = Math.sqrt((a*a)+(b*b))
```

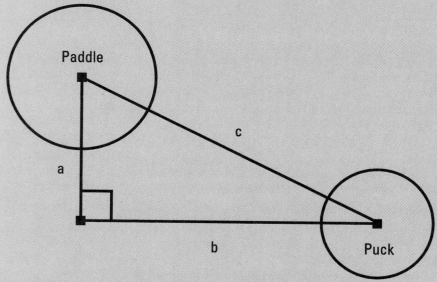

The Pythagorean Theorem can be used to calculate the distance of objects.

Continued

Continued

I put this all in a function that I could call at anytime from anywhere:

```
function checkCollision (source, target) {
    // Applying the Pythagorean theorem to
    // check for collision.
    a = target._y - source._y;
    b = target._x - source._x;
    c = Math.sqrt((a*a)+(b*b));
    dist = (target._width *.5)  +  (source._width*.5);
    if (c<=dist) {
        return true;
    } else {
        return false;
    }
}
```

When a function encounters the keyword `return`, it returns the value that follows the return statement and stops executing. To call the function, I have to reference the Movie Clip that contains it, the function, and then pass the required parameters in parenthesis like this (note that the ¬ indicates a continuation of the same line of code; this character does not appear in the actual code):

```
If (_root.functions.checkCollision(_root.paddle1, ¬
  _root.puck1)
    //Collision did occur!;
} Else {
    //Collision did not occur!;
}
```

Ricochet sound

Challenge: Animate the sound so that it adjusts the pan from left speaker to right speaker according to the horizontal location of the impact.

One of the new opportunities that Flash 5 affords us is the capability to control sound through ActionScript. This is accomplished with the new Sound Object, which enables us to adjust the panning of the ricochet sound based on where on the rink the sound occurs. The following function can be called from anywhere a ricochet occurs.

Author's Note: For another example of the new Flash 5 Sound Object, refer to Jay Vanian's Expert Tutorial "Sound Control," in Chapter 19, "Controlling Movie Clips."

```
function playSound(name,start,duration,vol,x){
    max=_root.dir_scene.right;
    inc=max/200;
    //The line below puts it on a scale of -100 to 100
    pan = (x/inc)-100;
    s = new Sound();
```

```
        s.attachSound(name);
        s.setPan(pan);
        s.setVolume(vol);
        s.start(start,duration);
}
```

Explanation of passed variables:

✦ name — The name specified in the Linkage properties for a sound

✦ start — The offset from the beginning of the sound

✦ duration — How long to play

✦ vol — Volume, how loud to play (range from 0 to 100)

✦ x — The horizontal position of the ricochet, which will be translated to −100 to 100 so that pan will be set appropriately

To get the panning to work correctly, we just need to pass _root.puck1._x for the x argument.

It is very convenient to organize your functions in a central place. Here is an example of the Functions Movie Clip used for this game.

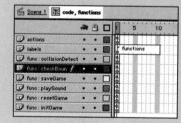

A Movie Clip can be used as a container for several functions.

Wrap Up

With a functional specifications sheet in front of us, a break down of each of the major elements required for the game, and some of the challenges identified and researched, you are now ready to open Flash and start making some ice.

Mark Burrs says that he found Flash when he "was looking for a Web-based diagramming solution I could integrate with Lotus Notes." He's from Stillwater, Minnesota, and is CEO and founder of CyBurrs Solutions, Inc. in White Bear Lake, Minnesota, and a member of the training staff at Lynda.com's Ojai Digital Arts Center in Ojai, CA. Some of his most impressive work includes www.cyburrs.com, www.swfstudio.com, and www.swfstudio.com/demo-lessons, which, "is a very extensive Flash-based training system that uses Lotus Notes as an organization and development tool." In the year that he graduated high school, "Total Eclipse of the Heart" was the big hit. What's Mark's single most favorite thing to do? "Play with my kids and spend time with my wife. Programming in Flash and Lotus Notes is great, too, but I couldn't list them first."

Managing Related Data: The Array Object

Have you ever had a bunch of variables that have a lot in common? For example, do you have variables such as name_1, name_2, name_3, name_4, and so on? These variables look like lists of common information, such as:

```
name_1 = "John";
name_2 = "Vanessa";
name_3 = "Jennifer";
name_4 = "Frank";
```

In programming languages, an array is a list of values that can be addressed by their position in the list. An array is created by using the Array constructor:

```
visitors = new Array();
```

The preceding code object simply creates the array container for data. You create an array with information already specified, such as:

```
visitors = new Array("John","Vanessa","Jennifer","Frank");
```

To access an item in visitors, you would use the array access operators with an array index number. To access the first position's data, you would use the following code:

```
message = "Hello " + visitors[0] + ", and welcome.";
```

Here, visitors[0] will return the value "John". If you traced the message variable, it would read:

```
Hello John, and welcome.
```

In most programming languages, the first index value (the starting position) is 0, not 1. In the following table, you'll see how the index number increases with our sample visitors array.

Index Position	0	1	2	3
Index Value	John	Vanessa	Jennifer	Frank

You can set and get the values within an array using the array access operators. You can replace existing array values by setting the index position to a new value, and you add values to the array by increasing the index number, as in:

```
visitors = new Array("John","Vanessa","Jennifer","Frank");
visitors[3] = "Nicole";
visitors[4] = "Candice";
```

In the example, "Nicole" replaces "Frank", and "Candice" is added to the end of the array. You can also add elements to the array using the push method of the Array Object, as in:

```
visitors = new Array("John", "Vanessa","Jennifer","Frank");
newLength = visitors.push("Nicole","Candice");
```

This code will add "Nicole" and "Candice" after "Frank", and set the variable newLength equal to the length of the visitors array. length is an Array property that returns the number of elements in the array. In the preceding example, newLength is equal to 6, because there are now six names in the array.

 You can read more about methods of the Array object on pages 214–224 of the Macromedia's *ActionScript Reference Guide*.

We look at arrays in a function example later in this chapter.

Emulating Arrays in Flash 4 Movies

In Flash 4, you could only emulate arrays, using expressions for variable names. In our array examples for Flash 5 ActionScript, you could create an arraylike structure for a Flash 4 movie by using the following code:

```
name_1 = "John";
name_2 = "Vanessa";
name_3 = "Jennifer";
name_4 = "Frank";
```

Then, you could use another variable, i, to indirectly refer to different name_ variables, as in:

```
i = 2;
currentName = eval("name_" add i);
message = "Hello " add currentName add ", and welcome!";
```

For Flash 4 compatibility, the add operator (instead of the + operator) and the eval() function are used to return the current value of the name_ variable we want to insert. If you traced the message variable, then the Output window would display:

```
Hello Vanessa, and welcome!
```

We only mention array emulation in this section because many Flash developers may encounter clients who wish to have Flash movies (or sites) that will work with the Flash 4 Player plug-in, because that plug-in version is likely to be installed on more computers.

Creating a Dynamic Reusable Flash Menu

In this section, we use arrays to create a dynamic code-built menu that you can adjust for any Flash movie. You create a Main Timeline with six sections for a photographer's site, and a menu that navigates to those four sections. While that sounds simple enough, we create the menu entirely from ActionScript code.

1. Create a new Flash movie (Ctrl+N or Command+N). In the Movie Properties dialog (Ctrl+M or Command+M), set the frame rate to 20 and the background color to white. Use any movie frame size you prefer.

2. Rename Layer 1 to **labels**. Create new keyframes (press F6) on frames 2, 10, 20, 30, 40, and 50. Select frame 60 and press F5.

3. Starting on frame 2 of the labels layer, assign the following label names to the keyframes you created in Step 2: **about**, **interiors**, **exteriors**, **landscapes**, **portraits**, and **editorial**.

4. Add a new layer, and name it **actions**. Add a keyframe on frame 2 of the actions layer. With that keyframe selected, open the Actions Panel and add a stop() action. In the Frame Panel, type **//stop** in the Label field. This will create a frame comment of stop. The stop() action on frame 2 will prevent the Main Timeline from playing past our about section, when the movie first loads.

5. Create another layer called **artwork**. Add keyframes on this layer, matching the keyframes in the labels layer. Insert some graphics in each keyframe for each section. As a starting point, you can simply add text headings to each section (for example, About the Company, Interior Photography, and so on). We need this artwork layer so that we have some indication that the playhead on the Main Timeline actually moves when an item in the menu is clicked.

6. Now we create an array that contains the names of each our frame labels. Add a new layer to the Main Timeline, and name it **menu actions**. Double-click the first keyframe on the menu actions layer. In the Actions Panel, add the following code (note that the ¬ indicates a continuation of the same line of code; do not insert this character into your actual code):

```
sectionNames = new Array("about", "interiors", ¬
   "exteriors", "landscapes","portraits", "editorial");
```

This line of ActionScript will create an array object named sectionNames. We can now refer to each section of our timeline using array syntax, such as sectionNames[0], sectionNames[1], and so on. We use this array to build the actual button text in our menu.

7. In the same block of code, add the following line to the Actions list for frame 1 of the menu actions layer:

```
sectionCount = sectionNames.length;
```

This code creates a new variable named `sectionCount`. The `length` property of an array will return the current number of elements inside of the array. Therefore, because we put six elements into the array (in Step 6), `sectionCount` will be equal to 6. You may be wondering why we just didn't manually insert the value 6 here. The point to using an array is that we can change the elements of the array at any point, and the rest of our code will update automatically to reflect the changes. In this way, we are building a dynamic menu system.

8. Save your Flash movie as **menuArray.fla**. At this point, your Flash movie should resemble Figure 22-1.

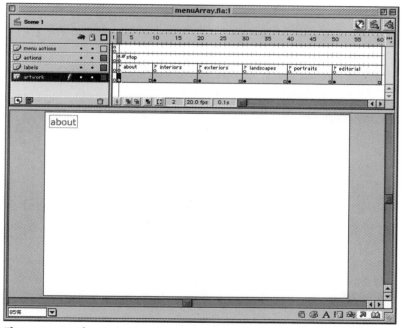

Figure 22-1: The Main Timeline has frame labels and artwork for each section of the presentation.

9. Now we need to create some menu elements that we can use to build a dynamic menu from ActionScript. First, we need to make a Movie Clip "container" for the menu items. This container will be a Movie Clip instance on the Stage. Press Ctrl+F8 (Command+F8) to create a new symbol. Name this symbol **menu**, and keep the default Movie Clip behavior. Flash automatically switches to Symbol Editing Mode.

10. Within the timeline of the menu symbol, rename Layer 1 to **menuItemBase**. This layer will hold a template Movie Clip instance for the menu item(s). Again, create a new Movie Clip symbol by pressing Ctrl+F8 (Command+F8). Name this symbol **menuItem**, and keep the default Movie Clip behavior.

11. Within the timeline of the menuItem symbol, rename Layer 1 to button. On this layer, create or add a Button symbol. In our example, we used the Pill Button from the Buttons Library (Window ➪ Common Libraries ➪ Buttons). This will be the actual button that appears in our menu. Make sure that the Button is wide enough to accommodate the names of our sections. We stretched our button, shown in Figure 22-2, to 175 percent. Also, center your Button instance on the Stage, using the Align Panel.

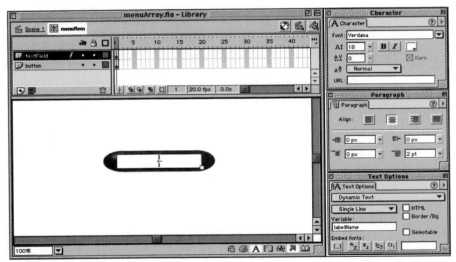

Figure 22-2: The menuItem instance will be used to create each button in the dynamic menu. Using ActionScript, the labelName text field will be filled with the appropriate section name.

12. Add a new layer to the menuItem symbol, and name it **textField**. On this layer, create a Dynamic Text field that is the length of the Button instance. In the Text Options Panel, give this Dynamic Text field the variable name labelName. Use whatever font face you prefer, in the Character Panel. In the Paragraph Panel, align the text to the center of the text field.

13. Add another layer to the menuItem symbol, and rename it **actions**. Add a stop() action and frame comment of //stop to the first frame of the actions layer. (See Step 4 for more information.)

14. Select the Button instance that you added in Step 10. Open the Actions Panel, and type the following code in the Actions list:

```
on(release){
    _root.gotoAndStop(labelName);
}
```

This code will use the value of the labelName text field as the frame label for the gotoAndStop() action. Notice that we will control the Main Timeline's playhead by indicating _root. Shortly, we will assign each instance of menuItem a unique labelName value.

15. Open the menu Movie Clip symbol by double-clicking it in the Library. Drag an instance of menuItem from the Library to the menuItemBase layer on the menu timeline. With this instance selected, open the Instance Panel and assign a name of **menuItemBase**, as shown in Figure 22-3. We will use this instance as a template for the real buttons in the menu symbol. Align this instance to the center of the Stage.

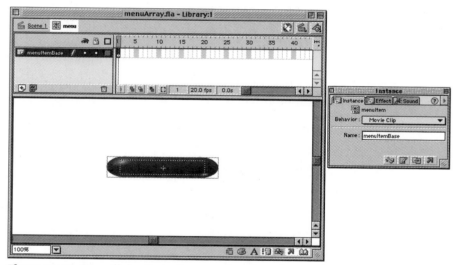

Figure 22-3: We will duplicate the menuItemBase instance in ActionScript, to build each button in the menu symbol.

16. Save your Flash movie.

17. Go back to the Main Timeline and create a new layer named **menu**. On this layer, place an instance of the menu Movie Clip symbol from the Library. In the Instance Panel, give this symbol the name **menu**.

18. Open the Actions Panel for frame 1 of the menu actions layer. At the end of the Actions list, type the following line:

```
menuItemSpacing = 10;
```

This line of code establishes a variable named `menuItemSpacing`. This value will designate the space (in pixels) to space each menuItem instance apart.

19. Then, add the following ActionScript to the Actions list for frame 1 of the menu actions layer (note that the ¬ indicates a continuation of the same line of code; do not insert this character into your actual code):

```
for(i=1;i<=sectionCount;i++){
    _root.menu.menuItemBase.duplicateMovieClip ¬
        ("menuItem_"+i, i);
    _root.menu["menuItem_"+i].labelName = ¬
        sectionNames[i-1];
        if(i != 1){
            _root.menu["menuItem_"+i]._y = ¬
            _root.menu["menuItem_"+(i-1)]._y + ¬
            _root.menu["menuItem_"+(i-1)]._height + ¬
            menuItemSpacing;
        }
}
```

This code inserts a `for` loop that will duplicate the menuItemBase instance (inside of the menu instance) for each element in the `sectionNames` array. It will also set the value of `labelName` in each duplicated menuItem instance to the name of the appropriate section name. Notice that we specify `i-1` for the index number of the `sectionNames` array because the position index of every array starts at 0 and our menuItem numbering starts at 1.

After an instance is duplicated for the section name, we then reposition the menuItem instance below the previous one. We only need to perform this operation for instances greater than 1 because the starting instance does not need to be moved down. Notice also that we use the `menuItemSpacing` variable add a buffer space between the menu items.

20. Before we can test the movie, we need to hide the menuItemBase template instance in the menu instance. After the `for` loop code, insert the following action:

```
_root.menu.menuItemBase._visible = false;
```

21. Save your Flash movie again, and test it (Ctrl+Enter or Command+Enter). Unless you had a syntax error in your ActionScript or forgot to name a Movie Clip instance, you will see a dynamic menu, built by ActionScript (as shown in Figure 22-4).

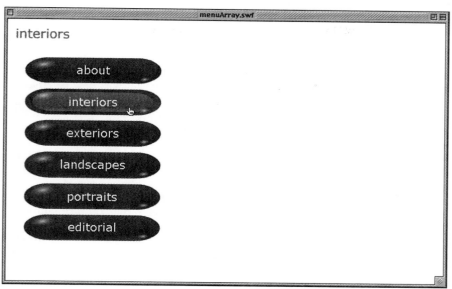

Figure 22-4: The ActionScript code in the menu actions layer duplicates the menuItemBase instance in the menu instance. Each duplicated instance has a unique labelName value, which is used in the gotoAndStop() action by each Button instance.

You can enhance this dynamic menu by adding animation to the menuItem symbol timeline. You can also restructure the ActionScript to work with separate Movie Clips for each `sectionName`, instead of frame labels. If used properly, you may never need to script a menu again! Simply change the Button instance artwork and text styles for unique menu interfaces.

On the CD-ROM In the ch22 folder of the *Flash 5 Bible* CD-ROM, you will find basic (menu Array_basic.fla) and advanced (menuArray_advanced.fla) implementations of the menu system. The advanced menu uses a function to check each button's animated state.

Functions as Methods of Objects

We've already discussed functions as subroutine mechanisms in Flash movies. Functions can be used to define a set of actions that are later executed when the function is invoked. In Flash 5, you can use also functions as methods of other code objects. Methods are actions specific to actions. Unlike properties and values, methods carry out a task with that object. In this section, we deconstruct a .FLA file that uses a function to create a menu completely from ActionScript.

On the CD-ROM Make a copy of the createMenu.fla file, located in the ch22 folder of the *Flash 5 Bible* CD-ROM.

Open a local copy of the createMenu.fla file in Flash 5. You'll notice that the Main Timeline has a setup similar to the arrayMenu.fla file that was discussed in the last section. We have a series of labels, indicating sections of the Flash movie. If you test this Flash movie, you'll see a dynamic menu display. Clicking each button takes you to the corresponding section of the Flash movie.

Unlike our previous arrayMenu.fla example, though, notice that we have different text on the menu buttons than the text used in the frame labels. For example, the Our Products menu button takes you to the products label on the Main Timeline. For this Flash movie, a function with multiple arguments enables you to specify the text of the menu buttons separately from the targeted labels (and timelines).

Double-click the first frame of the functions layer. In the Actions Panel, you'll see this function appear in the Actions list (note that the ¬ indicates a continuation of the same line of code; this character does not appear in the actual code):

```
function createMenu(names,targets,labels){
  this.itemName = names.split(",");
  this.itemTarget = targets.split(",");
  this.frameLabel = labels.split(",");
  _root.menuBase.duplicateMovieClip("menu_1",1);
  for(i=1;i<=this.itemName.length;i++){
    this.attachMovie("menuItem","menuItem_"+i,i);
    this["menuItem_"+i].name = this.itemName[i-1];
    this["menuItem_"+i].itemTarget = this.itemTarget[i-1];
    this["menuItem_"+i].frameLabel = this.frameLabel[i-1];
    if(i>1){
      this["menuItem_"+i]._y = this["menuItem_"+(i-1)]._y ¬
        + this["menuItem_"+(i-1)]._height;
    }
  }
}
```

The createMenu() function has three arguments: names, targets, and labels. The value for these arguments will be supplied as a method of a Movie Clip instance when the function is executed. Similar to our previous arrayMenu.fla example, we will use arrays to store the values of our frame labels (and section names). However, we'll also create an argument (and array) to store the button text that will appear on the menu buttons. In this way, we can create ActionScript that correctly uses frame labels in other Go To actions, without worrying about the text that is actually used as a button item. The targets argument is used to create an array of timeline targets for each button item.

The function also uses the `attachMovie` method (instead of `duplicateMovieClip`) to use the `menuItem` Movie Clip symbol in the instance timeline executing the function. In our example, there is a `menu` Movie Clip instance on the Stage. This empty Movie Clip instance is assigned the `createMenu()` function as a method, just as `duplicateMovieClip` or `attachMovie` is a method of the Movie Clip object:

```
_root.menu.createMenu = createMenu;
```

This line of code creates a new method called `createMenu`, specifically for the menu instance (object) on the Stage. It also set this method to use the function `createMenu` as its value. Therefore, whenever we evoke the `createMenu` method of the menu object, the actions within the `createMenu` function will run.

Caution   The act of creating and assigning a method name for an object does not actually execute the method or the function. We're simply defining a method for the object, so that it can be evoked later. Do not use parentheses for method (and function) assignment—doing so results in an error.

Note that you can use any method name you prefer—it need not match the name of the function as our example does. So, you could write:

```
_root.menu.customMenu = createMenu;
```

The function `createMenu` also uses the `this` syntax to make the function work in relation to the object that is executing it. `this` will equal `_root.menu` for the method assignment, `_root.menu.createMenu = createMenu`. However, if we had another menu instance, such as `menu_2`, that used the `createMenu` function as a method, then this would refer to its path for its method. Herein lies the power of a function as a method of an object—you can assign the same function (and arguments) to unique objects (or Movie Clip instances) on the Stage.

To execute the method `createMenu` for the `menu` instance, you need to specify the method and any arguments you will supply the method. In our example, the following line (note that the ¬ indicates a continuation of the same line of code; this character does not appear in the actual code) executes the `createMenu` method for the menu instance:

```
_root.menu.createMenu("Home,Our Products,Our ¬
    Services","_root,_root,_root","main,products,services");
```

In this line of code, the following arguments are passed to the `createMenu` function arguments:

```
names = "Home,Our Products,Our Services"
targets = "_root,_root,_root"
labels = "main,products,services"
```

When the `createMenu` method is evoked, the `createMenu` function parses this argument into the actions contained with the function. The split method (for String Objects) takes the values of names, targets, and labels, and makes each comma-delimited item (item separated by a comma) into a separate array element:

```
itemName[0] = "Home"
itemName[1] = "Our Products"
itemName[2] = "Our Services"
```

While you will never see those lines of code in the function, you will see references to these array items.

```
this.itemName[i-1]
```

is used to take each `itemName` element and put it on the proper `menuItem` Movie Clip instance in the menu object.

The `itemTarget` array is used to let the menuItem instances know to which time-line target to address the `gotoAndStop()` action (contained on the Button instance within the menuItem symbol in the Library). The `frameLabel` array assigns the proper frame label for the `gotoAndStop()` action for the Button instance.

This movie also uses a `resetMenu` function (and method) to delete the menuItem instances and arrays.

Functions as Constructors for Objects

Functions can also be used with the `new` constructor to create objects with properties and methods assigned by the function. This means that you can use a function to create unique objects, based on parameters that you pass as arguments to the function upon invocation. In this section, we deconstruct another function example that creates an entire Sound Library with ActionScript, without using any Movie Clip instances.

On the CD-ROM

Make a local copy of the soundObjects.fla file, located in the ch22 folder of the *Flash 5 Bible* CD-ROM.

Open your copy of the soundObjects.fla file in Flash 5. You'll notice that there aren't any Movie Clips and/or physical elements on the Stage. Double-click the first (and only) frame on the actions layer. In the Actions Panel, you'll see the following code:

```
function createLib(start,end){
    for(i=start;i<=end;i++){
        if(i==start){
```

```
            this.snd = new Array();
        }
        this.snd[i] = new Sound();
        this.snd[i].attachSound("sound_"+i);
    }
}
this.soundLib = new createLib(1,7);
this.soundLib.snd[1].start();
this.soundLib.snd[2].start();
```

There are three sections to this code: the function definition; the object creation and assignment; and the method execution of the Sound Objects.

Function definition

The `createLib` function has two arguments: start and end. Again, these are user-defined function names and arguments. You could rename the function and arguments to your own preferred terms. The for loop in the `createLib` function will create a `snd` array object within the calling object (`this`). This array will contain Sound Objects that use the .AIFF sound files in the Library. Note that each of the sounds in the Library have been set to export with the .SWF file, as defined by the Linkage Properties for each sound.

See Chapters 19, "Controlling Movie Clips," and 20, "Sharing and Loading Assets," for more information on Symbol Linkage.

Object creation and assignment

After the `createLib` function is defined, we can use it for new objects. In our example, a new object named `soundLib` is created after the function definition:

```
this.soundLib = new createLib(1,7);
```

First, the object is declared as being on the this timeline. This enables us to load this Flash movie into other Flash movies and retain proper targeting paths for the `createLib` function. If you test this movie on its own, `this` will simply be equal to `_root` or `_level0`. Using the new constructor, we create the `snd` array and Sound Objects relative to the `soundLib` object. We are creating a unique object with specific properties and values. This enables you to make as many objects as you desire, all from one function:

```
this.soundLib_1 = new createLib(1,3);
this.soundLib_2 = new createLib(4,7);
```

These actions (not used in our example) would create two separate `soundLib` objects, each using a specific range of Sound Objects from the Library.

The numbers specified in the parentheses indicate the sounds to use from the Library. Remember that in our function `createLib`, the `start` and `end` arguments are used to form the linkage identifiers:

```
"sound_"+i
```

where i is defined by the `start` argument, and incremented until the `end` argument value is reached.

Sound Object method execution

Finally, after the Sound Objects are created within the `soundLib` object, we can play the sounds with the Flash 5 built-in `start` method for Sound Objects:

```
this.soundLib.snd[1].start();
this.soundLib.snd[2].start();
```

These lines of code tell the Sound Objects located in the 1 and 2 index positions of the `snd` array (for example, `sound_1` and `sound_2` from the Library) to play.

This is just one example of using functions to create new objects. You can use functions to create other types of data-based objects for record storage and retrieval, as well as to create unique Color Objects to reference with more than one Movie Clip target.

Caution

During further testing, we discovered that the `setVolume` method of the Sound Object controls all Sound Object instances on a given timeline. This means that you should create one Sound Object instance *per timeline*. For example, if you wanted to separately control the volume of five individual sounds, then make sure you create each of those Sound Object instances on a separate Movie Clip instance.

Summary

✦ Flash 5 ActionScript has five data types: string, number, movieclip, object, and function.

✦ The data type of an ActionScript element can be checked using the `typeof` operator.

✦ The most common use of a function is as a subroutine, which is a set of actions that execute when the function's name is evoked.

✦ A subroutine function should be created when the same actions are repeated within a Flash movie, or when you want to avoid storing long action lists within Button instances.

✦ A function is defined with the `function` action, in the format `function name(arguments){actions}`.

✦ A function can be executed when the name of the function is evoked. The format of a function call is `targetPath.functionName(arguments);`, as in `_root.createLib(1,7)`.

✦ Arrays can manage related information, such as lists. An array is initiated with the `Array` constructor, as in `myArray = new Array();`.

✦ Array elements have an index number, indicating their position in the array. Array index numbers start with 0 and increment by 1 with each new element.

✦ Functions can be used as methods of ActionScript objects. A method is prescribed by creating a unique method name after the object and setting the method's value equal to a function name (for example, `_root.menu.createMenu = createMenu;`). Parentheses and arguments are omitted from the method assignment.

✦ Objects can be created with the function constructor. Functions intended for this use describe properties and methods for objects using the `this` target path. A new object is created by specifying an object name and setting it's value equal to a new instance of the function name, as in `myObject = new createLib(1,7);`.

✦ ✦ ✦

Understanding Movie Clips as Complex Objects

This chapter explores the ins and outs of advanced collision detection for Movie Clip Objects. If you've ever wanted to start building a space game with ships exploding upon the impact of a missile, then this is the place to start.

Movie Clip Collision Detection

Have you ever wanted to detect the intersection of two elements in a Flash movie? If two Movie Clip instances overlap on the Stage, how would you know? How would you tell ActionScript to look for an overlap? In Flash 5, there are two primary types of intersections (or collisions):

　　✦ User-dragged collisions

　　✦ Script- or time-based collisions

Using _dropTarget

A collision between two Movie Clip Objects can occur if the user drags one Movie Clip instance to the location of another Movie Clip instance. We first examined the `startDrag()` action and method in Chapter 19, "Controlling Movie Clips." In the dog movie, we used the `_dropTarget` property of a Movie Clip Object to detect whether the area of one Movie Clip

Object occupied the area of another Movie Clip Object. To recap, you can test the intersection of two Movie Clips with the following code:

```
on(press){
  this.startDrag(true);
}

on(release){
  if(eval(this._dropTarget) == _root.mcInstance2){
    trace("this MC instance overlaps mcInstance2");
  } else {
    trace("this MC instance does not overlap mcInstance2");
  }
  this.stopDrag();
}
```

This code could occur on a Button instance within the first Movie Clip instance. When the user clicks the Button instance, the Movie Clip startDrag method is invoked and the user can drag the Movie Clip instance on the Stage. When the user releases the mouse, the _dropTarget property (which returns target paths in Slashes notation) is evaluated to convert the target path to Dots notation. If the _dropTarget property returns the path to another instance, then the if condition will see whether the path matches _root.mcInstance2. If the paths match, then the trace action indicating an overlap is executed. Otherwise, a separate trace action will notify us that the instance is not on top of mcInstance2.

Cross-Reference

To see a fully functional example of the _dropTarget property in action, please review the section "Detecting the Drop Position: Using _dropTarget" in Chapter 19, "Controlling Movie Clips."

Collision detection with advanced scripting

You can also perform more advanced collision detection using the hitTest method of the Movie Clip Object. hitTest will do exactly what it says, it will test to see if a "hit" occurred between two elements. hitTest has two formats:

```
mcInstance.hitTest(anotherInstance);
```

or

```
mcInstance.hitTest(x coordinate, y coordinate, shapeFlag);
```

The latter method was demonstrated in Chapter 19, "Controlling Movie Clips," with the hit detection on the sliderBar Movie Clip instance. With this method, you can determine whether the X and Y coordinates are within the space occupied by the Movie Clip instance. onClipEvents such as mouseMove can be used to constantly check for a hit occurrence:

```
onClipEvent(mouseMove){
  if(this.hitTest(_root._xmouse, _root._ymouse, true)){
    trace("A hit has occurred");
  }
}
```

This code will report a trace action anytime the mouse pointer is moved within the artwork of the Movie Clip instance to which the onClipEvent action is attached. The shape flag attribute of hitTest defines the actual test area for the hit. If the shape flag is set to true, then a hit only occurs if the X and Y coordinates occur within the actual artwork of the Movie Clip instance. If the shape flag is set to false, then a hit will occur whenever the X and Y coordinates occur within the bounding box of the Movie Clip instance. In Figure 23-1, if the left circle uses a shape flag of true, then a hit is reported whenever the X and Y coordinates occur within the shape of the circle (not within the bounding box). If the right circle uses a shape of false, then a hit is reported when the X and Y coordinates occur within the bounding box.

Figure 23-1: The shape flag determines the boundary of the Movie Clip instance for the hitTest method.

 You can see a working example of shape flags and the hitTest method in the hitTest_xy.fla file, located in the ch23 folder of the *Flash 5 Bible* CD-ROM.

The other format for the hitTest method is to simply specify a target path to compare for a hit occurrence. With this syntax, you cannot use a shape flag option; if any area of the bounding box for a Movie Clip instance touches the bounding box of the tested instance, then a hit occurs. For example, you can modify the ActionScript used earlier to indicate a hit between instances, instead of X and Y coordinates:

```
onClipEvent(mouseMove){
  if(this.hitTest(_root.mcInstance2)){
    trace("A hit has occurred.");
  }
}
```

This code assumes that other actions are actually initiating a startDrag action. Also, we have omitted the other half of the if condition in both this example and the previous example. If you omit a condition operator and test condition, then ActionScript assumes that you are testing for a true result (as a Boolean value). The following if conditions are exactly the same:

```
myMouseClick = true;
if(myMouseClick){
  trace("myMouseClick is true.");
}
if(myMouseClick == true){
  trace("myMouseClick is true.");
}
```

Therefore, to test for a true value with any if statement, specify the variable (or method) that has a Boolean value. The hitTest method will yield either a true (a hit has occurred) or a false (no hit has occurred) result. Note that, with scripting languages, it is more common to use the former example for testing true conditions.

You can see a working example of targets and the hitTest method in the hitTest_target.fla file, located in the ch23 folder of the *Flash 5 Bible* CD-ROM.

Expert Tutorial: Using hitTest for Multiple Targets, *by Dorian Nisinson*

This tutorial teaches you one method for structuring a complex Flash 5 project. You also learn about the new Flash 5 Dots notation, and how to use the new onClipEvent handler and scripts attached to Movie Clips. In addition, you'll use the hitTest method of the Movie Clip Object and the getBounds method of the Movie Clip Object. But before we get started, it will be best if you launch Flash 5 and open the file redMaze.fla. Then, select Control ⇨ Test Movie to see how the completed movie plays and what it does.

In this tutorial, you learn how to structure a Flash 5 movie using the redmaze.fla as an example. You'll find the finished .FLA, together with the diagrams for this tutorial, on the CD-ROM in the ch23 folder.

Structuring a Flash 5 movie

When setting up a Flash project it is a good idea to create a diagram of the contents and how they relate to each other. The more complex the movie gets, the more helpful this diagram will be. This project gets very complex, so take some time to study the diagram.

The following figure is a diagram of the symbol elements and assets of this movie. The second type of diagram represents your ActionScript and how it flows between the different segments of code in the movie. First, decide what the movie has to be capable of doing and then decide the most efficient way to structure your ActionScript to achieve those goals.

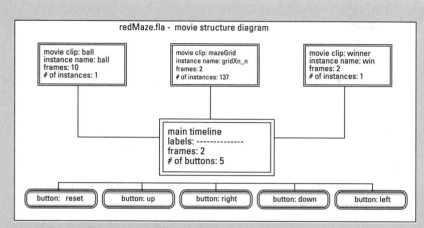

Movie layout diagram—the big picture

The ActionScript diagram, shown in the following figure, is the second thing to create during the planning stage of a Flash project. Combined, these two diagrams can make coming back to a project later very much easier. The more detailed the goals are to begin with, the less time that you will have to spend rethinking and reworking the movie.

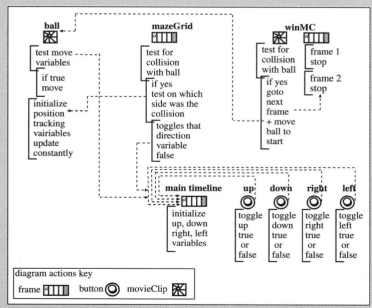

ActionScript diagram

Continued

Continued

Defining the goals of the maze game

Before we can start production within Flash, it's a good idea to also map out the primary goals of the game. For our example, we establish the following guidelines:

1. The user has to be able to control a small Movie Clip (ball) so that it can go left, right, up, or down by means of programming.

2. The movement of the ball should be as fluid and responsive as possible.

3. The ball should not be able to cross the boundaries of the maze, so some form of collision detection needs to be set up.

4. Any collision must be noted so that code can be added to stop the movement of the ball. It is crucial to the proper functioning of the maze game to know which side of a grid piece was collided with so that the ball's movement can be turned off in that direction as long as the ball is colliding with that side of the grid piece.

5. When the ball completes the maze, there should be recognition competition.

Now, we go over the goals that you need to implement to complete the project.

Goal 1. The User Controlled Game Piece.

Graphic assets:

✦ A small circle, eight pixels high and eight pixels wide, in a Movie Clip with the instance name of ball.

✦ An arrow button. Place four copies of the arrow button on the stage and rotate them individually so that you have an arrow button pointing up, down, right, and left.

✦ A rectangle, 4 pixels high by 20 pixels wide, in a Movie Clip with the instance name of gridH *or* Vn.

Each button will contain ActionScript that allows the ball to move. If we attached the code for moving the ball to the arrow button, the ball would move one pixel for each button press. As the ball should keep moving as long as an arrow button remains pressed, we create a variable that an arrow button press or release can toggle between two states, pressed or released. If the ball only needed to move in one direction, pressed would be a good choice for the variable name, but we need to know which direction button is pressed, so we will use variable names that give us that piece of information as well. The variable names are up, down, right, and left. Pressing the up arrow button changes the content of the variable up to `true`. All of the direction variables are initialized as set to `false` because we do not want the ball to move without a button being pressed. We define these four variables on the Main Timeline in a frame action to look like this:

```
up = false;
down = false;
left = false;
right = false;
```

To enter these lines of ActionScript in Normal Mode, you need to select and double-click evaluate from the Action Booklet in the Actions Panel for each line that you want to add. The following figure shows code in Normal Mode. The `evaluate` action enables you to type in a whole expression without predefining the fields for you. In Expert Mode, you can type whatever you want directly into the script pane with no prompting as you type.

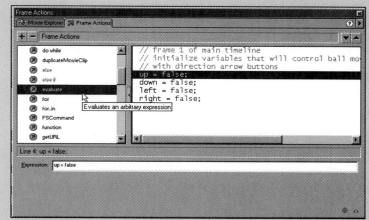

The button actions for the up direction arrow button that do this are:

```
on (press) {
    up = true;
}
on (release, releaseOutside) {
    up = false;
}
```

As long as the up button remains pressed, the value for the up variable will remain set to `true`. If the user releases the up arrow, the variable up will be reset to `false`.

The code looks different from Flash 4 ActionScript. We still have the mouse event handlers as in Flash 4, but now the actions to be executed when a mouse event occurs are contained in curly brackets. For those of you who are familiar with JavaScript, this way of formatting code will be very familiar. The curly brackets define the actions that relate to that particular segment of script.

The same script attaches to each direction arrow button except that the variable name must be changed to the correct direction for that arrow button. The ActionScript is now set up to know which button is being pressed so that it can tell in which direction to move. The next thing we need is ActionScript that actually moves the ball in the right direction.

Continued

Continued

Goal 2. Setting up the user controls to make the ball move.

onClipEvent **actions:**

So far, we have used button actions and frame actions, both of which existed in Flash 4. For the ball movement, however, we will use a new addition to Flash 5 ActionScript: Movie Clip actions. If you open redMaze.fla in Flash and click once on the ball Movie Clip on the stage and then right-click (PC) or Control+click (Mac) you will get a context-sensitive drop-down menu (see the following figure) that contains a new choice along with the expected ones. This new choice is Actions. Be sure that no other items are selected on the stage when you do this or you will not get the correct drop-down menu.

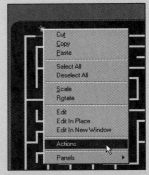

A context-sensitive drop-down
menu that contains the Actions
choice

The new onClipEvent has its own set of event handlers just as buttons do. The syntax for this action is:

```
onClipEvent ( movieEvent )
```

There are nine new Movie Clip events:

1. load

2. unload

3. enterFrame

4. mouseMove

5. mouseUp

6. mouseDown

7. keyDown

8. keyUp

9. data

Author's Note: onClipEvent is discussed in Chapter 19, "Controlling Movie Clips." The data event is discussed in Chapter 24, "Sending Data In and Out of Flash."

Putting a script in this new location enables the use of these new event handlers and takes advantage of the special features of the enterFrame event handler.

The entire contents of this enterFrame event are contained within curly brackets. These curly brackets define what lines of code are to be evaluated and executed when the specified event occurs.

The ActionScript for the ball Movie Clip is:

```
onClipEvent (enterFrame)   {
    if (_root.right == true)   {
        this._x+=1;
    }
    if (_root.left == true)   {
        this._x-=1;
    }
    if (_root.up == true)   {
        this._y+=1;
    }
    if (_root.down == true)   {
        this._y-=1;
    }
}
```

Line-by-line analysis: Line 1 of the onClipEvent **for the ball Movie Clip**

```
onClipEvent (enterFrame)   {
```

The event that this script uses is enterFrame. The enterFrame event handler executes whatever script is placed inside it each time the playhead enters the frame. Because a Movie Clip has its own separate timeline, it does not matter whether the Main Timeline is stopped. The enterFrame will repeatedly execute its script over and over as long as the movie that contains the Movie Clip and the Movie Clip itself exist on the Main Timeline. This has an application to the code that we want to set up for redMaze. We do not want to check only once to see if the user has pressed any of our buttons. We need to constantly check the state of those direction buttons and enterFrame will execute our test of the button state variable every time the Movie Clip enters a frame.

Continued

Continued

Line-by-line analysis: Line 2 of the onClipEvent **for the ball Movie Clip**

```
if (_root.right == true) {
```

The test to see what the contents of our direction-setting variables are is an `if` statement. Each `if` statement has its own set of curly brackets nested inside the event handler's curly brackets. These nested curly brackets define what to do if the result of the `if` test is `true`.

Next is the `==` sign. This is not the usual equal sign. This operator tests whether the element on the left of the `==` sign has the same value as the element on the right. If both items have the same value, it returns the value `true` and enables the code inside the `if` statement to be executed. This kind of comparison operator is called a Boolean operator. All `if` statements require a comparison that yields the results `true` or `false`. Do not be confused by the fact that the word `true` is on the right side of this comparison. The `==` operator only cares that the contents (value) of the variable named `right`, on the left side of the comparison, is the same as the expression on the right side.

Author's Note: When you are testing `true` conditions, you can omit the `== true`, and simply refer to the variable name, as in `if(_root.right){`. Remember also that all equality operators have two characters — do not use a single `=` in a comparison. This will actually set the variable to the value declared in the `if` statement.

The code wasn't written as `if (right == true)`. Instead, the word `_root` precedes the variable name. This is an example of the new Dots notation and `_root` refers to the Main Timeline. All of our direction variables were initialized (named for the first time) in the first frame of the Main Timeline. Thus, putting `_root` (separated by a dot) in front of the variable name tells the script to look for the variable `right` on the Main Timeline.

If the user has the right button pressed, triggering the change in the variable `right` on the Main Timeline, then the statement inside that `if` statement's curly brackets is executed and the ball moves. If the test result is `false`, then the statement inside is ignored. Flash then proceeds to the next `if` statement and evaluates it in the same manner. As long as no direction button is pressed, the instructions to move the ball are ignored.

Line-by-line analysis: Line 3 of the onClipEvent **for the ball Movie Clip**

In this section, we look at the following code:

```
this._x+=1;
```

At this stage of the ActionScript, the ball knows when it is all right to move in one of the four directions. Now we must tell the ball how much to move and in which direction. That happens in the previous line of code.

`this` is a new way of telling the script which Movie Clip to act on. It is a keyword that is a special kind of container for the target information of the Movie Clip in which it occurs. If this line of code was in an `onClipEvent`, or a frame action of a Movie Clip whose instance name was square, and that Movie Clip was inside another Movie Clip whose instance name was circle, and circle was on the Main Timeline, then `this` would be translated by Flash to mean `_root.circle.square`

In the example in the redMaze script, `this` is interpreted as `_root.ball`. Now we look at each part of the code from line three separately.

✦ `this`: Using `this` instead of the actual instance name of a Movie Clip allows for a lot of flexibility. It can make your scripts reusable. If you place those lines of code in another Movie Clip, Flash will then read `this` as the name of the Movie Clip to which it has moved.

✦ **Dot:** Next is the dot after the keyword `this`. The dot is used as a separator between an object and its properties or methods. A Movie Clip is an object in Flash 5, as are many other things. The dot is also used as a separator between the instance names of nested Movie Clips. Just as we use an actual space between words in English to make it more readable, dots define where one word (object, instance name, property, variable, expression, and so on) ends and another one starts. The order in which objects are written with dot syntax is crucial to the meaning of the script. As in English, *dog bites man* is very different from *man bites dog*.

✦ `_x`: The `_x` refers to the same property in Flash 5 as it did in Flash 4. It is the x position of whichever Movie Clip instance name precedes it. The x position property refers to the horizontal location. The 0,0 coordinates of the stage are at the upper-left corner of the stage. Both the right and the left arrow button move the ball on the horizontal plane so that the x position is the one to change for those buttons.

The x and y values of a Movie Clip are always measured from the center point of the Movie Clip. If you select the ball Movie Clip on the stage and open the Info Panel you will see the width, height, x, and y properties for that instance of ball on the stage. The x number tells where the center point of the Movie Clip is from the left edge of the stage to the right and y tells where the center point of Movie Clip is from the top edge of the stage to the bottom. The center point of the Movie Clip does not necessarily refer to the center of the artwork. A dotted line square is next to the x and the y boxes. This diagram has a black square at either the center of the dotted line square or at the upper-left corner, and a white square at the other position. Clicking one of these two squares will toggle it black and toggle the other one white. The black square tells Flash whether to use the center of the art or the upper-left corner of the art.

✦ `+=`: So far in this line of code, we have specified the x position of the ball Movie Clip instance on the Main Timeline. The next item in the code is `+=`. This is a compound assignment operator. It tells Flash to take the x position of the Movie Clip ball, add that number to the x position number on the right side of the equation, and then assign the total of those two numbers to the x position property of the ball Movie Clip. Thus, in one step you accomplish a task that would have taken 3 lines of code in Flash 4!

To sum up this line of code: It specifies the Movie Clip on which to act and tells Flash to move the x position of that Movie Clip 1 pixel to the right.

Continued

Continued

Line-by-line analysis: Line 4 of the onClipEvent **for the ball Movie Clip**

Look at the following code:

```
    }
```

Line 4 consists of only the closing curly bracket for the first of the four if test statements nested inside the onClipEvent. The closing curly bracket for the onClipEvent comes after all the other lines of code in this ActionScript.

Line-by-line analysis: Lines 5 to 13 of the onClipEvent **for the ball Movie Clip**

```
        if (_root.left == true)    {
            this._x-=1;
        }
        if (_root.up == true)    {
            this._y+=1;
        }
        if (_root.down == true)    {
            this._y-=1;
        }
```

These lines handle movement in the other three directions for the ball Movie Clip. They have the same structure as lines 2, 3, and 4 except that three elements need to be changed.

✦ The variable name: There must be a variable name for right, one for left, one for up, and one for down.

✦ The position property: _x is the horizontal position so we change the x position for right and left movement. _y is the vertical position so we change the y position for up and down movement.

✦ The compound assignment operator: If the x position should move to the right, or if the y position should move down, we use the += assignment operator. If the y position should move up, or if the x position should move left, we use the -= assignment operator.

Line-by-line analysis: Line 14 of the onClipEvent **for the ball Movie Clip**

```
        }
```

This is the closing curly bracket for the entire onClipEvent (enterFrame) code segment. If we were adding another type of onClipEvent (), for example load, we would use a separate set of curly brackets to enclose the code that should be executed on that movie event.

Goal 3. Creating the maze and defining the collision detection.

The ball Movie Clip must not move through any grid piece that makes up the maze. There needs to be a way to test whether the ball location on the Stage is already occupied by any grid piece. Collision detection needs to be set up for the maze and the ball; the new, built-in ActionScript function `hitTest` is does this. `hitTest` works by comparing the bounding box of the artwork of one Movie Clip with the bounding box of the artwork of another Movie Clip. See the `hitTest` examples that preceded this tutorial for more information on the area measured by the `hitTest` method.

Because each grid piece must detect a collision with the ball, it's necessary to construct the maze from many instances of the grid piece rectangles and scale and rotate them as needed. Making the grid pieces rectangular means the area occupied by the artwork will be exactly the same as the bounding box parameters tested by `hitTest`. The syntax for `hitTest` is:

```
anyMovieClip.hitTest(target);
```

`hitTest` has another way to specify the bounds of a Movie Clip, but that option is outside the scope of this tutorial. Please refer to the `hitTest` coverage that preceded this tutorial.

`hitTest` is a built-in function of the Movie Clip object. This function requires two Movie Clip instance names, let's call them the testerMC and the testeeMC. The testerMC is in front of `hitTest` and the testeeMC is enclosed within brackets after it.

Where to put the collision code

This code segment must be capable of constantly and repeatedly executing so that any collision is caught immediately. It would seem at first that we could put it in another `onClipEvent(enterFrame)` but this would require that we copy and paste our final collision detection code 136 times into each instance of the `mazeGrid` Movie Clip. Aside from the tedium of the task, that method of construction would make it very difficult to change the code if something wasn't working. We would have to fix the error in the code and make the same change 136 times. This would be arduous and it would increase the chances for further error. In this case, it is more efficient to put our code in a frame action inside the actual Movie Clip `mazeGrid`, and to make `mazeGrid` a two-frame movie with no `stop` actions in it. This will enable it to loop continually and therefore execute the code every time the playhead loops into frame 1. Thinking about coding in this way beforehand can save hours of troubleshooting later. To enter this code, we need to edit the actual `mazeGrid` symbol itself. To do this:

✦ Either double-click any instance of `mazeGrid` on the Stage to edit the Movie Clip in place on the Main Timeline Stage

✦ Or, select `mazeGrid` in the library and double-click the Movie Clip icon (not the Library name of the Movie Clip) to edit it as a separate symbol without the other content of the movie showing

Continued

Continued

The complete code for our collision detection script in frame 1 of mazeGrid

```
if (this.hitTest(_root.ball)) {
  trace ("ball intersects grid");
  location = this.getBounds(_root);
  if (_root.ball.nowBx < this.location.xMax -1) {
    _root.left = false;
    _root.ball._x -= 5;
  }
  if (_root.ball.nowBx > this.location.xMin-1) {
    _root.right = false;
    _root.ball._x += 5;
  }
  if (_root.ball.nowBy < this.location.yMax -1) {
    _root.up = false;
    _root.ball._y -= 5;
  }
  if (_root.ball.nowBy > this.location.yMin-1) {
    _root.down = false;
    _root.ball._y += 5;
  }
}
```

Line-by-line analysis: Line 1 of the `mazeGrid`

Look at the following code:

```
if (this.hitTest(_root.ball)) {
```

First, we set up an `if` statement to be the decision-maker or trigger for this code segment. We use the keyword `this` again and it is particularly necessary here. If the code reads:

```
if (_root.gridH2_V7.hitTest(_root.ball)) {
```

then no matter what grid piece the ball collided with, the `if` statement's test result would return `false` unless the grid piece that the ball collided with was the one that was named. Specifying `_root.ball` as the target is correct though, because that is the only moving Movie Clip and is therefore the only one that can cause a collision. The opening curly bracket at the end of this line signals the start of the code segment to be executed if the if statement returns `true`.

Line-by-line analysis: Line 2 of the `mazeGrid`

Now, for line 2:

```
trace("ball intersects grid");
```

This line does not contribute to or control any aspect of the collision detection ActionScript. Its purpose is as an information generator while testing the movie, using the Control ⇨ Test Movie command. Any element inside the parentheses is displayed in the output window during a test movie if Flash executes the `if` statement. In this case, it simply displays the words `ball intersects grid` whenever the ball Movie Clip collides with a grid piece. Notice that those three words are within quotes. Enclosing any words inside the parentheses in quotes tells Flash to treat those words *as* words, or strings, and to display them as written. If a keyword such as `this` was used and not enclosed in quotes, Flash would interpret the contents of `this`, which in this case is the instance name of the particular grid piece that had a collision with the ball. Try changing this line of code to:

```
trace("ball intersects" + this)
```

Be sure to check the Expression box to the right of the code entry box and do not omit the plus sign between the quoted text and the keyword `this`. The plus sign in this case concatenates (joins) the quoted text with the evaluated keyword. Trace can be a very useful tool in helping to see how your ActionScript is working and as an aid in debugging.

Line-by-line analysis: Line 3 of the `mazeGrid`

Now look at line 3:

```
location = this.getBounds(_root);
```

`location` is a new variable that is initialized within the collision detector to hold the results of the ActionScript method `getBounds`. A method is a function of a particular object. In this case, `getBounds` is a method of the Movie Clip Object. The syntax for this method is:

```
anyMoveClip.getBounds (targetCoordinateSpace)
```

✦ `anyMovieClip`: Defines the Movie Clip (instance name) whose bounding box coordinates we want to get.

✦ `getBounds`: Returns the minimum and maximum x and y coordinates of the specified Movie Clip. X minimum (`xMin`) and Y minimum (`yMin`) define the upper-left corner of the bounding box. X maximum (`xMax`) and Y maximum (`yMax`) define the lower-right corner of the Movie Clip's bounding box. The `getBounds` method returns these four coordinates for the instance of the grid piece that triggers the collision detection.

✦ `(targetCoordinateSpace)`: Defines which coordinate space is to be used.

Continued

Continued

The Main Timeline Stage has its own coordinate space but, less obviously, each Movie Clip has its own timeline as well as its own coordinate space. This difference in coordinate space is very important to keep in mind. Open the Info Panel, click once on a Movie Clip on the Stage, and look at the x and y position numbers in the Info Panel. If you then double-click that Movie Clip on the Stage to go into the Edit (Movie Clip) in Place Mode, and then click the object (graphic) on the Movie Clip's Stage, you will see that the x and y numbers showing in the Info Panel have changed. This is because Flash puts art that you convert into a Movie Clip on the Movie Clip's Stage with the upper-left corner of the art work's bounding box at the 0,0 point on the Movie Clip's Stage. You can change this placement by moving the art on the Movie Clip's Stage.

So, the actual code here specifies that the Movie Clip bounding coordinates to get are those of the grid instance that registered a collision. Remember that the code that contains the keyword `this` is inside a frame action of the Movie Clip `mazeGrid`. The coordinate space to be used is the `_root`, which always refers to the Main Timeline and its coordinate space, which is the Stage. As this code is contained in a `frameAction` of `mazeGrid` inside an `if` statement, it will be updated whenever a collision with the ball is detected. Therefore, the variable `location` will hold the current bounding box of grid piece that was hit.

Here's an example of why it is important to specify the `targetCoordinateSpace`. Select the top grid piece, second from the left, of the maze on the Main Timeline. In the Info Panel, look at its width and height numbers. They are w = 364 and h = 4. Now double-click that instance to go to Edit in Place Mode of the Movie Clip, which is an instance of `mazeGrid`. Click the graphic rectangle on `mazeGrid`'s Stage and look at the height and width numbers in the Info Panel now. They are w = 20 and h = 4. In this case, the reason for the difference is that all of the grid pieces on the Main Timeline's stage are made from the same Movie Clip, `mazeGrid` whose dimensions are w = 20 and h = 4. But the different lengths and widths needed to make up the entire maze are achieved by scaling and/or rotating instances of `mazeGrid` on the Main Stage; and the scaling and rotating occur within the coordinate space of the Main Timeline. Therefore, to get the correct size of any grid piece we need to use the coordinate space that contains the scaling and rotating that define what size a section of actual maze is.

Now a plan is needed to set up a test to compare the contents of `location` with the location of the ball when it hits a grid piece.

Setting up variables for lines 4 through 19 of mazeGrid to test against

After the `hitTest` inside the top level `if` statement has done its job, we need to nest four additional `if` statement tests to trigger one of the direction arrow buttons to stop allowing movement. As before, when a button is pressed it resets one of the direction variables (up, down, right, or left) to `true` allowing the ball to move. Then a collision creates an exception to disallowed movement. The information that is significant to the collision detection is not which grid piece collided with the ball, but with which *side* of a grid piece did the ball collide. Here's a summary of what the collision detection code needs to do after a collision is detected:

✦ If the ball hit a grid piece on the left side of the grid piece, the ball cannot be allowed to move right.

- ✦ If the ball hit a grid piece on the right side of the grid piece, the ball cannot be allowed to move left.

- ✦ If the ball hit a grid piece on the top of the grid piece, the ball cannot be allowed to move down.

- ✦ If the ball hit a grid piece on the bottom of the grid piece, the ball cannot be allowed to move up.

How do you test to determine on which side the collision occurred? First, a variable needs to be created that keeps track of the x and y position of the ball Movie Clip. For clarity, we will name these variables nowBx and nowBy.

- ✦ now: As a reminder that this variable's content is constantly updating

- ✦ B: For ball to remind us that it is the ball's position that we are tracking

- ✦ x or y: For the x position or the y position of the ball

Because these two new variables need to constantly update, it is easiest and clearest to put these two new variables within the onClipEvent action of the ball Movie Clip along with the other code that is constantly updating. Click evaluate in the actions toolbox and type in these two lines of code:

```
nowBy = _root.ball._y;
nowBx = _root.ball._x;
```

On the left side of the equal sign (assignment operator) is the variable's name; on the right side is a new Flash 5 ActionScript way of defining exactly what property of which Movie Clip is to be tracked. Don't use the keyword this in this instruction because there's only one Movie Clip (ball) that we want to track. Also notice that we specified the Movie Clip from _root. This tells Flash to get the x position of ball using the coordinate space of the Main Timeline's Stage. Because the coordinates of the grid location will be tracked in the Main Timeline coordinate space, the ball coordinates that we are comparing it to must be in that same coordinate space, or the results will not work as expected.

Line-by-line analysis: Lines 4 through 7 of the mazeGrid

Look at the following lines:

```
if (_root.ball.nowBx < this.location.xMax -1) {
  _root.left = false;
  _root.ball._x -= 5;
}
```

These are the first of four if statements that test which side of the grid piece the ball collided with and then set the appropriate direction variable to false. These if statements only need to be tested if a collision has been detected; therefore, they must be nested inside the if . . . .hitTest statement. These four *sub* if statement tests execute only if there has been a collision.

Continued

Continued

The if statement compares the x position of the ball to the contents of location, which is the xMax of the bounding box of the grid piece that registered the collision. xMax is the larger of the two x parameters that getBounds uses to determine the bounding box of the Movie Clip specified. There are four tests because you need one to test each side of the gird piece. The *sub* if test that is being analyzed checks whether the ball has collided with the grid on the right side of the grid piece.

Then, the -1 at the end subtracts 1 from the xMin number so that the x position of the ball matches the xMax position of the gird piece's x position of its bounding box just a bit ahead of time. Line 5 sets the ball movement variable for going left to false.

Line 6 subtracts 5 from the x position of the ball, which makes the ball appear to bounce off the grid when it touches the grid. Line 7 closes the curly bracket for this nested if statement

Line-by-line analysis: Lines 8 through 11 of the mazeGrid

```
if (_root.ball.nowBx > this.location.xMin-1) {
_root.right = false;
_root.ball._x += 5;
}
```

This next nested if test does the same job as the previous one, but it uses the xMin of the grid for the comparison test. It tests whether the ball has collided with the grid on the left side of the grid piece. Line 10 adds 5 to the x position of the ball, which makes the ball appear to bounce off the grid when it touches the grid. Line 11 closes the curly bracket for this nested if statement.

Line-by-line analysis: Lines 12 through 15 of the mazeGrid

```
if (_root.ball.nowBy < this.location.yMax -1) {
_root.up = false;
_root.ball._y -= 5;
}
```

This if uses the yMax of the grid for the comparison test. It tests whether the ball has collided with the grid on the bottom of the grid piece. Line 14 subtracts 5 from the y position of the ball, which makes it appear to bounce off the grid when it touches the grid. Line 15 closes the curly bracket for this nested if statement

Line-by-line analysis: Lines 16 through 20 of the mazeGrid

```
if (_root.ball.nowBy > this.location.yMin-1) {
  _root.down = false;
  _root.ball._y += 5;
}
}
```

This `if` uses the `yMin` of the grid for the comparison test. It tests whether the ball has collided with the grid on the top of the grid piece. Line 18 adds 5 to the y position of the ball, which makes the ball appear to bounce off the grid when it touches the grid. Line 19 closes the curly bracket for the nested `if` statement. Line 20 closes the curly bracket for the entire frame action.

Goal 4. The "You Win!" message on completing the maze.

The maze only needs a "you win!" acknowledgment for the completion of the maze. The ActionScript for `winMC` is a Movie Clip event:

```
onClipEvent (load) {
  this._alpha = 0;
}
onClipEvent (enterFrame) {
  if (this.hitTest(_root.ball )) {
    this.nextFrame();
    this._alpha = 100;
    _root.ball._x = 65;
    _root.ball._y = 25;
  }
}
```

Line-by-line analysis: Line 1 of the `winMC`

```
onClipEvent (load) {
```

The clip event here uses the loading of the Movie Clip to trigger this action because it contains instructions that must execute immediately and then do nothing after that. The `onClipEvent (load)` only executes once because the Movie Clip only loads once in this movie.

Line-by-line analysis: Lines 2 and 3 of the `winMC`

```
this._alpha = 0;
}
```

`winMC` is set to be 0 percent alpha to make it invisible but still active. Line 3 contains the closing curly bracket that defines the end of clip event.

Line-by-line analysis: Line 4 of the `winMC`

```
onClipEvent (enterFrame)
```

The second clip event uses `enterFrame` as the triggering event so this code will execute repeatedly.

Line-by-line analysis: Line 5 of the `winMC`

```
if (this.hitTest(_root.ball)) {
```

Continued

Continued

An `if` statement tests for the collision of the `winMC` and the ball. `winMC` is placed across the exit from the maze so that when the ball crosses over it, the maze has been completed.

Line-by-line analysis: Line 6 of the `winMC`

```
this.nextFrame();
```

This line tells `winMC` to go to the next frame in its own timeline and stop. The graphic in frame 2 of `winMC` contains the words, *"You Win!"* in big letters on the stage.

Line-by-line analysis: Line 7 of the `winMC`

```
this._alpha = 100;
```

Resets the alpha property of `winMC` to 100 percent so that it is no longer invisible. If we didn't do this, the *"You Win!"* would remain invisible.

Line-by-line analysis: Lines 8 and 9 of the `winMC`

```
_root.ball._x = 65;
_root.ball._y = 25;
```

These two lines move the ball back to its starting position ready to go again.

Line-by-line analysis: Lines 10 and 11 of the `winMC`

```
    }
}
```

Line 10 closes the `if` statement in `onclipEvent(enterFrame)` and line 11 closes the `onClipEvent` itself.

Now, test your version of the movie and compare its function to redMaze.fla, which is found on the CD-ROM.

For more information about Dorian, see her tutorial in Chapter 10, "Using Modify ⇨ Curves."

Expert Tutorial: Complex Hit Detection on the Z Axis, by *James Robertson*

In this section, we enter the third dimension and show you how to make the built-in Flash 5 collision detection work with your 3D creations. The first and most important lesson we need to teach you is this: *Don't panic!* Despite the title of this section, it's not that complex and you won't need to worry about detailed mathematical formulas or trigonometry—so, put down your scientific calculator and relax.

You'll find the source files for this tutorial, as well as a demo version of Edesign's *10-Pin Bowling Game* in the ch23 folder, on the accompanying CD-ROM.

Displaying 3D scenes

There are several ways to display a 3D scene on your computer screen, but in this section, we look at *vanishing point perspective*. This technique enables us to give the illusion of depth on your flat computer screen without too much effort or mathematical wizardry. So, what is it and how does it work? Imagine that you are standing in the middle of a flat desert area and this desert has a long, straight road running through the middle of it. If you were to stand on the road and look toward the horizon, what would you see? You should see something like the following figure, where the road would appear to get narrower as it nears the horizon and, eventually, it seems to vanish into a single point—hence the term, vanishing point perspective. Remember, if we were to stand on this road and watch a car driving away from us, it would appear to become gradually smaller as it moves away.

Continued

Continued

It's reasonably simple to recreate this scene in Flash. To give the illusion of a car driving into the distance all we have to do is move a car graphic slowly up the screen, gradually reducing the size of the image as it moves nearer to the vanishing point. Of course, that can be done as a tweened timeline animation, but let's take a look at using code for this. If we were to drive this car with code, how would we go about it? First, we need to set up the initial variables for the position and size of the car. We have the usual x and y coordinates, which you are already familiar with — but we will also define a z coordinate, which will tell us how far the car has moved into the distance. For this example, imagine the z coordinate to be like the odometer of the car — it tells us how far the car has moved. The start_size and end_size variables are used to scale the car as it moves away. In this example, it will start off at full size (100 percent) and, when it reaches the vanishing point, it will be just 1 percent. So, in frame 1, we have the following code:

```
car_x = 275;
car_y = 390;
car_z = 0;
start_size = 100;
end_size = 1;
car_size = start_size;
```

This next section works out the speed of the animation. The variable animationframes shows the number of steps it will take the car to move from it's starting position to the vanishing point. A larger number will slow down the animation and a smaller number will speed it up. The variable travel_distance is how far the car will move up the screen during the animation (or the length of the road). The variables size_factor and end_factor are calculated from the animation length and determine how much the car is moved and resized in each loop of the animation.

```
animationframes = 60;
travel_distance = getProperty("/road", _height);
size_factor = (start_size-end_size)/animationframes;
move_factor = travel_distance/animationframes;
```

Now for the actions for frame 2: With all the variables set up, we simply need to move and resize the car by subtracting the move_factor and size_factor variables, which we've just calculated. In addition, because the car has moved one step nearer the horizon, we increase the z coordinate by 1, as follows:

```
car_y = car_y-move_factor;
car_z = Number(car_z)+1;
car_size = car_size-size_factor;
```

Now that we've calculated the new size and position of the car, we simply move the Movie Clip and resize it.

```
setProperty ("/car", _y, car_y);
setProperty ("/car", _xscale, car_size);
setProperty ("/car", _yscale, car_size);
```

The last frame of this animation is frame 3, in which we insert the following actions: If the z coordinate is less than the number of `animationframes`, then the car has not reached the vanishing point on the horizon, so we simply `gotoAndPlay` frame 2 and repeat the animation. Otherwise, we `gotoAndPlay` frame 1 and restart the animation.

```
if (Number(car_z)<Number(animationframes)) {
    gotoAndPlay (2);
} else {
    gotoAndPlay (1);
}
```

See cardemo1.fla for the full source-code to the previous section. It's in the ch23 folder on the accompanying CD-ROM.

Collisions

Now that we have the basics in place, and our car is moving on the screen toward the horizon, we look at collisions. To have a collision, we need to add another animation that can collide with our original car. So, we'll add another car animation, which will move horizontally across the screen at a random distance and speed.

Much like the previous animation, we need to set up our initial variables for the position and size of this new car. The variable $sidecar\_x$ is the x coordinate of the car (it will start out of sight on the right side of our movie). $sidecar\_z$ is the z coordinate of the car (or the distance it has traveled toward the horizon). Although the formula may look slightly confusing, all we are doing is choosing a random number somewhere between 20 and the value of the variable `animationframes` (which was set to 60 in our original example). $sidecar\_y$ is our y coordinate and it is calculated from the z coordinate of the car (remember that as the z coordinate increases, the car moves up the screen). Additionally, `sidemove_factor` determines how quickly the car moves across the screen — again, this is randomized to make the movie more interesting. Finally, `sidecar_size` is the scale of the car. All of this code will go into the first frame of our movie, right after the code for the first car:

```
sidecar_x = 750;
sidecar_z = Number(random(animationframes-20))+20;
sidecar_y = car_y-(sidecar_z*move_factor);
sidemove_factor = 870/(random(animationframes*2)+40);
sidecar_size = 100-(size_factor*sidecar_z);
```

Now that we've defined all the variables, we can draw the car on screen at the correct size and position, by adding this code to frame 1:

```
setProperty ("/carside", _y, sidecar_y);
setProperty ("/carside", _xscale, sidecar_size);
setProperty ("/carside", _yscale, sidecar_size);
```

Continued

Continued

Next, in frame 2 of the movie, we need to modify the x coordinate of the second car and move it to its new position:

```
sidecar_x = sidecar_x-sidemove_factor;
setProperty ("/carside", _x, sidecar_x);
```

That's all we need. Our new car should be zooming across the screen at a random distance and speed. For the final ingredient, all we need to do is calculate when the two cars collide. Luckily for us, Flash 5 has built-in collision detection so it's not too difficult. In fact, we can tell whether the two cars collide by using the following command:

```
collision = _root.car.hitTest(_root.carside);
```

This checks whether the Movie Clip instance called `car` has hit the Movie Clip instance called `carside`. If the variable `collision` is `true` then the two cars have collided. However, remember that Flash 5 can only detect collisions in a two-dimensional scene and our scene is three-dimensional. What we need to do is check the z coordinates of each car to see if they are equal — if they are equal and the variable `collision` is `true`, *then* the cars have definitely collided. So, in order to determine whether we've had a collision on the z-axis, we need to add the following command to frame 2:

```
if (collision == true and car_z == sidecar_z) {
    result="CRASH!!!"
}
```

See cardemo2.fla for the full source-code to the previous section, it's in the ch23 folder on the accompanying CD-ROM.

Using depth in Flash

If you try the movie that we created in the previous section, you'll notice one small problem — the car moving horizontally *always* appears on top of the other car, which is not always right. To fix this, we need to use the depth facility in Flash. (Using depth is fully explained in this chapter; refer to the depth section to enhance your learning in this tutorial.)

By giving depth to a Movie Clip, you can determine which car appears on top when the two cars cross each other. To calculate the depth, we simply compare the z coordinates for each car. If the horizontal car has a larger z coordinate than the vertical car (that is, if it is nearer the horizon and, therefore, further away) then it should appear beneath the vertical car.

See cardemo3.fla for the full source-code to the previous section. It, too, is in the ch23 folder on the accompanying CD-ROM.

Using this technique

After you've mastered the basics of this technique, you can develop it further by having multiple objects and by doing collision detections on everything in the scene. The best method for this level of complexity is to use arrays to store the coordinates of each object and then use a loop to check for collisions.

Author's Note: You can read more about arrays in Chapter 22, "Creating Subroutines and Manipulating Data." For more information on loop actions, please refer to Chapter 21, "Planning Code Structures."

This guy came of age in Crowborough, East Sussex, England, when Madonna was singing "Vogue." His interests are, "Apart from the obvious, err . . . too many to mention. But I'll say, exploring the world — trips like the Galapagos, Amazon, or Machu Pichu come to mind. James was introduced to Flash by a demo version on the front of a magazine. Subsequently, according to Bill Turner, he's become "one of the sharpest Flash programmers around." This particular technique is only an indication of his "game." You can see this technique used in several productions such as *Walter's Been Framed* by Edesign and Turnertoons.

Reusing and Repurposing Code with Smart Clips

A new addition to the Library symbol types is the Smart Clip. A Smart Clip is a Movie Clip symbol that has been given a set of parameters that are easily accessed by the Clip Parameters Panel.

When would you want to use a Smart Clip? If you have any Movie Clip symbol that you use multiple times but would like to add unique settings (or properties) to, then a Smart Clip could be just what you need. For example, if you had a Button instance in a menu item Movie Clip and you want to reuse that same menu item symbol to point to different areas of your Flash movie, you have these options:

✦ Make duplicate menu items symbols in the Library, for each use of the symbol. Each Button instance will have a unique hard-coded Go To action, such as:

```
on(release){
    _root.gotoStop("products");
}
```

✦ Make a menu item symbol that uses an expression within the Button instance actions. Other ActionScripts will supply the values for this expression. (See our arrayMenu.fla example in the last chapter.) The actions on the Button instance would appear as:

```
on(release){
    _root.gotoAndStop(frameLabel);
}
```

where `frameLabel` was set on the Movie Clip timeline by some other ActionScript code.

✦ Create a Smart Clip menu item symbol that uses values from the Clip Parameters Panel to establish the values of expressions used within the Button instance code. The actions on the Button instance inside of a Smart Clip would appear as:

```
on(release){
    _root.gotoAndStop(frameLabel);
}
```

where `frameLabel` is defined by the Clip Parameters Panel for this specific instance. This method is by far the easiest for Flash designers who prefer not to get involved with complex ActionScripting. We demonstrate using a Smart Clip for a typical menu item symbol in the next section.

Usually, Smart Clips are most useful in a team production environment, in which the programmers on the staff design the ActionScripts, and Flash graphic artists create the movie elements and layout. The programmers would create the Clip Parameters for each symbol (and perhaps even a custom interface for the Clip Parameters Panel), and the designers would select and enter the values for each parameter in the Flash movie.

Adding parameters to a Movie Clip symbol

In this section, we create a Smart Clip symbol and then add a parameter to it. This symbol will be used for a menu system in a Flash movie.

On the CD-ROM As a starting point, you can use the smartClip_starter.fla located in the ch23 folder of the *Flash 5 Bible* CD-ROM.

1. Create a new Flash movie, and set its background color to white and its frame rate to 20 fps, in the Modify Movie dialog (Ctrl+M or Command+M). Use whatever frame size you prefer.

2. Save the Flash movie as **smartClip.fla**.

3. Create a Main Timeline that has four sections, with the frame labels **main**, **products**, **services**, and **contact** (as shown in Figure 23-2). Add some placeholder artwork to keyframes for each section, and insert a `stop()` action at the keyframe of the first section.

3. Make a new symbol by pressing Ctrl+F8 (PC) or Command+F8 (Mac). In the Symbol Properties dialog, type the name **menuItem** and keep the default Movie Clip behavior. Click OK. Flash automatically switches to Symbol Editing Mode.

4. On the menuItem timeline, rename Layer 1 to **button**. In frame 1 of this layer, create a rectangular Button symbol, using any of the drawing tools. Or, you can use a Button symbol from the Buttons Library (Window ➪ Common Libraries ➪ Buttons).

5. Create new layer on the menuItem timeline, and rename this layer **textField**. In frame 1 of this layer, create a Dynamic Text field whose length matches the Button instance that you created in Step 3. With this field selected, type **name** in the Variable field of the Text Options Panel, as shown in Figure 23-3.

Figure 23-2: The Main Timeline should demonstrate the layout of the Flash movie sections.

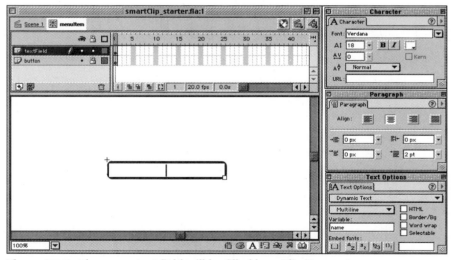

Figure 23-3: The name text field will be filled by a Clip Parameter.

6. Select the Button instance from Step 4, and open the Actions Panel. With the panel in Expert Mode, type the following actions into the Actions list:

```
on(release){
    _root.gotoAndStop(frameLabel);
}
```

In this code, we specify an expression for the label that the `gotoAndStop` action will use. The expression is a variable named `frameLabel`. This variable will be added to the `menuItem` symbol as a Smart Clip parameter.

7. Return to the Main Timeline of the Flash movie. Rename Layer 1 to **menuItems**.

8. Open the Library window, and select the menuItem symbol. In the Options menu of the Library window, choose Define Clip Parameters. The Define Clip Parameters dialog opens.

9. Press the plus (+) button at the top-left corner of the dialog. This will add a default varName parameter to the menuItem symbol (which is now a Smart Clip). Double-click the varName text, and replace varName with **name**. In the Value column, replace defaultValue with **[type button text here]**. Leave the Type column value set to Default. The Default value leaves this option as an editable text field in the Clip Parameters Panel, so that we can directly type the text for our menu item.

As shown in Figure 23-4, each parameter has three values: the name of the parameter (which is interpreted as an actual variable name in ActionScript), the value for that variable, and the type value which indicates how the value should be typed (string (default), array, object, or user-defined list).

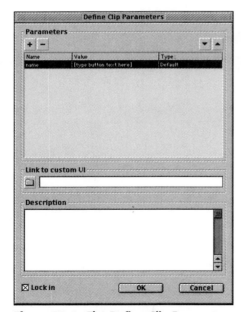

Figure 23-4: The Define Clip Parameters dialog enables you to enter name/value pairs for the Smart Clip.

10. Press the plus (+) button again, and rename the new varName entry to **frameLabel**. Then, double-click the Type column value for the frameLabel entry, and choose List from the drop-down menu.

11. Double-click the Value column value for the frameLabel entry. A Values dialog opens (see Figure 23-5). Click the plus (+) button to add each of the frame labels used on the Main Timeline. Surround each value with quotes — otherwise, Flash will look for variable names that have these names. Click OK to close the Values dialog when you are finished.

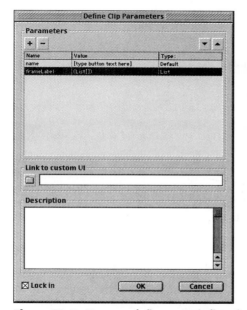

Figure 23-5: You can define a static list of values to choose from the Clip Parameters Panel for each instance of the menuItem.

12. You have now defined two parameters for the menuItem Smart Clip. These will be accessible by each instance of the menuItem symbol. Click OK on the Define Clip Parameters dialog.

You can continue to add more parameters to Smart Clip symbols, by going back to the Define Clip Parameters dialog and clicking the plug ("+") button. Use caution, though — if you place instances of a Smart Clip on the Stage and add more parameters later, then the old instances will not have those parameters available. You may need to delete the old instances and replace them with new instances to see the new parameters.

In the next section, you'll learn how to give unique parameter values to each Smart Clip instance in the Flash movie.

Assigning values to Smart Clip instances on the Stage

After you have created parameters for a Smart Clip symbol in the Library, you can start to use the Smart Clip in your Flash movie. The steps below will show you how to use the Smart Clip symbol we created in the last section.

1. On the Main Timeline, drag an instance of the menuItem Smart Clip to the menuItems layer. With the instance selected, open the Clip Parameters Panel (Window ➪ Panels ➪ Clip Parameters). In the Value column of the name parameter, type the text that you want to appear on the menu item button for the main section. For our example in Figure 23-6, we inserted the text Home. In the Value column of the frameLabel parameter, select main from the drop-down menu.

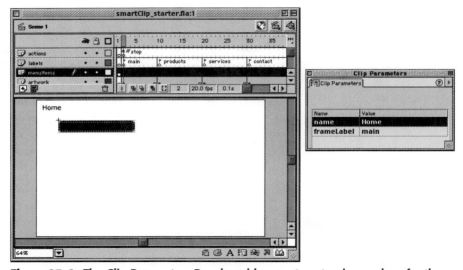

Figure 23-6: The Clip Parameters Panel enables you to set unique values for the parameters that you defined for the Smart Clip.

2. Repeat Step 1 for each section of the Flash movie. For our example, we will have four menuItem Smart Clips, one for each section.

3. Save your Flash movie, and test it (Ctrl+Enter or Command+Enter). Each button should show the proper text and take you to the appropriate section of the Flash movie.

The completed Flash movie, smartClip_finished.fla, is found on the *Flash 5 Bible* CD-ROM, in the ch23 folder. For more information on Smart Clips and custom interfaces for Smart Clips, you can read pages 119-224 of Macromedia's *ActionScript Reference Guide*.

Summary

✦ Collisions occur when two or more elements in a Flash movie touch each other. Whenever the space by one Movie Clip instance occupies the space of another, a collision, or "hit," has occurred.

✦ You can detect simple user-initiated collisions by using the `startDrag()` method and `_dropTarget` property of the Movie Clip object.

✦ Using the `hitTest` method of the Movie Clip object, you can detect the intersection of X and Y coordinates with a specified Movie Clip instance. You can also use `hitTest` in a similar fashion to `_dropTarget`, where the overlap of two specific Movie Clip instances is detected.

✦ Smart Clips are Movie Clip symbols that have been given user-defined parameters. These parameters can make some scripting routines a matter of selecting them from the Clip Parameter Panel.

✦ ✦ ✦

Sending Data In and Out of Flash

A powerful feature of Flash 5 is the extraordinary control of data acquisition and management it provides within a Flash movie. You can load external text data into Flash movies, making it possible to include fresh dynamic content every time a Flash movie is viewed over the Web.

Using Text Fields to Store and Display Data

Before we can discuss sending and receiving data with Flash movies, you need to know the basic mechanisms of input and output. Most of the time, unless you are using Macromedia Generator templates, your data in Flash will be text based, which means that you will gather information from the user and display new and updated information with text. In Flash 5, Input Text fields gather data from the user, while Dynamic Text fields can be used to display live and updated text to the user.

Input Text fields

Input Text fields are created with the Text Tool. In the Text Options Panel, the top drop-down menu must be set to Input Text for the selected text field. If you recall from Chapter 21, "Planning Code Structures," an Input Text field has a variable name because it *is* a variable. The text that is typed inside of an Input Text field is the value of that variable. For example, if you create an Input Text field and assign it the variable name `visitorInput`, anything that is typed into that text field during runtime will become the value of `visitorInput`. To test this, let's create a simple Input Text field.

1. By using the Text Tool, create a text field on the Main Timeline of a Flash movie. Make the box long enough to hold 20 characters. You can type a temporary word or phrase into the text field, but delete these characters before proceeding to the next step.

2. In the Text Options Panel, select Input Text in the top drop-down menu. In the Variable field, enter the text **visitorInput**. Check the Border/Bg option.

3. Save your Flash movie as inputText.fla, and test the movie (Ctrl+Enter or Command+Enter). In the .SWF movie, click the text field and type your first name into the field.

4. Choose Debug ➪ List Variables, and the `visitorInput` variable should display the value you typed in Step 3. In our example, we entered the name "Charlie." Therefore, the Output window displays:

```
Level #0:
   Variable _level0.$version = "MAC 5,0,30,0"
   Variable _level0.visitorInput = "Charlie"
```

The List Variables command always shows the `$version` variable and value, indicating the Flash Player version currently playing the movie.

5. If you change the text in the `visitorInput` text field, then the value will automatically update for the `visitorInput` variable. You need to choose List Variables from the Debug menu to see the updated value.

   Input Text fields not only accept input from the user, but they can also be set to an initial value or updated with a new value with ActionScript code. You can test this with the previous Flash movie example.

6. If you are viewing the `inputText.swf` from Step 5, then close the .SWF movie to return to the Flash authoring environment. Create a new layer, and rename it **Actions**. Double-click the first frame of the Actions layer to open the Actions Panel. Add the following code to the Actions list:

```
visitorInput = "enter your name here";
```

7. Save your Flash movie, and test it. You should see the text "enter your name here" in the `visitorInput` text field.

As you can see, Input Text fields can accept text input from the user, just like an HTML form. Later in this chapter, we use Input Text fields to create a fully functional Flash form that can send and receive information for a CGI (Common Gateway Interface) script.

Dynamic Text fields

If you want to display text information to people viewing Flash movies, you have two options: (a) create Static Text blocks whose contents can not be updated with ActionScript, or (b) create Dynamic Text fields that can be filled with internal Flash data or external text data.

Caution Do not use Input or Dynamic Text fields unless you need to accept or display live data to the user. Static Text is perfectly fine for text used for graphic purposes, where the text does not need to be changed during the presentation.

Dynamic Text fields are also variables, just as Input Text fields. The only difference between Input and Dynamic Text fields is that you can type into Dynamic Text fields. Dynamic Text fields are most useful for display of text information that doesn't need to be changed or updated by the user. Using Dynamic Text fields, you can display news articles that change on a daily (or hourly) basis, a player's score during a Flash game, and the system time and date, just to name a few.

New Feature Both Input and Dynamic Text fields use HTML text formatting tags to change the display of text. We discuss HTML use within text fields in Chapter 25, "Understanding HTML and Text Field Functions in Flash."

In the following steps, we create a Dynamic Text field that is updated with a Flash variable action. You can also load external variables for use in Dynamic Text fields, which we discuss in the next section. To insert text into a Dynamic Text field:

1. By using the Text Tool, create a text field on the Main Timeline of a Flash movie. Make a block large enough to accommodate multiple lines of text.

2. In the Text Options Panel, select Dynamic Text in the top drop-down menu. Select Multiline from the second drop-down menu. In the Variable field, enter the text **textOutput**. Check the Border/Bg and Word wrap options.

3. Add a new layer, and name it **Actions**. Double-click the first keyframe of the Actions layer, and, in the Actions Panel, enter the following action (note that the ¬ indicates a continuation of the same line of code; do not insert this character in your actual code):

```
textOutput = "WANTED: Flash Input & Output" + newline ¬
  + newline + "A start-up Dot com company is looking ¬
  for a qualified Web technology that will present text ¬
  input and output to Web visitors in a more compelling ¬
  animated and visually stunning environment than that ¬
  possible with HTML. Please call:" + newline + newline ¬
  + "1-800-555-CODE";
```

In this code, we specify string values (denoted with quotes) for the actual text we want to insert into the `textOutput` Dynamic Text field variable. To insert a carriage return in the text, the `newline` constant is inserted between string values.

4. Save the Flash movie as **dynamicText_internal.fla**.

5. Test the movie (Ctrl+Enter or Command+Enter). The `textOutput` Dynamic Text field updates with the value assigned to the `textOutput` variable in ActionScript.

You can also load text data into Input and Dynamic Text fields. This data can be returned from a simple text file (.TXT file) or from an application that resides on your Web server.

Defining a Data Process with States

When you manipulate text fields with internal Flash variables, then the data for the text fields is available for use immediately. Meaning, if you declare a variable and a value for that variable, that any text field can be given that value as well. When you want to load external data into a Flash movie, you need to create the appropriate steps, or "states," in your movie to make sure that the data is available for use in the Flash movie. For example, say you want to retrieve a news article from a Web server, and the text for that article is contained within a variable named article_1. You can't use or assign the value of article_1 to any other Flash element *unless* the article has fully downloaded to the Flash movie.

So, how do you know when data is available in a Flash movie? Any Flash movie that relies on data exchange between the Flash movie and the Web server should contain four separate steps, which are called *states*:

✦ An *input* state to gather the information from the user or the movie

✦ A *send* state in which a Flash action sends the data out of the movie

✦ A *wait* state during which the data downloads to the movie

✦ The *output* state in which the data can be used by the Flash movie in text fields and other ActionScript code

Input state

The first step for data exchange requires that you have something to send out of the Flash movie. The input can be a Flash form into which a user types text. The data could be environment variables, such as the time of the day or the Flash Player version. There could be various substeps in the input state, such as multiple forms or the completion of a quiz to calculate a test score that will be sent to the Web server.

Send state

Once the input data has been set in the Flash movie, you're ready to send the data to another host, such as an application or script on your Web server. The following actions can be used to send data out of the Flash movie:

✦ getURL

✦ loadVariables

✦ loadMovie

Of these actions, getURL is restricted to a one-way data path; that is, you can only send data out with getURL — you cannot receive external data with getURL. getURL must target the sought URL to the current browser (or frame) or a new browser window. In many situations, you may only need to send data out of the Flash movie without needing to receive any further data. To send information with the user's e-mail client, you can use a simple `mailto` URL in a `getURL` action on a Button instance:

```
on(release){
  email = "admin@server.com";
  subject = escape("Visitor Feedback");
  body = escape("Please let us know how you feel.");
  getURL("mailto:" + email + "?subject=" + subject + ¬
    "&body=" + body);
}
```

In the preceding code block, the variables `email`, `subject`, and `body` are inserted into the `getURL` action. Note that you can automatically set subject and body text for the e-mail message as well! To add specific variables to a URL string, you should use the `escape()` function in ActionScript, which converts illegal URL characters such as spaces and ? into URL form-encoded text (for example, a space is converted into `%20`).

Wait state

If you are sending data from the Flash movie with `loadVariables` or `loadMovie`, then you need to know when the requested data is received. The most common way to detect the download state of data into the Flash movie is to use a terminal tag — a name/value pair in the downloaded data that indicates the end of the data string. For example, if the `textOutput` variable that we used in the last section was converted to a name/value pair in a .TXT file (as URL form-encoded text), it would appear as the following (URL-converted characters are shown in bold, and the terminal tag is underlined):

```
textOutput=WANTED%3A%20Flash%20Input%20%26%20Output%0AA%20start
%2Dup%20Dot%20com%20company%20is%20looking%20for%20a%20qualifie
d%20web%20technology%20that%20will%20present%20text%20input%20a
nd%20output%20to%20web%20visitors%20in%20a%20more%20compelling%
20animated%20and%20visually%20stunning%20environment%20than%20t
hat%20possible%20with%20HTML%2E%20Please%20call%3A%0A%0A1%2D800
%2D555%2DCODE&success=1
```

At the end of this line of text (or at the very end of a long line of variables), we have inserted a terminal tag `success=1`. With this variable in place, we can set up a frame loop within our Flash movie to detect the existence (loading) of the terminal tag variable. After the terminal tag is loaded, the Flash movie will be directed to the appropriate output state.

Note   You can use GET or POST to send Flash variables to the URL for the .SWF file.

All wait states should have a timeout condition: If the data fails to load within a certain time frame, then we will assume the Web server (or script) is not functioning correctly. If the timeout condition proves `true`, then the Flash movie will go to the appropriate output state. We create a wait state for our Flash form in the next section.

New Feature   You can now avoid the use of terminal tags with the new Movie Clip `data` event, which is specified with the `onClipEvent()` action. We present this new alternative in the "Creating a Flash Form" section.

Output state

The final step in a data exchange is the actual display of any received data in the Flash movie. However, as indicated in the last state, there are two separate output states: a success display or an error display. If the data was properly received during the wait state, then the Flash movie will display the success output state. If the server failed to return any data to the Flash movie, then the movie will display an error output state, indicating that there was a problem with the server.

Creating a Flash Form

In this section, we create a Flash form that submits user-entered information to a server-side CGI script, which e-mails the data to an e-mail address that we specify with a Flash variable. By accessing a remote Perl CGI script, you make a Flash movie with five data exchange states: input, send, wait, output, and error. You learn how to submit name/value pairs from Flash to remote URLs, and learn how to check the receipt of variables from the CGI script using a multiple frame loop. We also use the new `onClipEvent(data)` action to detect the loading of the external variable data.

On the CD-ROM   You can find the Perl script (sendmail.cgi) and supporting Flash files for this section in the ch24 folder of the *Flash 5 Bible* CD-ROM. Note that you need to have Perl 5 installed on your Web server in order to configure and use the sendmail.cgi script.

Flash forms are user data entry forms (just like HTML forms) that are created in Flash using Input Text fields. When a user types information in these text fields, the information is stored as variables. The values of these variables are then sent to a specified Web server using standard GET or POST communication. These same variables are available to the Web server and can be processed there by a CGI program or script. CGI programs can be written to e-mail this information, manipulate it, store it in a database, or perform many other applications. The same CGI script can also return values to Flash — these can then be displayed or used by the originating Flash movie.

In this exercise, our Flash form solicits feedback from visitors, giving them an opportunity to submit comments, report bugs, or make suggestions for improvement.

As each form is submitted, it's e-mailed directly to the e-mail address you specify in the Flash movie.

1. Open a new Flash movie document (Ctrl+N or Command+N).

2. Rename layer 1 to **labels**. Create keyframes (F6) on frames 5, 15, 25, and 35. Give these keyframes the labels **input**, **wait**, **output**, and **error**, respectively. (Do not give frame 1 a label.) Select frame 45 and press F5 to insert more empty frames at the end of the layer.

3. Create a new layer, and name it **actions**. On frame 5 of the actions layer, insert a keyframe (F6) and double-click it. In the Actions Panel, add a **stop()** action. In the Frame Panel, add a comment of //**stop** in the Label field.

4. Create a new layer, and name it **text fields**. Insert keyframes on frames 5, 15, 25, and 35.

5. On frame 5 of the text fields layer, insert three separate Input Text fields. From top to bottom, assign the following variable names to the Input Text fields (in the Text Options Panel): **name**, **from**, and **comments**. The name and e-mail text fields should accommodate one line of text, while the comment field should be set to Multiline and Word wrap in order to hold multiple lines of text. All of the Input Text fields should have the Border/Bg option selected, unless you plan to create your own background graphics. Make each text field long enough to accommodate about 45 characters of text. The comments field should be able to show between five and ten lines of text. (See Figure 24-1.)

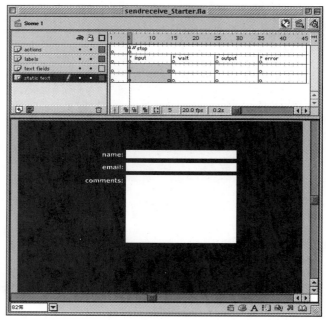

Figure 24-1: These text fields accept input from your site visitors.

6. Create a new layer, and name it **static text**. Insert keyframes on frames 5, 15, 25, and 35. On frame 5, add Static Text blocks to the left of the text fields, indicating the purpose of each field.

7. On frame 15 of the static text layer (underneath the `wait` label), insert a Static Text block indicating that the information is being sent to the server and that we're waiting for confirmation. In our example, we used the text "Checking the server. . . ."

8. On frame 25 of the static text layer (underneath the `output` label), insert a Static Text block containing a successful receipt of the visitor's information. In our example, we used the text "Thank you. Your feedback was received at:".

9. You can see that we are setting up the output state to display the time that the server received the data (Figure 24-2). The CGI script returns the time and date of the receipt to the Flash movie Main Timeline. On frame 25 of the text fields layer, create a Dynamic Text field named **serverTime**, and place it underneath the Static Text you just made.

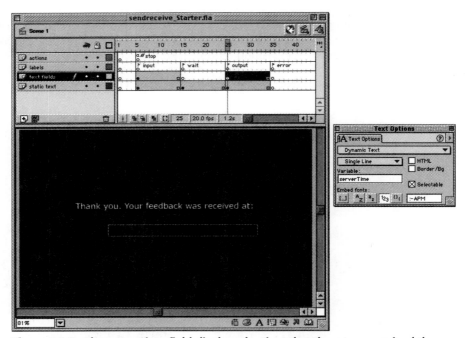

Figure 24-2: The serverTime field displays the time that the server received the Flash form data.

10. On frame 35 of the static text layer (underneath the `error` label), insert Static Text that indicates the data was not successfully received. In our example, we used the text "Sorry, the server is down."

11. Save your Flash movie as **sendReceive.fla**.

Now, we have all our states defined with placeholder artwork. You can go back later and refine the text and graphics to suit your particular needs. Next we need to add the interactive components to the Flash movie:

- A Flash action to define the e-mail address of the site administrator (or your own e-mail address)

- A Flash action to send the data in the Input Text fields (and the e-mail variables)

- A Flash action to wait for the server's response

These actions need to put on the appropriate Flash event handlers. We start by defining our e-mail address variable, and then adding a Button instance to the input state. This Button instance uses a `loadVariables` action to send the data from the Flash movie to the receiving script on our Web server. Then our wait state uses an `if. . .else` action to determine whether the server has received the data.

12. Create a new layer and name it **buttons**. Insert keyframes on frames 5 and 15. On frame 5, create a simple Button symbol or use one from the Buttons Library (Window ➪ Common Libraries ➪ Buttons). In our example, we used the Pill button from the Buttons Library. Place an instance of the Button symbol below your text fields. Then insert some Static Text on the Button instance, such as "Submit" or "Send."

13. Select the Button instance from Step 11, and open the Actions Panel. In the actions list, type the following code (note that the ¬ indicates a continuation of the same line of code; do not insert this character into your actual code):

```
on (release){
  to = "your@e-mail.com";
  subject = "Flash 5 Bible Form";
  loadVariables("http://www.themakers.com/cgi-bin/¬
    books/sendmail.cgi", _root, "POST");
  sendTime = getTimer();
  gotoAndPlay ("wait");
}
```

This code establishes the recipient's e-mail address (your e-mail address) and the subject line of the e-mail, and issues a `loadVariables` action that sends the `mailto`, `name`, `email`, and `comments` variables to the `sendmail.cgi` script on our Web server. `_root` indicates that any output from the `sendmail.cgi` script should be directed to the Main Timeline of our movie. Depending on the browsers of your target audience, you may want to use the GET method for `loadVariables`, as Internet Explorer 4.5 (or earlier) on the Mac does not support the POST method from plug-ins.

After the `loadVariables` action is executed, a new variable called `sendTime` marks the time that the `loadVariables` action occurred. The `getTimer()` function is a built-in Flash function that returns the current time, in milliseconds, of Flash movie playback. Thus, if the user clicked the Button instance after spending 2 minutes to fill in the form, the `getTimer()` will return a value of around 60,000 (milliseconds). Finally, the `gotoAndPlay` action will direct the Main Timeline playback to the `wait` label.

14. On frame 16 of the actions layer, insert an empty keyframe. In the Frame Panel, type a frame label (comment) of **//loop**. This keyframe contains the actions necessary to check the server's response to our `loadVariables` action. Open the Actions Panel, and type the following code:

```
if (success == "1") {
    gotoAndStop ("output");
} else {
    if( getTimer() > sendTime+25000 ) {
        gotoAndStop ("error");
    } else {
        gotoAndPlay ("wait");
    }
}
```

This code first tests whether a variable called `success` has been received by the Flash movie (from the CGI script). If `success` exists and it's equal to the string "1"", then the Main Timeline will go to the `output` label. If success has not been received, then a secondary `if. . .else` statement is evaluated. If the current time of the Flash movie is greater than 25 seconds from the `sendTime` value, then it sends the playhead to the `error` label. Otherwise, the playhead will loop back to the previous frame with the `wait` label.

Note   All variables received from an external source with `loadVariables` are typed as `string` data. Therefore, we need the quotes around our number 1. For more information on data types, see Chapter 22, "Creating Subroutines and Manipulating Data."

15. Finally, add a keyframe to frame 25 of the actions layer. With this keyframe selected, open the Actions Panel, and add the following action:

```
serverTime = timeDate;
```

This action takes the server's returned variable, `timeDate`, and use its value for the `serverTime` variable, which also updates the `serverTime` text field we created at this state.

16. Save your Flash movie again, and test it (Ctrl+Enter or Command+Enter). Type some information into the text fields, and click the Submit button. If the server script is available, you should see the output state display the time/date stamp from the server.

New Feature   Flash 5 now supports `loadVariable` actions to external data sources, right in the Test Movie environment!

You can modify this movie to work with as many text fields as you want. The server script supports either GET or POST methods. Remember, every data exchange with a Flash movie should use input, wait, output, and error states. Even if you are loading variables from a small .TXT file, you should confirm the download by checking for the presence (and value) of a terminal tag.

Only use the `sendmail.cgi` script on `www.theMakers.com` for development and/or testing purposes. Do not try to use the script for demanding, high-volume Web sites. The same Perl script is available on the *Flash 5 Bible* CD-ROM, in the ch24 folder.

Using onClipEvent(data) to Load Server Data

You can also detect the receipt of external data using the new Flash 5 `onClipEvent` handler for Movie Clip instances. To modify our sendReceive.fla example to work with this new action, do the following:

1. Add a new layer, and rename it **data**.

2. Create a new symbol (Ctrl+F8 or Command+F8). Name this symbol **dataDetect**, and keep the default Movie Clip behavior. Once you click OK, Flash automatically changes to the Symbol Editing Mode. Leave the symbol's timeline, and go back to the Main Timeline.

3. Drag an instance of the `data` Movie Clip to the data layer. In the Instance Panel, name the instance **data**.

4. With the instance selected, open the Actions Panel. Add the following code:

```
onClipEvent(data){
_root.gotoAndStop("output");
}
```

When the last variable from the server CGI script is loaded, any actions within the `onClipEvent(data)` curly braces are executed.

5. Now we need to change the Button instance code for the input state. Select the Button instance, and open the Actions Panel. Change the code to the following (note that the ¬ indicates a continuation of the same line of code; do not insert this character into your actual code):

```
on (release){
    to = "your@e-mail.com";
    subject = "Flash 5 Bible Form";
    loadVariables("http://www.themakers.com/cgi-bin/ ¬
        books/sendmail.cgi", _root.data, "POST");
```

Continued

Continued

```
        sendTime = getTimer();
        gotoAndPlay ("wait");
}
```

In this new code, we switch the target of the loadVariables **action to**
_root.data, instead of the Main Timeline (_root). The data **instance was**
created and given ActionScript code in Steps 2–4.

6. Next, we need to change the ActionScript on the //loop keyframe, which is frame 16
   of the actions layer. Select this keyframe, and open the Actions Panel. Change the
   code to:

```
if( getTimer() > sendTime+25000 ) {
    gotoAndStop ("error");
} else {
    gotoAndPlay ("wait");
}
```

In this code, we omit the initial if. . .else action because the variables are being
loaded into the data instance. We only need to check the time that has elapsed
since the loadVariables action occurred.

7. Finally, change the action on frame 25 of the actions layer to indicate the new path
   to the server's time/date stamp variable, returnTime:

```
serverTime = _root.data.timeDate;
```

After you have saved your Flash movie (with a new file name), test your .SWF file. When you
click the Submit button, the Flash data is sent to the email.cgi script. The Flash movie directs
the email.cgi output to the data instance, and the onClipEvent(data) event executes
when the data is finished loading.

Note that this new method only works with the Flash 5 Player. To retain compatibility with
Flash 4 Player, use the original method.

Using XML Data in Flash Movies

Flash 5 movies can now load (and send) external XML data. This is a very powerful
feature, as XML has quickly become a standard data structure for e-commerce purposes and for news services, as well as for easier control over HTML formatting
(and style sheets) in the Web browser. You can organize external data with simple
XML formatting, and use the XML data for text fields and ActionScript code in your
Flash movies.

Note It is beyond the scope of this book to give a thorough explanation of XML. We examine the basic structure of XML, and show you how to use XML data in a Flash movie. We recommend that you read the *XML Bible* by Elliotte Rusty Harold (IDG Books Worldwide, Inc., 1999; now Hungry Minds, Inc.) for more information on XML.

Understanding XML

XML is an acronym for eXtensible Markup Language. "Extensible," in this case, means that you can create your own markup tag names and attributes. While there are a few additional rules with XML, its structure very much resembles traditional HTML:

```
<tag name opener>Information here</tag name closer>
```

For basic XML-Flash usage, your XML document needs one "container" tag in which all other subordinate tags will be nested. Each opener and closer tag set is called a node. In the following XML example, the `<section>` tag is the primary container tag and the `<article>` tags are nodes of the `<section>` tag:

```
<section>
     <article>First article node</article>
     <article>Second article node</article>
</section>
```

You can create as many *child* nodes as you need. In the preceding example, the `<section>` tag has two child nodes: the first occurrence of `<article></article>` and the second occurrence of `<article></article>`. In the following example, the first `<article>` node has two child nodes:

```
<section>
     <article>
        <title>WANTED: New Computer</title>
        <description>Insert description here
        </description>
     </article>
     <article>Second article node</article>
</section>
```

`<title>` is the first child node of the first `<article>` node. The value of `<title>` is also considered a child of `<title>`. In the previous example, "WANTED: New Computer" is the child of `<title>`.

Caution The Flash 5 Player does not ignore white space in XML documents. For this reason, you should not format your XML documents with indented tags or carriage returns between tags.

Loading an XML document into a Flash movie

Once you have an XML document structured to use in a Flash movie, you can use the XML document tree in the Flash movie. When an XML document is loaded into a Flash movie, the structure and relationship of all nodes are retained within the Flash Player.

The XML Object

Before you can load an XML document into Flash, you need to make an object that will hold the XML data. To do this, use the XML() constructor function, as in:

```
myXML = new XML();
```

Just as we created new objects for the Color and Sound Objects in ActionScript, you can create as many new instances of the XML Object as you need for your movie. You can also use an XML Object to store Flash-created XML structures, and send them to a server for further processing.

The load method of the XML Object

After you have established an object, like the myXML variable in the previous heading, you can invoke built-in methods of the XML Object. The load method enables you to specify an external source (as a URL or file name) that holds the XML data. If you had an XML document called articles.xml in the same directory as your .SWF file, then you could load it by writing the following code:

```
myXML = new XML("articles.xml");
```

or

```
myXML = new XML();
myXML.load("articles.xml");
```

The onLoad() method of the XML Object

After the document is loaded into the Flash movie, you can specify another function (or action) to occur, using the onLoad method of the XML Object. The onLoad method simply defines a function to be executed when the XML document is finished loading — it does not actually execute the function (or actions) when the onLoad is first processed. In the following example, a function named loadArticles is executed when the XML document, articles.xml, is finished loading:

```
myXML = new XML();
myXML.load("articles.xml");
myXML.onLoad = loadArticles;

function loadArticles(success){
```

```
        if(success){
                //perform more XML methods upon the XML data
        } else {
                // indicate that the XML document (or data)
                // did not load.
        }
}
```

In this code example, the loadArticles function has one argument, success. The onLoad method returns a Boolean value of true or false. Therefore, our function loadArticles receives that value, too. If the previous load method successfully loaded the articles.xml document, then the onLoad method will be executed and will return a true value. This true value is passed to the loadArticles function, and inserted into the if condition. If success is equal to true, then the nested if actions will be executed. Otherwise, the else actions will be executed.

Check out the XML document load examples on the *Flash 5 Bible* CD-ROM, in the ch24 folder. These examples demonstrate how XML node values can be manipulated with Flash arrays. You may want to review Chapter 22's coverage of the Array Object before looking at these examples.

Expert Tutorial: Introduction to XML and Flash, by Christian Honselaar

The source .FLA for Christian's tutorial, and related assets, can be found in the ch24 folder of the Flash 5 Bible *CD-ROM.*

XML is rapidly being added to a wide range of development and client/server applications — and for good reasons. The ability to read and write any XML document in Flash means that you now have a robust and scalable way of exchanging data between Flash and the world. By expanding these methods, Flash can be used as a template with XML as the data-source, delivering basic client-side Generator functionality.

The new support for XML may be one of the best things that has happened to Flash 5. That's because this feature is more or less the missing link between Flash and the rest of the Internet. For those unfamiliar with XML, www.xml.com is a fine place to get started (and to stay up to date, for that matter).

Even if this is your first experience with XML, don't sweat it. This tutorial demonstrates the power of XML in a simple application. You learn how to use Flash to make a template for a little poem book that is linked to an XML file that fills in the actual details.

Continued

Continued

Starting with Flash 5, use the Text Tool to create two text fields to hold the poem title and the poem itself. With the first text field selected, open the Text Options Panel (Window ⇨ Panel ⇨ Text Options) for this first text field. From the ensuing drop-down menu, select Dynamic Text. Then, in the Variable field, enter **titletext**. Do the same for the second text field, but in the Variable field, enter **poemtext**. Also, for the second text field, select Multiline from the second drop-down menu of the Text Options Panel, and also check the Word wrap option.

Author's Note: For more information about working with text and text fields, refer to Chapter 7, "Working with Text," and Chapter 25, "Understanding HTML and Text Field Functions in Flash."

To keep things simple, we create an interface with one button that will skip to the next poem. For this example, I used the Oval-Play button located in the Common Library, which is accessible from Window ⇨ Common Libraries ⇨ Buttons. Create a new layer in the Main Timeline, label it Button, and position your button anywhere that makes sense to you. Now, right-click/Ctrl+click the Button instance and select Actions from the contextual pop-up. Enter this code in the ensuing Object Actions Panel:

```
on (release) {
   displayNextPoem();
}
```

Next, to spark your imagination about exotic ways to use XML, we'll add a Movie Clip that will play behind the poem, controlled by XML! To accomplish this, create another new layer, name it **Movie Clip**, and then, in order to ensure that the Movie Clips play below the text, move this Movie Clip layer to the bottom of the layer stack.

Now, to create an empty Movie Clip, proceed from the main menu, choose Insert ⇨ New Symbol ⇨ Movie Clip, and in the ensuing Symbol Properties dialog, give the Movie Clip a meaningful name, such as **Background Placeholder**, accept the default Movie Clip behavior, and click OK. This procedure lands you in Symbol Editing Mode, but because this is supposed to be an empty Movie Clip, simply exit Symbol Editing Mode via Edit ⇨ Edit Movie.

Next, create an instance of Background Placeholder in the top-left corner of the Stage by dragging this symbol from the library (Window ⇨ Library). Use the Instance Panel (Window ⇨ Panels ⇨ Instance) to name the instance placeholder.

Great! Our PUI (Poem User Interface) is complete. Now let's have a look at the XML document that drives the content to fill the text fields and placeholder. (As noted previously, this XML document and related assets for this tutorial are located in the ch24 folder of the CD-ROM.) You can edit it with a plain text editor, such as notepad (for Windows users) or any other text editor that saves to the .TXT format. You may also choose to produce an entirely new XML document. But first, I explain the basic XML layout. Here's the text (the white space between tags was omitted because Flash handles white space in a nonstandard way):

```
<poems>
<poem title="Kahlil Gibran" clip="poemclip2.swf">
```

```
Work is love made visible.
And if you cannot work with love but only with distaste, it is
better that you should leave your work and sit at the gate of the
temple and take alms of those who work with joy.
</poem>
<poem title="unix haiku" clip="poemclip1.swf">
wind catches lily
scatt'ring petals to the wind
segmentation fault
</poem>
</poems>
```

Even if you've never used XML, the terms "tag" and "attribute" may be familiar from the HTML world, where they serve equivalent functions. There are two tags here: <poems></poems> is our root tag. Every XML document should have one pair of tags in which all other tags are nested. Contained within the root are the tags, <poem></poem>, and you can have as many of these as you want. The <poem> tags are nodes within the greater root tags.

Author's Note: For more information on XML tag structures, refer to our XML coverage prior to this tutorial.

The <poem> tags have two attributes:

1. title="Kahlil Gibran" indicates that the first poem is called "Kahlil Gibran."

2. clip="poemclip2.swf" means that this poem should be displayed with the Movie Clip poemclip2.swf —thus, this Movie Clip appears in the empty Movie Clip, whose instance was named, placeholder.

Note that the actual poem text is contained within the <poem> opening tag and </poem> closing tag.

Now this is how we instruct the Flash movie to load the title, poem text, and Movie Clip from each <poem> tag: Return to the movie, add another layer at the top of the layer stack, label it actions, and then double-click the first frame to bring up the Frame Actions Panel. Insert the following script in the right pane:

```
poems = new XML();
poems.onload = poemsLoaded;
poems.load("poems.xml");

function poemsLoaded () {
    currentPoem = poems.firstChild.firstChild;
}

function displayNextPoem () {
    titleText = currentPoem.attributes.title;
    loadMovie (currentPoem.attributes.clip, placeholder);
```

Continued

Continued

```
        poemText = currentPoem.firstChild.toString();
        currentPoem = currentPoem.nextSibling;
    }
```

The first three lines of this script tell Flash to find, load, and parse the XML document. It also assigns it to the variable poems.

The next two lines tell Flash to call the function poemsLoaded. In turn, poemsLoaded initializes the variable currentPoem, which is a pointer to the part of the XML document currently showing.

Then the purpose of the next function, which begins with function displayNextPoem, is to extract the title, text, and associated clip of the current poem and to advance to the next poem.

Flash interprets this XML document by using a DOM, or Document Object Model. This means that the XML is represented as an object, with every tag a subobject, or child, which may also contain subobjects extending to any depth. Attributes are represented as properties of tag objects.

To cycle through all poems, the variable currentPoem is created. Initially, it points to the first child (the initial poem) of the first child (the poem's root) of the document. A simple logic of inheritance follows. Finally, toString() and nextSibling deliver the next object in a child list and all the XML text within that child, respectively. The script may be tiny, but it covers a lot of material. If it doesn't make much sense to you (particularly toward the end), read the topic of object-oriented scripting in the ActionScript manual and then have another look at the script and the XML code.

Final Note

To complete this tutorial, you need access to the .SWF files to which the .XML file refers. These files need to be located within the same folder as the .FLA and the .XML files. Although you can produce your own, just be sure to give them the same names as those listed in the .XML file, or edit the file names in the XML code. For testing purposes, you can use the .SWF files provided with the tutorial, located in the ch24 folder of the *Flash 5 Bible* CD-ROM.

A native of the City of Groningen, the Netherlands, Christian Honselaar claims to "like danger." His favorite activities include reading pulp SciFi, and mountain trekking in Asia. Perhaps this explains why the most memorable movie correlated with the year he graduated from the Gymnasium "would be *Jurassic Park*." Chris found Flash, he says, "while experimenting with digital video overlay. I tried it in Flash/QuickTime and immediately found bugs. Love at first sight. Thus, through no end of complaining to Macromedia, I began my relationship with Flash." During the daytime, he's an academic educational programmer, developing multimedia apps in C++ and for the Web platform. But by night, he works on his favorite project: htmwell.com, a company that develops informative software and Web sites. You can see their work at www.htmwell.com and www.liemo.nl.

Using the Flash Exchange

Within a few months of the Flash 5 release, Macromedia introduced the Flash Exchange. Like the Dreamweaver Exchange, the Flash Exchange enables you to download custom objects and libraries (ActionScripts, Smart Clips, user interface (UI) elements, and so on) for use in the Flash 5 authoring environment.

To use the Flash Exchange, you need to visit www.macromedia.com/exchange and have a Macromedia membership user ID and password. Click the Membership button on the Exchange home page to sign up for your free Macromedia membership. After you have established a membership, you can go back to the Exchange home page and enter the Flash Exchange portion. There, you need to download and install the Macromedia Extension Manager (approximately 2MB).

Note   The Extension Manager is a universal application for all of Macromedia's Exchange-compatible products, including Dreamweaver and Flash.

After you have installed the Extension Manager, you can download extensions for Flash 5 from the Flash Exchange. For the next tutorial by Branden Hall, you need to download and install the WDDX Serializer/Deserializer. To download this extension:

1. On the Flash Exchange page, select App Servers from the Find more extensions drop-down menu.

2. On the newly loaded page, click the WDDX Serializer/Deserializer link.

3. On the Extension Detail Page, click the Mac or PC download icon (depending on your OS), located on the right side of the page. Note the location on your hard drive to which the file is downloaded.

4. After the extension (.MXP file) has finished downloading, open Flash 5. Choose Help ⇨ Manage Exchange Items. This launches the Exchange Manager application.

5. In the Exchange Manager, choose File ⇨ Install Extension (Ctrl+O or Command+O). Browse to the location where you downloaded the .MXP file for the WDDX Serializer/Deserializer. After you have selected the file and clicked Open or OK, you are presented with a disclaimer dialog. Click Accept, and the extension installs into your Flash Common Libraries folder.

6. To use most Exchange extensions, open the extension's Library from the Window ⇨ Common Libraries folder. For the WDDX Serializer/Deserializer extension, an .AS file (ActionScript-coded text file) that defines functions and methods for the Serializer/Deserializer is copied into a new ActionScript folder located inside the Flash 5 application folder.

In the following tutorial, Branden Hall discusses the use of his WDDX Serializer/ Deserializer extension.

Expert Tutorial: WDDX and Flash, *by Branden J. Hall*

This tutorial introduces the WDDX Serializer/Deserialzer for XML Objects in Flash 5 movies. If you have not installed the Extensions Manager and the WDDX Serializer/Deserializer, then please read the preceding section describing the Flash Exchange.

WDDX stands for Web Distributed Data eXchange. Allaire Corporation created this subset of XML in 1998 to describe various types of data structures. Along with the specification for WDDX, Allaire also created a set of tools for using WDDX in Allaire's server-side programming language, Cold Fusion. These tools include a function that takes a data structure from Cold Fusion and turn it into a WDDX packet; this is known as serialization. There is also a function that does the reverse, turning a WDDX packet into a native Cold Fusion data structure; this is known as de-serialization. By themselves, these tools aren't particularly useful. However, Allaire also created a similar set of tools for JavaScript. This enables developers to create applications in which whole data structures are sent between the server and client with just XML.

Since that time, other languages have been WDDX-enabled, including Java, PHP, and Perl. Along with Dave Gallerizzo, vice president of consulting at Fig Leaf Software, I created a WDDX Serializer/Deserializer for Flash 5. Now, rather than having to send simple name/value pairs between Flash and server-side languages, you can send whole data structures. This includes arrays, structures, date/times, and recordsets in addition to basic data types such as strings and integers.

The Serializer/Deserializer is fully encapsulated, and using it inside of your own Flash applications is very simple. The actual toolset is inside of a single file, wddx.as. This file needs to be included in your movie either by importing it using the Import option in the Actions Panel or by using the include action (#include "wddx.as").

Author's Note: If you intend to use the #include action as shown in the following code, then you need to make a copy of the wddx.as file (located in the ActionScript folder of the Flash 5 application folder). If you wish to import the wddx.as file, then click the menu arrow located at the upper-right corner of the Actions Panel, and choose Import From File (Ctrl+I or Command+I, when the Action Panel is focused).

Let's take a simple array, serialize it, and then print out the results. The code looks like this:

```
// Include the WDDX class
#include "wddx.as"

// Create an instance of the WDDX class
myWDDX = new WDDX();

// Create an XML object to hold the serialized data
myXML = new XML();

// Create the array
students = new Array();
students[0] = "Bob";
students[1] = "Mary";
students[2] = "John";
```

```
    students[3] = "Sue";

    // Serialize the array and trace the resulting XML
    myXML = myWDDX.serialize(students);
    trace(myXML.toString());
```

When you run this code it prints the following XML to the output window:

```
    <wddxPacket version="1.0">
    <header />
    <data>
    <array length="4">
    <string>bob</string>
    <string>mary</string>
    <string>john</string>
    <string>sue</string>
    </array>
    </data>
    </wddxPacket>
```

Now that our array is in this form, we can send it to any other program that understands WDDX, and that program can turn it into its native array type. We don't have to worry about the name/value pairs where the variables are numerically ordered (for example, foo1, foo2, foo3, and so on) as we would have had to if we had wanted to do the same thing without WDDX.

Now, lets say that we have a packet of WDDX-formatted XML and that we want to turn it back into an actual data structure. The following code takes some XML and give us back our array. We can then trace out an element of the array.

```
    // Deserialize the XML and turn it into an array called bar
    bar = myWDDX.deserialize(myXML);

    // Trace out the 3rd element in the array
    trace(bar[2]);
```

In almost every case, the object that is created when you deserialize a WDDX packet is a built-in object in Flash 5, whether that is an array, string, structure, number, or something else. However, the recordset type of data structure that WDDX supports has no direct equivalent in Flash 5. Recordsets are used to hold the results of a database query, and are very important if you want to talk to a server-side program that is working with databases. So, included with wddx.as is an additional class, WDDXrecordset. It enables you to manipulate rows, columns, and fields of a recordset with a simple set of methods. The WDDXrecordset class and all of its methods are documented inside of the wddx.as file.

Raised in Hyattsville, Maryland, Branden Hall is a member of the extreme ActionScript Flasheratti. He is a senior interactive designer/instructor at Fig Leaf Software in Washington, DC. Branden tells us that Chrissy Rey, a friend and associate of his at Fig Leaf, introduced Flash to him. Besides figleaf.com, Branden lists randinteractive.com as a Flash site that he has worked on. When Branden graduated from high school, he recalls listening to "Before these Crowded Streets" by the Dave Matthews Band. Now, Branden's single most favorite thing to do is "laze around in bed with [his] fiancée."

Expert Tutorial: Using XMLSockets with a Flash 5 Movie, *by Shane Elliott*

In this tutorial, you learn to employ XMLSockets in a Flash movie. You will find all of the associated files on the Flash 5 Bible *CD-ROM. Be aware that this example utilizes a Java server, which requires the Java SDK in order to run and work with the Flash movie interactions.*

A new and long-awaited feature in Flash 5 is the capability to open a socket that connects to a back-end database or server and to keep an open line of communication between the Flash movie and the server. Previously, if we wanted to send data back and forth between a server and Flash, we would use the loadVariables action and connect to a back-end program such as a Perl script, JavaServlet, or some other middleware solution. With this older system, name/value pairs would be sent to and from the Flash movies to get a dynamic data flow, allowing data to be served on the fly. Feedback could be initiated by the user or by some system event (such as a timer or upon completion of a set of tasks). With XMLSockets in Flash 5, not only can we open a direct flow of data between our movie and the server, but we can receive the data as nicely formatted XML. This information structure is easier to handle and much more organized. Even though called XMLSockets in Flash, you don't have to send your data as XML to the server, nor do you have to receive it as such. Even though the XMLSocket object and methods are set up to handle XML elements, you have the option of sending String data as well, providing greater flexibility for database connectivity.

Now, you may ask, "When do I need to use these sockets, and, more importantly, how do I use them?" Even though you can still use loadVariables in Flash 5, you must make a request from within the Flash movie to be able to receive data from the server. With XMLSockets, you have a constant open connection. You can tell Flash to do a certain set of actions any time it detects data across this open socket. It's very useful for low-latency client-server applications, such as a chat room, where you want your messages to be sent immediately, or, in the case I describe next, for a Flash login movie. Now, instead of requiring a user to log in to my site or online resource using a standard form and CGI script, I can give the user a much better looking, and possibly more consistent, uninterrupted experience by allowing the user to log in using my Flash movie.

Before starting, you need certain graphic elements to be present on your Stage. I created a very simple login page that is focused completely on functionality — an aesthetically pleasing interface would follow this example in a real-world production environment. You need two Input Text fields: one for the username and one for the password. Name these input fields **userid** and **password** in the Variable field of the Text Options Panel. Include some Static Text to label these fields for the user. You also need a Dynamic Text field named **fromServer** to display the server response. Again, add some Static Text to identify the Dynamic Text field on the Stage. Last, but not least, you need a login button. I just grabbed one out of the Common Libraries (Window ➪ Common Libraries ➪ Buttons), but you can create one of your own if you prefer. You can put all of these graphic elements on one layer, or separate the graphics across multiple layers. When you're finished adding the graphic elements to the Stage, create a new layer for your actions. In our example, the actions layer is named action script.

At this point, there should be only one frame in the Main Timeline (for example, Scene 1). Now, go to the first frame of your actions layer, select that frame, and open the Actions Panel (Window ⇨ Actions). On this frame, we define our socket and tell Flash how to handle the events regarding it.

The code that goes here is:

```
function myOnConnect(success) {
    if (success)
        fromServer += newline + "Connected...";
    else
        fromServer += newline + "Unable to Connect...";
}
function myOnXML(doc) {
    trace("Im here");
    var e = doc.firstChild;
    if(e!=null && e.nodeName == "MESSAGE") {
        fromServer += newline + e.attributes.response;
        // Code here to take you into the protected area
    }
    else {
        fromServer += newline + e.attributes.response;
        // Code here to take you to an exit screen etc...
    }
}

myXML = new XML();
loginTag = myXML.createElement("login");
loginSocket = new XMLSocket();
loginSocket.onConnect = myOnConnect;
loginSocket.onXML = myOnXML;
loginSocket.connect("localhost",8080);
```

Now let's take a look at each line and go over what it's doing. Let's skip the function definitions for now and jump down to the following lines:

```
myXML = new XML();
loginTag = myXML.createElement("login");
```

The first line in the preceding code creates a new XML element on the Main Timeline. We will be sending the login information (username and password) in XML format to the Java server. The second line creates a new XML element named login, which is the equivalent to XML that looks like the following:

```
<login />
```

Continued

Continued

Now, we need to create a socket for communication with the server. That's where the following line of code comes in:

```
loginSocket = new XMLSocket();
```

When you create a new XMLSocket object, the constructor doesn't accept arguments. They're not needed at this point anyway. We don't define any of its options until we actually connect to the server. At this point, we have our XMLSocket object created and we're ready to move on to the next step. We need to define some of the callback functions that are built into the Flash ActionScript language.

Flash ActionScript recognizes three event handler methods for the XMLSocket Object. The Flash movie calls these functions at an internally known time or after a certain event whether you define them or not, but without indicating the event occurrence to you. If we don't define a set of actions to occur for these events, then these functions don't do anything in our Flash movie. They're simply there so that you can define (and, in a sense, override) them. Here are the three methods:

Method	Description
onConnect(*success*)	Executed when a connection request initiated through the XMLSocket.connect method either succeeds or fails (the success variable indicates true or false to tell you whether the connection was a success or not).
onXML(*object*)	Called when the specified XML object containing an XML document arrives over your XMLSocket connection. The *object* is an instance of the XML object containing the XML document received from the server.
onClose()	Initiated when an open connection is closed by the server.

Author's Note: Just as we use on(release) as an event handler for mouse events on Button instances, other objects have predefined event handlers and events. With data objects and methods, these events tend to occur when data is sent or received by the Flash movie.

The only two we use in this example are onConnect and onXML. Although Flash knows when to call these methods, there's nothing innately performed by them. Therefore, we must define our own methods to give them customized functionality.

```
loginSocket.onConnect = myOnConnect;
loginSocket.onXML = myOnXML;
```

These two lines simply assign these event handler methods to our customized versions of these methods. The myOnConnect and myOnXML functions tell our movie exactly what to do when a connection either succeeds or fails (onConnect), and what to do when data is received from the server through our socket (onXML), respectively.

Now let's go back to the two function definitions in the Flash movie. In frame 1 of the Main Timeline, we defined myOnConnect to execute some commands based on the status of the attempted connection. Flash sends the myOnConnect function a success argument, as a Boolean value (true or false) so that it knows whether a connection has been established. Then, we add an if. . .else statement to handle either case. The function sends a notification to the user by setting the fromServer variable (which we defined at the beginning of the movie) to give the user updates on the status of his/her login. You could add more lines of code here if you wanted to jump to another Movie Clip or perform some other action specifically designed for your application.

The myOnXML function is a bit more complex. This function is basically looking for data from the server in XML format and, when it detects that data (which has been sent to the Flash socket), it assigns it to doc or whatever argument you put into your custom version of onXML. In this example, I used doc for document. Whatever you choose, just know that it will be used as an XML object that's received from the server. Therefore, it must be treated as one throughout your function. You can convert it to a String object, or parse it like I did in the myOnXML function. Once e is set to be the doc.firstChild, I can access that node's elements and name, as you learned when using XML objects earlier in this chapter.

It's important at this stage of your development that you know the formatting of the XML data the server application will be sending you. If you're not writing the server application yourself, then make sure you stay in close contact with the XML developer.

The reason I know that I'm looking for the nodeName of MESSAGE is that I wrote my own Java server application to interact with my Flash movie. Again, I have an if statement that performs actions based on the server response. You could add more here as well.

Now, let's look at the last line of code, which is the most important line so far because it actually attempts to make the connection (open the socket) between our Flash movie and our server.

```
loginSocket.connect("localhost",8080);
```

To do that, I use the connect(host, port) method. The connect method takes two arguments: the host and the port. The host argument refers to one of the following:

✦ A fully qualified DNS name such as http://www.flash5bible.com

✦ An IP address such as 205.94.288.213

✦ A computer's name on a LAN, such as Zeus or Atlas

✦ null, which means to connect to the host server on which the movie resides

I use localhost for the host argument because that (like null) also refers to the machine that my Flash movie is running on, which happens to also be where my Java server is residing. Whatever you choose here, just remember the host must be the location of the server with which you'll be communicating.

Continued

Continued

The next argument is the `port`, which refers to the TCP port number on the host used to establish the connection. For security reasons, this number cannot be below 1024. I chose 8080 because I know my computer isn't using that port for anything significant. Some examples of commonly used ports for TCP connections are:

FTP Transfers = 21

HTTP = 80

Telnet = 23

POP3 = 110

Whatever you choose, remember the previous rules, and try to make sure nothing else on your computer is using that port number. Now, that last line of code automatically connects the Flash movie to my server when playback begins. Now that we have everything set up graphically and our code is ready to react to our socket events, we need to give some functionality to the login button so that our users can log in to the server. That code looks like this:

```
on (release, keyPress "<Enter>") {
    loginTag.attributes.username = userid;
    loginTag.attributes.password = password;
    myXML.appendChild(loginTag);
    loginSocket.send(myXML);
}
```

With the preceding code, we are detecting when the user clicks the button or presses the Enter key on the keyboard. When either event is detected, the username and password are sent to the server for verification. With those events detected, let's look at the nested code in the `on` handler.

Remember the `loginTag` XML element we made earlier? Here, we are giving that node some attributes and assigning those attributes to be the `userid` and `password` that the user has entered into our Input Text fields. Then, `loginTag` is appended as a child to the `myXML` object. The entire XML object is sent through the XMLSocket object named `loginSocket`.

When we use the `send` method, we don't necessarily have to have an XML object as its argument. In this case, we do (`myXML`), but we could just as easily put a string value in its place. As long as the server knows what to expect, we can use any data type or structure. If it's looking for an XML-formatted string and we send it something similar to `"hello"`, then the server might become confused. Either way, the `send` method is taking whatever it has as its argument, converting it to a string, and then sending it. So, let's say I, as a user, enter `shane` as my username and `flash` as my password and submit that information as my login. My server receives the following string value from the Flash movie:

```
<login password="flash" username="shane" />
```

I can choose to parse that string and compare the values in my server code, but now that it's left Flash I'm no longer responsible for what happens to it until the server sends back a response. When the server does send back a response, we have our `myOnXML` function set up to handle it and tell our user whether he/she got in or not.

You can see the final .FLA file of my Flash work on the *Flash 5 Bible* CD-ROM, in a file called XMLSignIn.fla, located in the ch24 folder. You need to run the Java program name loginServer.jar and then run the Flash movie that you created in order to try the login example. There is also a text file named data.txt on the CD-ROM that contains the usernames and passwords that the server recognizes as valid. If you'd like to modify this file so that you can try your own login info, feel free to do so. Just remember to put a semicolon at the end of every name/value pair.

Final Notes for Experts

When the Flash `send` method is used, it sends a `u\0000` termination character at the end of its string value to let you know when the data is completely sent. You must send this character back to Flash in order to get the `onXML()` function to recognize that it has received data. Without this termination character, you'll find yourself facing a few problems!

Shane Elliott was the senior technical director in the creative department of `Rampt.com`. There, he created the ActionScript architecture for later versions of the Rampt search interface. Shane has also created Flash and HTML designs for `benellis.com`, `apcadillac.com`, and `timberfish.com`. Currently, Shane develops integrated XML, Flash, and Java solutions in Los Angeles. His single most favorite thing to do is to write screenplays and novels. Shane pursues work as an actor, and enjoys painting, programming, and traveling. We should note as well that Shane was one of the technical editors of the *Flash 5 Bible*.

If you are a hardcore programmer in other object-oriented programming languages, you may be interested in using the new XMLSocket Object of Flash 5 with other server technologies. The next tutorial by Shane Elliott demonstrates the use of a Java server that can communicate with a Flash movie.

Summary

- ✦ Input Text fields can accept text data from anyone viewing the Flash movie (.SWF file) with the Flash 4 or 5 Player. Input Text fields are treated as ActionScript variables.

- ✦ Dynamic Text fields can display the string values of any variable in the Flash movie.

- ✦ Any data exchange between Flash and a remote application or server-side script should use four steps or states: input, send, wait, and output.

✦ A Flash form can be used to gather feedback from your site's visitors. The form's data can be sent to a properly configured CGI script for further data processing, such as sending the data in an e-mail to the site administrator.

✦ The getTimer() function returns the current time of the Flash movie. The Flash timer starts as soon as the movie is loaded into the Flash Player — it is not based on frames played or frame rate. You can use getTimer() to set variable values, and compare two different getTimer() variables for time tracking purposes.

✦ XML data structures are quickly becoming an interbusiness standard for data exchange over the Web. Now Flash can use XML data structures to send and receive data from your Web server.

✦   ✦   ✦

Understanding HTML and Text Field Functions in Flash

◆ ◆ ◆ ◆

In This Chapter

Using HTML tags
in text fields

Creating URL links
within Flash text

Accessing functions
with HTML tags

Selecting text in
text fields with
ActionScript

◆ ◆ ◆ ◆

This chapter shows you how to control text-field formatting and focus, using internal HTML tags and Action Script. Flash 5 has greatly enhanced the amount of control you have with text field formatting and selections within text fields.

Exploring HTML Usage in Text Fields

In the past few chapters, you may have noticed the HTML check box in the Text Options Panel. With Flash 5, you can now use HTML formatting tags within Input and Dynamic Text fields! In Flash 4 movies, you could not specify more than one set of formatting specifications for any text field. For example, if you created a text field that used black-colored Verdana text at 18 points in faux bold, then you could not insert any other typeface, color or size in that text field. With Flash 5, you can use ⟨FONT⟩ tags to specify multiple typefaces, colors, styles, and sizes within one text field. You can also use ⟨A HREF⟩ tags to link to internal Flash functions or external URLs!

New Feature

HTML support in Flash 5 text fields takes Flash movies one step closer to taking over traditional Macromedia Generator Server functionality. By using Generator templates, you can place environment variables in any text field or block (even Static Text!) in order to personalize Web experiences. Flash 5's HTML integration isn't as seamless as dynamic text and text formatting in Generator templates.

Supported HTML tags

You can use the following HTML tags to format your Flash text fields. You can insert these tags into ActionScript variable values, or you can apply them (without knowing or writing the syntax) using the Character and Text Options Panels.

Font and paragraph styles

The basic `<FONT>` and physical "faux" styles for text (bold, italic, and underline) can be applied to Flash text.

✦ **`<B>`:** Placing `<B></B>` tags around Flash text in string values for text field variables applies **bold** formatting to the enclosed text.

✦ **`<I>`:** Placing `<I></I>` tags around Flash string values *italicizes* the enclosed text.

✦ **`<U>`:** The `<U></U>` tags <u>underlines</u> the enclosed text.

✦ **`<P>`:** The `<P>` tag inserts paragraph break between lines of text. You can use the `ALIGN` attribute to specify `LEFT`, `RIGHT`, `CENTER`, or `JUSTIFY`, to apply the respective justifications to the Flash text.

✦ **`<BR>`:** The `<BR>` tag inserts a carriage return at the point of insertion. This is equivalent to the `newline` operator in ActionScript.

✦ **`<FONT COLOR='#HEX CODE'>`:** The `<FONT>` tag with the `COLOR` attribute can change the color of your Flash text. This color is specified in hexadecimal values, just like regular HTML. For example, `"<FONT COLOR='#FF0000>This is red text.</FONT>"` uses full red for the text color.

✦ **`<FONT FACE>`:** The `<FONT>` tag with the `FACE` attribute enables you to specify a specific typeface to the enclosed text. You can specify Flash device fonts for the `FACE` value, such as `<FONT FACE='_sans'>` to use the Sans Serif device font.

✦ **`<FONT SIZE>`:** The `SIZE` attribute of the `<FONT>` tag enables you to specify the point size of Flash text. You can use absolute values (in pt sizes), such as `<FONT SIZE='18'>`, or relative values, such as `<FONT SIZE='+1'>`, to change the size of text.

URL and ActionScript Linking

You can use the `<A>` tag with the `HREF` attribute to apply URL links within Flash text. For example, you can insert the following HTML into a string value for a text field variable, to link the text the Makers Web site to the appropriate URL:

```
<A HREF='http://www.theMakers.com'>the Makers Web site</A>
```

You can also specify a `TARGET` attribute for the `<A>` tag. The `TARGET` attribute determines which browser window or frame will display the URL link in the `HREF` attribute. As with regular HTML, You can use the default `_top`, `_parent`, `_self`, or `_blank` values, as described for the `getURL` action. Later in this section we see how you can also execute internal Flash functions from `<A HEF>` tags.

Caution   You cannot type HTML tags directly into any text block or field — the actual tags will show up in the text during .SWF playback. The formatting tags are specified in ActionScript code, or are "hidden" in Static Text (the Character Panel applies the formatting).

Formatting text with the Character and Text Options Panel

You don't necessarily need to write out HTML tags to apply them to your Flash text. You can use the Character Panel to assign HTML formatting to all Text types (for example, Static, Input, and Dynamic). For Input and Dynamic Text fields, you will need to use the Text Options Panel to enable HTML formatting, by checking the HTML option. In this section, we demonstrate the use of HTML formatting within Static and Dynamic Text fields.

1. Open a new Flash movie (Ctrl+N or Command+N). Set the background color to white in the Movie Properties dialog (Ctrl+M or Command+M). Save your Flash movie as **htmlText.fla**.

2. Select the Text Tool, and open the Text Options Panel. Make sure the top drop-down menu is set to Static Text. Click once on the Stage, and type the following text (with carriage returns) in the text block, using Verdana at 18 points:

   ```
   Flash 5 Bible
   by Robert Reinhardt & Jon Warren Lentz
   ```

3. With the text block still active, select the Flash 5 Bible text, and, in the Character Panel, change the point size to **24** and click the B (for bold) option, as shown in Figure 25-1. Enter the following URL in the URL field of the Character Panel:

   ```
   http://www.amazon.com/exec/obidos/ASIN/0764535153
   ```

4. With the text block still active, select the Robert Reinhardt text, and, in the Character Panel, enter the following text for the URL option:

   ```
   mailto:robert@theMakers.com
   ```

5. Now, select the Jon Warren Lentz text, and enter the following text in the URL option of the Character Panel:

   ```
   mailto:jon@theflashbible.com
   ```

   See Figure 25-2 for an example of how the URL-linked text will appear.

6. Save the Flash movie, and test the Flash .SWF file in your Web browser by choosing File ➪ Publish Preview ➪ HTML. When you click the Flash 5 Bible text, the browser loads the Amazon.com page for the *Flash 5 Bible*. When you click either author's name, your e-mail client opens a new message window.

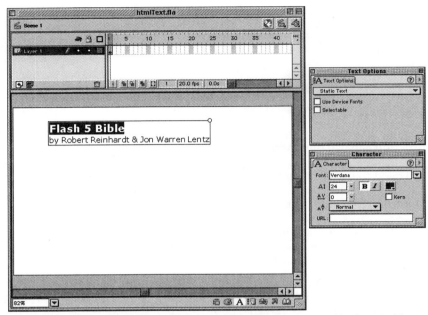

Figure 25-1: You can selectively change text within one text block or field.

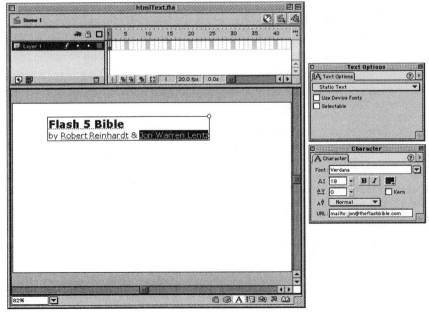

Figure 25-2: URL-linked text appears with dashed underlines. You will not see this dashed underline in the actual .SWF file.

Inserting HTML tags into Text Fields with ActionScript

In this section, we continue with the previous example that you created in the last section. We convert the Static Text block into a Dynamic Text field, and manipulate the formatting with ActionScript.

1. Resave your Flash movie from the last section as **htmlText_dynamic.fla**. We will convert this Static Text into a Dynamic Text field, so you'll want to keep your original Static Text example for future reference.

2. Select the text block, and open the Text Options Panel. Change the text type to Dynamic Text, and make sure the HTML option is checked. In the Variable field, type the variable name **book**. Now, this text field can be updated with ActionScript directed at the variable book. You can also uncheck the Border/Bg option if you don't want to see a bounding box around your text.

3. Save the Flash movie, and test it (Ctrl+Enter or Command+Enter). While the .SWF is playing back within the Flash 5 authoring environment, choose Debug ⇨ List Variables. You should see the HTML formatting tags displayed in the Output window (note that in the Output window, the book variable and the value will be shown on one continuous line):

```
Level #0:
  Variable _level0.$version = "MAC 5,0,30,0"
  Variable _level0.book = "<P ALIGN=\"LEFT\"><FONT
FACE=\"verdana\" SIZE=\"24\" COLOR=\"#000000\"><A
HREF=\"http://www.amazon.com/exec/obidos/ASIN/0764535153\"><B
>Flash 5 Bible</B></A></FONT></P><P ALIGN=\"LEFT\"><FONT
FACE=\"verdana\" SIZE=\"18\" COLOR=\"#000000\">by <A
HREF=\"mailto:robert@theMakers.com\">Robert Reinhardt</A>
&amp; <A HREF=\"mailto:jon@theflashbible.com\">Jon Warren
Lentz</A></FONT></P>"
```

You can observe the proper ActionScript syntax for HTML formatting in the Output window. Note that any quotes around values of tag attributes are preceded by a backslash, as in <FONT FACE=\"verdana\">. Because the value of book is already a string data type surrounded by quotes, any internal quotes need to be declared with a backslash character.

4. Close the .SWF movie window, and go back to the Main Timeline of your Flash movie. Create a new Dynamic Text field, and in the Text Options Panel, check the HTML and Word wrap options. Make sure the text field is set to Multiline. In the Variable field, type the name book2. The text field should be the same size as the previous text field.

5. Add a new layer, and name it **actions**. Double-click the first frame of the actions layer, and, in the Actions Panel, specify a HTML-formatted string value for the book2 variable, such as the following code:

```
book2 = "<FONT FACE=\"Verdana\" SIZE=\"24\" COLOR=\
"#0000FF\"><B><A HREF=\"http://www.amazon.com/exec/
obidos/ASIN/0764533568\">Flash 4 Bible</A></B></FONT>
```

```
<P><FONT SIZE=\"18\" COLOR=\"#000000\">by <A HREF=\
"mailto:robert@theMakers.com\">Robert Reinhardt</A>
& <A HREF=\"mailto:jon@theflashbible.com\">Jon Warren
Lentz</A>";
```

Note   This code should appear as one line of code in the Actions list of the Actions Panel.

6. Save the Flash movie and test it. The book2 text field will display the HTML-formatted value that you specified in the actions layer.

You can also use variables as values for HTML-formatted text fields, such as the following (note that the bookURL variable and value should appear on one line of code):

```
bookURL = "http://www.amazon.com/exec/obidos/ASIN/0764533568";
bookName = "Flash 4 Bible";
book2 = "<A HREF=\"" + bookURL + "\">" + bookName + "</A>";
```

By using other ActionScript variables and methods, you can apply specific text formatting to external data sources that have been loaded into the Flash movie, such as database records or lists. In the next section, you learn how to execute Flash functions from HTML-formatted text fields.

Using asfunction in <A HREF> tags

Not only can you use HTML formatting in Flash text, but you can also execute Flash actions from your text fields, using the <A> tag and a HREF attribute value of asfunction:function,argument. For example, if you wanted to link text to a function that loads a new Flash .SWF into a Movie Clip target, you can create a custom function that uses the loadMovie action and reference that action from your <A HREF> tag for a text field. See the following code (note that the ¬ indicates a continuation of the same line of code; do not insert this character into your actual code):

```
function myMovie(name){
  loadMovie(name, _root.mcHolder);
}
myText = "<A HREF=\"asfunction:myMovie,movie.swf\"> ¬
  Click to load movie</A>";
```

In this code example, the text within the <A></A> tags will execute the myMovie function, passing the string movie.swf as the name argument.

Tip   The asfunction can only pass one string value. You do not need to enclose the argument in quotes. If you need to pass another ActionScript variable for the value, then use the + operator to add it to the HTML text string.

If you need to pass more than one argument, then you will need to use send all the values as one string separated by a comma (or preferred character). Then, you would use the `split` method as follows (note that the ¬ indicates a continuation of the same line of code; do not insert this character into your actual code):

```
function myMovie(name){
    var tempArgs = name.split(",");
    var mcTarget = tempArgs[0];
    var swfUrl = tempArgs[1];
    loadMovie(swfUrl, mcTarget);
}
myArgs = "_root.mcHolder,movie.swf";
myText = "<A HREF=\"asfunction:myMovie," + myArgs + "\"> ¬
    Click to load movie</A>";
```

In this example, the `myMovie` function takes the `name` argument and creates an array with the `split` method. This array's name is `tempArgs`. The elements of the `tempArgs` array are the two string values separated by a comma in the `myArgs` variable.

You can see examples of HTML-formatted Flash text and the `asfunction` in the ch25 folder of the *Flash 5 Bible* CD-ROM.

Controlling Text Field Properties

Input and Dynamic Text fields have two properties that are accessible with Action Script: `.scroll` and `.maxscroll`. Using these properties, you can control the viewable area of a text field that has more lines of text than the text field can show.

- ✦ `.scroll`: This property can retrieve the current line number (from the top of the field), and it can also move to a new line number in a text field.

- ✦ `.maxscroll`: This property returns the maximum value of the scroll property for a given text field. You can only retrieve this value — you cannot set it.

To understand how these properties work, you need to see how lines are enumerated in a text field. Suppose you had ten lines of text, as a string value for a variable called `myText`. If you want to use this text in a Dynamic Text field named `article`, which only has a viewable area of five lines, then the remaining five lines of the `myText` variable will not be seen in the text field. To make the text field "scroll" to the next line of text by showing lines 2 to 6 (instead of lines 1 to 5), you can create a Button instance, such as a down arrow button, with ActionScript to advance the lines:

```
on(release){
    article.scroll = article.scroll + 1;
}
```

or

```
on(release){
    article.scroll += 1;
}
```

The .maxscroll property will return the maximum value for the top line number in a text field. In our previous ten-line text value example, the .maxscroll property would equal 6. If you had 20 lines worth of text in the article text field, then the .maxscroll property would return a value of 16.

In the ch25 folder of the *Flash 5 Bible* CD-ROM, you will find a Flash movie named scrollProp_simple.fla. This movie demonstrates the use of the .scroll property to view the entire Gettysburg Address within a text field. A more advanced scrolling mechanism can be found in the scrollProp_advanced.fla, which features a draggable scroll bar.

Manipulating Text with the Selection Object

The last text feature that we discuss in this chapter is the new Flash 5 Selection Object. The Selection Object is similar to the Mouse Object — you don't create instances of the Selection Object, as there can only be one active text field at any given time. In Flash 4 movies, we had no way of checking which text field was active. You could turn off a focus rectangle for Flash 4 text fields and Button instances, but you couldn't control tab order or automatically set a text field active.

Either Input or Dynamic Text fields can use the Selection Object. The Selection Object uses a string reference to the text field's variable name to perform its methods. We discuss the methods of the Selection Object in the following sections.

getBeginIndex

This method detects and returns the starting position of a highlighted selection in a text field. The method returns –1 if there is no active text field and/or there is no selection inside the text field. As with the Array Object, selection indexes start position values at 0. You do not need to specify a target path for this method — only one text field can have a selection at any given point. Therefore, as a variable startIndex, the getBeginIndex() method would look like:

```
onClipEvent(mouseMove){
startIndex = Selection.getBeginIndex();
trace("startIndex = " + startIndex);
}
```

In the Output window, the trace action would reveal startIndex = -1 until you made a selection within a text field in the movie, as shown in Figure 25-3.

In the ch25 folder of the *Flash 5 Bible* CD-ROM, review the getBeginIndex.fla to see how the getBeginIndex() method returns values for a text field. Each of the following sections also has a .FLA file to demonstrate its respective method.

test this text field with a selection

Figure 25-3: A text field with a starting selection index of 3

getEndIndex

Similar to the `getBeginIndex()` method, this method returns a number indicating the index position at the end of a highlighted selection in a text field, as shown in Figure 25-4. If there is no active selection, then a value of –1 will be returned.

test **this** text field with a selection

Figure 25-4: A text field with a starting selection index of 5 and an ending index of 9

getCaretIndex

This method of the Selection Object returns the current cursor position (as an index value) within an active text field, as shown in Figure 25-5. As with the two previous methods, if you use the `getCaretIndex()` method when there is no active cursor in a text field, it will return a –1.

test this text field with a selection

Figure 25-5: A text field with a caret index of 5

getFocus

This method returns the current active text field's name, as an absolute path; that is, if you have selected or inserted the cursor position inside a text field named `myOutput` on the Main Timeline, then `Selection.getFocus()` returns `_level0.myOutput`. If there is no active text field, then this method returns `null`.

setFocus

Perhaps the best enhancement to controlled text field activity is the `setFocus()` method. This method enables you to make a text field active automatically — the user doesn't need to click the mouse cursor inside the text field to start typing. To use this method, simply indicate the `setFocus()` method of the Selection Object, and the *absolute* path to the text field as its argument:

```
onClipEvent(load){
    Selection.setFocus("_root.testInput");
}
```

This code, when used on an empty Movie Clip instance, sets the current focus to the `testOutput` text field. If any text exists in the text field, it will be highlighted as a selection. You can only use string data types as the `setFocus()` argument. If you try the following:

```
myTextField = _root.testInput;
Selection.setFocus(myTextField);
```

the setFocus() method will not work. Why? The first line of code sets myTextField equal to the *value* of _root.testOutput, not to the text field's name itself. To remedy the situation, simply refer to the text field's name in quotes:

```
myTextField = "_root.testInput";
Selection.setFocus(myTextField);
```

setSelection

The last method available for the Selection Object is setSelection(). This method enables you make a specific selection within an active text field. The method takes two arguments: a start index and an end index. Using the same index numbering as getBeginIndex() and getEndIndex(). Note that this method will not work unless a text field is already active. The following code creates a selection span from index 5 to 9 of the testInput text field:

```
onClipEvent(load){
   Selection.setFocus("_root.testInput");
   Selection.setSelection(5,9);
}
```

On the CD-ROM   Daniel Szecket of Magritte's Cow (www.magrittescow.com) has provided several examples of the Selection methods. You can find these examples in the ch25 folder of the *Flash 5 Bible* CD-ROM. Daniel contributed an expert tutorial in Chapter 35, "Working with RealPlayer."

Summary

✦ You can use HTML text formatting within Flash text. Only basic HTML text formatting is allowed.

✦ You can insert HTML tags into the values of ActionScript variables that refer to Input or Dynamic Text fields. Any quotes used with HTML attributes should be preceded by a backward slash, \.

✦ The asfunction parameter for the HREF attribute of the <A> tag enables you to execute ActionScript functions from text fields. You can pass one argument to the specified function.

✦ The .scroll property of Input and Dynamic Text fields enables you to control the portion of a text field value that is displayed within the text field. .maxscroll returns the highest top line number for a given set of text in a text field.

✦ The Selection Object in Flash 5 ActionScript enables you to control the focus and highlighted selection spans of text fields in a Flash movie.

✦   ✦   ✦

Advanced Movie Clip Architecture and Beyond

In This Chapter

Moving objects along
scripted curves

Using innovative
scripted interfaces

Tracking time with the
new Date Object

We decided to end Part V with a chapter dedicated to three expert tutorials that introduced topics outside of the other scripting chapters. You learn a different ActionScript workflow with each tutorial.

Advanced Tutorials for Flash Interactivity

This chapter is comprised of three Expert Tutorials, all of which introduce advanced uses of ActionScript objects and functions. The following table summarizes the topics covered in each tutorial.

Tutorial	*ActionScript Topics*
Animation on Bézier Curves	`onClipEvent(load)`
	`onClipEvent(mouseDown)`
	`onClipEvent(enterFrame)`
	`_xmouse`
	`_ymouse`
	`Math.sqrt()`
	`Math.atan2()`
	`Math.pi`
	`Math.random()`
	`getTimer()`

Continued

Tutorial	ActionScript Topics
Scripting for Interfaces	`updateAfterEvent()`
	`String.length()`
	`Movie Clip.attachMovie()`
	`substring()`
	`onClipEvent(load)`
	A function with multiple arguments
Using `getTimer()` to make a Flash Clock	`getTimer()`
	`Date.getSeconds()`
	`Date.getMinutes()`
	`Date.getHour()`

Expert Tutorial: Animation on Bézier Curves, by Darrel Plant

While it's simple enough to create ActionScript routines that move objects along straight paths, wouldn't it be nice to know how to move paths along arcs or curves? Darrel's tutorial shows you how to do the math behind Bézier curves, and how to implement the proper equations into your ActionScript code.

In real life, most things don't move in straight lines. Even if they did, something that moves in a straight line wouldn't be nearly as interesting as another object that moves along a curved path. The curved path injects a bit of mystery and anticipation into a movement.

You probably already know that you can animate something on a motion guide in Flash, but motion guide animation paths are predefined. What if you want to have an object move randomly? What if you want it to move wherever the user clicks? What if you want it to look smooth and curvy instead of straight and dull?

One solution is to create an animation algorithmically—that is, by using a mathematical equation. The possibilities for which equations to use are infinite, but we should put a few requirements in place:

✦ The animation must happen along a curve.

✦ The animation must end exactly where we want it.

✦ The animation must take place over a definable period of time.

✦ The curve must be variable—it shouldn't travel the same path between two points unless we want it to.

One type of highly controllable mathematical curve that fits all of these requirements is the Bézier curve. You're probably already familiar with this type of curve from working with other programs (and now Flash 5). The Bézier curve has been used in graphics programs since Adobe introduced PostScript in the mid-1980s. You're probably already familiar with the types of shapes that it can draw — everything from a straight line to a loop that crosses over itself. What you might not be aware of are the simple mathematical equations behind it.

A Bézier curve is made up of four points: two end points and two control points, typically labeled p_0, p_1, p_2, and p_3. The end points of the curve are p_0 and p_3. The control points are p_1 and p_2. Most graphics programs draw lines between p_0 and p_1, and between p_3 and p_2. The curve described by the equations starts at p_0, moves toward p_1, and then moves toward p_2, ending up at p_3. It always intersects p_0 and p_3, but may not even come close to p_1 or p_2. A polygon drawn between the points in order encloses the curve completely. Each endpoint and control point has two components x_n and y_n.

Two equations are used to describe a Bézier curve:

$$x(t) = a_x t^3 + b_x t^2 + c_x t + x_0$$
$$y(t) = a_y t^3 + b_y t^2 + c_y t + y_0$$

The t in each equation is a floating-point number ranging from 0 to 1. When t is 0, the results of the equations equal x_0 and y_0, which is p_0, the origin point of the curve. When t is 1, the result is (x_3, y_3), or p_3, the destination point of the curve.

With this information as your basis, you need to know how to get values for the coefficients a_x, a_y and so on. These values are derived from the points used to describe the curve:

$$c_x = 3(x_1 - x_0)$$
$$b_x = 3(x_2 - x_1) - c_x$$
$$a_x = x_3 - x_0 - c_x - b_x$$
$$c_y = 3(y_1 - y_0)$$
$$b_y = 3(y_2 - y_1) - c_y$$
$$a_y = y_3 - y_0 - c_y - b_y$$

Because the values for the b and a coefficients are dependent on the c coefficient, the c coefficient should always be the first one that is derived.

In drawing programs, short segments of straight lines are drawn on the screen by evaluating t in increments that may range in value from 0 to 1. For instance, using steps of 0.05 (0.00, 0.05, 0.10, . . .) yields 21 points along the curve. Drawing lines between those points approximates the curve. The smaller the increment values of t are, the more steps you get, the shorter the line segments are, and the smoother a cure you get.

Instead of drawing, this same logic can be applied to an animation, thereby moving an object along the curve in a predefined number of steps. However, the third item on our list of requirements is that the animation has to take place over a defined period of time, so this project also requires that we use a timer to move our object.

Continued

Continued

The first project I ever used this for was a Ouija board done in Director, in which the planchette moves across the board in a spooky fashion, responding to clicks and keypress events. You can see that and other examples at my Bézier curve site (www.moshplant. com/direct-or/bezier/). In this shorter example, we make the planchette move to the position on the board where the user clicks. All of the movement code in the example movie is contained in a script attached to the Movie Clip named planchette. (You'll find the finished .FLA on the CD-ROM in the ch26 folder.)

Now that we've discussed the concept and you've (hopefully) viewed a few of my samples, it's time to develop the scripts to adapt this effect in Flash 5. First, we need to define some variables when the planchette first appears, in an onClipEvent (load) handler:

```
onClipEvent (load) {
    // initialize the activity flag
    active = false;

    // define period of movement
    period = 2500;
}
```

The active variable is used to determine whether the planchette is in the middle of a movement. The period of 2500 is in milliseconds, so this is defining a movement period of 2.5 seconds. At this point, the planchette would just sit there.

The next handler is where most of the work is done. Here, an onClipEvent (mouseDown) is used to find where the mouse has been clicked, define that point as the destination of the Bézier curve, and then derive the coefficient values needed for the animation (in the following code, the ¬ character indicates a continuation of the same line of code; do not insert this character in your actual code):

```
onClipEvent (mouseDown) {

    // set the activity flag
    active = true;

    // define the destination point
    x3 = _root._xmouse;
    y3 = _root._ymouse;

    // define the origin point
    x0 = _x;
    y0 = _y;

    // derive the vector between the origin and destination
    vectorX = x3-x0;
    vectorY = y3-y0;
```

```
    // find a point 1/3 of the way from origin to destination
    // for control 1
    x1 = x0 + vectorX / 3;
    y1 = y0 + vectorY / 3;

    // find a point 2/3 of the way from origin to destination
    // for control 2
    x2 = x0 + 2 * vectorX / 3;
    y2 = y0 + 2 * vectorY / 3;

    // variability is determined by the distance from origin
    // to destination
    variability = Math.sqrt(vectorX * vectorX + vectorY * ¬
      vectorY)/ 1.5;

    // perturb the control points by a random value
    // ranging between - (destination / 2) and
    // (destination / 2)
    x1 = x1 + Math.random()*(variability+1) - variability/2;
    y1 = y1 + Math.random()*(variability+1) - variability/2;
    x2 = x2 + Math.random()*(variability+1) - variability/2;
    y2 = y2 + Math.random()*(variability+1) - variability/2;

    // derive the coefficients of the Bezier equations
    cx = 3 * (x1 - x0);
    cy = 3 * (y1 - y0);
    bx = 3 * (x2 - x1) - cx;
    by = 3 * (y2 - y1) - cy;
    ax = x3 - x0 - cx - bx;
    ay = y3 - y0 - cy - by;

    // set the timer
    originTime = getTimer();
  }
```

Most of the preceding code is a straightforward interpretation of the original equations into ActionScript. The derivation of the control points, however, might need some explaining. Here's how those control points are derived.

We start with control point p1 placed one-third of the way from p0 to p3, and p2 is two-thirds of the distance. (This is actually how you can draw a straight line with a Bézier curve, and one of the only times the curve will pass through all four points.)

Continued

Continued

Next, to get a variable curve (requirement 4) we change the coordinates of the two control points by a random number. In this case, the distance from p0 to p3 determines the range of the random number. The total range (represented by the variable `variability`) is about two-thirds of the total distance. That value (ranging between 0 and ⅔) is shifted (by subtracting half of the variability: ⅓) to a range of −⅓ to +⅓, and added to the original position of the coordinates in the four lines that perturb the control points. As an example, if the distance between p_0 and p_3 is 350 units, the variability factor will be 233.333. In the perturbation lines, the original coordinate will have a random value that may range anywhere between 0 and 233.333 added to it, and have 116.666 subtracted from it. If the original coordinate value is 200, the result could be anywhere from 83.333 to 316.666. By increasing or reducing variability, the curve can be more or less controlled. For example, if `variability` is 0, the curve will become a straight line.

Then, once the points have been determined, the coefficients of the equations are a cinch to derive. The last thing to do is set the timer.

Nevertheless, the planchette won't yet move. One more handler, an `onClipEvent (enterFrame)` takes care of that:

```
onClipEvent (enterFrame) {

  // check activity flag
  if (active) {
    var t;
    var dX;
    var dY;
    var modangle;

    // derive value of t from ratio of elapsed time to period
    t = (getTimer()-originTime) / period;

    // check to see if timeout has occurred
    if (t >= 1) {

      // timeout; set object to final position
      _x = x3;
      _y = y3;

      // turn off activity flag
      active = false;

    } else {

      // object is still moving; plug t into equations
      newX = ax * t * t * t + bx * t * t + cx * t + x0;
      newY = ay * t * t * t + by * t * t + cy * t + y0;
```

```
    // set object position
    _x = newX;
    _y = newY;
  }

  // rotate to point at the pointto movie clip
  // derive vector from planchette to pointto
  dX = _x -_root.pointto._x;
  dY = _y -_root.pointto._y;

  // use the atan2 function to get a rotation angle
  // from the vector
  modangle = 270 + (Math.atan2 ( dY, dX) * 360 / 2 / Math.PI);
  // rotate the body and shadow of planchette
  body._rotation = modangle;
  shadow._rotation = modangle;
  }
}
```

To set the timer, first check whether the planchette is active. If it's not active, nothing happens.

If the planchette is active, set the timer as follows: The value we plug into the equations is the number of milliseconds that have elapsed since the mouse press, divided by the total movement period. That will be a positive floating-point number ranging from 0 up. When the t value is 1 or greater, then the elapsed time is greater than the period. At that point, the object is placed in its final position, and the activity flag is turned off.

If t is less than 1, then we simply plug it into the equations. It's almost too simple — it's just multiplication and addition. You'll notice that for the cube and square values of t I just multiply rather than use the `Math.exp` function. It's just simpler. Then the position properties of the Movie Clip are changed. You're done!

One additional goodie that I've added as a final embellishment doesn't have anything to do with the movement on Bézier curves. That's the mechanism to point the planchette at a specific point on the Stage. The last part of the handler uses an invisible clip called pointto (near the top of the Stage) as its target, figures out the angle between the planchette and the target, and then rotates the planchette body and shadow so that it looks as if some supernatural force is running the show.

The entire animation is event driven; if you click while the planchette is moving, it automatically recalculates a new curve based on the click and its own current position. It's also independent of the movie frame rate. This version always takes 2.5 seconds to move from origin to destination no matter whether the frame rate is 5 or 100. Slower frame rates will only mean that the animation isn't as smooth; while speeding up the movie won't make the animation too fast, just smoother. (Note that, by changing the value of the period, which was set in the third line of the `onClipEvent (load)`, the apparent swiftness of the planchette's movement can be either quickened or retarded.)

Continued

Continued

You can do many more things with Bézier curves and animation. My original Director version let you type in a key and moved the planchette to the appropriate position on the screen to cover the typed letter (by using an array of points on the Stage associated with keys). Change the period at the same time as you define the curve by varying it with the distance between p_0 and p_3. Animations that move continuously are easy to do by defining a new destination and curve instead of turning off the activity flag. If you put the curve definition statements into a function instead of the `onClipEvent` handler, then you can send messages from anywhere in the movie, passing parameters for the destination instead of just using the mouse click location.

A resident of Portland, Oregon, Darrel says, "I've lived all my life in Oregon, rarely going beyond the confines of even the city I live in." In the year that he graduated from high school, he saw *Alien* six times in the theater. Darrel's credits as an author include *Shockwave: Breathe New Life into Your Web Pages* (n.p.: Ventana, 1996), and *Flash! Creative Web Animation* (Berkeley: Peachpit Press, 1997). Daniel was also lead author of *The Lingo Programmer's Reference* (n.p.: Ventana, 1997) and *Special Edition Using Macromedia Flash 5* (New York: Macmillan, Que, 2001). Yet his favorite thing to do is "Read. Not computer books. Oh, and *Battlebots*." Regarding his entry to Flash, he relates, "I've been a vector guy for over a decade, and doing multimedia programming since the early '90s, so when Flash was folded into the Macromedia family, it was a natural progression."

Expert Tutorial: Scripting for Interfaces, *by Nik Schramm*

Since Flash 4 (which introduced the impressive scripting capacity which has been so powerfully enhanced with the release of Flash 5) it's become increasingly common for developers to build Flash movies that consist of very few keyframes on the Main Timeline. Instead, they move all the scripting and animation action to the timelines of the Flash movie's Movie Clip components. In the realm of interface design, where screen action is normally dependent on some form of user interaction, there is hardly any other way to operate. Because this is my main area of interest, you can imagine my delight with the improvements to the Flash 5 scripting engine. In this tutorial, I show you some of the new possibilites of Flash 5.

It is now *very* easy to create reusable Movie Clips for navigational systems, complete with built-in generic actions. This can be done by using the new Functions and Object Actions, with which a given Movie Clip can initialize its own independent set of `onLoad` variables and perform a series of actions `onEnterFrame`. The key to making this work is to write reusable functions at the root level and access them from each independent clip that wants to perform the actions contained therein; this is similar to the `call` action in Flash 4, but far more flexible. To illustrate how to employ some of these new techniques, I dissect the main navigational menu of `www.industriality.com`, a site I recently designed with Flash 5.

The interface shown in the following figure was designed in Illustrator 9, exported as a .SWF, and imported into Flash. Following import, I optimized by removing unnecessary duplicate elements and reusing symbols in as many places as possible, which reduced the file size of all graphics in this interface to 19KB, leaving plenty of space for some heavy-weight scripting. To fully exploit the new ObjectActions in Flash 5, I also converted all the graphic symbols to Movie Clips.

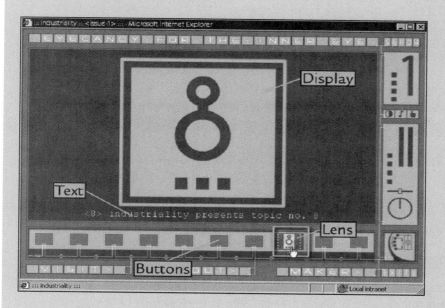

Objective

The Main Timeline has only one keyframe, in which all root-level scripting, such as global variables and functions, is initialized. The main navigation consists of a lens that follows the mouse when it is over a menu comprised of ten identical buttons, which is an effect similar to a slide rule. On `rollOver`, a button begins a short animation to display the index number of the selected topic inside the lens.

Additionally, the large display at the top scrolls from its rest position, displaying the Industriality logo, to the number representing the selected menu item, thus echoing and magnifying the smaller number inside the lens. To top off the effect, a descriptive text line is dynamically generated, animated using random calculations, and placed on the stage between the main menu and the large display. The (`rollOut`) event must return everything to its original positions; thus, all functions must be designed to accommodate this. So, let's have a closer look at the component elements that make up this navigation and how they work, starting with the animated effects and concluding with the actual buttons.

Continued

Continued

The Lens

The lens is contained by itself in a Movie Clip called `_root.menuLens`. As you will recall, it is set to follow the mouse when it is over the main menu. Rather than using `dragMovie` to achieve this effect, I opted to write a short function at root level that matches the x positions of mouse and lens, which frees me to use `dragMovie` in other ways, proof of the fact that Flash 5 often has many options available to achieve the same result. The function is very simple:

```
function lensMenu() {
  // set variables for the current x and y positions of the mouse
  mouseX = _root._xmouse;
  mouseY = _root._ymouse;

  // restrict the active area to the main menu
  if(mouseY>421 && mouseY<489 && mouseX>43 && mouseX<655) {
  //  set the x position of menuLens MC to that of the mouse
  _root.menuLens._x = mouseX
  }

  // stop lens on button 1 if mouse is too far left
  if(mouseY>421 && mouseY<489 && mouseX>9 && mouseX<44) {
    _root.menuLens._x = 43
  }

  // stop lens on button 10 if mouse is too far right
  if(mouseY>421 && mouseY<489 && mouseX>654 && mouseX<688) {
    _root.menuLens._x = 655
  }
}
```

Of course, a function by itself does nothing, so the `menuLens` Movie Clip needs to call this function to update its position every time the mouse is moved. This is achieved with ease in Flash 5 by assigning the following Object Action to the `menuLens` Movie Clip on the Main Timeline:

```
onClipEvent (mouseMove) {
  _root.lensMenu();
  updateAfterEvent();
}
```

In the final line, `updateAfterEvent` updates the screen independent of the actual movie frame rate, so it is useful to reduce the inevitable lag involved in dragging anything in Flash.

The Rollover Text

Every bit of text in this interface is dynamically generated at runtime, using only one neat root-level function. This function is sent a series of variables by each calling event handler to describe in detail what, where, and how it is to generate and display. All of the button labels were created in this manner, as well as the descriptive text line for the Rollover effect.

To be able to do this, I made a Movie Clip for each of the fonts I wanted to use. Inside this Movie Clip, there is an empty text field set to the appropriate font, color, and size, which is addressed by the variable `letter`. These text Movie Clips will be generated by the function `_root.createText`, using the new `attachMovie` action, so that there are no instances of these Movie Clips physically present on the Stage at design time. Therefore, the export linkage properties of these Movie Clips have to be set in the Library to ensure that they will be exported along with the .SWF. Thankfully, that is as easy as right-clicking the Movie Clips and choosing Linkage, giving them each a unique identifier, and then selecting Export this symbol in the Linkage options.

Author's Note: Linkage properties are discussed in Chapter 19, "Controlling Movie Clips," and Chapter 20, "Sharing and Loading Assets."

Okay, now lets build the function on frame 1 of the Main Timeline that generates this text. The function is sent the following variables by the event handler that calls it, in our case the buttons: The text string to display, a base Movie Clip to which the text Movie Clips will be attached, the screen area it is to be centered in, an x position, a y position, basic kerning info, and — of course — the linkage name of the font. The idea here is to split the text string into separate Movie Clips, one for each character, and position them as specified by the variables. In this particular case, the separate characters will begin a random growth animation, built into the actual font Movie Clips but undocumented here, once they appear on the Stage (in the following code, the ¬ character indicates a continuation of the same line of code; do not insert this character in your actual code):

```
function createText(text,base,area,xpos,ypos,kern,font) {
    // initialize local variables
    this.text = text;
    this.base = base;
    this.area = area;
    this.xpos = xpos;
    this.ypos = ypos;
    this.kern = kern;
    this.font = font;
    var textString = this.text;

    // compute the required amount of characters
    letterCount = textString.length;

    // make a new array out of the input text string
    arrayNumbering = letterCount - 1;
    textArray = new Array(arrayNumbering);
```

Continued

Continued

```
    // assign one text character to each position
    // within the array
    for (i = 0; i < letterCount; i ++) {
      textArray[i] = substring (textString, i+1, 1);
    }
    // use attachMovie to create one Movie Clip per character
    // in the array
    for (i = 0; i < letterCount; i++) {
      eval(this.base).attachMovie(this.font,"clip"+i ,i+1);

      // do basic 20 pixel kerning on the x axis and
      // set y position
      eval(this.base)["clip" + i]._x += this.xpos +(i * 20);
      eval(this.base)["clip" + i]._y = this.ypos;

      // set the variable "letter" in each clip to display the
      // desired character
      eval(this.base)["clip" + i].letter = ¬
        substring (textString, i+1, 1 );
    }

    // center all the clips in the target screen area
    // and kern as specified
    for (i = 0; i < letterCount; i++) {
      x = ((this.area -(letterCount * this.kern))/2)+50;
      pos = ((x)+(i*this.kern));
      eval(this.base)["clip" + i]._x = pos;
    }
  }
```

Now we just need a short function to remove these clips for the rollOut event:

```
function removeText() {
  // we can reuse our variables from createText() !!
  for (i = arrayNumbering; i >= 0; i--) {
    removeMovieClip (eval(this.base+".clip"+i));
  }
}
```

Author's Note: Using array access operators, you can rewrite the removeMovieClip method shown above as:

```
removeMovieClip(this.base["clip"+i]);.
```

That's it, short and sweet. Later, we see how the menu buttons call these functions to achieve the desired RollOver/RollOut effects.

The Display

Actually, the display is 11 times as wide as the visible display area and functions like a sideways slot machine, if you will. It consists of the numbers 0 to 9 as well as the Industriality logo side-by-side and is set to scroll to the relevant number after the corresponding button in the main menu receives an `on(rollOver)` event. It then returns to the logo view `on(rollOut)`. This is achieved by dynamically setting the x position of this Movie Clip, which is called `_root.mask.container.content`.

Okay, so how does it know where to scroll to? Each of the buttons in the menu controls a global variable called `_root.windowTarget`, which is equal to the desired target number, 0 being the logo. All we have to do is use the value of this variable in the scrolling script. Here's the code for the instance `_root.mask` on the Main Timeline:

```
onClipEvent (enterFrame) {
    // make display show logo (position 0) by default
    // by subtracting half the total # of poss.targets
    // and adjusting _root.windowTarget accordingly
    interim = _root.windowTarget - 5.5;
    final = 5.5 - interim;

    // final is now the adjusted target number
    // find the new x position by multiplying final
    // with the visible width (315.4)
    // subtract half the total width of all 11 targets (1892.4)
    xTarget = (final * 315.4) - 1892.4;

    // find out where the display is at the monent
    xIs = this.container.content._x;

    // if the new position is further to the right
    if (xTarget > xIs) {
        // make speed dynamic for realistic slow-down/speed-up effect
        // set basic scroll factor to 3.5
        speed = (xTarget - xIs) / 3.5

        // gradually increase x position by speed
        this.container.content._x += speed
    }

    // the same as before if new position is further left
    if (xTarget < xIs) {
        speed = (xIs - xTarget) / 3.5

        // gradually decrease x position by speed
        this.container.content._x -= speed
    }
}
```

Continued

Continued

Now, we're ready to program our buttons to set off this chain of events.

The Buttons

The buttons in the main menu are actually Movie Clips that contain an invisible button and a 15-frame rollOver/rollOut animation. The advantage of this technique is that all elements inside the Movie Clip remain fully scriptable. To compensate for this, our button scripts will have to include code to control the actual button Movie Clip as well as the other elements we have discussed.

By now, we have set up a variety of functions and events just waiting for the word GO from any of these buttons, each button achieving a slightly different result within itself, in the descriptive text, and in the display window on rollOver. However, that does not mean that we have to use ten different buttons with ten times the amount of code and file size here, because we *can* use ten instances of the very same button instead.

How does that work? Each Movie Clip instance can have its own object Actions in `onClipEvent` handlers. If we initialize variables using `onClipEvent(load)` for each instance, we end up with ten different sets of variables, one for each button, and we can design the button Movie Clips so that the variables are unique and distinguish one button from another. In contrast, the actual actions, which are common to all of the button Movie Clips, can be hard coded into the actual Movie Clip — that is, they will appear within each instance. Combine these two strategies and you get hard-coded actions that contain local instance variables to achieve multiple rollOver effects from the very same button!

So what are the actions we need to assign to the instance of our invisible button inside the button Movie Clip so that the various targets behave as planned? The lens is fine by itself, but the display is using a variable called `_root.windowTarget` to compute its scrolling movement, so our buttons need to set this variable to their respective index number for the display to begin scrolling toward it. Therefore, we could set a variable `indexNumber` using an `onClipEvent(load)` event handler for each button Movie Clip instance and use that to set `_root.windowTarget` accordingly. That would work . . . but why not use the built-in properties of our button Movie Clip object instead?

This is crucuial: Each Movie Clip in Flash 5 is an object and each object has certain inherent properties available at all times, such as `_x`, `_y`, or `_name`. Because we have cleverly placed our invisible buttons inside Movie Clips, we *can* assign instance names to these Movie Clips and — if these instance names happen to be equal to their respective index numbers (for example, `_root.1`, `_root.2`, and so on) — then these would be available at any time without any unnecessary variable setting. In the same way, we can load additional .SWFs into higher levels once the button is pressed, we just have to name them accordingly (`content1.swf`, `content2.swf`, and so on). Of course, that is what was done.

Next, for the text animation, we need to call the function `_root.createText` and send it the specified variables `text`, `base`, `area`, `xpos`, `ypos`, `kern`, and `font`. The positioning data will involve a mixture of trial, error, and math, so for now let's just say that `area` = 600, `xpos` = 10, `ypos` = 405, and `kern` = 12. The base I want to use is `_root`. Thus, all positioning data will be relative to the entire Stage and the targeting address of these clips will be `_root.clip0`, `_root.clip1`, and so forth.

The linkage name of the font that I want to use is `twLetterClip`. All these variables will be the exact same for all ten buttons, so we don't have to set button-specific variables for them. The text string and the content to be loaded, however, will differ from button to button, so we do need to define what they will be. Each button Movie Clip instance sets the text string and content variables in an `onClipEvent (load)` handler. I also want to use the index number of the menu item in `<>` brackets to precede each button's descriptive text, so I need to account for this, too:

```
onClipEvent (load) {
  // assemble the text string
  header = "<";

  // add the index number
  header += this._name;

  // close the bracket and add the text string
  // which will of course differ from button to button
  header += "> industriality presents topic no. ";

  // add the index number again
  header += this._name;

  // for button # 8 this.header will now read "<8> industriality
  // presents topic no.8"

  // set a variable to define which content swf is loaded
  // onRelease
  content = "content";
  content += this._name;
  content += ".swf";
}
```

Now we have two variables for each button Movie Clip instance, each of which defines the text string and the content that we want to load with this button later on. Thus, the final code for the invisible button should read as follows (in the following code, the ¬ character indicates a continuation of the same line of code; do not insert this character in your actual code):

```
on (rollOver) {
  // begin rollover animation inside the button
  play ();
```

Continued

Continued

```
    // make the buttons grow in size
    this._xscale = 160;
    this._yscale = 140;

    // make the display window scroll to this index number
    _root.windowTarget = this._name;

    // call the function to generate the descriptive text
    _root.createText(this.header, "_root", 600, 10, 405, 12, ¬
      "twLetterClip");
}
on (releaseOutside, rollOut, dragOver, dragOut) {
    // make the display scroll back to the logo
    _root.windowTarget = 0;

    // call the function to remove the descriptive text clips
    _root.removeText();

    // begin rollout animation inside the button and reset its size
    gotoAndPlay ("out");
    this._xscale = 100;
    this._yscale = 100;
}
on (release) {
    // load a SWF based on the variable "this.content"
    // into the level that is equal to the instance name of
    // this MC (1-10)
    loadMovieNum (this.content, this._name);

    // reset the button to the off position
    gotoAndPlay ("off");
}
```

Final Notes

The technique used to set up the scripting for the buttons is very similar to the concept of Smart Clips, which lend themselves to hard-coded content coupled with user-definable instance variables. If the buttons had become any more complicated than they are now, I would definitely have employed that technique here. As it is, normal clips did the job just fine.

It pays to plan ahead in Flash. Designing movies to reuse code wherever possible is and will remain an absolute must until the entire globe has broadband connections (that is, never), and it has just become easier than ever with the new Flash 5 scripting engine. Functions, Object Actions, Smart Clips, and Shared Libraries all help to keep the file size down and the entertainment factor up where it belongs, so use them.

A native of Hamburg, Germany, Nik Schramm's, Flash career "began with an OEM copy of CorelDraw 4, unlimited enthusiasm, MS FrontPage, and major frustration at not being able to translate my designs from the one to the other. I was designing a site to promote music and needed vivid graphics, animation, tight typographic control, and support for sound integration. So I ditched those other apps and went with Flash, which was the obvious and most suitable solution." Since then he's established an indelible reputation with his sites www.industriality.com and www.nae.de. We've media-dated Nik with this bit; in the year that he graduated from high school, "the world was a-boppin to "Let's Go Crazy" by TATVMSKAP (The artist then and very much still known as Prince)." His single most favorite thing is, "Spending time with my two sons Noah (3) and Ruben (1)." Apparently, he didn't take Prince's advice.

Expert Tutorial: Using getTimer to make a Flash Clock, by *Jake Smith*

My first reaction to Flash 5 ActionScripting was fear. But soon I found myself pondering scenarios of "what ifs . . ." and "wonder if that would work . . .?" — when nowhere near a computer! This Flash clock is one such "what if . . ." with a bit of simple math thrown in to make it work. Honestly, after having the initial idea on the way to work, it took about two minutes to get a second hand moving. The rest followed quite easily, as you'll see.

Objective: To create an authentic, real-time analog clock.

First, I created a clock face piece of art in Freehand 9. Nothing fancy, but it basically had to have all 12 points of a clock face. This was a simple job in Freehand. It involved drawing a line across the diameter of the clock circle, and then cloning and rotating it by 30 degrees, successively. This process was repeated 5 times, to create a starburst with 12 points. Next, a smaller circle was dropped on top, in the center, to mask out all the line intersections near the middle of the clock face. (The rotating by 30 degrees is because we have 12 hours in a clock face and 360 degrees in a circle. Basic math tells us that the hour indicators are each separated by 30 degrees from the center of the clock.)

Importing the Clock Artwork into Flash

Use Flash 5's facility to import Freehand 9 files (File ⇨ Import) to bring your clock artwork into Flash. Next, center the clock on the stage, because we need a definite reference point in order to add the clock hands. At this point, you can either lock the layer with your art on it or make a Movie Clip out of the clock face and then lock the layer. It's up to you — but the Movie Clip route is the most efficient method.

Continued

Continued

Second Hand

Now, create a new layer and draw a thin, tall rectangle using the Rectangle Tool. The second hand should be just a little longer than the radius of the clock face, from center to the edge. Select the rectangle that you've drawn and make a Movie Clip out of it. Name it **Second hand**. If the hand isn't dead center on the Stage, use the Align function to align the hand with the middle of the Stage.

Click once on the hand and press Ctrl/Command+E to edit the Movie Clip. The hand should be in the center of the screen, with the crosshairs in the middle of the rectangle. These crosshairs are the point around which everything is rotated by Flash. If we leave the rectangle as it is, the second hand will look like a propeller. What we need to do is select the rectangle and move it upwards, until the crosshairs are close to the bottom of the rectangle. How close to the bottom they are is up to you—but with a small amount of the rectangle below the crosshairs, the clock will look more authentic. (Note that you won't need to move the rectangle to the left or right, just up. It was centered when we made it into a Movie Clip.)

Press Ctrl/Command+E to exit editing the Movie Clip and return to the Main Stage. The hand should look like it's pointing to 12 o'clock. Finally, we need to give the instance a name. With the hand selected, locate the Instance Panel and give this instance a name of **second_hand**.

Make the Seconds Pass

On the Main Timeline of your clock movie, create three frames on all the existing layers (and if you haven't already, start labeling the layers so that you know what they are later). Now, create a new layer and label it **Actions**. This will only contain the actions that control this movie. It helps to keep actions on a separate layer so that you can find them easily if your project starts to get huge.

Now, in the Actions layer, create a keyframe on frames 1, 2, and 3. Then open the Frame Actions Panel because it's time to get technical! One of Flash 5's new features is the capability to return values for the day, date, time, and year. By creating a new Date Object, the .SWF can find out what time it is on the computer. It will return this information by hours, minutes, and seconds, which is just what we want.

In the Frame Actions Panel, type the following:

```
mySecs = new Date();
secs = mySecs.getSeconds();
```

This code creates a new Date Object, called `mySecs,` and sets the value of `secs` equal to the seconds count on the host computer. This is all we need in frame 1 for the time being; on to frame 2.

The trick to keeping this clock running is another Flash 5 command called `getTimer`. This command returns the amount of time that the Flash movie has been running since the command was executed, measured in 1/1000 of a second. Using this call, we have a means of continuously incrementing the seconds count, and thus the minutes and hours as well.

Now, we want to create a new variable and set it equal to the integer value of `getTimer`. To do this, the first line in the second frame of the Actions layer should be:

```
mytime = getTimer();
```

Because the value returned is measured in thousandths of a second, we'll perform a quick sum to derive the exact seconds; thus, the next line should read:

```
seconds = mytime / 1000;
```

The new variable `seconds` contains, well, the seconds! Not in thousandths but as a digital watch would display seconds. This value is good, but it's only the amount of time that the movie has been running, it isn't the correct time (in seconds) when the computer started the Flash movie. So, to obtain the time, we take our `secs` value from the first frame, which grabbed the time according to the computer, and add it to the `seconds` value derived from the `getTimer`:

```
clocksecs = seconds + secs;
```

Here's what we've accomplished so far: If the movie were played now, the position where the second hand would start would be just as the computer's clock dictates. If the computer says that its time says 30 seconds, then the Flash movie will think the initial seconds value is 30 and continue to count time from there.

Well, the movie knows what time it is, but we need it to move the second hand correspondingly so that we can see it. I talked about rotation points earlier because that's the command we're going to use to move the hand in time, to the match the current time. This is easily achieved in Flash with a single line of ActionScript:

```
setProperty ("second_hand", _rotation, ((clocksecs/60)*360));
```

Although this may look complex, it's easily divided into components. The `setProperty` alters the physical characteristics of the `second_hand` Movie Clip instance; the property that's being set (or changed) is `_rotation`; and, finally, we need to assign a new value to the `_rotation` property. For the clock to work correctly, we use some basic statements to deduce where the second hand should be. Next, we'll explore the reasoning behind the equation (clocksecs/60)*360.

A circle has 360 degrees, and a second hand has to travel through 60 seconds to complete a full rotation of the clock face. Therefore, the rotation value of the second hand is attained by dividing the time — or `clocksecs` — at any instance, x, by 60 (because seconds can only be anywhere from 1 to 60 before being reset to 1). Multiplying that value by 360 (which is the number of degrees in a circle) tells us exactly how far the second hand is to be rotated, denoted as

```
((clocksecs/60)*360)
```

Continued

Continued

Lastly, to obtain a continuously rotating second hand, we add one final action to the third frame on the Actions layer:

```
gotoandPlay (2);
```

You can now preview your movie to see a second hand sweeping round the clock.

Adding Minutes

You'll be pleased to know that the process for the minute hand follows a very similar method, and only requires changing a few variables along the way. First, create a new layer below the seconds layer and name it **minutes**. Draw a black minute hand on the Stage, tall and thin, although not quite as long as the second hand. Convert it to a Movie Clip, and center this new clip on the Stage.

Now, press Ctrl/Command+E to edit the minute hand. Then select all and move the hand up (as was done with the second hand) so that the crosshairs are near the bottom of the rectangle. Then return to the Main Timeline. The minute hand should point straight up toward 12 o'clock. Finally give the minute instance a name, such as **minute_hand**.

In the first frame of the Actions layer, add this code:

```
myMins = new Date();
mins = myMins.getMinutes();
```

This creates a new Date Object specifically to retrieve the minutes value held in the computer's clock.

Then, move to frame 2 of the Actions layer and enter the following code directly after the code `seconds = mytime / 1000;`

```
minutes = (secs + seconds) / 60;
```

This line keeps the minute count going by adding the known values (seconds at the beginning of the movie) + (the amount of seconds the movie has been running).

The next code, to be added after `clocksecs = seconds + secs`, is:

```
clockmins = minutes + mins;
```

That code sets the starting minutes value for our Flash movie.

Then, finally, to move the minute hand according to `clockmins`, the last line of code on frame 2 of the Actions layer, is:

```
setProperty ("minute_hand", _rotation, ((clockmins/60)*360));
```

Here, the rotation of the minute hand is set using the same principle as the second hand, because minutes also pass through 60 minutes on a 360-degree clock face.

Adding Hours

Now, create a new layer under the minutes layer, and name it **hours**. Then draw a short, thin, black rectangle on the Stage. This will be the hour hand. Turn it into a Movie Clip and center the hour hand on the Stage. As before (for the seconds and minute hands) edit the hour hand so that the crosshairs are near the bottom of the rectangle. Then return to the Main Stage and, in the Instance Panel, name the instance **hour_hand**.

Following the same method as used for minutes and seconds to set the hours from the computer, we create a third Date Object in the ActionScript of frame 1 of the Actions layer:

```
myHrs = new Date();
hrs = myHrs.getHours();
```

At frame 2 of the Actions layer, after the line `minutes = (secs + seconds) / 60;`, we add this line of code:

```
hours = (minutes + mins) / 60;
```

Then, after the minutes version `clockmins = minutes + mins`, we add this line of code:

```
clockhours = hours + hrs;
```

The very last line to add at the bottom of the ActionScript for frame 2 is:

```
setProperty ("hour_hand", _rotation, ((clockhours/12)*360));
```

You may notice that this is different from the two previous `setProperty` commands because it divides by 12 instead of 60. That's because the hour hand can only go to 12 before being reset to 1.

The movie is now finished and ready for export.

Authors' Note: The finished .FLA for this clock, as well as Jake's example of a digital display (which includes the day), are in the ch26 folder on the CD-ROM.

Jake Smith is a member of the esteemed Subnet and has worked on an impressive roster of clients, including www.kelloggs.co.uk, www.foxkids.co.uk, www.wotsits.co.uk, and www.capri-sun.co.uk. A son of Liverpool, he reports that, in the year he graduated from high school, the most memorable movie was, "err, umm, *Wayne's World*, I think." Jake boasts a huge collection of video arcade machines, as his favorite thing to do is "play video games." In addition, he loves "music, kung-fu films, designing, and Bacardi, too. . . ." Regarding his introduction to Flash, Jake recalls, "Many years back we first saw FutureSplash used on the Fox site for *The Simpsons*. Really basic, just rollovers and very simple animation, but I was blown away by moving vectors and the small file sizes."

Summary

✦ Natural movement doesn't usually occur along a straight line. Variation in a motion path can yield more life-like animation.

✦ You can script movement algorithmically and define parameters for the algorithm: the shape, end point, and duration can be randomly assigned.

✦ Many experienced Flash developers use Movie Clip timelines to separate ActionScript code and animation action from the Main Timeline.

✦ By using onClipEvent() handlers, a given Movie Clip instance can initialize its own independent set of variables and perform a series of actions.

✦ By learning to create reusable menu interfaces, you can recreate aesthetically different interfaces in less time.

✦ By using the Date Object, you can initialize a Flash clock's time. Then you can use getTimer() to update the time displayed by the clock, at regular intervals.

✦   ✦   ✦

Using Flash with Generator and Other Server Technologies

In Parts IV and V, you learned how to use ActionScript to add enhanced interactivity and functionality to your Flash movies. For the most part, our examples were confined to internal Flash movie structures — everything used Movie Clips, ActionScript variables, and methods of Objects. In Part VI, we introduce the external environment (and dynamic power) of Macromedia Generator. As you'll see, Generator involves two steps: adding Generator Objects and variables to Flash movies, and serving Generator Templates from a Web server that utilizes the Generator Server software. Chapters 27 and 28 teach you how to add Generator functionality to your Flash movies, while Chapter 29 discusses other dynamic server environments, such as .ASP documents.

What Is Generator?

Despite the new capabilities that ActionScript has brought to Flash 4 and 5, the Flash Player plug-in still can't directly import "raw" dynamic media — at least not without a little help. That's where Macromedia Generator 2 comes to the rescue. For example, if you want to dynamically insert or update bitmap graphics in Flash movies, then you need Generator. Generator can do a whole lot more, so without further ado, let's get started.

Many thanks to Mike Jones, who supplied the Generator information for the *Flash 4 Bible*. Mike Jones is one of the original team members of Spooky and the Bandit, which is a Flash design and development team (www.spookyandthebandit. com). We have updated and revised his material to reflect the new enhancements of Generator 2.

An Overview of Generator 2

Macromedia Generator 2 is both a tool and a server application used to develop and deploy automated and/or personalized Web-based graphics. The Web graphics can be .SWFs, .GIFs, .JPEGs, .PNGs, image maps, QuickTime Flash movies, or animated .GIFs. All of these can be produced by Generator to deliver personalized content for individual users. They can also be produced by Generator for inclusion within scheduled, updated interactive Web applications such as banner ads, stock market tickers, scrolling lists, 3D pie charts, maps, calendars, and headliners. Generator 2 release 2 adds support for Flash 5 movies and three new Generator Objects: Multipage List, Radio Button, and Insert MP3.

Caution This entire chapter is based on Generator 2 release 2. Generator release 1 is not compatible with Flash 5 movies. Generator 1.0 is not compatible with Flash 4 and 5 movies. Do not try to reinstall Generator 1.0 to use with Flash 4 and 5.

Macromedia's concept behind Generator was to separate the design-based elements from the actual content, which gives the developers greater flexibility and control when updating or altering graphics on the Web. Generator takes a given set of data elements and applies them to a given list of variables. For example, Generator can convert a template that has a placeholder for a dynamic weather map .GIF image and serve a .SWF with an always-up-to-date weather map. This saves developers time and money in the management of content, and leaves the designers to do what they do best — design!

To do this they created a "hybridized" application. To create Generator content you need the free Generator authoring extensions. These extensions are automatically installed with Flash 5. The installer files can also be downloaded from Macromedia's Web site. To dynamically serve these Generator "templates" from your site, you also need to own and install the Generator Server application on your Web server. The Generator Server is available for Windows, Solaris, and Linux operating systems.

Developing Generator-driven Web sites is a two-part process. First, the Generator authoring extensions in Flash 5 are used to design and incorporate graphical Web templates. Then, when implemented, the Generator Server takes these templates and combines them with data provided from an external source to create "live" Web graphics (.SWF, .GIF, .GIF89, .JPEG, .PNG, or .MOV).

Before we discuss the Generator authoring extensions, let's take a brief look at the Generator Server application.

Generator Server

As mentioned previously, if you want to serve Generator content you have to purchase and install the Generator Server application for your Web server. This is truly the Generator: It sits on your Web server, takes the templates (.SWT files) that you designed with the authoring extensions and published in Flash 5, applies the specified data sources that are used in the template, and then delivers a .SWF file (or another image format) to the user. See Figure 27-1 for a diagram of this process.

Generator is not only capable of producing interactive content solely based in Flash; the Generator Server application can also convert this Flash content (or any .SWT) into a .GIF, .JPEG, or .PNG image, or even a QuickTime Flash movie. Generator can also remove all textual elements from a .SWF file and its data source and save these elements to a standard text document. (Note, however, that Generator doesn't format the text.) Generator can create image maps — both client and server side. All of these items can be produced in either a "per-user" (online), or a scheduled (offline), capacity.

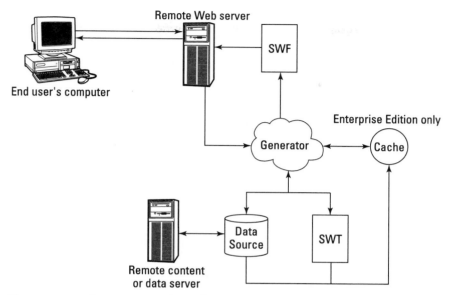

Figure 27-1: When a request is made for a .SWT file on a Generator-enabled Web server, Generator 2 will create a custom .SWF file (from the .SWT file and data sources) and deliver it to the end user.

Generator editions

Just before Flash 5 was released to the public, Macromedia announced that the Generator product would be split into two editions: the Enterprise Edition and the Developer Edition. As the names imply, Generator's two flavors are geared to high-end production use (Enterprise) or low-demand production and development (Developer). On a price level, Enterprise is much more expensive and slated for corporate budgets (starting price is $30,000). The Developer Edition can be purchased for $999, or lower if you purchase it as part of a combo software upgrade.

For the most part, both editions perform the same primary task: convert .SWT files and data sources into customized .SWF files. The biggest difference between the two editions is the potential speed with which the Generator Server can create the .SWF files. Although the Developer Edition can only utilize one processor on a server, the Enterprise Edition can scale across multiple processors and handle many more simultaneous requests for .SWT files than can the Developer Edition. The Enterprise Edition can also utilize a server cache that stores frequently accessed content. When this content is requested, Generator will serve the faster cache content. The Enterprise Edition also has more robust administration and logging features that the Developer Edition does not have.

If you want to plan, develop, and test Generator content, then you won't need the Enterprise Edition. You can even use the Developer Edition to serve live Generator content on your Web site—just don't expect it to dynamically generate 50 or more .SWF files per second. On average, the Developer Edition can serve three to five .SWF files per second, depending on network conditions.

> **Note**   To use Generator Server software, you need access to your own personal Web server. Most virtual Web servers that offer Web hosting will not provide Generator services. At the time of this writing, some Internet Presence Providers offered Generator-enabled hosting. If you have a high-speed Internet connection (such as a cable or DSL modem) for your LAN (Local Area Network), you can install the Developer Edition on a local machine and access it remotely over the Web to test your Generator Templates.

Online/Offline?

So, what exactly are online/offline, and how do they differ? Basically the online functions of Generator are employed when you need to update dynamic content on a per-user basis. Examples of this might be stock market tickers, weather maps, booking information, and that sort of thing. An online process is evoked every time a user calls a .SWT from the server, or when a script is run that returns updated information that is constantly changing minute by minute.

> **Note**   Online deployment of content for navigation links, nondated textual information, and any files that are not changed frequently are a waste of the Generator resource. Because serving Generator-driven content can be demanding, you should not unnecessarily strain your Web server. Infrequent content updates should be handled by offline functions.

Offline functionality schedules Generator to create files locally and place them wherever required, such as a remote Web server. When Generator operates in offline mode, it builds a static .SWF file that is loaded by every user of your Web site. In this method of production, you don't make requests for .SWT files—you won't put calls for .SWT files in your Flash movies or HTML documents. Offline mode would be equivalent to you manually going into a Flash movie (a .FLA file), updating the images or text, publishing the file, and uploading the new .SWF file to your Web server. However, offline Generator can do all of this for you, so that you are free to do other things (such as design new Web sites!). You can set up command lines for offline Generator using standard DOS commands, switches, and arguments that evoke the Generator executable file, directing it to the .SWT files you wish to use. You can schedule these commands to be run only when necessary or once a week. These command lines can be placed directly on the Web server.

>   **Caution**   Only the Generator Server software can provide online functionality. Because this server software is only available for Solaris, Linux, and Windows operating systems (primary NT Server with IIS 3.0 or 4.0 or Windows 95/98 Personal Web Server), Macintosh Flash developers can only design—not serve—dynamic content with the Flash 5 authoring extensions.

Pseudo-offline functionality

You can fake offline Generator functionality by using Generator objects with static URLs (local or remote) or file paths. What does this mean? As you'll see in the next section, you can add Generator Objects to your Flash movies with the free Generator authoring extensions. Even if you don't purchase the Generator Server software, you can place image or chart objects that use local (or remote) data sources (such as a .JPEG file) and publish a .SWF file that contains the data-source information as it applies to the placed object.

For example, if you have an image file called test.jpg at:

```
http://www.theMakers.com/books/f5bible/test.jpg
```

Then you can place a JPEG Object into your Flash movie, specify the preceding URL, and, when you publish the .SWF file from Flash, it will retrieve the image and embed it in your .SWF file! This type of pseudo-Generator functionality is useful for quickly creating pie chart graphics or updating a few graphics in a static Flash movie. You'll see how to use the Generator Objects and data sources in the remainder of this chapter.

Generator authoring extensions

Now that you've been introduced to the concepts of serving Generator Templates, all you need to know is how to make them. The Generator authoring extensions, in conjunction with Flash 5, are used to make Generator Templates. These extensions can be used to create content for Generator 2, and will work with Flash 3, 4, and 5. Although some content can be created for Flash 2, it will have limited functionality.

Caution   The new Generator Objects that ship with Flash 5, Multi-page List, Radio Button, and Insert MP3, will not work with the original Generator 2 release. Also, Flash 5-specific ActionScript may not be translated appropriately by earlier releases of Generator 2. You will need to download and install the release 2 updater, from the Macromedia site in order to use these objects and the Flash 5 .SWF format.

Unlike other products that Macromedia develops, Generator doesn't have its own front-end application or GUI (graphical user interface). You can access Generator elements from a variety of places within the Flash 5 authoring environment. The main Generator element appears as an additional file type in the Formats tab of the File ➪ Publish Settings dialog (see Figure 27-2). When you enable the Generator Template (.SWT) check box in the Formats tab, you'll be able to access another Publish Settings tab called Generator. This is shown in Figure 27-3. If you do not have the Generator authoring extensions installed, then the Generator Template file format is disabled in the Formats tab.

Cross-Reference   The settings in the Generator tab of the Publish Settings dialog are discussed in the next chapter.

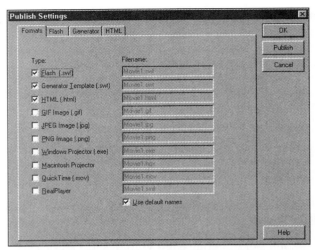

Figure 27-2: The Publish Settings dialog, with the Generator format enabled

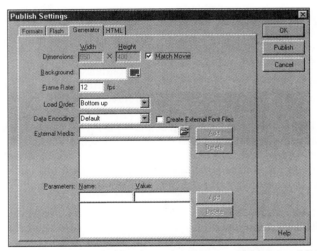

Figure 27-3: The Generator tab appears within the Publish Settings

There's also a Generator Panel in Flash that is accessed with Windows ➪ Panels ➪ Generator. Unless you have the authoring extensions installed, the Generator Panel will display an advertisement, shown in Figure 27-4.

Figure 27-4: If the Generator extensions are not installed, you see an advertisement that promotes Generator (left image). If you have the extensions, the Panel is blank until a Generator Object is selected on the Stage.

We're ready to start using Flash to create Generator Templates, which are referred to as .SWT files. But before looking at an example of how Generator content is created, let's look at the Generator Objects that are available after the extensions are installed. You can access a tool window for Generator Objects (see Figure 27- 5) by using the Windows ➪ Generator Objects command.

Figure 27-5: The Generator Objects tool window

The Generator Objects tool window is used to place dynamic content placeholders into Flash movies. You can drag objects from the window to the Stage. The following objects are available with Generator 2 release 2:

✦ **Basic Charts:** This template facilitates the creation of charts, which come in various "flavors": Bar, Stacked Bar, Line, Stacked Line, Area, Stacked Area, Scatter, and Scatter Line.

✦ **Insert Flash Movie:** This option enables the insertion of a Flash movie from another source directly into the .SWT. In the output, Generator merges the two files into one. The source files can be external to the .SWT, either locally or remotely.

✦ **Insert GIF:** As mentioned previously, .GIF files can also be acquired from their native format and inserted directly into the .SWT.

✦ **Insert JPEG:** Same as Insert GIF.

✦ **Insert MP3 File:** Just as you can import custom compressed MP3 files into Flash 5 movies, you can now dynamically pull MP3 files from your server and embed them in your Generator-created .SWF files.

✦ **Insert PNG:** Same as Insert GIF.

✦ **Insert Sound:** This option enables sounds to be merged into a .SWT.

✦ **Insert Symbol:** This option enables a symbol to be taken from the .SWT's Library and inserted directly into the .SWT file. Symbols don't have to be taken from the same .SWT; they can be held in separate .SWTs.

✦ **List:** Enables the display of information in either a vertical or horizontal orientation.

✦ **Multi-page List:** This new Generator Object will make a set of pages from large lists of information. Navigation buttons (Next, Previous, and Home) are automatically added to the list.

✦ **Pie Chart:** Enables data to be fed into a pie chart format, which can even be 3D (and exploded) to show breakdown of data.

✦ **Plot:** Plot enables the placement of an element from the Library onto the canvas at specified coordinates. Scaling and rotation can also be applied via this template.

✦ **Radio Button:** This new Generator Object will make a series of radio buttons that reference existing Flash symbols (that you have created in the Library) for on and off states, as well as text characteristics.

✦ **Scrolling List:** A scrolling version of the List template. This is like the List template except that it uses one symbol to replicate information, which can be displayed either as a vertical or horizontal scrolling template.

✦ **Stock Chart:** This option facilitates the display of data pertaining to stock market quotes. This template is able to display figures in various data sets as either: High-Low-Close, Open-High-Low, or Candlesticks.

✦ **Table:** The Table template enables the display of textual information such as calendars and scheduling information

✦ **Ticker:** Based on the Scrolling List, this template is especially useful for a banner header or quote ticker. The data can be displayed either vertically or horizontally.

Your First Generator Template

So, you have the authoring extensions and you're ready to make a template. First you need to decide on your data source. This can be either a humble text file, or a middleware solution — such as output from Perl/CGI scripts, ColdFusion, Active

ActionScript or Generator?

A common question among Flash developers is: "When should I use Generator for dynamic content?" The simple answer is: "Whenever you need dynamic graphic content where non-textual data (for example, image files) is changed frequently." Basically, if you only need to change text information in a Flash movie, then you may be better off using `loadMovie` and `loadVariables` actions within your Flash movies to update content.

Since Flash 4, we have the ability to load dynamic text content into Flash movies (.SWF files) without the use of Generator. A major problem, however, is that a Flash 4 text field had to have a uniform font style, size, and color. With Generator, you could dynamically inserted blue text with black text, all in the same text block. Now, with Flash 5, you can accomplish the same effect with HTML tags in Dynamic Text fields, without the use of Generator. However, Generator templates still makes this task much simpler.

You can even simulate dynamic content by creating multiple .SWF files for content areas on your site. If you have a lot of JPEG images that you want to use in your site, you don't necessarily need Generator to put them into .SWF files for you. You can create archives of .SWF files that simply contain the JPEG image file(s). While this may be a bit labor intensive, if you have a slow growing (or static) number of images (or sounds, or other assets) in your site, then you will only have to create this files once and be done with it. With a little work, you can create a data layout and naming convention for all your assets, and load them into Flash movies with `loadMovie` actions.

However, if you need to pull content or data from remote servers, or continually update graphics within your Flash movies, then you'll want to use Generator 2. You won't be able to create a dynamic weather map for each person across the country if you're using static .SWF files on your Web server. Generator, however, can take the user's regional information (in the form of Flash and/or Generator variables) and produce a custom weather map for each person who visits the site.

Again, if you primarily need to update text in your Flash movies, you may not need Generator. If you need to update or create custom graphics in your Flash movies, then you'll need Generator.

Server Pages (ASP), or a direct link to a database. For this simple example we use a text document.

> **Tip**
>
> You can specify Generator variables as your data source. These variables can be declared and set by other Flash movies that use `loadMovie` (with Send Variables) to fetch .SWT files from the Generator-enabled Web site.

1. Create a directory on your local machine. The exact location is up to you. Call it **GenDev** and in this folder make three more folders: one called **data**, another called **swt**, and a third named **fla**.

2. Create an empty text file in an ASCII editor, either Notepad (PC) or SimpleText (Mac). Save the text file in the data folder as **info.txt**.

3. At the top of the text document, type the following words — make sure you observe the syntax carefully:

   ```
   name, value
   ```

4. Save the text file and close it.

5. Open Flash 5, and save a new empty Flash movie (.FLA file) as **lesson1.fla** in the fla directory.

Now's a good time to explain the logic behind the folder structure that we've just created. Using relative paths for your data source makes it very easy to migrate the final files to your Web server for final deployment. Also, the current folder configuration affords the extra advantage that the final .SWT files can easily find other source files. The exported .SWF files that are created with Flash's Test Movie and Scene commands are also saved to the .FLA source folder, where the final .SWTs can find them.

To set your data source, look to the top-right corner of the Flash Timeline window, where — as shown in Figure 27-6 — you see the Generator logo. Its presence on the Timeline window indicates that the Generator extensions are installed. It also opens the Generator Set Environment dialog. To insert Environment parameters, click this button and a dialog opens.

Click to insert a Generator
environment variable

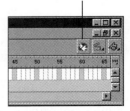

Figure 27-6: The Generator Environment button (to the left of the Scenes pop-up menu)

Note In Generator 1, the environment parameters were set in the timeline. Other changes in Generator 2 are that specific selections for `Set Environment` and `Set SQL Environment` no longer exist. Both of these have been combined in the new Set Environment dialog. Once you have made your settings in this box you can check them at any point by clicking the Generator Environment button.

As shown in Figure 27-7, two icons appear at the top-right corner of the Set Environment dialog: Column Name/Value Data Layout and Name/Value Data Layout. Basically, these variable containers enable you to input names and values in the same manner as we are going to in our text file. You can browse to a data source via the small folder icon in the top left. Remember to keep the paths *relative*.

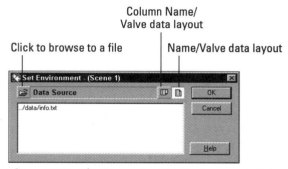

Figure 27-7: The Generator Set Environment dialog

Let's enter the data source we have just saved as a text file. If you aren't there already, switch back to Flash and click the Generator logo. When the dialog opens, type this directly into the text field:

    ../data/info.txt

Click OK and save the Flash file. That's the path to the data source set in the text file, named info.txt. Remember that if you used the browser icon you need to crop off the front part of the absolute path and enter a relative one instead. The following path would need to be cropped to match the preceding relative path example:

    C:\gendev\data\info.txt

Now you're ready to make your mark on the Flash Stage. Select the Text Tool and change the font to Arial (PC) or Helvetica (Mac). Select a black fill color in the Toolbar, and select a 20-point text size in the Character Panel. Then, click the stage to create a Static Text block, and type the following: **{btext}{ntext}**. Unlike Flash 5 ActionScript variables, all Generator variables are written between curly braces ({ }). Refer to Figure 27-8 for more information on the position and size of the text.

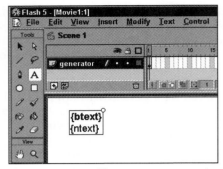

Figure 27-8: Making Generator Text in Flash

Tip Note that {btext} is bold in the editor. If you want particular formatting for elements of text, you'll need to add these to the variable, as they can't be added via the data source.

As you can see, the text layout properties are still active. If we just left it like this, our data source information would have a very small text block—letters may wrap to the next line upon generation. That's because there's only space for seven characters. To resolve this, set the size of the text box by "grabbing" the circle icon at the top-right corner of the text block and drag while the mouse button is still pressed, as shown in Figure 27-9.

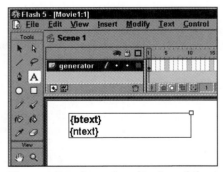

Figure 27-9: Resetting the size of the text box

Now save the file—make sure that it's saved in the fla folder of the GenDev folder. As we continue adding more and more information to this file, you'll need to keep backing it up. Therefore, it's recommended that you make an incremental save to the file *before* you make any major changes to it. If these new changes are successful, then you should save the file as the next file in order, as follows: gen_01.fla, gen_02.fla, and so on.

Switch to your text editor and open the text file called info.txt. This file should only contain the two words that we entered at the very beginning. To recap, these should be:

```
name, value
```

Under this entry, we'll insert a carriage return and — on the next line down — we'll add our first variable, {btext}, and then on the next line we'll add our second variable, {ntext}:

```
name, value
btext,
ntext,
```

Note that a comma follows each of the variables and that the curly braces (that surrounded the equivalent variable in the Flash movie) have been removed. The comma is what is known as the delimiter — that means that Generator treats anything appearing after the comma as a variable value.

Knowing this, you might imagine that problems arise when you need to include a whole sentence or a string of characters that may or may not be separated by a comma. We solve this by putting the value of the variable in double quotes. The downside of this solution is that you can't put double quotes inside a value — because it would have the same effect as placing a comma outside double quotes, which would cause the text to end abruptly. You can, however, use single quotes inside double quotes with no adverse effects. Then, if you need to use double quotes, use a \ as a delimiter. Therefore, to double quote within a set of quotes, write the sentence thus:

```
This section of \"text\" is in quotes.
```

Tip If only part of the text is being generated from your template, Generator is not at fault. It is more likely to be a syntax error is in your text source than an error in the generation process itself. If no text is generated, check all elements before looking at Generator as the source of the problem. Remember a lot of user elements can cause a template to fail — especially the old "forgot to set my file as a Generator Template" one. That's not saying Generator is foolproof though!

Now let's add values for both variables. The first variable, btext, has the value:

```
Generator
```

Our second variable, ntext, has the variable:

```
Welcome to Personalization
```

Our final text document should look something like this:

```
Name, value
btext, Generator
ntext, Welcome to Personalization
```

Finally, save the file and close your text editor. That's all the text manipulation we need to do. Now, if you closed Flash while working on the text you'll need to open it again. So let's go back into Flash for our last time.

Now, we test our file to see if it works. Open lesson1.fla and double-check your Set Environment dialog box one more time to make sure that it's pointing to your text document. Select Publish Settings in the File menu and make sure that Generator is checked in the Formats tab. This box is the equivalent to the Settings dialog box that you encountered in Generator. Ignore the rest of the Generator settings for this exercise. Click OK. Now, *save* the file! Choose File ➪ Publish Preview (F12) or use the Control ➪ Test Movie command. Behold . . . it worked.

Why does this work if you don't have the Generator Server on your local machine? As mentioned earlier in this chapter, when Flash publishes a .SWF file from a .FLA file with Generator Objects and variables, it will locate the data sources at the time of publishing and fill in the template where necessary. Therefore, you'll see the data source information in the actual .SWF file. Don't be fooled though. This isn't dynamic generation. If you change the info.txt to indicate new text, it will not show up in the .SWF file until you publish a new one from Flash 5.

To dynamically repopulate the text block with updated information, you'll need to upload the .SWT and info.txt files (with the same directory structure) to your Generator-enabled server. You've taken your first step on the dynamic road of Generator. In the next chapter, we explore some creative uses of Flash and Generator content.

Summary

✦ Creating Generator content is a two-part process: creating the template with the Generator authoring extensions in Flash 5, and serving the template with data-source information from your Generator-enabled Web server.

✦ Generator can dynamically update images, sounds, charts, and lists within single Flash movie. Generator can also render Flash content as a static .JPEG, .GIF, or .PNG image, as a .GIF imagemap or animation, or as a QuickTime Flash movie.

✦ There are two editions of Generator: Enterprise and Developer. The Enterprise Edition is designed (and priced) for large corporate Web sites that deliver personalized content to millions of visitors. The Developer Edition can deliver the same dynamic content that the Enterprise Edition can — just not as fast.

✦ Generator has two modes: online and offline. In online mode, Generator dynamically creates a custom .SWF file from a .SWT file and a data source each time the template is requested. In offline mode, Generator creates updated .SWF content on a scheduled basis, and uploads the files to the Web server, which delivers the .SWF content normally (not dynamically).

✦ You can set up a simple text file as the data source for a static Flash text block. Generator variables are enclosed in curly braces ({ }) in Flash text fields, Generator Panels, and Flash ActionScript.

✦   ✦   ✦

Revving Up Generator

I
In the last chapter, you learned what Generator is and when to use it. Now we explore how to use some Generator Objects to create more Generator Templates (.SWT files) to use with Generator Server. This chapter teaches you how to deploy several kinds of Generator Objects, including Charts, Lists, Scrolling Lists, Tickers, Tables, Multipage Lists, and MP3 sounds. We assume you are already read the previous chapter, and are able to deploy a simple text replacement object that calls data from a text file.

We would like to thank Christian Buchholz for the awesome insight he provided to us for this chapter. Christian also created an Expert Tutorial on Multipage List Objects.

An Overview of Data Representation

In our text replacement example from the last chapter, you learned that data can be represented in a text document (or as output from a server script or application) as `name, value`. With Generator variables and values, there are two methods of feeding data into Templates: Name/Value layout, and Column Name/Value layout.

Name/Value data

Specifying the variable's name and its value on the same line of the text file or output represents this type of data. Similar to Flash 5's URL-encoded variables (see Chapter 24, "Sending Data In and Out of Flash," for more information), the variable's name and value are declared side by side. The following URL form-encoded variables:

```
firstName=Derrick&lastName=Fullerton
```

or the Flash 5 ActionScript equivalent:

```
firstName = "Derrick";
lastName = "Fullerton";
```

would appear as:

```
name, value
firstName, Derrick
lastName, Fullerton
```

in a Generator data source.

This method of data representation is useful when you have nonrepeating variable names. If you had several firstName variables and lastName variables, then you would need to either number each variable (for example, firstName_1, firstName_2, and so on) or use a Column Name/Value data layout.

Column Name/Value data

The other type of data representation is Column Name/Value, in which the first text line describes the variable names, and each line of text thereafter becomes a unique instance with values. The line position and count determines the order and frequency of the data (respectively). You may have already guessed that this description sounds a lot like an Array Object in Flash 5.

The following Flash 5 Array Objects:

```
firstName = new Array("Derrick","Cathy","Alonzo","Sean");
lastName = new Array("Fullerton","Jones","Silver","Nicks");
```

could be represented in Column Name/Value form as:

```
firstName, lastName
Derrick, Fullerton
Cathy, Jones
Alonzo, Silver
Sean, Nicks
```

As you can see, Column Names enable you to quickly specify new values for the same data element. In the preceding example, we can very easily add new names to the Column Name/Value layout.

Generator can use both types of data representation. Some objects, such as the Chart Object, require the use of Column Name/Value layout. However, Generator text variables can use Name/Value layouts to dynamically insert data into Flash Text blocks and fields (as demonstrated in the last chapter).

The Chart Object

Generator offers several types of commonly used charts. Using the Chart Object, you can make an impression by displaying your data in a high-impact visual presentation — and you can do it quickly and easily.

Four different types of Chart Objects are included, each with two variations:

✦ Bar

✦ Line

✦ Area

✦ Scattered (not covered in this book)

Basic Charts, like most Generator Objects, need their own data source. However, charts have somewhat more complex Generator Panel settings than other types of objects. See Figure 28-1 for the options of the Basic Charts Object.

Figure 28-1: All Generator Objects are modified in the Generator Panel. The options in this panel will change according to the object type.

Before you decide which type of Basic Chart (Bar, Line, or Area) that you would like to create, you should analyze your data source and determine the outcome that you would like to achieve.

✦ **Bar Charts** are ideal for change in one data value over time. For example, you can use a Bar Chart to compare the number of products sold in each month over the course of a year. Because there is a discrete number of products sold and a definitive evaluation period (for example, the end of each month), we can make comparisons of monthly sales rather quickly with a Bar Chart. As a Generator Object, Bar Charts require a Value column in the data source. The value column specifies the relative height of the bar. In a Column Name/Value layout (specified in a simple text file), our Bar Chart variable names would be described as:

```
value, color, url
```

where `value` would indicate the bar's relative value, `color` would indicate that bar's color, and `url` would be the URL that the bar jumps to when it is clicked.

✦ **Line** and **Area Charts** can display growth data over extended periods of time, visually depicting minor fluctuations (or incremental changes). For example, you can plot the values of a stock's price over a week, month, or year with a Line or Area Chart, seeing general trends of increased stock activity. The properties of Line and Area Charts are similar to those of a Bar Chart but only require a Value Column to define the heights of the Line Chart. You can create multiple lines in a Line Chart by specifying more than one data source; separate each data source with a semicolon character (;), as in chart_1.txt; chart_2.txt;chart_3.txt, which will create three lines using these text files as data sources.

✦ **Stacked Bar**, **Stacked Lines**, and **Stacked Area** require a Color column as well as a series of Values columns (value1, value2, and so on). These types of charts can similar to multidimensional arrays, in that you can plot multiple values and multiple items within one data source. You can use a Stacked Bar Chart to compare your product sales to the sales of a competitor (for a given amount of time), or to compare the sales of one product line to those of another product.

The properties for Basic Charts can be found on pages 41–44 of the *Using Generator* manual that ships with the software. If you are using a trial version of Generator Server, then you can download the complete manual in PDF format from the Generator support area of the Macromedia site at `www.macromedia.com/support/generator`.

Some notable properties of Basic Chart Objects are:

✦ **Data Source:** All charts require a Column Name/Value data source, which specifies the value of each node (such as a bar or a point in a line) of the chart.

✦ **Plot Symbol:** Even before you could use `attachMovie` methods in Flash, Generator enabled you to specify a symbol in the Flash file's Library to use as the graphic for plotting points in a Scatter Chart.

✦ **Depth:** You can create 3D charts by specifying a depth amount. One unit of depth is equal to 1/20 of a pixel (20 depth units = 1 pixel). The depth property works on all charts except Scatter Charts.

✦ **External Symbol File:** Generator Chart Objects can use another external Generator Template, which contains the symbols to use for chart labels and values.

✦ **Instance Name:** You can give a Chart Object (and most Generator Objects) an instance name so that it can be targeted like a Movie Clip instance with ActionScript.

Unlike Lists, Tables, or Tickers, Bar Charts don't require any additional Movie Clips to define their layout. Bar Charts are generated completely from the values that you set inside the Generator Panel and the data source.

Creating a Bar Chart

With these properties in mind, let's create your first Bar Chart Template. In this lesson, you create a Bar Chart that graphs the populations of several major world cities. The data will be pulled from a simple text file.

1. Create a new directory on your local hard drive and name it **barchart**.

2. Inside this directory, create a second directory and call it **data**. When working with Generator, it is a good idea to keep all of your data files in one folder.

3. Open a text editor, such as Notepad in Windows or SimpleText on the Mac, and create a new plain text file.

4. Enter the following in the first line, noting the syntax:

   ```
   value, color, hlabel
   ```

5. Save this text file as **barchart.txt** inside your data directory.

6. Open Flash 5 and create a new file.

7. Select File ➪ Publish Settings, and check the Generator Template option in the Format tab.

Basic Charts can be exported as static image files, but they will lack the interactive capabilities of the .SWF format.

8. Open your Generator Objects tool window (Window ➪ Generator Objects) and drag a Basic Chart Object onto the Stage.

9. With the Chart Object selected, use the Arrow Tool with the Scale modifier to resize the Object to fill about two-thirds of the Stage. Chart Objects can be sized as needed.

Tip If you would prefer to have your Bar Chart aligned horizontally instead of vertically, simply rotate the object 90 degrees clockwise and change the Horizontal Label Orientation in the Generator Panel to Vertical.

10. Double-click the Chart Object to open the Generator Panel. Set the properties to those listed in Figure 28-2. Make sure you correctly set the data source as data/barchart.txt.

Figure 28-2: You can control the look and feel of your Bar Chart Object in the Generator Panel.

11. Save the .FLA file in the barchart directory.

12. Open your text file and fill in the following data. Be sure to type in the syntax exactly:

```
COLOR, HLABEL, VALUE
#ffcc33, "Sydney", 3.71
#33ff00, "New York", 7.33
#00c9ff, "London", 6.96
#ff6633, "Berlin", 3.47
#ff3399, "Tokyo", 8.12
```

You can designate color values with hexadecimal code or by name (Red, Green, and so on). Values must be numeric; any other values will be ignored and result in an error.

13. Save barchart.txt in the data folder.

14. Return to Flash and test the movie (Control ⇨ Test Movie). Your results should resemble the Chart shown in Figure 28-3.

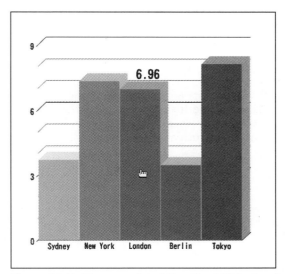

Figure 28-3: The completed Bar Chart Object as it appears in a generated .SWF file.

You can experiment with other color values and use the Depth control in the Generator Panel to customize the look of your Chart.

Lists and Tickers

Since Flash 4, developers have been able to create dynamic scrolling lists via the loadVariables() action, which loads variables from text files. Why, then, should anyone use Generator to create Lists, Scrolling Lists, or Tickers?

First, Generator creates lists and tickers from databases or text files on the server side, rather than on the client side, which the loadVariables() action does. More importantly, Generator provides superior designing and formatting of lists and tickers, as it enables you to create dynamic links and insert images.

Using Generator Variables as Property Values

You can set your absolute values for Chart Objects (as well as other Objects) in as Generator variables and call them in a separate global text data source. For example, in our previous Bar Chart example, you could set the Max Y-Pos Type to Absolute instead of Relative Percent. Then, for the Max Y-Pos property, you could use the value:

```
{max_ypos}
```

which specifies a Generator variable named max_ypos for the maximum Y position in the Bar Chart Object. In a separate text file, you can then set the maximum Y position value in a Name/Value layout. Be sure to add an appropriate buffer to the maximum data value for the Bar Chart Object so that the data can be framed nicely. This buffer value will vary depending on the data. For our Bar Chart example, our largest value is 8.31. Our maximum Y position value should be something higher, such as 10. So, the global text data source file would read:

```
Name,value
max_ypos, 10
```

You can use this technique for any value in the Bar Chart properties listed in the Generator Panel. In general, it is a good way to set data dynamically within any Generator Object. Don't forget to refer to this data source in the Set Environment dialog, which is accessed by clicking the Generator icon at the top-right corner of your Timeline window.

Now that we've got your attention, let's have a look how List and Ticker Objects are built. Generator can create four different list types:

✦ **List** (a basic list)

✦ **Scrolling List** (a scrollable list)

✦ **Multipage List** (a manageable series of pages for large list data)

✦ **Ticker** (a scrolling list that continuously loops)

For the most part, all four List types share the same property settings in the Generator Panel. The only difference is that there is an additional field in the Scrolling List, shown in Figure 28-4, and the Ticker called Step Size.

How do List and Ticker Objects work? Generator preconfigures a custom Movie Clip instance that builds itself from the data in the data source. You don't have to worry about spending time developing buttons and ActionScript to control movement of list content!

.SWF versus .SWT Files

For each of these examples (and our previous ones), you will publish both .SWF and .SWT files. You only need to upload the .SWT to your Generator-enabled server for live production use. Flash "generates" a .SWF at the time of publishing so that you can preview the data source as it will be formatted from the .SWT file. As we stated earlier, though, you can use this static .SWF file for use on your Web server, even if Generator is not installed there. However, changes to your data source will not be reflected in the static .SWF file — only the Generator Server will build customized .SWF files on the fly from a data source.

Figure 28-4: Properties for the Scrolling List Object

Basic Lists

In this tutorial, you create a Generator List Object. Unlike a Flash 5 ActionScript-driven list that would need to use `loadVariables()` to bring in dynamic content, we see how Generator can build the list from a predefined data source and serve it to the user without waiting for a `loadVariables()` action to finish. We start by creating a data source, and then building the List Object in our Generator Template.

1. Create a new directory (folder) on your local hard drive and name it **list**.

2. Inside this directory, create another directory and name it **data**.

3. Next, let's create a data source for your list. Open a text editor, create a new text file, and save this text file as **basicList.txt** inside the data folder.

4. The only defined value you need inside this text file is the variable name `clip`. The `clip` variable defines the symbol name that you want to use for a given item in the list. This symbol can contain graphics and text that you want to appear for each item in the list. Give all of the other variables meaningful names to help yourself remember them. For now, let's use the following structure:

```
clip, header, textvalue, url
```

Besides the required `clip` variable, we'll also use three more variables, all of which will need to be reflected inside your Movie Clip symbol (defined by the `clip` variable).

5. Save the text file in the data folder, and create a new Flash movie file in Flash 5. Save the .FLA file in the list folder.

6. As always, be sure to enable the Generator Template format in the Publish Settings dialog. Usually, this format is automatically checked as soon as you add a Generator Object to a Flash movie, but it's always a good idea to check the Publish Settings.

7. Drag the List Object from the Generator Object tool window to the Stage. Select the Object, and use the Arrow Tool with the Scale modifier to resize the List Object so that it is nearly as tall as the Stage and about 210 pixels wide.

Tip   If you decide to change the List type later in the project, you can retain the original shape and location of the initial List Object by simply changing the List Object type in the drop-down menu at the top of the Generator Panel. You will need to assign a new data source (and possibly other properties).

8. Next, we prepare the format of the list, as it will be displayed in the Flash movie. We need to create a Movie Clip to use within the List Object. Choose Insert ➪ New Symbol, name it **clip_1** and leave the Symbol behavior at the default Movie Clip. Generally, you can give your clips any name you like, but you should use meaningful names, so that you can remember to refer back to them in your data source text file.

9. With the clip_1 Movie Clip open in Symbol Editing Mode, type the following in two separate text fields, making sure that the first variable, `header`, is bold:

```
{header}
{textvalue}
```

Set the text location below and to the right of the center point. This way, when you align your symbol, you don't need to change the default value in the Generator Panel. Notice also that the more space you leave between the center point and the first line of text, the more space that you have between your first list item and the top. It is also a good habit to set the width of the text field to the width of your list (see Figure 28-5), so that Generator does not wrap the text to the next line.

Notice that you are essentially doing the same task here that you did in the text-replacement exercise from the previous chapter, except that you are placing the variables in a Movie Clip symbol, rather than on the Main Timeline.

Two of the three variables in our text file data source have been added to the clip_1 Movie Clip symbol. The last one, `url`, will be used in the actions of a Button instance described in the next section.

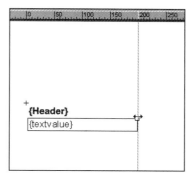

Figure 28-5: In Flash 5, you can drag a guide to the X axis at 210 pixels, because this is the width of our List Object on the Main Timeline. Make sure each text field area extends to this guide.

Now we add another level of sophistication, so that you can really see what Generator can do. We are going to add an invisible Button instance to our Movie Clip. This button will contain ActionScript that will reference the url Generator variable. Technically, this can be done with ActionScript and the loadVariables() action — however, unlike loadVariables(), we won't have to make sure the data has loaded before we can use it. Because Generator delivers the Flash .SWF file with everything already in it, we won't have to wait for any additional data to be delivered.

Strictly speaking, invisible Buttons are not needed for List Objects in Generator. Also, if you want to create buttons for the text, complete with rollover states, you could do that as well. For this example, we use the invisible Button to link to a new URL.

10. Create a new Button symbol (Ctrl+F8 or Command+F8) and name it **invisibleButton**.

11. Insert a keyframe in the Hit frame.

12. Draw a rectangle shape approximately 200 pixels wide and 50 pixels high on the Stage. Use the Info Panel to size up the shape.

13. Open the clip_1 Movie Clip in Symbol Editing Mode.

14. Create a new layer, and move it to the bottom of the stack. Name this layer **button**.

15. Drag an instance of the invisibleButton symbol onto the Stage and place it directly on top of the {header} variable text block. Scale the button so that it is the same height as the {header} variable text block (see Figure 28-6).

16. Select the Button instance and open the Actions Panel.

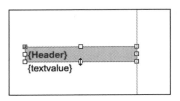

Figure 28-6: Cover the entire {header} text block with the invisibleButton instance, scaling as necessary to make it fit.

17. To create a dynamic URL link, you need to set a Generator variable inside your ActionScript. This is where we will use the url variable from our data source text file. Add the following ActionScript to the Button instance:

```
on(release){
     getURL ("{url}", "_blank");
}
```

Caution You must always use quotation marks for Generator variables in ActionScript, even if you use an expression; otherwise, Generator will not be able to recognize these values as Generator Variables and the ActionScript editor will report an error.

You can also use window and method as Generator variables in the same way that you use the url variable. You only need to add these Name/Values to your text file, such as:

```
clip, header, textvalue, url, window, method
```

and the ActionScript would appear as:

```
on(release){
     getURL ("{url}","{window}","{method}");
}
```

Now we are ready to move beyond what loadVariables() lists are capable of producing.

18. Select the clip_1 Movie Clip symbol in the Library, and choose Duplicate from the Options menu, located at the top right corner of the Library window. Name this new duplicate symbol **clip_2**.

19. Delete the {header} text block and the invisibleButton instance, but keep the {textvalue} text block.

20. Return to the Main Timeline (Scene 1), select the List Object, and open the Generator Panel.

21. In the Data Source field, define your data by either browsing to the local folder where your text file is located, or by typing the relative path:

```
data/basicList.txt
```

22. In the Orientation field, define the direction of your List by selecting Vertical (top to the bottom).

23. The Mask to Box option lets you define whether your List should be masked. Usually you leave it set to true, unless you want your list to expand beyond the defined space. For this example, leave it set to true.

24. Spacing can be either Fixed or Automatic. When Fixed, each clip takes the amount of space in pixels you define in the Item space field. If spacing is set to Automatic, it will take as much space as the clip needs from your data source. For this exercise, set this option to Fixed.

25. Item Space specifies the amount in pixels between clips. Enter **40**.

26. The Horizontal and Vertical Alignment options define how the clip should be aligned inside the list area. Items are always aligned on the center point of the Movie Clip. Leave the options at the default Left and Top, respectively.

27. Instance Name identifies the object so it can be used with Actions such as with() and print(). Name this instance **basicList**.

Tip   Always use instance names so that you are able to identify your Generator Objects in ActionScript.

After setting all the values for your Basic List, you should have object properties identical to Figure 28-7.

Figure 28-7: These List values will properly format our Basic List Object.

28. The .FLA file is ready, but we don't yet have any values in the data source! Open your data source text file and enter the following values:

```
clip, header, textvalue, url
clip_1, "Your Header1", "Insert text1", "http://url1.com"
clip_2, "Your Header2", "Insert text2", "http://url2.com"
clip_1, "Your Header3", "Insert text3", "http://url3.com"
```

You might be curious as to why we are reusing clip_1. One advantage of Generator Lists is that you can reuse clips inside your Template as many times you like and fill it with different information. If you test your Flash movie, you will see that the first line in your list has the same look and feel like the as the third one.

Tip You can create and reuse an entire library of clips with different appearances, Buttons or other symbols, and you can use every one of them or just a specific clip, depending how you want your List to appear in your .SWF. This is especially advantageous if you have a long scrolling list (such as a list of player statistics for a sports team) and you want to customize certain sections. If your text is larger than the given text field, it will wrap itself to the next line. Generator will move the following clip appropriately to make room.

If you have a clip that does not contain one of the variables (in our case `header` or `url`), your data source would look like this:

```
clip, header, textvalue, url
clip_1, "Your Header1","Your text1","http://url1.com"
clip_2," ","Your text2"," "
clip_1,"Your Header3","Your text3","http://url3.com"
```

You still need to account for the general data source, but you can leave these fields empty and they will be ignored.

As you will see, the value of using Basic Lists in Generator over Scrolling Lists that use `loadVariables()` in normal Flash movies is that you can build custom graphics and formatting for each item in the list. In this way, you can make items belong to category types, and assign the appropriate category formatting to each item in the list.

Note It is entirely possible to use the new Flash movie `attachMovie` method, combined with `loadVariables()`, to dynamically build custom item types in a list. However, this method is very time intensive. Furthermore, you can't dynamically insert .JPEG images (or other bitmap formats) into regular Flash movies. With Generator, you could insert a .JPEG Object into a Movie Clip symbol that is used for the list item.

Scrolling Lists

Now that you know how Column Name/Value layouts work with Basic Lists, let's move on to Scrolling Lists. Of course, the primary difference between a Basic List and a Scrolling List is that a Basic List has a finite length (the size of the List Object on the Stage), whereas a Scrolling List can continue indefinitely past the frame of the List Object. By using scroll buttons, we can navigate the items in the list.

To make a Scrolling List, the steps are similar to the Basic List procedure, with a few exceptions:

✦ Choose Scrolling List, rather than Basic List from the Generator Object Panel.

✦ The Scrolling List has an additional parameter, Step Size, that you need to set in the Generator Panel.

✦ Scrolling Lists require an additional Button symbol instance that controls the scrolling of the list items.

To add scrolling functionality to a Scrolling List Object:

1. Drag a Scrolling List Object from the Generator Objects tool window to the Stage. Set up a data source text file in the same manner as the Basic List data source. Set the other object properties in the Generator Panel so that they resemble those of the Basic List from the previous section. Create Movie Clip instances that contain the formatting (and interactive functionality) for each list item.

2. Create a new Button symbol containing artwork of an arrow pointing down, and place two instances of it on the Stage. Rotate one of the instances so that it points up. These Buttons will target the Scrolling List Object, thus enabling the scrolling function.

3. Position the Button instances next to the Scrolling List Object on the Stage.

4. In the Generator Panel, name the Scrolling List instance **scroll_down**.

5. To create a simple Scrolling List, highlight the Button instance with the arrow pointing down, and open your Actions Panel. Add the following script:

For Flash 5 compatibility:

```
on (release) {
    with (scroll_down) {
        nextFrame();
    }
}
```

For Flash 4 compatibility:

```
on(release){
    tellTarget("scroll_down"){
        nextFrame();
    }
}
```

You now have a down button for your Scrolling List.

Caution

The `with()` action is only understood by Flash 5 player and higher! If you develop for Flash 4, use `tellTarget()` instead.

6. Select the Button instance with the arrow pointing up, and, in the Actions Panel, modify the ActionScript so that it reads as follows:

For Flash 5:

```
on (release) {
    with(scroll_down) {
        prevFrame ();
    }
}
```

For Flash 4:

```
on(release){
     tellTarget("scroll_down"){
          prevFrame();
     }
}
```

You now have up and down Buttons for your Scrolling List.

Tip You can create any scrolling functionality depending on your level of expertise in ActionScript, but you must always refer to the Scrolling List's instance name.

Tickers

Ticker Objects work the same as Scrolling Lists, with these differences:

✦ Tickers play as a continuous loop. Therefore, they do not need buttons.

✦ Select the Ticker Object from the Generator Objects tool window, rather than from the Scrolling List Object.

Otherwise, you can use the same settings for the Ticker and the Scrolling List. The formatting for their data sources is identical as well.

Expert Tutorial: Using the Multipage List Object, by Christian Buchholz

Christian supplied much of the information for this chapter. In this tutorial, you learn to use the new Multipage List Object that was introduced with Flash 5 and Generator Server 2 release 2.

The Multipage List Object has been introduced along with the Radio Button Object with the latest version of Generator. To use these objects in a Template or to serve them from your Web server, you need the Developer's Edition or Enterprise Edition installed on your server.

How does a Multipage List differ from other Lists? A Multipage List Object creates a series of pages in order to display a large list of data that you can browse with forward, backward, and home buttons. An example could be the player statistics of a soccer team, where each player is displayed in a separate window. To avoid creating each player one at a time, you use the Multipage Object.

In this tutorial, we create a Multipage List Object in a Flash movie.

1. Create a new folder named **multipage** on your local hard drive, and make another folder called **data** inside of the multipage folder. Again, the data folder will store all of your data source files and .SWT Template files.

2. Like the Basic, Scrolling, and Ticker Objects described in previous sections, the Multipage Object needs its own data source to function properly. However, the structure of this data source is more expansive. Create a new text file called **multiList.txt** and type the following Column Names:

text, symbol, channel, show, times, description, image

Instead of a `clip` column used in the other lists, the Multipage List needs a `text` column. You can also add `url`, `window`, and `symbol` as column name variables. The `url` variable would define the URL to be loaded when you click an item in the Multipage List, just like in our example in the Basic List. The `window` variable targets an HTML window name (`_target`, `_blank`, `_self`) into which the URL will load.

3. Save your text file as **multiList.txt** inside the data folder.

4. Open Flash and create a new Flash movie. Be sure that your Publish Settings have the Generator Template format enabled, and save the .FLA file in the multilist folder.

5. Open the Generator Object tool window (Window ➪ Generator Objects) and drag the Multipage List Object to the Stage. It is not necessary to change the size of the Multipage Object — if you change the size you will get strange layout results, so for now, just leave the size of the Generator Object at its default.

The next steps create the several items that you want to see inside your Multipage List.

6. Create a new Movie Clip symbol and name it **info**.

7. In Symbol Editing Mode, create two Generator text variables in Flash text blocks, placing the text blocks just below and to the right of the symbol's registration point. As you may recall, these variables are referenced in your data source text file:

```
{times}
{description}
```

8. Create a second Movie Clip symbol and name it **header**.

9. On the `header` timeline, add the following variables, positioned just below and to the right of the center point:

```
{channel}
{show}
```

10. Drag an Insert JPEG File Object into the `header` timeline, and position it below the two variables.

11. Double-click the .JPEG Object, and the Generator Panel opens. Set the .JPEG Object's data source value to:

```
{image}
```

Continued

Continued

12. For this example, you should place several small .JPEG files (around 200×200 pixels) into your data folder. The data source text file (multiList.txt) should have values for the `image` column that indicate the path to the image file(s):

```
data/image1.jpg
```

Author's Note: You can specify images that reside on your Web server, or on any other remote server. This is a very powerful feature of Generator Image Objects. If you need to use material from a separate server (one that doesn't hold the .SWT files), you can have Generator fetch the image file and place it in the Template.

You should now have two symbols in your Flash Library: `info` and `header`. Just like the List Objects, we don't need to physically place any instances of these symbols on the Main Timeline of our Flash movie. The Multipage List Object will grab these symbols from the Library automatically (because we'll specify them in the data source), just like `attachMovie` can grab Movie Clips from the Library. Unlike the use of `attachMovie`, Generator does not use or refer to the Linkage identifier name. Generator uses the name of the symbol in the Library.

13. Return to the Main Timeline, and select the Multipage List Object. In the Generator Panel, set the Data Source, Items Per Page, Text Symbol, and Instance Name values to match those of the following figure. Use the default values for the remaining properties. For a description of all Multi-List Object properties, please refer to the *Using Generator* manual, pages 36–38.

The default color for the prebuilt Home, Next, and Previous buttons is black. If you use a black background color for your Flash movie, you should build your own custom buttons, and specify the symbol names as the values of the Home symbol, Next symbol, and Previous symbol properties in the Generator Panel. You can even store these symbols in another .SWT file. If you do this, then specify that .SWT's path and filename as the value of the External Symbol File property.

The Home, Next, and Previous buttons for the Multipage List object will always display at the top-left corner of your list. You cannot change the location of these buttons.

14. Now, we need to specify some information in our data source text file. Open multiList.txt and enter the following information (Note: The ¬ indicates a continuation of the same line of text. Do not insert this character into your actual text.):

```
text, symbol, channel, show, times, description, image
, header, CH 1, Movie_1, 4:15 PM, A movie about ¬
Nothing, data/image1.jpg
, header, CH 2, Movie_2, 6:15 PM, A movie about ¬
Something, data/image2.jpg
, header, CH 3, Movie_3, 8:15 PM, A movie about ¬
Everything, data/image3.jpg
```

You might be wondering about the comma that starts each item entry in the text file. This comma, shown before the header symbol, is a placeholder for the text column variable. Because we specified the `info` symbol as the value of our Text Symbol property in the Generator Panel, we do not need to specify one here. However, you could define a different Text Symbol for each item entry in the data source.

15. Save your text file and your Flash movie (.FLA file). Then, test the movie. The .SWF file that you see will have a list with multiple pages.

At this point, you may want to go back and adjust the formatting within the `info` and `header` Movie Clip symbols. You can also adjust the .JPEG Image Object formatting to suit your needs, or even add more JPEG (or other format) Image Objects.

Christian Buchholz was born in Moscow, Russia, and then grew up in East Germany. After the wall came down, he moved to Munich, where he studied ballet for nine years and then spent three years in photography and advertising. Christian came of age when *Basic Instinct* was the top film. He says, "Flash is my tool of choice to create highly interactive, elegant Web sites." A few of these sites are www.elle.com.au, www.toyota.com.au, www.news.com.au, and www.bromide73.com. Christian now lives in Sydney, Australia. His favorite pastime is cooking.

Using Generator Templates in Production

So far, you have learned how to create Generator Templates and preview their look and feel by viewing the static .SWF file that Flash 5 creates for you. We have not discussed how to actually implement .SWT files into a live production environment. In this section, you learn to use Generator Templates in HTML and in other Flash movies.

Publishing Generator Templates (.SWT files)

If you add a Generator Object or set a Generator environment variable, then a Generator Template (.SWT file) will automatically be created whenever you publish your Flash movie. If you are using dynamic graphics or data sources, then you will need to publish a .SWT file and upload it to your Generator Server. You can select a Generator Template file in the Publish Settings dialog (File ⇨ Publish Settings), and define its settings in the Generator tab. Most of these settings mirror those found in the Flash format tab of the Publish Settings dialog and the Movie Properties (Modify ⇨ Movie) dialog.

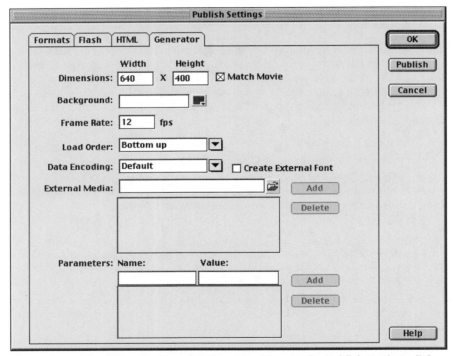

Figure 28-8: The Generator Template format settings in the Publish Settings dialog.

Dimensions

You can specify the width and height (in pixels) of the Flash movie that will be created from the Generator Template. If Match Movie is checked (the default), then the width and height will reflect the current settings in the Movie Properties dialog (Modify ⇨ Movie).

Background

This option enables you to enter a hexadecimal value for color, or select a color from the pop-up color chip menu. Note that you can also type Web-safe color names into this field, such as blue, black, or white.

Frame Rate

In this field, you can enter a frame rate that differs from the setting in the Movie Properties dialog. The frame rate controls how fast the Flash movie is played. The higher the frame rate, the faster the movie plays.

Load Order

This option controls how the layers in a Flash movie load into the Flash Player. The default setting, Bottom up, loads the lowest layer first and progressively loads higher layers. You can also choose Top down, which loads the highest layer first and then progressively loads lower layers.

Data Encoding

From this drop-down menu, you can select the data encoding method used for your Generator data sources. The Default option uses the data encoding for the operating system with which you are using the Flash authoring application. Most data sources use ASCII encoding (the standard encoding for Windows and UNIX text). If you're using the Mac version of Flash, the Default option is the same as selecting MacRoman encoding. UTF8 is version of Unicode encoding, and is used by many applications. SJIS (a Japanese character encoding) and EUC_JP (Extended UNIX Code for Japanese) are available for data sources that use Japanese text.

Create External Font

This check box creates .FFT files with your published Generator Template (.SWT file). Each typeface (font) that you use in Static, Dynamic, or Input Text will be saved in a separate file. These font files should be in the same directory as the .SWT file on the Generator-enabled Web server. If you use Generator variables in Flash text, then you should always create external font files.

External Media

With this setting, you can choose one or more .SWT files, whose symbols can be referenced by the current Flash movie you are authoring. By linking to external media in other .SWT files, you can create custom symbols in Flash template "libraries" and use those symbols in multiple Generator Templates.

Parameters

You can test Generator environment variables by adding them in the Parameters area of the Generator tab. Type the variable's name and value into the provided text fields, and click the Add button. When you publish the .SWT file, the accompanying

.SWF file will show the Generator variable in use, as if a live Generator Server served it. Note that you should only use these area of the Generator tab to test Generator environment variables — use standard data sources for live Web delivery.

Using Generator Templates in HTML

Quite simply, you refer to Generator Templates in HTML `<EMBED>` and `<OBJECT>` tags just as you would any other .SWF file. We discuss integration of Flash movies and HTML in Chapter 41, "Integrating Flash Content with HTML.". You can also use the HTML templates in Flash 5 to automatically publish the HTML required to use a Generator Template.

New Feature   Flash 5 has added four HTML templates specifically for Generator Templates: Generator Ad Any Banner (for dynamic ad serving), Generator Image Output (for static .JPEG, .GIF, or .PNG images), Generator Only (Default) (for straight template use), and Generator QuickTime (to serve QuickTime Flash movie versions of your Generator Template). We discuss this template in Chapter 40, "Publishing Flash Movies."

To create an HTML document that uses the Generator Template (.SWT file), follow these steps:

1. Open the Publish Settings dialog, and check HTML in the Format tab.

2. In the HTML tab, choose Generator Only (Default) in the Template drop-down menu. Also, if you want the returned Flash .SWF to scale to fill the Web browser window, then select Percent in the Dimensions drop-down menu. The width and height values automatically change to 100 percent.

3. Click the Publish button in the Publish Settings dialog. Flash publishes three files: the .SWF file, the .SWT file, and the HTML file. You only need to upload the .SWT and HTML files to your Generator-enabled Web server.

If you open the HTML document that Flash 5 publishes for you, you'll notice that it refers to the .SWT file instead of the .SWF file (the formatting of the following code has been modified to fit this page; the ¬ character denotes a continuation of the same line of text):

```
<OBJECT
    classid="clsid:D27CDB6E-AE6D-11cf-96B8-444553540000"
    codebase="http://download.macromedia.com/pub/¬
        shockwave/cabs/flash/swflash.cab#version=5,0,0,0"
    WIDTH=100% HEIGHT=100%>
    <PARAM NAME=movie VALUE="basicList.swt?type=swf">
    <PARAM NAME=quality VALUE=high>
        <EMBED src="basicList.swt?type=swf"
            quality=high
            WIDTH=100% HEIGHT=100%
            TYPE="application/x-shockwave-flash"
            PLUGINSPAGE="http://www.macromedia.com/¬
```

```
                    shockwave/download/index.cgi?¬
                    P1_Prod_Version=ShockwaveFlash">
              </EMBED>
        </OBJECT>
```

You'll see that Flash also inserts a query string (a question mark followed by URL form-encoded text) after the .SWT file name, as in:

```
basicList.swt?type=swf
```

The `?type=swf` is the query string appended to the Generator Template name. When the Generator Server receives the request for the basicList.swt Template file, it will see the `type=swf` string. It then returns a .SWF format file to the Web browser. The types are:

- ✦ **type=swf**, which returns a .SWF file.

- ✦ **type=jpg**, which returns a .JPEG image. Use an <IMG> HTML tag instead of an `<OBJECT>` or `<EMBED>` tag, with the Generator Template listed as the value of the SRC attribute. If you choose the Generator Image Output Template in the HTML tab of Publish Settings, then Flash will automatically create the appropriate HTML formatting.

- ✦ **type=gif**, which returns a .GIF image. See the preceding .JPEG description.

- ✦ **type=png**, which returns a .PNG image. See the preceding .JPEG description.

- ✦ **type=mov**, which delivers a QuickTime Flash movie to the Web browser. If you use this query string manually, then make sure that you use the `<EMBED>` tag to call the .SWT template file. The Generator QuickTime HTML Template automatically creates the appropriate formatting for you.

Caution Because Generator uses the type variable for content creation, do not use type as variable in your Generator Templates unless you want to show the content type in a text block.

Using Generator Templates in other Flash movies

You can also load Generator Templates into other Flash .SWF files. You don't actually even download the .SWF file itself (as mentioned earlier) — Generator creates a .SWF file from the .SWT request, and delivers that new .SWF file to the Web browser or the Flash movie that requested it.

As you learned in Part V of the *Flash 5 Bible*, you can use the `loadMovie()` action to incorporate other .SWF files into a "master" .SWF file. Likewise, you can load Generator content into any Flash movie, such as:

```
loadMovie("basicList.swt", "movieHolder");
```

which loads the .SWF output from the basicList.swt file into the Movie Clip instance named `movieHolder`.

And just as you can pass variables with HTML to Generator Templates, you can send establish data sources directly in Flash movies with the `loadMovie()` action:

```
firstName = "Robert";
loadMovie("welcome.swt", "movieHolder", "GET");
```

This sends the following query string to our Generator Server:

```
welcome.swt?firstName=Robert
```

You may recall from our earlier discussions in Chapter 24, "Sending Data In and Out of Flash," that the `GET` method appends Name/Value pairs to the end of the requested URL. You could also send a Generator data source as:

```
firstName = "Robert";
loadMovie("welcome.swt?firstName=" + firstName, "movieHolder");
```

which omits the `GET` option from the `loadMovie()` action. Because the variable is declared in the actual URL option, we do need to have Flash add the query string for us. This method is useful if you only want to send specific variables on the current Flash timeline. The previous `loadMovie()` method would send any and all Flash variables declared on the current timeline.

You can try this `loadMovie()` method with a Generator Template that uses an MP3 Object. In the Generator Template file, select the MP3 Object and, in the Generator Panel, set its Data Source to `{soundURL}`. Save the Flash file (.FLA file) and publish a .SWT file (for example, `mp3.swt`). Then, in a separate Flash movie (a .FLA file) — one in which you want to load the Generator Template — add the following actions on a keyframe or Button instance:

```
soundURL = "/data/sound_1.mp3";
loadMovie("mp3.swt?soundURL=" + soundURL, "movieHolder");
```

Make sure that you have a Movie Clip instance named `movieHolder` on the current timeline. When these actions are executed in the Flash movie, a request will be made for the Generator Template called mp3.swt. Generator will see the `soundURL` string, and fill in the Data Source for the MP3 Object in the mp3.swt file. It will retrieve the MP3 file named sound_1.mp3 in the data folder on the server, and return a custom .SWF to the `movieHolder` instance in the original .SWF file.

The next expert tutorial by premiere Generator expert Mike Jones shows you another way to use `loadMovie` actions in a Flash movie, so that you can load images from your Webcam.

Expert Tutorial: Flash, Generator, and Webcams, *by Mike Jones*

In this tutorial, we look at extending Flash into the real world by connecting Flash via Generator to a Webcam. Participation in this tutorial assumes that you have access to a Generator Web server as well as having the Generator authoring extensions installed in Flash. Before we get started, there are two questions to answer. First, what type of Webcam? Second, what type of server?

The Webcam used in this tutorial is a Logitech Quickcam Pro (USB version). You can run this on Windows 95, Windows 98, and Windows 2000. (To run this Webcam in Windows 2000, you need to download the latest drivers from the Logitech site.) Unfortunately, this Webcam does not run on Macs. Of course, you don't have to use this particular Webcam—this is just the model used here. Your Webcam only needs to be capable of uploading an image to a Web server without incrementing the image file name.

The Web server needs to have FTP access—as this is how this particular Webcam uploads the images, even if they are on one and the same machine. Sadly, this rules out Windows 95 and 98, because these only come with a cut down "Personal Web Server—PWS," which has no FTP capabilities. This means that you need access to an NT or 2000 Web Server on Windows or an Apache Server on Linux. Finally, your Webcam server doesn't have to be the same server as your Generator Server—although that will make the job easier because of upload/download times.

Enter the Webcam

OK, with the preliminaries covered, let's get down to the nitty-gritty. First we discuss setting up the Webcam to broadcast to the Web server. We won't discuss installing and setting up the Webcam on your machine, because the manufacturer's manual should cover this! If you're using the Logitech Quickcam Pro (USB version), then you can follow this directly; otherwise, you have to ad lib, although the process will be similar.

1. Start up the Webcam software.

2. Select Create a Webcam from the icons on the menu bar. You should now have two windows in the main window area:

3. The left-hand pane is the Webcam's live view. The right-hand pane displays status information for the Webcam, or what the Webcam is currently doing.

4. Starting with the left pane, we need to set how we want the images captured. To do this, locate the Settings button, which you'll find at the bottom right, next to the large Start button. Press the Settings button.

5. A dialog opens with four tabs across the top: Web Page, Image, Schedule, and General. Ignore the General tab, because we only deal with the first three.

Continued

Continued

6. First, click the Web Page tab and then deselect Create and Upload a Web page. . . . Next, click the Image tab to access optional settings to drop the image quality in order to up the compression — the choice is yours. However, I do recommend that you leave the Image filename as Image.jpg.

7. Now we need to set how long the Webcam waits between each image it snaps. To do this, click the Schedule tab. Again, this is somewhat optional — although for this tutorial we set it to five seconds.

8. Click OK at the bottom of the Settings dialog to apply these settings.

So, now we've nearly finished adjusting the capture settings. All we have left is to set the resolution of the image that will be captured. To do this, find the little camera icon on the left hand, Webcam Live View, pane — it's located just above the Settings button. On this particular Webcam we have the choice of three sizes:

✦ Small: 160×120

✦ Medium: 320×240

✦ Large: 640×480

I recommend either small or medium for optimal upload/download speeds. The rest of the information on this panel can be ignored.

Webcam to Web server

Now we set the server details for the Webcam and then we can begin in Flash. Still in the Webcam's main window, we click another button named Settings — note, however, that this one is located in the status bar area of the Webcam's main window. The first setting to sort out is the connection from this machine to the Web. Select Internet Connection from the drop-down, which has two connection options: Modem and LAN.

Choose the one relevant to your connection and click OK. Now, the final task is to set the Web server information. In the Status pane, under the Web account drop-down, is an option for Internet Connection. Once this dialog opens, you have three text fields to fill in: FTP, HTTP, and Optional directory folder.

✦ FTP: This is where you enter the FTP settings of the Web server where you want to upload the captured image files (for example, ftp.myserver.com). So, enter the relevant details here. You will be prompted for a username and password to access this.

✦ HTTP: This is the URL, plus directory extension, that the FTP settings are mapped to (for example, http://www.myserver.com/mydirectory).

✦ Optional directory/folder: Use this if you have a specific directory in which you want to place your images. We'll leave it blank.

Finally, before we click OK, we need to test the connection to check that it works. So, press the Test button — if you are using a dialup connection, make sure that you are connected first. If all goes according to plan, the Webcam will connect via the FTP settings and within moments you should see both a smiley and the successful message. With that success, we are done with the Webcam for the moment. (If it fails to connect, review the preceding steps to ascertain at which point the failure occurred; the error dialog should assist you here.)

Loading it into Flash

Open Flash because it's time to start making the files that we will place on our Generator Web server. We will create two files for our Flash element:

✦ The *holding* file — this is the Flash interface and will be used to load in the generated .SWF's

✦ The *image* loader — this is the Generator Template into which the captured images will be placed

The holding movie

Open a new Flash file, and create four layers and name them, in order, from top to bottom: **Graphics**, **Variables**, **Actions**, and **Labels**. After you have created and named the four layers, save the file! As a working procedure, I cannot over emphasize the importance of this: Every time you alter your file, save it incrementally. That way, if we ever have a problem, or if Flash crashes, you won't lose anything more than the latest update. So, save it now and call it **flashcam_01.fla** — and increment the file with each subsequent save. Why increment? Because sometimes a version will corrupt; if you have a prior increment, you only lose a small amount of work, rather than all of your work. Next from Modify ⇨ Movie, in the Movie Properties dialog, set your initial movie settings to:

✦ Frame rate — 12 fps

✦ Stage Size — 800 × 600

Now with your file set up, we can get started.

1. There should only be one frame in timeline.

2. Unlock the Label layer and lock the rest. Then put a label in the first frame called **default**.

3. Lock the other layer and unlock the Variables layer, set a variable and call it **image_num**. Give it the value of **1**.

4. Follow the same process for the Actions layer and place a `Stop()` action in its first frame.

5. Lock all layers but the Graphics layer. On this layer, draw a rectangle with the dimensions: Width 320 × Height 240, use the Info Panel to get the dimensions exact.

Continued

Continued

6. With the rectangle selected, use the Info Panel to place the rectangle at these coordinates: x = 400, y = 300.

7. This rectangle will form the basis of our window interface, so we need to turn it into a symbol. Do that now, just remember to name it something meaningful — I suggest **Cam Interface**.

8. Set this symbol's behavior to Movie Clip and then, if isn't still selected, select it on the stage again.

9. With this instance of the Cam Interface Movie Clip selected, open the Actions Panel and add the following actions:

```
onClipEvent (load) {
    loadMovie ("image_" + _root.image_num + ".swt", 1);
}
```

This will act as our initial `loadMovie` call to load the first Movie Clip — we needn't create the string via concatenation, as we could have just typed in `loadmovie n.swf`, but by doing it this way, we are immediately using our `image_num` variable.

10. Save the file. Now the loader is done, so we are well on the way to getting this working!

11. Export the .SWF to a file called flashcam.swf and place it in a folder ready to upload to your Web server/Generator Server once you have finished creating the .SWT's.

The Image Loader

For the Image Loader, we need to follow the same initial setup as for the Holding Movie. So, create four layers and name them, in order, from top to bottom: **Graphics**, **Variables**, **Actions**, and **Labels**. After you have created and named the four layers, save the file as webimage_01.fla. Again, in the Movie Properties dialog, set your initial movie settings to:

✦ Frame rate — 12 fps

✦ Stage Size — 800×600

Now with your file set up, we can add the content.

1. This time you need 91 frames in the timeline.

2. Unlock the Label layer and lock the rest. Then, put a label called default in the first frame.

3. Follow the same procedure for the Actions layer and place a `Stop()` action in its last frame.

4. Lock the other layers, unlock the Variables layer, and then set a variable in frame 1; call it **image_num**, giving it the value of **level0.image_num**. (All we are doing here is passing the Global variable to the local clip.) Then, on frame 49 of the Variables layer insert this block of code:

```
if (image_num == 1) {
    loadMovie ("image_" + image_num + ".swt", 2);
    _level0.image_num = "2";
} else {
    loadMovie ("image_" + image_num + ".swt", 1);
    _level0.image_num = "1";
}
```

This block of code checks whether the current value of image_num is equal to 1, if it is, it loads the movie clip image_1.swt into itself and then sets the holding movie's value to 2. Otherwise, it loads in the movie clip image_2.swt and sets the holding movie's value to 1.

5. Now, lock all of the layers except the Graphics layer and open the Generator Objects Panel.

6. Finally, save the file.

Generator Objects

We are going into Generator territory now, so we should make a slight introduction before we press on. What are Generator Templates? These Templates are prebuilt objects that enable the linkage of a data source with Flash graphics to create flexible, but reusable components with the minimum of fuss and time. (Plus they help you develop wacky ideas or just get things done if you're crazy, like me.) So, which Template(s) are we going to use? Well just one this time round—the Insert JPEG Template.

1. Just click and drag the Insert JPEG Template icon from the panel and onto the stage area. Select the Info Panel again and, with the Insert JPEG Template still selected, alter the Template's dimensions and coordinates to match those of the rectangle that we initially created for our Holding Movie.

2. Then, double-click the Template to open the Generator Properties dialog. The options in the dialog are:

   • **File Name:** The name or dynamic location of the file to be used within this Template. Set this to point to the designated directory to which you are uploading your captured images (for example, www.myserver.com/webcam/myimages/image.jpg).

   • **Cache:** Check this item if want to cache this item to alleviate strain on your Generator Server; otherwise, you can ignore it.

Continued

Continued

- **Scale to Fit:** Set this to true; it does what it says—it scales the image to the size of the Template.

- **Export as:** Set this to JPEG.

- **JPEG Quality:** The higher you make this the larger the file, but the better the quality—your call.

- **Instance name:** We're not going to need this but it's worth noting that you can treat the image as a target in an ActionScript.

3. After we've set the options, we need to turn our Template into a symbol. Give it a meaningful name so that the files will make sense when your grandchildren want a demo. I recommend naming it **Generator Image Template.** Assign it the behavior of Graphic.

4. Now that it has been assigned the properties of a graphic, we can tween it. So first, make sure that there is nothing else in the Graphics layer timeline, and that our Template symbol is in frame 1. Then, tween this instance of Generator Image Template from an Alpha of 0 percent to an Alpha of 100 percent—extending from frame 1 to frame 31. (You'll find the Alpha controls on the Effects Panel.)

5. Now repeat the same process but in reverse from frame 61 to frame 91.

6. What we should have now is an Alpha Tween from invisible to solid (frames 1 to 31), followed by an Alpha Tween from solid back to invisible (frames 61 to 91). Thus, there should be point between frames 31 and 61 where the Template is visible.

7. Save the file—we're done!

All that's left for you to do now is export the .SWT for this file *twice*—call the exported files **image_1.swt** and **image_2.swt**, and upload them to your Generator Server along with the flashcam.swf that we exported earlier. With that done, fire up your Webcam and start capturing and uploading. Then open your Web browser, point it to the site location of your uploaded Flash files, and let the good times roll.

A final note:You may need to manipulate the quality settings on the template/capture setup, as well as the length of the tweens that were set to load in each file. This usually depends upon several factors, such as whether you are uploading from one machine to another, or whether you are on a slow dialup or a fast pipe such as ADSL. But you can't anticipate these finer tunings; you need to deal with them creatively and intelligently at the end.

After you've got your Webcam running, enjoy the Webcam experience and think about these extensions to your setup:

✦ Create multiple Webcams and have them load into the interface via a drag-and-drop style flash icon—enabling users to switch cameras graphically and dynamically.

✦ Load the .SWT's into movie clips, which will give you greater control over their placement and interaction within the Flash environment — dragging, `setProperty()`, and so on.

✦ Consider using the `getTimer()` property to load the files in through a user-defined control, slider, knob, or other device, instead of loading automatically.

Mike Jones, creator of FlashGen.Com, `www.flashgen.com`, has been using Flash since it first appeared as the little known FutureWave Splash Animator. A founding member of Spooky and the Bandit, `www.spookyandthebandit.com`, Mike says he, "Took to Generator like a fish to batter, spending far too many nights messing with Flash and Generator when he should have been spraying walls or hanging around alleys!" Perhaps that explains why this derelict Londoner recalls little more of school matriculation other than, "Max Headroom was the film of the year . . . trés cool!" In addition to Generator, Mike's other passion is drinking beer *down tha pub*, with Spooky cohorts — Chris Glaubitz, `www.testbild.com`, and Dave Williamson, `www.oldskoolflash.com` — arguing weirdly elaborate ideas for Flash creations. Now Mike and Dave work at Quidnunc, `www.quidnunc.com`, leaving Chris as the only Spooky member. Both Mike and Dave are threatening to emigrate from the U.K. to the U.S. to live and Flash in San Francisco. Right that's the bio done, now off to the pub. . . .

Summary

✦ Generator data sources can represent information in two ways: Name/Value layout or Column Name/Value layout. Name/Value layouts specify a Generator variable and its value in each line of the data source. Column Name/Value layouts are similar to arrays: The position of each value in any given line indicates which variable the value is assigned to.

✦ You can create several types of Chart Objects with Flash 5 and the Generator authoring extensions. Charts can visually plot multiple values in bars, line, or scatter graphics.

✦ List Objects display dynamic text and graphics in a sequential item list. You can specify Scrolling Lists or Tickers as List Objects.

✦ When you publish or test a Flash movie that contains Generator Objects or variables, the .SWF file will show the current data source information as applied to the Generator Template (.SWT file). You only need to upload the .SWT (and your data sources) to your Generator Server for dynamic content publishing.

✦ Generator Templates are referenced in HTML and `loadMovie()` actions as if they were regular .SWF files. You can send variables to the Generator Template with HTML query strings or Flash actions with query strings.

✦ ✦ ✦

Working with Third-party, Server-side Applications

This chapter explores other server-side applications that use Flash movies. You learn how to add ASP (Active Server Pages) functionality to your Flash movies. We take a quick look at other Generator-like applications that can create dynamic Flash content.

Using ASP with Flash Movies

ASP is a technology from Microsoft (see Note) that enables Web developers to produce dynamic content within the convenience of a markup environment. ASP is one of several technologies that combine the power of server-side processing with the ease of HTML-like syntax. The structure of ASP is that of HTML with VBScript or JScript (Microsoft's version of JavaScript) placed within special tags. When an ASP page is requested on a Web server that supports ASP, it is first interpreted by the ISAPI (Internet Server Application Programming Interface) filter, then the interpreted output is sent back to the requesting client. This model is different from that of client-side scripting such as JavaScript, which cannot take advantage of the power of the server. It is also different from CGI (Common Gateway Interface) programs in that ASP enables the developer to provide a server-side solution just as CGI programs do, but often with much greater ease.

 Note   ASP technology works with Microsoft's IIS (Internet Information Server). IIS is the most common way to deploy ASP, but that there are other interpreters for other platforms, such as Chilisoft (www.chilisoft.com).

The following tutorial by James Baker shows you how to create a login system with ASP and Flash movies.

Expert Tutorial: Creating a Simple Login with ASP, by *James Baker*

The Flash 4 and 5 .SWF format gives developers the ability to develop Flash past simple motion graphics into the realm of systems and GUI development. Flash now has the capability to be anything from a slick navigation system to the front-end for an e-commerce system. While Flash itself does not have database connectivity without the use of Generator, by combining your Flash movie with a server-side programming language such as ASP, you can harness power of server applications and Flash's graphical abilities.

Flash and ASP

Using external programming, we can take advantage of all the strengths of whatever language you wish to use. ASP provides an easy-to-learn and easy-to-implement language on the NT platform. While we may use ASP in this tutorial, interfacing any back-end language with Flash works on the same principles.

The basic way in which you interface your server-side scripts with your Flash movie is through the `loadVariables()` command. This command enables you to execute a page on the server and to return its output either into a level in Flash or into a Movie Clip. It also enables you to send variables to the server-side script either through a POST or GET method. (If you do not need to send variables, you have the option not to.) You can also send variables manually by using a URL, as we do in this example. After the server-side page executes, Flash is capable of accessing the variables that it returns. Flash requires that you return name-value pairs for Flash to properly use them. If you want to return a user number variable called `UserNum` to Flash, you will want your ASP page to return a result such as `UserNum=2`.

Building the Flash login

We are building a simple login page for a Flash 5 site. You might build a login into your site for any number of reasons, including:

- ✦ Retrieve preferences
- ✦ Participate in chat
- ✦ Participate in BBS
- ✦ Ordering goods

In the FlashChallenge site (www.flashchallenge.com), we use a simple login page to make sure that users are unable to vote for their site repeatedly, and thus cheat. If people want to vote on a site or to comment on someone else's site, we require them to log in. That way we can stop people from anonymously voting hundreds of times for themselves or anonymously flaming other sites.

Creating the Flash file

The Flash file is set up with 4 layers and 20 frames. The top layer is called Actions and is where all the frame labels and frame actions will reside. We do this for ease of readability and because Flash executes each frame from the bottom up. If the actions are on the top frame, we can be sure that Flash has loaded all the elements on the layers below it. Sometimes I set up the scene to have multiple action layers, but I always put them at the top of the layer order.

There are 20 frames divided into 4 sections. This Movie Clip could be just four frames long, but because Flash does not add any file size for frames that aren't doing anything, I like to spread the frames out for better legibility of the frame labels.

The four sections, as shown in the figure that follows, are:

✦ Frames 1 to 4: Ready

✦ Frames 5 to 9: Logging

✦ Frames 10 to 14: Error

✦ Frames 15 to 19: Success

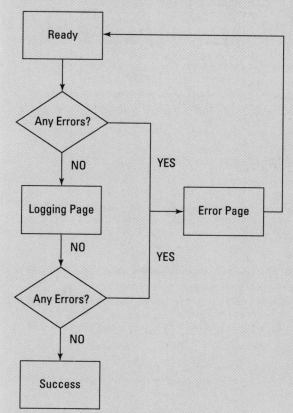

The flow of logic for the login system

Continued

Continued

Frame 1: Ready

This is the first frame of this Movie Clip. This frame is where we have users input their username and password so that they can log in. We have a simple script on the actions layer that sets sError equal to nothing and stops the timeline.

```
sError = "";
stop ();
```

We have two Input Text fields, one for the username and one for the password—sUserName and sPassword, respectively. The following figure shows the sUserName properties on the left and the sPassword properties on the right.

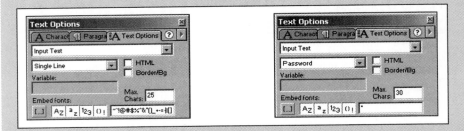

For input text fields, we generally include every character on a standard U.S. keyboard. To do this, we click the second, third, fourth, and fifth buttons on the bottom row of the text options palette. We also put the following characters into the field on the bottom row:

```
~`!@#$%^&*()_+-={|[]\:";'<>?,./
```

Why don't we just click the first button to add all fonts? If you do that, many unnecessary characters from the chosen font will be included with the .SWF file—increasing its file size. Many fonts sets include hundreds of special characters for foreign keyboards, so including them will bloat your file size.

We also have a Submit button for submitting the fields and a Clear button for clearing the text fields, as shown in the following figure.

This is what the user will click to submit `sUserName` and `sPassword` to the back-end ASP Page. The ASP page will check whether it is a valid username/password combination, but in order to take some strain off the servers, we will do a couple of quick validations in Flash first. We will check for glaring errors such as leaving blanks for your username or password.

You should have the following actions on the Submit Button instance:

(Note: The ¬ indicates a continuation of the same line of code. Do not insert this character into your actual code.)

```
on (release, keyPress "<Enter>") {
  sError = "";
  // validate the UserName
  sUserName = _root.Trim(sUserName);
  if (sUserName eq "") {
    sError = sError + "Please enter your UserName." ¬
      + newline;
  }
  // Validate the password
  if ((substring(sPassword, 1, 1) eq " ") or ¬
    (substring(sPassword, length(sPassword), 1) eq " ")){
    sError = sError + "Your Password does not begin or end ¬
      with a space" + newline;
  }
  if (sPassword eq "") {
    sError = sError+"Please enter your Password." + newline;
  }
  // load variables or display error
  if (sError == "") {
    gotoAndStop ("Logging");
    loadVariables ("Login.asp?UserName=" + sUserName + ¬
      "&Password=" + sPassword, "VariablesMC");
  } else {
    gotoAndStop ("Error");
  }
}
```

Author's Note: The `Trim()` function is a custom function designed by James to check for extra white space around the text entered for the `sUserName`. You can see this function on the first keyframe of the Login.fla included on the *Flash 5 Bible* CD-ROM.

If there is an error, we jump to Frame 10 Error and where the value of `sError` will be displayed. If there is no error, we construct the proper ASP page name. In this case, we are attaching `sUserName` and `sPassword` onto the URL. I like to do this when there are only a couple of variables that need to be sent to the ASP page. Because the Flash Player on Internet Explorer Mac tends to have problems passing data through the `POST` variables, I find that it is more reliable to send short variables through the URL.

Continued

Continued

We could be using GET here, but we don't need to be sending all the variables from this Movie Clip to the ASP page — the ASP page only needs sUserName and sPassword.

We are loading the output of the ASP page Login.asp into a target Movie Clip. In this case, it is called VariablesMC. Then we jump to the Logging frame. What we are doing here is waiting for the data that our ASP page will return to arrive.

In this case, there is some specific logic that we need to perform after the ASP page gives us the results. Flash calls to ASP pages through loadVariables() in an asynchronous fashion, which means that it will not wait for the variables to be returned before going to the next line of ActionScript. In Flash 4, we would attach a flag to the end of the returned variables string and wait until that flag had been changed, indicating that the variables had been returned.

In Flash 5, we have the onClipEvent() action, which we will use to check whether our variables have been returned from our ASP page. We use the onClipEvent(data) command on the variablesMC Movie Clip to specify that we want to do some special processing after the ASP page has returned its data. OnClipEvent(data) will fire after the ASP page that we are loading fully executes and returns its data.

variablesMC Movie Clip

This is the blank movie clip that we are loading our variables into. It contains no graphics and is only used to check whether our ASP page has returned its data and then to execute its script.

This ActionScript is executed immediately after the data from our loadVariables() script is returned. This ActionScript then checks whether the ASP page returns anything for the sError variable. If the ASP page encounters an error, such as not finding the username or finding the username, but not having the appropriate password, the ASP page will return something for the sError variable. If not, because we set sError equal to nothing on the first frame of this timeline, the ActionScript sends us to the Success frame:

```
onClipEvent (data) {
    if (sError != "") {
        _parent.gotoAndPlay ("Error");
        _parent.sError = sError;
    } else {
        _parent.gotoAndPlay ("Success");
    }
}
```

Frame 5: Logging

This is just a simple frame, shown in the following figure, to tell the user that we are currently accessing our servers and attempting to log in. This helps the user because it indicates that something is going on behind the scenes. The only ActionScript here is a simple stop() command. It is hoped that the variables will load quickly and that the user won't have to sit at this frame for very long.

Frame 10: Error

This frame is another simple frame in which we tell the user what is going on. In this case, we are telling the user that there has been an error. We have one text field, sError which, when sError is populated, will display its value. You can see the properties of the sError text field in the following figure.

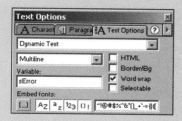

There is a "Retry" button, shown in the following figure, which resets sError back to nothing and sends the user back to the first frame.

Retry Button Actions:

```
on (release) {
    sError = "";
    gotoAndStop ("Ready");
}
```

Continued

Continued

Frame 15: Success

This is another simple frame, shown in the following figure, which tells the user that they have successfully logged in. We reach this frame only if the ASP page has processed correctly and has not returned an error.

In this example, we don't need to do anything with the data that was returned by our ASP page, but if there were some additional processing that might need to be done, this frame would be a good place to do it. On the FlashChallenge site, at this point, we set a global flag that the user has successfully logged in, and we tell the menu to go to the advanced menu.

Overview of the ASP

This ASP page is a simple login script. On an advanced site, I wouldn't recommend using a text file to store your usernames and passwords, but ASP really isn't the focus of this book, so we're just using a simple script that you don't need to set up any database connections to use. For the FlashChallenge, we use an SQL Server to store all our data from the site, which provides much better reliability, more security, and greater speed than using a text file.

This ASP page takes the username and password sent to the ASP pages and checks for them in a simple text file (users.txt). If it finds a matching username and password combination, it sends the `usernum` back to the Flash Movie. If it does not find any match, or encounters any other errors, it returns `sError`.

Because Flash sends variables through the `loadVariables()` ActionScript via `POST` or `GET`, we can code our ASP as is the variables were coming through a normal HTML form. So, there is nothing special that we need to do to capture variables passed from Flash to ASP. However to return variables back to Flash we need to properly format our variables. To do that we must return name-value pairs delimited by ampersands. Also, the only thing that Flash needs to have returned to it is those variables, so there is no need to add any HTML formatting to the data returned. All we need is the data itself.

Variables must be formatted in name-value pairs for Flash to be capable of using them. An example of proper formatting is this:

```
Variable=something&variable2=something
```

Now we typically add ampersands to the front and back of this to avoid accidentally sending Flash a carriage return or extra space.

```
&Variable=something&variable2=something&
```

As you see, each pair is separated by an ampersand and each variable name is unique. You do not want variables with the same name because Flash will only recognize the last one returned. Also, if you have any & in the strings that you are returning to Flash, your returned string will break. Make sure to convert any & not used to separate name-value pairs into the proper hex code '%26'.

So if the value of a variable called names that you need to return to Flash was

```
"Leonard & Nathan"
```

You would want to return:

```
&Names=Leonard  %26 Nathan&
```

The Login.asp page

This ASP page takes the username and password sent to the ASP pages and checks for them in a simple text file (users.txt). If it finds a matching username and password combination, it sends the usernum back to the Flash movie. If it does not find any match, or encounters any other errors, it returns sError.

Author's Note: You can examine this code more closely (and easily) by copying the Login.asp file from the ch29 folder of the *Flash 5 Bible* CD-ROM.

```
' ****************************************************************
'               Process the data and log in
' ****************************************************************

If (Request.Querystring.Count > 0) Then

   Dim strUsername 'User's username
   Dim strPassword 'User's password
   Dim strFile 'The text file path and filename
   Dim strTextLine 'One line of the text file
   Dim strError 'Stores the error message if there is one
   Dim bolUsernameMatch 'Flag to determine if the username matches
   Dim bolPasswordMatch 'Flag to determine if the password matches
   Dim objFSO 'File System Object
   Dim objUserFile 'File containing all the username and passwords
   Dim nUserNum 'UserNum to be returned to flash on success

   ' Populate variables
   strFile = Server.MapPath("users.txt")
   strUsername = Request.Querystring("Username")
   strPassword = Request.Querystring("Password")
```

Continued

Continued

```
      bolUsernameMatch = false
      bolPasswordMatch = false
      nUserNum = ""

      ' Create an instance of the file system object
      Set objFSO = CreateObject("Scripting.FileSystemObject")

      If (fxValidateForm) Then
        ' Create an instance of the user text file
        Set objUserFile = objFSO.OpenTextFile(strFile)

        Do While Not (objUserFile.AtEndOfStream Or (bolUsernameMatch
      And bolPasswordMatch))
          ' increment a line
          strTextLine = objUserFile.ReadLine
          If (strTextLine <> "***") Then
            ' Compare the usernames with no case sensitivity
            If (StrComp(strUsername, strTextLine, 1) = 0) Then
              bolUsernameMatch = true
            End If
              ' increment a line
              strTextLine = objUserFile.ReadLine
            ' Compare the passwords with case sensitivity
            If (StrComp(strPassword, strTextLine, 0) = 0) Then
              bolPasswordMatch = true
            End If
              ' increment a line
              strTextLine = objUserFile.ReadLine
              if bolUsernameMatch And bolPasswordMatch Then
                nUserNum = strTextLine
              end if
          else
              ' reset both flags on moving to a new login set
              bolUsernameMatch = false
              bolPasswordMatch = false
          End If
        Loop

        ' Set the object to nothing
        If IsObject(objFSO) Then
          Set objFSO = Nothing
        End If
        If IsObject(objUserFile) Then
          Set objUserFile = Nothing
        End If
```

```
      ' Set the sError variables.
     If Not (bolUsernameMatch And bolPasswordMatch) Then
        strError = " The username and password combination is
invalid."
     End If

  End If

Else

    ' for some reason no password or username were entered
    ' this shouldn't happen, so it is a critical error
    strError = "An error has occurred, please contact system
administrator."

End If
```

Now after we have processed the inputted username and password and checked it against the list of users in the users.txt file, we need to return the results back to Flash.

```
' ****************************************************************
'                   Return data to Flash
' ****************************************************************


%>&sError=<%=FlashFormat(strError)%>&nUserNum=<%=nUserNum%>&<%
```

Finally there are a couple of functions that we use. The FlashFormat() function removes ampersands from the text and replaces them with the appropriate hex code. The second function, fxValidateForm() is used to validate the username and password that were sent to the ASP page.

```
' ****************************************************************
'                       Functions
' ****************************************************************


Function FlashFormat(sTextString)
     sNewString = ""
     if sTextString <> "" Then
         ' this is for getting & into the flash movie....
         sNewString = trim(replace(sNewString,"&","%26"))
     end if
     FlashFormat = sNewString
end Function
```

Continued

Continued

```
Function fxValidateForm()
   If not objFSO.FileExists(strFile) Then
      ' if we cannot find the users.txt file we say that the site
is shut down
      strError = strError & "The login system is temporarily
unavailable."
   End If

   If (strUsername = "") Then
      strError = strError & "The Username field must be filled in."
   End If

   If (strPassword = "") Then
      strError = strError & "The Password field must be filled in."
   End If
   ' return true or false
   If (strError <> "") Then
      fxValidateForm = false
   Else
      fxValidateForm = true
   End If
End Function
```

Here is the format of the users.txt file. The first line is the username, the next line is the password, and the third line is the `usernum`. The *** is used to separate the entries. Again, this is very simple, and I suggest using some database to hold and manage your data. Microsoft Access is easy to learn and will suit most simple sites just fine.

```
<usename>
<password>
<usernum>
***
james
brown
```

Conclusion

There you have it! After you have a database set up with the proper formatting for user entries, you can use the Login.asp page to accept data from the Flash movie and to validate login entries more securely.

Originally from Palm Beach, Florida, James Baker loves to "make people wonder what the hell [he is] thinking." James is the Creative Director at the WDDG (wddg.com), a multimedia company in Manhattan, where he has created Flash experiences for the photographer John Mark Sorum (www.johnmarksorum.com), Cinnamon Altoids (www.toohot.com), and Campari (www.campariusa.com), among other award-winning presentations. In his free time, James makes sure FlashChallenge (www.flashchallenge.com) is on top of the best Flash sites in the world. During his final year of high school, James remembers watching *Pulp Fiction*.

Flash Generation Utilities

While Macromedia Generator 2 is by far the most powerful tool for dynamic Flash movies (and dynamic .GIF, .JPEG, .PNG, and QuickTime Flash movies), there are other options for creating .SWF movies on the fly. Most third-party Flash server tools use proprietary scripting languages or syntax to enhance content generation and management. Just as you can use Column Name/Values to specify environment variables for .SWTs served by Generator, each generation tool has its own way to pass information to the .SWT (or .SWF) files for processing.

This section provides an overview of the more popular third-party Flash utilities on the market. The primary benefit of these utilities is cost — they're significantly cheaper than Macromedia Generator. However, you won't find comprehensive technical support for most of these third-party utilities.

Swift Tools' Swift Generator

Perhaps the best known "competition" to Macromedia Generator 2, Swift Generator (www.swift-tools.com) can produce .SWF movies from .SWT template files. Unlike Macromedia Generator, Swift Generator cannot create alternative output from .SWT files (for example, .GIF, .JPEG, .PNG, .QuickTime Flash, and so on). As of this writing, Swift Generator is fully compliant with Flash 5 ActionScript and is available for these server platforms: Linux, Windows, FreeBSD, Solaris, BSDi, and Mac OS X Server.

SwiffPEG by SwiffTOOLS

SwiffPEG (www.swifftools.com) is a utility that converts MP3 audio files into Flash .SWF files. You can batch-process several MP3 files, saving yourself the time of importing MP3 sounds into Flash and publishing them as .SWF files. While this isn't a real server application, you could potentially operate the program with scripts. At the time of this writing, SwiffTOOLS had a SwiffPEG Server in beta development.

Blue Pacific's Flash Turbine

Flash Turbine (www.blue-pac.com) dynamically generates .SWF files from .SWT files. Unlike Swift Generator or Macromedia Generator, Flash Turbine uses a scripting language called Draw Script that enables you to dynamically draw shapes or text and place images and Movie Clips. There are several versions of Flash Turbine, most notably ASP Flash Turbine, which, as the name implies, works with ASP pages.

Form2Flash

Jeroen Kessels, Internet engineer, created this CGI utility that serves as a Flash text-replacement utility. Form2Flash (www.kessels.com/Form2Flash) cannot generate dynamic images like Macromedia Generator, Swift Generator, or Flash Turbine. This application uses `<macro name>` variable formatting instead of Macromedia Generator's `{environment variable}` formatting. The name of the macro is declared with form input, as in:

```
<FORM ACTION="/cgi-bin/form2flash.exe">
<INPUT TYPE="HIDDEN" NAME="myText" VALUE="Hello Flash.">
<INPUT TYPE="SUBMIT" VALUE="Submit">
</FORM>
```

When the form is submitted to the `form2flash` application, it will look for the macro `<macro myText>` in your Flash text and ActionScript, and replace it with the value "Hello Flash." This application is available for Windows and UNIX servers.

Note You can use internal Flash 4 or 5 ActionScript to do the same thing, as outlined at `www.kessels.com/Form2Flash/Flash4/`.

OpenSWF.org

You can create your own Flash generation utilities if you have the will and the know-how. The best site to find information about the open standards with the .SWF file format is `openswf.org`. You can also find official Macromedia information about the .SWF file format at `www.macromedia.com/software/flash/open/licensing/`.

A Note about CGI Scripts

There is a whole world behind server-side technology that can apply to Flash movie management and control. As we demonstrated in Chapter 24, "Sending Data In and Out of Flash," you can create e-mail applications that gather information from a Flash movie and send it as an e-mail to an address specified in ActionScript (or as a CGI script parameter). You can modify many Perl, ASP, or PHP scripts to work with Flash movie data. CGI scripts are useful for:

✦ Redirection of `loadVariables`, `loadMovie`, or `XML load` requests from a Flash movie. The `loadVariables` or `XML load` action can only load data from the same remote URL where the Flash .SWF resides. With a CGI script, you can send requests through the script and redirect the query to another remote server.

✦ Returning database information to the Flash movie. A CGI script can process a query from a Flash movie to search a database and return record sets to the Flash movie.

Summary

✦ Flash movies can tap into ASP scripts and linked server-side resources (for example, databases) to send and receive dynamic information.

✦ Several third-party applications can create .SWF files on the fly. These utilities are more affordable to purchase (some are free) but lack the advanced technical support services that are available for Macromedia Generator.

✦ You can modify CGI scripts to send and receive output to Flash movies.

✦ ✦ ✦

Using Flash with Other Programs

◆   ◆   ◆   ◆

In Parts I through VI, you learned that Flash can tackle some of the most complex graphic, animation, sound and interactive projects. But, as we all know, no one program can do it all — every computer application (or *app*) fits into a workflow with other apps. Unlike most computer books, this Bible seeks to find a place for Flash amongst all those other applications that you use in your multimedia work.

Part VII shows you how to use Flash with everything from Macromedia Fireworks to Discreet 3D Studio MAX to RealPlayer to Macromedia Director. This section has been broken into chapters of application families. At this point, you can skip around to different chapters to study a certain aspect of Flash content creation more closely. If you want to get back to working solely with the Flash authoring environment, jump to Part VIII, where we discuss how to publish Flash movies for use on the Web or in stand-alone projectors and players.

◆   ◆   ◆   ◆

Working with Raster Graphics

Flash 5 is an amazingly versatile application that can import and export just about any raster (a.k.a. *bitmap*) image format. This chapter shows you how to create bitmaps for Flash in image applications such as Fireworks and Photoshop. You also learn how to create alpha-masking channels, simulated 360-degree object movies, and natural art with Painter.

Optimizing Images in Fireworks 4

Although Flash can hold its own for vector art creation, you need another application to acquire, finesse, and export bitmap images for use in Flash. The newest release of Macromedia Fireworks has upped the ante on what you can expect from a Web-imaging application. Many of the new features of Fireworks 4 enable you to do more of your Web-image production from start to finish without ever going to another application. Here's a quick overview of some of those features:

  ✦ **Macromedia common user interface (UI):** Just like Flash 5, all the tools and options are laid out in panels that are distinguished by unique icons and names. Also, the document window provides a Launcher Bar in the lower-right corner.

  ✦ **Batch Processing improvements:** It's easier to run the same processes with a group of images, thanks to the new user interface for Batch Processing. Scott Brown's tutorial in the next section shows you how to use this incredible feature. You can also run scripts during a batch process.

  ✦ **Selective JPEG compression:** Fireworks 4 enables you to add a JPEG Mask to an area of your image. This mask can have a different JPEG compression setting than the rest of the image.

✦ **Better Dreamweaver integration:** You can more easily edit .PNG image files while authoring HTML documents in Dreamweaver 4. When a .PNG image is opened in Fireworks from another application, Fireworks will let you know that you're in "Launch and Edit" mode.

✦ **Director export:** Fireworks can now export its files in a format suitable for Director use. This export requires an additional plug-in for Director.

✦ **FreeHand reader:** You can import FreeHand files from versions 7, 8, and 9 into Fireworks 4.

There's plenty more to Fireworks 4, and we get you on your way by introducing some solutions for Fireworks and Flash integration.

Expert Tutorial: Fireworks and Flash, *by Scott Brown*

Scott's tutorial provides you with a solid foundation for using Fireworks to produce better quality images for use in Flash. Also, you learn where and when to use Fireworks for your Web production needs.

How Fireworks fits into the Web design process

Fireworks is an essential production tool for Flash projects in which bitmaps are involved. Furthermore, if you're trying to get any kind of graphic out onto the Web, whether via Flash movies or .GIFs and .JPEGs for HTML Web pages, Fireworks is the optimal Web graphic processing center. With Fireworks, designers have the freedom to import work that they have created in Photoshop, Illustrator, FreeHand, Flash, Poser, After Effects, LiveMotion, or even 3D Studio Max—yet still be able to edit the files. Or, a designer can work from start to finish all within Fireworks! Unlike other Web graphic design programs, Fireworks combines the ease of vector-based editing with the breadth of bitmap editing. Along with its advanced, yet familiar tools, Fireworks also sports a superior optimization engine for exporting files, and for the automation of custom command batch processing, and even includes the capability to implement a find and replace for elements within a graphic project. Moreover, the files remain editable.

How does Fireworks work with Flash? For designers working in Flash, one of Fireworks' most powerful features is its capability to prepare (and optimally compress) huge quantities of bitmap files for import. Going the other way, Fireworks is equally capable of receiving files from Flash and optimizing them for inclusion on HTML sites.

In this tutorial, I guide you through two workflows between Flash and Fireworks. One is the preparation and implementation of bitmapped animations for Flash. The second is teaming the strengths of both programs—Flash for animation and Fireworks for graphics compression—to make some amazing .GIF banner ads.

Optimizing a bitmap sequence for Flash

Consider a Flash project—a catalog or a portfolio, for example—that requires many bitmaps and bitmap animations. How do we get all those nicely rendered images into Flash? Suppose you have an animation created in a bitmap program such as Adobe After

Effects, 3D StudioMax, QuickTime Pro, or Poser; all of these programs have an option to export the animation as a sequence of files, usually as a sequence of .PICT, .PNG, or .BMP images. Often, this will be a sequence of filename_01, filename_02, filename_03, and so on. The obvious challenge of working with such file sequences is that they have the potential to add up to hundreds of individual files, all needing to be prepared and optimized for Flash import. Often, in dealing with such a sequence, the files are the wrong dimension, or need to have other changes made! It's daunting to consider the laborious tedium of massaging so many files! Luckily, there is Fireworks. Fireworks, with its batch-processing capabilities coupled with its capability to run custom commands during such batch processes, easily save the day (and your wrists).

You'll find all of the required assets for this project in the ch30 folder of the CD-ROM. To work through this example, copy the provided QuickTime movie and the exported .PICT sequence to a separate folder on your hard drive.

Setting up Fireworks to batch process

To batch process efficiently, we first need to consider the several changes that might be required to prep the file sequence for Flash:

1. All of the files are the wrong dimensions. For the animation to fit nicely into our Flash project, we need to change the dimensions from 500×300 to 300×200.

2. We also want to change the hue and saturation of those files to match the color scheme of the Flash project.

3. The art director decided to shake things up; he actually wants you to flip the animation horizontally.

4. Finally, we need to convert all those files from the PICT format to JPEG format, so that they will perform most efficiently in Flash.

Let's get started. Open the first file of the sequence and make a copy. Then, working on just this one file, make all of the changes that need to be done, per your list (as explained previously). This will be your test file.

If you're familiar with the Actions Palette and the batch file feature in Photoshop, you might be thinking that you could do all those functions in Photoshop. Well, you would be right, but the truth is that Fireworks has the inside track for working with Flash. When a JPEG from Fireworks is imported into Flash, Flash recognizes the compression that was set in Fireworks and knows not to recompress it. However, when a JPEG that was made in Photoshop is imported into Flash, Flash doesn't recognize the JPEG settings. Unless care is taken with the Flash JPEG compression settings — in both the Library and the Publish Settings — Flash will attempt to apply its own JPEG compression to the previously compressed file. And we all know that JPEGing a JPEG is bad practice: Hello, blocky graphic! So that's another reason for doing this batch processing in Fireworks.

Creating a Fireworks command

Let's assume that you found the perfect settings and are completely pleased with the results on your test file. If not, undo and repeat the process until it comes out just right.

Continued

Continued

Then, the next step is to use the History Panel to create a Fireworks command. To make this custom command we need to make the necessary changes to the file, with optimal results:

1. Resize the image to 300 pixels wide.

2. Change the hue/saturation to a cool color.

3. Flip the image horizontally.

In case you didn't notice, the History Panel has kept track of every action or event that's been done to the file. This is how Fireworks commands are created. However, here's a word of caution about the History Panel: Not every step in Fireworks can be used in a command. When you select steps that cannot be translated into a command, Fireworks will notify you with a dialog. Fireworks also gives you two visual clues for steps that cannot be applied as commands: One is the step icon with a red X over it, and the other is not so obvious — it's a horizontal line break in between steps. But there are work-arounds. To get around these glitches, we'll just make two commands for the batch process.

To create the first command:

✦ In the History Panel, select the first two steps (by Shift-clicking) and repeat.

✦ Click the save icon at the bottom of History Panel

✦ Save the new command as **Resize & Colorize**, and click OK

You've just made a custom command in Fireworks. The custom command can then be accessed in the Command menu for future use.

For the second command, while still in the History Panel, select the last step, flip horizontal, and save it as **Flip**.

With these two custom commands saved, the next step is to customize the compression settings for the .PICT sequence.

Creating custom export settings

Fireworks ships with two default preset settings for exporting JPEGs: better quality (80 percent), and smaller file (60 percent). However, we need more compression than 60 percent. So, we simply create our own custom export setting:

1. Select the Preview View tab on the document window and experiment with the JPEG compression settings in the Optimize Panel, until you finally conclude that 50 percent is ideal for this project

2. Set the JPEG quality to 50 percent

3. Select the Save icon at the bottom of the Optimize Panel

4. Save this new setting as **JPEG 50%**

Launching the batch process

Now that we have two custom commands and a custom compression setting, we're ready to initiate the Fireworks batch process. Here's how:

1. Go to File ⇨ Batch process and navigate to the folder that contains the files to be processed.

2. Select the files to batch by opening the folder where all the images reside, clicking Add All, and then clicking Next.

3. This invokes the Batch Options dialog. Here, we can choose what commands to apply to the selected files. A word of caution though: To get the desired effect, the commands need to be arranged in chronological order. The order of the commands should be (a) Resize &Colorize, (b) Flip, and (c) Export. Select a command and click the Add button. Note that more options become available in the bottom half of the window if you select the command on the right side. Although the two custom commands don't have any extra options, the Export command does. With the Export command selected, click the drop-down menu for Export Settings, and then select the JPEG 50% setting that we created earlier. Click Next.

4. This last step of the batch process asks where to place the new files and what to do with the originals. We also have the option to save these batch process settings, which is useful if there's even a remote possibility that there may be more than one set of files to batch. For now, just click the Go button. While batch processing, Fireworks opens a feedback window indicating how many files are completed and how many files have yet to be processed.

Now that we've size, flipped, and optimized all of our files, we're ready to import them into Flash.

Importing a file sequence into Flash

1. In Flash, create a new Movie Clip symbol and select the first frame of that symbol's timeline.

2. From File ⇨ Import, navigate to the folder containing the optimized files. Double-click the first file of the sequence, which adds it to the import list.

3. Click OK. Flash automatically detects that this file is the first file in a sequence and will ask if you'd like to import the rest of the sequence. The correct response is yes. (Notice how the sequence of files extends along the timeline of the Movie Clip.) The bitmap sequence now resides in Flash, within a Movie Clip, and is a Web-ready animation.

   In the Library, check the imported settings for an image of this sequence. Note how Flash acknowledges the Fireworks .JPEG settings, as the **Use imported JPEG data** option is available and checked. This means that when the Flash movie is exported, Flash will not apply any further compression to the files.

Fine-tuning

After experimenting with the new Movie Clip, you may find it necessary to redo the batch compression in order to get smaller file sizes. Or, maybe the animation looks too chunky because the compression is too extreme. Either way, it's easy enough to go back to Fireworks to experiment with the compression settings and then rebatch and reimport the file sequence.

Continued

Continued

In the near future, as the Flash plug-in nears 95 percent ubiquity, we'll start to see Flash banner ads gain in popularity. Meanwhile, we'll be in a transitional period between animated .GIF banners and rich-media banners. So, we will still need to turn Flash ad banners into animated .GIFs.

Creating Flash/.GIF ad banners

Not only does Fireworks excel at preparing file sequences for Flash, but also it's equally capable of importing Flash animations. It really is a two-way street with these programs. So, if you're already comfortable creating animations in Flash, why waste time learning how to animate in any other program, when Fireworks can import anything you've done in Flash!

Before we make a cool animated banner with Flash, we need to know the basic restrictions on banners. Here are some simple guidelines for animated banners: Target file size ranges from 12KB on the high end, to an acceptable 5KB, and on down to the ideal of a mere 3KB. Typical dimensions are 468×60, 392×72, and 125×125.

Now we need to create an exciting animated banner ad that will work on all browsers. (That means it has to be an animated .GIF.) The dimensions of the movie are 468×60 and the file size limitation is that it can be no more than 12KB.

With these limitations in mind, we can begin designing our banner in Flash:

1. In the Movie Properties dialog, which is accessed from Modify ⇨ Movie, set the movie size to the specified dimensions.

2. Also in the Movie Properties, set the frame rate to no more than 10 fps. That's because we know we have to make this animation into an animated .GIF and, to stay within our file size limit, the lower the frame rate, the better our chances.

3. While creating the animation, watch out for file size: Try to design a simple animation with few colors and few frames. Fewer colors with fewer frames make it more likely to land within our target file size.

Which format is best for export?

Once the animation works to your liking, the next step is to decide how to export it. If the animation has a lot of colors or images, then the best option is usually to export the animation as a .PNG sequence with File ⇨ Export Movie. But if the animation has very few colors, it's often best to export it as an animated .GIF, either from the Publish Settings or with Export Movie.

Colorful animation export

Because the hypothetical animation is very colorful, we choose to export a .PNG sequence. .PNG is ideal for this, due to the amount of information that the format can hold, which is 24-bit color plus an alpha channel.

1. Still in Flash, choose File ⇨ Export Movie.

2. In the Export Movie dialog, choose .PNG sequence from the File Format drop-down menu. Then, name the animation, choose a location for the exported file sequence, and click OK.

3. Now, to import the sequence into Fireworks as one file, choose File ⇨ Open, and then navigate to the folder containing the .PNG sequence. The next step is important.

4. If, at this point, we were to shift-click all the files that we want to open and then open them, Fireworks would open each file individually, which would make it more difficult to create our animated .GIF. So, we need to make sure to check the Open as Animation Option, *before* we click OK. With this option, Fireworks places each selected file in its own frame within a single Fireworks file, in numerical order. Now click OK.

5. This new Fireworks file has the file sequence set for export as an animated .GIF. But we're not done yet. To reduce the file size, we still have to go to work with the color palette.

6. Select the Preview tab to see how our animation will look when exported. In preview mode, Fireworks indicates the file size that will result with the current compression settings. Now it's necessary to focus on the Optimize Panel, which is where the file type is chosen.

7. Select animated .GIF in the Optimize Panel. Once a file type is selected, various optimization options appear. For an animated .GIF, we begin by editing the number of colors, either (a) choosing from a range of default color settings, with 128, 64, 32, 16, 8, 4, or 2 colors in the color palette, or (b) entering a specific number of colors. Note that, with every change to the color range or adjustment to the Optimize Panel, the preview window updates with the file size. To ease comparison, Fireworks gives the option to view compression schemes with the 2-up and 4-up preview modes, viewing either two or four settings side by side.

The trick to compression is finding a balance between appearance and file size. Too much compression, and the graphic looks like dirt, although the file size is ideal; too little compression and, while the graphic looks beautiful, the file size threatens to choke the fastest connections. So what can you do after trying to find that balance between image quality and file size, without success? What to do when the image quality can't go any lower, but the file size is still way too large? As mentioned earlier, there is a second factor to the file size of animated .GIFs: the number of frames. When image optimization fails, change your focus from the Optimize Panel to the Frames Panel.

The Fireworks Frames Panel is used to control several animation playback settings. These are:

✦ The number of frames in the animation.

✦ The frame delay for each frame — should this frame hold for a second or two or just breeze right through as quickly as possible.

✦ The loop settings for the animation. Will the animation loop ten times, five times, never, or forever?

Continued

Continued

To further reduce the file size of an animated .GIF, remove some frames. To remove a frame, simply select the frame in Fireworks' Frames Panel, and then click the trash can icon at the bottom of the panel.

Keep deleting frames, judiciously, and continuously preview the animation, until you've brought the animation down to the required file size. Throughout this process, the preview mode will update its display of the file size every time a change is made. Unfortunately, you will find that, as you delete frames from the animation, the animation will not play back as smoothly as originally designed and intended. But that's just a limitation of animated .GIFs and a compelling reason to start creating Flash banner ads!

When the file's been brought down to an acceptable size, the next step is to edit the timing of each frame. Each frame in the Frames Panel has a name on the left and a number on the right. The number signifies the delay length for each frame, measured in 100ths of a second. The default setting is 20 — or 20/100 of a second. So, to pause a frame for 3 seconds, set the frame delay to 300.

The last adjustment to set is the looping of the animation. At the bottom left of the Frames Panel is a loop icon. Select it and choose a loop setting. Finally, it's time to export this file as an animated .GIF and send it off to the Web. Use File ⇨ Export Preview. In the Export Preview window, select "Animated GIF" from the format pull-down menu. Now press the Export button to name the file and place it within the desired location. Click Save and you will be ready to go.

Alternative workflow

If an animation is created in Flash with few colors, there's no need to export it as a .PNG sequence. Instead, export the animation as an animated .GIF, either from the File Menu with File ⇨ Export, and choose GIF; or from the Publish Settings, by first choosing the .GIF check box, and then from the .GIF tab, choose Animated. In either case, use the largest possible color palette in order to defer color crunching to Fireworks, where the controls over the color palette are both more accurate and robust.

The exportedanimated .GIF is easily imported into Fireworks by choosing File ⇨ Open, and then selecting the single animated .GIF file. Fireworks imports each frame with the frame delay settings intact. From here, the animation may be optimized per the previous instructions, proceeding from color palette, to the number of frames and loop settings.

In the year that Scott Brown graduated from high school, the most memorable song was, "Losing My Religion" by REM. Prior to that, he'd lived "all over the place: Santa Maria, Boston, Phoenix, Austin, then Switzerland, and finally Los Angeles. A few years later, he graduated from Art Center College of Design with a degree in product design. Immediately after graduation, he began working at www.guess.com as their new media designer. It was there that he discovered Flash, while "trying to learn Director so that I could make a simple game for the Guess e-commerce site." Scott recently began working on the redesign of the Rampt.com site while also teaching an evening class in Web design at Art Center College of Design. His single most favorite thing to do is, "waste time on the Playstation when not trying to keep on top of all these new software developments."

Preparing Images for Flash with Photoshop 6

Adobe Photoshop 6 is an exciting upgrade to this premiere image-editing program. When you're preparing bitmaps for use in Flash, Photoshop 6 adds some extremely useful and powerful Web features that make saving high-quality .JPEGs and .PNGs a snap. The PNG-24 format is a great format to use with Flash, because this file format supports lossless compression and can use an alpha channel (a.k.a. *transparency mask*). In this section, we show you how to export a Photoshop image (.PSD file) as a PNG-24 image to use in Flash, and how to create a 3D-object simulation with image sequences from Photoshop.

Creating alpha channels for .PNG files

Photoshop has excellent selection and masking tools for the most complex images. Although some third party plug-ins can make the task a lot simpler, a little know-how with Photoshop tools can also go a long way toward simplifying your task. In the following tutorial, we take an image of some houses along the beach and mask the background sky. This lesson assumes that you have a working knowledge of Photoshop layers and layer masks.

On the CD-ROM
Use the sample image beachhouses.psd in the ch30 folder of the *Flash 5 Bible* CD-ROM for this section. The completed .PSD and .PNG versions of the masked image titled beachhouses_masked.psd and beachhouses_masked.png are also on the CD-ROM.

1. Open the beachhouses.psd file from the CD-ROM. If you receive a message about a color profile mismatch, choose Don't Convert. For more information about color profiles and Flash, see the "Color Management in Photoshop 6" sidebar in this section.

2. To more easily separate the color tones of the sky from the foreground, add a Levels adjustment layer to Layer 0 (the layer with the actual image). Do *not* use the regular Levels command, which permanently applies its effect to the image. We only need a temporary Levels effect to increase the contrast. See Figure 30-1.

On the CD-ROM
You can achieve the correct level values in the Levels dialog by loading the separation.alv file into the dialog, using the Load button. This file is in the ch30 folder of the *Flash 5 Bible* CD-ROM.

3. Select the Magic Wand tool in the Photoshop Tools palette. In the Magic Wand settings of the Option bar, enter **15** in the Tolerance field, and make sure Anti-Aliased and Contiguous are checked. Click the uppermost area of the now-darkened sky to select it. Shift+click additional areas with the Magic Wand tool until the entire sky is selected. If you grab anything in the foreground, either undo or start over (Select ➪ None). See Figure 30-2.

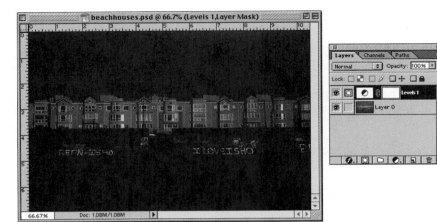

Figure 30-1: The image with a Levels adjustment layer

Figure 30-2: When you're creating your selection, pay particular attention to the edges of the rooftops.

4. With Layer 0 highlighted in the Layers window, Option+click (Mac) or Alt+click (PC) the Add a mask icon at the bottom of the Layers window. This uses the selection of the sky as a mask (see Figure 30-3). If the Add a mask icon was clicked without holding Alt or Option, then the foreground elements would have been masked instead.

Figure 30-3: Option+ or Alt+clicking the Add a mask icon uses the active selection as the black area of a layer mask.

5. Now that we have masked out the sky, we don't need the Levels effect anymore. Turn off the Levels adjustment layer, or delete it.

6. Before we save this image as a PNG-24 file, we should crop all unnecessary information from the image. In this example, the masked sky should be nearly eliminated. See Figure 30-4.

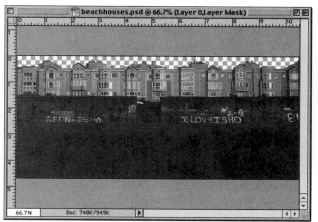

Figure 30-4: It's always a good idea to crop unnecessary information (especially if it's hidden by a mask) from the image before importing it into Flash.

7. In Chapter 12, "Using Bitmaps and Other Media with Flash," the effects of larger-than-necessary bitmaps were discussed. Because the image width is currently larger than the default Flash movie width, we also use the Image ⇨ Image Size command to change the width from 755 to 550. Be careful when using the Image Size command. For this example, the Constrain Proportions and Resample Image: Bicubic options should be checked.

Caution   Make sure you double-check the layer mask by viewing it separately in the Channels window. If any faint gray lines appear along the top edges of the mask, paint over them with a black brush. If any gray appears in the black area of the mask, it shows up in the Flash movie.

8. We're ready to save the image as a PNG-24 file, using the Photoshop 6 Save for Web command (Option+Shift+Command+S or Ctrl+Shift+Alt+S), located in the File menu. After you have chosen this command, the image appears in Live Preview mode within the Save for Web dialog (see Figure 30-5). Click the 2-Up tab to view the original image with the optimized version. In the Settings section, choose the PNG-24 preset. Make sure the Transparency option is checked—this exports the layer mask as an alpha channel in the .PNG file. Do not use the Interlaced or Matte options for Flash import. Click OK and Photoshop asks you to specify a location and filename for the PNG-24 image. Note that the .PNG image format is already selected in the Save as Type drop-down menu. It is not necessary to check the Save HTML File option for Flash use.

Tip   The Save for Web dialog has many other cool features. While the 4-Up effect is not necessary for PNG-24 files (there are no compression options to worry about), you can preview your original with three different .JPEG or .GIF versions, each at a different compression setting. You can use the Preview Menu to see the effect of 8-bit browser dither (by checking the Browser Dither option), and you can use color profiles using Photoshop Compensation or Uncompensated Color. For PNG-24 files, always use the Uncompensated Color preview, because it is the most accurate for Flash use. See the sidebar titled Color Management in Photoshop 6 for more information on color compensation. Note that you can also resize the optimized image in the Image Size tab, instead of performing this action in Step 7.

9. We're ready to import the .PNG file into Flash, which recognizes the alpha channel in the PNG-24 version of our image. Open a movie in Flash (or create a new one), and choose File ⇨ Import (Command+R or Ctrl+R). Select the .PNG image and Flash places the image on the current frame of the active layer. Remember that all bitmaps are stored in the Flash Library. If you delete the instance of the bitmap on the Stage, you can always replace it with the bitmap in the Library. That's it! You've successfully imported an image with an alpha channel into Flash (see Figure 30-6).

On the CD-ROM   Check out the sample Flash movie, alphabitmap.fla, in the ch30 folder of the *Flash 5 Bible* CD-ROM.

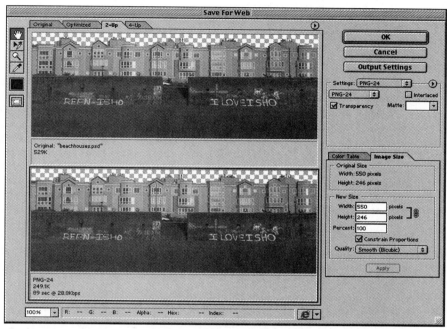

Figure 30-5: The Save for Web command enables fast Web image previews in Photoshop 6. You may need to resize this dialog in order to display horizontal images on top of each other, as shown in this figure.

Figure 30-6: Using a bitmap with an alpha channel enables you to seamlessly place other elements behind the bitmap in a Flash movie.

Color management in Photoshop 6

Many strategies exist for color calibration on desktop computer systems. Macintosh computers have had a leg up in this area of graphics creation and output ever since the development of ColorSync. Apple's ColorSync software provides one of the most complete system-level color management solutions for desktop publishing. Unfortunately, while Windows 98 and Windows ME do include ICC profile support, it's not as comprehensive as Apple's ColorSync system. Since Photoshop's 5.0 release, ICC color profiles can be specified and attached to most image file formats. In a nutshell, ICC profiles describe the color capabilities of a given input or output device, such as a computer monitor, printer, or scanner. When an ICC profile is attached to an image, the profile tells the application that is using the image how the colors in the image should be interpreted. If every program in your workflow supports ICC profiles, then, theoretically, this provides a consistent display and output of all graphics.

However, while Photoshop and most page-layout programs recognize ICC profiles, the majority of applications do not. Some Web browsers do not support embedded image profiles, although Apple has proposed many ICC tags to make color management a reality for the Web (see www.apple.com/colorsync/benefits/web). More importantly, Flash 5 does not support ICC profiles. Neither does the current implementation of the PNG-24 format. The .JPEG file format is the only current Web image format that supports embedded profiles. Moreover, ICC profiles typically add about 500 to 800 bytes to an image's file size.

Herein lies the problem for serious graphic designers who routinely work under tight color management. If you specify an RGB space in the Color Settings preferences (Edit ⇨ Color Settings in Photoshop 6, or File ⇨ Color Settings ⇨ RGB Setup in Photoshop 5.5) *other than* sRGB IEC61966-2.1 (Photoshop 6), or Monitor RGB or sRGB (Photoshop 5.5), *and* have Display Using Monitor Compensation checked (Photoshop 5.5 only), then what you see in Photoshop is *not* what you see in Flash when you import the image. This is why Photoshop 6's Save for Web feature and its Preview Menu are so invaluable. They enable you to see how the .JPEG, .GIF, or .PNG looks without Photoshop Compensation.

If you work primarily with Web or screen graphics, then you should use Photoshop 6's new Color Settings presets to quickly switch color spaces. For Web work, always use Web Graphics Default. For ColorSync management on the Mac, choose ColorSync Workflow. On the PC, choose a setting that best matches your printing needs (ColorSync is an Apple-only management system).

In Photoshop 5.5, change your RGB working space to sRGB, or turn off Display Using Monitor Compensation if you continue to use other RGB spaces. Either method enables you to work with your images so that the Photoshop Compensation and Uncompensated Color settings render the image exactly the same within the Save for Web preview panes. Also, disable ICC profile embedding in the Profile Setup preferences (File ⇨ Color Settings ⇨ Profile Setup) by unchecking all the boxes under the Embed Profiles heading.

Expert Tutorial: Simulating 360-degree Turnarounds, by *Jay Vanian*

In this tutorial, you learn a useful technique for representing products on a clients' site — a believable simulation of a 360-degree turnaround. This tutorial is intended to help familiarize you with the new Flash 5 panel layouts, while teaching an effective way to emulate video through the use of keyframe animation with bitmaps. (You'll find the source .FLA file, procedural screen grabs, and related assets for this tutorial in the ch30 folder on the accompanying *Flash 5 Bible* CD-ROM.)

1. If you don't already have a lazy susan, or utility turntable (commonly used in a kitchen pantry or on the kitchen table), you'll need to buy or borrow one. Measure the diameter, and then set 25 to 35 numbered markers evenly spaced around the circumference of the turntable. If you have any more or less markers, your Flash movie will be too slow or too fast. If you're borrowing the turntable, it might be a good idea to use labels or erasable ink.

2. Set up your turntable next to a wall of the same color, or tape up a sheet of colored paper to match your turntable. This will simplify your work with the images in Photoshop. Center the object that you want to turnaround on the turntable.

3. Set the turntable to the first numbered marker and, using a tripod, take a picture of the object. Carefully move the turntable to the next number and snap another shot. This can't be done without a tripod — and the tripod must remain stationary throughout the process. Continue rotating and shooting until you've returned to the original marker.

4. If you've used a digital camera, you're ready to move your images onto your hard drive. Otherwise, you'll need to have the film developed and get scans before you can open them with Photoshop.

5. Use the Lasso, or other Photoshop tools, to cut the images out from their background, and then copy and paste each of these cut-out images into successive numbered layers of a single .PSD image — take care to maintain the proper order. The background should be transparent for all layers. If necessary, crop and then save your image as a layered .PSD file (this helps if you later have to resize your images).

6. Save each individual layer as a numbered .PNG (for example, 01.png, 02.png, 03.png, and so on)

7. Open Flash 5 and insert a new Movie Clip symbol (Ctrl+F8 or Command+F8). Give it a meaningful name, such as **mov_360**. Stay in Symbol Editing Mode.

8. Use File ➪ Import to select the first .PNG in your image sequence, and Flash automatically detects that you've selected a numbered file. Flash then asks whether you want to import the remaining numbered files. Choose Yes and Flash displays your .PNG files frame-by-frame on the Movie Clip's timeline. If necessary, center your images on the Stage using the Align Panel (Window ➪ Panels ➪ Align, or Ctrl+K/Command+K). It helps to use a guide to ensure that your images don't jump around too much. Choose View ➪ Rulers, and then pull a guide down from the top ruler in the Stage window.

Continued

Continued

9. While still in Symbol Editing Mode, hold down the Ctrl key (or Command key on the Mac), select all of the keyframes in the timeline, and drag them to start at frame 20. Note that there should be one keyframe for each image in the sequence. This allows you a comfortable working space in the timeline of the movie clip.

10. Now add two layers—one for your actions, one for your labels. Label the layers with meaningful names.

11. On the labels layer, add keyframes at frames 20, 34, and 51. Use the Frame Panel (Window ➪ Panels ➪ Frame, or Ctrl+F/Command+F), to label these, respectively, **next**, **start**, and **previous**. Save the .FLA file.

12. Now, add a keyframe to frame 20 on the actions layer. Add a stop action here by double-clicking the keyframe, and then choosing Stop from the Basic Actions menu. Copy this stop action to frames 21 to 51 by holding down the Alt key and dragging the keyframe over to each frame, up to frame 51.

13. Still working with the actions layer, add a keyframe at frame 19. Give this frame a gotoAndStop("previous"); action by (a) double-clicking the keyframe, (b) choosing Go To under Basic Actions, (c) selecting Frame Label in the Type options menu, and (d) typing **previous** in the Frame field.

14. Repeat this procedure with frame 52 of the actions layer, substituting **next** for previous. Save the .FLA file.

15. Now, on the bitmap layer, drag the keyframe at 20 back to 19, so that the first frame of the bitmap sequence will appear for two frames: 19 and 20.

16. For the finishing touch on the Movie Clip, go to the first frame of the actions layer and add a gotoAndStop("start"); action. Then exit the Movie Clip. (If you still haven't saved the .FLA file, you are courting disaster.)

17. Now, back at the Main Timeline, drag the 360 Movie Clip from the Library onto the Stage and access the Instance Panel, using either Window ➪ Panels ➪ Instance or Ctrl+I/Command+I, and name this instance **360**.

18. Insert a new Movie Clip symbol (Ctrl+F8 or Command+F8) and name the new Movie Clip **mov_buttons**. Now add four layers (for a total of five layers) to the new Movie Clip timeline, and from the top down, name these layers: **A** (for Actions), **Left2**, **Left1**, **Right2**, and **Right1**.

19. On frames 1 and 3 of the Left1 layer, insert or create a button with the following action:

```
on (release, dragOver) {
  tellTarget ("/360") {
    prevFrame ();
  }
}
```

Remember to highlight each frame before proceeding to the Actions Panel. After you have selected the frame, open (or draw focus to) the Actions Panel (Ctrl+Alt+A or Option+Command+A), and then add actions from the Actions booklets or menus.

20. Repeat Step 19 for frames 2 and 4 of the Left2 layer.

21. Repeat Step 19 again for frames 1 and 3 of the Right1 layer, and also for frames 2 and 4 of the Right2 layer — except, this time, substitute the action `nextFrame();` for `prevFrame();`.

22. Then, on the actions layer, add keyframes to the first three frames and give each one a `stop();` action.

23. At the fourth frame of the actions layer, add another keyframe with the action `gotoAndPlay(1);`. Exit the Symbol Editing Mode (Edit ➪ Edit Movie).

24. Then, back at the Main Timeline, add and name two additional layers — one for actions (with the name **A**), one for the **buttons** Movie Clip instance.

25. Now, on the buttons layer, drag an instance of your buttons Movie Clip onto the Stage and position it below the mov_360 instance.

26. Then, on the actions layer, add a `stop();` action to frame 1. (This isn't really necessary, because Movie Clips play, once loaded, without relation to the Main Timeline and we only have one frame in our Main Timeline anyway; but for the sake of consistency, I always maintain an actions layer.)

27. Finally, publish your movie. The finished project is shown in the following figure.

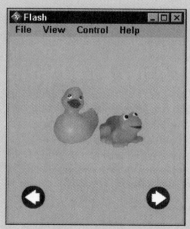

The animals can be viewed in a 360-degree turnaround.

Continued

Continued

Experiment with the JPEG export settings to bring down your file size. For more information about JPEG settings refer to Chapter 9, "Checking Out the Library: Symbols and Instances," and Chapter 12, "Using Bitmaps and Other Media with Flash."

Jay Vanian was inspired to learn Flash because he "saw two sites that really stood out — Balthaser's, and Shiny Entertainment's." He's worked on a number of sites, including: 11th Hour (www.hourtogo.com), THQ/Evil Dead (www.evildeadgame.com), Rhythmcraft (www.rhythmcraft.com), Crave Entertainment (www.cravegames.com), 2thebiz (www.2thebiz.com), Irvine Barclay Theatre (www.thebarclay.org), Ghosts (www.vanian.com/ghosts), and Alien Dog (www.alien-dog.com). Jay is billed as a Multimedia Artist with Pixelpushers, Inc. Jay's single most favorite thing to do is actually three things, foremost of which is "taking pictures of buildings." He's also prone to "plan world strategies," and also enjoys Krav Maga, which includes frequent visits to the emergency room. Perhaps these interests explain why he has no memories of popular culture from the year (1992) that he graduated high school in Newport Beach.

Creating Image Effects with Corel Painter

Corel Painter (formerly owned by MetaCreations) is a unique image-creation tool. Unlike other image-editing tools, Painter has a wide selection of tools that are more familiar to the traditional artist. Not only are the tools more identifiable, but the look and feel of the output from the tools resembles that of real-life art materials. While Painter may not be the tool to use for every job (what application is?), you can produce some amazing effects that aren't possible with other applications.

Expert Tutorial: Using Painter with Flash, *by Arena Reed*

Arena is a natural at Painter (and the Wacom tablet) and has used Flash extensively for artistic effects. As a member of the Painter development team, she has firsthand knowledge of what this tool can do to produce artwork for Flash.

The evolution of Painter

In this tutorial, we explore ways of using Corel Painter to add the look and feel of Natural Media to Flash. The initial idea behind Painter was Mark Zimmer's attempt to emulate a pencil sketch, which led to the paper texture model and the dye-concentration models, which simulate how different colors interact with each other. From there, Painter grew into a program that emulates a wide range of traditional mediums. Painter then branched into supernatural media that opened new outlets of expression to artists. As increased computing power and advances in input devices continue to erase technical boundaries, Painter will become even more realistic/surrealistic in the hands of Corel, Mark Zimmer, Tom Hedges, and John Derry.

Fun and exciting ways to use Painter with Flash include:

✦ Creating large collages that blend together with a look that you can only get by using Painter

✦ Creation of patterns

✦ Using Painter's scripting capabilities to record the creation of an image

✦ Cloning video to create a myriad of beautiful effects

✦ Collages, paintings, and image editing with Painter

Painter is an excellent tool for image creation! The most obvious thing to do with Painter is paint, to use the huge selection of brushes and art materials to create an image that has the look and feel of a traditional medium. Oil paint, pencil, watercolor, chalk, airbrushes, spray paint, ink, crayon, and markers are some of the standard mediums Painter emulates. However, Painter's capabilities go beyond this to offer a set of tools that are unlike anything in the traditional art-supply world. To name a few:

✦ The famous Distorto brush that smears everything all over the place in psychedelic streaks

✦ F/X brushes that create fire and fairy dust

✦ Image Hose that allows you to paint with photographic elements such as flowers and leaves, Liquid-Metal, Water, and Shattered Glass

✦ Pattern Pen that scales and rotates a continuous pattern

✦ Impasto brushes that create the illusion of raised thick paint strokes

Aside from creating images with Painter's Natural Media tools, the Cloning Brushes are fantastic for creating collages or photo manipulations, because they allow you to scale, rotate, and systematically distort on the fly.

Creating patterns with Painter

Painter is the best tool that I know of for creating seamless patterns because of the vast array of painting tools at your fingertips and the ease of wraparound painting. Here's how to create a seamless pattern with Painter:

1. Open Painter and then open a new file.

2. Define it as a pattern by opening the Art Materials Palette, selecting the Patterns Palette, and then, from pop-up menu, choose Define Pattern. Although you may also offset the pattern with the slider on the Patterns Palette, neither HTML nor Flash supports offset patterns. See the following figure for an example of the Art Materials Palette and its options.

Continued

Continued

Select Define Pattern from the Pattern Palette of the Art Materials Palette to define an image as a pattern.

3. You'll notice that, after defining the image as a pattern, a brushstroke that goes off the page will wrap around onto the other side of the page, as shown in the following figure.

Wrap-around painting enables the creation of seamless patterns.

4. Shift the pattern by holding down the spacebar+Shift and dragging.

5. When you've completed your pattern, save the pattern as a .JPEG and use it as a background.

Scripting the painting of an image

As you paint an image it's possible to record your process and then play back the process as an animation. Scripting in Painter is the process of recording a series of brushstrokes, menu commands, and choices of art materials (color, paper texture, pattern, and so on). Follow the steps outlined below with a quick, little image first to make sure that you are following the steps properly. This is a somewhat advanced use of Painter, so the steps should be followed carefully in order to achieve the proper results. Here are the steps to record the creation of an image with Painter:

1. Open a new file. Pay attention to the dimensions of your file, which will translate into file size. Unless you're using a supercomputer with lots of hard-drive space, you should keep the size of this file reasonably small, because this will be the size of each frame of your final animation. Write down the dimensions of this file, because you will need to know it later.

2. Open the Scripting Panel of the Objects Palette. Select Window ⇨ Show Objects ⇨ Scripting to expand this part of the Objects Palette.

3. Adjust the Script Options. Select Scripting Menu ⇨ Script Options and select Record Initial State. This assures that your painting will look the same every time you play it back, if you want it to look different every time because you have a different brush or color selected you can deselect this option. See the following figure for the Script Options dialog.

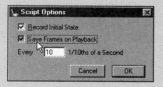

4. Press the Record button, which is the red circle button on the Scripting Panel.

5. Begin painting, this is the fun part! (Note: Do not save during the recording process, as it will cause the file to be saved again and again and again—each time the script is played back.)

6. When you're finished press the Stop button, which is the black square button.

7. Painter will ask you to name your Script; give it a name and click OK. It's a good idea to include the size of your image in the name of the script, in case you want to play it back as an animation later.

Continued

Continued

8. The script will now appear as an item in the drop-down list of scripts and also as an icon in the expanded view of the Scripting Panel.

9. After a script has been created it can be played back to a special kind of Painter file known as a Frame Stack file. Frame Stacks are saved upon opening and are continually saved to disk as you work with them. Therefore there is no reversion, but this usually doesn't matter in the case of playing back a prerecorded script. However, if you are working with frame stacks to create a frame-by-frame animation, you'll be wise to occasionally close the file and duplicate it for back-up purposes.

Here are the steps for playing back a script and then bringing a sequence of numbered files into Flash:

1. Adjust the Script Options. Select Scripting Menu ⇨ Script Options (see the following figure), and check Record Frames on Playback.

2. Open a new file with the same dimensions as the image that you recorded the script from. Select the script that you just recorded and click Play.

3. Now Painter will ask you to:

   a. Name the Frame Stack file

   b. Choose the number of onion skin layers to display

   c. Choose a bit depth (use 24-bit with 8-bit mask)

This file can have a tendency to get very large depending on the frame-rate of play back, the size per frame and the bit-depth chosen. Save it to a location that has plenty of free space.

4. Watch it play back frame-by-frame, each time adding to the image.

5. When this Play process is done, choose File ⇨ Save As. Then Choose the Numbered Files option from the Save As dialog.

6. Give these files a name that ends with the beginning of a numbered sequence such as, myFile0001, and choose a format that is compatible with Flash, such as JPEG.

7. Finally, to import these frames into Flash, open a Flash file and choose File ⇨ Import. Choose the first file in the sequence of numbered files. Flash will alert you with the message: This file appears to be part of a sequence of images. Do you want to import all of the images in the sequence? Choose Yes. Now, all of the images will appear as keyframes in a layer of the timeline.

Cloning video to create beautiful effects with Painter

The process of cloning video involves importing video into Painter, then creating a blank Frame Stack file of the same size and length, and then referencing the imported video to set the color or size of the brush you are using. This technique can be utilized to create video that has the texture of a pencil sketch, oil painting, silk screen, or any of a vast variety of mediums Painter emulates. The Painter manual has detailed instructions on cloning video. To get a cloned video sequence into Flash, follow the previous steps to save the frames as numbered files, and then import them into Flash.

Above all, when working with Painter, it is important to enjoy yourself — so have fun!

Originally from San Francisco, Arena Reed left high school when she was 16 and went to college. She recalls that, "The song I remember from that year is 'Cold Hearted,' by Paula Abdul — I remember dancing to it while wearing hot-pink high-tops." After studying art and biology at the University of California at Santa Cruz, she became a member of the Painter development team, contributing content to Painter 4, 5, and 6. She claims to have "found Flash one day when I was digging in the dirt with my HTML shovel." Projects that Arena has worked on include: www.beema.com, www.visualarena.com, www.living-arch.com, www.missioncreek.org, www.lorikay.com, http://mckenna.sccoe.net, and content for Painter and Expression. Her current interests include teaching art and science to children, watercolor painting, bicycling, gardening, learning Chinese, and Flashing.

Exporting Raster Images from Flash

If you've been wondering how to use your artwork in Flash with other raster-based applications, then this section is for you. Many people prefer to use Flash as their primary drawing and illustration tool, thanks to Flash's uniquely intuitive set of vector drawing tools in combination with the (new) more traditional Pen Tool. Combined with a pressure-sensitive graphics tablet, Flash can indeed be a powerful illustration program.

Why would you want to export raster-based images from a vector-based application? The answer is quite simple: Some applications work better with raster (or bitmap) images than they do with vector images. As you see in Chapter 36, "Creating Full-Motion Video with Flash," video-editing applications usually prefer to work with bitmaps instead of vectors. If the application in which you want to use Flash artwork supports vector file formats such as .EPS or .AI, then you most likely want to use those instead of bitmap-based formats such as .BMP or .PCT.

Cross-Reference We discuss using external vector applications in Chapter 31, "Working with Vector Graphics." If you want the best quality artwork exported from Flash, jump to that chapter.

If you are unsure of the format to use in your graphics program, refer to Table 30-1. Afterward, we show you how to export a frame's artwork as a static raster image.

Table 30-1 Raster Image Formats for Flash Export		
Flash Export Format	**File Extension**	**Comments**
BMP (PC only), Windows Bitmap	.BMP	Can be used with all PC and some Mac applications. Variable bit depths and compression settings with support of alpha channels. Supports lossless compression. Ideal for high-quality graphics work.
CompuServe GIF, Graphics Interchange File	.GIF	Limited to a 256-color (or less) palette. Not recommended as a high-quality Flash export format, even for Web use.
JPEG, Joint Photographic Experts Group	.JPG	Supports 24-bit RGB color. No alpha channel support. Recommended for most high-quality graphics work. Note that this format does throw out color information due to its lossy compression method.
PICT (Mac only), Picture	.PCT	Can be used with many PC and all Mac applications. Variable bit depths and compression settings with support of alpha channels. Supports lossless compression. Can contain vector and raster graphics. Ideal for high quality graphics work.
PNG, Portable Network Graphic	.PNG	Supports variable bit depth (PNG-8 and PNG-24) and compression settings with alpha channels. Lossless compression schemes make it an ideal candidate for any high-quality graphics work.

To export a raster image format from Flash 5:

1. Move the Playhead in the Flash timeline to the frame that contains the artwork that you wish to export.

2. Choose File ➪ Export Image.

3. Select a destination folder and enter a file name. Select your preferred raster image format in the Save as Type drop-down menu.

4. Depending on the file format you selected, you are presented with an export dialog with options specific to that file format. We look at the general options and at some file-specific settings next.

General export options in raster formats

Every raster image format in Flash's Export dialog box has the same initial options. All of these options (as seen in Figure 30-7) pertain to the image size, resolution, and bit depth. You can also trim any unused stage area from the final exported image.

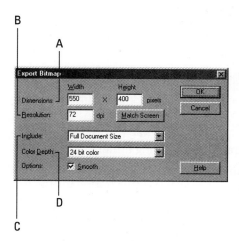

Figure 30-7: The general options of the Export dialog for raster image formats

A. **Dimensions.** The Width and Height options control the image's width and height, respectively, in pixels. Note that the aspect ratio of these values is always locked. You cannot control the Width value independently of the Height value.

B. Resolution. Measured in dpi (dots per inch), this setting controls the quality of the image, in terms of how much information is present in the image. By default, this setting is 72 dpi. If you want to use Flash artwork in print or high-resolution graphics work, enter a higher value, such as 300 or 600. If you change this setting accidentally, pressing the Match Screen button reverts the value to 72 dpi, the resolution of most computer monitors. Note that changing the value for this setting also changes the Width and Height values in the Dimensions setting.

C. Include. This drop-down menu determines what Flash content is included in the exported image.

- **Minimum Image Area.** When this option is selected, the image size (a.k.a. *dimensions*) is reduced to the boundary of Flash artwork currently on the Stage. This means that, if you only have a circle in the middle of the Stage, then the dimensions of the exported image match those of the circle — the rest of the Flash Stage or background is be included.

- **Full Document Size.** When this option is selected, the exported image looks exactly like the Flash stage. The entire frame dimensions and contents are exported.

D. Color Depth (or Colors). This drop-down setting controls the color range of the raster image. The higher the bit depth, the wider the color range. Depending on the file format, not all options are identical. We define the most frequently occurring options here. This option is not available for the .JPEG format, as that format must always be 24-bit.

- **8-bit grayscale.** This option limits the image to 256 levels, or values, of gray. It is equivalent to a typical scan of a black and white photograph.

- **8-bit color.** This option reduces the image to 256 colors. You may notice unsightly dithering in the image as a result. See Chapter 40, "Publishing Flash Movies," for more information regarding dither.

- **24-bit color.** This option enables the image to use any of the 16.7 million colors available in true RGB color space. Use this option for the best color quality.

- **32-bit color w/ alpha.** This image enables the same range of colors as 24-bit color, but also adds an alpha channel using the Flash movie's background color as a guide. If your raster image program can read alpha channels, then the Flash background color is transparent.

Other raster file format options

Each file format may have additional export options. In this section, we look at the additional options available for .BMP (PC only), .PCT or .PICT (Mac only), and .GIF. These options have not changed from the previous release of Flash. In fact, you may have more control with export file formats using the Export Image command instead of the Publish Settings/Publish commands.

The .JPEG, .GIF, and .PNG format options are discussed in Chapter 40, "Publishing Flash Movies." Because a problem exists with publishing adaptive .GIFs in the Macintosh version of Flash, however, we explore the .GIF export options here.

.BMP (PC only) options

The Windows Bitmap (.BMP) file format has numerous options. In addition to the general export settings, the .BMP Export dialog has an Options setting containing a check box for Smooth. When this option is checked, Flash antialiases all Flash artwork, making the edges nice and smooth. If this option is unchecked, then Flash artwork is rendered in an aliased fashion, in which edges appear jagged and rough.

In most external graphics applications, the 32-bit w/ alpha option in the Colors drop-down menu is not supported. You should use the 24-bit option if you experience difficulties using 32-bit .BMP files. If you need to export an image with alpha channel support, use the .PNG format in the Windows version of Flash.

.PICT (Mac only) options

The .PICT (short for Picture) format is a standard Macintosh graphic file format. Any Macintosh application that uses graphics can use it, and, with QuickTime, you can use .PICT (or .PCT) files on Windows computers. .PICT files can contain both vector and raster (bitmap) information. Usually, only raster-based .PICT files are truly cross-platform. See Figure 30-8.

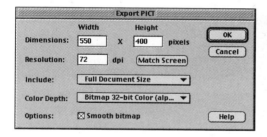

Figure 30-8: The .PICT format has a unique Objects option (in the Color Depth drop-down menu) in addition to traditional raster-based options.

✦ **Color Depth.** This drop-down menu is the same as the Colors setting for other raster-image file formats. It has a few peculiarities that are defined next.

- **Objects.** Due to the transgender nature of .PICT files, you can specify Objects to export Flash artwork as vector-based images. Note that selecting this option enables you to select Use PostScript in the Options setting. Use PostScript that contains .PICT output with caution, as it can produce undesirable results. If you need PostScript output, it is better to use Illustrator or .EPS as the format.

- **Bitmap 1-bit B/W.** This option converts all colors to either black or white, with no between values of gray. It is equivalent to the Bitmap image mode in Photoshop, and gives a fax document look to your Flash artwork.

- **Bitmap 8-bit Gray.** This option converts your Flash artwork colors to 256 values of gray.

- **Bitmap 8-bit Color.** This option creates an adaptive palette of 256 colors for the exported image.

- **Bitmap 24-bit Color.** This option produces the highest-quality raster-based .PICT files, enabling any color in the RGB color space to be represented. By default, you should use this option for graphics work in other applications.

- **Bitmap 32-bit Color (alpha channel).** This option has the same color depth as 24-bit color, with the addition of an alpha channel (or transparent mask). An unoccupied area of the Flash Stage is used to determine the transparent areas of the alpha channel.

✦ **Options.** The .PICT Export dialog displays one option. The option displayed varies depending on the Color Depth setting.

- **Smooth bitmap.** If you chose any of the Bitmap color options in Color Depth, then you have the option of antialiasing (or smoothing) Flash artwork. Smoothing produces cleaner edges on Flash vector-based artwork.

- **Include PostScript.** If you choose Objects from the Color Depth menu, then you can enable the Include PostScript option. This option optimizes the file's settings for output to a PostScript-compatible printer.

.GIF options

The majority of the options listed in the Colors section of the .GIF Export dialog are discussed in Chapter 40's section "Using the GIF settings." The Colors drop-down menu is slightly different, however. Also, as mentioned in a previous note, the Publish settings in the Macintosh version of Flash 5 do not create adaptive .GIF images (even if you have selected the option to do so). You can, however, create suitable .GIF images in both Windows and Macintosh versions of Flash 5 using the Export Image command. See Figure 30-9.

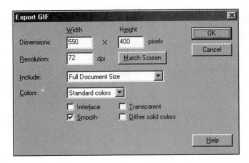

Figure 30-9: Options that are specific to the .GIF format.

On the CD-ROM

You can see the effect of each of these color options by looking at a series of .GIF images created from a test Flash movie, gifcolors.fla, located in the ch30 folder of the *Flash 5 Bible* CD-ROM. Each .GIF color depth setting was applied to this movie, and saved as a separate .GIF image.

✦ **Colors.** As stated in the discussion regarding general options, this setting controls the range of colors contained in the exported image. .GIF images can use a variety of bit depths with the overall 8-bit color depth setting. The fewer colors, the smaller the resulting .GIF file.

- **Black & White.** This option is equivalent to a 2-bit color depth, and converts all Flash colors to one of three colors (Web hex in parentheses): black (#000000), middle gray (#808080), or white (#FFFFFF).

- **4, 8, 16, 32, 64, 128, or 256 colors.** These options create the respective color ranges within the .GIF format. Flash determines which colors are used for each setting, similar to the adaptive palette type in Photoshop.

- **Standard Colors.** This option creates .GIF images that use the 216 Web-Safe Palette.

Summary

✦ Flash 5 is a vector artwork tool, and cannot create bitmap images from scratch. You need to use an image-editing application such as Macromedia Fireworks to create, modify, and optimize bitmap images for Flash.

✦ Macromedia Fireworks 4 has batch processing features that optimize your Web production workflow. Fireworks and Flash share a common UI, making it simpler to learn the tools in Fireworks.

✦ Adobe Photoshop 6 can be used to create a PNG-24 image with an alpha channel. Flash renders the black area of an alpha channel transparent (or semi-transparent) on the Flash Stage, so that other elements in a Flash movie can show through the foreground bitmap.

✦ You can mimic QuickTime VR objects using a lazy susan turntable and a camera. Using an image-editing application, you can isolate each object view and place the images in a Flash Movie Clip as an image sequence.

✦ Corel Painter can create fluid bitmap effects that you can use in Flash. Painter also offers unique video-cloning tools that can be imported as frame sequences into Flash.

✦ Flash 5 can export a variety of raster image file formats, so that you can transfer your Flash artwork to other graphics programs. You can specify the exported image's quality in the Export Image dialog.

✦ ✦ ✦

Working with Vector Graphics

Although Flash 5 has effective drawing tools, don't be mislead: It is not a replacement for a full-featured illustration program such as Macromedia FreeHand. Creating complex artwork can be accomplished much more easily in drawing and illustration programs — and integrating the final artwork with Flash is a cinch.

Preparing Vector Graphics for Flash Movies

Earlier in this book, we discussed the use of external media in Flash movies. However, not all vector graphics are created the same. Some vector graphics may be simple objects and fills, while others may include complex blending or paths that add significant weight to a Flash movie. Even though most vector graphics are by nature much smaller than raster graphic equivalents, don't assume that they're optimized for Flash use.

Cross-Reference Please read Chapter 12, "Using Bitmaps and Other Media with Flash," for details on importing all types of external media, including vector artwork, into Flash movies.

Guidelines for using external vector graphics in Flash

Because Flash is primarily a vector-based application, using vector graphics from other applications is rather straightforward. However, because most vector graphics applications are geared for print production (for example, publishing documents intended for press), you need to keep some principles in mind when creating graphics for Flash in external graphics applications:

✦ Limit or reduce the number of points describing complex paths. This chapter looks at using FreeHand's Simplify command and Illustrator's Pathfinder window to accomplish this task.

✦ Limit the number of embedded typefaces (or fonts). Multiple fonts add to the final .SWF movie's file size. This chapter shows you how to convert fonts to outlines in both FreeHand and Illustrator.

✦ To insure color consistency between applications, use only RGB colors (and color pickers) for artwork. Flash can only use RGB color values, and converts any CMYK colors to RGB colors. Color conversions usually produce unwanted color shifts. This chapter shows you how to set up FreeHand and Illustrator to avoid this.

✦ Gradients created in other drawing applications are not converted to Flash gradients when the file is imported. Unless you're using Macromedia FreeHand, you may need to replace externally created gradients with Flash gradients, or to accept the file size addition to the Flash movie. This chapter teaches you how to redraw gradients in Flash.

✦ Some vector formats can use layers, and Flash recognizes these layers if the graphic file format is correctly specified. Layers keep graphic elements separate from one another.

Reducing path complexity

All vector graphics are made up of paths in one shape or another. A path can be as simple as a straight-line with 2 points, a curved line with 2 points, or 500 or more points along an irregular shape or fill. This is why vector graphics are well suited for noncontinuous tone images such as logos, architectural drawings, clip art, and so forth. Fonts are also made up of paths. As we've seen with Flash-drawn graphics, you can scale them to any size without any loss of resolution. You learned in the last chapter that raster (bitmap) artwork cannot scale larger than its original size without loss of resolution.

Note   Vector graphics are eventually *rasterized*, so to speak. The vector formatting for drawn shapes and text is more of a simplified storage structure that contains a mathematical description (that is, smaller than a bit-for-bit description) of an object or set of objects. When the vector graphic is displayed, especially with antialiasing, the video card needs to render the edges in pixels. Likewise, the PostScript RIP (Raster Image Processor) of a laser printer needs to convert the vector information, or an EPS (Encapsulated PostScript) file, into printer "dots."

When you use imported vector graphics in Flash movies, you should minimize the number of points describing curved lines or intricate outlined graphics (for example, "traced" raster images). A big problem with creating cool graphics in vector-based applications such as Illustrator, FreeHand, and 3D Studio Max is the number of points used to describe lines. When these graphics are imported into Flash, animations are slower and harder to redraw (or refresh) on the computer screen. In addition, the file size of the Flash movie grows considerably.

Simplify paths in FreeHand

Complex artwork can be "simplified" in FreeHand. Simplifying reduces the number of points to describe a path (or a set of paths). To simplify any artwork, select the paths that describe the object and choose Modify ➪ Alter Path ➪ Simplify (see Figure 31-1).

Figure 31-1: The Simplify dialog in FreeHand 8 can reduce the complexity of vector artwork.

The slider and/or text field of the Simplify dialog controls how much information is discarded from the original artwork. Although it might seem tempting to use the highest setting (10), you may end up drastically changing the look of the original artwork. See Figure 31-2 for an example.

a) Original artwork   b) Simplify "5"   c) Simplify "8"

Figure 31-2: Compare the effects of the Simplify command at different settings.

Although the visual difference between the Simplify settings may not be readily apparent, the resulting .SWF file sizes are noticeably different. The original artwork's .SWF file (when copied, pasted, and exported from Flash 5) was 48.4K.

The simplified "5" version of the original produced a 31K .SWF file, and the simplified "8" version resulted in a 29.8K .SWF file.

On the CD-ROM To see the differences for yourself, check out seashell_normal.swf, seashell_ simplify_5.swf, and seashell_simplify_8.swf in the ch31 folder of the *Flash 5 Bible* CD-ROM.

Granted, those are still large .SWF movies, but it does illustrate the file-size savings that the Simplify command can accomplish.

Optimize curves command in Flash

You can also reduce the complexity of paths within Flash 5, by using the Modify ⇨ Curves ⇨ Optimize command. This has the same effect as the Simplify command in FreeHand, with a couple of extra options. Be sure to use the Modify ⇨ Break Apart command before you use the Optimize command — you can't optimize groups or symbols. Figure 31-3 shows the effect of maximum smoothing on the seashell_ simplify_5 graphic from the previous section.

Figure 31-3: Flash 5's Optimize Curves dialog enables you to specify multiple passes, which means that Flash will optimize the graphic at a given setting as much as it possibly can.

On the CD-ROM You can test the Optimize Curves effect on the seashell_simplify_5.fla file, located in the ch31 folder of the *Flash 5 Bible* CD-ROM.

Using the Pathfinder window in Illustrator 9

You can use the Pathfinder window in Illustrator 9 to join overlapping paths. Not only does this reduce the complexity of the path, but it makes the graphic easier to handle as a group.

Select the overlapping paths by Shift+clicking each object. In the Pathfinder window, select an operation that is suitable for the overlapping elements. In Figure 31-4, the Unite command is used to combine the individual components of the crosshair into one unified path.

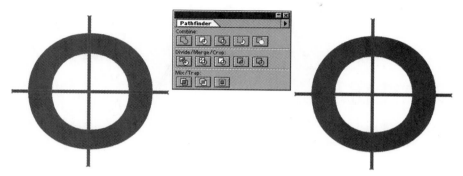

Figure 31-4: Combine paths into single path by using the Pathfinder window.

Tracing complex vector artwork in Flash

Many graphics programs, such as Discreet 3D Studio Max and Adobe Dimensions, can create some astonishing vector-based graphics. However, when you import EPS versions of those graphics into Flash, they either fall apart (display horribly) or add unrealistic byte chunks to your Flash movie. Does this mean that you can't use these intricate graphics in Flash movies?

You can try several different procedures with intricate vector artwork, including using the methods described previously, to make intricate graphics more Flash-friendly. Depending on the needs of the artwork, you may be able to output small raster equivalents that won't consume nearly as much space as highly detailed vector graphics. Or you can try redrawing the artwork in Flash. Sound crazy and time-consuming? Well, it's a bit of both, but many Flash designers spend hour after hour getting incredibly small file sizes from "hand-tracing" vector designs in Flash.

For example, if you made a highly detailed technical drawing of a light bulb, and wanted to bring into Flash, you could import the original EPS version of the drawing into Flash, place it on a locked layer, and use Flash drawing tools to recreate the object (see Figure 31-5).

Note   Many new Flash .SWF tools have been released since Flash 4. Electric Rain's Swift 3D can simplify 3D models and output .SWF files. We take a closer look at Swift 3D in Chapter 33, "Working with 3D Graphics."

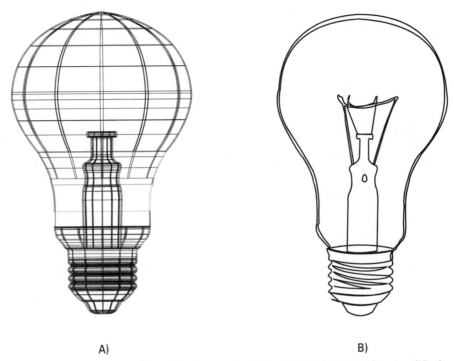

A)   B)

Figure 31-5: Compare the original artwork of the light bulb (A) to the simplified version drawn in Flash (B).

Converting text to outlines

Another aspect of vector graphics that you need to keep in mind — especially when working with other designers — is font linking and embedding. With most vector file formats such as Illustrator, FreeHand, or EPS, you can link to fonts that are located on your system. However, if you give those files to someone else who doesn't have those fonts installed, then he/she won't be able to see or use those fonts. Some formats enable you to embed fonts into the document file, which circumvents this problem. However, whether the fonts are linked or embedded, you may be unnecessarily bloating the size of the vector graphic.

You can convert any text into outlines (a.k.a. *paths*) in any drawing or illustration program (see Figure 31-6). In FreeHand 9, select the text as a text block (with the Arrow Tool, not the Text Tool) and choose Text ➪ Convert to Paths. In Illustrator 9, select the text as an object and choose Type ➪ Create Outlines.

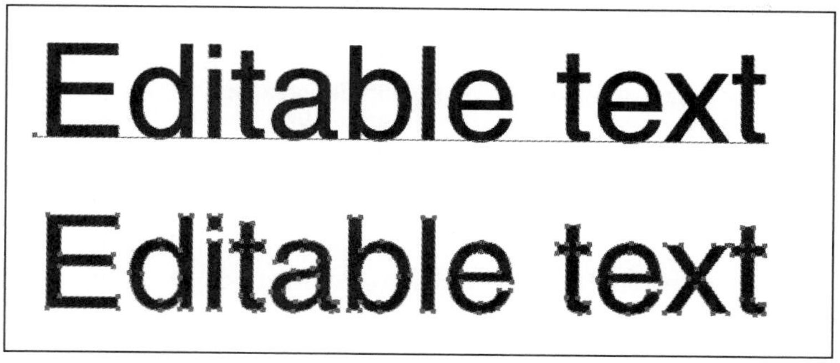

Figure 31-6: Make sure that you have finished editing your text before converting the text to outlines. The text at the top can be edited, whereas the text at the bottom (the same text converted to outlines) cannot be edited.

If you have a lot of body text in the graphic, you may want to copy the text directly into a Flash text box and use a _sans, _serif, or _typewriter device font. These fonts do not require any additional file information (unlike embedded fonts) when used in a Flash movie.

Controlling color output

Flash 5 can only use an RGB color space, meaning that it renders colors in an additive fashion — full red, green, and blue light added together produce white light. Whenever possible, use RGB color pickers in your preferred drawing application. If you use CMYK (subtraction colors), then you will notice color shifts when the artwork is imported into Flash 5. If you're using FreeHand 9 or Illustrator 9, be sure that you specify colors with the RGB color picker; doing so ensures that both copied-and-pasted objects and exported files will appear as you see them in the Illustrator workspace. If you're using Macromedia FreeHand 9, then you have a wider range of clipboard options.

Setting up preferences in FreeHand

Macromedia FreeHand 9 has controllable clipboard options, accessible via File ➪ Preferences. In the PC version of FreeHand, click the Import/Export tab of the Preferences dialog. In the Mac version of FreeHand, click the Export category of the Preferences dialog. There, you find a Convert Colors To drop-down menu. If you are using a mix of CMYK and RGB color in a FreeHand document, then choose CMYK and RGB. However, this may render CMYK artwork differently in Flash 5. To have WYSIWYG (What You See Is What You Get) color between FreeHand and Flash, opt to use the solitary RGB option. This option converts all artwork to RGB color space, regardless of the original color picker used to fill the object(s).

Saving in the proper file format

Some vector file formats cannot save artwork color values in RGB space. If you are using Adobe Illustrator 8 or 9, make sure you specify Illustrator 7 in the Illustrator document options when saving. If you choose the Illustrator 6 or lower format, then RGB values will not be saved and color shifts will result. If you are exporting EPS files from FreeHand 8, use the Setup (PC) or Options (Mac) button in the Export Document dialog to access the same color options available in the FreeHand Preferences, discussed previously. Because FreeHand 9 supports direct export to .SWF files, you should use this route (instead of EPS files) to insure complete color compatibility with Flash 5. We see more discussion of color space in the next section.

Using FreeHand 9 with Flash

Macromedia's print and design application, FreeHand 9, adds many features that make coexistence with Flash 5 much simpler. Actually, as we'll see, Flash 5 does most of the work by natively supporting FreeHand files as an import file type. If you're not familiar with FreeHand 9, then take a look at its capabilities:

✦ Blending effects that automatically produce intermediate steps between two pieces of artwork

✦ A Perspective Grid that believably distorts the scale of artwork

✦ Native .SWF export

✦ Preview with Flash antialiased display mode

✦ Transferable symbols that work in Flash 5

This section explores these features in two expert tutorials from leading Web specialists, Bentley Wolfe and Todd Purgason.

Expert Tutorial: Marrying Flash and Freehand, *by Bentley Wolfe*

Bentley was highly recommended to us by Macromedia FreeHand product manager Brian Schmidt. This tutorial provides an excellent overview of FreeHand and Flash developments, and teaches you how to use FreeHand's unique features to integrate FreeHand artwork into Flash 5 movies.

Why Get Married?

A long time ago, there was FreeHand, which you used to draw vector illustrations. Then, there was Flash for vector animations. Vectors are vectors are vectors, right? Something like a line with a point at each end, right?

Well, not exactly. The vectors inside previous versions of FreeHand were built on an engine dating back to the medieval times of desktop publishing. Although that engine was good for drawing in FreeHand, it didn't always play well with others. Because FreeHand's vectors were largely designed for PostScript printing, there weren't usually problems going to print-design applications such as Illustrator or CorelDraw.

However, when the destination was a newer application such as Flash, it wasn't always easy to make the two formats line up correctly. Flash's drawing engine, an infant in Internet years, was significantly different than the venerable FreeHand code base. It would have been natural to assume that two Macromedia vector-based products could swap information with one another.

Because of the disparity in the rendering engines, it wasn't as easy as that. Flash and FreeHand were in the seventh grade: The boys get along with the boys and the girls get along with the girls. Both are curious about the other, but nobody knows where to start. So they stumbled around, copying and pasting vectors into Flash with mixed results, losing our arrowheads, always having trouble with the dashed lines, trying the EPS and Illustrator exports—just as awkward as the first seventh-grade dance.

Along comes FreeHand 7, and it's time to move to high school. FreeHand 7.02 adds the capability to export .SWF files directly from FreeHand, a step in the right direction. The original goal of this development was to enable FreeHand users to use Flash technology, even if they didn't own the Flash authoring tool. While .SWF export from FreeHand was an improvement, there still wasn't a way to retain FreeHand-based data in Flash. Importing .SWF into Flash didn't maintain layering. Groups didn't map to a single symbol, which would seem logical. Rather they broke into a zillion small symbols and had to be recombined. Dashed lines disappeared. Some fill types just plain weren't compatible. Like every couple, Flash and FreeHand had their share of problems.

The lack of a true interchange format between Flash and FreeHand was the root of the problem. Flash was designed to export .SWF files, not to import them. The .SWF format was designed to be as compact as possible for fast streaming playback and quick downloads. Because .SWF files are the end product of a process, they're not the ideal format for import back into Flash (or anything else for that matter). So, odd things happened. However, it was usually better than the junior high days of copy and paste.

Sooner or later, every application grows up. Along comes FreeHand 9, ready to go off to college. It still likes Flash, and it's gotten a bit more sophisticated about exporting .SWF files, but FreeHand doesn't open any more doors for Flash.

Don't lose hope, though, because Flash wants to grow up, too. Flash has decided that it likes FreeHand best, and those old flames Mr. Clipboard and Mr. EPS file can fade into the background. Flash wants to get married, and FreeHand is Mr. Right. Flash 5 adds the capability to directly import the FreeHand file format. This is a huge event! Because we have a major event worth celebrating, you'd better get some rice so that you have something to throw.

Continued

Continued

The pre-basics

Before we discuss the basic need-to-knows of getting FreeHand to work with Flash after the wedding, let's look at something important. Think of this as the wedding night talk. I'm the bride's father, you're the groom. You do want to pay close attention.

If I could telepathically implant one lesson into every user's head, it would be this: Always, always, always get the latest patch or updater! It doesn't matter what the product is, or what company made it. No software is perfect, and if it's been a month or two after the product hit the streets, then it's likely that some bugs have been found. Luckily, this usually means a patch exists to fix some of those bugs.

In this case, I'm specifically talking about the FreeHand 9.02 updater for Windows (or the 9.01 updater for Macintosh) available at www.macromedia.com/support/freehand. Why is this update important? Well, there's usually a Readme file. That's where the secrets lie.

". . . Macromedia Flash SWF export now more accurately autotraces dashes when the Trace Dashed Strokes option is chosen in the Export Options dialog box."

". . . FreeHand page links are now supported when exporting as Flash (SWF)."

See? Some of this won't affect all of your FreeHand-Flash projects, but if you hadn't downloaded the updater and read the Readme file how would you know?

The real basics

Which FreeHand versions can we import into Flash 5? Well, there is a broad range. We can directly import FreeHand versions 7, 8, and 9. So, if you've got any version of FreeHand made in the last 4 years or so you should be in good shape. What exactly can we import? All kinds of good stuff, some of which we had no way of importing into Flash before:

✦ Symbols

✦ FreeHand layers

✦ FreeHand Lens fills (with exceptions)

✦ Gradient fills

✦ Imported TIFF, GIF, JPG, and PNG bitmaps

✦ Blended and composite paths

✦ FreeHand clipping paths

✦ Text blocks as editable Flash text

✦ Arrowheads

✦ Dashed lines (using a little trick)

We can import all kinds of things into Flash from a FreeHand file. However, there are a few caveats — and it's important to know what we can't import:

✦ Fills. FreeHand illustrations can contain many fills that are designed for PostScript printing and that are built with the PostScript drawing engine. These fills require a PostScript interpreter to display correctly; Flash doesn't use PostScript. Consequently, the following fills won't import into Flash: Tiled, Custom, PostScript, Pattern, Textured, and Lens fills (other than simple transparency).

✦ Dashed strokes, Pattern strokes, PostScript strokes

✦ Certain types of fonts, including bitmapped and locked outline fonts

✦ Text effects that don't preview or export as .SWF

✦ EPS files, which do not preview or export as .SWF

✦ Multiple-layered objects with Lens fills. Lens fills only affect underlying artwork that exists on the same layer.

Setting the page size in FreeHand

You can simplify your life by setting up the FreeHand page to match your Flash movie. This makes it significantly easier to position elements when imported into Flash. The easiest way to do this is to set FreeHand's ruler measurement to either points or pixels (which are basically the same for multimedia sizing purposes), and then choose a custom page size that matches your Flash movie frame size. It's usually helpful to set the page orientation to landscape as well, because most Flash movies are wider then they are tall.

If you choose not to resize the page, then draw in the upper-leftmost corner of the pasteboard, or resize the FreeHand page to match the size of the object after drawing it. Because Flash uses the upper-left corner of its Stage to position all imported objects, your FreeHand artwork will map appropriately.

Strokes, fills, and blends

Some of you may be thinking, "Why bother using FreeHand in the first place? I can draw perfectly well in Flash." OK, maybe you can — many talented Flash illustrators and animators manage fine without FreeHand. However, FreeHand can bring a few tricks to the process that you just can't do in Flash. Have you ever tried to draw an acute-angle eight-pointed star in Flash? What about a Mollusk shell? No? Although Flash has a very good natural drawing engine, some of its drawing tools aren't particularly sophisticated, which is where FreeHand comes in. FreeHand has had the benefit of a long development history, and has enhanced drawing tools for complex illustrations.

FreeHand brings three qualities to the process: (a) the capability to create sophisticated artwork such as multisided polygons, stars and starbursts, and quick and dirty triangles; (b) the world's coolest spirals in any possible shape; and (c) the capability to apply strokes and fills to that artwork. Sure, you can draw basic shapes with fills and strokes in Flash, but, if you throw FreeHand into the mix, then you can put vectors into overdrive.

Continued

Continued

After you're comfortable with FreeHand's "release to layers" feature, you can even build animations of these complex images for use in Flash. Let's walk you through an example:

1. In FreeHand, use the spiral tool to draw a basic spiral (see the following figure). If you're new to FreeHand, double-click the spiral tool to set spiral options before drawing the path. For this particular example, I've closed the spiral using the Object Inspector and given it a gradient fill between two RGB colors (see "Color Conversion" later in this sidebar for more information).

2. In the preceding figure, we have a basic spiral. Now, clone the spiral so that you have two of the same (Edit ⇨ Clone). Select only the new copy. Double-click FreeHand's Rotation Tool. This opens the Transform dialog. Enter 180 degrees in the Rotation field and click the "Rotate" button. This gives you something unsightly that is similar to the following figure.

3. Now for the fun part. Select both images by clicking one and Shift+clicking the other. Choose Xtras ⇨ Create ⇨ Blend. This creates a blend between the two spirals. If you've never created blends and want to know more about them, you can read about them in the FreeHand manual.

4. With that blend still selected, choose Xtras ⇨ Animate ⇨ Release to Layers. Release to Layers is well documented in the FreeHand manual and online help, so I won't go into detail about it here. Basically, Release to Layers puts each step of the blend on its own layer.

5. Save the FreeHand file, and switch to Flash 5.

   Generally, if you're going through the trouble to animate something in FreeHand, then you're going to be using it in a symbol. You *could* be using FreeHand to create static vector artwork for Flash, but what fun is that?

6. In Flash 5, choose Insert ⇨ New Symbol (Ctrl+F8 or Command+F8). When we import the FreeHand file, the artwork will go directly into the new symbol. In most cases, this symbol will be a Movie Clip, but it could be a Graphic or Button symbol, too.

7. While in the Symbol Editing Mode, the first keyframe is ready for some artwork. Import the FreeHand file (Ctrl+R or Command+R). You should see a dialog similar to this:

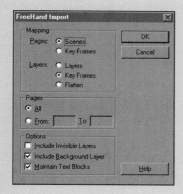

Despite the myriad options available, just look at the Layers section. Remember that we released all those steps to layers in FreeHand. Therefore, we don't want everything on one keyframe on separate layers in Flash, at least not for this type of animation. We want the images to import as a series of keyframes so that we can animate the blend in our Flash movie.

8. For this example, choose to have each separate FreeHand layer import to a new keyframe in Flash. All of the keyframes will be on the same Flash layer that was active or selected before you initiated the import.

That's it. Once you've completed the import, exit the symbol's timeline (Edit ⇨ Edit Movie) and use this new symbol in your movie. What you should see is an interesting morph between the original spiral and the final spiral. Of course, you could do a Shape Tween in Flash that might be similar, but it would be significantly more difficult to build a composite spiral shape with Flash drawing tools. Through experimentation, you can develop some interesting effects with FreeHand's drawing tools.

Color conversion: Be careful

All colors in Flash are described in RGB color space. Flash's primary presentation mode is onscreen display. Although the Flash Player now has the capability to print (since later releases of the Flash 4 Player), Flash movies aren't designed to see a printing press. On the other hand, FreeHand was designed for print purposes. It's likely that you'll be designing comps in FreeHand that may be used for both print and Web spaces. Therefore, you'll initially be working in CMYK color space.

Continued

Continued

When Flash imports a FreeHand file, all CMYK color items convert to RGB, including any grayscale bitmaps that you may have in the file. The problem is that this conversion process isn't always perfect, and the colors that you see in Flash may not exactly match the colors with which you started in FreeHand. Usually the Flash colors appear more muted than the FreeHand colors.

The safest course of action is to convert the colors to RGB in the FreeHand artwork *before* you import it into Flash. If you need to keep the CMYK version of the FreeHand file for print purposes, then do a Save As to preserve the original file. Convert the colors to RGB, save the new file, and import it into Flash. Voilà, matching RBG colors.

Symbols

Finally, you can create symbols in FreeHand! Symbols in FreeHand are fundamentally the same symbols that you use in Flash: Create a master symbol and use it as many times as you like in the document. Each child instance maintains the attributes of the parent symbol. Making changes to the shape, stroke, or fill of the object(s) within the parent symbol affects all the symbol instances of the parent. Therefore, multiple-use elements in your FreeHand document (and Flash movie) can be updated painlessly and in a straightforward manner.

Creating symbols is simple in FreeHand. Unlike Flash, FreeHand has only one symbol type. Before you create a symbol in FreeHand, you need to draw something: multiple objects, groups, blends, and so on.

  1. Let's make a symbol that contains a basic black triangle. Turn on the page rulers and set the zero point (see the following figure). You'll be using the zero point as the axis of rotation. In this example, I've added two blue guides to help you see where the zero point is.

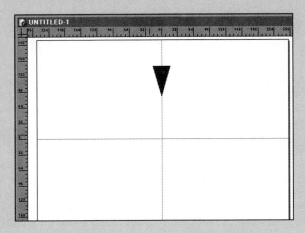

2. Now, select the black triangle. Open Window ⇨ Panels ⇨ Symbols and drag the triangle into the Symbol Panel. This creates a parent symbol of the triangle. You may now delete the original triangle from the Stage.

3. To use instance of the symbol in FreeHand, drag the symbol from the Symbol Panel and drop it on the Stage. Place the instance of the triangle in roughly the same position as it appears in the preceding illustration.

4. Select the black triangle and clone it (Edit ⇨ Clone).

5. Double-click the Rotation Tool to open the Transform Panel. We want eight total triangles in this step. Therefore, we need each triangle to be 45 degrees from the previous triangle (8 triangles × 45 degrees = 360 degrees). Enter **45** degrees for the rotation angle. Make sure to set both the x and y center numbers to **zero**. These numbers inform FreeHand to use that point (0,0) as the axis of rotation. You'll see what I mean in the next few steps.

6. Click Apply in the Transform Panel. This creates the second triangle 45 degrees to the left of the first.

This is a great time to show you another helpful FreeHand feature, Power Duplicate. Some of you may know this as Step and Repeat in other programs. In any case, it's a feature that Flash doesn't have. Power Duplicate is best for making repetitive geometric shapes, which can be awkward in Flash.

7. To Power Duplicate, press Ctrl+D (PC) or Command+D (Mac) repeatedly. Each time you press these keys, another clone is made with the same offset. When you've done that seven times, you should have something similar to the following figure. Remember that each of these items is an instance of the original parent symbol.

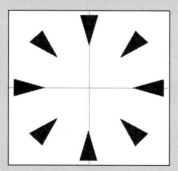

8. Save this file in FreeHand 9 format. Open Flash 5 and import the file. In this case, you want to choose Flatten for the Layers option.

Continued

Continued

Look at the Flash Library. Notice how the FreeHand symbol came into Flash as a Flash symbol, and how each triangle imported as an instance of that symbol? As with any other Flash symbol, you can now make changes to the symbol that will affect all the instances. Additionally, Flash 5 mapped the FreeHand guides into Flash guides. Excellent!

When I published this Flash movie (with just this one symbol), the file size was a miserly 2K. Sure, you could do this in Flash with instances, moving the instances around and rotating them. However, it could take up to five times longer. Who has time? With a little creativity using this technique, you can make Flash and FreeHand sing. You'll be more productive, you'll bill more hours, and you'll be better looking!

Well, OK. Maybe you won't be better looking, but you'll definitely be a Flash and FreeHand guru. Which is better than just a Flash guru, right? After you become comfortable with this technique, you can very quickly create symmetrical shapes that would have taken much longer in Flash. When I envision this technique, I think about clock faces and watch dials. I leave more examples up to your imagination.

You can use power duplicate to create instances, as you saw in this example. However, you can't use instances to build a blend. The steps of a blend in a FreeHand file will import into Flash as separate objects. The final .SWF file will be larger than our previous example.

Layers

The FreeHand Import dialog in Flash 5 has an option for handling FreeHand layers. Direct importation of .SWF files never allowed us to keep our layer formatting. Now, Flash 5 can map FreeHand layers into Flash layers. While this may not seem very important, it is extremely useful. Consistent organization and proper resource management will save you a lot of time that you might otherwise have invested in converting copied-and-pasted vectors into symbols and organizing them on your Flash layers.

Lens fills

Lens fills are cool. There's no other way to say it. Macromedia has pulled off a neat trick with Lens fills. If you want to apply alpha-channel transparency to a Flash element, what do you have to do? You have to convert the artwork into a symbol and apply the alpha transparency to the symbol.

As an alternative, try this in Freehand: Make a transparent Lens fill on a closed object. It doesn't matter what's underneath it — just make sure that you don't use any imported EPS graphics with this trick. Embedded EPS graphics won't import into Flash. If you want to use external graphics, try using a JPEG image. This effect can achieve some amazing results with a JPEG image. Also, don't make the combined Lens fill and graphic into a symbol. Save the FreeHand file and import it in Flash. What happens? Even though we didn't make the object a symbol, the Flash import maintains transparency! The transparency remains, just as it appeared inside FreeHand.

If you try the same effect with the Lens-filled object, a symbol *in FreeHand*, then you get another interesting effect. You lose the transparency, but you get a clipping path of the bitmap that was underneath the object.

If you import this FreeHand file into Flash and edit the symbol, you'll see that the Lens-filled object has automatically become a mask of the bitmap. Although this might adversely affect file size, it can be useful to have access to the separated mask.

With the exception of monochrome fills, all of the Lens fill types are supported. Monochrome fills will not import into Flash 5. However, the Transparency and Magnify Lens fills both work very well, and provide effects that would more difficult to get in Flash. As with all work involving complex visual information, watch those file sizes!

Gradient fills

You need to know two tips about FreeHand Gradient fills and Flash: (a) You can use them interchangeably, and (b) you should use them sparingly. Flash 5 can only handle a gradient with no more than eight colors. If you use more than eight colors in a FreeHand gradient, Flash will break up the fill into separate shapes with clipping paths. You'll get the same basic effect, but the file size will be much bigger.

Here's another cool tip. What if you made the world's coolest gradient in FreeHand, and you wanted to use it again with other Flash artwork? Import the FreeHand file, and then double-click the item with the Gradient fill. Open the Color Mixer in Flash. The gradient should be displayed in the fill pop-up menu. If it's not showing, then you've selected the wrong gradient or piece of artwork. Access the Color Mixer Panel's options menu in the upper right and choose Add Swatch. Now you can reapply that gradient to any other fill in the Flash movie.

Clipping paths

Clipping paths, created using the Paste Inside feature in FreeHand, are directly imported into Flash. The clipping path comes into Flash as a Graphic symbol containing the clipping object on a Mask layer and the clipped artwork on a nested layer. If there's a stroke on the clipping path, then the stroke will have its own Flash layer above the other two. Remember that, when working with clipping paths, Flash imports all of the information *outside* the clipping path, too! If your Flash movie file size is extraordinarily large after you've imported clipping paths from FreeHand, then clipping paths are probably the culprit. Make sure that you trim all the areas that won't be seen in the clipping area *before* importing the FreeHand file into Flash.

Although you can create masks in Flash using the new Pen Tool (and Bézier curves), FreeHand has much better control over what's inside the path. After you have a workflow in place, FreeHand can save you time and effort.

Text blocks and preferences

Flash 5 only has one preference option that affects FreeHand import. In the Clipboard tab of the Flash Preferences dialog is an option for FreeHand Text, a check box named Maintain Text as Blocks. This option has no effect on FreeHand files *imported* into Flash. Rather, it controls what happens when a block of text from FreeHand is *pasted* into Flash 5. If this preference is checked, then the text block will paste into Flash as editable text. If it's unchecked, the outlines of the letters will be pasted and you won't be able to edit the text in Flash.

Continued

Continued

A similar check box in the FreeHand Import dialog performs the exact same function. If you want to preserve editable text boxes when importing a FreeHand file, check this box.

Those crazy dashed lines

In the past, we could never manage to get dashed lines from FreeHand into Flash. Flash has dashed lines and FreeHand has dashed lines. So, why couldn't we import them? Flash 5 fixed the problem. Flash 5 automatically converts dashed lines in a FreeHand file into a group of outlined paths. Even though it doesn't become a Flash dashed line, it does look like one.

Achieving the impossible with the Perspective Grid

Now here's a trick that FreeHand can do that Flash cannot do: FreeHand can build vector artwork with true perspective. This is a new feature in FreeHand 9 and is thoroughly covered in the FreeHand documentation. This type of artwork isn't particularly useful for animation because there is no way to automate the process, and blends on a Perspective Grid cannot be released to layer. However, you can create some amazing singular images for use in Flash, which doesn't have a Perspective Grid. See the following figure for some examples.

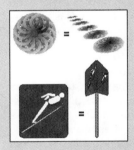

"Flash found me. I was on the tech support teams for FreeHand and Director when Macromedia bought Futuresplash. After years of phone support, I was offered the opportunity to become a unique online support evangelist, focusing only on Flash . . . it's been pretty interesting. Just for the record, my work would be nearly impossible without Colin Moock's `moock.org`, `flashkit.com`, Amanda's `virtual-fx.net`, Chrissy Rey's `flashlite.net`, and `were-here.com`." Which explains why Bentley can't enumerate the sites he's worked on. By helping Flash users online, he's "made contributions to thousands of Flash sites." When Bentley was finishing high school, the Star Wars series was still a major force and, in "the coal mine regions of northeastern Pennsylvania—Hazleton, to be exact," he recalls "listening to John Cougar's *American Fool* a lot. (Of course, it's embarrassing now to admit I listened to that more than the Clash. What was I thinking?)" Now an established family man in Richardson, Texas, Bentley Wolfe's single most favorite thing is to, "Ride anything with two wheels. I'm a full-time single father of three girls 7, 9, and 10. They all ride motorcycles, too. Remember: Parenting is a tough job, but it's an easy job to get."

FreeHand 9 can do more than just create vector artwork more quickly than Flash 5. With FreeHand, you can create mockups and presentation boards for Web clients and have Flash-ready artwork ready for interactive development. The next tutorial by Todd Purgason explains this concept more thoroughly.

Expert Tutorial: Streamlined Workflow: FreeHand 9 and Flash 5 *by Todd Purgason*

Todd contributed to the last edition of the Flash Bible. Because he is a leading FreeHand-Flash authority with award-winning Flash design work, we invited him to add his workflow wisdom to this edition.

Flash 5 is a powerful tool for developing intelligent, sophisticated Web sites and interactive environments. But as most of us in the digital design arena know, no single tool does it all. We've all mastered many applications that enable us to design and produce the images and interfaces that are imagined in our mind's eye. The old cliché, "the right tool for the job," holds just as true in the digital arena as it does in your grandpappy's garage. By adding FreeHand to your Flash toolbox, you go from having four drawers of specialized tools to having eight drawers of specialized tools. FreeHand is an extremely powerful illustration and typography tool that brings more than 10 years of research, design and refinement to all your Flash projects. By tapping the strengths of FreeHand, your Flash 5 applications can be that much more effective.

What advantages can FreeHand give to Flash 5 projects?

For starters, familiarity: Flash 5 is a new tool with a new paradigm for creating vector-graphic artwork. It works with vectors but often feels like a raster-based authoring application. Many of us are very used to objects with lines, curves, points, and fills that are the foundations of applications such as FreeHand and Illustrator. We've become quite proficient in this working model, and setting these skills aside would be a terrible waste. FreeHand brings much more than familiarity to the table. It has very powerful tools for illustration and — my personal favorite — typography.

A huge benefit of using FreeHand in the Flash design process is conceptualizing a design. Using FreeHand's multipage format, you can lay out moments in time or keyframes to visualize and study the interface and motion graphics that you will be executing in Flash. This is a big advantage of using FreeHand, instead of Illustrator, for your conceptualizing needs: Illustrator is limited to one-page documents. In addition, Macromedia has spent a great deal of time and effort on features such as the Animate to Layer Tool and .SWF export in FreeHand, which enable FreeHand to live symbiotically in the same design space as Flash.

I think that the greatest asset that FreeHand brings to the Flash table is *print*. Ooooo . . . that nasty word: the old medium of print. Don't we live in the paperless society yet? Not quite. While developing your design in FreeHand, you're actually doing production and composition at the same time.

Continued

Continued

After you have visualized an animation over several pages in FreeHand, it is a very simple task to bring those pages together onto a large format presentation board that you can output to a printer. These presentations blow the clients away! After you get approval, it's on to Flash, where you breathe life into the design that you've been carefully planning in FreeHand. If your clients are like mine, they'll come back and want you to do print promotions, ads, and even identity materials based on the Web site. You already have all the print assets developed in your page compositions. What a bonus! I just hate getting more billable work, don't you?

Developing a process model

Because the complexity of this process would require several chapters, I walk you through the key steps, using visuals from one of my recent projects, an in-house marketing project titled "The Process." It's a reflection of our creative philosophy at Juxt Interactive. Visit this project at www.juxinteractive.com/theprocess.

Design

Many Flash projects are orchestrated over one or more layouts that are called *scenes*. The term *scene is* appropriate because oftentimes they are just that — scenes in a Flash movie. After I've developed a concept in my head and scribbled sketches on paper, I go to FreeHand and start sketching out scenes. The following figure is an example of such scenes.

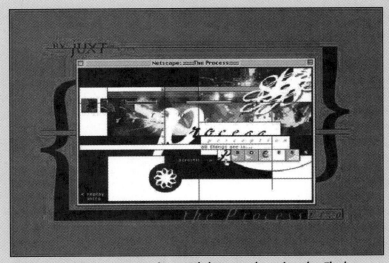

The Process scene, as seen in a Web browser by using the Flash Player plug-in.

Next, I start building moments in time, or keyframes, that bring elements (characters) into the scene to be laid out and experimented with. I typically start by developing a moment in time that is very heavy visually—often the end of the first major scene. Once I am happy with the scene and the way the elements or characters are working together, I duplicate the page in FreeHand. Then, working with the duplicated page(s), I experiment with the relationships of all the characters. During this step, I'm mindful of the motions that will get me to and from each moment in time. I continue to develop a number of keyframes that form the framework of what I intend to do. The renowned film title designer, Kyle Cooper, of Imaginary Forces, has been a great inspiration to me. He once said, "I think that, in the end, I should be able to pull any frame out of my title sequences and it should be able to stand on its own as an effective illustration." By studying my design as snapshots in time in FreeHand I hope to ensure that the motion won't destroy the concept, but rather, that it will enhance its effectiveness.

Realness of presentation

Now, I have many pages that help me understand just how to pull this project off. I take those keyframe pages and lay them out onto a large format sheet that will be printed on our large format HP Design Jet at roughly 30"×40". Many people ask me why I continue to print in this day and age. I will tell you why: communication. Half of the job of design is selling the design you create, especially if you are asking the client to take risks pushing the envelope that they are accustomed to. A digital presentation has many advantages, but so does a good old tangible printed piece.

We have developed a presentation process at Juxt that I affectionately call the 2×4 approach. It is based on the old aphorism, "How do you get the attention of a donkey? Hit him over the head with a 2×4." Don't get me wrong—I'm not insulting any clients, but the point is to make an impact. When we go into a presentation, we intend to exceed the client's expectations and to make the client very happy. With a presentation board, I can show many keyframes or screens simultaneously as I walk the client through the animation, explaining the process of the motion or the interaction of the interface without, at this early stage, committing the resources to create an actual working prototype.

However, as a communication tool, the advantages are far greater than saving time. Here's why: The digital medium is abstract, whereas print is tangible and real. With a presentation board, the clients can absorb the design when it is all laid out for them. They can see how their brand is working across the piece. Because the print piece is so very tangible, they can grasp the wholeness of it—which means that they can take ownership of it emotionally. But most importantly, it communicates to the client that you are good at what you do. Consequently, they'll have more faith in the decisions that you'll make for them during the process of creating the project. Refer to the following figure.

Continued

Continued

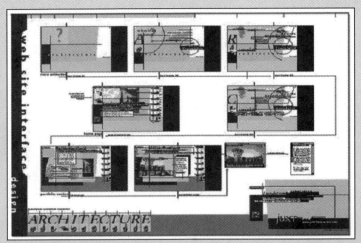

Here's an example of the presentation board, which is used as a printed presentation for clients.

Instant changeability

So you've finished presenting the project, your client is sold on your design, but then his partner walks in and says, "Eww . . . I just hate that green." You try to explain its purpose and the importance of that color to the design, but he won't budge. If you'd completed a prototype in Flash, you would have to go back and spend many hours tediously changing that green to tan. But because you laid it out in FreeHand, you can change that green to tan across the entire piece — in about 5 seconds. You simply select the new tan color in FreeHand's Web-Safe Color Palette, drag and drop it on top of the banished green in the color list, and voilà, every instance of the green is now tan. No matter where there were green lines, files, patterns, text, or colored bitmaps, all are now tan.

Before you have time to gloat, the client's graphics guru tells you that you were given the old corporate design standards manual. Instead of Franklin Gothic (the font you used on 75 percent of the typography), you are supposed to be using Meta Plus. Well, because you still have all your pages in FreeHand, you can simply use the graphic search-and-replace feature to instantly change every bit of Franklin Gothic to Meta Plus. After a few minutes of double-checking kerning effects, you are back to where you started. Now go ahead and feel proud of yourself. Your client will love that these changes won't cost the company a dime.

Moving artwork from FreeHand to Flash

You have four ways to get your artwork from FreeHand to Flash: the .SWF export feature from FreeHand, copy-and-paste, drag and drop, and now — in Flash 5 — you can open FreeHand 9 files directly in Flash.

Using the .SWF export for static Flash movies

Opening Freehand files directly into Flash 5 is very convenient because it retains a good deal of structure. However, the .SWF Export feature is still a very good method for outputting FreeHand files as Flash movies, because it not only creates the most optimized result, it also does much of the tedious work for you. For instance, if you have a tinted black-and-white TIFF image pasted inside a circle shape in a FreeHand drawing, you can export an optimized .SWF movie. When you import that .SWF file into Flash, your image will open as a Flash bitmap image with a mask of the circle shape.

You can access the .SWF Export feature by choosing File ⇨ Export (Shift+Command+R or Shift+Ctrl+R), and selecting Flash (.SWF) (PC) or Flash .SWF (Mac) in the Save as Type (PC) or Format (Mac) drop-down menu. Click the Options button (Mac) or the Setup button (PC) to access the conversion properties used for the Flash .SWF file (see the following figure).

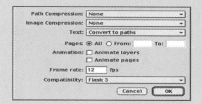

The Export Document dialog gives you access to the .SWF file settings by clicking the Options button (Mac) or Setup button (PC). Note that you can only choose Flash 3 as the .SWF version format, which is perfectly fine for Flash 5 artwork. The Flash 5 .SWF format has not changed any artwork specifications that were used in Flash 3 or 4.

In this section, we output a set of FreeHand objects as the basis of a Flash scene. Before you export a FreeHand document as a Flash file, you need to prepare the FreeHand artwork for optimal export. In the FreeHand file, select all the objects on a "moment in time" page that has the scene completely built and some of the elements or characters on the stage. Copy that page and paste it into a new FreeHand document, aligning the upper left-hand extents of objects with the upper left-hand extents of the page. If you have some complex typography elements with special kerning as well as body text, you will want to select the illustration text elements and convert them to paths using the Text ⇨ Convert to Paths command.

You will lose kerning of text if you export with the Maintain blocks option enabled. Always convert type elements that use special kerning or FreeHand-specific text effects. If you do *not* have body text, I recommend setting the text option of the .SWF Export dialog to Convert to Paths. This converts the characters to paths and creates symbols of each character in the process.

Now access the Flash file properties in the Export Document dialog. Because you are exporting a particular moment in time, turn off the Animate Pages and Animate Layers options in the Animation setting. Because this export is a transition from FreeHand to Flash and *not* a final file, you will want to eliminate any file degradation by setting the Path Compression and Image Compression drop-down menus to None. Export the file import it into Flash 5.

Continued

Continued

Once in Flash, you will want to go through a process of organizing your file and optimizing the imported artwork. The objects exported from FreeHand come into Flash as a group—often, objects are in nested groups. You need to move key elements to separate Flash layers. As you do this, ungroup the objects and create logically named Flash symbols out of them. After the scene is organized with the objects regrouped as symbols and arranged on their own layers, you are ready to animate.

Using the .SWF export for animating Flash movies

Another avenue for small simple animations is to use FreeHand's Release to Layers process to build a frame-by-frame animation in Flash. Try this process for yourself by following these steps:

1. Create a circle and a square in FreeHand. Keep some distance between the two objects.

2. Select both objects and blend them together using the Modify ⇨ Combine ⇨ Blend command (Shift+Command+B or Shift+Ctrl+B), or Xtras ⇨ Create ⇨ Blend. Open the Object Inspector window. With the blend selected, change the Number of Steps value to **30** steps.

3. Select Xtras ⇨ Animate ⇨ Release to Layers. This releases each blend step to a unique layer.

4. Choose File ⇨ Export, and access the Flash .SWF options. Check the Animate Layers option, and set the Frame Rate to 15 fps. Click OK and export the .SWF file.

5. Open Flash and import the .SWF file. You will see 30 keyframes in the Flash timeline, each containing a step in the blend (see the following figure). Although this is a cool trick, this is a frame-by-frame animation, which results in larger file size than if this same animation were developed within Flash 5.

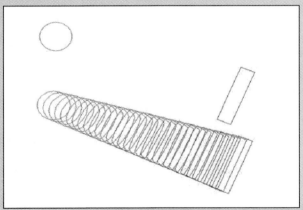

This FreeHand document shows the outlines of the two individual shapes, as well as the outlines of the 30-step blend between them.

Author's Note: Although the Release to Layers function can be a quick way to produce shape-morphing animations, it's not necessarily the best method. Prior to Flash 3, this feature was extremely useful, because shape morphing with hints was not supported within the Flash authoring environment — but now, this kind of work is best handled within Flash, using shape morphing and hints. That's because of the file size consequences of frame-by-frame animation.

General guidelines when using the .SWF export from FreeHand

After you become familiar with the process of exporting artwork to Flash, you'll discover that it's relatively simple. However, you want to keep in mind some guidelines:

✦ If you are using Flash, you must set the Import/Export tab (or the Export category in the Mac version) of the FreeHand Preferences dialog to use RGB color conversion (in the Convert Colors To drop-down menu). If you fail to do so, unexpected color shifts appear in your FreeHand and Flash artwork.

✦ When exporting .SWF files from FreeHand, do not include large amounts of body text. Recreate the body text (for example, copy and paste the text into a text box) in Flash.

✦ Remember that elements from FreeHand will be put into groups, often stacked or nested within other groups. If you can't edit an element, ungroup it or break it apart.

✦ Organize your FreeHand artwork into logical Flash layers. Develop a consistent system that you and others on your team can recognize and implement.

✦ You must be using FreeHand 8.01 or greater to export Flash .SWF files.

Opening FreeHand files directly into Flash 5

Macromedia has invested a lot of development time to its quest to create a seamless workflow between FreeHand 9 and Flash 5 — and it shows! The result is that it's much easier and more efficient to use these applications together. The best example of this workflow is the ease of copy and paste and drag and drop between FreeHand 9 and Flash 5. (These processes, which in the past only worked in the most optimal environment, now work in any environment.)

Caution: If you plan to open your FreeHand files directly in Flash, be aware of the following issues while working in FreeHand: Use symbols in FreeHand to start the optimization process. Only use Type 1 PostScript fonts. You may have problems with True Type Fonts. Only use image formats supported by Flash — JPG, PICT, BMP, and PNG.

With the recent release of FreeHand 9, followed by the introduction of Flash 5, the starting point for Flash development and concept design is more firmly grounded in FreeHand. For example, FreeHand 9 introduced symbols, which function much like symbols in Flash. Consequently, symbols that are created in Freehand 9 will be maintained — along with their layers and guides — when the FreeHand file is opened in Flash 5. Let's take a look at just how this works, as it really is very simple.

1. Open a new Flash file and set the movie size to match the page size of the FreeHand file that you will be importing.

Continued

Continued

2. Use File Í Import to select your Freehand 9 File.

3. A dialog appears (see the following figure) with a number of options to control how you want your file translated. Select the desired options and click OK.

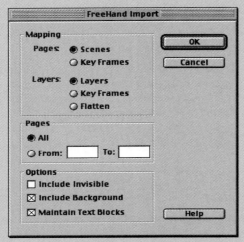

The new Flash 5 Freehand Import dialog

4. Now that you have your FreeHand artwork in Flash (intact and organized just as it was in the Freehand), you are ready to develop your Flash project.

In summary

Starting your Flash project by using FreeHand gives you huge advantages that won't detract from Flash as a tool. Instead, FreeHand can enhance your understanding of animation and interactive concepts. With FreeHand, you'll have a fast, powerful tool to study your design and develop it, without investing countless hours in work that may or may not make the final cut. Furthermore, you will have fantastic print deliverables to sell your design approach. For me, this is the icing on the cake — I have print-ready materials if the client needs anything from the FreeHand concepts. That means I don't have to create my artwork or designs twice — which means that I have more time to dedicate to design.

A native Southern Californian, Todd Purgason is the principal of the highly regarded, award-winning Juxt Interactive. Juxt Interactive's portfolio includes these Web sites: www.billabong-usa.com, www.omniskywireless.com, http://shorn.com, and http://lundstromarch.com. Other Web sites are listed at www.juxtinteractive.com.

Todd recalls the album, Queen is Dead, by the Smiths, as a notable relic from his final year of high school. His single most-favorite thing to do is to "hug my two little girls." He also enjoys spending time with his wife, designing, playing volleyball in the sand, and reading. Todd first saw Futuresplash in 1996; but when Macromedia bought it, he said he "knew what would happen, so I dove in head first."

Exporting Artwork from Illustrator

You can also repurpose Adobe Illustrator artwork to use in Flash 5. If you use Adobe Illustrator 9, you can export your artwork for Flash as:

1. EPS format (.EPS file)

2. Adobe Illustrator format (.AI file)

3. Flash format (.SWF file)

If you use Illustrator 8, then you can still export artwork as .SWF files if you download and install Macromedia's free Flash Writer plug-in, which is available at `www.macromedia.com/support/flash/download`. Depending on the nature of your artwork, you may choose to use any of the three file formats listed previously. You'll see examples of using layered FreeHand and Illustrator files later in this chapter. For most purposes, you will want to export directly to the .SWF format from Illustrator.

Using the Macromedia Flash Writer plug-in

Shortly after Flash 4 was released, Macromedia wrote a Flash Writer plug-in for Illustrator 8 that enabled the direct export of .SWF files. This free download from the Macromedia Web site bypasses many problems with using .EPS and .AI files in Flash 4 and 5. Notably, the Flash Writer plug-in can convert EPS blends into Flash gradients. After you download the plug-in from Macromedia, you'll receive an e-mail with a serial number so that you can run the installation on your system. To export .SWF files in Illustrator 8, follow these steps:

1. Run the Illustrator application and open your artwork file.

2. Access the Export command in the File menu, and select Flash Player .SWF in the Format drop-down menu of the Export dialog. Select a folder or directory to store your .SWF file, and type a name for the file. Make sure you specify .SWF at the end of the filename. Click Save.

3. In the Flash Writer dialog (shown in Figure 31-7), select the options for your .SWF file. The dialog contains these options:

   • **Image Settings:** These options control the compression of any placed bitmaps in your Illustrator file. We recommend setting the compression type to JPEG (lossy) at Medium or Medium-High quality, and the dpi setting at 72 to reduce file size.

   • **File and Objects:** Use these options to set the Flash version (2, 3, or 4), and to control how the artwork structures are mapped to Flash gradients and frames. If you're not planning to bring the .SWF back into Flash for further editing, you'll want to enable the Export File as Protected option.

You can also choose to export each layer of your Illustrator document as a unique .SWF file, using the Export Layers as Separate Files option. The remaining options determine how Illustrator artwork translates into Flash. If you are using Gradient Meshes, Patterns and Brushes, Text Objects or Chart Items, then enable them as needed.

• **Movie Size:** Usually, you'll want to export the .SWF to match the size of the artwork on the page. By default, the Match to Content option is selected. To output the .SWF with the dimensions of the page layout, select Preserve Artboard Bounds. If you want a border to appear around the edge of the Flash movie frame, then select Add Border to Content.

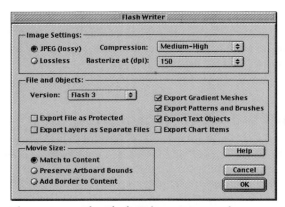

Figure 31-7: The Flash Writer export settings

4. Click OK, and you now have a new .SWF file. You can import the .SWF file into an existing Flash movie, or publish it on your Web site.

Again, the Flash Writer plug-in is available only for Illustrator 8. If you want to export .SWF files from Illustrator 9, proceed to the next section.

Tip
Be sure to read the help files that install with the Flash Writer plug-in. You can access these HTML files by clicking the Help button within the Flash Writer dialog. Among other guidelines, the Help documents indicate that some text settings, such as leading, kerning, and tracking, will not export properly with the Flash Writer plug-in. You should convert your text to outlines before using the Flash Writer plug-in if you alter any of these text settings.

Using .SWF Export from Illustrator 9

A new feature of Adobe Illustrator 9 is the capability to export .SWF files without the use of an additional plug-in. The options for the Flash Format are nearly identical to the Macromedia Flash Writer plug-in, with some important additions. To export a .SWF file from Illustrator 9, follow these steps:

1. In Illustrator 9, open your Illustrator or EPS file.

2. Select Export from the File menu, and choose Flash (.SWF) from the Format drop-down menu. Type a name for your new .SWF file, and choose a folder to store the file.

3. In the Flash (.SWF) Format Options dialog (shown in Figure 31-8), you can choose how you want your artwork to export. With the exception of choosing Baseline (Standard) or Baseline Optimized for JPEG compression, the Image Options are nearly identical to those of the Image Settings in the Flash Writer plug-in (see previous section). The Export options have these settings:

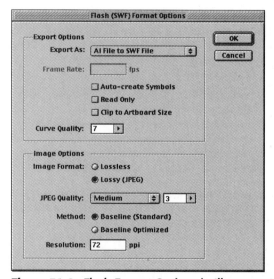

Figure 31-8: Flash Format Options in Illustrator 9

- **Export As:** The main addition to Illustrator 9's .SWF export is the Export As drop-down menu options. If AI File to .SWF File is selected, all of your artwork will appear on one keyframe and one layer in the Flash movie. AI Layers to .SWF Frames will export each layer as separate sequential keyframes on the Flash movie timeline. If this option is selected, then you can enter a Frame Rate as well. AI Layers to .SWF Files exports a separate .SWF file for each Illustrator layer.

- **Frame Rate:** As mentioned in the Export As section, you can specify a frame rate for your .SWF animation if you chose the AI Layers to .SWF Frames option. By default, this option is 12 fps. For faster animations, enter a higher frame rate.

- **Auto-create Symbols:** This setting converts each piece (or group) of Illustrator artwork into a Flash symbol that can be accessed from the Flash Library. Use this setting if you want to import the .SWF file into Flash for further editing and for reuse in other Flash movies. This feature will add a duplicate keyframe for each symbol when imported into Flash. As odd as this may seem, it's necessary for Flash to recognize the symbols on import. Make sure that you remove the second keyframe before you publish your final .SWF from Flash 5.

- **Read Only:** To prevent your .SWF file from being imported into the Flash authoring environment, enable this check box.

- **Clip to Artboard Size:** This option forces the .SWF's movie dimensions to match the page size of your Illustrator document, even if your artwork doesn't occupy the whole page.

- **Curve Quality:** This setting enables you to specify the accuracy of paths exported from Illustrator. Higher settings (up to 10) result in better accuracy but larger file sizes. Lower settings produce smaller file sizes, at the expense of line quality. We recommend that you use the default setting of **7**.

4. Click OK, and Illustrator exports a new .SWF file. You can use the new file in another Flash movie or publish it to the Web.

Replacing Blends with Flash Gradients

If you're using a drawing application that doesn't support .SWF export, then you can still work around EPS blends in Flash 5. Replacing externally rendered "blends" with Flash gradients, an old trick among 3D Flash designers, drastically cuts down on Flash movie (.SWF) file sizes. Unless you're using a program that supports Flash gradients in .SWF export, gradients or blends created in drawing, illustration, or 3D programs will not be converted to Flash gradients when the graphic(s) are imported into Flash.

 Use the 3Dgraphic.eps file, located in the ch31 folder of the *Flash 5 Bible* CD-ROM, if you need a sample image for the following steps.

Because the vast majority of applications do not render Flash-style gradients, it's up to you to decide to accept the file size "weight gains" of shaded blends or to recreate the blends with Flash gradients after the artwork has been imported into the Flash authoring environment. Here's the general process for replacing externally created blends in Flash:

1. After the artwork has been rendered as an EPS or AI file, open Flash 5. Create a new graphic symbol and open this symbol in the Symbol Editing stage. Import the EPS graphic into the first frame of the symbol.

2. Break apart (Command+B or Ctrl+B) or ungroup the imported vector artwork to the point where you isolate the blend separately from the rest of the graphic. If you break apart the imported vector graphic, then it should be reduced to "symbol" parts and groups in one step as seen in Figure 31-9. Note that Flash will convert EPS blends to symbols (accessible from the Flash Library). These symbols will contain a mask layer and a blend layer.

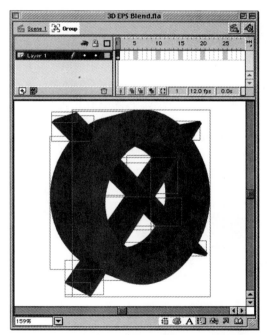

Figure 31-9: When the Break Apart command is applied to the imported graphic, you can access the individual groups within the graphic.

3. Access the timeline of each symbol that contains a blend, and erase the "blend" graphics. Keep the original Mask Layer intact, but replace the Blend Layer contents with a Flash gradient. You may need to make a three- or four-color gradient, and use the Transform Fill modifier of the Paint Bucket Tool to modify the direction and size of the gradient.

Refer to Figures 31-10 and 31-11 for more details.

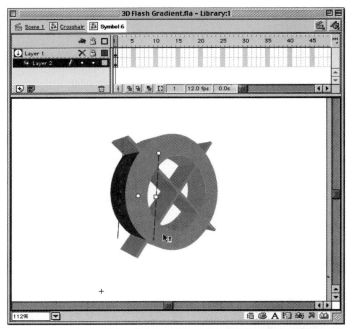

Figure 31-10: Double-click a selected symbol to enter Symbol Editing Mode. Replace the blend in the lower layer of the symbol with a Flash gradient.

Figure 31-11: The Flash version of the blended EPS graphic

When you are done replacing each blend's symbol with a Flash gradient, you'll have a better looking (and slightly smaller) Flash movie. If you are working with multiple imported vector graphics that have blends, you'll end up with much smaller Shockwave Flash movies — which means Web visitors will spend less time waiting to see your movies.

Tip

Remember that gradients created in Macromedia FreeHand 8.0.1 can be directly exported to .SWF files as Flash gradients. FreeHand's transparent colors will also convert to Flash alpha colors.

Using Layered FreeHand, EPS, or Illustrator Files

A handy feature of many popular illustration programs is support for layers. Just like layers in a Flash movie (.FLA file), layers in illustration programs enable you to keep individual groups of graphics separate from one another. A simple technique with animating vector graphic files is to animate or tween each layer separately in the Flash authoring environment.

A quick example of an easily converted illustration movie is a business card. If you have laid out any promotion materials in FreeHand or Illustrator and have kept the elements separated by layers, then you can create an interactive business card.

On the CD-ROM

You can use the sample business card, businesscard.fh9 or businesscard.eps, in the ch31 folder of the *Flash 5 Bible* CD-ROM for this exercise.

1. Create a layered graphic in FreeHand or Illustrator. Before a new element is created, make a new layer for it.

2. If you used extensive text controls (such as kerning, leading, tracking, and so on), then convert the text to outlines (or paths).

3. Save the layout as a FreeHand file, an EPS file, or an Illustrator file. If you have used RGB colors in an Illustrator document and want the colors to appear the same in Flash 5, make sure you save it as an Illustrator 7 file; artwork saved as an Illustrator 8 or 9 file may not import correctly into Flash. Because Flash 5 supports direct import of FreeHand documents, we recommend that you save artwork as a FreeHand 9 document (.FH9 file).

Caution

CMYK colors shift when imported into the RGB color space of Flash. Moreover, some masking and cropping information (for bleeds) may not be interpreted by Flash.

4. Import the FreeHand, .EPS, or .AI file into Flash 5. You may want to create a new scene or symbol to contain the imported graphic(s). Otherwise, the layers from the imported file will be stacked on top of or below your current layers. See Figure 31-12 for reference.

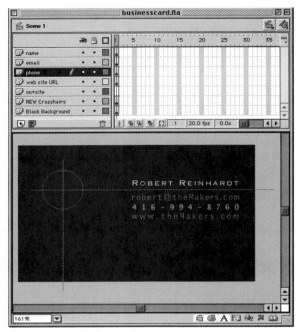

Figure 31-12: When a layered .EPS or .AI file is imported into the Flash, the layers are converted to Flash layers.

5. Even though Flash recognizes the layers in the .EPS or .AI file, it will not group elements on each layer. So, select any one layer and lock the others. Select everything on the active unlocked layer (Command+A or Ctrl+A) and group it (Command+G or Ctrl+G). Alternatively, you can convert the selection into a symbol for easier manipulation later. You need to make button symbols for any element that you want to use interactively (such as clicking the name to e-mail the person, and so on). Repeat this step for every layer.

6. Now add any Flash tweens or actions to the groups or symbols in each layer. At this point, continue creating a full Flash movie with other components, or export a Flash movie (.SWF file).

As you can see, in just six straightforward steps, you can create an interactive business card that can be put on a floppy disk or in an e-mail. Whenever you're developing complicated layered work in an illustration application such as FreeHand or Illustrator, you can take advantage of those layers in Flash.

Check out the completed interactive business card, businesscard.fla or businesscard. swf, located in the ch31 folder of the *Flash 5 Bible* CD-ROM.

Going Wild with Expression

Creature House owns the vector-image creation application called Expression, which was formerly owned by MetaCreations. Expression is similar to Painter, with the exception that it works with vectors, not bitmaps. At the time of this writing, Expression 2 was near the end of its beta phase. Arena Reed, an expert whose Painter tutorial is featured in the previous chapter, shows you how this amazing program can work with Flash .SWF files.

Expert Tutorial: Vector Painting: Using Expression 2 with Flash, *by Arena Reed*

Arena is quite fond of her Wacom Intuos tablet. Most illustrators and animators prefer to work with tablets for computer-generated artwork. Many applications, including Flash 5, provide support for pressure-sensitive input devices such as pen tablets.

What is Expression?

Expression is a sophisticated and unique vector-based painting tool that can enhance a Flash project with imagery that has an artistic look that differs from other vector-based art-work out there. That's because Expression is a painting application that utilizes Skeletal Stroke technology, which gives an artist the ability to paint a single, pressure-sensitive stroke that's based on a more complex image such as a beautiful brush stroke, a flame, a biological structure, or other intricate forms (see the following figure). Skeletal Strokes may contain multiple views that will export as an animation to the Flash (.SWF) format. Expression features a suite of interesting shape-creation tools that are much more fun than the usual pen tool (which it also has). Expression also enables you to automatically assign motion and color behaviors to objects that can be controlled by mouseover states when exported to the Flash format.

The theme I've chosen for this tutorial is plankton. Often, the art we create for the Internet is like plankton, because the Internet is such a vast and ever-changing sea of information. (In fact, our word, plankton, derives from the Greek *plankthos,* which means adrift. It was a common epithet for a wanderer, such as Odysseus. — jwl)

Author's Note: You can find assets and examples for this tutorial in the ch31 folder. In the file, planktonAnimation.xpr, there are examples of objects that have Flash motion settings applied to them, and the result of these behaviors are visible in the file, planktonAnimation.SWF.

Creating images with Expression

Painting with Skeletal Strokes is the heart and soul of Expression. To paint with skeletal strokes, select the brush tool and begin painting with different strokes from the Stroke Warehouse. Make sure to explore all of the different categories within the Stroke Warehouse. Skeletal Strokes can either emulate the kind of brush strokes created by a paintbrush, or they can contain a graphical image such as a fish or a pattern (see the following figure).

Continued

Continued

In the *planktonAnimation.xpr* example, all of the planktonic creatures were created either with a single brush stroke or a couple of primitive shapes.

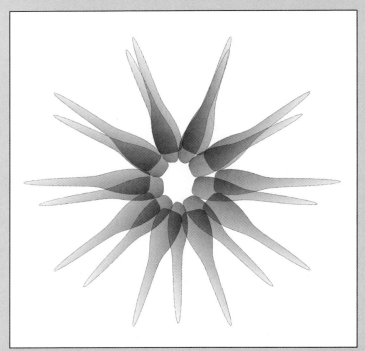

An image that was created by drawing two circles with a skeletal stroke.

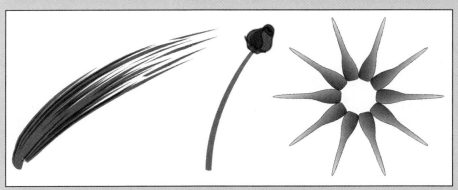

Each image was created with a single brushstroke that references a more complex image.

Expression also features unique drawing tools for creating vector elements (see the following figure). Using the B-Spline Tool is like drawing with a piece of elastic string that curves between the points you set. It's a great tool for quickly and easily creating smooth, organic shapes. The PolyLine Tool is great for creating sharp, clean shapes with curved accents. Expression also has the standard vector-drawing tools, such as the Pen Tool, which draws with the familiar Bézier curve.

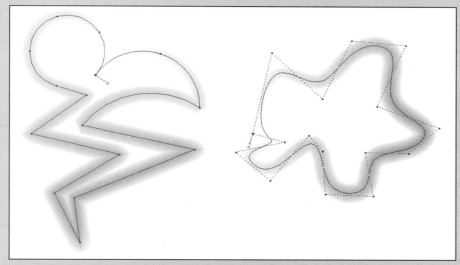

Expression has unique drawing tools, such as the B-Spline and PolyLine tools.

Creating your own Skeletal Strokes is easy. All that's involved is creating the image that you want to paint with so that it is on its side (sideways), selecting it, and defining it as a stroke. In this manner, you can turn just about anything into a skeletal stroke. Skeletal strokes can be composed of bitmap images or vector images, including text. In the *planktonAnimation* example, the text *Creating Plankton with Expression* was turned into a Skeletal Stroke to give it the effect of varied width and rotation along a path. Follow these steps to create a Skeletal Stroke:

1. Draw an object from which you want to create a stroke.

2. Select the object and proceed from the menu bar, Stroke ➪ New Stroke Definition.

3. Make sure that the object fits neatly within the boundaries of the red box and that it is oriented to be in line with the red arrow in the center of the box.

4. Press the Define Stroke button at the lower-left hand corner of the Stroke Definition Window (it looks like a little dashed arrow).

5. Name your stoke and categorize it.

Continued

Continued

6. Finally, use your new stroke by selecting the Paintbrush and painting with it. If it appears too thin, use the Node Tool to increase it's width by dragging the width handle at the head of the stroke.

The following figures provide an example of a stroke definition and a brushstroke that uses that definition.

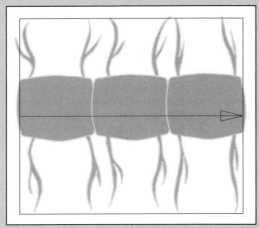

Here's an example of a Stroke Definition.

This is the resulting brushstroke.

A special case of a skeletal stroke is a *multiview stroke*. Multiview strokes add variety to an illustration, or they become an animation when exported to the Flash .SWF format.

To add views to a stroke, simply open an existing stroke, add a view to the top bar of the stroke definition window by pressing the + button, and then alter the image to create the additional view. The amoebalike creature at the bottom right-hand corner of the plankton Animation was created by using a multiview stroke. Here's how to add additional views to a Skeletal Stroke:

1. Open an existing stroke.

2. Press the Add View button (the + symbol at the top of the Stroke Definition Window).

3. Alter the image in the new view.

4. Add as many views as you like.

5. Define the stroke and give it a new name.

Assigning Flash behaviors to elements of your composition

The *Object List Palette* contains a list of every object or group of objects that's included in an image (see the following figure). Any one of these objects can be given Flash behaviors by double-clicking the object and then clicking the Flash Settings button.

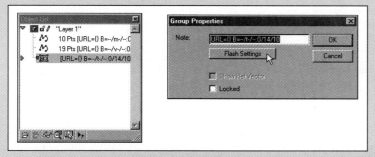

The Object List palette contains a list of every object and group of object in an Expression file. Double-click an object to get to the Flash Settings dialog.

Using the Flash Settings is the fun part—where you get to animate something without setting a single key frame. Rather, you just choose a behavior and your exported .SWF file will contain moving elements, that move according to whichever effect you've chosen. You may also specify a URL to link to in the Flash Settings dialog (shown in the following figure), which is an easy way to create a vector-based image map with automatic rollover effects. The different behaviors are Animated (this only appears if the selected stoke is a multiview stroke), Pulsate, Horizontal-Vertical Pulsate, Rock, X/Y Vibrate, Rotate, Enlarge, Shrink, Fade, Blink, Brighten, and Darken.

Continued

Continued

The Flash Settings dialog enables the assignment of various motion behaviors based on mouseover states.

Exporting a Flash (.SWF) file from Expression

Exporting a Flash movie from Expression is easy. Simply choose File ⇨ Export ⇨ Flash File. However, consider these settings:

✦ Frame rate

✦ The area of the animation (object bounding box or paper size)

✦ Whether or not you want to emulate caps and joints that are not supported by Flash (emulation increases your file size)

✦ Protection from editing

Because Flash does not support the same level of sophistication as Expression, there are some limitations to what you can export. For example, you cannot export blending methods, embossed/soft-edged fill, paper textures, fully colored bitmapped strokes, or graphics that use the non-zero winding rule. However, if you stay with purely vector-based strokes and transparency effects, you should have good results.

See the files planktonAnimation.xpr and planktonAnimation.swf in the ch31 folder on the CD-ROM for examples of an exported Expression image.

What to do with an exported Flash (.SWF) file

Your resulting .SWF file can be used as a stand-alone graphic embedded in an HTML document. The advantages of using graphics in the .SWF format are their compact size, their scalability, and their motion capabilities.

Some good applications of Expression for stand-alone graphics are banners with waving text, scientific illustrations that have moving elements, and anything quick, expressive, and whimsical that has motion. But your Expression .SWF's can also be imported into the Flash Editor or accessed by Flash as an external .SWF file with `loadMovie`.

You may also choose to use the exported .SWF as a loaded movie in a larger Flash project. See Chapter 20 for more information about using the `loadMovie` command

To get your loaded movie to interact with the rest of your project, you should use instances of an invisible button that have ActionScript attached to them. See Chapter 18's piano keys exercise for more information on attaching code to invisible buttons.

Arena Reed also submitted the Expert Tutorial "Using Painter with Flash," located in Chapter 30, "Working with Raster Graphics." Refer to that tutorial for her biographical information.

Converting Rasters to Vectors

Have you ever wanted to take a scan of a "real" pen-and-ink drawing that you made and turn it into a vector graphic? It's not incredibly hard to do, and the results are usually pretty close to the original (see Figure 31-13). You can also turn continuous tone or photographic images into vector art, but the converted version will not likely bear much resemblance to the original. However, this can be useful for aesthetic effects.

Figure 31-13: Compare the raster version (on the left) of the sketch to its traced vector version (on the right).

A handful of applications, including Flash 5, let you trace raster artwork. In the following sections, we compare the tracing capabilities of Flash, FreeHand, and Adobe Streamline. With all of these tracing applications, keep in mind these points:

✦ Higher resolution images always yield better "traced" vector artwork. With more pixels to define edges, the application can better detect shapes.

✦ Sharper images (such as clearly focused images) and higher contrast images produce better-traced artwork. Oftentimes, applying Photoshop art filters to an image can reduce the complexity of a photographic image, making it easier to trace.

✦ One-color images or scans, like those of hand-drawn sketches with pencil or ink, produce the best-traced artwork.

Caution   Ironically, the results of some traced raster images can produce even larger vector images. Remember that vectors were designed for solid colors, blends, lines, and points. Every file format has its purpose, and sometimes raster images are smaller than their traced counterparts. With a little practice, you'll be able to judge what kind of images will produce small "traced" versions.

Flash's Trace Bitmap command

After you have imported a bitmap into Flash, you can use the Modify ➪ Trace Bitmap command to convert the image into Flash lines and fills. This method is by far the simplest and quickest method of tracing artwork to use in Flash movies. The benefits are that you can perform it directly in Flash 5 without the aid of external applications, you have moderate control of the conversion settings, and, most importantly, the artwork is converted directly into Flash lines and fills (see Figure 31-14 for an example).

If the results of the Trace Bitmap command are less than desirable, then use as many undo steps as necessary to get back to your original bitmap image.

Cross-Reference   See Chapter 12, "Using Bitmaps and Other Media with Flash," for more information on the Trace Bitmap settings.

FreeHand's Trace Tool

Macromedia FreeHand 9 also has tracing capabilities, and arguably, they are more expansive than Flash's Trace Bitmap command. The Trace Tool now works like a magic wand, and you can selectively trace areas of a bitmap. You can access the Trace Tool in the FreeHand toolbox (see Figure 31-15). By double-clicking it, you can adjust the sensitivity of the Trace Tool for imported bitmapped artwork.

Figure 31-14: The Trace Bitmap command can be used to convert bitmap images into vector Flash artwork. Higher Minimum Area and Color Threshold values reduce the complexity of the resulting Flash artwork, which means smaller Flash movies.

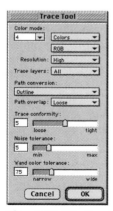

Figure 31-15: FreeHand's Trace Tool has an array of options for precise tracing.

When you're ready to trace the bitmap, you can do the trace in one of two ways: (a) selectively trace bitmap image areas, or (b) trace the entire bitmap. To use the first method, click the desired area with the Trace Tool. Once a selection is made, click inside the selection. FreeHand shows you the Wand options dialog, and you can choose whether you want to trace everything inside the selection (Trace Selection) or just the edge of the selection (Convert Selection Edge). Click OK after you have chosen an option, and FreeHand traces that area. To use the second method of tracing, simply click-drag a marquee selection with the Trace Tool, and FreeHand traces everything in the selection area.

Tip Use the magic wand method if you want to extract a traced image from an image that contains multiple elements. For example, if you have a picture of many people, and you want to trace just one of them, the magic wand can help you isolate that one person. If you want to trace all the people and the background matter, trace the entire image using the second method described previously.

Because the nature of bitmapped artwork varies by subject matter, we recommend that you use a "trial and error" method for using the FreeHand Trace Tool. If the results are not satisfactory, then simply undo the trace. Or refer to Deke McClelland's coverage of the Trace Tool in the *FreeHand 8 Bible* (from IDG Books Worldwide, now Hungry Minds).

Note FreeHand retains the original bitmapped artwork behind the traced vector artwork. If you no longer need the bitmapped version, delete the bitmap image after you have moved the traced objects to a new location. Group the traced objects for greater ease in moving them.

Tracing with Adobe Streamline

Although you can trace images in Adobe Illustrator, Adobe has a stand-alone product that is designed for tracing raster artwork — Streamline 4.0. With Streamline, you have the most conversion options, and, more importantly, you can optimize the results with smoothing commands. See Figure 31-16 for an example of Streamline 4.0.

After you have converted a bitmap image to vector artwork, you have the option of "smoothing" the results. Smoothing means eliminating redundant or excess points to create simpler shapes and curves. By reducing the complexity of points in vector artwork, you can reduce the overall file size dramatically.

In the Edit menu, you can access two types of smoothing: Smooth Paths and Smooth Direction Points. Smooth Paths eliminates anchor points within selected paths, and Smooth Direction Points changes hard-edged corners into rounded edges. Each command has a Minimum, Normal, and Maximum setting. For more information on the exactness of these settings, refer to the online Streamline help.

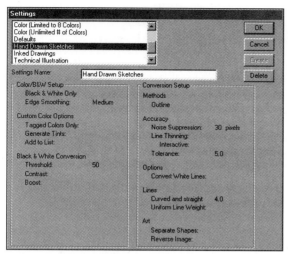

Figure 31-16: Streamline 4.0 hosts a wide range of presets in the Settings dialog.

Caution

Be extremely careful of "over smoothing." While we all would like smaller file sizes, don't lose sight of the effect of smoothing on image quality.

Exporting Vector Graphics from Flash

In the previous chapter, you learned to export raster image formats from Flash. If you've created artwork in Flash that you want to share with other drawing applications, then you can export any frame (or series of frames) from Flash — in any of the popular vector file formats.

Why would you want to export vector-based images from Flash? If you're a design or graphics professional, then you probably need to reuse your artwork in a number of different media for print, multimedia, or broadcast delivery. As such, you don't like wasting valuable time recreating the same artwork twice. Most Flash artwork exports flawlessly to the file formats listed in Table 31-1.

Cross-Reference

If you want to export a series of vector images from a Flash movie to use with video or other multiframe applications, check out Chapter 36, "Creating Full-Motion Video in Flash."

If you are unsure of the format to use in your graphics program, then refer to Table 31-1. Afterward, we show you how to export a Flash frame's artwork as a static vector image.

Table 31-1
Vector Image Formats for Flash Export

Flash Export Format	File Extension	Comments
EPS 3.0 (Encapsulated PostScript)	.EPS	Universal vector format recognized by most applications. However, any gradients created in Flash will not export well with this format.
Illustrator (Adobe Illustrator)	.AI	Proprietary file format mainly used by Adobe applications. However, any gradients created in Flash will not export well with this format.
DXF (Drawing eXchange Format)	.DXF	AutoCAD 2D/3D file format.
PICT — Mac only (Picture)	.PCT	Strange as it may seem, the Macintosh PICT format can contain vector and raster information.
WMF/EMF — PC only (Windows Meta File/Extended Meta File)	.WMF, .EMF	Only some Windows applications support these formats. These formats are not widely used on either Mac or PC systems.

To export artwork as a vector file format from Flash 5, follow these steps:

1. Move the Current Frame Indicator in the Flash timeline to the frame that contains the artwork you wish to export.

2. Choose the File ⇨ Export Image command.

3. Select a destination folder and enter a file name. Select your preferred raster image format in the Save as Type drop-down menu.

4. Click Save, and use the new vector file in your drawing or illustration program.

Note   Unlike exported raster image formats from Flash, the exported vector file formats do not have any additional settings for image quality, contents, or size. This is due primarily to these settings not being necessary for vector file formats. By their nature, vector graphics can be scaled at any size.

A word of caution: Using vector formats from Flash

Generally, the quality of exported vector files from Flash is less than desirable. Although it would seem that Flash's vector exports would be better than its raster exports, this simply isn't the case. Because RGB color space (as the "end" product) is relatively new to the world of print-based production, most vector file formats need to encode color information as CMYK. This presents a couple of problems, as you'll see in the following sections.

Color consistency

Flash works within an RGB color model, which means that all color is defined by three numbers, one assigned to each color channel of the image (for example, red, green, and blue). Most standard vector file formats do not encode the color information in this manner. Rather, they use CMYK (cyan, magenta, yellow, and black) colors that have a much more restricted color gamut (range) than RGB.

As such, most, if not all, of your Flash artwork will display quite differently when exported as a vector file format such as .EPS or .AI. Is this yet another reason to start projects intended for multiple media in Macromedia FreeHand? Yes and no. While starting projects in FreeHand lends itself to greater flexibility for the reuse or repurposing of artwork, you have an alternative to exporting vector files from Flash: good old copy and paste. If you select Flash artwork, choose Edit ➪ Copy, switch to your illustration program and choose Edit ➪ Paste; the newly pasted artwork should match your original Flash artwork.

Why is this so? Most likely because Flash's export file formats (or the versions of these formats) don't seem to support RGB colors. However, the clipboard can support a multitude of data types, and Adobe Illustrator and FreeHand can recognize RGB colors. Therefore, the copied-and-pasted colors show up as RGB colors in these programs.

Note

Interestingly, if you choose Adobe Illustrator (.AI) as the export file format from Flash, you can only choose up to and including Illustrator 6 formats. RGB color support was first introduced to Adobe Illustrator in version 7. It is also likely that the EPS 3.0 format is an older version of the format that does not support RGB colors.

Flash gradients

Another troublesome spot for exported vector files from Flash is the re-rendering of Flash gradients as CMYK "blends." Depending on the vibrancy of the original gradient in Flash, the exported vector equivalents might end up very muddy or brownish — especially in the middle range of the gradient. Again, you can avoid this color shifting by copying and pasting the Flash gradients directly between applications. Note that this still converts Flash gradients to blends, but it will retain the RGB color values of the original Flash gradient.

Tip   If you need perfect exported material from Flash, you might consider exporting high-resolution bitmap (a.k.a. *raster*) files instead.

Summary

✦ You can use other programs such as Macromedia FreeHand to create vector artwork for use in Flash.

✦ Before you import vector artwork into Flash, make sure you have optimized it in the parent application.

✦ Always use RGB colors for your vector artwork. Flash 5 uses the RGB color space, not CMYK as printing presses do.

✦ FreeHand 9 can work closely with the Flash for streamlined Web production. Among other things, FreeHand documents can now be imported directly into Flash 5.

✦ You can export .SWF files from Illustrator 8 with the Macromedia Flash Writer plug-in. .SWF file export is native to Illustrator 9.

✦ Layer names and formatting in .EPS or .AI files will be retained when imported into Flash 5.

✦ Many applications are adding support for the .SWF file format. Expression 2 can export amazing artwork as a .SWF file.

✦ You can convert bitmap artwork into vector artwork with Flash 5's Trace Bitmap command. FreeHand has superior tracing capabilities when compared to Flash 5.

✦ Flash 5 can export many vector formats for use in print and video applications.

✦   ✦   ✦

Working with Audio Applications

Although Flash has rudimentary sound-editing controls, those who are serious about integrating sound and music in their projects should consider purchasing other audio applications. Using professional-quality sound editors such as Peak (for Macintosh) or Sound Forge (for PC) can facilitate the manipulation and optimization of high-quality audio in your Flash projects.

In this chapter, you learn how to prepare your multimedia sounds for use in Flash. Because of the limited number of options for editing audio in Flash, we recommend that you optimize and experiment with your sound clips in an external application before importing them into the Library. When creating or editing audio for use in Flash, we *cannot stress enough* the importance of starting out with the highest sample and bit conversion rates possible. Remember that sound quality in general is simple to degrade, but can be difficult or impossible to restore, so it's not a good idea to skimp from the beginning. Ideally, your original files are 16-bit 44.1 kHz. From this point on, we assume that your audio clips are of reasonable quality and were captured or created from a good 16-bit source, such as an audio CD or a sound effects application such as Propellerhead's Rebirth (discussed later in this chapter).

Sound-editing and Creation Software

Just about every multimedia or video software package includes a sound-editing application. For the most part, you'll find limited edition (a.k.a. *LE*) versions of popular sound applications bundled with Macromedia Director or video application suites such as Digital Origin's EditDV.

For a price, you can upgrade these LE versions to full versions, or purchase them separately if you don't need or want a multimedia production software package. While very few of the following applications are available on both Macintosh and Windows platforms, their functionality is virtually identical.

Several software companies produce excellent sound-editing software. Many of these companies offer a software suite of their flagship products bundled with several supporting products that specialize in different areas of audio editing and creation. The following is a list of some of the most popular software developers that offer audio editing and creation applications.

Note   You can perform the same basic functions described in this chapter in either the LE or fully featured versions of the sound-editing application. LE versions usually have less effects-oriented controls such as sound filters and enhanced noise reduction.

Sonic Foundry's suite (PC only)

Sonic Foundry (www.sonicfoundry.com) provides the best-known sound-editing solutions for the Windows operating system. From simple editing to powerful looping effects, Sonic Foundry has a tool to work with any sound project.

Sound Forge

Sound Forge is a powerful, yet easy-to-use waveform sound editor for the PC environment. A great feature of Sound Forge is nondestructive editing. Sound Forge can also be integrated with Sonic Foundry's ACID software.

Sound Forge supports all three of the Flash-compatible audio import formats, .AIFF, .WAV, and .MP3. In addition, it has the capability to save in the RealAudio G2 streaming format. You can open an existing sound file, edit it, and save it as .WAV, .MP3, or .AIFF at several different sampling and bit rates.

Vegas

Another application in the Sonic Foundry's suite is the multitrack recording and editing software, Vegas. The strength of Vegas lies in its capability to perform multitrack editing and recording. A great added feature is that Vegas can synchronize your audio composition with a video clip within the program. This is a very handy feature when trying to match sound with your animation. Furthermore, Vegas also supports an unlimited number of tracks and a vast array of effects and plug-ins for some funky sounds.

ACID Pro

ACID is a powerful, loop-based sound-editing program that is ideal for use with Flash (see Figure 32-1). With ACID, you can very easily take loops created in other programs and arrange them on multiple tracks. One of ACID's great features is its capability to change the speed of the loop without changing the key. ACID Pro also comes with over 100 ready-to-use loops, so you can arrange an audio track in a pinch.

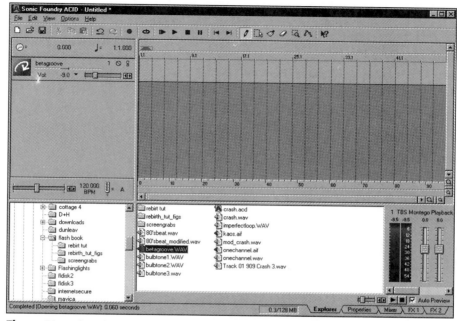

Figure 32-1: In ACID, you can very easily preview an audio clip, add it as a track, and move it around a timeline.

Bias suite (Mac only)

Bias (www.bias-inc.com) creates sound-editing applications for the Macintosh operating system. When Macromedia stopped developing SoundEdit 16 and Deck, Bias picked up the products and started to fine-tune them for new Web technologies.

Peak

Peak specializes in getting down and dirty with editing stereo tracks while supporting a large number of file formats. Some of the other features of Peak are its capability to execute batch file processing, burn CDs directly from a play list, export in RealAudio G2 streaming format, and nondestructive editing. Peak is rapidly becoming one of the most widely used audio-editing applications for multimedia on the Macintosh. It is available in both full and LE versions.

Deck

Deck is a powerful multitrack editor, also with nondestructive editing, for the Macintosh platform. In addition to being capable of playing back up to 64 tracks simultaneously, Deck can also function as a multitrack recorder, enabling you to create your own music or sound effects. It is less expensive than other similar software packages, and can be closely integrated with Bias Peak.

SFX

SFX is an amazing little tool that enables you to create your own sound effects. This program will keep you entertained for nights on end, especially with its randomizer mode that creates a new sound with every click. Of course, SFX ties in very neatly with the other Bias programs, Peak and Deck.

Cakewalk Pro suite (PC only)

Cakewalk (www.cakewalk.com) manufactures top-of-the-line audio software for the sound professional. Their software is designed for serious users who need to master audio for broadcast and CD applications.

Pro Audio is comparable to the multitrack editors/recorders from Bias's Deck and Sonic Foundry's Vegas. With Pro Audio, you can record and mix up to 256 tracks of MIDI and digital audio. It supports 24-bit audio hardware (that's above CD quality), and it enables you to export your audio in the standard .WAV and .AIFF formats along with .MP3, RealAudio G2, and Windows Media Player. Of course, Pro Audio doesn't come alone in the Pro Suite. Cakewalk packs the suite with a long list of programs such as Nemesys GigaSampler, GigaPiano, Audio FX 1, Audio FX 2, Audio FX 3, and Musicians Toolbox. If you would like more information on the programs packaged in the suite just hop on over to Cakewalk's Web site.

Studio Vision Pro (Mac only)

Studio Vision Pro (www.opcode.com) is probably the best deal out there for anyone on a tight budget but who needs all the advanced features from the more expensive programs. Studio Vision Pro is a multitrack editor/recorder with the capability to work with MIDI information and digital audio.

Cubase (Mac/PC)

Cubase (www.us.steinberg.net) is one of the very few programs available on both platforms. Cubase is a top-of-the-line multitrack editor/recorder. Cubase has the capability to edit and print musical scores and to handle both MIDI and digital audio. It is capable of 16- to 24-bit audio and has a built-in virtual synthesizer.

Macromedia SoundEdit 16 (Mac only)

SoundEdit has had a relatively long history with Macintosh users as a sound-editing workhorse, especially for use with multimedia. Although still widely used, SoundEdit 16 is no longer being produced by Macromedia, and Mac users are slowly migrating to the more robust, full featured Peak.

Digidesign's Pro Tools (Mac/PC)

Last, but not least, is Pro Tools (www.protools.com), the industry standard. If we were to walk into just about any major recording studio, we would see Pro Tools displayed on their massive monitors. Naturally, the professionals will have more than just Pro Tools on their system. In fact, the audio engineers will usually have several of the programs mentioned earlier because they might require a feature or two that only another program supports. In comparison, Flash can't do everything we want, so we use other programs to help get that desired effect. But in the end, the reality is that the Pro Tools system is their primary tool for audio editing and mixing.

Not only do the makers of Pro Tools make software products, but they also make a bit of the hardware for sound studios, including computer peripherals. Once you bring hardware into the equation for setting up a system, the cost can go sky-high. Thankfully, Digidesign is aware of this fact and has developed two home studio kits for all those people who love to make music but just don't have a major studio budget or a degree in audio engineering.

Starring in both of Digidesign's home studio package's is Pro Tools LE. This LE version is far from skimpy though. This multitrack editor/recorder is capable of playing back 24 tracks of 16- or 24-bit audio and 128 tracks of MIDI. It also supports Real Time Audio Suite (RTAS) effect processing and sample-accurate editing of audio and MIDI simultaneously, along with being capable of exporting .MP3 and RealAudio G2 files. The full version of Pro Tools is capable of 64 tracks of simultaneous recording and playing back plus a lot more. The full version is beyond the scope of this chapter.

Expert Tutorial: Building a Home Sound Studio, by Scott Brown

While you can do a lot with a standard sound card and sound-editing software, you might want to expand your multimedia skills and your computer's capabilities with additional audio equipment. Scott's tutorial tells you what you need to get started.

The day may come when you would like to import your own guitar track or a keyboard melody into your Flash project. How would you do it? It used to be that the process of turning the analog signal (tape recording) into a digital signal (CD/DAT) required the help of the local audio engineer—you know, the guy with a sound studio that had the look and feel of a starship control center. Well those days of turning your tape in to a studio to be converted to a digital format are—as you guessed it—gone. With a mixture of some hardware and software, and a lot less money than previously needed, you can record and mix music tracks in your home before you know it.

Continued

Continued

With both of these intro studio systems, there are some computer hardware requirements. For both of these packages to work smoothly, your computer must be either a Power Mac or a Pentium III system, contain either an IDE or SCSI hard drive, and have at least 128MB of RAM.

The first system is called the Digidesign Toolbox, developed by Digidesign. This package comes with a sound card called the Audiomedia III and Pro Tools LE as the software. The Audiomedia III sound card is placed into a PCI card slot in your computer and contains two pairs of analog I/O (input/output) ports that enable you to connect the computer to a small mixing board. Along with the analog ports, the sound card also contains a pair of S/PIDIF I/O ports. These S/PIDIF's are digital ports for your computer to hook up with either a DAT player/recorder or a CD player (not a CD burner) with optical output. Please consult your computer's user manual before installing any type of hardware.

As I mentioned earlier, the analog I/O ports connect the computer to a mixer, but what does the mixer do? Well, think of the mixer as a hub for all your analog equipment: a guitar, keyboard, microphones, speakers, headphones, synthesizer, and so forth. The mixer handles all the signals coming from these devices and preps them for input into your computer.

So far, we have two pieces of hardware that we need for your home system, the sound card and the mixer. These two pieces are essential for getting the sound from its source to the computer, for recording the audio signal, and for editing the track. However, we are still missing two elements that are more important for our studio. We need something that will create the sound, an input device (keyboard, guitar, microphone), and something that will enable us to hear the sound that we have created, an output device (speakers, headphones). With these hardware elements (sound card, mixer, input, and output) coupled with audio editing/recording software, you will possess the basic equipment needed for your first home audio studio.

Continuing with our first system, one day you might find that all the music you have been creating is taking up a lot of space on your hard drive. Now would be the time for a dedicated hard drive to store all those audio files. It's not impossible to run a studio system without a dedicated hard drive, but it will make your recording life easier in the long haul. To set up this dedicated audio drive, we need some additional hardware. First, you need to install a SCSI Ultra Wide, Ultra2 Wide, or Ultra160 accelerator card. This card is placed in another PCI slot, just like the sound card before it. After the SCSI card is installed, the next level of business is to hook up an External SCSI A/V hard drive to the SCSI accelerator card in your computer. (A/V stands for Audio/Video drive, which is fine-tuned to handle the performance demands of large data transfers to and from the hard drive. Make sure you choose a hard drive with high RPMs [7,200, 10,000, or higher] for the best playback of your music.)

Eventually, if you just happen to catch the music bug, you might want to be able to give your friends some of your creations or create high-quality multimedia presentations for distribution. What's the best medium for high-quality music and presentations? Yep, you guessed it—the good ol' CD. And the only tool missing in your studio, right now, is a device to create your own CDs, otherwise known as a CD burner. Because you already have a SCSI accelerator card in your computer (and perhaps a FireWire connection), you can easily plug in a CD burner to your system, thereby satisfying all your current musical needs. But what if you want more expandability in your studio?

The next level in the home studio set up gives you just that — the ability to expand the amount of devices to be plugged into the computer. This second system is based on Digidesign's 001 (pronounced double O one) home system. This system differs slightly from Digidesign's Toolbox package. Instead of using a mixing board as the hub (the mixer is not included in the Toolbox package) for all your connecting devices, Digidesign provides its own hub called the 001. The 001 hub is also called a I/O (input/output) box. Included in the 001 I/O box are inputs for two microphones complete with adjustable gain and phantom power.

Also included in the 001 package is the 001 sound card that contains 18 I/Os, compared to the Audiomedia III card that has 6 I/Os. The 001 sound card has a port for a light pipe. What is a *light pipe*? Light pipe is a fiber-optic cable that provides the cleanest way to transfer digital data. Because the Digidesign 001 system is a Digidesign product, Digidesign also includes Pro Tools LE to complete the package. And finally, this system, just like the previous system, wouldn't be complete until the addition of a dedicated external hard drive for all your audio, a CD burner, some type of input device (multiple devices for the 001 system), and last, but not least, some speakers. With all this power at your fingertips, the only limitation is your imagination.

Scott Brown wrote the Fireworks tutorial for Chapter 30, "Working with Raster Graphics." You can find his biographical information there, along with his advice on using Fireworks 4 in a Flash 5 Web production workflow.

Setting In and Out points

One of the first things you will want to do with your audio file before you bring it into the Flash environment is set its In and Out points. These points, respectively, control where the sound will start and end. By precisely placing In and Out points, you can minimize the sound's file size (see Figure 32-2), making it less cumbersome to move around, and reducing the amount of time that you'll have to spend using Flash's less-than-full-featured interface. You can set In and Out points in most, if not all, audio applications.

In Sound Forge, Peak, and SoundEdit 16, follow these steps to set the In and Out points of a sound:

1. Highlight the area you want to keep.

2. Test your selection by pressing the Play Loop or Play Normal button (Sound Forge).

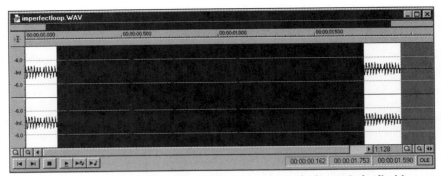

Figure 32-2: You can greatly reduce the file size of a Flash movie by limiting an audio track to its essential portion.

To create a new audio file with your selection:

1. Select File ➪ Copy (Command+C or Ctrl+C).

2. Select File ➪ New (Command+N or Ctrl+N).

3. A new window opens. Select Edit ➪ Paste (Command+V or Ctrl+V).

4. Your selection will now be a new audio file.

Normalizing audio levels

You can use the Normalize function to optimize your sound levels and to prevent your audio file from "clipping." (Digital clipping occurs when an audio clip is recorded at too high a level. The clipping sound is distorted, resulting in an undesirable crackling or buzzing sound.) Normalize can also be used to boost levels when your audio file was recorded too low. Normalize is an option available in most audio applications.

Tip

If you are gathering sound samples from a number of different audio sources (such as audio CD, direct recordings with a computer microphone, DAT recordings, DV camcorder audio, and so on), it's best to normalize all of them to a consistent audio level.

To normalize in Sound Forge:

1. Select part or all of the clip to be normalized.

2. Choose Process ➪ Normalize

3. The Normalize Window appears (see Figure 32-3). You can click Preview to see what the default settings do.

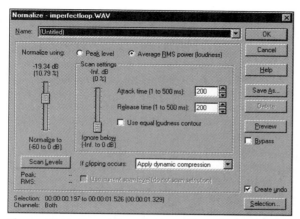

Figure 32-3: Sound Forge's Normalize window enables you to preview the settings before you apply them to the audio clip.

Watch the Play Meter on the right side of the screen. If the levels seem high (constantly in the red), lower the levels with the slider bar on the left side of the Normalize Window. If your levels are too low, gradually raise the slider bar. Click OK, and your file is now Normalized. Note that many other options exist in the Normalize Window. If you like, you can experiment with these settings to get the result you are looking for.

To normalize in Peak and SoundEdit:

1. Select part or all of the clip to be normalized.

2. In Peak, choose DSP ➪ Normalize; in SoundEdit, choose Effects ➪ Normalize.

In Peak's Normalize dialog, you can move the slider bar back and forth to choose the normalization percentage. The number you choose will normalize to a percentage of the maximum level. After you click OK, you can listen to the normalized selection by pressing Option+spacebar. Watch the levels for any clipping.

Caution

If you are recording your own sounds with a microphone attached to your computer's sound card, make sure that you have adjusted the microphone's volume level (or gain) in the sound-recording application. If the levels are too high during recording, you won't be able to normalize the sound — the resulting sound will be very distorted and "clip" on playback.

Expert Tutorial: Optimizing Sound for Flash in Sound Forge, *by William Moschella*

While we already explained how to perform basic normalization on sound files, Bill explains how and why to optimize sound levels and sampling within Sound Forge. Most of the sound-editing applications we mentioned earlier can perform similar operations as well. Refer to your sound-editing software manual for the specific menu commands that are necessary for normalization and sampling rate.

In a perfect Web world, we would be using stereo files at their highest sample rate. As the creator, you must decide which is more important: download time or sound quality. The settings I discuss in this tutorial are tools that can be used to decrease file size while maintaining decent sound quality. However, if your original sample sounds bad, these settings will make it sound worse. A little bit of sound advice: Bad in = Bad out!

Although it is true that .MP3 offers the best sound compression, for ideal results it helps to know a few tricks that will enable you to reduce your file size before you import your sounds into Flash — which will result in even smaller sound files with better sound quality. Another bit of sound advice: Smart sound = Better, smaller sound.

Although a number of excellent programs may be used for sound editing, I use Sonic Foundry's Sound Forge to explain these procedures. The two main categories of focus are *normalizing* and *resampling*.

Normalizing a sound file

Normalizing is used to increase the volume of a sound file without fear of clipping. You can also set specific parameters so that certain areas can be ignored or intensified. Start by opening your sound file in Sound Forge. If you like, you can drag and drop the file right into the workspace. Then choose Normalize from the drop-down menu, Process ➪ Normalize. Make sure that your file is completely deselected. This allows the normalization process to be applied to the whole file. Don't be intimidated by all the settings. Here is a walk-through of each control in the Normalize dialog.

✦ **Normalize using: Peak level or Average RMS?** Choose Average RMS. This will enable you to save a setting so that if you have more than one sound file, you can maintain and compare volume between audio files.

✦ **Normalize to:** This sets the level of your normalized sound. I recommend a value of 16 to 20 percent. These settings mean that you are reducing the sound volume by a factor of 16 to 20 percent. Remember that when the final .SWF is played, the Flash player will boost your gain by several decibels.

✦ **Scan settings:** The best feature of this is the Ignore below slider. This enables you to choose a level at which the normalization will bypass. Simply put, you might have sections of silence in your file. If you boost the gain in these sections, you might bring out unwanted frequencies (noise) that you could not hear previously. After you have scanned your selection you can use the RMS calculations to gauge what level to set the slider at.

In most cases, anything under 5 percent is a good starting point. Be careful though! If your file is already at a low decibel, these settings could bypass the whole normalization process. If you are confused, leave the slider at 0 percent. You can leave the default settings for attack and release time at 200 and leave the use equal contour box checked.

✦ **If clipping occurs:** Select Apply dynamic compression. This is your safety net. Although you may have a situation in which the normalization settings are exactly where you need them to be, some sections may still peak. Applying dynamic compression prevents any peaks from exceeding the threshold.

After you've set the parameters, you can audition (preview) your selection. If you're using multiple audio files in your Flash project and want to maintain a consistent volume throughout, you can use the Save as button to save a preset for future use.

Resampling

Most of the audio files you work with are probably set to stereo 44.1 kHz. This may be fine for CD-ROM applications, but the Web is a different area. You may disagree with this, but my philosophy is this: Whenever possible, before importing to Flash, optimize your sound as mono 22.05 kHz. When you import to Flash, you can then continue to decrease your file size with MP3 compression. A third-party sound editor, such as Sound Forge, gives you the advantage of higher-quality filters and high-end processing. Although Flash *can* resample PCM files, it will not process them with the same level of quality that a program such as Sound Forge offers. Furthermore, Flash prevents you from resampling in .MP3 format. Your ideal situation is to resample while introducing as little audible change as possible. Again, your ear will be the best judge.

Author's Note: PCM stands for Pulse Code Modulation. It is a standard sound-sampling mechanism for audio — it is a digital representation of sound.

To begin Resampling, with your sound open in Sound Forge, select Resample from the drop-down menu, Process ➪ Resample. Then make your choices from the settings that follow:

✦ **New Sample Rate:** Select a new sample rate from the New Sample Rate drop-down or else type the rate into the field yourself. The next two items are the most important. These filters maintain your sound quality.

✦ **Interpolation accuracy:** This determines the range of number crunching, or the complexity of the calculations that will be used to resample the sound. A higher number results in a more accurate resample calculation. A setting of 4 takes longer to process than a setting of 1, but will come closer to your original sample. This setting will not change your file size; it only affects the quality of the resample.

✦ **Antialias filter:** When you are resampling you might notice distortion or a loss in the high end. Applying an antialias filter helps prevent these high frequencies from distorting. Preview your sound and resample accordingly.

Continued

Continued

Final notes

You should always normalize your sound file before you resample because this order pre-serves the best sound quality. I highly recommend that you keep the Create Undo box checked at all times, because this type of editing drastically alters your file, and it can be very nice to have that Undo available. Similarly, it can be advantageous to use the Save as command (and save to a new name) after you have made your changes. This procedure preserves the original file so that you can go back to it later.

Bill Moschella has contributed a number of Expert Tutorials on sound-related topics. His biographical infor-mation can be found (together with his sound advice) in Chapter 16, "Optimizing Flash Sound for Export."

Fade in and fade out

As discussed in Chapter 15, "Importing and Editing Sounds in Flash," fading in means increasing the volume of a sound over time and fading out means decreasing it. Most audio-editing applications have more sophisticated fading effects than Flash.

To fade audio in Sound Forge:

1. Select the part of the audio that you wish to fade in or out.
2. Choose Process ⇨ Fade ⇨ Graphic.
3. The Graphic Fade Window appears (see Figure 32-4).

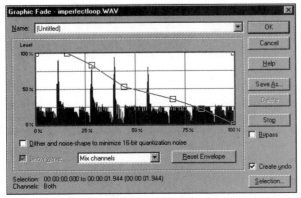

Figure 32-4: Sound Forge enables you to save custom fade effects to apply to other sounds.

You should now see your selected sound as a waveform (that is, a graphic representation of sound waves). The interface for customizing your fade is vaguely similar to the one used in Flash. You create envelope handles by clicking points on the envelope line at the top of the waveform. Drag these handles around to create your desired volume/fading effects. The lines themselves show the volume level of the sound. Thus, when you drag an envelope handle down, the line slopes down, indicating a decrease in the volume level. Click Preview to hear your custom fade. Click OK when you are satisfied.

Using Peak to fade audio:

1. Select the section of audio that you want to fade in or out.

2. Choose Preferences ⇨ Fade In Envelope or Fade Out Envelope. The Fade In Envelope or Fade Out Envelope Window appears.

3. You can use the default fade shape, or create your own by using a similar technique to the one described previously in the Sound Forge instructions.

4. Choose DSP ⇨ Fade Out. Peak will apply the fade to your selection.

5. To hear your Fade, press Option+spacebar.

Fading with SoundEdit:

1. Select the section of audio that you want to fade in or out.

2. Choose Effects ⇨ Fade In or Effects ⇨ Fade Out.

3. Create your fade using a similar technique to the one described in the Sound Forge instructions. SoundEdit also has Slow, Medium, or Fast fade presets. Click OK when finished.

Creating a reverb effect

Adding reverb to a sound file can create an interesting effect. Reverb creates the auditory illusion of acoustic space. For example, you could simulate the sound of water dripping in a cave.

To add a reverb to an audio sample in Sound Forge:

1. Select the section of sound that you want to add reverb to.

2. Choose Effects ⇨ Reverb.

3. The Reverb Window appears.

4. Select a Reverberation Mode from the drop-down menu. To create the dripping-water sound, choose Cavernous Space.

5. Press the Preview Button to hear how it sounds. Play with some of the sliders and other options until you achieve the desired effect. When done, click OK.

Peak does not come with a reverb effect. However, a variety of third-party effects plug-ins are available on the market that are compatible with Peak.

SoundEdit 16 has a similar effect to reverb called Echo. To add Echo to a selection, choose Effects ⇨ Echo.

Other effects

Many other effects and processes are available in these audio-editing applications, and to list them all would be beyond the scope of this book. A great feature of many of these software packages is nondestructive editing. You can make as many changes to your audio clips as you like without destroying the original source files. Set aside some time to experiment and let your creativity take over.

If you don't have any source sound material for adding effects, you can create your own super-synth techno music with Propellerhead's Rebirth. The next tutorial by Justin Jamieson shows you how to create a soundtrack with Rebirth.

Expert Tutorial: Using Propellerhead's Rebirth to Create Loops for Flash, *by Justin Jamieson*

If you don't want to invest time and money in audio hardware, you can use Rebirth to create electronic music. Justin's tutorial walks you through the basic process of mixing samples and beats in Rebirth.

Rebirth is an innovative sound-creation tool that accurately replicates vintage analog synthesizers and drum machines. Simply put, it enables you to easily create electronic music without investing tons of money in hardware.

With Rebirth, you can create looping music for Stream or Event sounds in Flash. You can also create some weird effects by tweaking the various knobs and adding distortion. Prepare yourself to spend long hours and sleepless nights experimenting with this program. That's not to say that it's extremely difficult — it's not. Rebirth is actually quite easy to get the hang of, but you'll soon be keeping the neighbors awake at night with heavy bass and spacey frequencies.

Rebirth emulates two synthesizers, Roland 303s, and two drum machines, a Roland 808 and a Roland 909. Countless Mods (modifications) are available on the Internet, with different graphics and sample sets. Some of these sample sets specialize in certain types of electronic music, such as drum and bass, dub, industrial, and so on. For the purposes of this tutorial, however, we use the default Mod, which has controls that are easy to use (and that provide that sought-after 1980s Electro sound.)

Getting started with Rebirth
First, familiarize yourself with some of Rebirth's controls. See the following figure for the main Rebirth window. A fair number of them exist, and the Rebirth manual describes them very well. You should have a basic knowledge of Rebirth for the purposes of this tutorial.

The main Rebirth Window

Although you can use the demo version of this software for the purposes of this tutorial, it lacks the capability to save any final audio files and shuts down after 15 minutes.

Creating your first simple beat in Rebirth

In Pattern Mode, press Play and look at the 909 at the bottom of the screen. You'll notice red lights moving from left to right over the 16 step buttons. This represents one musical measure. To modify the beat that is playing, you can clear some or all of the buttons and add your own. You can also select premade beats by pressing the pattern buttons on the left side of the screen.

Author's Note: To clear an entire pattern, move the red Focus Bar down to the bottom of the screen using the down arrow key and then choose Edit ➪ Clear.

To begin creating your own beat, or to modify an existing one, you will want to "solo" the 909, so the other sections don't get in the way. To do this, click the Mix buttons to turn off the green lights in all but the 909 section. You should now only hear the 909. You can also select the number of beats per minute by altering the number on the BPM selector at the top left of the screen.

More advanced musicians may want to change the time signature by altering the number in the value display on the left side of the 909 (see the following figure). When you change the number, you are altering the total of sixteenth notes within a bar. Thus, if you change it to 14, there will be 14 sixteenth notes between the beginning and end of a bar.

Continued

Continued

The 909 is "soloed" in the main Rebirth window.

To select different drum sounds to play, you can either use the rotary dial on the right side, or you can click the sound names above the 16 step buttons. Each step button also has two instance levels. The first time that you click a step button, a faint red light appears, indicating a lighter drum hit. The second time that you click the same step button, the heavier red light appears, indicating a heavier hit. The third time that you click the same button, you clear it. No sound is produced.

The 909 also has a Flam feature that simulates the sound of a percussionist hitting a drum with both sticks at slightly different intervals (see the following figure). To use this feature, click the Flam button on the 909, and choose the step button that you want to hear the Flam on. The dial above the Flam button adjusts the "width" of the Flam — the actual time interval between the two simulated "stick hits."

This figure shows the various instance levels of the 909. The faint light indicates a "light hit." The heavier one indicates a "heavy hit." The green light indicates a "Flam," which is similar to the sound of a drummer hitting a drum with both sticks at slightly different intervals.

The process of creating your own beat involves clearing all or some of an existing drum pattern by manually clicking the step buttons for the various drum sounds, and clicking in new ones. After you have found a suitable bar of beats, at a suitable speed, you are now ready to add some 303 synthesizer.

Adding sound from the 303

The two top sections are digital replications of the vintage Roland TB 303 analog synthesizer. These are a little bit more difficult to program than are the 808s, and those new to Rebirth may find it a little frustrating. A good way to begin is to customize an existing pattern.

Use the up arrow keys to move the focus bar to the 303 that you want to use. Solo it the same way that you soloed the 808 previously. Press play, and begin the process of choosing a pattern.

You can choose the pattern either by using the Pattern Selector on the left side of the 303 (see the following figure), or by pressing Ctrl+R to randomly "surf" the patterns. After you find a suitable pattern, you can begin to modify it using the synthesizer sound controls.

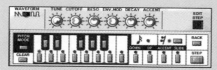

The various synthesizer sound controls on the 303. Experiment with these knobs and buttons to achieve interesting results.

The synthesizer sound controls can create interesting results. For a detailed description of what each control does, consult the Rebirth manual. Keep in mind that experimentation is key. Set aside some time to create the perfect synthesizer lick by playing with these controls.

Using the 808

The 808 drum section, above the 909, is similar to the 909, but with several differences. For one, the drum sounds are different. Also, the controls aren't quite the same. When you are creating or editing beats in the 808, you only have one instance level on the key buttons. The 808 instead uses the Accent (AC) feature to create heavier beats. The Accent feature is located over the first key button, and when chosen you can add accents just like you would add a sound or beat. When you add an accent to a key button, all other sounds that occur on the same key button are emphasized.

Continued

Continued

Other controls in Rebirth

Other effects and controls in Rebirth can help you find the sound you are looking for. Here are some of the basic ones:

✦ **Distortion (Dist):** Distortion is an effect similar to cranking up a guitar amplifier to full volume. It creates a harsher, louder sound. Clicking the Dist button on the right side of any of the four sections uses Distortion. Although distortion can be applied to any or all of the sections at the same time, only one master control exists for all sections. It is located on the right side of the Rebirth window.

✦ **Pattern Controlled Filter (PCF):** The PCF is a versatile filter that can be applied to one section at a time. It has a master control on the right side of the Rebirth window. The PCF radically modifies the sound, essentially by reshaping it. To experiment with the PCF controls, move the four slider bars up and down.

✦ **Compressor (Comp):** The Compressor evens up the audio signal, making it sound tighter. You can use the Compressor for either one individual section or for the Master Output.

✦ **Delay:** The Delay creates an echo effect for a given sound. You'll find delay knobs on the right side of each section and one master control on the right side of the Rebirth window.

✦ **Level Controls:** You can control the sound Levels that are going out to mix by using the mix slides to the right of each section. Remember that as discussed in earlier sound chapters, Levels are important to consider before you import your final sound or music loop into Flash. A Master Output slide also exists that controls the Levels going out. Make sure that the meter isn't spending too much time in the red or clipping will occur.

Preparation, mixing, and exporting Rebirth loops

At this point you should have a loop created that you want to export to .AIFF or .WAV format. Before you do, you should take a few steps to ensure good quality output.

✦ **Final Mixing:** Make sure that all the sections you want to mix are no longer soloed. To do this, make sure that all of your sections are set to go to the mix (green light on.) Set the Levels on your sections individually to your liking by adjusting the Level Controls, as described previously. Bring them down if they are too "hot" (too much in the red), and set the Master Output Levels in a similar way.

✦ **Switch to Song Mode:** To export your Rebirth loop to .AIFF or .WAV, you need to switch to Song Mode. To do this, click Song Mode at the top of the screen. In Song Mode, choose Edit ➪ Initialize Song from Pattern Mode. Press Play to test your loop.

✦ **Exporting:** To export your loop, choose File ➪ Export Loop as Audio File. You will be given the option to save your loop as a .WAV or .AIFF file. The quality is automatically set to 44.1 kHz, 16-bit.

You should now have a one bar loop in .AIFF or .WAV format. You can test it in another audio application, such as Peak or Sound Forge, and make any necessary changes, or add additional effects, or import it directly into Flash.

Advanced methods to create multiple bar loops in Rebirth

Once you get the basics down, you will no doubt want to work on more complex sounds. Creating a one-bar loop in Rebirth is just the beginning—you can use Rebirth's recording and loop features to make complex songs. Rebirth can also be integrated with other audio applications, such as Cubase VST. For more information on how to create a more complex sound in Rebirth, see the very comprehensive Rebirth manual.

With the greatly improved MP3 compression available with Flash 5, an incentive now exists to create complex, high-quality electronic music by using an application such as Rebirth without having to worry as much about file size. And the rewards for creating your own samples, loops, and songs are tremendous.

Rebirth is available for Macintosh and Windows platforms. You can download a demo version of Rebirth from the Propellerhead Web site at www.propellerheads.se/demo. You can also find information about Rebirth at www.steinberg.net.

Justin Jamieson started using his first computer when he was eight years old. Years later, after studying design and cinematography, he combined his training with his computing knowledge to cofound mediumLarge (www.mediumLarge.com), a new media design firm in Toronto. Justin remembers listening to "A Rollerskating Jam Named Saturdays" by De La Soul when he graduated from high school. In 1997, while developing a Web site for a local Toronto rap group, Justin began his research into the use of sound on the Internet and there's been no turning back. Justin's dream is "to create an old-school MP3 ghetto blaster."

Expert Tutorial: ACID Loops to and from Flash, *by William Moschella*

As in any creative field, there are certain basic guidelines. At the same time, any truly creative person knows that creative ideas often come out of breaking these guidelines. This tutorial only presents some basic ideas to follow if you're looking for a starting point in using Sonic Foundry's ACID to make sound loops for use in Flash. The following tutorial also assumes that you have at least beginner-level experience with ACID—you'll need to know how to use the basic ACID tools and must be familiar with the faders, tempo, and pitch functions.

About the library disks

Sonic Foundry ACID software comes with a disk titled *Essential Sounds vol. 1*. This disk contains enough loops to keep you busy for quite some time. You can purchase additional disks from Sonic Foundry. (For more information, check Sonic Foundry's Web site: www.sonicfoundry.com/acid.html.)

Choosing the loops

Choosing the files for your loops is something everyone does differently. Although there is no right or wrong way to arrange a song, there are a few things to keep in mind.

Continued

Continued

Not everyone has a subwoofer! If you decide to crank some serious bass and drums be aware that it might sound awful coming through a tiny set of built-in speakers. You can also lose many high frequencies because of poor speakers

Tempo and key changes

The tempo of a loop is up to the creator. However, some loops might seem to drag or speed up when played with other loops. Loops are usually best when placed within a limited range of beats per minute (BPM) above and below their original tempo. If the loop is pushed outside this range, it can lead to bad sound. Although there is no set rule for this threshold, it helps to know the original tempo when you are pushing a sound in this manner. The original tempo of a loop can be found in the Properties dialog. Just right-click/Ctrl+click over the file and choose Properties from the contextual menu. Speeding up and slowing down a loop will bring out human errors that aren't easily noticed at the original tempo. Don't assume that all Sonic Foundry loops are cut precisely either! Again, your ear is the best judge. As for key change, just be sure that you change all the tracks if you change one track. Otherwise, this might result in some disharmonious music. Yet, if that's your thing, by all means experiment.

Mixing

The key to mixing in ACID, or any environment, is consistency. Because each loop was probably recorded in a different environment, you will want to mix all the tracks smoothly to make it sound as if they were all playing together. Also, a combination of like instruments (such as four tracks of drums, or two bass tracks) can lead to an overload in one particular frequency or a muddy mix. When mixing, test at least three different levels. If you only mix with your speakers cranked all the way up to 10, you will be inconsistent with the same mix at a lower level. Try to find a mix that sounds equal at a low, medium, and loud volume. This ensures that the listener has a pleasant experience with whatever speaker they are using.

Exporting

When you've finished mixing your loop you can export it in a number of different formats. Make sure that your loop region is marked at the beginning and end of the selection you will want to export. (To be safe, you may choose to erase all existing audio outside of the loop region.) From the File menu choose Save as and check the option Save only the audio within the current loop region. The drop-down menu to the right of your new filename will give you a number of combinations for sample rates in both .WAV and .AIFF formats. Save your file to a new name and then import it into the Flash Library.

Bill Moschella is a principal of STEP2Production, which is an audio, web, and multimedia design firm. Bill has been involved in music since age 4 — in fact, playing and recording music is his single most favorite thing to do. Since he's not "into newer music," the most memorable song from the year that he exited High School in Prospect Connecticut was "Because," from the Beatles' Abbey Road. After aquiring a degree in the 20th century mucis theory and composition he opened a recording studio, where he applied his engineering techniques to the computerand web. After college, he started scoring music for radio and television advertising. However, after discovering Flash (while browsing the web), he was able to apply his expertise to websites and interactive CD – ROMS. Bill has worked on websites for: www.functionfirst.com, www.deluxesounds.com, www.timeritemedia.com, www.vdmlaw.com, and www.step2production.com

Expert Tutorial: Why Use Beatnik Audio? An Introduction to Structured Audio, *by Doug Loftus*

Coverage of Beatnik, Mixman, and Flash is an exciting addition to our sound coverage in the Flash 5 Bible. Doug Loftus and Andreas Wagner provide the in-depth coverage. In this first tutorial, Doug explains why and how to use Beatnik Audio files with your Flash movies. Then, Andreas goes under the hood, showing you how to enable Beatnik with JavaScript in HTML and FSCommand actions in Flash.

As a Flash developer, you may be aware that Beatnik audio can be used as an alternative to native Flash audio. However, it may not be clear why, or under what circumstances, it makes sense to pair Flash with Beatnik. In this tutorial, we look at what Beatnik audio has to offer when used with Flash to create media-rich presentations.

Although the term "vector audio" would be a misnomer, the Beatnik Player handles audio in a manner similar to Flash's handling of graphics; as such, Beatnik might be considered Flash's "sonic cousin." Just as a Flash .SWF combines instructions for displaying vector graphics and permits inclusion of bitmapped graphics, a Beatnik Rich Music Format (.RMF) file contains instructions for playing sounds and can include digital audio data. This latter feature adds greatly to the versatility and quality of the audio experience offered to end-users. Before elaborating further on why Beatnik might be considered Flash's "sonic cousin," we briefly examine the key features of Beatnik's audio technology.

MIDI and RMF

.RMF is a MIDI (Musical Instrument Digital Interface)-based file format, albeit with a powerful twist: .RMF files can contain custom audio samples. When embedded in a Web page, .RMF files are played back by the Beatnik Player, which exists either as an ActiveX Control (for Internet Explorer/Windows) or as a browser plug-in (for Netscape Navigator under Windows or Mac OS). .RMF is not a streaming format; these files are downloaded and cached by a browser.

For the uninitiated, here's a quick rundown on MIDI. A standard MIDI file (with the extension .MID) doesn't contain audio information. Instead, a .MID file holds music performance data, specifying to a playback device what instruments to play, together with the pitch, duration, and loudness of the notes to be played on the musical timeline. In the simplest case, up to 16 independent channels of such performance instructions can be simultaneously played back on a MIDI device. Audio playback devices that conform to the General MIDI (GM) standard contain a minimum of 128 instruments and sound effects, each assigned to a given program or *patch* number. For instance, on a GM device, patch number 1 is always a piano sound, patch number 40 is always a violin, and so on. A separate bank of drum and percussion sounds is also part of the GM standard.

Continued

Continued

Because MIDI files only contain performance instructions, their size is typically quite small. And because most of the sound cards found on today's computers are GM-compatible playback devices, the MIDI format might seem like an ideal audio delivery solution for the Web. However, MIDI hasn't exactly taken the Internet by storm for three good reasons. First, a GM soundbank, consisting largely of (often ersatz) acoustic/orchestral instrument sounds, constricts composers to a rather limited sonic palette that isn't well suited to creating music in contemporary styles. Second, sample quality can vary widely among the plethora of sound cards found on PCs. Thus, a painstakingly crafted sax solo that may sound passable, perhaps even soulful on one sound card, can sound like a wounded goose on another. Third, the lack of a cross-browser, cross-platform approach to programmatically controlling playback of MIDI audio limits its ability to integrate well with Web pages to such an extent that sophisticated scoring and interactivity is not practically possible. The Beatnik Music System alleviates these problems by providing the following:

✦ The Beatnik Editor, an application that links to MIDI sequencing software and permits incorporation of custom samples into MIDI-based compositions. The Editor exports both MIDI and digital audio (uncompressed or MP3 compressed) data together in a single, encrypted .RMF file.

✦ An independent GM soundset plus additional sounds and effects that permanently reside with the Beatnik Player (after a one-time download and install). When composing for the Beatnik Player, regardless of whether you're using the Player's built-in sounds, custom sounds, or both in combination, what you hear is what the end-user hears.

✦ A JavaScript-based API — the Music Object — that provides cross-browser, cross-platform control over numerous .RMF file playback parameters. This enables developers to readily integrate interactive music and sound with other Web page elements such as text, images, and Flash movies.

Of course, a full examination of the features and techniques available when authoring .RMF audio is beyond the scope of this tutorial. The intent here is to expose some of the key concepts underlying *structured audio*, as RMF is sometimes referred to, versus *linear audio* — digital audio that is fixed with respect to the majority of its playback parameters, and whose constituent sounds are not accessible as individual elements (as, for example, audio as customarily used in Flash).

Structured and linear audio

Typically, Flash developers use audio in a few discrete ways. Short sounds are sometimes given to navigation elements or triggered by frame events to synchronize with a changing visual element. Background music often consists of a two- or four-bar audio loop — percussion or other rhythmically well-defined loops lend themselves well to this task — that repeats for the duration of a scene or even for an entire presentation.

Of course, your intentions may be adequately served by using a few short sounds and an audio loop (or two) in linear format. In that case, you honestly don't have much to gain by using an alternative approach; snagging a few sound effects and hip-hop loops off the Internet is easy (as long as they're royalty-free), and the skill and time required to incorporate these sounds into a Flash movie is minimal. However, if your audio ambitions are more complex, then structured audio may be the right solution.

The better Flash developers (and content developers in general) tend to be rather obsessive about both file size and about making economical use of graphic assets. Even when bandwidth isn't an overriding concern, if one adheres to the notion that the Web is an *ecosystem* of sorts, then it's never good form to use more resources than necessary. Structured audio enables a developer to make economical use of audio assets while attaining high quality results.

Example: A structured versus linear approach to an audio problem

As a knowledgeable Flash artist, if you want an animated circle to grow in diameter over several seconds, you'd never import a sequence of bitmap images for this purpose—you'd use a symbol and let Flash do the work by tweening. As an audio equivalent, consider the case in which you'd like to use a high, whistle-like tone that smoothly ascends in pitch by one octave over ten seconds. A linear audio approach would involve either finding or constructing an audio sample of the ascending tone. An acceptable result (with a minimum of audible artifacts) can be obtained starting with a 22.05 kHz mono sample and MP3 compressing with a bit rate of 56Kbps, with the resulting file size of about 68KB.

A structured audio approach, using the Beatnik Music System, would be to link the Beatnik Editor to your MIDI sequencing software and to choose a suitable sound and pitch as a starting point (the Editor makes the Beatnik Player's soundbanks available in the composition environment). By applying a one-octave pitch bend to a note that sustains for ten seconds, the desired effect is achieved. This latter operation is akin to an *audio tween*. The size of the resulting .RMF: 600 bytes, which is a 100-fold reduction compared to the linear equivalent.

Synchronization

It's often desirable to have visual and audio elements relate to each other. Because Flash can support a two-way dialog with JavaScript, it can also communicate with the Beatnik Player. MIDI (and .RMF) files can incorporate special nonperformance data—known as metaevents—that can be placed along the Music timeline in the composition environment. The Beatnik Player can read these cue points, and the ensuing JavaScript call can be used to trigger events and set properties in Flash. Conversely, ActionScript can make a JavaScript call from any frame or button, making it possible to trigger changes in a playing .RMF file.

Continued

Continued

Conclusion

The benefits of authoring with Beatnik audio go well beyond those described here, especially when sophisticated interactivity is desired. When your Flash projects call for audio, consider whether structured audio might be a better solution for your needs than that provided by linear audio. Further documentation and tutorials are available at www.beatnik.com. Also note that Beatnik maintains a discussion forum for developers who use Beatnik audio and Flash together, at http://discussion.beatnik.com.

Currently living in San Francisco, Doug Loftus recalls the Devo remake of "Satisfaction" as a prominent feature of his final year of compulsory education. Not surprisingly, in response to our question, "what is your single most favorite thing to do?," Doug responded, "creating grooves for my own amusement and hypnosis." He also told us that he "gravitated to Flash because it's an ideal medium for creating sophisticated, great-looking interfaces." Among his finer accomplishments, Doug's credited for much of the work on both www.mubu.com and www.mixman.com.

Expert Tutorial: Mixman in a Web page, *by Andreas Wagner*

Now that you know what Beatnik audio is all about, Andreas shows you how to enable the Beatnik plug-in in your HTML documents and how to control Beatnik audio from your Flash movies.

The Mixman Studio Pro software is a very powerful music creation, remixing, and performance system that lets you create professional-sounding music on your PC or Mac. For those not familiar with Mixman Studio, the interface consists of a 2-turntable metaphor, with 8 buttons on each record symbolizing the 16 tracks of digital audio that can be loaded and triggered live. Additionally, it has a ton of features too numerous to list here.

For more information visit www.mixman.com.

The recent release, Mixman Studio Pro 4, features an option for exporting your Mixman creation to the Beatnik sound file format .RMF, making it possible to publish your music on a Web page through the use of the Beatnik plug-in. For more in-depth information on the .RMF format, see Doug Loftus' entry "Why Use Beatnik Audio?"

Mixman in a Web page was made, in Flash 4, for the mymixzone community, where users can promote themselves, uploading their music for others to remix online (www.mixman.com/mymixzone). Needless to say, the Flash interpretation of Mixman Studio is miles away from the original software. Still, Mixman in a Web page is a little revolutionary. Sixteen tracks can be triggered, tempo changes can be made (without changing the pitch!), and 11 different reverb types can be set — all in real-time.

When you are done with this tutorial, you will be capable of creating a Flash 5/Beatnik Web page with the ground elements of Mixman in a Web page, which are the 16 buttons that can trigger the audio channels of a .RMF file. You will furthermore be equipped and prepared to experiment with the power of the Beatnik plug-in. I recommend that you download the *Beatnik Web Authoring Documentation* available at www.beatnik.com.

The following are the JavaScript library files necessary for Beatnik communication. They are found in the ch32 folder on the *Flash 5 Bible* CD-ROM.

```
/java/

        music-object.js
        music-object-x-flash.js
```

A demo .RMF file exported from the Mixman Studio Pro 4 software:

```
/rmf/

        mixman.rmf
```

Tutorial Flash 5 movie and source:

```
/tutorial_movie/

        index.html
        tutorial.swf
        tutorial.fla
```

Mixman in a Web page "Lite" version source code.

```
/mixman_lite/

        index.html
        lite.swf
        lite.fla
```

Preparing the HTML

Beatnik has created JavaScript library files (.js) to make life easier for Beatnik authors. They contain the comprehensive JavaScript code needed to make our connections to the Beatnik plug-in. It is not necessary to fully understand the code in these .js files, but it is a good idea to whip out the text editor and take a look at what is in the code.

To build the foundation for a Flash/Beatnik Web page, source these two JavaScript's in the HTML body.

```
<SCRIPT SRC="../java/music-object.js"></SCRIPT>
<SCRIPT SRC="../java/music-object-x-flash.js"></SCRIPT>
```

Continued

Continued

Briefly, the music-object.js (Music Object) is the stairway to the Beatnik plug-in. Without this code, controlling and communicating with the Beatnik plug-in would be really challenging. The Music Object handles requests such as play, volume, and stop between Flash and the Beatnik plug-in. The Music Object should be seen as a layer between the Beatnik plug-in (handles the audio output) and the Flash Movie (the graphical front end).

The Music Object can be expanded with extensions such as music-object-x-flash.js. This extension connects the *wires* between the Beatnik player and Flash, which enables messages to be transmitted to the Music Object from Flash, using the Flash ActionScript `fscommand()` action.

Create a new Music Object instance and name it **MMplayer**. This name is passed on to the Music Object's constructor method (`new Music();`).

```
<SCRIPT LANGUAGE = JavaScript>
<!-- //
MMplayer = new Music();
MMplayer.magicEmbed ('SRC="../rmf/mixman.rmf" HIDDEN ¬
    VOLUME=0 AUTOSTART=true');
MMplayer.onPlay('getSampleNames();getSongInfo(); ¬
    startFlash()');
Music.embedFlashMovie ('SRC="lite.swf" NAME="mixman" ¬
    WIDTH=550 HEIGHT=400');
// -->
</SCRIPT>
```

The `magicEmbed` is our standard way to embed a Beatnik Player instance in a cross-browser HTML page. We assign it the following properties:

✦ The correct path to the .RMF file

✦ The player interface is HIDDEN

✦ `VOLUME` is set to zero (later, the volume is turned up in Flash with a `fscommand`)

✦ The `AUTOSTART` Boolean is set to `true`.

The reason that `AUTOSTART` is `true` is that we have a chance to execute JavaScript functions each time the Music Object instance enters playing state, using Beatniks `onPlay` callback method. (Other callbacks are available, such as `onLoad`, `onReady`, `onStop`, `onMetaEvent`, and so on.) These callback methods can take JavaScriptSTR or a JavaScript function as their parameters. Our three functions `getSampleNames()`, `getSongInfo()`, and `startFlash()` are executed when the player hits the playing state.

Finally, the Flash movie is embedded with these properties: Path, Name, and the movie's Width and Height.

If Music Object is made visible (`HIDDEN=false WIDTH=144 HEIGHT=44`), the standard Beatnik player interface appears. Essentially, what we are doing here is building a remote control for this player.

This concludes the embedding. Now, its time to build three functions that will be executed when the player instance is in the playing state. In order for it to work properly, these should be placed above all the embedded code.

When running, the Beatnik Player receives and holds significant information about the loaded .RMF (see "An Introduction to Structured Audio") file, which is distributed in fields called composer, song name, copyright, and so on.

```
function getSampleNames(){
    var trackData = new String(MMplayer.getInfo('notes'));
    var tracks =  trackData.split(",");
    for ( var i = 0; i <= 15; i++){
        window.document.mixman.SetVariable("sample" ¬
            + (i + 1), "" + tracks[i]);
    }
}
```

This is useful because the `MMplayer.getInfo()` Beatnik method returns these fields as a string value, giving us information about our .RMF file according to the specific parameter that we have assigned.

When exporting as .RMF from Mixman Studio Pro 4, all sounds assigned to the separate channels are in the field "notes." So, for example, to retrieve the instrument names assigned for each channel, we use the parameter `notes`. The received information is split (between the commas) and made equal to the variables generated in the `for` loop (sample1 up to sample16).

However, we want this information to be passed on to our Flash movie, which is named "mixman." To do this, we use `window.document.mixman.SetVariable`, which is the way to address objects and their functions or variables, embedded in Web pages. In a more elaborate way, it could be described, in more natural language, as: "In the `window`, find the `document` object. In the `document` object, find the `mixman` object. In the `mixman` object, use the function `SetVariable`."

So with that clear, let's get our hands on both the song title and on the name of the artist, too.

```
function getSongInfo(){
    window.document.mixman.SetVariable("songTitle", "" ¬
        + MMplayer.getInfo('title'));
    window.document.mixman.SetVariable("artist", "" ¬
        + MMplayer.getInfo('composer'));
}
```

Again, to accomplish this, we use `getInfo`. The variable `songTitle` should be equal to the string returned when we set the `getinfo()` parameter to `title`. The `artist` variable should be equal to `getInfo` together with the parameter `composer`.

Continued

Continued

Finally, we need the Flash movie to react when the instance is playing.

```
function startFlash(){
    window.document.mixman.GotoFrame(4);
}
```

In this case, the Flash movie should progress to frame 4.

The Flash 5 ActionScript

Frame number 5 is the base for our Flash 5 ActionScript functions. Let us look at the essential `fscommand()` action in Flash, and how to control volume for each of our 16 channels.

```
function tellBeatnik(channel,controller,volume){
    fscommand("MMplayer.setController," + channel + "," ¬
        + controller + "," + volume + "");
}
```

The `fscommand` action has two parameters: command and arguments. We are sending the command `setController` with the arguments `MidiChannel0` to `16`, `ControllerNumber0` to `127`, and `ControllerValue0` to `127` to our player instance (`MMplayer`). The ActionScript function `tellBeatnik()` has been built to send parameters and change the arguments of the `fscommand` action more simply:

✦ The `channel` parameter enables a MIDI channel number (1–16).

✦ The `controller` parameter specifies a MIDI controller for the channel. (We use the controller for volume, which is number 7.)

✦ Finally, the `volume` parameter lets us set the value of the MIDI controller. (0–127). For example, we want channel 9 to use the MIDI controller number 7 and give it the value 127:

```
tellBeatnik(9,7,127);
```

Author's Note: Beatnik supports MIDI controllers such as Modulation (number 1), volume (number 7), Pan (number 10), Reverb Type (number 90), Reverb Level (number 91) and others (listed in the Beatnik Web Authoring Documentation).

Our `tellBeatnik()` ActionScript function is used in our next initialization function that is designed to turn down the volume for our 16 channels.

```
function initMixman(){
        var i = 1;
        while (i <= 16) {
            tellBeatnik(i,7,0);.
        i++;
        }
    if( i == 17){
```

```
        play();
        }
    }
```

The loop executes `tellBeatnik()` with the channel parameter `i`, controller 7 and value 0. Now, when all the channels are silent, we should the movie start with the `play()` method. Before we leave frame 5, remember that the `initMixman()` function is called here:

```
stop();
initMixman();
```

We let the movie play to frame 10, and turn up the overall volume (range 0–100) of the `MMplayer`. (Initially, we embedded the player with the volume set to zero.)

```
fscommand ("MMplayer.setVolume(100)");
stop();
```

This does not affect the value of the MIDI Controller 7; it will remain as it is. Although this might seem weird, it removes a short, loud noise that sometimes occurs when the loop is not quick enough to turn down all the 16 channels.

In frame 10, we build a function that can change the color of a Movie Clip instance when required:

```
function colorChange (myChannel,myColor){
    cleverLight = new Color (eval("_root.ch"+myChannel));
    cleverLight.setRGB(myColor);
}
```

We use the constructor `new Color()` to create a new Color Object. We call this Color Object `cleverLight` and make it possible to set the RGB value (in hexadecimal) with the `myColor` parameter. Calling `colorChange` with parameter `(3, 0x666666)` will make a new Color Object with Movie Clip `ch3` as target, and set the RGB value to `0x666666` (gray).

We need two more functions in frame 10; these will handle the channel volume change (`unMute` and `mute`), put the responding sample names in a dynamic text field, and change the color a Movie Clip.

```
function unMute(myChannel) {
    tellBeatnik(mychannel,7,127);
    sampleName = eval("_root.sample"+mychannel);
    colorChange (myChannel,0x33FF00);
}
function mute(myChannel) {
    tellBeatnik(mychannel,7,0);
    sampleName = eval("_root.sample"+myChannel);
    colorChange (myChannel,0x666666);
}
```

Continued

Continued

In function unMute(), the channel number we use as its parameter is passed on to the tellBeatnik() function. The string in the text field, sampleName, is equal to the content of the variable sample + myChannel number. This gives us the name of the sample, retrieved by the JavaScript function getSampleNames() on the HTML page. Finally, our colorChange() function is called with the parameters myChannel and color hex code 0x666666. This will change the color of the Smart Clip, which we create in the next section, to green.

Before making the Smart Clip to trigger the mute and unMute functions, we should create our three dynamic text fields and name them sampleName, songTitle and artist.

The Smart Clip

In the Flash 4 version of Mixman in a Web page, 16 individual Movie Clips had to be created, making it very time-consuming if the boss wanted a feature added or changed. The improvement of ActionScript in Flash 5 simply prevents too many ulcers in these situations. We only need to make one Movie Clip, define a clip parameter, drag it to the Stage, and change its parameter. Even though we have to do that 16 times, we still only have one Movie Clip, making it leisurely if we want to add a new look to the clip or change some code.

Let's create a Movie Clip symbol, and name it **superClip**. Open the Library, select the new Movie Clip, and choose Define Clip Parameters in the Library Options menu. Here, you should create a new parameter and change the varName to **myChannel**. Create a list of values that range from 1 to 16.

In the first frame of the new Smart Clip timeline, add these frame actions:

```
this._name = "ch" + myChannel;
muted=true;
stop();
```

Here we set the name of the Smart Clip semiautomatically using the _name **property and the value "ch" + myChannel. This will help our colorChange() function to locate its Color Object (for example, ch1..ch16). We also initialize our muted Boolean to true. This Boolean is used by our button to check which state the Smart Clip is in.

Draw a gray (hex 666666) masterpiece of a button in the first frame of the Smart Clip and convert it to a Button instance. Highlight it and give it these actions in the Actions Panel:

```
on (press) {
    if ( muted ){
        _root.unMute(MyChannel);
        muted=false;
    }
    else if ( muted == false){
        _root.mute(MyChannel);
        muted=true;
    }
}
```

When we mouse "press" the button, the actions will be executed in the following manner: If the Boolean `muted` is `true`, call the `unMute()` function in the root of the main movie. Call `unMute()` with a parameter that corresponds to this Smart Clip's `MyChannel` variable (which is set in the Clip Parameters Panel). Now, this channel is playing. So, we set the `muted` Boolean to `false`. On the second mouse "press," the `else if` action executes. This nest calls the `mute()` action and resets the `muted` Boolean. Now we can toggle our channels, as soon as the Smart Clip is on the Stage.

Go to the root of the movie in frame 10. In the Library, highlight the Smart Clip and drag it onto the stage. With the Smart Clip selected, go to Window ➪ Panels ➪ Clip Parameter. In the Clip Parameters Panel, choose a value for the `myChannel` clip parameter. Repeat this 16 times, giving each Smart Clip a `myChannel` parameter value ranging 1 to 16.

Now, all of the ground elements for Mixman in a Web page will be functioning. Save your Flash movie and test it in your HTML page in a Web browser.

Final Notes

If you want to go a step further, you can either look at the source for the mixman_lite.fla on the CD-ROM (it explains the keycodes and solostate macros), or download the *Beatnik Web Authoring Documentation* available at `www.beatnik.com`.

I would like to thank Jason "Mouse" Bard, Steve Markovich, Sal Orlando, and everyone at Mixman/Beatnik, the *Flash 5 Bible* team, and Morten Wagner.

In the year that Andreas Wagner graduated from High School, "Asleep At The Wheel," by Suicidal Tendencies, was the most memorable song. A native of Copenhagen, Denmark, currently residing on the Spanish Isle of Mallorca, Andreas is true pioneer of distant employment — he works on contract for Mixman of San Francisco. Oddly enough, his most favorite thing to do is, "Compressing Gifs" and he claims to have discovered Flash at the "Space Invaders" School of Multimedia Design. Sites that Andreas has worked on include: `www.mixman.com/mymixzone`, `www.koalition.net`, and his own `www.invaders.dk/andreas`.

Summary

✦ There are a number of sound-editing applications that you can use on your Windows or Macintosh computer. Some software bundles use proprietary audio hardware and computer peripherals.

✦ Every sound-editing application can perform basic edit functions for sound files. Among other things, you can change In and Out points, normalize, and resample sound files.

✦ Sonic Foundry's ACID can be used to create seamless loops for Flash soundtracks.

✦ The Beatnik plug-in enables you to use both sound samples and MIDI audio with Flash movies.

✦ Mixman Studio can export sound mixes as .RMF files, which can be explicitly controlled with FSCommands from Flash movies.

✦   ✦   ✦

Working with 3D Graphics

Although Flash has no true 3D art tools, with a little time and effort, you can effectively simulate depth. If you have other 3D applications, you'll learn how to export optimized EPS or bitmap sequences to use as Movie Clips in a Flash movie. Because interest in 3D Flash artwork is growing, developers are including direct .SWF output capabilities with their applications.

Introduction to 3D Modeling

Computer monitors have only two dimensions, width and height, which makes working with three-dimensional objects a bit unnerving for someone who is a novice to 3D-computer modeling. That's because 3D artwork occurs in what is called 3D space, which is a simulation of real space. Three-dimensional space has three axes: X (width), Y (height), and Z (depth). While conceptualizing three dimensions may not be difficult, controlling views of objects and cameras, or rotating objects with a mouse and keyboard can prove to be an arduous task. Likewise, most 3D graphics are displayed on flat computer screens. So, what makes a graphic appear to have depth in a two-dimensional space? See Figure 33-1 for an example.

Art history teaches us that several factors can give the illusion of depth on a flat surface. All of these factors are central to the arrangement of subject matter within a frame, also known as the composition. Most artwork achieves the appearance of depth through the use of perspective, wherein the proportion of the composition's foreground and background spaces lend a perceived depth. With linear perspective, parallel lines are drawn as converging lines, usually to a single vanishing point on a horizon line (see Figure 33-2). The diminution of scale is integral to the concept of linear perspective. Objects closer to the viewer appear larger, while objects farther from the viewer appear smaller. Similarly, atmospheric perspective adds to a composition's sense of depth by reducing the visibility of objects as they approach the horizon.

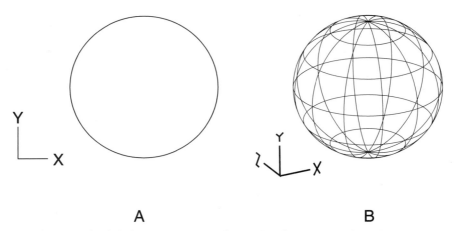

A   **B**

Figure 33-1: The left diagram is a two-dimensional representation of space, whereas the right diagram depicts three-dimensional space.

In most 3D computer applications, you can also choose a viewpoint known as orthographic perspective, in which objects and scenes are shown from a strict mathematical viewpoint — without any sense of depth (see Figure 33-3). Technically, because orthographic views do not use perspective, this viewpoint should be referred to as orthographic projection. That's because an orthographic view renders an object or scene with mathematical accuracy instead of perspective accuracy. Some applications may also have an *isometric* view. As far as 3D computer-drawing programs are concerned, *isometric* and *orthographic* views are the same.

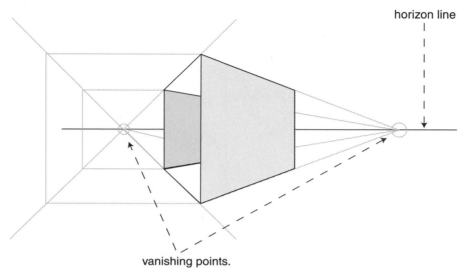

Figure 33-2: The line drawing illustrates the concept of linear perspective. The image created in MetaCreations Bryce 3D shows linear and atmospheric perspective.

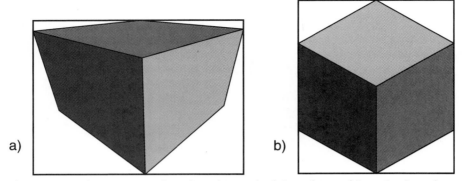

Figure 33-3: Linear perspective of a cube on the left; orthographic projection of a cube on the right

With the advent of photography, depth-of-field effects have also become factors that can be used to contribute to a sense of perceived depth within a two-dimensional plane. *Depth of field* refers to the range of clear focus in either the foreground or the background of a composition. A low depth of field means that objects appear in focus only within a short distance range from the viewer (see Figure 33-4). For example, if a camera lens is focused on a person with mountains in the distance, then the person is in focus, while the mountains are not. A high depth of field means that objects can be farther apart from one another while maintaining the same focus clarity. Using the same previous example, a high depth of field enables both the near person and the distant mountains to appear in focus.

Most 3D-creation programs not only strive to render scenes with accurate perspective, but also strive for a sense of near-photographic realism. Given the nature of Flash's vector-based framework, most highly textured 3D artwork won't mesh well with small vector file sizes. Nevertheless, simpler 3D objects and animations can be imported into Flash while maintaining reasonable file sizes (less than 60KB). The 3D programs use the following processes or enhancements to add realism and depth to artwork:

✦ **Extruding.** This is the process of importing a two-dimensional vector graphics file (such as Illustrator EPS) into a 3D modeling program and giving depth to an otherwise flat object — usually by extending vertices or edges along the Z axis (see Figure 33-5).

✦ **Lighting.** The most important factor in creating the illusion of spatial depth is adding and positioning light sources. A well-lit 3D model emphasizes planar depth; poorly lit 3D objects look flat (see Figure 33-6).

Figure 33-4: Low depth of field on the left; high depth of field on the right

Figure 33-5: A flat 2D graphic on the left; an extruded 2D graphic on the right

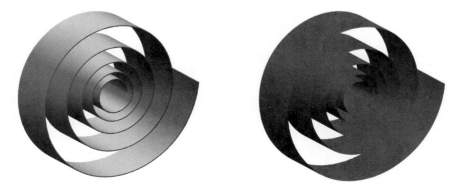

Figure 33-6: A well-lit 3D object on the left; a poorly lit object on the right

✦ **Texture Mapping.** Textures (images of patterns or surface materials) can be stretched across an object's surface(s) or faces (see Figure 33-7). Through the use of color contrast, pattern, and opacity, texture mapping gives an object unique, realistic attributes.

✦ **Wireframe.** A wireframe is the most basic model structure of a 3D object. It renders objects using lines to represent the edges of polygons and faces (see Figure 33-8).

Figure 33-7: A texture-mapped object

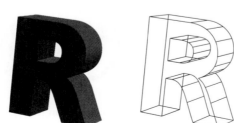

Figure 33-8: A PostScript view of an extruded letter R in Adobe Dimensions; a wireframe view of the same model

✦ **Inverse Kinematics.** Kinematics is the study of the motion of objects or of a system of objects. Inverse kinematics (IK) refers to how motion in one area of the system effects the movement of other parts in the system. For example, in respect to the human body, movement of the hip necessarily involves repositioning the legs to accommodate that motion. Early 3D programs didn't incorporate IK very well. Most high-end 3D applications such as 3D Studio MAX have advanced control of IK effects, while most prosumer 3D applications, such as Curious Labs Poser, have some level of IK support. Although IK support doesn't necessarily affect the three-dimensional feel of an object, it adds automated realism to animated figures and complex objects.

Several cross-platform 3D file formats exist: .3DS (3D Studio), .DXF, and .VRML. However, Flash 5 only recognizes two-dimensional .DXF files, such as those created by CAD programs. Consequently, for most 3D artwork imported into Flash, we recommend that you export either .EPS/.AI files (on the vector side) or .PICT/ .BMP files (on the raster side) from the parent 3D application.

At the time of this writing, only two plug-ins for Kinetix 3D Studio Max provide for direct export of 3D objects or animations to the Flash .SWF format — Digimation's Illustrate! 4 and Vecta3D by Ideaworks. Because Macromedia has opened the Flash .SWF source code to the public, we expect to see more applications that can either save as or export to the .SWF file format.

A variety of 3D applications are on the market, and they vary greatly in price and quality. Although a program such as Kinetix 3D Studio Max offers the broadest range of advanced controls, you might not need (or want) to take the time to learn it. Simpler programs, such as Adobe Dimensions or Curious Labs Poser, sacrifice the finer controls but offer the ease of use that Web designers expect from other graphics applications. Without further introduction, let's get started with some simple yet effective 3D work created in Flash with the help of FreeHand or Illustrator.

Simulating 3D with Flash

In this section, Manuel Clement, foremost master of Flash 3D graphics, shows you how to create a 3D vortex.

If you'd like to see the fully constructed Flash (.FLA) file for this tutorial, see vortex.fla in the ch33 folder on the *Flash 5 Bible* CD-ROM.

Expert Tutorial: Vortex: The Illusion of 3D with Flash, *by Manuel Clement*

It's not necessary to own expensive 3D applications to create interesting 3D animations. In Mano's tutorial, you learn to create the 3D-like artwork entirely with the drawing tools of Flash.

Illusion: The Vortex

A common drawback to 3D animation delivered over the Web is that the results can vary widely due to variables of systems and connections. Yet this animation has been tested over many connections on systems ranging from 200 MHz to 450 MHz and is drawn smoothly even on slower systems.

The vortex is a 3D effect created without an external modeler, using only the Flash drawing tools, timeline, and layers. After this tutorial, you'll be able to create similar effects using the same technique, which is to simulate 3D with one object of the library, a semivisible ring, by decreasing the size of the symbol on successive layers. As you'll see, the possibilities are endless.

To begin, create a new movie and modify it using Modify ⇨ Movie ⇨ Background so that it has a black background. (Save this new movie, and don't forget to save your work using Ctrl+S [Command+S] each time you complete a step.) Next, select the Oval Tool and set Fill Color to neutral, Line Color to white, and Line Thickness to H (thinnest setting). Now, draw a large circle at the default keyframe 1, as shown in the following figure.

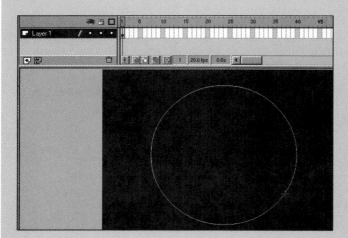

Select the circle. Copy it using Ctrl+C (Command+C) and then Paste it using Ctrl+V (Command+V) into the same (first) keyframe, as seen in the following figure.

With the circle still selected, use the Arrow Tool with the Scale Modifier to first reduce the size of the new circle, and then to drag it to the middle of the original circle as seen in the following figure.

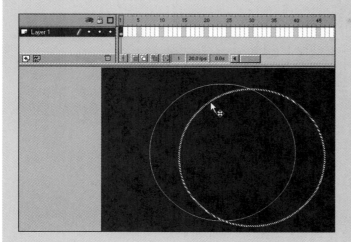

Be careful when you are drawing more than one shape on the same layer—if you accidentally deselect a shape that is over another shape, then the two shapes will be joined.

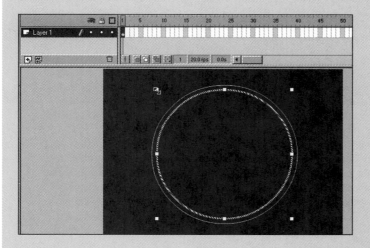

Choose the Paint Bucket Tool and create a new color with a 30-percent Alpha. For this example, a blue with a 30-percent Alpha was used. The Alpha setting is important for the optical illusion that we are creating. (Be sure to press the New button to add your new color to the Current Colors pop-up menu.) Now fill the space between the two circles.

Continued

Continued

We now have a filled shape with two outline circles. Delete these outline circles by selecting each circle with the Arrow Tool and then pressing the Delete key. You should now have a transparent ring that looks like this figure:

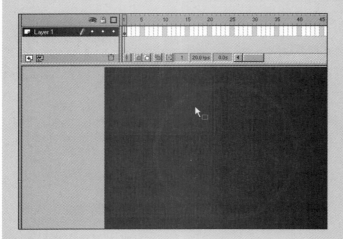

Select the ring and convert it to a movie clip (Insert ➪ Convert to Symbol). In the ensuing Symbol Properties dialog, type the Name of the symbol, and select Movie Clip as the Behavior.

Now, with the Arrow Tool and the Scale Modifier, select the ring and reduce its size — we're going to need a lot of space to create the vortex (see the following figure). If you haven't saved your project yet, do so now.

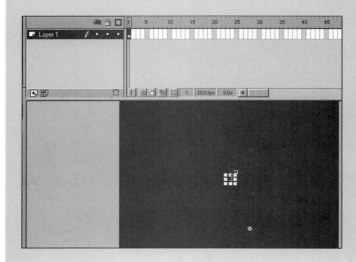

Select the keyframe and copy it by right-clicking the keyframe and selecting Copy Frames from the ensuing pop-up menu. Create a new layer with Insert ⇨ Layer (or by clicking the Add Layer button on the timeline). Now Select the first keyframe of the new layer and paste the previously copied keyframe with a right-click into the keyframe followed by selecting Paste Frames from the ensuing pop up menu. At this point, there should be two layers with identical keyframes, as shown. Lock the previous layer to prevent future mistakes.

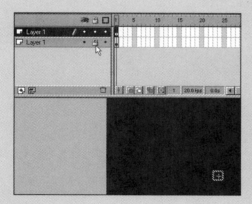

In order to see exactly what you are doing, go to the Zoom control and select Show All (alternately, use View ⇨ Show All). With the original layer locked and the new layer active, use the Scale Modifier of the Arrow Tool to select the ring and enlarge it slightly. This becomes the basic procedure: Each time we create a new layer with its new ring, we make that layer larger than the previous one. In the figure that follows, you can see that the ring in the second layer is larger than the circle in the lower layer.

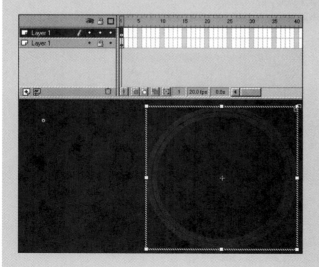

Continued

Continued

Mimic the previous procedures to copy the latest keyframe, create a new layer, and then paste the frame on the newest layer's first keyframe. Again, lock the previous layer to prevent future mistakes. Finally, enlarge the newest ring and save.

Repeat the previous steps a few more times, until you have about 21 rings (on 21 layers). Note that, although the process remains the same, the effect varies depending on the number of rings: The more rings you add, the bigger the vortex. The following figure shows the completed set of rings.

Now we're going to animate the vortex. Select frame 20 of *all* the layers: To do this, start at the bottom of the timeline, click frame 20, and hold the Shift key while selecting all remaining layers. Now, with all the frames that you've selected still selected, make frame 20 of each layer into a keyframe by pressing F6.

As shown in the following figure, all of the rings should still be selected and you should be at keyframe 33. If not, Shift+click to select keyframe 33 of all layers and select all of the rings simultaneously with Edit ➪ Select All.

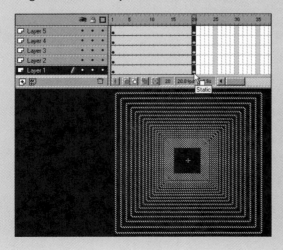

Now, use the Scale Modifier of the Arrow Tool to reduce the width of the rings on the X-axis, as shown in the following figure. Then, lock the top layer.

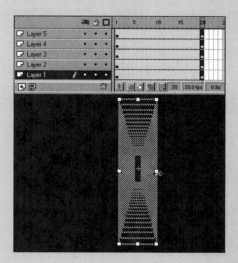

If they are not selected, reselect all of the rings again and then press the right arrow key 10 times. This moves all the selected rings (except for those rings on layers that are locked) toward the right along their X-axes. Finally, lock the topmost layer of the unlocked layers, as shown in the following figure.

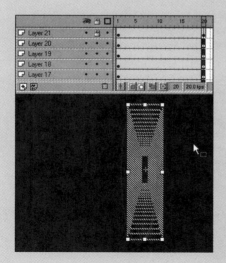

Continued

Continued

Again, reselect all of the rings (if they are not selected) and press the right arrow key ten times. This moves the selected rings (on all unlocked layers) farther to the right along the X-axis. (You can see the shape of the vortex starting to appear.) Lock the topmost, unlocked layer.

Repeat the previous procedure until all layers are locked, and the vortex is drawn. Your vortex should look just like the one shown here.

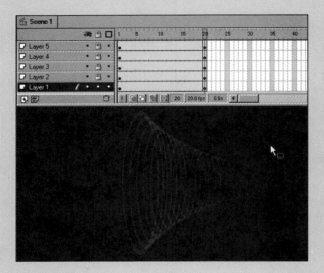

Now select the first keyframe of all layers by starting at the bottom layer and shift-clicking the first keyframe of each layer until you've selected the first keyframe of each layer. With all first keyframes still selected, open the Frame Panel (Ctrl+F or Command+F). Select Motion in the Tweening menu.

An arrow appears between keyframes, passing through the frames of each layer to indicate a Motion Tweening transition between frame 1 and frame 20. Save, and then press Enter to see the vortex animate! The following figure shows the vortex as it appears halfway through the tween.

The file size of this seemingly complex animation is only 6KB. That's because it's built from a single, simple ring symbol. With more rings or keyframes, your file size might be a little larger, but not much. Although this vortex animation is only a transition between two keyframes, once you understand the principle, you can create your own varied effects. You may get some interesting results by editing the ring Movie Clip in the gallery and changing its shape or color, or maybe even by animating the clip itself. The vortex differs with each change made to the ring symbol.

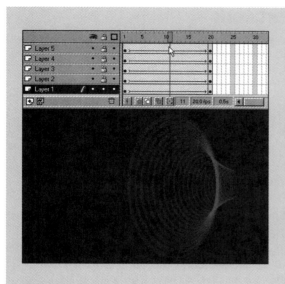

Manuel Clement, affectionately known as "Mano" to friends and colleagues, is the designer behind `mano1.com`. With seven years of classical piano and music theory training, he also runs `onlinedj.com`, an emerging site for the music industry. Winner of two Macromedia Shocked Site of the Day awards in 1999, Manual is passionate about design, technology, and has spoken at conferences in San Francisco, New York and London. Manuel says this of his recent work; "I am influenced by the artist Victor Vasarely, who is distinguished in contemporary art for the exceptional results that he brought [to] geometrical abstract painting, under the name of kinetism." (Vasarely's work can be viewed online at `www.netprovence.com/fondationvasarely/`) "This vortex," Manuel continues, "reminds me of his paintings."

Using Adobe Dimensions to Create 3D Objects

Many Flashers create 3D designs and animations for Flash movies with Adobe Dimensions 3.0. That's because Dimensions offers an intuitive interface for elementary 3D design. If you've never used a 3D program before, then Adobe Dimensions is a great place to start. The interface has familiar tools found in other 2D drawing programs. These include Pen, Text, and Object Tools. Although Dimensions' support of animation isn't as advanced as that of other applications (such as 3D Studio MAX or even Macromedia Extreme 3D Version 2) you can use it to create great-looking 3D animations to use in Flash—while maintaining small file sizes! This section shows you how to turn an existing 2D design into a simple—yet effective—3D sequence that can be imported into Flash. (If you aren't acquainted with the basic interface of Dimensions, please read Chapter 1 of the *Adobe Dimensions 3.0 User Guide,* which comes with the software, before proceeding with this section.)

How to extrude vector artwork

In Dimensions 3.0, you can create 3D artwork from scratch using the various drawing tools in the toolbox. You can also use Dimensions to generate dimensional artwork from any vector file, such as .EPS or .AI files. In this section, we describe how to extrude an imported Illustrator file.

✦ Make sure that you have installed Dimensions 3.0 on your Windows or Macintosh computer. Open the application.

✦ In the Render Mode drop-down menu of the Untitled-1 document window, choose PostScript.

✦ Open the Extrude window by choosing Operations ➪ Extrude or Command ➪ Ctrl+E. This command or shortcut can hide the Extrude window as well.

✦ In the lower-left corner of the Extrude window, click the New Base button.

✦ With the Extrude base window active, import an .EPS file that you want to turn into animated 3D artwork for Flash. To do this, choose File ➪ Import (Command+Option+I or Ctrl+Alt+I), and select a vector file. (You can use the crossHairs.eps file in the ch31 folder on the *Flash 5 Bible* CD-ROM.)

Tip   You can export an .EPS or Illustrator file from Flash to use in Dimensions. For more information on exporting vector file formats from Flash, see Chapter 31, "Working with Vector Graphics."

In the Extrude window, enter a value in the Depth text field. By default, all values in Dimensions are in points. After you enter a value, click the Apply button in the lower right-hand corner of the Extrude window (see Figure 33-9). A value of 75 points was used for the crosshairs sample file.

Figure 33-9: Using the Extrude window, you can convert a two-dimensional vector file to a three-dimensional object.

With the object selected in the document window, open the Camera window (Window ➪ Show Camera), which controls the view angle of the 3D window. Enter **75** for the Lens value, and **0** for Lon, Lat, and Roll.

Open the Move window (Operations ➪ Transform ➪ Move). Choose Absolute for the Coordinates property, and enter **0** for X, Y, and Z values. Click Apply. If you're using the crosshair sample file, your object should resemble Figure 33-10.

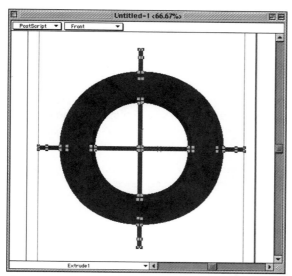

Figure 33-10: After applying a new Camera view and object coordinates, the crosshairs object has a much more dynamic look.

The next step is to generate a series of still images from Dimensions to use in Flash. (The process is similar to using the Auto-Distort command in the Paint window of Macromedia Director.) To do this, we use Dimensions to record the position and scale of the object as it is rotated and moved in the 3D window. A start point and an end point are specified. Then Dimensions creates the in-between keyframes for the sequence.

With the 3D object selected and in a starting position, choose Operations ⇨ Generate Sequence. The alert box shown in Figure 33-11 appears.

Figure 33-11: After you select the Generate Sequence command, move, scale, or rotate the 3D object to a new position or size. The Operations menu item remains high-lighted to remind you that you are generating a sequence.

Now, move and rotate the object to the final position of the animation. Note that you won't be able to preview the animated sequence. So, if you want to be precise, use any of the Operations ⇨ Transform windows to specify the end position. To create a rotating crosshair, open the Rotate window (Operations ⇨ Transform ⇨ Rotate) and enter **180** for the Y axis. Click Apply.

Choose Operations ⇨ End Sequence to stop the recording process. The Sequence dialog (see Figure 33-12) automatically opens, and you can specify the number of frames (in the sequence), the file type, and the filename prefix.

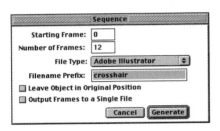

Figure 33-12: Specify the image output settings in the Sequence dialog.

To keep the final Flash file size as small as possible (for optimal transmission over the Web), try to limit the number of frames to as few as possible. Depending on the range of motion and scaling, you may be able to use as few as five or six frames. For the 180-degree crosshair rotation, a series of 12 frames was generated by Dimensions in the Adobe Illustrator (.AI) format, which Flash can import.

Note   You may want to experiment with .PICT or .BMP file types and use the Trace Bitmap command in Flash to reduce the complexity of the imported bitmaps. It may seem counterintuitive, but small bitmaps in a series are often smaller than their vector equivalents.

Most 3D applications have a filename prefix property that enables you to specify the name that precedes the numbers in the sequence. For example, if you use crosshair as the filename prefix, then the first frame's filename is crosshair0000. You can insert spaces or underscores (for example, "crosshair " or "crosshair_") to separate the number from the prefix.

Tip   The Sequence dialog box has two additional options, Leave Object in Original Position and Output Frames to a Single File. The first option, if checked, keeps the object in the center of each frame generated. If it is not checked, then the object's center varies depending on the starting and ending positions. Because you can tween the imported sequence as a Movie Clip in Flash, you may find this first option very useful, because broad and general movements can be created with a Movie Clip symbol by applying a motion tween to it.

Click the Generate button, and Dimensions starts processing each frame in the sequence. When it is finished rendering all the frames, you are ready to bring the sequence into Flash.

Bringing a sequence into Flash

With a Flash movie (.FLA) open, create a new layer and import the Dimensions sequence. Refer to the "Importing Poser Sequences into Flash" section in this chapter to see how to contain an imported sequence as a movie clip.

Some 3D animations make excellent rollovers for Flash buttons. Refer to the crossButton.swf file in the ch33 folder on the *Flash 5 Bible* CD-ROM for a rollover button example. You can see how this .SWF was made from the accompanying file, crossButton.fla.

Animating Figures with MetaCreations Poser

MetaCreations Poser 4.0 is a 3D figure-generation and animation application. With Poser, you can create lifelike human and animal characters to use in illustrations or animations. Poser 4.0 sports a sophisticated user interface with dozens of options for every tool and component. In this section, we walk you through the process of making a running mannequin figure that is then imported into Flash. While you need not be an advanced user of Poser to understand this example, you will benefit from reading the Tutorial section of the *Poser 4.0 User Guide* (which ships with the Poser software package) before starting this example. However, if you don't want to concern yourself with advanced functionality, it's possible to simply read and follow the guidelines in the following paragraphs.

Creating a walking figure in Poser

Here's how to create walking motion in Poser:

1. If you open Poser with its default factory settings, a clothed male figure should appear in the center of a 350×350 view window. Using the Translate/Pull tool, position the figure to the upper portion of the 350×350 window. The figure's shadow needs some room to fully display during the walk cycle.

2. Next, open the Poser figure and object libraries through the Window ➪ Libraries command (Shift+Command+B or Shift+Ctrl+B).

3. In this window, select Figures, then Additional Figures, and then Mannequin.

4. Access the Mannequin figure for the Additional Figures library.

5. Click OK to the following dialog. This alert box appears whenever you change the current figure. Do not check the Keep Current Proportions option.

6. Your Poser screen should now resemble Figure 33-13.

Figure 33-13: The new mannequin figure on the stage

7. Open Window ⇨ Walk Designer (Shift+Command+S or Shift+Ctrl+S). In the Walk Designer window, set the Blend Styles Run slider to 52 percent. Click the Walk button to preview the current settings, and then select different angles (¾, side, front, top) to see the walk from varying viewpoints. Click Apply. You'll then be presented with frame settings for the animation. Make sure the End Frame is set to frame 10 and that the Walk in Place option is checked. See Figure 33-14. Click OK, and Poser generates a complete walk cycle with ten frames.

8. To preview your figure's new walk, open the Animation Controls window (Shift+Command+ P or Shift+Ctrl+P) and drag the playback head (see Figure 33-15) through each frame. If you press Enter or Return, Poser plays back the entire frame sequence. To stop playback, press Enter or Return.

9. *Before* outputting the animation frames, make a new folder on a local drive to store the files. Do this now, because Poser won't give you the option to create a new folder during the save process.

10. Next, to output the animation, go to the Animation menu, and select Make Movie (Command+J or Ctrl+J). Set an end time of eight frames. Because Poser counts time zero as a frame, we'll have nine frames. Furthermore, because frame 10 is exactly the same as frame 1, we won't need it in Flash. For this example, use Display Settings. This means the exported frames look the same as the figure appears in the workspace of Poser. (You can add more detailed texture and bump maps to figures in Poser, but that's beyond the scope of this tutorial.) Also, if you want smoother-looking edges in the bitmap sequence, make sure the Antialias option is checked. If you're using the Mac version of Poser, you'll want to use PICT files as the Sequence Type instead of QuickTime. On the PC version, you'll want to use BMP or TIF files. Use the TIF format if you need to use an alpha channel. Refer to Figure 33-16 for the correct settings.

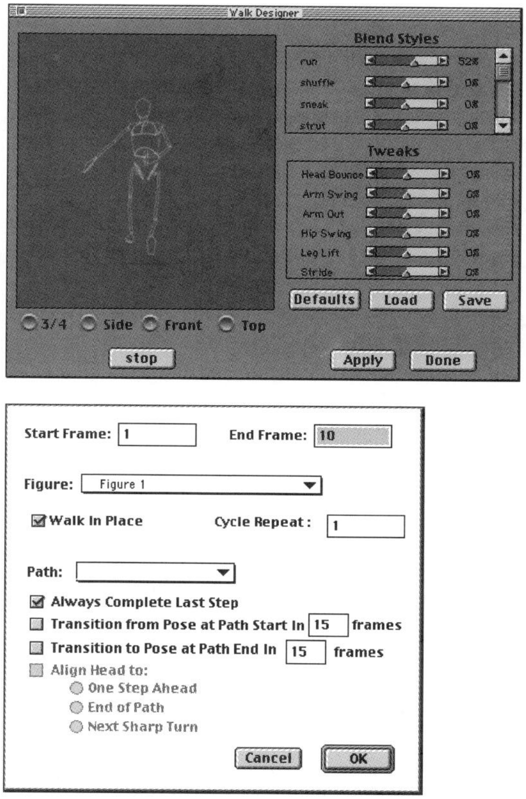

Figure 33-14: The Walk Designer in Poser 4.0 can create full-motion walks for any Poser figure.

Playback Head

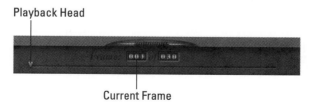

Current Frame

Figure 33-15: Animation controls

Using lower resolutions for Flash movies on the Web

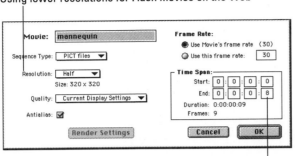

Specify an end frame of 8

Figure 33-16: Export settings for Poser image sequences

11. Click OK to proceed to the Save dialog, which prompts you to select a folder and filename for the sequence. Because Poser automatically adds the number extension to your filenames, just type the base filename. For example, typing **mannequin** generates successive filenames beginning with mannequin.0001 on the Mac or mannequin_0001.tif on the PC. Click Save, and Poser renders this little nine-frame animation. Save your Poser project and exit Poser.

Preparing Poser sequences for Flash

It would be nice if we could just directly import our .PICT or .TIF sequence into Flash, but first a number of small nuisances must be addressed.

To begin with, on the Mac, Flash doesn't seem to like the way Poser creates .PICTs — if you're using a PC, see the following note. This means that if you import a .PICT from Poser directly into Flash, Flash displays the file as a collection of horizontal and vertical lines. Furthermore, Poser creates inverted alpha channels, while Flash expects straight alpha channels, with black indicating hidden areas and white indicating shown areas. (See Chapter 17, "Understanding Actions and Event Handlers," for more discussion on alpha channels in Flash.) So, in order to make the Poser files read correctly in Flash, the alpha channels of the Poser .PICT files must be inverted and the file format saved correctly. To facilitate this transition, we've created a Photoshop action (located on the CD-ROM) that properly converts a sequence of Poser files into images that Flash understands.

Caution

PC Users: The alpha channels of exported .TIF sequences are correctly formatted for Flash use. However, while Flash 5 can now import .TIF files, Flash 5 on the PC will not recognize alpha channels in .TIF files. Therefore, you need to convert the .TIF files to the .PNG format in Photoshop or another graphics application. The .PNG format is the only alpha-channel-enabled raster-image format that Flash on the PC can use. .PNG images saved from Photoshop 5 or earlier may appear much darker when imported into Flash. If you have Photoshop 5.5 or later, use the new Save for Web feature to export .PNG images with more accurate color.

To load this Photoshop action, first pop the *Flash 5 Bible* CD-ROM into your computer. Then launch Adobe Photoshop (you need version 4 or greater) and open the Actions palette (Window ⇨ Show Actions). Make sure that the Actions Palette is *not* set to Button Mode. Then, on the palette's pop-up menu, choose Load Actions. Browse to the Photoshop folder in the ch18 folder on the *Flash 5 Bible* CD-ROM, and choose Flash 5 Actions.atn.

Now choose File ⇨ Automate ⇨ Batch. In the Set property, choose Flash 5 Actions, and select Poser Alpha Inversion for the Action property. For the Source, choose the folder that you specified for your Poser sequence files. For the Destination, choose Save and Close. Now click OK, and Photoshop fixes the .PCT or .BMP alpha channels so that Flash recognizes them properly. There's also a Poser Alpha + Image Inversion action that can be used to invert the RGB channels as well as the alpha channels — this is useful for converting Poser's white silhouettes into black ones.

Depending on your Photoshop color profile setup, you may encounter a dialog that interrupts the automate process. If you are presented with a Missing Profile dialog (as shown in Figure 33-17), choose Don't Convert. Photoshop continues with the automated processing of your image sequence. Note, however, that, if you receive this message for the first file, you'll keep getting it for every file in the sequence. Just stay with it and repeatedly press Return (on the Mac) or click Don't Convert when the Missing Profile dialog box pops up.

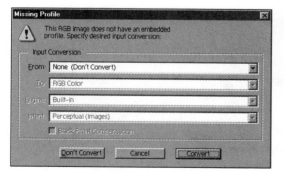

Figure 33-17: Depending on your specific color settings in Photoshop 5 or 6, you may receive a Missing Profile alert when an image without an ICC profile is opened.

If you're using the PC versions of Poser, Flash, and Photoshop, then you can skip to the next section. The Macintosh version of Flash won't recognize the 0001, 0002, or 0003 extension as an image sequence. You need to add a .PCT extension to the end of each of your .PICT files. This can be a time-consuming task for large sequences, so let the FileMunger shareware application (which can be downloaded from www.download.com) do all the work for you. FileMunger is a great little tool that is used to batch process file-creator types, filename extensions, and file date names. After you've installed the application, run FileMunger, and click the Filename Extensions button on the left (see Figure 33-18). This changes its operating mode to exclusively work with filename extensions.

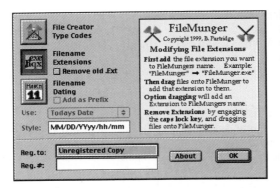

Figure 33-18: Use the Filename Extensions mode of FileMunger to automatically add extension suffixes to a group of files.

Close the FileMunger application, and rename the actual FileMunger application file to FileMunger.pct. This causes FileMunger to work in what is called Filename Extensions mode, meaning that it adds the .PCT extension to any file (or group of files) that is dropped on the FileMunger application icon. Now open the folder with the mannequin sequence, select all the files in the window by pressing Command+A, and drag them to the FileMunger application icon (Figure 33-19); FileMunger adds a .PCT extension to all your files. Thus, mannequin.0001 is now mannequin.0001.pct. Now the Mac version of Flash recognizes the Poser images as a sequence.

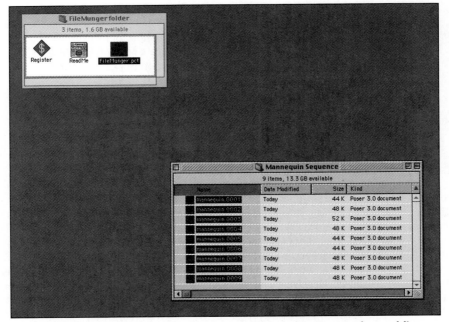

Figure 33-19: FileMunger can perform timesaving operations such as adding extensions to multiple files.

Importing Poser sequences into Flash

Okay, now we can get back to Flash. Open an existing Flash (.FLA) file or create a new one. Make a new symbol (Insert ⇨ New Symbol; Command+F8 or Ctrl+F8), and set it to the Movie Clip type. Give it the name **mannequin** or something similar. Automatically, Flash changes the stage to Symbol Editing Mode. Choose File ⇨ Import (Command+R or Ctrl+R), browse to the folder containing the Poser sequence, and double-click the first filename in the sequence (such as mannequin.0001.pct or mannequin_0001.bmp). Now click Import. You should receive an alert from Flash 5 that asks if you want to import all of the images in the sequence. Click Yes to this dialog, and Flash imports all the images associated with this sequence. When the import is completed, as indicated by the progress bar, the mannequin symbol has nine frames — and each of these frames is a keyframe.

Next, because Flash auto-aligned the top-left corner of the imported bitmaps to the center of the symbol, we need to change the symbol center to match the center of the bitmaps. Click the Edit Multiple Frames button on the timeline, and drag the End Onion Skin marker to frame 9. Select all the bitmaps in the symbol by pressing Command+A or Ctrl+A, or by using the Edit ⇨ Select All command. Press Command+K or Ctrl+K to bring up the Align dialog; set both vertical and horizontal align properties to center, check the Align to Page option, and click OK.

Your Movie Clip should resemble Figure 33-20.

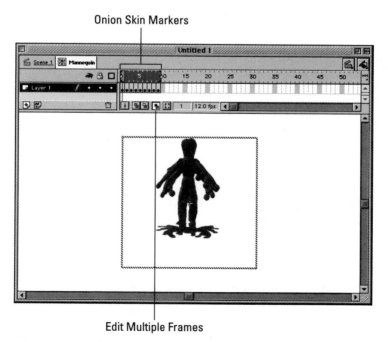

Onion Skin Markers

Edit Multiple Frames

Figure 33-20: The Mannequin Movie Clip

Caution

Don't neglect to turn off Edit Multiple Frames so that you don't accidentally displace all of these element(s).

Now you need to make a critical decision. Is it better to trace the bitmap files imported from Poser? Or are there advantages to leaving them as is? If you want to preserve the detail currently displayed by the imported sequence, then tracing the bitmap makes the Flash .SWF larger. If you want to minimize detail and can accept a loss of detail in your imported sequence, then use the Modify ⇨ Trace Bitmap command on each frame of the mannequin Movie Clip symbol at whatever quality settings you desire. But before you leap to tracing those bitmap files, here's a surprising comparison: The mannequin example was exported from Flash as is (with default .SWF settings) with a file size of 54.5KB. But the traced bitmap mannequin (using 10 for the Color Threshold, 8 for the Minimum Area and Normal for both Curve Fit and Corners) exported with a file size of 83.6KB!

Note that the traced bitmap version doesn't even look as good as the regular bitmapped version. Granted, we could have used many other procedures in Poser, Photoshop, FreeHand, or Streamline to optimize the quality of the bitmap or its converted vector counterpart. The point here, however, is that vector equivalents aren't *always* better than the original bit-for-bit raster graphics. (Here's a related example of a situation in which the vector equivalents *would* have been better: a silhouette figure generated in Poser with one solid color fill. Tracing those bitmaps would have yielded better results because the figure has only one color and a relatively simple outline. Remember, for the most part, vector graphics are ideal for illustrations with solid color fields and lines. Raster or bitmap graphics are ideal for continuous tone or photo-quality images.)

Cross-Reference

Macromedia FreeHand and Adobe Streamline are discussed in Chapter 31, "Working with Vector Graphics." We discuss Adobe Photoshop in Chapter 30, "Working with Raster Graphics."

Now you have a running mannequin Movie Clip that can be referenced from your Flash Library and placed anywhere in your Flash movies. Once placed in a scene, this Movie Clip can be scaled, rotated, or tweened to any position or size.

Exporting Animations from Kinetix 3D Studio Max

Discreet 3D Studio Max (3DS MAX) is one of the most popular, powerful, and professional 3D modeling and animation programs. The R3.1 release does not support direct export to Flash .SWF files. It can, however, export to the .EPS vector format. This file format can be imported into Flash, but the file sizes and vector information are usually too weighty for easy Internet transmission. Digimation's Illustrate! 4 and Ideaworks3D's Vecta3D-MAX plug-ins are available for 3D Studio MAX, enabling the program to export straight to Flash files. The following expert tutorial shows you how use Swift 3D, a standalone program with similar functions, enabling you to export optimized Flash files from 3D models.

Note Swift 3D does not convert texture maps into Flash gradients or bitmap fills. For this reason, 3D Studio MAX material textures are collapsed to the most predominant color of the material when imported into Swift 3D.

On the CD-ROM This tutorial requires both 3D Studio MAX and Swift 3D version 1.00. There were no demo versions available for either application at the time this book was written. You'll find the source folder for this tutorial in the ch33 folder on the *Flash 5 Bible* CD-ROM.

Expert Tutorial: From 3D Studio MAX to Vectors in Flash, by *Daniel Cluff*

Although you can create 3D artwork with many tools, 3D Studio MAX is a leading 3D software application for high-end professional artwork. In this tutorial, Daniel shows you how to integrate a MAX model into a Flash movie with the help of the Electric Rain's Swift 3D.

Overview

Creation of any project takes planning. You need to have a clear idea of the desired outcome and be aware of the steps that will be taken to achieve that desired outcome. You must know the tools you will need to proceed with those steps and how much time it will take. If you are following along with this tutorial on your own project and are not too familiar with all of the applications used, you will not finish in one day. Don't try to rush it, just take your time and make sure everything looks the way you want it to.

This tutorial covers a few effective ways to deliver "3D" graphics via Flash. The tools used in this tutorial are 3D Studio MAX Release 3.1, Swift 3D Version 1.0, and Flash 5. There were no available trial versions of either 3D Studio MAX or Swift3D at the time this tutorial was written. This is considered an expert tutorial; it presumes an understanding of all the applications involved.

3D Studio MAX is a 3D modeling and animation program with a unique plug-in structure, making it an extremely versatile tool. This plug-in structure, in combination with its complex but immensely effective and meticulously thorough user interface, provides for an enormously powerful 3D modeling and animation solution that can be the backbone of any number of various projects. It is for these reasons that 3D Studio MAX was chosen as the modeling tool for this tutorial.

Swift 3D is a standalone software application that has the capability to create and convert 3D models and animations to vector-based graphics and animations. Swift 3D will import 3D Studio (.3DS) models, respecting materials (sans maps), camera views, lighting schemes, and animations. It will also accept Encapsulated PostScript (.EPS) files and Adobe Illustrator files (.AI). The user interface is relatively simple and easy to use. A key feature of this program is the accurate way it handles geometry and lighting/shading.

Continued

Continued

This tutorial has three parts. The first part covers procedures and tips for preparing your 3D Studio MAX model/animation to be brought into Flash. The second part discusses two effective ways (pic sequence and Swift 3D) to export and optimize your 3D project for integration into the Flash movie, and compares and contrasts the two methods. The third part focuses on the actual integration into the Flash movie and covers any further necessary optimization.

The Beginning Step

Open the file mace_anim.max found on the CD-ROM. Play the animation. The mace will rotate 60 degrees over a span of 20 frames. As the animation continues to play, it appears as if the mace is rotating a complete 360 degrees. Because the mace is symmetrical 6 ways at 60-degree increments, it needs only to rotate 60 degrees. Stop the animation and return the time slider to zero. Open the Time Configuration dialog by clicking the Time Configuration button at the bottom right of the MAX window. Notice that under Frame Rate, the Custom option is selected and that the Frame Rate is set to 20 fps (see the following figure). I typically work in Flash at this frame rate. It is important to keep the frame rate constant throughout this process so that the animation plays the same speed in all three programs. I wanted the mace to rotate slowly, so over the course of 6 seconds, or 120 frames, the mace will appear to have rotated one complete revolution. Close the Time Configuration dialog.

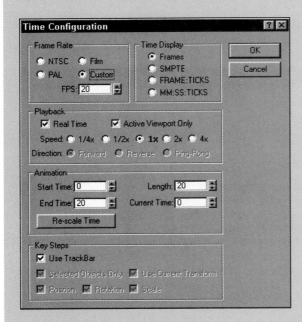

If you plan to export to Swift 3D, it isn't necessary animate in MAX. Swift 3D has many simple, ready-to-use animations that can be applied after the scene has been imported. For the pic sequence export, however, animation in Max is necessary.

The geometry in this animation has a rather high polygon count (more than 800 polygons) for a project of this type. Depending on the type of export you use, this will determine how the finished product will look. If you plan to export to Swift 3D, I recommend a much lower polygon count (between 400 and 500) so that "mesh shading" can be applied effectively without creating a 200KB animation. If you go the pic sequence route, you can use more complex geometry, but as a rule of thumb, do your best to never exceed 1000 polygons per object.

There are three lights applied to this animation. One white light that hits the mace in front, a medium blue light that hits the mace from the lower left, and a third red light that hits the mace from above and slightly to the right. This lighting scheme looks fantastic in a rendered pic sequence, and the lights translate perfectly into Swift 3D. The geometry may be far too complex to use lit shading in Swift 3D. This topic is discussed in the next section of the tutorial.

The materials assigned to the mace mesh are all basic MAX materials and can be found in the Material Library in Max's Material/Map Browser. To locate these materials, open the Material Editor (shown in the figure that follows) by pressing the M key.

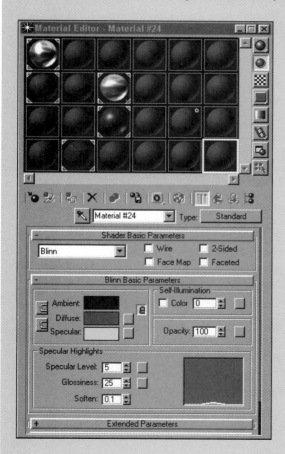

Continued

Continued

Click the Get material button. When the Material/Map Browser opens (shown in the following figure), make sure Mtl Library is selected in the Browse From section. You can drag and drop the materials that you want into the material editor. The head and spikes have a highly reflective chrome material applied to them. This will create a polished metal surface appearance when rendered. The shaft of the mace has a wood material applied to it, showing wood grain for added realism. The ring on the shaft, the hilt, and the pommel, all have a gold material, similar to the chrome material used on the head, but darkened slightly to look more like brass. The handle has a gray, low "gloss" metallic material assigned to it. For details on creation of this mace, please refer to mace.pdf found on the CD-ROM.

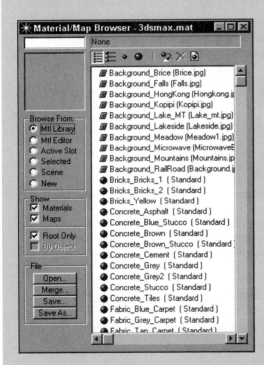

The Middle Step

Buckle your seat belts and prepare to export. The following procedure should be used if exporting a sequence of image files. On the main toolbar in MAX, click the Render Scene button. This will bring up the Render Scene dialog (shown in the figure that follows).

From here, you have options to control which frames are rendered, the pixel size of the animation, and whether or not you want to save the animation as a file or files. Under the time Output rollout, select the Active Time Segment option. This renders all of the frames in the scene. In the Every Nth Frame box, enter the value of 2.

This will render every other frame. The reason this is done is to avoid rendering frames that must later be taken out because of file size. In the Output Size section click the 320×240 button. This is a decent size that will look good, while being relatively flexible in file size. In the Render Output section, click the Files button, set the location where you want the files to be saved, and give them a name. The best file type to use is Portable Network Graphics (.PNG). It's the only file format that you can import into Flash using alpha transparency. MAX will automatically attach frame numbers to the end of each file name in sequence. Once this is done, make sure that the desired view port is selected at the bottom of the dialogue window and then click Render. It shouldn't take more that one minute to render the animation.

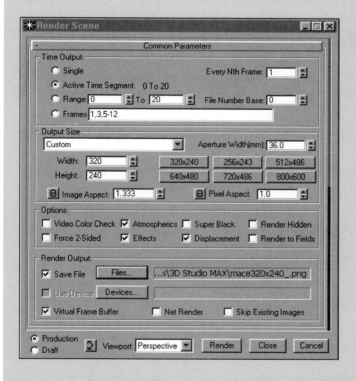

Now on to the Swift 3D Export. When the Animation has finished rendering, close the Render Scene dialog and go to File ⇨ Export. The Select File to Export dialog appears. Set the location and filename and make sure that the file type being exported is .3DS (3D Studio) format. Save the file. Boom! You have finished the MAX portion of this project.

Continued

Continued

Remember that .PNG sequence we rendered? Time to optimize. Macromedia Fireworks is the best application to use for this operation. For optimization techniques, please refer to Fireworks and Flash tutorial by Scott Brown found in Chapter 30, "Working with Raster Graphics," of this book. I have had the most success optimizing the sequence from a series of .PNG graphics to .GIF format, with a 128 Web Snap Adaptive color palette, and alpha transparency. This should reduce file size from approximately 74KB per frame to about 6KB per frame, a much more manageable number. You can get an even lower file size by converting to .JPEG files instead of to .GIF files, but you sacrifice background transparency. File optimization, essentially, is finding a comfortable balance between file size and appearance. That balance varies widely per project.

Let's turn our focus back to the 3D Studio file that was exported just a moment ago. Open the Swift 3D application. At the very top-left of the program window, click the New button. The New File Wizard should now be visible. You have two choices at this point: to create a new and empty Swift 3D document or to create a new Swift 3D document by importing a 3D Studio file. Select the latter and the Wizard will change pages. There will now be a browse button in the center of the Wizard. Click this button and locate your 3D Studio file that you previously exported. Once this is done you can click Finish. The scene will open just as you last saw it in MAX. The animation and lighting was already completed, so all that needs to be done is export to .SWF format.

First things first. Set the frame rate (right below the timeline on the left side) to the same rate that you used in MAX. Next let's take care of that horrid, white background. At the top left of the program window and underneath the buttons, there is a box containing the words Layout and Environment (see the following figure).

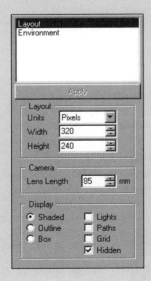

Underneath that window are the settings for the currently highlighted selection. Layout should currently be highlighted. Select Environment in the Settings selection window and then double-click the Background color box (see the figure that follows). Choose black in the color picker, and click OK. Then, click Apply to set the changes. Now select Layout in the Settings selection window. Below, change the pixel size to 320×240 and then click Apply. This changes the output size of the .SWF file. Play with the Camera Lens Length setting until the mace roughly reaches the edges of the active view. Click Apply again to set the changes.

Now let's export the animation. Under the File menu, select Export. The Export Vector File dialog will appear. Give your vector file a name and location. In the Export Options section, there are settings that affect the way your 3D model is "traced" (stroked) and filled. You can choose to include edges with either outlines or entire mesh. *Outlines* will create a line around the outermost edge of each element of the mesh. *Entire Mesh* will trace every edge in the mesh. With the Fill Objects box checked, several options are presented. Flat Shading is the first option. It fills each area of the mesh with a flat color. In this case, the head of the mace will be filled with a flat gray, the hilt, ring, and pommel with a flat gold color, and so on. Area shading will take each area and mimic the lighting with gradient fills. This option works excellently for some models, but the combination of the polygon count, the three lights, and the animation in this scene make this a bad choice. Go ahead and export using this setting to see what happens. The final option is the Mesh Shading Setting, which will fill every polygon with it's own gradient, mimicking the lighting in a much more accurate way. Export the file with this setting and view the results. It looks great but the file size is huge. This setting works best on low-polygon animated models or on higher polygon stills. The settings I chose to use were Outlines and Flat Filled. This set the file size of the animation at about 60KB, pretty close to the size of the pic sequence.

Continued

Continued

On the left side of this Export Vector File window (shown in the following figure) are settings that enable you to render only certain frames. This is handy when you have animation but would like to render a still. You can also select a range of frames to render if you don't want to render the entire animation. To the right of the window, near the bottom, you have the ability to change the file version of the exported .SWF file. Swift 3D Version 1.00 is only able to make .SWF files in Flash 3 and 4 formats. Version 4 will work fine and is the best choice. Experiment with different combinations of settings and use what works best for you.

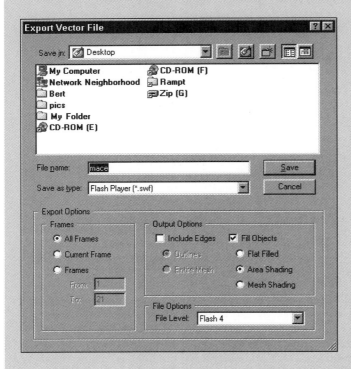

The Final Step

This section discusses importing the animation into Flash 5, so it is relatively short. Generally before I import an animation, I create a symbol and import the file (or files) directly into the symbol. This practice generally saves time over importing files, arranging them, and then converting to symbols or moving frames into the symbol.

On that note, open Flash 5. Press Ctrl+M (or Command+M on the Mac) to bring up the Movie Properties dialog. Set the Frame Rate to the rate that you used in MAX and Swift 3D. Change the Height and Width to accommodate your artwork. Make sure the background color is the same color as the background of the .SWF file and the pic sequence if you did not use transparency. Click OK to close the dialog and then press Ctrl+F8 (or Command+F8 on the Mac) to create a new symbol. Give it a name and make it a Movie Clip symbol.

Clicking OK places you in Symbol Editing Mode for the symbol you just created. Press Ctrl+R (or Command+R) to import a file. Find the pic sequence you rendered and select the first file (MAX should have put a 0000 after the name you typed). When you click OK, you should get a dialog that says, "This file appears to be part of a sequence of images. Do you want to import the entire sequence?" Click Yes and Flash will import each image and place them one after another (as separate keyframes) on the timeline. If you press the Enter key, you can watch the animation play through one time. You may notice that the animation plays faster than it did in MAX. This is because you rendered every other frame. To fix this, add a frame after every keyframe to extend the animation to the correct length. At this point, you can leave the sequence as it is, or create Graphic symbols with the first and last pics to create entrance and exit animations. It's only necessary to convert the pics that you need to control alpha, tint, brightness, and so on to Graphic symbols.

If you export this animation by itself, the .SWF file should be between 60KB and 75KB. If you have gone overboard, retrace your steps and see where you might have done something that would increase file size. Don't forget that you can apply further JPEG compression inside Flash.

Now lets shift gears back to the .SWF animation that was exported from Swift 3D. Check the file size. If you used the Outline and Flat Shading settings, it should be around 60KB. If the file size is near 250KB, you probably used the Mesh Shading setting. Again, try different export settings until you find the perfect balance between file size and visual clarity.

There are two ways to put this animation into your Flash movie. You can create a Movie Clip in the main movie and use the `loadMovie` action to load it into the clip. Another way is to import the .SWF file into the current Flash movie using the File ⇨ Import command. This way will give you the ability to manipulate the animation on a frame-by-frame level if you want to avoid using the entire animation. After the frames are in Flash, you can do what you want to them. They are vectors after all! Try spicing them up a bit. Throw in a gradient here or there. See what you can do. You are limited only by your imagination. Of course, there is download time, too.

Conclusion

I hope that this tutorial was useful. If you want to send me comments on this tutorial or have problems with its execution, feel free to e-mail me at dcluff@mailcity.com. All the necessary files to this tutorial are located on the CD-ROM. There is a MAX file of the complete scene, light, materials, and animation. A 3D Studio (.3DS) file, a pic sequence (optimized), and a Swift 3D Scene (.t3D) are included as well. I also built two Flash movies, one with the Swift export and one with a pic sequence, so that you can view and compare the end products. Both .FLA files are included. If you are unsure of anything, check out the files first. I've always found that finding my own answers provided the most gratifying results. Enjoy and Flash hard.

Born in Salt Lake City, Utah, and raised in Torrance, California, Daniel Cluff found Flash "by accident." A true computer gamer at heart, Daniel likes to spend most of his time modeling in 3D Studio MAX and playing various video games. Daniel created 3D artwork for the Rampt.com interface, and, in his free time, he maintains his site, www.houseofsinboy.com. Daniel doesn't remember any movies from high school — he claims his memory is too clouded. He does, however, remember the anticipation of leaving high school and the near-simultaneous release of Pantera's "Far Beyond Driven" and Slayer's "Divine Intervention."

Summary

✦ All 3D effects are achieved by creating the illusion of spatial depth. In art history, there are several methods that have been developed to illustrate three dimensions within a two-dimensional space.

✦ You can create spatial effects within Flash with the use of scaling artwork, as demonstrated by Mano Clement's tutorial.

✦ Basic 3D artwork and animations can be created with Adobe Dimensions. While this application doesn't have the powerful feature sets of more professional 3D applications, you can quickly render 3D text and shapes, extrude two-dimensional line drawings, and export frame-by-frame animations.

✦ Curious Labs' Poser is a 3D figure-modeler and animation tool. Poser has many figures in its libraries to create walk cycles, combat moves, and facial expressions (including phonemes).

✦ Discreet 3D Studio MAX is a powerhouse 3D modeling and animation tool. Used by serious professional 3D artists, 3D Studio MAX has advanced lighting and camera functionality, as well as an extensible plug-in architecture. Combined with Electric Rain's Swift 3D, you can convert MAX models into .SWF files.

✦   ✦   ✦

Working with QuickTime

CHAPTER

34

This chapter explains how to use QuickTime (QT) media with Flash. Flash expands the definition of desktop video by adding a new track type to QuickTime 4. We explore the integration of QuickTime movies with Flash interactivity, as well as distinguishing the different types of QuickTime movies (Flash, video, and VR).

QuickTime 4 introduced a new media track to QuickTime movies: the Flash track. A Flash track is just one of the many multimedia tracks available for use in QuickTime. Flash has the capability to import QuickTime movies, add Flash content on layers above or below the QuickTime (QT) movies, and to reexport the whole product as a QuickTime Flash movie. QuickTime Flash movies are basically the same file type (.MOV file) as other QuickTime movies — QT Flash movies simply have a stored or referenced Flash movie (.SWF file).

QuickTime versus Video for Windows

Because QuickTime has the powerful capability to store a combination of multimedia tracks, Flash supports the QuickTime format with its Export and Publish commands. Although PC Flashers can also export Video for Windows files, these files don't support a Flash track. The differences between these two formats are intricate. But before we talk about the intricacies, how do you recognize one from the other? The QuickTime file extension is .MOV (from the Macintosh File Type MooV), while the Video for Windows' file extension is .AVI (Audio-Video Interleaved format).

Video content is usually delivered in wrapper formats for distribution. Two primary system-level container formats or *wrappers* exist for video content on computer systems today: QuickTime and Video for Windows. Although both can be considered architectures for multimedia content, QuickTime has the most advanced architecture of the two. (Technically, RealSystems' RealPlayer is also a container format for multimedia, but it's only used for delivery—it cannot be used for editing and reediting material.) Before Windows 95, multimedia developers relied on the QuickTime architecture on the Macintosh to make their multimedia components work together harmoniously. That's because QuickTime for Windows lacked many of the Mac's QuickTime features until its 3.0 release, which finally delivered to Windows the same multitrack interactivity that Mac users had enjoyed from the start. With QuickTime 4, both Windows and Mac versions can play Flash 3 content—Flash 4 and 5 features are not supported by QuickTime 4. Flash 3 content can be embedded as an interface to control another QuickTime video or audio track, or even as an enhancement to Sprite animation.

Caution   Unfortunately, Video for Windows (VfW) wasn't developed along the same lines as QuickTime. Video for Windows is just that—video that's designed to play on Windows machines. It can't contain other media tracks (such as Flash tracks) like QuickTime can. Luckily, newer versions of the Windows Media Player can play QuickTime content, and QuickTime 3.0 (or higher) can play Video for Windows movies, provided that the necessary codecs are installed. Both QuickTime and Video for Windows can read most of the software-based codecs, such as Cinepak or Indeo. When you get stuck, usually it's not difficult to translate a QuickTime file to a Video for Windows file using a video-editing application such as the PC version of Adobe Premiere, or vice versa with the Mac version.

The only difference between QuickTime files on the Mac and the PC is that movies made on the Macintosh can internally reference media content from either a resource or data fork, whereas movies made on the PC cannot. Because the two operating systems have different file and directory structures, this referencing system can't be carried over to the PC. Consequently, most Mac movies need to be *flattened* in order to work properly on the PC—*flattening* means that all material referenced in the resource fork of the Mac QuickTime is compiled into one data fork, which is then accessible by all operating systems. Usually, when you are rendering video content on the Mac, you are given an option to flatten (or not flatten) the final movie. A movie can also be flattened with QuickTime Player by selecting Make Movie Self-Contained when you save (or resave) the movie.

Note   Since version 4 of QuickTime, Apple has renamed the MoviePlayer application to QuickTime Player. You need the professional version of QuickTime Player to edit or recompress QuickTime movies. Luckily, you only need to purchase an unlock key code from Apple to transform the regular player into the pro player, as well as download a few extra components using the QuickTime Updater. Use the QuickTime control panel to enter your unlock key. The application name, however, remains QuickTime Player. Even though we refer to QuickTime Player Pro, you won't see the Pro suffix in the application name.

The major limitation of Video for Windows is that it only supports two tracks of multimedia content: video and audio. QuickTime, however, supports multiple media tracks: video, audio, Flash, text, Sprite, and time code tracks. Furthermore, using QuickTime Player, you can set up many options for each movie's track, such as preloading into memory and enabling high quality. QuickTime 4, which is the latest version, also enables you to create reference movies specifically designed for the varying speeds of Internet connections. Using the free Apple utility, MakeRefMovie, you can create different versions of the same movie with a range of file sizes. Depending on the visitor's QuickTime plug-in settings, the proper movie downloads to the computer. For example, if the connection speed setting of the plug-in is set to ISDN, the visitor receives the ISDN-version of the movie, which is of better quality and — as you've learned in this introduction — also bigger in file size. (MakeRef Movie is available at `http://developer.apple.com/quicktime/quicktimeintro/ tools/` along with many other QuickTime tools and utilities.)

Tip Terran Interactive's Media Cleaner Pro can take the guesswork out of video compression. It has optimized presets for CD-ROM and Web delivery. Find it at `www. terran-int.com`.

QuickTime Support in Flash

Flash 5 provides the amazing capability to import QuickTime movie files into the Library. If you want to synch your Flash movie with a preexisting QT movie, you can bring the QT movie into a Flash scene and play both movies simultaneously in the authoring environment of Flash. When you're finished, you can export the Flash movie as a QuickTime Flash movie, using either the Export or Publish commands. The result is a QT movie with video, audio, and Flash tracks. At the time of this writing, you need QuickTime 4 to pull off this stunt — with the unfortunate limitation that you can't use any Flash 4 or higher actions yet. QuickTime 4 can only interpret Flash 3.0 or earlier actions. This means that any ActionScripting (as described in Parts V and VI of this book) is not recognized. Furthermore, you can't export a Flash movie (.SWF file) from Flash 5 with both Flash content and imported QuickTime movies. To play QuickTime movies with Flash content, you need to use the QuickTime format (.MOV).

When you import a QuickTime file into Flash, you need to keep your original QuickTime movie file independent of the Flash (.FLA) file. Flash does not make a copy of the QuickTime file inside the movie. Rather, it links to the external QuickTime movie file for playback and rendering purposes.

QuickTime 4 Supported Actions in Flash Movies:

FSCommand	getURL
gotoAndPlay	gotoAndStop
ifFrameLoaded	loadMovie
nextFrame	nextScene
on	play
prevFrame	prevScene
stop	stopAllSounds
tellTarget	toggleHighQuality
unloadMovie	

You should have the latest version of QuickTime 4 installed (4.1.2). If you already installed the original 4.0 release of QuickTime, run the QuickTime Updater application that is installed with QuickTime 4 to check and update your current version.

Note At the time of this writing, QuickTime 5 was available as a Public Preview release. QuickTime 5 will support Flash 4-compatible actions. It is our understanding, though, that the `loadVariables` action will not be able to load data into a QuickTime Flash track.

Importing QuickTime into Flash

To bring a QT movie into Flash, use the File ⇨ Import command (Command+R or Ctrl+R) and select a QuickTime movie from the file dialog. QuickTime movies usually have a QuickTime logo icon and end with the MOV extension, although they sometimes end with QT. Prior to import, make sure you've selected the layer in which you wish to import the QT. It's often a good idea to create a new layer to hold the imported QT. After you've imported the QT movie, the first frame of the QT movie displays in the current frame of the Flash movie. You also see a new symbol type in the Library window — this is a Video (see Figure 34-1), not to be confused with a Movie Clip.

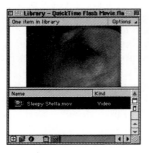

Figure 34-1: Imported QuickTime movies have a movie camera icon. This file, Sleepy Stella.mov, can be found on in the ch34 folder of the CD-ROM.

The timeline in Flash displays the QT's movie length relative to the duration (in time, *not* frames) of the Flash movie. Note that one second of the Flash movie equals one second of the QT movie: This means that one frame of QT video is *not* equivalent to one frame of a Flash movie — unless your Flash frame rate matches the QuickTime video frame rate. You can see this for yourself. After you have imported a QT, use the F5 key to add more frames to the layer of the QT movie. Then, scrub the timeline to preview the QT movie. Stop on any discernable frame, and change the frame rate of the Flash movie via the Modify ⇨ Movie command (Command/Ctrl+M). After you click OK, you notice that the QT movie frame has changed even though the Flash frame marker is still on the same frame. How do you deal with this variability? Usually, if you intend to export the Flash movie as a QuickTime movie with a Flash track, you want to set the frame rate of your Flash movie to match the frame rate of your QT movie. If you have a Flash movie frame rate that's different from the video track of the QuickTime, you may run into slow or jerky playback. QuickTime Flash movies can theoretically have any number of Flash scenes. If you have more than one scene, the QuickTime Player may continue to briefly play any running QT movie from the previous scene. For this reason, you may want to add a few blank buffer frames at the beginning of any transition point (for example, going from one scene to the next). This seems to depend on how large the imported QuickTime movies are — the QuickTime Player needs to unload one movie before it proceeds with the next.

With regards to movie length, no built-in limitations exist. You can make the scene as long as you wish in order to accommodate any range of interactivity or animation. If you plan to have continuously running Flash and video layers (for example, a Flash animation moving on top of the video track), add enough frames to view the entire length of the QT movie within the Flash timeline. Please see Figures 34-2 and 34-3 for examples.

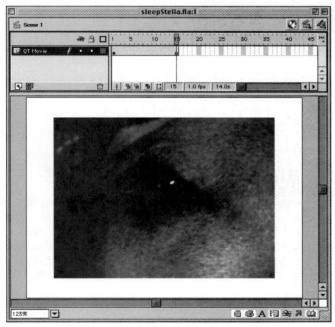

Figure 34-2: This timeline does not have enough frames to show the entire QT movie — only 15 frames have been assigned to the layer. The Flash movie has a frame rate of 1 fps, and the QT movie is 28 seconds long.

The problem to avoid is this: If you don't add enough frames to accommodate the entire QuickTime movie, then the duration of the Flash movie determines the duration of the video track. This means that your imported QT movie may be arbitrarily cropped or trimmed to the length prescribed in the Flash editor document (.FLA file).

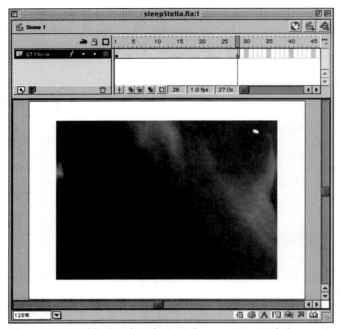

Figure 34-3: This timeline has 28 frames — enough frames to accommodate the entire QT movie.

Combining Flash and QuickTime Movies

After you've created a Flash movie synched to an imported QT movie, you can export a fully self-contained QuickTime movie that stores both the Flash and imported QT movie. However, you don't need to use Flash to put Flash content into QuickTime movies. If you want to layer Flash movies into preexisting QuickTime movies, you can import .SWF files directly into the QuickTime Player. But you need the latest Player that installs with QuickTime 4 to import Flash material. Prior versions of the QuickTime Player cannot do this.

Creating QuickTime Flash movies

After you've created a Flash movie with an imported QT movie, you can export or publish the entire Flash scene as a self-contained QT Flash movie that can be played with the latest QuickTime Player.

To create a quick and simple QuickTime movie from Flash, choose File ➪ Export Movie (Command+Option+Shift+S or Ctrl+Alt+Shift+S). Browse to a folder where you want to save the QuickTime, type a filename, and click Save (see Figure 34-4). You are then presented with the Export QuickTime dialog.

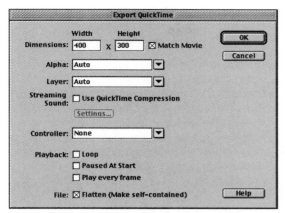

Figure 34-4: For a quick look at a QuickTime Flash version of your Flash document, accept the defaults in the Export QuickTime dialog.

To check out the quality of the QuickTime movie, open the new QuickTime movie with QuickTime Player.

Caution   Be careful with the controller type setting. If you select None, you won't even be able to stop the movie by using the space bar once it's started.

While you can use the Export Movie command to produce independent QuickTime movies, the Publish Settings command enables you to create QuickTime movies as well as other linked file formats. Go to the File menu, and choose Publish Settings (Command+Shift+F12 or Ctrl+Shift+F12).

In the Format tab, make sure that you have a checkmark next to the QuickTime option, and deselect the others. Each time you check or uncheck an option in the Publish Settings dialog, the corresponding Settings tab appears or disappears, respectively.

For the purpose of exporting QuickTime, you should only have the Format, Flash, and QuickTime tabs showing (see Figures 34-5 and 34-6). If Use Default Names is checked, the resulting QuickTime movie has the same name as the .FLA file that is currently open in Flash. Otherwise, you can uncheck this option and specify a different name in the text fields next to the corresponding format types. Unfortunately, you can't control the location of the new files that are generated via the Publish command — all files produced via Publish are saved to the same location as the .FLA file.

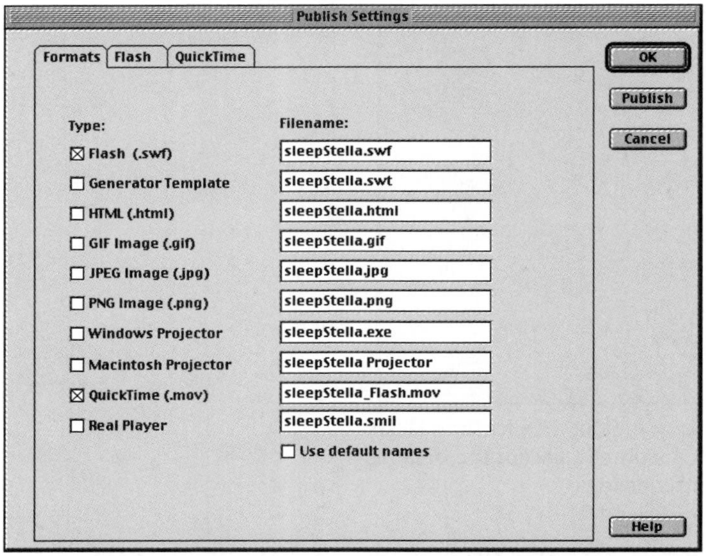

Figure 34-5: The Publish Settings dialog for QuickTime-only publishing. Click the QuickTime tab to access the movie's properties. The Flash tab is available to set the version to Flash 3, which is the highest version currently supported by QuickTime.

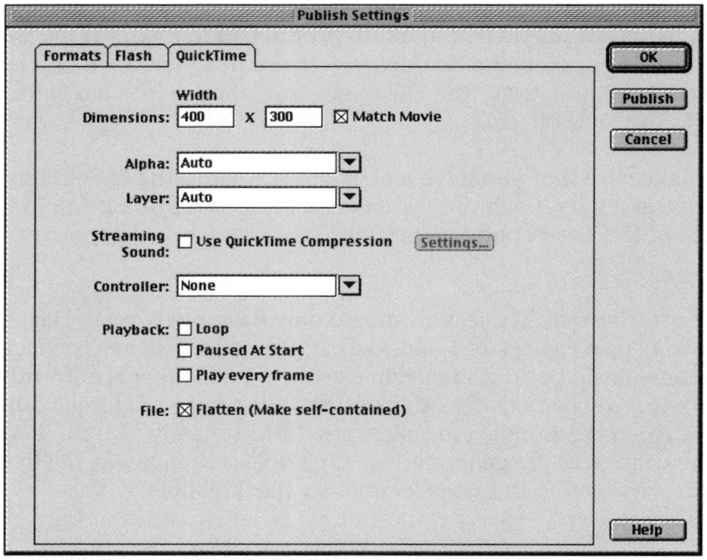

Figure 34-6: Use the Publish Settings' QuickTime tab to control QT movie settings.

Tip   Use the Export Movie instead of Publish to save QuickTime movies to specific folders or locations.

The following sections describe all of the QuickTime settings and how each setting is used.

Dimensions

The Dimensions setting controls the size of the QuickTime Flash movie frame. Although you've probably already set the correct movie size in the Modify ⇨ Movie dialog to conform to your specific output needs, it's good to note here that you can resize your QuickTime movie with the Dimensions properties to export a movie at alternate dimensions.

Alpha

For the Alpha property, you can decide whether you want the Flash track's background to be transparent or opaque. If want your Flash material to display together with underlying QuickTime video content, choose Alpha-Transparent. If you don't want the underlying QuickTime video to show through the Flash track, choose Copy. The Auto setting makes the Flash background transparent if Flash artwork exists on top of other content. If a QuickTime movie is stacked above the Flash artwork, then Auto makes the Flash background opaque. If you export a QuickTime Flash movie with only Flash artwork, Auto uses an opaque background.

Layer

For the Layer property, you can decide whether you want the Flash track to be layered on top of or below the QuickTime content. If you want the Flash content to play on top of the QuickTime movie, choose Top. If you designed an interface or animation to appear underneath the QT movie, choose Bottom. The Auto setting for the Layer property places the Flash track in front of QuickTime material if Flash artwork appears on top of the QuickTime anywhere in the Flash editor document. If you placed QuickTime movies on top of Flash artwork layers, then Auto places the Flash track behind the video track.

Streaming Sound

If you want Flash-enabled sounds to be converted to an additional QuickTime sound track, check the Use QuickTime Compression option for the Streaming Sound property. Any and all sounds that are used in the scenes are recompressed into a separate sound track. This sound track is separate from any other sound tracks that may be present in imported QuickTime movies. The Settings button enables you to define the parameters of the audio compression. You may want to match the audio characteristics of the imported QuickTime movie used in the Flash movie if you choose to use this option. Because this property converts Flash audio into QuickTime audio, you can use any sound compressor that is available to QuickTime. For more sound advice on Flash 5's audio compression settings, refer to Chapter 14, "Understanding Sound for Flash," Chapter 15, "Importing and Editing Sounds in Flash," and Chapter 16, "Optimizing Flash Sound for Export."

Controller

The Controller property determines whether a controller (control panel for playback) is shown with the movie in the QuickTime Player application, and if one is shown, what kind of a controller. None disables the display of a control panel, and, subsequently, it is the default setting for the Export Movie command. If you have created your own Flash buttons to play and stop the timeline, you may want to disable the display of the regular QuickTime controller. The Standard option presents the QuickTime movie with the standard QuickTime Player 4 interface, enabling play, pause, frame forward and backward, and volume level, among other controls. The QuickTime VR option displays the specialized control panel for QuickTime panorama or object movies. We discuss QTVR later in the "A Word about QuickTime VR Movies" section of this chapter. To compare the different controllers, see Figures 34-7 through 34-9.

Figure 34-7: A QuickTime movie with no controller: This was made with the Controller property set to None.

Figure 34-8: A QuickTime movie with the standard controller

Figure 34-9: The QuickTime VR controller used with a Flash-enabled QTVR panorama

Playback

The Playback property controls how the movie plays when it's first opened in the QuickTime Player. Check the Loop option if you want to the QuickTime to automatically replay the movie when it's reached the end. Check the Paused at Start option if you don't want the QuickTime movie to automatically start playing as soon as it opens in the QuickTime Player. Note that if any controller (other than None) is specified, the movie is always paused when it loads in the QuickTime Player. The Play Every Frame option, when checked, overrides the frame rate setting to playback every frame contained in the video. Usually, this is not recommended because the QuickTime audio track is silenced.

File

The File property has only one option, Flatten (Make self-contained). Checking this option forces Flash to write one QuickTime movie that contains any and all referenced material. If you imported a 10MB QuickTime movie into Flash and created a few layers of Flash content to work with the QT movie, flattening creates one QuickTime movie that copies the imported QT movie and Flash material to video, audio, and Flash tracks, respectively. If you do not check Flatten, Flash creates a reference QuickTime movie that looks for (and require the presence of) the Flash .SWF file and other QuickTime file(s) on playback. While this reference movie has a very small file size, you need to make sure all the referenced material is readily available for playback. This means that the Format tab of the Publish Settings dialog should have a checkmark next to Flash (.SWF) as well as QuickTime (.MOV). Furthermore, you may run into linking problems over the Internet due to connection latency or if the referenced files aren't together in one location. For this reason, you may prefer to package everything into one flattened QuickTime movie.

Export Movie or Publish?

Although the Export QuickTime dialog is identical to the QuickTime tab of the Publish Settings dialog, one important difference exists. The File property, which controls linking to external files, creates different results with each command.

If Flatten (Make self-contained) is unchecked in the Export QuickTime dialog, then only the imported QT movie is referenced externally—it is not stored in the new QuickTime Flash movie.

If you check both the Flash (.SWF) and QuickTime (.MOV) options in the Formats tab of the Publish Settings dialog *and* uncheck the Flatten (Make self-contained) option in the QuickTime tab, then the Publish command creates a QuickTime Flash movie (.MOV file) that links to the .SWF file as well as the original imported QuickTime movie (.MOV). Neither the Flash content or the imported QT movie is stored in the new QuickTime Flash movie— the QuickTime Flash movie, .SWF file, and original QuickTime(s) need to be in the same location in order to play.

Click OK to accept your current Publish Settings and return to the Flash scene. Make any final adjustments to your movie. When you're ready to test drive your new QuickTime movie, you can preview the QuickTime movie by using the Publish Preview menu, and selecting QuickTime. QuickTime Player Pro should automatically start and load the movie. If you like the results, run the File ➪ Publish command (Shift+F12). Flash saves a QuickTime movie to the same directory where your .FLA file has been saved. You can also publish the movie by using the Publish button directly in the Publish Settings dialog.

Note   For those who want to maximize the built-in functions of QuickTime Player Pro, QuickTime video filters and graphics modes can be applied to Flash tracks.

So far, you've seen how to combine existing QT movies with your Flash content. You don't need to import other QuickTime content into Flash in order to export QuickTime material from Flash. With QuickTime 4, you can create QuickTime movies that are essentially repackaged .SWF files. Using Flash 4 or 5, .FLA movies can be exported to QuickTime formats. At the time of this writing, QuickTime Player recognizes only Flash 3 actions. To export QuickTime Flash movies from Flash 4 or 5, follow the same steps described previously without importing any external QuickTime movie files.

Creating QuickTime video with Flash

If you own the Macintosh version of Flash 4 or 5, then you can also export QuickTime Video via the Export Movie command. QuickTime Video is raster- or bitmap-based animated movement. Remember, QuickTime Flash movies contain a new Flash media track, which is exactly the same file format as a Flash movie (.SWF file). As such, the Flash track uses antialiased vector graphics to store and display information. Quick Time Video, however, uses only raster information—each frame in the movie is described as collection of pixels. This method of storage is much more byte inten-sive. For this reason, QuickTime Video files are usually several megabytes large, and time-consuming to download over slower Internet connections.

Tip   Why would you want to use QuickTime Video if it creates larger file sizes than QuickTime Flash? Unfortunately, QuickTime Flash movies can only be played with QuickTime 4.0 or greater. If you want to be sure that your QuickTimes can be played with older versions of QuickTime, then the movies need to be QuickTime Video.

In the Mac version of Flash 4 or 5, you have the option of creating either QuickTime Video or QuickTime Flash movies. If you want to use your Flash animations in home videos or videotaped presentations, then you should export Flash movies as Quick Time Video movies. These movies can then be edited with your other digitally cap-tured video.

To save a Flash movie as a QuickTime Video movie, choose File ⇨ Export Movie and select QuickTime Video as the Format type. After you specify a filename and a loca-tion to save the movie, click Save. Next, you see the Export QuickTime dialog (Figure 34-10), where you can specify how Flash should rasterize the Flash movie.

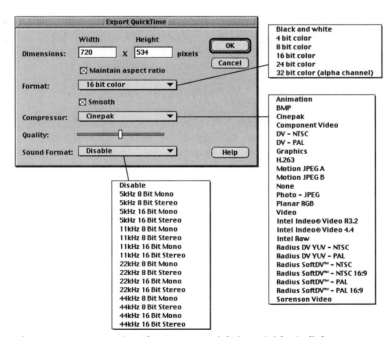

Figure 34-10: By using the Export QuickTime (Video) dialog, you can specify Dimensions, Format, Compressor, Quality, and Sound Format.

Dimensions

This property performs exactly the same way as the Dimensions property of QuickTime Flash movie exports. See our coverage of Publish Settings and QuickTime Flash earlier in this chapter. Because Flash vector can maintain high quality at any size, you can scale the dimensions of the QuickTime Video file to match the requirements of your video project. For example, if you want to use this QuickTime Video with DV format video, then scale the movie dimensions to 720×534.

 See Chapter 36, "Creating Full-Motion Video in Flash," for more detailed information on frame dimensions.

Format

Use the Format property to control the bit-depth of the QuickTime Video movie. For most high-quality video work, use 24-bit or 32-bit color formats. For Web distribution of QuickTime Video movies, lower color formats yield smaller file sizes. Refer to Table 34-1 for a quick breakdown of each color format. If the Smooth option of the Format property is checked, Flash artwork is converted to antialiased bitmap information. Otherwise, curved lines may exhibit the "jaggies" — jagged or staircased steps on curves or gradients.

Table 34-1 QuickTime Video color formats		
Format	*Number of Colors*	*Description/Use*
Black and white	2	Fax-like image quality
4-bit color	16	Similar to the 16 system colors used by Windows in Safe mode
8-bit color	256	Indexed Color mode, like GIF
16-bit color	65,536	High Color in Windows 95/98 or Thousands of Colors on the Mac
24-bit color	16.7 million	True Color in Windows 95/98 or Millions of Colors on the Mac
32-bit color	16.7 million + 8-bit alpha channel	Same as 24-bit color; supports 256 levels of transparency

Compressor

This menu determines which video codec (*compressor-de*compressor) is used for the bitmap frames in the QuickTime Video movie. Because QuickTime Video is more bandwidth-intensive, bitmap information needs to be condensed in some manner. Compressors, or codecs, reduce the amount of information that needs to be stored for each frame. For general distribution, you may want to use Cinepak or Intel Indeo Video codecs. For high-quality video output for editing or broadcast purposes, use the hardware codec used by your specific video capture card. Chapter 36, "Creating Full-Motion Video in Flash," explores codecs more deeply.

Quality

This unmarked slider (which apparently has no units) controls how the compressor selected in the previous menu works. As you drag the slider to the right, less compression is applied to the QuickTime Video, which results in higher-quality video. As you drag the slider to the left, more information is discarded from each frame of video (more compression, lower quality).

Sound format

If your Flash movie contains any audio, then you can choose to convert those audio samples to a QuickTime-compatible audio track. QuickTime can use any major sampling rate (such as 22 kHz), bit-depth (such as 8 or 16), or channel (such as mono or stereo). Usually, you won't want to use anything lower than 22 kHz 16-bit stereo for quality audio. If you don't need to use Flash audio in the QuickTime Video file, then choose Disable.

Cross-Reference

See Chapter 14, "Understanding Sound for Flash," and Chapter 16, "Optimizing Flash Sound for Export," for more information on sampling rates and file formats.

A word about QuickTime VR movies

If you are familiar with QuickTime VR's amazing panorama and object movies, then you should be happy to know that Flash supports QuickTime VR (QTVR) movies as well. Because QTVR movies aren't strict linear playback video movies, you need to keep a few points in mind when you use QTVR movies in Flash. Note that you cannot create QTVR movies from scratch in Flash. You first need to create a QTVR movie with VR equipment and software, like Apple's QuickTime VR Authoring Studio. Flash can then import these movies and add Flash artwork and actions to them.

On the CD-ROM

The QTVR folder of the ch34 folder on the *Flash 5 Bible* CD-ROM contains sample Flash editor documents (.FLA files) and QuickTime VR movies (.MOV files) to use with this section. Paul Nykamp, a QTVR specialist in Toronto, Canada, provided the QTVR movies. He can be reached at pnykamp@focusvr.com.

Panoramic movies

QuickTime panoramic movies enable you to view a physical or virtual space by stitching a series of images into a 360-degree view. You navigate the space by clicking and dragging the mouse inside the movie frame. When you import a QTVR panoramic movie (a.k.a. *pano*) into Flash, it only displays the first frame of the QTVR movie on the stage, regardless of the frame marker's position. It's very important to make sure that your Flash timeline's frame span doesn't extend beyond the length of the QTVR movie. Playback beyond the length of the QTVR causes the QTVR to disappear until the Flash frame playback loops back to the starting frame. The best solution, whenever possible, is to limit your timeline to just a few frames (one frame would be ideal), and use movie clips with Tell Target commands to provide longer frame length animations.

Caution   QuickTime VR panos are particularly sensitive to Flash movie frame rates. The default setting of 12 fps may result in incomplete panoramas with missing sections. If a problem occurs, try changing the Flash movie frame rate to 1 fps and reexporting the QuickTime VR movie.

Due to limitations of the QTVR controller, there's no way to rewind a movie or return to frame 1 of the Flash track. Technically, because each media track has its own timeline of frames, if the Flash track plays beyond the QTVR track, you lose the QTVR movie. You can prevent this from happening by ensuring that you can always view the QTVR's first frame within the Flash authoring environment. Another clue is this: If you go beyond the length of the QTVR movie, the extended area is represented by a struck-through rectangular box, as seen in Figure 34-11.

Figure 34-11: If your Flash movie plays beyond the length of an imported QTVR panorama or object movie, it disappears from the stage and is replaced with a struck-through box.

To export or publish QTVR pano movies, specify the QuickTime VR Controller type in the Export QuickTime dialog or in the Publish Settings' QuickTime tab.

Object movies

You can also make QTVR object movies in Flash 5. QTVR object movies let you rotate or spin an object — photographed or 3D modeled — by dragging the mouse inside the movie frame (see Figure 34-12). With Flash, you can expand the multimedia capabilities of object movies. Adding Flash buttons, audio, and artwork to an object movie can provide a different navigational interface for the object, and provide call-out information to the object movie.

Figure 34-12: QTVR object movies with Flash tracks can have more impact than regular QTVR movies.

Unlike QuickTime pano movies, object movies can be fully viewed within the Flash authoring environment. Each frame of the object movie shows a different viewing angle of the object. Again, like regular QuickTime movies, make sure you add enough frames to view the entire object movie. Keep adding frames until the stage displays the object movie with a struck-through box. Then, subtract any frames that show the movie as a struck-through box.

Our tests with object movies have also shown that the frame rate of the Flash movie is a critical setting. Most of our test exports with QTVR object movies played back very poorly — the object's rotation movement was not very smooth. However, when we specified a controller type of None and added a Flash button to provide a *play* action, the object movie played back very smoothly.

Tip

For Flash-controlled playback of QTVR object movies, you need to add a Go to and Play action to the last frame of the scene, which loops back to the first frame of the scene. However, the QuickTime Player does not recognize a Flash Stop action on the first frame. To start a QTVR Flash movie in a paused state, select the Paused at Start option in the Playback section of the Export QuickTime dialog or in the QuickTime tab of Publish Settings.

Using Digital Video in Flash Movies

Because the strength of Flash lies in its vector animation capabilities, it makes sense that Flash prefers vector-based material. Most Web-site visitors prefer quicker download speeds, and vector animations are much easier to store as small files than are raster graphics. As a result, Flash handles raster-based material with JPEG or lossless (a.k.a. PNG) compression schemes. In the past, Flash didn't let you import digital video files into a Flash movie because they added too much to the file size, which prevented efficient compression and delivery on the Web. So, what do you do if you want to showcase your next blockbuster feature in your Flash movie? You compromise. If you want visitors to get a taste of some raster-based animation, it's best to select a short section of the overall movie and extract frames from that selection. In contrast to the next chapter, which discusses the process of exporting sequences from Flash movies, this section describes how to create still image sequences in other applications and bring them into Flash. If you want to accommodate visitors who are willing to wait for larger full-length movies, then you can then link the preview in Flash to load the entire QuickTime movie (or QuickTime movie reference), via HTML and the QuickTime plug-in, into its own window or frame. Generally, though, this method of digital video integration into Flash is used for visual effects or just really cool raster content you snagged on video, such as water ripples or textures.

Note   We explained earlier in this chapter the process of creating new QuickTime Flash movies. This is a new alternative to adding Flash content to existing QuickTime movies, and, therefore, distributing Flash and QuickTime content simultaneously on the Web. In this section, we discuss the process of embedding raster material derived from video into a Flash (.SWF) file, not into a QuickTime Flash (.MOV) file.

This section covers a basic method of converting digital video content into a Flash-friendly sequence of frames. If you want to recreate the movement of original video via the converted vector-based art in Flash, we recommend that you read this section first and then check out WebMonkey's tutorial on Converting Animations to Flash at www.hotwired.com/webmonkey/98/42/index3a.html.

Even though Flash 4 or 5 enables you to place QT movies in a Flash movie, they do not export or link with a .SWF file. If you want to embed frames from a QuickTime movie in your Flash movie for playback on the Web, read the rest of the section. If you want to synchronize your Flash animations and interactivity with a QuickTime movie to use in a final QuickTime 4 movie, then refer to "Importing QuickTime into Flash," earlier in this chapter.

Extracting frames from digital video clips

The premise of frame extraction is simple: Instead of downloading large video files with Flash content, reduce the video in frame size, rate, and length to something that Flash (and slow Internet connections) can handle.

Although QuickTime video cannot be imported into Flash as one video file (because Flash does not store video files in the current implementation of the .SWF format), Flash does support image sequences in bitmap formats. So, we can convert any video clip into a short sequence of still images that can play as an animation or movie clip in Flash.

The following tutorials/workshops assume that you have some working knowledge of the applications described herein. Also, you must have some existing digital video material; we do not create or edit any video in these tutorials.

We recommend that you have QuickTime 4 or higher installed on your computer, as well as any updates to your video-editing application(s). At the time this book went to press, QuickTime 4.1.2 was available for both Windows and the Macintosh.

QT Player Pro

You don't need an expensive video-editing application to extract frames from video clips. In fact, you can do it for less than $30! Apple's QuickTime Player Pro (see Figure 34-13) can export any QuickTime movie as a series of individual still frames, which can then be imported to Flash. You need the latest version of the QuickTime software (currently 4.0) to export image sequences.

On the CD-ROM If you want to use a sample QuickTime movie, choose a QuickTime movie from the ch34 folder on the *Flash 5 Bible* CD-ROM.

After you have some QuickTime movie footage that you want to use in a Flash .SWF file, you can begin the process of selecting a range of frames and exporting them as a bitmap sequence. This sequence will then be imported into our Flash movie .FLA file.

1. **Making a Selection:** First, decide how much of the QuickTime movie you want to import into Flash. Do this sparingly. Remember that raster animation is heavy on file sizes, and people generally like faster-loading content on Web pages. Restrict your selections to movie clips of very short duration, less than five seconds if possible. If you want the visitor to see more than that, consider linking to the entire QuickTime from the smaller clip that you import into the Flash SWF file.

2. **Define Your Selection:** Use the In and Out markers to define your selection. Unfortunately, QT Player Pro does not show frame numbers in the time code display. As a result, you need to eyeball your selection. You can also use the additional video controls to move through the video clip frame by frame. The selection is indicated by a gray bar between the In and Out points. Using Movie ⇨ Get Info and selecting Time from the pop-up you can view the time code of where your selection starts and its duration. In Figure 34-14, a two-second selection is made from a QuickTime video clip.

Time Display

Playback Head

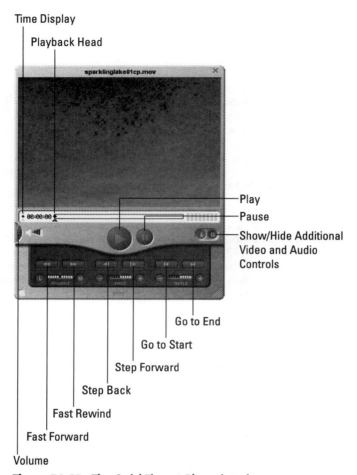

Play

Pause

Show/Hide Additional
Video and Audio
Controls

Go to End

Go to Start

Step Forward

Step Back

Fast Rewind

Fast Forward

Volume

Figure 34-13: The QuickTime 4 Player interface

In point

Out point

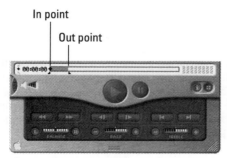

Figure 34-14: Keep your selections as short
as possible. Longer selections add substantial
weight to the file size of the Flash .SWF file.

3. **Trimming the Movie:** After you've defined a selection, you need to delete the rest of the video track. If we don't delete it, QT Player Pro exports the entire movie as an image sequence. Again, we only need the short selection for use in Flash. Hold down the Ctrl and Alt keys (PC) or Command and Option keys (Mac), and click Edit on the QT Player Pro menu bar. Now click Trim. This command discards everything but your selection from the movie clip. (Don't worry about losing this content. As long as you don't resave your QuickTime movie at this point, your video clip file won't be altered in any way, because we simply want to export this selection as an image sequence and then close the QuickTime movie *without saving*.) After you execute the Trim command, the In and Out markers automatically reset to encompass the entire remaining video, and the QuickTime movie only contains the selection that you defined previously.

4. **Exporting an Image Sequence:** Now you're ready to export the QuickTime as an image sequence. Choose File ➪ Export (Command+E or Ctrl+E), and you see the Save Exported File As dialog (see Figure 34-15). Select a folder (or create a new one) to store your image sequence, specify a filename, and choose Movie to Image Sequence in the Export drop-down menu. Next, click the Options button to define the format settings to be used for the image sequence. You see the Export Image Sequence Settings dialog. If you are using the PC version of Flash, choose .BMP (Windows Bitmap) for the Format property. If you're using the Mac version of Flash, choose the .PICT format. For the Frames Per Second property, choose a value from the drop-down menu (or type one) that's appropriate to the length of the clip. For a two-second clip, a value of 4 or 5 is adequate, rendering a total of 8 or 10 frames. Click the Options button to select a bit-depth for the .BMP or .PICT sequence.

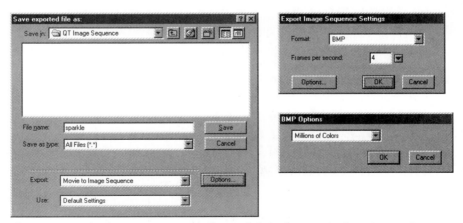

Figure 34-15: In the Save Exported File As dialog, choose Movie to Image Sequence as the Export type.

In the Export Image Sequence Settings, you can access the file type-specific settings, such as color depth or compression. Choose Millions of Colors if you don't want to prematurely limit the color palette used for the image sequence.

Note   The Options dialog displays the settings applicable for the file format chosen. Some file formats, such as JPEG, enable you to define compression levels in addition to bit-depth.

Click OK to the BMP or PCT Options dialog, and then click OK again on the Export Image Sequence Settings dialog. Finally, click Save on the original Export Image Sequence to render your image sequence. QT Player Pro adds consecutive numbers to the end of each filename generated in the sequence. Flash can recognize file sequences with this kind of numbering.

Now you have a collection of still images that can be imported into Flash. See "Importing a Sequence into Flash" later in this chapter for instructions.

Adobe Premiere 5.1

Adobe Premiere is a cross-platform video-editing application used by serious hobbyists and professional videographers. Unlike proprietary video systems such as Avid, Premiere uses the QuickTime and/or the Video for Windows architecture for processing video. Premiere's functionality extends from creating Web-based video to CD-ROM video to professional broadcast-quality video. You can also use Premiere to generate image sequences from existing projects or movies.

On the CD-ROM   Use the dogs_small.mov QuickTime file on the *Flash 5 Bible* CD-ROM if you need some material for this section.

1. Open Premiere 5.1, and start a new project. If you've left the preferences for Premiere at their defaults, you are automatically presented with a New Project Settings dialog as soon as Premiere finishes loading.

2. Specify the settings for the new project. See Figure 34-16 for reference. The following list delineates the various settings.

   • **General Settings, Timebase:** For NTSC video, use a timebase of 29.97 fps; use 25 for PAL/SECAM video.

   • **General Settings, Time Display:** For most consumer video material, including mini-DV, use Drop-Frame Time Code. You may want to use Non Drop-Frame Time Code for DVCAM or other professional video types, if that's how the source footage was recorded.

   • **Video Settings, Compressor:** Even though you may have used other video compressors (or codecs) for your video footage, the None type configures our export settings correctly for image sequences.

   • **Video Settings, Depth:** If you have video that includes an alpha channel or matte, use Millions+ for the Depth setting.

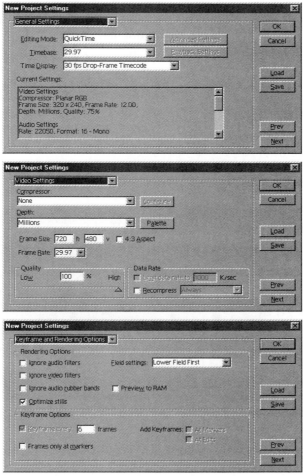

Figure 34-16: Use these Project Settings for DV format video that you want to export as an image sequence.

- **Video Settings, Frame Size:** All DV-captured material is 720×480. Some MJPEG video capture cards, including the Iomega Buz, capture at 720×480 as well. You need to uncheck the 4:3 Aspect box for this frame size. Most MJPEG video capture cards use a 640×480 frame size.

- **Video Settings, Frame Rate:** Use 29.97 for NTSC video; if you are using PAL/SECAM, use 25. For a thorough explanation of frame rates and time-bases, see page 336 of the *Premiere 5 User Guide*.

- **Keyframe & Rendering Options, Field Settings:** Lower field first (for most DV-captured material. Check your video capture card's user manual to confirm your card's field dominance).

3. In the Project window, import an existing QuickTime (.MOV) or Video for Windows (.AVI) file. To maintain true cross-platform compatibility, you should use QuickTime movies. To import a movie, double-click in the Project window, and select a file in the following Import dialog.

4. Next, you need to determine the length of the clip. Double-click the imported movie in the Project window. Premiere loads the clip into the Monitor window (see Figure 34-17). Using the Mark In and Mark Out buttons, set the In and Out points of the clip to reflect the selection you want to bring into Flash. You want to keep the duration of the clip fairly short, around a few seconds. The longer you make the selection, the larger your Flash file.

Figure 34-17: Use the Monitor window to set the In and Out points of the Movie Clip.

5. Put the clip into the timeline. Open the timeline window with the Window ⇨ Timeline menu item (see Figure 34-18). Set the Time Units pop-up menu to two seconds. Click and drag the movie from the Project window onto any Video track in the timeline window. Make sure you place it at the very beginning of the timeline, at frame marker 00:00:00:00. If you can't see the clip in the timeline, you might have to select a smaller time unit, such as two, four, or eight frames. If you are not sure that your clip is at the zero point, click and drag the clip in the video track as far left as possible To check this, click the time ruler and drag the edit line to the zero point. Whenever you drag the edit line along the video in the timeline, the Monitor window automatically pops up and plays the video as you drag.

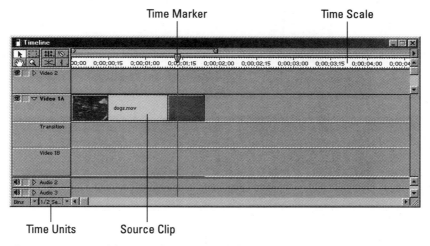

Time Marker   Time Scale

Time Units   Source Clip

Figure 34-18: Build your video project in the timeline window. For an image sequence, put your Movie Clip on any video track at time 00:00:00:00, which is at the very beginning (far left) of the time scale.

Note

Do not drag the clip into the timeline more than once. If you dragged a clip into the timeline but don't see it, chances are it's in there somewhere. You can always check how many times a given clip is used in the timeline by checking the Video Usage and Audio Usage columns in the Project window. So far, you should only have one video and one audio use of your clip in the timeline.

6. Now you're ready to export this selection as a sequence of individual images, which we can animate in Flash. With either the Monitor or Project window highlighted, select File ⇨ Export ⇨ Movie (Command+M or Ctrl+M). In the Export Movie dialog, click the Settings button in the lower-right corner.

7. Specify the export settings. See Figure 34-19 for reference. A summary of key settings follows.

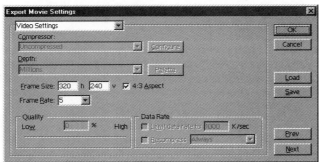

Figure 34-19: Use these settings to export an image sequence that Flash can import.

- **General Settings, File Type:** On the PC, choose Windows BMP Sequence. On Mac, use PICT Sequence. You can also try Animated GIF if you don't mind having the color palette of the sequence limited to 256 colors.

- **Video Settings, Depth:** If you have an alpha channel that you wish to also export with each image in the sequence, select Millions+.

- **Video Settings, Frame Size:** If you want a smaller Flash movie file size and are willing to sacrifice some image quality, shrink the frame size to 320×240 for both DV and MJPEG captured material. Sequences are rendered in square pixel formats. Because DV uses nonsquare pixels, you need to resize the actual frame to achieve the correct aspect ratio. That is, if you have 720×480 captured clips, you need to export 640×480 (or some 4:3 variation) for proper still images.

- **Video Settings, Frame Rate:** The frame rate depends on the length of your clip. If you have a 2-second clip, then a setting of 6 fps results in a 12-frame sequence, which is imported into Flash. Higher frame rates equal more individual frames that Flash needs to animate. Basically, you want to obtain a balance between a minimum number of frames and a smooth, believable sense of movement — without the sequence becoming too jerky or jumpy.

- **Special Processing:** Because the Special Processing dialog gives you a live preview of each effect, you may want to experiment with different settings. Noise reduction can smooth pixilated edges, while the de-interlace option averages the lower and upper fields for each frame rendering. Otherwise, the field you specified in the New Project settings is used as when rendering the frame. De-interlacing is not recommended if you are scaling down any DV-format video that you want to convert to an image sequence. Meaning, if you're outputting an image sequence at 720×480 (normal DV frame size), then you should turn de-interlace on. If you are outputting at any size smaller than the original interlaced video, then leave the de-interlace option off.

8. After you specify the settings for the export, you should create a new folder or choose an existing folder to store the image sequence. When you name the export, don't worry about adding a number to the file name. Premiere does this automatically. For example, typing apple_ for the filename directs Premiere to call each frame of the sequence as follow: apple_01, apple_02, apple_03, and so on. In Windows, the appropriate file extension is added as well, such as apple_01.pct.

9. Click OK and Premiere generates a still image sequence from the clip. You're now ready to import the still images into Flash. See "Importing a Sequence into Flash," later in this chapter, for more details.

Adobe After Effects 4.1

Adobe After Effects is an extremely powerful video-compositing tool. You can think of After Effects as Photoshop for video. You can add custom filters and motion control to any graphic or video with After Effects. After Effects comes in two versions: regular (Standard) and professional (Production Bundle). The Production Bundle version of After Effects uses the exact same interface as the regular version, but it has superior filters for compositing video. While it's easier to use Premiere or QT Player Pro to extract frames from a video clip, you can also use After Effects to do it. If you've already constructed a project in After Effects, it's much easier to use it to extract a few frames from a larger project. Otherwise, you need to render the entire project and then go to another application, such as Premiere, to extract those frames from an already rendered (and possible very large) movie file.

Before we begin the steps to extract frames in After Effects, we briefly discuss the workflow in After Effects. Like Premiere, After Effects uses a Project window that links all your graphics, sounds, and video clips to compositions, or comps. A composition can be thought of as the *real* project container, but you can have more than one composition for a project. In fact, for some killer effects and presentations, comps are often nested within another comp. If you've used After Effects primarily for full-motion video effects, then this section shows you how to repurpose your video content for Flash.

1. Open an existing After Effects project file (.AEP), or create a new project. If you have an existing After Effects project, then open the Time Layout window of the comp you wish to render and skip to Step 5.

2. Import the video clip that you want to use in Flash, via the File ➪ Import ➪ Footage File command (Ctrl/Command+I). Note the duration and frame size of the clip you have imported.

3. Create a new composition (Command+N or Ctrl+N), and conform the settings of the comp to those of the imported Movie Clip. For example, if the clip's frame size is 320×240 at 15 fps, then make the comp's setting 320×240 at 15 fps.

4. Drag the video clip from the Project window to the new composition's Time Layout window. If it's not showing, then double-click the composition's name in the Project window. By default, the comp's name is Comp 1. Once you drag the video clip into the Time Layout window, it shows up as a layer in the composition.

   Now, you have to define the work area in After Effects. All extracted frames are drawn from this area. You should keep the length of the work area quite short (a few seconds or less) as each extracted frame adds a lot of weight to the Flash movie.

5. Move the Time Marker in the Time Layout window to the desired In point of the composition. The In point is where we start extracting frames. Make sure your Composition window is also open, so you have a visual reference for the Time Marker. If it's not showing, double-clicking the comp's name in the Project window reopens it.

6. In the Time Layout window, click and drag the Work Area Start tab while holding down the Shift key. Drag the tab to the Time Marker's position, and the tab snaps to it.

7. Move the Time Marker to the Out point of the composition, and shift-drag the Work Area End tab to this position (see Figure 34-20).

   You've now defined the work area in After Effects, and we're ready to render a series of frames from the comp.

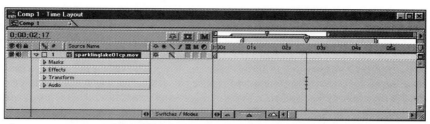

Figure 34-20: Use the Work Area tabs in the Time Layout window to set the In and Out points of the image sequence.

8. Choose Composition ➪ Make Movie (Command+M or Ctrl+M). In the Save Movie dialog, browse to the folder where you want to store your frames, enter a prefix filename for the frame sequence, such as comp, and click Save. After Effects automatically numbers the sequence by adding _0000, _0001, _0002, and so on to the filename on the PC version, or .0000, .0001, .0002, and so on to the filename on the Mac version. If you're using the PC version of After Effects, you get an automatic .AVI extension to the filename. Even though we're rendering frames as individual files, don't worry about the .AVI extension. You then see the Render Queue window.

9. Click the underlined Current Settings text field next to Render Settings, and adjust the frame size and rate to match the size you want for your Flash movie (see Figure 34-21). In the following example, a DV format clip at 720×480 is halved in size by choosing Half in the Resolution setting. Choose Work Area Only for the Time Span setting, and note the length of the duration information listed directly beneath this setting. Hopefully, your comp's work area isn't longer than five seconds. For the Frame Rate setting, click the Use this Frame Rate option and type a value that won't overgenerate frames. For a 3-second comp, 4 frames per second will yield 12 frames that can be imported into Flash. Then, click OK to proceed to the next setting dialog.

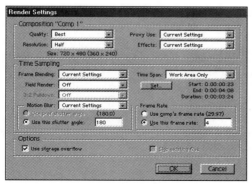

Figure 34-21: Use the Render Settings options to control resolution, time span, and frame rate for image sequences.

10. Click the underlined Lossless text field (or whatever your default may be) next to Output Module. In the Output Module Settings dialog (see Figure 34-22), choose BMP Sequence (if you're using a PC) or PICT Sequence (if you're using a Mac) from the Output Module, Format setting. Don't change the default settings in the Video section. If you are using nonsquare pixel video such as DV, you may want to resize the frame for each still image extracted. For a 360×240 (half-resolution DV) frame size, check the Stretch option and choose Medium, 320×240 in the drop-down menu. Select High for the Stretch Quality. Click OK to proceed to the next step.

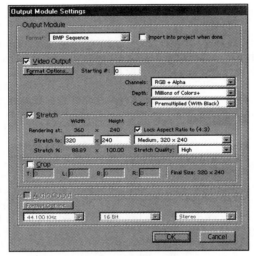

Figure 34-22: The Output Module Settings control the file format, video, stretch, and audio characteristics for a queued composition.

11. Click the underlined filename field next to the Output To setting of the Render Queue window. Make any changes to the filename structure to meet your preferred formatting. On the Mac version of After Effects, you need to add a .PCT extension to the filename. By default, the Mac version outputs a series beginning with Comp 1 Movie.[#####], but Flash won't recognize this as the beginning of a sequence without a .PCT extension. So, you should change the format of the filename to Comp 1 Movie.[#####].pct. Click Save to proceed.

12. When you're ready to render a sequence of frames from After Effects, click the Render button in the Render Queue window. After Effects then generates a series of frames ready to bring into Flash.

Using Audio from Digital Video Movies

If you want to bring the audio portion of this shortened video clip into Flash, then you can choose QuickTime as the Output Module format. Turn off the Video section, and turn on the Audio section with the sampling rate and bit-depth at the settings you want. Then render the audio-only QT movie, open it in QT Player Pro, and export it as a .WAV or .AIF file. You can then import the .WAV or .AIF into Flash and synchronize it with the bitmap sequence. You need to use the Stream audio setting in order for the audio to synch with the bitmap sequence. If audio and video synch is a critical issue, you may want to forego the replication of bitmap sequences within .SWF movies. Because QuickTime 4 now supports Flash tracks, you can output QuickTime Flash movies that use regular QuickTime movies, complete with video, sound, and Flash tracks.

Importing a sequence into Flash

After you have created an image sequence from another application, you can import the sequence into Flash as a series of keyframes with bitmaps. Flash can autoimport an entire sequence of numbered stills and place them frame by frame on the timeline.

Movie Clip storage

Rather than import an image sequence directly into a layer within a scene, you can import the sequence into a Movie Clip symbol. This makes it easier to duplicate an image-sequence animation through the Flash movie in any number of scenes.

1. Create a new Flash (.FLA) file or open an existing one.

2. Create a new symbol of the Movie Clip type (Insert ➪ New Symbol), and give it a descriptive name.

3. Choose File ➪ Import and browse to the folder containing your image sequence. Select the first image of the image sequence, and click OK.

   You are presented with the message shown in Figure 34-23.

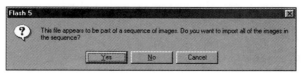

Figure 34-23: Whenever you import a file whose names contains a number, Flash asks you whether you want to import the entire numbered sequence of files.

4. Click Yes in the dialog shown in Figure 34-23 and Flash automatically imports every image in the numeric sequence.

5. Go back to the Stage and drag the Movie Clip into a scene.

6. Use `tellTarget` actions (for Flash 3 or 4 compatibility) or Movie Clip methods (in Flash 5 Dots notation) to control the Movie Clip if necessary. For more information on intramovie interactivity, see Part IV, "Adding Basic Interactivity to Flash Movies."

Optimizing bitmaps

Like any imported bitmap, you can trace each bitmap in the image sequence. Tracing effectively converts raster information into vector information. Depending on the complexity of the bitmap image, though, the efficiency of tracing can vary wildly. Refer to Chapter 17, "Understanding Actions and Event Handlers," for more information on optimizing bitmap images.

Tip If you plan to trace bitmaps in an imported image sequence, you may want to consider applying an art filter (for example, Extract, Posterize, or Solarize) to the original footage in Adobe Premiere or After Effects. Some art filters create more solid areas of color in the image, making the traced bitmaps in Flash less complex with smaller file sizes.

Summary

✦ QuickTime 4 has added a new media layer, the Flash track. With this new feature, Flash can export QuickTime movies with Flash tracks that control playback of QuickTime movies.

✦ Flash movies can be exported as Flash-only QuickTime movies. As of this writing, the QuickTime Player can currently play Flash 3 content only.

✦ Digital video needs many megabytes of disk storage. For this reason, there are some limitations and precautions involved when using digital video with Flash.

✦ By extracting frames at low frame rates from digital video files such as QuickTime or AVI, small video clips can be imported into Flash movies and played back from .SWF files. The results can be of astonishingly high quality with relatively fast transmission.

✦   ✦   ✦

Working with RealPlayer

One of Flash's most powerful capabilities is exporting to other media formats. In this chapter, we look at using Flash content with RealPlayer. Earlier versions of Flash and RealPlayer required extensive production to export Flash files to translated RealMedia formats. Flash 5 is now capable of publishing streaming audio and Flash files directly to the RealMedia formats.

Flash to RealPlayer

RealPlayer is the multimedia player and plug-in created by RealSystems, Inc. RealPlayer can play all Real formats, such as RealAudio (for streaming music and radio broadcasts) and RealVideo (for streaming video). RealPlayer can also play Flash .SWF files, provided that they are properly formatted for true streaming playback. RealPlayer version 8 is capable of reading Flash 3 and 4.SWF files — it will understand Flash actions in a Flash 3- or 4-published .SWF file. Versions 6 and 7 of RealPlayer can only read Flash 2 files.

While RealPlayer can display the visual portion of a Flash .SWF file, it will not play the audio portions of a .SWF file. The Real playback system looks for a separate RealAudio file to synchronize with the graphics and animation of a Flash .SWF file. Prior to Flash 5, the process to create separated Flash and RealAudio files required the use of production utilities from RealSystems. Now, we can create RealAudio and Flash .SWF files directly from the Flash application. Using the Publish Settings dialog, you can export the files necessary for Flash movie playback in RealPlayer:

✦ **.SWF** file (without audio), a special one created by the RealMedia exporter, which creates a "tuned" file by stripping the audio and resampling the Flash movie timeline for streaming playback. The degree of resampling depends on the bit rate selected in the Publish Settings dialog.

✦ **.RM** (RealAudio) file containing an streamed version of the stripped Stream audio from the .SWF file.

✦ **.SMIL** file that controls the synchronization between the tuned .SWF and .RM files.

Note This chapter provides an overview of combining Flash animation with Real content. For more documentation on content creation for RealPlayer 8 or earlier, see http://service.real.com/help/library/encoders.html.

Flash Versions and Content Considerations

You can only use Flash 4 or earlier version .SWF files with RealServer 8 and Real-Player 8. If your Web server uses RealServer 6 or 7, then you can only use Flash 2 .SWF files with RealPlayer 8 or earlier. As you see later in this chapter, you can change the Flash .SWF version in the Flash tab of the Publish Settings dialog.

RealPlayer G2 and RealPlayer 7 will prompt users to update to RealPlayer 8 when Flash 3 or 4 .SWF content is encountered. Before playing Flash 3 or 4 .SWF content, RealPlayer 8 downloads a Flash plug-in that is not part of the standard RealPlayer installation.

Caution RealPlayer 8 and RealServer 8 do not support Flash 5 .SWF files. If you are developing with new Flash 5 ActionScript, then some interactive functionality will be lost when the movie is exported as a Flash 4 or earlier .SWF file.

Realistically, we advise you to only use appropriate Flash content for use in Real Player productions. RealPlayer is best suited for the following types of linear Flash content:

✦ Animated shorts or trailers

✦ Instructional media

✦ Simple interactive demonstrations

✦ Flash forms that gather information from the user and send it to your server

✦ Enhanced presentation or user interfaces for streaming music

As you can see, RealPlayer likes Flash movies that use basic navigation controls, like play and stop. Do not use convert complex games and entire site files made in Flash for use in RealPlayer — the Flash Player plug-in was developed to handle highly interactive and animated content on the Web.

Caution

We strongly recommend that you develop most, if not all, of your linear Flash movie content on the Main Timeline. The playback timeline displayed within the RealPlayer interface only shows the length of the Main Timeline of your Flash movie. While Movie Clip timelines will play in the RealPlayer, you will not be able to control their playback with the RealPlayer controller. You will need to add your own Flash buttons or frame actions that control Movie Clip timelines. Also, Movie Clips can continue to play even if the RealPlayer timeline has finished playing.

Finally, Flash background transparency is not supported in any RealPlayer version. If you want to superimpose Flash animation with any other content, you need to do it within Flash. You cannot overlay a Flash track with RealVideo.

We recommend that you convert appropriate Flash movies to Real-compatible formats for use on Web sites that already require the RealPlayer plug-in for other content (for example, streaming radio broadcasts, streaming music videos) on the site.

Controlling RealPlayer Playback

If you use ActionScript in a Flash movie to control playback of the movie's timeline (for example, `gotoAndPlay()` and `stop()`), then you'll lose synchronization with your RealAudio track. Although RealPlayer will recognize Flash actions that are compatible with .SWF version 4 or earlier, it will not apply those actions to other tracks that are running simultaneously. To control the RealPlayer, you need to use a special `getURL` action on a Flash event handler (for example, a keyframe or a Button instance).

To send playback commands to RealPlayer from your Flash movies, do the following:

1. In Flash 5, open a Flash movie that you want to convert to a tuned Flash .SWF.

2. Select (or add) a Button instance that will control both the Flash movie timeline and any other tracks that will play along with your Flash content in RealPlayer. Or, you can select a keyframe on your Flash timeline.

3. Open the Actions Panel (in Normal Mode). If you used a Button instance in Step 2, then add an `onMouseEvent` action and choose your desired mouse event (for example, press, release, and so on). If you selected a keyframe in Step 2, then you don't need this action.

4. Add a `getURL` action, and for the URL option, use one of the following RealPlayer commands:

   - `command: pause()`: This halts playback of all content playing in RealPlayer. All timelines in the Flash movie, including those of Movie Clips, stop on the current frame.

- command: play(): This command tells RealPlayer to resume playback of all content.

- command: stop(): This command stops playback and rewinds all content tracks to their respective starting points.

- command: seek(time): The seek command sends all content tracks to the specified time and resumes playback. Time is denoted in the format dd:hh:mm:ss.xyz, where dd is the day, hh is the hour, mm is the minute, ss is the second, and xyz are the fraction of the second. If you omit the decimal point, then RealPlayer reads the last two digits as the seconds. For example, command:seek(1:00) sends all playing tracks to the point where 1 minute has elapsed. command:seek(1:00:00) sends all playing tracks to the point where 1 hour has elapsed.

If you add the following getURL action to a Flash keyframe or Button instance, the RealPlayer will go to the timeline position at 45 seconds on the Flash and RealAudio tracks:

```
getURL("command:seek(45)");
```

However, if you add a gotoAndPlay() or gotoAndStop() action to a keyframe or Button instance*, then only the Flash track will proceed to the new time position. All other Real tracks will continue to play from their current positions.

We discuss how to publish the Flash movie with the RealAudio and .SMIL files later in this chapter.

Evaluating Media Quality for RealFlash Movies

When you decide that you want to convert a Flash movie into a RealPlayer-compatible format, you will need to consider the audio quality and bandwidth that your target audience's connection speed will require. This next section will explain how to properly set up the RealPlayer files for use on the Web.

Audio requirements

The most important RealPlayer authoring consideration within Flash movies is the use of audio. RealPlayer only supports Flash audio that uses Stream Sync mode. Event Synch audio cannot play in RealPlayer. Flash Stream audio needs to be set for raw compression that uses a sample rate of 11 kHz, 22 kHz, or 44 kHz.

---

*If you are exporting Flash 2 .SWF files, then Flash playback actions will control RealPlayer playback of other tracks as well.

Because the Real Encoder will be compressing the Flash sounds, we recommend that you begin your Real Flash movie production with uncompressed audio files. If you have imported .MP3 sound files into your Flash movies, the Real Encoder will recompress them for use in RealPlayer. Recompressed audio usually sounds worse than the original compressed audio.

Caution Avoid using sounds on Flash Button symbols. Even if you nest a Movie Clip symbol instance that uses Stream sound on the Over keyframe of a Button instance, RealPlayer will not play the sound.

To set the output format of Flash Stream audio:

1. Open the Publish Settings dialog (File ➪ Publish Settings).
2. Select the Flash tab.
3. Click the Set button next to the Audio Stream option.
4. In the Sound Settings dialog (shown in Figure 35-1), choose the Raw option in the Compression drop-down menu, and pick a Sample Rate that is appropriate for your Flash audio. (See Chapters 14 through 16 for more information on digital audio and Flash sound use.) If you are using Stereo Stream sounds, then do not check the Convert Stereo to Mono option — let the Real Encoder merge the sound channels on export. Click OK.

Figure 35-1: The Sound Settings dialog enables you to change the default compression used for Stream and Event Audio in Flash movies.

5. If you still have Event Sync audio in the Flash movie, you should prevent its export by clicking the Set button next to the Audio Event option and selecting Disable in its Compression drop-down menu.
6. Finally, just in case you have given unique compression settings to Stream sounds in the Library, check the Override sound settings option in the Flash tab.

Note RealAudio cannot encode 5.5 kHz audio. If you have imported source audio files that use a sample rate at or below 5.5 kHz, make sure you use the Update or Import button in the Sound Properties dialog (for each sound in the Library) to select a higher sample rate file.

Bandwidth considerations

Because RealPlayer can stream two or more media tracks simultaneously, you need to watch the file sizes of all the tracks that will play in the RealPlayer. You need to decide how much bandwidth each media track (the Flash or the RealAudio track) will consume. In the RealPlayer tab for the Publish Settings dialog, you can select a bit rate for the tuned Flash .SWF file and choose an audio format for the RealAudio file. You must balance bandwidth usage between the tuned Flash file and RealAudio file based on the target audience settings.

SureStream and Single Rate RealMedia files

Before you can decide how to divide the bandwidth between Flash and RealAudio files, you need to know the difference between Singe Rate and SureStream as it applies to RealMedia. When you produce Real content, you need to know what kind of RealServer your Web provider (or server) has installed.

If you have access to RealServer G2 or RealServer 8, then you'll be able to use SureStream files on your site. A SureStream file can be streamed at various bit rates, depending on the connection preferences of the user's RealPlayer and the current network conditions. All SureStream files need to use RTSP (Real Time Streaming Protocol) instead of HTTP (Hypertext Transfer Protocol), the standard protocol for the Web. If you try to stream a SureStream file over HTTP, the lowest bit rate version that you selected for publish will stream to your users.

If you use an earlier RealServer and/or use HTTP to serve your Real files, then you can use Single Rate Real files that are published for specific connection speeds. With this method of distribution, you would create a separate Single Rate file for each connection speed that you want to support. Then, you would specify the source file for each connection speed in the SMIL document. For more information on the use of SMIL for RealPlayer files, see

```
http://service.real.com/help/library/guides/production8/htmfiles/
smil.htm
```

Determining bit rate

To select the proper bit rate for the tuned Flash file, subtract the bit rate of the RealAudio file from the total bit rate available for your target audience's Internet connection speed. The formula to find the bit rate for the tuned Flash .SWF file is:

Connection speed – RealAudio bit rate = Flash .SWF bit rate

The average bit rate available for 56KB modem users is about 37 Kbps (in practical testing). A RealAudio file using the Music codec set for Single Rate streaming over a 56KB modem connection requires 20 Kbps. Therefore, the bit rate for the tuned Flash .SWF file should be around 17 Kbps:

37 Kbps – 20 Kbps = 17 Kbps

The typical bandwidth available for target audiences is generally lower than the connection rate. Table 35-1 lists the practical limits for each target audience.

Table 35-1 Average Connect Speed of Standard Modem Rates				
Connection Type	**Practical Throughput Recommendations**			
	Real Systems	**Apple***	**Macromedia****	**Average**
28 Kbps Modem	20 Kbps	16 Kbps	18.4 Kbps	18 Kbps
56 Kbps Modem	34 Kbps	32 Kbps	37.6 Kbps	34.5 Kbps
64 Kbps Single ISDN	45 Kbps	40 Kbps	N/A	42.5 Kbps
112 Kbps Dual ISDN	80 Kbps	80 Kbps	N/A	80 Kbps
Corporate LAN	150 Kbps	280 Kbps	N/A	215 Kbps
256 Kbps DSL/Cable	225 Kbps	N/A	N/A	225 Kbps
384 Kbps DSL/Cable	350 Kbps	240 Kbps	N/A	295 Kbps
512 Kbps DSL/Cable	450 Kbps	N/A	N/A	450 Kbps

*As quoted from Apple's book, *QuickTime for the Web*, by Steven Gulie.

**As calculated by the default connection speeds listed in the Flash 5 Bandwidth Profiler.

If you choose to use SureStream RealAudio and multiple target audiences, we recommend that you use the bit rate of the lowest target audience (see Table 35-2) to calculate the bit rate for the tuned Flash file. This ensures that all targeted connection speeds will be capable of playing the presentation with greater success.

Alternatively, you can create several individual combinations of tuned .SWF files and Single Rate RealAudio streams, using SMIL to deliver the appropriate files to each target audience. This method enables you to create larger (and higher quality) tuned .SWF files for faster connection speeds.

Table 35-2 RealAudio Codecs and Bit Rates				
Internet Connection Speed	**Format Choices in Flash 5 (in Kbps)**			
	Voice Only	**Voice with Background Music**	**Music**	**Stereo Music**
28 Kbps (18 Kbps)	8.5	8.5	8	N/A
56 Kbps (34.5 Kbps)	16	16	20*	20
Single ISDN (42.5 Kbps)	16	32	32*	32
Dual ISDN (80 Kbps)	32	32	32*	32
Corporate LAN (215 Kbps)	32	32	32*	32
256K DSL/Cable (225 Kbps)	32	32	64	64
384K DSL/Cable (295 Kbps)	32	32	64	96
512K DSL/Cable (450 Kbps)	32	32	64	96

*Indicates High Response, with 44.1 kHz sampling rates. 64 Kbps and 96 Kbps Stereo Music codecs also use 44.1 kHz sampling rates; 32 Kbps Stereo Music codecs sample audio at 22 kHz; and 20 Kbps Stereo Music uses 11 kHz.

For more information on RealAudio codecs and sampling rates of each codec, see http://service.real.com/help/library/guides/production8/htmfiles/audio.htm.

Note   Bit rates are selected automatically based on your Format and Target Audience choices; you cannot set (or choose) a bit rate for a RealAudio codec.

Publishing RealPlayer Presentations

Now that you know how to tailor your content to RealPlayer, and how to calculate the available bandwidth for tuned Flash files, we show you how to publish RealPlayer content directly from Flash 5. We walk-through the format settings within the Publish Settings dialog.

1. In Flash, create or open the movie that you want to publish. Make sure you have removed or disabled all Event Sync audio.

2. Choose File ➪ Publish Settings.

3. In the Format tab, check Flash and RealPlayer. You cannot publish RealPlayer files without having the Flash .SWF format checked.

4. Click the Flash tab. In the Version drop-down menu, select Flash 4 or Flash 3 if your Web server has RealServer 8 installed. If you have an earlier version of RealServer, then you will need to select Flash 2. Change the Audio Stream settings to export Raw audio with a sample rate of 11, 22, or 44 kHz

5. Click the RealPlayer tab of the Publish Settings dialog, shown in Figure 35-2. In the Flash Bandwidth Tuning area, check Export Tuned Flash. The tuned .SWF file will automatically be given a "t" suffix at the end of the filename, before the .SWF extension. Then select (or type) a bit rate for the tuned Flash file. This can be any value between 1 and 100. Finally, if you want to be able to reselect (or reenter) a bit rate at the time of publishing, check the Adjust Bit Rate on Publish option. If this is checked, then Flash will prompt you to select a bit rate each time you publish your Flash movie. Otherwise, it will use the setting here for the tuned Flash file.

Tip One reason to use the Adjust Bit Rate on Publish option is to see the amount of time required to buffer (or preroll) the Flash movie with RealPlayer. The Publish Settings dialog will not show you this information.

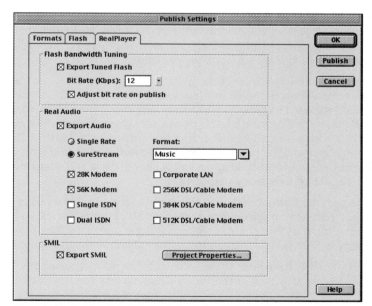

Figure 35-2: The RealPlayer tab of the Publish Settings dialog

6. In the RealAudio section of the RealPlayer tab, select Export Audio. Depending on your distribution method, choose a RealAudio streaming file type:

- Single Rate streams sound for one target audience only. You can only check one connection speed with this file type.

- SureStream streams sound for multiple target audiences. SureStream automatically switches to a lower bit rate during poor network conditions and/or for slower connection speeds.

7. In the Format menu, select a codec to use for the streaming sound compression:

- **Voice Only** applies compression suitable for voiceover soundtracks. If you choose a target audience option of 28.8KB, then the audio track will be sampled at 8 kHz. If you choose target audience option of 56KB or Single ISDN, then the audio will be sampled at 16 kHz. All higher connection speeds will sample the audio track at 22 kHz.

- **Voice With Background Music** uses the same codec as Voice Only. The only difference from Voice Only is that the Single ISDN target audience option will also produce 22 kHz audio.

- **Music** should be used for mono music soundtracks. The Music codec requires more bandwidth bit rate than the Voice codecs at all speeds except 28.8KB. If you select 28.8KB as the target audience, then this codec will sample audio at 8 kHz. At all other speeds, the audio will sample at 44 kHz with a frequency response of 20 kHz.

- **Stereo Music** lets you encode the left and right channels of the audio track separately. At 56KB modem speeds, Stereo Music will sample the audio track at 11 kHz with a low frequency response of 5 kHz. At Single ISDN through Corporate LAN speeds, this codec will sample audio at 22 kHz with a slightly higher frequency response of 8 kHz. A 256KB DSL/cable modem speed will sample the audio at 44 kHz with a frequency response of 16 kHz, and all higher speeds will sample at 44 kHz with a 20 kHz frequency response.

8. Depending on the Format and available bandwidth, choose a target audience option (the connection speed that audiences will connect at). If you selected SureStream you may select more than one target audience. RealServer G2 or 8 can compress SureStream files on the fly to maximize the available bandwidth.

9. Select Export SMIL to export a .SMIL file with the published movie. The SMIL file synchronizes playback of the tuned Flash file and the RealAudio stream in the RealPlayer. If you exported RealAudio, you will need to export a .SMIL file. The .SMIL file is an XML (extensible markup language)-based file that the RealPlayer reads to layout the RealMedia tracks. This text file can be further edited in Dreamweaver or in a text editor such as BB Edit. Click the Project Properties button to add information about the project with the published movie. In the Project Properties dialog, enter information in the specified text fields to identify the movie by title, author, copyright data, keywords, and description, and click OK.

10. At this point, you can publish the files immediately by clicking the Publish button, or you can click OK and return to the Flash authoring environment to further edit your Flash movie. When you're ready to publish, choose File ⇨ Publish (Shift+F12).

If you place all files associated with the RealPlayer movie (the .SWF, .RM, and .SMIL files) in the same directory on your RealServer-enabled Web site, then the SMIL generated by Flash 5 contains all the code needed to stream the movie. However, if you place the .SMIL file on the HTTP server and the .RM and .SWF files on the RealServer, you need to modify the links in the .SMIL file to reference the content files on the RealServer.

For more information, see the *RealSystem 8 Production Guide* at: http://service. real.com/help/library/guides/production8/realpgd.htm

For information on Flash production and bandwidth considerations, see the section titled "Producing Animation" at: http://service.real.com/help/library/guides/ production8/htmfiles/animate.htm

Expert Tutorial: Rotoscoping Video Frames with Flash, by *Daniel Szecket*

The files for Daniel's tutorial can be found in the ch35 folder of the Flash 5 Bible *CD-ROM. You may want to review the previous chapter on QuickTime, as well as the chapters on drawing and animation in the front end of the* Flash 5 Bible *before proceeding with this tutorial. We thank Dr. Octo (a.k.a. Steve Barber) in Toronto, Canada, for supplying the cool audio track used in this tutorial.*

Overview

In this tutorial, we show you how to create a presentation that uses Flash animation on top of a sequence of JPEG images, synchronized to a RealAudio track. We are going to convert the provided QuickTime movie on the CD-ROM to a series of image files. This image sequence will be imported into Flash and used as a background for our Flash animation and artwork. We will rotoscope on top of the image sequence. Rotoscoping is the process of drawing on film or video frames, to add special effects, funky text, or anything else that you couldn't have photographed. After we finish the rotoscoping, we add some synchronized sound and export all of our work to RealPlayer.

Image sequence considerations

The *Flash 5 Bible* explains how to export frames from video files in Chapter 34, "Working with QuickTime." For purposes of integrating video frames into a tuned Flash file, we should keep a few points in mind.

Continued

Continued

When you're choosing a file format for the image sequence, you'll have a variety of formats to choose among in Flash 5. .PNG images can be small in file size and can contain an alpha channel, which can be useful for vector conversion or to overlay your video content with other content. .PNG images also don't throw away color information — it uses lossless compression to minimize file size.

JPEG images usually compress much more than .PNG images compress. However, this compression only applies to the saved file size. When a JPEG is viewed on the computer screen, the image is uncompressed in RAM. For example, if your entire sequence of JPEG images takes up 4.5MB of hard disk space, the RAM it will occupy could be as much as 60MB. However, this 60MB of RAM will not be allocated all at once — as each frame plays, it will occupy its uncompressed size in RAM.

If your presentation is built for people with low-end computers, it might be better to export an animated .GIF file from your video file. When you import the animated .GIF into Flash, make sure you keep the Library settings in each image to GIF/PNG/uncompressed. This is the default compression setting when you import a .GIF file.

The last consideration for converting the video file to an image sequence is the frame rate. When you view the QuickTime file, you may notice that it was already reduced to 15 fps from the original 29.97 fps that broadcast video uses. Because we would like to view the whole clip in Flash, and it is approximately 25 seconds long, it would be difficult to manage all 375 frames. Because of this, we converted the video to an image sequence at 6 fps, which gives us approximately 150 frames. Luckily, because our footage depicts a slow-moving snail, we won't notice extreme jerkiness during playback.

Creating the Graphic symbol for the image sequence

After we have exported the frames from the QuickTime movie, we need to import them into our Flash movie. If you don't want to worry about converting the video file to an image sequence, you'll find the image sequence on the *Flash 5 Bible* CD-ROM. Also, our Flash movie has a frame rate of 24 fps and a frame size that matches the video frame, 320×240.

1. In your Flash movie, create a Graphic symbol (Ctrl+F8 or Command+F8). Give it the name **snail** and click OK. You'll already be on that symbol's timeline in Symbol Editing Mode.

2. Now, import either your converted image sequence or the JPEG snail images provided on the *Flash 5 Bible* CD-ROM.

   If you import the sequence of snail JPEG images and play the timeline, you will notice that they play faster than the original .MOV file. Because our Flash movie has a frame rate of 24 fps, our snail sequence is playing at 24 fps, too. To get the real 6 fps of the image sequence, we need to add three frames of space between each image in the sequence. You can space out the frames one by one to the desired timing.

3. For the purposes of this tutorial, put a frame between each image in the sequence — effectively doubling the fps of the sequence to 12 fps. You should have 303 frames filled when you are done.

If you converted the images to an animated .GIF, you will notice that the image sequence imports perfectly, spaced to the original timing.

4. After all the images are in the graphic, go back to the Main Timeline of your Flash movie. Place an instance of the snail Graphic symbol in the first frame of your timeline.

5. Extend the timeline to frame 303, which is the length of our Graphic symbol, by pressing F5 at frame 303.

6. Now we import our audio track. You can use the octo.wav file on the *Flash 5 Bible* CD-ROM or use one of your own sound files. Using the File ⇨ Import command, import the sound file into your Flash movie.

7. Create another layer at the top of your layer list. Name this layer **sound**. In the Sound Panel, select octo.wav as the sound, as shown in the following figure. Because this sound will be used for a RealPlayer presentation, set its Sync mode to Stream.

8. Let's edit the sound clip length, and add a fade at the end of the clip. Click the Edit button in the Sound Panel. Select the Frames button (last one in the lower right of the dialog, to the right of the Help button) to display the time units in frames. Scroll to the end of the waveform display and drag the Out point (shown as a small gray bar between the two waveform displays; see the following figure) to frame 153. Then, create a new volume node at frame 303 and at frame 220. Lower the volume of the frame 303 node to 0, on both channels. Click OK.

9. Now it's time to add some rotoscoping effects to the movie. Create a few layers in the Main Timeline, and start drawing some vector artwork and animation. If you want to make frame-by-frame vector animation, you might want to select a range of frames and create empty frames (Modify ⇨ Frames ⇨ Convert to Blank Key Frames). You will notice that, as you scrub the playhead through the scene, you can both hear the music and see the frames animate. For more information on drawing and animation in Flash, see the chapters in Part II of the *Flash 5 Bible*.

Continued

Continued

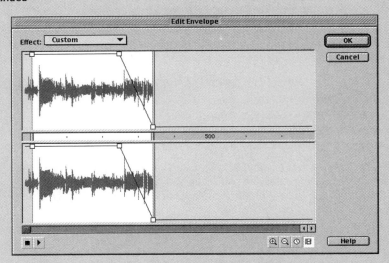

10. When you're finished with your artwork, save the Flash movie.

Preparing the RealMedia files

After you have created the Flash movie presentation, you're ready to set up the RealPlayer options in the Publish Settings dialog of Flash 5.

1. Open the Publish Settings dialog (File ➪ Publish Settings).

2. In the Format tab, check both Flash and RealPlayer.

3. In the Flash tab, select a Player version between 2 and 4, depending on the RealServer version installed on your Web server.

4. Click the Set button next to Audio Stream, and select either 11, 22, or 44 kHz for the Sample Rate. (Refer to the sections preceding this tutorial for more information on RealAudio codecs and sample rates. You should choose a sample rate that doesn't exceed your original source material.) Make sure Compression is set to Raw. Click OK.

5. Click the Set button next to Audio Event. Choose Disable in the Compression menu of the Sound Settings dialog, and then click OK.

6. Select Override sound settings in the Flash tab. This option will force all audio in the Flash movie to honor the Audio settings in this Flash tab.

7. Select the RealPlayer tab of the Publish Settings dialog.

8. Set the bit rate of the tuned Flash file to the result of the following formula, which was explained earlier in this chapter:

Tuned Flash Bit Rate = Average Bit Rate – Audio Bit Rate

9. Deselect the Adjust Bit Rate on Publish option.

10. If you have RealServer G2 or higher installed, select SureStream in the RealAudio section and check the target audiences you want to reach. If you have an earlier RealServer installed, select Single Rate, and select at least one target audience option.

11. Make sure Export SMIL is checked. If you want to add information about the presentation to the SMIL document, then click Project Properties and fill in the appropriate information. Note that the files used in this tutorial are copyrighted. Please do not distribute these files.

12. Click the Publish button on the right hand side of the Publish Settings dialog. Flash will publish all four files (the normal .SWF file, the tuned .SWF file, the RealAudio file, and the .SMIL file) to the same location as your saved .FLA file.

After the files have been published, you'll need to upload the files to your RealServer. You only need to upload the tuned .SWF file to your Web site or RealServer. The tuned file will have a "t" at the end of its name. If you change any of the filenames, you'll need to update the SMIL document to reflect the changes. After they're on the server, try accessing the .SMIL directly from the RealPlayer window by typing: **rtsp://www.yourdomain.com/ realfiles/realfile.smil**

This will make all the files stream over RTSP instead of HTTP.

If your RealServer is behaving properly, you should see your Flash and audio files streaming over the Web!

Daniel Szecket is quite the Renaissance man. He has traveled and lived more than six countries, and speaks five languages fluently (Spanish, English, Hebrew, French, and Portuguese — and is learning Italian). Born in Argentina, Daniel now resides in Los Angeles with his wife. With Ronen Lasry, they run Magritte's Cow (www.magrittescow.com), a company specializing in innovative new media content. Even though he's at his computer most of the time, Daniel's single most favorite thing to do is "hang out with my wife, dogs, and friends."

Summary

✦ Publishing your Flash movies in the Real format is a fast and effective way to expand the reach of your Flash content to other media players on the Web.

✦ .SMIL controls the synchronization between the tuned Flash file and the RealAudio file.

✦ Only RealPlayer 8 and RealServer 8 support Flash 3 and 4 files. All other versions of RealPlayer and RealServer use Flash 2 files.

✦ Transparency in Flash files is not supported by any RealPlayer version.

✦ If you want to control all tracks of a RealPlayer presentation from a Flash 3 or 4 .SWF file, you'll need to use a `getURL` action that specifies a RealPlayer command for the URL, such as `command:stop()`, `command:play()`, `command:pause()`, or `command:seek(time)`. Regular navigation Flash actions such as `gotoAndStop()` and `gotoAndPlay()` only control the Flash track, not the RealAudio track.

✦ Before you publish a tuned Flash file for RealPlayer playback, you need to determine its bit rate by subtracting the RealAudio bit rate from the practical throughput bit rate of your target audience(s).

✦ ✦ ✦

Creating Full-Motion Video with Flash

Flash isn't just a vector graphics tool for the Web — using Flash, you can create amazing video effects for your home videos or professional productions. This chapter explains how to use digital video with Flash. It also shows you how to export high-quality material from Flash to use in your video-editing applications.

High-Quality Video Output from Flash

While Flash is primarily used to create interactive animations and presentations on the Web, you can also generate high-quality output for other media uses. Macromedia began as a company called MacroMind, specializing in frame-by-frame video animation tools for desktop computers. Their flagship product, VideoWorks, eventually became Director, which was the first widely used Macromedia authoring product. Like Director, Flash also has some "hidden" video animation capabilities. You can use Flash to create spinning logos for your own corporate, creative, or home videos. Or, you could export those shape morphs — so difficult to create elsewhere — to layer over other video content. As we have seen in the previous chapter, Flash can output in QuickTime multimedia files. Flash can also generate numbered still sequences for use in other video-editing applications.

In previous Mac versions of Flash, 100 percent video-based (a.k.a. raster-based) QuickTime (QT) files could be directly rendered via the Export Movie command. Macromedia has added a more robust solution — based on QuickTime 4 — that exports Flash material directly to a Flash track for use in conjunction with video and audio tracks from other sources. This is wonderful if you want to create QTs for QuickTime 4-enabled applications. At the time of this writing, most Mac and PC applications that use the QuickTime architecture — such as Adobe Premiere and Adobe After Effects — will import QuickTime Flash movies. Some DV-only NLE (nonlinear editing) software, such as Digital Origin EditDV, will not allow you to import QuickTime Flash movies. For the best video results, you will want to export still image sequences from Flash instead of using QuickTime Flash files, or export traditional QuickTime Video files (available only on the Macintosh version of Flash) or .AVI files (available only on the PC version of Flash).

Note Because the export process for sequences uses generic vector or raster formats, you lose all interactivity that you have created in Flash. But that's perfectly fine because we're transferring our Flash movie to a linear viewing environment like video — we're simply making something to watch on a television or on a computer monitor without any involvement from the audience.

In the near future, it's possible that animated material intended for higher bandwidth media such as television or film can be created and generated from Flash. Flash artwork is completely scalable and flexible for just about any media use. Combined with the QuickTime architecture, Flash artwork can be output to DV tape or motion picture film. If you think your project looks good in Flash, you should be able to repurpose that hard work into another format very easily.

A Quick Video Primer

If you're a neophyte to digital video, then you need to know some basic terms and procedures involved with digital video. The following section will be useful if you've never used digital video or used it without really knowing what you were doing.

A brief history of digital video

In the past, digital video on the desktop computer was almost impossible. It required expensive hardware such as superfast processors, huge hard drives, video-capture boards, and professional-quality video decks and cameras. Beginning at $15,000, such systems were out of reach for most users. But like most technology after it has been around for a while, digital video equipment has become much more affordable for the average user. Although digital video still requires fast and efficient computers to work well, it isn't nearly as expensive anymore. You can get 30GB hard drives for under $500! Since the advent of the DV (Digital Video) format (a.k.a. DVCAM or miniDV), consumer-level video cameras and decks are almost as good as their professional-level counterparts.

The need for space

Why does digital video require so many resources? To begin with, digital video is entirely raster-based. This means that, unlike Flash and other vector file formats, each frame of digital video requires that almost every pixel on the screen is remembered and stored. Vector formats, on the other hand, use mathematical descriptions of objects on the screen and compute their movement very efficiently. The resolution of an average television set is roughly equivalent to a 640×480 resolution at 24-bit color depth on your computer monitor. Mathematically speaking, one frame of digital video at this resolution is nearly 1MB!

$$640 \times 480 \times 3^* = 921{,}600 \text{ bytes} = 900\text{KB} = 0.88\text{MB}$$

If that isn't bad enough, consider that 1 second of video contains 30 frames. That's 26MB for just 1 second of video! Only the fastest systems and hard drives on the market could deliver such performance. One solution to this performance bottleneck was to compress the data. Thus, most digital video now employs some form of compression (for storage) and decompression (for playback). The short form of this expression is *codec* (*co*mpression and *dec*ompression). You may have already heard of many codecs in use today, but what you probably don't know is that there are three kinds of codecs: software, hardware, and hybrid.

> **Note**
>
> Cinepak, Indeo, RealVideo, and Sorenson are all software-based codecs, meaning that the computer processor has to decompress each frame of compressed video. These differ from hardware-based codecs, such as MJPEG (Motion JPEG, based on the Joint Photographic Experts Group compression scheme), which need video-capture cards to compress and decompress each frame of video.
>
> The latest breed of codecs today are hybrids, both software and hardware based, such as the MPEG (Moving Picture Experts Group) and DV codecs. MPEG currently has two versions, MPEG-1 and MPEG-2. Originally, MPEG-1 and MPEG-2 video needed special hardware to playback, but as computer processors got faster, software-based players could handle the decompression tasks. Today, MPEG-2 is standard for DVD.

DVD, or digital versatile/video disc, is a new storage medium that can handle feature-length movies in a snap. DVD should not be confused with DV. DV refers to true Digital Video, in which the source video originates as binary (zeros and ones) data. Furthermore, the general term *digital video* should not be confused with *DV*. *Digital video* usually refers to the any video that has been stored as binary data, although it most likely originated from an analog source such as a regular VHS or BetaCam video camera. *DV* refers to video that originated from a digital (a.k.a. *binary*) source and that remains digital through any number of edits on a digital system.

---

*Each byte has 8 bits. Therefore, 24 bits is equivalent to 3 bytes.

With the current implementation of DV, using IEEE-1394 (a.k.a. *FireWire* or *iLink*) technology, video is transferred from digital tape to your computer hard drive with virtually no loss of quality. The DV footage is not recompressed unless the image in the footage is changed during editing by adding effects or transitions. But like any digital video, DV still requires a lot of hard drive space — about 2GB for every 9 minutes.

Note Most operating systems have a maximum file size limit of 2GB. This means that you cannot have more than nine minutes of DV-compressed footage in one QuickTime or .AVI file. However, you can string many movies together during playback for continuous recording. New versions of the Mac OS (version 9.0.4 or higher) and of the Windows OS support files that are larger than 2GB. Even so, some applications may not be capable of using these larger files unless they've been updated to do so.

Codec, frame size, and frame rate: The keys to manageable video

Before you begin any digital video project you should have a clear understanding of codecs. Most software-based codecs are intended for computer playback and distribution, while hardware-based codecs are intended for capturing and editing original footage to be used for television broadcast or feature films. You can repurpose hardware-based codec video by compressing it with a software-based codec. Most video developers take high-quality video and shrink it, in both frame and file size, to fit onto multimedia CD-ROMs or the Web.

Three variables can be applied to digital video to make it more manageable for most consumer computer systems: frame size, frame rate, and compression. Developers often use all three variables to shrink huge 9GB video projects down to 3 to 5MB, which may lead to undesirable results.

First, let's talk about frame size. Although most professional video uses a 640×480 or greater frame size, you may have noticed that most video on multimedia CD-ROMs only takes up a quarter or less of your entire computer monitor. Most video on the Web or CD-ROMs is rendered at 320×240 resolution, half the resolution of broadcast video. Actually, this is only slightly less than the horizontal-line resolution of your VHS recordings.

What about frame rate? You may have also noticed that video on multimedia CD-ROMs often looks a little jerky or choppy. Although this may be due to a slow processor, it's more likely that — in order to cut the file size — the frame rate of the video was reduced. It's not uncommon to find CD-ROM frame rates as low as 12 or 15 fps (frames per second) — about half of the original frame rate of broadcast video. This slower frame rate is also the default frame rate of a new Flash movie, to ensure consistent playback on slower machines. Despite the drop in video quality, the lower frame rates result in much smaller file sizes with fewer frames for the processor to play within each second, which delivers better CD-ROM performance.

Finally, how does compression affect video? You've probably noticed that Web and multimedia CD-ROM video is often blocky looking. This is due to the software-based compression that has been used on the video. Codecs look for areas of the frame that stay consistent over many frames, and then log those areas and drop them from subsequent frames. The result is that no unnecessary repetition of data exists that needs to be continually decompressed. But, depending on the level of compression used, the properties of the codec itself, and the settings used in running that codec, the video varies in quality.

Keeping with the trend of better and faster, digital video continues to improve dramatically. This is well illustrated by the fact that many popular Web sites, such as Apple's QuickTime Web site (`www.apple.com/quicktime`), now enables visitors to download larger, higher-quality videos (upwards of 15MB) for playback on newer, faster systems.

Playback bottlenecks

Digital video needs to be kept small for two reasons: storage and playback. So far, we have largely discussed storage issues. But playback (or transfer rate) further complicates the creation of digital video. Despite the relatively large capacity of CD-ROMs (650MB), most CD-ROM readers have limited transfer rates of about 600KB/second. It's important to note that each second of video cannot exceed the transfer rate, otherwise the video will drop frames to keep up with the audio. So if the video is distributed via CD-ROM, this factor results in serious limitations.

Let's look at some of the math involved under ideal (choppy) playback conditions: If you use 15 fps for compressed video, you are limited to a maximum of roughly 40KB per frame. (Remember, though, that the playback stream usually includes an audio track as well, which means that less than 40KB is available for the video component of each individual frame.)

 For more information on audio formatting and compression, see Chapter 14, "Understanding Sound for Flash," and Chapter 16, "Optimizing Flash Sound for Export."

Unfortunately, the Web still affords less than ideal playback conditions for video. On the Web, transfer rates can be as slow as 500 bytes/second. On average, a 56KB modem downloads around 4KB/second. The ideal Web video streams to the user while loading the page. If you intend to stream video quickly, you have to keep this very small transfer rate in mind. Large videos simply will not stream! This is why most Web sites offer larger videos as a download file. But you do have an alternative. Later in this section, you can learn how to extract a minimal number of frames in order to simulate digital video motion with Flash, yet keep your Flash files streaming quickly. As modem technologies get faster, though, we'll most likely see bigger and better video delivered across the Web. The ADSL (Asymmetrical Digital Subscriber Line) modem was developed with the MPEG-1 and -2 standards in mind.

Adjusting Flash Movies for Video Output

By default, Flash uses a frame rate of 12 fps for all new movies. Unless you have changed this setting with the Modify ➪ Movie command (Command+M or Ctrl+M), this is the setting for any Flash movie you have created so far. As mentioned earlier in this chapter, broadcast (NTSC) video needs 30 fps (29.97 fps to be exact) for motion to be smooth and fluid. It may be necessary for you to add more blank frames between each of your tweened keyframes to accommodate a faster frame rate. Your 5-second intro to your Web site may have been possible with 70 or fewer frames, but now you need 300 frames for the same amount of time in full-motion video. Flash doesn't support interlacing (or field-ordering) with any export method (see the "What Is Interlacing?" sidebar for an explanation of interlacing). As a result, you need twice the number of frames (double the frame rate) used for every second of NTSC video — 59.94 fps to be exact — to properly render full-motion video from Flash. It's easier to use 60 fps in Flash and then conform the rendered sequence to 59.94 fps in the video-editing application.

If you are using the PAL or SECAM video systems, which are video systems used outside of North America, then you need to use different frame sizes and frame rates to accurately render Flash content. Use the same methods described here, but adjust any values to fit within PAL or SECAM specifications.

If possible, restrict your Flash movie to one scene for video-editing purposes. Flash exports all scenes within a Flash movie into a sequence or QT/AVI movie, which may complicate the editing process later. It's easier to make more Flash movies and render them independent of each other.

Frames stored in Movie Clips do not export with sequences. Make sure that you have either removed any Movie Clip symbols or that you have replaced them with the actual frames contained within the Movie Clip.

To replace a Movie Clip symbol with the actual frames contained within it:

1. Open the Movie Clip in the library, select the frames in the timeline.

2. Copy the frames with the Copy Frames command (Command+Option+C or Ctrl+Alt+C) in the Edit menu.

3. Go back to the Scene and paste the frames with the Paste Frames command (Command+Option+V or Ctrl+Alt+V). Paste the frames on their own layer, so that they won't conflict with any tweens or settings in other layers.

Remember that, unlike regular Flash movies, the exported sequence will not have any interactivity. The sequence is simply a collection of still images that will be compiled later in your video-editing application. (So don't mistakenly overwrite or delete your original Flash movie!)

What Is Interlacing?

Most computer monitors are non-interlaced, which means that each "frame" of video is fully displayed with each screen refresh. Most TV sets, though, are interlaced displays, which means that each frame of video consists of two fields, one upper and one lower, and each screen refresh shows one field then the other. Therefore, each second of video contains 60 fields, or 30 frames. Because Flash doesn't export field-ordered sequences, you have to compensate the lack of individual fields by using two Flash frames for every regular frame of video.

You may also need to adjust your Flash movie's pixel width and height. Depending on the type of video-editing software you are using, this setting needs to be 640×480, 720×534, or something else. Again, use the Modify ⇨ Movie command to adjust the size of your Flash movie. You can notice that adjusting pixel sizes of the Flash movie doesn't have the same effect as changing pixel heights or widths of raster-based images. Usually, adjusting pixel sizes will distort or change the shape of elements. With Flash, the movie's pixel size is independent of the pixel sizes of any elements it may contain. You're simply adding or subtracting space to the movie area. If you intend to bring the sequence into another video-editing application such as Premiere and you are outputting with the DV format, a movie size of 720×534 should be used. Why? The DV format uses nonsquare pixels delivering the same 4:3 aspect ratio with 720×480 as other video formats do with only 640×480 square pixels. By using 720×534 movie sizes, the frame can be stretched to fit a 720×480 DV workspace without losing any resolution quality. It's better to adjust the size before you export any material intended for broadcast video delivery (or for transfer to any NTSC recording media), especially with raster formats. Not only does this ensure optimal quality, it could easily lessen the time during video rendering in other applications.

Note The movie sizes just listed should work equally well for MJPEG video hardware and DV hardware. If you use these baseline settings, you can then accommodate either MJPEG or DV specifications in your video-editing application.

Not only do you need to have the proper frame size for high-quality video output, but you also need to be aware of overscanning. TV sets overscan video images, which means that information near the edges of the frame may be cropped and not visible. Because the amount of overscan is inconsistent from TV to TV, some general guidelines have been developed to make sure vital information in the frame is not lost. The crux of the guidelines is simple: Don't put anything important (such as text) near the edges of the frame. Video has two safe zones: title-safe and action-safe. To see these zones on a sample movie in Flash, refer to Figure 36-1.

The action-safe zone is approximately 90 percent of the 720×534 (or 640×480) frame size we're using in Flash, which calculates into 648×480 (or 576×432). All of your Flash artwork should be contained with the limits of the action-safe zone. The title-safe zone is about 80 percent of the total frame size. For a 720×534 frame size, any text on the Flash stage should fall within the borders of a 576×427 centered frame. With a 640×480 frame size, this centered frame size would be 512×384.

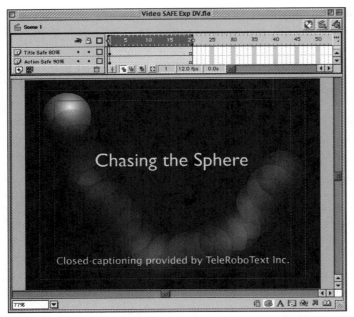

Figure 36-1: While designing for broadcast content in Flash, you should always be aware of the safe-zone boundaries for NTSC video playback.

Finally, you may need to adjust the colors and artwork you used in your Flash movie. NTSC video, while technically 24-bit, doesn't display some colors very well. In general, bright and saturated RGB colors tend to bleed on regular TV sets. Here are some guidelines for using broadcast (and WebTV)-safe color:

✦ Avoid one-pixel-wide horizontal lines. Because NTSC is interlaced, this line flickers constantly. If you need to use thin lines, try blurring a one-pixel line or simply never use anything less than a two-pixel stroke width.

✦ Do not use very fine textures as they may flicker and bleed at the edges. Because most NTSC monitors have low-quality resolutions, the fine details are lost anyway.

✦ Avoid using any color that uses any color channel's maximum intensity. Use a NTSC color filter on any bitmap art, such as the NTSC Colors filter in Adobe Photoshop. Full red (R: 255, G: 000, B: 000) displays horribly on TV sets. Replace a full red with R: 181, G: 000, B: 000. Pure white backgrounds should also be avoided and replaced with R: 235, G: 235, B: 235. Like red, pure white can cause annoying screen flicker, especially if high contrast objects are placed against the white. As a rule of thumb, keep your RGB values within the 16 to 235 range, instead of 0 to 255. Although Photoshop's NTSC Colors filter actually allows certain 255 values to be used, you should *only* use these values if they do not occupy large solid areas in the Flash movie.

✦ Use the NTSC & Web Safe color set (ntsc_web_179.act file) on the *Flash 5 Bible* CD-ROM (see Chapter 6, "Applying Color," for more information on importing or switching color sets). Of the 216 Web-safe color palettes, only 179 of them are NTSC/WebTV safe. NTSC TV sets are capable of displaying more colors than that, but if you're used to working with Web color palettes, then you may find this optimized palette handy. There's another color set file, ntsc_213_colors.act on the CD-ROM that you can use if you're just taking Flash content to video, which has 213 NTSC-safe colors, converted from the 216 Web-safe colors. Because 35 colors of this set are outside of the Web-safe colors, you should not use this palette for Web and broadcast work.

✦ If you are using video-editing software that allows both color and levels corrections on imported clips, then you might avoid time-consuming adjustments to your Flash movie. After you have generated a Flash sequence and imported the sequence into your video-editing application, restrict the gamut of the sequence clip using the values in the preceding tips.

Tip

In After Effects, use the Broadcast Colors filter to perform NTSC color adjustments on imported sequences or movies. This filter can adjust either luminance or saturation values to bring out-of-gamut colors into the NTSC color gamut. Use caution, however, as reducing the luminance may cause artifacts from MJPEG or DV compression to become more obvious. Reducing saturation is preferred method for using the Broadcast Colors.

Refer to Table 36-1 to see how Photoshop's NTSC Colors filter remaps the saturated values of the Web-safe color palette.

Table 36-1 NTSC Color Conversion Chart					
Original Web HEX Value	**Original RGB Web Value**			**Converted RGB NTSC Value**		
	R	**G**	**B**	**R**	**G**	**B**
FF0033	255	000	051	227	000	045
CC6699	204	051	153	204	102	153
FF00FF	255	000	255	210	000	210
FF00CC	255	000	204	219	000	175
FF0099	255	000	153	226	000	136
FF0066	255	000	102	230	000	092
CC00FF	204	000	255	199	000	248
00CCCC	000	204	204	000	170	170
00FFFF	000	255	255	000	170	170

Continued

Table 36-1 (continued)

Original Web HEX Value	Original RGB Web Value			Converted RGB NTSC Value		
	R	G	B	R	G	B
33FFFF	051	255	255	045	225	225
66FFFF	102	255	255	101	253	253
00CCFF	000	204	255	000	160	201
0099FF	000	153	255	000	147	245
00FFCC	000	255	204	000	178	143
33FFCC	051	255	204	047	237	190
00FF99	000	255	153	000	188	113
33FF99	051	255	153	050	249	150
00CC66	000	204	102	000	193	096
00FF00	000	255	000	000	210	000
00FF33	000	255	051	000	210	042
00FF66	000	255	102	000	198	079
33FF00	051	255	000	047	234	000
66FF00	102	255	000	088	220	000
99FF00	153	255	000	122	203	000
99CC00	153	204	000	142	190	000
FFFF66	255	255	102	252	252	101
CCCC00	204	204	000	170	170	000
CCFF00	204	255	000	148	185	000
FFCC00	255	204	000	191	153	000
CC9900	204	153	000	197	148	000
FF9900	255	153	000	216	130	000
FF6600	255	102	000	248	099	000
FF0000	255	000	000	181	000	000
CC0000	204	000	000	181	000	000

You can find Flash movies (.FLA files) containing grid layers for the safe-zones of NTSC video on the *Flash 5 Bible* CD-ROM.

Creating Sequences from Flash Movies

A sequence is a series of still images that simulate full-motion video when played back continuously. Think of a sequence as a regular QuickTime or AVI broken down into individual frames. Another analogy would be that of a flipbook made of individual sketches that animate when you thumb through the pages quickly. Flash can export a scene or movie as a series of still images as well, with quite a bit of flexibility.

Because Flash is vector-based, it supports all the major vector formats to use in other applications: EPS 3.0, Illustrator, and .DXF formats. On the PC version of Flash, you can also export metafile sequences in the .WMF and .EMF formats. Most likely, all of these vector formats will retain the scalable quality that Flash offers for the Web; that is, you can shrink or expand the size of vector formats, displaying equal richness and quality at all sizes. Most vector formats can embed raster content, and any raster content will always have a finite resolution capacity. You will notice degradation on any raster elements if you scale the entire vector graphic beyond its original fixed pixel size.

You can also export a still sequence in raster-based formats such as .PICT (Mac only), .BMP (PC only), .GIF, .JPEG, or .PNG. We can look at the benefits of each format and the particular uses each can have, but first, we should look at how to the process of exporting individual frames works in Flash.

Export process in Flash

After you have opened your Flash movie, make sure that your movie falls within the guidelines described in the last section. All of these settings are critical for flawless video playback: 60 frames per second, 640×480 (or greater) movie dimensions, limitations of scenes and Movie Clips, and color gamut considerations. When you're all ready to go, the actual export process is quite simple.

1. Select File ⇨ Export Movie (see Figure 36-2).
2. Choose or create the folder in which you wish to store the sequence.
3. Choose the type of file you want Flash to create.
4. Specify a filename and click Save.

For the highest quality video rendering, use a vector file format for export. The next section details each file type and its particular uses.

Uses of each sequence format

Flash can export in a variety of file formats, and each one has a particular purpose. While vector formats allow the most scalability, some Flash artwork does not display properly in them. Raster formats usually maintain the highest fidelity to Flash artwork, but their file sizes can be rather large.

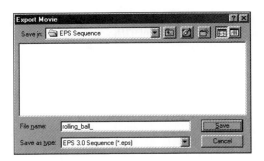
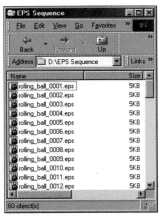

Figure 36-2: When you export a Flash movie as a sequence, Flash generates a still image (that is, one file) for each frame in the Flash movie.

Vector sequence formats

Use a vector format type for your sequences when you want the highest quality re-rendering in applications such as Adobe After Effects or Premiere (see Table 36-2 for a list of formats supported in Flash). Flash exports vector sequences very quickly, although the sequence files themselves may take longer to re-render in your video-editing application than raster formats. Once you see the smooth edges of vector-rendered sequences, though, you can see that it is worth the wait. Vector formats automatically matte out the Flash background color and make superimposing Flash material supereasy.

Mask layers (and the artwork that they mask) will not export properly in EPS sequences. The artwork in the mask layer will show up in the exported EPS file(s). If you use mask layers in your Flash movie, export raster image sequences instead.

Table 36-2
Flash-Supported Vector Sequence Formats

Flash Export Format	File Extension	Application Support	Comments
EPS 3.0; Encapsulated PostScript	.EPS	AE, PR	Universal vector format recognized by most applications. However, any gradients created in Flash will not export well with this format.
Illustrator; Adobe Illustrator	.AI	AE, PR	Proprietary file format mainly used by Adobe applications. However, any gradients created in Flash will not export well with this format.

Flash Export Format	File Extension	Application Support	Comments
DXF; Drawing eXchange Format	.DXF	3S	AutoCAD 2D/3D file format.
WMF/EMF; Windows Meta File/ Extended Meta File	.WMF, .EMF	PR (WMF only)	There's no reason to use these formats over the other vector formats. While some non-Microsoft applications support them, they aren't widely used on either Mac or PC systems.

AE = Adobe After Effects; PR = Adobe Premiere; 3S = Kinetix 3D Studio MAX

Raster formats

All raster formats can export at variable pixel widths, heights, and resolutions. As long as your Flash movie is in the proper aspect ratio for video (usually 4:3), you can size up your Flash movie on export (see Table 36-3 for a list of formats supported in Flash). This will save time during the re-rendering process in the video-editing application. Not all file formats support alpha channels, which are necessary if you intend to superimpose exported Flash material on top of other video material. Refer to Chapter 17, "Understanding Actions and Event Handlers," for more detailed information on the options associated with each raster file format.

Table 36-3
Flash-Supported Raster Sequence Formats

Flash Export Format	File Extension	Application Support	Comments
PICT (Mac only); Picture	.PCT	AE, PR, QT, 3S	Can be used with many PC and all Mac applications. Variable bit-depths and compression settings with support of alpha channels. Supports lossless compression.
BMP (PC only); Windows Bitmap	.BMP	AE, PR, QT, 3S	Can be used with all PC and some Mac applications. Variable bit-depths and compression settings with support of alpha channels. Supports lossless compression.

Continued

Table 36-3			
Flash Export Format	**File Extension**	**Application Support**	**Comments**
GIF; Graphics Interchange File	.GIF	AE, PR, QT, 3S	Limited to a 256-color palette. Not recommended for full-motion NTSC video.
JPEG; Joint Photo-graphic Experts Group	.JPG	AE, PR, QT, 3S	Only supports 24-bit RGB color. No alpha channel support. Recommended for full-motion NTSC video, but this format does throw out color information due to its lossy compression method.
PNG; Portable Network Graphic	.PNG	AE, QT	Supports variable bit-depth and compression settings with alpha channels. Lossless compression schemes make it an ideal candidate for NTSC video.

AE = Adobe After Effects; PR = Adobe Premiere; QT = Apple QuickTime Player Pro; 3S = Kinetix 3D Studio Max

Creating .AVI Files on the PC

If you want a quick-and-dirty 100-percent raster-based video version of your Flash movie, and you use the PC version of Flash, then you can export your Flash movie as a Video for Windows (.AVI) file. If you want the best video quality for output to videotape, you should not use this method for rendering video. Flash doesn't support interlaced video and won't create the smoothest possible video content directly. This export file format is used primarily for digital video intended for computer playback, not NTSC playback.

You can render a Flash movie at twice the frame rate of NTSC video (29.97×2 = 59.94 fps) using the necessary codec for your video hardware. If you want to play the .AVI through your IEEE-1394 (a.k.a. *FireWire, iLink*) hardware, you need to resize the 720×534 AVI movie to 720×480 in a video-editing application or by using the Dimensions property of the Export AVI Settings dialog. Do not change the Flash movie properties via Modify ➪ Movie! DV uses nonsquare pixels, and shapes will be stretched if you use a 720×480 movie size in Flash.

Choose Export Movie from the File menu. Select a folder (or create one) to store the .AVI file, type the filename, and click Save. You will then see the Export Windows AVI dialog box with the following options (see Figure 36-3).

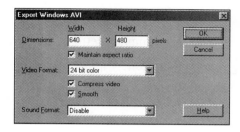

Figure 36-3: Adjust the values of the Windows AVI settings to accommodate your playback needs.

Dimensions

This property enables you to scale your .AVI movie. If you wish to scale the movie's width separate from the height, uncheck the Maintain Aspect Ratio box for this property. This may be necessary if you need to accommodate nonsquare pixel formats such as DV or D1.

Video format

The drop-down menu associated with this property enables you to choose a bit-depth for the .AVI movie. For serious video work, you'll want to choose 24-bit color or greater.

✦ **8-bit color:** Limits the rendered movie to 256 colors that are determined on the fly by Flash.

✦ **16-bit color:** Limits the movie to 65,536 colors; also known as High Color in Windows or Thousands of Colors on the Mac.

✦ **24-bit color:** Enables the movie to use full RGB color (16.7 million colors); also known as True Color on the PC or Millions of Colors on the Mac.

✦ **32-bit color w/ alpha:** Enables the movie to use full RGB color and store an alpha channel for compositing effects. Not all video codecs can store alpha channel information.

✦ **Compress video:** If this option is checked, you are given the option to select a video compressor (codec) after you click OK on the Export Windows AVI dialog. If you do not check this box, Flash generates uncompressed video frames, which can take over 1MB of file space per frame. In general, you do not want to use uncompressed video, as it takes very long to re-render uncompressed video into the hardware codec used by your video setup.

✦ **Smooth:** Using the smooth option antialiases the Flash graphics. This adds more time to the export process, but your .AVI file looks much better. If you just want a rough .AVI movie, then uncheck Smooth for faster exporting.

Sound format

This drop-down list enables you to specify the audio sampling settings. If you didn't use any audio in your Flash movie, then choose Disable. For a description of each of the sampling rates and bit-depths, please see Chapter 10, "Drawing in Flash," and Chapter 12, "Using Bitmaps and Other Media with Flash."

Video compression

When you've chosen the options you need, click OK. If you specified Compress Video, you'll see the dialog shown in Figure 36-4:

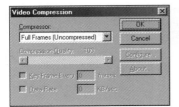

Figure 36-4: Choose the proper video codec for your video output hardware, or select a software-based codec for computer playback and distribution.

In the Video Compression dialog, you can select a software- or hardware-based codec to use for the .AVI movie. By default, Flash chooses Full Frames (Uncompressed). This option is the same as deselecting Compress Video, which forces Flash to render full-frame video. Because you probably want manageable file sizes, choose the codec you need to use for your video hardware. If you want to simply review your Flash work as an .AVI movie, use Cinepak or Indeo codecs. Adjust the codec settings as necessary for your needs. Smaller files and lower quality will result from using compression qualities less than 100 percent, the use of keyframes, and data-rate limiting. For high-quality rendering using hardware-based codecs, make sure that the hardware codec (such as MJPEG or DV) is set to 100 percent compression quality with no keyframes or data-rate limiting. Click OK.

Flash then exports an .AVI movie file to the folder you specified earlier. Depending on the length of your Flash movie and the video codec used, the export process could take less than a minute or many hours. Unfortunately, Flash doesn't give you an estimated time for completion like Adobe Premiere or After Effects does. When Flash has finished exporting the file, you can view the video with Windows Media Player or with the software that your video hardware uses.

Importing Sequences into Video Applications

Now that you've created a sequence or QuickTime movie with Flash's Export or Publish command, you can bring the newly generated material into most video-editing applications. Not all video-editing applications will accept still image sequences and automatically treat them as one movie clip like Adobe Premiere or After Effects do. Just about any video application will accept QuickTime movies. In this section, you see how to prepare either a raster QuickTime movie or an image sequence for video output.

Adobe Premiere 5.1

Adobe Premiere is one of the most popular video-editing applications available for desktop computers. Just about every major video-capture card comes with Adobe Premiere (or Premiere LE), and it offers a very intuitive interface for editing video. While not as advanced as Adobe After Effects for visual effects or compositing, it can be used for a variety of tasks, from CD-ROM video to animated GIFs to DV-ready output.

Note   This section assumes that you have a working knowledge of Premiere 5.1 and that you know how to set up a project with optimized settings for your video hardware. If you haven't used Premiere, refer to the Premiere section of "Extracting frames from digital video clips" in Chapter 34.

To import a numbered sequence of still images generated from Flash, double-click in the Project window or choose File ➪ Import ➪ File (Ctrl+I/Command+I). Browse to the folder that contains the image sequence and select the first image in the sequence. Check the box for Numbered Stills underneath the filename field. This option tells Premiere to automatically look for consecutively numbered filenames and treat the group of them as one Movie Clip.

Click OK, and Premiere adds the image sequence to the Project window as a Movie Clip. As shown in Figure 36-5, it displays the first frame of the clip as an icon, and includes the duration of the clip and its pixel size.

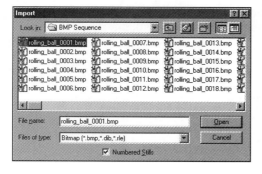

Figure 36-5: The Project window displays useful information about the clip, such as duration and frame size.

If you followed the guidelines in the "Adjusting Flash Movies for Video Output " section, then you've already anticipated a 59.94 fps playback speed. Because NTSC video uses 29.97, we need to adjust the speed of the imported sequence. Select the clip in the Project window, and choose Clip ⇨ Speed (Command+Shift+R or Ctrl+ Shift+R). Enter **200** percent for the New Rate setting, as shown in Figure 36-6.

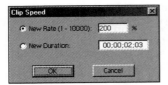

Figure 36-6: Use the New Rate setting to adjust the speed at which Premiere plays the clip. Because Flash does not create interlaced frames, you need to mimic the effect of interlacing by doubling the number of frames in the Flash movie.

Note If you are using the DV format, you should have made the image sequence from a 720×534-sized Flash movie. Premiere automatically stretches the imported sequence (now a clip) to fill the 720×480 frame size of DV. Because the DV format uses nonsquare pixels, elements in the clip may appear distorted along the horizontal axis. Circles will look like ovals, and squares will look like rectangles. This appearance is normal on computer monitors, which use square pixels. When you play your movie back to tape through the FireWire, i.Link, or IEEE-1394 connection, this distortion will no longer be noticeable.

Drag the imported sequence from the Project window to the timeline window. Place the clip at the desired insertion point. If you intend to superimpose the image sequence over another video track, place the image sequence clip on the Video 2 track.

Adobe After Effects 4.1

As mentioned in the previous chapter, After Effects is the Photoshop equivalent to video production. After Effects works with moving images in the same way that Photoshop works with still images. Although After Effects is a complex program with innumerable settings, you can use it for simple tasks as well.

Using After Effects, you can achieve the highest quality video from your Flash-generated image sequence. That's because After Effects offers subtle controls for video clip and composition settings that deliver crisp, interlaced, frame-accurate video.

After Effects can continuously rasterize any vector content — meaning that After Effects can re-render each vector frame into a raster frame. Most video applications, such as Premiere, rasterize the first frame of a vector image and continue to reuse that first rasterized version for the entire render process.

What does that mean? Simply put, if you have a small vector circle in the first frame of a project that grows larger in subsequent frames, then the circle appears very jagged at the larger sizes. Although both Premiere and After Effects render a Flash-generated image sequence at the same quality, please note that if you want to do special effects with just one frame (or still) from a Flash movie (not an entire image sequence), then After Effects does a much better job. Also note that this can be confusing because there are two potential uses of material imported from Flash into either After Effects or Premiere. These are either single frame imports or multi-frame imports. The big point is this: After Effects does a consistent high-quality job with both types, whereas Premiere only handles the latter type (multiframe) well.

Caution

While .EPS and .AI image sequences offer the most scalability for digital video production, Flash poorly translates their gradients into common PostScript-defined colors. As a result, gradients appear as solid color fills in After Effects. If you are using gradients in your Flash artwork, then export the movie as a raster sequence. After Effects can import a .PNG sequence, which has superior compression to .JPEG.

Please refer to the earlier discussion of After Effects in this chapter, if you are not familiar with its interface and controls.

To import a sequence into After Effects:

1. Open an existing After Effects project file (.AEP) or create a new project (Command+Option+N or Ctrl+Alt+N).

2. Double-click in the Project window to import the image sequence. In the Open dialog, browse to the folder containing the image sequence. Select the first file of the sequence (for example, ball_0001.png) and check the Sequence option (such as PNG Sequence, JPEG Sequence, EPS Sequence, and so forth). Click Open.

3. If After Effects detects an alpha channel in the imported file(s), then an Interpret Footage dialog opens, as shown in Figure 36-7. You must tell After Effects how to treat the alpha channel. For any image or image sequence with an alpha channel imported from Flash, use the Treat As Straight (Unmatted) setting.

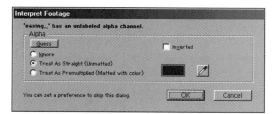

Figure 36-7: After Effects automatically detects the presence of an alpha channel in imported file(s). For alpha channels that Flash creates, use the Treat As Straight (Unmatted) setting.

4. Select the imported sequence (now shown as one footage item) in the Project window and choose File ⇨ Interpret Footage ⇨ Main. This time, the Interpret Footage dialog (see Figure 36-8) displays the complete settings for the selected footage file. In the Frame Rate section, enter the correct frame rate in the "Assume this frame rate" field. If you followed the guidelines given earlier in this chapter, then you used a 59.94 fps for your Flash movie. Enter that value here. Also, make sure Square Pixels is selected in the Pixel Aspect Ratio section.

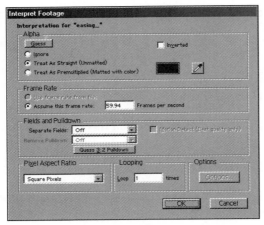

Figure 36-8: In the complete Interpret Footage dialog, you can set the frame rate and pixel aspect ratio for the Flash image sequence.

5. Create a new composition via the Composition ⇨ New Composition command (Command+N or Ctrl+N). Depending on your video hardware, the settings for a new composition will vary. For the Duration section, enter a value greater than or equal to the length of the imported Flash sequence. See Figure 36-9 for a DV-specific composition.

6. Drag the Flash sequence footage file from the Project window to the Time Layout window.

You now have a Flash sequence ready to integrate with other video in After Effects. See the After Effects section in "Extracting frames from digital video clips" in Chapter 34 for more information on exporting image sequences from After Effects. Use Render Settings and Output Module settings specific for your video hardware.

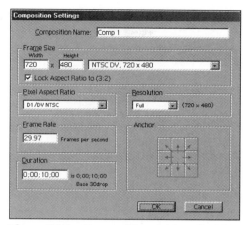

Figure 36-9: Composition settings for DV-format (for example, mini-DV, DVCAM) video

Summary

✦ Desktop digital video systems have become more affordable with the advent of the DV format, used by miniDV and DVCAM camcorders and decks. Because DV material is binary from start to finish, there is virtually no loss of video quality during the editing process.

✦ Because Flash is designed for optimal playback on the Web, Flash movie properties (frame size, frame rate, and the number of total frames) need to be adjusted to work with high-quality digital video.

✦ Flash can export high-quality raster-based .AVI and QuickTime movies. It should be noted, however, that these movie files will not contain any Flash interactivity or Flash tracks.

✦ NTSC television sets and WebTVs have color signal limitations. Avoid using highly saturated colors and thin lines in Flash movies intended for interlaced video delivery.

✦ Flash can create high-quality animations as an image sequence. An image sequence is a series of numbered still images. Certain video-editing applications, such as Adobe Premiere and After Effects, can import raster and vector sequences. These sequences can be composited with other video tracks and output to videotape — which opens up a whole new realm of motion techniques, all generated in Flash!

✦   ✦   ✦

Creating Cartoon Animation with Flash

Flash is a powerful tool capable of creating high-quality cartoons much like those you might see on Nickelodeon, Cartoon Network, and so on. This is due to Flash's unique drawing tools, file format, and scalability. By scalability, we mean that a Flash cartoon can be scaled up to the size and quality of the finest video or even film resolution cartoons. Because the subject of creating broadcast cartoons can be extremely complex (and could even fill a book of it's own) we focus on some fundamental techniques and tricks that will start you on the way to becoming the next Tex Avery.

Working with Large File Sizes

Because Flash output is usually intended for the Web, Flash file size is often a dominant concern. But when creating cartoons for broadcast output, this concern is thrown to the wind. In cartoon land, you create for digital video output via QuickTime or .AVI and these file sizes can be huge. It's common for such projects to expand into the gigabytes, so it's important to have the equipment to handle this kind of work. This means large, fast hard drives and plenty of RAM. The extensive use of bitmaps and full-fidelity 16-bit 44 kHz stereo audio tracks means that Flash itself will require a great deal of RAM. Your machine should have at least 128MB of RAM with at least 90 MB available to Flash. Even with this configuration, however, you may — like some nefarious cartoon character — paint yourself into a corner and find that you need more RAM in order to render (export raster video) your scene. In addition, the time required to perform a render can often exceed 45 minutes. This may cause you to think that the machine has crashed. . . . Sometimes it has, sometimes it has not. Sometimes, very annoying results can happen. When rendering complex scenes that take a long, long time, it may seem that all is proceeding just fine, but then Flash may hiccup and report that there isn't enough memory to finish. That's when patience is required. Remember that, although some amazing cartoon animations can be created in Flash, it was engineered to create small, compact files for the Web; our cartoon use is pushing it far beyond its calling. Keeping this in mind may save a brick from going through your monitor.

Caution You'll spend many hours working on your animation, so back it up as much and as often as you can! The project file is precious. Make a habit of keeping incremental backups on various disks so that you won't lose everything when disaster strikes (it will). A good plan is to make a new copy on a different disk after each major change, rotating through two or three different disks. This way if Flash eats your project file, you can always go back to the version you saved an hour ago (which should be on a different disk) without loosing much time.

The Storyboard

Let's assume that you already have characters and a story (why else would you want to create a cartoon show?) and that you want to build a cartoon based on that small beginning. In this section, we touch on some of the tips that you need to think about in the storyboard phase. Although it's OK to play around, never start a serious cartoon project without a storyboard. The storyboard is your roadmap, your plan, your menu of things needed, your best friend when your project gets complicated — without it, you are lost.

On the CD-ROM You'll find a storyboard template on the CD-ROM, in the ch37 folder. It's an EPS (storyboardMAC.eps or storybPC.eps) template form that includes all the essentials of a basic storyboard. Print it out as is, or import it into FreeHand, Illustrator, or Flash, and modify it to suit your needs.

First, break up the story into workable cartoon scenes. In creating a broadcast cartoon, we use the terminology a bit differently. Long before Flash, cartoonists used the terminology of a scene to describe something quite different than a Flash Scene. By scenes, we mean a cartoon scene, which is much like a movie or TV scene — not a Flash Scene. Remember that cartoons are fast-paced adventures. Most cartoon scenes last less than 30 seconds. A cartoon scene is usually a section of dialog or action that tells a part of the story. Generally, a cartoon scene can stand-alone, but it needs other scenes to complete the story. Because of the length of time required for most cartoon scenes, it would become unruly if we were to rely solely upon

Flash's Scene function. You'd scroll through the timeline forever, just trying to cover a 45-second scene. But as you'll learn in this section, there's still use for the Flash Scene function.

After your cartoon scenes are established, break each of these scenes into shots. A shot is a break in the camera focus. For example, a soap opera (they are famous for this) will have a scene of dialog, but the camera will cut back and forth to whoever is talking at the time — which means that one scene may have many shots. Although the art of cinematography is beyond the scope of this book, that is what's involved when deciding shots in a cartoon scene.

Never create an entire cartoon in one Flash project file! Even trying to load the huge files created can create problems for Flash. Instead, use Flash's Scene function for shots. (This may seem confusing at first, but the utility of this method will become clear as you work on your masterpiece.) Make a separate Flash file for each storyboard scene of your cartoon; then, within each of these Flash files, assign a Flash Scene for each of the shots within a storyboard scene. Think of it this way; the Flash project file is the Storyboard Scene, nested within that project file is the Flash Scene, or shot. Although this may seem contrary to the way in which you usually work with Flash, we are trying to reconcile the traditional terminology of cartoon animation with the recent terminology of the Flash program. Besides, the creation of broadcast cartoons isn't an advertised use of Flash.

On the CD-ROM

The Weber cartoon (QuickTime version included on the CD-ROM, in the ch37 folder) runs for 6 minutes and contains about 32 shots spread over 13 scenes. The project files (scenes) alone are over 170MB. Loading one 170MB file into Flash is flirting with disaster.

The single most important work you'll do in your cartoon is not the drawing but the voices of your characters; the voices are what make the character. Obtaining a voice can be as simple as your speaking into a microphone or as complex as a highly paid professional acting into a microphone. The key here is not the voice, but the emotion put into it. The right mix of unique voice and emotion can be taken into a sound program, such as Peak or Premiere, and tweaked with the proper plug-ins to render the cartoon sound that you're looking for. Voice effects can always be added digitally, human emotion cannot. Some online voice resources are:

✦ www.voicecasting.com

✦ www.voice-choice.com

✦ www.voicetraxwest.com

Another important part of the cartoon is the use of sound effects. Try to imagine Tom and Jerry or Road Runner without them. There's nothing like a good CLANK, followed by the tweeting of birds, when the old anvil hits Wile E. Coyote's head. Many good sound effects collections are available on CD-ROM and online. These collections, used primarily by radio stations, come on CD-ROM and can easily be imported into the digital realm. One resource for such collections is www.radio-mall.com, which has a range of effects at a broad range of prices; furthermore, most of their collections have Real Audio links, which means that you can audition them online.

Sometimes, though, you just can't buy the sound you need. So, when you need that special CLANK, it's time to set up the microphone and start tossing anvils at unsuspecting heads. Really, though, it's not difficult to setup your own little foley stage or sound effects recording area. A good shotgun microphone (highly directional for aiming at sound) and DAT recorder are ideal, although you can get by with less.

Tip   If you have to scrimp, don't pinch pennies on the microphone. A good microphone can make an average capture device sound better.

The capture device (audio tape, DAT, miniDV, MD, and so on) should be portable not only in order to get it away from the whirring sound of hard drives and fans but also to enable you to take it on location when needed. Another advantage of a battery-powered portable device is that static from power line voltage won't be a problem. After you get started and begin playing around, you'll be surprised at the sounds that you can create with ordinary household objects. Be creative—innovate! Sound effects are an art form unto itself. Although your dinner guests may think you've gone mad as they regard your meditative squeezing of the dish soap bottle, don't worry about it. You know you are right! When amplified, it will make a nice whoosh. Great for fast limb movement of that character doing a karate chop.

Backgrounds and Scenery

In Flash, you work in an area that is called the Stage (or Movie) area. For broadcast (or any other kind for that matter) animation it is better to think of it as the viewfinder of a camera. The main difference between this camera and the traditional kind, or even those used in 3D animation, is this: *You can't move it.* So, to give the illusion of camera movement, everything within the view must move. This is not as hard as it might seem with Flash's capability to use animated graphic symbols. A good example is in the Weber cartoon, in the scene where there's a malfunction in the control room and everything is shaking. Here's how this effect was created (as shown in Figure 37-1):

1. A graphic symbol of the entire scene of animation that was larger than the camera's view was made (so that white space wouldn't show at the edges),

2. The symbol was placed in the Main Timeline.

3. Every frame was keyframed and moved in a jarring fashion to give the jerking look needed to convey that everything had run amok.

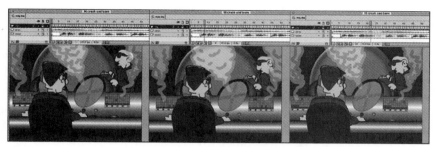

Figure 37-1: Here are a few shots from the control room scene of the Weber cartoon.

Bitmaps

As mentioned previously, when designing with Flash for the Web, the use of raster (bitmap) images should be kept to an absolute minimum. But for broadcast output there's no limit. Not only can you use as many images as you'd like (within system constraints), but doing so will make a richer, far more attractive finished product. And, unlike the .SWF format, when output as raster video, animations built with such bitmap image intensity will always play at the proper frame rate. So move, animate, scale, and rotate them — even play sequences of them. The sky and RAM are the only limits.

QuickTime limitations

With Flash 4, Flash expanded its import capabilities to include raster video — QuickTime and .AVI. When using video output for broadcast you can export to these formats too, but video that's been imported into Flash will not show up when output to the .SWF format. Unfortunately, Flash does not recognize alpha channels embedded in the QuickTime 32-bit animation codec (which supports traveling mattes, or alphas). However, you can use Mask layers on the video in Flash. Remember that Flash doesn't save the video file within the project file (thank goodness) — it makes a pointer to it instead. This addition brought tremendous functionality to Flash because animations can be keyed (composited) over (or behind) live video without having to recomposite in After Effects. To take advantage of this, keep your live video at the same frame rate as the Flash project. Note, however, that Flash will only export the video — audio from the video clip will need to be reapplied in a video-editing application. An alternate solution is to bring the video and audio tracks into Flash separately and to synchronize them there.

Building layered backgrounds in Flash with Photoshop

By using layers in Photoshop, multiplane shots are easily accomplished in Flash. Using layers is very important to the organization of the animation. Some shots in Weber employ more than 20 layers to keep things where they need to be. When designing backgrounds (or scenery, to be more precise) remember that, at some point, background elements may need to be foreground elements. For instance, in the introduction to Weber, the sky will always be in the background so it is on a layer furthest down in the stack. Unlike the sky, however, the pier, which is also a background object, may sometimes need to be in the foreground to facilitate movement of the character either in front or behind it. Thus, the pier gets a layer (actually a group of layers) of it's own, placed further up in the layer stack, above the sky. When creating such backgrounds, use of Photoshop and alpha channels delivers the most versatility. When using Photoshop for scenery elements, it's mandatory to work in layers and to save a master file with all layers intact. Elements can then be exported to individual files (with alpha channels) as needed. (Retaining the master layered Photoshop file gives you maximum options later, if edits or changes occur. It can also be used as a resource for subsequent animations, so don't flatten or discard your master layered Photoshop file. Instead, number and archive it!) Why the alpha channels? When translating the Photoshop elements into Flash vector scenery they automatically mask themselves — so a little preplanning in Photoshop can save lots of time later.

Flash Mask layers

Whoops! You got to a point where you didn't use layers and now you need a mask. Some situations may be either too complicated or else unforeseeable in the original design. Flash Mask layers can come to the rescue. Here's the good news: You can mask (and animate the mask) interactively with the other elements while in Flash. The bad news is that you can't feather (soften the edges) the mask. In the Weber cartoon, an example where masks are used to good effect is the ending, where black circles in as the scene closes.

Long pans

Long pans are a standard device of animated cartoons, as when Fred Flintstone runs through the house and furniture keeps zipping past (that must be one looooong living room, it just keeps rockin'). This can be done in a couple of ways in Flash. For landscape backgrounds, it's usually best to first create a very wide bitmap of the landscape and then to Motion Tween it horizontally, with keyframes for stopping and starting as needed within the tween. If something is either falling or ascending, use a tall bitmap and Motion Tween vertically. Another solid technique is to create art of the objects that will pan (such as clouds) and then loop them as the background layer, across the view. A good example of this is the chase scene from the Weber cartoon, which is shown in Figure 37-2. To get smooth results when using looping, don't use easing in or out with the tween setup. Also, to maintain constant speed, maintain the exact number of frames between the keyframes. Then, copy the tween by Alt (Option) dragging the selected tween frames to the desired area in the timeline. Repeat copying until you've covered the time needed.

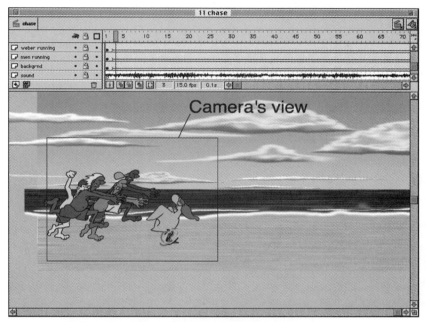

Figure 37-2: The chase scene from the Weber cartoon

Multiplane pans

To provide 3D-motion depth during the pan, keep this rule in mind: An object that is further away appears to move slower (than a nearer object) as it moves across the view. This takes some experimenting to get it right, but once mastered, this will add a professional touch to your animations. For example, in a 100-frame pan:

✦ The sky moves very slowly, 100 pixels total

✦ The water moves more quickly, 125 pixels total

✦ The character on the beach moves more quickly than the water, 150 pixels total

✦ A parked car in the immediate foreground moves most rapidly, 250 pixels total

Blurring to simulate depth

The multiplane camera was used in early Disney films to give a feeling of depth in the animation of flat artwork. There was physical space between the individual cels when photographed. By using a short depth of field lens, the artwork that was further away from the lens lost focus slightly. (You may have noticed this in still photography yourself.) If you set up your scenery using bitmaps, you can recreate this effect. A good example of this is the pier scene from the Weber cartoon, which is shown in Figure 37-3. In Photoshop, it's a simple case of using incrementally higher doses of Gaussian blur on the layers of your scenery that are further way. The further the object is, the more blur that is applied—just be sure that the blur is applied to the alpha channel that Flash will use in compositing. Use this technique as a photographer brings attention to the element in the shot that is in focus. Using it in animation tends to generate the illusion of depth. However, using it in the foreground can also portray various elements such as fog.

Figure 37-3: The opening pier scene from the Weber cartoon

Some Cartoon Animation Basics

In the world of film, movies are shot at 24 fps (frames per second), while in video and 3D animation 30 fps is the norm. But for cartoons 12 to 15 fps is all that's needed. The cartoon language of motion that we've all learned since childhood has taught our minds to expect this slightly jumpy quality of motion in a cartoon. As an animator, this is good for you, because 15 fps means half the amount of hand drawing work that 30 fps requires. It also means that you can get your cartoon done within your lifetime and maybe take a day off here and there. Actually, there are a lot of scenes in which as few as three drawings per second will suffice—depending on how well you can express motion with your art or drawing. The rule of motion here is that things that move quickly require fewer frames (drawings), while things that move slowly require more frames. This is the main reason you'll hardly ever see slow-motion sequences in cartoons. Broadcast cartoons have lots of fast-paced motion. Fewer drawings are produced more quickly and are less costly. These are very significant factors when battling budgets and deadlines.

Expressing motion and emotion

The hardest part of animation is expressing motion and emotion. Learn to do this well and it will save you time and make your work stand out above the rest. One of the best exercises you can do in this respect is to simply watch the world around you as though your eyes were a camera, clicking off frames. Videotaping cartoons and advancing through them at single-frame speed is also a revealing practice. (If you have digitizing capabilities, there's nothing better than capturing a cartoon to your hard drive and then analyzing the results, as you get a more stable frame this way.) If you employ Flash's capability to import raster video, you can use actual video as your guide and even practice drawing on top of it. While this is good for getting the mechanics of motion down, it's really just a start.

Exaggerate everything! After all, this is what makes it a cartoon. Tex Avery, whom we mentioned earlier, created cartoons that revolutionized animation with overblown and hilarious motion. You can read about him at `www.brightlightsfilm.com/22/texavery.html`.

Anticipation

Anticipation is a technique that is used when characters are about to do something, like take off running. Before lunging into the sprint, characters slowly back up, loading all their motion into their feet until their motion reverses and sends them blasting off in the other direction. In a more subtle form, this is shown in Figure 37-4, when Weber takes flight from his perch on the pier.

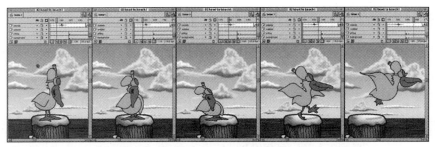

Figure 37-4: Anticipation is used to accentuate Weber's take off

Weight

Keep the weight of objects in mind. This helps to make your cartoon believable. A feather falls more slowly than the anvil. The feather also eases out (slows down) before landing gently on the ground, while the anvil slams the ground with such force as to make a gashing dent in it. Humor can play a role here by giving extreme weight to things that do not have it (or vice versa) thereby causing a surprise in the viewer's preconceived notion of what should happen — and this is the seed of humor.

Overlapping actions

Visualize a jogging Santa Claus, belly bouncing up and down with each step. Because of its weight, the belly is still on a downward motion when the rest of the body is being pushed upward by the thrust of the push-off leg. This opposing motion is known as *overlapping actions*. Another good example of overlapping actions is the scene in which the muscle-man bully catches Weber and wrings his neck. A good example of this is shown in Figure 37-5. Note that, as the bully thrusts forward, Weber's body reacts in the opposite direction . . . only to catch up just in time for the thrust to reverse and go the other way.

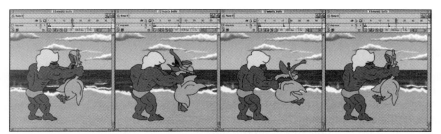

Figure 37-5: Overlapping actions are often used to accentuate movement.

Blurring to simulate motion

Blurring is a technique or device that animators use to signify a motion that's moving faster than the frame rate can physically show. In film, this manifests itself as a blurred out of focus subject (due to the subject moving faster than the camera's shutter can capture). You may have already employed this effect in Photoshop, with the motion blur filter. In cartoon animation, blurring is often (and easily) described with blur lines. Blur lines are an approximation of the moving subject utilizing line or brush strokes that trail off in the direction that the subject is coming from. When used properly, this great device can save hours of tedious drawing. A good example of animated motion blur can be seen in Figure 37-6, which shows the opening sequence in which the word *Weber* turns into Weber the pelican.

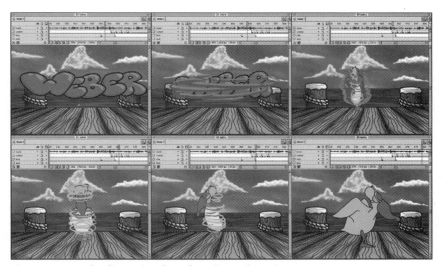

Figure 37-6: Blur lines simulate the effect of motion.

Animator's Keys and Inbetweening

Earlier in this book you learned about two Flash animation methods: frame-by-frame and tweening. This section focuses on traditional cartoonist frame-by-frame techniques together with traditional cartoonist's keys and inbetween methods to accomplish frame-by-frame animation. Despite the similarity of terminology, this topic heading does not refer to a menu item in Flash. Instead, it should be noted that animation programs such as Flash have derived some of their terminology (and methods) from the vintage world of hand-drawn cel animation. Vintage animators used the methods of keys and inbetweening to determine what action a character will take in a given shot. It's akin to sketching, but with motion in mind. In this sense, keys are the high points, or ultimate positions, in a given sequence of motion. Thus, in vintage animation:

✦ Keys are the pivotal drawings or highlights that determine how the motion will play out.

✦ Inbetweens are the fill-in drawings that smooth out the motion.

In Flash, the usual workflow is to set keyframes for a symbol and then to tween the intervening frames, which harnesses the power of the computer to fill the inbetweens. Although this is fine for many things, it is inadequate for many others. For example, a walk sequence is too subtle and complex to be tweened by a computer. So, let's take a look at the traditional use of keys and inbetweens for generating a simple walk sequence that starts and ends according to a natural pace, yet will also generate a walk loop.

Walk cycles (or walk loops)

Earlier in the book, you learned about using Poser to create a walk loop using a 3D model. 3D animation is a wonderful practice that is coming of age in films such as *Jurassic Park, A Bug's Life,* and *Toy Story.* But perhaps you've noticed that a focus on humans is missing from such films. That's because humans are incredibly difficult to animate convincingly in 3D. Why? Because computers are too perfect — too stiff. Human movement is delightfully sloppy — and we are keenly aware of this quality of human movement, both on a conscious and a subconscious level. (Another term for this is body language.) This factor drives the 3D animators nuts when they try to create human characters. Interestingly, these same factors lead to a plus for the 2D hand-drawn animator: Because our hands are also sloppy when drawing, we find that there's emotion in the imprecision of a hand-drawn stroke — which brings us back to keys. Keys should be loosely sketched and then refined and inbetweened. Refer to the following diagrams, which express this concept in visual terms.

Notice that these keys are quickly drawn ovals approximating a woman at the high points in a walk cycle. This was drawn on a layer in Flash with a light gray pencil. Next, we'll lock that layer and create a new layer on top of it. Then, using the pencil in Ink Mode with black as our color to ink it in, we'll refine this character to a more finished look, as shown in Figure 37-7. Once we're satisfied with the look, the Fast Sketch layer can be discarded.

Now the keys for the finished walk cycle are set. However, upon playback (although she walks!) it's an extremely jerky and unnatural gait. So, where do we start if we want to "fix" the walk? Do you remember the rule discussed earlier, that the slower the movement the more frames (or drawings) would be needed? A good starting point for a normal walk cycle is about 1.5 seconds or 24 frames at 15 fps. This is timed from when the left foot pushes off the ground until just before it returns to its original position. Why not go back to its original position? Because this would cause two frames to be almost the same and — in a loop — would introduce a stutter to the walk. (Of course, that might be OK if you're animating a stumbling drunk, but here we want smooth.) So, depending on the speed that you want the subject to walk, you can determine the amount of inbetweens you need to draw.

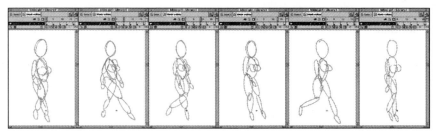

Figure 37-7: Here are some rough finished keys from a walk cycle prior to playback.

Repeaters

You may notice there are some blank, nonkeyed frames (repeaters) in the timeline. These were used to economize drawing time and to slow the walk of the character in the previous figure even more. If a speedier walk were called for, we would simply delete these repeater frames. A good basic rule about repeaters is to add no more than one repeater frame between keys; adding more causes the smoothness of motion to fall apart. If the motion must proceed more slowly, then you have to draw more inbetweens. Fortunately, with Flash onion skinning (the capability to see before and after the current time in a dimmed graphic), which is discussed in Chapter 8, "Exploring the Timeline," the addition of a few more inbetweens is not an enormous task. In fact, onion skinning is indispensable for doing inbetweens, and even for setting keys. One pitfall of onion skinning is the tendency to trace what you're seeing. It takes practice to ignore the onion lines and use them only as a guide. You need to remember that the object is to draw frames that have slight, but meaningful differences between them. Although it can mean a lot more drawing, it's well worth it. Because you'll use your walk (and running) cycles over and over during the course of your cartoon, do them well.

Tip

One real time-saver in creating a walk cycle is to isolate the head and animate it separately via layers or grouping. This trick helps to prevent undesirable quivering facial movements that often result from imperfectly traced copies. Similarly, an accessory like a hat or brief case can be isolated on a separate layer. Finally, if the character will be talking while walking, make a copy of the symbol and eliminate the mouth. Later, the mouth will be added back as a separate animation. We cover this later in the section on lip-synching.

Types of walks

So far, we've covered the mechanics of a walk cycle. But for animators, the great thing about walking — in all its forms — is what it can communicate about the character. We read this body language constantly every day without really thinking about it. We often make judgments about people's mood, mission, and character based on the way that they carry themselves. Picture the young man, head held high, confidently striding briskly with direction and purpose: He is in control of the situation and will accomplish the task set before him. But if we throw in a little wristwatch checking and awkward arm movements, then that same walk becomes a stressful "I'm late." This late gait suggests a very different story of the person who didn't plan ahead. Or, witness the poor shlub — back hunched, arms dangling at his sides. He moves along, dragging his feet as if they each weigh a thousand pounds. That tells the sad story of a person who's a basket case. Finally, what about a random pace, feet slipping from side to side, sometimes crisscrossing, other times colliding, while the body moves in a stop-and-start fashion as if it were just going along for the ride? Is that someone who couldn't figure out when to leave the bar? Of course, these are extreme examples. Walks are actually very subtle and there are limitless variations on the basic forms. But if you begin to observe and analyze these details as they occur in everyday life, then you'll be able to instill a higher order in your animations. Simply take time to look. It's all there waiting for you to use in your next animation. Then remember that because it's a cartoon, *exaggerate!*

Coloring the art

Now, to color in the character between the inked lines. In traditional animation, this was the most tedious and time-consuming job of all: endless thousands of cels to be hand painted and dried. Most often, armies of low-paid workers in far away lands did it. But with Flash it's a snap! That's because of Flash's wonderful (and sometimes mysterious) gap-jumping fill tool, the Paint Bucket. With Flash, you never run out of paint, and it dries instantly — a real time-saver to be sure!

The model sheet

Here's a coloring time-saver that you can use for yourself within Flash: Use a fully colored model of your character at the start of a cycle or scene. This will serve as a color model and will be discarded when the cycle or shot is finished. It's very important to keep a model sheet, which is an archive of color models — finished, fully colored characters — to maintain consistent color across the span of the project. (It's also quite useful at the start of future projects.) "Why," you may ask, "is this necessary now that Flash has color sets?"

Even though Flash has the ability to save color sets, it's still difficult to remember which yellow was used on a certain area of the character, especially when there are ten different yellows in the palette. Such a color mistake — even a slight shade off — will cause unsightly flicker on playback. The Dropper makes no mistakes. So, to develop good animation habits, start a model sheet. When you begin a scene, copy the appropriate color model and paste it into the cycle, setting it off to the side of the active art in the first frame (if needed, ungroup it). Acquire the color that you need with the Dropper Tool and then set about the business of filling.

When filling, we've found that the most efficient method is to go through the entire cycle with one color, filling all objects of that color. Then go back to the beginning and sweep through again, doing the next color. This method saves you the tedium of constantly having to change the Paint Bucket's color, and also minimizes the possibility of mistakes. If some places fill while others don't, you'll probably need to adjust the Paint Bucket Gap Size Modifier.

Gap problems

There are, however, times when you can't find the gaps and the Paint Bucket just won't work. In this case, keep looking because the gaps are there. But if it just doesn't work, no matter how much you zoom in and click with the Paint Bucket, then you may need to zoom in and use the Arrow Tool to close the gap by adjusting a stroke. In a situation in which it's not aesthetically pleasing to do that, use the Brush Tool (set to the same fill color and to paint fills only) to fill the gaps manually. Perhaps this would be the case on a head and neck that you don't want connected to the body (remember earlier about the advantages of animating the head separately). You would paint a stroke of fill connecting the inked lines and then fill. This is a great tool, it's a huge time-saver, but a little mysterious at times.

Speed coloring

A good way to speed up the coloring process is to allocate one of the mouse buttons (if you have a programmable mouse) to perform the keyboard shortcut for step forward advancing (which is the > key). If you have a pressure-sensitive graphics tablet, then you can allocate a button on the pen to do the same. With a setup like this, you can leave the cursor in pretty much the same place and click-fill, click-advance; click-fill, click-advance . . . and so on.

Temporary backgrounds

Another problem that's easily solved is the process of filling areas with white. If you're like most people, you've accepted the default background color of white — which makes it impossible to distinguish when filling white areas. In this case, it's monstrously helpful to create a very light color that you don't plan to use in the final art, something like a light grayish puke-pink. While coloring, temporarily change the background color in the Movie Properties dialog (Modify ➪ Movie) to this "color" for the background of the entire movie. This makes it much easier to see what you're doing when using white as a fill color for objects such as eyeballs, teeth, and clouds. Then, when you're done coloring, you can set the background color back to white.

Flash Tweening

You can use Flash tweening to help your cartooning. Now that you've created some symbols, such as the walk cycle, here's where you can save a great deal of time making them slink and prance across the view without drawing every tedious frame. The hard hand drawing work is done, now you'll choreograph the character. Because once you've built a library of various walks, runs, turnarounds, and stand stills (a piece of walk cycle that ends with the character just standing still), you can use computer power to help you tell a story. Remember that you can always create more symbols of the character as needed — in fact, you can steal from other symbols to create new ones.

Panning

Use the panning techniques discussed earlier in this chapter to get your walking symbol looping, stationary in the middle of the view. Then move the background elements to give the illusion of the camera following alongside the walking character, a sort of dolly. It usually requires a little experimentation to get the motion of the background to match the stride of the step. If the timing isn't correct, you'll notice that the feet will seem to skate across the ground. To fix this, adjust the speed of the background by either increasing or decreasing the number of frames in the tween of the background. Another trick is to set the walking symbol to start at one end of the view and proceed to the other by tweening the symbol itself. What's really cool is to use a mixture of both. Again, to get it just right, experiment.

Instance swapping

There comes a time when the star of your show must stop walking (or running, or whatever he's doing) and reach into his pocket to pull out a hotrod car and make his getaway. This is where instance swapping comes in. At the end of the tween, create a keyframe on the next frame (the frame immediately following the last keyframe in the tween), and then turn off motion tweening for that keyframe in the Frame panel. This causes the symbol to stop at whichever frame the cycle ended on in the timeline. To swap the symbol, follow these steps:

1. Click the symbol to select it.

2. Open the Instance Panel (click the Instance tab on the Frame Panel that you have open).

3. Click the Swap Symbol button.

4. In the Swap Symbol dialog, select the symbol that you want to replace it with (in this case, the one where he reaches into his pocket).

5. Click OK.

If you loop the play of the symbol, you can also choose the frame on which the symbol's cycle will start. Other choices are limiting the symbol to play once and playing just a single frame (still). You must be sure that Synchronize is unchecked in the Frame Panel — otherwise your newly chosen instance will not show up; the old one will remain there instead.

This procedure may have been more easily accomplished in Flash 4. The new work flow is impacted by these considerations: (a) In the Frame Panel, under the options for Motion Tweens, the Synchronize option now replaces the former Synchronize Symbols option — but it does function the same. By Right-clicking/Ctrl+clicking a frame to invoke the contextual pop-up menu, and then selecting Create Motion Tween, you'll find that Synchronize and Snap checked by default in the Frame Panel. (b) *However*, if you select the frame and then navigate to the Frame Panel and create a motion tween there, then Synchronize and Snap are not checked by default. The second procedure is the preferred method for accomplishing the swap symbols technique described previously. To repeat, when you change a symbol instance on a motion tween, if the Synchronize box is checked, the old symbol instance will not be replaced with the new one — which is Swap Symbol failure. (c) Furthermore, double-clicking an instance will no longer bring up the desired instance controls. You must now fish those controls out of the Instance Panel. The Swap Symbol button is the little button at the far left with an icon of little arrows, a square, and a circle.

Finally, unless you've drawn all your symbols to perfect scale with each other, this new symbol may not fit exactly. No problem! To fix this, simply enable onion skinning from the Main Timeline, and set it to show the previous frame (the frame the tween ended on). Now you can align and scale the new symbol to match the ghosted image. We can't begin to tell you how much you'll use this simple instance swapping function when you create your cartoon. This is one of the unique functions that sets Flash apart from all other cel-type animation programs. After you have a modest library of predrawn actions, the possibilities for combining them are endless.

Motion guides

Although not terribly useful for tweening a walking character, the Flash motion guide function is tops for moving inanimate objects. If your character needs to throw a brick, a straight tween between points and some blur lines will do fine. If he needs to lob that brick over a fence to clang a pesky neighbor, then the use of motion guides is the ticket. Here's how:

1. Turn the brick into a graphic symbol if you haven't already. This makes it easier to make changes to the brick later.

2. Create a Motion Guide layer.

3. Draw an arch from start to destination. This is best done by drawing a line with the Line Tool and then retouching it with the Arrow Tool until you have bent it into the desired arch. This method keeps the motion smooth. (To use the Pencil Tool to draw the motion guide would create too many points and can cause stuttering in the motion.)

Although your brick is flying smoothly, something's wrong. Again, the computer made things too darned smooth. You could insert a few keyframes in the tween and rotate slightly here and there to give it some wobble. But that's still not convincing. You want this brick to mean business! Here's what to do: Because the brick is already a symbol, go back to the brick symbol and edit it, adding a few more frames. Don't add more than three or four frames, otherwise this will slow it down. At each of these new frames, mess up the brick a little here and there; differ the perspectives a little from one frame to another. Then, when you go back to your Main Timeline, the brick should be twitching with vengeance as it sails towards its target.

Lip-synching

Now, here's the part we've all been waiting for . . . a word from our character. If done properly, lip-synching is where a character can really spring to life. This is accomplished by drawing the various mouth positions that are formed for individual phonemes, which are the basic units of sound that make up a spoken word. Then these phonemes are melded together into morphemes, which are distinct units of a word, like a syllable. Morphemes are then strung together over the course of a sentence to present the illusion of a talking, animated character. Huh? Phonemes? Morphemes? What the devil are we talking about? Well, it's really not as complicated as all that but it's important to know how a spoken word is made. Most languages, although populated with thousands of words, are really made up from around 30 to 60 distinct sounds, or phonemes. For cartooning, these phonemes can be reduced to about 10 basic mouth positions. Some of these positions can be repeated for more than one sound because many sounds share roughly the same mouth positions. Although there are more subtleties in the real world, for cartoons, reliance upon transitions between mouth positions is convincing enough.

Earlier, we suggested that the face in an action (walk) cycle should be drawn without a mouth. That's because this method facilitates the use of layers (in the timeline) for the addition of the lip-sync. To do this, create a layer above the character so that you can freely draw in the mouth positions needed to add lip-sync. It's also very helpful to put the voice track on another separate layer directly beneath the Mouth layer. This makes it easy to see the waveform of the sound while you draw — which gives important clues to where and when the sound occurs visually.

Since Flash 4, Flash has had the capability to scrub the timeline, which means that you can drag the Playhead, or current frame indicator, and hear the sound as you drag. This functionality is limited to streaming sounds, which means that the sounds have their Sync option in the Sound panel set to Streaming. The capability to hear the sound and see the animation in real time is an important tool for lip-synching. This real-time feedback is critical for getting the timing just right. There's nothing worse than being plagued with O.G.M.S. (the Old Godzilla Movie Syndrome), in which the mouth doesn't match the sounds coming from it. To scrub most effectively, here's a hint: If you've been following this chapter's advice, then you've probably loaded a ton of moving bitmaps into your scene, which can be a serious hindrance to playback within the Flash authoring environment. To overcome this drag and to get real-time playback at the full-frame rate, simply hide all layers except the mouth layers and turn off antialiasing.

Shape morphing is not for lip-sync

You may be asking, "What about using shape morphing to save time in lip-synching?" Well, shape morphing is a wonderful tool but, for lip-sync, it's more hassle than it's worth. Your mouth drawings will become very complicated because they consist of lips, tongue, teeth, and facial features. Furthermore, because shape morphing only seems to work predictably on the simplest of shapes out of the box, shape hinting is required. Thus, by the time you've set all hinting (and even hinting heavily still leaves you with a mess at times), you might have had an easier time and obtained a better result (with greater control) if you had drawn it by hand.

Expression and lip-sync

As regards control and expression, it's important to remember to use the full range of expression when drawing the talking mouths. Happy, sad, or confused — these give life to your character. Furthermore, always emphasize mouth movements on those syllables that correspond with spikes of emotion in the voice track. These sections usually have a spike in the waveform that's easily recognized in the voice track. This device helps to convince the viewer that proper sync is happening.

Lip-sync tricks

There are a few more tricks to help ease the load. When characters talk, they do not always have to be looking you square in the face. Try lip-synching the first few words to establish that the character is speaking, and then obscure the character's mouth in some natural way. The relay man, shown in Figure 37-8, in Weber's intestine is a good example of this. The head and body bobs with the words being said, but the microphone obscures his mouth in a natural way. This saved a bunch of time but did not detract from his purpose in the story line. Here, a bit of design savvy saved a lot of work.

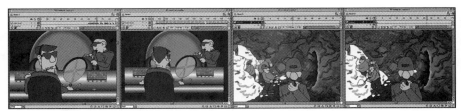

Figure 37-8: Lip-synching tricks include economy of effort, such as having the character begin to speak and then turn away naturally.

Many animators use a mirror placed nearby and mouth (act out) the words they are trying to draw. This is extremely helpful when learning to do lip-sync. It is also of great help in mastering facial expressions. Just try not to get too wrapped up in drawing every nuance you see. Sometimes less is more. After you get over feeling a bit foolish about talking to yourself in the mirror you'll be on your way to animating good expressive lip-synced sequences. Another trick that you can use to ease the load is to reuse lip-sync. Do this by copying frames from previous stretches of mouth movements to new locations where the words are the same, and then tweak the copied parts to fit the new dialog. Still, there is no magic lip-sync button. Even with all these tricks, effective lip-syncing is hard work. It's also one of the more tedious tasks in animation, as it demands a great deal of practice to get it right.

Synching with music and sound effects

In the introduction, Weber dances to the theme song, shuffling through a Michael Jackson moonwalk, and then spinning to the scratch of the synthesizer. This really helps to gel things because the action on screen syncs to the sound (music or effect) and helps to draw in the viewer. If you've already succeeded with lip-synching work, then this type of synching is easy. All that's going on here is a bit of instance swapping set to the beat of the music. Study your music waveform for visual clues then scrub it for the sound and you're sure to find the exact section where the change in action (instance swap) needs to go. You don't have to make your sync tight to every note. To keep the shot engaging, sync to the highlights, or hard beats.

Adding sound effects is really the fun part. It's easy and highly effective. Either working from your storyboard, or as you're animating, you'll know where you want to insert a sound effect. For example, when the anvil hits the head, a CLANK is needed there. If the effect you need is on hand, great! Just make sure it has the necessary duration, and then plug it in at the frame where it should start. For broadcast animation you'll set the sound sync pop-up of the Sound panel to Streaming for the soundtrack exclusively. In addition to the use of separate layers for each voice track, it's wise to confine your sound effects to a layer or two. This leads to less confusion; yet using two layers enables more than one sound effect to occur at a time.

For the following Expert Tutorial, we've supplied a short track for your use, lip_track.wav or lip_track.aif, which you'll find in the ch32 folder of the CD-ROM. These tracks include the major sounds used in the English language.

Expert Tutorial: Lip-synching Cartoons, *by Bill Turner*

These days, there's an abundance of Flash-authored cartoons on the Internet, so it's hard not to get caught up in the spirit and try one yourself—after all, cartooning is easy . . . just scribble some lines, color it, and there-you-go! Whoops—not so fast. "Houston, we have a *problem*." Too much of this animation looks like junk! Like a foreign film that's been dubbed, except worse, because all the actors' lips were numbed with Novocain.

For animated characters to really come alive, you need to know how to do lip-sync. To get quality lip-sync effects, you either need to draw them yourself or hire someone else to do it for you. Although this tutorial can't possibly cover every circumstance known to human communication, it can get you started on the road to lip service. There are some prequalifications: (a) you must be able to draw in Flash, which usually means drawing with a tablet, preferably a pressure-sensitive graphics tablet (such as a Wacom tablet), and (b) you need to have a recorded voice track on its own layer in Flash.

Because lip-sync can't be described in a simple a, b, c routine tutorial, you'll be required to improvise—in your style of drawing. I can't tell you how to do that. Style comes from years of practice and experimentation. But if you do know how to draw and you do have a style, then the intention here is to provide a context in which you might discover the basic trick of lip-sync.

The major sounds, known as phonemes, are less numerous than you might think. It's how these sounds meld together to become words and sentences that add an aura of complexity. Although one might surmise, from the alphabet, that there are 26 sounds, there aren't nearly that many. That's because many letters have the same basic mouth shape, movement, and pronunciation. And because we're now in the land of cartoons, we can simplify even further—the really great cartoons are often the simple ones built of tireless simple reinterpretation.

In this tutorial, to keep it simple, we'll deal with the two dominant views of talking heads (not David Byrne's): profile and face forward. A face forward talking head is probably the easiest to animate in Flash because the mouth can be animated on a layer that's situated in the layer stack above a drawing of a mouthless head. A talking head in profile is more difficult because of the need to redraw the portion of the face that extends down from the nose, to and including the chin, for *every* frame. Of course, including nose-to-chin movements can also enhance the animation of a face forward talker, and doing so would make for a more expressive animation. But we want to move quickly here.

In the figure, you see a mouthless head (provided on the CD-ROM for both demonstration and practice) in both of the basic orientations: face forward and profile. Note the playback head is at frame #12, at the beginning of the word, Meyers.

Continued

Continued

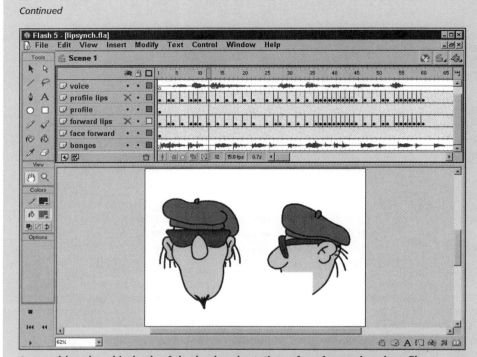

A mouthless head in both of the basic orientations: face forward and profile

To help get you started, I've supplied a fully functional .FLA file for you to work on, with the base character already drawn. The spoken test line reads, "Zinkle Meyers is very talented on the bongo drums. Flip Flap beats his hands on the smooooth skins. Dig the rhythm. Excellent!" Creating lip-sync for this line requires a number of mouth positions. To demonstrate the concepts, the first sentence of this test line is supplied, already drawn to lip-sync. It is your task to draw the mouth positions for the remainder of the spoken test.

The Sync Option

If you were setting this file up from scratch, you'd want to start by placing the voice sound track on its own layer on the timeline. You'd rename this layer with a meaningful name, such as voice, and then, in the Sound Panel, you'd set the Sync option to Stream.

Never use Event as the Sync option for any sound that must sync to the Flash timeline. Otherwise, the timing of the voice will not be locked to the frame rate, meaning that the mouth drawings may not appear simultaneously with their appropriate sounds, thus losing sync. (For a full explanation of the streaming versus event sound settings, refer to Chapter 15, "Importing and Editing Sounds in Flash.")

Getting into Sync

The best way to understand lip-sync is to have the sample file open. Note that there is a visible waveform (the little squiggly stuff) that shows where the peaks and valleys of the sound occur across the timeline. Note, too, that the voice is brought in as a separate asset. It's on it's own layer, separate from background sounds or music. Otherwise, it would be impossible to see the voice within the waveform if it were premixed with other sounds before bringing it into Flash. If you're producing a cartoon show, it's best to have each character recorded separately, particularly in cases in which they may talk over each other simultaneously. This separation gives you more control when animating. In fact, the entire animation is broken into layers for ease of editing. There's at least one layer for each major element. You might also note that the bongo sound track is set to event. This is useful while authoring because it mutes the track when scrubbing the timeline to listen for timings in the voice track. If both were set to streaming it would be more difficult to concentrate on the voice alone. (You must remember to reset this option to Stream when synching is completed, or you could just delete that layer until after you are done animating the mouth.)

The Phonemes

Now for the phonemes. There are several standard mouth positions for most of the major sounds. Although this is not a rigid rule, it does provide a good basis from which to expand into greater mastery of lip-sync. First, you'll note that the word Meyers begins on frame 12 of the animation. The mmmm sound is best represented with the bottom lip tucked slightly under the top lip. Try saying mmmm to see for yourself. In the word Meyers, this mmmm sound lasts two frames and is then followed by the long *i* sound. Notice that we didn't sync the word as it is spelled, e-y-e, because that's more complicated than it needs to be. The word Meyers is usually pronounced M-I-ER-Z, with the ER being just an ease-out (mouth holds shape but gets slightly smaller as phoneme trails off) of the long i sound. The word ends with the Z phoneme, which is simply drawn with the mouth slightly open, and the tongue at the top of the mouth.

In the next section of speech, the "very talented" part is a fast-moving set of syllables, so every available frame is needed to represent it. Here, you'll notice that most of the movement occurs when the tongue engages the roof of the mouth for both the T and L phoneme. Now, because the T and L are nearly the same mouth position, you can use the luxury of duplicating frames. Similarly, the V sound requires the same basic mouth formation as the M sound, so you could copy this one as well from the Meyers word. Although the B sound, in bongos, uses nearly the same mouth as M and V, we don't copy that one. Here, we draw a new mouth to add a bit of chaos because we don't want the mouth to look like a machine. The logic behind deciding which part to copy and which part to make new drawings for is a large part of the art of lip-sync. In short, it's all about balancing how much new artwork you really want to do, while avoiding obvious repetition.

Continued

Continued

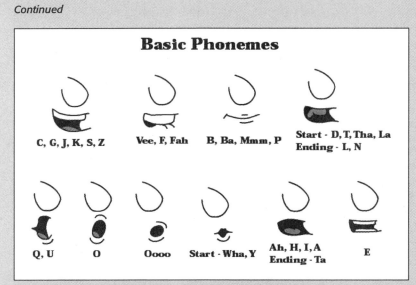

A few basic phonemes combine to create lip-synched speech.

Now that I've given you an insight into how this is done, I've left the rest of the phrase for you to complete. To accomplish this, you'll probably want to reuse many of the supplied mouth positions to sync the remaining voice. Remember that timing is the most crucial part. You can determine where a new mouth position is needed, or where the mouth needs work, by slowly scrubbing the timeline. Then, if you need new mouths, simply draw them in. We highly recommend doing this drawing yourself, because this practice will start you on your way to becoming a master of lip-sync.

Originally from Baltimore, Maryland, Bill remembers the Van Halen cover of "You Really Got Me" as the most memorable song of the year that he graduated high school. As the father of the Weber cartoon and the primary force behind the new cartoon series, *The Murky's* — both produced by Turnertoons Productions, of Melbourne, Florida — Bill's single most favorite thing to do is "to make people laugh and reflect at the same time." He was introduced to Flash by responding to an ad in MacWeek soliciting beta testers for a new program, which was then called Futuresplash. Bill was the contributing author for this chapter.

Finishing Up

When you have a shot done it's often helpful to see it play at full speed. Unfortunately, Flash is unable keep up with all of the sounds, bitmaps, and complicated vectors that go into broadcast-quality animation. Plus it's impossible — even with the most macho of processors — to play the shot at full speed, without hiding a bunch of elements. But, hey, you're the director of this masterpiece, it's time for dailies, and you need to see it all.

The best way to do this and to cut down on file size is to export a raster video at 320×240 pixels, using the standard QuickTime Video codec (Mac) or the Microsoft Video 1 codec. These codecs are for draft purposes only, so it may have banding and artifacts from compression, but the point is to generate something that even a machine that's ill-equipped for high-end video output can display easily at full frame-rate speed. This method will be of great help in revealing those areas of the animation that still need further tweaking and work before going out to the final published version. The general movement and pace of the shot will make itself known. Look for errors such as unintended jumpiness in frames, and color shifts or inconsistencies between views. Furthermore, your lip-synching efforts will either be a glory to behold or a disaster in need of medical attention. Other things, such as sound clipping (pops in high volume sound) also become apparent here. To put it bluntly, if the preview makes you cringe, then it needs work — if not, you're ready for final output.

Final output

Now, after checking endlessly you're ready for the final video file of the shot to be rendered. Back it up one more time. Then, when you've safely archived your final project file, it's time to choose the codec that your playback equipment can use and render one out for the tube. Then, when you have rendered all your shots at full screen, you can take them into Premiere or After Effects for more detailed editing and tweaking, utilizing all the power that these applications offer. For example, you might want music to play gently in the background across all of your scenes. Although this would be impossible to piece together with separate Flash project files, it's a snap in Premiere. Again, the possibilities are endless.

Expert Tutorial: 2D Character Animation, by *Richard Bazley*

Until recently, the process of creating animation has been labor intensive and extremely expensive. I've worked on many successful animated films that cost millions of dollars, and have required several years and hundreds of artists to complete. Similarly, an animated short would have also involved numerous artists and high costs. Yet, with advancements in technology and the speed and efficiency of computers, much of this has changed. Now, with Flash 5, one artist can be the producer, director, animator, effects artist, layout artist, scene planner, color stylist, and editor.

Continued

Continued

A few years ago, I storyboarded a short film. I had British cartoonist Ronald Searle's particular illustrative style in mind, which involves having the characters drawn with a very fluid line with a lively thick and thin quality to it. To create this look with the tools of traditional animation and to animate those lines would be a nightmare. Although it has been done for the occasional commercial, the animator's original rough drawings would have to be painstakingly copied by specialist inkers. As well as being very time-consuming, the look of the line would also boil or shimmer, because it is practically impossible for a human to repeatedly copy this type of line without there being a difference.

However, I found that I could create this look almost effortlessly in Flash by drawing directly on the Wacom tablet. It was very spontaneous, as my own personal drawings are often in this style. I found that once you've drawn a line like this with Flash, you can create a motion tween and then scale, or roll, or do almost anything with the line—effortlessly. You can also copy and paste an image in seconds, whereas if you had to draw it again, it would take some time. When I found Flash, I immediately knew that I'd found a way to make my film the way I wanted to and that it would be groundbreaking in many ways. Once I'd found Flash, I began work on my animated short, *The Journal of Edwin Carp*, almost without delay.

There are two main approaches to creating 2D character animation: Full Animation and Limited Animation. Full Animation, also known as Classical Animation, is the type of animation found in all the Disney films. There, the movements are very fluid and the animator is more interested in the dynamics of motion as well as strong character acting. It often requires complete drawings for every frame of film, at the rate of 24 frames per second. (It is possible to do 12 drawings per second, but any fast movements require 24.) This is the most expensive form of animation. Limited Animation is just that—you limit the number of drawings that you do to save both time and money. Hannah and Barbara refined it, and their best example is *The Flintstones*. There you can see that parts of the body are separated and animated separately, so that other parts can be held for many frames at a time. The Japanese employ a slightly different technique where they might animate on "eights" which creates a kind of jerky movement so often found in anime. There are times when both techniques can be employed for artistic reasons, such as in *Peter Pan*. When Captain Hook is playing the piano, his body is held, his arms are on "twos," and his fingers are on "ones." The animator decided that the arms were fine on "two's" and that there would be no benefit in drawing them on "ones," so he employed a time-saving device. In creating my short film, I often employed this technique because it is so easy in Flash and yet it's still possible to maintain high artistic quality. Flash has so many strengths, especially in the interactive area, but those were not what interested me. I chose Flash because of its animation tools and its capability to manipulate shapes. Because I'm not designing for the Web, I don't worry about file size. I simply use Flash as an animator's tool to get what I want.

(Richard was kind enough to permit us to include the .SWF's of several scenes from his groundbreaking animated short, *The Journal of Edwin Carp*. You'll find them on the CD-ROM, in the Bazley folder, which is nested within the ch37 folder—if you refer to them as you read this tutorial, many of the principles that Richard describes will become much more clear.)

Reuse

One feature of Flash that is most useful for animation is the Library. For instance, I drew a moose head once from a front view and once from the side. I was then able to repeatedly drag this from the library to use in scene after scene without having to redraw it. With one side view drawn, I can use the Transform Tool to flip it vertically and then use it in another scene in which he faces the other way. When used intelligently, it's unlikely that the audience will notice, and for those classical animation purists, this does not affect the quality. (Just look at *Jungle Book*. You'll see plenty of reuse there.) I even created one scene in my movie for which I drew no new drawings; instead, I drew them all from my Library.

"Cheating" a Head Turn

I did this scene using three drawings! First, I drew the body on one layer, which is held. The background is simply a color on another level. I did one profile drawing and, using Transform, flipped it to face the other way. Then I drew one inbetween drawing. Instead of being a halfway drawing, although, this is a drawing of multiples in which it appears that the character has many eyes. (If you stop-frame *Who Framed Roger Rabbit* or any of the old Tex Avery shorts, you will see a lot of this technique.) Because this multiple drawing only shows for one frame, you won't actually see it, but you will *feel* it. Then to soften the movement into the next key, I copied the profile drawing and placed it two frames after the key, and then used the Scale Tool to narrow the face a little so that it appears to inbetween on the way out of the multiple. Then I did the same process before the next key. This is a little bit of a "cheat," because a little volume is lost in the scaling, and because the volume is something that you should try to maintain. But this is a quick scene and it delivers the desired effect. Rules can be broken, but it is best to know them first so that you know when and if you are creating a "cheat."

This drawing of multiples appears for only one frame, yet it contributes powerfully to the feeling of this scene.

Continued

Continued

Beauty in Simplicity

Sometimes less really is more. In the scene in which Edwin's mother runs down the stairs, I worked economically but to great effect by creating her run from six basic keys. First, I created the camera pan as it moves down the stairs. Then I drew one drawing of her facing right. Then, I created a Motion Tween and set her next keyframe out of shot on the right. This way I don't have to show her turn, but it also enhances the action to have her move in and out of camera. Then I used the Transform Tool to flip her the other way for the next keyframe. I repeated this going the other way down the next flight of steps, and then I repeated it once more. All this motion was created with only two drawings! I managed to get away with this because I used other elements to add interest, such as her shawl and dress blowing behind her. These were animated on single keyframes, but this sort of secondary action doesn't take long. I only economize on scenes like this if I think the result will work well. There are other occasions when it might be necessary to do a full run, but this is up to the discretion of the artist and filmmaker. Choose your shots and where you want to invest your energy. It can save you time and money.

Layers

One of the useful ways of creating apparently quite complex scenes in Flash is to use multiple background layers. By separating the components of your background, you can create a variety of camera moves, such as the pan discussed in the scene in which Edwin's mother runs downstairs. In another scene, I created the effect of a multiplane Truck-in, which is where the camera appears to zoom in. In the days of *Pinocchio* and *Fantasia* this effect was achieved with a complex multiplane camera that separated the different background levels onto different planes located at different distances from the camera. These background planes would be moved toward the camera at different speeds to create the illusion of depth. The problem with this process was that if any kind of mistake were made, it would all have to be shot again — often at the expense of several days work. This effect can be created in Flash in only a few minutes and, if you change your mind, you can go right back and change it. For this scene, I drew one line drawing of the attic, while separate drawings for the foreground elements, such as the bottles and other knick-knacks, were arranged on two subsequent levels. I returned to the first frame of the first attic level and created a motion tween. Then, on the last frame, I scaled the drawing up to where I wanted it. I then did this individually for each of the other elements, but made the nearer objects move more quickly, thus giving the illusion of movement through depth.

Animation Approach

For many reasons, I decided to use the Motion Tween as much as possible in my film. One, it is a very fast and economical way to animate. Two, it maintains the line quality, which was important to me. Three, the computer tweens with such ease! I occasionally use the Shape Tweens, but I found that, for my purposes, I have to keep the shapes as simple as possible; otherwise, Flash generates unacceptable inbetweens.

Although shape hints may help to a certain degree, if the shape becomes complex the result is very hit and miss. It is a shame because you can get a better squash and stretch look using the Shape Tween—but only on a simple shape. Because the characters in my film are fairly complex, I chose to use the Motion Tween. For any squash, stretch, or shape change, I simply drew it myself, in single frames.

This shot is from a Truck-in, where the illusion of complex depth was achieved by moving different objects on separate layers at varied rates. As the camera pulls into the scene, the objects feel as though they are coming toward the camera.

There's one scene in *Edwin Carp* in which Edwin climbs up into the attic and then stumbles backward onto a tailor's dummy. This is a very complex movement and requires what animators call straight-ahead animation. This means that instead of making one key drawing, and then making another key eight frames later, and then going back to inbetween those two keys, you simply draw one drawing after another to create a very free-flowing animation. This is normally best for things such as a walk or run, where a motion is continuous with no pause. So, for this scene, the straight-ahead technique worked best. I first created a rough layer with enough frames to contain the stumble. This was a series of crude and sketchy drawings wherein I could rough out the action. Once I was happy with the motion I then drew on another layer over the top of the rough and cleaned up the action, drawing the character properly over the form of the working motion. When you try this, remember that on the rough level, draw with a light color and keep it rough, because your only concern is movement.

If a Motion Tween had been used here, the character might appear as if he were cut out of paper and moved around. This can be done on other scenes in which the action is simpler, by separating enough elements of the body and then touching up the effect with clothing moving fluidly on "ones" so that the viewer won't notice the more rigid parts. This was the technique used for the scene of Edwin's mother running out of the house.

Continued

Continued

Another combination of techniques was used for the spider scene. Here, I created the usual motion path for one drawing of the body of the spider and Flash did the work for me. That was easy. Now for the legs! I created six drawings of legs. Then all I had to do was copy each individually on each successive frame and rotate them up on one frame and down on the next frame, making sure that each leg was different from the one next to it. I also had to throw in some randomness by holding some legs up and other legs down for maybe two frames. The result is a scurrying spider! As a final touch, I threw the shadow on the same motion path as the body.

Edwin's backward stumble in the attic was drawn as what animators refer to as a straight-ahead animation sequence. To accomplish this, Flash's layers were indispensable.

Using a Stagger

A stagger is an effect whereby a character shakes, shivers, or makes some other jerky movement giving the character the appearance of being cold, frightened, stretching, or even applying force to something. For example, Tramp in *Lady and the Tramp* stretches out his leg and it appears to quiver. Similarly, when Sir Kaye draws back his bow in *The Sword and the Stone*, there's a tension introduced to the pull by the use of a stagger. This can be achieved by randomly offsetting the drawing so that there's a slight shimmer to the line. After you've created a drawing, simply copy and paste it into the next frame and then shift it just a little. This is what was done to various parts of the body in the scene in which Edwin's mother walks down the hall rattling a tea tray. Her arms are on a separate layer apart from the body so that a stagger could be applied to them while her body moves slowly forward. I also applied a stagger to the tray, teapot, and teacups, which were all animated on separate layers. They all vary a little, which adds texture to the scene.

This scene, in which Edwin's mother rattles down the hallway with her tea tray, is a perfect example of the use of Flash layers, as well as cut and paste, to accomplish an effect that is much more difficult to achieve with traditional drawn animation.

Performance and Acting

Here's something you'll learn over time: Observe everyday life. Use your own experiences and put them into your characters. It's the little things and seemingly inconsequential actions that a character does that makes her believable. That's why the old Disney classics have so much depth. Those animators often studied live actors for nuances that they could use to bring their characters to life. This doesn't mean rotoscope, which is where the animator traces a live-action film and leaves it at that. But even that can be a starting point if you retime and reanimate the scene using the rotoscope as just a point of departure. If you choose to use this technique, you can do it in a series of passes, or generations. With the first pass over a rotoscoped scene, you might retime a little. Then you might pull out a few drawings and make them more extreme. Then you might add some new drawings. Each time you run back through the sequence, it enhances the look and complexity of the animation, which might have been hard to initiate without the live-action, although — in the end — it will not look traced. (This is how the character animation was achieved for the magnificent Captain Hook character in *Peter Pan*.) Remember that to animate doesn't just mean to move something around; it must come to life, so that the audience can relate to the character.

Continued

Continued

Timing, Phrasing, and Texture

With some practice, you'll begin to get a feel for good timing. In animation, timing is every-thing. It's like telling a good joke — if it is not delivered properly and the timing is off, it doesn't work. The veteran Disney animators all studied the great comics, such as Buster Keaton, Charlie Chaplin, and Laurel and Hardy, because their impeccable sense of timing was so visual. There are occasions where a motion is continuous, but usually there are pauses, stops, and starts, and then a flurry of activity.

This is what adds interest to a scene. If everything moves at the same time and is very even, it appears mushy, as if it's occurring underwater. So, vary your timing and use Flash's easing in and easing out wherever you can. Flash also has the advantage of easily splitting things off onto layers, with varied timing on different parts. Another nice feature of Flash is that you can add layer upon layer without causing problems. Years ago when animation was copied onto clear cels and painted, additional layers meant that the lower layers would appear lighter: therefore, the cel painter had to paint compensating colors on the upper lev-els so that they would all match. (Do you need to know this? Yes! So that you'll use Flash layers to best advantage.)

Dialog Diagram

This technique should be used as a guide to help you get your dialog timing. Write a line of spoken dialogue on a piece of paper. Then, listen to the sound track very carefully and decide where the major emphasis is; for example the line, "It's a sunny day," could have an emphasis in any of these variations: "IT'S a sunny day," "It's A sunny day," or "It's SUNNY day." Next, above the sentence draw a line, almost like you are drawing a tent, with the highest point above the word that's pronounced with the strongest emphasis. Then, as you're animating, refer back to this diagram, and when you get to the key word or words, exaggerate the action. More often than not, the character's head will rise on this word, or other factors will be brought into play to augment the dialog.

Animation Business

To create the most interesting character animation, avoid static talking heads. What the vet-eran animators called business is nearly a lost art. Think of Baloo, the bear, in *Jungle Book*, when he pulls out a tree and starts to scratch his back with it, while he's delivering his song. Think how much less engaging this would have been if he'd just stood there singing. Or, consider Medusa, in *The Rescuers*, in the scene in which she talks to Penny while she's plucking her eyebrows. This action informs us about her character and makes her much more engaging to watch. Look for these opportunities; it will transform your moving graphic image into a real character.

Artists Animate, Computers Don't

Flash is a great tool, but that's all it is — a tool. It will not animate for you. As they say at Pixar, "artists animate, not computers." With only a little artistic experience it is possible to do minimal graphics and simple animation, but for complex character animation there's no escaping the fact that you'll need to do a lot of other studying. This doesn't mean that it has to be a hard grind, because it can be a lot of fun. Effective study ranges from sketching at the zoo to videoing various things that might be used for later reference. Sketching is good because you build a visual memory bank that you can recall at any time. You will be surprised at what your subconscious stores away. I once designed a character for a movie that looked very much like my dad, but I had no idea until someone pointed it out. You may have observed something from many years ago that may appear in a scene you are currently animating.

Artists draw from their experiences and much this shows in their work. It's a little like handwriting: We are all taught the forms of each letter, yet everyone has distinctly different handwriting. In the hands of an accomplished animator, it's the same with the Flash animation tools. Although there are set rules and guidelines, within those constraints we can create something unique and individual.

Richard Bazley has no memory of popular songs from the year in which he graduated from Exeter High School in his native Devon, England (it was 1979). We surmise that's because he was so focused upon becoming an animator. A short list of Richard's early credits includes work on *Who Framed Roger Rabbit* and *Pocahontas*. More recently, he was a lead animator on *Hercules, The Iron Giant,* and *Osmosis Jones*. Richard discovered Flash by visiting www.shockwave.com. His favorite thing is to drink a pint of Boddingtons at the Double Locks Hotel and Pub, located by the Exeter Canal in the Devonshire countryside. Jon learned of Richard, and his groundbreaking Flash animation *The Journal of Edwin Carp*, through a fortuitous e-mail correspondence.

Summary

✦ Flash can be a powerful tool for the creation of broadcast-quality cartoons. In such cases, many of the usual file-size concerns related to Flash development are set aside because work in this genre leads to big files.

✦ There are many ways to create effective backgrounds and scenery. These techniques include the use of bitmaps, layers, multiplane pans, blurring to simulate depth, and innumerable combinations of these basic techniques.

✦ The task of a cartoon animator is to express motion and emotion. Anticipation and overlapping actions are basic tools used by cartoon animators to express motion and emotion.

✦ Coloring the art is critical to the final quality of the cartoon — the model sheet, speed coloring, and the use of temporary backgrounds ease the task and lead to greater consistency.

✦ Flash tweening, including instance swapping and motion guides, is one of the most useful aspects of Flash as a cartoonist's tool.

✦ Lip-synching, which is critical to fine cartoon animation, is not a push-button task — even with Flash, an animator must understand the relationship between expression and lip-synch, and have a working knowledge phonemes, and synching with music and sound effects.

✦ After a cartoon is created in Flash, final output may include a trip to either Premiere or After Effects for the final polish.

✦ Veteran animator Richard Bazley has compiled a number of insightful tricks from his use of Flash to create his animated short, *The Journal of Edwin Carp*. These include the judicious reuse of drawings, knowing when and where to "cheat," the advantages of simplicity, the power of layers, and the process of making a stagger. He also shared some thoughts about the relevance of performance and acting to animation, timing, diagramming dialog, and animation business.

✦ The key point of this entire chapter is this: Artists animate, computers don't.

✦　　✦　　✦

Planning Flash Production with Flowcharting Software

One of the most important steps — if not *the* most important step — to producing great Flash content is *knowing* what steps you'll have to take to move from the concept or idea of the Flash movie to the finished product. This chapter explores the basics of Flash production, and shows you how to use Inspiration to build flowcharts. Whether you are a freelance Web consultant (or designer) or a member of a large .com creative department, knowing how to manage the Flash content production will save you plenty of headaches, time, and money.

Workflow Basics

No matter what the size or scope, every project in which you choose to participate should follow some type of workflow. Whether it's for print, film, video, or Web delivery (or all four!), you should establish a process to guide the production of your presentation.

Before we can explore the way in which Flash fits into a Web production workflow, we need to define a holistic approach to Web production in general. Figure 38-1 shows a typical Web production with an Internet production company.

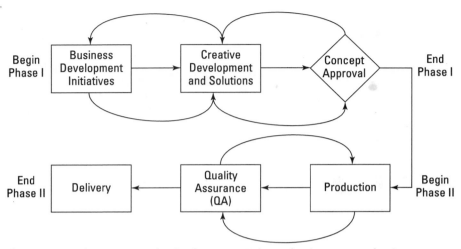

Figure 38-1: There are two basic phases to Web production: preproduction (shown here as Phase I) and production (Phase II).

Phase I: Establishing the concept and goals

As a Web developer or member of a creative team, you will be approached by companies (or representatives for other departments) to help solve a problem with a project. The problem may or may not be well defined by the parties coming to you. Phase I's goal is to thoroughly define the problem, offer solutions for the problem, and approve one (or more) solutions for final production.

Defining the problem

Before you can help someone solve a problem, you need to determine what the problem is, and whether there is more than one problem. When we say "problem," we don't mean something that's necessarily troublesome or irritating. Think of it more as a math problem, where you know what you want — you're just not sure how to get there. When you're attempting to define a client's problem, you should keep in mind the following:

✦ What's the message they want to deliver? Is it a product that they want to feature on an existing Web site?

✦ Who's their current audience?

✦ Who's their ideal audience? (Don't let them say, "Everyone!")

✦ What branding materials (logos, colors, and identity) do they already have in place?

✦ Who are their competitors? What do they know about their competitors?

Information Architects

You may have already been bombarded by the idea of information architecture. Information architecture is the method by which sought data is represented and structured. Good information architecture is usually equivalent to intuitive user interface design—visitors to a well-organized Web site won't spend much time to find what they came for.

We mention information architecture because the steps in Phase I are similar to the steps that traditional architects take to build a comprehensive design and production strategy *before* they start building any structure. While this may seem obvious enough, the sad fact remains that most Internet sites (or projects) are planned as they're constructed. Indeed, we are told that production must move at Internet speed—directives can be given without thorough research into other solutions to the problem.

The last question points to a bigger picture, one in which the client may already have several emotive keywords that define their brand. Try to define the emotional heart and feeling of their message—get them to be descriptive. Don't leave the meeting with the words "edgy" or "sexy" as the only descriptive terms for the message.

Tip   Never go into a meeting or a planning session without a white board, or a big pad of paper. It's always a good idea to document everyone's ideas and let the group see the discussion in a visual format.

You can also start to ask technical questions at this point:

✦ What type of browser support do you want to have?

✦ Do you have an idea of a Web technology (Shockwave, Flash, DHTML, SVG) that you want to use?

✦ Does the message need to be delivered in a Web browser? Can it be in a downloadable application such as a standalone player? A CD-ROM? DVD?

✦ What type of computer processing speed should be supported? What other types of hardware concerns might exist (for example, hi-fi audio)?

Of course, many clients and company reps will look to you for the technical answers. If this is the case, then the most important questions are:

✦ Who's your audience?

✦ Who do you want to be your audience?

Your audience will determine, in many ways, what type of technology to choose for the presentation. If they say that ma and pa from a country farm should be able to view the Web site with no hassle, then you may need to consider a non-Flash presentation (such as HTML 3.0 or earlier), unless it's packaged as a stand-alone player that's installed with a CD-ROM (provided by the client to ma and pa). However, if they say that their ideal audience is someone who has a 56KB modem and likes to watch mature cartoons, then you're getting closer to a Flash-based presentation. If the client has any demographic information for its user base, then ask for it up front. It's difficult to put on a show for a crowd if you don't know who's in the crowd.

 Stand-alone players are discussed in Chapter 42, "Using Players, Projectors, and Screensaver Utilities."

Determine the project's goals

The client or company rep came to you for a reason — they want to walk away with a completed project. As you initially discuss the message and audience for the presentation, you also need to get a clear picture of what the client expects to get from you.

✦ Will you be producing just one piece of a larger production?

✦ Do they need you to host the Web site? Or do they already have a Web server and a staff to support it?

✦ Do they expect you to market the presentation? If not, what resources are in place to advertise the message?

✦ When does the client expect you to deliver proposals, concepts, and the finished piece?

✦ Will they expect to receive copies of all the files you produce, including your source .FLA files?

✦ What are the costs associated with developing a proposal? Will you do work on speculation of a potential project? Or will you be paid for your time to develop a concept pitch? (You should determine this *before* you walk into your initial meeting with the client.) Of course, if you're working with a production team in a company, you're already being paid a salary to provide a role within the company.

At this point, you'll want to plan the next meeting with your client or company rep. Give them a realistic time frame for coming back to them with your ideas. This amount of time will vary from project to project, and will depend on your level of expertise with the materials involved with the presentation.

Creative exploration: Producing a solution

After you leave the meeting, you'll go back to your design studio and start cranking out materials, right? Yes and no. Give yourself plenty of time to work with the client's materials (what you gathered from the initial meeting). If your client sells shoes, read up on the shoe business. See what the client's competitor is doing to promote their message — visit their Web site, go to a store and compare the products, and read any consumer reports that you can find about your client's products or services. You should have clear understanding of your client's market, and a clear picture of who your client is.

After you (and other members of your creative team) have completed a round of research, sit down and discuss the findings. Start defining the project in terms of mood, response, and time. Is this a serious message? Do we want the viewer to laugh? How quickly should this presentation happen? Sketch out any ideas you and any other member of the team may have. Create a chart that lists the emotional keywords for your presentation.

At a certain point, you need to start developing some visual material that articulates the message to the audience. Of course, your initial audience will be the client. You are preparing materials for them, not the consumer audience. We assume that you are creating a Flash-based Web site for your client. For any interactive presentation, you need to prepare the following:

1. An organizational flowchart for the site

2. A process flowchart for the experience

3. A functional specification for the interface

4. A prototype or a series of comps

Cross-Reference To see how Inspiration can be used to make flowcharts, skip to the "Using Inspiration to Create Flowcharts" section later in this chapter.

An *organizational flowchart* is a simple document that describes the scope of a site or presentation. Other names for this type of chart are site chart, navigation flowchart, and layout flowchart. It will include the major sections of the presentation. For example, if you are creating a Flash movie for an animation site, you might have a main menu and four content areas: parody, slapstick, anime, and mature. In an organizational flowchart, this would look like Figure 38-2.

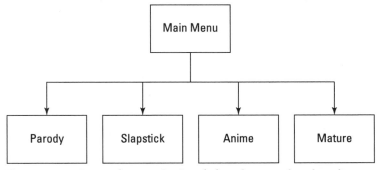

Figure 38-2: A sample organizational chart for an animation site.

A *process flowchart* constructs the interactive experience of the presentation, and shows the decision-making process involved for each area of the site. There are few types of process charts. A basic process flowchart will display the decision-making of the end-user (for example, what type of options does a user have on any given page of the site?). Another type of flowchart will show the programming logic involved for the end-user process chart. For example, will certain conditions need to exist before a user can enter a certain area of the site? Does he/she have to pass a test, finish a section of a game, or enter a username and password? Refer to Figure 38-3 for a preliminary flowchart for the believeGOSSIP.com Shockwave Web site. We discuss the actual symbols of the flowchart later in this chapter.

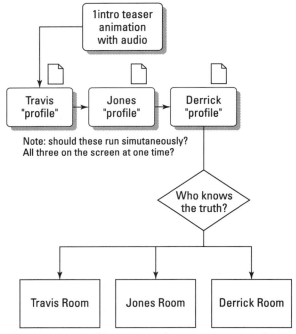

Figure 38-3: In this process chart, you can see that the user watches a teaser animation, which is followed by three linear animations of the characters for the site. After all the animations have finished playing, the user can decide which room to explore.

A *functional specification* (see Figure 38-4) is a document that breaks down the elements for each step in the organizational and/or process flowchart. This is by far the most important piece of documentation that you can create for yourself and your team. Each page of a functional specification (or functional spec) will list all the assets used on a page (or Flash scene, keyframe, Movie Clip) and indicate the following information for each asset:

✦ **Item ID:** This is part of the naming convention for your files and assets. It should be part of the filename, or Flash symbol and instance name. It should also be used in organizational and process flowcharts.

✦ **Type:** This part of the spec defines the name you are assigning to the asset, in more natural language, such as Home Button.

✦ **Purpose:** You should be able to clearly explain why this element is part of the presentation. If you can't, then you should consider omitting it from the project.

✦ **Format:** This column will indicate what technology (or what component of the technology) will be utilized to accomplish the needs of the asset. In an all-Flash presentation, list the symbol type or timeline component (frames, scene, nested Movie Clips) necessary to accomplish the goals of the asset.

PROJECT: Flash Interface v2.0			SECTION: 1 of 5 (Main Menu)	
No.	**Type**	**Purpose**	**Content**	**Format**
1.A	Navigation Bar	To provide easier access to site content		A menu bar that is fixed at the top edge of the browser window
1.A.1	Directory Access	To provide a means of accessing any of the animation sections	Names of each content area (for example slapstick, parody, an so on)	Flash Horizontal menu list or drop-down menu
1.A.2	Home Button	Allow user to always get back to the opening page	The text "Home"	Flash Text button
1.A.3	Search Field	To provide a means of entering a specific search word or phrase	A white text field with the word "search" next to it.	Flash Dynamic Text field
1.A.4	Login/Reg	To capture user's e-mail address	Text field(s) to enter name and e-mail address	Flash pop-up menu (or box) OR HTML/JavaScript pop-up window
1.A.5	Back Button	Allow the user to see the last page viewed without using menu items	The text "Back"	Flash Text button
1.A.6	Conpany Logo/ID	Provide means of company branding	Company name in Officina Sans Bold, with tag line	Flash graphics

Figure 38-4: This functional spec displays the six components of a Flash-based navigation bar, which will appear on the main menu of our animation content site.

Finally, once you have plan for your project, you'll want to start creating some graphics to provide an atmosphere for the client presentation. Gather placement graphics (company logos, typefaces, photographs) or appropriate "temporary" resources for purposes of illustration. Construct one composition (or comp) that represents each major section or theme of the site. In our animation content site example, you might create a comp for the main page and a comp for one of the animation sections. Don't create a comp for each animation section. You simply want to establish the feel for the content you will create for the client. We recommend that you use the tool(s) with which you feel most comfortable creating content. If you're better at using FreeHand or Photoshop to create layouts, then use them. If you're comfortable with Flash for assembling content, then use it.

Caution Do not use copyrighted material for final production use, unless you have secured the appropriate rights to use the material. However, while you're exploring creative concepts, use whatever materials you feel best illustrate your ideas. When you get approval for your concept, improve upon the materials that inspired you.

Then, you'll want to determine the time and human resources required for the entire project or concept. What role will you play in the production? Will you need to hire outside contractors to work on the presentation (for example, character animators, programmers, and so on)? Make sure you provide ample time to produce and thoroughly test the presentation. When you've determined the time and resources necessary, you'll determine the costs involved. If this is an internal project for your company, then you won't be concerned about cost so much as the time involved — your company reps will want to know what it will cost the company to produce the piece. For large client projects, your client will probably expect a project rate — not an hourly or weekly rate. Outline a time schedule with milestone dates, at which point you'll present the client with updates on the progress of the project.

It's beyond the scope of this book to explore the workflow process any further. However, there are many excellent resources for project planning. One of the best books available for learning the process of planning interactive presentations is Nicholas Iuppa's *Designing Interactive Digital Media*. We strongly recommend that you consult the *Graphic Artists Guild Handbook of Pricing and Ethical Guidelines* and the *AIGA Professional Practices in Graphic Design*, edited by Tad Crawford, for information on professional rates for design services.

Note You can search for recommended design, computer, and art books at the Makers' Web site, www.theMakers.com/resources.

Approving a final concept and budget

After you have prepared your design documents for the client, it's time to have another meeting with the client (or company rep). Display your visual materials (color laser prints, inkjet mockups, and so on), and walk through the charts you have produced. In some situations, you may want to prepare more than one design concept. Always reinforce how the presentation addresses the client's message and audience.

Cross-Reference See Todd Purgason's Expert Tutorial on Flash and FreeHand, in Chapter 31. He offers excellent suggestions for creating presentation boards in FreeHand.

When all is said and done, discuss with the client the options that you presented. Gather feedback. Hopefully, the client prefers one concept (and its budget) and gives you the approval to proceed. It's important that you leave this meeting knowing that:

1. The client has signed off on the entire project or presentation.

2. The client wants to see more exploration before committing to a final piece.

In either case, you shouldn't walk away not knowing how you'll proceed. If the client wants more time or more material before a commitment, negotiate the terms of your fees that are associated with further conceptual development.

Expert Tutorial: Designing for Usability, *by Scott Brown*

As mentioned earlier in this chapter, the first step in developing a Flash site, or any other type of site, is to define the information architecture. In this tutorial, you learn how to define the goals and mission of the site.

Define the goals and mission of the site

Defining the mission and goals is to lay the foundation upon which to build your project. To create a solid project foundation we must begin by questioning everything, especially the company's business model. Start with these questions:

1. What is the mission or purpose of the organization?

2. Why does this organization want a Web site?

3. Will the Web site support the mission of the organization?

4. What are the short- and long-term goals of the Web site?

5. Who are the intended audiences?

6. Why will people come to the site?

7. Are we trying to sell a product?

8. What is the product or products?

9. Do we have a unique service?

10. What makes the service different?

11. Why will people come to the site for the first time?

12. Will they ever come back?

13. Why would they come back?

Continued

Continued

The list of questions can go on forever. After we have gathered a list of questions we need to get the answers. Ask around the organization, ask your friends, ask strangers, just ask people. After the answers have been collected it is time to filter through them to create a list of goals that are based on the responses. From this list of goals, we must define further the answer to the question, "Who is the audience?"

Define the Audience

The audience can be defined as the potential users of the site and by their intentions or tasks that they might have when they come to your site. Are they kids or adults? Are they generation x, y, or z? Are they into rave music or country music? So, who is your audience? It's not an easy question, because there are so many possibilities. Start with a list of all the possible audiences that the organization would like to reach, and then rearrange the list in a ranking order, of most important audience to least important audience. From the audience ranking list, create a list of possible goals and needs of each audience.

Create Character Scenarios

With the list of possible goals take the process one step further by creating scenarios of the users. Think of it as writing a screenplay for your Web site. Create multiple characters that represent the majority of visitors with hobbies, likes, dislikes, and, most importantly, a task to complete on the site. The object of the scenario game is to get into the characters' heads to learn why and how they would use your site. From their view point you will have an easier time creating a list of needs and wants for the character, a wish list if you will.

After the scenarios are written, the next step in the process is to gather the team together and analyze the Web sites of the competition.

Analyze the Competition

Studying the competition gives us the chance to generate a list of what kind of features they are offering and to determine whether our feature list, the one that we created from the scenarios, is missing anything. If our wish list is lacking anything in comparison to our competition, now is a good time to expand the user's functionality requirements, and to return to the scenarios to determine whether the competition's functionality matches your character's needs. If it does you should try to elaborate on their functions and create new functions of your own — the classic case of outdoing your competition.

Reach a Consensus on What Good Design Is

At this time in the process, have the team come together to develop a definition of what is "good site design." This step is most beneficial for any contract designer trying to gain an understanding of your client's design viewpoint. To create this "good design" definition, the team should observe a good number of sites and document everybody's likes and dislikes for each site. From the documentation of this exercise, everyone on the team will have a better understanding of what to strive for and what to try to avoid.

Structure the Content

Now you should have several documents to refer to—the project mission statement, the user functionality needs (wish list), and the organization's definition of good design. With these three documents in hand, the next step is to blend them into one master menu of content inventory. Think of each item on this list as a building block. We now have all the blocks needed to construct the site. The only problem is that these blocks are in a big pile with no organization (structure). Naturally, the next step is to begin creating layouts of the site, therefore providing structure. But before we can begin the page layout process, we need to educate ourselves on some Web site usability issues.

Factors of Usability

Designing for usability is just that, designing a site that is usable by a user. A usable site aims to be a natural extension of a user's expectations and needs. A user-friendly site will try to mirror its structure to that of the user's experience and goals. Just to make the task at hand a little more complex, keep in mind that user expectations learned in other areas of life affect how the user will think your site works. So, how can we design a site to meet our user's expectations? Well, if you did your homework on your audience and wrote the character scenarios, you should have a pretty good idea of the targeted audience's expectations. By knowing the general background of a user, you could include metaphors into the structure of the site. Using metaphors is a great way to help users draw upon knowledge they already have, thereby making the site easier to use. By matching the site structure to the user's experience, the amount of time it takes for the user to learn how to operate or navigate the site is minimized. The shorter the learning curve for the site, the better. If you come to a site when you have a specific goal in mind and it takes you ten minutes to figure out how to achieve your goal, would you call that a positive experience? Most likely not!

The goal of the designer is to create an attractive site without distracting the users from their goals. Forcing the user to spend a noticeable amount of time trying to learn how to achieve their goal is very taxing on their patience, and is a good path to creating a negative experience. If you are trying to sell something, chances are you want customers to be happy not annoyed. One way to make your customers experience more enjoyable is to make their experience as easy as possible. So, how do you create a positive experience? Let's start with the most basic of a user needs, the ability to navigate.

Users need to know at all times where they are in the site, where they have been, and where they can go. When developing a navigation system, be sure to keep the navigation visually consistent. Inconsistency in the navigation can cause the user to be confused and frustrated. A great concept for a navigational aid is the use of a breadcrumb trail. The breadcrumb system is a visual way to show the user the path they took to get to their current position in the site. Beyond displaying the path of the user, the system gives the user the ability to back track to any page displayed in the path. However, remember that navigation is not the goal of the user, only an aid. The user is there to find or buy something; the user is there for the content. So, make the content the first read on all your pages. Navigational elements are there to support the content, not eclipse it.

Continued

Continued

Of course, navigation is not the only factor to considerwhen designing for usability. Other variables such as the length of text on a page can affect the usability of a site tremendously. It doesn't take a usability expert to know that people prefer to read long sections of text on paper instead of the screen. When users come across large articles, they usually print the page or pages and then read the printout. It's a fact that reading text on a monitor is far more taxing on the eyes than reading text on paper. Therefore, people are less inclined to read large amounts of text on the Web. As designers, we must accommodate these changes in reading patterns. Keep these simple guidelines in mind when writing text for the Web. Try to make the text scannable, because readers skim Web content. Bold the important ideas or bullet list the information. But most of all, keep the text short.

In addition to the treatment of text, there are several other tips to help improve the usability of a site. The concept of redundant links is an excellent method to support users with different backgrounds and goals. With redundant links a user has more than one way to get to the desired content. The user might have the option to click a text link, a graphic link, or even a text link that is worded differently. Each redundant link should be designed to accommodate a wide range of users. So, where on the page should all these usability elements go?

I can't tell you where you should place your navigation system or your redundant links. However, I can provide you with some information on eye-tracking studies that will help you make an educated decision. Yes, it is true that usability researchers are able to actually monitor and record what you are looking at when viewing a Web site. Based on the research they have found that when a Web page loads, our eyes are looking at the center of the page then move over to the left and then sometimes to the right. Of course, these findings are dependent on the user's cultural background. Nevertheless, the scary finding is that the users rarely look to the right! This is most likely because most sites use the right side of the page as a place to add sidebar elements, items of lesser importance. This is also a good example of how user's past experience can affect their future experiences. So, how does Flash fit into Web site usability factors?

Flash is a great design tool to create amazing interfaces. Flash gives the designer the freedom to create almost anything they desire. But the flexibility given to the designer is also Flash's greatest weakness from a usability perspective. Flash is a great tool for creating animation but when used by an inexperienced Web designer the amount of animation can easily go overboard. Just because you can animate an object doesn't mean that you should. The eye is very sensitive to the smallest amount of animation or movement in its peripheral view, pulling the eyes' attention away from the site's main content. On the plus side, animation used as a transitional element is very beneficial for the user. Animated transitions enable the user to follow the navigation process, therefore gaining a better understanding of how the site might work.

Along with the problems of animation abuse, Flash enables the designers to create their own graphical user interface (GUI) elements. This is great for the designers, but the users are often left out in the cold with all this newfound freedom.

This design freedom is forcing the user to learn, almost from scratch, how to operate a scroll bar or a navigation bar. If you recall, earlier I mentioned the importance of a short learning curve for the users. These extreme creative versions of standardized GUI elements might rank high on the "cool" scale but they really throw a monkey wrench into the users goal and expectations. GUI standards are developed to help create a consistent experience across all platforms in an effort to eliminate any unpleasant surprises. Again these usability problems can be avoided in Flash by educating the designers about the issues at hand and finding solutions based on the set standards.

Other usability issues with Flash concern the actual plug-in nature of Flash. Unfortunately, because Flash requires a plug-in to work in the browsers the Flash movies are unable to take advantage of some of the browsers built-in capabilities such as the browser's Back button and the capability to display history for the links by changing the color of the links that have been clicked. The history feature can actually be simulated in Flash by capturing a history variable in the ActionScript to display a history state for the button (refer to Chapter 21, "Planning Code Structures," for more information on ActionScripting). As for the browser's Back button, the problem is that when the button is pressed, the browser will take the user back to the previous HTML page, not to the previous state in the Flash movie. It's a nice little surprise to unsuspecting users. One solution to this problem is to pop up the Flash movie in a new browser window (via JavaScript) with all the browser's navigation elements removed (in other words, no toolbar, no location bar, no menus, and so on). No Back button on the browser, no problem right?

Build Mockups of the Site

We are now ready to begin mocking up the site structure using index cards, sticky notes, and other common office supplies. Creating these paper mockups will save the development team a large amount of time. The beauty of the paper mockups is that you can quickly create a navigational system and find the major flaws without spending long hours developing a beautiful rendering of a structure that might be flawed. There is nothing worse than spending months developing a product with a faulty structure only to discover the mistake just before launch! Which brings me to the final topic, test your site.

Test the Site on Real Users

Testing the site is the most important step in creating a usable site. The key to testing the site is to *not* test it on people of the organization, but to test it on people in the target audience that was defined in the second step of this tutorial. Test the site on the real users. It's usually easier to test the site by using people who are familiar with the project. The problem with that practice is that the people are familiar with the project. You want to test fresh eyes and minds in order to get optimum feedback. For testing purposes, create a list of several tasks to complete on the site. The tasks should be pulled from the list of possible users' goals defined in the early steps of the project. After the test subject has completed a task, or tried, give them a post-task questionnaire with questions such as:

"How would you rate the quality of the content on this site?"

unacceptable −3 −2 −1 0 1 2 3 excellent

Continued

Continued

Also, leave some room for the test subject to elaborate on the questions. After the testing is finished, review your findings and determine what needs to be fixed. After the problems are fixed, test the site again, but on new users. Repeat the process until you have a product that meets the defined goals of the organization and the users. Keep asking yourself this question, "Is the interface helping the users accomplish their goals?" When all else fails you can always depend on the greatest guideline of the century, Keep It Simple. Oh, so true.

Scott Brown contributed a Fireworks tutorial in Chapter 30, "Working with Raster Graphics." You can find his biographical information there.

Phase II: Producing, testing, and staging the presentation

Once your client or company executives have signed off on a presentation concept, it's time to rock and roll! You're ready to gather your materials, assemble the crew, and meet an insane production schedule. This section provides a brief overview of the steps you need to take to produce material that is ready to go "live" on your Web site.

Assembling assets

The first step is to gather (or start production of) the individual assets required for the Flash presentation. Depending on the resources you included in your functional spec and budget, you may need to hire a photographer, illustrator, animator, music composer (or all four!) to start work on the production. Or, if you perform any of these roles, then you'll start creating rough drafts for the elements within the production. At this stage, you'll also gather high-quality images from the client for their logos, proprietary material, and so on.

Making the Flash architecture

Of course, we're assuming that you're creating a Flash-based production. All the resources that you have gathered (or are working to create) in Step 1 will be assembled into the Flash movie(s) for the production. For large presentations or sites, you'll likely make one master Flash movie that provides a skeleton architecture for the presentation, and use `loadMovie()` to bring in material for the appropriate sections of the site.

Before you begin Flash movie production, you should determine two important factors: frame size and frame rate. You don't want to change either of these settings midway through your project. Any reductions in frame size will crop elements that weren't located near the top-left portion of the Stage — you will need to recompose most of the elements on the Stage if you used the entire Stage. Any changes in your frame rate will change the timing of any linear animation and/or sound synchronization that you have already produced.

Staging a local test environment

As soon as you start to author the Flash movies, you will create a local version of the presentation (or entire site) on your computer, or a networked drive that everyone on your team can access. The file and folder structure (including the naming conventions) will be consistent with the structure of the files and folders on the Web server. As you build each component of the site, you should begin to test the presentation with the target browsers (and Flash Player plug-in versions) for your audience.

HTML page production

Even if you're creating an all-Flash Web site, you need a few basic HTML documents, including:

✦ HTML frameset document (if you're creating a scalable Flash movie). The frameset has two frames: One displays the Flash movie at 100 percent of the browser window size, and the other one is hidden. Colin Moock explains this browser window technique in Chapter 41, "Integrating Flash Content with HTML."

✦ A plug-in detection page, that directs visitors without the Flash Player plug-in to the Macromedia site to download the plug-in.

✦ HTML page(s) to display any non-Flash material in the site within the browser.

You will want to construct your basic HTML documents holding the main Flash movie as you develop the Flash architecture of the site.

Staging a server test environment

Before you can make your Flash content public, you will need to set up a Web server that is publicly accessible (with login and password protection) so that you can test the site functionality over a non-LAN connection. This also enables your client to preview the site remotely. Once quality assurance (QA) testing has finished (the next step that follows), then you will move the files from the staging server to the live Web server.

We have noticed problems with larger .SWF files that weren't detected until we tested them from a staging server. Why? When you test your files locally, they're loaded instantly into the browser. When you test your files from a server (even over a fast DSL or cable modem connection), you can test your .SWF files over slower network conditions. Especially with preloaders or loading sequences, timing glitches may be revealed during tests on the staging server.

Quality assurance testing

In larger corporate environments, you'll find a team of individuals whose sole responsibility is to thoroughly test the quality of a nearly finished production (or product). If you are responsible for QA, then you should have an intimate knowledge of the process chart for the site. That way, you know how the site should function. If a feature or function fails in the production, QA will report it to the creative production team. QA teams will test the production with the same hardware and conditions of the target audiences, accounting for variations in:

✦ Computer type (PC versus Mac)

✦ Computer speed (top-of-the-line processing speed versus minimal supported speeds, as determined by the target audiences)

✦ Internet connection speeds (as determined by target audiences)

✦ Flash Player plug-in versions (and any other plug-ins required by the production)

✦ Browser application and version (as determined by target audiences)

If you are a freelance designer or operate a small company, then you should realize that there is no such thing as a useless computer — recycle your older computers as test platforms for target audiences.

After QA has finished rugged testing of the production, then, pending approval by the client (or company executives), the material is ready to go live on the site.

Maintenance and updates

After you've celebrated the finished production, your job's not over yet. If you were contracted to build the site or presentation for a third party, then you may be expected to maintain and address usability issues provided by follow-ups with the client and any support staff they might have. Be sure to account for periodic maintenance and updates for the presentation in your initial budget proposal. If you don't want to be responsible for updates, make sure you advise your clients ahead of time to avoid any potential conflicts after the production has finished.

You should have a thorough staging and testing environment for any updates you make to an all-Flash site, especially if you're changing major assets or master architecture files. Repeat the same process of staging and testing with the QA team that you employed during original production.

Using Inspiration to Create Flowcharts

Inspiration 6 is a flowcharting application for Windows and Macintosh. By using Inspiration, you can create the flowcharts with a variety of artwork symbols, including ANSI chart graphics that work with the Gantt system of flowcharting.

For the purposes of this chapter, we show you how to create an organizational chart (a.k.a. orgchart) and a process chart.

You can find trial versions of Inspiration 6 at `www.inspiration.com`.

Building an organizational chart

To create an organizational chart (site chart) for your Flash or Web concepts, you need to have a list of all the sections within the concept. For this example, we make an organizational chart for an animation site that has:

✦ A main menu screen

✦ Dedicated sections for parody, slapstick, anime, and mature animations

✦ A submission form for new animations

✦ The featured animation for each section

✦ Subsection categories for each section that contain top ten, visitors' choice, and archived animations

With that, let's build an organizational chart.

1. Open Inspiration 6. By default, the Tip of the Day dialog will appear. Click Close to dismiss the window.

2. A new untitled document window will already be open, with the basic library of symbols available in the Symbol Palette. Each library has a specific set of predefined symbols. You can change the library set by clicking either the left or right arrow located at the top of the Symbol Palette. The down arrow will display the entire list of libraries available in Inspiration.

3. In the File ➪ Page Setup dialog (Mac) or the File ➪ Print Setup dialog (PC), change the document's orientation to Landscape.

4. Select the Main Idea symbol, which is already within the document window. Click the Rectangle symbol, located in the first row of symbols in the Symbol Palette. This will change the shape of the existing Main Idea symbol in the document. Then, click the New Look button in the document toolbar. This will change the default new symbol type to the Rectangle symbol.

5. Click once inside the Main Idea symbol to change or add the text. The text cursor will automatically become active inside the Rectangle symbol. Type the text **Main Menu**.

6. With the Rectangle symbol still selected, click the RapidFire button, located in the toolbar at the top of the document. The RapidFire feature enables you to quickly create new symbols by typing text into a parent symbol and pressing the Return key to move the new text into a child symbol. Once the RapidFire button is depressed, a lightning bolt icon will appear next to your Main Menu text. Type the text **Parody**, and press the Return key. A new lightning bolt icon will appear after the Parody text, and, after a few seconds, a new symbol with the Parody text will show up below the Main Menu symbol. By default, the new symbol will be an Oval shape. We'll change this shape in a later step.

7. With the RapidFire button still depressed, type **Slapstick** in the Main Menu symbol, and press the Return key. Then, type **Anime** and press the Return key. Use this same process to create **Mature** and **Submission Form** symbols from the Main Menu symbol. At this point, turn off the RapidFire feature by clicking its button in the toolbar.

8. Now, we'll reposition the symbols so that they're organized in a more readable layout. Press Ctrl+A or Command+A to select all of the symbol, and click the Arrange button on the document toolbar. Make sure that the Diagram Type is set to Top Down Tree, and that the Links menu is set to Auto-90. Click OK, and Inspiration will place all of the child symbols below the Main Menu symbol.

9. Now we will remove the arrowheads from the connecting lines — orgcharts should not display flow directions like a process chart does. Select the connecting line between the Main Menu and Parody symbols. Then Shift+click the other connecting lines between the Main Menu and remaining symbols. Then choose Link ➪ Arrow Head Ending Point ➪ None. When you're finished, your chart should resemble Figure 38-5.

10. Save your Inspiration document as **orgchart.ins**.

11. Next, we will create child documents for each of the site sections. Select the Parody symbol, and choose File ➪ Family ➪ Open Child (F6). Inspiration will create a new diagram for the document. This diagram is contained with the orgChart.ins file, but it will be printed on a separate page.

12. In the new diagram, select the Parody symbol, and click the RapidFire button in the document toolbar. Again, create four Rectangle symbols below the Parody Menu: Featured Animation, Top Ten Animations, Visitors' Choice, and Archived Animations (as shown in Figure 38-6). Then turn off the RapidFire feature.

13. Save your Inspiration document.

14. Because our example has the same format for each section of the movie, it's not necessary to repeat Steps 11 and 12 for the other categories. However, if each section had a different format, then you would want to define the content within each section at this point.

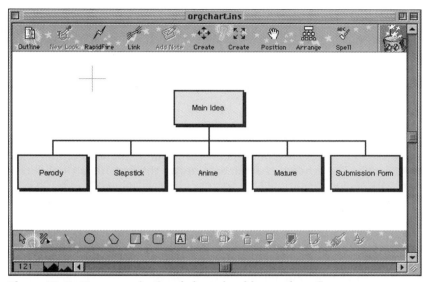

Figure 38-5: Your organizational chart should now show five separate sections of your Flash movie.

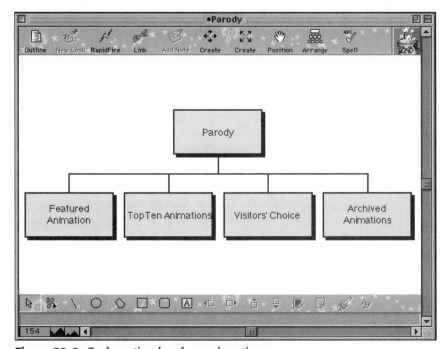

Figure 38-6: Each section has four subsections.

That's all there is to building an organizational chart. When you print the document, the top-level drawing (the main document) will print first, followed by each drawing in the document.

You can view the completed orgchart file named orgChart.ins, located in ch38 folder of the *Flash 5 Bible* CD-ROM.

Creating a process chart

In this section, we create a process chart for our animation content site, which is an all-Flash site. The process chart demonstrates the experience and decision-making steps with the presentation. Our process chart will show:

✦ An intro animation with a "skip intro" button

✦ The Main Menu screen with a showcase animation window

✦ Navigation links to other content areas in the site

✦ The steps to submit an animation to the site

For this example, we will not continue with the orgchart file we created in the last section. Close that file before you start the steps in this section.

1. Open Inspiration 6, or, if it's already open, create a new document. Open the Process ⇨ Flowchart1 symbol library, from the drop-down menu accessible from the down arrow at the top of the Symbol Palette. Also, make sure Utility ⇨ Grid Snap is turned on.

2. Select the Main Idea symbol in the document, and click the Rounded Rectangle symbol in the first row of symbols in the Symbol Palette.We will use this symbol to indicate an animated sequence in our process chart. Type **intro animation** in the Main Idea symbol.

3. Because we will give the user the option to skip this animation, we will insert a decision point into the process chart. Click the right arrow of the Create button in the document toolbar. This will add a new Rounded Rectangle symbol to the right of the intro animation symbol. Select the Decision symbol (the diamond-shaped one located in the left column of the Symbol Palette), and click once to the right of the intro animation symbol. Type **skip intro** in the Decision symbol.

4. Click the right diagonal of the Create button in the document toolbar, and select the Rectangle symbol. Type **Home Screen** in this new symbol.

5. Click the down arrow of the Create button, and select the Rounded Rectangle symbol. Type **Showcase Animation** in the new symbol.

6. Reselect the Home Screen symbol, and click the diagonal left-down arrow of the Create button. Select the Decision symbol. Type **Main Menu** in the new symbol.

7. Click the right-down arrow of the Create button in the document toolbar. Type **Parody** in the new symbol. Now, we'll change the active library for the Symbol Palette, in order to select a new symbol type for the Parody symbol. Click the right arrow at the top of the Symbol Palette to advance to the next library, Flowchart2. Select the Document symbol, which is located in the leftmost symbol in the first row of Flowchart2 symbols.

Note The Document symbol is used to indicate a continuation of the process chart on another page. There will not be enough room to show the processes of the Parody section within this drawing.

8. Reselect the Main Menu symbol, and repeat the first part of Step 7 for the Slapstick, Anime, and Mature sections of the site.

9. Select the Main Menu symbol with the Arrow Tool, and click the left arrow of the Create button. Type **Submission Form** in this new symbol. Then click the Rectangle symbol in the Symbol Palette to change its shape.

10. Click the down arrow of the Create button and type **Request info** in the symbol. Click the left arrow of the Symbol Palette to access the symbols from the Flowchart1 symbol library and select the Decision symbol to change the shape of the Request info symbol.

11. Click the right-down arrow of the Create button, and, in the new symbol, type **Visitor Name**. Change its symbol shape to the short, rounded rectangle, found in the lower left of the Symbol Palette (third row from the bottom).

12. Reselect the Request info symbol, and repeat Step 11 for two more short rounded rectangle symbols, **Animation Title** and **Animation URL**.

13. Now, our flowchart symbols are complete. At this point, Shift+click all of the diagonal connecting lines for your chart. Choose Link ⇨ Auto-90. Then, using the Arrow Tool, click and drag the arrowhead end points of each line to connect to the appropriate side of each symbol. Use Figure 38-7 as a reference for the direction and flow of the connecting lines. You may need to reposition the symbol shapes to prevent the symbols from overlapping.

14. Save your Inspiration file as **processChart.ins**.

After you have a process flowchart, you are ready to start building the functional specification for your Flash movie. Refer to the earlier sections of this chapter for more information.

On the CD-ROM You will find the completed process chart file, processChart.ins, in the ch38 folder of the *Flash 5 Bible* CD-ROM.

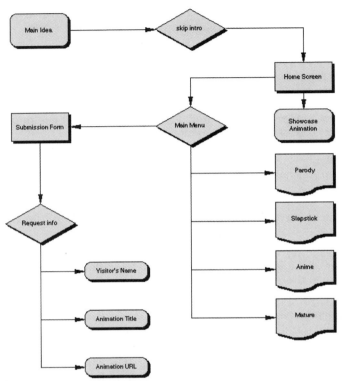

Figure 38-7: This process flowchart maps the user's experience of the animation site.

Expert Tutorial: Storyboarding and Planning Interactivity, *by MD Dundon*

MD Dundon is a filmmaker and experience designer who found Flash when it was still known, "as FutureSplash, while I was working in Director doing interface design and CD-ROM work." She's credited with having taught the first Flash classes in the world, at San Francisco State University. She's the founder of Paradox Productions (film) and a design consulting business, Flash411.

Planning your interactivity. Sounds boring, huh? In reality, it's one of the most exciting parts of the process. How else do you save yourself sleepless nights, accomplish enormous projects with minimal stress, *and* keep your clients stunned and happy with both your progress and your bug-free development?

I've always been amazed at how few people in our business make the time for a preproduction phase in their workflow. I've heard some great excuses: "My client doesn't want to pay for me to do that extra stuff." "They just want me to build it." "They don't want to answer all those questions." "I'm not a designer, I can't draw. I'm best if I just jump in and do it and create as I go." All these are perfectly valid excuses, but completely beside the point.

A preproduction process is absolutely necessary—not because your client or director wants it, but because it speeds and calms your own process of development. If you don't know how to draw or design, then you need to figure out creative ways around that while still getting your planning finished. Or, if you really do work better by just jumping in, then reverse the order in which you do the processes: Try functionality tests and prototyping first, and then go back through to make your interaction storyboards.

Most of the storyboards and examples discussed in this tutorial are located in the tutorial folder in the ch38 folder of the *Flash 5 Bible* CD-ROM. Although we've included a few examples within the text, we think that you'll find them much more usable as files that you can open on you own machine. Anticipating potential font problems, we've also exported these as .SWFs.

Preproduction Process

Know your project—because, if *you* don't, who will? That may seem like an obvious statement, but several years ago I realized that I kept expecting everyone else to know what was going on, when the reality was that I still had to figure it out for myself. I realized that if I wanted to be really good at developing multimedia projects, and if I also wanted to deliver them on time, on budget, and with my sanity intact, then I'd better be able to answer all of my own and my client's questions about every aspect of the project. I've discovered the easiest way to do this is with a really solid preproduction process. In the following flowchart, you can see an overview of the process, which I'll break out into each step in the balance of this tutorial.

This is a basic preproduction flowchart, which is useful to a Flash developer because the flowcharting process ensures that you will know what's going on.

Continued

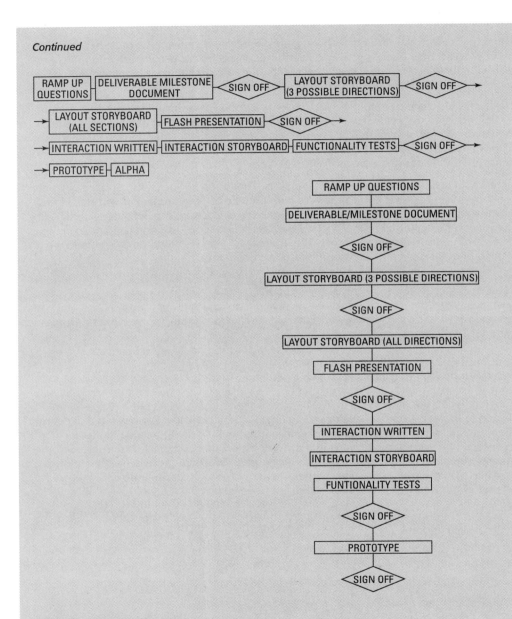

Continued

Ramping Up the Project

Even if you do no other planning, I still suggest that you write down all of the functionality, deliverables, and milestones that you and your client or project managers have decided on. If you don't have enough information to write this document, then you'll be hard pressed to bid on the project or to plan realistically how long the project might take.

So, ask a lot of questions and get as many specifics as possible *before* you agree to the project. At the very least, you should be able to answer these prep questions:

✦ Where is the project going to be displayed? (Web, local drive, kiosk, video, or multiple media)

✦ What is the target audience? Who's using this? (Age, usability skills, browsers, processor speed, user goals, other user information or experience)

✦ Are there other projects like theirs that they admire? Why? (Look, feel, information design, experience, stability) Get URLS, printouts, screenshots, or pictures of such examples.

✦ If this is a Web project, do they want to build dual sites (Flash and HTML) or do they want to use a plug-in detection strategy? (This determines the number of pages in the site and whether you'll need to program or hire someone to program your detection.)

✦ For presentations and animation projects, are they going to provide the source illustrations or do you need to produce these yourself? Is this a character animation project? (Developing character animations *always* costs more time and money to the developer.)

✦ What information *must* be included? Is this divided into sections? List them.

✦ Does the client want the source files at the completion of the project? (Usually increases the bid and/or the hourly rate.)

If you've done your research and you can answer all of these questions, then you should be able to produce a pretty accurate deliverable bid or project milestone document for them, by listing this information and citing your prices based on:

a. Per page

b. Section quotes

c. Length of presentation (usually bid in seconds)

Its important to your planning that your bid include a list of deliverables so that it's very clear what work you are bidding on. Even within companies, most production managers and directors of projects are aided by developing this documentation so everyone on the team is clear about the goals—from the start.

Storyboarding

Now you're ready for the next step, which is to figure out the look of the project. Storyboarding is the most common way to approach this part of the process. However, many developers don't realize that there are several types of storyboards to choose from, and that each one is tuned for handling a specific set, or type of information. These types include Layout Storyboards, Animation Storyboards, Interaction Storyboards, Visual Interaction Storyboards, and Flowchart Storyboards for Complex ActionScript.

Continued

Continued

Layout Storyboards

When starting a project, the first presentation that I make is usually with printed or displayed concepts that I've either mocked up in a program such as FreeHand or Flash, or that I've hand sketched. Layout Storyboards are a simple way to present the first set of visual concepts for the client to decide a direction. They are also specific to projects that involve an interface system of some sort (Web page or interactive project). Graphic designers almost always use this type of storyboard for developing their printed work. For our purposes, we use the storyboard to show the client or art director two or three choices of style, color and the arrangement of interactive and display elements. To review, here are the purposes of Layout Storyboards:

✦ Use for interface system projects (Web or interactive)

✦ Create in FreeHand, Illustrator, Flash, or sketch in a sketchbook

✦ Use as your first point for the client to sign off on your progress

To see an example of a Layout Storyboard, find the tutorial folder in the ch38 folder on the CD-ROM and open the layout_storyboard.pdf document.

A Layout Storyboard needs to show the position and look of button elements, title elements, and informational spaces. You also need to specify the color palette. I usually do this with a small set of color squares on the page. After you get the top-level page general layout, you'll need to layout any interactive elements such as open menus, avatars, logos, or transitions that occur before the hypothetical user goes on to another section.

Depending on his or her skill sets, each designer will have a different approach to this. I have a friend who cuts pictures out of magazines and pastes them into interesting layouts on large sketchpads. Then she creates a color copy and presents them to her client. Others use colored pencils and a sketchpad, while others might take screenshots and then cut them up and arrange them in Fireworks.

I tend to approach the layout storyboard by beginning with a pencil sketch on a sketchpad, often first working with the client, so that my client can give me a general direction. Then I proceed by jumping into FreeHand to develop the top-level page. I like FreeHand because I can create several pages in the same document and because I can export a .SWF movie, as well as create symbols that can then be imported directly into Flash.

After I've mocked up two or three conceptual directions for the general look and feel, I'll have another meeting to present these ideas and have the client or project director sign off (again) on the direction we're going to take. The next step is to complete a detailed layout for each section, which should carefully note changes of color, submenu structure, and informational areas for each section.

Flash Concept Presentation

When you're done storyboarding a detailed layout for each section of the project, you are ready for your second presentation. This can be a breeze if you've followed my advice and generated most of your concepts in an illustration program. Simply export your document as a .SWF movie and import it into Flash. You can do this from *both* FreeHand and Illustrator 8 (by getting the FlashWriter addition from `www.macromedia.com`).

However, FreeHand 9 has this added advantage: It also enables you to create symbols and export directly to a .SWF movie. Once in Flash, add frame labels, stop actions, and buttons to take you forward and backward through each storyboard. Your client (or boss) will think this is stunning and credit you for having spent a number of hours preparing your presentation.

Author's Note: Flash 5 can import FreeHand files, and Illustrator 9 now offers direct export of Flash .SWF files.

Animation Storyboarding

The primary purposes of creating a storyboard for Flash animation projects are as follows:

✦ Use for logo or character animations within a project

✦ Create by using a printed or illustrated template in FreeHand or Illustrator

✦ Draw or illustrate specifics

Animation storyboarding is the most common type. Anyone who wants to produce anything — from a splash logo animation to a full character animation — will usually need to develop this type of storyboard. To do this, you only need to be able to draw stick figures; if you lack even that skill, you can draw circles, squares, and triangles. As you become more advanced you'll be able to specify camera angles, cuts in the action, and transitions. An animation storyboard template is a page with three rectangles, representing frames, and with space to the side for writing down the description of the action, other notes, and the sound cue — if you are using sound.

However, let's figure out the basics first. Begin by writing out a series of *very* short, simple sentences that tell the *action* that you want to storyboard. For example:

Woman appears under a streetlight from left.

Woman walks right to a green door.

Sign on door says "Pet Shop."

Woman opens the door by the knob.

A frog jumps out.

The frog knocks the woman over.

Continued

Continued

It's usually best to limit each sentence to a description of one *character* and one *action*. With these descriptions, all you need to do is print out the template, and assign one sentence to the description area of each frame of the storyboard template. Then simply draw the scene that you are describing in the sentence.

To see an example of an Animation Storyboard, find the tutorial folder in the ch38 folder on the CD-ROM and open the animation_storyboard.ai document.

This procedure helps you to make many, many decisions. "Woman appears under a streetlight from left" suggests that we are able to see the woman and the street, which means we have a wide view. We call this an establishing shot or a wide shot. You set the mood of your scene here. In the rectangle to the left, draw the scene out, making sure to show exactly what will be in the frame when the woman appears. Depending on your illustration ability and time constraints, you could develop your character and scene's look. Otherwise, just hammer it out. Use a triangle to mark your person, a circle for the light and rectangle for the door. The value of this work is that you will already *know* where you are going when you finally start building the animation in Flash—which translates into an incredible savings of time!

At this point, many students (and even developers) ask, "So, what if I'm just making a little splash logo animation?" Well, simply change your mindset (or the storyboard concept) to *transition*. Then, work out each transition the logo will take with a short description.

1. Logo fades up.

2. Logo spins three times.

3. Logo pulses.

4. Logo sends out a shock wave.

5. Wave fills screen to white.

6. Interface fades up.

Then, storyboard those descriptions before you start animation!

Interaction Storyboards

Are you a visual person who is attempting to communicate to your programmer or project engineer what you want to have happen in a project? Are you attempting to make broad functionality changes across an entire project? Are you designing a project all by yourself and needing to turn it around in 24 hours? Well, interaction storyboards may be your salvation.

✦ Use for any interactive project, including complex ActionScripting.

✦ Create using an outline version of your layout storyboard *or* by using the interaction storyboard template provided on the CD-ROM.

To see an example of an interaction storyboard, locate the tutorial in the ch38 folder of the CD-ROM, and then open the interaction_storyboard.pdf document.

Interaction storyboarding is most important to the Flash development process. I began creating this type of storyboard back when I developed Director CD-ROMS and I've carried it over to my user interface and prototype design work in Flash. There are several styles of interaction storyboard, which are suitable for different situations. You could choose one style or even combine them for use in different situations.

Written Interaction Description

All interaction storyboards start in the same manner as layout and animation storyboards: You must be able to write down in short sentences *what* you want to have happen. This can be easier if you reverse the equation by asking yourself, at each point of interactivity, "what do I want the user's experience to be?" The answers to these questions will provide the backbone of your interactive storyboard. In programming, this style of describing actions in sentences and then later turning it into actual code is called PDL, Programming Description Language. Advanced programmers may not find this very useful but for those who are either learning scripting or else handing our design to someone else (in hopes that they will script it for us), it's a great skill to have. Here's an example of a simple interaction description:

- ✦ Play an opening logo animation while preloading content.

- ✦ Have a menu that shows choices on click.

- ✦ (The menu will be present at all times.)

- ✦ Rolling over causes the icon and word to highlight.

- ✦ The icons and words are ____.

- ✦ Clicking any section of the menu shows submenu choices or loads subsection.

- ✦ As you get more familiar with Flash and its structures and actions you can give more detailed information:

- ✦ LOGO ANIMATION Plays while a Preloader downloads our BASE INTERFACE, MENUS and SOUND.

- ✦ On Rollover of LOGO, Target to Play a logo animation.

- ✦ On Click of LOGO, Go To base interface and Unload all submovies

- ✦ When Over BUTTON of each MENU CHOICE, highlight the icon.

- ✦ On Click of each MENU CHOICE, open a set of submenu choices.

Here is the logic to the way the information is presented: I CAPITALIZE the names of the objects I'm acting on or need to create. I capitalize the first letter of each action I need to create. "On Rollover" indicates that the action occurs by using an ActionScript command and Target tells me I'm going to Tell Target (Flash 4) or use a with command (Flash 5) to talk to a Movie Clip. In the next line, "When over," indicates that the highlight occurs in the OVER frame of a button timeline. Load means I'm going to load a .SWF movie or text document into a level above my base movie, movie clip or a text field. I hope that you get the idea!

Continued

Continued

Here's an ideal workflow for complex ActionScript interfaces:

✦ Create a detailed description of what you want to happen.

✦ Create an interaction storyboard, which breaks out:

- Where you will to store your objects and methods
- What the variable names will be
- Whether you want to access the script from several places
- Any variables that you will use

✦ Create a list of naming conventions

Most of my scripting takes place on paper so that either I, or my production person, can quickly set up all of the elements, the Main Timeline, layers, Movie Clips, and buttons that will be needed. Naming conventions should be established early so that your production people always know whether you're talking about a frame label (error_test), variable name (maxWidth), Movie Clip instance name (controller) or a symbol library name (mc_controller). You might also consider color-coding your document as you write it. Little snippets of code could be blue, variable names red, and so on. This is a *very* quick way to simplify the task of actually writing your own code or to facilitate having a programmer code it for you.

Visual Interaction Storyboard

Now I give you a visual way to storyboard this interaction. After you've figured out what you want, and why, then you can get really specific with a Visual Interaction Storyboard. For simple projects, I usually open my Layout Storyboard, which I've created in either FreeHand or Flash, turn the display to outlines, and then I take a screenshot and print it. This page will display all of my elements without cluttering the storyboard with colors or solid elements. But for really complex storyboarding, I go to a large sketchpad and distill my elements to their basics. At the top of the sketch, I draw a set of lines for my Main Timeline; below I draw my interactivity using signs; for example, rectangles = buttons, squares = Movie Clips, and so forth.

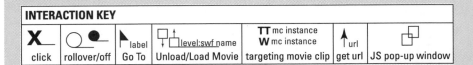

Here's the key to my shorthand for interactive storyboards. It's always a good idea to print a key like this along with your storyboards so that if someone else is trying to decipher them, they'll know what you are communicating.

I have identified five main types of interaction design in Flash. These are:

1. Go To structures

2. Get URL structures

3. Load Movie structures

4. Tell Target (in Flash 5 called "with" structures because of the change in Movie Clip behaviors) structures

5. Complex ActionScript structures

I need to be able to indicate what happens when I rollover an element, when I click it, or when I enter a frame on the timeline. In Flash 5, I can also interact with Movie Clips, which may also have actions attached to them. In Flash 4, only buttons could have actions attached.

To see an example that maps one type of interface, locate the tutorial folder within the ch38 folder of the CD-ROM, and then open the interaction_key_+_storyboard.ai document.

Flowchart Storyboarding for Complex ActionScript

The most difficult interactivity to storyboard visually is a complex ActionScript interface. Yet e-commerce sites and database-driven or interactive-driven projects can be particularly important to hammer out in written and visual form. I find it easiest to use a very old form of engineering flowcharting to map these complex interactions. Get URL structures are also easily mapped with this type of storyboard. Most other forms of interactivity can be mapped out with a modified flowchart.

Authors' Note: The written description from Dorian Nisinson's Expert Tutorial, "Using hitTest for a Multiple Targets," located in Chapter 23, is a perfect example of the kind of documentation that is needed in order to create a visual storyboard to map out complex ActionScript interactivity.

Were you able to figure out what was supposed to happen throughout each phase of the interactivity? If I have done this much preplanning on a project, and then followed that planning with a couple of storyboards, it rarely takes me more than three or four hours to set up the first prototype of the alpha version.

Before you jump right into development you might consider taking one more step. This involves taking small pieces of your interaction storyboard and trying them out. For instance, if you have a specific type of menu in your interaction storyboard, you might want to try out an example of that menu so your client can see what the functionality will be. It's much easier to change a small piece now rather than having to go through and change the entire interface later. Other than menus, I always test transition animations, game-play elements, and small ActionScript subroutines.

Continued

Continued

Prototyping

At this point, you are ready to create a full prototype of the project. You can quickly build-out your Main Timeline, Movie Clip, animation, and button structures using your interactive storyboard. To add your scripting you can use your written description. Make sure that you continuously save different versions of your prototype, recording in a version document what changes you made since the first save (for example, nav03a.fla: changed base font to mini; added images to button over states; tested with .JPEG or .PNG images; used .PNG). While prototyping, you'll also want to keep your interaction storyboard and interaction description current with changes that need to be applied to the whole project, especially if you are working with a large group of people. If you need to move really quickly, then at least keep a sketchpad to jot notes about what you are doing so that you can come back through the project after you've finished and create updated versions of the documents. This may seem stupid, but when you have to come back—six days, weeks, or months later—to make changes, I promise that you'll be very happy that you did this.

If you set up a preproduction process like this for yourself, it will be a rare project that you can't prototype in a single day of production. In addition, you have a great paper trail that other people can follow, that you can use to manage clients and production cycles, and that you can return to months later to make changes easily. See? It wasn't that difficult and you've made yourself a very happy Flash camper.

Curiously, while MD Dundon claims to be from "earth," she lists "live" as her singular favorite thing to do. "Red Corvette," by Prince, and the *Star Wars* theme were the big hits when she graduated high school. She's consulted for and worked on many noteworthy sites, including: www.stonecircledesign.com, www.casioresearch.com, and www.indiansunset.com.

Summary

✦ You are responsible for making sure that you understand the production process involved with Flash content creation. We introduced you to a two-phase production model that involves six milestones: Business Initiative, Creative Solutions, Approval, Production, QA, and Delivery.

✦ During the production period, keep six concepts in mind: asset assembly, a master Flash architecture, a local test environment, HTML page layout, a server staging environment, and proper QA testing. After production is finished, you need to develop a systematic maintenance routine.

✦ Inspiration can be used to create organizational and process flowcharts. After you have developed these flowcharts, you can more easily create the functional specification for your Flash site.

✦ No one workflow is absolute. As MD Dundon's tutorial demonstrates, you should work within the parameters of each project, and answer key questions with the client before you commence intense Flash production.

✦   ✦   ✦

Working with Authoring Applications

Dreamweaver and Director are Macromedia's most popular authoring solutions for Web and CD-ROM presentations. As the last chapter to Part VII, this chapter teaches you how to integrate advanced Flash movies, created from lessons in other sections of this book, into final production with these two applications.

Flash movies (as .SWF files) have the amazing capability to be embedded in other applications. The best — and the best known — example of this is the Flash Player plug-in for Web browsers. To take more control over the usage of Flash movies in Web browsers, you can use Macromedia Dreamweaver to customize plug-in settings. However, the fun doesn't stop there. You can import Flash .SWF files into Macromedia Director. Director is the premiere multimedia authoring application on the market. With Director's scripting language Lingo, interactive commands can be passed between the Flash movie and the Director movie. In some cases, you can do more with Flash movies in Director than you can with even the most advanced ActionScripts in Flash 5 alone.

Caution

You need to know how to export your Flash editor documents (.FLA files) as Flash movies (.SWF files). You may want to read Chapter 40, "Publishing Flash Movies," and Chapter 41, "Integrating Flash Content with HTML," before proceeding with this chapter.

Integrating .SWF Files into Dreamweaver

Although Flash 5's Publish feature takes a lot of the guesswork out of placing Flash movies into HTML pages, you might want to add HTML graphics and text to the page, too. Macromedia Dreamweaver has been a huge hit with Web designers — its roundtrip HTML feature keeps your HTML code just the way you like it. Roundtrip HTML refers to Dreamweaver's capability to transfer HTML code back and forth between applications, keeping your preferred formatting intact — Dreamweaver will not write over your own code. New features of Dreamweaver 4 include:

✦ A fully integrated text editor complete with syntax coloring capabilities

✦ The Layout view, which allows you to draw HTML tables and cells directly on the page with the Table tool and the Cell tool

✦ Custom Flash Buttons and Flash Text creation tools

✦ Roundtrip image editing with Fireworks

In this section, we look at the fundamentals of using Flash movies with Dreamweaver and HTML.

For more information on using the Publish feature of Flash 5, see Chapter 40, "Publishing Flash Movies."

Working with your Flash movie

After you have created an interactive animation and have exported the file into the .SWF format, it's time to put the file into your HTML document. (For more information on exporting a Flash animation to the .SWF format, refer to Chapter 40, "Publishing Flash Movies.")

Let's get started. First, create a new document in Dreamweaver, using File ➪ New (Command+N or Ctrl+N). Next, insert the Flash file by selecting Insert ➪ Media ➪ Flash, or by using the Objects Panel, and clicking the Flash icon, as shown in the following figure. If you prefer to use keyboard shortcuts, try Option+Command+F (or Ctrl+Alt+F on the PC). The Select File dialog appears. Now, browse your folders until you find a .SWF file to import.

Select a Flash .SWF file and click Select. You should see a gray rectangle with a small Flash symbol in your Dreamweaver document, indicating that this is a Flash movie (see Figure 39-1).

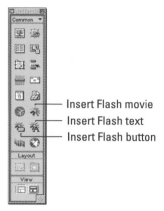

Insert Flash movie
Insert Flash text
Insert Flash button

Figure 39-1: Click the Flash object icon on the Objects Panel to insert a Flash movie.

You should also notice that your Flash file now appears in the Dreamweaver Properties Inspector, as shown in Figure 39-2, which displays the properties most commonly used in Dreamweaver (see Table 39-1 for a description of those properties). If the Properties Inspector is not visible, access it with Window ⇨ Properties (Command+F3 or Ctrl+F3). If all of the properties are not displayed, click the expand arrow in the lower-right corner or double-click the inactive areas of the inspector. The inspector hosts many options and controls:

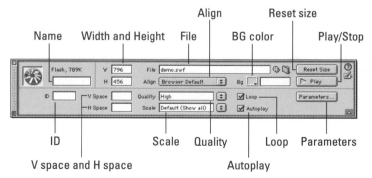

Figure 39-2: The Properties Inspector in Dreamweaver 4

Table 39-1
Flash Properties in the Property Inspector

Property	Description
Name	The first field is used to identify the movie for scripting purposes. As always, it is a good habit to name all your elements in Dreamweaver.
W and H	Represents the movies dimension in default pixels. The dimensions can also be set to pc (picas), pt (points), in (inches), mm (millimeters), cm (centimeters), or %. This information is automatically set to the movies original dimensions.
File	The file's path/location. This information should already appear in this field.
Reset Size	Returns the selected movie to its original size.
Align	Determines how the movie is aligned on the page (left, middle, right). The default is align left.
Bg Color	Specifies a background color for the movie area. This color also appears while the movie is not playing (while loading and after playing). This setting can also be set within Flash 5 in the Movie Properties dialog (Modify ➪ Movie).
ID	Defines the optional ActiveX ID parameter. This parameter is most often used to pass information between ActiveX controls.
V Space and H Space	Specifies the number of pixels for white space around the movie. V Space pertains to the white space above, and below, while H space defines the space on the left and right sides of the movie.
Quality	Sets the quality parameter for the object and embed tags that run the movie. The settings to choose from are Low, Auto Low, Auto High, and High.
Scale	Sets the scale parameter for the OBJECT and EMBED tags that place the movie. Scale defines how the movie is placed within the browser window when the width and height values are percentages.
Loop	This option makes the Flash movie automatically loop if no Stop actions occur on the Main Timeline.
Autoplay	Plays the movie's Main Timeline automatically when the page loads.
Parameters	Opens a dialog for entering additional parameters to pass to the movie. The movie must be created in Flash to receive these parameters.

Positioning your movie

The easiest way to center your Flash movie within the browser window is to surround the <EMBED> and/or <OBJECT> tags with the <CENTER></CENTER> tags. This method will not cause the movie to stretch or expand, thereby revealing the workspace of the Flash movie. There is, of course, another way to center the Flash movie in the browser—all you need to do is set the width and height dimensions to 100 percent.

Note   This method also might cause some unwanted effects to your movie by revealing the work area of the Flash movie. For example, if you had objects in the Flash environment that bleed off the stage area and into the work area, those parts of the objects that bleed off the stage would regularly be "cropped" by the dimensions of the movie. By importing the Flash movie into Dreamweaver, Dreamweaver adheres to the original dimensions, giving you the clean edge appearance. But when the width and height are set to 100 percent, the movie will show everything that was meant to be cropped, giving you a possible "sloppy" edge to the movie.

Although most Web sites are viewed in full-screen capacity, some users scale their browser to their own desired size, which may adversely impact the aspect ratio (the height and width ratio) of your movie. The scale option enables you to select three options to achieve the desired perspective. These options are:

✦ **showall:** Makes the entire movie visible in the specified area. The aspect ratio of the movie is maintained, and no distortion occurs. Borders may appear on two sides of the movie.

✦ **noborder:** Forces the movie to fill the specified area. The aspect ratio of the movie is maintained, and no distortion occurs—but portions of the movie may be cropped.

✦ **exactfit:** Forces the entire movie to fill the specified area. The aspect ratio of the movie is not maintained, and distortion may occur. For this example, we used the exactfit option to enable users to resize their windows and still see the entire movie.

Inserting a Flash Button

New to Dreamweaver 4 is the capability to create Flash Button objects based on predetermined button styles. These styles look much like the Button Library that ships with Flash 5. Dreamweaver actually lets you edit the text labels and links of these buttons. Dreamweaver will also create a .SWF file that is placed in the same directory as the current HTML document.

Note   You must save your document first before inserting a Flash button or text object. If you have not saved your document, Dreamweaver will prompt you to do so at that time. Dreamweaver needs to know where the HTML file resides before it can create the .SWF file.

Select the Flash Button icon within the Objects Panel, or select Insert ➪ Interactive Media ➪ Flash Button. Alternatively, you can drag the Flash Button icon from the Objects Panel and into the document window. Using either method will enable you to access the Insert Flash Button dialog, shown in Figure 39-3.

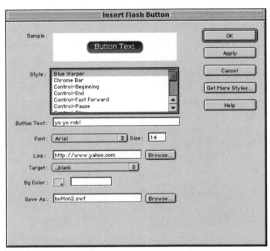

Figure 39-3: Scroll through the library of available button styles

Now select a Button style from the list provided. Dreamweaver provides you with a preview of the Button style. You can also click and rollover the Button style to preview how the Button will behave. However, you will not be able to preview any changes to the text or Bg color in this window.

Next, in the Button text field, type the text that you would like to see. This field doesn't work for every button style. If the button preview has the words Button Text on the button, then you will be able to type in your own text. Also, the amount of text is limited to the width of the Button.

For the Font field (optional), select a font for the text and the font size from their respective drop-down menus.

For the Link field (optional), type a file name (or URL) or click the Browse button to locate the file to link to. The link can be either a document-relative or absolute link for the button. If you try to type in a site-relative link, Dreamweaver will prompt you with a error message. This error occurs due to the manner in which that Flash files have to be saved in relation to the HTML document files.

The Target field (optional) enables you to choose a target frame or target window from the drop-down menu.

The Bg field (optional) enables you to choose a background color for your Flash button within a rectangular area. You can either type in a hexadecimal color value (for example, #0066FF) or use the color well to select a background color.

For the Save As field, type in a name to save your new .SWF file as, or accept the default button name. You could also choose a different location for the SWF to be saved by clicking the Browse button and then finding the folder to place your Flash button (for example, flash_assets/green_arrow.swf).

If you can't find a Button style that suits you, click Get More Styles to connect to the Macromedia Exchange site to download even more button styles.

Finally, click Apply or OK to insert the Flash button into the document window. If you clicked Apply, you will not leave the Button dialog; instead, you will be able to preview your new Button on the page.

Editing a Flash Button

There are two ways to open the Edit dialog for Flash Buttons: (a) you can double-click the Flash button, or (b) you can select the Flash button and click the Edit button in the Property Inspector.

More options are available within the Properties inspector. Bg color and File source are the only two options that are repeated from the Edit dialog.

Inserting a Flash Text Object

The Flash Text Object enables you to insert a body of Flash Text with a simple rollover effect. Inserting the Flash Text Object is very similar to inserting the Flash Button. Simply select the Flash Text icon in the Objects Panel, or choose Insert ⇨ Interactive Media ⇨ Flash Text. This brings up the Insert Flash Text dialog, shown in Figure 39-4.

Then follow these steps to format and insert your text:

1. Select a font face from the Font drop-down menu.
2. Enter a font size (in points) in the Size field.
3. Select style attributes by clicking the Bold, Italic, and Text Alignment buttons.
4. Choose a text color by entering a hexadecimal color (for example, #0066FF) or by choosing a specific color from the color pop-up menu.

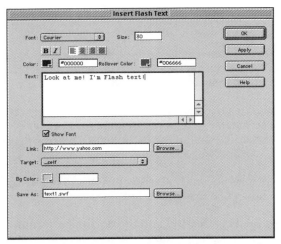

Figure 39-4: Dreamweaver 4 enables you to place antialiased Flash Text within an HTML document. Dreamweaver will create the necessary .SWF file for the HTML document.

5. Type in your desired text in the Text field.

6. Enter a document-relative or absolute HTML link.

7. Choose an HTML target window or target frame (optional).

8. Choose a background color (optional).

9. Type in a file name for the Save as field or accept the default name (for example, text1.swf).

10. To preview all of your settings, click Apply to insert the Flash Text without leaving the dialog.

11. To insert the Flash Text and exit the dialog, click OK.

Editing a Flash Text Object

There are two ways of opening the Edit dialog for Flash Text: (a) you can double-click the Flash Text Object, or (b) select the Flash Text object and click Edit in the Property inspector.

Directing the browser to the Flash plug-in

Perhaps one of the greatest timesaving features of Dreamweaver 4 is to its automatic inclusion of plug-in download locations for both Netscape and Internet Explorer (ActiveX). The following example of code will appear in your HTML document (note that the ¬ indicates continuation of the same line of code) — it simultaneously places the Flash movie in your document and also directs the browser to the download location of the Flash Player plug-in if it is not installed:

```
<object classid="clsid:D27CDB6E-AE6D-11cf-96B8 ¬
    -444553540000"
    codebase="http://download.macromedia.com/pub/shockwave/¬
    cabs/flash/swflash.cab#version=4,0,2,0"
    width="100%" height="100%">
    <param name="SRC" value="flashmovie.swf">
    <param name="SCALE" value="exactfit">

<embed
    src="flashmovie.swf"
    pluginspage="http://www.macromedia.com/shockwave/¬
        download/"
    type="application/x-shockwave-flash"
    width="100%" height="100%"
    scale="exactfit">
</embed>
</object>
```

Caution   Dreamweaver still uses the Flash 4.0 ActiveX download location. Change the 4 in the CODEBASE attribute of the `<OBJECT>` tag to 5,0,41,0 to ensure that the latest Flash 5.0 ActiveX control is downloaded.

Expert Tutorial: Exploring the JavaScript Integration Kit for Flash 5, *by Joseph Lowery*

When it comes to Dreamweaver expertise, we didn't need to think twice about asking fellow Bible author Joseph Lowery to contribute his techniques for using Dreamweaver's new JavaScript Integration Kit for Flash 5. You'll find a version of the JavaScript Integration Kit for Flash 5 on the Flash 5 Bible CD-ROM in the ch39 folder.

With an eye toward smoothing the integration between Flash and Dreamweaver, Macromedia released the JavaScript Integration Kit for Flash 5 (JIK). The JIK is a suite of commands and behaviors installable in Dreamweaver—versions 3 and above—via the Extension Manager. You can download the current version from the Macromedia Exchange; choose Help ⇨ Flash Exchange to go directly online.

The JavaScript Integration Kit for Flash 5 has four main components:

   ✦ **Macromedia Flash Player Controls:** Enables the designer to include interactive control over Flash movies in a Web page. New Dreamweaver behaviors assign play, stop, rewind, fast-forward, pan, and zoom actions to any graphic element. In addition, an HTML drop-down menu can be turned into Flash movie selector.

Continued

Continued

✦ **Advanced Form Validations:** Ensures that your visitors are entering in the proper type of information in your Flash form. You can apply any of 18 client-side form validations — everything from a required, nonblank to an International Phone Validation.

✦ **Browser Scripts for Flash:** Embeds up to ten different JavaScript functions in the Dreamweaver page, which functions are callable from any Flash 5 movie. With these functions, your Flash movie can control form elements such as text fields and select lists, open remote browser windows, set cookies, and swap images on the Web page.

✦ **Flash Dispatcher Behavior:** Detects the visitor's Flash Player version and redirects to a suitable Web page.

The beauty of the JIK is that it's various components can be mixed and matched to achieve a wide range of effects and control. The resulting Web page offers a greater degree of interactivity for the visitor as well as for the Flash designer.

Macromedia Flash Player Controls

One method of engaging your Web page visitors is to give them more control over their viewing experience; rather than just displaying a movie from beginning to end, allow the viewer to pause, rewind, and play the animation at will. Flash's vector-based nature even enables them to zoom in and out, without loss of image clarity.

While all of this functionality is available through Flash ActionScripting, not all designs require the controls to be maintained within a Flash movie. The Flash Player Controls enable all of the common VCR-like functionality — and then some — to be assigned to HTML elements such as images or hotspots.

When the JavaScript Integration Kit is installed, ten different behaviors are grouped under the MM Flash Player Controls:

Fast Forward Flash	Go To Flash Frame
Go To Flash Frame Based on Cookie	Load Flash Movie
Pan Flash	Play Flash
Rewind Flash	Set Flash by List
Stop Flash	Zoom Flash

As with any other Dreamweaver behavior, the player controls must be assigned to a target: a text link, an image map hotspot, or a graphic with a link attached. Typically, such a graphic button would use a false link, such as # or `javascript:;` so that it may act as a trigger but not actually open a URL.

You must have at least one Flash movie in the page before the Flash Player Controls become available as shown in the following figure. Once activated, the user interfaces for the Flash Player Controls vary according to their function as detailed later. With the Play, Stop, and Rewind Flash behaviors, you just pick the Flash movie that you want to control from the drop-down list. All the other behaviors include this option as well, so you can affect any movie on the page.

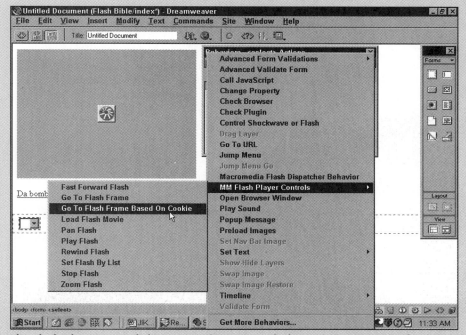

The Flash Player Controls become active once a Flash movie is present in the current Dreamweaver document.

To use the Flash Player Controls, follow these steps:

Step 1: Insert at least one Flash movie by choosing an animation from the Assets panel or applying the Insert Flash object.

Step 2: Enter a unique name in the ID field of the Flash Property Inspector for each movie. A distinct ID avoids browser compatibility problems; if one is not initially supplied, Dreamweaver offers to make one for you when any of the behaviors are applied.

Step 3: Select the text link, hotspot, or image to trigger the behavior. If you'd like to apply the Set Flash by List behavior, select a form list object.

Continued

Continued

Step 4: Choose Window ⇨ Behaviors to open the Behaviors Panel, if necessary. Alternatively, you can select the Behavior icon from the Launcher or use the keyboard shortcut F8.

Step 5: Choose the Add button from the Behaviors Panel and select the desired behavior under the MM Flash Player Controls heading. The chosen behavior's dialog appears, similar to the one shown in the following figure.

With the Pan Flash behavior, your viewer can move around a Flash movie in any direction. As shown, this behavior would pan in a diagonal direction, down and to the right, every time it was triggered.

Step 6: Select the parameters for your behavior.

✦ For the Play Flash, Rewind Flash, and Stop Flash behaviors, select the desired animation to affect from the Movie drop-down list.

✦ For the Fast Forward Flash behavior:

   1. Select the desired animation to affect from the Movie drop-down list.

   2. In the first blank field, enter the desired value you want the movie to advance by.

   3. Select either Frames or Percent from the drop-down list.

   For example, to advance the movie by 5 percent each time the behavior is called, enter 5 in the first field and choose Percent from the list.

  Author's Note: You can use a negative number to rewind one or more frames at a time.

✦ For the Go To Flash Frame behavior:

   1. Select the desired animation to affect from the Movie drop-down list.

   2. Enter the frame number to move to in the Go To Frame field.

✦ For the Go To Flash Frame Based on Cookie behavior:

   1. Select the desired animation to affect from the Movie drop-down list.

   2. Enter the name of the cookie to read in the Cookie Name field.

3. Enter the value to look for in the Cookie Value field.

4. Enter the frame number to advance to when the cookie name and value are read in the Go To Frame field.

✦ For the Load Flash Movie behavior (As Dreamweaver warns you, this behavior is not supported for Netscape browsers):

1. Select the desired animation to you want to replace from the Replace Movie drop-down list.

2. Enter the filename for the movie to load in the With Movie field or locate the movie by selecting the Browse button.

3. Input the level to load the movie into in the Level field. To replace an existing movie with the loaded movie, enter a level number that is currently occupied by another movie. To replace the original movie and unload every level, choose 0 for the Level.

4. To begin playing the movie immediately, set the Play option to Yes; otherwise, set Play to No.

✦ For the Pan Flash behavior:

1. Select the desired animation to affect from the Movie drop-down list.

2. Choose the Horizontal and/or Vertical direction — up, down, right, or left — to pan to from the drop-down lists.

3. Select the degree of the pan by entering a value in the fields below each direction.

You can pan diagonally by entering nonzero values for both the Horizontal and Vertical direction.

4. Choose whether you'd like the pan values to operate in either Pixel or Percent Mode.

✦ For the Set Flash by List behavior (As Dreamweaver warns you, this behavior is not supported for Netscape browsers.):

1. Select the desired animation to affect from the Movie drop-down list.

2. Choose the list object from the Select Box drop-down list.

3. Input the level to load the movie into in the Level field. To replace an existing movie with the loaded movie, enter a level number that is currently occupied by another movie. To replace the original movie and unload every level, choose 0 for the Level.

4. To begin playing the movie immediately, set the Play option to Yes; otherwise, set Play to No.

Continued

Continued

5. For the Set Flash by List behavior to work properly, you'll also need to set the values of each of the list items to a relative or absolute file URL pointing to a .SWF file. Click the Parameters button on the List/Menu Property Inspector to enter new labels and their corresponding values.

✦ For the Zoom Flash behavior:

1. Select the desired animation to affect from the Movie drop-down list.

2. Enter the value desired in the Zoom field.

   To zoom in, enter a number greater than 100; to zoom out, enter a number below 100. To reset the movie to the original zoom level, enter 0.

Step 7: After you've chosen all the desired parameters from the dialog, select OK to close it. The Behaviors Panel displays the event and action for the behavior just applied.

Step 8: By default, `onClick` is the selected event. To change the triggering event to `onMouseOver` or `onMouseOut`, select the down arrow between the event and the action and choose the desired event from the list.

Advanced Form Validations

HTML forms can be tricky: The more use you put forms to gathering information from your visitors, the greater the possibility for user error. In a sense, forms are a classic double-edged sword and a few people taking advantage of Flash's increased interactivity are getting nicked by them. If, for example, your online form includes two fields for a telephone number, one for the United States, and one for international visitors, you'll want to be sure that the proper data is entered in the correct field. To ensure that a user enters the type of information you're expecting in your Flash form, that information needs to be validated. The JavaScript Integration Kit includes methods for validating 18 different types of data.

For the Advanced Form Validations to work, you'll need to work both with your Flash movie and with the Dreamweaver page the movies is embedded in. Here's an overview of the process:

On the Dreamweaver side:

✦ Create a form with hidden fields — one for each of the Flash fields you want to validate.

✦ Attach the Advance Validate Form behavior to the form itself.

✦ Add one of the Browser Scripts for Flash functions, `FDK_setFormText`, to the page.

✦ Attach the desired validation behavior to the `<body>` tag of the current document.

On the Flash side:

✦ Make sure every form field has a unique variable name assign to it.

✦ Add a `getURL` action to the `on (press)` event of the submit button, calling the `FDK_setFormText` function inserted into the Dreamweaver page.

✦ Add another `getURL` action to the `on (release)` event of the submit button which invokes the `FDK_Validate` function — which was put on the Dreamweaver document by the Advance Validate Form behavior.

You'll need to keep track of the names of the Hidden field inputs inserted in Dreamweaver, as well as the name of the form itself; they both are referenced when the functions are added in Flash.

Now that you've got an overview, let's go through the process with a little more detail. Again, we start with the Dreamweaver page:

1. Choose Insert ➪ Form to add a form to your document.

   In Dreamweaver 4, the form is automatically named, but you'll need to add a name in the Property Inspector if you're using Dreamweaver 3.

2. Within the form, add a Hidden form field (Insert ➪ Form Objects ➪ Hidden Field) for every Flash field that you'd like to validate. Give each Hidden field a unique name and leave the Value blank.

3. Select the <form> tag in the Tag Selector and, from the Behaviors panel, choose the Advance Validate Form behavior.

   The Advance Validate Form dialog appears, as shown in the figure that follows.

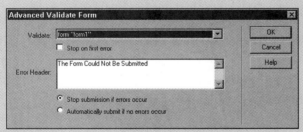

The Advance Validate Form behavior controls how validations overall are applied.

4. In the Advance Validate Form dialog:

   • Select the form containing the Hidden elements you want to use from the Validate drop-down list.

   • To stop validating when an incorrect entry is encountered, check the Stop on First Error option.

   • Enter any desired message in the Error Header text area. The Error Header is displayed in addition to any validation-specific error messages.

Continued

Continued

- If your behavior is assigned to an `onSubmit` event (the default) choose the Stop Submission If Errors Occur option; otherwise, select the Automatically Submit If No Errors Occur option.

- Select OK to close the dialog when you're done.

5. Choose Commands ⇨ Browser Scripts for Flash.

The Browser Scripts for Flash commands, discussed in more detail later in this section, embeds functions in the Dreamweaver page for communicating with Flash.

6. When the Browser Scripts for Flash dialog opens, select the FDK_setFormText option; close the dialog when you're done.

Our final preparation in Dreamweaver is to add the individual validation behaviors required

7. Select the <body> tag from the Tag Selector and choose the Add button in the Behaviors panel. From the drop-down list, select a validation behavior from the Advanced Form Validations category.

Most of the Advanced Form Validation behaviors have similar dialogs in which you can choose the particular form element (the Hidden field relating to the Flash form field) affected, make the field required, and set the error message. The differences between the various behaviors are detailed in the table that follows.

8. Repeat Step 7 for each validation that you'd like to apply in the form.

Behavior	*Description*
Alphanumeric Validation	Displays an error if nonalphanumeric characters are entered.
Credit Card Validation	Removes any spaces or hyphens and then displays an error message if the card number is not valid. This behavior does not authorize credit card purchases.
Date Validation	Optionally enables dates in the future, in the past, or in a particular range and specific format.
E-mail Validation	Makes sure that the entry contains an @ and a period.
Entry Length Validation	Accepts a defined number range of characters; for example, from 5 to 10.
Floating Point Validation	Displays a error if a non-number is entered; floating point numbers can contain decimals.
Integer Validation	Displays the message if a non-number or a number with decimals is entered. You can also set an acceptable number range.

Behavior	Description
International Phone Validation	Removes parentheses, spaces, and hyphens, and then makes sure at least six digits are entered.
Like Entry Validation	Checks one form field entry against another; typically used for password verification.
Mask Validation	Enables the designer to require a specific pattern of text, and numbers to be entered. Use A to indicate a letter, # for numbers, and ? if the entry could be either a letter or a number. For example, the mask A###?? would require a letter followed by three numbers, followed by two other alphanumeric characters.
Nonblank Validation	Displays a message if the field is left empty.
Radio Button Validation	Ensures that at least one option in a specified radio button group is selected. Note: This behavior is only used with HTML form elements.
Selection Made in List Validation	Displays an error if the user does not make a selection from a specific drop-down list. Note: This behavior is only used with HTML form elements.
Social Security Validation	Removes any hyphens, checks for a proper length and then reformats the number into a 3-2-4 configuration, as in 123-45-6789.
Time Validation	Displays an error if a valid time with minutes within a certain range is not entered. Military time and most variations of a.m. and p.m. are accepted.
URL Validation	Looks for valid URL protocols and displays an error message if one is not found at the start of the entry. Accepted URLs include: ftp://, http://, javascript:, file://, gopher://, https://, mailto:, rlogin://, shttp://, snews://, telnet://, tn3270://, swais://
US Phone Validation	Verifies that the entered information is either seven or ten digits after removing any parentheses and hyphens.
Zip Code Validation	Requires the entry to be either five or nine digits.

Now that the Dreamweaver page is prepped, we're ready to prepare the Flash movie:

1. In Flash, add the required form fields as text input fields.

2. In the Text Options Panel, enter a unique name in the Variable field.

3. Make sure your form has a graphic that acts as a submit button.

Continued

Continued

4. Select the Submit button graphic and open the Action Panel.

5. Add an `on (press)` event and attach a `getURL` function to the event.

6. In the `getURL` function, call the `FDK_setFormText` function that was embedded into the Dreamweaver page. The `FDK_setFormText` function takes three arguments: the name of the form, the name of the field to be validated, and variable name assigned to the corresponding field in Flash.

For example, let's say the form is named `theForm`, that you've created a field for gathering an e-mail address, and that you have given it a name in Dreamweaver such as emailHidden. In Flash, the variable assigned to the corresponding text field might be called emailField. In this case, the `getURL` function would read:

```
getURL("javascript:FDK_setFormText('theForm','emailHidden','" ¬
emailField add "');");
```

Note the addition of the word `add` on either side of the variable name as shown in the code and in the following figure. This syntax is required for the parameters to be passed correctly.

Enter an FDK_setFormText function for every Flash field that you need to qualify.

7. Continue adding as many `FDK_setFormText` functions as you have fields to validate to the same `getURL` action. Separate each function with a semicolon.

After you've entered all the required `FDK_setFormText` functions, you'll need to add one last event and function.

8. In the Action Panel for the Submit button graphic, add an `on (release)` event and attach a `getURL` action to it.

9. In the `getURL` action, insert the `FDK_Validate` function. This function takes four arguments that correspond to the options available in Dreamweaver's Advanced Validate Form dialog: FormName, stopOnFailure, AutoSubmit, and ErrorHeader. Both stopOnFailure and AutoSubmit are Booleans and accept either `true` or `false`.

For example, suppose the form is again called theForm, that you'd like the form to stop processing when an error is encountered as well as automatically be submitted, and that your general error message reads, "Attention!! I found an error on the form!" Here, the `getURL` function would look like this (note that the ¬ indicates continuation of the same line of code):

```
getURL("javascript:FDK_Validate('theForm',true,true,¬
'Attention!! I found an error on the form!!\n\n');");
```

The `\n\n` after the function call acts as a hard return in the alert box to separate the generic message header and the specific validation error.

The final step is to cross the bridge again from Flash to Dreamweaver, bringing your exported Flash movie into the Dreamweaver page. Be sure to give it both a name and ID (which can be the same) in the Property Inspector.

Browser Scripts for Flash

With the JavaScript Integration Kit, integration is a two-way street: Not only is it easier to control Flash movies, but also the Flash movies can also affect the HTML page. The JIK includes one overall command called Browser Scripts for Flash which offers five different types of control:

✦ Setting a form element's value

✦ Setting a cookie

✦ Opening a remote browser window

✦ Swapping image for rollovers

✦ Setting list menu items

Implementing these functions in Dreamweaver is simplicity itself: Just choose Commands ⇨ Browser Scripts for Flash and check off the desired options you see in the figure that follows. The various functions are grouped into five different categories. If you open a page with these functions already in place, you'll find the option already selected; deselecting the checkbox removes the function from the page when the dialog is closed.

Continued

Continued

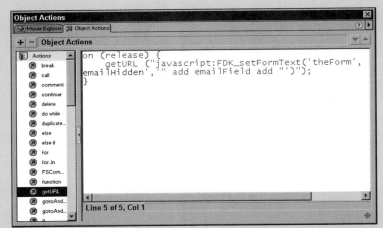

The Browser Scripts for Flash lets you easily insert or remove functions that you can call from Flash.

Like the form validations, using the Browser Scripts is a two-program process. After you've installed them in Dreamweaver, you need call the function in a Flash action. Each of the functions takes it's own series of parameters and, typically, each is invoked using an action such as getURL. The functions and their arguments are explained in the following table.

Function	Arguments	Description
FDK_setFormText	form, name, text	Sets the value of a form element.
FDK_newWindowable	URL, name, width, height, status, directories, location, toolbar, menubar, scrollbars, resize	Opens a remote browser window. The width and height values are entered in pixels; for all other parameters (except URL and windowName) enter a 0 to disallow the element and a 1 to include it.
FDK_setCookie	namevalue, expires, path, domain, secure	Sets a cookie from within a Flash movie and can be used in conjunction with the Go To Flash Frame Based on Cookie behavior.
FDK_swapImage	imageName, [blank], replacementPath, 1	Performs a image swap in the HTML document. The second parameter is intentionally left blank.

Function	Arguments	Description
FDK_swapImgRestore	n/a	Restores an previously executed image swap. For complex pages using multiple image swaps, it's best to explicitly swap the image from it's replacement to it's original source rather than use the FDK_SwapImRestore behavior.
FDK_findObj	n/a	Used in conjunction with the FDK_SwapImage behavior.
FDK_AddValueToList	ListObj, TextString, ValString, Position	Inserts a new value into a form list element.
FDK_SetSelectionByValue	ListObj, ListVal	Determines the selection of a list item with a given value.
FDK_SetSelectionByPosition	ListObj, ListPos	Determines the selection of a list item in a particular list position.
FDK_SetSelectionByText	ListObj, ListText	Determines the selection of a list item with a given label.

Flash Dispatcher Behavior

The final component of the JavaScript Integration Kit, the Flash Dispatcher Behavior, is designed to smooth visitor access to your Web-based Flash content. The Flash Dispatcher checks whether the visitor to your site already has the Flash player and, if the visitor does have a player, what version the player is. If the proper version — or no player at all — is found, this behavior allows you several options. The visitor's browser can be redirected to a Flash-less page or to a site for downloading an appropriate version, if an automatically down-loaded version is not possible.

To apply this behavior, select the <body> tag from the Tag Selector and, from the Behaviors panel, choose Macromedia Flash Dispatcher Behavior. In the dialog, you have the following options:

✦ **Macromedia Flash Content URL:** Enter or locate the path to the page containing the Flash movie.

✦ **Alternate URL:** Enter or locate the path to a Web page the visitor should go to if the proper Flash player was not found.

✦ **Macromedia Flash Version:** Choose the lowest permissible version from 2.0, 3.0, 4.0, or 5.0

Continued

Continued

✦ **Require Latest Plugin:** Select this option to require the latest version of the Flash Player.

✦ **No Player Options:** Any visitors who do not have the Flash Player installed will be sent to a selectable download page or use the Alternate URL.

✦ **Improper Version Options:** Any visitors who do not have the required version of the Flash Player installed will be sent to a selectable upgrade page or use the Alternate URL.

The Flash Content URL can be the same page that the behavior is applied to or, in the case of what is referred to as a gateway script, another page.

Publishing the HTML document

When you're ready to see your HTML document in a Web browser, save your Dreamweaver HTML document by selecting File ➪ Save (Command+S or Ctrl+S). To preview the page in a browser, use File ➪ Preview In Browser ➪ IE or Netscape, or press F12 to preview the page in your primary browser (as set in Dreamweaver's preferences). Although Flash 5 is able to publish supporting HTML documents for .SWF files, Dreamweaver is best used to achieve more advanced integration of Flash in HTML and JavaScript, as you see in the Expert Tutorial by Joseph Lowery, author of the *Dreamweaver Bible*.

Animation techniques using layers

The window mode parameter for Flash movies currently only works with the Windows 95/98/NT versions of Internet Explorer 4.0 or higher. The window mode parameter, wmode, lets the background of a Flash movie drop out, so that HTML or DHTML content can appear in place of the Flash movie background. Because support for this option is not broadly supported, you are unlikely to find very many Web pages that use it. However, if you want to try it out, it's pretty simple.

First, make sure that your Flash movie is on its own DHTML layer — if you want to animate other material behind or in front of the Flash movie. In the Dreamweaver Properties Inspector for Flash movies, click the Parameters button. In the Parameters dialog, click the + button above the Parameter column. Enter **wmode** in the left column. Click under the Value column, and enter one of the three options:

✦ **Window:** This is the "standard" player interface, in which the Flash movie plays as it would normally, in its own rectangular window on a Web page.

✦ **Opaque:** Use this option if you want the Flash movie to have an opaque background and have DHTML or HTML elements behind the Flash movie.

✦ **Transparent:** This option "knocks out" the Flash background color so that other HTML elements behind the Flash movie shows through. Note that the Flash movie's frame rate and performance may suffer on slower machines when this mode is used, because the Flash movie needs to composite itself over other non-Flash material.

The `wmode` parameter is only recognized by 32-bit Windows versions of Internet Explorer 4 or higher. If you are using browser detection on your Web pages, you can divert visitors using these browsers to specialized Flash and DHTML Web pages.

Using .SWF Files in Macromedia Director

Macromedia Director 8.5 is *the* multimedia authoring application used to create dazzling multimedia-rich DVD-ROMs, CD-ROMs, and Shockwave-enhanced Web experiences. The most exciting news for the 8.5 release is the under-the-hood Intel 3D technology that enables Shockwave to use high-impact, textured, 3D graphics and models. Since version 6.5, you can import Flash movies (as .SWF files) via the Flash Asset Xtra. With version 8.5, you can take even more control of your .SWF movies in Director. Moreover, the latest versions of the Shockwave plug-in automatically install the Flash Asset Xtra on Web browsers. That means that you can count on Shockwave-enabled visitors being able to view your Flash-Director Shockwave content. But why would you want to use Director in combination with Flash in the first place? We answer that question next.

Caution

If you want to use Flash 5 .SWF files, you need to have Director 8.5. Director 7.02 and 8.0 can use Flash 4 or earlier. You can find more product update information by going to the Director Web site at `www.macromedia.com/support/director/downloads.html`.

Benefits and limitations of Flash movies in Director

Flash 5 has been another monumental leap forward for Flash interactivity. With the additional advanced ActionScripting that Flash can now employ, many of the previous Flash-Director scenarios or workarounds are no longer needed. However, if you're already familiar with Director and Lingo (Director's scripting language), then you may find integrating .SWF files into Director projects easier than learning advanced scripting with ActionScript in Flash 5. The following list reviews some of the benefits and drawbacks of using Flash movies in Director projects.

✦ **Vector control:** Even though Director has vector shape-drawing tools, it doesn't use the same intuitive drawing mechanism that Flash does. Use Flash for any complex vector drawing and animation, and then bring it into your Director project.

✦ **Implement existing projects:** With the ability to use Flash movies in Director, you need not duplicate efforts if material already exists in one format or the other. Thus, if you've already developed some cool animations in Flash for your company's Web site, you can reuse the same Flash .SWF files in your Director projects.

✦ **Use media types that are not available in Flash:** Director's architecture can be expanded with the use of Macromedia's (or a third party's) Xtras. Even though Flash 4 and 5 can import QuickTime movie files, it can only export QuickTime Flash movies — it can't export .SWF files that contain QuickTime movies. However, you can import QuickTime movies, as well as many other media types, such as 3D Studio MAX models, into Director and that can be viewed and controlled in Shockwave Director movies. (Check out http://www.believeGOSSIP.com for an example of Director and Flash integration.) Some audio file formats, such as AU and MIDI, are not supported by Flash 5. Director 8.5 natively supports AU import. With the proper Xtras, you can use MIDI music with your Flash movies in Director.

✦ **Audio support:** In versions of Director before 7.02, Flash audio could not play simultaneously with Director sound channels. Now, you can control the global property soundMixMedia to mix Flash sounds with Director score sound channels.

✦ **Flash frame rate control:** Ironically, you have more control over a Flash movie's frame rate in Director than you do natively within Flash 5. In Flash, the movie's frame rate is fixed throughout the entire movie — once it is set in the Modify ➪ Movie dialog, it cannot be updated or changed during playback. Flash movies also seem to play more smoothly at higher frame rates when played within a Director projector.

✦ **Similar scripting environments:** Both Flash and Director use a form of Dots notation for their scripting languages. Flash ActionScript resembles JavaScript much more closely than Director Lingo does. Director Lingo uses a different model of command and event control than Flash 5 does.

Flash and Director intermovie activity is a two-way street: You can send events from Flash to Director (via Lingo), or you can control Flash movie playback from Director (via Lingo). Just as Flash Movie Clips can be self-contained interactive modules within one overall .SWF file, Flash .SWF files can be components of a much larger and media rich Director movie. To get you started with Director-Flash interactivity, the next section shows you how to send events from Flash movies to Director movies.

Note The following sections are intended for readers who already know the basics of Director movie production. If you need more information on the Director authoring environment, please refer to the *Director 8 Bible*.

Creating Director-specific actions in Flash

You can use Flash .SWF files in any number of ways with Director. If you simply want to use a Flash animation for graphic content within a Director presentation, you can simply use the same .SWF you generated for the Web. Use the Flash Asset Xtra import box (see the more in-depth discussion later in this section) to set the parameters of playback without needing any Lingo. However, if you want Flash actions (in frames or on buttons) to do something in your Director movies, then you need to know how to get Lingo's attention. The drawback to this type of "dual" interactivity is that you need to plan ahead with both your Flash and Director movies. As with any project, you should outline a storyboard before embarking on a task such as this.

Cross-Reference

Use a project planner such as Microsoft Organization Chart (included with Microsoft Office) or Inspiration (included on the *Flash 5 Bible* CD-ROM) to plan an interactive project. By creating interactive hierarchies and flow-charts (for example, determining which scenes will link to other scenes), you can manage projects with greater ease. We discussed the importance of interactive project planning in Chapter 38, "Planning Flash Production with Flowcharting Software."

You have three methods to use within the Flash authoring environment, all involving the getURL action. You can assign any of these methods the same way you would with any other Flash interactivity—attach these actions to buttons, frames, or ActionScript conditions.

Caution

If you experience crashes in Director using any of the getURL commands listed in this section, please see the sidebar "Quirks with Flash Sprites and Lingo go Commands" later in this chapter.

Standard GetURL command

On a Flash Button or frame, open the Actions Panel and assign a getURL action. This is the preferred method of sending information to Director movies because you can deal with the result of the action in Director—you do not need to specify what Director does with the string from Flash. When a Button instance is selected *and* the Actions Panel is in Normal Mode, Flash 5 automatically creates a default on (release) action to contain the getURL action. In the URL setting, create a string to be passed to an event handler in Lingo. In Figure 39-5, a getURL action is assigned to a frame in Flash. The string ProjectOne is entered in the URL text field. This string, in turn, is received by Lingo.

In Director, you need to attach a behavior script to the Flash Sprite so that the getURL action and string can be received by Lingo. We discuss the actual implementation of this example later in the "Controlling .SWF files in Director" section. In Figure 39-5, the string ProjectOne was assigned to getURL. In Director, we could tell Lingo to go to the frame marker called ProjectOne:

```
on getURL me, FlashString
  go to frame FlashString
end
```

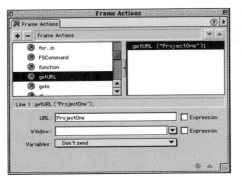

Figure 39-5: You can enter any word or series of characters (that is, a *string*) in the URL field. This string is then passed to Lingo.

When the Flash Sprite plays in Director and the `getURL` action is executed, the `ProjectOne` value of `getURL` is passed as the `FlashString` argument of the Lingo event handler, `on getURL`. Lingo will direct the playback of the Director movie to the frame marker `ProjectOne`.

Event: command

You can also specify an `event:` handler in the URL field of the `getURL` action. This method is useful if you would like to describe an event that is repeatedly used in Flash, but needs customized settings with each use. For example, if you want to add a mouse click to go to a different Director frame depending on which button was clicked, you could use the following URL in the `getURL` action:

```
event: FClick "ProjectOne"
```

In Director, you then write a behavior that would receive the `FClick` event:

```
on FClick me FlashString
   go to frame FlashString
end
```

How is this different from the last example? If you want to have several events in one script that perform different Lingo commands, you need to label each one with a separate event, such as:

```
on FClickButton01 me FlashString
   go to frame FlashString
end

on FClickButton02 me FlashString
   quit
end
```

In the preceding example, we have two defined Flash events, FClickButton01 and FclickButton02, which do different things. If we had used the standard getURL action, we could only pass the string to one Lingo command.

Tip   With a bit more programming in Lingo, you could pass one argument string to multiple Lingo commands by testing the string with if...else statements.

Lingo: command

The last getURL method of sending events to Lingo is the most direct method of communicating with Director movies. In the URL field, a lingo: handler is used to specify a Lingo statement. This is the most inflexible method of sending events to Director — insofar as you cannot do anything in Director to modify or direct the event. For example, if you added the following code to an on (release), getURL button event in Flash:

```
lingo: quit
```

then the Director movie quits (or the Director projector closes) when that button was clicked.

With lingo: statements in getURL actions, you do not need to specify any further Lingo in the Director movie, unless you are setting the value of prescripted variable or executing a event described in the Director movie script.

Controlling .SWF files in Director

You can import and use Flash movies (.SWF files) into Director just as you would any other cast member. Director controls Flash movies with the Flash Asset Xtra.

Quirks with Flash Sprites and Lingo go Commands

In Director 6.5, you may experience crashes if you send Flash events to Lingo that make a Director movie go to a frame where the Flash Sprite is no longer on the Stage. For example, if you start a Director movie with a Flash animation, and you have a frame action on the last frame of the Flash animation that directs playback to a new section of the Director score, the Flash Sprite duration needs to be extended all the way to the frame that the Director movie is jumping to. Use a Lingo command such as:

```
set the visible of sprite X to false
```

(where X designates the Flash Sprite number) to make the Flash Sprite invisible on that frame if necessary. If you don't want to extend the Sprite to that frame and/or you are jumping to a new movie, see the advanced workarounds at www.macromedia.com/support/director/ts/documents/flash_asset_xtra_go_issue.htm.

This section shows you how to import Flash movies and use them in the Director Score window. You should already be familiar with the Director authoring environment and basic Behavior use.

The Flash Asset Xtra: Importing Flash movies

Since Director 6.5, the Flash Asset Xtra has enabled Flash movies to play within a Director movie. Again, make sure you have Director 8.5 in order to use Flash 5 movies. If you have Director 8.0 or 7.0.2, you'll need to export your Flash 4 .SWF files from Flash 5. Director 7.0.1 supports Flash 3 or earlier movies. If you have Director 6.5, you need to export your Flash movies as Flash 2 movies.

Caution If you are using a version of Director earlier than 7.0.2, then be extremely careful with the use of Flash audio. In older versions of Director that support Flash movies, Flash audio cannot play simultaneously with Director score sounds. Macromedia's tech notes advise turning sound off when using earlier versions of the Flash Asset Xtra.

To import a Flash movie (.SWF file), do the following:

1. Start a new Director movie (.DIR file) or open an existing movie.

2. Use the File ➪ Import command (Command+R or Ctrl+R) to select a Flash movie (.SWF file). Double-click the file name in the upper portion of the Import dialog (see Figure 39-6), or select the file name and choose Add. You can select several files of different types and import them all at once. When you are done adding files, click Import to bring the Flash movie(s) into the Internal Cast.

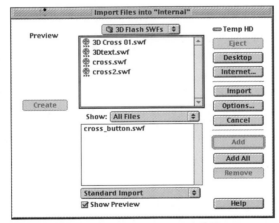

Figure 39-6: You can import several files at once with the Import command. (The Mac version is shown here.)

You can use any of the .SWF files on the *Flash 5 Bible* CD-ROM for this example. For this section, we use the file crossButton.swf, which is located in the ch33 folder on the *Flash 5 Bible* CD-ROM.

3. Open the Cast window (Command+3 or Ctrl+3). Double-click the Flash movie that was imported. This brings up the Flash Asset Properties dialog (see Figure 39-7). The top section of the dialog is used to link to external or remote Flash movies (see following tip and sidebar), while the lower section sets the playback attributes:

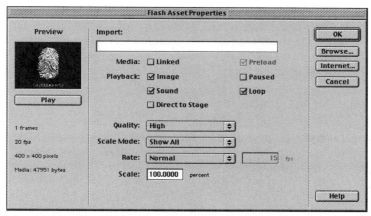

Figure 39-7: The Flash Asset Properties dialog enables you to specify how the Flash movie functions in the Director movie.

- **Media:** This setting has two options, Linked and Preload. If you don't want to store a Flash movie within the Director movie, check Link and specify the path to the Flash movie. Unless you want to link to a Flash movie on the Internet, you should store the Flash movie in the Director movie — Flash movies are usually very small due to their vector structure. If Link is checked, then you can also enable Preload. Preloading will force Director to load (or download) the entire .SWF file before it starts playing the Flash movie. Otherwise, Director will start playing the Flash movie as soon as it starts to stream the Flash cast member. See the sidebar at the end of this section for more information on linked Internet files.

- **Playback:** This setting has five options that control how Director displays the Flash movie.

  The Image option, checked by default, determines whether Director shows the graphic content of a Flash movie.

  The Sound option determines whether Director plays the audio content of a Flash movie.

The Direct to Stage option tells Director to give priority to the Flash movie Sprite over all other Sprites currently on the Stage. Although this option may enable Flash movies to playback more smoothly, Director ignores any ink effects applied to the Sprite (see the "Flash Movies as Sprites" section for more information on ink effects), and the Flash movie always displays on top of other Sprites.

The Paused option is akin to adding a `stop()` Flash action to the first frame of the Flash movie — you can force Director to display the movie in a paused state.

The Loop option enables continuous playback of the Flash movie. If this option is checked, the Flash movie repeats as soon as it reaches the last frame unless the last frame has a `stop()` Flash action. It continues to repeat while the Flash Sprite is present in the Director Score, or until it is paused by a Lingo command.

- **Quality:** This setting has a drop-down menu with the exact same settings as the Quality setting in the Flash 5 Publish Settings. By default, this setting is High. For more information on the Quality property of a Flash movie, see Chapter 40, "Publishing Flash Movies."

- **Scale Mode:** By default, this setting uses Auto-Size, which enables Director to automatically resize the Flash movie's width and height according to the Sprite's bounding box on the Director stage. Meaning, if you resize the Sprite, then the Flash movie should fit the size of the Sprite box. Auto-Size automatically sets the Scale setting to 100 percent. Conversely, No Scale keeps the Flash movie at the size specified by the Scale setting (covered in a moment) and any subsequent resizing of the Sprite bounding box may crop the Flash movie. The remaining options, Show All, No Border, and Exact Fit operate the same as the Publish Settings options in Flash 5 (see Chapter 40, "Publishing Flash Movies").

- **Rate:** Perhaps one of the most powerful settings in the Flash Asset Properties dialog, Rate controls how fast or slow the Flash movie plays in a Director Scores — irrespective of the Tempo setting used in the Score. The Flash Asset Properties' Rate setting has two options: a drop-down menu and an fps text field. If Normal or Lock-Step is selected, then the fps text field is disabled. Normal plays the Flash movie at its native frame rate, as set in the Flash application via the Modify ➪ Movie dialog.

Lock-Step plays one Flash movie frame for every Director frame that its Sprite occupies (for example, if the Flash movie occupies four frames of the Director score, then only the first four frames of the animation plays back in Director). Therefore, Lock-Step inherits the frame rate of the Director movie as established in the Tempo setting in the Score.

Fixed Rate enables you to specify a new frame rate for the Flash movie, independent of the original frame rate specified in Flash 5 (via Modify ➪ Movie) or the Director Tempo setting in the Score.

- **Scale:** This setting works hand-in-hand with the Scale Mode setting. If anything other than Auto-Size is selected in Scale Mode, you can specify what percentage of the original Flash movie is used for the Flash Sprite. If 50 percent is used for the Scale of a 550×400 Flash movie and Exact Fit is chosen in Scale Mode, then the movie displays at 225×200 in the original placed Flash Sprite on the Stage. If you resize the Sprite box, then it continues to maintain a 50 percent portion of the Sprite box area.

Tip You can also use the Insert ➪ Media Element ➪ Flash Movie command to import Flash movies via the Flash Asset Properties dialog. Simply click the Browse button and select a Flash movie (.SWF file). Both the File ➪ Import and Flash Asset Property dialogs enable you to enter Internet URLs for the filename path.

After specifying the settings you wish to use for your Flash movie, you can then place the Flash cast member as a Sprite on to the Director Stage.

Using Lingo to Preload Flash Movies

Like other Director Cast Members, you can control how a Flash movie Cast Member is loaded into a Shockwave movie or standalone Director projector. While you author a Director movie with a Flash movie Cast Member, it's useful to have a linked .SWF file included in the Internal Cast. However, when you launch a Shockwave movie on the Web, you may want to make changes to the .SWF file only and leave the Director .DCR file unchanged. Moreover, the path of a locally linked file is different from a file linked remotely over the Internet. This problem is easy to fix with a little Director Lingo.

For any Director movie that uses .SWF files that you intend to update on a regular basis, you should dynamically set the `filename` property of the Flash Cast Member with Lingo. The following steps show you how to detect where the Director movie is being played (for example, from a standalone projector or from the Shockwave Player), and how to change the source of a linked Flash Cast Member.

1. Create or add the following Lingo to the Movie Script for your Director movie (note that the ¬ indicates continuation of the same line of code):

```
on prepareMovie
    global URLRootPath
    global shockPlayer
    if (the runMode contains "Projector") OR (the ¬
    runMode contains "Author") then
        shockPlayer = false
    else
```

Continued

Continued

```
              shockPlayer = true
              URLRootPath = "http://www.theMakers.com/flash5/"
        end if
    end prepareMovie

    on initLoad me
        global URLRootPath
        global myNetID
        global flashPath
        flashPath = URLRootPath & "sliders.swf"
        set myNetID = preloadNetThing(flashPath)
    end initLoad
```

For the variable URLRootPath, change the value to the path to your Flash files on your Web server. Don't forget the ending forward slash character, as a filename is appended to this path in the initLoad handler. In the initLoad handler, change the flashPath variable to specify the filename of the .SWF movie that you want to load into the Director movie.

2. In the Director Score window, reserve a section of ten frames at the very beginning of the Score. Create a frame marker named initPreload on frame 1, and on frame 5, create a marker named loadLoop. Also, make sure that you have a marker on the frame where your Director movie's first interactivity takes place (for example, wherever the movie starts beyond these first ten frames for the preload sequence). In this example, we use the name intro.

3. On frame 1, add the following Frame Script:

```
on enterFrame
    global shockPlayer
    if shockPlayer = true then
        initLoad
    else
        go to "intro"
    end if
end
```

Here, we check whether the prepareMovie handler returned a true or false value for the shockPlayer variable. If the movie is being played in a Web browser, then shockPlayer will equal true. If that's the case, then execute the initLoad handler (in the Movie Script). Incidentally, handlers in Lingo work much like functions in ActionScript and JavaScript.

If the movie is being played in the authoring environment or a projector, then shockPlayer will equal false. Therefore, the else condition will execute, moving the Director playhead to the intro marker.

4. On frame 10, add the following Frame Script:

```
on exitFrame
    global myNetID, flashPath
    if netDone(myNetID) = true then
        member("sliders").fileName = flashPath
        go to "intro"
    else
        go to "loadLoop"
    end if
end
```

Here, we check whether the `preloadNetThing` command that was executed in the `initLoad` handler has finished loading the Flash .SWF file. If it has, then the path of the linked (or stored) Cast Member `sliders` is changed to the Internet path described in `flashPath`. Then, the Director playhead moves to the `intro` frame marker to start the movie. If the .SWF file isn't finished loading, then the Director playhead moves back to the `loadLoop` frame marker. The playhead will continue looping the frames between `loadLoop` and frame 10 until the .SWF file loads.

You will want to change the name of the Cast Member sliders to the name of your Flash movie Cast Number that was used in your Director movie.

These are the basic steps to preloading and changing the source file for Flash Cast Members. We didn't include error handling in the frame 10 script. As you may well know, Web servers can crash, Internet connections may falter, or a file has been deleted or moved to another location. Refer to the Lingo Dictionary included with Director 8.5 to see the various `netDone` and `netError` return values.

Using Director's Property Inspector

Director 8.0 introduced a new look-and-feel to the authoring environment. In addition to a resizable Stage window, you can change the Cast window to view by list or thumbnail, and you can quickly modify Sprite, Cast Member, and Movie attributes (among others) with the Property Inspector.

The Property Inspector (shown in Figure 39-8) enables you to quickly change all of the Flash Asset Properties for any Flash Cast Member. You can click the More Options button on the Property Inspector to access the traditional Flash Asset Properties dialog, which enables you to change Import (for example, path to remotely or locally linked .SWF files) and Media (Linked and Preload) properties. You cannot preview Flash movies in the Property Inspector.

Figure 39-8: Director's new Property Inspector

Tip

You may have noticed that the Flash Asset Properties dialog takes a few seconds to load, as it requires the entire Flash Asset Options Xtra to load into memory. Why? In order to use the Play button in the Flash Asset Properties dialog, the Flash Player contained within the Flash Asset Options Xtra must be loaded. Because the Property Inspector doesn't include a preview/play option, you can change Flash movie settings much more quickly in the Inspector.

Flash Movies as Sprites

In Director, any item that is used in a movie becomes part of a Cast, and is referred to as a Cast Member. When a Cast Member is placed on the Stage, it becomes a Sprite. A Sprite is an instance of the Cast Member used in the Score. The relationship between a Flash Symbol and a Symbol instance is similar to the relationship between a Director Cast Member and its Sprite(s).

To place a Flash Cast Member on the Director Stage, simply click and drag its Cast Member icon (or thumbnail) from the Internal Cast window to the Stage or the Score. If you drag a Cast Member to the Stage (see Figure 39-9), it automatically becomes a Sprite on the first Sprite channel. If you drag a Sprite to the Score (see Figure 39-9), it is automatically centered on the Stage.

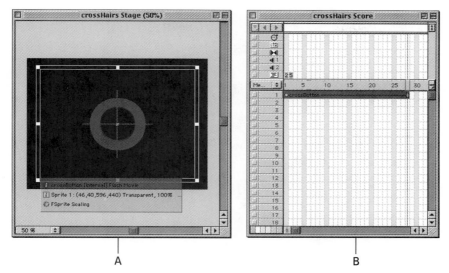

Figure 39-9: (A) A Flash Sprite on the Director stage. (B) A Flash Sprite in the Director score.

Although Flash Sprites perform almost the same as other Director Sprites, you should be aware of certain Sprite properties before proceeding with Lingo Behaviors and Flash Sprites. For more information on basic animation features of Director, please consult the *Using Director 8* manual that comes with the Director software.

✦ **Sprite Duration:** Every Sprite has a duration in the Score. By default, every Sprite dragged to the Score or Stage has a duration of 28 frames. Like digital video and sound Sprites, Flash Sprites only play for as long as their frame duration allows them. For example, if a Flash movie that is 30 Flash frames long (and has a Lock-Step rate) is inserted as a 15-frame Flash Sprite in Director, then Director only shows the first half of the Flash movie.

✦ **Sprite Inks:** Of all the inks available to Sprites, only Copy, Transparent, and Background Transparent have any noticeable effect on Flash Sprites. Copy makes the Flash movie background opaque, in the same color that you specified in the Flash authoring environment. Transparent or Background Transparent (see Figure 39-10) hide the background of a Flash movie, so that the Director movie background (and other Director Sprites) show through.

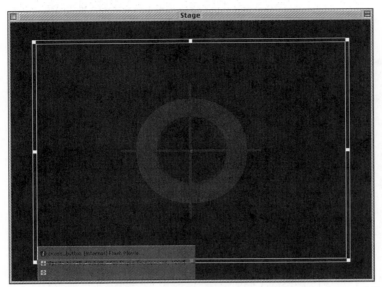

Figure 39-10: With an ink effect of Background Transparent, the white background of the crosshairsButton Flash Sprite drops out.

Controlling .SWF files with Lingo

Not only can you send events from Flash movies to Director movies, but you can also control Flash movies from Director with Lingo. More than 70 Lingo commands exist that are specific for Flash movie assets in a Director movie. Unfortunately, it is beyond the scope of this book to explore so many different commands. This section provides an overview of the new Lingo commands for Flash movie, and shows you how to alter the size and rotation of Flash Sprites.

Lingo and ActionScript

For a complete listing of Flash-specific Lingo commands that can be used with Flash Cast Members and Sprites, access the Help ➪ Lingo Dictionary in Director 8.5 and search for Flash. Some of the more powerful Lingo commands are `getVariable` and `setVariable`, which give you access to any variables inside a Flash 4 or 5 movie. Make sure that you specify the variable name as a string in Director Lingo (unless it's also the name of a Lingo variable), as in:

```
on beginSprite me
    sprite(me.spriteNum).setVariable("/globals:currentURL",¬
        "http://www.theMakers.com")
end
```

This Lingo code will give the variable `currentURL` in the globals Movie Clip of the current Sprite (me.spriteNum) the value of `http://www.theMakers.com`. Therefore, you can use Slashes notation to access nested variables in Movie Clip instances.

Note   Notice the similarities of Director's Dots notation to Flash 5's new ActionScript syntax. Both Director and Flash can use Object references followed by methods or properties.

Similarly, the `getFlashProperty` and `setFlashProperty` Lingo commands can use Slashes notation to access Movie Clip or Main Timeline properties:

```
on enterFrame me
    global dog_ScaleX
    dog_ScaleX = sprite(1).getFlashProperty("/dog_1",¬
        #scaleX)
end
```

This Lingo code will retrieve the current X scale of the _root.dog_1 Movie Clip instance and make it the value of a global Director variable named `dog_ScaleX`. Table 39-2 details the Flash Movie Clip and Main Timeline properties that can be retrieved and set by Lingo.

<table>
<tr><td colspan="3" align="center">Table 39-2
Lingo and ActionScript Property Conversion Chart</td></tr>
<tr><td>*Lingo*</td><td>*ActionScript*</td><td>*Definition*</td></tr>
<tr><td>#posX</td><td>_x</td><td>The current X coordinate of the specified Flash target.</td></tr>
<tr><td>#posY</td><td>_y</td><td>The current Y coordinate of the specified Flash target.</td></tr>
<tr><td>#scaleX</td><td>_xscale</td><td>The current percent value of the target's X scale.</td></tr>
<tr><td>#scaleY</td><td>_yscale</td><td>The current percent value of the target's Y scale.</td></tr>
<tr><td>#visible</td><td>_visible</td><td>Determines whether the target is shown or hidden.</td></tr>
<tr><td>#rotate</td><td>_rotation</td><td>The current degree value of the target's rotation.</td></tr>
<tr><td>#alpha</td><td>_alpha</td><td>The current percent value of the target's opacity.</td></tr>
</table>

Continued

		Table 39-2 (continued)	
Lingo	*ActionScript*	*Definition*
#name	_name	The name given to the Movie Clip instance in the Instance Panel or with a duplicateMovieClip (or attachMovie) Flash action.
#width	_width	The current width (in pixels) of the specified Flash target.
#height	_height	The current height (in pixels) of the specified Flash target.
#target	_target	The full Flash path (in Slashes notation) to the specified Flash target. The path starts from the root (Main Timeline) and ends with the Instance name.
#dropTarget	_dropTarget	The full Flash path (in Slashes notation) of a dragged-over Flash target. See Chapter 19 for more information on _dropTarget.
#url	_url	The full location path of the Flash target, in HTTP syntax (for example, http://www.theMakers.com/flash5/sliders.swf or file://Macintosh%20HD/Internet/Shared/load.swf).
#totalFrames	_totalFrames	The total number of Flash frames in the specified Flash instance.
#currentFrame	_currentFrame	The current position (frame number) of the playhead in the Flash instance's timeline.
#lastframeLoaded	_framesLoaded	The number of the last frame (of the specified target) to have fully loaded into the Director movie.
#focusRect	_focusRect	This global property controls the visibility of focus rectangles for Flash Button instances. The target should be specified as an empty string (" ").
#spriteSoundBufferTime	_soundbuftime	This global property controls how much audio should stream from a Flash movie before playback begins. The target should be specified as an empty string (" ").

Macromedia has expanded the Lingo `hitTest` command (which can be used to detect whether an arbitrary point in the Flash movie is the transparent background area, a normal "fill" area, or a Flash button) to include an `#editTest` return value to detect Flash 4 and 5 editable text fields. The Lingo `hitTest` method works much like the `hitTest` ActionScript method. For more information on Director's `hitTest` method, refer to the Help ➪ Lingo Dictionary. Refer to Chapter 23, "Understanding Movie Clips as Complex Objects," for more information on Flash's `hitTest` method.

Finally, Director 8.5 adds five new Lingo commands to work with Flash movies:

✦ `call`: This command works just like the call(frame) action in Flash 5. It executes the actions on the specified Flash timeline keyframe.

✦ `print` and `printAsBitmap`: These commands print the contents of a target Flash timeline. See Chapter 19, "Controlling Movie Clips," for more information on the print actions.

✦ `sendXML`: This is a new event handler in Director 8.5 that catches any `sendXML` events from a Flash 5 movie. You can define an `on sendXML` handler on a Flash Sprite that will execute whenever a `sendXML` action is executed in the Flash movie. For more information on the XML Object in Flash 5, see Chapter 24, "Sending Data In and Out of Flash."

✦ `tellTarget` and `endTellTarget`: These commands work like the Flash 4 equivalent actions. However, in Lingo, you nest the actions in a slightly different manner. Also, you can only use the following actions within a `tellTarget` Lingo group: `stop`, `play`, `gotoFrame`, `call(frame)`, `find(label)`, `getFlash Property`, and `setFlashProperty`. You use a `tellTarget` Lingo action in the following way:

```
on exitFrame me
   sprite(1).tellTarget("/nestedMovie")
   sprite(1).setFlashProperty("",#ScaleX,200)
   sprite(1).setFlashProperty("", #ScaleY, 200)
   sprite(1).goToFrame(2)
   sprite(1).endtellTarget()
   go to frame 5
end
```

This Lingo code targets the nestedMovie Movie Clip instance located on the Main Timeline and sets its scale to 200 percent and moves its playhead to frame 2. Then, Director's Score moves to frame 5.

Changing the size and rotation of Flash Sprites

The previous section listed the properties of internal Flash Movie Clips that can be manipulated with Lingo. You can also control the Flash Sprite properties with Lingo, which will affect everything in the Flash movie. With the crossButton.swf example used earlier, we can rotate and zoom the Flash movie in Director. Because the crossButton Sprite is a Flash button that already plays a 3D rotation sequence, we disable the Flash button by using a Lingo script in the first frame of the score:

```
on enterFrame
  sprite(1).buttonsEnabled = false
end
On exitFrame
  go the frame
end
```

The `sprite(1)` line of code refers to the Sprite occupying the first Sprite channel, which in our example is the crosshairs_button Flash Sprite. Adding the `.buttonsEnabled` property lets Director know what property we want to change with the Sprite — in this case, Flash button activity. Setting this property to `false` means it is being turned off.

Next, add the following behavior script to the Flash Sprite:

```
on mouseEnter me
  repeat while sprite(1).rotation < 720
    sprite(1).rotation = sprite(1).rotation + 10
    updateStage
  end repeat
end

on mouseLeave me
  sprite(1).rotation = 0
end
```

This Behavior causes the Flash Sprite to rotate a full 720 degrees — two revolutions — when the mouse enters the Flash Sprite. Here, the `.rotation` property is called and manipulated. Notice that when the mouse leaves the Sprite, the rotation is reset to 0.

To change this to a zooming behavior, simply change the script to the following:

```
on mouseEnter me
  repeat while sprite(1).scale < 800
    sprite(1).scale = sprite(1).scale + 10
    updateStage
  end repeat
end

on mouseLeave me
  sprite(1).scale = 100
end
```

For a cool effect, reenable the Flash button by removing the `on enterFrame` section, containing the `sprite(1).buttonsEnabled` line, from the frame 1 script. Now, as the Flash movie zooms, the button continues to rotate on a 3D axis.

To view the current Flash Sprite properties in Director's Message window, you can add the following line of Lingo to the Frame Script:

```
on exitFrame
    sprite(1).showProps()
    go to frame 2
end
```

Then, on frame 2, create the following Frame Script:

```
on exitFrame
    go the frame
end
```

The `showProps()` command shows you the current properties of the Flash Sprite and Cast Member, as shown in Figure 39-11.

Figure 39-11: Director's Message window, displaying the current Flash Sprite properties

Open the crossHairs.dir file in the ch39 folder of the *Flash 5 Bible* CD-ROM to see the rotation and scaling Lingo actions.

Expert Tutorial: Flash Avatars for Multiuser Apps in Director, *by Robert Walch*

You'll find the source .FLA, Director files, screen shots, and other assets related to this tutorial in the Avatar *folder of the ch39 folder of the* Flash 5 Bible *CD-ROM.*

There are many great uses for Flash content in Director. If you like using Flash to make interfaces, you could surely make some great ones for those Director presentations. However, if you like using Flash to make cartoons, or if, like me, you want to make games with Flash or Director, why not make all your characters in Flash?

On the other hand, when developing content for the Web, one of the factors that would make me choose Director over Flash is Director's MultiUser Xtra. Here's why: I found a great site one day that had a multiuser chat. It's located at http://poppy.macromedia.com/~sallen/multiuser. The Shockwave movie allowed you to import your own avatar into the chat, and allowed you to update your avatar's mood on everyone else's machine by telling it to go to a specific frame label. So let's take a look at how to set up your Flash animations, and how to get Director to make a list of all those labels in your Flash file.

In Flash 5, create a series of Flash mood animations along one timeline. At the beginning of each animation (or mood) place a label, naming it according to what you avatar is doing in this part of the animation. You can include actions to loop certain parts or sequences of the animation.

When you're done animating, make sure to export your avatar as a Flash 4 format .SWF file if you're using Director 8 or 7.0.2. Flash 5 .SWF's are only supported in Director 8.5. For the purposes of this tutorial, name it **avatar.swf**.

Open Director and import your avatar.swf file. Make a new text member and title it **MoodList**. Place your avatar in the score, so that it's starting in frame 1 of Sprite channel 1. Then, place the text member MoodList in the Score under your avatar Sprite. In a new Movie Script, use the following code to call the labels in your Flash file:

```
--//The following is code from the source file

on startmovie
  member("MoodList").text = GetFlashLabels(1)
end

on GetFlashLabels FlashSpriteNum
  theLabelList = "Mood List:"
  FlashSprite = sprite(FlashSpriteNum)
  if FlashSprite.member.type = #flash  then
    frameCount = FlashSprite.member.frameCount
```

```
      repeat with frameNum = 1 to frameCount
        theLabel = FlashSprite.getFrameLabel(frameNum)
        if theLabel <> "" then
          theLabelList = theLabelList & Return & theLabel
        end if
      end repeat
    end if
    return theLabelList
  end
```

Now, attach a behavior with the following code to the `moodlist` Sprite:

```
property spritenum

on mouseup me
  clickline = sprite(spritenum).pointToLine(the mouseloc)
  if clickline > 1 then
    theMood = sprite(spritenum).member.text.line[clickline]
    if theMood <> "" then
      theFrame = sprite(1).findLabel(theMood)
      if theFrame then
        sprite(1).goToFrame(theFrame)
      end if
    end if
  end if
end
```

Play the file in Director. (Make sure playback is looping in the control panel.) Now you can click an item in the list to go to that frame!

As a final note, you can also experiment with setting variables in the Flash avatar, and the avatar could then respond with ActionScript that internally changes its look-and-feel and/or sends information back to the Director movie. Try using your avatars in Flash movies as well. And have fun!

Based upon this answer, "All I listened to in high school was Jimi Hendrix," we know that Robert Walch may be a genius. "I remember going to see *Pulp Fiction* as a freshman in college," tells us that he was diggin' long after Jimi had moved on to a harp. This young New Yorker's favorite thing is developing and playing multiuser games because "It's so much fun to be in a world were you can act however you want, and talk, play or compete with others. I want to see content like this developed with Director and Flash." Robert says about starting with Flash: "When Macromedia released Flash 4, and Web sites started displaying the potential for animated Web sites and online cartoons, I got hooked."

Summary

✦ Dreamweaver 4 now has the capability to insert three types of Flash objects: a standard Flash movie created with the Flash authoring tool (any version), and two new Dreamweaver-native objects, Flash Buttons and Flash Text. When Flash Button and Text Objects are inserted into the HTML, Dreamweaver actually generates a .SWF file with custom text and links.

✦ The JavaScript Integration Kit (JIK) extends the power of Flash by giving Dreamweaver the capability to use JavaScript to control advanced features. JIK provides more Flash Player controls, advanced form validation for Flash forms (for example, checking whether you typed in enough numbers for a phone number), and more browser scripts for Flash to open browser windows, set cookies, and swap images. Finally, the Flash Dispatch behavior detects a visitor's Flash Player version and then redirects them to the appropriate page.

✦ Macromedia Director 8.5 and Flash 5 make a powerful scripting combination. Director 8.5 supports new Flash 5 methods, enabling you to pass more information between Flash assets and the Director movie.

✦ Director 8.5 can integrate most multimedia file formats, and play them within a Shockwave movie over the Web.

✦ Director 8.5 can harness the power of the Shockwave MultiUser Server, which enables real-time connections between Internet visitors to your Web sites. Combined with lightweight Flash .SWF assets and the new 3D imaging technology of Shockwave, you can create amazing Web experiences.

✦   ✦   ✦

Distributing Flash Movies

After you've created Flash movies that dazzle the eye with morphing Shape Tweens, soothe the ear with MP3-encoded sound, and interact with mouse movements using ActionScript, you'll need to convert your Flash movie (.FLA file) to the Flash .SWF format so that other people can view the content on a Web browser using the Flash Player plug-in or ActiveX control. You can also publish your movies as QuickTime 4 movies with Flash tracks (discussed in detail back in Chapter 34), as stand-alone projectors, or as .SWF files that use the stand-alone Flash Player. Stand-alones are discussed in Chapter 42.

Chapter 40 will walk you through the process of optimizing your Flash movie, testing your movies within Flash, and using the Publish commands that create preformatted HTML documents to display Flash movies. If you prefer to hard-code your own HTML or if you want to create a detection system for the Flash Player, then jump to Chapter 41, where we show you how to use <OBJECT> and <EMBED> tags for Flash movies. Chapter 41 also explains how Flash movies can interact with JavaScript and DHTML to change the page attributes on the fly.

Publishing Flash Movies

If you have read the entire book to this point, then you're probably more than ready to get your Flash movies uploaded to your Web server to share with your visitors. This chapter shows you how to create .SWF files from Flash 5 so that your Flash movies can be played with the Flash Player plug-in for Web browsers.

Optimizing Flash Movies

Before you create a .SWF file from your Flash movie (.FLA file), you should read through this section to determine whether you can optimize your Flash movie. Optimizing can mean finding anything redundant in the final movie — extra points in a line, repeated artwork, and so on — to breaking apart your large .FLA file into several smaller .FLA files that will be loaded into a primary Flash movie. As you should see, symbols are the key to eliminating unnecessary repetition with Flash artwork. Optimizing can also entail the restricted use of bandwidth-heavy items, such as bitmapped artwork or lengthy sound tracks.

Simplify artwork

Although Flash can do some pretty amazing things with vector shapes and animation, you don't want to overdo it — at least not if you want 28.8 Kbps modem users to see your work without too much waiting. Keep the following tips in mind while creating your Flash artwork or reviewing your final production:

> ✦ Use tweens for animations wherever possible. If you need complicated paths for objects to follow, use a motion guide layer instead of using a series of keyframes — the fewer keyframes, the better.

✦ Custom line types (such as dashed, dotted, ragged, and so on) take up more file space than regular solid lines. Strokes created with the Brush Tool also use more memory than lines created with the Pencil Tool. Artwork created with the Brush Tool is actually a fill—not a stroke. The boundary of a fill is more complex than a simple line or stroke.

✦ Reduce the number of points and/or lines used to create a shape. In Flash, you can use the Modify ➪ Optimize command, which joins line segments in a line or shape. Note that you need to ungroup any grouped lines to use this command. The Use Multiple Passes option optimizes the selection to the fullest extent possible.

For tips on optimizing vector artwork created outside of Flash, see Chapter 31, "Working with Vector Graphics."

✦ Gradients are more complex than a solid fill for a computer processor to handle. Try to minimize the number of simultaneous gradients shown in any given frame, and avoid any complex animation with gradient shapes or symbols. Gradients add more bytes to a .SWF's file size than does a solid color. See Table 40-1 for a study of gradient color and .SWF file sizes.

✦ Don't use many different fonts (typefaces) or font styles (such as Oblique, Bold, Condensed, and so on) in your Flash movies. Most elegant designs use complementary typefaces that occur in the same typeface family, or use a balanced and restricted number of sans serif or serif fonts. Font characters can require a lot of file space, from 81 bytes to over 191 bytes *per character*. Generally, more elaborate serif fonts (such as Garamond) take up more room per character than sans serif fonts (such as Arial). For text fields, make sure that you embed only what is necessary from a font for the given field. For example, if a text field needs to use only lowercase characters of a font for a login or name field, then specify this in the Text Options Panel for that text field. Ultimately, use device fonts (_sans, _serif, and _typewriter) whenever possible, as they do not need their outlines stored in the .SWF file.

You cannot use device fonts underneath a Mask layer. Any font that is in a Mask layer nesting needs to be embedded in the .SWF file.

✦ Keep bitmap or raster images to a minimum. Flash's strength is its vector-based technology. Animated bitmap sequences inflate your Flash file sizes. Unless the content you are creating needs to be photorealistic (as in a photographer's portfolio), don't use 24-bit color bitmaps.

If you want to mimic full-motion video effects in Flash with as little file overhead as possible, see Chapter 36, "Creating Full-Motion Video in Flash." If you want to optimize bitmaps before you bring them into Flash, see the "Fireworks and Flash" tutorial by Scott Brown in Chapter 30.

✦ Use alpha effects on symbol instances sparingly with Motion Tweens. Alpha options can be found in the Effect Panel. In a sample three-keyframe Motion Tween, adding an alpha effect to a symbol instance on the start keyframe added 85 bytes to the .SWF file size. Adding another alpha effect to a symbol instance on the end keyframe added 175 bytes to the original alpha-free Motion Tween. Alpha effects can also slow frame rates during complex animated sequences. If you need to fade in or out a symbol, try using the Tint option in the Effect Panel first.

Table 40-1
Effects of Gradient Colors on .SWF File Size

Artwork Type	Colors	.SWF Size	Percent Increase
Circle Shape	1	115 bytes	n/a
Circle Shape	2	130 bytes	13%
Circle Shape	3	134 bytes	16.5%
Circle Shape	4	140 bytes	21.7%
Graphic Symbol	4	140 bytes	21.7%
Graphic Symbols*	4	152 bytes	32.7%
Movie Clip Symbol	4	162 bytes	40.9%
Circle Shapes*	4	225 bytes	95.6%
Graphic Symbols**	4	248 bytes	115.7%
Movie Clip Symbols**	4	272 bytes	136.5%
Circle Shapes**	4	923 bytes	702.6%

*Two instances or shapes with the same gradient fill.

**Ten instances or shapes with the same gradient fill.

Although some of these optimization tips may not seem to have a drastic effect on file size, realize that most Flash movies on the Web don't just use one or two elements, or one or two Motion Tweens. When you start to compound the file size reductions over several Movie Clips or .SWF files, you'll find that you can cut many kilobytes from your Flash .SWF files.

Use symbols

Anything in Flash can be turned into a symbol. When the Flash movie is exported as a .SWF file, the symbol's contents are stored on the first frame that uses that symbol. Symbol instances are similar to <A HREF> tags in HTML: They link data to a given frame, rather than copying or storing it there. After a symbol's contents are downloaded to the Flash player, it is easily available for any subsequent reuse in the Flash movie. After you've completed a Flash movie, you want to review your Flash production and perform the following optimizations:

✦ If any element is used in more than one keyframe or scene, consider making a symbol out of it. Just about every professional Flash designer uses nested symbols: An element is drawn, converted to a symbol, and then used in another symbol such as a Button or Movie Clip. Symbol instances reduce the resource overhead in .SWF files. Unlike grouped shapes, symbols need only refer to the original resource in the .SWF file rather than storing a new resource for every occurrence of it. You can, however, make a grouped shape into a symbol.

✦ If you want to use the same shape in a variety of colors, then make that shape a symbol. For each instance of the symbol, use the Effect Panel to change the color.

✦ The contents of a symbol are downloaded when the Flash Player encounters the first frame that uses the symbol. Given this, put any heavy symbol (for example, a symbol with bitmaps or sounds) in its own Flash movie, and start preloading the .SWF file near the beginning of the main Flash movie.

✦ Avoid using linked symbols from large Shared Library .SWF files (as discussed in Chapter 20, "Sharing and Loading Assets"). Any Flash movie that links to a Shared Library .SWF file will not start to play until the entire Shared Library .SWF has downloaded.

✦ Avoid setting large symbols or assets to be exported as Linked Symbols (to use with `attachSound` or `attachMovie` methods) in the movie's native Library. All Linked Symbols must be downloaded before playback of the .SWF can begin.

✦ If you are streaming your Flash movies (and not preloading them), then streaming playback can be interrupted when the playhead reaches a frame with a large symbol. Flash will not play a frame until the entire contents of any symbol on that frame are fully downloaded.

Cross-Reference

You can preload movies into a browser by using either the `ifFrameLoaded`, `_framesLoaded`/`_totalFrames` or the `getBytesLoaded()`/`getTotalBytes()` method. See Chapter 20, "Sharing and Loading Assets," for more information.

Manage assets in the Flash Library

Bitmaps and sound files that have been imported into Flash automatically become items stored in the Flash Library. As later sections of this chapter show you, you can specify the sound quality of audio events and streams in the Export Movie or Publish Settings dialog. However, these settings control the audio quality for the entire movie unless a specific encoding scheme is specified for individual sound clips in the Flash Library. Use the Library to assign specific compression methods to any given media element. For audio, Flash's MP3 encoding provides the best compression-to-quality ratio available. Specify MP3 compression on as many sounds in the Flash Library as possible.

Check out Chapter 12, "Using Bitmaps and Other Media with Flash," and Chapter 16, "Optimizing Flash Sound for Export," for detailed information regarding compression of Flash media in the Library.

Testing Flash Movies

You have three ways to test your Flash movies: in the authoring environment of Flash 5 using the Test Movie and Scene commands, in a browser using the Publish Preview command, or in the standalone Flash Player using Flash files (.SWF) made with the Export Movie command. There are several reasons why you should test your Flash movie before you transfer Flash movies to your Web server (or to the intended delivery medium):

✦ Flash .FLA files have much larger file sizes than their .SWF file counterparts. To accurately foretell the network bandwidth that a Flash movie requires, you need to know how large the final Flash movie will be. If the download demand is too overwhelming for your desired Internet connection speed (for example, a 28.8 Kbps modem), then you can go back and optimize your Flash movie.

✦ The Control ➪ Play command in the Flash authoring environment does not provide any streaming information. When you use the Test Movie or Scene command, you can view the byte size of each frame, and how long it will take to download the .SWF from the Web server.

✦ Movie Clip animations and actions targeting Movie Clip instances cannot be previewed using the standard Control ➪ Play command (or the Play button on the Controller) in the Flash authoring environment.

You can temporarily preview Movie Clip symbol instances within the Flash authoring environment (for example, the Timeline window) by changing the Symbol instance behavior to Graphic instead of Movie Clip. Do this by selecting the instance, opening the Instance Panel and choosing Graphic in the Behavior drop-down menu. However, when you switch the behavior back to Movie Clip, you will have lost the original instance name of the Movie Clip.

✦ Most scripting done with Flash 5 actions, such as `loadMovie`, `loadVariables`, and `startDrag`, cannot be previewed with the Play command. Enabling Frame Actions or Buttons in the Control menu has no effect with new scripting actions. You need to use Test Movie to try out most interactive functions in a Flash movie.

New Feature   Any actions that require the use of remote CGI (Common Gateway Interface) scripts to load variables, movies, or XML data, will now work in the Test Movie environment. You do not need to view your .SWF files in a browser to test these actions.

✦ Accurate frame rates cannot be previewed with the Play command (Control⇨ Play) in the authoring environment. Most complex animations appear jerky, pausing or skipping frames when the Play command is used.

Using the Test Scene or Movie command

You can test your Flash movies directly within the Flash 5 interface by using the Control⇨ Test Movie or Test Scene command. When you choose one of these commands, Flash opens your Flash movie in a new window *as a Flash .SWF movie*. Even though you are only "testing" a Flash movie, a new .SWF file is actually created and stored in the same location as the Flash .FLA file. For this reason, it is a good idea to always save your Flash file before you begin testing it.

Caution   If your movie is currently titled Untitled1, Untitled2, and so on in the application title bar, then it has not yet been saved. Make sure you give your Flash movie a distinct name before testing it.

Before you use the Test Scene or Movie command, you need to specify the settings of the resulting Flash .SWF movie. The Test Scene or Movie command uses the specifications outlined in the Publish Settings dialog to generate .SWF files. The Publish Settings dialog is discussed later in this chapter. For the time being, we can use the Flash 5 default settings to explore the Test Scene and Movie commands.

Test Movie

When you choose Control⇨ Test Movie (Command+Enter or Ctrl+Enter), Flash 5 generates a .SWF file of the entire Flash .FLA file that is currently open. If you have more than one Flash movie open, Flash creates a .SWF file for the one that is currently in the foreground and that has "focus."

Test Scene

If you are working on a lengthy Flash movie with multiple scenes, you want to test your scenes individually. You can do this by using Control⇨ Test Scene (Option+ Command+Enter or Ctrl+Alt+Enter). The process of exporting entire movies via Test Movie may require many minutes to complete, whereas exporting one scene will require a significantly smaller amount of time. As is shown in the next section, you can analyze each tested scene (or movie) with the Bandwidth Profiler.

Tip   You can use the Test Scene command while you are in Symbol Editing Mode to export a .SWF file that contains the current symbol timeline. The .SWF will not contain anything else from your Flash movie. Note that the symbol's center point will become the top-left corner of the playback stage.

How to use the Bandwidth Profiler

Do you want to know how long it will take for a 28.8 Kbps modem to download your Flash movie or scene? How about a 36.6 Kbps modem? Or a 56 Kbps modem? Or a cable modem? The Bandwidth Profiler enables you to simulate any download speed.

On the CD-ROM   In the ch40 folder of the *Flash 5 Bible* CD-ROM is a .FLA file called bandwidth.fla. We use that Flash movie for this section.

To use the Bandwidth Profiler, you first need to create a test movie or scene. When you create a .SWF file with the Control ➪ Test Movie or Scene commands, Flash opens the .SWF file in its own Player window.

One Reason to Use Imported .MP3 Files

If you have imported raw audio files (.WAV or .AIFF files) into your Flash movie, you may notice lengthy wait times to use the Test Movie or Publish commands in Flash 5. Why? The MP3 encoding process consumes much of the computer processor's power and time.

Flash has three MP3 compression qualities: Fast, Medium, or Best. Fast is the default MP3 quality setting—this is by far the fastest method of encoding MP3 sound. Because MP3 uses perceptual encoding, it compares a range of samples to determine how best to compress the sound. Fast compares over a smaller range of samples than either Medium or Best. As you increase quality, the sampling range increases.

This process is similar to building 256-color palettes for video files; it's best to look at all the frames of the video (instead of just the first frame) when you're trying to build a palette that's representative of all the colors used in the video. While MP3 doesn't quite work in this fashion, the analogy is appropriate. So, at Best quality, the MP3 encoding scans more of the waveform to look for similarities and differences. However, it's also more time intensive.

If you want to avoid the wait for Flash to publish .SWF files that use MP3 compression, we recommend that you compress your source audio files to the MP3 format (including the newly supported VBR—Variable Bit Rate—compression in Flash 5) and import those .MP3 files into Flash 5. Unless the .MP3 sound file is used for Stream Synch audio, Flash 5 will export the audio in its original MP3 compressed format.

View menu

The Test Movie or Scene viewing environment changes the View and Control menus. The first four commands in the View menu are the same as those of the Flash Player plug-in viewing controls:

✦ **Zoom In:** Selecting this option enlarges the Flash movie.

✦ **Zoom Out:** Selecting this option shrinks the Flash movie.

✦ **Magnification:** This submenu enables you to change the zoom factor of the movie. The .SWF movie is displayed at the original pixel size specified in the Modify ➪ Movie dialog when 100 percent (Ctrl+1 or Command+1) is the setting. For example, if the movie size is 500×300 pixels, it takes up 500×300 pixels on your monitor. If you change the size of the viewing window, the movie may be cropped. The lower section of this submenu enables you to change the viewable area of the Flash movie. Show Frame (Ctrl+2 or Command+2) will show only the frame boundary area in the Player window. Show All (Ctrl+3 or Command+3) shrinks or enlarges the Flash movie so that you can view all the artwork in the Flash movie, including elements off stage.

✦ **Bandwidth Profiler:** To view the Bandwidth Profiler in this new window, use View ➪ Bandwidth Profiler (Ctrl+B or Command+B). The .SWF movie shrinks to accommodate the Bandwidth Profiler.

 • The left side of the profiler displays three sections: Movie, Settings, and State. Movie indicates the dimensions, frame rate, size (in KB and bytes), duration and preload (in number of frames and seconds). Settings displays the current selected connection speed (which is set in the Debug menu). State shows you the current frame playing and its byte requirements, as well as the loaded percent of the movie.

 • The larger right section of the profiler shows the timeline header and graph. The lower red line beneath the timeline header indicates whether a given frame streams in real-time with the current modem speed specified in the Control menu. For a 28.8 Kbps modem, any frame above 200 bytes may cause delays in streaming for a 12 fps movie. Note that the byte limit for each frame is dependent on frame rate. For example, a 24 fps movie has a limit of 120 bytes per frame (for a 28.8 Kbps modem connection).

 • When the Bandwidth Profiler is enabled, two other commands are available in the View menu: Streaming Graph (Ctrl+G or Command+G) and Frame-By-Frame Graph (Ctrl+F or Command+F).

✦ **Show Streaming:** When Show Streaming is enabled, the Bandwidth Profiler emulates the chosen modem speed (in the Control menu) when playing the Flash movie. The Bandwidth Profiler counts the bytes downloaded (displayed in the Loaded subsection of the State heading), and shows the download/play progress via a green bar in the timeline header.

✦ **Streaming Graph:** By default, Flash opens the Bandwidth Profiler in Streaming Graph mode. This mode indicates how the Flash movie streams into a browser (see Figure 40-1). Alternating light and dark gray blocks represent each frame. The size of each block indicates its relative byte size. For our bandwidth.swf example, all the frames will have loaded by the time our playhead reaches frame 22.

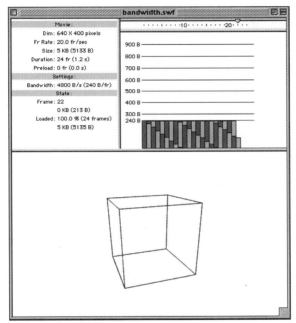

Figure 40-1: The Streaming Graph indicates how a movie will download over a given modem connection. Shown here is our bandwidth.swf as it would download over a 56 Kbps modem.

✦ **Frame-By-Frame Graph:** This second mode available to the Bandwidth Profiler lays each frame side by side under the timeline header (see Figure 40-2). Although the Streaming Graph enables you to see the real-time performance of a .SWF movie, the Frame-By-Frame Graph enables you to more easily detect which frames are contributing to streaming delays. If any frame block goes beyond the red line of the graph (for a given connection speed), then the Flash Player halts playback until the entire frame downloads. In the bandwidth.swf example, frame 1 is the only frame that may cause a very slight delay in streaming. The remaining frames are right around 200 bytes each — below our threshold of 240 bytes per frame for a 56 Kbps modem connection playing a 20 fps Flash movie.

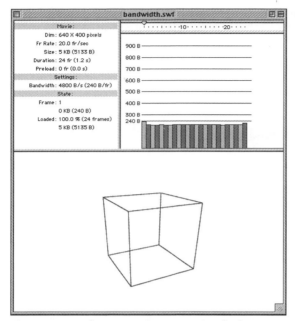

Figure 40-2: The Frame-By-Frame Graph shows you the byte demand of each frame in the Flash movie.

Control menu

Use the Control menu to play (Return) or rewind (Option+Command+R or Ctrl+Alt+R) the test movie. Rewinding pauses the bandwidth.swf movie on the first frame. Use the Step Forward (>) and Step Backward (<) commands to view the Flash movie frame by frame. If a Flash movie doesn't have a stop( ) action on the last frame, the Loop command forces the player to infinitely repeat the Flash movie.

Debug menu

The Debug menu also features commands that work in tandem with the Streaming and Frame-By-Frame Graphs:

✦ **14.4, 28.8, 56K:** These settings determine what speed the Bandwidth Profiler uses to calculate estimated download times and frame byte limitations. Notice that these settings use more practical expectations of these modem speeds. For example, a 28.8 modem can theoretically download 3.5 kilobytes per second (KB/sec), but a more realistic download rate for this modem speed is 2.3KB/sec.

✦ **User Settings 4, 5, and 6:** These are user-definable speed settings. By default, they are all 2.3KB/sec.

✦ **Customize:** To change the settings for any of the modem speeds listed previously, use the Customize command to input the new value(s).

Note The Control menu also contains List Objects and List Variables commands. List Objects can be used to show the names of Movie Clip instances or ActionScript Objects in the Output window, while the List Variables command displays the names and values of any currently loaded variables, ActionScript Objects, and XML Data.

Using the size report

Flash also lets you view a text-file summary of movie elements, frames, and fonts called a size report. In addition to viewing Frame-By-Frame Graphs of a Flash movie with the Bandwidth Profiler, you can inspect this size report for other "hidden" byte additions such as font character outlines. This report can only be generated when using the Export Movie or Publish commands.

A sample size report, called bandwidth_report.txt, is included in the ch40 folder of the *Flash 5 Bible* CD-ROM.

Publishing Your Flash Movies

After you've made a dazzling Flash movie complete with Motion Tweens, 3D simulations and ActionScripted interactivity, you need to make the Flash movie usable for the intended delivery medium — the Web, a CD-ROM (or floppy disk), a template for Macromedia Generator, a QuickTime Flash movie or a RealPlayer presentation, to name a few. As we mentioned in the introduction to this book, you need the Flash 5 application to open .FLA files. Because the majority of your intended audience won't have the full Flash 5 application, you need to export or publish your .FLA movie in a format that your audience can use.

You can convert your Flash movie (.FLA) files to .SWF files by using either the File ➪ Export Movie or File ➪ Publish/Publish Settings commands. The latter command is Flash's Publish feature. You can specify just about all file format properties in one step using the File ➪ Publish Settings command. After you've entered the settings, the File ➪ Publish command exports any and all file formats with your specified parameters in one step — all from the Flash 5 application.

A Word about the Export Movie Command

Even though Flash 5 has incredibly streamlined the process of creating .SWF movies with the Publish commands (discussed in the next section), it is worth mentioning that the File ➪ Export Movie command provides another route to creating a simple .SWF file. Although the Publish command is the quickest way to create HTML-ready Flash movies, the Export Movie command can be used to create updated .SWF files that have already been placed in HTML documents, or Flash movies that you intend to import into Macromedia Director movies (see Chapter 39, "Working with Authoring Applications").

The Export Movie command is discussed throughout the book. For more information on exporting still images in raster/bitmap formats, see Chapter 30, "Working with Raster Graphics." To export vector formats, see Chapter 31, "Working with Vector Graphics." To export QuickTime or .AVI files, see Chapter 34, "Working with QuickTime," and Chapter 36, "Creating Full-Motion Video in Flash."

Three commands are available with the Publish feature: Publish Settings, Publish Preview, and Publish. Each of these commands is discussed in the following sections.

Publish Settings

The Publish Settings command (File ⇨ Publish Settings) is used to determine which file formats are exported when the File ⇨ Publish command is invoked. By default, Flash 5 ships with Publish Settings that will export a Flash (.SWF) file and an HTML file with the proper markup tags to utilize the Flash plug-in or ActiveX control. If you want to customize the settings of the exported file types, you should familiarize yourself with the Publish Settings before you attempt to use the Publish command.

Selecting formats

Select File ⇨ Publish Settings to access the Publish Settings dialog, which is nearly identical for both PC and Mac. The dialog opens to the Formats tab, which has checkboxes to select the formats in which your Flash movie will be published (see Figure 40-3). For each Type that is checked, a tab appears in the Publish Settings dialog. Click each type's tab to specify settings to control the particulars of the movie or file that will be generated in that format.

The Use default names checkbox either enables or disables default names (disabled means that the Filename entry boxes are unavailable or grayed out). For example, if your movie is named intro.fla, then, if Use default names is selected, this is the base from which the names are generated in publishing. Thus, `intro.swf`, `intro.html`, `intro.gif`, and so on would result.

By unchecking Use default names, you can enter non-version–specific filenames for .FLA files that you incrementally save as you work. For example, if you have a .FLA file named main_100.fla, uncheck Use default names and set the Flash .SWF filename to main.swf, then every new .FLA version you save (for example, main_101.fla, main_102.fla, and so on) will still produce a main.swf file. This way, you can consistently refer to one .SWF file in your HTML code and incrementally save your Flash movies.

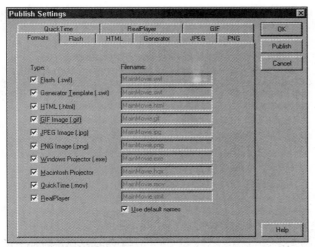

Figure 40-3: The Formats tab of the Publish Settings dialog enables you to select the published file formats and to use default or custom names for these published files.

Using the Flash settings

The primary and default publishing format of Flash 5 movies is the Flash (.SWF) format. Only .SWF movies retain full support for Flash actions and animations.

Here are your options in the Flash tab:

✦ **Load Order:** This option determines how Flash will draw the first frame of the Flash movie as it is downloaded to the plug-in or player. When Bottom up (the default) is chosen, the layers load in ascending order: The lowest layer displays first, then the second lowest, and so on, until all of the layers for the first frame have been displayed. When Top down is selected, the layers load in descending order: the top-most layer displays first, then the layer underneath it, and so on. Again, this option only affects the display of the first frame of a Flash movie. If the content of the first frame is downloaded or streamed quickly, you probably won't notice the Load Order's effect.

✦ **Generate size report:** As discussed earlier in this chapter, the size report for a Flash movie can be very useful in pinpointing problematic bandwidth-intensive elements, such as font characters. When this option is checked, the Publish command exports a SimpleText (Mac) or TXT file (PC) to view separately in a text-editor application.

✦ **Omit Trace Actions:** When this option is selected, the Flash player ignores any trace actions used in Flash ActionScripting. Trace actions will open the Flash Output window for debugging purposes. In general, if you used Trace actions, you will want to omit them from the final .SWF file — they can't be viewed in the Flash Player anyway.

✦ **Protect from import:** This option safeguards your Flash .SWF files on the Internet. When enabled, the .SWF file cannot be imported back into the Flash 5 authoring environment, or altered in any way.

The Protect from import option will *not* prevent a Web browser from caching your .SWF files. Also, Macromedia Director can import and use protected .SWF files. Hacking utilities called *swiffers,* can break into any .SWF file and extract artwork, sounds, and ActionScripted code. Even Notepad can open .SWF files and see variable names and values. For this reason, you should always use CGI scripts to verify password entries in Flash movies, rather than internal ActionScripted password checking with if . . . else conditions. Don't store sensitive information such as passwords in your source files!

✦ **Debugging Permitted:** If this option is checked, then you can access the Debugger Panel from in the Debug Movie environment, or from a Web browser that is using the Flash Debug Player plug-in or ActiveX control.

To install the Flash Debug Player plug-in or ActiveX control, go to the Players folder in your Macromedia Flash 5 application folder. There, you will find a Debug folder. Run the Flash 5 Player Installer file (Netscape for Mac and/or Internet Explorer for Mac), the flash32.exe file (Netscape for Windows), or the InstallAXFlash.exe (Internet Explorer for Windows) file located there.

✦ **Password:** If you checked the Debugging Permitted option, you can enter a password to access the Debugger Panel. Because you can now debug movies over a live Internet connection, you should always enter a password here if you intend to debug a remote Flash .SWF file. If you leave this field empty and check the Debugging Permitted option, Flash will still ask you for a password when you attempt to access the Debugger Panel remotely. Simply press the Enter key if you left this field blank.

✦ **JPEG Quality:** This slider and text-field option specifies the level of JPEG compression applied to bitmapped artwork in the Flash movie. The value can be any value between (and including) 0 to 100. Higher values apply less compression and preserve more information of the original bitmap, whereas lower values apply more compression and keep less information. The value entered here applies to all bitmaps that enable the Use document default quality option, found in the Bitmap Properties dialog for each bitmap in the Flash Library. Unlike the audio settings discussed in a moment, no "override" option exists to disregard settings in the Flash Library.

✦ **Audio Stream:** This option displays the current audio compression scheme for Stream audio. By clicking the Set button (see Figure 40-4), you can control the compression applied to any sounds that use the Stream Sync setting in the Sound tab of the Frame Properties dialog. Like the JPEG Quality option discussed previously, this compression value is applied to any Stream sounds that use the Default compression in the Export Settings section of each audio file's Sound Properties dialog in the Flash Library. See Chapters 14 through 16 for more information on using Stream sounds and audio compression schemes.

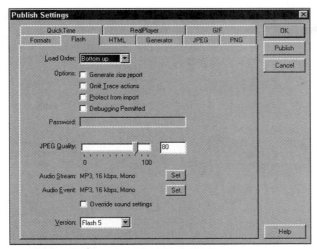

Figure 40-4: The Flash tab of the Publish Settings dialog controls the settings for a movie published in the Flash format.

✦ **Audio Event:** This setting behaves exactly the same as the Audio Stream option, except that this compression setting applies to Default compression-enabled Event sounds. See Chapter 15, "Importing and Editing Sounds in Flash," for more information on Event sounds.

Flash 5 now supports imported MP3 audio that uses VBR (Variable Bit Rate) compression. However, Flash 5 cannot compress native sounds in VBR. If you use any imported MP3 audio for Stream Sync audio, Flash will recompress the MP3 audio on export.

✦ **Override sound settings:** If you want the settings for Audio Stream and Audio Event to apply to all Stream and Event sounds, respectively, and to disregard any unique compression schemes specified in the Flash Library, then check this option. This is useful for creating multiple .SWF versions of the Flash movie (hi-fi, lo-fi, and so on) and enabling the Web visitor to decide which one to download. See Figure 40-5.

✦ **Version:** This drop-down menu provides the option to publish movies in any of the Flash .SWF formats. To ensure complete compatibility with all of the new Flash 5 features, select Flash 5. If you haven't used any new Flash 5 ActionScript commands or Dots notation, then you can use Flash 4. Flash 1 and 2 support only basic animation and interactive functions. Flash 3 will support just about all animation and artwork created in Flash 5, but it doesn't recognize any of the ActionScripts introduced with either Flash 4 or 5, editable text fields (such as form elements), or MP3 audio. If in doubt, you should test your choice of version in that version's Flash Player.

Figure 40-5: Click the Set button for Audio Stream or Audio Event, and the Sound Settings dialog appears.

Tip   You can download older versions of the Flash Player from the Macromedia site at: www.macromedia.com/support/flash/ts/documents/oldplayers.htm

When you are finished entering the settings for the .SWF movie, you can proceed to other file-type settings in the Publish Settings dialog. Or, you can click OK to return to the authoring environment of Flash 5 so that you can use the newly entered settings in the Test Movie or Scene environment. You can also export a .SWF file (and other file formats currently selected in Publish Settings) by clicking the Publish button in the Publish Settings dialog.

Using the HTML settings

HTML is the language in which the layout of most Web pages is written. The HTML tab of the Publish Settings dialog (see Figure 40-6) has a number of settings that control the way in which Flash will publish a movie into a complete Web page with the HTML format.

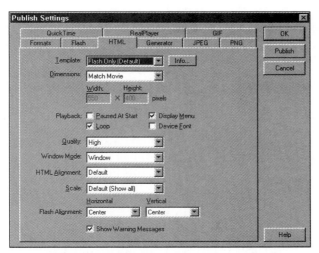

Figure 40-6: The HTML settings tab controls flexible Flash movie options — you can change this options without permanently affecting the Flash .SWF movie.

The settings available in the HTML tab include:

✦ **Template:** Perhaps the most important (and versatile) feature of all Publish Settings, the Template setting enables you to select a predefined set of HTML tags to display your Flash movies. To view the description of each template, click the Info button to the right of the drop-down list (shown in Figure 40-6). All templates use the same options listed in the HTML dialog — the template simply places the values of those settings into HTML tags scripted in the template. You can also create your own custom templates for your own unique implementation of Flash movies. Figure 40-7 shows the description for the Flash Only (Default) template.

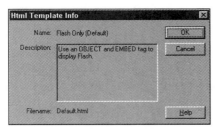

Figure 40-7: Clicking the Info button shown in Figure 40-6 summons a brief description of the HTML template that has been specified in the Template drop-down list.

You can view the "source" of each template in the HTML folder of the Flash 5 application folder. Although these template files have.html extensions, use Notepad (PC) or SimpleText (Mac) to view the files. All of the preinstalled templates include HTML tags to create an entire Web page, complete with <HEAD>, <TITLE>, and <BODY> tags.

- **Ad 3 Banner:** With this template, Flash creates an HTML document that checks for the Flash 3 Player plug-in. If JavaScript or VBScript detects the plug-in, then the Flash .SWF file will be served. If there is no Flash Player, then a GIF or JPEG will be loaded into the page. You must choose either the GIF or JPEG option in the Format tab of the Publish Settings dialog. As the name of the template implies, this template is useful for serving Flash ad banners. You can, however, use any of the Ad templates for any Flash movie version checking. Make sure that you have selected Flash 3 as the .SWF version in the Flash tab.

- **Ad 4 Banner:** Same as the Ad 3 Banner, except that the JavaScript and VBScript check for the Flash 4 Player plug-in. You need to change the .SWF Version option to Flash 4 in the Flash tab of the Publish Settings. Use this template only if you are using Flash 4-specific ActionScripts, such as variable declarations or loadVariable actions.

- **Ad 5 Banner:** Same as the Ad 3 Banner, except that the JavaScript and VBScript check for the Flash 5 Player plug-in. Change the .SWF version option to Flash 5 in the Flash tab of the Publish Settings dialog. If you are serving Flash ad banners, you may not want to serve the Flash 5 format. Unless your Flash 5 movies use Flash 5-specific ActionScripts (Dots notation, XML data, and so on), choose one of the previous Banner templates.

- **Ad Any Banner:** This template checks whether the Flash 3, 4, or 5 Player plug-in is installed. If any of these players is installed, then the published .SWF file will load into the HTML document. Otherwise, the published JPEG or GIF will be served. Use this option only if you are publishing Flash 3-compatible .SWF files, and want to serve a .SWF file to everyone who has a Flash 3, 4, or 5 Player plug-in.

- **Flash Only (Default):** This template simply inserts the <OBJECT> and <EMBED> tags for a Flash 5 movie. It does not perform any browser or plug-in detection.

- **Flash with FSCommand:** Use this template if you are using the FSCommand action in your Flash movies to communicate with JavaScript in the HTML page. The FSCommand is discussed in the next chapter. The necessary <OBJECT> and <EMBED> tags from the Flash Only (Default) template are also included.

- **Generator Ad Any Banner:** This template is similar to the Ad Any Banner template. If you have used Generator Objects or Generator Environment variables to your Flash movie, then this template will create an HTML that checks for the Flash 3, 4, or 5 Player plug-in. If any of those versions are installed, then a request will be made for a dynamic .SWF file (?type=swf) from the Generator template (.SWT file). Otherwise, a JPEG, GIF, or PNG image will be made from the Generator template. You need to specify an image format (JPEG, GIF, or PNG) in the Formats tab for this template. However, you will not need to upload the published image file — the Generator Server is responsible for creating the static image on the fly.

- **Generator Image Output:** This template creates a simple <IMG> tag with a SRC attribute that contains the template's filename and the desired image format, as in <IMG SRC="templateFile.swt?type=gif">, which will tell the Generator Server to create a GIF image from the templateFile.swt file. You need to check the desired image format in the Formats tab of the Publish Settings dialog. As with the Generator Ad Any Banner template, you will not need to upload the published image file.

- **Generator Only (Default):** This template makes an HTML document that is similar to the Flash Only (Default) template. It will include <OBJECT> and <EMBED> tags that refer to the Generator template file (.SWT file) and a Flash output format (?type=swf).

- **Generator QuickTime:** The HTML document published with this template will create an <EMBED> tag that references the Generator template file (.SWT file) and a QuickTime Flash output format, as in <EMBED SRC= "template.swt?type=mov" . . .>. Note that this output format will require the QuickTime 4 (or higher) Player plug-in.

 For more information on Generator output, refer to Chapter 28, "Revving Up Generator."

- **Image Map:** This template does not use or display any .SWF movie. Instead, it uses a GIF, JPEG, or PNG image (as specified in the Publish Settings' Format tab) as a client-side image map, via an <IMG> tag with a USEMAP attribute. Use a frame label of #map in the Flash editor document (.FLA file) to designate which frame is used as the map image. See "Using the GIF settings" later in this chapter for more details.

- **Java Player:** Instead of using the Flash Player or an image map, this template creates the necessary <APPLET> tags to use the Flash Java Player. To use this player, you must select the Publish Settings' Flash tab and specify a version 2 .SWF format. The Flash Java Player needs to access Java class files (found in the Players folder of the Flash 4 application folder). Make sure that you have uploaded the class files to your Web server. You may need to add a CODEBASE=[URL of class files] to the <APPLET> tag created by this template.

- **QuickTime:** This template creates an ⟨EMBED⟩ tag to display QuickTime Flash movies. You need to enable the QuickTime file type in the Publish Settings' Format tab. A QuickTime Flash movie is a special type of QuickTime movie, playable with QuickTime 4 or higher. QuickTime 4 can only recognize Flash 3 features. You must choose Flash 3 as the Version option in the Flash tab. Depending on the options selected in the QuickTime tab of Publish Settings, the Flash movie may or may not be stored within the QuickTime movie file. See Chapter 34, "Working with QuickTime," for more information.

Note

At the time of this writing, the QuickTime 5 Public Preview had been released. This version of QuickTime supports Flash 4 ActionScripts.

- **User Choice:** Often the scripter's testing tool, this template creates an HTML document with Flash 5 plug-in detection and a JavaScript cookie that enables you to choose three loading options for the Flash .SWF file: automatic plug-in detection, standard plug-in usage (via direct non-JavaScript–written ⟨OBJECT⟩ or ⟨EMBED⟩ tags), or substitute image (for example, GIF, JPEG, or PNG).

✦ **Dimensions:** This setting controls the WIDTH and HEIGHT values of the ⟨OBJECT⟩ and ⟨EMBED⟩ tags. The dimension settings here do not change the original .SWF movie, they simply create the viewport through which your Flash movie is viewed on the Web page. The way that the Flash movie "fits" into this viewport is determined with the Scale option (discussed later). Three input areas exist: a drop-down menu and two text fields for width andheight.

- **Match Movie:** If you want to keep the same width and height that you specified in the Modify ➪ Movie dialog, then use this option in the drop-down menu.

- **Pixels:** You can change the viewing size (in pixel units) of the Flash movie window by selecting this option and entering new values in the Width and Height text fields.

- **Percent:** By far one of the most popular options with Flash movies, Percent scales the movie to the size of the browser window — or a portion of it. Using a value of 100 on both Width and Height expands the Flash movie to fit the entire browser window. If Percent is used with the proper Scale setting (see the description of the Scale setting later in this chapter), then the aspect ratio of your Flash movie will not be distorted.

- **Width and Height:** Enter the values for the Flash movie width and height here. If Match Movie is selected, you shouldn't be able to enter any values. The unit of measurement is determined by selecting either Pixels or Percent from the drop-down menu.

✦ **Playback:** These options control how the Flash movie plays when it is downloaded to the browser. Each of these options has an ⟨OBJECT⟩ and ⟨EMBED⟩ attribute if you want to control them outside of Publish Settings. Note that these attributes are not viewable within the Publish Settings dialog — you need to load the published HTML document into a text editor to see the attributes.

- **Paused at Start:** This is equivalent to adding a Stop action on the first frame of the first scene in the Flash movie. By default, this option is off — movies play as soon as they stream into the player. A button with a Play action can start the movie, or the Play command can be executed from the Flash Player shortcut menu (by right-clicking or Control+clicking the movie). Attribute: PLAY=true or false. If PLAY=true, the movie will play as soon as it is loaded.

- **Loop:** This option causes the Flash movie to repeat an infinite number of times. By default, this option is on. If it is not checked, the Flash movie stops on the last frame unless some other ActionScripted event is initiated on the last frame. Attribute: LOOP=true or false.

- **Display Menu:** This option controls whether the person viewing the Flash movie in the Flash Player environment can access the shortcut menu via a right-click (PC) or Ctrl+click (Mac) anywhere within the movie area. If this option is checked, then the visitor can select Zoom In/Out, 100 percent, Show All, High Quality, Play, Loop, Rewind, Forward, and Back from the menu. If this option is not checked, then the visitor can only select About Flash Player from the menu. Attribute: MENU=true or false.

- **Device Font:** This option only applies to Flash movie played in the Windows version of the Flash Player. When enabled, this option replaces fonts that are not installed on the Player's system with antialiased system fonts. Attribute: DEVICEFONT=true or false.

✦ **Quality:** This menu determines how the Flash artwork in a movie will render. While it would be ideal to play all Flash movies at high quality, slower processors may not be able to redraw antialiased artwork and keep up with the frame rate.

- **Low:** This setting forces the Flash Player to turn off antialiasing (smooth edges) completely. On slower processors, this may improve playback performance. Attribute: QUALITY=LOW.

- **Auto Low:** This setting starts in Low quality mode (no antialiasing), but will switch to High quality if the computer's processor can handle the playback speed. Attribute: QUALITY=AUTOLOW.

- **Auto High:** This setting is the opposite of Auto Low. The Flash Player starts playing the movie in High quality mode, but, if the processor cannot handle the playback demands, then it switches to Low quality mode. For most Web sites, this is the optimal setting to use because it favors higher quality first. Attribute: QUALITY=AUTOHIGH.

- **Medium:** This quality produces antialiased vector graphics on a 2×2 grid (in other words, it will smooth edges over a 4-pixel square area), but does not smooth bitmap images. Artwork will appear slightly better than the Low quality, but not as smooth as the High setting. Attribute: QUALITY=MEDIUM.

New Feature The Medium quality option is new to Flash 5. You can now specify this intermediate quality in order to achieve smoother playback and smoother graphics quality.

- **High:** When this setting is used, the Flash Player dedicates more of the computer's processor to rendering graphics (instead of playback). All vector artwork is antialiased on a 4×4 grid (16-pixel square area). Bitmaps are smoothed unless they are contained within an animation sequence such as a Motion Tween. By default, this setting is selected in the HTML tab of the Publish Settings dialog. Attribute: QUALITY=HIGH.

- **Best:** This mode does everything that High quality does, with the addition of smoothing all bitmaps — regardless of whether they are in Motion Tweens. This mode is the most processor-intensive. Attribute: QUALITY=BEST.

✦ **Window Mode:** As discussed in the "Animation techniques using layers" section of Chapter 39, the Window Mode setting only works with the Flash ActiveX control. Therefore, it only applies to 32-bit Windows versions of Internet Explorer. If you intend to deliver to this browser, then you can animate Flash content on top of DHTML content. Refer to Chapter 24, "Sending Data In and Out of Flash," for more information. Attribute: WMODE=WINDOW, or OPAQUE, or TRANSPARENT.

✦ **HTML Alignment:** This setting works much like the ALIGN attribute of <IMG> tags in HTML documents, but it's used with the ALIGN attribute of the <OBJECT> and <EMBED> tags for the Flash movie. Note that these settings may not have any effect when used within a table cell (<TD> tag) or a DHTML layer (<DIV> or <LAYER> tag).

- **Default:** This option horizontally or vertically centers the Flash movie in the browser window. If the browser window is smaller than a Flash movie that uses a Pixel or Match Movie dimensions setting (see Dimensions setting earlier in this section), then the Flash movie will be cropped.

- **Left, Right, Top, and Bottom:** These options align the Flash movie along the left, right, top, or bottom edge of the browser window, respectively.

✦ **Scale:** This setting works in tandem with the Dimensions setting discussed earlier in this section, and determines how the Flash movie displays on the HTML page. Just as big screen movies must be cropped to fit the aspect ratio of a TV screen, Flash movies may need to be modified to fit the area prescribed by the Dimensions setting.

- **Default (Show all):** This option fits the entire Flash movie into the area defined by the Dimensions setting without distorting the original aspect ratio of the Flash movie. However, borders may appear on two sides of the Flash movie. For example, if a 300×300-pixel window is specified in Dimensions and the Flash movie has an aspect ratio of 1.33:1 (for example, 400×300 pixels), then a border fills the remaining areas on top of and below the Flash movie. This is similar to the "letterbox" effect on widescreen video rentals. Attribute: SCALE=SHOWALL.

- **No border:** This option forces the Flash movie to fill the area defined by the Dimensions setting without leaving borders. The Flash movie's aspect ratio is not distorted or stretched. However, this may crop two sides of the Flash movie. Using the same example from Show All, the left and right sides of the Flash movie are cropped when No Border is selected. Attribute: SCALE=NOBORDER.

- **Exact fit:** This option stretches a Flash movie to fill the entire area defined by the Dimensions setting. Using the same example from Show All, the 400×300 Flash movie is scrunched to fit a 300×300 window. If the original movie showed a perfect circle, it now appears as an oval. Attribute: SCALE=EXACTFIT.

✦ **Flash Alignment:** This setting adjusts the SALIGN attribute of the <OBJECT> and <EMBED> tags for the Flash movie. In contrast to the HTML Alignment setting, Flash Alignment works in conjunction with the Scale and Dimensions settings, and determines how a Flash movie is aligned within the Player window.

- **Horizontal:** These options — Left, Center, and Right — determine whether the Flash movie is horizontally aligned to the left, center, or right of the Dimensions area, respectively. Using the same example from the Scale setting, a 400×300-pixel Flash movie (fit into a 300×300 Dimension window with SCALE=NOBORDER) with a Flash Horizontal Alignment setting of Left crops only the right side of the Flash movie.

- **Vertical:** These options — Top, Center, and Bottom — determine whether the Flash movie is vertically aligned to the top, center, or bottom of the Dimensions area, respectively. If the previous example used a Show All Scale setting and had a Flash Vertical Alignment setting of Top, then the border only occurs below the bottom edge of the Flash movie.

✦ **Show Warning Messages:** This useful feature alerts you to errors during the actual Publish process. For example, if you selected the Image Map template and didn't specify a static GIF, JPEG, or PNG file in the Formats tab, then Flash returns an error. By default, this option is enabled. If it is disabled, then Flash suppresses any warnings during the Publish process.

Using the GIF settings

The GIF (Graphics Interchange File) format, developed by CompuServe, defined the first generation of Web graphics, and is still quite popular today, despite its 256-color limitation. In the context of the Flash Publish Settings, the GIF format is used to export a static or animated image that can be used in place of the Flash movie if the Flash Player or plug-in is not installed. Although the Flash and HTML tabs are specific to Flash movie display and playback, the settings of the GIF tab (see Figure 40-8) control the characteristics of a GIF animation (or still image) that Flash will publish.

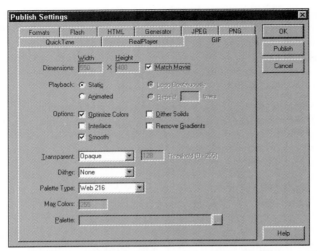

Figure 40-8: Every subtle aspect of a GIF animation or still image can be finessed with these settings of the GIF tab of the Publish Settings dialog.

The settings in the GIF tab include the following:

✦ **Dimensions:** This setting has three options: Width, Height, and Match Movie. As you might surmise, Width and Height control the dimensions of the GIF image. These fields are enabled only when the Match Movie checkbox is unchecked. With Match Movie checked, the dimensions of the GIF match those of the Flash Movie that is being published.

✦ **Playback:** These radio buttons control what type of GIF image is created and how it plays (if Animated is chosen).

• **Static:** If this button is selected, then Flash exports the first frame of the Flash movie as a single still image in the GIF format. If you want to use a different frame other than the first frame, use a frame label of #Static on the desired frame. Alternatively, you could use the File ⇨ Export Image command to export a GIF image from whatever frame the Current Frame Indicator is positioned over.

• **Animated:** If this button is selected, then Flash exports the entire Flash movie as an animated GIF file (in the GIF89a format). If you don't want to export the entire movie as an animated GIF (indeed, a GIF file for a Flash movie with over 100 frames would be most likely too large to download easily over the Web), you can designate a range of frames to export. Use a frame label of #First on the beginning frame of a given range of frames. Next, add a frame label of #Last to the ending frame of the desired sequence of frames. Flash actually does a pretty good at optimizing animated GIFs by only saving areas that change over time in each frame — instead of the entire frame.

Scott Brown discusses optimized animated GIFs in his "Fireworks and Flash" Expert Tutorial in Chapter 30.

- **Loop Continuously:** When the Animated radio button is selected, you can specify that the animated GIF repeats an infinite number of times by selecting the Loop Continuously radio button.

- **Repeat __ times:** This option can be used to set up an animated GIF that repeats a given number of times. If you don't want the animated GIF to repeat continuously, then enter the number of repetitions here.

✦ **Options:** The options in the Options settings control the creation of the GIF's color table and how the browser displays the GIF.

- **Optimize Colors:** When you are using any palette type other than Adaptive, this option removes any colors preexisting in the Web 216 or custom palettes that are not used by the GIF image. Enabling this option can only save you precious bytes used in file overhead — it has no effect on the actual quality of the image. Most images do not use all 216 colors of the Web palette. For example, a black and white picture can only use between 3 and 10 colors from the 216-color palette.

- **Interlace:** This option makes the GIF image download in incrementing resolutions. As the image downloads, the image becomes sharper with each successive "scan." Use of this option is usually personal preference. Some people like to use it for image maps that can provide basic navigation information before the entire image downloads.

- **Smooth:** This option antialiases the Flash artwork as it exports to the GIF image. Text may look better when it is antialiased, but may want to test this option for your particular use. If you need to make a transparent GIF, then smoothing may produce unsightly edges.

- **Dither Solids:** This option determines if solid areas of color (such as fills) are dithered. In this context, this type of dithering would create a two-color pattern to mimic a solid color that doesn't occur in the GIF's color palette. See the discussion of dithering later in this section.

- **Remove Gradients:** Flash gradients do not translate or display very well in 256 or less colors. Use this option to convert all Flash gradients to solid colors. The solid color is determined by the first color prescribed in the gradient. Unless you developed your gradients with this effect in mind, this option may produce undesirable results.

✦ **Transparent:** This setting controls the appearance of the Flash movie background, as well as any Flash artwork that uses alpha settings. Because GIF images only support one level of transparency (that is, the transparent area cannot be antialiased), you need to exercise caution when using this setting. The Threshold option is only available if Alpha is selected.

- **Opaque:** This option produces a GIF image with a solid background. The image has a rectangular shape.

- **Transparent:** This option makes the Flash movie background appear transparent. If the Smooth option in the Options setting is enabled, then Flash artwork may display halos over the background HTML color.

- **Alpha and Threshold:** When the Alpha option is selected in the drop-down menu, you can control at what alpha level Flash artwork becomes transparent by entering a value in the Threshold text field. For example, if you enter 128, then all alphas at 50 percent become completely transparent. If you are considering an animated GIF that has Flash artwork fading in or out, then you probably want to use the Opaque transparent option. If Alpha and Threshold were used, then the fade effect would be lost.

✦ **Dither:** Dithering is the process of emulating a color by juxtaposing two colors in a pattern arrangement. Because GIF images are limited to 256 colors (or less), dithering can often produce better-looking images for continuous tone artwork such as gradients. However, Flash's dithering seems to work best with the Web 216 palette. Dithering can increase the file size of a GIF image.

- **None:** This option does not apply any dithering to the GIF image.

- **Ordered:** This option applies an intermediate level of dithering with minimal file size overhead.

- **Diffusion:** This option applies the best level of dithering to the GIF image, but with larger file size overhead. Diffusion dithering only has a noticeable effect when the Web 216 palette is chosen in Palette Type.

✦ **Palette Type:** As mentioned earlier in this section, GIF images are limited to 256 or less colors. However, this grouping of 256 is arbitrary: Any set of 256 (or less) colors can be used for a given GIF image. This setting enables you to select predefined sets of colors to use on the GIF image. See Chapter 2, "Exploring the Interface: Panels, Settings, and More," for more information on the Web color palette.

- **Web 216:** When this option is selected, the GIF image only uses colors from the limited 216 Web-color palette. For most Flash artwork, this should produce acceptable results. However, it may not render Flash gradients or photographic bitmaps very well.

- **Adaptive:** With this option selected, Flash creates a unique set of 256 colors (or fewer, if specified in the Max Colors setting) for the GIF image. However, these adapted colors fall outside of the Web-Safe Color Palette. File sizes for adaptive GIFs are larger than Web 216 GIFs, unless few colors are chosen in the Max Colors setting. Adaptive GIFs look much better than Web 216 GIFs, but may not display very well with 8-bit video cards and monitors.

- **Web Snap Adaptive:** This option tries to give the GIF image the best of both worlds. Flash converts any colors close to the 216 Web palette to Web-safe colors and uses adaptive colors for the rest. This palette produces better results than the Adaptive palette for older display systems that used 8-bit video cards.

- **Custom:** When this option is selected, you can specify a palette that uses the .ACT file format to be used as the GIF image's palette. Macromedia Fireworks and Adobe Photoshop can export color palettes (or color look-up tables) as .ACT files.

✦ **Max Colors:** With this setting, you can specify exactly how many colors are in the GIF's color table. This numeric entry field is only enabled when Adaptive or Web Snap Adaptive is selected in the Palette Type drop-down menu.

✦ **Palette:** This text field and the "..." browse button are only enabled when Custom is selected in the Palette Type drop-down menu. When enabled, this dialog is used to locate and load a palette file from the hard drive.

Using the JPEG settings

The JPEG (Joint Photographic Experts Group) format is just as popular as the GIF format on the Web. Unlike GIF images, though, JPEG images can use much more than 256 colors. In fact, JPEG files must be 24-bit color (or full-color RGB) images. Although GIF files use lossless compression (within the actual file itself), JPEG images use lossy compression, which means that color information is discarded in order to save file space. However, JPEG compression is very good. Even at its lowest quality settings, JPEG images can preserve quite a bit of detail in photographic images.

Another significant difference between GIF and JPEG is that GIF images do not require nearly as much memory (for equivalent image dimensions) as JPEG images do. You need to remember that JPEG images "uncompress" when they are downloaded to your computer. While the file sizes may be small initially, they still open as full-color images in the computer's memory. For example, even though you may get the file size of a 400×300-pixel JPEG image down to 10KB, it still requires nearly 352KB in memory when it is opened or displayed.

Flash publishes the first frame of the Flash movie as the JPEG image, unless a #Static frame label is given to another frame in the Flash movie. The limited settings of the JPEG tab of the Publish Settings dialog (see Figure 40-9) control the few variables of this still photoquality image format:

✦ **Dimensions:** This setting behaves the same as the GIF Dimensions setting. Width and Height control the dimensions of the movie. But these fields are enabled only when the Match Movie checkbox is unchecked. With Match Movie checked, the dimensions of the JPEG match those of the Flash Movie.

✦ **Quality:** This slider and text field work exactly the same way as the JPEG Quality setting in the Flash tab of Publish Settings. Higher values apply less compression and result in better quality, but create images with larger file sizes.

✦ **Progressive:** This option is similar to the Interlaced option for GIF images. When enabled, the JPEG image loads in successive scans, becoming sharper with each pass.

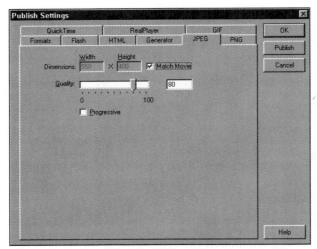

Figure 40-9: The settings of the JPEG tab are limited because JPEGs are still images with relatively few variables to be addressed.

Using the PNG settings

The PNG (Portable Network Graphic) format is another still-image format. It was developed quite recently and is an improvement over both the GIF and JPEG formats in several ways. Much like JPEG, it is excellent for transmission of photographic quality images. The primary advantages of PNG are variable bit-depths (images can be 256 colors or millions of colors), multilevel transparency, and lossless compression. However, most browsers do not offer full support for all PNG options without some kind of additional plug-in. When in doubt, test your PNG images in your preferred browser.

The settings of the PNG tab (see Figure 40-10) control the characteristics of the PNG image that Flash will publish.

The PNG tab options are:

✦ **Dimensions:** This setting works just like the GIF and JPEG equivalents. When Match Movie is checked, you cannot alter the Width and Height of the PNG image.

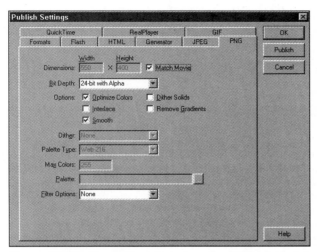

Figure 40-10: The settings found on the PNG tab closely resemble those on the GIF tab. The PNG was engineered to have many of the advantages of both the GIF and JPEG formats.

✦ **Bit Depth:** This setting controls how many colors are created in the PNG image:

- **8-bit:** In this mode, the PNG image has a maximum color palette of 256 colors, similar to the palette function of GIF images. When this option is selected, the Options, Dither, Palette Type, Max Colors, and Palette settings can be altered.

- **24-bit:** When this option is selected, the PNG image can display any of the 16.7 million RGB colors. This option produces larger files than 8-bit PNG images, but renders the Flash artwork most faithfully.

- **24-bit with Alpha:** This option adds another 8-bit channel to the 24-bit PNG image for multilevel transparency support. This means that Flash will treat the Flash movie background as a transparent area, so that information behind the PNG image (such as HTML background colors) shows through. Note that, with proper browser support, PNG can render antialiased edges on top of other elements, such as HTML background images!

Caution Flash's PNG export or publish settings do not reflect the full range of PNG options available. PNG can support transparency in both 8-bit and 24-bit flavors, but Flash only enables transparency in 24-bit with Alpha images.

✦ **Options:** These options behave the same as the equivalent GIF Publish Settings.

✦ **Dither, Palette Type, Max Colors,** and **Palette:** These settings work the same as the equivalent GIF Publish Settings. Because PNG images can be either 8- or 24-bit, these options are only apply to 8-bit PNG images. If anything other than 8-bit is selected in the Bit Depth setting, then these options are disabled. Please refer to the previous section for more information.

✦ **Filter Options:** This drop-down menu controls what type of compression sampling or algorithm the PNG image uses. Note that this does not apply an art or graphic "filter effect" like the filters in Adobe Photoshop do, nor does it throw away any image information — all filters are lossless. It simply enables you to be the judge of what kind of compression to use on the image. You need to experiment with each of these filters on your Flash movie image to find the best filter-to-file size combination. Technically, the filters do not actually look at the pixel data. Rather, they look at the byte data of each pixel. Results vary depending on the image content, but here are some guidelines to keep in mind:

- **None:** When this option is selected, no filtering is applied to the image. When no filter is applied, you usually have unnecessarily large file sizes.

- **Sub:** This filter works best on images that have repeated information along the horizontal axis. For example, the stripes of a horizontal American flag filter nicely with the sub filter.

- **Up:** The opposite of the sub filter, this filter works by looking for repeated information along the vertical axis. The stripes of a vertical American flag filter well with the up filter.

- **Average:** Use this option when a mixture of vertical and horizontal information exists. When in doubt, try this filter first.

- **Paeth:** This filter works like an advanced average filter. When in doubt, try this filter after you have experimented with the average filter.

Creating Windows and Macintosh projectors

To export a Mac standalone projector, check the Macintosh Projector option in the Formats tab. To publish a PC standalone projector, check the Windows Projector option in the Formats tab.

The process of creating and using Flash standalone projectors is described in Chapter 42, "Using Players, Projectors, and Screensaver Utilities."

Using the QuickTime settings

Now that QuickTime 4 (and the forthcoming QuickTime 5) includes built-in support for Flash tracks and .SWF files, you may want to publish QuickTime 4 movies (.MOV files) in addition to your Flash movies (.SWF files). The QuickTime publish settings are discussed at length in Chapter 34, "Working with QuickTime." If you want to enable QuickTime movie output via the Publish command, make sure that it is selected in the Formats tab of the Publish Settings dialog.

Producing RealPlayer presentations

Flash 5 can now automatically create tuned .SWF files and RealAudio files from your Stream Sync audio used in your Flash movie file. To create the tuned .SWF, RealAudio, and .SMIL files necessary for playback in RealPlayer, check the RealPlayer option in the Formats tab of the Publish Settings dialog.

Cross-Reference

To learn the ins and outs of RealPlayer Flash presentations, please read Chapter 35, "Working with RealPlayer."

Publish Preview and Publish Commands

After you have entered the file format types and specifications for each in the Publish Settings dialog, you can proceed to preview and publish the file types you selected.

Using Publish Preview

The Publish Preview submenu (accessible from File ➪ Publish Preview) lists all of the file types currently enabled in the Publish Settings dialog*. By default, HTML is the first file type available for preview. In general, the first item enabled in the Formats tab of Publish Settings is the first item in the submenu, and can be executed by pressing F12. Selecting a file type in the Publish Preview menu launches your preferred browser and inserts the selected file type(s) into the browser window.

Note

When you use Publish Preview, Flash 5 actually creates real files in the same location as the saved Flash movie. In a sense, previewing is the same as running the Publish command, except that Publish Preview will save you the steps of opening the browser and loading the files manually.

Using Publish

When you want Flash to export the file type(s) selected in the Publish Settings, choose File ➪ Publish (Shift+F12). Flash creates the new files wherever the Flash movie was last saved. If you have selected an HTML template in the HTML tab of Publish Settings, then you may receive a warning or error message if any other necessary files were not specified. That's it! After you've tested the files for the delivery browser and/or platforms of your choice, you can upload the files to your Web server.

---

*RealPlayer files can not be previewed from this menu.

Summary

✦ To achieve the smallest possible file size for quick download over the Internet, make sure that you have optimized your Flash movie. Reducing the use of bitmapped artwork and the number of points in a line or shape, and using nested symbols, can help reduce wasted space in a Flash movie.

✦ For audio, we recommend that you use Flash's MP3 encoding. MP3 provides the best sound quality with the smallest byte requirements. However, you will want to experiment with different audio codecs, depending on your source audio.

✦ Test your Flash movies and scenes within the Flash authoring environment. The Bandwidth Profiler can provide vital information about frame byte requirements, and can help you find problematic streaming areas of the Flash movie.

✦ The size report that can be generated from the Export Movie or Publish commands for .SWF movies lists detailed information regarding any and all Flash elements, such as audio, fonts and frame byte size.

✦ The Publish Settings dialog box enables you to pick any number of file formats to export at one time. You can control just about every setting imaginable for each file type, and use HTML templates to automate the insertion of Flash movies into your Web pages.

✦ Publish Preview will automatically launch your preferred browser and load the selected publish file(s) into the browser window.

✦   ✦   ✦

Integrating Flash Content with HTML

◆ ◆ ◆ ◆

In This Chapter

Adding Flash movies with raw HTML

Filling the entire browser window with a Flash movie

Detecting the Flash Player plug-in

Using JavaScript with Flash movies

◆ ◆ ◆ ◆

I f you're not one for automated HTML production using templates, then this chapter is for you. This chapter teaches you the ins and outs of the `<OBJECT>` and `<EMBED>` tags, as well as some secrets to using `<FRAMESET>` tags to display Flash movies. At the end of this chapter, we examine how Flash movies can interact with JavaScript and DHTML by using `FSCommand` actions from Flash.

Writing Markup for Flash Movies

In Chapter 40, you learned how to use the new Publish feature, which included automated HTML templates. These templates created the necessary HTML tags to display Flash movies on Web pages. This section discusses the use of Flash movies in your handwritten HTML documents. You can also use this knowledge to alter HTML documents created by the Publish feature.

Note   In the following code examples, we use an asterisk (*) when displaying optional parameters that are not in the default setting of the Flash Only (Default) HTML template.

Two tags can be used to place Flash movies on a Web page (such as an HTML document): `<OBJECT>` and `<EMBED>`. You need to include both of these plug-in tags in HTML documents, as each tag is specific to a browser: `<OBJECT>` for Internet Explorer on Windows, and `<EMBED>` for Netscape on Windows and Mac (and Internet Explorer on Mac). Each tag works similarly to the other, with some slight differences in attribute names and organization. Remember that if both sets of tags are included with the HTML, only one set of tags is actually read by the browser, depending on which browser is used to view the Web page. Without these tags, Flash movies cannot be displayed with other HTML elements such as images and text.

Tip   You can, however, directly link to .SWF files as an alternative method for displaying Flash content. That method, however, precludes the use of parameters to control the look and playback of the Flash movie — it would be the same as loading the .SWF movie straight into the standalone Flash Player. See Colin Moock's tutorial later in this chapter for more information on direct linking.

Using the <OBJECT> tag

Microsoft Internet Explorer for Windows uses this tag exclusively to enable the Flash ActiveX control. When the Flash Only (Default) HTML template is used in Publish Settings, the HTML document that is published uses the <OBJECT> tag in the following way:

```
A. <OBJECT
B.      classid="clsid:D27CDB6E-AE6D-11cf-96B8-
        444553540000"
C.      codebase="http://download.macromedia.com/pub/
        shockwave/cabs/flash/swflash.cab#version=5,0,0,0"
D.      ID=home
E.      WIDTH=550 HEIGHT=400>
F.      <PARAM NAME=movie VALUE="home.swf">
G.      <PARAM NAME=quality VALUE=high>
H.      <PARAM NAME=bgcolor VALUE=#FFFFFF>
I.*     <PARAM NAME=scale VALUE=noborder>
J.*     <PARAM NAME=play VALUE=false>
K. </OBJECT>
```

A. <OBJECT: This is the opening tag containing the ID code and locations of the ActiveX control for Flash. Note that this opening tag includes the attributes lettered B through E.

B. classid: This lengthy string is the unique ActiveX identification code. If you are inserting the <OBJECT> tag by hand in a text editor, make sure that you copy this ID string exactly.

C. codebase: Like the codebase attribute of Java <APPLET> tags, this attribute of the <OBJECT> tag specifies the location of the ActiveX control installer as a URL. Notice that the #version=5,0,0,0 portion of the URL indicates that the Flash Player version 5 should be used. You can also specify specific minor releases, such as #version=5,0,29,0, which would install the Flash 5.0 r29 ActiveX control. If the visitor doesn't have the ActiveX control already installed, then Internet Explorer automatically downloads the control from this URL.

D. `ID`: This attribute of the `<OBJECT>` tag assigns a JavaScript/VBScript identifier to the Flash movie, so that it can be controlled by HTML JavaScript/VBScript functions. By default, this attribute's value is the name of the actual of .SWF file, without the .SWF extension. Each element on an HTML page should have a unique `ID` or `NAME` attribute. The `NAME` attribute is discussed in the next section.

E. `WIDTH` **and** `HEIGHT>`: These attributes control the actual width and height of the Flash movie, as it appears on the Web page. If no unit of measurement is specified, then these values are in pixels. If the % character is added to the end of each value, then the attribute adjusts the Flash movie to the corresponding percent of the browser window. For example, if 100 percent was the value for both `WIDTH` and `HEIGHT`, then the Flash movie fills the entire browser, except for the browser gutter. See Colin Moock's tutorial later in this chapter to learn how to minimize this gutter thickness.

F. `<PARAM NAME=movie VALUE="home.swf">`: This is the first set of `<PARAM>` subtags within the `<OBJECT></OBJECT>` tags. Each parameter tag has a unique `NAME=` setting, not to be confused with JavaScript `NAME`'s or `ID`'s. This parameter's `NAME` setting `movie` specifies the filename of the Flash movie as the `VALUE` attribute.

G. `<PARAM NAME=quality VALUE=high>`: This parameter has a `NAME` attribute-setting quality that controls how the Flash movie's artwork renders within the browser window. The VALUE can be `low`, `autolow`, `autohigh`, `high`, or `best`. Most Flash movies on the Web use the `autohigh` value, as this forces the Flash Player to try rendering the movie elements antialiased. If the processor of the machine can't keep up with the Flash movie using antialiased elements, then it turns off antialiasing by switching to a `low` quality. For a full description of each of the `quality` settings, please refer to the section "Using the HTML settings" in Chapter 40.

H. `<PARAM NAME=bgcolor VALUE=#FFFFFF>`: This last parameter name, `bgcolor`, controls the background color of the Flash movie. If you published an HTML document via the Publish command, then the `VALUE` is automatically set to the background color specified by the Modify ⇨ Movie command in Flash. However, you can override the Movie setting by entering a different value in this parameter tag. Note that this parameter, like all HTML tags and attributes concerning color, uses hexadecimal code to describe the color. For more information on color, see Chapter 6, "Applying Color."

I. `<PARAM NAME=scale VALUE=noborder>`: This optional parameter controls how the Flash movie scales in the window defined by the `WIDTH` and `HEIGHT` attributes of the opening `<OBJECT>` tag. Its value can be `showall`, `noborder`, or `exactfit`. If this entire subtag is omitted, then the Flash Player treats the movie as if the `showall` default setting was specified. The `showall` setting fits the Flash movie within the boundaries of the `WIDTH` and `HEIGHT` dimensions without any distortion to the original aspect ratio of the Flash movie. Again, refer to "Using the HTML Settings" section of Chapter 40 for a complete description of the `scale` settings and how they work within the dimensions of a Flash movie.

J. `<PARAM NAME=play VALUE=false>`: This optional parameter tells the Flash Player whether or not it should start playing the Flash movie as it downloads. If the `VALUE` equals `false`, the Flash movie loads in a "paused" state, just as if a "stop" action was placed on the first frame. If the `VALUE` equals `true`, Flash starts playing the movie as soon as it starts to stream into the browser.

K. `</OBJECT>`: This is the closing tag for the starting `<OBJECT>` tag. As is shown later in this chapter, you can put other HTML tags between the last `<PARAM>` tag and the closing `</OBJECT>` tag for non-ActiveX–enabled browsers, such as Netscape. Because Internet Explorer is the only browser that currently recognizes `<OBJECT>` tags, other browsers simply skip the `<OBJECT>` tag (as well as its `<PARAM>` tags) and only read the tags between the last `<PARAM>` and `</OBJECT>` tags.

Tip

The `<OBJECT>` tag can use other parameter tag names such as `WMODE`. This parameter only works on 32-bit versions of Windows 95/98/NT Internet Explorer. See the end of the Dreamweaver section in Chapter 39, "Working with Authoring Applications," for more information regarding its use.

Using the `<EMBED>` tag

Netscape Communicator (or Navigator) uses the `<EMBED>` tag to display non-browser native file formats that require a plug-in, such as Macromedia Flash and Shockwave Director or Apple QuickTime.

```
A.  <EMBED
B.      src="home.swf"
C.      quality=high
D.*     scale=noborder
E.*     play=false
F.      bgcolor=#FFFFFF
G.      WIDTH=550 HEIGHT=400
H.*     swLiveConnect=false
I.      TYPE="application/x-shockwave-flash"
J.      PLUGINSPAGE="http://www.macromedia.com/shockwave/
        download/index.cgi?P1_Prod_Version=ShockwaveFlash">
K.  </EMBED>
```

A. `<EMBED`: This is the opening `<EMBED>` tag. Note that lines B through H are attributes of the opening `<EMBED>` tag, which is why you won't see the `>` character at the end of line A.

B. `src`: This stands for "source," and indicates the filename of the Shockwave Flash movie. This attribute of `<EMBED>` works exactly like the `<PARAM NAME= movie VALUE="home.swf">` subtag of the `<OBJECT>` tag.

C. `quality`: This attribute controls how the Flash movie's artwork will display in the browser window. Like the equivalent `<PARAM NAME=quality>` subtag of the `<OBJECT>` tag, its value can be `low`, `autolow`, `autohigh`, `high`, or `best`.

D. `scale`: This attribute of `<EMBED>` controls how the Flash movie fits within the browser window and/or the dimensions specified by `WIDTH` and `HEIGHT` (F). Its value can be `showall` (default if attribute is omitted), `noborder`, or `exactfit`.

E. `play`: This attribute controls the playback of the Flash movie. If set to `false`, the Flash movie does not automatically play until a Flash action tells the movie to play (such as a Flash button or frame action). If set to `true`, then the Flash movie plays as soon as it starts to stream into the browser.

F. `bgcolor`: This setting controls the Flash movie's background color. Again, this attribute behaves identically to the equivalent `<PARAM>` subtag of the `<OBJECT>` tag. See that tag's description in the previous section.

G. `WIDTH` and `HEIGHT`: These attributes control the dimensions of the Flash movie as it appears on the Web page. Refer to the `WIDTH` and `HEIGHT` descriptions of the `<OBJECT>` tag for more information.

H. `swLiveConnect`: This is one attribute that you can't find in the `<OBJECT>` tag. This unique tag enables Netscape's LiveConnect feature, which enables plug-ins and Java applets to communicate with JavaScript. By default, this attribute is set to `false`. If it is enabled (for example, the attribute is set to `true`), the Web page may experience a short delay during loading. The latest versions of Netscape don't start the Java engine during a browsing session until a Web page containing a Java applet (or a Java-enabled plug-in such as Flash) is loaded. Unless you use FSCommands in your Flash movies, it's best to leave these attribute set to `false`.

I. `TYPE="application/x-shockwave-flash"`: This attribute tells Netscape what MIME (Multipurpose Internet Mail Extension) content-type the embedded file is. Each file type (.TIF, .JPG, .GIF, .DOC, .TXT, and so on) has a unique MIME content-type header, describing what its content is. For Flash movies, the content-type is `application/x-shockwave-flash`. Any program (or operating system) that uses files over the Internet handles MIME content-types according to a reference chart that links each MIME content-type to its appropriate parent application or plug-in. Without this attribute, Netscape may not understand what type of file the Flash movie is. As a result, it may display the broken plug-in icon when the Flash movie downloads to the browser.

J. `PLUGINSPAGE`: Literally "plug-in's page," this attribute tells Netscape where to go to find the appropriate plug-in installer if it doesn't have the Flash plug-in already installed. This is not equivalent to a JavaScript-enabled autoinstaller. It simply redirects the browser to the URL of the Web page where the appropriate software can be downloaded.

K. `</EMBED>`: This is the closing tag for the original `<EMBED>` tag in line A. Some older or text-based browsers such as Lynx are incapable of displaying `<EMBED>` tags. You can insert alternate HTML (such as a static or animated .GIF with the `<IMG>` tag) between the `<EMBED>` `</EMBED>` tags for these browsers.

Caution

You may be surprised to learn that all versions of Internet Explorer (IE) for the Macintosh cannot read <OBJECT> tags. Rather, IE for Mac uses a Netscape plug-in emulator to read <EMBED> tags. However, this emulator does not interpret all <EMBED> tags with the same level of support as Netscape. As a result, the swLiveConnect attribute does not function on IE for Mac browsers. This means that FSCommands are not supported on these browsers.

Expert Tutorial: Filling the Browser Window by Using the <FRAMESET> Tag, *by Colin Moock*

Colin's biographical information can be found in his expert tutorial, Making GWEN!'s Eyes Shut When She Yawns, *located in Chapter 18, "Navigating Flash Timelines." Perhaps one of Colin's most famous (and often read) tutorials is this* <FRAMESET> *technique that forces the Flash movie to fill nearly all of the browser window.*

Filling the Gap

Many Flash designers have experienced the problem that Flash movies don't default to fill the entire viewing space of a browser window. This results in wasted screen space, or, what's worse, an unsightly gutter, or gap, between the edge of the Flash movie and the edges of the browser.

In the following figure, the browser on the left sports an unsightly white gutter around a Flash Movie. On the right, the same movie is displayed with a minimal gutter around a framed Flash Movie. For designers who prefer the effect shown on the right, two options work with most browsers. One solution depends on the use of frames, and is therefore limited to frames-capable browsers. The other solution requires that the Flash Player plug-in be detected before serving pages built with this method — so it's not appropriate for a splash page.

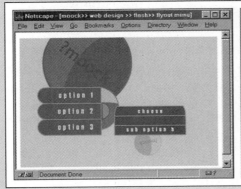 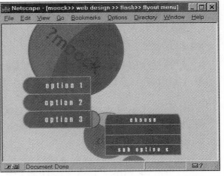

Single-frame frameset

With the attributes a frameset set correctly, framed Flash content can stretch to within one or two pixels (depending on the browser) of the edge of the browser window. To do this, first make the page (yourmovie.html) in which your movie is embedded. Then when embedding the movie, set the width, height, and scale for the desired effect. The SCALE parameter has three options:

✦ **HEIGHT="100%" WIDTH="100%" SCALE="EXACTFIT":** This combination forces every edge of your movie to the edge of the browser, and distorts your movie to fit the aspect ratio (proportion of height to width) of the browser.

✦ **HEIGHT="100%" WIDTH="100%" SCALE="SHOWALL":** This combination fits the width or height of your movie to the smaller of either the width or height of the browser. Your movie is not cropped or skewed to fit the browser window, but there are borders on either the top and bottom or right and left of your movie.

✦ **HEIGHT="100%" WIDTH="100%" SCALE="NOBORDER":** This combination adjusts either the height or width of your movie to the larger of either the width or height of the browser. When the dimensions of your movie do not match the dimensions of the browser, your movie is matted with additional background space on either the vertical or horizontal axis.

Your embedded movie code will look something like this. (The ¬ symbol indicates a continuation of the same line of code. Do not insert this character in your actual code.)

```
<OBJECT
CLASSID="clsid:D27CDB6E-AE6D-11cf-96B8-444553540000"
CODEBASE="http://download.macromedia.com/pub/ ¬
    shockwave/cabs/flash/swflash.cab#version=5,0,0,0"
WIDTH="100%"
HEIGHT="100%">
<PARAM NAME="MOVIE" VALUE="moviename.swf">
<PARAM NAME="PLAY" VALUE="true">
<PARAM NAME="LOOP" VALUE="true">
<PARAM NAME="QUALITY" VALUE="high">
<PARAM NAME="SCALE" VALUE="SHOWALL">

<EMBED SRC="yourmovie.swf"
        WIDTH="100%"
        HEIGHT="100%"
        PLAY="true"
        LOOP="true"
        QUALITY="high"
        SCALE="SHOWALL"
        PLUGINSPAGE="http://www.macromedia.com/shockwave/¬
            download/index.cgi?P1_Prod_Version=ShockwaveFlash">
</EMBED>
</OBJECT>
```

Continued

Continued

Now you're ready to make the single-frame frameset. Actually, it's a two-frame frameset, but you only use one of the frames for displaying your page. The first frame is allotted 100 percent of the browser area, and the second frame is allotted "*" (meaning whatever is left, which is nothing). The SRC of the first frame of the frameset will be the page (yourmovie.html) with your Flash Movie, while the SRC of the second frame will be an empty HTML page with a matching BGCOLOR. Then real trick is to specify the attributes of the frameset and frames so that the Flash movie will extend to the edges of the browser. Here's an example of code with the correct settings:

```
<HTML><HEAD><TITLE>Your Flash Movie Title</TITLE></HEAD>

<FRAMESET ROWS="100%,*"
          FRAMESPACING="0"
          FRAMEBORDER="NO"
          BORDER="0">

  <FRAME NAME="top"
         SRC="yourmovie.html"
         FRAMEBORDER="0"
         BORDER="0"
         MARGINWIDTH="0"
         MARGINHEIGHT="0"
         SCROLLING="NO">

  <FRAME NAME="hidden"
         SRC="empty.html"
         FRAMEBORDER="0"
         BORDER="0"
         MARGINWIDTH="0"
         MARGINHEIGHT="0"
         SCROLLING="NO">

</FRAMESET>
</HTML>
```

Now let's look at some of the code in detail:

✦ As an attribute of `<FRAMESET>`, FRAMEBORDER is either `true` or `false`, but as an attribute of `<FRAME>`, FRAMEBORDER is a pixel value for setting the width of the space between the browser edge and the page content.

✦ On `<FRAMESET>`, BORDER refers to the number of pixels between frames, while on `<FRAME>`, BORDER is simply a now-obsolete version of FRAMEBORDER.

✦ The SCROLLING attribute must be set to NO, otherwise, if the content is not larger than the browser window, a gap will appear on the right and bottom of the frame where the scroll bars would normally appear.

As a final option, to reduce the gutter as much as possible in Internet Explorer 4 (or higher) and Netscape Communicator 4 (or higher), you can set the margin values on the movie page (yourmovie.html). To accomplish this, Netscape 4 or higher uses `MARGINHEIGHT` and `MARGINWIDTH`, while Internet Explorer 4 or higher uses `TOPMARGIN`, `BOTTOMMARGIN`, `LEFTMARGIN`, and `RIGHTMARGIN`. So, to accommodate both browsers, use these values:

```
<BODY MARGINWIDTH="0" MARGINHEIGHT="0" LEFTMARGIN="0"
RIGHTMARGIN="0" TOPMARGIN="0" BOTTOMMARGIN="0">
```

Directly Linking to the Flash Movie (.SWF File)

An alternate method to the single-frame frameset described previously is to link directly to the Flash movie and let the browser display it inline. So, if your movie mymovie.swf is normally embedded in mymovie.html, then:

```
<A HREF="mymovie.html">View my movie</A>
```

would be changed to:

```
<A HREF="mymovie.swf">View my movie</A>
```

This method is easier to implement than the frames method, but should only be used after Flash has been successfully detected, because the browser won't have access to any of the HTML instructions that would normally tell it where to get the plug-in if the plug-in is not present. Thus, this method should not be used for a splash page.

If you use the Direct Link method, it's also important to remember to set the `QUALITY` of your movie to "high" from inside your movie using the Toggle High Quality action (Flash 3+ only). To do this, select your first keyframe, open the Actions Panel (in Normal Mode), and then add a `toggleHighQuality` action.

If you'd like to learn more about Colin Moock, please see his bio in Chapter 18, "Navigating Flash Timelines."

Detecting the Flash Player

What good is an awesome Flash experience if no one can see your Flash movies? Because most Flash content is viewed with a Web browser, it's extremely important to make sure that your HTML pages check for the existence of the Flash Player plug-in before you start pushing Flash content to the browser. There are a variety of ways to check for the Flash Player, and this section provides an overview of the available methods.

Plug-in versus ActiveX: Forcing content without a check

The Flash Player is available for Web browsers in two forms: the Flash Player plug-in (as a Netscape-compatible plug-in) and the Flash Player ActiveX Control (for use only with Microsoft Internet Explorer on Windows 95/98/NT/2000).

If you directly insert a Flash movie into a Web page with the <EMBED> tag (for Netscape browsers), then one of two scenarios will happen:

1. The browser has the Flash Player plug-in and will load the Flash movie.

2. The browser does not have the Flash Player plug-in, and displays a broken plug-in icon.

If scenario 2 occurs and the PLUGINSPAGE attribute of the <EMBED> tag is defined, the user can click the broken plug-in icon and go to the Macromedia site to download the Flash Player plug-in. If no PLUGINSPAGE attribute is specified, then clicking the broken plug-in icon will take you to a generic Netscape plug-in page.

If you insert a Flash movie into a HTML document with the <OBJECT> tag (for Internet Explorer on Windows only), then one of two scenarios will happen:

1. The browser has the Flash Player ActiveX Control and will load the Flash movie.

2. The browser does not have the Flash Player ActiveX Control, and will autodownload and install the ActiveX Control file from the Macromedia site.

The ActiveX Control will only autodownload and install if the classid and codebase attributes of the Flash movie's <OBJECT> tag are correctly specified. Depending on the user's security settings, the user needs to grant permission to a Security Warning dialog (shown in Figure 41-1) in order to commence the download and install process.

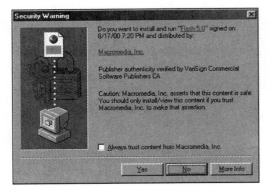

Figure 41-1: The Flash 5 Player ActiveX Control will automatically download if Microsoft Internet Explorer for Windows encounters an HTML page with Flash content.

Although using the <OBJECT> and <EMBED> tags by themselves is by far the simplest method for integrating Flash content into a Web page, it's not the most user-friendly method of ensuring that the majority of your Web visitors can view the Flash content. The most common way to detect Flash movies is by using JavaScript and VBScript, as we see in the next section.

JavaScript and VBScript player detection

The use of scripts written into an HTML document is very popular for Flash Player detection. If you're getting familiar with Flash 5's new ActionScript syntax, then you'll find that JavaScript detection code isn't all that complex. JavaScript is a universal scripting language that most 3.0 or higher Web browsers can employ to some capacity. Microsoft's implementation of JavaScript, called JScript, isn't exactly the same as Netscape's JavaScript. For this reason, you can translate some JavaScript functionality into Microsoft's proprietary Web-scripting language, VBScript.

You'll find the HTML, .FLA, .SWF, and .GIF files for this section in the ch41 folder of the *Flash 5 Bible* CD-ROM.

In this section, we look at how to create an HTML document that checks for the presence of the Flash Player plug-in with JavaScript, and the Flash ActiveX Control with VBScript. We use two images of a traffic light — one .SWF image with a green light on, and one .GIF image with a red light on — to display the results of our plug-in and ActiveX detection. Many Web sites employ a similar mechanism: Before an HTML page with Flash content can be accessed, the visitor will be presented with a screen telling them if they have the Flash Player installed. If they don't have it, then they can click a link to get the plug-in or ActiveX Control.

The Flash Player can be detected with most JavaScript-enabled Web browsers, by using the JavaScript array `navigator.mimeTypes`. **The value for this array is** always empty for Internet Explorer browsers, including IE 4.5 on Macintosh. IE 5.0 for Macintosh now supports this array. While we can use VBScript to detect for IE on Windows, there is no script plug-in detection available for IE 4.5 on Macintosh. You can however, use the Flash Sniffer method, discussed in the next heading, to detect Flash on IE 4.5 on Macintosh.

Detecting the plug-in with JavaScript

By rearranging the JavaScript code that is created by the Ad 5 Banner template in the Publish Settings, we can set up a testing mechanism that delivers one of two graphics to the visitor's Web browser. Copy the `scriptDetection.html` document located in the ch41 folder of the *Flash 5 Bible* CD-ROM, and open it in your preferred text editor (SimpleText, Notepad, BBEdit, and so on). Look at lines 10 to 15 (The ¬ indicates a continuation of the same line of code. It should not be written in the actual JavaScript code in the HTML document.):

```
10. var plugin = 0;
11. var activeX = 0;
12. var plugin = (navigator.mimeTypes && ¬
    navigator.mimeTypes["application/x-shockwave-flash"]) ¬
    ? navigator.mimeTypes["application/x-shockwave- ¬
    flash"].enabledPlugin : 0;
13. if ( plugin ) {
14.    plugin = parseInt(plugin.description.substring ¬
    (plugin.description.indexOf(".")-1)) >= 5;
15. }
```

Line 10 initializes a variable `plugin` to indicate the presence of the Flash 5 Player plug-in on Netscape (or IE 5.0 Mac). Line 11 initializes a variable called `activeX` to indicate the presence of the Flash 5 Player ActiveX Control. At this point, we create them with a value of 0, meaning that the plug-in and ActiveX Control are not installed.

Line 12 is borrowed from the Ad 5 Banner HTML template output. It uses the `mimeTypes` array of the navigator JavaScript Object to determine whether the Flash Player (in any version) is installed. If the Flash Player plug-in is installed, then the variable `plugin` is now equal to the value `[object Plugin]`. If this is `true`, then lines 13 and 14 will execute. Using the `description` property of the Plugin Object, we can determine whether the Flash Player is the correct version. In this example, we check whether it's greater than or equal to 5. Notice that we can use a comparison as the value of the `plugin` variable. If the Flash 5 Player (or higher) is installed, then `plugin` will equal `true` (or 1); if a lower version is installed, then `plugin` will equal `false` (or 0).

Creating a test object in VBScript

At this point, if the visitor is using Netscape (on any operating system) or Internet Explorer on the Macintosh, then the variable `plugin` will have a value of either 0 or 1. However, we still need to check for the ActiveX Control, if the visitor is using Internet Explorer for Windows. Line 11 already initialized a variable called `activeX`. Lines 16-21 check to see if VBScript can create a Flash Object in the document (The ¬ indicates a continuation of the same line of code. It should not be written in the actual JavaScript code in the HTML document.):

```
16. else if (navigator.userAgent && ¬
      navigator.userAgent.indexOf("MSIE")>=0 && ¬
      (navigator.userAgent.indexOf("Windows 95")>=0 || ¬
      navigator.userAgent.indexOf("Windows 98")>=0 || ¬
      navigator.userAgent.indexOf("Windows NT")>=0)) {
17.    document.write('<SCRIPT LANGUAGE=VBScript\> \n');
18.    document.write('on error resume next \n');
19.    document.write('activeX = ( IsObject(CreateObject ¬
      ("ShockwaveFlash.ShockwaveFlash.5")))\n');
20.    document.write('<' + '/SCRIPT>');
21. }
```

Line 16 determines whether the visitor is using Internet Explorer on Windows 95, 98, or NT. If that's the browser they're using, then lines 17 to 21 will execute. These lines of code create the VBScript that is necessary to check for the existence of the Flash 5 Player ActiveX Control. Using the `IsObject` and `CreateObject` methods, VBScript can determine whether the ActiveX Control is installed. If it is installed, then the variable `activeX` will equal `true` (or 1). Note that this variable is available to both JavaScript and VBScript. This section of code is also borrowed from the Ad 5 Banner HTML template.

Inserting the graphics

After the variables plugin and activeX have been set appropriately, we can use these variables to either display a Flash .SWF graphic or a .GIF image graphic. In the body of the HTML document, we can reuse the `plugin` and `activeX` variables to insert either the Flash or .GIF graphics. Lines 31 to 36 of the HTML document will write the tags to display the .SWF or .GIF image for Netscape (on any platform) or IE on the Mac (The ¬ indicates a continuation of the same line of code. It should not be written in the actual JavaScript code in the HTML document.):

```
31. if ( plugin ) {
32.     document.write('<EMBED SRC="trafficLightGreen.swf" ¬
        WIDTH="105" HEIGHT="185" SWLIVECONNECT="FALSE" ¬
        QUALITY="HIGH"></EMBED><BR><FONT ¬
        FACE="Verdana,Arial,Geneva" SIZE=2>Flash 5 ¬
        Player<BR>Plug-in detected.</FONT>');
33. } else if (!(navigator.appName && ¬
        navigator.appName.indexOf("Netscape")>=0 && ¬
        navigator.appVersion.indexOf("2.")>=0)){
34.     document.write('<A HREF="http://www.macromedia.com ¬
        /shockwave/download/index.cgi ¬
        P1_Prod_Version=ShockwaveFlash">');
35.     document.write('<IMG SRC="trafficLightRed.gif" ¬
        WIDTH="105" HEIGHT="185" BORDER="0"></A><BR> ¬
        <FONT FACE="Verdana,Arial,Geneva" SIZE=2>Flash ¬
        5 Player<BR>Plug-in not installed.</FONT>');
36. }
```

If the `plugin` variable is not equal to `false` (line 31), then line 32 will execute. Line 32 uses the `<EMBED>` tag to insert a Flash .SWF file, depicting a green light that animates to a full green color, and the HTML text "Flash 5 Player Plug-in detected." If the `plugin` variable is equal to `false` and the browser is Netscape 2.0 or higher (line 33), then lines 34 and 35 will create `<A HREF>` and `<IMG>` tags, depicting a static .GIF image of a red traffic light that links to the Macromedia download area. Then, JavaScript will create the HTML text "Flash 5 Player Plug-in not installed."

Lines 43 to 52 perform the same functionality for Internet Explorer for Windows. If the `activeX` variable is `true`, then an `<OBJECT>` tag is written and a green traffic light will animate on. If it's not installed, then a static .GIF image of a red traffic light will be displayed.

Finally, we should do two more things:

1. Tell IE 4.5 (or earlier) Mac users that we can't detect the Flash 5 Player plug-in.

2. Tell other users that they can either (a) proceed to the main Flash site, or (b) click the appropriate traffic light to download the plug-in or ActiveX Control.

Lines 59 to 62 tell IE 4.5 (or earlier) Mac users that we can't detect their plug-in settings. We can either leave it to them to decide whether they should download the plug-in, or we could direct them to a sniffer movie (discussed in the next section) to determine if the plug-in is installed.

Lines 63 to 65 check whether either the plug-in or the ActiveX Control is installed. If it is, then we tell the visitor to proceed to the main Flash site. Note that you would want to insert more JavaScript code here that includes a link to your Flash content.

Lines 66 to 74 check whether the plug-in and the ActiveX Control are both absent. If neither is installed, then we tell them which traffic light (lines 67 to 74) to click.

Although you'll most likely want to spruce up the look and feel of this page to suit your particular site, you can use this scripting layout to inform your visitors about their plug-in or ActiveX Control settings.

Using a Flash Swiffer movie

If you would prefer to avoid JavaScript and VBScript, then you can also use small Flash movies known as *swiffers* to detect the Flash Player. Swiffers are virtually hidden from the visitor, and direct the HTML page to a new location (using a `getURL` action) where the real Flash content (or site) exists. If the Player is not installed, then the movie won't be able to play and direct the HTML page to a new location. If this happens, then a special `<META>` tag in the `<HEAD>` of the HTML document will direct the browser location to a screen that informs the visitor to download the plug-in or ActiveX Control.

Making the Swiffer movie

The Swiffer movie is a small Flash movie that has the same background color as the HTML document. We do not need any artwork or symbols in this movie.

1. Open Flash 5, and in a new Flash movie document (.FLA file), rename Layer 1 to **actions**.

2. Add a keyframe on frame 2 of the actions layer. Double-click this new keyframe to open the Actions Panel.

3. In the Actions Panel, we create some ActionScript that checks for Flash 3 (or earlier), 4, and 5 Player versions. We can direct each version of the Player to a unique URL. The basic principle of this ActionScript is to use Flash version-specific actions to determine which Player is displaying the movie:

```
// create a Flash variable, whose value is equal to the
// $version environment variable in Flash 4 or 5. This
// action line will not be read by Flash 3 (or earlier)
// Players.
```

```
player = eval("$version");

/* The $version value will be in the format:

    abc 1,2,3,4

    where abc is the operating system (e.g. WIN, MAC)
    and 1 and 2 are the major version designations
    (e.g. 4.0, 5.0, etc.) and 3 and 4 are the minor
    version designations (e.g. r20, r27, etc.)

    By default, Flash 5 ships with a Player version equal
    to WIN 5,0,30,0 or MAC 5,0,30,0

    We just need the major version designation, at
    placeholder 1. Using substring(), we can extract this
    number. The major version starts at the 5th character
    of the version value. The Flash 3 Player will
    disregard this line.
*/

player = substring(player, 5, 1);

// player will be equal to either 4 or 5 in Flash 4 or 5
Player, respectively.

if (player eq ""){

    // Flash 3 Player will execute this code
    // automatically, because it will need interpret the
    // if action.

    getURL("flash3.html");

} else if (player eq "4"){

    // Flash 4 Player will execute this code.

    getURL("flash4.html");

} else if (player eq "5"){

    // Flash 5 Player will execute this code.

    getURL("flash5.html");
}

// We will prevent the movie from accidentally looping.

stop();
```

4. Change the size of the movie frame to **18 px×18 px**, in the Modify ➪ Movie dialog. This is the smallest size a Flash movie can have. Change the background color of the movie to match the background color of the HTML document. Click OK.

5. Save the Flash movie as **swiffer.fla**.

6. Open the Publish Settings dialog (File ➪ Publish Settings). Check the Flash and HTML options in the Formats tab. Uncheck the Use default names option, and rename the HTML file to swiffer_start.html.

7. In the Flash tab, select Flash 4 in the Version drop-down menu.

Note   We are using the Flash 4 format because the Flash 3 Player will ignore all Flash 4 or higher actions, and the Flash 4 Player will recognize the formatting of the variable and ActionScript structures. Flash 5 .SWF files restructure variables and ActionScript (even Flash 4-compatible code) in a manner that doesn't work consistently in the Flash 4 Player.

8. In the HTML tab, select the Flash Only (Default) template. Click the Publish button located on the right side of the Publish Settings dialog.

9. When the files have been published, click OK to close the Publish Settings dialog. Save your movie again.

You now have swiffer.html and swiffer.swf files in the same folder as your swiffer.fla file. In the next section, we add some additional HTML tags to the swiffer.html document.

Integrating the Swiffer movie into an HTML document

After you have made the swiffer.swf and the swiffer.html files, you can modify the HTML document to guide the browser to a unique URL where plug-in information and download screen will be shown. Remember that the ¬ indicates a continuation of the same line of code. Do not insert this character into your HTML document.

1. Open the swiffer.html file in your preferred HTML document editor. Macromedia Dreamweaver, Notepad (PC), SimpleText (Mac), or BBEdit will do just fine.

2. Somewhere between the 〈HEAD〉 〈/HEAD〉 tags, insert the following HTML 〈META〉 tag:

```
<META http-equiv="Refresh" content="5; ¬
URL=download.html">
```

This 〈META〉 tag has two attributes, http-equiv and content. The http-equiv attribute instructs the hosting Web server to add the value of http-equiv as a discrete name in the MIME header of the HTML document. The value of the content attribute becomes the value of the MIME entry. Here, the Web browser will interpret the META tag as:

```
Refresh: 5; URL=download.html
```

in the MIME header. This name/value pair tells the browser to reload the browser window in five seconds, with the file download.html. After testing, you may decide to increase the time the browser waits before reloading a new URL. On slower connections (or during peak Internet hours), you may find that five seconds is not long enough for the Flash movie to initiate its getURL actions.

Caution

Some older browsers may require an absolute URL in the content attribute. This means that you may need to insert a full path to your HTML document, such as http://www.yourserver.com/download.html, as the URL in the content attribute.

3. Save the HTML file. At this point, you need to create a download.html file. As a temporary measure, you can use the scriptDetection.html file from the previous detection method. You also need to create flash3.html, flash4.html, and flash5.html files for the getURL actions in the swiffer.swf movie.

On the CD-ROM

We have included sample flash3.html, flash4.html, and flash5.html files on the *Flash 5 Bible* CD-ROM. These are simple placeholder documents that do not contain any Flash movie URLs.

When you have your HTML documents ready, you can load the swiffer.html document into a browser. If the Flash Player is not installed, then the META tag should transport the browser location to the download.html URL. If the Flash Player is installed, then the Flash ActionScript will direct the browser to the appropriate page.

Expert Tutorial: Flash Player Detection (a.k.a. the moock fpi), *by Colin Moock*

While there are several ways to check for the existence of the Flash Player plug-in, no one has developed as comprehensive a strategy as Colin's strategy. We are pleased to present an introduction to his moock fpi.

Producers of Flash content live with an undeniable, often frustrating truth: Flash content is not always immediately viewable by the audience for which it is intended. Because Flash is normally viewed as a secondary application to a Web browser, a user attempting to view a Flash site may not have the Flash player installed in his or her browser, or may have an older version of the Flash player that won't allow the user to view the site.

Continued

Continued

The first time I dealt directly with the accessibility (or inaccessibility) of Flash content was in 1997, when I embarked on my first large-scale production in Flash — the Levi's Canada Web site. Throughout the project, the issue of accessibility was a matter of great concern for both the client, Levi's, and the agency producing the site, ICE (where I work). How should the site handle visitors without Flash installed in their browser? Should it simply tell everyone to get Flash? Should it only tell visitors without Flash to get Flash? What if a visitor had never heard of Flash?

After various discussions, it was decided that the best approach was to use JavaScript to automatically detect the presence of Flash in the user's browser. If the user had Flash, we sent the user to the Flash content. If not, we sent the user to equivalent non-Flash content. If detection failed, we sent the user to a page describing Flash, and offering installation instructions.

Since the Levi's project, I have yet to encounter a project that did not revisit the issue of Flash accessibility, deployment, and detection in some way. The factors have changed somewhat over the years, but the issue is always there. After countless hours of testing, thinking, and meeting, I have come to a single conclusion: No matter what the script or publication model, a site must never, ever cause its audience to feel lost.

Thus, with that single philosophy in mind, I decided to build a standard system for detecting and publishing Flash content: the moock fLASH pLAYER iNSPECTOR (a.k.a. the moock fpi). The moock fpi is a scripted system for detecting Flash. The use of a scripted detection system offers users with Flash-enabled browsers seamless access to our content, and users with non-Flash browsers a controlled and customized experience.

The behavior of the moock fpi is simple: Supply the user with Flash content if appropriate, and with alternate content if not. This premise translates to the following scripted behavior:

✦ If we can undeniably detect that a user has the correct version of Flash installed, we deploy Flash content.

✦ If we can undeniably detect that the user has an old version of Flash installed, we either ask the user to upgrade, or simply deploy non-Flash content.

✦ If we can undeniably detect that a user does not have Flash, or if our attempt to detect Flash fails, we deploy non-Flash content.

By following these three rules, the moock fpi should, in theory, never strand a user, and will always provide a user with the smoothest path to a site's content. Luckily, with the help of heavy testing by the Internet community, the theory seems to be working so far.

The moock fpi is posted for public use at: `www.moock.org/webdesign/flash/detection/moockfpi/`.

My research notes and thoughts on detection and publishing Flash content are posted at: `www.moock.org/webdesign/lectures/ff2knyc/`

If you'd like to learn more about Colin Moock, please see his bio in Chapter 18, "Navigating Flash Timelines."

Using Flash Movies with JavaScript and DHTML

The new ActionScripting features in Flash 5 have greatly increased the range of interactive and dynamic possibilities for Flash movies on the Web. In previous releases of Flash, Flash movies could only interact with external HTML or scripts through the FSCommand action. This meant mapping commands and variables to JavaScript, which, in turn, passed information to the document object model of DHTML, Java applets, or CGI (Common Gateway Interface) scripts. Now that Flash movies can directly send and receive data to server-side CGI scripts, just about anything can be done within the Flash movie. However, if you want to directly communicate with the Web browser or the HTML document, you need to use FSCommands or `getURL` actions with `javascript:` statements. Because all JavaScript-capable browsers do not support these methods, we're limiting our discussion to FSCommands and JavaScript-controllable Flash movie properties.

A word of caution to Web developers

This section covers FSCommands, which, when used in Flash movies on Web pages, are only supported by a handful of browsers. Currently, not one version of Internet Explorer for Macintosh (up to version 5.0) can interpret FSCommands (see the Caution note in "The <EMBED> Tag" section earlier in this chapter). Only Netscape 3.0 (or higher) offers cross-platform support for FSCommands. Internet Explorer 3 and higher for Windows 95/98/NT also support FSCommands. Our coverage of the FSCommand assumes that you have basic knowledge of JavaScript and Flash ActionScript. If you don't know how to add Actions to frames or buttons, please read Chapter 17, "Understanding Actions and Event Handlers." If you don't know JavaScript, you can still follow the steps to the tutorials and create a fully functional Flash-JavaScript movie. However, because this isn't a book on JavaScript, we don't explain how JavaScript syntax or functions work.

How Flash movies work with JavaScript

As mentioned earlier, Flash has an action called `fscommand`. FSCommands are used to send a command (and an optional argument string) from a Flash movie to its hosting environment (such as a Web browser or standalone Flash Player). What does this mean for interactivity? The FSCommand offers the capability to have any Flash event (Button instance, `onClipEvent`, or frame actions) initiate an event in JavaScript. Although this may not sound too exciting, you can use FSCommands to trigger anything that you would have used JavaScript alone to do in the past, such as updating HTML-form text fields, changing the visibility of HTML elements, or switching HTML background colors on the fly. Most Flash-to-JavaScript interactivity works best with dynamic HTML (DHTML) browsers such as Netscape 4 or higher and Internet Explorer 4 or higher. We look at these effects in the next section.

Flash movie communication with JavaScript is not a one-way street. You can also monitor and control Flash movies with JavaScript. Just as JavaScript treats an HTML document as an object and its elements as properties of that object, JavaScript treats Flash movies as it would any other element on a Web page. Therefore, you can use JavaScript functions and HTML hyperlinks (<A HREF> tags) to control Flash movie playback. At the end of this chapter, we show you how to make an HTML form menu that can jump to various scenes of a Flash movie.

Note   In order for JavaScript to receive Flash FSCommands, you need to make sure that the attribute swLiveConnect for the <EMBED> tag is set to true. By default, most Flash HTML templates have this settings set to false.

Changing HTML attributes

In this section, we show you how to dynamically change the BGCOLOR attribute of the <BODY> tag with an FSCommand from a Flash movie while it is playing in the browser window. In fact, we change the background color a few times. Then, once that has been accomplished, we show you how to update the text field of a <FORM> tag to display what percent of the Flash movie has been loaded.

On the CD-ROM   Open the Flash movie countdown.fla located in the ch41 folder of the *Flash 5 Bible* CD-ROM. This is quite a large .FLA file (over 14MB) as it uses many imported bitmap images and sounds to demonstrate slow-loading movie. If you are using the Mac version of Flash 5, you may want to increase the memory allocation for the Flash 5 application file to 64MB or higher.

Adding FSCommands to a Flash movie

Open a copy of the countdown.fla Flash movie from the *Flash 5 Bible* CD-ROM, and use Control ⇨ Test Movie to play the Flash .SWF version. You should notice that the filmstrip countdown fades to white, and then to near-black, and then back to its original gray color. This countdown contains to loop until the entire first scene has loaded into the Flash Player. When the first scene has loaded, playback will skip to a Movie Clip of two dogs (in "negative") and a title sequence. There's more to the Flash movie, but for now, that's all we need to deal with.

Our goal for this section of the tutorial is to add FSCommand frame actions to specific keyframes in the countdown.fla Flash demonstration movie. When the Flash Player plays the frame with the FSCommand action, the Player sends a command and argument string to JavaScript. JavaScript then calls a function that changes the background color to the value specified in the argument string of the FSCommand (see Figure 41-2). To be more exact, you add an FSCommand to the frames where the color fades to white, black, and gray. When the Flash movie changes to these colors, so will the HTML background colors.

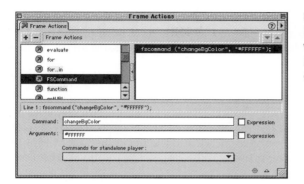

Figure 41-2: Frame 16: FSCommand of changeBgColor with an argument of #FFFFFF (the hexadecimal code for the color white)

Here's the process:

1. On frame 16 of the Introduction scene, add a keyframe on the actions layer. With the keyframe selected, open the Actions Panel. Make sure the Panel is in Normal Mode. Add an FSCommand action from the + pop-up menu (located in the top-left corner of the panel). In the Command field, type **changeBgColor**. In the Arguments field, type **#FFFFFF**. The command changeBgColor is mapped to a JavaScript function called changeBgColor later in this tutorial. The argument string #FFFFFF is passed to that function, changing the HTML background color to white.

2. On frame 20, add another FSCommand action to the corresponding keyframe on the actions layer. Again, insert **changeBgColor** in the Command text box. In the Arguments text box, type **#333333**. This argument changes the HTML background color to a dark gray.

3. On frame 21 of the actions layer, follow the same instructions for Step 2, except use **#9E9E9E** for the argument string. This changes the HTML background color to the same color as the Flash movie countdown graphic.

4. On frame 66 of the actions layer, add another changeBgColor FSCommand action to the empty keyframe. This time, use an argument string of **#000000**, which changes the HTML background color to black.

5. Now that we've added several FSCommands, let's try them out in the browser. Save the countdown.fla Flash movie to a folder on your hard drive, and open the Publish Settings dialog (for more information on Publish Settings, refer to Chapter 40, "Publishing Flash Movies"). In the HTML tab, select the template Flash with FSCommand. Click OK to close the Publish Settings dialog. Select the File ➪ Publish command to export the Flash .SWF movie and HTML document.

Next, we look at the automated JavaScript code that the HTML template created. While the basic code structure has been set up, we need to make some alterations and additions to the JavaScript in order for our FSCommands to work.

Note   You may have noticed that some FSCommands have already been entered on other keyframes of the countdown.fla movie. These have been placed to ensure that the background color stays consistent with other settings, regardless of where playback occurs.

Enabling JavaScript for Flash movies

Although the Flash with FSCommand template does a lot of the JavaScripting for you, it doesn't automatically map out the commands and arguments (args) to JavaScript-defined functions. In this section, we add the necessary JavaScript to make the FSCommands work in the browser. What follows is the JavaScript code that Flash 5 generates.

Note   Any numbered line of code marked with an asterisk (*) is custom JavaScript code that Flash 4 does not create. Also, remember that the ¬ indicates a continuation of the same line of code. Do not insert this character into your HTML document.

```
1.    <SCRIPT LANGUAGE=JavaScript>
2.    <!--
3.    var InternetExplorer = ¬
      navigator.appName.indexOf("Microsoft") != -1;
4.*   var stringFlash = "";
5.    // Handle all the FSCommand messages in a Flash movie
6.        function countdown_DoFSCommand(command,args){
7.            var countdownObj = InternetExplorer ¬
                ? countdown : document.countdown;
8.*          stringFlash = stringFlash + args;
9.*          if(command=="changeBgColor"){
                changeBgColor();
              }
          }
10.*     function changeBgColor(){
11.*         document.bgColor = stringFlash;
12.*         stringFlash = "";
          }
13.    // Hook for Internet Explorer
          if (navigator.appName && ¬
            navigator.appName.indexOf("Microsoft") != -1 ¬
            && navigator.userAgent.indexOf("Windows") != -1 ¬
            && navigator.userAgent.indexOf("Windows 3.1") ¬
            == -1){
          document.write('<SCRIPT LANGUAGE=VBScript\> \n');
          document.write('on error resume next \n');
          document.write('Sub countdown_FSCommand(ByVal ¬
            command, ByVal args)\n');
          document.write('   call ¬
            countdown_DoFSCommand(command,args)\n');
          document.write('end sub\n');
          document.write('</SCRIPT\> \n');
```

```
        }
      //-->
14.   </SCRIPT>
```

The following is a line-by-line explanation of the code:

1. This HTML tag initializes the JavaScript code.

2. This string of characters is standard HTML comment code. By adding this after the opening `<SCRIPT>` tag, non-JavaScript browsers ignore the code. If this string wasn't included, text-based browsers such as Lynx might display JavaScript code as HTML text.

3. This variable simply condenses the JavaScript code that detects Internet Explorer into a single term, `InternetExplorer`.

4. We added this line of code to declare a variable called `stringFlash`. Its value is set to nothing by putting two straight quote characters together. This variable is necessary for FSCommand arguments to pass cleanly into JavaScript functions on both Netscape and Internet Explorer.

5. This is comment code added by the Macromedia team to let us know that the following JavaScript code is designed to catch the FSCommands from a Flash movie.

6. This is the initial JavaScript function that works exclusively with Flash FSCommands. The function's name is the value of the `NAME` attribute of the `<EMBED>` tag (or the value of the `ID` attribute of the `<OBJECT>` tag) followed by a underscore and `DoFSCommand(command,args){`. In this sample, the Flash movie `NAME` is `countdown`. Notice that the command and arguments that were specified in Flash are passed to this function as `(command,args)`, respectively.

7. This is a handy optional variable that the Flash with FSCommand template created. Strangely, it is not necessary unless you need to refer to the differing document object models between Internet Explorer and Netscape. Instead of testing for either browser, you can insert the `countdownObj` variable in your own JavaScript code. For this example, though, it is not needed.

8. This code makes the `stringFlash` variable called in line 4 equal to the argument string (`args`) from the Flash FSCommand. Because stringFlash was equal to nothing (`""`), `stringFlash` is now the same as the original argument string. This isn't necessary for Internet Explorer, but Netscape doesn't recognize arguments straight from Flash without it.

9. This compares the passed command string from the Flash FSCommand to the string `changeBgColor`. If they're the same, then JavaScript executes the code contained within the `if` statement. Because we only made one unique command in Flash for this sample, we only have to map the Flash FSCommand `changeBgColor` to the JavaScript function `changeBgColor()`.

10. This is where the function `changeBgColor()` is defined. Remember that line 9 maps the Flash FSCommand `changeBgColor` to this JavaScript function.

11. This line of code passes the variable `stringFlash` to the `document.bgColor` property, which controls the HTML background color. When the Flash FSCommand sends the command `changeBgColor`, the JavaScript `change Bgcolor()` function is invoked, which passes the argument string from the Flash FSCommand to `document.bgColor`.

12. This resets the variable `stringFlash` back to nothing (" "), so that future invocations of the FSCommand don't use the same argument from the previous execution.

13. This section of code detects the presence of Internet Explorer for Windows and maps the JavaScript functions to VBScript (which is used exclusively by Windows-only versions of Internet Explorer).

14. The closing `</SCRIPT>` tag ends this portion of JavaScript code.

Caution   For some reason, the Flash with FSCommand template omits the `NAME` attribute for the `<EMBED>` tag. Make sure that you add this attribute to the `<EMBED>` tag. Set its value equal to the name of the Flash .SWF movie, without the .SWF file extension. For example, in the sample used for this section, the `<EMBED>` tag should have a `NAME` attribute equal to `countdown`.

That's it! Once you've manually added the custom lines of JavaScript code, you can load the HTML document into either Internet Explorer or Netscape (see the caveats mentioned at the beginning of this section). When the Flash Player comes to the frames with FSCommands, the HTML background should change along with the Flash movie. Next, we add a `<FORM>` element that displays the percentage of the Flash movie that has loaded into the browser window.

On the CD-ROM   You can find the completed version of the countdown.fla movie on the *Flash 5 Bible* CD-ROM. It is called countdown_complete.fla and is located in the ch41 folder. You will also find countdown_complete.swf and a fully JavaScripted HTML document called countdown_complete.html. The JavaScript and HTML reflect the usage of the countdown_complete filename.

Using the PercentLoaded() method

JavaScript can control several Flash movie properties. It's beyond the scope of this book to describe each JavaScript method for Flash movies. If you want to see a complete list of Flash JavaScript methods, see the Macromedia Flash tech support page (The ¬ indicates a continuation in the URL. Do not type this character into the browser location field.):

```
http://www.macromedia.com/support/flash/ts/documents/¬
tn4160.html
```

In this section, we use the `PercentLoaded()` method to display the Flash movie's loading progress update as a text field of a `<FORM>` element. First, we add the necessary FSCommand to the Flash movie. HTML `<FORM>` elements, and then we add the appropriate JavaScript.

1. Open the countdown.fla movie that you used in the previous section. There should already be an empty keyframe present on frame 1 of the percentLoaded actions layer. Add an `FSCommand` action to this keyframe. Insert **PercentLoaded** in the Command field. This command has no arguments. Add the same FSCommand to the keyframes on frames 10, 20, 30, 40, 50, 60, and 67 of the percentLoaded actions layer. Export a Flash .SWF movie called countdown.swf with the File➪Export Movie command. Make sure you place the new .SWF file in the same folder as the HTML document that we were using in the previous section.

2. In a text editor such as Notepad or SimpleText, open the HTML document showing the countdown.swf Flash movie.

3. Add the following HTML after the `<OBJECT>` and `<EMBED>` tags:

```
<FORM METHOD="post" ACTION="" NAME="flashPercent"
STYLE="display:show">
  <INPUT TYPE="text" NAME="textfield" SIZE="5" STYLE =
"display:show">
</FORM>
```

The code in Step 3 uses two `NAME` attributes so that JavaScript can recognize them. Also, the DHTML `STYLE` attribute assigns a `display:show` value to the both the `<FORM>` and `<INPUT>` tags.

Caution

Netscape 4's implementation of the document object model (DOM) doesn't allow styles to be updated on the fly unless the page is reformatted (for example, the user resizes the window). It could be possible to write more JavaScript code that would insert JavaScript styles for the `<FORM>` elements, but that's beyond the scope of this section.

4. Now we need to map the `PercentLoaded` FSCommand to a JavaScript function. Add the following JavaScript to the `if` statement(s) in the `function countdown_DoFSCommand` of the HTML document:

```
if(command=="percentLoaded"){
        moviePercentLoaded();
}
```

5. Add the following JavaScript after the `function changeBgColor()` section. This function tells the browser to update the `<FORM>` text field with the percent of the Flash movie currently loaded. When the value is greater than or equal to 99, then the text field reads 100 percent and disappears after 2 seconds. As mentioned earlier, Netscape is unable to change the `style` of the

<FORM> elements on the fly. (The ¬ indicates a continuation in the URL. Do not type this character into the browser location field.)

```
function moviePercentLoaded(){
    var m = InternetExplorer ? countdown_complete : ¬
       document.countdown_complete;
    var Percent = m.PercentLoaded();
    var temp = 0;
    if(Percent >= 99 ){
     document.flashPercent.textfield.value="100 %";
     if (navigator.appName.indexOf("Microsoft") != -1){
        setTimeout("document.flashPercent.¬
           textfield.style.display = 'none'",2000);
        setTimeout("document.flashPercent.style.¬
           display = 'none'",2000);
           }
    }
    else {
        temp = Percent;
        document.flashPercent.textfield.value = temp ¬
           + " %" ;
    }
}
```

6. Save the HTML document and load it into a browser. If you run into errors, check your JavaScript syntax carefully. A misplaced ; or } can set off the entire script. If you continue to run into errors, compare your document to the countdown_complete.html document on the *Flash 5 Bible* CD-ROM.

Okay, that wasn't the easiest task in the world, and, admittedly, the effects might not have been as spectacular as you may have thought. However, now that you know the basics of Flash and JavaScript interactivity, you can take your Flash movie interactivity one step further.

Expert Tutorial: Java Script and FSCommands, *by Christian Honselaar*

Flash has changed the way we see and experience the Web; and with the increased power and functionality of Flash 5, this trend will only continue. Yet one underutilized capability is Flash's capability to talk with HTML to coordinate an interface. That is, Flash is capable of sending data and instructions to HTML by means of FSCommands. Similarly, JavaScript in the HTML document can be used both to get and to set Flash variables as well as perform operations in Flash. To facilitate this, Macromedia developed JavaScript methods for Flash objects. In this tutorial, you learn how to use both communication paths in one Web page.

The .FLA source file for this Flash project is on the CD-ROM in the ch41 folder. So, before we get started, please locate and open this example file, bothways.FLA.

Looking at the Main Timeline, you'll see two keyframes with ActionScripts in each one. Plus, there's a third ActionScript that is hidden from view.

The first ActionScript is located in frame 1:

```
var goalNumber=0, i=0;
fscommand("flashloaded","true");
```

The first line of code initializes the variables, goalNumber and i, and sets their value at zero. The second line issues a fscommand "flashloaded" to the JavaScript and VBScript of the HTML page.

The second script, located in the last frame looks like this:

```
if ((i==1)&&(goalNumber==0)) fscommand ( "ballGone", "dfgf");

if (i<=goalNumber){
    surface.attachMovie( "cBall", "Ball_"+i, i );
    setProperty ( "surface.Ball_"+i, _yscale, i*10 );
    setProperty ( "surface.Ball_"+i, _xscale, i*10 );
    i++;} else goalNumber=0;
gotoAndPlay (2);
```

This script uses an if statement to check whether a limit defined by the variable goalNumber hasn't yet been reached. If goalNumber hasn't been reached, then the script copies a Movie Clip instance (the ball symbol) to the Stage. You should notice that goalNumber is not assigned a proper value anywhere in this script. That's because goalNumber will be set externally, by the Web page! Also note that the other variable i tracks the current number of balls. Both of these variables were initialized in the first frame script.

There's just one more script to discuss:

```
This.removeMovieClip();
_root.i--;
if (_root.i==0) fscommand ( "ballGone" );
```

This script is in the last frame of the Movie Clip, ballAnim. The first line of this script deletes the ballAnim Movie Clip instance. With the next two lines, the script checks whether any balls are left. If not, the fscommand is evoked, sending a message to the Web browser that hosts the Flash Player.

Here's how an fscommand is constructed: The first parameter of the fscommand is the command name itself, while the second parameter can contain any arguments. Both are strings that you can pick arbitrarily. The fscommand sends a message to the Web browser, which, in turn, passes it to JavaScript or VBScript in the document. A special event handler in the script then processes the fscommand. Let's see how to do it for our example.

Continued

Continued

Open the finished HTML document that is located in the ch41 folder of the *Flash 5 Bible* CD-ROM. The JavaScript/VBScript is broken into four sections:

Section 1: Internet Explorer automatically links any fscommand from the Flash movie to a VBScript procedure with a specific name, which must look like this: the name (ID) you gave it in the <OBJECT> tag, with _FSCommand appended to it. The parameters are equal to those in the Flash movie fscommand. Not that we do anything with them. Our sole purpose here is to reveal the <DIV> or <LAYER> element containing our message. We create these tags in the next section.

This setup works fine on Internet Explorer 3.0 and up, on PC and MAC platforms. To make it work with Netscape 3.0+, you create a JavaScript function to receive the FSCommand. Its name is a little different: replace _FSCommand with _DoFSCommand. In addition, you need to add two attributes to the <EMBED> tag, found after the <BODY> tag:

```
NAME=flash and SWLIVECONNECT=true
```

That's right, Flash is controlling the HTML!

Section 2: Because each browser has its own way of using DHTML layers, we write code that will create the appropriate HTML tag for each browser. Internet Explorer will use a <DIV> tag, and Netscape will use a <LAYER> tag. This element will display the text "Flash to control center: no balls!"

Section 3: A function called hideMessage will be executed when the user clicks the Form button. This function will change the visibility of the <DIV> and <LAYER> tags to false.

Section 4: The showMessage function will execute when the Flash movie sends an fscommand to the HTML document. This will occur when the last remaining ballAnim symbol is removed from the Flash movie.

HTML can control the Flash movie by invoking JavaScript methods of the Flash object. We added a text box where the user can input the desired number of balls, and a button that will send this input to the Flash Movie. Here's the text box:

```
number of balls:<input id="nBalls" name="nBalls" value=20
type="text"></input>
```

nBalls now contains the desired number. By making use of the Flash method SetVariable, we set the variable goalNumber in the Flash movie to this value. But first we hide the "no balls" message. The following <INPUT> tag will execute the hideMessage function (in Section 3), which will use the nBalls value for the goalNumber value:

```
<input type="button" value="Allright Flash, do a ball trick!"
onmouseup="hideMessage(); "></input>
```

The following figure shows the form fields, as they appear beneath the Flash movie.

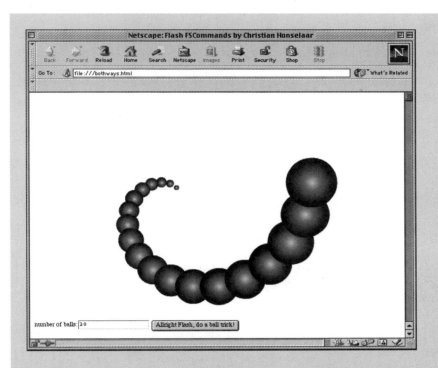

Now, when the button is pressed, the `nBalls` value is sent to Flash, updating the variable `goalNumber`, which Flash checks to see if it should create any more balls! This was just a simple example of Flash methods. In real-world situations, you'll probably find Flash methods/FSCommands most useful for synchronization purposes, such as updating navigation bars. In fact, there are many more Flash methods, and you can find documentation on them at: `www.macromedia.com/support/flash/publishexport/scriptingwithflash`

Christian's biography can be found in his expert tutorial, "Introduction to XML and Flash," located in Chapter 24.

Summary

✦ You can customize many Flash movie attributes by adjusting the attributes of the `<OBJECT>` and `<EMBED>` tags in an HTML document. Scaling, size, quality, and background color are just a few of the Flash movie properties that can be changed within HTML without altering the original .SWF file.

✦ Even though you can set the `WIDTH` and `HEIGHT` attributes of a Flash movie to 100 percent, the browser window will still show a small border around the Flash movie. To minimize this border effect, place the Flash movie in a single frame within the `<FRAMESET>` tag.

✦ You can detect the Flash Player plug-in or ActiveX Control in a variety of ways: by using the `<OBJECT>` and `<EMBED>` tags alone, by using JavaScript and VBScript to check for the presence of the plug-in or the ActiveX Control, or by inserting a Flash swiffer movie into an HTML document with a special `<META>` tag.

✦ Flash movies can interact with JavaScript and DHTML elements on a Web page. This type of interactivity, however, is limited to the 3.0 or higher versions of Internet Explorer (on 32-bit Windows versions) and Netscape (on Windows and Macintosh).

✦ Flash movies can send commands to JavaScript with the Flash action, `fscommand`. An FSCommand consists of a user-defined command and argument string.

✦ Although the Flash with FSCommand HTML template will set up the initial JavaScript to enable FSCommand support, it won't find the FSCommands you specified in the Flash and map them to JavaScript functions. You have to do this manually.

✦ FSCommands can be used to change HTML document attributes or styles.

✦ The Flash Player plug-in has JavaScript-specific methods that can be used to send or receive information to a Flash movie. For example, JavaScript can query a Flash movie to determine how much of it has downloaded to the browser.

✦   ✦   ✦

Using Players, Projectors, and Screensaver Utilities

✦ ✦ ✦ ✦

In This Chapter

Using the stand-alone player or projector

Controlling a projector with FSCommands

Understanding the Flash Player plug-in

Creating screensavers from Flash movies

✦ ✦ ✦ ✦

This last chapter explores alternative means of distributing your Flash movies, as self-contained executable applications for CD-ROMs or floppy disks. Also, we look at the broad support available for the Flash Player plug-in for Web browsers.

The Flash Stand-alone Player and Projector

The Flash Stand-alone Player and Projector let you take your Flash right off the Web and onto the desktop without having to worry whether users have the plug-in. In fact, you don't even need to worry about them having browsers! Stand-alone Players and Projectors have similar properties and limitations, although they're slightly different.

✦ **Stand-alone Player:** This is an executable player that comes with Flash. You can open any .SWF file in this player. The Stand-alone Player can be found in the Macromedia/Flash 5/Players folder (Windows) or the Macromedia Flash 5:Players folder (Mac) where you installed Flash 5.

✦ **Projector:** A Projector is an executable copy of your movie that doesn't need an additional player or plug-in to be viewed. It's essentially a movie contained within the Stand-alone Player. The Projector is ideal for distribution of Flash applications on floppy disks or CD-ROMs. Figure 42-1 shows a Flash movie played as a Projector.

Figure 42-1: This movie is being played as a Projector.

For the sake of simplicity, we refer to both Projectors and movies played in the Stand-alone Player as stand-alones in this discussion. Because both the Projector and Stand-alone Player have the same properties and limitations, you can apply everything discussed here to either one you choose to use.

Creating a projector

When you have finished producing a Flash movie, it's fairly simple to turn it into a projector. You have two ways to create a self-contained projector. Turning your Flash movies into self-contained projectors typically adds 368KB (Windows projectors) or 500KB (Mac projectors) to the final file size.

Note   As each new version of Flash is released, the projector size will likely increase. Flash 4 projectors added 280KB to a .SWF's file size (Windows projector), or 316KB to the file size (Mac projector). Because Flash 5 has an extended scripting language, the projector sizes need to store more code to playback .SWF files.

Method 1: Using the Publish command

The simplest way to make a Flash projector file is to use the Publish feature of Flash. In three short steps, you can have a stand-alone Flash movie presentation.

1. Select File ➪ Publish Settings from the main menu.

2. When the Publish Settings dialog opens, select the Formats tab and then check the projector formats. Publish both Windows and Macintosh projectors using this method. Figure 42-2 shows the Publish Settings dialog with the appropriate formats selected.

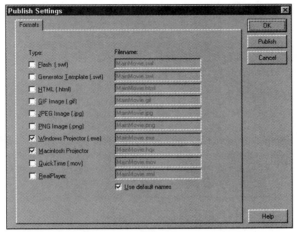

Figure 42-2: Select the projector formats in the Publish Settings dialog.

3. Press the Publish button in the Publish Settings dialog, and your Flash movie will be published in all of the formats (for example, .SWF, .GIF, .JPG, and projector formats) specified with Publish Settings.

Method 2: Using the Stand-alone Flash Player

You can also create a Flash projector file using the Flash Player executable file that ships with Flash. You can find the Stand-alone Flash Player in the Players folder of the Flash application folder.

1. Export your Flash movie as a .SWF file using File ➪ Export Movie from the main menu. Alternatively, you can use the Publish feature to create the .SWF file.

2. Open the exported Flash movie (.SWF file) in the Stand-alone Player.

3. Choose File ➪ Create Projector from the Stand-alone Player menu, as shown in Figure 42-3.

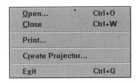

Figure 42-3: Choose File ⇨ Create Projector from the Stand-alone Player menu.

4. When the Save As dialog opens, name the Projector and save it.

Tip

If your movie is set to play at full screen (see FSCommands later in this chapter), press the Esc key to make the Stand-alone Player menu bar appear. If the .SWF movie is set to play without the menu, you should use the Publish method to create a projector.

Distribution and licensing

Distribution of stand-alone projectors or the Flash Player is free; you don't have to buy a license to distribute either the Stand-alone Player or Projector. However, according to Macromedia, you need to follow the "Made with Macromedia" guidelines for distributed Flash Players and projectors. Among other requirements, you need to include the "Made with Macromedia" logo on your product's packaging and credits screen. The runtime license agreement and Macromedia logos can be downloaded from the Macromedia Web site. For more information, check out www.macromedia.com/support/programs/mwm.

Distribution on CD-ROM or floppy disk

Flash has become increasingly popular for use on multimedia CD-ROMs, especially as embedded .SWF files in larger Macromedia Director projectors. Stand-alones can be used as front-ends for installations, splash screens for other programs, or even as complete applications. When you combine the good looks of a Flash interface with a few FSCommands (see "FSCommands" in the next section), some simple scripting (BAT and AppleScript), and put them together on a CD-ROM that's programmed to start automatically on insertion, you have a first-class product.

Because Flash movies can be very small (even when packaged as a projector), you can fit interactive multimedia presentations on 3.5-inch 1.44MB floppy disks! This is truly revolutionary, as floppy disks can be copied very easily on any system with a floppy drive — you don't need a CD recorder to distribute your Flash movies in promotional mailers to clients.

Cross-Reference

Read William Moschella's tutorial on creating autorun CD-ROMs for Flash presentations at the end of this section. Also, check out Chrissy Rey's excellent "Flash for CDs" resource at www.flashlite.net/help/cd.

FSCommands

FSCommands can be used to provide greater functionality to your stand-alones. These actions can turn a simple Flash movie into something spectacular! When combined with additional scripting and executables, you can make fully functional applications. Table 42-1 lists FSCommands for stand-alones.

	Table 42-1	
	FSCommands for Stand-alones	
FSCommand	**Arguments**	**Function**
fullscreen	true/false	True sets the stand-alone to full-screen mode, without a menu. False sets it to the size specified by the Movie Properties.
allowscale	true/false	Allows for scaling of the movie. False sets the movie to the size specified by the Movie Properties. This doesn't actually keep the stand-alone from being resized, it only the keeps the movie inside of it from being scaled.
showmenu	true/false	Toggles the menu bar and the right-click/control-click menu. True enables them; false turns them both off.
trapallkeys	true/false	Captures all key presses, including those that would normally control the player. If you have turned off the menu with the showmenu command, then you will need to manually create a quit command to exit the player or projector.
exec	Path to executable (BAT, COM, EXE, and so on)	Opens an executable from within the stand-alone player. The application opens in front of the projector.
quit		Closes the stand-alone.

When an FSCommand action is added in the Actions Panel, you can access stand-alone– specific commands from a drop-down menu (see Figure 42-4). Refer to Chapter 17, "Understanding Actions and Event Handlers," for more information on adding actions to Flash frames or buttons.

New Feature The FSCommand in Flash 5 has a new player/projector command, trapallkeys. This command is useful for creating kiosk presentations where you don't want to allow access to the system beyond the Flash projector or player.

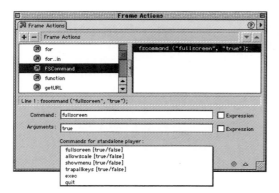

Figure 42-4: Flash 5 adds a convenient drop-down menu for FSCommands specific to the stand-alone Flash Player or projector.

Make sure you list FSCommands and their arguments as strings, not as expressions (unless you purposely want to refer to an ActionScript variable). If you do not encapsulate the FSCommand in quotes, as in `fscommand("allowscale","true");`, then it will not be interpreted by the stand-alone.

Expert Tutorial: Opening Web Pages from Stand-alones, by Chrissy Rey

The source file for this tutorial, which is located in the ch42 folder of the Flash 5 Bible *CD-ROM, contains three examples that use the Get URL action in a stand-alone projector.*

One of the great improvements delivered with Flash 4 was the ease with which an external URL can be opened from the Stand-alone Projector. The functionality is still the same in Flash 5, except that we now have the easily accessible Actions Panel to add our FSCommands. You'd surely appreciate this, too, if you labored endlessly with Flash 3, trying to find a way to open Web pages from the Stand-alone Projector . . . only to learn that there was no easy solution. (Furthermore, if you threw cross-platform compatibility needs into the mix, you had to spend considerable time writing BAT files and AppleScripts to get everything to work.) Happily, Flash 4 solved this problem, and it's as simple as adding a Get URL action to your movie — in fact that's exactly what we're going to do here.

Step 1: Create your movie as you normally would.

Step 2: When you get to the button or keyframe where you want to open a Web page, simply use the `getURL` action, with the URL value set to the local HTML file or Web site that you'd like to open. In the Frame Actions Panel (shown in the following figure), you can add a `getURL` action that opens a Web page in the default browser.

You can also use the `getURL` action to create an e-mail link from the stand-alone. Just type the e-mail address preceded by `mailto:` in the URL box (for example, `mailto:userID@domain.com`). You don't need to worry about the Window settings when using the `getURL` action in the stand-alone. Each time the action is called, it will open the URL in the user's default browser. The Variables setting is only important if your stand-alone will be communicating with a back-end script.

Step 3: Export the movie and open it in the stand-alone or publish the movie as a projector. Test your actions to see how nicely they work.

Unfortunately, this method doesn't let you open anything locally but HTML files. In order to open other file types, you still need to use the FSCommand Exec in conjunction with a BAT file, AppleScript, or another trick to open these files. Refer to the section on FSCommands, earlier in this chapter, for more information on stand-alone specific commands.

Originally from College Park, Maryland, Chrissy Rey was among the first with in-depth Flash tutorial sites on the Web — www.flashlite.net. She found Flash when she was working at the Department of Justice; she was given a copy of Flash 3 and told to make a CD-ROM presentation with it. She did as she was told: "It worked, and there was much rejoicing." Like many overworked Flash experts, Chrissy's single most favorite thing to do is sleep — something the authors of this book certainly miss as well.

Expert Tutorial: CD-ROMS and Projectors, by *William Moschella*

Bill Moschella has contributed a number of Expert Tutorials on sound-related topics. His biographical information can be found (together with his sound advice) in Chapter 32, "Optimizing Flash Sound for Export."

The Flash 5 Publish Settings includes a tab for both Windows and Macintosh Projectors, which publish self-inclusive Stand-alone Players. When published as such, these are actually applications/programs. These players enable viewers to see your Flash movies without worrying about downloading the latest version of the Flash Player. While the default Flash .SWF format is cross-platform, these projectors have either a Macintosh or a Windows version.

Continued

Continued

The following tutorial shows you how to use this feature of the Publish Settings to make an autostart cross-platform CD-ROM.

Some Guidelines

Before we get started, you should be familiar with the limitations of playing Flash content from an auto start CD-ROM. You should follow these guidelines:

✦ The projector will strain the processor if you ask it to read a large file. Try to break up your presentation using the load/unload movie command. I've made CD-ROMs that contain a combined totals of up to 50MB of .SWF's and projectors. However, the largest .SWF that the projector can play smoothly — one at a time — is approximately 1MB.

✦ For smooth presentations, avoid situations that require the projector to process multiple actions at once. If you decide that your whole presentation needs to be divided into multiple .SWF files, you must be careful where and when you command these actions.

✦ If you're streaming animation with audio and attempt to simultaneously execute commands to load other .SWF's, the player will hiccup, meaning that you will see blips in the animation.

✦ If you are loading other .SWF's into your projector, be sure that they have the same Movie Properties as your projector. To maintain functionality and consistency, all .SWF's need the same background color and window sizes.

✦ If you want to load a new .SWF with different background colors, first stop your original — or root — movie at a final keyframe. The content of this keyframe should be a square that fills the workspace window with the same color as the background of movie you're about to load in. This will smooth the transition.

✦ If your movie has different settings than the projector, don't fret. Simply create another projector and use the FSCommand exec to load the new projector in front of your existing one. Your script will look like this:

```
fscommand("exec", "yourmovie.exe");
```

Using CD Recording Software

After you've published your projectors and .SWFs, and have tested their performance from your hard drive, you will be ready to burn them to a CD-ROM. Although .SWF's can be shared on multiple platforms, it is a good idea to create a set of .SWF's for your Macintosh projector and a separate set for your Windows projector. Because we want to create a cross-platform CD-ROM, it's important to check the specs of the CD burner; some burners can't burn a cross-platform disk. (Sony's Discribe and Adaptec's Toast are great for cross-platform compatibility.) By using a MAC/ISO HYBRID format, your Mac files will remain hidden from Windows users and your Windows files will be unreadable on the Mac.

First, create an HFS volume for your Mac files. This is a separate disk/drive where all your files are stored. If you don't have a secondary drive on your Mac, you'll need to trick the computer. Open your hard drive and find your Utilities folder. Launch your Disk Copy application. Choose Image from the pull-down menu and select Create New Image. This will create a new partition on your Mac Desktop, which will act as a separate hard drive. Now, choose a size for your new disk copy—but be careful about the size you choose, because this drive takes it's space from your initial hard drive. Now, place your Mac projector files and related .SWF's on the new disk image.

(These next steps assume that you are working with Adaptec's Toast, which is a CD recording application. If you do not have Toast, you will need to find similar controls in your CD recording application.) Next, launch your CD recording application and choose Mac/ISO Hybrid from the menu. It will ask you to choose a drive for the HFS volume. Choose your newly created disk copy. On the check-off list, choose Don't Copy Free Space. This setting ensures that you will only burn the files from the disk, rather than the entire disk, including free space. Open the ISO window by double-clicking your CD title in Discribe or by choosing the ISO tab in Toast. Now place your ISO (Windows) files into the data window—you can drag and drop them. You have the option to make your files invisible so that the user cannot access them, so double-click the files and check off invisible. When you are finished making these modifications, you can burn your files to disk.

Autostart

You'll probably want to have a specific projector autostart upon insertion of the disk. To accomplish this, you must include an `autorun.inf` file in your ISO portion. Open your word processor and type the following code:

```
[autorun]
open=yourfile.exe
```

Save this file as autorun.inf and burn it to the ISO partition of the CD-ROM. This file will cause the named projector, `open=yourfile.exe`, to autostart.

Unfortunately, there is no file that we can include to make this happen on a MAC platform. To my knowledge, Adaptec's Toast is the only method for including this option. When choosing the HFS volume, there is a check box for Auto-start. With this option checked, Toast will ask you to choose a file to autostart from your HFS volume in your new disk image. Select the file that you want to autostart and continue with the steps as explained previously. This will act the same as your autorun.inf file in Windows. These two techniques, combined, will create a cross-platform autostart CD-ROM.

Stand-alone Limitations and Solutions

When you distribute your Flash movies as stand-alones, you may think that you won't have to worry about streaming and download. As a consequence, stand-alones are often made considerably larger than a typical Flash movie—which can be a mistake! Very large movies (1MB or more) may not play on slower computers.

Remember that Flash requires the computer processor to compute all of those vector calculations. When you try to give a slower computer 1MB worth of Flash at once, it may not be able to handle it.

Tip   One way to get around this limitation is to break your movies into several smaller movies. You can use the `loadMovie`/`unloadMovie` actions to open and close other movies within the original movie. You should use these actions in your stand-alones.

You should also test your movies on a variety of computers, especially if you plan to put a lot of money into distributing them on CD-ROM. Some processors handle the movies better than others, and you often have to decide which processor you want to target as the lowest common denominator.

Expert Tutorial: Distributing PR on the Flash Player, by Cam Christiansen

You can download the files for Cam Christiansen's tutorial from the Flash 5 Bible Web site at www.flash5bible.com/ch42.

This tutorial describes two methods of using Flash for promotional purposes. One uses the Flash stand-alone projector and the other is a HTML page with a JavaScript full-screen function. At Anlanda, we've used Flash as an effective method for promoting our company, staying in touch with our clients, and showcasing our creativity. We have found it a cost-effective method of spreading the message of our business to existing clients as well as prospective ones. To date we have used the Flash projector as our main method of delivery for our promos. Some of the reasons why we chose this method are:

✦ It scales full-screen (no ugly browser to contend with). This helps to define the promo as something *more* than just another Web site.

✦ It performs very well because it's already downloaded onto the users computer when they play it.

✦ The user values the presentation more than if they'd simply received a URL via e-mail, because they feel like they've received something tangible that they can, in turn, pass on to others.

But there's also a downside to the Flash projector: Because of the monotonous regularity of executable virus scares, some people are understandably reluctant to open these executable (.EXE) e-mail attachments, and many larger companies set up filters that thwart them all together. Another, minor, downside is that the projector adds to the overall file size, making an original file that may have been quite tiny, much larger.

So most recently, in an effort to work around these downsides while maintaining the full-screen aspect, we're now using an HTML page and attaining the full-screen aspect by using a JavaScript that I discovered at www.flashgen.com. The benefits of this approach are that the user does not have to wait for the e-mail to download—it comes up like any Web site and there are no worries about e-mail attachments. Plus, it can link seamlessly to other HTML files. However, the downside of this approach is that it only works on the PC, using the Explorer 4 and up.

For the purposes of this tutorial, I thought I would give you a taste of what we have done in the past and demonstrate the steps with our promotion, *Wasabi lunch*, which was developed from four earlier promotions that had been originally distributed as Stand-Alone Projectors (SAP). There are two versions of this movie: One is an SAP and the other is an HTML page deployed using JavaScript.

Version One: The Stand-Alone Player

Now, we show you how to create a projector that plays full-screen and offers an option to exit (or quit) the movie. In the first three steps that follow, we add the appropriate FSCommand to enable full-screen functionality. Later, a Quit button will be added to the movie.

1. Begin by adding an action to the first frame of your movie.

2. As shown in the following figure, click the + sign in the Frame Actions Panel, navigate to Basic Actions, and then click FSCommands.

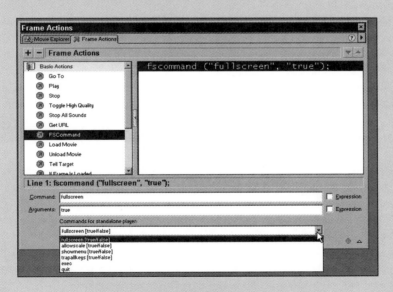

3. There's a drop-down menu at the bottom of this panel labeled Commands for standalone player. Click the arrow button to open the drop-down menu, and then select fullscreen [true/false]. This command will launch your movie full-screen when the user clicks the projector icon.

Continued

Continued

About a few of the other FSCommands in the drop-down menu:

✦ **quit** — Quit is used to close the projector (we will get to this in one second).

✦ **allowscale** — When used along with the false argument, this doesn't let the movie scale and is shown at the movie dimensions. With the true argument, it sets the projector back to its default mode, show all, which is not full-screen.

✦ **showmenu** — The true argument enables the user to see a full list of menu items by right-clicking (PC), whereas false removes the menu option.

✦ **exec** — Exec enables you to execute another application from within a projector.

After you've created the full-screen frame action, you need to make a Quit button. This is very important because once you're viewing a full-screen Flash movie, the only way to get out of it is to press the Esc key, which isn't user friendly because it gives the impression that you have thoughtlessly created a movie that has taken over the prospective client's computer.

Here's how to create a button and assign an FSCommand called `quit`:

1. Create a button with the text Quit on it. In the Frame Actions Panel, click the + sign and navigate to Basic Actions, and then click FSCommands.

2. At the bottom return to the menu called Commands for standalone player, click the arrow button to open the drop-down menu, and then select quit. Your Actions list for the Button instance should contain the code shown in the figure that follows.

3. As long as your button remains visible on the timeline, the user can click Quit to stop the playing of the movie at full-screen.

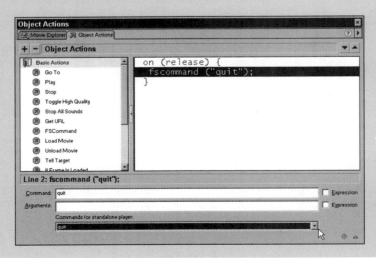

Finally, we're at the last step to create the projector:

1. Go to Publish Settings, File ➪ Publish settings.

2. Then click the Formats tab. Next, to create SAPs for both the Mac and the PC, check both Windows Projector [.EXE] and Macintosh Projector.

3. Click the Publish button and you are done! You've created a self-contained movie, which can be viewed on any Mac or PC, regardless whether or not they have the Flash Player installed on their computer.

Version Two: The JavaScript/HTML approach

As I said earlier, there's another way to achieve an effect similar to that of the full-screen projector. This second way uses JavaScript in an HTML document and is limited to PCs using Explorer 4 and up. (This script is distributed free from www.flashgen.com. They indicate that they are happy to let others use the script as long as you leave credits for them in the HTML). Although I'm not a JavaScript wizard (yet), I can reiterate the explanation I received from flashgen.com. If you want a more detailed explanation, please visit their site. You will need three HTML pages to create a full-screen Flash promotion.

1. A quick-switch screen that launches the full-screen HTML page.

2. An HTML file that has the final Flash file, with a Quit button, that you wish to present full-screen.

3. An HTML file that will be viewed by those unable to see the full-screen (Mac and PC users with Internet Explorer below version 4).

Stage 1: The First HTML Page

1. Create an HTML file that will be your quick-switch page. This can have any content that you want, but remember, it will only be shown for a split second.

2. Next, open the quick-switch HTML file in an editor such as Dreamweaver.

3. Copy the script (supplied at the end of this section) into the document after the `<head>` tag

4. Replace the line `nonfullscreen.html` with the title of the HTML file that you wish to be viewed by users who are unable to view the full-screen promotion.

5. Replace the line `yesfullscreen.html` with the title of the HTML file that will be seen by users who are able to view the full-screen promotion.

This is used to determine what platform the viewer is using. It sends the Mac users to a non-full–screen HTML page that you have defined in the line `location.href= nonfullscreen.html`. Then as the script continues, it sifts out Netscape and all other browsers except Internet Explorer 4+. Finally, it takes those using Internet Explorer 4+ to the page defined as `yesfullscreen.html`. (In the following code, the ¬ indicates a continuation of the same line of code.)

Continued

Continued

```
<script LANGUAGE="Javascript">
<!-- //
function intro()
{
    if ((navigator.appVersion.indexOf("Mac")!=-1) && ¬
      (navigator.userAgent.indexOf("MSIE")!=-1) && ¬
      (parseInt(navigator.appVersion)==4))
    {
    skip()
    }
    else
    {
    popup()
    }
}
function skip()
{
    location.href="nonfullscreen.html";
}
function popup()
{

    version =    parseFloat(navigator.appVersion.substring ¬
      (navigator.appVersion.indexOf('.')-1,navigator. ¬
      appVersion.length));
    if (version >= 4)
    version = parseFloat(navigator.appVersion.substring¬
      (navigator.appVersion.indexOf('.')-1,navigator. ¬
      appVersion.length));
    if (version >= 4)
    {
    if (navigator.appName=="Netscape")
        {
            location.href=" nonfullscreen.html";

        }
        if (navigator.appName=="Microsoft Internet ¬
          Explorer")
        {
            window.open("yesfullscreen.html","screen", ¬
            "fullscreen=yes");
        }
    }
    else
```

```
            {
                location.href=" nonfullscreen.html";
            }
        }
}
// -->
</script>

<body LINK="#000000" BGCOLOR="#000000" onLoad="intro()">
</body>
</html>
<!-- Copyright 1999 FlashGen.Com If you wanna submit work to
FlashGen.Com, send your emails to: info@flashgen.com -->
```

Stage 2: The Second HTML Page

The next step is to create an HTML file to contain your Flash movie with a Quit button. This will be the Flash file that you want to be viewed full-screen. For the purpose of this tutorial, we have called it yesfullscreen.html. The purpose of the Quit button within the Flash movie is to enable viewers to close the window and quit the movie. As was stated earlier in the context of Stand-alone Projectors, it's very important to do this so that the user feels in control of what they are viewing. Let's get started.

1. Open your movie and create a button labeled Quit. Add the button to the movie interface.

2. Select the button and, in the Frame Actions Panel, click the + button. Then, from the Basic Actions, choose get URL. The following code will appear in the right pane of the Frame Actions Panel: getURL ("");.

3. Then, at the bottom of the dialog, type **Javascript:closer()** in the URL field. Your action list should look like the following figure.

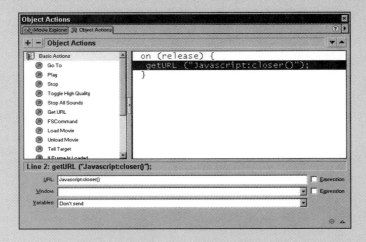

Continued

Continued

4. Next, use File ⇨ Publish to publish this Flash movie (which has the Quit button in it) and generate the HTML page named yesfullscreen.html. To do this, be sure that the HTML [.html] option is checked on the Formats tab.

5. Then, open the HTML file yesfullscreen.html in an editor such as Dreamweaver and insert the following script between the `<HEAD>` tags:

```
<script LANGUAGE="Javascript">
<!--//
function closer()
{
parent.close();
}
// -->
</script>
```

Author's Note: Internet Explorer 4.5 (or earlier) on the Macintosh will not support the use of direct `javascript:` calls in `getURL` actions.

Now if the user clicks the Quit button in the Flash presentation, the button will call the function from the Flash Player and close the window.

Stage 3: The Third HTML Page

Publish a Flash movie to an HTML format (or create a regular HTML file) and name it **nonfullscreen.html**. This page can be anything—the only purpose of this HTML file is to offer those using Macs, Netscape, and versions of Internet Explorer below 4 an alternative path to view your presentation.

That's it! You're done. Now, when a visitor arrives at the first quick-switch HTML page, the script will check the system and send your visitor to the appropriate page. If the visitor has Internet Explorer 4+, they get the full-screen! Others are served the alternative. After they're finished viewing the full-screen movie, all they have to do is click Quit and full-screen mode quits.

"I am not sure what year it was from, but my favorate late '80s album was Soul Mining, by The The. I was definitely listening to it during my last year of school; it's still awsome," says Cam, who is a native of Calgary, Alberta, Canada, where he is one of two partners in the Anlanda design firm. Of his introduction to Flash, Cam relates, "I was introduced to it by a classmate at university." Now, he uses Flash to craft amazing sites and to develop distributable PR. Some of his work can be seen at www.anlanda.com, www.jawzinc.com, and www.madison-page.com. What's his single most favorite thing to do? "Travel with my wife, Mo, to Italy; where we eat expensive porcini mushrooms, drink lots of red wine, and plot ways to become honorary Italian citizens."

Using the Flash Player Plug-in for Web Browsers

Flash movies can only be played in Web browsers that have the Flash Player plug-in or ActiveX control installed. Macromedia has made huge strides in making the plug-in prepackaged with newer Web browsers and operating system installation programs, eliminating the need for users to manually download and install the plug-in themselves. Unfortunately, the Flash 5 version of the plug-in will only be included in future releases of Web browsers and operating systems. Remember that the Flash 3 and 4 Player plug-ins can *try* to play Flash 5 movies — however, new features in Flash 5 movies will not be available (such as new ActionScript syntax and features).

Note For up-to-date information on the Flash Player plug-in, see Macromedia's download page at www.macromedia.com/shockwave/download/alternates.

Supported operating systems

Since Flash 3, Macromedia has greatly expanded its platform support for the Flash Player plug-in. At the time of this writing, you can download Flash 5 Players for Windows 95/98/ME/NT/2000 and for Mac Power PCs. By the time this book is published, version 5 players should be available for Sun Solaris and Linux *x*86. At the FlashForward2000 March conference, the Flash Player was demonstrated on Windows CE! While this was an "unofficial" player that is not publicly available (it was a "proof of concept" demo), Macromedia has proven that Flash graphics can be ported to a variety of GUIs (graphical user interfaces) and operating systems. We've also heard reports of Flash 3 graphics showing up in add-on applications for the Sega Dreamcast.

Supported browsers

The Flash Player plug-in works best with Netscape and Internet Explorer browsers. Any browser that is compliant with Netscape Navigator 2.0's plug-in specification or Internet Explorer's ActiveX technology can support the Flash Player plug-in or ActiveX control. Note that Mac versions of Internet Explorer use a Netscape plug-in emulator to use the Flash Player plug-in rather than an ActiveX control.

For AOL subscribers, any version of AOL's 3.0, 4.0, 5.0, or 6.0 browsers (except for the earliest 3.0 release that used a non-Microsoft Internet Explorer shell) will support Macromedia plug-ins.

Caution The Flash action FSCommand, which can be used to communicate with JavaScript, will only work with certain browser versions. Currently, all versions of Internet Explorer on the Macintosh (up to version 5.0) do not support the FSCommand action. Netscape 3.01 or greater (on both Macintosh and Windows) or Internet Explorer 3.0 or greater for Windows 95/98/NT is necessary for FSCommand implementation.

For a comprehensive list of supported browsers (and Flash compatibility), please see the Macromedia tech note at www.macromedia.com/support/flash/ts/documents/browser_support_matrix.htm

Plug-in and Flash movie distribution on the Web

Anyone can download the Flash Player plug-in for free from the Macromedia Web site. You can direct visitors at your Web sites to Macromedia's Flash Player download page, www.macromedia.com/shockwave/download/index.cgi?P1_Prod_Version=ShockwaveFlash. In fact, according to Macromedia's licensing agreement, if you're publishing Flash movies on your Web site, you need to display the "Get Shockwave Player" logo or "Get Flash Player" logo on your Web site. This logo should link to Macromedia's download page, just listed. However, you need to license the right to distribute any Shockwave plug-in installer from Macromedia. For more details on licensing, see www.macromedia.com/shockwave.

You can find the official Macromedia button graphics at www.macromedia.com/support/programs/mwm/swb.html

Plug-in installation

In Chapter 40, "Publishing Flash Movies," we discuss the Publish feature of Flash and the use of preformatted HTML templates to deliver your Flash movies to your Web site. The template and/or handwritten HTML that you use for your Flash-enabled Web pages determines the degree of difficulty your visitors will have upon loading a Flash movie.

Cross-Reference We added an entire section on plug-in detection to the *Flash 5 Bible*. See Chapter 41, "Integrating Flash Content with HTML," for more information.

Because Web browsers vary dramatically between operating systems (for example, Internet Explorer for the Mac behaves very differently from Internet Explorer for Windows), you should make the plug-in process as invisible as possible. The following are the possible outcomes of each HTML template that Flash 5 uses:

✦ **Flash Only (Default):** This template doesn't use any JavaScript detection for the Flash Player plug-in. It simply places the <OBJECT> and <EMBED> tags for the Flash movie into an HTML document. The CODEBASE attribute of <OBJECT> will direct Internet Explorer for Windows to the download location of the Flash ActiveX control. This process should be relatively straightforward for Windows users. For visitors using Netscape 3.0 or greater (on any platform), the PLUGINSPAGE attribute of <EMBED> provides the browser with the plug-in location, and prompts the visitor to go there.

✦ **Ad 5 Banner:** This template inserts an <OBJECT> tag for Internet Explorer (just as the Flash Only template will) and JavaScript detection code for the presence of the Netscape plug-in. When a Netscape browser loads the HTML page, JavaScript checks for version 5 of the Flash Player plug-in. If the plug-in is installed, then JavaScript writes the proper <EMBED> tag and attributes for the Flash movie. If the plug-in is not installed, then JavaScript writes HTML code for a static .GIF image.

✦ **Ad 4 Banner:** This template works in the same way as the Ad 5 Banner template, except that it checks for the Flash 4 Player plug-in or ActiveX control. Note that the Flash 4 format should be selected in the Flash tab of the Publish Settings.

✦ **Ad 3 Banner:** This template uses the same HTML code as the Flash 4 with Image template, except that it checks for version 3 of the Flash Player plug-in. Note that the Flash 3 format should be selected in the Flash tab of the Publish Settings.

✦ **Flash with FSCommand:** This template does not employ any JavaScript plug-in detection. The JavaScript inserted by this template is solely for the Flash action, FSCommand.

✦ **Java Player:** This HTML template will use an <APPLET> tag with <PARAM> subtags to employ the Flash Player Java edition. It does not use <OBJECT> or <EMBED> tags. See the next section for more information.

✦ **QuickTime:** This template will create an HTML document containing the <EMBED> tag information to display a QuickTime Flash movie — a .MOV file, not a .SWF file. The QuickTime Player is discussed in the next section.

 Cross-Reference For information on other templates, including those that support Generator template files, please refer to Chapter 40, "Publishing Flash Movies."

Unfortunately, you can never predict with any certainty how visitors will encounter a Flash plug-in installation. Most of the automated HTML coding from earlier versions of Flash (3.0 and earlier) and/or Aftershock may make an "upgrade" installation very difficult for Web visitors. For example, if an HTML document uses JavaScript to detect the Flash Player version 3 plug-in and the visitor's browser is using the version 4 or 5 plug-in, the browser may return a false value for the plug-in and direct the visitor to a non-Flash page. The older JavaScript code doesn't know that the Flash 4 or 5 Player plug-in is perfectly capable of playing older Flash movies. If you have created Web pages and Flash movies with Flash 3.0 or earlier, see Macromedia's tech note at www.macromedia.com/support/flash/ts/documents/flash4_detection.htm for more information on updating JavaScript code to detect Flash Player version 4 or 5.

Alternative Flash-Content Players

While Flash 5 movies play back best with Macromedia's Flash Player plug-in (or Stand-alone Player), Macromedia has developed Java class files (available in the Flash application folder) so that Java-enabled Web browsers can play Flash movies.

Macromedia has also teamed up with RealSystems and Apple to enable Flash content in RealPlayer and the QuickTime Player, respectively. By enabling Flash content in other players, Macromedia is promoting the acceptance of Flash as the de facto vector standard for Web graphics. Moreover, with so many alternatives for Flash playback, it is more likely that your Web visitors can see your Flash content.

Flash Player Java edition

You can use the Java Player HTML template to enable the Flash Player Java edition in Web browsers. This player will work on any Java-compatible Web browser. However, you need to do a bit of work to make sure that the Flash class files are available on your Web server. The Java Player HTML template inserts the following <APPLET> and <PARAM> tags into a Web document:

```
<APPLET CODE=Flash.class ARCHIVE=Flash.jar WIDTH=550
HEIGHT=400>
<PARAM NAME=cabbase VALUE="Flash.cab">
<PARAM NAME=movie VALUE="home.swf">
<PARAM NAME=quality VALUE=high>
<PARAM NAME=bgcolor VALUE=#FFFFFF>
</APPLET>
```

You may need to adjust the CODE and ARCHIVE paths to indicate where the class files are located relative to the HTML document. You can find the Java class files (as well as Netscape .JAR and Internet Explorer .CAB files) in the Flash Player Java Edition folder, located inside the Players folder of the Flash 5 application folder. Upload the .CLASS, .JAR and .CAB files to a folder located on your Web server.

Tip   You may have noticed another folder called FlashSmall inside the Flash Player Java Edition folder. The class files inside of the FlashSmall can be used instead of the regular .CLASS, .JAR, and .CAB files if your Flash movie does not contain any bitmaps or sounds. The FlashSmall class files are smaller and easier for visitors to download. You'll need to change any reference to Flash.*xxx* files in the <APPLET> and <PARAM> tags to FlashSmall.xxx. For example, Flash.class should be changed to FlashSmall.class.

You can only use Flash 2-format .SWF files with the Java Player. To export Flash 2 movies, select Flash 2 in the Version drop-down menu of the Publish Settings' Flash tab. Flash 2 movies cannot use many of the features available to Flash 3, 4, and 5 movies, such as:

✦ Alpha channel effects (transparent colors)

✦ Shape tweening

✦ Mask layers

✦ Movie Clip symbols

✦ Many Flash actions such as `tellTarget, if, loadMovie,` and `loadVariables`

RealPlayer 8.0 with Flash playback

With a little effort, you can repackage your Flash .SWF movies as RealFlash presentations over the Web. Web visitors can use the RealPlayer G2 or RealPlayer 8 to play Flash, RealAudio, or RealVideo (among a long list of RealMedia types) content. RealPlayer movies stream from a RealServer (special server software running concurrently with Web server software) into the RealPlayer plug-in (Netscape) or ActiveX control (Internet Explorer).

Cross-Reference   We added a new chapter to the *Flash 5 Bible,* Chapter 35, "Working with RealPlayer." Please read this chapter for more information on the creation of RealPlayer Flash movies.

QuickTime Player

Apple introduced playback support for Flash movies with QuickTime 4. Better yet, Macromedia included QuickTime Flash export options with Flash 4. A QuickTime Flash movie (.MOV file) is essentially a Flash .SWF file packaged as a QuickTime media type.

Cross-Reference   The QuickTime architecture and QuickTime Flash format are discussed at length in Chapter 34, "Working with QuickTime." The QuickTime HTML template is discussed in Chapter 40, "Publishing Flash Movies."

You can use the QuickTime HTML template in Publish Settings to create an instant Web page that uses the QuickTime Player plug-in. It uses the `<EMBED>` tag to prescribe the name, width, height, and plug-in download location:

```
<EMBED
  SRC="flashmovie.mov"
  WIDTH=550 HEIGHT=400
  BGCOLOR="#FFFFFF" BORDER="0"
PLUGINSPAGE="http://www.apple.com/quicktime/download/">
</EMBED>
```

QuickTime 4 can only support Flash 3 graphics and actions. Remember that Flash 4 only added new interactive components such as ActionScript to the Flash milieu — all Flash graphics, including Mask layers and Movie Clips, are supported by the QuickTime Player. Flash movies can act as a timeline navigator for other QuickTime media, such as video or audio.

Note   At the time of this writing, QuickTime 5 Public Preview had just been released. QuickTime 5 will support Flash 4–compatible actions.

For interactive Flash content, you should limit yourself to the following Flash 3-compatible actions:

```
play();
stop();
gotoAndStop();
gotoAndPlay();
toggleHighQuality();
stopAllSounds();
getURL(url, window);
loadMovie(url, level);
unloadMovie(level);
tellTarget(instance){}
ifFrameLoaded(frameLabel){}
on(mouseEvent){}
```

Tip   Check out Apple's QuickTime Sprites overview page at `www.apple.com/quicktime/overview/sprites.html` for a demo of QuickTime Flash.

Shockwave Player

Since Director 6.5, you can include Flash movies (as .SWF files) in your Director movies, either as stand-alone Director projectors or as part of Shockwave movies (.DCR files) on the Web. The Flash Asset Xtra is automatically installed as part of the default Shockwave plug-in installation process. Among other benefits, Shockwave movies enable you to integrate Flash movies with QuickTime video and use Flash assets with Macromedia's Multiuser Server (which is part of the Director Internet Studio software package).

Cross-Reference   For more information on Director and Flash interactivity, please read the latter half of Chapter 39, "Working with Authoring Applications."

Screensaver utilities

You can also reformat Flash movies as screensavers for both Windows and Macintosh. A few software companies create applications specifically designed to modify Flash movies:

✦ FlashJester.com

✦ LivingScreen.com

We are pleased to have Christian Kocholl from Living Screen present the following tutorial on Flash screensavers.

Expert Tutorial: Living Screen's Screensavertool, by Christian Kocholl

Christian's tutorial discusses the creation of screensavers with the Mac version of the Living Screen Screensavertool. This utility is also available for Windows.

The value of imaginative, animated, and interactive screensavers as a public relations tool is beyond argument. Screensavers carry brands and images to those users that normally would not be reached by other distribution channels. The Living Screen Screensavertool was developed for every Flash designer who wants to painlessly create screensavers — within minutes — that contain Flash animations. This is guaranteed by the structured set up of our Screensavertool, which can utilize a Wizard mode.

The tool supports every feature of Macromedia Flash, and therefore offers an ideal basis for almost limitless interactions and exciting concepts. A Living Screen screensaver is the platform for interactive experiences. Animated games, superior applications, and active description fields are easily integrated with our Screensavertool. The tool also supports Flash Layer technology. This is the premise for translating the most demanding movies into individual screensavers.

Now I'll show you how easy it is to create a screensaver from an existing Flash animation using the Living Screen Screensavertool.

Step 1: After starting the Living Screen Screensavertool, a welcome screen appears. By clicking the Continue button, you will see the Personal Data page. Here, you insert general information such as your company name, an e-mail address, or your URL. You can also add a picture in .PICT format, with 320×240 dimensions. This information will be displayed in the About screen, accessible by the clicking the About button in the LS Control Panel (Mac). Click the Continue button.

Continued

Continued

Step 2: On the next page of the wizard (shown in the following figure), you can choose between a Full version or a Demo version for your screensaver application. If you choose Demo version, then indicate the length of the trial period (in days). Click the Continue button. *Note: If you are using the Trial version of Screensavertool, then you will only be able to select Demo version.*

Step 3: On the next page of the wizard (shown in the following figure), you must select the .SWF file to be used as a screensaver. You should also enter a name for your screensaver in the field provided. If you using the `loadMovie` or `loadVariables` action as a method to load more .SWF files (or text information), then you will need to select the option Embed additional SWF or text files. You can optionally define whether the screensaver can be deactivated with the keyboard and/or a mouse click. Click the Continue button.

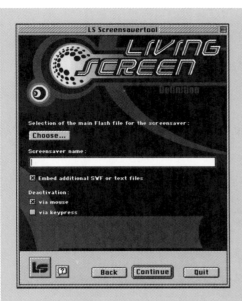

Step 4: If you selected the option Embed additional SWF or text files in the previous step, you will now be able to choose those files from the interface shown in the following figure. These files need to be in the same directory as the starter .SWF file of the screensaver or in a subdirectory. Make sure that your Flash actions use relative paths to these files. Click Continue.

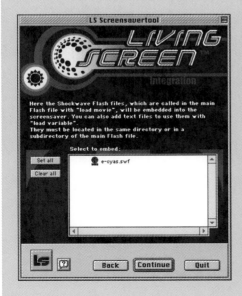

Continued

Continued

Step 5: On the last page of Living Screen wizard, you can review the screensaver options. If you need to change anything, simply click the Back button. When you're ready to create the screensaver, click the Complete button. Your screensaver will automatically be compressed and BinHex-coded (as an .HQX file) so that it can delivered over the Internet.

To install the screensaver, decompress the .HQX file with StuffIt Expander. Double-click the installation file named LS Screensaver Installer. On the Mac, a new control panel called LS Screensaver will be installed in the Apple system folder. This control panel can manage several screensavers created with the Living Screen Screensavertool. Each screensaver is referred to as a Module in the control panel. Remember that you will need to restart your computer after installation.

The LS Screensaver control panel (shown in the following figure) enables the user to regulate the time after which the screensaver should be started. The control panel offers the option of a password safety feature. If a password is specified, the screensaver will only shut down after the correct password is entered. You can also choose a sleepcorner, which will force the activation of the screensaver when the user clicks that corner of the desktop screen. The Information area of the control panel enables the user to delete Modules, read the About information (which you supplied in Step 1 of this tutorial), or test the selected Module.

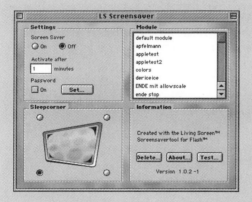

Through the About dialog (see an example in the following figure), the user can go directly to your Web site or send an e-mail to your e-mail address. This is a wonderful way to drive traffic to your site and other products (or services).

The user-friendly license regulation of this tool is an added bonus. With only one license, you are able to distribute as many screensavers as you like! Because the Screensavertool is also available for Windows, you can create screensavers for most of your Internet users.

Born and raised in Heidelberg, Germany, Christian Kocholl works as a technical production manager for I-D Media AG in Stuttgart, Germany. He discovered Flash 2 when he started working for the company. Besides the Living Screen home page (www.livingscreen.com), Christian has worked on the Sony Europe Digital Camcorder site (www.sony-europe.com/com/camcorders) and the home page of the Amateur Radio Club (www.darc.de/distrikte/a/19/). When Christian graduated from high school, he recalls listening to the Red Hot Chili Peppers' Blood Sugar Sex Magik album. In his spare time, he enjoys kiting.

Future players, future features

Who can predict where Flash content will show up next? While the Flash Player plug-in has made its way into the browser installations all over the world, there are still other possible avenues for Flash content. Currently, there is no .SVG output from the Flash authoring environment — nor are there any conversion utilities to translate .SWF files into .SVG files (at the time of this writing). Or, maybe you would like to see Flash content supported in some other authoring application, as an additional asset. If you have feature requests or general comments regarding the Flash authoring application or the Flash .SWF format, you can send feedback to Macromedia at wish-flash@macromedia.com.

Summary

✦ Flash movies can be viewed in Web pages with the Flash Player plug-in or ActiveX control. You can also play .SWF files with the Flash Player Stand-alone Player included with the Flash 5 application, or publish a Macintosh or Windows projector that packages the Stand-alone Player and .SWF file into one executable file.

✦ You can freely distribute a Flash movie projector or Stand-alone Player as long as you adhere to the "Made with Macromedia" guidelines outlined at Macromedia's Web site.

✦ Flash movies can be distributed with other multimedia presentations such as Macromedia Director projectors. Your Flash movies may be small enough to distribute on a 1.44MB floppy disk.

✦ The Actions Panel of Flash 5 has a stand-alone–specific submenu to the FScommand action. FSCommands can control playback and execute external applications from a stand-alone.

✦ Flash movies can be viewed best with Macromedia's Flash Player plug-in or ActiveX control. However, you can also view Flash movies with third-party products, such as Java, RealPlayer, or QuickTime Player.

✦ You can enhance your Flash movies with third-party tools such as Living Screen's Screensavertool for Flash.

✦   ✦   ✦

Using the CD-ROM

The CD-ROM included with this book aids you with many examples and tutorials by providing many useful files, including the following:

✦ Trial versions of Macromedia Flash 5, Dreamweaver 4, Fireworks 4, FreeHand 9, and Director 8.

✦ Evaluation versions of many .SWF-compatible applications and utilities, including Swift3D, SWiSH, Swift-Inspector, and Swift-Generator.

✦ Demo versions of Sonic Foundry's audio applications, Sound Forge 4.5, and ACID Pro 2.

✦ Limited-edition version of Joey Lott's sendmail.cgi Perl script, to be used in conjunction with the Flash form lesson in Chapter 24.

✦ Just about every .FLA and .SWF file that is discussed in the book, including those used in Expert Tutorials.

✦ QuickTime movies and QTVR panorama and object movies. Many thanks to Paul Nykamp from Focus VR for the QTVR samples.

Installing and Using Plug-Ins and Applications

In the software folder of the CD-ROM, you'll find the trial versions of the many applications discussed in this book, particularly those from Part VII.

On a Macintosh, go to the specific application's folder and double-click the installation file. Then follow the installer's instructions to proceed.

On a PC, go to the specific application's folder and either unzip the installation .ZIP file or double-click the installation .EXE file.

Installing and Using sendmail.cgi

To use Joey Lott's sendmail.cgi Perl script (the .cgi file), you need to have Perl 5 installed on your Web server. You may need the assistance and permission of the system administrator of your Internet service provider (ISP) or Internet presence provider (IPP) to install (or use) Perl 5. Once it is installed, upload the script file, sendmail.cgi, to a directory or folder that is accessible by Perl. This folder may need to have proper permissions in order for Web users to execute the script file.

In a text editor such as Notepad, SimpleText, or BBEdit, you may need to edit the first line of the script to indicate the path to the Perl files on your server. On line 19, you can remove the comment code (#) and specify a default e-mail to which output from the script will be sent. Meaning, if you wish to omit a variable in the Flash movie ActionScript, then you can specify an e-mail address on line 19. If you are receiving errors from the script during trials, you may need to adjust the location parameter of the Web server's sendmail program (*not* the script file, but the actual program the server uses to send e-mail), specified in line 24.

Once you have the script installed, you should be able to follow the "Creating a Flash Form" section in Chapter 24 to create a fully functional form in your Flash movies. You can modify the loadVariables action to refer to your script's URL instead of theMakers.com's script URL.

✦   ✦   ✦

Contact Information for Contributors and Expert Tutorialists

Contributors

Bardzell, Jeffrey
Bloomington, Indiana, USA
jb@uncom.com
www.eHandsOn.com

Expert Tutorialists

Baker, James
WDDG
New York, New York, USA
james@wddg.com
www.wddg.com

Bazley, Richard
Bazley Films
Hollywood, California, USA
richard@bazleyfilms.com
www.bazleyfilms.com

Brown, Scott
Los Angeles, California, USA
sbrown@artcenter.edu
www.spicybrown.com

Buchholz, Christian
Bromide73
Sydney, Australia
christian@bromide73.com
www.bromide73.com

Burrs, Mark
CyBurrs Solutions, Inc.
White Bear Lake, Minnesota, USA
mburrs@cyburrs.com
www.cyburrs.com
www.swfStudio.com

Christiansen, Cam
anlanda inc.
Calgary, Alberta, Canada
cam@anlanda.com
www.anlanda.com

Cluff, Daniel
sinderblok
Hollywood, California, USA
dcluff@mailcity.com
www.sinderblok.com

Debreuil, Robin and Sandy
Debreuil Digital Works
Miami, Manitoba, Canada
admin@debreuil.com
www.debreuil.com

Dundon, MD
Flash411
Oakland, California, USA
info@flash411.com
http://www.flash411.com

Elliott, Shane
Timberfish
Studio City, California, USA
greyson4@pacbell.net

Fierlinger, Philip
Turntable
Emeryville, California, USA
philip@turntable.com
www.turntable.com

Finkelstein, Ellen
Author of Flash 5 for Dummies
ellenfinkl@bigfoot.com
www.ellenfinkelstein.com

Franklin, Derek
Coauthor, Flash 5 Creative Web Animation
Bloomington, Indiana, USA
derek@derekfranklin.com
www.derekfranklin.com

Hall, Branden
Fig Leaf Software
Washington, D.C., USA
bhall@figleaf.com
www.figleaf.com

Holzschlag, Molly E.
Author, Instructor, Designer
Tucson, Arizona, USA
molly@molly.com
www.molly.com

Honselaar, Chris
HTMwell Holistic Multimedia
Groningen, the Netherlands
flash@htmwell.com
www.htmwell.com

Jones, Mike
FlashGen.Com
London, England
San Francisco, California, USA
flashgen2000@yahoo.com
www.flashgen.com

Jordan, Eric
Design Insites
Laguna Beach, California, USA
ejordan@2advanced.com
www.designinsites.com
www.2advanced.com

Kocholl, Christian
Technical Production Manager
I-D Media AG — Living Screen
Stuttgart, Germany
christian.kocholl@
livingscreen.com
www.livingscreen.com

Kunst, Merien Q.
BSUR Concepting & Communications
Amsterdam, The Netherlands
quintus@quintus.org
www.quintus.org

Larry D. Larsen
the Alien Containment Facility
St. Petersburg, Florida, USA
777@greenjem.com
www.greenjem.com
www.ehandson.com

Loftus, Doug
Beatnik, Inc.
San Francisco, California, USA
dloftus@beatnik.com
www.mixman.com

Lott, Joey
North Hollywood, California, USA
joey@cleardigital.com

Lowery, Joseph
Author, *Dreamweaver 3 Bible* and
Fireworks 3 Bible
New York, New York, USA
jlowery@idest.com

Moock, Colin
ICE Integrated Communications &
Entertainment
Toronto, Canada
colin_moock@iceinc.com
www.moock.org

Moschella, William
Timerite Media Services
Cheshire, Conneticut, USA
trm01@earthlink.net
www.deluxesounds.com

Nisinson, Dorian
Dorian Nisinson Design
New York, New York, USA
dorian@nisinson.com
www.nisinson.com
www.flashcentral.com

Parameswaran, Viswanath
Media Arts
Singapore
vish@media-arts.net
www.media-arts.net

Plant, Darrel
Moshofsky/Plant
Portland, Oregon, USA
dplant@moshplant.com
www.moshplant.com

Purgason, Todd
Juxt Interactive
Newport Beach, California, USA
toddhead@juxtinteractive.com
http://juxtinteractive.com

Pursehouse, Gareth
Carlsbad, California, USA
gareth@infinovation.com
www.infinovation.com

Reed, Arena
Santa Cruz, California, USA
arena@visualarena.com
www.visualarena.com

Rey, Chrissy
FlashLite
College Park, Maryland, USA
webmistress@flashlite.net
www.flashlite.net

Richards, Mike
Macromedia
San Francisco, California, USA
miker@macromedia.com
www.macromedia.com

Robertson, James
EDesign.uk.com Ltd
Crowborough, England
james@edesign.uk.com
www.edesign.uk.com

Schramm, Nik
nae interactive
Hamburg, Germany
nik@nae.de
www.nae.de
www.industriality.com

Smith, Jake
Subnet
Nelson, Lancashire, England
jake@subnet.co.uk
www.subnet.co.uk
www.systemerror.co.uk

Szecket, Daniel
Magritte's Cow
Los Angeles, California, USA
daniel@magrittescow.com
www.magrittescow.com

Turner, Bill
Turnertoons Productions, Inc.
Melbourne, Florida, USA
bill@turnertoons.com
www.turnertoons.com

Vanian, Jay
Pixelpushers, Inc.
Newport Beach, California, USA
jvanian@pixelpushers.com
www.vanian.com
www.pixelpushers.com

Andreas Wagner
Mixman Technologies Inc.
San Francisco, California, USA
andreas@mixman.com
wagner@koalition.net
www.mixman.com
www.koalition.net

Walch, Robert
entermation
New York, New York, USA
rwalch@entermation.com
www.entermation.com

Wolfe, Bentley
Macromedia
Richardson, Texas, USA
bwolfe@macromedia.com
www.macromedia.com/support

✦   ✦   ✦

Index

Continued

Continued

Continued

Continued

Continued

Continued

Continued

Continued

Continued

Continued

Continued

Hungry Minds, Inc.
End-User License Agreement

READ THIS. You should carefully read these terms and conditions before opening the software packet(s) included with this book ("Book"). This is a license agreement ("Agreement") between you and Hungry Minds, Inc. ("HMIN"). By opening the accompanying software packet(s), you acknowledge that you have read and accept the following terms and conditions. If you do not agree and do not want to be bound by such terms and conditions, promptly return the Book and the unopened software packet(s) to the place you obtained them for a full refund.

1. **License Grant.** HMIN grants to you (either an individual or entity) a nonexclusive license to use one copy of the enclosed software program(s) (collectively, the "Software") solely for your own personal or business purposes on a single computer (whether a standard computer or a workstation component of a multiuser network). The Software is in use on a computer when it is loaded into temporary memory (RAM) or installed into permanent memory (hard disk, CD-ROM, or other storage device). HMIN reserves all rights not expressly granted herein.

2. **Ownership.** HMIN is the owner of all right, title, and interest, including copyright, in and to the compilation of the Software recorded on the disk(s) or CD-ROM ("Software Media"). Copyright to the individual programs recorded on the Software Media is owned by the author or other authorized copyright owner of each program. Ownership of the Software and all proprietary rights relating thereto remain with HMIN and its licensers.

3. **Restrictions On Use and Transfer.**

   (a) You may only (i) make one copy of the Software for backup or archival purposes, or (ii) transfer the Software to a single hard disk, provided that you keep the original for backup or archival purposes. You may not (i) rent or lease the Software, (ii) copy or reproduce the Software through a LAN or other network system or through any computer subscriber system or bulletin-board system, or (iii) modify, adapt, or create derivative works based on the Software.

   (b) You may not reverse engineer, decompile, or disassemble the Software. You may transfer the Software and user documentation on a permanent basis, provided that the transferee agrees to accept the terms and conditions of this Agreement and you retain no copies. If the Software is an update or has been updated, any transfer must include the most recent update and all prior versions.

4. **Restrictions on Use of Individual Programs.** You must follow the individual requirements and restrictions detailed for each individual program in Appendix A of this Book. These limitations are also contained in the individual

license agreements recorded on the Software Media. These limitations may include a requirement that after using the program for a specified period of time, the user must pay a registration fee or discontinue use. By opening the Software packet(s), you will be agreeing to abide by the licenses and restrictions for these individual programs that are detailed in Appendix A and on the Software Media. None of the material on this Software Media or listed in this Book may ever be redistributed, in original or modified form, for commercial purposes.

5. Limited Warranty.

(a) HMIN warrants that the Software and Software Media are free from defects in materials and workmanship under normal use for a period of sixty (60) days from the date of purchase of this Book. If HMIN receives notification within the warranty period of defects in materials or workmanship, HMIN will replace the defective Software Media.

(b) HMIN AND THE AUTHORS OF THE BOOK DISCLAIM ALL OTHER WARRANTIES, EXPRESS OR IMPLIED, INCLUDING WITHOUT LIMITATION IMPLIED WARRANTIES OF MERCHANTABILITY AND FITNESS FOR A PARTICULAR PURPOSE, WITH RESPECT TO THE SOFTWARE, THE PROGRAMS, THE SOURCE CODE CONTAINED THEREIN, AND/OR THE TECHNIQUES DESCRIBED IN THIS BOOK. HMIN DOES NOT WARRANT THAT THE FUNCTIONS CONTAINED IN THE SOFTWARE WILL MEET YOUR REQUIREMENTS OR THAT THE OPERATION OF THE SOFTWARE WILL BE ERROR FREE.

(c) This limited warranty gives you specific legal rights, and you may have other rights that vary from jurisdiction to jurisdiction.

6. Remedies.

(a) HMIN's entire liability and your exclusive remedy for defects in materials and workmanship shall be limited to replacement of the Software Media, which may be returned to HMIN with a copy of your receipt at the following address: Software Media Fulfillment Department, Attn.: *Flash 5 Bible*, Hungry Minds, Inc., 7260 Shadeland Station, Ste. 100, Indianapolis, IN 46256, or call 1-800-762-2974. Please allow three to four weeks for delivery. This Limited Warranty is void if failure of the Software Media has resulted from accident, abuse, or misapplication. Any replacement Software Media will be warranted for the remainder of the original warranty period or thirty (30) days, whichever is longer.

(b) In no event shall HMIN or the authors be liable for any damages whatsoever (including without limitation damages for loss of business profits, business interruption, loss of business information, or any other pecuniary loss) arising from the use of or inability to use the Book or the Software, even if HMIN has been advised of the possibility of such damages.

(c) Because some jurisdictions do not allow the exclusion or limitation of liability for consequential or incidental damages, the above limitation or exclusion may not apply to you.

7. **U.S. Government Restricted Rights.** Use, duplication, or disclosure of the Software by the U.S. Government is subject to restrictions stated in paragraph (c)(1)(ii) of the Rights in Technical Data and Computer Software clause of DFARS 252.227-7013, and in subparagraphs (a) through (d) of the Commercial Computer — Restricted Rights clause at FAR 52.227-19, and in similar clauses in the NASA FAR supplement, when applicable.

8. **General.** This Agreement constitutes the entire understanding of the parties and revokes and supersedes all prior agreements, oral or written, between them and may not be modified or amended except in a writing signed by both parties hereto that specifically refers to this Agreement. This Agreement shall take precedence over any other documents that may be in conflict herewith. If any one or more provisions contained in this Agreement are held by any court or tribunal to be invalid, illegal, or otherwise unenforceable, each and every other provision shall remain in full force and effect.

CD-ROM Installation Instructions

The *Flash 5 Bible* CD-ROM is packed with tutorials, plug-ins, and examples from almost all of the .FLA and .SWF files that are discussed on the book. You'll find all kinds of useful things so you can easily learn — and master! — in Flash 5.

The CD-ROM that accompanies this book can be used on both Windows and Macintosh Systems. To make sure that your computer can run the CD-ROM, please check the system requirements that are found on the back of the book.

For more information on installing and using the programs on the CD-ROM, please read Appendix A.